Encyclopedias
Atlases *&*
Dictionaries

Encyclopedias Atlases & Dictionaries

Marion Sader
Amy Lewis
Editors

Charles A. Bunge
April Carlucci
Kathleen Malanga
Marilyn Miller
Consultants

R. R. Bowker®
A Reed Reference Publishing Company
New Providence, New Jersey

Published by R. R. Bowker®
A Reed Reference Publishing Company
Copyright © 1995 by Reed Reference Publishing
All rights reserved
Printed and bound in the United States of America

Library of Congress Cataloging-in-Publication Data

Encyclopedias, atlases, and dictionaries / Marion Sader, Amy Lewis,
   editors.
      p.   cm.
   Includes bibliographical references and index.
   ISBN 0–8352–3669–2
    1. Encyclopedias and dictionaries—History and criticism.
2. Atlases—History. I. Sader, Marion. II. Lewis, Amy.
AE1.E48   1995
031—dc20   95–6195
                                       CIP

All copyright notices can be found under "Acknowledgments," on page 485.

**Editorial Development
by Visual Education Corporation,
Princeton, New Jersey**

ISBN 0 - 8352 - 3669 - 2

Contents

List of Titles Reviewed

Electronic Atlases *(pp. 433–439)*

Electronic Dictionaries *(pp. 441–455)*

Large-Print Atlas *(pp. 457 459)*

Large-Print Dictionaries *(pp. 459–474)*

Consultants, Reviewers, and Contributors

Consultants

Charles A. Bunge
 Professor
School of Library and Information Studies
University of Wisconsin–Madison
Madison, WI

April Carlucci
 Assistant Chief
Map Division
New York Public Library
New York, NY

Kathleen Malanga
 Head of Reference
Sarah Byrd Askew Library
William Paterson College
Wayne, NJ

Marilyn Miller
 Professor and Chair
Department of Library and Information Studies
University of North Carolina at Greensboro
Greensboro, NC

Subject Consultants

Bernard D. Blaustein
 Retired, Senior Scientist
U.S. Department of Energy
Washington, DC

Mark Dignan
 Professor
Department of Family and Community Medicine
The Bowman Gray School of Medicine
Wake Forest University
Winston-Salem, NC

Paul G. Lewis
 Assistant Professor
Department of Political Science
Florida International University
North Miami, FL

Derrick H. Pitts
 Vice President
Fels Planetarium and Tuttleman Omniverse Theater
The Franklin Institute Science Museum
Philadelphia, PA

Lawrence R. Poos
 Associate Professor
Department of History
The Catholic University of America
Washington, DC

Reviewers and Contributors

Barbara M. Bibel
 Reference Librarian
Science, Business, and Sociology Department
Oakland Public Library
Oakland, CA

Ken Black
 Head of Public Services
Rebecca Crown Library
Rosary College
River Forest, IL

Jerry Carbone
 Director
Brooks Memorial Library
Brattleboro, VT

Ron Chepesiuk
 Associate Professor and Head of Special Collections
Dacus Library
Winthrop University
Rock Hill, NC

Brian E. Coutts
 Coordinator of Collection Development
Helms-Craven Library
Western Kentucky University
Bowling Green, KY

Carolyn B. Duffy
 Associate Professor, ESL
Center of International Programs
St. Michael's College
Winooski, VT

Marie Ellis
English and American Literature Bibliographer
Main Library
University of Georgia
Athens, GA

Abbie Vestal Landry
Head, Reference Department
Watson Library
Northwestern State University
Natchitoches, LA

Carolyn Mulac
Assistant Head
Information Center
Chicago Public Library
Chicago, IL

Elizabeth B. Nibley
Reference Librarian
The American University Library
The American University
Washington, DC

David N. Pauli
Director
Missoula Public Library
Missoula, MT

David Schau
Reference Librarian
Kanawha County Public Library
Charleston, WV

Christopher J.J. Thiry
Reference Librarian
Map Division
New York Public Library
New York, NY

Fannette H. Thomas
Coordinator of Collection Development
James A. Newpher Library
Essex Community College
Baltimore, MD

Editorial Consultants

Donna J. Gelagotis
Princeton Junction, NJ

Diane S. Kendall
Editor, "Children's Software: A Newsletter for Parents"
Houston, TX

Charles O. Roebuck
Editor, "Children's Software: A Newsletter for Parents"
Montgomery, NY

Elizabeth West
Boxborough, MA

Jessamyn West
Seattle, WA

Preface

Encyclopedias, Atlases, and Dictionaries is the newest publication in the Bowker Buying Guide Series, a venture begun in 1988 with the publication of *Reference Books for Young Readers* and *General Reference Books for Adults* and continued in 1991 with the appearance of *Topical Reference Books.* These volumes provided reference librarians and consumers who were considering the purchase of a reference book with a resource containing thorough reviews in standardized formats for ease of comparison. This new volume continues that valuable service.

New Features

Encyclopedias, Atlases, and Dictionaries is an update of the first two books in the Bowker Buying Guide Series. It combines the coverage of those two earlier works, embracing works aimed at preschool to school-age users, which had been reviewed in *Young Readers,* and the more advanced titles (such as the *OED*) that were covered in *Adults.*

In some ways, however, *Encyclopedias, Atlases, and Dictionaries* goes beyond the two earlier works in terms of coverage of the field and ease of use. In this new edition, electronic reference works—a burgeoning area of publishing—now enjoy a far more prominent place than before, occupying a separate part of the book. This part begins with a valuable guide to the new media—a chapter entitled "What to Look for in Electronic Reference Works." That useful introduction is followed by three chapters devoted to reviews of specific types of electronic works—encyclopedias, atlases, and dictionaries. We believe that this approach provides the librarian and patron who seek guidance in purchasing electronic works with the same kind of accessible, reliable information found on print materials in both this new volume and previous Buying Guides.

Another feature new to this book is a more convenient organization. While the volume is still divided into parts devoted to the major types of general reference works—encyclopedias, atlases, and dictionaries—each part is now subdivided into chapters that group reviews of works intended for users of the same level. Thus, reviews of dictionaries are divided into four chapters: children's dictionaries, middle school dictionaries, secondary and adult dictionaries, and special dictionaries. The other parts of the book are similarly organized. This structure, we believe, makes it easier for the librarian

and patron to move from the review of one title to that of its main competitors—because all will be located in close proximity.

Other Features

Along with these changes, this Buying Guide builds on the strengths of the earlier works:

- Comparative charts at the beginning of the book summarize the statistical information on each book reviewed to help the user focus on a few titles at the desired scope, level, and cost.
- "Facts at a Glance" features at the beginning of each review conveniently summarize the relevant information about a title.
- Facsimile pages or partial pages, which accompany the reviews of most encyclopedias and dictionaries, provide a glimpse of the organization and appearance of the book being reviewed and, through the use of annotations, highlight special features.
- Full coverage is provided for large-print reference works, an important and often overlooked area of publishing.

The main feature of the book is, of course, the material at its heart: systematic, clearly organized, comparative reviews follow consistent criteria that are fully explained in regard to each type of reference book.

This work begins with a brief overview entitled "Using This Book." We urge the reader to spend some time on this introduction before proceeding further, as it details the structure of the book and suggests how the user can navigate through the material efficiently and profitably.

Scope of the Work

In *Encyclopedias, Atlases, and Dictionaries,* we have chosen to limit coverage to the three main classes of general reference books: general encyclopedias, world atlases, and general English-language dictionaries. We include such works whether they appear in traditional print, electronic, or large-print format. We have avoided covering more specialized reference works. Reviews of the best of such works, organized topically, can be found in another volume in the Bowker Buying Guide Series—*Topical Reference Books.*

To qualify for inclusion in this book, a work had to be available in the United States, be in print as of the spring of 1994, and sell for $10 or more. We decided on the $10 cutoff for this volume on the grounds that any work of a lower price is not likely to require the kind of detailed analysis that is provided for the works reviewed here. We nevertheless urge all consumers who are considering the purchase of any reference book, regardless of price, to read the appropriate "What to Look for" chapters in this volume and apply the criteria outlined there to the work under consideration.

We have undertaken a painstaking search to identify the reference works to be included in the volume. This search involved perusing professional journals and catalogs, compiling many lists of titles, and making countless telephone calls to publishers. The result is a list of about 200 general encyclopedias, world atlases, and general dictionaries—in print and in electronic format. We have made every effort to identify all appropriate general reference works and have given publishers every opportunity to submit information about and copies of their publications for inclusion in this guide. We apologize for any titles that may have been overlooked.

Acknowledgments

The editors would like, first of all, to thank the many publishers who cooperated with us in our efforts to build a list of titles and prepare the reviews.

We extend another hearty thanks to the specialists who assisted us. The librarians who served as consultants—Charles Bunge, April Carlucci, Kathleen Malanga, and Marilyn Miller—were of tremendous help in sharpening the guidelines for reviewers and reading and commenting on the reviews themselves. A number of academics provided a special service by lending their expertise to our assessments of the encyclopedias; we thank Bernard Blaustein, Mark Dignan, Paul Lewis, Derrick Pitts, and Lawrence Poos for their thoughtful and informed observations.

We owe a great debt to the many librarians and academics who contributed their time and effort by providing thorough, careful reviews. These individuals are too numerous to list here, but all appear in the list of "Consultants, Reviewers, and Contributors." They should feel proud of their efforts.

Finally, we want to thank our colleagues at Visual Education Corporation and R. R. Bowker for their highly professional efforts in editing, checking, designing, proofreading, and checking yet again. We are especially grateful to Dale Anderson and Linda Perrin for their guidance and support throughout the project and to Suzanne Murdico and Stacy Tibbetts, who provided outstanding aid. Special thanks must be given to Carol Ciaston, whose patience and persistence on the telephone cannot be overlooked.

Encyclopedias, Atlases, and Dictionaries presents the most extensive, systematic, consistent, and objective reviews of general reference titles gathered into one volume. We are confident that these reviews will prove useful to anyone—librarian or patron—engaged in the important task of selecting an encyclopedia, atlas, or dictionary.

Marion Sader
R. R. Bowker

Amy Lewis
Visual Education Corporation

Using This Book

Encyclopedias, Atlases, and Dictionaries is divided into six main parts: Part One, Introduction; Part Two, Encyclopedias; Part Three, Atlases; Part Four, Dictionaries; Part Five, Electronic Reference Works; and Part Six, Large-Print General Reference Works. In addition, there is a Selected Bibliography, a list of Publishers and Distributors, and an index.

Part One provides broad overview material that will orient the reader to the world of general reference books. Chapter 1, "Choosing General Reference Works," notes the criteria that the reader may wish to consider when selecting a reference book. We recommend that any user of this book begin by reading Chapter 1 to reach an understanding of the scope and nature of the works in question.

The next chapter of Part One presents comprehensive charts that compare each title reviewed in this book on a number of statistical categories. The charts are grouped by type of book and by market; for instance, all children's encyclopedias are grouped together, followed by all adult encyclopedias. These groupings correspond to the evaluation chapters in the book. Titles are listed alphabetically in the appropriate chart, following the same sequence in which the actual reviews appear. Charts include such information as the page count, number of entries and illustrations, and price. By consulting these charts at the beginning of the selection process, the reader can identify titles with similar scope within a desired price range, thus narrowing choices quickly. He or she can then read the reviews of those books that seem attractive.

The initial chapters in parts two, three, four, and five describe the specific criteria used for evaluating the titles in that part, as well as present the structure that those reviews will take. Each of these "What to Look for" chapters ends with a glossary of terms appropriate to that type of reference work. Chapter 6, "What to Look for in Atlases," contains an added feature—generic maps that illustrate some of the concepts and technical concerns that are peculiar and important to the evaluation of atlases.

The body of the book consists of the reviews that appear in parts two through six. Reviews are organized alphabetically (ignoring initial articles) within a sequence of titles of comparable type. Those types are determined by the ability level of the intended audience. Thus, one chapter in Part Two, on encyclopedias, covers children's encyclopedias; the other chapter covers encyclopedias for readers from secondary school through adulthood.

Each review begins with a "Facts at a Glance" listing that details the essential statistical and editorial data of the title. This information is similar to that found in the comparative charts, though additional facts (such as the publisher's discount and revision policies) are given in "Facts at a Glance."

Each review within a category follows a standard format. Subheadings vary from category to category, but generally include such essential elements as scope, format, authority, clarity, accessibility, and special features. Criteria that are specific to a given type of work—such as search capabilities for electronic works—are included when needed. Each review concludes with a summary, which judges the book's overall quality and usefulness to readers. In the summary—and indeed throughout the body of the reviews—comments compare each title to significant related titles when appropriate. For easy identification, all references to titles reviewed in this volume are printed in capital and small capital letters (for example, WORLD BOOK ENCYCLOPEDIA).

Many reviews are enhanced by the inclusion of facsimile pages—reproductions of typical pages or entries annotated to highlight the work's features. These facsimiles will be of special value to anyone using this guide to comparison shop prior to making a purchase. Readers of this guide should note that the facsimiles are often photoreduced to fit on our pages; a note near the facsimile indicates the amount of photo reduction. Facsimiles have been specially selected to illustrate representative samples of design and editorial features of the various titles. The reproduction process necessarily results in some loss of image quality from the original, especially when converting a color page to black and white. The facsimiles therefore do not represent the quality of the image in the original work, but are meant only as a guide to the general look and features of the book. We urge any librarian or consumer who is considering the purchase of a reference book to try to peruse a copy of the real item.

The Buying Guide does not include facsimile pages for the atlases reviewed. Color is essential to the maps in these atlases, and black-and-white reproductions simply do not do justice to these works.

Encyclopedias, Atlases, and Dictionaries concludes with a bibliography; an alphabetical list of publishers whose works are reviewed here, with their addresses; and a comprehensive index. The bibliography includes titles of related reference works and professional journals that regularly review the kinds of books reviewed here. The list of publishers includes all publishers and distributors cited in the reviews; addresses are current as of the summer of 1994. The index cites page references for all titles reviewed in this volume as well as for any other titles (such as historically important or out-of-print works) mentioned in the text.

This Buying Guide can be used in a variety of ways. A librarian or lay reader interested in an overview of a given type of work could read the appropriate "What to Look for" chapter and the reviews of the major works of that type. A librarian who is considering the addition of a new dictionary to the collection will probably want to turn right to the review of that work, perhaps consulting the reviews of comparable works as well. For a parent or student considering, for example, which world atlas to purchase, we recommend beginning with the comparative charts and using the information there to focus the search on titles that seem appropriate in terms of level, size, and price. From there, the next step is to read "What to Look for in Atlases" and then consult the appropriate reviews. Both librarians and consumers will probably want to give special attention to the chapter entitled "What to Look for in Electronic Reference Works"; this chapter should clarify murky and confusing concepts in a technical and rapidly changing field.

Whatever the approach taken to the material in this book, we are confident that both librarians and patrons will find *Encyclopedias, Atlases, and Dictionaries* to be authoritative, objective, and highly readable—an indispensable tool in the selection of general reference books.

Encyclopedias Atlases *&* Dictionaries

Introduction

Chapter 1
Choosing General Reference Works

General encyclopedias, world atlases, and general dictionaries are manufactured to withstand extended use and are generally expensive. Because of their expense, they are often kept in use for many years. The expense and longevity of these works make it important for the shopper, whether a librarian or someone seeking such a work for the home or office, to follow a careful selection process. The increasing availability of electronic reference works, the features and capabilities of which may confuse the librarian or other consumer who is more accustomed to traditional print media, is another factor suggesting use of a careful selection process. This chapter offers suggestions that will help librarians and other potential purchasers of general reference works to clarify their needs for these works. It also explores, in a general way, the features and characteristics of each type of these resources.

This book is written with two principles in mind. First, no single reference work is capable of satisfying a universal readership. Each individual who consults one of these works has specific needs, and each work has its own approach, making it more or less suitable for those needs. Second, however varied these works may be individually, there are defined standards against which each can be judged. In this chapter, we examine each of these principles.

Identifying What Is Needed from General Reference Works

Someone considering the purchase of a general reference work must begin by determining how the work will be used—what information is being sought and for what purpose. Without clarifying these needs, the potential purchaser has no basis on which to identify alternatives or to make choices among them. The parent seeking a home encyclopedia that a sixth grader can refer to when writing school reports has a far different use in mind than does the office worker who needs an encyclopedia to provide ready-reference information on people and places. The teacher looking for a children's atlas with basic world maps and a discussion of fundamental map skills seeks a different resource than does a travel agent who wants detailed maps of the world. The librarian, of course, must determine a whole range of reasons that patrons will have for using these works and make selection decisions to ensure that the reference collection meets that variety of purposes.

No outside source can identify the particular needs of a librarian or individual—the librarian or other consumer must make that determination. However, we can list some questions that a librarian or individual may ask as part of this process:

- What kinds of information are likely to be sought in the reference work?
- What are the characteristics of the population needing the works? In the case of a library, this means evaluating the ages and ability levels of patrons.
- Why will users seek that information? Among the possibilities are to prepare reports, to answer ready-reference questions, to explore the nuances of language, and to satisfy curiosity. This list, hardly exhaustive, suggests the kind of thinking that the prospective purchaser must pursue.

- What are the current levels of knowledge and skills of the people who will use the work? There are different requirements for young children, adolescents, and adults—as well as differences within each group. A home library may be adequately served by a world atlas that offers basic maps of the world. A library reference section is more likely to need an atlas that supplements those basic maps with more specific information on the population, economic resources, or cultures of the world's nations. A library serving a population with limited English-speaking skills has unique needs in its reference collection.

- What might be the *future* abilities of the work's users? This is a crucial question, particularly for the consumer seeking a work for his or her children, who must consider buying an encyclopedia, atlas, or dictionary not just for today but also for tomorrow. Some of these works are substantial investments. It would be shortsighted to spend several hundred dollars on a work that a child will outgrow in a year or two. Of course, this consideration must be balanced against the preceding one, for it is equally undesirable to spend the money on a work that the child cannot use at the time of purchase. Electronic works, which may be less expensive than print versions, can be valuable in light of this factor.

- What are the research capabilities of the work's potential users? The sophisticated user can take advantage of the lengthy entries in a scholarly encyclopedia or the detailed word studies in an unabridged dictionary. A younger student is likely to need a work that contains less advanced research aids.

- How familiar with computers are the people who will use the work? What effective use could they make of electronic reference works? These questions have arisen because of the increased availability of electronic works. Computers are revolutionizing the delivery of basic information—and the kind of information that can be delivered. While electronic reference works are not right for everyone, they can provide powerful and effective research aids. And these tools, with their multimedia features, can be very appealing to young users. Of course, familiarity with electronic tools is not a static condition; it is an ability that grows with practice. Still, the user's level of experience with computers at the time of purchase is an issue to consider in terms of the usefulness of an electronic work.

After using these questions—and any others that he or she can identify—to clarify individual needs, the prospective buyer can use the resources provided in this book to focus on a number of alternative titles that may meet those needs.

Reference Works in Libraries. A librarian selecting general reference books for a public library must meet the needs of a broad range of patrons, including very young readers, older students, parents, business people, and older people who may prefer large-print works. One way to accomplish this task is to select a range of atlases, dictionaries, and encyclopedias that complement and supplement each other.

Because patrons rely on them for current information, librarians need to keep their reference collections up-to-date. Currency may not be the most critical factor, however. Most information in a general reference book remains accurate for many years.

One way of ensuring currency is to alternate encyclopedia purchases from year to year, adding a new edition of a few multivolume sets one year and a few others the next.

One approach to avoid investing in an entirely new edition is to purchase a publisher's yearbook. These supplements to encyclopedias, whether focusing on science or health, or offering a general update of a year's events, can be housed near the set. They provide patrons with additional, more current information.

It is also important to consider the characteristics of the work itself. An encyclopedia that is strong on historical data and general background information that does not change rapidly with time may be worth retaining for a relatively longer time, especially if the library has other encyclopedias that have been updated more recently. The library's budget is, of course, an important factor in these considerations.

A typical small public library might have three or four multivolume adult encyclopedias and one or two one-volume works. It might also have one or two children's encyclopedias. Such a library probably also has one or more abridged dictionaries, a selection of unabridged or college dictionaries, and children's dictionaries and picture word books in the children's section. A public library often has more than one atlas, supplementing general world atlases with any thematic atlases that fit the broad general interests of its patrons. Increasingly, these libraries also contain electronic versions of encyclopedias, atlases, and dictionaries.

Most school libraries, or school library media centers, probably need more than one multivolume encyclopedia; whether to select higher-level or lower-level works depends on the age of the student population. The number also depends on the size of the student body and the demands made by the school's curriculum. A school library should also have several school dictionaries and atlases. A high school's reference collection could include more advanced works (for example, an unabridged dictionary). In selecting reference books, many school library media specialists consider the advice of teachers and curriculum requirements as well as conclusions from their own research. Unlike most public libraries, many school libraries need to have several copies of particular reference works to satisfy the needs of a large number of users who may all need to use these resources at the same time.

The same factors for evaluating a work's worth apply to electronic reference works—a growing field. An additional significant factor is the equipment available and who has access to it. If computers are made accessible to the library's patrons, any electronic reference works purchased should be sufficiently user-friendly for a variety of people with vastly differing levels of computer experience to be able to use them effectively. The librarian also must be aware of the demands on staff time if patrons frequently need to ask for help.

Electronic reference works can be extremely economical, allowing the library to conserve dollars for other uses or more easily fit acquisitions into tight budgets. Librarians must remember, however, that these tools are limited to one user at a time unless they are networked.

Reference Works in the Home.   One or two dictionaries, a world atlas, and a general encyclopedia will meet the reference-book needs of most families. Many families can meet their needs with less.

Encyclopedias are major purchases and, while many are impressive and illuminating works, every family does not need one. A number of dictionaries offer much more than lexicographical information. With basic charts and tables (metric and standard measure equivalents, for instance) and those biographical and geographical entries that are likely to meet the most frequent ready-reference questions, these dictionaries are somewhat encyclopedic. If family members do not need to consult an encyclopedia frequently, these works may be adequate, with the understanding that they can consult an encyclopedia at the library when necessary. This not only saves the family a substantial cost; it also offers the occasional researcher access to sets that are likely to be more current.

Families with children must be concerned with an issue raised earlier—the importance of balancing the children's current abilities and needs with their future ones. Budgetary constraints generally dictate that a purchase be made carefully. It is not a bad idea to buy something that a child can grow into, as long as the gap between the child's current ability level and the level at which the work is written is not too great.

This is more of a concern with encyclopedias than dictionaries; the latter are much less expensive. Indeed, given their size and the amount of information they contain, dictionaries are bargains. Because they are more affordable, it may not be inappropriate to have a dictionary at the right level for each child in the house.

Atlases, like encyclopedias, may be seen as optional purchases. The maps found in some dictionaries—or even in almanacs, which are quite inexpensive—are enough to meet many families' needs to answer the occasional geographical question. Because of the many changes in national boundaries in the past few years, however, it is important to ensure that these maps are up-to-date. Other families, who have an encyclopedia, may feel that the maps in that resource provide enough geographical information. For those who want more, however, a world atlas is a good resource. It can offer a wealth of detail not found in an encyclopedia and, depending on the features, provide information on the solar system or world cultures as well.

In evaluating any of these reference works, it is important for consumers—especially those with children—to consider the format of the work. The size and weight of the volume or volumes can make the resource easier or harder to use. Legibility, too, can promote or inhibit use. If a goal of the family is to encourage children to acquaint themselves with reference works, these are important issues.

Finally, of course, price will be a factor. Options such as deluxe bindings, slipcases, and other supplementary materials and research services can add considerably to the cost of a multivolume encyclopedia. Consumers should bear in mind, though, that the purpose of a price comparison is to determine the lowest price for the best reference book in a given category—not just the lowest price. The prospective purchaser should look for the best combination of desirable features and price.

Dictionary shoppers should be particularly wary of great bargains, which sometimes can be a waste of money. These bargain dictionaries are often reprints of earlier works that have become obsolete and have simply been repackaged to look new.

There are other ways to reduce the cost of acquiring reference books. Taking advantage of bookstore specials is one, although this can mean buying the title that happens to be on sale rather than the one that, after careful consideration, seems most suitable. Buying secondhand books can help. Reading classified ads and watching for garage sales will often lead to true bargains. Such purchases may be adequate for most home use, although the buyer should remember that currency is probably being sacrificed.

Before purchasing any reference work—new or used—it is wise to examine the goods. Some of this investigation can be done at the bookstore, where a few minutes comparing one dictionary with another can help finalize a decision. Electronic sources can be tested at a computer store. The consumer can also use the resources of the local library, where more than one encyclopedia can be easily compared. This can be valuable time spent before making a purchase.

Evaluating General Reference Works

Reference books differ from one another; certain works are more suitable than others to meet certain reference needs. Many people may believe that all encyclopedias, atlases, and dictionaries are alike, but while all works of a type may share certain characteristics, each is unique. We attempt, in the reviews published here, to meet the twin goals of giving a sense of the character of each work being reviewed and of assessing its quality by stating its strengths and weaknesses.

We try to meet these goals by identifying the standards against which each type of general reference work may be judged. These criteria are explained in detail in the various chapters entitled "What to Look for . . ." and then applied in the reviews. In this chapter, we examine the broad issues related to each type of reference work.

Encyclopedias. Encyclopedias are in widespread use. It is estimated that encyclopedias are found in one of every four homes in the United States. The average public library provides anywhere from 4 to 12 different sets on its shelves. The sale of encyclopedias and supplementary material generates about $500 million in revenues each year. This figure represents a large investment for the publishers and a substantial expense for the purchaser—especially considering that many sets are revised annually.

In the few years since the publication of the first volumes in the Buying Guide series, the encyclopedia market has changed dramatically. The field is still dominated by four major publishers of multivolume encyclopedias: Encyclopaedia Britannica, World Book, Grolier, and Macmillan. These firms have seen significant changes in recent years, however, and many other companies now compete for encyclopedia purchasers' dollars.

Britannica recently sold its Compton's line to the Times-Mirror Company, which now publishes COMPTON'S ENCYCLOPEDIA AND FACT-INDEX, COMPTON'S PRECYCLOPEDIA, and COMPTON'S INTERACTIVE ENCYCLOPEDIA (the electronic version, available on CD-ROM). Grolier has increased its offerings by adding two new multivolume sets—THE NEW GROLIER STUDENT ENCYCLOPEDIA and the GROLIER ENCYCLOPEDIA OF KNOWLEDGE. Publishers have also begun to provide their information in an electronic format. World Book publishes its encyclopedia, packaged along with the WORLD BOOK DICTIONARY, on a CD-ROM called the INFORMATION FINDER. Grolier offers an online version of its ACADEMIC AMERICAN ENCYCLOPEDIA as well as a CD-ROM version; it also has a CD-ROM index to a number of its sets. In early 1994, Encyclopaedia Britannica announced that its encyclopedia would be available online through the Internet. While this new resource became available too late for us to review in this volume, it is clearly a research tool that should be considered. Of the four major encyclopedia publishers, Macmillan seems to be the only one contracting its efforts. This company has ceased publication of the *Merit Students Encyclopedia* and as yet has announced no plans for computerizing COLLIER'S ENCYCLOPEDIA.

The number of other publishers interested in encyclopedias is growing rapidly. Standard Educational Corporation (NEW STANDARD ENCYCLOPEDIA) and Funk & Wagnalls (FUNK & WAGNALLS NEW ENCYCLOPEDIA) continue to publish economical multivolume sets. They have been joined by Oxford University Press, with two recently inaugurated multivolume works, one aimed at children (OXFORD CHILDREN'S ENCYCLOPEDIA) and the other at the older user (OXFORD ILLUSTRATED ENCYCLOPEDIA). Random House has continued publishing its one-volume adult encyclopedia and added a work suitable for children, the RANDOM HOUSE CHILDREN'S ENCYCLOPEDIA. The one-volume encyclopedia market has become quite crowded now, with two entries each from Columbia University Press, Simon & Schuster (in its *Webster's New World* line), and Cambridge University Press joining the Random House work. Finally, Barron's, EDC, Kingfisher, and Troll, all publishers of many products for young children, have recently issued encyclopedias. Microsoft is pursuing its strategy of aggressively entering the reference market with two electronic works, including its impressive ENCARTA.

It is not entirely clear why the competition is suddenly so great. Certainly publishers saw that there previously was a dearth of children's encyclopedias and have filled that void—fully two-thirds of the children's encyclopedias reviewed here did not appear in *Reference Books for Young Readers*. Given the quality of a number of these new children's encyclopedias, their addition is welcome. Among the adult works, the most recent entries involve the computerization of major works and the growth of one-volume works. In other words, publishers have approached new markets prudently. Either they have taken advantage of an existing base of information, converting from the print format to the electronic approach, or they have invested modest amounts of money creating a single-volume work rather than a multivolume one. No new major multivolume encyclopedia has appeared since ACADEMIC AMERICAN in the early 1980s.

With so much to choose from, prospective purchasers may not know how to start. Of all the factors on which to base an encyclopedia purchase, four are probably key: scope, currency, accuracy, and price. (These factors and others are examined in greater detail in Chapter 3, "What to Look for in Encyclopedias.")

The issues involved in scope are depth and breadth of coverage. Obviously, multivolume encyclopedias treat their subjects in far greater depth than do one-volume sets. One-volume works are useful for ready-reference information, such as a capsule biography or a quick look at the geographical details about a country. The major sets can go well beyond this, with detailed studies of the person or place, extensive information on a wide range of subjects, and thousands of elaborate illustrations. The prospective purchaser must first determine whether a one-volume or multivolume resource is most appropriatc for his or her needs, then examine individual entries in that class to select the most desirable work.

Revision is essential if an encyclopedia is to remain current, although there is a limit to the value of a new edition if it contains a high proportion of information that can be found in less-expensive resources such as almanacs or yearbooks. Some publishers revise their titles only sporadically, but a responsible publisher makes a long-term commitment to keeping its works as current as possible. The major multivolume encyclopedia publishers revise their sets every year. (It will be interesting to see if the newer publishers are as dedicated to maintaining their works' currency.) Continuous or annual revision typically means that a portion of the set (around 10 percent) is replaced with new material or brought up-to-date with more current information. Every few years, the publisher may also undertake a substantial revision that involves the rewriting, addition, or removal of hundreds or even thousands of articles. The reviews in this book and in professional journals can convey a sense of the thoroughness with which revisions were treated at a certain time, but the encyclopedia shopper should always examine the existing edition before making a purchase. The reviews in this book assess currency based on an analysis of a standard set of articles (see Chapter 3, "What to Look for in Encyclopedias"). The revision policies of electronic works, where publishers speak of upgrades rather than updates, are less clear-cut than in print media. However, the potential for maintaining currency is tremendous.

Buyers expect encyclopedias to be substantially accurate, but no encyclopedia is absolutely error free. Many critics feel that encyclopedias err more often by omitting important information than through mistakes in the information that they do include, particularly in regard to complex or controversial subjects. Still, the reviews here can convey a sense of the general reputation (authority) and accuracy of the work in question. Any comments about slipshod writing or editing should be taken as a warning.

Many children's encyclopedias differ from their adult counterparts in more than the level of their prose or the conceptual level of their content. In this volume, we have placed the encyclopedias intended for older students—such as WORLD BOOK, COMPTON'S, and THE NEW BOOK OF KNOWLEDGE—in the category of secondary and adult works. These sets are primarily intended for serious reference use, even if they may be written at a lower level than the scholarly encyclopedias (AMERICANA, NEW BRITANNICA, and COLLIER'S). By "children's encyclopedias," we mean those works that are appropriate for an audience from preschool through the upper elementary grades. These works are not, obviously, as comprehensive as either adult works or the upper-level multivolume sets. Some arrange the information topically rather than alphabetically. Some are encyclopedias in name only; they are really collections of stories, fairy tales, things to do, and rhymes and riddles, with some basic facts. COMPTON'S PRECYCLOPEDIA and CHILDCRAFT are examples of this type. Others have the content range of an encyclopedia but are quite brief. A prospective purchaser should examine a children's encyclopedia closely to ensure that he or she is getting the kind of reference work that is desired.

Children's encyclopedias are most attractive to their readers when they are richly illustrated. Their usefulness is enhanced when they are structured so that entries on specific topics can be found quickly. Since students are usually instructed to use encyclopedias to gain an overview of a subject, a set that includes bibliographies or study guides listing other sources of information offers a valuable feature.

Atlases. Atlases are collections of maps of a specified area (such as a region, a nation, the lands and oceans of the world, or the solar system). This Buying Guide evaluates only world atlases. These atlases have three typical kinds of maps: political maps show the boundaries of nations, territories, cities, or towns; physical maps show natural features such as elevations; and thematic maps show populations, facts about economic activity, and other specialized data.

Atlases are usually arranged to show a large area (such as a continent), and then smaller segments of the same area (such as individual countries or regions). They may contain a number of supplementary features such as tables of the countries of the world or lists of the world's largest cities.

The three most significant factors on which to judge an atlas (other than price) are currency, legibility, and accessibility. These factors—and other criteria on which to judge atlases—are discussed in detail in Chapter 6, "What to Look for in Atlases," but some comments are appropriate here.

People rely on atlases for geographical information, and they expect the information portrayed to be current. While extensive world changes have increased the burden on atlas publishers in recent years, this need for currency is still a fact of life. An atlas that shows old borders or out-of-date country names is not worth the money. The currency of an atlas cannot simply be judged by its copyright date, however. Atlas publishers often update their map stock to show current world borders in a new printing without giving their work a new copyright date. Careful examination of the work itself is required to judge atlases in this regard.

Legibility encompasses such issues as the range of scales employed, the amount of detail on the maps, the type styles and sizes used for labels, and the color distinctions used to show different countries, elevations, or other cartographic features. The larger the scale of the maps, the more detail can be included. Especially for younger users, a consistent use of scales throughout the atlas is desirable; a wide variation can lead to distorted pictures of the relative size of different areas. Atlas maps often show many details, including lakes, rivers, highways, railroad lines, airports, and extremely small towns. Children's atlases are much less detailed, including only the main physical and political features of an area.

Accessibility is a very important factor. People consult atlases to find where something is—to locate a city or a mountain or an airport. A detailed index is essential to help users find the features they seek. Equally important is the presence of some kind of grid system, whether latitude and longitude or a specially devised alphanumeric grid, that can be used to pinpoint locations on the maps. Unfortunately, many children's atlases have spotty indexes and no grid, making it difficult for less-informed users to locate information on the maps.

Although there are dozens of world atlases on the market, most of the maps they include are produced by a relatively small number of cartographic firms. In the United States, Rand McNally and Hammond are the leading mapmakers, with National Geographic also enjoying a reputation for making high-quality maps. The premier cartographers in England are John Bartholomew & Son, Ltd., and George Philip & Son, Ltd. Both of these firms supply maps for a number of atlases reviewed in this volume that are published in the United States.

If a prospective purchaser is choosing an atlas from among a number of books that employ maps reflecting the same cartography, he or she should be aware of what differences to look for. While the maps may reflect the same cartography, the selection, order of presentation, and number included in the various atlases may vary. In addition, the atlases may differ in terms of other features (additional text, statistical tables, and supplementary photographs) and format (overall size of the book, quality of the paper, and binding) as well as price.

Dictionaries. Dictionaries are broadly classified according to the number of entries they contain as *unabridged, semi-unabridged, abridged,* and *paperback* or *pocket-sized.* The largest unabridged dictionary is, of course, the OXFORD ENGLISH DICTIONARY, newly revised in 1989. Other unabridged dictionaries include THE RANDOM HOUSE UNABRIDGED DICTIONARY, SECOND EDITION, and WEBSTER'S THIRD NEW INTERNATIONAL DICTIONARY, both of which were revised in 1993. A semi-unabridged dictionary contains roughly 200,000 entries; two examples are THE AMERICAN HERITAGE DICTIONARY OF THE ENGLISH LANGUAGE and WORLD BOOK DICTIONARY. An abridged dictionary ranges from 50,000 entries for a concise or desk edition to 130,000 or more for a college dictionary. Paperback dictionaries weigh in at the bottom end of that range, with pocket dictionaries containing even fewer

words. (Because a work must sell for more than $10 to be reviewed in this Buying Guide, few paperback or pocket dictionaries appear here.)

Publishers achieve the reduced levels of coverage by omitting thousands of entries for obscure, technical, or archaic words. They also make other changes in the work. They may reduce the number of meanings provided for each entry, eliminate synonyms and antonyms, cut biographical or geographical entries, and decrease the number of special features.

These ranges offer a broad sense of the types of dictionaries available for adults and upper-level students. They need to be used cautiously, however. The number of entries can vary widely between two dictionaries that, based on publishers' claims, appear to be nearly the same size. Some publishers count every form and variant of a word as a separate entry; others count only the main entry.

Generally speaking, only librarians, scholars, teachers, writers, and language aficionados need unabridged dictionaries. The average adult recognizes only about 20,000 words and customarily uses far fewer than this number in both writing and speech, so an abridged dictionary will be adequate for most households. High school and college students should use college dictionaries; younger students will probably find that a school or student's dictionary suits their needs and language skills. School and children's dictionaries are usually written for junior high or elementary school reading levels, and the entries are selected on the basis of the frequency of their appearance in the textbooks and literature prevalent at the appropriate grade level. Etymologies are often omitted or simplified, and definitions emphasize standard usage.

Children's dictionaries come in three main classes: word books, picture dictionaries, and children's dictionaries. Word books offer pictures and labels for specific objects in the context of a related scene (for example, swings, slides, and ponds at a park); picture dictionaries begin to alphabetize all entries, although most (or all) are still accompanied by illustrations; and children's dictionaries seem like true dictionaries, with several thousand words and definitions.

Word books and picture dictionaries are intended for children before and in the early years of school. Many require that an adult work with the child in using these books; they are more like vocabulary learning tools than true reference works. These books are quickly outgrown, but can be valuable until that occurs.

Picture dictionaries can provide young children with important early experience in looking up words. However, special care must be used in their purchase; there is a wide variation in quality among them. Attractive illustrations alone do not make a good picture dictionary. It is also important to consider such details as the correlation between art and text, the suitability of the concepts and words included, and the accurate presentation of words. Picture dictionaries must also be constructed of durable materials, since they must withstand extensive use that is often less than gentle.

Dictionaries are produced by staffs of editors and specialists who decide which new words have entered the standard lexicon, how technical words are defined, what new meanings have been attached to old words, how pronunciations are shown, and other similar matters. Most new dictionary entries come from files of citations, which are continuously updated collections of words that the publisher's staff cull from current books, periodicals, newspapers, and other sources. Most dictionaries provide standard words and meanings and also include colloquial or slang words and usage commonly employed in newspapers, on radio, or on television.

Lexicographers continually debate whether a dictionary should provide authoritative guidance to correct English or describe current usage. Most dictionaries try to strike a balance between the two extremes of description and prescription. Works that have extensive usage notes provide valuable guidance for the user.

Some dictionaries have more components than others, but a standard entry in an abridged dictionary provides the spelling, pronunciation, syllabication, parts of speech, basic definitions, plurals, and inflected forms for each word. In more comprehensive dictionaries, the main entries may also include etymologies, synonym and antonym studies, and usage labels. These labels indicate whether or not a word is current in a particular field or science or if it is archaic or peculiar to one region or profession. Finally, many dictionaries include several examples or quotations showing how the word is used in standard written English. Some dictionaries use invented examples; others employ real quotations.

Some dictionaries tout themselves as encyclopedic, offering much more than words and definitions. They may contain tables of weights and measures, proofreading marks, biographical and geographical entries, a table of alphabets, maps, and other useful facts.

It is the treatment of words on which dictionaries are judged, however, and the work's scope and the quality and clarity of its entries are the keys to a good dictionary. Many publishers issue a family of dictionaries—the Merriam-Webster, *American Heritage,* and *Webster's New World* line are just a few examples. Each work in the family is drawn from the same database of words, meanings, and illustrative examples. Publishers then fashion the breadth, depth, and features of each individual dictionary to reflect their estimate of the features desired by a particular purchaser. Thus, the dictionary shopper may have a number of different titles that seem satisfactory in terms of approach to language and clarity of definitions.

Electronic Reference Works. Much of what can be said about electronic reference works depends on what kind of work is being discussed—electronic atlases have different features than do electronic dictionaries. The key issue is whether the purchaser would prefer electronic or print media to access the information. Print offers a number of benefits, including ease of access (no equipment is necessary), the ability to scan more material at a given time, and access by multiple users (when comparing computerized encyclopedias with multivolume ones). On the other hand, electronic reference works can provide audio and video to supplement text and offer quicker access to information, a feature that will undoubtedly revolutionize research.

Currently, most electronic reference works are computerized versions of material already available in print. In such a situation, because the core content is the same, the user can simply decide which format and set of features is more congenial. In the future, it is likely that publishers will develop reference materials meant primarily for the computer. It will be interesting to see what shape these works take and what features they offer.

Chapter 2
Comparative Charts

The following comparative charts provide basic factual information about every reference book or set evaluated in *Encyclopedias, Atlases, and Dictionaries.* Organized for quick and easy reference, the charts break down titles according to the broad age and grade levels for which the books are intended. Within each category, works are listed alphabetically by title. The charts include such information as the publisher, the edition reviewed, the page and illustration counts, and the price.

There are two **Encyclopedia** comparative charts. The first of these includes all titles in the *Children's* category. The second lists titles appropriate for the *Secondary and Adult* level. There are two **Atlas** comparative charts, which are divided into these same two categories. The four **Dictionary** comparative charts comprise the following categories: *Children's, Middle School, Secondary and Adult,* and *Special.* This last category includes both English as a second language (ESL) dictionaries and visual dictionaries. Finally, three comparative charts for **Electronic Reference Works** are simply organized by their respective type: *Electronic Encyclopedias, Electronic Atlases,* and *Electronic Dictionaries.*

One suggested method of using these charts is for the prospective buyer to consult them at the outset of the decision-making process. The various categories in the comparative charts for each type of reference book will help the user to focus on titles that are similar in scope (that is, in number of pages, entries, illustrations, and so on). The buyer can also locate titles that are priced within a range that will fulfill other budgetary criteria.

The information given in the charts has been compiled from fact information request forms sent to the publishers of the respective titles, and in many cases from additional direct contact with the publishers. We have made every effort to ensure that this information is complete and up-to-date. When publishers were unable to provide us with precise figures about their books, we have relied on their estimate or on the careful estimates of our reviewers.

ENCYCLOPEDIAS

Title	*Publisher*	*Edition Reviewed © Date*	*Volumes*	*Entries*	*Pages*
Children's Encyclopedias					
Barron's Junior Fact Finder: An Illustrated Encyclopedia for Children	Barron's Educational Series	1989	1	134	304
Childcraft—The How and Why Library	World Book	1993	15	3,000	4,000
Children's Britannica	Encyclopaedia Britannica	1993	20	4,200+	6,832
Compton's Precyclopedia	Compton's Learning Company	1988	16 + teaching guide	445	2,928
The Kingfisher Children's Encyclopedia	Kingfisher Books	1992	1	1,300	816
My First Encyclopedia	Dorling Kindersley	1993	1	370	80
My First Encyclopedia	Troll Associates	1992	1	12	32
The New Grolier Student Encyclopedia	Grolier	1992	22	3,000	2,700
Oxford Children's Encyclopedia	Oxford University Press	1991	7	2,000	1,641
Random House Children's Encyclopedia	Random House	1993	1	450	644
Student Encyclopedia	Troll Associates	1991	1	2,000	128
Usborne Children's Encyclopedia	EDC Publishing	1987	1	59	128
The Young Children's Encyclopedia	Encyclopaedia Britannica	1988	16	642	2,560
Secondary and Adult Encyclopedias					
Academic American Encyclopedia	Grolier	1993	21	28,950	9,864
Barron's New Student's Concise Encyclopedia	Barron's Educational Series	1993	1	15,000	1,170

Contributors[a]	Illustrations	Maps	Index Entries	Price[b]
one author	2,500	80	612	$ 19.95 I S/L discount available
none listed	4,275 color 225 b/w	0	20,000	$249.00 I, S/L $199.00 w/*World Book Encyclopedia*
900+	3,100 color 3,100 b/w	300+	30,000	$459.00 I $369.00 S/L
48	2,600 color 400 b/w	10	2,147	[c]
none listed	2,000 color	260	4,000	$ 31.95 I, S/L
17	450 color	0	400	$ 16.95 I, S/L
one author	110 color	0	126	$ 12.79 I, S/L $ 4.95 paperback
none listed	4,500+	400+	20,000	$319.00 I, S/L
112	28,500 color 1,500 b/w	200	15,000	$200.00
18	3,325 color 175 b/w	40	5,600+	$ 50.00 I, S/L
none listed	182 color	5	0	$ 14.89 I, S/L $ 9.95 paperback
7	650 color	17	1,050	$ 17.96 I, S/L $ 14.95 paperback
none listed	2,675	17	0	$149.50
2,500[d]	16,980 (most in color)	1,090	201,000	$798.00 I, S/L
19	500+	49	15,000	$ 29.95 I, S/L

(*Continued*)

ENCYCLOPEDIAS *continued*

Title	Publisher	Edition Reviewed © Date	Volumes	Entries	Pages
Secondary and Adult Encyclopedias *continued*					
The Cambridge Encyclopedia	Cambridge University Press	1992	1	30,000	1,488
The Cambridge Paperback Encyclopedia	Cambridge University Press	1993	1	19,000	928
Collier's Encyclopedia	Macmillan	1992[e]	24	25,000	19,844
The Columbia Encyclopedia	Columbia University Press (dist. by Houghton Mifflin)	1993	1	50,000	3,048
Compton's Encyclopedia and Fact-Index	Compton's Learning Company	1993[g]	26	34,596	10,692
The Concise Columbia Encyclopedia	Columbia University Press (dist. by Houghton Mifflin)	1989	1	15,000	920
The Encyclopedia Americana	Grolier	1993	30	52,000	26,740
Funk & Wagnalls New Encyclopedia	Funk & Wagnalls	1993	29	25,000	13,056
Grolier Encyclopedia of Knowledge	Grolier	1991	20	22,000	8,320
The New Book of Knowledge	Grolier	1993	21	9,063	10,576
The New Encyclopaedia Britannica	Encyclopaedia Britannica	1993	32	64,128 (Micropaedia) 672 (Macropaedia)	31,919
New Standard Encyclopedia	Standard Educational Corporation	1993	20	17,456	10,292
Oxford Illustrated Encyclopedia	Oxford University Press	1993	9	20,000	3,376
The Random House Encyclopedia, New Revised Third Edition	Random House	1990	1	25,000	2,912
Webster's New World Encyclopedia	Prentice Hall	1992	1	25,000	1,248

Contributors[a]	Illustrations	Maps	Index Entries	Price[b]
100	77 color 750 b/w	700+	0	$ 49.95 I, S/L
100	300 b/w	270+	0	paperback $ 19.95 I, S/L
4,800[d]	4,034 color 10,374 b/w	1,600	450,000	$1,499–$1,699[f] $ 995.00 S/L
100	500+ b/w	500+	0	$ 125.00 I, S/L
500[d]	14,625 color 7,875 b/w	1,360	69,083	$ 395.00 I, S/L
59	150 b/w	16 color 24 b/w	0	$ 39.95 I, S/L
6,500[d]	4,600 color 18,400 b/w	1,300	353,000	$1,168.00 I, S/L
1,056[d]	4,255 color 4,995 b/w	257 color 60 b/w	130,000	$ 170.00–$299.00[f] I, S/L
2,000	11,400 color 600 b/w	1,000	90,000	[c]
1,813[d]	22,632 color 1,968 b/w	1,193	85,000	$ 758.00 I, S/L
6,800[d]	7,150 color 16,685 b/w	1,283	228,274	starting at $1,599[f]
630	12,000 color and b/w	636	103,000	I prices determined by distributor S/L $549.00
400+	1,400 color 1,400 b/w inc. maps	N/A	54,000	$ 265.00 I, S/L
number not given[d]	11,325 color 2,475 b/w	300	0	$ 129.95 I, S/L
61	1,875 color 625 b/w	0	0	$ 75.00 I, S/L

(*Continued*)

ENCYCLOPEDIAS   *continued*

Title	Publisher	Edition Reviewed © Date	Volumes	Entries	Pages
Secondary and Adult Encyclopedias *continued* °					
Webster's New World Encyclopedia, Pocket Edition	Prentice Hall	1993	1	15,000	928
World Book Encyclopedia	World Book	1993	22	17,000	14,000+

[a] Articles unsigned unless otherwise noted

[b] Hardcover unless indicated; I indicates individual price; S/L indicates school/library price

[c] Contact publisher for price information

[d] Some or most articles signed; in case of *Britannica*, signed articles appear in Macropaedia only

[e] Statistics apply to 1993 edition

[f] Cost depends on binding chosen

[g] Statistics apply to 1994 edition

Contributors[a]	Illustrations	Maps	Index Entries	Price[b]
37	0	0	0	paperback $14.00 I, S/L
3,000+[d]	23,200 color 5,800 b/w	2,300+	150,000+	I $599.00–$899.00[f] S/L discount available

ATLASES

Title	Publisher	Edition Reviewed © Date	Pages	Maps	Index Entries	Price [a]
Children's Atlases						
Discovering Maps: A Children's World Atlas	Hammond	1992	80	75	217	$ 11.95[b,c]
The Doubleday Children's Atlas	Doubleday	1987	93	37	1,480	$ 14.00
The Doubleday Picture Atlas	Doubleday	1989	63	26	570	$ 11.99
The Facts On File Children's Atlas	Facts on File	1993	96	56	2,000	$ 15.95
The Gage Atlas of the World	Gage Educational Publishing	1985	192	170	10,500	$ 19.35
Giant Atlas of the World	Rand McNally	1993	13	12	0	$ 27.95
The Global Atlas	Gage Educational Publishing	1993	100	150	2,660	$ 24.20
The Kingfisher Reference Atlas	Kingfisher Books	1993	216	500[d]	8,300	$ 19.95
The Macmillan First Atlas	Macmillan	1991	40	17	182	$ 12.95
The Macmillan School Atlas	Gage Educational Publishing	1993	140	96	2,350	$ 19.35
My First Atlas	Troll Associates	1992	30	13	240	$ 12.79 $ 4.95[b]
National Geographic Picture Atlas of Our World	National Geographic Society	1993	276	58	3,200	$ 27.50[e]
Rand McNally Children's World Atlas	Rand McNally	1992	93	60	480	$ 14.95
Rand McNally Picture Atlas of the World	Rand McNally	1993	80	50	1,850	$ 19.95
The Reader's Digest Children's World Atlas	Reader's Digest	1991	128	61	3,795	$ 20.00
Student Atlas	Troll Associates	1991	128	30	3,500	$ 14.89 $ 9.95[b]
Secondary and Adult Atlases						
Atlas of the World	Oxford University Press	1993	400	238	75,000	$ 65.00
Bartholomew Mini Atlas World	Bartholomew (dist. by Hammond)	1993	192	112	20,000	$ 15.95

Title	Publisher	Edition Reviewed © Date	Pages	Maps	Index Entries	Price[a]
Secondary and Adult Atlases *continued*						
Britannica Atlas	Encyclopaedia Britannica	1992	560	286	170,000	$ 99.50
Concise Atlas of the World	Oxford University Press	1993	264	80	44,000	$ 30.00
The Economist Atlas	Henry Holt	1992	384	48	28,500	$ 47.50
The Great World Atlas	American Map Corporation	1992	367	120	100,000	$ 49.95
Hammond Atlas of the World	Hammond	1994	304	230	115,000	$ 69.95[c]
Hammond Atlas of the World, Concise Edition	Hammond	1993	232	156	60,000	$ 39.95 $ 24.95[c]
Hammond International Atlas of the World	Hammond	1994	168	90	45,000	$ 27.95[c] $ 15.95[b]
Hammond Nova World Atlas	Hammond	1991	176	174	0	$ 10.95[b,c]
Hammond World Atlas, Collectors Edition	Hammond	1993	224	182	7,400	$ 15.95[c]
National Geographic Atlas of the World	National Geographic Society	1992	412	350	150,000	$100.00[e] $ 80.00[b,e]
The New Cosmopolitan World Atlas	Rand McNally	1993	344	236	69,000	$ 60.00[c]
The New International Atlas	Rand McNally	1993	564	286	170,000	$125.00[c]
The New York Times Atlas of the World, New Family Edition	Times Books/Random House	1992	224	84	30,000	$ 37.50
The New York Times Atlas of the World, Paperback Edition	Times Books/Random House	1993	132	54	30,000	$ 22.50[b]
The New York Times Atlas of the World, Third Revised Concise Edition	Times Books/Random House	1993	288	146	100,000	$ 75.00
Rand McNally Goode's World Atlas	Rand McNally	1993	384	422	34,000	$ 29.95 $ 14.00[b]
The Random House Compact World Atlas	Random House	1992	192	112	20,000	$ 12.00
Reader's Digest Atlas of the World	Reader's Digest	1993	240	86	42,000	$ 39.95[c]

(Continued)

ATLASES   *continued*

Title	Publisher	Edition Reviewed © Date	Pages	Maps	Index Entries	Price[a]
Secondary and Adult Atlases *continued*						
Reader's Digest–Bartholomew Illustrated Atlas of the World, Revised Edition	Reader's Digest	1992	176	90	30,000	$ 24.00
Student Atlas of the World	Tuttle	1993	264	75	40,000	$ 30.00[c]
The Times Atlas of the World, Ninth Comprehensive Edition	Times Books/Random House	1994	514	123	210,000	$175.00
Today's World	Rand McNally	1993	200	85	52,000	$ 29.95
World Atlas of Nations	Rand McNally	1993	256	85	52,000	$ 39.95
The World Book Atlas	World Book	1992	432	284	67,000	$ 89.00[c,f]

[a] Hardcover unless otherwise indicated
[b] Paperback
[c] Discount available to schools and libraries
[d] Total includes maps, graphs, charts, and diagrams
[e] Discount available to National Geographic Society members
[f] Discount available when sold with *World Book Encyclopedia*

DICTIONARIES

Title	Publisher	Edition Reviewed © Date	Pages[a]	Entries	Illustrations	Price[b]
Children's Dictionaries						
The American Heritage Children's Dictionary	Houghton Mifflin	1994	864	37,000	800 color	$14.95
The American Heritage First Dictionary	Houghton Mifflin	1994	368	1,800	650 color	$13.95
The American Heritage Picture Dictionary	Houghton Mifflin	1994	144	900	650 color	$10.95
Beginning Dictionary	Macmillan	1987	816	30,000	1,200 color	$35.16[c]
The Doubleday Children's Dictionary	Doubleday	1989	319	8,000	500	$14.95
The Doubleday Children's Picture Dictionary	Doubleday	1986	199	1,500	199 pgs full color	$16.00
The First Thousand Words: A Picture Word Book	EDC Publishing	1989	63	1,000	1,080 color	$11.95
Macmillan Dictionary for Children	Macmillan	1989	896	35,000	1,100 color	$14.95
Macmillan First Dictionary	Macmillan	1990	416	2,200	550 color	$12.95
My Big Dictionary	Houghton Mifflin	1994	40	170	170 + 10 vignettes (color)	$18.95
My First Dictionary	Dorling Kindersley	1993	96	1,000	1,000 color	$16.95[c]
My First Dictionary	Scott, Foresman (dist. by HarperCollins)	1990	448	4,000	1,000 color	$12.95
My First Dictionary	Troll Associates	1992	32	350	350 color	$12.79 $ 4.95[d]
My First Picture Dictionary	Scott, Foresman	1990	312	1,500	1,100 color	$13.95 $10.95[d]
My Pictionary	Scott, Foresman	1990	144	850	850 color	$11.95 $ 8.95[d]
My Second Picture Dictionary	Scott, Foresman	1990	448	4,000	1,000 color	$15.95 $12.95[d]
Round the World Picture Word Book	EDC Publishing	1980	47	600	586 color	$11.95
Scott, Foresman Beginning Dictionary	Scott, Foresman	1993	832	28,000	860 color 215 b/w	$17.95
The Sesame Street Dictionary	Random House	1980	253	1,300	all full color	$15.95

(Continued)

DICTIONARIES *continued*

Title	Publisher	Edition Reviewed © Date	Pages[a]	Entries	Illustrations	Price[b]
Children's Dictionaries *continued*						
Thorndike-Barnhart Children's Dictionary	Scott, Foresman (dist. by HarperCollins)	1991	832	28,000	860 color 215 b/w	$14.95
Webster's Elementary Dictionary	Merriam-Webster	1986	600	32,000	600 color	$14.95
Webster's New World Children's Dictionary	Prentice Hall	1991	896	33,000	700 color	$16.00
Words for New Readers	Scott, Foresman (dist. by HarperCollins	1991	312	1,500	1,100 color	$10.95
Young People's Dictionary	Troll Associates	1991	128	1,248	250 color	$14.89 $ 9.95[d]
Middle School Dictionaries						
The American Heritage Student's Dictionary	Houghton Mifflin	1986	992	70,000	2,000 b/w	$16.95
The Christian Student Dictionary	Bob Jones University Press	1982	864	13,000	700 color 700 b/w	$19.95
HBJ School Dictionary	Harcourt	1990	1,088	60,000	1,600	$24.99
The Lincoln Writing Dictionary	Harcourt	1989	934	35,000	700	$28.26
Macmillan Dictionary	Macmillan	1987	1,184	95,000	1,800	$36.16[e]
Macmillan Dictionary for Students	Macmillan	1984	1,216	90,000	1,800	$16.95
Macmillan School Dictionary	Macmillan	1987	1,136	65,000	1,500	$35.28[e]
Scott, Foresman Advanced Dictionary	Scott, Foresman	1993	1,328	100,000	1,442	$17.95
Scott, Foresman Intermediate Dictionary	Scott, Foresman	1993	1,098	68,000	1,240	$17.95
Thorndike-Barnhart Student Dictionary	Scott, Foresman	1993	1,302	100,000	1,500	$16.95
Webster's Intermediate Dictionary	Merriam-Webster	1986	960	65,000	1,000	$13.95
Webster's New World Dictionary for Young Adults	Prentice Hall	1992	1,040	47,500	600+	$18.00
The World Book Student Dictionary	World Book	1993	900	30,000	1,000	$23.00

Title	Publisher	Edition Reviewed © Date	Pages[a]	Entries	Illustrations	Price[b]
Secondary and Adult Dictionaries						
The American Heritage College Dictionary	Houghton Mifflin	1993	1,630	200,000	2,500 b/w	$ 19.95[f]
The American Heritage Desk Dictionary	Houghton Mifflin	1981	1,184	100,000	1,500 b/w	$ 12.95
The American Heritage Dictionary of the English Language	Houghton Mifflin	1992	2,140	350,000	4,000 b/w	$ 45.00
The American Heritage High School Dictionary	Houghton Mifflin	1993	1,630	200,000	2,500 b/w	$ 21.95
Cassell Giant Paperback Dictionary	Cassell (dist. by Sterling)	1993	1,600	160,000	0	$ 16.95[c,d]
Cassell Student English Dictionary	Cassell (dist. by Sterling)	1993	1,024	110,000	0	$ 14.95[c]
The Compact Oxford English Dictionary	Oxford University Press	1992	2,416	290,500	0	$ 325.00
The Concise Oxford Dictionary of Current English	Oxford University Press	1991	1,504	120,000	0	$ 27.50[g]
Fearon New School Dictionary	Globe/Fearon	1987	1,267	70,000	0	$ 17.90
The Little Oxford Dictionary of Current English	Oxford University Press	1986	720	34,000	0	$ 11.95
Merriam-Webster's Collegiate Dictionary, Tenth Edition	Merriam-Webster	1993	1,559	160,000	700 b/w	$ 19.95[f,g,k]
The New Shorter Oxford English Dictionary	Oxford University Press	1993	4,000	97,600	0	$ 125.00
Oxford American Dictionary	Oxford University Press	1980	832	35,000	0	$ 21.00 $ 9.95[d]
The Oxford Encyclopedic English Dictionary	Oxford University Press	1991	1,824	70,000	200 most b/w	$ 35.00
The Oxford English Dictionary, Second Edition	Oxford University Press	1989	22,000[h]	290,500	0	$2,750.00
The Oxford Modern English Dictionary	Oxford University Press	1993	1,287	90,000	0	$ 19.95
The Pocket Oxford Dictionary of Current English	Oxford University Press	1990	900	49,000	0	$ 14.95

(Continued)

DICTIONARIES   *continued*

Title	Publisher	Edition Reviewed © Date	Pages[a]	Entries	Illustrations	Price[b]
Secondary and Adult Dictionaries *continued*						
The Random House Unabridged Dictionary, Second Edition	Random House	1993	2,520	315,000	2,400	$ 100.00
Random House Webster's College Dictionary	Random House	1992	1,600	180,000	700	$ 18.00[g]
Webster Comprehensive Dictionary: Encyclopedic Edition	J. G. Ferguson	1992	1,728[j]	90,000	1,500	[i]
Webster Comprehensive Dictionary: International Edition	J. G. Ferguson	1992	1,536[j]	90,000	1,500	[i]
Webster Illustrated Contemporary Dictionary: Encyclopedic Edition	J. G. Ferguson	1992	1,149	85,000	970	[i]
Webster's Encyclopedic Unabridged Dictionary	Random House Value Publishing	1993	1,854	270,000	2,000	$ 14.00
Webster's New Ideal Dictionary	Merriam-Webster	1989	671	60,000	100 b/w	$ 12.95
Webster's New World Dictionary, Third College Edition	Prentice Hall	1994	1,574	150,000	650	$ 18.00[g]
Webster's School Dictionary	Merriam-Webster	1986	1,184	85,000	953	$ 15.95[c]
Webster's Third New International Dictionary of the English Language, Unabridged	Merriam-Webster	1993	2,764	460,000	3,105 b/w 2 color plates	$ 99.95[k]
Webster's II New Riverside University Dictionary	Houghton Mifflin	1988	1,536	200,000	400 b/w	$ 17.95
The World Book Dictionary	World Book	1993	2,430[j]	225,000	3,000 b/w	$ 99.00[k,l]
Special Dictionaries						
Collins COBUILD English Language Dictionary	HarperCollins	1992	1,728	40,000	0	$ 40.00
The Facts On File Junior Visual Dictionary	Facts On File	1989	160	5,000	800	$ 18.95
The Facts On File Visual Dictionary	Facts On File	1986	800	3,000	3,000	$ 29.95

Title	Publisher	Edition Reviewed © Date	Pages[a]	Entries	Illustrations	Price[b]
Special Dictionaries *continued*						
Longman Dictionary of American English: A Dictionary for Learners of English	Longman/ Addison-Wesley	1983	792	38,000	15 pages	$ 15.95[d]
Longman Dictionary of Contemporary English, New Edition	Longman/ Addison-Wesley	1987	1,229	56,000	500	$ 25.95[d]
Longman Dictionary of English Language and Culture	Longman/ Addison-Wesley	1992	1,528	80,000	500	$ 29.95[d]
Longman Language Activator	Longman/ Addison-Wesley	1993	1,587	1,052	12	$ 29.95[d]
The Macmillan Visual Dictionary	Macmillan	1992	892	25,000	3,500	$ 45.00[c]
Oxford Advanced Learner's Dictionary of Current English	Oxford University Press	1989	1,598	57,100	1,820	$ 23.95 $ 15.95[d]
Oxford-Duden Pictorial English Dictionary	Oxford University Press	1981	820	28,000	28,000	$ 15.95[d]
Oxford Elementary Learner's Dictionary of English	Oxford University Press	1981	303	10,000	450	$ 11.95[d]
The Oxford ESL Dictionary	Oxford University Press	1991	752	35,000	140	$ 10.95[d]
Webster's Basic English Dictionary	Merriam-Webster	1990	600	32,000	600 color	$ 14.95

[a] One volume unless otherwise indicated
[b] Hardcover unless otherwise indicated
[c] Discount available to schools and libraries
[d] Paperback
[e] School discount available
[f] Deluxe edition(s) priced slightly higher
[g] Thumb-indexed edition priced slightly higher
[h] 20 volumes
[i] Contact publisher for price information
[j] 2 volumes
[k] Cost depends on binding chosen
[l] Discount when purchased with *World Book Encyclopedia*

ELECTRONIC REFERENCE WORKS

Title	Publisher	Edition Reviewed © Date	Platform Reviewed	Media
Electronic Encyclopedias				
Compton's Interactive Encyclopedia	Compton's NewMedia	1994 (version 2.01VW)	*Windows*/MPC	CD-ROM
The Concise Columbia Encyclopedia, Second Edition (in Microsoft Bookshelf '94)	Microsoft	1994	*Windows*	CD-ROM
Information Finder (Encyclopedia)	World Book	1993 (version 2.40)	DOS	CD-ROM
Microsoft Encarta Multimedia Encyclopedia	Microsoft	1994	*Windows*/MPC	CD-ROM
The New Grolier Multimedia Encyclopedia	Grolier	1993 (version 6.01)	*Windows*/MPC	CD-ROM
The New Grolier Multimedia Encyclopedia (online)	Grolier	1994	Apple Macintosh	online
The Random House Encyclopedia: Electronic Edition	Microlytics	1990	DOS	floppy disk
Electronic Atlases				
Hammond Intermediate World Atlas (in Microsoft Bookshelf '94)	Microsoft	1994	*Windows*	CD-ROM
PC Globe Maps 'N' Facts	Brøderbund	1993	DOS	CD-ROM
Picture Atlas of the World	National Geographic (dist. by Karol Media)	1992	DOS	CD-ROM
The Software Toolworks World Atlas	Software Toolworks	1993	Apple Macintosh	CD-ROM
Electronic Dictionaries				
The American Heritage Dictionary (in Microsoft Bookshelf '94)	Microsoft	1994	*Windows*	CD-ROM
The American Heritage Illustrated Encyclopedic Dictionary	Xïphias	1990–1993 (version 4.3)	DOS	CD-ROM

Entries	Illustrations	Video	Audio	Price
33,000 (encyclopedia) 70,000 (dictionary)	7,000	yes	*yes*	$149.95
15,000+	1,300+	yes	yes	$ 99.95 [a,g]
17,000	0	no	no	$599.00 [a,c,h]
26,000	8,400	yes	yes	$139.00 [a]
33,000	4,000	yes	yes	$395.00
12,197	0	no	no	varies [b]
20,000	0	no	no	$ 69.95 [a]
N/A	160 [d]	no	yes	$ 99.95 [a,g]
N/A	700 [d]	no	no	$ 49.95
N/A	800 [d]	yes	yes	$ 99.00
300+	5,000+	yes	yes	$ 69.95 [a]
350,000+	2,000+	no	yes	$ 99.95 [a,g]
180,000	4,000	no	yes	$ 39.95

(*Continued*)

ELECTRONIC REFERENCE WORKS   *continued*

Title	Publisher	Edition Reviewed © Date	Platform Reviewed	Media
Electronic Dictionaries *continued*				
Funk & Wagnalls Standard Desk Dictionary	Inductel	1992 (version 2.0)	DOS	floppy disk
Information Finder (Dictionary)	World Book	1993 (version 2.40)	DOS	CD-ROM
Macmillan Dictionary for Children— Multimedia Edition	Macmillan New Media	1993	*Windows*	CD-ROM
The Oxford English Dictionary: Second Edition on Compact Disc	Oxford University Press	1992	*Windows*	CD-ROM
The Random House Unabridged Dictionary, Second Edition	Random House	1993	DOS, *Windows*, Macintosh[e]	CD-ROM
Webster's Ninth New Collegiate Dictionary	Highlighted Data	1989 (version 1.2)	Apple Macintosh	CD-ROM

[a] School discount available
[b] Price varies with online service
[c] Discount available with *World Book Encyclopedia*
[d] Number indicates map count
[e] All platforms contained on same disc
[f] $159.00 for both disc and print version
[g] Price for entire *Microsoft Bookshelf* package
[h] Price for entire *Information Finding* package

Entries	Illustrations	Video	Audio	Price
100,000	0	no	*no*	$ 79.95[a]
225,000	0	no	no	$599.00[a,c,h]
12,000	1,000	yes	yes	$ 39.95
290,500	0	no	no	$895.00
315,000	0	no	no	$ 79.00[f]
160,000	600	no	yes	$199.95[a]

PART TWO

Encyclopedias

Chapter 3
What to Look for in Encyclopedias

After many years in which the encyclopedia market was dominated by just a few publishers—World Book, Encyclopaedia Britannica, and Grolier, primarily—encyclopedia publishing has now become a field of increased activity. Grolier has issued two new sets, as have such major publishers as Random House and Oxford University Press. Where once the COLUMBIA ENCYCLOPEDIA stood virtually alone as a one-volume reference work, it now faces competition from three reputable publishers—Cambridge University Press, Random House, and Simon & Schuster. Other titles—notably Macmillan's *Merit Students Encyclopedia*—are now no longer published. With the growing availability of computers, there has been a boom in the publication of computerized encyclopedias, offering automatic searching capabilities as well as the excitement of audio and video. (For a discussion of electronic encyclopedias, see Chapter 14 of this Buying Guide; for reviews of electronic encyclopedias, see Chapter 15.) Meanwhile, the traditional encyclopedia publishers have continued to update and improve their works.

In this newly dynamic area of publishing, librarians desiring to purchase encyclopedias for their general or children's reference collections and consumers thinking of buying an encyclopedia for home use are more confused than ever. What makes a good encyclopedia? How can one work be compared with another? These questions plague the potential purchaser, who often does not have access to the many competing works to be able to make thorough judgments on his or her own. This chapter and the following two chapters (which offer reviews of children's encyclopedias and secondary and adult en-

cyclopedias) attempt to give that confused buyer some guidance when considering such a purchase. This assistance is especially important because many encyclopedias require a substantial investment.

Characteristics and Uses of Encyclopedias

The reviews in this Buying Guide consider only general encyclopedias. Such topical works as *The Baseball Encyclopedia* or *The Encyclopedia of the Confederacy* are excluded. (For reviews of such works, see *Topical Reference Books,* New Jersey: R. R. Bowker, 1991.) While the works reviewed here differ widely, virtually all share a common goal: to present an encapsulation of our knowledge of our world in all fields of study. Size, scope, and intended audience, as well as the financial resources allocated to the task, create many different approaches to this goal. Indeed, it is fascinating to see how similar information can be organized or presented in such varying ways.

The value of each encyclopedia, then, depends on how well its approach meets the information needs of the individual user. No matter how good it may be, no one work can satisfy the needs of all users. The first issue in considering an encyclopedia purchase must be to determine its intended use.

The many possible uses tend to cluster in two broad areas. Some works are designed for ready reference, answering such questions as how many moons Jupiter has and who has served as Chief Justice of the Supreme Court. Others offer sophisticated discussion of complex subjects such as subatomic particles or the history of mathematics, often complete with suggestions for further reading. Librarians, who serve many and varied patrons, need to select works for their reference shelves that meet both these needs. Consumers, with more limited resources and more focused needs, usually can choose one of these uses as more important—though many encyclopedias now available do not completely sacrifice one for the other.

In addition to these two broad areas, encyclopedias differ in other ways, such as the relative coverage devoted to various subject areas, the extent and nature of the illustration program, and the use of finding aids. We attempt to reveal these differences through our reviews.

Structure of the Reviews

Encyclopedias may be assessed according to a number of criteria. In the reviews that appear in the next two chapters, we evaluate each work using these criteria, allowing the prospective buyer to make informed decisions based on their importance to him or her. This chapter details what those criteria are and the specific issues our reviewers addressed related to each. The result is a guide to what a librarian or consumer should look for when shopping for an encyclopedia.

In preparing these reviews, we have followed a standard structure to facilitate comparison from work to work. Indeed, the reviewers often directly compare one work with another. Care was taken to ensure that such comments are made between truly comparable works. It is unreasonable to judge the RANDOM HOUSE ENCYCLOPEDIA as wanting because it doesn't have the depth of WORLD BOOK or to challenge the NEW BRITANNICA as inappropriate for young children. Such comments betray a misunderstanding of the fundamentally different editorial directions of these works. Judicious comparisons of works in the same category, however, can shed light on the nature and merits of each work.

The following section explains the structure of the reviews and explores the issues addressed within each topic.

Facts at a Glance. Beginning each review is a listing of basic factual information about the work, such as the names of the publisher and editor; the number of volumes, pages, entries, words, cross-references, index entries, and illustrations; the intended readership (in terms of ages or grade level); the trim size, binding, and price; and ordering information. This information was supplied by the work's publisher and was accurate at the time it was given. When the publisher did not supply the information, the data printed here is followed by the notation (reviewer estimate).

Because many encyclopedias are revised annually, the specifications of a more current edition may differ from those printed here; price, too, is subject to change.

Introduction. The body of each review begins with a general statement about the intended purpose of the encyclopedia under discussion. This overview states the work's size (in volumes, pages, entries, words, and illustrations), intended audience, and general aims. In many cases these aims are quoted directly from the publisher's or editor's description of the work. This introduction also indicates which edition was reviewed.

Authority. Many readers assume that an encyclopedia—*any* encyclopedia—is necessarily a trustworthy source of information and that the authors of encyclopedia articles are well qualified to write about their chosen subjects. In reality, however, there is no guarantee that what is printed in an encyclopedia is any more authoritative than the opinion expressed by the average person on the street. An encyclopedia is the result of a massive collaborative effort involving hundreds of scholars, writers, editors, artists, and other specialists. The excellence of any encyclopedia, then, depends on the knowledge and communication skills of those who participated in that effort.

For this Buying Guide, *authority* refers to the reputation of the publisher and the qualifications of the work's editors and contributors. In this section, therefore, reviewers briefly comment on the history of the encyclopedia under consideration, summarizing its general reputation and noting any recent changes in ownership or editorial policy that may have an impact on its trustworthiness.

The second most important criterion for evaluating authority is to judge the qualifications of those who participated in the work. Some encyclopedias contain articles written by experts; others use freelance writers and editors to create the text. The use of freelancers should not be interpreted as a mark against the work. Professional writers and editors frequently are able to convey the essence of a subject more clearly to laypeople in the intended audience than could experts. It is crucial to the authority of an encyclopedia, however, that outside experts at least authenticate articles and illustrations for accuracy and clarity. Generally speaking, the use of academics in this expert role adds more authority than reliance on individuals from corporations or professional organizations. Should the names of such interested parties constitute a substantial number of the contributors, it may be fair to doubt the work's objectivity. Our reviewers examine the credentials of the contributors in light of these factors.

The reviewers also note the extent to which the contributors' or consultants' work is clearly identified. Signed or initialed articles offer the reader some assurance that the cited authority has, theoretically at least, read the article prior to publication and verified its accuracy or suggested revisions. Many encyclopedias do not have signed articles but do identify what subjects were submitted to the scrutiny of individual experts. The willingness of these experts to link their names to specific topics provides the prospective purchaser with a degree of comfort in the work's reliability.

Scope. This section provides an important overview of the encyclopedia's range and contents. Reviewers report some basic statistics about the encyclopedia, such as the average length of typical articles and the general maximum and minimum length. This information provides a sense of whether the work favors broader, more inclusive general entries or shorter, more focused specific entries.

In this section reviewers also try to indicate the general extent of coverage in the work, grouping entries according to broad subject areas (such as the humanities, geography, and science), and noting the percentage of entries given to biographies. Reviewers also comment on the extent to which these biographies profile women and members of "minority" groups. These estimates are based on the reviewers' perusal of a randomly chosen 50-page segment of the work. Reviewers attempt to point out relative strengths and weaknesses of coverage in these areas. They include a partial list of the articles found in this analysis, to give the reader some flavor of the range of subjects covered.

Reviewers also comment on whether the work leans more toward traditional, historical, and academic coverage or more toward high-interest topics. This issue may be of particular importance in the reviews of children's encyclopedias. An important function of these works is to pique the young user's interest by supplying background to enable him or her to understand familiar topics such as the seasons, animals, and means of transportation.

To provide a further perspective on the work's scope, reviewers examined a randomly chosen 25-page segment of the work to determine the extent to which entries reflect non-American subjects. Here, too, they reproduce representative article titles.

Reviewers report on depth of coverage by indicating the amount of space devoted to certain standard topics in each work. For children's encyclopedias, the entries examined are **Louisa May Alcott, dinosaurs, Martin Luther King, Jr., Mexico, Middle Ages, painting,** and **soccer.** For adult encyclopedias, the entries are **castle,** *Hamlet,* **Impressionism, Nelson Mandela, Mexico, Elvis Presley,** and **Tyrannosaurus rex.** By comparing the length of these articles in different encyclopedias, the reader can develop a sense of the balance of coverage in each work. Reviewers may also discuss the depth of coverage of other topics of their own choosing.

Currency. Unlike newspapers, magazines, and specialized journals, encyclopedias are not intended to provide newsworthy information. However, an encyclopedia should reflect current understanding of the subjects it

covers and include significant recent developments. This is particularly important in entries on contemporary figures, ongoing political events, and scientific subjects.

Most of the multivolume encyclopedias reviewed here are revised and reissued annually. The extent of the revision—whether major or minor—varies from publisher to publisher and may take one of several forms. Some publishers focus on a few volumes in each revision, making major changes in topics that appear in those volumes (although they may also change major articles in other volumes that must be updated due to new developments). Others revise articles more generally throughout the set. Virtually all publishers update statistics and other factual information regardless of the volume where that information appears.

These issues are particularly important given the volatility of the political world in the past five years. Recently, for instance, encyclopedia publishers have faced the need to update coverage of Germany, the Soviet Union, and South Africa, among other countries. The difficulty of reflecting currency in an encyclopedia is compounded by two factors. First is the fact that any encyclopedia contains multiple appearances of major subjects like these countries. It is not enough, then, to change the article on Germany to reflect its reunification. Related entries such as **communism, NATO,** and **Europe** must also be updated, and all maps that contain either of the two former German states must be fixed to note the reunified nation. Second is the fact that the encyclopedia must often go to press before the changes are fully developed. For instance, this edition of the Buying Guide reviews the 1993 editions of most encyclopedias. These works were published during the breakup of the former Yugoslavia. As a result, each encyclopedia editor had to describe a fluid situation—a difficult task.

The way in which articles are revised also varies from work to work. Some articles reflect new information only in their introductory lines and an illustration or two; others undergo a thorough rewriting that makes the revised version, in effect, a new article. Thoroughness of changes is thus an important factor in determining the currency of an encyclopedia.

With an understanding of the complexity of these issues, our reviewers assessed the currency of each encyclopedia. They analyzed the coverage of the following topics in children's encyclopedias: **Bill Clinton,** the **food pyramid** (the federal government's new standard for presenting nutritional guidelines), the **Persian Gulf War, Russia,** and **space exploration.** Reviews of adult encyclopedias examined **Bill Clinton,** the **food pyramid,** the **Hubble Space Telescope, Frida Kahlo, Lithuania,** the **Persian Gulf War,** and **Russia.** Both children's and adult encyclopedias were examined to ensure that maps reflected the unification of Germany and of Yemen and the breakups of Czechoslovakia, the Soviet Union, and Yugoslavia. (Reviewers could also choose other entries to check for currency.) The evaluation of the work's currency was also based on how up-to-date statistics and illustrations were.

It is important to use the comments on currency in these reviews fairly. If you are reading this book some years after its publication, it is quite possible that a lapse in currency noted here has since been corrected and brief entries on current topics have been expanded. The minor coverage of Bill Clinton in this edition, for example, is likely to be expanded in the future. The comments here, then, are to be taken as an accurate picture of the currency of a particular edition at a specific time, not a statement about a permanent condition. They do, however, provide a suggestion of the thoroughness with which the editors of a given work approach updating. Of course, the comments on currency about works that are not revised annually still apply in the future. If a reviewer found an encyclopedia lacking in currency on a given topic when the review was written in 1994, it will be even less current in later years.

Accuracy. As educational tools and self-styled repositories of human knowledge, encyclopedias have a responsibility to present accurate information. An encyclopedia that is inaccurate has no value other than as a curiosity. Of course, no reference book, no matter how carefully written, reviewed, and edited, is entirely error free. In a well-edited encyclopedia, however, any errors or inconsistencies will generally be so slight as to be insignificant.

Apart from honest mistakes, other factors may contribute to an encyclopedia's lack of accuracy. These can include oversimplification, generalization, and imprecise writing. A set's currency and scope may also affect accuracy.

To determine the general accuracy of each encyclopedia reviewed, the editors of the Buying Guide have drawn on the expertise of a number of subject specialists, each of whom read the entries for a particular subject in all of the encyclopedias. The entries reviewed for accuracy in children's encyclopedias included **cancer, comet, Congress, Henry VIII,** and **oxygen.** For adult encyclopedias, these subject specialists examined the entries for **cancer, comet, Henry VIII, House of Representatives,** and **oxygen.** Their findings are presented in the body of the review. Generally they found that encyclopedia editors are to be congratulated for the correctness of their information. The reviews of children's encyclopedias, however, revealed a tendency to ignore and obscure important facts out of the desire to make articles brief and understandable. This is one area in which the editors of the Buying Guide hope that encyclopedia publishers will improve their efforts. We understand the need to shape information in terms of length, complexity, and diction to match the young user's abilities and

interest level. Nevertheless, to emphasize brevity at the expense of accuracy—and clarity—is to shortchange children and give them little credit for their very real intellectual curiosity.

In addition to reporting the findings of our content specialists, reviewers were invited to examine articles about topics within their own range of knowledge. They also conducted a spot check of randomly selected statistics, dates, and names.

Clarity. Clarity derives from the internal structure of an encyclopedia's entries as well as from the overall quality of the writing and readability.

Internal structure involves the organization of information within the entry. Reviewers assess whether extended articles begin with a general overview of the subject and then move on to consider more complex details. They comment on whether subheads divide longer articles into logical, well-defined component parts. They note the presence of an outline or other feature that gives the user an overview of the structure of lengthy articles.

Clarity also involves readability, of course. Whatever the specific subject being looked up or the age level of the reader, the encyclopedia user tends to approach the work from the point of view of the nonspecialist. The adult wanting to read an overview of cancer or the fourth grader who wants to know about spiders for a school paper both come to the work with little background in the field. Thus an important criterion for judging an encyclopedia is how clearly it conveys information to its intended audience. Are specialized terms well defined? Can each article be understood on its own terms, or is it necessary to seek clarification by consulting related entries? Of course, a degree of cross-referencing is necessary—even desirable—but readers, especially young ones, can be frustrated by an endless chain of searches for enlightenment.

In addition to discussing these aspects of clarity, reviewers also describe the general writing style and its benefits and drawbacks. To convey a flavor of the works, we reprint a small portion of an entry. The topics—**fingerprints,** for children's encyclopedias, and *Titanic,* for adult works—were chosen to offer representative subjects of general interest that required the presentation of basic facts and some technical information.

Objectivity. People consult encyclopedias primarily to learn particular facts and to find background information on specific subjects. These works are intended to inform, not persuade, the reader; an encyclopedia article is not the same as a newspaper editorial and serves its purpose only if it presents accurate information without bias.

The responsible encyclopedia editor filters out writers' biases, whether they are intentional or unconscious. However, when controversy is part of the subject, it should be noted and explained. One way to test the objectivity of an encyclopedia, then, is to examine how it deals with controversial issues. Our reviewers evaluate whether each work takes a particular stand on such issues or presents information from a particular perspective, whether blatant or subtle. Where more than one side exists on an issue, the content should fairly present the arguments of each opposing view. Reviewers also point out when controversy is completely ignored.

An encyclopedia can reflect bias in other ways as well. Contributors may express personal opinions. If so, the reviewer must determine how this affects the overall objectivity of particular articles. It is possible that these opinions, clearly expressed as such and reasonably substantiated by supporting evidence, can provide a refreshing breath of spontaneity in a work that is otherwise so balanced as to be bland.

Our reviewers examined a number of entries in each encyclopedia for objectivity. These articles included **discrimination, Northern Ireland,** and **ozone layer** for the children's works and **AIDS** (particularly issues related to demographics, access to treatment, and civil rights), **capital punishment, Northern Ireland,** and **ozone layer** for the adult works. Of course, these are not the only subjects that could be used for this purpose, but they are representative of those subjects likely to provoke debate. Reviewers also note instances of exceptional objectivity or bias in other articles.

Accessibility. Encyclopedias contain thousands of entries and often millions of words. The organization of entries and the inclusion of other features to allow readers to find those words quickly are very important factors in the usefulness of an encyclopedia. One key factor is whether the items chosen as entries are logical and clear and likely to be points of access for the intended audience. A children's encyclopedia should have a different list of entry words than a work meant for an older, more knowledgeable audience.

The preface generally contains information about the work's finding aids, such as the guide words typically found at the top of each page. Many works contain an introductory section on how to use these finding aids. The clarity and comprehensiveness of this information is important in determining the work's accessibility and is an area on which the reviewers comment.

Two other features—cross-references and an index—generally aid access. Cross-references are vital aids that can lead the user to unanticipated connections, pursuit of which can expand or clarify the reader's understanding of the entry originally consulted. Some single-volume works lack an index and rely exclusively on cross-references to notify the reader of related topics. Reviewers comment on the effectiveness and consistency of cross-references in each work.

The most important aid to accessibility is the index, which helps users who know what they want to look up but may not know where to find it. Reviewers assessed the comprehensiveness of the index, spot-checking entries for accuracy and analyzing cross-references for consistency. They also noted whether illustrations and other special features are indexed.

Special Features. Nearly all general reference encyclopedias attempt to enhance their usefulness with a number of special features. Those most commonly found are illustrations and bibliographies.

The illustration program may contain a wide variety of images, including photographs, art reproductions, drawings, schematic diagrams, maps, charts, graphs, and tables. The reviewers assessed the clarity, attractiveness, variety, and quality of these images. (Currency and accuracy of illustrations are addressed under the appropriate headings.) These issues are particularly important in children's encyclopedias, where so much information is conveyed visually. In addition to evaluating the illustrations in terms of these factors, reviewers also looked at the people depicted in illustrations to determine whether women and members of minority groups are shown in reasonable numbers and in varied roles.

The illustration programs of single-volume encyclopedias (except for the RANDOM HOUSE ENCYCLOPEDIA) are generally less extensive and less colorful than those of the multivolume works. It would be unfair to criticize these works for not competing with the multivolume sets in this regard, as the choice was a deliberate decision related to their scope and pricing. Nevertheless, the quality of the illustrations that they *do* contain is an appropriate area of comment.

Encyclopedias are generally not intended as the last word on a given subject, but rather represent a starting point for further research. As such, encyclopedia editors recognize the importance of providing guidance for more advanced study and often provide bibliographies. Reviewers evaluate the strength of these bibliographies by looking at where they appear (they are more useful when they follow the article, rather than being gathered in a separate, easily overlooked, spot), how extensive they are, whether the reading level of the listed sources is indicated, and how up-to-date they are.

While many encyclopedias contain illustrations and bibliographies, the inclusion of other special features is more idiosyncratic. Some children's encyclopedias include information of special interest in the margins or offer special how-to projects that enable the young reader to carry out simple scientific experiments or perform some other activity. Reviewers comment on these and other special features, noting their nature, frequency of appearance, and effectiveness.

Format. The size, number of volumes, and durability of the binding may be determining factors for the prospective buyer, especially the librarian. In this section, reviewers assess the ease with which the reader can use the set and comment on the durability of its binding.

Layout and design can enhance—or hinder—accessibility. Reviewers comment on the clarity and functionality of the design by describing the typographical treatment of entry headings, subheads, and other features.

Summary. Each review concludes with a brief summary that reviews the encyclopedia's major strengths and weaknesses. The summary indicates the readership that the encyclopedia would best serve and makes general comparisons of the work with similar, competitive encyclopedias when appropriate. References to reviews in other published works are also provided in the summary.

Derived Works. Some encyclopedias are derived from longer works, employing the same basic organization but condensing the number of entries, the coverage within entries, or both. Reviews of these encyclopedias are shorter and are organized under subheads as follows:

Facts at a Glance
Introduction, Format, and Authority
Scope and Special Features
Summary

These reviews refer the reader to the review of the main work for a full discussion of such issues as currency, accuracy, legibility, and accessibility, noting only any differences between the derived and main works on these points. The main thrust of these derived reviews is the "Scope and Special Features" section, in which the reviewer explains the content of the derived work and assesses its appropriateness for the target audience.

Facsimiles. Accompanying most encyclopedia reviews is a page reproduced from the work in question. These facsimiles, photoreduced to fit on the pages of our book, give the reader a feel for what the work looks like and allow us to highlight the special features and typical structure of the work. The pages are selected to provide a general sense of how the information is organized, but the reader should note that no one page could possibly do justice to the variety of information, illustrations, and page designs that an encyclopedia must employ. Also, because color originals have been transferred to black-and-white pages in our book, these facsimiles offer only the most general sense of the look of an encyclopedia—they obscure the quality of reproduction of illustrations in the encyclopedia and cannot possibly convey color. Nevertheless, we think that they provide a useful first glance at the works being reviewed, although we urge prospective purchasers to leaf through an actual copy of the encyclopedia before making a final decision.

Glossary

For users of this guide who may be unfamiliar with some of the terms employed in these reviews, the following glossary is provided:

annual revision. The practice of most multivolume encyclopedia publishers, in which major and minor changes are made in the content of a publication each year.

authenticate. To establish any article or information contained in an encyclopedia as being genuine, accurate, and authentic.

authenticator. A qualified authority responsible for critically examining an article and ensuring its reliability and accuracy. See also **consultant; contributor.**

completely revised edition. Any edition of a previous work that has been critically reviewed, authenticated, revised, brought up-to-date, reedited, and typographically reset.

consultant. An expert or specialist who provides professional advice, reviews original entries on specific topics, and makes recommendations to the editor. See also **authenticator; contributor.**

contributor. A person (such as a consultant, freelance writer, or staff writer) who provides written information for inclusion in an encyclopedia. See also **authenticator; consultant.**

cross-reference. A finding aid. A word or phrase, often in italic or boldface type or small capital letters, that directs the reader to another related entry or article for additional information. Cross-references may appear within, alongside, or at the end of the article in question. A *main-entry cross-reference* is found as a separate entry in the main alphabetical sequence; it indicates that information on the topic is found under another name.

editor. The person who is responsible for the contents and organization of a written work. The main editor of an encyclopedia will usually manage a staff of editors who carry out the actual editing of the entries.

entry. A self-contained article, listed under a subject heading (also called the *entry word*) and dealing with that subject.

general entry. A broadly focused entry that deals with a large subject (such as an entire historical period or artistic movement rather than a single historical figure or artist). Often lengthy and discursive, general-entry articles may include interpretations of the subject in addition to specific facts. Compare **specific entry.**

guide words. The word or words at the top of a page that repeat the first or last entry words on that page.

major revision. For reference books, an edition that is changed beyond the regularly scheduled program of changes. A major revision requires reediting, resetting of type, new illustrations, and extensive inclusion of new material. May also refer to an extensive overhaul of individual entries; see **minor revision.**

minor revision. Slight changes in the content of a reference work. May also refer to minor updates of this nature to individual entries; see **major revision.**

multivolume. A word describing any encyclopedia in which information is presented in more than one volume.

ready-reference. A phrase describing a reference work that provides concise, easily accessible, factual information.

revise. To change or edit material in order to improve or update it. If material in an encyclopedia has been checked and reviewed and changes are actually made, it has been **revised;** if the material is checked and reviewed but no changes are made, it is **authenticated.**

revised edition. A work that has been changed in some way from an earlier edition. These alterations can range from minor corrections in typography and minor revisions to a **completely revised edition.**

specific entry. An entry that focuses on a single, narrow subject or on a single aspect of a broader subject (such as one historical figure or artist rather than an entire historical period or artistic movement). Usually concise rather than discursive, specific-entry articles concentrate on the main facts related to a subject. Compare **general entry.**

subhead. A heading within an entry that indicates a major subdivision of a topic.

Chapter 4
Evaluations of Children's Encyclopedias

Barron's Junior Fact Finder: An Illustrated Encyclopedia for Children

Facts at a Glance

Full title: **Barron's Junior Fact Finder: An Illustrated Encyclopedia for Children**
Publisher: Barron's Educational Series
Author: Jean-Paul Dupré
Edition reviewed: © 1989

Number of volumes: 1
Number of articles: 134
Number of pages: 304
Number of words: 52,392
Number of cross-references: none
Number of index entries: 612
Number of maps: approximately 80
Number of illustrations: approximately 2,500
Intended readership: ages 7 to 11
Trim size: 7" × 10¼"
Binding: hardcover

Price: $19.95; discount available to schools and libraries
Sold directly to libraries and schools; also sold in bookstores and other retail outlets
ISBN 0-8120-6072-5
No stated revision policy

Introduction

Barron's Junior Fact Finder is a one-volume illustrated encyclopedia for children ages 7 to 11. First published as a one-volume encyclopedia in France in 1987, under the title *Visa Junior,* it was translated by Marguerite and Albert Carozzi and repackaged for an American market by Barron's in 1989. Its 304 pages contain 134 articles and approximately 2,500 color illustrations. The publisher's ambitious claim is that students will find in this volume answers to all their more commonly asked questions, from school or elsewhere.

Authority

The encyclopedia was first published in France by Editions Fernand Nathan in 1987 and is the work of a single author, Jean-Paul Dupré. The preface, entitled "A Few Words to Young Readers," cites "an entire team of experts" as having contributed to the book, although they are not listed by name. Barron's, although best known for its academic test-preparation guidebooks, is also the publisher of BARRON'S NEW STUDENT'S CONCISE ENCYCLOPEDIA, reviewed in this guide.

Scope

The encyclopedia contains 134 articles grouped into eight broad categories. History is covered in the longest section (about 22 percent of the text). This is followed by coverage of physical science (18 percent), geography (15 percent), mathematics (13 percent), natural science

Barron's Junior Fact Finder: An Illustrated Encyclopedia for Children

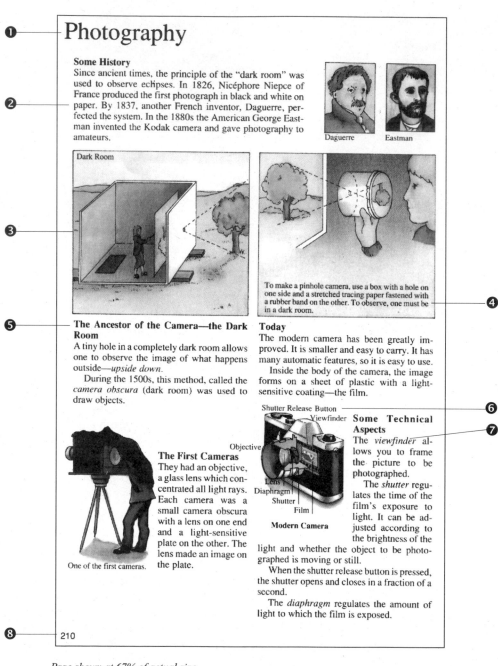

Photography

Some History

Since ancient times, the principle of the "dark room" was used to observe eclipses. In 1826, Nicéphore Niepce of France produced the first photograph in black and white on paper. By 1837, another French inventor, Daguerre, perfected the system. In the 1880s the American George Eastman invented the Kodak camera and gave photography to amateurs.

Daguerre   Eastman

Dark Room

To make a pinhole camera, use a box with a hole on one side and a stretched tracing paper fastened with a rubber band on the other. To observe, one must be in a dark room.

The Ancestor of the Camera—the Dark Room

A tiny hole in a completely dark room allows one to observe the image of what happens outside—*upside down*.

During the 1500s, this method, called the *camera obscura* (dark room) was used to draw objects.

Today

The modern camera has been greatly improved. It is smaller and easy to carry. It has many automatic features, so it is easy to use.

Inside the body of the camera, the image forms on a sheet of plastic with a light-sensitive coating—the film.

Objective

The First Cameras

They had an objective, a glass lens which concentrated all light rays. Each camera was a small camera obscura with a lens on one end and a light-sensitive plate on the other. The lens made an image on the plate.

One of the first cameras.

Shutter Release Button
Viewfinder
Lens
Diaphragm
Shutter
Film

Modern Camera

Some Technical Aspects

The *viewfinder* allows you to frame the picture to be photographed.

The *shutter* regulates the time of the film's exposure to light. It can be adjusted according to the brightness of the light and whether the object to be photographed is moving or still.

When the shutter release button is pressed, the shutter opens and closes in a fraction of a second.

The *diaphragm* regulates the amount of light to which the film is exposed.

210

Page shown at 67% of actual size.

❶ Boldface main entry heading is on a line by itself, making it easy to find

❷ Illustrated introduction explains the subject

❸ Four-color illustration

❹ Caption explains the illustration

❺ Subentry gives information about a related topic

❻ Diagram with callouts

❼ Important words italicized

❽ Page number

(11 percent), language and its uses (10 percent), English grammar (6 percent), and arithmetic (5 percent).

Virtually all articles are identical in length, spanning two pages (including illustrations). The brief entries in this encyclopedia are intended as general introductions to topics frequently studied by elementary school children.

Currency

Published in 1989, this encyclopedia is now badly out-of-date in some sections. Articles like **Emerging World Powers, East-West: The Two Blocs,** and **Major Changes in the Post-War World** now seem quite ancient in light of events in the former Soviet Union and Eastern Europe. Statistical data in various articles in the geography section is also out-of-date.

Since all of the illustrations are color drawings, they tend to date more slowly than photographs. The illustration of the Berlin Wall now seems out of place, however, and the map of Asia shows the Yemens as separate countries and the U.S.S.R. as it existed prior to 1991. Under **Human Rights Today,** South Africa is described as having a white government that "rules over the black majority of the country with a policy of *apartheid.*"

Accuracy

The information presented in the encyclopedia is generally accurate but very brief. For example, only two countries, Canada and the United States, receive separate articles in the geography section; all others are treated in one of five continent articles. These show a country's location on the continent map and highlight its flag, area, population, capital, monetary unit, and principal language.

The map of major languages in the section "Language and Its Uses" is not well reproduced, making it difficult to distinguish French-speaking areas from those where Italian or Portuguese is the main language. On this same map, it is unclear which countries have more than one major language group.

Exploration is treated in an article entitled **The Age of Great Discoveries.** Only four explorers are mentioned: Columbus, da Gama, Magellan, and Cartier. Of Columbus it says only that in 1492 he searched for the western route to India; there is no mention of his other voyages or of the significance of his discoveries.

The illustrations in the "Natural Science" section on **How Life Begins, Respiration, Blood—Stream of Life,** and **The Sense of Touch** are excellent and will engage children in the desired age group. One inaccuracy, however, stems from the book's French origin: a drawing labeled "Pollution of the Hudson River" shows the Eiffel Tower.

Clarity

Entries are written in a clear, readable style with short, declarative sentences predominating. While written using a simple vocabulary to appeal to school children in the elementary grades, the tone is rather academic and pedestrian. Few attempts are made to provide a lighter touch or some humor. One notable exception is the black-and-white drawing of recent world leaders done in caricature with a pipe-smoking Stalin leading the procession.

Objectivity

The encyclopedia is objective but somewhat limited in its coverage. For example, in the article **Four Great Religions,** equal space is given to Judaism, Christianity, Islam, and Buddhism. Coverage of Africa includes an article on **Colonialism,** and under **Human Rights Today,** there is a brief discussion of racism, torture, and refugees. There is also discussion of the debate over **Nuclear Power.** Many other controversial issues, such as AIDS, are ignored.

Accessibility

Since the encyclopedia is organized by subject groupings rather than alphabetically, it will be more difficult for students to use than traditionally organized volumes or sets. Topics are principally found by using the "Contents" section at the beginning of the book or by using the index. The latter is very short (seven pages with only 612 entries). Random checks of selected subjects turned up no errors in the index.

Special Features

An important special feature is the large number of lavish illustrations. Those of trees, mushrooms, common plants, and flowers are outstanding. Almost all 2,500 illustrations are in color and were drawn especially for this encyclopedia. The article **Signs and Symbols** contains illustrations of sign language, U.S. road signs, Morse code, semaphore signals, and Braille.

Another special feature is the inclusion of problems and answers in mathematical sections. Puzzles to solve, including a crossword puzzle and box of letters, appear in the section **Playing With Words.**

The work contains no cross-references, lists of sources for additional reading, or bibliography.

Format

Children in this age group will be able to hold the volume easily. The sewn bindings allow it to be opened easily and lie flat, even at the beginning and end of the book.

The design is attractive, with key words printed in boldface or italics and illustrations nicely organized on the pages.

Summary

For another opinion about *Barron's Junior Fact Finder,* see *Booklist (Reference Books Bulletin),* March 1, 1990.

Barron's Junior Fact Finder, while attractively packaged, is now badly in need of updating and revision to reflect the dramatic changes that have occurred in the world in recent years.

In addition, because of its subject arrangement, it is less accessible for students than traditional alphabetically arranged one-volume and multivolume encyclopedias, such as THE KINGFISHER CHILDREN'S ENCYCLOPEDIA or CHILDREN'S BRITANNICA. Finally, while brevity may be an advantage for the youngest students in the intended market for this work, it will certainly cause irritation for older students who need additional information.

Childcraft—The How and Why Library

Facts at a Glance

Full title: **Childcraft—The How and Why Library**
Publisher: World Book
Editor: Dominic Miccolis, Executive Editor
Edition reviewed: © 1993

Number of volumes: 15
Number of articles: 3,000 (reviewer estimate)
Number of pages: more than 4,000
Number of words: 750,000 (reviewer estimate)
Number of cross-references: none
Number of index entries: 20,000 (reviewer estimate)
Number of illustrations: 4,500 (reviewer estimate), 95 percent in color
Intended readership: preschool to grade 6; volume 15 is for parents of young children
Trim size: 7¼″ × 9¾″
Binding: hardcover

Price: $249 (when sold separately); $199 (with *World Book Encyclopedia*)
Sold directly to schools and libraries; also sold door-to-door
ISBN 0-7166-0193-1
Revised periodically; preparation of new edition begun in December 1993

Introduction

Childcraft—The How and Why Library has been continuously published by World Book (under various titles) since 1934. This is not an encyclopedia in the traditional sense; rather, it is an attractively illustrated and informative set of books to inspire a joy of learning in children from preschool through the elementary grades. It is de-signed so that adults and children can work together in exploring each volume.

The 1993 edition, with more than 4,000 pages, is published in 15 volumes. This set introduces young children to literature, natural and physical science, mathematics, social studies, and themselves. The volumes include not only information, but also activities, experiments, and crafts for preschool and school-age children.

Authority

The World Book publishing company is known for WORLD BOOK ENCYCLOPEDIA, one of the most popular encyclopedias. Its reputation and the longevity of *Childcraft* indicate a tradition of producing quality products. *Childcraft's* editorial staff is headed by William H. Nault, the publisher, and Dominic Miccolis, the executive editor. Nault was also the chair of the advisory board for the most recent edition of the WORLD BOOK ENCYCLOPEDIA. The team includes seven editors and nine specialists in research and library science.

Volumes 1 to 3 contain excerpts from the works of many well-known writers of children's literature. Articles in volumes 4 to 14 were researched, written, and edited chiefly by *Childcraft's* staff, and are unsigned. Nine special consultants (listed in volume 15) provided technical assistance and advice in preparing six of those volumes. Volume 15, intended for parents, lists more than 40 specialists who wrote or reviewed the articles.

Scope

Childcraft is divided into 15 volumes. Volumes 1 to 3 contain literature. The first volume consists of nursery rhymes, poems, fairy tales, and fables that adults can read aloud to children. Volume 2 is designed for both reading aloud and for the child to read. It introduces many familiar characters, such as Pippi Longstocking, Frog and Toad, Paddington Bear, and Amelia Bedelia. The third volume, which includes legends, folktales, fantasy, and poetry, is for children who are more advanced readers. The legends are multicultural and include a Native American story, an Australian legend, and a West African folktale.

Volumes 4 to 7 deal with topics about the world and space, including the earth, outer space, animals, plants, and the sea. Articles in volume 8 are about the people in over 50 nations and their lifestyles, beliefs, customs, foods, and houses.

Most of the encyclopedia's biographical and historical information is contained in volume 9, which covers birthdays of famous men and women, national celebrations, and religious holidays.

Volume 10 presents well-known places from the "Seven Wonders of the Ancient World" to famous landmarks, buildings, parks, and historical sites.

Childcraft—The How and Why Library

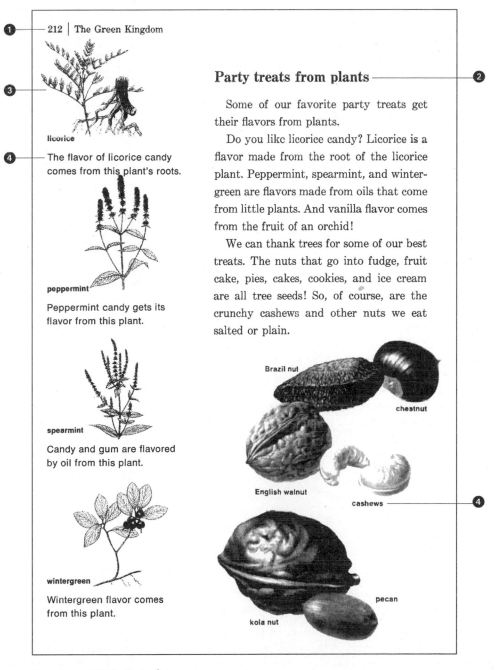

1 212 | The Green Kingdom

3 licorice

4 The flavor of licorice candy comes from this plant's roots.

peppermint

Peppermint candy gets its flavor from this plant.

spearmint

Candy and gum are flavored by oil from this plant.

wintergreen

Wintergreen flavor comes from this plant.

Party treats from plants — **2**

Some of our favorite party treats get their flavors from plants.

Do you like licorice candy? Licorice is a flavor made from the root of the licorice plant. Peppermint, spearmint, and wintergreen are flavors made from oils that come from little plants. And vanilla flavor comes from the fruit of an orchid!

We can thank trees for some of our best treats. The nuts that go into fudge, fruit cake, pies, cakes, cookies, and ice cream are all tree seeds! So, of course, are the crunchy cashews and other nuts we eat salted or plain.

Brazil nut

chestnut

English walnut

cashews — **4**

pecan

kola nut

Page shown at 72% of actual size

1 Page number and guide words (volume title on left-hand pages, section title on right hand pages)

2 Main entry heading in boldface type
3 Four-color illustrations include both drawings and photographs

4 Caption

Volume 11 has more than 300 projects for children, ranging from woodworking to nature crafts. Volume 12 explains how things work, including machines, sound, light, heat, motion, and electricity. Volume 13 includes games, puzzles, and facts that involve mathematics (with answers included for all problems and puzzles).

Volume 14 deals with how people are alike and yet different. It explores the human body, what makes a family, growing, learning about the world, and understanding feelings.

Volume 15 contains four sections for parents. The first is on children's growth and development; the second contains topics, such as divorce and moving, for special consideration; the third is a medical guide; and the fourth shows how to use *Childcraft* at home and in the classroom.

Because of *Childcraft*'s unique thematic organization, it is difficult to compare it with other encyclopedias reviewed in this Buying Guide. However, since 6 of the 15 volumes are devoted to the world around us, and a further 3 are devoted to literature, it is clear that the work is strongly weighted toward science, social studies, and the humanities. Much effort has been made in the text to present cultures from around the world in the coverage of religion, customs, food, housing, games, holidays, and historical figures. The illustration program also reflects various racial, cultural, and ethnic groups.

In general, the work is aimed at a younger readership than other multivolume children's sets such as the CHILDREN'S BRITANNICA or THE NEW GROLIER STUDENT ENCYCLOPEDIA. The children's literature in volumes 1 to 3 and the activities in volumes 11 to 13 also make *Childcraft* more entertaining and interactive than traditional encyclopedias.

Currency

Many of the topics used by the Buying Guide to measure currency are not included. Neither Bill Clinton nor Boris Yeltsin is mentioned. The breakup of the Soviet Union, the reunification of Germany, and the Gulf War are not included. Good nutrition is covered, but the food pyramid is not.

Information on Russia concentrates on the Russian people and culture as well as on special holidays and festivals. However, updating is evident in this excerpt from "Maypoles and parades": "in Russia and some other countries, Communist governments have changed to other kinds of governments."

Much of volume 4 covers the earth and solar system, but little attention is paid to space exploration. *Voyager I* and *II* are mentioned as sources of information about the planets, but little text is devoted to the subject. A photograph of the Hubble Space Telescope is included as well as photographs of astronauts.

Modern technology is not given much coverage either. Although computers, telephones, and radios are discussed, modems, fax machines, compact discs, and global communication are not. *Childcraft* also fails to cover such current topics as drugs, diseases, violence, discrimination, war, and political unrest.

Many of the illustrations in the children's volumes are timeless—for example, pictures of wild animals, or illustrations for poems—so currency is not a factor. However, some of the photographs in volume 15 (for parents) are dated, and the drawn art in that volume looks old-fashioned.

Accuracy

Although the information in *Childcraft* is accurate, some topics that are important for this age group are omitted. For example, the article on **D-day** says that it was a military secret, it was delayed because of weather, and it was the beginning of the end of the war. The problem with the article is that there is no cross-reference to information on World War II, which is necessary for a thorough understanding of the subject.

The **cancer** article is essentially correct. However, in the final paragraph, *surgery* is misrepresented. The article states that physicians may prefer to remove both benign and cancerous tumors surgically. In fact, surgery is done to remove malignant tissue. If malignant tissue remains, the cancer is still present and *will* grow unless treated by other means.

The two paragraphs on **comets** are accurate, but one sentence is misleading because it compares the orbits of comets to the orbits of planets.

Oxygen is covered in two articles: **Kinds of Matter** and **Building Blocks.** All of the material in these articles is correct and written at a level appropriate for its intended audience.

Clarity

Childcraft is written in a simple and clear style. Only volume 15, written for adults, varies from the upbeat, conversational tone that characterizes the work. The following excerpt from the article on **mirrors** in volume 12 offers an example of this style:

> Who is that person in the mirror? It seems to be another you, doing exactly what you are doing. How can a mirror "copy" you?
>
> A mirror is very smooth. The front of a mirror is flat, polished glass. Behind the glass is a thin layer of silver or some other kind of shiny material.
>
> As you stand in front of a mirror, light bounces off you and passes through the glass. When the light hits the shiny layer behind the glass, it bounces straight back. This is why you can see yourself.

In the text, difficult words are defined and accompanied by pronunciation guides. Volumes 4 to 8 and 12 to

14 contain alphabetical lists of "New Words" at the back, with definitions and pronunciations.

Objectivity

Childcraft avoids most controversial topics. There are no entries for *Northern Ireland, discrimination,* or the *ozone layer.* Of the potentially controversial topics selected by the Buying Guide for examination, *pollution* is the only one discussed, and it is handled in a matter-of-fact manner in the volumes about animals, plants, and the sea.

Major world religions, including Christianity, Judaism, Islam, and Buddhism, receive balanced coverage. There are also stories from various racial and ethnic groups such as Native Americans, Africans, Russians, Chinese, and Japanese. Creation myths from various cultures are also included in a simple and straightforward manner.

Accessibility

Twenty-two indexes are provided in the 15 volumes. Volumes 1 to 3 have indexes of authors, titles, and first lines, which make locating a particular story or poem easy. Volume 1 also has a subject index. Volumes 4 to 14 have subject indexes at the end of each volume. Volume 15 has a comprehensive subject index for all of the volumes.

The indexes make use of *see* and *see also* references to direct the user to alternative terms or related topics. For example, under **vision** one is instructed to *"see* **sight,"** and under **sight** one is directed to *"see also* **eye."** Illustrations are also indexed. Before each index, there is a brief explanation on how to use it to find information.

Special Features

One of the strengths of *Childcraft* is the number of special features included. For instance, the illustrations are outstanding. There are works by famous artists, such as Frederic Remington's "Custer's Last Stand" and Raphael's frescoes. Drawn art, such as the star charts of the constellations in **Planets, Stars, and Galaxies,** complements many entries. Illustrations reflect different races, ethnic groups, and cultures. Males and females are equally represented throughout.

The list of "Books to Read" at the end of Volumes 4 to 14 is a special feature of this work. The titles provide additional in-depth information about subjects discussed in the volume. These are arranged by age, with the first group for ages 5 to 8 and the second for ages 9 to 12. All citations are up-to-date, ranging from 1980 to 1990.

The guide to *Childcraft* in volume 15 is another noteworthy feature. The editors explain how the volumes are organized, the skills they are trying to help children develop, and the best ways to introduce the volumes to children and to make use of them. Although most of the information given is oriented toward adults who will be using the books with their children at home, a 14-page set of "Curriculum enrichment guides" links specific sections of the encyclopedia to a typical primary school curriculum. These guides may be of use to teachers.

Format

Childcraft is a handsome, hardcover set of books. The bindings are sturdy, and the pages are durable enough to stand up to heavy use. The type size varies from volume to volume, depending on the intended readership. Most volumes have single-column text, many illustrations, and well-laid-out pages with wide margins and plenty of white space.

Summary

For another opinion on the 1991 edition, see *ARBA 93,* Carol L. Noll, pp. 24–25.

Childcraft—The How and Why Library is a beautiful set of books for the preschool and elementary age child to explore. The illustrations are excellent, and the simple approach to learning is appealing. The use of literature in the form of poems, stories, fairy tales, folk legends, and well-chosen excerpts from popular authors will help children to develop a love of reading. The wide range of subjects opens up a world of learning to children. The lack of maps is a major weakness, especially in the volumes on exploration and famous places, and some controversial topics, such as discrimination, should be covered in an encyclopedia of this size. For parents who want a traditional format, CHILDREN'S BRITANNICA might be a better choice. However, in terms of color and interesting things to read and do, *Childcraft* is unsurpassed.

Children's Britannica

Facts at a Glance

Full title: **Children's Britannica**
Publisher: Encyclopaedia Britannica
Editor: James Somerville
Edition reviewed: © 1993

Number of volumes: 20
Number of articles: more than 4,200
Number of pages: 6,832
Number of index entries: 30,000
Number of maps: 2 atlases with 152 pages of maps in volume 19; about 250 additional maps throughout the encyclopedia
Number of illustrations: 3,100 four-color; 3,100 black and white
Intended readership: upper elementary to middle school (reviewer estimate)
Trim size: 7½" × 9¼"

Binding: hardcover
Price: $459; discount available to schools and libraries
ISBN 0-85229-237-6
Revised annually

Introduction

The 20-volume *Children's Britannica* is a general encyclopedia for children. The articles, arranged in alphabetical order, have been prepared by authorities in the various subject areas. According to the encyclopedia's preface, "Many biographies are included, their subjects representing most fields of human endeavor through the ages and around the world."

Authority

Children's Britannica is published by Encyclopaedia Britannica, best known as the publisher of THE NEW ENCYCLOPAEDIA BRITANNICA and its predecessors.

The first edition of *Children's Britannica* was published in the United Kingdom in 1960 and revised twice. The work was extensively revised for its fourth edition in 1988 "to adapt the encyclopedia for young students living in the technological age of the late 20th century and to do so on a broad, international basis." This edition was the first to be published in the United States and has been updated yearly.

James Somerville heads *Children's Britannica's* editorial staff. The team includes seven associate editors, four contributing editors, and two editorial consultants.

The encyclopedia's entries are not signed, but a list of more than 900 "text authorities" who wrote and critiqued the articles appears in the final volume. This wide-ranging list includes such names as the Boy Scouts of America; dance critic Walter Terry; D. Elizabeth Martin-Clarke, the author of *Culture in Early Anglo-Saxon England;* Roscoe Pound, former Dean of Harvard University's Law School; and the Ford Motor Company.

Scope

Children's Britannica contains about 4,200 entries, but, as the publisher notes, "it also has information on some 35,000 subjects." The length of individual articles in the set varies considerably; for example, about one-third of a page is devoted to an article on **albino,** three-quarters of a page to **fencing,** 2½ pages to **family,** 10 pages to **American literature,** and 15 pages to **Rome, Ancient.** The average article covers about three-quarters of a page.

After checking a 50-page sample in volume 7, we found that the encyclopedia gives greatest weight in its coverage to history and social studies (33 percent) and science (30 percent). About 18 percent of the articles focus on geography, and the rest deal with the humanities, popular culture, and other subjects. About 12 percent of the entries in this sample were biographies.

For the most part, the articles focus on topics that are relevant to 8- to 14-year-olds (the target audience). The emphasis, however, is more on traditional and historical subjects than on contemporary ones. Although the work is suitable for the U.S. market—it has good European and historical coverage—there is definitely a British orientation. For example, 2½ pages are devoted to **fife,** a local government region in Scotland and ancient Scottish kingdom. The article entitled **lift** begins with the statement: "In the United States and Canada lifts are known as elevators." Roughly 30 percent of the articles are devoted to topics not related to Britain, Canada, or the United States, such as the mythological Greek king **Agamemnon** and the French actor and playwright **Molière.**

The question of allocating appropriate space to topics according to their importance is certainly a subjective one. However, the 4¾ pages devoted to **boxing** and the 7½ pages given to **soccer** seem excessive, while the space accorded to **fat** (one-half page) and **dinosaur** (1½ pages) seems inadequate. Our list of standard entries gives an indication of the relative weight accorded to various topics in *Children's Britannica:* **Louisa May Alcott** receives ⅓ page, **Martin Luther King,** ⅔ page, **dinosaur** and **Middle Ages** 1½ pages each, **Mexico** 6⅓ pages, and **painters and painting** 16½ pages.

Currency

The 1993 edition of *Children's Britannica* is the fifth annual updating of the 1988 major revision. In many cases, the updating of articles is superficial. A sentence or two has been added about major developments of the past few years, but the body of the article remains unchanged. The large percentage of black-and-white and old photographs in the illustration program gives an overall dated look to the encyclopedia.

A review of such current topics as the United Nations, the Gulf War, Russia, and the food pyramid reveals that the record on updating since 1990 is spotty. For example, the article on the **United Nations** lists 160 member countries, whereas at the end of 1992, there were 178 members.

There is no article on the Gulf War. Coverage of the war and its repercussions is scant—14 lines in the **Iraq** article, 15 lines in **Kuwait,** and 3 lines in the **George Bush** article.

There is an 11¾-page article on **Russia,** but the coverage of events after the breakup of the Soviet Union is extremely limited, and the article contains no photographs relating to any events or people after 1917. More detail about the events leading up to the end of the

Children's Britannica

182 MYNAH

in 1789 on board the British ship HMS *Bounty*; for more about it, see the article BOUNTY, MUTINY OF THE.

A mutiny may sometimes be caused by political discontent. This was one of the causes of the Indian Mutiny, or War of Independence, of 1857. Indian soldiers refused to obey the orders of their British officers and this mutiny led to a more general uprising by Indians against British rule (see INDIAN MUTINY).

Those who take part in a mutiny are usually brought to trial before a military court, or court martial. Throughout history, the death penalty has frequently been imposed for mutiny, particularly for mutiny during time of war.

MYNAH. The mynahs are birds of the starling family. They are native to Asia, though they have been introduced into other countries.

The common, or Indian, mynah (*Acridotheres tristis*), is about 20 centimetres (8 inches) long and is brown and black, with white in the wing and tail, orange skin around the eyes, and heavy dark wattles. It can be taught to talk, but the true talking mynah is the hill mynah (*Gracula religiosa*) of southern Asia, called the grackle in India. A little bigger than the Indian mynah, the grackle is glossy black in colour, with white wing patches, yellow wattles, and orange bill and legs. It can

NHPA/E. Hanumantha Rao

The common mynah is a noisy bird that feeds on the ground in open country, often in small flocks.

imitate the human voice better than any other bird.

The crested mynah (*Acridotheres cristatellus*) is black with white wing patches and yellow legs. Native to China, it has been introduced to Vancouver Island, British Columbia, Canada.

MYRTLE. The myrtles are shrubs or small trees with sweet-scented, evergreen leaves growing in pairs opposite each other, on short stalks or on the plant stems themselves. If a leaf of the common myrtle (*Myrtus communis*) is held up to the light, tiny holes like pin-pricks will be seen all over it. These are the little oil glands where the scent of the shrub is produced.

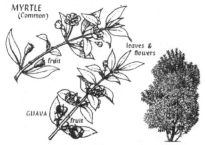

MYRTLE
(Common)

leaves & flowers

fruit

GUAVA fruit

The myrtles belong to the family Myrtaceae, and are therefore relations of the eucalyptus, another plant with scented leaves. There are about 16 species of myrtles, and they grow all over the warm and tropical parts of the Earth. The common myrtle is a very leafy bush. It is from 3 to 4.5 metres (9.5 to 15 feet) high and it has sweet-scented white flowers which blossom during summer. The berries are roundish and purple-black. It grows wild in western Asia but was brought to Europe a very long time ago. It is about the hardiest species and therefore best for growing in English gardens. The Chilean guava (*Myrtus ugni*) comes from Chile and has white flowers and edible red berries.

The myrtle was a tree of Venus, the goddess of love, and so the chief temple of Venus at Rome was surrounded by a myrtle grove. In

Page shown at 72% of actual size.

❶ Page number and guide word

❷ Interior cross-references indicated by small capitals and usually placed within parentheses

❸ Capitalized main entry word in boldface type

❹ Scientific name given in italics

❺ Illustrations include photographs and drawings with callouts

❻ Caption gives additional information

❼ Measurements given in both metric and standard systems

U.S.S.R. can be found in an article entitled **Union of Soviet Socialist Republics, History of,** but this article is not cross-referenced in **Russia.** However, the maps are up-to-date.

There is no reference in the encyclopedia to the food pyramid. The **nutrition** article is vague and somewhat dated. It does not even mention cholesterol or different types of carbohydrates or fats. There is a separate article on **fat** and one on **carbohydrate,** but the only explanation of cholesterol is in the index.

Accuracy

The information presented in *Children's Britannica* seems to be accurate. There are lapses—the date for the launching of the Hubble Space Telescope is given as 1991 in the **telescope** article rather than 1990; **John Hancock** is introduced as "the person to sign the Declaration of Independence," though his role as the first signer is correctly stated later in the article; and the article on **Geological History** erroneously states that "The Paleozoic Era lasted 45 million years" (instead of 345 million).

On the whole, though, misleading or dated information is more common than outright error. In **cancer,** for example, the text states that the most common form of treatment for cancer is surgery; in fact, the most common treatment today is a combination of surgery, chemotherapy, and radiation. Also, information presented on the most common types of cancer in men and women is now obsolete.

Henry VIII contains no factual errors, but the article occasionally borders on distortion in an attempt to simplify the material—as in the statement that "people were discontented with the church's preoccupation with making money rather than giving spiritual guidance." The article on **oxygen** is technically correct, but there are a few instances where vague wording obscures the writer's intended meaning. In the **Congress of the United States** entry, everything is accurate.

Our astronomy adviser, however, was disappointed with *Children's Britannica*'s treatment of the **comet** article, finding numerous inappropriate word choices and confusing or unnecessary paragraphs.

Clarity

Children's Britannica is written in a somewhat discursive style with longer and more convoluted sentences than American schoolchildren are accustomed to. The following one-sentence description of Henry VIII's adviser makes the point:

> Thomas Wolsey, who soon became Cardinal Wolsey and the king's chief adviser, was a very clever man who saw that England could become important by taking advantage of the fact that France and Spain hated each other and

were more eager to gain the support of England against the other.

Although the articles are organized logically, they are not highly structured. As a rule, only the longer articles (two or more pages) have subheads. The tone of the writing seems appropriate for middle school children, though fifth graders may find the reading heavy going. American spelling is used. Weights and measures are given first in metric form with pounds, inches, and so on in parentheses.

A quotation from **fingerprints** offers another typical example of the style in which *Children's Britannica* is written:

> No one in the world has fingertip patterns exactly like anyone else's in every detail. Even the fingerprints of identical twins are not exactly the same. Sir Francis Galton, a noted scientist of the 19th century, discovered that the patterns never change throughout life, although the skin may become wrinkled and cracked with old age.

Objectivity

The general impression is one of evenhandedness. The articles do not generally reflect a strong point of view. The difficult topics of **prejudice** and **racism** are handled with sensitivity and some sophistication. The discussion of the ozone layer in **oxygen** and **atmosphere** is brief and noncommittal. The article on **Northern Ireland** describes the issues dividing the warring parties and the years of violence but remains fairly uninvolved.

There are a few lapses, however, in the tolerant, balanced approach. The **Jehovah's Witnesses** article takes a slightly condescending tone toward the group and its beliefs, and a photograph in the article shows two Jehovah's witnesses importuning a woman in the doorway of her home. In **Indonesia,** a caption proclaims blithely: "Every day in Bali a bright and cheerful Hindu ceremony is taking place somewhere on the island."

Accessibility

The entry words are clear but, as noted earlier, the choice of topics is somewhat slanted toward British readers. Cross-references are indicated by capital letters within parentheses in the text "(see ASTRONOMY)" or by the phrase "See also" at the end of an article.

Cross-references are logical but not entirely consistent. As noted earlier, the article on **Union of Soviet Socialist Republics, History of** has no cross-reference to a separate article in the encyclopedia on **Russia;** nor does **Russia** contain a cross-reference to **USSR, History of.** There are no references to **Yeltsin** in the articles on **Gorbachev, Russia,** or **USSR, History of,** and the **Yeltsin** article contains no references to **Gorbachev, Russia,** or **USSR, History of.**

The index in volume 20 is an integral part of the encyclopedia. It contains 30,000 words, many with capsule entries. It starts off with a six-page introduction, "How to Use the Index," that describes the index as a "miniencyclopedia." If illustrations appear with a topic, they are so indicated in the index.

The index is clear and very helpful in guiding the reader to appropriate articles, but it also suffers from some lapses. The headings of the **Union of Soviet Socialist Republics** and **Russia,** for example, include a reference to the entry **Yeltsin** but not to **Gorbachev** or **Stalin.**

Special Features

Almost every spread in *Children's Britannica* has illustrations—photographs, drawings, diagrams, charts, or maps. All of the volumes (except the index volume) contain signatures with four-color illustrations (about 20 percent of the pages) and two-color illustrations (about 10 percent). Most of the drawings are two-color or black and white. Those of the *how it works* type are quite clear.

The illustrations do not always relate well to the article. **Dinosaur,** for example, includes drawings of six types of dinosaurs—not one of which is discussed in the text. There are more pictures of males than of females throughout the set, but this is partly a result of the many historical topics in the encyclopedia. The overwhelming majority of the illustrations show white people. The captions are generally very thorough and explain or describe, rather than simply name, the object shown.

Most of the maps are two- or four-color. The two-color maps within the text have very little detail. The four-color political-physical maps in the Atlas (volume 19) are extremely detailed, but on some of them the type is quite small and difficult to read (France and Spain); on others there is so much type that it is hard to make sense of the map (Florida). The world physical map is illegible.

There are no bibliographies in the encyclopedia.

Format

The volumes are small enough to make them easy for a middle school child to handle. The type is easy to read and printed on good-quality stock. The page is nicely laid out but a bit dense for younger children. Entry words, set in boldface in capital letters, are easy to find; subheads stand out well. Pages that are in the color section are quite attractive. The black-and-white pages with the older illustrations are dull by comparison.

Summary

For other opinions regarding *Children's Britannica,* see *ARBA 92* (Bohdan S. Wynar), page 15; and *Booklist (Reference Books Bulletin),* September 15, 1993, page 174.

Despite its British orientation, spotty updating, and occasional inaccuracies, *Children's Britannica* may be a useful work for middle school children. Its articles tend to provide more historical background and more analysis than comparable articles in THE NEW GROLIER STUDENT ENCYCLOPEDIA. On the other hand, the articles in GROLIER'S are generally shorter, more straightforward, easier to read, better illustrated, and more attuned to American children. *Children's Britannica*—its title notwithstanding—is suitable for slightly more sophisticated readers. It would be a good library addition to a collection that already has a basic American encyclopedia such as GROLIER'S; it is half again as expensive as that work, however, and as a result is not recommended for home purchase.

Compton's Precyclopedia

Facts at a Glance

Full title: **Compton's Precyclopedia**
Publisher: Compton's Learning Company
Editors: David L. Murray; Howard L. Goodkind
Number of contributors: 48
Edition reviewed: © 1988

Number of volumes: 16, plus teaching guide
Number of articles: 445
Number of pages: 2,928
Number of words: 800,000
Number of cross-references: 400 (reviewer estimate)
Number of index entries: 2,147
Number of maps: 10
Number of illustrations: 3,000; 87 percent in color
Intended readership: ages 4 to 8
Trim size: 8″ × 9½″
Binding: hardcover

Price: contact publisher for price information
ISBN 0-85229-479-4
No stated revision policy

Introduction

Compton's Precyclopedia is designed for children in kindergarten through fourth grade. Published in 1988, the work contains 445 articles arranged in alphabetical order. The work is divided into 16 volumes and contains 2,928 pages and 800,000 words. Each volume begins with 24 pages of activities that, according to the explanatory note in volume 1, "will contribute to the development of the whole child—intellectually, socially, emotionally, and physically." The work contains 3,000 illustrations, 87 percent of which are in color. Because this encyclopedia is intended to be used by teachers, a paperback teaching guide, which contains a subject index and a curriculum index, accompanies the set.

Authority

Compton's Precyclopedia is based on THE YOUNG CHILDREN'S ENCYCLOPEDIA, published by Encyclopaedia Britannica. Since *Compton's* contains the complete text of that work as well as supplementary material, the work is reviewed in its entirety here. It was first published as *Compton's Young Children's Precyclopedia* in 1971 and was designed for children ages four to eight. Compton's is probably as well known for children's encyclopedias as is its major competitor, World Book. Along with the editors, there were two curriculum consultants: Lois N. Hodgson, the chairman of the Department of Special Education at the University of Toledo; and Mary Alice Weller, Associate Professor of Elementary Education, Slippery Rock State College. In addition to Dr. Weller, four other specialists in early childhood education, kindergarten, and curriculum critically reviewed parts of the sections of activities that begin each volume. The authors of the articles are not named.

Scope

The volumes in this set are arranged alphabetically, as are the articles. The individual articles range from one to several pages and provide broad information on the person, place, or thing covered. An examination of a 50-page sample in volume 9 reveals that 48 percent of the articles cover science; 24 percent history and social science; 16 percent humanities; 8 percent geography; and 4 percent popular culture. Although science topics dominate this encyclopedia, that is true of most children's reference works.

The work tends to favor U.S. topics; however, other geographical regions also receive a fair amount of coverage. For example, in volume 2, 54 percent of the articles are on the United States, 33 percent total are on Europe, Asia, and South America; and 13 percent are about Great Britain. The editors have included articles from many different ethnic groups and nationalities.

The coverage of selected individuals and subjects is standard for this type of encyclopedia. The writer **Louisa May Alcott** receives two pages. The **dinosaurs** article is ten pages long with cross-references to **brontosaur** and **tyrannosaur.** The articles on **Mexico** cover ten pages with a cross-reference to Hernando Cortés in **exploring.** The articles entitled **painting** take up six pages in volume 12. Painting is also mentioned on three pages in volume 1 and is discussed in individual articles on famous painters.

The topic *Middle Ages* is mentioned in the cross-reference under **castles** and **knights** but is not defined in either article. There is no entry for *soccer,* although **baseball, swimming,** and the **Olympics** are covered.

The omission of an entry on *Martin Luther King, Jr.,* is a major weakness. Although African Americans such as **Benjamin Banneker, George Washington Carver, Jean Baptiste du Sable,** and **Harriet Tubman** receive coverage, King does not.

Currency

This edition was published in 1988, and it contains none of the standard topics checked for currency.

The articles on space exploration provide fairly recent information. A section on space stations theorizes about how they will be used, and theories about life on other planets are also mentioned.

Modern technology receives some general coverage. There are articles on **newspapers, radio, television,** and **telescopes. Computers** occupy four pages in volume 3. However, the coverage is basic, concentrating on the problem-solving applications of computers. In volume 13, there is a four-page article on **robots.** Fax machines and modems are not mentioned anywhere, despite the fact that they existed when the encyclopedia was published. If currency is important to the purchaser, a more up-to-date multivolume set such as the WORLD BOOK ENCYCLOPEDIA or the OXFORD CHILDREN'S ENCYCLOPEDIA might be a better purchase.

Accuracy

The articles in *Compton's* are generally accurate. Our expert thought that the **comets** entry was brief and well written for young children. The subject *oxygen* was mentioned in five articles; each time the information was correct.

There are problems in *Compton's,* however, as a result of omissions. *Cancer* and *Congress* were not covered. The article **Davy Crockett** mentions most of his career except his death at the Alamo. Since this is one of the most famous battles in history and Crockett was its most famous participant, this is a serious omission. In the entry on **Abraham Lincoln,** there is no mention of his assassination.

Clarity

The overall writing style of the articles is very good. The descriptive phrases are vivid, and the vocabulary is appropriate for the age level. Longer articles are divided into sections. The entry on **reading,** for example, is 16 pages long but is broken down into four independent sections. The sections teach children about the adventure of reading, how poems are written, the parts of speech, and foreign languages.

The article on **roads** is typical of the writing style:

Did you ever travel on a wolf trail?

Did you ever follow an Indian hunting path through the woods?

You might have, without even knowing it!

A long time ago, there were no roads anywhere in the world. There were only paths made by the hooves and paws of animals. Wild creatures, such as the deer, the wolf, and the mountain lion, knew where to find water. Some animals knew where to find salt. Some knew where the berries were juicy and the fish were fat, and where the plants were most tender.

The animals went back and forth to these places so often that they wore paths through the forest and across the land. Men learned to follow these paths.

Words that may be new to students are italicized, but *Compton's* does not have a glossary of these words.

Objectivity

Compton's tends to avoid controversial topics. For example, discrimination, Northern Ireland, and the ozone layer are not mentioned at all. Pollution is covered in the entries **air** and **water.** However, in sections on dirty air and dirty water, *Compton's* communicates the optimistic belief that science and technology can cure these problems.

Another area of concern in this work is the portrayal of women. For example, the picture of the newsroom in the article **newspapers** shows only men. Although nine male artists are covered in articles, no female artists are discussed. In the **airplanes** entry, there are four pages on Charles Lindbergh but none on Amelia Earhart.

The most sexist and dated text occurs in the article on **jobs.** The article states that, although mother does most of the cooking at home, most bakers and chefs are men. It also states that fathers build things, but some women can work in factories putting together irons and wristwatches. The article also includes statements such as "Most of the time, girls play girls' games and boys play boys' games."

Articles on women such as **Marie Curie, Louisa May Alcott, Elizabeth Blackwell,** the **Brontë Sisters,** and **Emily Dickinson** help to balance the gender bias, but many articles reinforce traditional sex roles and should be revised.

Compton's does, however, cover a variety of racial and ethnic groups quite well. The illustrations reflect a number of different groups such as Asians, African Americans, Africans, and Native Americans. Tales from African and Native American folklore appear frequently. Slavery in the context of the American Civil War receives coverage in the **Underground Railroad** and **Abraham Lincoln,** but the modern struggle for civil rights is not mentioned.

Accessibility

One of the greatest strengths of this work is its many points of access. Each volume has a detailed table of contents following the activity pages. The subject headings are easy for young children to understand. The pairing of some entry words, such as **kings and queens** and **plus and minus,** is logical. In the table of contents, the main headings are in red type and the subheads are in black type. In the articles themselves, the main heading appears in a rectangular box with the subheads in large type underneath.

Cross-references appear at the end of selected articles. These references (approximately 400 in all) state where the reader can find related information. For example, a reference to related areas is handled like the one at the end of the entry for **newspapers:** "You may read about other ways people find out the news under **Radio** in Volume 13 and **Television** in Volume 15."

Cross-referencing is also used in each volume on the page following the table of contents. A list of topic words that begin with the letter or letters covered by that volume directs the reader to related articles in other volumes where more information on those topics can be found.

The paperback *Teaching Guide and Index to Compton's Precyclopedia* contains two indexes. The first is a comprehensive listing of the subjects covered in the entire work. The main entry is in boldface type followed by the volume number (also in boldface), and the page number or numbers in roman type. Subheads are listed with the volume number in boldface and the page numbers in roman type. Topics that appear in "Activity" sections are identified by a square, which is followed by the article title, volume number, and page numbers. Topics in the *Teaching Guide* are identified by a blue box with the item number in it. The general index also contains cross-references to related articles. For example, "**Zoology** *see* **animals.**" Illustrations are not indexed.

The second index is the *Teaching Guide* index, which is divided into 13 topics frequently taught in grade school, such as **Pioneers, Exploring, Animals,** and **Getting Ready for Mathematics.** Related articles are listed under each main heading.

Special Features

Compton's contains a number of special features, including the separate *Teaching Guide.* Children and adults can use this guide to locate information on specific subjects or topics within broad themes.

Another noteworthy feature is the "Activity" pages at the beginning of each volume. Activities range from rhymes, games, and puzzles to projects and experiments. Answers to the quizzes and puzzles are provided within the section. Activities can also be found within articles. For example, in **farming,** directions for growing sweet potatoes, carrots, and lemon trees are provided.

The illustrations are bright and colorful, but many of them look out-of-date. For the most part, they reflect various racial, cultural, and ethnic groups, but they are weak in depicting females. The lack of maps is another drawback. Only ten maps are included, most of which are simple outlines of countries with principal cities marked.

Format

Compton's Precyclopedia includes 16 hardcover volumes with a paperback index and teaching guide. The volumes' binding is sturdy enough to stand up to heavy use, and the pages are thick enough to withstand years of handling. The type is large enough so that young children can read it. Subject headings and subheads are in large boldface type, making them easy to distinguish.

Summary

Compton's Precyclopedia provides training for young children in how to use encyclopedias as well as knowledge of more than 445 subjects. In addition, the activities help students to practice what they learn.

However, this work is badly in need of updating, correction, and a major revision. The lack of current information is further aggravated by the illustrations, many of which appear outdated, and specific articles that reinforce traditional sex roles. In addition, this work contains very few maps. Because of this, other sets such as CHILDCRAFT and CHILDREN'S BRITANNICA would be a better choice for parents or educators who want to introduce children to multivolume encyclopedias. This work is not recommended for purchase.

The Kingfisher Children's Encyclopedia

Facts at a Glance

Full title: **The Kingfisher Children's Encyclopedia**
Publisher: Kingfisher
Editor: John Paton
Edition reviewed: © 1992

Number of volumes: 1
Number of articles: 1,300
Number of pages: 816
Number of words: more than 250,000
Number of cross-references: 975 (reviewer estimate)
Number of index entries: more than 4,000
Number of maps: 10 full-color; 250 two-color (reviewer estimate)
Number of illustrations: more than 2,000
Intended readership: ages 8 to 14
Trim size: 7½″ × 10¼″
Binding: hardcover

Price: $31.95
Sold directly to libraries and schools; also sold in bookstores and other retail outlets
ISBN 1-85697-800-1
No stated revision policy

Introduction

The Kingfisher Children's Encyclopedia is a one-volume encyclopedia created for children in the middle and upper elementary grades. First published as a multivolume work in England in 1989, and in the United States as the *Doubleday Children's Encyclopedia,* the work was revised and repackaged in one volume in 1992. Its 816 pages contain over 1,300 entries and more than 2,000 illustrations, predominantly in color. Its "one overriding aim," as stated in the editor's foreword, is to "be a work that children will find easy to use and will *enjoy* using."

Authority

The encyclopedia was created in England in 1989 by Grisewood & Dempsey, a firm well established in the field of reference material for children. Articles are all unsigned, and no content experts are listed by name. The foreword does cite the efforts of "writers, editors, consultants, reviewers, [and] authenticators," but as none of these individuals is identified, their number and qualifications cannot be evaluated.

Scope

The encyclopedia contains about 1,300 entries grouped into 16 subject areas. The largest category embraces geographical units—countries, states and provinces, cities, and other regional entities. There are more than 270 such entries (about 21 percent of the total). The next largest category is "Animals," with about 160 entries (12 percent). "Science" (about 10 percent) follows, with "Peoples and Government," "Our Earth," and "History" at about 8 percent each. The remaining categories, in descending order, are "Plants and Food," "Human Body," "Language and Literature," "The Arts," "Religion," "Machines and Mechanisms," "Astronomy and Space," "Sports and Pastimes," "Travel and Transportation," and "Buildings."

About 190 (15 percent) of the entries are biographical. The biographies are largely historical rather than contemporary. There are no entries for entertainers and only one for an athlete (**Jesse Owens**). Political and military leaders predominate. There are entries for all presidents of the United States up to and including **George Bush,** as well as for a sprinkling of other U.S. political figures (such as **Daniel Boone, John Brown,** and **Martin Luther King, Jr.**). Major explorers and scientists also appear. It is, however, a predominantly white male list of subjects. Women and minority group members constitute only a small fraction of those profiled, although biographies appear for **Harriet Tubman, Indira Gandhi,** and **Margaret Thatcher.**

The nonbiographical entries also take a traditional approach, presenting basic information about academic

The Kingfisher Children's Encyclopedia

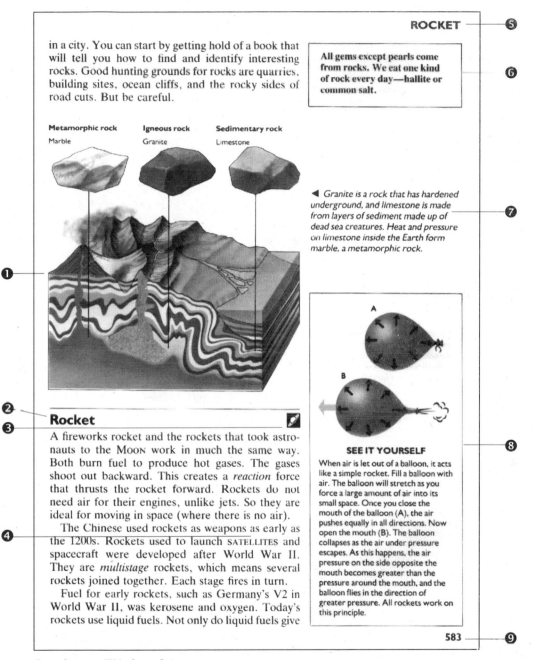

ROCKET

in a city. You can start by getting hold of a book that will tell you how to find and identify interesting rocks. Good hunting grounds for rocks are quarries, building sites, ocean cliffs, and the rocky sides of road cuts. But be careful.

All gems except pearls come from rocks. We eat one kind of rock every day—hallite or common salt.

Metamorphic rock
Marble

Igneous rock
Granite

Sedimentary rock
Limestone

◄ *Granite is a rock that has hardened underground, and limestone is made from layers of sediment made up of dead sea creatures. Heat and pressure on limestone inside the Earth form marble, a metamorphic rock.*

Rocket

A fireworks rocket and the rockets that took astronauts to the Moon work in much the same way. Both burn fuel to produce hot gases. The gases shoot out backward. This creates a *reaction* force that thrusts the rocket forward. Rockets do not need air for their engines, unlike jets. So they are ideal for moving in space (where there is no air).

The Chinese used rockets as weapons as early as the 1200s. Rockets used to launch SATELLITES and spacecraft were developed after World War II. They are *multistage* rockets, which means several rockets joined together. Each stage fires in turn.

Fuel for early rockets, such as Germany's V2 in World War II, was kerosene and oxygen. Today's rockets use liquid fuels. Not only do liquid fuels give

SEE IT YOURSELF
When air is let out of a balloon, it acts like a simple rocket. Fill a balloon with air. The balloon will stretch as you force a large amount of air into its small space. Once you close the mouth of the balloon (A), the air pushes equally in all directions. Now open the mouth (B). The balloon collapses as the air under pressure escapes. As this happens, the air pressure on the side opposite the mouth becomes greater than the pressure around the mouth, and the balloon flies in the direction of greater pressure. All rockets work on this principle.

583

Page shown at 67% of actual size.

❶ Four-color illustration with callouts

❷ Boldface main entry word on a line by itself

❸ Subject symbol appears near main entry word to designate area of interest

❹ Interior cross-reference indicated by small capitals

❺ Guide word appears in boldface capitals

❻ Boxes containing interesting facts and additional information located in the outer margins of most pages

❼ Caption explains the illustration

❽ "See It Yourself" boxes provide illustrated activities related to main entries

❾ Page number printed at foot of page

subjects. Some entries, such as **dinosaur, hurricane, volcano, echo, pulse,** and **witch,** are clearly intended to appeal to the child user. Many of the entries within academic subjects are aimed at the user's interest. Authors include **Aesop, Alcott, Hans Christian Andersen, Brontë Sisters,** and **Lewis Carroll.**

A check of the 47 entries from **rubber** to **ship** (covering 25 pages) shows about half to be political units (including **St. Kitts and Nevis** and the **Seychelles**), animals, and plants. Almost ten more are science related (such as **salt** and **Saturn**). The remaining entries include a variety of interesting subjects: **sailing, saint, satire, school, science fiction, scouting, sculpture, Shakespeare,** and **Shinto.**

The work's longest entries cover about a full page each (these include major topics such as **Canada, church, galaxy,** and **nuclear energy**). Twenty-four topics are treated as "Special Features" and presented on two-page spreads. These features are highly illustrated and should appeal to children. These topics range from **aircraft** to **battles** to **prehistoric animals** to **The Vikings.**

Most entries are of the brief, ready-reference type, as can be seen from the coverage allotted our list of standard entries. **Louisa May Alcott** receives 7 lines, **dinosaur** 32 lines (plus two high-interest features), **Martin Luther King** 16 lines, **Mexico** 14 lines (plus a fact box), **painting** 27 lines (plus an activity), and **soccer** 10 lines.

Currency

Revised in 1992, the edition under review reflects updating. **Germany** is unified, and **South Africa** includes steps to liberalize apartheid. While **Yugoslavia** is presented as one country, the independence of Slovenia and Croatia in 1991 is mentioned, as is the fighting that resulted. Articles on **Bulgaria, Czechoslovakia, Hungary, Poland,** and **Romania** include the fall of communism. (The division of Czechoslovakia took place after publication.)

Treatment of the breakup of the Soviet Union, however, is muddled. The entry **Soviet Union** discusses the splintering of that country and the formation of the Commonwealth of Independent States. Separate entries appear for **Baltic States** and **Russia,** but not for any of the other new republics. No country fact box accompanies either **Russia** or **Soviet Union,** however, making the status of either as a nation unclear, and the **Soviet Union** article speaks primarily of conditions in Russia rather than those in any of the other former constituent members. In addition, the map in **Soviet Union** mistakenly labels the entire expanse of the former U.S.S.R. (except for the Baltic states) as *Russia,* not the *Soviet Union.* (The "Asia" map repeats the error.)

Bill Clinton does not appear as president since his election came late in the year of publication. There is no entry for the *food pyramid* or the *Gulf War* (although that conflict is mentioned in a caption). The entry on **space exploration** is current in spite of its brevity; *Voyager II*'s departure from the solar system is noted. Some other recent developments are noted in entries or sidebars. The *Channel Tunnel* is mentioned in the entry **tunnel,** there is an entry for **fiber optics,** and *fax machines* appear in **telecommunications.** On the other hand, there is no mention of *compact discs* or *cellular telephones.*

The photograph program is up-to-date, as are the illustrations in general, but there are exceptions. The diagram of a basketball court uses a dated version of the lane extending from the free throw line to the end line; the drawing of a personal computer shows a dated look and outmoded technology. On the whole, though, the work is fairly current. Because of the large number of historical subjects depicted, men are featured more prominently in the illustrations than are women. The photographs do not reinforce job-related gender stereotypes.

Accuracy

The Kingfisher Children's Encyclopedia is fairly accurate, but the work suffers from its brevity. The entry **Congress,** for instance, defines the term *legislature* early on and adequately explains the role of Congress in the United States government, but its last sentence may imply that presidential signing of a bill is automatic. However, any potential misunderstanding is clarified in the caption for the accompanying illustration, where the presidential veto—and the congressional override—are mentioned.

The **cancer** entry is somewhat misleading because it does not make clear that all tumors are not cancerous. It also neglects to mention the concept of *metastasis,* a central issue in understanding the disease.

Comet sums up what is known about these phenomena appropriately for children, providing enough information to differentiate comets from other bodies and to answer basic questions.

Our reviewer found **oxygen** to be a clear and readable account that is good for its length. The article is accompanied by an activity that our reviewer liked, although he questioned whether a young reader could understand it.

These entries highlight the basic nature of the work. Entries are generally accurate, but because they are short and written at a fairly low level, they sometimes suffer from a fuzziness that borders on inaccuracy. Generalizations can lead to nonsense, such as this opening to the entry **battles:** "Some battles have played an important part in the history of the world. Others are important only to the countries that fought them." Despite such lapses, the work provides a useful introduction for children to most topics.

The illustrations are generally accurate. Drawings of animals (which abound throughout the work) are correct in look and coloration. The drawings give an impression of cuteness rather than wildness, and when different animals appear together their relative sizes are not always accurately conveyed, but the reader gets a clear idea of what each animal looks like. Some of the likenesses of famous people are less successful. *Fred Astaire* (in the **dance** feature) looks like Stan Laurel, and a few presidents (**Lyndon Baines Johnson, Franklin Delano Roosevelt,** and **Woodrow Wilson,** for example) might not be recognized. The black-and-white representations of authors and other famous people are more accurate. Diagrams of machines show interesting cutaway views with many parts labeled.

There are about ten large, detailed maps—one of each continent, plus additional subjects such as the "United States" and the "Soviet Union." (The work also includes small locator maps for each country, state, and province entry.) Borders and physical features are generally shown accurately, although some city locator symbols are slightly misplaced.

Clarity

Entries are written in a clear, readable style. **Skeleton** offers a good explanation of the differences between internal and external skeletons and describes the functions of the human skeleton quite well. The entry yeast is clear on how **yeast** is processed, what it is used for, and why it works. **Fruit** makes a nice distinction between the common and scientific uses of the term. As with accuracy, the clarity sometimes suffers from brevity, but these lapses are the exception.

The tone is somewhat pedantic, albeit at a low level. The writers do not attempt to entertain the reader with jazzy writing or fun facts. Sidebars do provide more entertaining informational nuggets, but the focus in the text itself is to be interesting by being informative.

The entry **fingerprints** conveys the tone and style of the majority of entries in this work. It clearly establishes that fingerprints are the marks we leave, not the skin grooves themselves, and explains how they are used:

> Fingerprints are marks we leave behind whenever we touch something. You can see them by pressing your fingertips into an ink pad and then onto a sheet of white paper. Everybody has patterns of lines and swirls on their fingers. But each person's fingerprints are different from everybody else's. Because of this, police officers use fingerprints to help identify criminals. They keep files of thousands of different prints. By comparing those on file with those found at the scene of a crime, they can often trace the guilty person. Computers can now hold details of the fingerprints of half a million people. In a few seconds, the computer will match any of these prints with those of a suspect.

Objectivity

With so much of the book devoted to basic information, *The Kingfisher Children's Encyclopedia* is generally objective. Its coverage, as noted above, is fairly well balanced except in the biographies. Indeed, the editors are to be applauded for the variety of entries on religious groups, which draw on a range of cultures.

Controversial issues are generally avoided. The editors seem to wish to take a fairly positive view of the world, probably an understandable stance for a work at this level. On the other hand, the result is a somewhat tame product. **Civil rights** defines the concept (largely in terms of *Bill of Rights* issues) and concludes by saying that civil rights "became an important issue" for blacks in the 1950s, thus obscuring the depth of discrimination against blacks and the intensity of their struggle to secure rights. **Discrimination** acknowledges the existence of discrimination based on race and sex, but does not present either as a serious issue in the contemporary United States. **Northern Ireland** mentions sectarian conflict, but spotty writing obscures the fact that both Protestants and Catholics are responsible for violent attacks. **Ozone layer** accepts the view that the ozone layer is being depleted but does not address the arguments of those opposed to that view.

Accessibility

The editors have skillfully phrased entries in terms that the reader is most likely to use to seek information. For example, they use **cereal** and **clothing** as entry words instead of *grain* and *fashion*. Information can be accessed in a number of ways: by following guide words at the outer corner of each page, by consulting the main index, or by using the subject index. Cross-references point to related subjects.

The main index of more than 4,000 entries includes the 1,300 entry words, plus hundreds of other terms that appear in the text and illustrations. All entry words are printed in boldface in the index, and references to pages with illustrations are in italic. The index contains some *see* and *see also* references to other forms of a word or to related items. The index seems comprehensive and accurate.

The subject index lists all of the entries alphabetically within the 16 main subject classifications, although page numbers on which entries appear are not given. This index is not as well prepared as the main index. The subject areas are not listed alphabetically, nor do they follow the order given in the book's front matter, so locating the desired subject area will require page turning. Moreover, about 100 entries are missing. The subject index does offer an additional way to locate some related entries, but this index needs revision in the next edition of the encyclopedia.

Within the text of an entry, references to topics that appear as their own entries are printed in small capitals. These cross-references occur with useful frequency. Spot checks revealed two (to nonexistent entries on *Roald Amundsen* and *Hundred Years' War*) that are clearly wrong; these are perhaps vestiges of the work's multivolume original. Others that were checked were accurate.

When an entry may be consulted in a variant form, a cross-reference entry head appears. **Air cushion vehicle** is only a cross-reference to **hydrofoil. Crocodile** sends the reader to the joint entry **alligator and crocodile.**

Special Features

The most special feature of *The Kingfisher Children's Encyclopedia* is the lavish illustration program. The more than 2,000 illustrations are predominantly in color; fewer than 10 percent are black and white. About one-third of the nonmap illustrations are photographs; the remainder are commissioned drawings done especially for this work. Nonhistorical images reflect an even distribution of male and female subjects and a good representation of individuals from minority groups. The illustrations are attractive and well placed in relation to the entry they supplement. Captions are informative; as with the text, there are occasional inaccuracies, but the majority are correct. The illustrations make the work attractive and appealing.

Other features appear throughout the book. Each country, state, and province entry is accompanied by a colored fact box that provides such information as the size and population. Country boxes include the nation's flag, chief language, and currency. State boxes include the state bird, flower, and tree, as well as date of entry into statehood.

The encyclopedia includes about 200 brief marginal features that provide interesting facts (such as stories of famous diamonds) that supplement information in the main text. In addition, about 25 "See It Yourself" activities are scattered throughout the book. These describe simple projects that children can perform to learn more about such areas as growing plants, day and night, and friction. Parental participation may be needed in some cases (for example, putting together an aquarium), but that point is never explicitly made.

The work contains no bibliography.

Format

The thick volume is bulky to hold; children would probably prefer to rest the book on a table to use it. Fortunately, the book lies flat when open (except in the earliest pages).

The design and layout of the book is pleasing. Entry words stand out, and the type size is quite readable. The size of the page provides adequate scope for large illustrations. Margins are used for many illustrations, which stand alongside the text entry in a helpful arrangement.

Summary

For another opinion about this work, see *Booklist (Reference Books Bulletin),* October 15, 1992, pages 456–57.

The Kingfisher Children's Encyclopedia is an attractive, colorful work suitable for children. It sometimes suffers from vagueness or inaccuracy caused by generalizations, but on the whole the work provides a good introduction to a variety of standard academic topics written at an appropriate level. While it cannot compete in coverage with multivolume encyclopedias, it represents a much better value than the slight one-volume USBORNE CHILDREN'S ENCYCLOPEDIA or Troll's STUDENT ENCYCLOPEDIA. It is a better value than the RANDOM HOUSE CHILDREN'S ENCYCLOPEDIA, although it is not as well illustrated as that work. *The Kingfisher Children's Encyclopedia* is recommended for purchase by parents and libraries as a quick-reference tool for older children.

My First Encyclopedia

Facts at a Glance

Full title: **My First Encyclopedia**
Publisher: Dorling Kindersley
Editor: Sheila Hanly
Number of contributors: 17
Edition reviewed: © 1993

Number of volumes: 1
Number of articles: 370 (reviewer estimate)
Number of pages: 80
Number of cross-references: none
Number of index entries: 400 (reviewer estimate)
Number of maps: none
Number of illustrations: 450 (reviewer estimate), all in full color; 50 percent photographs, 50 percent drawings
Intended readership: beginning readers
Trim size: 10″ × 13″
Binding: hardcover

Price: $16.95
Sold directly to schools and libraries; also sold by direct mail and in bookstores and other retail outlets
ISBN 1-56458-214-0
No stated revision policy

Introduction

This one-volume, 80-page encyclopedia is aimed at beginning readers. Its oversized pages are filled with brightly colored photographs and line drawings. According to the preface, the accompanying text has been

My First Encyclopedia (Dorling Kindersley)

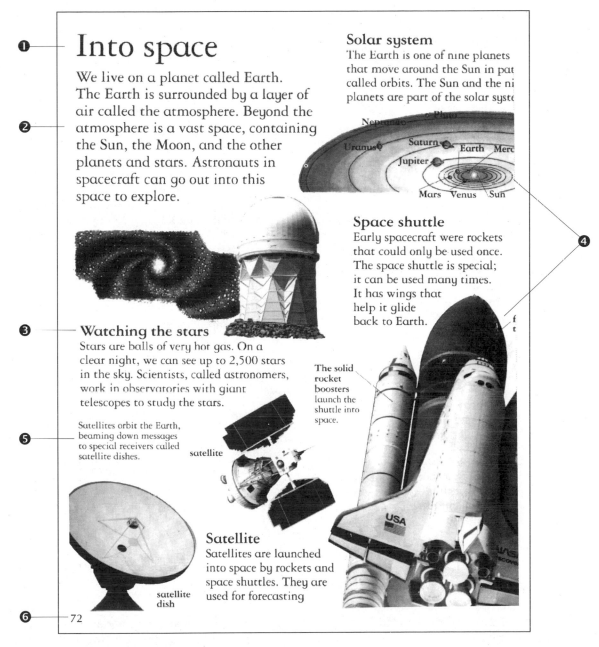

❶ Into space

❷ We live on a planet called Earth. The Earth is surrounded by a layer of air called the atmosphere. Beyond the atmosphere is a vast space, containing the Sun, the Moon, and the other planets and stars. Astronauts in spacecraft can go out into this space to explore.

Solar system
The Earth is one of nine planets that move around the Sun in pat called orbits. The Sun and the ni planets are part of the solar syste

Neptune — Pluto
Uranus — Saturn — Earth — Merc
Jupiter
Mars — Venus — Sun

❹

Space shuttle
Early spacecraft were rockets that could only be used once. The space shuttle is special; it can be used many times. It has wings that help it glide back to Earth.

❸ Watching the stars
Stars are balls of very hot gas. On a clear night, we can see up to 2,500 stars in the sky. Scientists, called astronomers, work in observatories with giant telescopes to study the stars.

The solid rocket boosters launch the shuttle into space.

❺ Satellites orbit the Earth, beaming down messages to special receivers called satellite dishes.

satellite

Satellite
Satellites are launched into space by rockets and space shuttles. They are used for forecasting

satellite dish

USA

❻ 72

Page shown at 55% of actual size.

❶ Main entry word in large, boldface type, on a line by itself
❷ Introduction explaining topic
❸ Subentry giving information about related topic
❹ Four-color illustrations with callouts
❺ Caption explaining illustration
❻ Page number

specially designed to answer many of the questions children ask and introduce them to the exciting world of books—as a source of information about themselves and their world.

The work is arranged by themes, starting with "a child's immediate daily experiences" and extending to "an exploration of the wider world, covering topics such as animals, climatic regions, the people of the world, and even outer space." *My First Encyclopedia* bears a 1993 copyright date.

Authority

Dorling Kindersley is well known for its high-quality illustrated children's books, which include the companion books to the 13-part PBS *Eyewitness* natural history series and a popular series of *cross-sections* books illustrated by Stephen Biesty. *My First Encyclopedia* benefited from the advice of several specialist consultants, including Professor Elizabeth Goodacre, language consultant; Professor Willam E. Nagy, U.S. language consultant; Steve Parker, natural history consultant; Dr. T. Kramer, medical consultant; and James Mills-Hicks, geography consultant. The book does not list institutional affiliations for any of the consultants except James Mills-Hicks, who is a member of Dorling Kindersley's cartography staff.

Scope

My First Encyclopedia contains 33 two-page spreads of information, each based on a particular theme. The earliest spreads are entitled "The human body," "Families," "Houses and homes," "Pets," "All in one day," and "Games and sports." The work proceeds through topics such as "Clothes we wear," "Jobs people do," "Plants," "Trees," "In the ocean," "Children of the world," and ends with "Traveling on land," "Traveling on water," "Traveling by air," and "Into space." By comparison, Troll's MY FIRST ENCYCLOPEDIA has only eight two-page spreads and three single pages of information.

A typical spread includes a large heading and introductory sentences surrounded by brightly colored photographs of related objects. Each photograph is accompanied by a boldface entry and a sentence or two of text describing the object. For example, the "Foods we eat" spread has large photographs of a sandwich, a piece of chocolate cake, a salad, a baked potato, a cup of hot chocolate, a glass of orange juice, a soft-boiled egg in an eggcup, a bowl of rice with chopsticks, a forkful of spaghetti, and a series of pasta shapes. Also included are color line drawings of a girl pouring milk onto a bowl of cereal, a mother and son baking bread, a boy eating an apple from a plate of mixed fruit, a tin of sardines, and a plate of lamb chops and chicken. Some photographs bleed into the margins and off the page, giving the work a relaxed, playful feel appropriate for this age group.

Typical entries include words and phrases such as **Bread, Sweet things, Fish and meat,** and **Fruit.** The passage under **Bread** reads: "Bread is an important food in most countries of the world. Many people eat bread as a sandwich. They take two or more slices of bread and put a filling, such as cheese, between them." The passage for **Drink** reads: "People need to drink water every day. Fruit juice is a tasty cold drink. Hot drinks made from milk give you plenty of energy."

Although it was originally produced in Great Britain, the work shows only minimal signs of cultural bias. (A bus, for instance, is labeled a **Coach** on the "Traveling on land" pages.) In fact, the work has a distinctly multicultural approach. The child models used in the photographs throughout represent a broad ethnic mix. For example, on the "Clothes we wear" pages, two of the children are Asian, one is Indian, one is African, and one is European. Sections on "In the desert," "In the grasslands," "In the rain forest," "In the mountains," and "In cold lands" include boxed features on the **Tuareg people, Xhosa people, Yanomami people, Alpine farmers,** and **Inuit people,** respectively.

Currency

My First Encyclopedia is very up-to-date. A mountain bike and a high-speed train, for example, are depicted on the "Traveling on land" pages. The work includes no geographical or biographical information, other than passing references to a handful of countries. All place names are current.

The illustrations and design of the book itself are notably contemporary: the bold colors leap off the page, and the edges of the photographs are so precisely cut as to make them stand out clearly from the white pages. Shadows have been added occasionally to make the subjects appear to be standing on the page itself. The typeface of the text is contemporary and easily read. Neither Troll's MY FIRST ENCYCLOPEDIA nor the USBORNE CHILDREN'S ENCYCLOPEDIA uses photographs, and the typeface in each is smaller and more difficult to read.

Clarity

The text is written at an appropriate level for beginning readers. The preface notes that "the pages dealing with children's everyday experiences are addressed to the reader, but the more impersonal, instructional style of information books is also introduced." For example, the entry for **Hearing** in "The human body" section reads: "You hear with your ears. They collect sounds from the air and send them to your brain. Your brain then tells you what the sounds mean." The final entry, **Moon landing,** reads: "On July 21, 1969, two American astronauts were the first people to walk on the surface of the Moon. They traveled to the Moon in a huge rocket called *Apollo.* There have been five more Moon landings since then."

Some of the entries actively encourage appropriate behaviors for children: **Pet care,** for instance, tells children that "All pets need to be kept clean. A dog's coat should be gently brushed to remove loose hair and dirt." The entry for **Sweet things** tells children that "Many people enjoy eating sugary food such as cake, candy, and cookies. But eating too much sugar can be bad for you."

Accessibility

This encyclopedia should be easily accessible to young readers. A table of contents appears in large print at the beginning of the book. In addition, a three-page index appears at the end of the book, with references to entry words and other important words from within the text. Although it is printed in a small typeface, which may make it difficult for younger readers to use, the index includes rudimentary pronunciations for some of the more difficult words such as *chrysalis (kriss-sal-liss)* and *guinea pig (gin-nee)*.

My First Encyclopedia contains no guide words or page indexes, but its scope is limited enough that children will be able to flip to a desired page quite easily. The book's hardcover binding should stand up to heavy use.

Summary

The Dorling Kindersley *My First Encyclopedia* is a high-quality reference work for beginning readers. Most striking about this work are the quality and clarity of the photographs and illustrations, which are in bright, bold colors that will appeal to both children and adults. Although it is more expensive than either the USBORNE CHILDREN'S ENCYCLOPEDIA or Troll's MY FIRST ENCYCLOPEDIA, this work's large print and simple vocabulary make it more enjoyable and appropriate for very young children than either of those volumes. Its 80 pages make it less comprehensive than the USBORNE CHILDREN'S ENCYCLOPEDIA, which contains more historical, geographical, and sociological entries than this work. Parents seeking a modern, bright, multiculturally oriented volume that clearly depicts and explains a variety of objects of interest to children will appreciate Dorling Kindersley's *My First Encyclopedia*.

My First Encyclopedia

Facts at a Glance

Full title: **My First Encyclopedia**
Publisher: Troll Associates
Author: Alan Snow
Edition reviewed: © 1992

Number of volumes: 1
Number of articles: 12
Number of pages: 32
Number of words: 7,500 (reviewer estimate)
Number of cross-references: none
Number of index entries: 126
Number of maps: none
Number of illustrations: 110 (reviewer estimate), all in color
Intended readership: kindergarten to grade 3
Trim size: 8½" × 11"
Binding: hardcover; paperback

Price: $12.79 (library binding); $4.95 (paperback)
Sold directly to schools and libraries; also sold by direct mail, in retail outlets, and by dealers
ISBN 0-8167-2519-5 (hardcover); ISBN 0-8167-2520 (paperback)
No stated revision policy

Introduction

Children cannot be introduced to reference works too soon, and several one-volume encyclopedias are available for students in kindergarten through third grade. *My First Encyclopedia,* first published in 1992 by Troll Associates, is a lavishly illustrated work with more than 100 cartoon illustrations designed to fascinate the young child. The purpose of the work, explained in the opening section, is to provide "one convenient book source of different facts about people, places, ideas, events, and things." The work is a manageable size (32 pages) for reading from cover to cover. Broad concepts such as *plants, animals,* and *space* cover areas of interest to young children, and the index can help the user find information on a number of subjects.

Authority

The author, Alan Snow, also serves as the illustrator of the encyclopedia. The publisher, Troll Associates, publishes several one-volume reference works, including an encyclopedia for older children, dictionaries, and atlases. No mention is made of other contributors, nor are educators, librarians, or other experts cited.

Scope

The encyclopedia is divided into 11 one- or two-page subject areas: "Your Body," "People of the World," "Keeping in Touch," "Transportation," "Prehistoric World," "Animals Today," "More Animals," "Plants," "Earth," "Space," and "It's the Greatest." Short entries, most two or three sentences long, are spread across each page and surround the illustrations. The work begins with a brief explanation called "What is an Ency-

My First Encyclopedia (Troll Associates)

Prehistoric world

Dinosaurs and other prehistoric creatures lived long before there were people. Dinosaurs ruled the Earth for about 140 million years. They all died out millions of years ago.

Pteranodon
27-foot (8-meter) wingspan
Pteranodon was a flying reptile. It had leathery wings but could not fly very well.

Diplodocus
90 feet (27 meters) long

The **biggest dinosaurs** were twice the length of a tennis court. They were plant-eaters with huge, heavy bodies and very long necks.

Tyrannosaurus
50 feet (15 meters) long

Diplodocus was one of the larger dinosaurs. It was a plant-eater.

Tyrannosaurus was the largest meat-eater. It was very fierce. It might have caught other dinosaurs and killed them with its sharp teeth.

Triceratops had three horns, and a shield of bone around its neck. It was very strong.

Fossils (see below) are the remains of ancient plants and animals left behind in rocks. They help show us what prehistoric creatures looked like.

Triceratops 30 feet (9 meters) long.

The **smallest dinosaurs** were the size of chickens. They ate insects and ran fast on their back legs.

Dinosaurs were reptiles. Their babies hatched out of eggs.

Compsognathus
2 feet (½ meter) long

baby dinosaur

Page shown at 67% of actual size.

❶ Main entry word or phrase in bold-face type

❷ Boxed introduction explains the general topic

❸ Four-color cartoon illustrations

❹ Informative caption describes each illustration

❺ Measurements given in both standard and metric systems

❻ Subentry gives added information

clopedia?" and concludes with a puzzle section and a subject index.

No biographies are included in the work. The only historical figures mentioned are Aristotle and Orville Wright. Presidents, political leaders, generals, and writers are outside the scope of this book.

The work shows a definite bias toward scientific information. About 68 percent of the information is scientific, 15 percent popular culture, 7 percent history, 6 percent physical geography, and 4 percent humanities. The areas of science include a page on the **prehistoric world** (illustrated mostly with pictures of dinosaurs) and the two-page section on **space** that focuses on space exploration. Popular culture is spread throughout the work, especially on the last page, "It's the Greatest," which lists world records such as the tallest humans and fastest animals. Historical subjects are mostly limited to the history of technology and development of communication. The humanities are restricted to the development of language and cave paintings.

Currency

The coverage of modern technology in this work is excellent. The "Space" section includes the **space shuttle, astronauts,** and **space stations.** "Keeping in Touch" shows modern technology such as **fax machines, computers,** and **communication satellites.** "Transportation" has **jumbo jets,** the **Concorde,** and a **hydrofoil.** The reader will find **rain forests** and **acid rain** in the "Plants" section. The illustrations all have a modern, even timeless, look.

Accuracy

Our content experts could not comment on **cancer, comet, Congress,** or **Henry VIII** because the encyclopedia does not cover these topics. **Oxygen** is mentioned in the discussion of lungs in "Your Body" and in the discussion of plants. The information under the discussion of **lungs** is incorrect, however. (The author states that "the oxygen passes into your blood where it is used as fuel.")

The statistics provided are presented in a way that will keep the volume current for some time. For example, in the "People of the World" section, a fact box explains that the population of the world increases by 223,285 a day, or 155 people per minute. Although the information is generally accurate, it is so simplified that a child wanting to know how something works would need to consult a different type of encyclopedia. For those users who already know how a fax machine or computer is used, the information is adequate; for those who do not, the coverage will be frustrating.

Clarity

The writing style and the vocabulary are appropriate for the intended audience. Explanations are simple and short. This paragraph on **wheat** is typical:

> Many **farmers** grow plants for people to eat. These farmers are growing **wheat** in huge, flat, fields. When the wheat is ripe, a machine called a combine harvester cuts it and takes out the wheat seeds. The seeds are taken to a mill where they are ground up into a powder called flour. Flour is an important food. It is used to make bread, pasta, and cookies.

More difficult concepts, such as **acid rain, communication satellites, fold mountains,** and **amphibians,** are covered with simple explanations that a child can easily understand. Parents or teachers might need to help with the pronunciation of some terms.

Objectivity

The encyclopedia attempts to include all parts and peoples of the world. The historical sections, however, definitely emphasize western European, with Egyptian, Greek, and Roman cultures receiving the bulk of the coverage. Other cultures are occasionally represented through foods and by pictures of mud huts, houseboats, and tents in the desert. The "People of the World" section is illustrated by pictures of children representing a wide variety of ethnic and cultural groups. The fact that more people speak Chinese than any other language is also mentioned.

The illustrations, which are cartoonish, avoid stereotypes. Most of the illustrations are fairly generic pictures of children that can be either male or female and almost any racial or ethnic group. There are specific pictures of cave dwellers, Swiss mountaineers, and Native Americans.

The work is generally balanced on controversial subjects. The article on **acid rain,** for instance, states, "Some chemicals from air pollution mix with water in clouds. This can cause **acid rain** which is harmful to trees and animals." However, the article on **rain forests** takes a definite stand, ending with the admonition, "It is important to stop people from cutting down too much of the forests."

Accessibility

This encyclopedia is designed to give the young user a number of access points. The table of contents leads to the general articles; a 126-item alphabetical index leads to specific information. The index is fairly easy to use, but some problems are evident. **Snakes** is correctly indexed to page 17, but an additional reference to the picture of a snake on page 21 is missing.

A more important problem concerns the indexing of section headings. Some of the general topics in the table of contents such as "Plants" and "Space" are covered in the index, but "Animals," "People," and "Transportation" are not.

Special Features

This work is loaded with a number of special features that make it a singularly attractive and interesting work. The informative opening section on "What is an Encyclopedia?" explains to the young user the history and purpose of an encyclopedia. This helps place in context what the author is attempting to do.

Each page is covered with colorful and interesting illustrations, with six to ten on a page. The illustrations are done in a cartoon style that will seem familiar to the young user. Although the illustrator has sacrificed some detail, readers should not have difficulty identifying what is portrayed. Most illustrations are labeled or appear next to the entry they illustrate.

This work does not have maps in the traditional sense. The few representations of the world show very stylized outlines of the continents; they are not labeled.

The author has included materials that make using the encyclopedia fun and educational. The section on communication includes a table with the **Morse Code** and a message to be deciphered. The last section of the work, called "Encyclopedia Fun," has five puzzles to solve. Each question is based on information in the encyclopedia. A page of answers follows the questions.

Format

The format of the work fits the age group of the intended audience. The type is large enough to be easily read, and the main subject terms are in boldface type. Many of the explanations are placed in colored boxes to set them off from the rest of the page. The introduction to each section is also set off by a box with a differently colored background. This arrangement, which is very different from the traditional columns, is both attractive and effective.

The paper used is sturdy and will stand up to handling. The paperback edition was reviewed. The publisher also has a hardcover version, which a prospective purchaser should examine for durability, especially if the work is being obtained for a library.

Summary

My First Encyclopedia is a fascinating work that should entice the young reader into exploring every section. Children with reading skills higher than a third-grade level, however, will find it too simple and will prefer works such as the STUDENT ENCYCLOPEDIA (also by Troll Associates), the USBORNE CHILDREN'S ENCYCLOPEDIA, or THE KINGFISHER CHILDREN'S ENCYCLOPEDIA. *My First En-*

cyclopedia would not be an appropriate purchase for most libraries; they would be better advised to spend their money on more substantial single-volume works such as the RANDOM HOUSE CHILDREN'S ENCYCLOPEDIA. But for parents desiring to introduce young children to encyclopedias, this is an inexpensive, attractive, and useful work.

For other opinions about this work, see *School Library Journal,* May 1992, page 28; and *Booklist,* June 15, 1992, pages 1884–1885.

The New Grolier Student Encyclopedia

Facts at a Glance

Full title: **The New Grolier Student Encyclopedia**
Publisher: Grolier
Editor: Rita D'Apice Gould, Senior Project Editor
Edition reviewed: © 1992

Number of volumes: 22, plus an unnumbered atlas volume
Number of articles: more than 3,000
Number of pages: 2,700
Number of words: more than 1 million
Number of cross-references: approximately 10,000 (reviewer estimate)
Number of index entries: 20,000
Number of maps: more than 400, including those in separate atlas volume (reviewer estimate)
Number of illustrations: more than 4,500, most in color
Intended readership: grades 2 to 7
Trim size: 8½″ × 11″
Binding: hardcover

Price: $319 (library binding); $299 (multiple set pricing)
Sold directly to schools and libraries; also sold to individuals through direct sales staff
ISBN 0-7172-7142-0
Usually revised annually
Next scheduled revision: July 1994

Introduction

The New Grolier Student Encyclopedia is a 22-volume set designed for use by students in grades 2 to 7. The 1992 edition contains more than 3,000 entries, 4,500 illustrations, and 1 million words. This work was first published in 1972 as the *Young Students Encyclopedia* by Weekly Reader Books. Grolier, the current publisher, states that the encyclopedia

has been written especially for children to enable them to keep pace with the world in which they live. . . . Children

The New Grolier Student Encyclopedia

uses two of these, as he or she takes turns curling against a player from the opposing rink. When all the stones of both rinks have been played, this is called an *end* (inning), and scores are totaled. Ten ends usually make a game.

① Curling stones are made of real stone. Each stone usually weighs 38 pounds (17 kg), but they can weigh as little as 35 (16 kg) or as much as 50 (23 kg). The stone is about 36 inches (90 cm) around. The top and bottom of the stone are flat and slightly scooped out. A handle is attached through a hole that is drilled through the stone from top to bottom.

To slide a stone, a player holds it by its handle and tries to give it a slight twist as he or she slides it forward. The twist makes the stone spin, or *curl*, as it slides, which gives the game its name. Each rink tries to aim its stones to knock its opponents' stones out of the target boundaries. The players all carry brooms with them to sweep frost from the ice ahead of a rinkmate's sliding stone.

② ALSO READ: BOWLING, GAMES, SPORTS.

③ **CURRENT** see OCEAN.

④ **CUSTER, GEORGE** (1839–1876) George Armstrong Custer was a blond-haired army officer and Indian fighter. Historians do not agree whether he was a hero. He died in the battle of the Little Big Horn.

Custer was born in New Rumley, Ohio. He dreamed of becoming a soldier and graduated from West Point in 1861. In the Civil War he fought as a cavalry officer at Bull Run, Gettysburg, and Richmond. He became the youngest general in the Union Army.

Settlers swarmed westward after the war, killing the buffalo and driving the Plains Indians from their homes. The Indians fought back. The army began to force them onto reser-

vations. Custer, who held the rank of lieutenant colonel, commanded the famous Seventh Cavalry in many attacks—often brutal ones—on the Sioux and Cheyenne tribes.

In 1876 he led a column of soldiers in search of Sioux who had left their Black Hills reservation to hunt buffalo. He found them at the Little Big Horn River in Montana. He was supposed to wait for reinforcements, but he attacked on June 25, before other troops could arrive. About 2,500 braves, led by chiefs Sitting Bull and Crazy Horse, surrounded "Yellow Hair," as the Indians called him, and his soldiers. Custer and all his men were killed.

There were arguments after the defeat. Some thought Custer was a fool who disobeyed orders. Others honored his memory. The argument may never be settled.

ALSO READ: INDIANS, AMERICAN; INDIAN WARS.

CUSTOMS Why do many people shake hands when they meet? Why do Japanese bow to each other in greeting? They are following customs. Customs are ways of acting and living—learned and followed by a great many people—that have come down from generation to generation. Customs often change as time goes by and the lives of people change.

How does a custom start? Many develop because people find them the easiest, most convenient way to do things. For example, it is a custom to close schools during the summer. This practice was begun so that children could help with the harvest. Some customs begin because some people believe certain ways of behaving are proper and good. Other customs come from religious beliefs.

Some are taken more seriously than others. Some have become laws of the land. These are sometimes called *mores*, the Latin word for "customs."

⑥ ⑦ ▲ *George Custer, the famous U.S. Army officer who lost his life, and those of several hundred of his soldiers, in a battle with the Sioux Indians.*

▲ *It is the custom in some Muslim countries for women to wear veils over their faces whenever they are in the presence of men other than their husbands, fathers, or brothers.*

Page shown at 66% of actual size.

① Measurements given for standard and metric systems

② Cross-references indicated by small capitals, following the phrase: "ALSO READ"

③ Cross-reference entry

④ Main entry word in boldface capitals, set off by boldface rule, and easy to locate on page

⑤ Guide word

⑥ Illustrations include both photographs and drawings

⑦ Caption

⑧ Page number appears at foot of page

will find these books accessible, stimulating, activity-oriented, and most important, especially for primary-grade youngsters, non-threatening.

Authority

Grolier is a respected firm that also publishes THE NEW BOOK OF KNOWLEDGE, ENCYCLOPEDIA AMERICANA, and ACADEMIC AMERICAN ENCYCLOPEDIA. All articles are unsigned, and there are no lists of contributors or writers. The editorial staff is listed at the beginning of volume 1, but no credentials are provided.

Scope

The New Grolier Student Encyclopedia's 3,000 entries cover a wide variety of subjects related to school curriculum and children's interests. About 27 percent of the articles cover science and technology. These include articles about flowers and plants and the human body, and entries such as **nuclear energy, nutrition, space,** and **numbers.** The next largest categories cover geography and history, at about 24 percent each. These include articles on cities, states, Canadian provinces, countries and continents, biographies, and historical subjects such as the **Hundred Years' War** and the **Ottoman Empire.** The arts and humanities, with articles on **actors and acting,** the **novel, orchestras and bands,** and various religions, account for about 19 percent. Social sciences and popular culture account for the rest, with articles on occupations (**nursing**), **opinion polls,** and the **Olympic Games.**

Biographical entries include both historical and contemporary figures from many cultures, such as **Blaise Pascal, Mao Tse-tung, George Washington Carver, Martin Luther King,** and **Mikhail Gorbachev.** Women are well represented; entries include **Annie Oakley, Marian Anderson, Sandra Day O'Connor, Mother Teresa,** and **Margaret Thatcher.**

Articles tend to be brief, ranging from one paragraph to a maximum of five pages. The approach is traditional, presenting basic, factual information at a level appropriate for the intended users. The subjects reflect the interests of elementary school students. A sample of entries from **anthropology** to **architecture** demonstrates the variety of topics included. Among them are **antibiotic; antimatter; antique; Apache Indians; ape; Appalachian Mountains; Appleseed, Johnny; Arabia; Arabian Nights; archeology, archery,** and **Archimedes.**

The encyclopedia comprehensively covers the sample topics. **Louisa May Alcott** receives half a page, **dinosaurs** one and one-quarter pages of text and two pages of illustrations, **Martin Luther King** two pages, **Mexico** three and a half pages, the **Middle Ages** two and a half pages of text and two pages of illustrations, **painting** four pages, and **soccer** two pages.

Currency

Although the edition reviewed here has a 1992 copyright date, many articles do not reflect information that was current at that time. The publisher claims that the set is revised annually but does not mention the extent of the revision. A major revision of 90 percent of the set is planned for July 1994, according to the publisher.

Articles on countries, states, cities, and provinces are written without listing government officials or economic information. Populations are included, but no date or source is given. These figures are not current when compared with the 1990 U.S. census and the *1992 Statistical Abstract of the United States.* There is no article on *Russia* since the breakup of the U.S.S.R. occurred in late 1991, presumably while the work was in production. **Yugoslavia** and **Czechoslovakia** also remain intact in this work. Maps within the text (as well as those in the separate atlas that comes with it, *Discovering Maps: A Young Person's World Atlas*) are out-of-date. Germany is united, as is Yemen, but other changes in Europe are not reflected. *Yemen* does not have its own article. It is included in the article on **Arabia.**

Bill Clinton is not mentioned in this encyclopedia, and *George Bush* is still listed as President of the United States. The *food pyramid* is not included in the article on **nutrition,** which cites four food groups. The **Gulf War** receives a half page as a main entry with related information in the articles on **Iraq** and **Israel** and brief mentions in the articles on **George Herbert Walker Bush, oil, sanctions,** and **conservation.** Space exploration is covered in the articles on **space research** (three pages) and **space travel** (five pages). The photographs in this encyclopedia are reasonably current, although the picture in the entry **computer** shows old hardware with external disk drives and an outdated printer. The illustrations of dinosaurs still call the *apatosaurus* the *brontosaurus.*

Accuracy

In general, our content specialists found the information in *The New Grolier Student Encyclopedia* to be well written, accurate, and appropriate for the intended age level. The entry **oxygen,** for example, is factually correct and covers most of the topics that should be covered in an article in a multivolume work. Our astronomy adviser commented that the **comets** entry has the best description for students of those that he read and is well balanced and well organized for young readers.

In the **Congress, United States** entry, however, some information, including a discussion of why the House is the lower house and the Senate the upper house, is misleading and confusing.

The text on Henry VIII, found in the **Henry, King of England** article, is confusing and incomplete. It concentrates on his marriages and ignores almost everything else.

Some articles on complex subjects lack substance. The treatment of diseases such as **cancer** and **AIDS** underestimates the seriousness of these conditions. Cancer is actually many different diseases that require different therapeutic approaches, but the article does not convey this. The **AIDS** article implies that a cure is forthcoming, which unfortunately is not the case.

In some entries, the encyclopedia suffers from both lack of revision and oversimplification. For example, the list of countries in the article on **Africa** provides the wrong capitals for both Nigeria (*Lagos* rather than *Abuja*) and Tanzania (*Dodoma* rather than *Dar es Salaam*).

Clarity

Articles are written in a clear, readable style that conveys the necessary information. The placement of illustrations and activity sections sometimes breaks up articles, making them difficult to follow. The **fingerprints** article, for example, begins with a "Learn by doing" exercise before presenting any text material. The text begins with history:

> Sir Francis Galton, a British scientist, developed a system in the 1800's for comparing fingerprints. Impressions of a person's fingerprints can be taken by placing each fingertip on an ink pad and then pressing it on a card. A person's fingerprints are also left on any smooth surface he or she touches even if they are not visible to the eye.

Although the writing is understandable, the article does not convey the essential facts about the way fingerprints are collected and analyzed. WORLD BOOK ENCYCLOPEDIA offers a better explanation.

Other articles provide adequate coverage of their subjects. **Digestion** explains the process and the differences between human and animal digestive tracts. **Fencing** demonstrates the movements and equipment used in the sport. Although some information is sacrificed for simplicity and brevity, the basic concepts appear.

Objectivity

The New Grolier Student Encyclopedia provides basic information on a wide variety of subjects. Controversial topics, such as abortion, do not appear. There is no obvious bias in the writing, although controversial aspects of some subjects are not fully presented.

A sampling of potentially controversial articles demonstrates the encyclopedia's tendency to avoid controversy. **Discrimination** begins with a false premise:

> If pupils in your school start a club for stamp collectors, anyone who is not a stamp collector is excluded. We say that the club's members are *discriminating* against non-stamp collectors.

It later states, "In the United States, blacks were discriminated against for many years," as if the problem had been solved. The article on **Northern Ireland** takes a straight historical approach, stopping in 1985 and failing to mention the fact that both Catholics and Protestants are responsible for the violence. There is no article on the *ozone layer*.

Accessibility

This encyclopedia is easy to use. Main entry terms are logical and well chosen. Entries are arranged alphabetically. Guide words on each page help users find desired information. An introduction in volume 1 explains the organization of the set. Each volume has its own table of contents, listing all of its main entries.

A system of cross-references helps users locate related material. They appear at the end of the article in small capitals with the heading "Also Read." There are also *see* references to refer readers to material located in other articles for subjects that do not have their own entries, such as "Achilles, see Trojan War."

The index in volume 22 contains 20,000 entries. Illustrations, maps, and material in "Information nuggets" and "Learn by doing" exercises are included. Main entries for articles appear in boldface. Entries for illustrations are in italics and those for "Learn by doing" material have an asterisk after the page number. Detailed instructions for using the index appear at the beginning of the section. The index does not contain any cross-references but seems comprehensive and accurate.

The atlas (*Discovering Maps: A Young Person's World Atlas*) that comes with this encyclopedia is not directly connected to it. No references to the atlas are made in the "Introduction" to the encyclopedia, and the atlas's function seems to be simply to teach basic map skills to students. The content of the atlas is identical to that of DISCOVERING MAPS: A CHILDREN'S WORLD ATLAS, which is reviewed in Chapter 7.

Special Features

The New Grolier Student Encyclopedia is profusely illustrated with color and black-and-white photographs, drawings, diagrams, charts, and maps. Approximately 75 percent of the illustrations are in color. The placement of illustrations sometimes breaks up the articles. A few are misplaced, such as a full-page color plate of New Guinea peoples at the beginning of the **Nevada** article. The quality of the pictures varies. Most are acceptable, but some are grainy. Reproductions of paintings are poor. Captions are clear and often describe the depicted object, rather than simply naming it. Illustrations are multicultural, and women such as Sarah Bernhardt, the French actress, and Mary McLeod Bethune, the American educator, are depicted.

Fact boxes accompany articles on states and countries, and contain information such as the official flag, flower, bird, tree, motto, song, language, and money.

"Information nuggets," set off by colored bars at the side of the page, contain interesting facts related to the main text of the article. In a 50-page sample, there were 25 nuggets, such as this one on **Newton, Sir Isaac:**

> Newton made his three momentous discoveries in a burst of inspiration from 1665 to 1667. He was not yet 26 years of age when he achieved this.

"Learn by doing" exercises show users how to perform simple experiments that reinforce the information presented (for example, building an abacus). None of the articles have bibliographies, and there are no supplemental reading lists in the introduction or index sections.

Format

The slim 8½" × 11" volumes are easy for young students to hold. The typeface is very readable and the margins adequate. The book lies flat when open. The paper is of good quality and the binding is very sturdy. The overall layout is reasonably attractive but old-fashioned.

Summary

The New Grolier Student Encyclopedia is a simple, colorful beginning reference tool for elementary school students. It suffers from oversimplification and is more out-of-date than its copyright would suggest. It is, however, more straightforward, better illustrated, and more attuned to American children than CHILDREN'S BRITANNICA. *The New Grolier Student Encyclopedia* is adequate for home use, and will be the best available set intended strictly for children after its 1994 revision. Schools and libraries should invest in one of the more comprehensive sets, such as WORLD BOOK, that is aimed toward both children and older students.

For another opinion, see D. A. Rothschild's review of the 1991 edition in *ARBA 1993,* page 28.

Oxford Children's Encyclopedia

Facts at a Glance

Full title: **Oxford Children's Encyclopedia**
Publisher: Oxford University Press
Editor: Mary Worrall
Number of contributors: 112
Edition reviewed: © 1991, 1993 printing

Number of volumes: 7
Number of articles: 2,000
Number of pages: 1,641 (reviewer estimate)
Number of words: 100,000 (reviewer estimate)
Number of cross-references: 6,000 (reviewer estimate)
Number of index entries: 15,000
Number of maps: 200 (reviewer estimate)
Number of illustrations: 3,000; 95 percent in full-color

Intended readership: ages 8 to 13
Trim size: $8^5/_8" \times 10^7/_8"$
Binding: hardcover

Price: $200
Sold directly to school libraries; also sold in bookstores
ISBN 0-19-910136-6
No stated revision policy

Introduction

The *Oxford Children's Encyclopedia* is the first encyclopedia published by Oxford University Press (OUP) for 8- to 13-year-olds since the now out-of-print *Junior Encyclopedia* was published in the 1950s. This seven-volume set consists of five volumes of subject entries in alphabetical order, a sixth volume of biographical entries, and a seventh volume containing the index. The biographical volume covers 500 individuals. The work has 2,000 articles and 3,000 illustrations, half of which are photographs. According to the work's introduction, the encyclopedia is designed to be a "starting point from which [children] can find out about animals, plants, people, places, science, technology, the Earth, the universe, history, religions, music, painting, and many other topics." This very recent work was copyrighted in 1991, revised in 1992, and reprinted in 1993.

Authority

The subject experts who helped to draw up the article list for the encyclopedia included a physicist, a geographer, two educators, and two scientists. All are from England, and most are affiliated with British universities. Groups of children from six schools in England were asked to suggest topics about which they were curious, and the final article list reflected a balance between the experts' and the children's ideas. Fifty-three other consultants are identified in the work as well, the majority of whom hold Ph.D.s and/or are professors.

Oxford University Press, publisher of the renowned OXFORD ENGLISH DICTIONARY, has an excellent reputation with regard to reference works. This encyclopedia is no exception to the high quality expected from this publisher.

Scope

The articles in the *Oxford Children's Encyclopedia* tend to favor specific topics, although broad subjects such as the **Renaissance** also receive coverage. Since children in the target age range helped in selecting topics, the articles will definitely appeal to 8- to 13-year-olds. The articles cover both current topics such as the **Cold war** and **microprocessors** and historical subjects such as **Midas** and the **Aztecs.**

As its introduction states, this work is weighted toward science and technology. Fifty pages in volume 5,

Oxford Children's Encyclopedia

❶ Magnets

198

Magnets

There are probably lots of magnets in your house. They hold refrigerator and wardrobe doors shut and they attract can-tops to the can opener. There are other magnets you cannot see: in the door bell, the telephone, the television and the electric motors in food mixers and drills.

Magnetic materials

Tin is not attracted to magnets. Magnets attract 'tin' cans because these are mainly steel. The tin is just a thin coating.

Magnets attract some metals, but not all. They attract iron, nickel, cobalt and most types of steel. But there are many metals they do not attract, including copper, aluminium, brass, gold, tin, silver and lead.

Materials which are attracted to magnets can be *made* into magnets. If you put a steel needle next to a magnet, it too becomes a magnet. And it stays magnetized when you take the magnet away. An iron nail also becomes magnetized near a magnet. But it quickly loses its magnetism when the magnet is removed. Steel keeps its magnetism, but iron does not. Magnets which keep their magnetism are called permanent magnets. Most are made of steel, special alloys (metal mixtures) or materials called ferrites. They can be made in the shape of bars, horseshoes and rings.

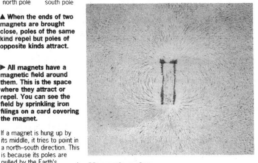

north pole   south pole

▲ When the ends of two magnets are brought close, poles of the same kind repel but poles of opposite kinds attract.

▶ All magnets have a magnetic field around them. This is the space where they attract or repel. You can see the field by sprinkling iron filings on a card covering the magnet.

If a magnet is hung up by its middle, it tries to point in a north–south direction. This is because its poles are pulled by the Earth's magnetic poles. With a magnet, 'north pole' really means 'north-seeking pole'. This is the end that tries to point north.

◉ See also

Compasses
Iron and steel
Metals

Biography
Faraday

Magnetic poles

The forces from a magnet seem to come from two points near its ends. These points are called the poles of the magnet. One is a north pole; the other is a south pole. If you hold two magnets with their north poles close, they push each other apart: they repel. The same happens with two south poles. But a north pole and a south pole attract. Poles of the same kind repel; poles of opposite kinds attract.

When a piece of iron or steel enters the magnetic field of a magnet, it becomes magnetized with poles that are opposite to those of the permanent magnet. This is why they are attracted to each other.

Nobody knows for certain how magnets work. Scientists think that, in materials like iron and steel, each atom is a tiny magnet. Normally, the atoms point in all directions and their magnetic effects cancel. But when a material is magnetized, its atoms line up in the same direction, and it becomes one big magnet.

Electromagnets

An electromagnet is a type of magnet which can be switched on and off. This is manufactured by winding specially insulated wire round an iron core. An electric current is then passed through the wire, which magnetizes the iron. The iron loses its magnetism when the current is switched off. If a steel core is used instead of iron, it keeps its magnetism when the current is switched off. This is the way most permanent magnets are made.

Electromagnets are used in scrap-yards for separating iron and steel from other materials. Surgeons use them to remove iron and steel splinters from eyes.

Flashback

The ancient Greeks knew about magnetism 2,500 years ago. They knew that lodestone was a naturally magnetic rock. The Earth itself behaves like a big magnet. It pulls on lodestone and other magnets so that they always try to point the same way. The idea was later used in compasses.

In 1820, Hans Christian Oersted, a Danish scientist, found that electric currents could have an effect on magnets.

In the 1830s, Michael Faraday discovered that an electric current could be produced by moving a magnet about in a coil of wire. For the first time, electricity could be made without batteries. The idea is still used in the power-stations of today. ■

Something to do

Hang paper-clips from a magnet. Where can you hang most clips, the ends or the middle?

Magnetize a blunt needle by stroking it with a magnet. Always stroke it the same way, with the same end. What can it pick up?

Page shown at 77% of actual size.

❶ Guide word and page number

❷ Boldface main entry word on a line by itself

❸ Subheads divide longer entries into more manageable sections

❹ Additional interesting facts located in outer margin

❺ Four-color illustration includes call-outs and informative caption

❻ Cross-references indicated by eye symbol

❼ "Something to do" lists related projects

covering the entries from **submarines** to **trade unions,** were selected for content-area analysis. Over 49 percent of the entries were science- and technology-related, 18 percent were about geography, 16 percent about history and social studies, 10 percent about popular culture, and 7 percent about the humanities.

The work's British bias comes through strongly in the selection of topics and vocabulary. For example, the article **averages** uses cricket for an example where an American writer would have used baseball. Decimal points are centered, in the British style (for example, 3·5 meters), and topics such as **tyres** (tires), **Georgian England, cricket,** and **snooker** all show a British orientation. Although **baseball, American football,** and **American Indians** are included, young readers may be confused by entries such as **hedgerows,** where a sidebar instructs readers to "Find your old parish boundary on a historical map and count the different types of trees and shrubs along a stretch of hedgerow there."

The amount of coverage per article is balanced and appropriate for the topics. The entry for **Louisa May Alcott** occupies one-third of a page; **dinosaurs,** five pages; **Dr. Martin Luther King,** three-fourths of a page; **Mexico,** one page including a map; the **Middle Ages,** four pages; and **painting,** six pages including illustrations. The two-page article on *soccer* can be found under **football,** as the game is called in Europe. This is one of the few children's encyclopedias that contains all of the Buying Guide's test entries.

THE NEW GROLIER STUDENT ENCYCLOPEDIA, which is similar in scope to this work, has very comparable coverage of each of the previously mentioned entries. Only **Mexico,** represented in NEW GROLIER by four pages of text and illustrations, differs significantly. This difference reflects NEW GROLIER's more thorough coverage of geography.

Currency

The introduction states that the work was begun in 1987 and was checked and updated in March 1992. This revision was done prior to the most recent U.S. presidential election, so George Bush is the last president identified. *Food pyramid* is not included, which is not surprising since it is an American concept. However, the article on **diets** includes a food pie chart that identifies which foods to eat more of and which to avoid.

Gulf War is covered briefly in the article on **Iraq.** The breakup of the U.S.S.R. is covered in the articles on **Russia** and the **Union of Soviet Socialist Republics,** although a list of the "Republics of the Union of Soviet Socialist Republics" is still appended to the index volume. The reunification of Germany is handled under **German history.** The division of Czechoslovakia occurred after the encyclopedia's revision date, so it is not included.

The coverage of **space exploration** is quite extensive, covering more than four pages. The coverage of other current technology is also comprehensive: **computers** and **robots** have their own entries, and *compact discs* and *fax machines* are mentioned elsewhere.

The photographs and illustrations all have a contemporary look. For example, in the article on **singing and songs,** Michael Jackson is featured in a photograph. One of the photographs for **architects** shows the Lloyds building in London, which was completed in 1986.

Accuracy

Entries for **Henry VIII, Congress,** and **cancer** are generally accurate, although some factual errors have crept in. For example, a 1990 reapportionment has changed the number of representatives to Congress from certain states, but this change is not reflected in the article. The entry for **cancer** states that "Cancers can be cured if they are found and treated at an early stage of development," but neglects to mention that some cancers are incurable. The entry for **comet** is both accurate and appropriate for a young audience. **Oxygen** describes the element as being the most plentiful one "on this planet," when in fact it is only the most common element in the earth's crust.

Unlike many children's encyclopedias, this work generally does not oversimplify subjects or soften the information given. For example, the article on **sex** includes a detailed description of human intercourse, and **birth** is accompanied by a photograph of a woman giving birth.

Clarity

The work is designed for children 8 to 13 years old, but the vocabulary and level of information would also be appropriate for young people up to age 17. The articles are well structured, beginning with general information and adding specific details and facts in later sections. Longer articles, such as those on countries, are divided by subheads in bold type.

The authors of the articles do not hesitate to use advanced vocabulary, which is then explained in the text, in a sidebar, or in the caption of an illustration. The entry for **earth** mentions the term "remote sensing," which is explained as using satellites to study the earth from great distances.

The last paragraph in the **fingerprints** entry provides a good example of the complexity of the writing style and vocabulary:

> When you touch anything, you leave a trace of sweat from sweat glands in your fingerprint pattern. After a crime, the police dust aluminum powder over any fingerprints to make them show up. In Britain the fingerprints of every convicted criminal are kept at New Scotland Yard, and fingerprints found after a crime are compared with them. They must match in sixteen different ways before they can be used as evidence.

Objectivity

The editor and writers of the *Oxford Children's Encyclopedia* are not afraid to deal with controversial issues. The term **apartheid** has its own entry and is also covered in the articles on **South Africa** and **Nelson Mandela. Civil rights** are covered generally in their own entry and are also mentioned in articles on **Dr. Martin Luther King** and **Mahatma Gandhi.** The complicated situation leading to the "troubles" in Northern Ireland is covered in **Ireland's History, Ulster,** and **Northern Ireland.** *Discrimination* is not an entry word.

Controversial scientific topics are also discussed, and the coverage afforded to each is very similar to that of THE NEW GROLIER STUDENT ENCYCLOPEDIA. The article on **ozone** explains that scientists are concerned about the ozone layer, and the articles on the **greenhouse effect** and **aerosols** elaborate these concerns. An article on **Brazil** contains information on the destruction of the rain forest. This important issue, however, deserves a separate entry.

Accessibility

The first five volumes are arranged in alphabetical order by subject. A table of contents in each one identifies every entry in that volume and gives its page number. Each volume has a section entitled "How to use the Oxford Children's Encyclopedia," which gives examples of how to locate articles, use the work's many cross-references, and negotiate the index volume.

The title of each entry that begins on a page appears in the upper outside corner of that page as a guide word. Each volume's first and last entries are printed on the spine of the book, along with the letters of the alphabet covered therein.

The biographical entries in volume 6 contain dates and accomplishments in a green box and information about the person's life in several paragraphs. This volume has its own "How to use . . ." page. Volume 7 contains the 15,000-entry index to the set. A detailed explanation of its use is given in the front of the volume. Works of art that appear in the text, such as George Stubbs' *Horses* in the article on **painting,** are indexed, but general illustrations are not. A special index following the general index lists the people in the biography volume grouped by occupation.

In general, young readers will find this work more accessible than NEW GROLIER, which is divided into 22 slim volumes. NEW GROLIER incorporates biographical entries into the main lexicon, rather than grouping them in a separate volume.

Special Features

The encyclopedia has outstanding illustrations that are more up-to-date than those of THE NEW GROLIER STUDENT ENCYCLOPEDIA. More than 3,000 are included, half of which are photographs. Most of the 2,000 articles are illustrated, and many have more than one picture. The photographs are fascinating: goats that climb trees to forage for food are shown in the entry for **goats,** and a rock python swallowing a whole antelope appears under **snakes.**

The illustrations show men, women, boys, girls, and various ethnic and racial groups. The physically challenged are represented in pictures such as the illustration for **archery,** which shows a contestant shooting from a wheelchair. Although many of the photographs are British, other countries and cultures are well represented.

The maps contained in this work are excellent. Nearly every country covered has a general map indicating its location in the hemisphere and a boundary map showing neighboring countries, major cities, and (on larger maps) geographical features. Unlike in many children's encyclopedias, historical maps are used extensively with the historical articles. The maps help to show the extent of the Roman Empire, the spread of ice during the Ice Age, and the concept of plate tectonics, for example.

The biography volume contains special sections on the British royal family, film actors and actresses, pop and rock figures, and athletes. The index volume provides lists of countries and their capitals, U.S. states and their capitals, prime ministers of Britain, Canada, Australia, and New Zealand, historical rulers of England and the United Kingdom, presidents of the United States, states and territories of Australia, provinces and territories of Canada, counties of the United Kingdom, and Republics of the U.S.S.R.

Some of the encyclopedia's articles have special features entitled "Something to Do." These include such activities as experiments with **magnets** and instructions for *Klondike,* a **card game** similar to solitaire.

Format

The *Oxford Children's Encyclopedia* is particularly well designed. The volumes are packaged in a cardboard storage case and are easily handled. The type size is legible and the paragraphs are well spaced on the page. The margins are 1 inch at the top and bottom and ½ inch on the sides. The paper is thick and will stand up to heavy use. Captions and subheads are clear and easy to read. Blue fact boxes are especially useful for locating specific facts about countries quickly.

Summary

The *Oxford Children's Encyclopedia* is an excellent seven-volume reference set for children and young adults. OUP has an outstanding reputation in publishing, and the writing styles and level of complexity of this work will appeal to 8- to 13-year-olds as well as to older children who need general information.

The encyclopedia's British bias may confuse some young readers. The review of this work in *Booklist (Reference Books Bulletin)* (June 15, 1992, pp. 1886–87), however, points out that it gives "more of a world view than traditional American sources."

The *Oxford Children's Encyclopedia* is very comparable in scope to THE NEW GROLIER STUDENT ENCYCLOPEDIA. That work has more thorough coverage of geography and a slightly more advanced writing style; it is, however, more expensive and less attractively illustrated. Some other multivolume sets, such as the CHILDREN'S BRITANNICA and the adult WORLD BOOK ENCYCLOPEDIA, are more comprehensive than this work. Despite their higher prices, these works may be more valuable in the long run for families, since children will eventually grow out of a set such as the *Oxford Children's Encyclopedia*. Nonetheless, this work is a very appealing, contemporary multivolume reference tool that has broad appeal.

Random House Children's Encyclopedia

Facts at a Glance

Full title: **Random House Children's Encyclopedia**
Publisher: Random House/Dorling Kindersley
Editors: Ann Kramer, Senior Editor; Regina Kahney, U.S. Editor
Number of contributors: 18
Edition reviewed: © 1993, second American edition

Number of volumes: 1
Number of articles: 450
Number of pages: 644
Number of words: 75,000 (reviewer estimate)
Number of cross-references: 2,250 (reviewer estimate)
Number of index entries: 5,600 (reviewer estimate)
Number of maps: 40 (reviewer estimate)
Number of illustrations: 3,500; 95 percent in full color
Intended readership: ages 7 to 12
Trim size: 8½″ × 10¾″
Binding: hardcover

Price: $50
Sold in bookstores; also sold through children's book clubs
ISBN 0-394-83852-1
No stated revision policy

Introduction

This work was originally published in 1991 by the British firm of Dorling Kindersley as the *Dorling Kindersley Children's Illustrated Encyclopedia*. It was also adapted for an American audience and sold by Random House. The one-volume work contains 644 pages (140 of which have been revised from the 1991 edition), with 450 main entries. It has 3,500 illustrations, most in color. Designed for a readership of 7- to 12-year-olds, the work is arranged alphabetically by subject and has a comprehensive 14-page index. It is one of the largest single-volume children's encyclopedias available.

Authority

Sixty-three subject-area advisers and consultants contributed to this work. They include NASA (for space science), the International Olympic Committee (for sports), and the British Royal Air Force (for transportation). Individual contributors, many with advanced degrees, are also indicated on the encyclopedia's copyright page. Ruth I. Gordon, M.L.S., Ph.D., and Sachem Publishing Associates are listed as U.S. consultants, but no child or reading specialists are indicated. Both Dorling Kindersley in Great Britain and Random House in the United States are known for their quality work.

Scope

Most of the articles are one or two pages long, and they cover a broad range of topics. As with many children's encyclopedias, topics on science predominate. An examination of the 50 pages beginning with **crocodiles** and ending with **explorers** shows that 68 percent of the entries are science related, 19 percent cover history and the social sciences, 8 percent deal with the humanities, and 5 percent are about geography. Except for sports, very little popular culture is covered. An evaluation of the 25 pages from **oceans and seas** to **Pilgrims** reveals that only 29 percent of the articles represent uniquely British or American topics, while 71 percent represent other countries and cultures.

The number of pages accorded specific subjects is appropriate for the importance of the subject. For example, **dinosaurs** receive two pages, as do **Mexico,** the **Middle Ages,** and **painting. Martin Luther King** is accorded one page, while soccer receives a brief mention in the illustration captions of two articles; one of the pictures is a diagram of a soccer field. However, American writer *Louisa May Alcott* is not mentioned.

Currency

Because 22 percent of the *Random House Children's Encyclopedia* was revised for the 1993 edition, this work is very current. **Bill Clinton** is listed as the current president of the United States in the "Fact Finder." The **Gulf War** receives a brief mention under **Middle East Wars.** The new **Russian Federation** is one of the largest sections, covering four pages. Space exploration is covered in the article **space flight,** which includes the space

Random House Children's Encyclopedia

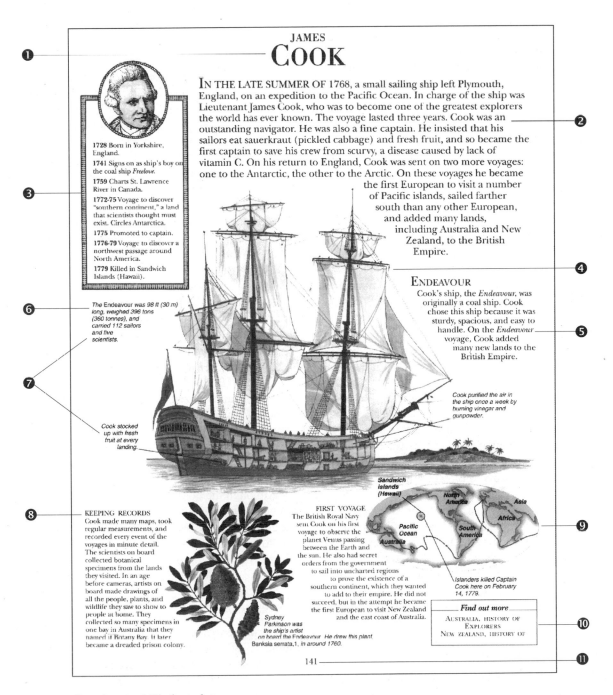

JAMES
COOK

IN THE LATE SUMMER OF 1768, a small sailing ship left Plymouth, England, on an expedition to the Pacific Ocean. In charge of the ship was Lieutenant James Cook, who was to become one of the greatest explorers the world has ever known. The voyage lasted three years. Cook was an outstanding navigator. He was also a fine captain. He insisted that his sailors eat sauerkraut (pickled cabbage) and fresh fruit, and so became the first captain to save his crew from scurvy, a disease caused by lack of vitamin C. On his return to England, Cook was sent on two more voyages: one to the Antarctic, the other to the Arctic. On these voyages he became the first European to visit a number of Pacific islands, sailed farther south than any other European, and added many lands, including Australia and New Zealand, to the British Empire.

1728 Born in Yorkshire, England.

1741 Signs on as ship's boy on the coal ship *Freelove*.

1759 Charts St. Lawrence River in Canada.

1772-75 Voyage to discover "southern continent," a land that scientists thought must exist. Circles Antarctica.

1775 Promoted to captain.

1776-79 Voyage to discover a northwest passage around North America.

1779 Killed in Sandwich Islands (Hawaii).

ENDEAVOUR
Cook's ship, the *Endeavour*, was originally a coal ship. Cook chose this ship because it was sturdy, spacious, and easy to handle. On the *Endeavour* voyage, Cook added many new lands to the British Empire.

The Endeavour was 98 ft (30 m) long, weighed 396 tons (360 tonnes), and carried 112 sailors and five scientists.

Cook purified the air in the ship once a week by burning vinegar and gunpowder.

Cook stocked up with fresh fruit at every landing.

KEEPING RECORDS
Cook made many maps, took regular measurements, and recorded every event of the voyages in minute detail. The scientists on board collected botanical specimens from the lands they visited. In an age before cameras, artists on board made drawings of all the people, plants, and wildlife they saw to show to people at home. They collected so many specimens in one bay in Australia that they named it Botany Bay. It later became a dreaded prison colony.

Sydney Parkinson was the ship's artist on board the Endeavour. He drew this plant, Banksia serrata, 1, in around 1760.

FIRST VOYAGE
The British Royal Navy sent Cook on his first voyage to observe the planet Venus passing between the Earth and the sun. He also had secret orders from the government to sail into uncharted regions to prove the existence of a southern continent, which they wanted to add to their empire. He did not succeed, but in the attempt he became the first European to visit New Zealand and the east coast of Australia.

Sandwich Islands (Hawaii)

North America

Asia

Africa

Pacific Ocean

South America

Australia

Islanders killed Captain Cook here on February 14, 1779.

Find out more
AUSTRALIA, HISTORY OF
EXPLORERS
NEW ZEALAND, HISTORY OF

141

Page shown at 64% of actual size.

❶ Main entry heading in large, bold-face type
❷ Introduction explains the subject
❸ Illustrated time line
❹ Four-color illustration
❺ Caption explains the illustration
❻ Measurements given in both standard and metric systems
❼ Additional captions offer more interesting details about the illustration
❽ Subentry gives information about a related topic
❾ Map gives travel route and specific location
❿ "Find out more" box directs readers to related entries
⓫ Page number

shuttle and various planetary probes. The map of Europe shows the Russian Federation, a united Germany, the Czech Republic and Slovakia, and a fragmented Yugoslavia. There is no entry for *food pyramid,* however.

The photographs and drawings are colorful and have a modern look. The ones for **cars** are especially good in this respect, as are those for **air forces** and **aircraft.** The article on **computers** also has contemporary illustrations as well as coverage of scanners and color printers.

Accuracy

Coverage of specifics is sometimes lacking in the *Random House Children's Encyclopedia. Henry VIII* is mentioned only in passing within the **United Kingdom** article, and *Congress* is discussed only as a type of governing body under **governments.** The use of microscopy to reveal *cancer* cells is mentioned briefly in the article on **health,** but the topic *cancer* is discussed nowhere else in the encyclopedia.

The information about **comets and meteors** is accurate, but the article on **oxygen** is less so. Oxygen is described as "the most common substance on Earth," but it is only the most common substance in the earth's crust. During the process of burning, oxygen is said to combine with wood to give off heat. This oversimplifies a reaction that involves carbon and hydrogen atoms in the wood and the release of carbon dioxide and water. The article states that plants "produce energy for growth by the process of photosynthesis"; they actually *capture* energy for growth from sunlight through this process. In addition, the article's statement that "sea water contains dissolved oxygen" may lead readers to believe that *only* sea water contains dissolved oxygen. In fact, all water contains some oxygen in solution.

Other oversimplifications also occur. For example, the coverage of the **English Civil War** does not mention religion as a cause, despite the fact that Cromwell and most of his followers wanted to purify the Anglican church of remaining Catholic influences. This is not a major flaw in the work, but it does show a tendency to oversimplify complicated and multifaceted events and processes.

Clarity

The writing style of the articles is very lucid and concise. The articles begin with a general overview of one to three paragraphs and give more specific information in sidebars and extensive paragraph-long illustration captions. The vocabulary and writing style are appropriate for the target audience, especially the upper age range.

Information on *fingerprints* appears under the heading **police** in three captions surrounding photographs of a fingerprint-dust brush and a page of fingerprints as they would appear in a criminal's record. The captions

read: "Police keep fingerprint records of every known criminal," "Brushing special powder onto shiny surfaces reveals fingerprints," and "The pattern on the skin of every person's hands is unique. Detectives look for the fingerprints of the suspect at the scene of the crime."

Objectivity

In many ways, the *Random House Children's Encyclopedia* is very objective. The illustrations are remarkably free of gender and racial bias. For example, the pictures for **doctors** show women as physicians, and the article on the **human body** shows African, Hispanic, Oriental, and European figures.

The encyclopedia takes an evenhanded view of most controversial subjects. For example, balanced coverage of the *civil rights movement* appears under the article on **Martin Luther King.** An explanation of *apartheid* appears in the article on **Africa** next to a picture of Nelson Mandela.

The most unsatisfactory coverage is accorded the topic *Northern Ireland.* The region is mentioned in separate entries for the **United Kingdom** and **Ireland,** but the reasons for the division of Ireland are not covered at all. The article makes the split seem to be a whim of the British rulers, when in fact it was primarily a religious issue. Although the "History of Ireland" section describes the "Planting of Protestant English and Scottish people on lands seized from the Irish" and mentions the suppression of Catholic civil rights marches in 1968, coverage of the religious controversy is inadequate. As with the **English Civil War** entry, the editors show an unfortunate tendency to downplay this key factor in human history.

Although the book was revised for an American audience, some British bias is evident. The fact that the English Civil War receives the same amount of space as the American Civil War will strike an American readership as odd. The time line for the Industrial Revolution also has a distinctly British slant.

Accessibility

The arrangement of the work in alphabetical order by subject heading is a familiar and easily understood concept to the target audience. A three-page introductory section entitled "How to Use This Book" employs circles, arrows, and photoreduced sample pages to explain how the articles are organized and how to find information.

"See" references appear at the top of each page on which a new entry begins: on the **New Zealand** page, for example, "**New deal** *see* Roosevelt, Franklin D." and "**New York City** *see* United States of America" appear. Cross-references to related articles appear in a box in the lower right-hand corner of the last page of each entry. Usually three to five references are given.

The 14-page index is quite extensive. Subentries are indented under the main entries. Bold page numbers indicate a main entry, numbers in roman refer to information within a main entry, and italicized numbers indicate that the topic is found in the "Fact Finder." "See also" references are extensively employed in the index. Illustrations are not indexed.

Special Features

This work is loaded with special features to attract and inform the user. Typical of Dorling Kindersley's publications, the vivid illustrations are very effective in enhancing the textual explanations. For example, the illustration of how a color printing press works is very informative. Diagrams and charts also help to clarify the articles. Large maps of countries and continents are especially well done and are clear, accurate, and up-to-date. The full-page map of Africa, for example, shows countries, geographical features, and major cities.

A 21-page "Fact Finder," located before the index, includes time lines; lists of historical events, U.S. presidents, kings and queens of Great Britain, and prime ministers of Great Britain; a world map; superlatives such as largest countries and biggest cities; Olympic events; wildlife facts; conservation organizations; star maps; the periodic table; and time zones. This part of the work is also indexed.

Format

The *Random House Children's Encyclopedia* is a large and hefty volume, weighing well over 5 pounds. This means that a smaller child will have to prop the book up on a table or on a stand to use it. The type is very legible, the paper is thick enough to withstand heavy use, and the binding is sturdy.

Summary

The *Random House Children's Encyclopedia* is a very attractive and informative reference work. It is particularly well done for a single-volume work, and it compares favorably to some multivolume encyclopedias. In length and coverage of information, it is far superior to Troll's STUDENT ENCYCLOPEDIA and the USBORNE CHILDREN'S ENCYCLOPEDIA. Although not enough information is included here for long reports, this is an excellent resource for short factual research. Its bold and contemporary illustrations encourage browsing and will fascinate both children and adults.

For other opinions about the *Random House Children's Encyclopedia,* see the *School Library Journal,* May 1992, page 28, and *Booklist (Reference Books Bulletin),* Oct. 15, 1991, page 467, for information on the 1991 edition. See *Booklist (Reference Books Bulletin)* January 1, 1994, page 852, for a review of the 1993 revision.

Student Encyclopedia

Facts at a Glance

Full title: **Student Encyclopedia**
Publisher: Troll Associates
Editors: Michael Dempsey; Keith Lye
Edition reviewed: © 1991

Number of volumes: 1
Number of articles: 2,000 (reviewer estimate)
Number of pages: 128
Number of words: 82,000 (reviewer estimate)
Number of cross-references: none
Number of index entries: none
Number of maps: 5
Number of illustrations: 182 (reviewer estimate), all in color
Intended readership: grades 1 to 8
Trim size: 8½″ × 10¾″
Binding: hardcover; paperback

Price: $14.89 (hardcover); $9.95 (paperback)
Sold directly to schools and libraries; also sold in bookstores and other retail outlets, and by dealers
ISBN 0-8167-2257-9 (hardcover);
    ISBN 0-8167-2258-7 (paperback)
No stated revision policy

Introduction

The *Student Encyclopedia* is a one-volume, 128-page work designed to help children from elementary through junior high school satisfy their curiosity about their world, both past and present. According to the opening section entitled "How to Use this Book," young people "can use this book to find out about people, places, events, animals, ideas, and things you might have wondered about." The work contains 2,000 entries, ranging from science to art to music to history to entertainment. Approximately 182 color illustrations will encourage the curious child to browse.

Authority

The editors of this encyclopedia are Michael Dempsey and Keith Lye. No biographical information is included about them, nor are any contributors mentioned. The publishers, Troll Associates, have several works in print, including an atlas aimed at the same audience as this encyclopedia. No information is provided on the criteria used to include or exclude information. Whether subject authorities, educators, or librarians were consulted in the production of this work is not indicated.

Student Encyclopedia

❶ HADDOCK

❷ H

❸ ❹ Haddock An important food fish belonging to the cod family. Large schools of haddock are found in the northern Atlantic Ocean. The fish weighs about 3 pounds (1.4 kilograms).

Hades God of the underworld in Greek mythology. He ruled over the souls of the dead. The Romans called him Pluto.

Hair One of many of the threadlike growths on the skin of people and animals.

Halloween Festival celebrated on October 31, the eve of All Saints' Day. Once a pagan celebration before the beginning of winter, it is still associated with ghosts and witches.

Hamilton, Alexander (1757-1804) US statesman and first secretary of the treasury. He was killed in a duel with Aaron Burr.

Hamster A short-tailed rodent. It is considered a pest in the wild but is popular as a pet.

Hancock, John (1737-1793) US statesman. He was one of the leaders of the American Revolution and the first to sign the Declaration of Independence. He became the first governor of Massachusetts.

Handel, George Frideric (1685-1759) German-born British composer. He wrote more than 40 operas and over 30 musical compositions called oratorios. His most famous oratorio is *The Messiah* (1742). Handel also wrote organ and orchestral music, including the popular *Water Music* (1717).

Hannibal (247-183 BC) General of Carthage, an ancient city in northern Africa. He conquered southern Spain, then led his army and elephants across the Alps into Italy. Hannibal won a series of brilliant victories against the Romans. He was later defeated by the Romans in 202 BC.

Hanoi Port and capital city of Vietnam, on the Red River.

Harding, Warren G. (1865-1923) Twenty-ninth president of the United States. A Republican, he was a senator from Ohio. As president from 1921 to 1923, his administration was marked by political scandals. Harding died of pneumonia before completing his term of office.

Brown hare

Hare An animal with long ears and long legs. It is related to the rabbit. It can run very fast and lives in open fields. The jackrabbit is actually a hare, not a rabbit.

Harrison, Benjamin (1833-1901) Twenty-third president of the United States. He was the grandson of William Henry Harrison, the ninth president. Harrison was a lawyer. He served in the Union Army during the Civil War. After the war, he returned to his law practice and later was a senator from Indiana. A Republican, he was president from 1889 to 1893.

Harrison, William Henry (1773-1841) Ninth president of the United States. He had a distinguished army career. From 1800 to 1812 he was governor of the Indiana Territory. He was a member of the House of Representatives and the Senate from Ohio. A member of the Whig Party, Harrison died of pneumonia one month after he was inaugurated as president in 1841.

Hawaii The 50th state to join the United States. It is a group of about 130 volcanic islands in the central Pacific Ocean. Area: 6,450 square miles (16,705 square kilometers). Capital: Honolulu.

Hawthorne, Nathaniel (1804-1864) US writer. He wrote many children's stories, as well as short stories and novels. The novels include *The Scarlet Letter* and *The House of the Seven Gables*.

Haydn, Franz Joseph (1732-1809) Austrian composer. He wrote over 100 symphonies, over 80 string quartets, 20 operas, and a number of other musical works.

Hayes, Rutherford B. (1822-1893) Nineteenth president of the United States. He was a general in the Union Army during the Civil War. A Republican, Hayes entered politics after the war. He served three terms as governor of Ohio. He was president of the United States from 1877 to 1881. During his presidency, federal troops were withdrawn from the South.

Heart A muscular organ that

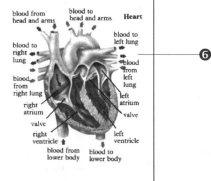

blood from head and arms — blood to head and arms — **Heart** — blood to left lung — blood to right lung — blood from left lung — blood from right lung — left atrium — right atrium — valve — valve — right ventricle — left ventricle — blood from lower body — blood to lower body — **❻**

Page shown at 66% of actual size.

❶ Guide word
❷ Guide letter set off by rules
❸ Main entry word in boldface type
❹ Measurements given in both standard and metric systems
❺ Page number appears at foot of page
❻ Four-color illustrations include detailed drawings with callouts

Scope

The encyclopedia contains 2,000 entries, arranged in alphabetical order. The majority of entries (about 38 percent) cover the area of science. Most of the scientific articles are about animals, although botany, space, and geology are also well represented. Scientific subjects include **beetle, dew point, lichen, microscope, oxidation,** and **solar system.** The second largest group (about 25 percent) contains geographical entries on cities, states, countries, and provinces. Physical geographical features such as **volcano, island,** and **mountains** are also covered. The third largest group of entries covers history and the social sciences. These range from political and historical figures to explanations of political offices such as the **President of the United States** and philosophies of government such as **fascism** and **socialism.** Entries on art, music, sports, literature, and popular culture round out the encyclopedia. Entries on **Leonard Bernstein, football, table tennis, Charlie Chaplin, Mark Twain, Renaissance,** and **Rembrandt** exemplify coverage of the humanities and popular culture.

Fifty sample pages containing entries from **Iceland** to the **solar system** were analyzed to determine the percentage of articles in each of these fields. Science is given 46 percent, geographical entries 24 percent, history and social sciences 22 percent, humanities 6 percent, and popular culture 2 percent.

Of the pages analyzed, 24 percent of the entries are biographical. About two-thirds of these entries are mainly political and historical figures. Of the remainder, 22 percent are in the humanities and 14 percent in science. Males predominate at 92 percent, with females at only 8 percent. African Americans (at 4 percent), and other groups (at 8 percent) had little representation.

The lack of coverage of important contemporary African-American writers is a problem. No mention is made of Alice Walker, Maya Angelou, or Toni Morrison—all prominent writers whom many students might wish to study. In general, only the most well-known authors, such as Edgar Allan Poe and William Shakespeare, are included in this work.

The encyclopedia has well-balanced coverage of the world. In a randomly selected 25-page segment, 44 percent of the entries covered U.S. subjects, and 7 percent covered topics related to Great Britain, 1 percent topics related to Canada, and the rest (48 percent) topics related to other areas of the world. Very little information about Asian or African countries is included, however.

Entries are quite brief, averaging about 35 words each. The standard entries used for comparison purposes in these reviews had the following word counts: **dinosaurs,** 50 words; **Martin Luther King,** 46 words; **Mexico,** 27 words; **Middle Ages,** 27 words; **painting,** 38 words; and **soccer,** 37 words. The author *Louisa May Alcott* did not have an entry. Such short entries would

limit their effectiveness for students in middle elementary grades—the intended readership.

Currency

The edition reviewed was published in 1991, which makes **George Bush** the last U.S. president covered. The dismantling of the Berlin Wall is mentioned within the entry on **Berlin.** *Mikhail Gorbachev* is not mentioned. The *food pyramid* is not covered. *Space exploration* is not an entry, but the **space probe** article covers the *Voyager II* flyby of Neptune in 1989. The article on **space station** covers *Salyut I* and *Skylab* but not the controversy concerning NASA's plans for a permanent space station. The 1989 California earthquake is discussed under **earthquake.** The entry on **smallpox** indicates that the disease has disappeared due to a worldwide vaccination program.

Current technology is well represented in the entries for **fiber optics, silicon,** and **hovercraft.** Illustrations accompanying **submarine** show the *USS Los Angeles.* Terms such as *compact disc, modem,* and *telecommunications* are not covered, but given how quickly technology changes, the omission of these terms is not a fatal flaw.

The *Student Encyclopedia* does not contain any political maps. The five that are included show ocean currents, prevailing winds, the earth's tectonic plates, the Native American nations in 1880, and world climates. The photographs appear new, with no out-of-date automobiles or clothing. Most of them show subjects such as the Hoover Dam or Mount Rushmore, which have not changed and are not likely to change in the future. The illustrations do not reflect cultural or gender stereotypes.

Accuracy

For the most part, the brevity of the articles in the *Student Encyclopedia* affects the work's accuracy. Our content adviser felt the two-sentence definition of **cancer** should be changed to reflect the concept that tumors disrupt normal body processes, which include not only the destroying of cells, but also other harmful effects to the body. Two of the four sentences about **Congress** are devoted to those that met in America prior to the founding of the United States. The only facts presented about the Congress of the past 204 years is that it is the "lawmaking assembly" and has two houses. Our adviser found the basic facts about **Henry VIII** to be correct, but questioned the article's ability to convey to children why Henry was a significant king in English history. The **comet** article is factually correct, but needs an illustration. The chemical symbol for **oxygen** gas is incorrectly given as O instead of O_2.

No serious inaccuracies as to facts or dates were found; however, the need for brevity has caused some of the entries to be so oversimplified that the user will definitely need to consult a different source for more details. For example, the entry for **ballet** reads: "A popular entertainment with dancing, music, scenery, and costumes." This could also describe modern musicals and some operas.

The term **civil rights** is defined, but the struggle for civil rights in the United States and in countries such as South Africa are not mentioned. The terms *Black Codes, Reconstruction,* and *Jim Crow laws* do not have entries. The majority of African-American history covered here deals with **slavery, the Underground Railroad,** and the **Civil War.** The term *apartheid* is not given an entry, nor is it mentioned in the coverage of **South Africa.** *Nelson Mandela* is not mentioned either.

The illustrations accompanying the entries are extremely clear and give an excellent sense of the subject. The illustrations of plants and animals give enough detail to make identification easy. The one for **spiders** shows five different types and the relative size and markings of each. The picture of the black widow spider, however, does not show the classic red hourglass. The illustrations for the **sun, solar system, Rome,** and **clouds** are most impressive and each covers up to one-third of a page. In general, though, most pictures are about 2 inches square. The drawings of people, such as those of **Hernando Cortés** and **Charles Darwin,** are small but detailed. Details from photographs are used for some individuals, such as **Winston Churchill** and **Joseph Stalin.** The illustrations are located near the entries they depict. Captions are often only a single word; some, however, give a brief description of the subject.

Clarity

The writing in the encyclopedia is clear and direct. Most sentences are short and to the point. Entries define or identify the subject, then follow with facts, dates, examples, or explanations. For example, the entry for **nuclear weapons** gives a brief explanation followed by the dates of the first explosion and the first atomic bombs dropped on Japan to end World War II. In other entries, such as the one on **nuclear fusion,** an illustration helps explain the process by which "the four atoms of hydrogen fuse to form one atom of helium." The overall tone of the writing would best fit the middle elementary grades, which is the target audience. The vocabulary in some cases may be too complex for primary grades and the entries are far too simple for high school.

The **fingerprints** entry is a typical example of the writing style and formula for most entries. Unfortunately, the entry confuses the ridges on the fingers that cause the prints with the marks left when a person touches some surfaces.

> **Fingerprints** The pattern of ridges on a person's finger pads. The pattern is unchanging and unique to each per-

son. The prints provide an almost foolproof method of identifying people and are useful in criminal investigations.

Objectivity

The *Student Encyclopedia*'s coverage is well balanced among time periods, nations, races, and religions. In the area of biography, white males predominate, but the editors make an honest attempt to include women and minorities in their coverage. While applauding the attempt, one does wonder why *Margaret Thatcher* or *Elizabeth II* were not accorded entries. One might also wonder why **Charlotte Brontë** merited an entry while *Emily Brontë* did not.

The coverage of political conflict is not as evenhanded. Although the sectarian violence between Protestants and Catholics in Northern Ireland is mentioned, the racial violence in South Africa is not. The articles on **American Indians** [sic], **Geronimo,** and **Sitting Bull** do not deal with the issue of relations between the United States and Native Americans in any but the most superficial terms.

In the articles dealing with science, the editors have avoided controversy. The article on **ozone** states that "some pollutants are destroying the ozone layer" without mentioning any other view. *Acid rain* is not even mentioned as a heading, nor is pollution of any type. The **AIDS** virus is covered but no mention is made of how it is transmitted. The article is misleading, making it seem that **AIDS** can be caught like the flu.

The pictures and illustrations also lack a balanced approach. Females appear in only three illustrations, for the entries: **ballet, gymnastics,** and **weaving.** No prominent women are illustrated even though over a dozen males are shown.

Accessibility

Entries are arranged in alphabetical order. Guide words at the tops of pages enable the user to easily locate subjects. The biggest disappointment in the work is the lack of cross-references. In the opening section, "How To Use This Book," the editors indicate that by looking up **Abraham Lincoln,** clues to related topics—**President; United States; slavery; Civil War;** and **Booth, John Wilkes**—can be found. Indeed, all these are terms in the encyclopedia but no typographical distinctions within the entry **Abraham Lincoln** enable the reader to know that. Cross-references to the illustrations would also have been useful. For example, **Mount Rushmore** has an entry but the picture appears in the **South Dakota** entry. Unless a reader happened upon the entry or thought to look there the picture would be missed. The lack of an index is another drawback that limits this work's usefulness.

Special Features

The illustrations in the encyclopedia are especially noteworthy. Illustrations range from color drawings to photographs, schematics, and five maps. The captions often add additional information to the entry. For example, the subject **erosion** is accompanied by a drawing of an Oklahoma farm in the Dust Bowl in the 1930s. The illustration accompanying the entry **beaver** shows a cross-section of a beaver lodge. Diagrams of the heart, the digestive system, and skin all help clarify the text of the articles.

In addition to drawings, paintings are used to illustrate subjects. For example, Edwin Chenan's painting of Niagara Falls and Emmanuel Leutze's painting of Washington crossing the Delaware are used. It would have been useful to have the dates of the paintings included in the captions. Photographs of geographical features (such as the Badlands of North Dakota and the Rocky Mountains of Colorado) and buildings (such as the White House and Independence Hall) are mixed in with the other illustrations. The photographs are clear and of good quality.

No political maps are included in the work. It would have been useful to include maps at least of the continents. The lack of historical maps showing **Alexander the Great**'s conquests, the **Roman Empire,** the **Louisiana Purchase,** Europe in the **Middle Ages,** or routes of the world explorers such as **Magellan** is mystifying. The editors opted instead for maps of the climate, Native Americans in 1880, tectonic plates, ocean currents, and winds. The maps are simple, with only key details indicated. Neither countries nor continents are labeled.

No bibliographies are included in this encyclopedia, nor are lists of recommended or related readings. The inclusion of a bibliography with each article would not have been practical in a work such as this, but one might have been appended to the text.

Format

The encyclopedia pages are arranged in three 2-inch columns with one or two illustrations per page. The type style is legible and large enough to be easily read. The boldface subject headings overhang the text. Margins on all four sides of the page are ample.

The type for the captions of the illustrations is smaller than the type for the entries but is still easy to read. The full-color illustrations are large enough to be clear yet do not overwhelm the page.

The paper is of good enough quality that the print on the back of the page does not show through. The work is fairly large, but should be manageable by even small children. The paperback edition was reviewed. The publisher also has a hardcover version, which a prospective purchaser should examine for durability, especially if the work is being obtained for a library.

Summary

For another opinion about the *Student Encyclopedia,* see *Booklist,* September 1, 1991, page 84.

The *Student Encyclopedia* is a good ready-reference work for students in the primary to middle grades, although it is slight. The easy-to-use arrangement, attractive illustrations, and reasonable price will make it appealing to students. The size of the book, the print style, and the layout make the work easy to handle for most students. The very brief entries would preclude students from using the *Student Encyclopedia* as a source for reports or school assignments, and the omission of many major biographical figures is a serious flaw. Users would find works such as BARRON'S JUNIOR FACT FINDER or THE KINGFISHER CHILDREN'S ENCYCLOPEDIA more suitable for classroom assignments. The lack of cross-references and political maps are also major flaws, but do not necessarily inhibit the usefulness of this inexpensive volume as a starting point for research.

Usborne Children's Encyclopedia

Facts at a Glance

Full title: **Usborne Children's Encyclopedia**
Publisher: EDC Publishing
Editors: Jane Elliott; Colin King
Number of contributors: 7
Edition reviewed: © 1987

Number of volumes: 1
Number of articles: 59
Number of pages: 128
Number of words: approximately 28,000
Number of cross-references: none
Number of index entries: 1,050
Number of maps: 17
Number of illustrations: more than 650, all color line drawings
Intended readership: ages 8 to 12
Trim size: 8" × 10"
Binding: hardcover; paperback

Price: $17.96 (hardcover); $14.95 (paperback)
Sold directly to libraries and schools; also sold in bookstores and other retail outlets and by home business division at home parties, book fairs, and fund-raisers
ISBN 0-88110-265-2 (hardcover);
 ISBN 0-7460-0000-6 (paperback)
No scheduled revision

Usborne Children's Encyclopedia

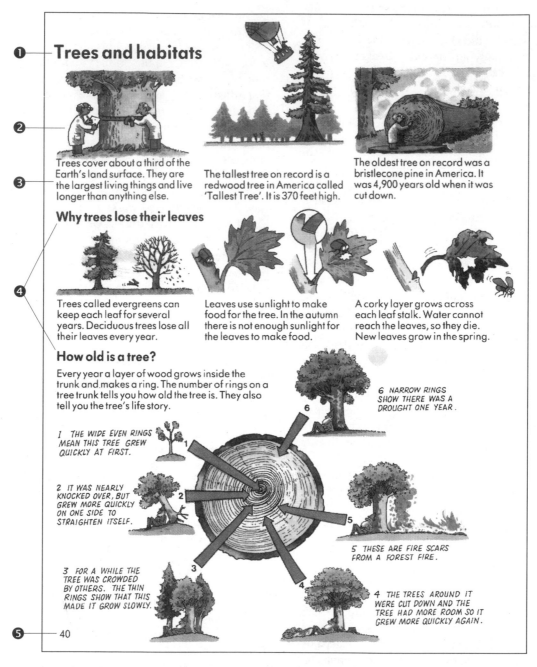

❶ Trees and habitats

❷

❸ Trees cover about a third of the Earth's land surface. They are the largest living things and live longer than anything else.

The tallest tree on record is a redwood tree in America called 'Tallest Tree'. It is 370 feet high.

The oldest tree on record was a bristlecone pine in America. It was 4,900 years old when it was cut down.

Why trees lose their leaves

❹ Trees called evergreens can keep each leaf for several years. Deciduous trees lose all their leaves every year.

Leaves use sunlight to make food for the tree. In the autumn there is not enough sunlight for the leaves to make food.

A corky layer grows across each leaf stalk. Water cannot reach the leaves, so they die. New leaves grow in the spring.

How old is a tree?

Every year a layer of wood grows inside the trunk and makes a ring. The number of rings on a tree trunk tells you how old the tree is. They also tell you the tree's life story.

1   THE WIDE EVEN RINGS MEAN THIS TREE GREW QUICKLY AT FIRST.

2   IT WAS NEARLY KNOCKED OVER, BUT GREW MORE QUICKLY ON ONE SIDE TO STRAIGHTEN ITSELF.

3   FOR A WHILE THE TREE WAS CROWDED BY OTHERS. THE THIN RINGS SHOW THAT THIS MADE IT GROW SLOWLY.

6 NARROW RINGS SHOW THERE WAS A DROUGHT ONE YEAR.

5 THESE ARE FIRE SCARS FROM A FOREST FIRE.

4 THE TREES AROUND IT WERE CUT DOWN AND THE TREE HAD MORE ROOM SO IT GREW MORE QUICKLY AGAIN.

❺ 40

Page shown at 67% of actual size.

❶ Boldface main entry heading on a line by itself

❷ Four-color humorous illustration

❸ Informative caption describes the illustration

❹ Subentries include series of illustrations and captions that explain a process

❺ Page number at foot of page

Introduction

The *Usborne Children's Encyclopedia* is a one-volume, 128-page work designed to provide simple explanations linked to key concepts of everyday life for children ages 8 to 12. This edition was published in 1987 for sale in the United States. It is divided into 59 articles that are grouped thematically. The work is illustrated with more than 650 drawings and 17 maps, most of which are in color. Although the information is conveyed mainly in pictures, 28,000 words of text are included. The work ends with an index containing 1,050 entries.

Authority

This work was originally published in 1986 by Usborne Publishing in London. The American edition was published by EDC Publishing (Educational Development Corporation), located in Tulsa, Oklahoma. Only the cover was changed for sale in the United States. No editorial work was done to make any changes for the U.S. market. No biographical information is included about the editors or the other people listed on the contents page. Articles are unsigned, and no consulting board or content experts are listed.

Scope

The encyclopedia contains 59 articles grouped under the following headings: "Our planet," "Natural Life," "History," "People," "Science around us," and "Appendix."

Science has the largest representation, with 31 articles (53 percent of the total); history and social science are next, with 13 articles (22 percent); geography and humanities are tied, with 6 articles each (10 percent each); and popular culture has only 3 articles (5 percent). No bias is evident toward topics relating to the United States, Canada, or Great Britain.

Coverage of our sample topics was scant. Information on *dinosaurs* receives a half page, most of which is an illustration. *Mexico* is mentioned briefly in three articles. The article on the **Middle Ages** covers two pages. The topic *painting* can be found in **art,** with nine illustrations and about as many lines of text. *Soccer* does not appear in the index, but it receives one illustration and two sentences in **sports** (given the British spelling *sport* on the page). The encyclopedia does not devote much space to biographics. Neither *Louisa May Alcott* nor *Martin Luther King* are mentioned.

Currency

Since this work was published in 1987, the standard topics checked for currency are not included.

The appendix is mostly devoted to technology, such as computers, robots, and lasers. However, the information on plastic phonograph records is outdated, since compact discs have all but replaced them. If currency is important to the purchaser, more up-to-date single-volume encyclopedias such as Dorling Kindersley's My First Encyclopedia or the Random House Children's Encyclopedia (both © 1993) might be better choices.

Accuracy

Our content experts found the encyclopedia to be fairly accurate. Comets are briefly described in **stars:** "Comets sometimes appear as they orbit the Sun. They are made of ice and rock and have long tails." Our astronomy expert says that this description is fine for its indicated use but that comets *sometimes* have long tails. The discussion of oxygen in **air and water** is technically correct; however, the writing is too simplistic for 12-year-olds. Because the work contains no information on the topics *cancer* and *Congress,* our subject experts were not able to comment on these topics.

Some information, such as that on Christopher Columbus in **explorers,** is misleading and lacks the latest scholarship. The article says, "Christopher Columbus wanted to find a new sea route to India. . . . Instead he found America." In fact, he was trying to reach Japan and landed at San Salvador.

Omissions plague the work. For example, in **flying machines** the Wright brothers, Louis Blériot, and Amy Johnson are mentioned, but Charles Lindbergh and Amelia Earhart are not.

The inaccuracies and omissions impair the overall quality of the work, especially considering that some children may use *Usborne* as a reference tool for writing reports.

Clarity

In general, the writing style is clear and concise, and the vocabulary is appropriate for 8- to 12-year-olds. Most of the text is in the form of two- to six-sentence captions under illustrations. There is no entry for our sample term *fingerprints,* but the following explanation of why the wind blows in the **weather** article gives an example of the encyclopedia's writing style:

> When the air is warm, it rises and cold air flows in beneath it. When air moves around like this it makes wind. Some winds blow right across the world as hot air from the Equator rises and is replaced by cold air from the Poles.

Objectivity

The work avoids any controversy because of the brevity of its articles and its limited scope. The encyclopedia does not discuss the standard topics checked for objectivity.

One bias is that only one woman, Amy Johnson, is mentioned by name. This is somewhat offset by the illustrations of female scientists in **education** and the coverage of women's rights in **modern times.** The illustrations seem evenly balanced between males and females, and minorities are well represented.

Accessibility

A table of contents lists the broad subject fields ("Our planet," "History," and so on) and the articles under each field. A seven-page index provides a second access point. Illustrations are not indexed, but one can usually find pictures by looking up the desired subject. There are no traditional cross-references, but directions at the bottom of a few pages indicate where to find related information. Unfortunately, those directions are poorly edited. For example, the reader is directed to see pages 104/5 for more information on rainbows when, in fact, the correct page reference is 102.

The index also contains many errors. For instance, the reference to Christianity on page 86 is one of many blind references. Such sloppiness severely hinders a child's ability to use this work effectively.

Special Features

The most outstanding feature of the work is the use of color illustrations, which employ humor to entertain and to inform. However, some of the illustrations may be inappropriate for this age group, such as one that shows dead bodies heaped in a wagon in **The Black Death** and another in **cavemen** of a man lying in a pool of blood.

The illustrated maps of continents are very well done. A globe is used to indicate the location of the continent in the world; a political map shows the countries in different colors; and another map includes key cities, geographical features, and information about industry, clothing, houses, and farming. Unfortunately, the maps' lack of currency limits their overall usefulness.

The work does not contain any bibliographies or research sources.

Format

The small size of this work makes it easy for children to use. The type is very legible (except on two pages where the print is placed over a dark background). The paper is of good quality and heavy enough so that type from one page cannot be seen on another. The paperback edition was reviewed. The publisher also has a hardcover version, which a prospective purchaser should examine for durability, especially if the work is being obtained for a library.

Summary

The inexpensive *Usborne Children's Encyclopedia* has a number of good features including the maps, illustrations, subjects covered, and readability. Unfortunately, the errors in the index, the misinformation in some of the entries, and the outdatedness are serious shortcom-

ings and prevent us from recommending this work. Furthermore, *Usborne* simplifies information so much so that the intended readership should be younger than its suggested 8- to 12-year-old range. Troll's STUDENT ENCYCLOPEDIA, which is comparable in scope and price and gives better coverage of famous individuals, might be a better selection for young children. THE KINGFISHER CHILDREN'S ENCYCLOPEDIA, which is six times larger, is a better reference work for older elementary school students.

For another opinion about this work, see the *Times Educational Supplement,* May 22, 1987, page 24.

The Young Children's Encyclopedia

Facts at a Glance

Full title: **The Young Children's Encyclopedia**
Publisher: Encyclopaedia Britannica
Editor: Howard L. Goodkind
Edition reviewed: © 1988

Number of volumes: 16
Number of articles: 445
Number of pages: 2,560
Number of words: 700,000
Number of cross-references: 400 (reviewer estimate)
Number of index entries: none
Number of maps: 10
Number of illustrations: 2,675
Intended readership: ages 4 to 8
Trim size: 8" × 9½"
Binding: hardcover

Price: $149.50
ISBN 0-85229-478-6
No stated revision policy

Introduction

The Young Children's Encyclopedia is designed for children in kindergarten through fourth grade. Published in 1988, it contains 445 articles arranged in alphabetical order. It is divided into 16 volumes and contains 2,560 pages, 700,000 words, and 2,675 illustrations. This encyclopedia is identical to COMPTON'S PRECYCLOPEDIA, except that COMPTON'S also has a paperback teaching guide volume (which includes an index) and a 24-page activity section that precedes the entries in each volume.

Authority

Although no experts are listed, it can be assumed that the same contributors and editors were used as with COMPTON'S PRECYCLOPEDIA. See the review of COMPTON'S PRECYCLOPEDIA for a discussion of that work's authority.

Scope

The volumes in this set are arranged alphabetically, as are the articles. An explanation in volume 9 reveals that 48 percent of the articles cover science; 24 percent, history and social science; 16 percent, humanities; 8 percent, geography; and 4 percent, popular culture.

The work tends to favor U.S. topics. In volume 2, 54 percent of the articles are on the United States; 33 percent are on Europe, Asia, and South America; and 13 percent are on Great Britain.

For a more detailed discussion of scope, see the review of COMPTON'S PRECYCLOPEDIA.

Currency

Since this edition was published in 1988, the standard topics checked for currency are not included. See the review of COMPTON'S PRECYCLOPEDIA for more information on currency.

Accuracy

The articles are generally accurate. For example, our expert thought that the **comets** entry was well written for young children. The subject *oxygen* is mentioned in five articles; each time the information was correct. The topics *cancer* and *Congress* are not covered.

Clarity

See the review of COMPTON'S PRECYCLOPEDIA for a discussion of clarity.

Objectivity

For a discussion of objectivity, see the review of COMPTON'S PRECYCLOPEDIA.

Accessibility

See the review of COMPTON'S PRECYCLOPEDIA for a discussion of accessibility.

Special Features

Although the illustrations are bright and colorful, many of them appear out-of-date. For the most part, they reflect various racial, cultural, and ethnic groups. For example, the article on the **Amazon** depicts Bernardo, a fictional Brazilian boy who is "part Indian, part Portuguese, and part Negro." Women, however, are often depicted in traditional roles. The lack of maps is another drawback—only 10 maps are included in the whole set. They depict countries such as Mexico, Italy, and Israel, but not continents such as Africa.

Unlike COMPTON'S PRECYCLOPEDIA, *The Young Children's Encyclopedia* does not contain activities, a teaching guide, or an index.

Format

The encyclopedia includes 16 hardcover volumes with bindings sturdy enough to stand up to heavy use and pages thick enough to withstand years of handling. The type is large, and headings are easy to distinguish from one another.

Summary

The Young Children's Encyclopedia provides training for young children in how to use encyclopedias as well as knowledge on hundreds of subjects. Like COMPTON'S PRECYCLOPEDIA, however, this work is badly in need of updating. Because of this, other sets such as CHILDCRAFT—THE HOW AND WHY LIBRARY and CHILDREN'S BRITANNICA would be better choices for parents and librarians seeking a multivolume encyclopedia.

Chapter 5
Evaluations of Secondary and Adult Encyclopedias

Academic American Encyclopedia

Facts at a Glance

Full title: Academic American Encyclopedia
Publisher: Grolier
Editor: K. Anne Ranson, Editor-in-Chief
Number of contributors: more than 2,500
Edition reviewed: © 1993

Number of volumes: 21
Number of articles: 28,950
Number of pages: 9,864
Number of words: 9,160,000
Number of cross-references: 67,000
Number of index entries: 201,000
Number of maps: 1,090
Number of illustrations: 16,980
Intended readership: junior high school and up
Trim size: 8" × 10"
Binding: hardcover

Price: $798
Sold directly to libraries and schools
ISBN 0-7172-2047-8
Revised every year

Introduction

The *Academic American Encyclopedia* is a 21-volume encyclopedia designed, according to the editor's preface (volume 1), to meet four objectives: (1) to provide "quick access to definitive factual information"; (2) to offer a "readily intelligent general overview of a subject"; (3) to provide "a starting place for further research"; and (4) to allow the user to "visualize and recognize people, places, objects, and processes." This review is based on the 1993 printing of the work; the 1994 printing was not available at the time of review.

Authority

Academic American was first published in 1980. At that time, it established itself as an excellent source of both current and time-tested information supplemented by a profusion of clear and attractive illustrations. Originally published by a subsidiary of a Dutch publishing giant, *Academic American* was acquired in 1982 by Grolier (publisher of ENCYCLOPEDIA AMERICANA and THE NEW BOOK OF KNOWLEDGE), which has maintained its quality and attractiveness.

The front matter of volume 1 lists the names and affiliations of the content experts who work on *Academic American.* The 25-person advisory board approves the entry list and reads selected articles. Members come primarily from the sciences, history, and the arts; curiously, none represent literature. The board includes such luminaries as psychologist Roger Brown, historian John Garraty, anthropologist Ashley Montagu, and musicologist Gunther Schuller. There are more than 2,500 contributors. About 80 percent are academics; the rest are nonacademic specialists. Distinguished contributors include paleontologist John Ostrom and critic René Wellek.

Academic American Encyclopedia

won high critical praise for its protrait of a woman whose life reflects the pointlessness and destructiveness of her society. Didion's style is almost devoid of exposition; her moral horror is communicated in concrete images. Other novels include *A Book of Common Prayer* (1977) and *Democracy* (1984). Nonfiction works include a book of essays, *Slouching Towards Bethlehem* (1968), *Salvador* (1983), and *Miami* (1987).

❶ ### Dido   [dy'-doh]

In Roman mythology, Dido was the daughter of a king of Tyre. She fled to the African coast with large provisions and many followers after her brother PYGMALION murdered her husband. There she founded Byrsa, a fort that developed into the city of CARTHAGE. The *Aeneid* by VERGIL describes the arrival of AENEAS and the Trojan refugees, seeking hospitality at Queen Dido's court. Dido fell in love with Aeneas, and when he left Carthage for Italy, she killed herself.

❷ ### Didrikson, Babe: see ZAHARIAS, BABE DIDRIKSON.

Diebenkorn, Richard   [dee'-ben-korn]

Richard Diebenkorn, b. Portland, Oreg., Apr. 22, 1922, is an artist whose paintings have alternated between figurative compositions and abstracted landscapes, both usually exuding a calm, pensive atmosphere. He attended Stanford University and the California School of Fine Arts, where he was influenced by Clyfford STILL and his teacher David Park. He is considered an important member of the California group of expressionist realists, which included Park and Elmer Bischoff. In the mid-1950s he abandoned ABSTRACT EXPRESSIONISM to paint still lifes and interiors, often revealing an admiration for Henri MATISSE. In 1967, Diebenkorn began the *Ocean Park* series, harmonious geometrical abstractions that have only vestigial reminders of perspective and landscape.

❸ **Bibliography:** Buck, R. T., ed., *Richard Diebenkorn: Paintings and Drawings 1943–1980* (1982); Nordland, G., *Richard Diebenkorn* (1987).

Diefenbaker, John G.   [dee'-fen-bay-kur]

John Diefenbaker, prime minister of Canada from 1957 to 1963, secured the largest majority in Canadian history for his Progressive Conservative government in 1958. Recession contributed to the loss of that majority in 1962, but Diefenbaker led a minority government until his indecision over whether Canada should have nuclear warheads resulted in defeat in 1963.

❹
❺

John George Diefenbaker, b. Sept. 18, 1895, d. Aug. 16, 1979, was a Canadian political leader. A lawyer in Saskatchewan, he ran several times for the House of Commons as a Conservative before being elected in 1940. He was a candidate for the leadership of the Conservative party in 1942 and 1948, and he finally became leader in 1956. The next year he succeeded Louis ST. LAURENT as prime minister. A passionate believer in Canada, Diefenbaker generated support that won his party an overwhelming victory in the parliamentary election of 1958. His great majority was dissipated by indecision, however, and he was defeated in 1963.   P. B. WAITE

❻ **Bibliography:** McIlroy, T., *Diefenbaker: Remembering the Chief* (1985) and *Personal Letters of a Public Man: The Family Letters of J. G. Diefenbaker* (1986); Robinson, H. B., *Diefenbaker's World* (1989).

dieffenbachia   [dee-fen-bak'-ee-uh]

❽ *Dieffenbachia amoena is a common, decorative houseplant with long (up to 50-cm/20-in), attractive leaves.*

The genus *Dieffenbachia* of the arum family, Araceae, comprises about 30 species of tropical American shrublike evergreen plants with fleshy stems. Species of *Dieffenbachia* are commonly used as houseplants, particularly *D. amoena*, which has leaves that are dark green with irregular creamy-white zones radiating from the midrib. The bitter sap of the mother-in-law's tongue, *D. sequine*, is reported to cause the tongue and throat to swell; hence the common name "dumb cane."

❾ ### dielectric   [dy-uh-lek'-trik]

A dielectric is an electrical insulator that may be polarized by the action of an applied electric field. Dielectric materials include all materials that are not conductors, which is to say all materials except condensed metals.

Under the influence of electric fields, electrons move freely through conductors, whereas in dielectrics, or insulators, the fields displace electrons only slightly from their normal positions. Within each molecule of a dielectric, therefore, electric fields cause a separation of negative charges (electrons) from positive charges (protons in the atomic nuclei). Each molecule thus becomes an electric dipole, and the material is said to be polarized. Dielectrics such as water possess permanent dipole moments, and the applied electric field tends to align these dipoles along its own direction. This is called the orientation effect.

The induced dipoles are aligned so as to produce an overall dipole moment—the product of one of the charges and the distance separating the charges—and this moment reduces the strength of the applied electric field. (The reason for the reduction is that the dipole moment has polarity opposite to that of the field.) The factor by which the induced dipoles reduce the electric field is called the dielectric constant, which is a measurable characteristic for each material.

Dielectric materials are widely used in the manufacture of electric circuit elements called capacitors, which store electric charge. When a dielectric is placed between the plates of a CAPACITOR, the CAPACITANCE (ability to store charge) is increased by a factor equal to the dielectric constant. The measurement of the dipole moment of dielectric materials provides two kinds of information about their molecular structure: the extent of permanent-polarized bonding, or ionic bonding, and the angles between chemical bonds.

Diels, Otto Paul Hermann   [deels]

The German chemist Otto Paul Herman Diels, b. Jan. 23, 1876, d. Mar. 7, 1954, was awarded the Nobel Prize for chemistry in 1950 jointly with Kurt ALDER for his contribution to the discovery of the diene synthesis reaction. The reaction involves joining a diene (a compound with two conjugated double bonds) with another substance to form a compound with a

Page shown at 70% of actual size.

---

❶ Main entry words printed in boldface
❷ Cross-reference entry
❸ Bibliography
❹ Illustrations include photographs and drawings
❺ Captions often add to the information presented in the text
❻ Contributor's credit
❼ Guide words and page number
❽ Measurements given in both metric and standard systems
❾ Pronunciations given for foreign or unusual entry words

The preface states that 90 percent of the articles were written by experts, and 75 percent are signed. Most unsigned articles are short biographical or geographical entries.

Scope

Academic American is a short-entry encyclopedia; the editors state that over half of the content is presented in articles of fewer than 500 words. The length of our sample entries gives a sense of the brief coverage accorded most topics. **Castle** receives over a page. **Tyrannosaurus** receives about a half page, including a drawing. **Nelson Mandela,** at 11 lines, **Hamlet,** at 22 lines, and **Elvis Presley,** at 20 lines, are quite short. The entry on **Impressionism** is five and a half pages, five pages of which are illustrations. **Mexico** receives six pages, supplemented by another five pages on **Mexico, history of.** Virtually all of these entries are shorter than those in THE WORLD BOOK ENCYCLOPEDIA and COMPTON'S ENCYCLOPEDIA FACT INDEX. On the other hand, *Academic American*'s articles generally contain more informative and attractive illustrations. The diagram in *Academic American*'s **castle** is superior to the art in the other two sets; the 20 reproductions in **Impressionism** dwarf the number in the other works.

The preface estimates that articles are divided into the following subject areas: humanities and the arts (includes history), 36 percent; science and technology, 35 percent; social sciences, 14 percent; geography, 13 percent; and sports and contemporary life, 2 percent. The editors state that about 35 percent of the entries are biographical.

The small proportion of space devoted to "sports and contemporary life" obscures the contemporary flavor of the work. Technology entries include **cable TV; compact disc; and publishing, desktop.** Music entries include the **Marsalis** family, **Bette Midler,** and **rap music;** literature has **Michael Crichton, Alice Walker,** and **Donald Westlake;** and movies offer **John Sayles** in addition to **George Lucas** and **Stephen Spielberg.** Reflecting current issues, *Academic American* provides articles on **health-care systems, Hezbollah,** and **Intifada.**

Academic American's entry list was devised with "the curriculum of American schools and universities" in mind (Preface). The set abounds in topics within science, history, and literature and the arts. Entries reflect an acceptable range of non-American subjects. Those on pages 46 to 72 of volume 13, which range from **Mafeking** in South Africa to the **Main River** in Germany, include **Magellan, Maghrib** (in North Africa), **magi, Alessandro Magnasco, Magnitogorsk** (in Russia), **Magnus VI** and **VII** of Norway, **Magyars, Mah-Jongg, the *Mahabharata*** (an ancient Indian epic), **Mahathir Mohammed** (from Malaysia), **mahdi, Naguib Mah-**fouz, Gustav Mahler, Antonine Maillet** (a Canadian writer), and **Maimonides.** Coverage of non-American subjects tends to be more European than African, Asian, or Latin American—the articles **costume** and **house,** for instance, contain only European examples. The editors do cover such topics as **Hinduism** and **Islam** with extensive articles that are supplemented by many additional shorter entries.

Currency

Academic American is revised each year, and the 1993 printing maintains its well-earned reputation for currency. The editors estimate that about 2,000 pages (22 percent of the set) were affected in this revision, with almost 100 new entries, 74 replacement entries, and more than 200 entries with major revisions. New entries reflect recent arrivals on the international scene (**Boutros Boutros-Ghali**), cultural figures (**Madonna**), newly recognized issues (**sexual harassment**), and topics affected by recent changes (**arms control, national defense**). Replacement articles and major revisions are not limited to current events.

The newer biographical entries tend to be brief, but changes in other articles are extensive. **Gulf War** received a replacement article that expanded on earlier coverage to assess the aftermath of that conflict; the article is superior to those in COMPTON'S and WORLD BOOK. **Automobile** now includes information on antilock brakes (although **brake** still lacks such coverage). A new article—**sexual harassment**—is disappointingly brief.

Germany is treated as a unified country, and each of the new republics that grew out of the U.S.S.R. is accorded its own complete country entry. (The article **Union of Soviet Socialist Republics** is retained as a historical entry.) These articles are up-to-date; **Lithuania** mentions the 1992 elections.

The handling of Yugoslavia is less successful. **Yugoslavia** states that the article is about the former Balkan state, but a country fact box and map treat the six regions as constituent republics instead of independent states. Still, each region receives a separate entry, up-to-date as of 1992. **Czechoslovakia,** too, is still treated as one entity although the plan to separate into the Czech Republic and Slovakia is noted. Curiously, most maps show these two areas as independent. Maps reflect the breakup of the Soviet Union.

Bill Clinton does appear as president, and coverage of the 1992 election appears in **Democratic Party** and **presidential elections** as well. The food pyramid is discussed in **nutrition, human** (and is listed in the index), but the information is poorly presented; the text does not specify serving recommendations. **Space telescope** describes the Hubble telescope and its post-launch problems, as well as the plan to use a future shuttle flight to solve the mirror problem. **Frida Kahlo** has a brief entry with a good overview of her significance.

The illustrations are generally up-to-date. Most photographs are carefully chosen to avoid issues of datedness. Some new pictures are added in each revision; this year's group includes photographs from the 1992 Olympics. Some older photographs remain; the pictures in **computers in education** look dated, and the sole color photograph in **baseball** is from the 1983 World Series.

Accuracy

As befits a work backed by a distinguished panel of advisers and contributors, *Academic American* is accurate. **House of Representatives of the United States** offers an accurate account of the membership, organization, and functions of the House, but one that reflects little or no revision in recent years. It refers to Tip O'Neill's assumption of the post of Speaker of the House, but two others have held that post since O'Neill retired in 1987. **Oxygen** is a good comprehensive discussion of this element, although it does contain some minor errors, misplacing oxygen in Group V-A, not VI-A, of the periodic table, and misidentifying bauxite as a mineral rather than an aluminum-bearing ore. The article is complex, however, and suffers from a proliferation of technical terms. **Cancer** is well written and mostly correct; our content expert would have preferred seeing more up-to-date information on screening recommendations and on tests for prostate cancer. **Comet** is a model of well-organized, well-explained information that is both accurate and up-to-date. **Henry VIII** offers a useful summary of the monarch's marriages, but one that provides little background on the Reformation and slight information on his domestic policies, which are receiving increasing attention among scholars.

Not surprisingly in a work of this size and scope, some lapses do occur. The caption to the illustration in **apes** mistakenly says that these primates are "more intelligent than other monkeys"; the article itself correctly points out that apes are *not* monkeys. The entry on **Corazon C. Aquino** notes her "continuing popularity," a curious comment given the number of attempted coups against her government. But these are minor quibbles in a work that, all in all, offers a model of accuracy.

Clarity

Entries are usually clear, relying primarily on the well-organized transmission of the relevant facts about a given subject. The entry **bookkeeping** presents the basics about double-entry accounting in a careful and thorough way that would be intelligible to any average reader. The greatest difficulty in clarity arises in scientific or technical subjects. Formulas are frequently used, requiring a familiarity with higher-level mathematics or chemical formulas (see the earlier comments on **oxygen**). The set is probably not appropriate as a home reference if family members do not have a basic understanding of science.

Longer articles are subdivided into sections by up to two levels of subheads. These are typically used for entries on countries, states, and provinces as well as other topics receiving substantial coverage (**mass media** and **muscle**). On the whole, *Academic American* is quite clear. The entry *Titanic* exemplifies the encyclopedia's style:

> The *Titanic,* a British passenger liner, struck an iceberg off Newfoundland on the night of Apr. 14–15, 1912, and sank. The ship, the largest and most luxurious built up to that time, was on its maiden voyage from Southampton to New York, carrying more than 2,200 people; about 1,500 drowned.
>
> Official inquiries determined that the *Titanic* was traveling too fast for the known icy conditions; it rammed the iceberg at a speed of 22 knots (41 km/h; 25 mph). The large loss of life was partly because of the failure of a nearby ship, the *Californian,* to respond to the distress signals, and the insufficient number of lifeboats on the *Titanic.* The shipwreck, considered by contemporaries to be the worst in history, prompted international agreements to improve safety procedures at sea. The sunken vessel was located (1985) by a team of U.S. and French researchers using a surface-towed submersible camera-sled.

Objectivity

The preface notes the editors' efforts to represent diverse points of view. Articles dealing with controversial subjects—such as **capital punishment** and **greenhouse effect**—address both sides of the question. A certain liberal bent emerges occasionally from the writing, however. **Sex education,** for instance, fairly presents contrasting views of the appropriateness of teaching the subject in schools but describes what a "comprehensive curriculum" on sexuality should include, which undercuts the claim of objectivity.

In some cases controversies are essentially ignored. The entry on **AIDS** mentions issues of cost and civil rights in relation to AIDS testing, but spends little space debating either point. **Northern Ireland** mentions the conflict between Protestant and Catholic but does not elaborate. **Ozone layer** accurately describes the human activities that are causing problems for the ozone and the steps being taken to reduce the release of CFCs. The article does not, however, mention that some scientists question the pessimistic view of the situation.

Accessibility

Guide words show the first and last entries on a spread. Entries beginning with *Mc* are alphabetized as *Mac;* those with *St.* are inserted as though the word were spelled out. Entries with a shared keyword include a parenthetical identifier—**mass (musical setting)** and **mass (physics)**—to help the reader locate precisely which entry is desired.

Cross-references (presented in SMALL CAPITALS) to other entries are liberally sprinkled throughout articles; some articles list related entries at the end. The cross-references are generally helpful, but they can be hard to see because of the typography, making the system less effective than the parenthetical, boldface "see" references used in WORLD BOOK. When an entry may be consulted in a variant form, a cross-reference entry head appears. **Maltese cross** simply directs the reader to **cross.**

The index in volume 21 contains over 201,000 entries, including both entry words (printed in capitals and in boldface) and other key concepts. Index entries specify volume number (in boldface) and page number. Major locations on maps are found in the index (along with latitude and longitude coordinates); minor villages and sites on city maps are not included. Illustrations are shown by italicizing the page reference. The presence of a bibliography is also noted in the index. Preceding the index is a clear explanation of how the index is organized.

Many index entries contain a comprehensive list of all related entries. Thus, *novel* is followed by a list of about 900 articles on individual novelists, national literatures, and related topics. This feature provides useful overviews on a subject.

Special Features

A major feature of *Academic American* is the excellent illustration program, perhaps the most attractive of any of the major encyclopedias and second only to WORLD BOOK's in terms of size. The set contains almost 17,000 illustrations, including nearly 1,100 maps, the vast majority of which are in full color. The selection of photographs reflects an appealing mix of contemporary and historical images. Drawings include hundreds of animal species (showing both males and females when coloring differs) and plants, musical instruments, anatomical structures and processes, and machines. Earlier comments (on **Impressionism** and **castle**) pointed out how the scope and detail of the illustrations make *Academic American* superior to competing works. These examples are typical. *Academic American* uses its illustrations to convey information effectively and attractively.

Fact boxes with all country, state, and province entries provide good basic statistical information at a glance.

The publisher estimates that bibliographies accompany about 40 percent of the entries. They provide further information for entries as basic as **birthstone** and

as technical as **aerodynamics.** Longer bibliographies (for example, those for **United States, history of the**) are divided into categories. That bibliography has 32 titles, although 3 or 4 is more typical. Works cited tend to be from the 1980s, but some 1990s titles are included. Bibliography entries tend to be appropriate for high school to adult readers; there seems to be no effort to list readings suitable for junior high users (COMPTON's bibliographies are superior in this regard).

Format

Most volumes are devoted to one letter of the alphabet, although *A, C,* and *S* are split into two volumes and some volumes combine letters. Length of volumes ranges from 370 to 700 pages. Each is easy to hold and lies open when placed on a surface. Margins are ample, and the overall use of white space helps create a clean and attractive look; the ragged right margin of each column helps create a comfortable look as well. Entry words, larger than the text and in bold type, clearly stand out.

The type—a sans serif face—may be troublesome for some users to read; it can be light on the page, and sans serif faces are generally considered more difficult for those whose reading skills are not well developed. The look is suitable for the junior high to adult audience, however.

The pages are colorful due to the extensive illustration program. Illustrations occupy about a third of the set's space.

Academic American is available in two electronic formats—online and on CD-ROM (as the NEW GROLIER MULTIMEDIA ENCYCLOPEDIA). See Chapter 15 for reviews of these versions.

Summary

For other opinions regarding *Academic American,* see the review of the 1992 edition in *ARBA 93* (Anne Grace Patterson) and a review of the 1993 edition in *Booklist (Reference Books Bulletin),* September 15, 1993.

Academic American Encyclopedia is a worthy competitor among multivolume encyclopedias. Up-to-date and factual, it amply fills the need for ready-reference use in the library. While not as comprehensive as COLLIER's ENCYCLOPEDIA, ENCYCLOPEDIA AMERICANA, or NEW BRITANNICA, it does offer brief, generally intelligible entries on myriad topics. Clear and attractive, it would also find heavy use in the home library, where it stacks up quite nicely with WORLD BOOK except, perhaps, regarding coverage of science. The purchaser looking for greater detail and a slightly lower reading level should consider WORLD BOOK; the purchaser who wants quick information and an attractive illustration program might well consider *Academic American.*

Barron's New Student's Concise Encyclopedia

Facts at a Glance

Full title: **Barron's New Student's Concise Encyclopedia**

Publisher: Barron's Educational Series

Editors: Grace Freedson, Managing Editor; Lorraine DePietro, Project Editor

Number of contributors: 19

Edition reviewed: © 1993, second edition

Number of volumes: 1

Number of articles: 15,000 (reviewer estimate)

Number of pages: 1,170

Number of cross-references: 1,530 (reviewer estimate)

Number of index entries: 15,000 (reviewer estimate)

Number of maps: 35

Number of illustrations: more than 500

Intended readership: high school to adult

Trim size: 6¾″ × 9¼″

Binding: hardcover

Price: $29.95

ISBN 0-8120-6329-5

No stated revision policy

Introduction

Barron's New Student's Concise Encyclopedia is a copiously illustrated one-volume student's encyclopedia. Because it contains several unique features such as sections on "Health and Medicine" and "Life Skills," *Barron's Encyclopedia* purports to serve not only as a desk-reference tool, but also as "a survival guide for young people living on their own—away from home and family."

Authority

Barron's New Student's Concise Encyclopedia is published by Barron's Educational Series, publishers of study guides, college directories, and handbooks. Contributors are listed, but no academic affiliations or areas of expertise are given. The book's editors are staff members of Barron's. The *New Student's Concise Encyclopedia* is a revised second edition of *Barron's Student's Concise Encyclopedia,* published in 1988.

Scope

Barron's New Student's Concise Encyclopedia is organized thematically. Twenty-four alphabetically arranged sections cover topics from "Art" to the "World at a Glance." Most of these sections contain a conventional alphabetical entry list of words and phrases. Some, such as "Language Arts," contain subsections of narrative, organized in textbook style. Others, such as the "United States at a Glance" section, consist solely of maps and tables.

A majority of the encyclopedia's entries favor the social sciences and science; 794 pages of the work are devoted to disciplines such as "Government," "Economics and Business," "Chemistry," "Physics," "Psychology," and "Law." Two special sections directed at "young people living on their own" are the 60-page "Health and Medicine" section, which includes information on nutrition and meal planning; and the 41-page "Life Skills" section, with information on traveling abroad, simple banking skills, and study tips. Very little space is devoted to popular culture: no section exists for sports, and no popular artists appear in the 37-page "Music" section.

Entries emphasize the historical over the contemporary. For example, in the "Literature" section there is an entry for **Lessing, Gotthold Ephraim** but not for *Doris Lessing;* there is an entry for **Lindsay, Vachel** (1879–1931), a modern-day American troubadour, but no entry for *Stephen King,* one of the most popular writers among the young.

There are no entries for *Elvis Presley* or *women's rights,* yet there are two entries for **impressionism,** one each for the movements in art and music. **Hamlet** rates a longer than average entry of 175 words, and the entry for **Nelson Mandela** is an average 75 words long. Unfortunately, the only information on countries is provided in a list of six entries per page, which gives 14 basic facts about each country, but no historical narrative.

Currency

Information on **Bill Clinton** is up-to-date through the end of 1992. There is no entry or mention of *Frida Kahlo,* but there are two entries for the **Persian Gulf War;** one each in the "History of the World" and "History of the United States" sections. A brief mention of the *Hubble Space Telescope* is made in the "History of Technology" section under "Space Travel," but no reference is made to the telescope's problems.

The *food guide pyramid* appears along with tables entitled "What Counts as One Serving?" and "How Many Servings Do You Need Each Day?" The information provided here exceeds what most other one-volume encyclopedias present on this topic. The color maps for Yugoslavia, Yemen, Germany, the former U.S.S.R., and the Czech Republic and Slovakia are all up-to-date (as of 1992) and accurate.

Accuracy

Entries are generally accurate, but their brevity sometimes results in oversimplifications. The entry for **House of Representatives,** for example, is only two

Barron's New Student's Concise Encyclopedia

❶

Direct current   PHYSICS   **Efficiency**

Any quantities can be multiplied or divided, and the outcome is always a new dimensionality. For example, volume is always the product of three linear measures, so its dimensionality is cubic meters (m^3). This is not the same dimensionality as meters (m), and lengths cannot be added to volumes. Volumes can also be expressed in liters, cubic centimeters, acre-feet, or cubic miles, however, and any of these measurements can be converted to cubic meters. All have the dimensionality m^3.

Most physical quantities have complex dimensionality, with several different basic quantities combined. For example, a force is a mass times an acceleration, so its dimensionality is $kg\,m/s^2$. Specific heat is energy per unit mass per unit temperature change, and its dimensionality works out this way:

$$\frac{kg \cdot m^2}{s^2} \div kg \cdot K = \frac{m^2}{s^2 \cdot K}$$

Dimensional analysis provides an extremely useful means of checking the results of a theoretical calculation.

For example, an engineer does some theoretical work and concludes that the pressure (force per unit area) in a pipe can be found as the product of the density of the fluid in the pipe and its velocity. He can check his result this way:

$$\frac{force}{area} = density \times velocity.$$

$$\frac{kg \cdot m}{s^2} \div m^2 = \frac{kg}{m^3} \times \frac{m}{s}$$

Since the dimensionalities on the two sides of the equation are different, the equation cannot be true.

❷ Direct current (DC)   Electric current flowing steadily in one direction. All batteries produce direct current, flowing steadily from the high potential to the low potential terminal. In a generator, the current in the armature is always alternating. If a generator is to produce direct current, the output of the armature must be fed through a commutator, which will reverse its connections every half-cycle.

Dispersion   The sorting out of waves according to the speed at which they travel. In most media, higher frequency waves travel slower. In glass, red light travels faster than violet. As shown in the figure, **❸** white light entering the prism is bent toward the normal (*see* **Refraction**). The violet is bent more than the red. On emerging from the prism, the light speeds up and bends away from the normal. However, because the sides of the prism are not parallel, the rays bend twice in the same direction. This amplifies the dispersion effect, and the light is sorted out into a full spectrum.

❹

PHYSICS

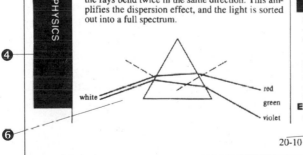

white   red

green

violet

❻

Doppler effect   The change in frequency of a wave due to the motion of the source or of the observer. The figure shows that if a moving object emits a sound wave, the crests will be crowded together on the side toward which the object is moving. This means that the wavelength is shorter on that side, so the frequency is higher. Conversely, the frequency heard by the observer on the other side will be lower than the frequency emitted by the source. If a car moves past the observer while sounding its horn, the observer will hear a sudden drop in pitch as the car passes.

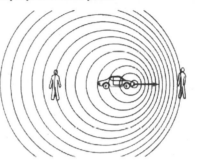

A similar effect is noted if the source is at rest and the observer is moving. If the observer is moving toward the source, his or her ear will intercept crests of the wave at a higher frequency than the one at which they are being emitted.

The Doppler shift of the frequency of light plays an important role in cosmology. Astronomers note that the light from distant galaxies is "red-shifted." This means that the frequencies received are lower than those emitted by the galaxies. Since all galaxies are thus seen to be moving away from us, the whole universe must be expanding.

Double-slit interference   The pattern of alternate bright and dark bars produced by constructive and destructive interference of the light passing through two slits close together. Many slits close together form a diffraction grating, which produces the same pattern.

Dry cell   The cell of an electric battery made in such a way that its electrolyte is a paste instead of a liquid, so that it will not spill. *See* **Cell**.   **❺**

E **ffective value**   A measure of current or potential difference, applied to an alternating current, indicating that it produces the same heating effect as a direct current with that value. For example, if a sine-wave current constantly changes from +5 A to –5 A and back, it produces the same heat as a 3.5 A direct current. Its effective value is therefore 3.5 A.

If an alternating current registers on a meter as 7.0 A, that is its effective value. Its maximum is found by multiplying the effective value by $\sqrt{2}$. Thus a 6.0 A alternating current is constantly changing from +8.5 to –8.5 A and back. AC potentials follow the same rule.

Efficiency   For a system, the ratio of the useful energy output to the energy input. Every device that   **❼**

20-10   **❽**

Page shown at 80% of actual size.

❶ Guide words
❷ Boldface main entry word
❸ Boldface cross-reference in parentheses

❹ Section marker
❺ Large-print alphabet break marker
❻ Black-and-white illustration includes callouts

❼ Topical section number
❽ Page number

lines long; one could consult a dictionary and find as much information. The entry for **cancer** estimates that "one-third of those patients with newly diagnosed cancers are ultimately permanently cured"; this figure oversimplifies the matter. Also, the relationship between **melanoma** and the more general **skin cancer** is not clearly explained.

The entry for **Henry VIII** is very brief, but factual. It focuses on the main political issues of Henry's reign, downplaying his marriages and personal life. There is no entry for *oxygen* except for a brief reference to the percentages of the element in the earth's crust, atmosphere, and hydrosphere. Several aspects of oxygen chemistry are covered under various topics, but the information presented is fragmented and ultimately confusing. The entry for **comet** includes no factual errors.

Clarity

The writing style is clear and concise. The tone is unpretentious and nonacademic; it is appropriate for a wide range of students, high school age and older. The following entry is typical:

> **African National Congress** Major political force in the Union of South Africa. Led by Nelson Mandela, it is moving the current white-dominated government toward the elimination of all vestiges of apartheid and toward black majority rule. *See* **Apartheid; Mandela, Nelson.**

Objectivity

Information is presented in an evenhanded way, although the work avoids most controversial topics. There is only a one-sentence description of **capital punishment,** no mention of *sexism,* and only a cursory mention of problems with the **ozone layer.** The only mention of *Northern Ireland* is contained in entries for the **Irish Republican Army (IRA),** and **Home Rule,** neither of which mentions the religious aspects of the fighting. Information on **AIDS** is balanced and appears in two places—within the "Biology" and "Health and Medicine" sections.

Accessibility

Accessibility is one of the biggest weaknesses of *Barron's New Student's Concise Encyclopedia.* The lack of a single alphabetical entry listing necessitates frequent use of the index. Cross-references are sparse, and the user may have to look up several entries in different sections of the book to find complete coverage of a topic (for example, **AIDS** and *Northern Ireland*). Although black section markers are printed at the edge of each page, it is still difficult to locate a section rapidly. Recessed thumb indexes would be a big improvement to this encyclopedia.

Special Features

Illustrations, most in black and white, are widely used. A set of color plates in the "Biology" section rivals the illustrations in many multivolume encyclopedias. More than 100 exhibits, such as the "Krebs Citric Cycle" (for "Biology"), the "Beaufort Wind Scale" (for "Earth and Space Sciences"), and "Racial Groups by Geographic Location" (for the "World at a Glance" section), supply added information.

Both color and black-and-white maps appear. All include longitude and latitude lines and major cities and towns. The table of contents contains a "Map-Reading Basics" essay, an attractive feature that provides information about map projections, grids, and scales.

Format

The 6¾" × 9¼" trim size is approximately the same as that of a typical college dictionary. The typeface is legible and easy to read; boldface entry words stand out clearly on the page.

Summary

Because of its casual style, libraries will find *Barron's New Student's Concise Encyclopedia* inappropriate for a research-oriented setting. As a ready-reference desk encyclopedia for students in high school or on their way to college, however, it is an economical and up-to-date choice. Its clear, informal writing style; eclectic and often fascinating range of information; and informative maps, exhibits, and illustrations are its greatest strengths. Its drawbacks are its inaccessibility and its lack of comprehensiveness compared with other one-volume sources such as WEBSTER'S NEW WORLD ENCYCLOPEDIA and THE CAMBRIDGE ENCYCLOPEDIA, which have more than 25,000 entries each. Its scope is similar to that of THE CONCISE COLUMBIA ENCYCLOPEDIA, and in other respects it compares favorably with that work: it has about 300 more pages, costs $10 less, and is more up-to-date. If *Barron's New Student's Concise Encyclopedia* is revised on a regular schedule, it should continue to be a recommended purchase.

The Cambridge Encyclopedia

Facts at a Glance

Full title: **The Cambridge Encyclopedia**
Publisher: Cambridge University Press
Editor: David Crystal
Number of contributors: more than 100
Edition reviewed: © 1990, 1992 printing

Number of volumes: 1
Number of articles: more than 30,000 (25,000 main
   entries; 7,000 "Ready Reference" entries)
Number of pages: 1,488
Number of words: 1.5 million
Number of cross-references: 75,000
Number of index entries: no index
Number of maps: more than 700
Number of illustrations: 750 black-and-white line
   drawings; 16 pages of color plates
Intended readership: general reader
Trim size: 7½" × 10¼"
Binding: hardcover

Price: $49.95
Sold directly to libraries and schools; also sold in
   bookstores and by direct mail
ISBN 0-521-43176-X
Revised edition to be published in late 1994

Introduction

According to the editor's preface, the aim of *The Cambridge Encyclopedia* is "to provide a succinct, systematic, and readable guide to the facts, events, issues, beliefs, and achievements which make up the sum of human knowledge" for a general audience. The 1992 work is an updated reprint of the 1990 edition. A new edition of *The Cambridge Encyclopedia* will be published in late 1994.

This one-volume encyclopedia has 1,488 pages, 1,334 of which contain about 25,000 alphabetical entries. There are 5,500 biographical entries and 4,000 gazetteer entries. In addition to the 25,000 main entries, about 7,000 other topics, persons, and important places are listed in the 128-page "Ready Reference" section at the end of the book. The entries are linked together by 75,000 cross-references.

Authority

As in the 1990 edition, the editor is David Crystal, a British linguist whose other work is *The Cambridge Encyclopedia of the English Language.* The entries were written by more than 100 contributors and consultants. Most are from British academic institutions such as the University of Lancaster, the Science Museum (London), and the University of Edinburgh. Only three of the contributors are from American academic institutions. Entries are not signed, but contributors are listed with their academic title and institution, or by their area of expertise. Access to the W. & R. Chambers *Biographical Dictionary* and *World Gazetteer* databases lends additional authority to the work. Recognizing the limitations of a one-volume encyclopedia of this size, the editor encourages feedback from users on the coverage and treatment of its entries.

Scope

The editor states that the key feature of *The Cambridge Encyclopedia* is the rapid answers it gives to specific queries about people, places, or topics. According to the preface, over half of the articles average 125 words in length, 45 percent average 50 words in length, and 5 percent average 500 words in length. Three articles on **Impressionism** summarize the movement in art, literature, and music in separate entries of 100 to 130 words each, while **Nelson Mandela** contains 160 words and **Elvis Presley** has approximately 180 words. There are no entries for *castle* or *Hamlet,* although the play is mentioned under the entry for **William Shakespeare,** where a table of Shakespeare's plays is given with title, year written, and well-known characters. The entry on **Mexico** has approximately 560 words.

Topics favor science, biography, and geography, and entries on these topics comprise about 76 percent of the articles. The biographical entries are heavily weighted toward British people in various disciplines, such as **George Cadbury** (British businessman), **James Callaghan** (British Labour party statesman), and **James Cameron** (British journalist). This bias is logical given the publisher's access to the Chambers biographical and geographical databases. Humanities and social sciences have the next largest total (23 percent of all entries). Brief entries on art and music abound (as in the entry on **capriccio**), but may extend to longer essays of 150 to 200 words for entries such as **Caribbean literature.**

There are scant entries—fewer than 1 percent of those surveyed—on popular culture. Coverage of popular culture is more accessible from a biographical perspective than from a topical one; for example, there are entries for **The Rolling Stones, Meryl Streep, Dustin Hoffman, Wilt Chamberlain,** and **Barbra Streisand.** Many of these entries contain cross-references that lead the reader to related subjects; for example, the entry on **The Rolling Stones** has cross-references to **The Beatles, blues,** and **rock music.**

The editor states in the preface that *The Cambridge Encyclopedia* emphasizes international coverage: more than 60 percent is British, U.S., and European (overwhelmingly British and European) coverage. The other 40 percent includes the rest of the world. A surprisingly small percentage—roughly less than 1 percent—of entries relate to Canada.

Currency

The version of *The Cambridge Encyclopedia* reviewed is a 1992 updated printing of the first edition, published in 1990. Unfortunately, updates for the U.S. presidential election were not included in this edition. There is no mention of *Bill Clinton* either as a main entry or in the "Ready Reference" section, where other world leaders are noted. The entry on the **Gulf War 1 (1980–88)** dis-

The Cambridge Encyclopedia

leaves stay green in the autumn. (*Nasturtium officinale*. Family: *Cruciferae*.) » perennial; pinnate; vitamins ⓘ

Waterford (county), Gaelic **Phort Láirge** pop(1981) 88 591; area 1 839 sq km/710 sq ml. County in Munster province, S Irish Republic; bounded S by Atlantic Ocean, with coastal inlets at Youghal, Dungarvan, Tramore, and Waterford; Knockmealdown Mts in the W; watered by Suir and Barrow Rivers; apple growing, cattle, glass making; popular resorts such as Tramore on S coast. » Irish Republic ⓘ; Waterford (city)

Waterford 52°15N 7°06W, pop(1981) 39 636. Seaport, county borough, and capital of Co Waterford, Munster, S Irish Republic; on R Suir at its mouth on Waterford harbour; railway; technical college; shipyards, food processing, footwear, paper, glass and crystal; remains of city walls, cathedral (1793), Blackfriars priory (1226); light opera festival (Sep). » Irish Republic ⓘ; Waterford (county)

Watergate (1972–4) A political scandal that led to the first resignation of a president in US history (Richard Nixon, in office 1968–74). The actual 'Watergate' is a hotel and office complex in Washington, DC, where the Democratic Party had its headquarters. During the presidential campaign of 1972, a team of burglars was caught inside Democratic headquarters, and their connections were traced to the White House and to the Committee to Re-elect the President. Investigations by the Washington Post, a grand jury, and two special prosecutors revealed that high officials who were very close to President Nixon were implicated, and that Nixon himself was aware of illegal measures to cover up that implication. A number of officials were eventually imprisoned. Nixon himself left office when it became clear that he was likely to be impeached and removed. » Irangate; Nixon, Richard M

Waterhouse, Alfred (1830–1905) British architect, born in Liverpool. He studied at Manchester, where he designed the town hall and assize courts, then in London built the romanesque Natural History Museum (1873–81). He also designed many educational buildings, and from his great use of redbrick came the name 'redbrick university'. He died at Yattendon, Berkshire.

Waterloo, Battle of (1815) The final defeat of Napoleon, ending the French Wars and the Emperor's last bid for power in the Hundred Days. A hard-fought battle, in which Blucher's Prussian force arrived at the climax to support Wellington's mixed Allied force; a number of crucial blunders by the French contributed to their defeat. » Blücher; Hundred Days; Napoleon I; Napoleonic Wars; Wellington, Duke of

Waterloo Cup » bowls; coursing

Watling Street » Roman roads ⓘ

Watson, James (Dewey) (1928–) US geneticist, born in Chicago. Educated at Chicago and Indiana, he worked in Copenhagen and then Cambridge, where with Crick and Wilkins he helped to discover the molecular structure of DNA, for which he shared the 1962 Nobel Prize for Physiology or Medicine. He became professor of biology at Harvard in 1961, and director of a molecular biology research centre at Long Island, New York in 1968. » DNA ⓘ

Watson, John B(roadus) (1878–1958) US psychologist, born at Greenville, South Carolina. Educated at Chicago, he became professor of psychology at Johns Hopkins (1908–20), where he established an animal research laboratory, and became known for his behaviourist approach, which he later applied to human behaviour. In 1921 he entered advertising, and wrote several general books on psychology. He died in New York City. » behaviourism

Watson, Tom, properly **Thomas (Sturges)** (1949–) US golfer, born in Kansas City, Missouri. He turned professional in 1971, and has since won 32 tournaments on the US tour, with career winnings second only to Jack Nicklaus. He has won the British Open five times (1975, 1977, 1980, 1982–3), the US Open (1982), and the Masters (1977, 1981). » golf; Nicklaus

watt SI unit of power; symbol W; named after British inventor James Watt; the production of 1 joule of energy per second corresponds to a power of 1 watt; commonly used as **kilowatts** (kW, 10³ W) or **megawatts** (MW, 10⁶ W). » kilowatt-hour; power; units (scientific); Watt; RR71

Watt, James (1736–1819) British inventor, born at Greenock, Renfrewshire, Scotland. He went to Glasgow in 1754 to learn the trade of a mathematical-instrument maker, and there, after a year in London, he set up in business. He was employed on surveys for several canals, improved harbours and rivers, and by 1759 was studying steam as a motive force. In 1763–4, in the course of repairing a working model of the Newcomen engine, he hit upon the expedient of the separate condenser. After other improvements, he went into partnership with Matthew Boulton (1728–1809), and the new engine was manufactured at Birmingham in 1774. Several other inventions followed, including the design of a steam locomotive (1784). The term *horse-power* was first used by him, and the metric unit of power is named after him. He retired in 1800, and died near Birmingham. » Industrial Revolution; steam engine; watt

Watteau, (Jean) Antoine [vatoh] (1684–1721) French Rococo painter, born at Valenciennes. In 1702 he went to study in Paris, where he worked as a scene painter and a copyist. His early canvases were mostly military scenes, but it was the mythological 'L'Embarquement pour l'île de Cythère' (1717, Embarkation for the island of Cythera) which won him membership of the Academy. He is also known for his 'Fêtes galantes' (scenes of gallantry), quasi-pastoral idylls in court dress which became fashionable in high society. He died at Nogent-sur-Marne. » French art; Rococo

wattle A large group of mainly trees or shrubs, native to many tropical and subtropical areas, but notably Australia where (together with the eucalypts) they form the dominant tree vegetation. The leaves are divided into numerous tiny leaflets or, in many species, reduced in the adult form to a flattened leaf-stalk (*phyllode*) resembling a leaf-blade. The flowers are mostly yellow, very small but numerous, in rounded or catkin-like clusters. Many species are planted as shade trees and for ornament. The foliage may be used as fodder for livestock. Many are useful timber trees, producing very hard tough wood. The bark and pods are employed for tanning. Some yield gum arabic. Several species are widely cultivated for stabilizing sandy soils. Commonly cultivated species include the **blue-leaved wattle** (*Acacia cyanophylla*) from W Australia, a small tree growing to 10 m/30 ft; leaf stalks bluish-green, up to 30 cm/12 in long, often pendulous; flowers in heads to 1.5 cm/0.6 in across, arranged in long leafy clusters; pods brown, constricted between the seeds. Also common is the **silver wattle** (*Acacia dealbata*) from SE Australia and Tasmania, a tree growing to 30 m/100 ft; leaves finely divided with 20–50 pairs of narrow leaflets, silvery-white when young; flowers deep yellow, fragrant, in rounded heads. It is the 'mimosa' of florists. (Genus: *Acacia*, 1 200 species. Family: *Leguminosae*.) » gum arabic/tree; shrub; tree ⓘ

wattle and daub A framework of interlaced twigs and rods plastered with mud or clay. The walls of timber-framed houses were often made of wattle and daub. If protected from the weather by good overhanging eaves to the roof, these walls can last for hundreds of years.

wattmeter An instrument for measuring electric power. Many types are used, the most common being the *electrodynamic*

Page shown at 70% of actual size

① Guide words indicate the first and last entries on the page
② Main entry words printed in boldface
③ Cross-reference
④ Cross-reference entries
⑤ Page number
⑥ Illustration
⑦ Caption
⑧ Pronunciations given for foreign or unusual entry words
⑨ Measurements given in both metric and standard systems
⑩ This symbol used to indicate an illustration

cusses the earlier war between Iraq and Iran and adds brief information on the invasion of Kuwait and the beginnings of the second Gulf War, up to the capping of the Kuwaiti oil wells in November 1991. No biographical entries are included for Colin Powell or H. Norman Schwarzkopf, leaders of the U.S. forces in the war. The entry for **Russia** mentions the breakup of the Soviet Union, and the entry for **Lithuania** refers to its declaration of independence in 1990. Cross-references to the "Ready Reference" section on world political leaders confirm the correct heads of state for these countries. There are no entries for *Frida Kahlo* or the *food pyramid;* searching further under the heading **nutrition** did not reveal any information on this last topic.

There are more than 700 maps in this edition of *The Cambridge Encyclopedia.* The current national boundaries created after the dramatic changes in Europe in 1989 are reflected in the maps containing **Germany, Yugoslavia,** and **Czechoslovakia.** The entry for Russia does not include a map, but the entries for **Yemen, Czechoslovakia,** and **Yugoslavia** do. A map of Russia is found under the entry for **Soviet Union** to show the constituent republics of the Commonwealth of Independent States, but there is no physical detail—only political boundary lines are given. A large, full-color world map correctly shows the changes in Eastern European boundaries and in the Commonwealth of Independent States.

Accuracy

Our content expert found the entry for **House of Representatives** useful, concise, and clearly written. Likewise, the **Congress** entry is unique for a one-volume encyclopedia because of its comparative perspective on that body; interpretive statements (often absent from multivolume encyclopedias) are accurate in light of the scholarly literature. According to our medical consultant, **cancer** is well written and factual. The only improvement might be to change the focus from the singular *cancer* to *cancers* in the sentences dealing with causes of the disease. This would help to convey the notion that cancer is a collection of many different diseases, each of which may have a separate cause.

Oxygen contains a few mistakes, probably due to faulty copyediting. The first sentence incorrectly states, "By far the commonest element in the Earth's crust, of which it makes up nearly 50%; in various combined forms it also constitutes 21% of the atmosphere as diatomic molecules." Instead, it should read, "By far the commonest element in the Earth's crust, of which it makes up nearly 50% in various combined forms; it also constitutes. . . ." A sentence reading, "The element boils 13°C higher than does nitrogen" should instead say "13C° higher," since it refers to a temperature difference, not a temperature.

The **comet** entry is accurate except that it overgeneralizes about the size of comet nuclei. Our astronomy consultant also felt the entry's writing style was rough and disjointed, making it hard to read. Similarly, our history consultant found the **Henry VIII** entry generally accurate in the facts it presents, but the facts are stated without appropriate context and could mislead the reader. For example, the significance of Henry's membership in the Holy League or his victory at the Battle of Spurs is unexplained. The article also focuses heavily on the king's marriages, at the expense of the impact of Henry's reign on domestic and foreign affairs.

Clarity

As the editor states in the preface, the level and style of writing were determined by a collaboration of editorial staffs of both W. R. Chambers and Cambridge University Press. This collaboration produced a writing style that is clear, economical, and understandable for its intended audience. Explanations, especially for scientific and technical subjects, are well presented in a logical and nontechnical way.

Each entry includes the following: the entry word(s) in boldface followed by a pronunciation (if necessary) in parentheses. (The pronunciation guide is found in the "How to Use The Cambridge Encyclopedia" section located after the preface. This section also explains abbreviations used in the main text.) The main text then follows in a paragraph or more; longer entries are divided by italicized subheads. Following the text are cross-references to other entries; use of the symbol ⓘ after a cross-reference denotes that the entry has an illustration or panel.

Because it is a British venture, *The Cambridge Encyclopedia*'s style does use some conventions not usually seen in the United States, as in the word *whilst* seen below in the entry for the **Titanic:**

> **Titanic** [tiytanik] White Star Line's 46,329 gross tons passenger liner, which collided with an iceberg in the N Atlantic on her maiden voyage in April 1912. Lifeboat capacity was inadequate, and just over 700 people were saved, whilst 1500 went down with the ship. The vessel was rediscovered in 1985, explored, and photographed on the sea bed. As she was found to be broken into two unequal pieces, each severely damaged, it is unlikely that she will ever be raised. The task is not impossible, but it would be prohibitively expensive.

One aggravation for American readers might be the English style of spelling: *center of gravity* is found under **centre of gravity,** *edema* under **oedema.** The editor has taken this into account and provides cross-references when the first three letters of the entry are different. Both spellings of the word are given, however, at the entry word.

Objectivity

By nature of their length, the entries in a one-volume encyclopedia can give only the facts; space does not allow room for opinions or points of view. The entries for **AIDS, capital punishment, Northern Ireland,** and **ozone layer** rely on facts and description to convey information for the most part, ignoring whatever controversies may exist for these subjects. The only exception to this evenhanded treatment may be in the entry for **AIDS.** In this 200-word essay, no mention is made of civil rights issues, funding, treatment availability, or the potential for heterosexual transmission. The entry goes seriously astray in noting the risks of contracting the disease for those "persons who have had casual sexual relationships especially in sub-Saharan Africa, San Francisco, or New York." Articles on Northern Ireland mention the conflict between Protestants and Catholics, noting that most of the violence is aimed at the British force that occupies the territory. The article on the ozone layer notes the harmful effects of chlorofluorocarbons (CFCs) on the loss of the ozone layer and the steps taken by the international community to reduce these emissions. A cross-reference to the **greenhouse effect** discusses the theory that global temperature increase may melt the polar ice caps, but the entry adds that there are many uncertainties concerning the possible effects of this temperature increase.

Accessibility

The short-entry, one-volume encyclopedia allows the user the luxury of searching for more specific terms, as in a dictionary. Over 3,000 guide words help the reader locate entries. The use of cross-references is the best feature of *The Cambridge Encyclopedia.* According to the preface, almost as much editorial time was spent creating the cross-references as the actual entries. The cross-references at the end of the entry on **violin,** for example, direct the reader to other instruments in this family, such as **viola, kit,** and **kinnor,** and to the family of instruments in **string instrument.** Cross-references also lead users to illustrations, color plates, and the "Ready Reference" section.

Special Features

The Cambridge Encyclopedia uses 700 maps and drawings, both black and white and two-color, throughout the text. The front- and endpapers display 189 flags of the world in full color. These are up-to-date as of the book's 1992 printing date. Use of tables, charts, and panels also allows the concise depiction of information that *The Cambridge Encyclopedia* excels at providing. For example, a panel following the entry on **vestments** shows clergy and definitions of the religious vestments worn.

A special section of 16 color plates is found at the end of the alphabetical main entry section. This section is used to illustrate the varied uses of color in the physical, natural, and social world. The plates range from computer graphics to Lord Nelson's famous telegraph flag signal sent at the Battle of Trafalgar. Some inconsistency occurs in cross-referencing the color plates. In the example above, a cross-reference is made from the plate to **Horatio Nelson** but not vice versa.

The "Ready Reference" section is the most significant special feature of *The Cambridge Encyclopedia.* The last section in the work, its 7,000 entries are organized under 11 broad categories: "The Earth in Space," "Space Exploration," "Earth: General Data," "Times and Distances," "Nations of the World," "Political Leaders 1900–1990," "Measurement," "Communication Systems," "Names and Titles," "Competitive Sports and Games," and "Common Abbreviations." This section contains the most up-to-date entries for *The Cambridge Encyclopedia,* with most of the information current through 1990 or 1991. All pertinent entries in the main text are cross-referenced to this section. For example, the entries **dactylology** and **sign language** send the user to a one-page chart of the British and American deaf alphabet in the "Ready Reference" section. An index to the "Ready Reference" section helps the user access its information.

Another interesting feature makes *The Cambridge Encyclopedia* a quasi-online tool. Users are invited to send a request for a "datasearch" on any term to the publishers. The output will provide a listing of every entry in *The Cambridge Encyclopedia* that refers to the selected topic. This is a free service, and results are returned within 14 days.

The Cambridge Encyclopedia does not include bibliographies, although principal works are listed with the entries for various authors in the main alphabetical section.

Format

The Cambridge Encyclopedia has a durable binding and its pages spread out nicely when the book is opened and laid flat. Guide words are presented in bold type in capital letters over a red line, which separates them from the entries on a page. Each entry is in bold type, upper- and lowercase, and the very readable text follows underneath, slightly indented from its main entry word. Entry arrangement is done on a word-by-word indexing basis. The "Ready Reference" section is presented on tinted paper, distinguishing it from the main alphabetical section.

Summary

For other opinions regarding *The Cambridge Encyclopedia,* see *Booklist (Reference Books Bulletin),* November 1, 1990, pages 558–559; and *Library Journal,* April 15, 1991, pages 40–42.

The Cambridge Encyclopedia offers libraries and individuals fast access to accurate facts written in an easy-to-understand, intelligible style. While its more than 30,000 entries make it less exhaustive than the new one-volume fifth edition of THE COLUMBIA ENCYCLOPEDIA or the third edition of THE RANDOM HOUSE ENCYCLOPEDIA, its ease of use, accessibility, and reasonable price ($49.95) make it very attractive. Geographical and biographical data are its strong points because of access to the W. & R. Chambers databases, but *The Cambridge Encyclopedia* is weak on contemporary life and popular culture. Potential buyers should be aware of the decidedly British slant and of dated material relating to the U.S. presidential elections of 1992. If price is not a consideration, then the first choice—especially for an American audience—would probably be THE COLUMBIA ENCYCLOPEDIA. If budget is a factor, however, or if the purchaser wants a British viewpoint, *The Cambridge Encyclopedia* is an excellent choice.

The Cambridge Paperback Encyclopedia

Facts at a Glance

Full title: **The Cambridge Paperback Encyclopedia**
Publisher: Cambridge University Press
Editor: David Crystal
Edition reviewed: © 1993

Number of volumes: 1
Number of articles: more than 19,000
Number of pages: 928
Number of words: more than 750,000
Number of cross-references: 26,000
Number of index entries: no index
Number of maps: more than 270 (reviewer estimate)
Number of illustrations: more than 300 black-and-white line drawings (reviewer estimate)
Intended readership: general reader
Trim size: $6\frac{1}{8}'' \times 9\frac{1}{4}''$
Binding: paperback

Price: $19.95
Sold directly to libraries and schools; also sold in bookstores and through direct mail
ISBN 0-521-43762-8
Revised edition to be published in late 1994

Introduction

According to the editor's preface, the aim of the *Cambridge Paperback Encyclopedia* is the same as its parent volume, THE CAMBRIDGE ENCYCLOPEDIA: "to provide a succinct, systematic, and readable guide" to basic facts for a general audience. This first paperback edition, published in 1993, is 526 pages shorter than the hardcover edition and contains about 6,000 fewer main entries than the parent work. A new paperback edition will be published in late 1994.

Authority

Since the paperback edition is derived from the same databases as the hardcover volume, the authoritativeness is the same. (See the review of THE CAMBRIDGE ENCYCLOPEDIA for a full discussion.)

Scope

The number of words devoted to each entry appears to be about one-half of the hardcover edition. Three articles on **Impressionism** summarize the movement in art, literature, and music in separate entries of 72 words each (the hardcover edition devoted 130 words), while **Nelson Mandela** contains 78 words (hardcover, 160 words) and **Elvis Presley** has approximately 99 words (hardcover, 180 words). The entry on **Mexico** has approximately 295 words (hardcover, 560 words). **Hubble Space Telescope** contains about 100 words with information giving its size, date of launch, and mention of the problem in its main optical system.

For a full discussion of scope, see the review of THE CAMBRIDGE ENCYCLOPEDIA.

There are scant entries (less than 2 percent of those surveyed) on popular culture, but this total has doubled from the hardcover edition. Entries related to popular culture tend to be biographical rather than topical: there are entries for **The Rolling Stones, Madonna, Dustin Hoffman,** and **Wilt Chamberlain.**

The editor states in the preface that the *Cambridge Paperback Encyclopedia* emphasizes international coverage; however, more than 69 percent is British, U.S., and European coverage. This is an increase of 9 percent from the hardcover edition total. Coverage of Africa and Asia increased from 6 percent in the hardcover edition to over 16 percent in the *Cambridge Paperback Encyclopedia*. The surprisingly small percentage of Canadian entries in the hardcover edition (roughly 1 percent of the total) was increased in the *Cambridge Paperback Encyclopedia* to 2 percent.

Currency

The 1993 edition of the *Cambridge Paperback Encyclopedia* is based on the hardcover edition published in 1990 and updated to reflect changes through 1992. The shorter work has an entry on **Bill Clinton;** the hardcover had none. The entry in the "Ready Reference" section on political rulers and leaders is not updated for the United States. The entry for **Czechoslovakia** includes the division into the Czech Republic and Slovak Repub-

Cambridge Paperback Encyclopedia

① **CLOSED SHOP**   **CLUJ-NAPOCA**

and its display screen are directly linked, even at a considerable distance, rather than by broadcast transmission or intermediate recording. Applications include surveillance, surgical and scientific demonstration, and industrial remote examination. ≫ interactive video; television

closed shop A company or works where the work force is required to belong to one or more officially recognized trade unions; the opposite situation is known as an **open shop**. The advantages of the closed shop system are that negotiations between a company and its workforce are simplified. However, problems arise for the company if negotiations break down, as the unions can close down operations more easily where all the workforce are members.

Clostridium A genus of rod-shaped bactera that are typically motile by means of flagella, and produce spores (*endospores*). They are widespread in the soil and in the intestinal tract of humans and other animals. The genus includes the causative agents of botulism, gas gangrene, and tetanus. (Kingdom: Monera. Family: Bacillaceae.) ≫ bacteria ⓘ; intestine; spore

Clotho ≫ **Moerae**

cloud A visible collection of particles of ice and water held in suspension above the ground. Clouds form when air becomes saturated and water vapour condenses around nuclei of dust, smoke particles, and salt. Four main categories of clouds are recognized: *nimbus* clouds, which produce rain; *stratus* clouds, which resemble layers; *cumulus* clouds, which resemble heaps; and *cirrus* clouds, which resemble strands or filaments of hair. These names are further modified by an indication of cloud height: *strato* – low level clouds; *alto* – middle level clouds; *cirro* – high level clouds. Fog can be considered as cloud close to ground level. ≫ altocumulus / altostratus / cirrus / cirrocumulus/ cirrostratus / cumulonimbus / cumulus / nimbostratus/ nimbus/noctilucent/stratocumulus/stratus clouds; condensation (physics); dew point temperature; fog; nephanalysis; precipitation; thunderstorm

cloud chamber A device for detecting subatomic particles; invented by British physicist Charles Wilson in 1912. It comprises a chamber containing vapour prone to condensing to liquid. The passage of particles forms ions, which act as centres for condensation, and the particle paths become visible as trails of mist. The device has been superseded by

other particle detectors. ≫ bubble chamber; ion; particle detectors; Wilson, Charles

clouded tiger ≫ **tortoiseshell cat**   **⑥**

Clough, Arthur Hugh (1819–61) British poet, born in Liverpool. Experimental techniques in his long poem *The Bothie* (1848) and the ironic narrative *Amours de Voyage* (1849) have influenced modern poets.   **⑦**

clove tree An evergreen tree growing to 12 m/40 ft, native to Indonesia; flowers yellow, 4-petalled, in terminal clusters. The flower buds are dried to form the spice cloves. (*Syzygium aromaticum.* Family: Myrtaceae.) ≫ spice

clover A low-growing annual or perennial, occurring in both temperate and subtropical regions, but mainly in the N hemisphere; leaves with three toothed leaflets; small pea-flowers, white, pink, or red, clustered into often dense, rounded heads. Several species are extensively grown as fodder for cattle, and they are also valuable pasture plants. Yellow-flowered species are generally called **trefoils**. (Genus: *Trifolium*, 250 species. Family: Leguminosae.) ≫ **⑧** alsike; shamrock; trefoil

Clovis The earliest identifiable Indian culture of N America; hunter-gatherers exploiting the mammoth herds of the plains towards the end of the last glaciation, c.10 000–9 000 BC. It is characterized archaeologically by bifacially-flaked spear points found across the USA, notably near Clovis, NM, in 1963. ≫ hunter-gatherers

club foot A congenital deformity of one or both feet, in which the child cannot stand on the sole of the affected foot. The foot is pulled downward, and the heel turned inwards. Improvement may be achieved by the application of a series of graded splints, or in severe cases by surgical operation. ≫ congenital abnormality; foot

clubmoss A spore-bearing plant related to ferns and horsetails; stem long, regularly branched, clothed with numerous small leaves. It is found almost everywhere, many in heathland or similar habitats. (Genus: *Lycopodium*, 450 species. Family: Lycopodiaceae.) ≫ fern; horsetail; spore

clubroot A disease of cabbage-family plants (the Brassicaceae) that causes gall-like swellings of roots and discoloration of leaves; caused by the parasitic slime mould *Plasmodiophora brassicae*. ≫ cabbage; parasitology; slime mould   **⑨**

Cluj-Napoca or **Cluj** [kloozh napoka], Ger **Klausenburg** 46°47N 23°37E, pop (1986e) 310 000. City in NEC Rom-   **⑩**

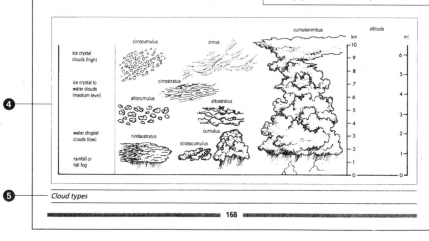

⑤   *Cloud types*

168

Page shown at 77% of actual size

① Guide words indicate the first and last entries on the page

② Cross-references

③ Main entry words printed in boldface

④ Illustrations include drawings with callouts

⑤ Caption

⑥ Cross-reference entry

⑦ Measurements given in both metric and standard systems

⑧ Scientific classifications given on flora and fauna entries

⑨ Pronunciations given for foreign or unusual entry words

⑩ Latitude and longitude locations given for countries and important cities

lic with separate entries for each. There are no entries for *Frida Kahlo, food pyramid,* or *virtual reality.*

There are approximately 570 maps in the *Cambridge Paperback Encyclopedia;* one-third fewer than in the hardcover edition of THE CAMBRIDGE ENCYCLOPEDIA. The current national boundaries created after the European revolutions of 1989 are reflected in the maps inspected for Germany, Yugoslavia, and Czechoslovakia. The maps for Yugoslavia and Czechoslovakia are updated to show the independent countries of the former Yugoslavia and the new Czech Republic and Slovakia. A map of Russia is found under the entry for Soviet Union to show the constituent republics of the Commonwealth of Independent States. It gives no physical detail, only political boundary information.

Accuracy

For information on the *Cambridge Paperback Encyclopedia*'s accuracy, see the review of THE CAMBRIDGE ENCYCLOPEDIA.

Clarity

For a full discussion of clarity, see the review of THE CAMBRIDGE ENCYCLOPEDIA. The *Cambridge Paperback Encyclopedia* carries forward the concise, understandable format used in the parent work in spite of the abbreviated entries, yet explanations for scientific and technical subjects are presented in a logical and non-technical way.

Objectivity

See the review of THE CAMBRIDGE ENCYCLOPEDIA for a full discussion of objectivity.

Accessibility

For a full discussion of accessibility, see the review of THE CAMBRIDGE ENCYCLOPEDIA.

Special Features

The *Cambridge Paperback Encyclopedia* uses more than 570 black-and-white maps and drawings throughout the text. All color plates have been deleted from the *Cambridge Paperback Encyclopedia.* Use of tables, charts, and panels also allows concise depiction of information. A few tables found in the parent edition have been deleted from the *Cambridge Paperback Encyclopedia.*

As in the parent volume, the "Ready Reference" section is the most significant special feature of the *Cambridge Paperback Encyclopedia.* Located after the main entries, it includes 6,000 entries in 100 pages under ten broad categories. The categories remain basically the same; categories missing in the *Cambridge Paperback Encyclopedia* are "Space Exploration," "Names and Titles,"

and "Common Abbreviations." New categories are "Signs and Symbols," "Prizes," and "New Nations." This section contains the most up-to-date entries for both the *Cambridge Paperback Encyclopedia* and THE CAMBRIDGE ENCYCLOPEDIA, with most information in the *Cambridge Paperback Encyclopedia* current through December 1992.

Format

The *Cambridge Paperback Encyclopedia* is slightly larger than a general almanac or desk dictionary. It has a durable binding and lies flat when open. Guide words are presented in bold type in capital letters over a gray line, which separates them from the entries on a page. Each entry term is in bold type, and the very readable text follows underneath, slightly indented from its main entry word. Entry arrangement is alphabetical and word by word. The margins of the "Ready Reference" section are tinted to distinguish it from the main alphabetical section.

Summary

The *Cambridge Paperback Encyclopedia* offers users fast access to accurate, up-to-date facts written in an easy-to-understand, intelligible style. About one-third to one-half the size of the hardcover CAMBRIDGE ENCYCLOPEDIA, it probably would not be a library's first choice for a one-volume encyclopedia. However, because of its currency (especially with its emphasis on the international scene) and low cost, the *Cambridge Paperback Encyclopedia* is a fine addition to a home library.

Collier's Encyclopedia

Facts at a Glance

Full title: **Collier's Encyclopedia**
Publisher: Macmillan Educational Company
Editors: Lauren S. Bahr, Editorial Director; Bernard Johnston, Editor-in-Chief
Number of contributors: 4,800
Edition reviewed: © 1992; statistics apply to 1993 printing

Number of volumes: 24
Number of articles: 25,000
Number of pages: 19,844
Number of words: 21 million
Number of cross-references: 13,000
Number of index entries: 450,000
Number of maps: 1,600
Number of illustrations: 4,034 four-color; 10,374 black and white
Intended readership: secondary and college students and adults (reviewer estimate)
Trim size: 8¼″ × 10⅝″
Binding: hardcover

Price: to individuals, $1,499 (regular binding); $1,699
    (deluxe binding); to schools and libraries, $995 +
    $35 shipping
Sold directly to libraries and schools; also sold door to
    door
ISBN 002-942548-4
Revised annually; next scheduled revision: February
    1994

Introduction

Collier's Encyclopedia is a 24-volume general reference
work that, according to the preface in volume 1, is "a
scholarly, . . . continuously revised summary of the
knowledge that is most significant to mankind." The set
includes "the essential content of the curricula of colleges and secondary schools, as well as the upper
grades" and is designed to meet the needs of "the most
exacting school and home users." Its main competitors
are THE NEW ENCYCLOPAEDIA BRITANNICA and ENCYCLOPE-
DIA AMERICANA.

Information is presented "comprehensively and in
depth" for nonspecialists and professionals.

This review is based on the 1992 printing.

Authority

The 1992 printing of *Collier's Encyclopedia* is published by Macmillan Educational Company. It was first
published in 1950 as a 20-volume set, expanding to its
present 24 volumes in 1962.

Collier's has three advisory boards (Library, Curriculum, and International), whose 22 members, many of
whom are librarians, contributed to the development of
the encyclopedia.

In addition, 145 senior editors and advisers are listed
in volume 1 under broad categories of specialization: biological sciences, humanities, physical sciences, regional studies, and social sciences. The senior editors
are complemented by a house editorial staff.

Almost all entries indicate the name of the contributor or contributors at the end of the article. When sections of long entries are written by different people,
individual sections are signed. The 4,800 contributors
are identified in volume 1 by the positions they held at
the time of their contribution. As with NEW BRITANNICA
and AMERICANA, most contributors are academics. Others
are journalists, industry and business specialists, and
government officials and agencies.

Scope

According to the preface, *Collier's* includes the "content
of the curricula of colleges and secondary schools, as
well as the upper grades," presenting the "major areas of
the physical sciences, life sciences, earth sciences, and

social sciences, as well as the humanities . . . comprehensively and in depth." Examination of a random 50-
page sample (volume 6, pages 415–465), which included
75 entries, shows broad coverage of the humanities (including history—45 percent of the entries) and of science (28 percent). Also well represented in the sample
are geography (17 percent) and the social sciences (9
percent). There are no entries from popular culture in the
sample and few throughout the series.

Like NEW BRITANNICA and AMERICANA, *Collier's* has
both broad-entry and specific-entry articles. However, it
differs from AMERICANA in that, as stated in the preface,
"Although there are numerous short articles, broad area
coverage is favored." For example, AMERICANA has individual entries on *Don Juan, Childe Harold,* and other
works of Lord Byron, whereas *Collier's* discusses them
within the **Lord Byron** article and in the article **history
of English literature.** It should be noted that *Collier's,*
with 25,000 entries and 21 million words, is considerably smaller than AMERICANA and NEW BRITANNICA.

Within *Collier's,* selected sample entries indicate the
following allocations of space: **castle,** 1¼ pages, including two photographs; *Hamlet,* the play, slightly more
than 3 pages, including one photograph; **impressionism**
(in art), ¾ page, including one illustration; **Nelson
Mandela,** ½ page; **Mexico,** 24 pages of text and photos
and 4 pages of map information; and **Elvis Presley,** 31
lines. *Tyrannosaurus* appears in the **dinosaur** entry,
where it receives 18 lines in an 11½-page article.

Collier's covers a broad range of both American and
international topics. Examination of a 25-page sample
(volume 8, pages 340–365) indicates coverage of 33
non-American topics out of a total of 55 entries. Of the
33, 17 are geographic entries. Other foreign articles in
the sample include **Domitian** (Roman emperor), **John
Donne, Fyodor Dostoevsky, Gaetano Donizetti** (19th-
century Italian opera composer), and **Paul Doumer**
(20th-century French statesman).

Currency

According to a policy that calls for the work to be "continuously revised," *Collier's* is updated yearly. The publisher's estimate of the extent of annual revisions is 10
percent to 18 percent.

The publisher provided the reviewers with the 1992
printing. Therefore, this review can address *Collier's*
coverage of events only up to that publication date. In
the 1992 printing, articles on the **Union of Soviet
Socialist Republics, Mikhail Gorbachev,** and **Boris
Yeltsin** cover the 1991 coup attempt in the U.S.S.R. The
Yugoslavia article includes the 1991 declaration of independence by Slovenia, Croatia, and Macedonia, and
the article on **Yemen** refers to the formation of the
Republic of Yemen in 1990. *Collier's* covers the
1990–1991 **Persian Gulf War** in an eight-and-a-half-

Collier's Encyclopedia

CREIGHTON, MANDELL   427

the terms of the act of Congress, Union Pacific's shares were to be sold for cash at par. But the railroad paid the Crédit Mobilier, which had built the road for less than $50,000,000, in securities worth in the market $70,000,000 among them shares of the common stock at about one third of their par value. In 1867, fearing that a Congressional investigation might question the affairs of the company, Oakes Ames, who had been a member of Congress since 1863, had a bloc of 343 Crédit Mobilier shares transferred to him for disposal to congressmen. In 1872-1873, an investigation traced 160 of these shares to senators and representatives, and found that Ames had sold them the stock at par, and even on credit, although it had, at the moment, a market value of $200. The investigation showed further that the Crédit Mobilier had, in 1868, distributed to its shareholders $60 in cash, Union Pacific first mortgage bonds at a face value of $230, and railroad stock worth $515 at face value. Among the congressmen investigated for dealings with Ames were Massachusetts' Senator Henry L. Wilson, New Hampshire's James W. Patterson, New York's Representative James Brooks, and Ohio's Representative James A. Garfield. Vice-President Schuyler Colfax was also implicated. The House of Representatives censured Ames and Brooks, but held that most of the congressmen who had taken the stock had done so without being aware of the impropriety of their acts. The Senate censured Patterson, but as his term was about to expire, did not expel him. The revelation of the Crédit Mobilier's methods did much to shake public confidence in the integrity and capacity of the Republicans, who were then in power.   WILLIAM B. HESSELTINE

CREED (Lat. *credo*, I believe), in ecclesiastical usage, a brief and authoritative statement of religious belief. A variety of creeds appeared in the second and third centuries in connection with the baptism of converts. The trinitarian formula common to them was gradually expanded to exclude divergent teachings and to distinguish true from false Christians and churches. The Apostles' Creed, so called because it once was believed to have been composed by the Apostles, but dating in its present form from the sixth century, is widely used in the West. The Nicene Creed, adopted at the Council of Nicaea in 325 and later modified, is used in the East and the West, but without the word *filioque* in the former. The Athanasian Creed, ascribed to Athanasius (c. 296-373) but actually dating from the fifth or sixth century, enjoys more limited use. Longer statements, called confessions, were prepared in the sixteenth and later centuries to supplement the creeds as doctrinal standards for most modern denominations. *See also* APOSTLES' CREED, THE; ATHANASIAN CREED, THE; NICENE CREED, THE.   THEODORE G. TAPPERT

CREEK WAR, a minor campaign between the United States and the Creek Indians in Alabama, then part of the Mississippi Territory, during the War of 1812. It was incited by Tecumseh, a Shawnee Indian chief, an ally of Great Britain, to halt encroachment on Creek lands by American settlers. On Aug. 30, 1813, the Creeks broke into the stockade at Fort Mims, and scalped most of the inmates. The governor of Tennessee authorized an emergency force of 2,500 men, led by Gen. Andrew Jackson, to be sent against the Indians. Following a series of forced marches, Jackson's troops met a large body of Creeks in the battle of Tohopeka, or Horseshoe Bend, on Mar. 27, 1814, and killed over 2,000 warriors. In the Treaty of Fort Jackson, Aug. 9, 1814, Jackson forced the Indians to cede to the United States over 20,000,000 acres (8,100,000 hectares), more than half of the old Creek country.   WALTON E. BEAN

CREEPER, a small songbird named for its habit of creeping up tree trunks, usually in a spiral path. Five species, belonging to the genus *Certhia,* are found in cooler regions throughout most of the northern hemisphere. The creeper is a brown bird, 5 to 7 inches (12-17 cm) long. Its stiff spine-tipped tail serves as a prop in climbing. Its bill is long, thin, and down-curved. The creeper feeds on insects and their eggs, which it captures by probing bark crevices with its bill. When it forages a tree, it starts at the base and works to the top. The nest is a shapeless mass of bark, wood chips, twigs, and moss wedged behind a piece of loose bark. The brown, or tree, creeper, *Certhia familiaris,* is the only species found in North America. It is dark brown above, with pale buff spots and stripes and a pale buff line over its eyes, and is gray below, shading to white on its throat. The brown creeper is found mainly in coniferous woods in most of the United States and in southern Canada. The creeper is classified in the order Passeriformes, family Certhiidae. *See color illustration in* BIRD.   HERBERT G. DEIGNAN

L. A. FUERTES FOR U. S. FISH AND WILDLIFE SERVICE
THE BROWN CREEPER

BROWN CREEPER

Breeding Range

Winter Range

CREEPING CHARLIE. *See* MONEYWORT.

CREEPING JENNY. *See* MONEYWORT.

CREIGHTON, MANDELL [krai'tn] (1843-1901), English historian and Anglican bishop, was born in Carlisle on July 5, 1843. He studied at Merton College, Oxford, where he took his B.A. in 1867, and was then appointed a fellow of that college. In 1875 he became a country vicar in Northumberland and there, for nearly ten years, he divided his time between pastoral work and historical research; in 1884 he became Dixie Professor of Ecclesiastical History at

Page shown at 72% of actual size

❶ Contributor's credit: most articles are signed

❷ Main entry words printed in capitals in boldface

❸ Cross-references

❹ Guide words and page number

❺ Illustrations include photographs and maps

❻ Measurements given in both standard and metric systems

❼ Caption

❽ Cross reference entries

❾ Pronunciations given for foreign or unusual entry words

page article, which includes the aftermath of the war. The **Germany** entry has been completely redone, including captions and maps.

The **sound reproduction and recording** article, criticized in a previous Buying Guide for not including information on digital technology, has been revised to include that information as well as data on compact discs and other laser technology.

There are lapses in currency in the set, however. For example, the maps in the **Somalia** and **Oman** articles show the old divisions of Yemen; maps in the **Sweden, Switzerland, Netherlands,** and **Belgium** articles still show the divided Germany; and the **United Nations** article makes no mention of the role of the United Nations in the Persian Gulf War. The Hubble Space Telescope, launched in April 1990, is mentioned in the **space astronomy** and **space exploration** articles only as an unnamed space telescope that is to be launched, contradicting photo and diagram captions that mention the telescope by name and state that it was launched. In the discussion of space shuttles in the **space exploration** article, there is no mention of the *Challenger* disaster of 1986. In the **nuclear fusion** article, cold-fusion experiments made in 1989 are not discussed. None of the Clean Air acts (the first of which dates back to 1970) are mentioned in the **air pollution** article.

The currency of population figures and other statistics is inconsistent: United States cities and states have 1990 census figures and some foreign cities and countries have recent figures. Many others, however, date from the early and mid-1980s or earlier. **Coal** and **sheep** production statistics extend to 1987, but **copper industry** production tables date from the early 1980s, and economic data tables in the **Europe** article are from 1979.

Some photographs, especially those in black and white, are dated; for example, photographs of the U.S. Congress in the **legislative process in the United States** article appear to be from the 1950s and 1960s and show only men. On the other hand, many of the color photos in the set (for example, those in the **Australia** article) provide up-to-date views of people and places.

Accuracy

The widespread use of experts as advisers and contributors helps ensure the accuracy of *Collier's Encyclopedia*. The **Henry VIII** article, written by the foremost living historian on Tudor England, is factually impeccable and includes up-to-date opinions of professional historians. The article could only have been enhanced by more attention to English domestic politics and government. The entry **legislative process in the United States** is factually accurate. The section "How a Bill Becomes a Law" is one of the most detailed and useful in any adult encyclopedia. However, some parts of the entry, such as the "legislative purpose" section, do not clearly distinguish between fact and opinion. The **cancer** entry is accurate but out-of-date in many respects, which affects the reliability of the article. The **oxygen** article is technically good and offers some helpful cross-references. However, it has some deficiencies, such as the incorrect melting point of ozone. Also, a cryptic statement that Los Angeles has a significant concentration of ozone in the air is never explained, and the stratospheric ozone layer is neither mentioned nor cross-referenced. The **comet** article, written by one of the leading authorities on comets, is clearly written and well illustrated, providing accurate information that is fully accessible to the lay reader.

Clarity

According to the preface, articles have been organized "to insure reader comprehension." A typical arrangement calls for "immediate definition, for simple explanation, and for presentation of the basic facts early in the article." A random examination of articles indicates that entries, especially longer ones, use this approach. Also according to the preface, when understanding the content of an article requires knowledge beyond the background of the average reader, "an attempt is made to prepare the reader by references to preliminary reading in more elementary related articles." This is accomplished through the study guide in volume 24, which lists articles under major headings according to degree of difficulty or complexity. Within specialized articles, however, cross-references are not identified specifically as articles that will give readers elementary information. Thus, the reader must know about and refer to the study guide for this information.

Although the tone is generally academic and the reading level is high, most articles are readily comprehensible to the lay reader. Glossaries of specialized terms appear at the end of many articles, and technical terms are often defined within an article as they are used.

The following extract from a typical short article illustrates the density of content and high reading level:

TITANIC, a British ocean liner lost in an extraordinary marine catastrophe. Just before midnight on Apr. 14, 1912, the White Star liner *Titanic* on its maiden voyage from Southampton to New York, while almost 1,300 (2,100 km) miles from its destination, struck an iceberg and sank, leaving 1,513 dead. Casualties were particularly heavy among the crew, only 24 percent surviving. None of the ship's band or of the engine crew was saved. Of the 534 women and children aboard 70 percent survived; of the 1,667 men only 20 percent. Among those lost were the ship's captain; the president of the Grand Trunk Railway, Charles M. Hays; the vice-president of the Pennsylvania Railroad, J. B. Thayer; John Jacob Astor IV; Benjamin Guggenheim; George D. Widener; and Isidor Straus, whose wife refused rescue.

When the tragedy occurred the sea was unusually calm and the night was clear and cold. Although the captain had received warning of icebergs ahead he had decided to follow the prevailing practice of relying on a sharp lookout rather than reducing speed. For this he was severely criticized by a London court of enquiry headed by Lord Mersey. Also castigated was the captain of the Leyland liner *Californian* for refusing prompt aid to the stricken vessel although his ship was less than 10 miles (16 km) away when distress signals were reported. . . .

Objectivity

According to the preface, to "insure objectivity, articles involving key issues are submitted to authorities representing all major points of view." In some of the articles sampled, controversial issues are presented in an even-handed way. For example, the article **nuclear power** presents a balanced view of the nuclear power industry, giving the views of both proponents and opponents as it discusses political, economic, and safety issues associated with nuclear power. **Northern Ireland** is a clearly written, in-depth article that discusses the conflicts between Protestants and Catholics in an evenhanded, balanced way.

Such balance is not always evident. **Sex education** identifies one of the groups who oppose sex education in schools as a "small, but well-organized and vocal minority" that sees sex education as a " 'scheme to demoralize youth.' " Contrary to the philosophy stated in the preface, this article does not seem to have been submitted to authorities who hold this point of view. The authors of the article are obviously proponents of sex education in schools, stating that "a classroom setting provides a learning atmosphere conducive to covering topics related to sex objectively." In the **AIDS** article, the treatment of demographics is slanted if not incorrect. The reader is told that the main victims of AIDS are homosexual men. The article downplays the growing evidence of and concerns about heterosexual transmission. Some topics, such as prevention methods and the surrounding controversy of abstinence versus "safe sex," are not discussed.

Topics such as the ozone layer and capital punishment are not given their own articles in the set, and controversies surrounding these issues are not discussed in any comprehensive way in the articles where they are mentioned. Some controversial issues are not even found in the index, which does include animal rights, gun control, and sexual harassment.

Accessibility

Guide words indicate the first and last entry on each two-page spread. Most entry words are logical and are ones the reader would be likely to look up. Entries are arranged alphabetically, letter by letter, up to the comma in an inverted item. The order of person, place, and thing is used when headings are identical. When pages are added because of a revision, extra pages are shown with a figure and a letter (131A, 131B).

Many articles are organized under one or more levels of subheads in bold or italic type. Long survey articles such as **automobile** and **U.S. Civil War** have boxes that describe the contents of the main headings and major subheads.

Cross-references, presented in large and small capital letters, are used within articles and at the ends of articles. They also appear as separate entries. Because there are only 13,000 cross-references (fewer than one per page), readers must rely heavily on *Collier's* index.

That index, which contains 450,000 entries (100,000 entries more than in the larger AMERICANA and 200,000 more than in the even larger NEW BRITANNICA), is comprehensive and indispensable. Entries are indicated by volume, page, and quadrant (*a, b, c, d*) on the page, a technique that facilitates locating topics. Articles are indexed in capital letters in bold type. Subjects treated within articles are indexed in capital and small letters in bold type. The index contains *see* and *see also* cross-references. Many entries are annotated in parentheses to describe the entry. This feature is particularly helpful in distinguishing entries with the same name. Within entries, maps, illustrations, and bibliographic entries are referenced.

Special Features

A special feature of *Collier's* is the annotated bibliography in volume 24. It contains 11,500 English-language titles, numbered and arranged under broad subject headings. Within each subject, titles are arranged in increasing order of difficulty and specialization. According to the editors, titles are appropriate for high school, college, and beyond. They are selected for their availability in libraries. These claims are true most of the time. The *Collier's* general bibliography is more comprehensive than the separate ones included at the ends of articles in AMERICANA and the NEW BRITANNICA "Macropaedia." *Collier's* also has bibliographic entries at the ends of selected articles. The index (see *Accessibility*) and the study guide (see *Clarity*) are other major features.

The illustration program includes photographs, diagrams, graphs, maps, and charts. Color photographs account for 28 percent of photos. Recent photographs do not reflect a conscious attempt to dispel sexual stereotypes. (See also *Currency*.) Color transparencies that show relationships between things and color plates are well executed and very effective.

On the whole, *Collier's* maps are of the highest quality. They include political, physical, historical, distribution, and locator maps. However, the shading on some of the small black-and-white distribution maps and black-and-white relief maps makes them difficult to read. Maps were prepared by Rand McNally.

A very helpful special feature is the inclusion of short biographical sketches of noted people at the end of related articles, such as a list of aviation pioneers at the end of the **history of aviation** article. The reader is told when there is a separate article about any of the people.

Format

The 24 volumes of *Collier's* use the split-letter system, as do AMERICANA and NEW BRITANNICA. Except for volume 24, which has 1,050 pages, all volumes contain between 700 and 800 pages. The two-column format, within a trim size of $8\frac{1}{4}'' \times 10\frac{5}{8}''$, is easy to read. Subheads are easy to locate and help to break up the running text.

Summary

For other opinions regarding the 1992 edition of *Collier's Encyclopedia,* see *Booklist (Reference Books Bulletin),* September 15, 1992.

Collier's, while not as comprehensive as AMERICANA or NEW BRITANNICA, presents accurate information on a broad range of topics. It offers many helpful devices, such as the liberal use of glossaries, that aid comprehension. It is suitable for high school and college students and adult general readers, although the reading level is rather high. Its bibliography is particularly comprehensive.

The Columbia Encyclopedia

Facts at a Glance

Full title: **The Columbia Encyclopedia**
Publisher: Columbia University Press
Editors: Barbara A. Chernow; George A. Vallasi
Edition reviewed: © 1993, fifth edition

Number of volumes: 1
Number of articles: 50,000
Number of pages: 3,048
Number of words: 6.6 million
Number of cross-references: 65,000
Number of index entries: no index
Number of maps: more than 500 (reviewer estimate)
Number of illustrations: more than 500 black-and-white line drawings (reviewer estimate)
Intended readership: general adult reader
Trim size: $9\frac{1}{2}'' \times 12''$
Binding: hardcover

Price: $125
Sold and distributed by Houghton Mifflin
ISBN 0-395-62438-X
No regular revision policy

Introduction

The fifth edition of *The Columbia Encyclopedia,* published in 1993, comes nearly 20 years after the fourth edition (entitled *The New Columbia Encyclopedia*), published in 1975. The fifth edition carries forward the aims and objectives of previous editions: "It is designed always to serve two purposes: for readers to check facts fast, and for readers to make their way into a subject, and to venture further if they wish to do so." The editors claim that the true "beauty" of the encyclopedia lies in its 65,000 cross-references, which allow people doing research or simply browsing to pursue information from entry to entry and explore how topics relate to each other.

Authority

The first edition of *The Columbia Encyclopedia* appeared in 1935. It was the result of an eight-year project at Columbia University performed under the utmost secrecy—no more than ten members of the Columbia faculty knew anything of it. For the 1993 edition, more than 100 subject area experts from Columbia University and other academic institutions served as advisers. A six-member board of consultants, each with distinguished credentials, directed the advisers' work. The encyclopedia was produced by a team of about 90 people, led by professional editors Barbara A. Chernow and George A. Vallasi. The individual articles are not signed.

Scope

The Columbia Encyclopedia is a short-entry encyclopedia. By our reviewers' estimate, article length ranges from 150 words to several thousand, with a typical entry having approximately 200 words. **Castle** receives 638 words, **Nelson Mandela** has 169 words, and **Elvis Presley** contains 282 words. **Impressionism** in art has 787 words (a shorter entry covers the movement in music). **Tyrannosaurus** has 166 words. The longest entry of the sample is **Mexico,** which has nearly 3,000 words. There is no entry for *Hamlet,* although the entry **Shakespeare, William** provides brief identifying information about the play.

Of 427 articles sampled, the topical breakdown is: geography, 27 percent; social sciences, 20 percent; biography, 19 percent; science, 17 percent; and humanities, 16 percent. A mere 1 percent of the entries surveyed cover popular culture topics such as **pop art, rap music,** and **sky diving.**

The preface states that *The Columbia Encyclopedia* "is more international than its predecessors, but it remains an American encyclopedia written for American readers." A 25-page sample suggests a broad international scope: of the 278 articles sampled, 25 percent relate to Europe, 22 percent to Asia, 19 percent to the

The Columbia Encyclopedia

❶ 963

FLIGHT SIMULATOR ❻

inent literary family, he began writing for the stage about 1606, first with Francis BEAUMONT, with whom his name is inseparably linked, later with Massinger and others. Fletcher may have collaborated with Shakespeare on *Henry VIII* and *The Two Noble Kinsmen*. Though there is great uncertainty in dating the plays of Beaumont and Fletcher, their chief works appeared between 1607 and 1613. In *Philaster, A Maid's Tragedy, A King and No King,* and *The Scornful Lady,* they developed the form of the romance tragicomedy, which came to characterize a whole generation of later plays. In these plays a potentially tragic situation is developed until, at the end, through a twist of plot a happy solution is effected. A prolific writer, he enjoyed great success in many genres because of his entertaining and accessible poetry, masterful use of sexual intrigue, and the refined composition of his work. See edition of the works of Beaumont and Fletcher by F. Bowers (5 vol, 1966–); studies by E. Waith (1952), A. E. Thorndike (1965), and J. H. Wilson (1968).

❷ **Fletcher, John Gould,** 1886–1950, American poet, b. Little Rock, Ark., educated (1903–7) at Harvard. After traveling throughout Europe, he became a leader of the IMAGISTS in England. His early collections of poetry are *Irradiations: Sand and Spray* (1915) and *Goblins and Pagodas* (1916). In later works Fletcher turned from free verse to more traditional forms. These include *The Black Rock* (1928), *Selected Poems* (1938, Pulitzer Prize), and *The Burning Mountain* (1946). Many of his poems reflect his youth in the Southwest. See his autobiography, *Life Is My Song* (1937).

Fletcher, Thomas Clement, 1827–99, governor of Missouri (1865–69), b. Herculaneum, Mo. A Democrat opposed to slavery, he became a Republican in 1856 and supported Lincoln for the presidential nomination in 1860. In the Civil War, Fletcher commanded a Missouri regiment and served in the Vicksburg, Chattanooga, and Atlanta campaigns. He was brevetted brigadier general of volunteers for his service in repulsing Sterling Price at Pilot Knob, Mo. (Oct., 1864). As governor in the difficult postwar period, he proved an exceptionally able administrator.

Fletcher vs. Peck, case decided by the U.S. Supreme Court in 1810, involving the YAZOO LAND FRAUD. The court ruled that an act of the Georgia legislature rescinding a land grant was unconstitutional because it revoked rights previously granted by contract. The decision was the first to declare a state legislative act unconstitutional.

❸ **Flettner, Peter:** see FLÖTNER, PETER.

Fleurus (flörüs'), town (1981 pop. 22,574), Hainaut prov., S Belgium. It is a coal-mining and manufacturing center; domestic appliances, furniture, and machinery are produced. At Fleurus, Mansfield and Christian of Brunswick defeated (1622) the Spanish in the Thirty Years War, the French under Marshal Luxembourg defeated (1690) the Dutch and their allies in the War of the Grand Alliance, and the French under Jourdan defeated the Austrians in a decisive battle (1794) of the French Revolutionary Wars.

❹ **Fleury, André Hercule de** (äNdrä' ĕrkül' də flörē'), 1653–1743, French statesman, cardinal of the Roman Catholic Church. Tutor of the young LOUIS XV, he became, at the age of 73, chief adviser to the king and virtual ruler of France (1726–43). Fleury restored order to the national finances, disorganized by the speculative schemes of John LAW. The currency was stabilized, roads were built, the merchant marine expanded, and a growth in commerce resulted. By his attempts to suppress the Jansenists (see JANSEN, CORNELIS) Fleury provoked opposition, particularly from the parlements [courts]. He strove for peace abroad but became involved in the War of the POLISH SUCCESSION; through it, however, he assured the eventual reversion of Lorraine to France and established a Spanish Bourbon on the throne of Naples. See A. McC. Wilson, *French Foreign Policy during the Administration of Cardinal Fleury* (1936, repr. 1972).

Fleury, Claude (klōd), 1640–1723?, French ecclesiastical historian, a Roman Catholic priest, confessor to Louis XV, and author of the learned and unbiased *Histoire ecclésiastique*. This great work, in 20 volumes, occupied him for 30 years. It was the first systematic history of the Church, its organization, doctrines, and rites.

Flexner, Abraham, 1866–1959, American educator, b. Louisville, Ky., grad. Johns Hopkins Univ., 1886. After 19 years as a secondary school teacher and principal, he took graduate work at Harvard and at the Univ. of Berlin. In 1908 he joined the research staff of the Carnegie Foundation for the Advancement of Teaching and in 1910 wrote a report, *Medical Education in the United States and Canada*, which is generally called the Flexner Report. It hastened much-needed reforms in the standards, organization, and curriculums of American medical schools. From 1912 to 1925, Flexner was a member of the General Education Board, serving as secretary after 1917. He was director of the newly organized Institute for Advanced Study at Princeton from 1930 to 1939. His influential works on education range from *A Modern School* (1916) and *The Gary Schools* (with F. B. Bachman, 1918) to *The Burden of Humanism* (the Taylorian Lecture at Oxford Univ., 1928) and his widely known study, *Universities: American, English, German* (1930). His biography of H. S. Pritchett was published in 1943. See his autobiography (rev. ed. 1960).

Flexner, Simon, 1863–1946, American pathologist, b. Louisville, Ky., M.D. Univ. of Louisville, 1889; brother of Abraham Flexner. He served with the Rockefeller Institute (now Rockfeller University) from 1903 to 1935 (as its first director, 1920–35) and was Eastman professor at Oxford from 1937 to 1938. He worked on experimental epidemiology and venoms and is known especially for his serum treatment of cerebrospinal meningitis and for his studies of poliomyelitis. He also isolated a bacillus of dysentery.

flicker: see WOODPECKER.

Fliedner, Theodor (tā'ōdôr flēt'nər), 1800–1864, German Protestant minister and philanthropist. In 1826 he organized the first prison society of Germany. Ten years later at Kaiserswerth he founded the pioneer deaconess house and hospital for the indigent sick, at which Florence Nightingale worked. Fliedner established schools and orphanages in Europe and from 1849 to 1851 stimulated the organization of mother houses for deaconesses in Europe, America, and Asia. See biography by Catherine Winkworth (1867).

flight, sustained, self-powered motion through the air, as accomplished by an animal, aircraft, or rocket. Adaptation for flight is highly developed in birds and insects. The bat is the only mammal that accomplishes true flight; flying squirrels, flying fish, and flying lizards glide rather than fly. Birds fly by means of the predominantly up-and-down motion of their wings. The flapping motion is not, however, straight up and down but semicircular, the wings generally moving backward on the upstroke and forward on the downstroke. That motion pushes air downward and to the rear, creating a lift and forward thrust. The leading edge of the slightly concave wings is rather sharp, and the feathers are small and close-fitting, so that a streamlined surface meets the air. On the trailing edge of each wing the interlocking of the larger feathers forms a surface that acts somewhat like the ailerons, or movable airfoils, of an airplane. In wing motion, the leading edge is twisted so as to be lower than the trailing edge in the downward stroke and above the trailing edge in the upward stroke. Besides flapping, some birds also use gliding and soaring techniques in flight. In gliding, a bird holds its outstretched wings relatively still and relies on its momentum to keep it aloft for short distances. In soaring, a bird uses rising warm air currents to give it lift. The form and size of wings vary in different birds. In woodland birds the wings are somewhat rounded and have a relatively broad surface area. Birds with well-developed gliding ability, such as gannets and gulls, usually have narrow, pointed wings. Especially noted for their soaring power are eagles, vultures, crows, and some hawks. In soaring flight the feathers on the wings of these birds separate at the tips, resembling opened fingers against the sky. It is thought that this movement diverts the airstream over the wing and aids the bird in turning, banking, and wheeling. There is disagreement as to the maximum speeds achieved by birds in flight. While the flight speeds of most birds range from 10 to 60 mi (16–100 km) per hr, some have been recorded at speeds reaching 70 mi (110 km) per hr, for ❼ long distances and near 100 mi (160 km) per hr, for short flights. Man's first attempts at flight were made with flapping wings strapped to his arms in imitation of birds, but these had no success. Machines designed to fly in this way, called ornithopters, date to antiquity (c.400 B.C.) and models that are capable of flight have been known for more than 100 years. However, there are no practical aircraft based on ornithopter designs, even though an ornithopter—which has no theoretical top speed limit—should be capable at least of efficient low-speed flight. In the 1930s an Italian model weighing approximately 50 lb (110 kg) and powered by a 0.5-hp motor was successfully flown. Airships and balloons owe their ability to ascend and remain aloft to their inflation with a gas lighter than air; this is an application of Archimedes' principle of flotation, i.e., that a body immersed in a fluid (liquid or gas) is buoyed up by a force equal to the weight of the fluid that it displaces. Aircraft, which are heavier than air, are able to remain aloft because of forces developed by the movement of the craft through the air. Propulsion of most aircraft derives from the rearward acceleration of the air. It is an application of Newton's third law, i.e., that for every action there is an equal and opposite reaction. In propeller aircraft the forward motion is obtained through conversion of engine power to thrust by means of acceleration of air to the rear by the propeller. Lift is obtained largely from the upward pressure of the air against the airfoils (e.g., wings, tail fins, and ailerons), on whose upper surface the pressure becomes lower than that of the atmosphere. In jet-propelled aircraft, propulsion is achieved by heating air that passes through the engine and accelerating the resultant hot exhaust gases rearward at high velocities. Rockets are propelled by the rapid expulsion of gas through vents at the rear of the craft. The high speeds that are produced by jet and rocket engines have brought about substantial changes in the science of flight. See AERODYNAMICS; ❽ AIRPLANE; JET PROPULSION; ROCKET. See bibliography under AVIATION.

flight simulator, device providing a controlled environment in which a flight trainee can experience conditions approximating those of actual flight. A simulator generally consists of an enclosure housing a working replica of the interior of the cockpit of an

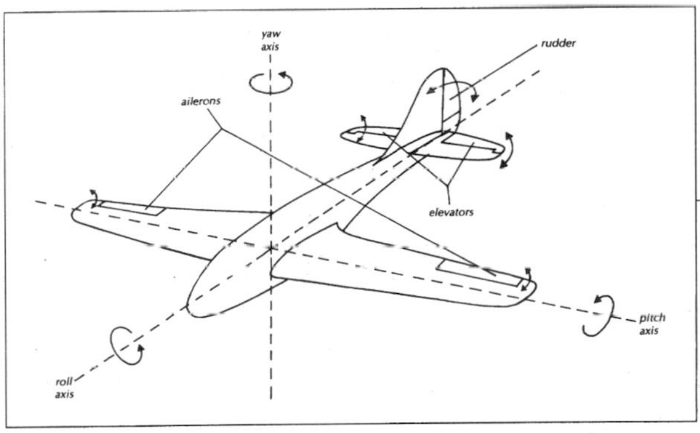

❾

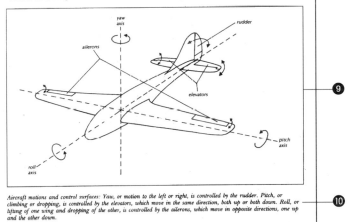

Aircraft motions and control surfaces: Yaw, or motion to the left or right, is controlled by the rudder. Pitch, or climbing or dropping, is controlled by the elevators, which move in the same direction, both up or both down. Roll, or lifting of one wing and dropping of the other, is controlled by the ailerons, which move in opposite directions, one up and the other down. ❿

❺ *The key to pronunciation appears on page xv.*

Page shown at 60% of actual size.

❶ Page number

❷ Main entry words printed in boldface

❸ Cross-reference entries indicated by small capitals

❹ Pronunciations given for foreign or unusual words

❺ Running foot repeated on every left-hand page reminds users about the punctuatin key; on the right-hand page, it reminds users about cross-references

❻ Guide words

❼ Measurements given in both standard and metric systems

❽ Cross-references

❾ Illustrations include diagrams with callouts

❿ Captions often add to the information presented in the text

United States, 13 percent to Africa, 7 percent to Latin America, and 5 percent to the United Nations. Surprisingly, only 6 percent of the articles relate to Britain and 3 percent to Canada.

Geographical entries are well represented and usually are the lengthiest, especially those relating to U.S. states and cities. A typical entry is **Indiana,** which has over 1,500 words and includes 1990 population figures and geographic, economic, historical, and political information about the state. U.S. state maps, continent maps, and some country maps typically note major cities, rivers, and major physical features. Most country maps, however, are outline maps with only the country labeled.

Biographical entries are international in scope and are weighted toward historical figures. Non-Western entries include **Ibn al-Arabi** (Muslim Sufi mystic); **Ibn Hanbal, Ahmad** (Muslim jurist and theologian); and **Ihara Saikaku** (Japanese writer of the 17th century). Contemporary figures include **Roy Innis, Senator Daniel Inouye** of Hawaii, **Donald Trump,** and **Ted Turner.** There seems to be an inconsistency in biographical coverage, however. For example, **Steven Spielberg** is included, but Frank Capra and Martin Scorsese are not. **Robert De Niro** appears but not Meryl Streep. **Carl Sagan** is discussed but not Stephen Hawking. And **Michael Milken** is included but not Peter Lynch.

Currency

The revision history of the encyclopedia follows no regular plan. The publishers issue revisions based on the significance and amount of global changes. The fact that there has been no revision for 20 years, a period that has seen major world events such as the end of communism as a dominant international force, engendered the publication of the fifth edition. According to the publisher, more than 60 percent of the entries have been revised for this edition to reflect changes in the world up to November 1, 1992. The 1992 U.S. presidential election is covered, and even some events in early 1993 are included. Many new articles have been included, and some old ones have been dropped to keep the size of the volume manageable.

An attempt has been made to assess the publisher's claim "to revise not only those entries on a place or system or idea that has changed, but virtually every other entry that happens to mention that place or system or idea." For the most part, the publishers have succeeded admirably in this goal. Thus, the entry **communism** has been updated to include the rise of Gorbachev and the abandonment of communism in Eastern Europe and Russia in the early 1990s. The article **Cold War** is the same as in the 1975 edition except at the end, where it notes the rise of Gorbachev, the reunification of East and West Germany, and the collapse of the Soviet empire. A completely revised bibliography accompanies the article.

Bill Clinton is a short biography that notes his election to the presidency. The well-written entry for **nutrition** includes an excellent illustration of the USDA food pyramid. A revised bibliography is appended, with five titles that have been published since 1980.

The **Persian Gulf War** article is approximately 300 words with cross-references to **Saddam Hussein, George Bush,** and **Norman Schwarzkopf.** Neither THE CAMBRIDGE ENCYCLOPEDIA nor the CAMBRIDGE PAPERBACK ENCYCLOPEDIA contain an entry for Schwarzkopf, one of the most notable persons of that war.

Hubble Space Telescope gives the accepted abbreviation used for the craft (HST), its size and launch date (mentioned only as 1990), and the telescope's designer. There is no bibliography. **Frida Kahlo** contains 175 words and is new to the fifth edition. It mentions her rejection of the surrealist label that has sometimes been applied to her. The bibliography contains two books with 1991 publication dates.

The 1,125 word article for **Lithuania** contains a small map of Europe with Lithuania situated among unlabeled countries. The text provides the history of the declaration of independence and the Soviet response, the ratification of the constitution, and the September 1991 election of Landsbergis as head of state. The article **Russia** is a major essay of 2,800 words, although updating is minimal since the entry only deals with the Russian state to 1917; one must go to the entry on **Russian Federation** for the status up to March 31, 1992, including information on the government of Boris Yeltsin and the Commonwealth of Independent States. (Yeltsin and the CIS also have separate entries.)

Maps of Germany, Yemen, countries of the former U.S.S.R., Czechoslovakia, and Yugoslavia all reflect the changes of the post-1989 world. However, there are a few problems. The map of Yugoslavia shows the country as constituting Macedonia as well as Serbia and Montenegro, although the text notes that only Serbia and Montenegro formed this new federation. The map of Yemen is poorly displayed, with no labels on the bordering states. There is no map under the **Union of Soviet Socialist Republics** entry; the reader must turn to **Russia** to see a map of the former republics. The reader must search under Europe to see a map of Czechoslovakia that shows all of the boundary changes (even though there are separate entries for both **Slovakia** and the **Czech Republic**).

There are other instances in which the revision has not done enough to update the material. The article **Oklahoma,** for example, mentions Platt National Park, which has not existed for some time. **Penobscot,** an article about Maine's Penobscot River, mentions that pulpwood is one of the principal freights on the river, but that has not been true for years. No mentions of recent efforts to build a new space station, the European space probe *Ulysses,* or the Cosmic Background Explorer (COBE) satellite are found in **satellite, artificial; space exploration; space probe; space shuttle;** or other related articles. **Turin** makes no mention of recent carbon-14 testing of the famous Shroud of Turin to determine its age.

Accuracy

Accuracy is a strong point of this fifth edition. A survey of entries ranging from **Dead Sea Scrolls** and **global warming** to **Sandra Day O'Connor** (who is not included in THE CAMBRIDGE ENCYCLOPEDIA) and **Thurgood Marshall** revealed no factual errors. The significance and context of the main subjects are also accurately presented. Entries on contemporary figures in popular culture, such as **Nolan Ryan** and **Pete Rose,** also provide accurate statistical information and are quite informative.

The well-written entry on **oxygen** covers the subject thoroughly and is accurate. There is no bibliography, but cross-references to other subjects are numerous. **Comet,** while brief, is accurate and complete. It is well organized and proceeds logically from point to point. **Henry VIII** does an excellent job of conveying a lot of information in a restricted space. Unlike many short articles about Henry that sensationalize his life, this one more accurately presents his life and reign within its proper context. Included is a good, up-to-date bibliography. Information on the House of Representatives can be found within the entry **Congress of the United States.** That entry also is accurate, useful, and complete. It ends with a good bibliography that is updated to 1991.

On the other hand, our content expert found the article on **cancer** to be in need of extensive revision. The examples used are ones that the readers cannot always identify with (for example, oral cancer in India). The descriptions of treatments are out-of-date and unnecessarily pessimistic.

A random check of other articles revealed few errors. However, a reviewer in *The Wall Street Journal* noted that the Kaiser plant in **Fontana,** California, does not produce steel any longer, despite that contention. And the notion that the people of **Hunza** are noted for their longevity has been discredited for some time. Other minor errors include statements that a junior college is located in **Evanston,** Illinois, and that the John Crerar Library is located in downtown **Chicago** (it is located at the University of Chicago).

Clarity

The publisher has aimed *The Columbia Encyclopedia* at the general adult reader. Most articles are clearly written, understandable, and straightforward. Longer entries are subdivided into sections (for example, **Henry VIII** has four sections). Section headings are difficult to detect, however, despite the fact that they are in italic. This is due primarily to a lack of extra spacing before section headings and to an absence of paragraphing. The result is that long articles are somewhat tedious to read.

The most difficult articles to understand conceptually are in the scientific realm, especially those on medical or chemical subjects. The **cancer** entry, for example, is unnecessarily dense, raising several tangential points that would be meaningful only to an expert. Although most scientific articles either define the technical terms used or provide a cross-reference for further explanation, a few, such as **thymine,** beg for more explanation.

In contrast, this excerpt from a new entry on **genetic engineering** reveals a fairly clear and concise style:

> **genetic engineering,** a group of new research techniques that manipulate the DNA (genetic material) of cells. The gene-splicing technique, which produces recombinant DNA, is a method of transporting selected genes from one species to another.

Long articles in other subject areas also are sometimes difficult to understand. The article **Thirty Years War,** for example, is a litany of place names and people that fails to explain adequately that disorganized period of history. Similar criticism can be leveled against the **Seven Years War** and the **Crusades.**

The article on **Evolution** presents another type of problem, which was criticized by a reviewer in *The Wall Street Journal.* Accompanying the article are illustrations of various hominid skulls, yet hominids are not discussed in the article. A cross-reference to **Man, Prehistoric** presents the reader with just another cross-reference to **Human Evolution.** This is where hominids finally are discussed, and the illustrations would be more appropriate there. A situation such as this results in confusion and frustration rather than clarity and comprehension.

Objectivity

Controversial topics are generally handled in an even-handed way. The article **capital punishment,** for example, presents the history of the practice dating back to 1750 B.C. and information on executions to September 1992. Along with the facts, both sides of the issue as debated in contemporary American society are fairly presented.

More than two-thirds of the article **Ireland, Northern** is from 1968 on. The essay presents attempts by the Irish Republic and Great Britain to reach a compromise during the 1970s and 1980s, while Catholic and Protestant violence flared. This is a well-balanced and factual article.

Information on the ozone layer is found under the entry **global warming.** The controversies are cited as well as explanations for global temperature rise given the magnitude of the threats. This is a fair and thorough discussion.

There are, however, omissions in the article on **AIDS.** Although the entry contains general information on the disease, citing statistics on its worldwide spread, there is no information on the civil rights issues or other controversies, such as alternative therapies.

Accessibility

In addition to its many short entries, *The Columbia Encyclopedia* contains numerous entries that are longer than those in any other one-volume encyclopedia. Despite this, the work is not indexed. There are 65,000 cross-references, but a case such as **Evolution** mentioned above reveals that cross-referencing can confuse rather than clarify. A work of this size requires more points of access than cross-referencing alone can supply. An index could have provided those points of access.

Most entries have at least one cross-reference, and the longer entries may have five to ten. Cross-references appear in small capital letters.

Special Features

The fifth edition of *The Columbia Encyclopedia* includes about 500 black-and-white illustrations. They tend to be quite simple, and generally serve to clarify entries or provide information in a convenient tabular format. Accompanying **orchestra and orchestration,** for example, is a simple diagram of the seating plan of a symphony orchestra. The entry **rose** shows one type of rose. In the scientific areas, the illustrations do a particularly good job of illuminating the topics.

The encyclopedia includes numerous maps, but these maps are, for the most part, not very good. Maps of U.S. states, continents, and a few countries show major cities, bodies of water, and some physical features. These maps are barely adequate. Maps for smaller or less important nations are very poor. They merely show the outline of the country with its name labeled, similar to a locator map. Surrounding countries are unmarked and no cities or other features are shown. Such maps provide no context for readers; they are almost useless for people unfamiliar with geography.

The Columbia Encyclopedia's best special feature—and the one that makes it stand out above all the other one-volume encyclopedias—is its use of bibliographies. Forty percent of the entries have at least one bibliographic citation; there are 40,000 citations listed. The extent and range of these citations is impressive and an effort has been made to include current works. In some cases, however, bibliographic citations are dated. In the entry **Plath, Sylvia,** for example, the latest work cited is from 1989, despite recent interest in her life and work. The most recent citation in the entry **Faulkner, William** is a 1984 reprint of a 1974 work. This is surely inadequate for such a major American author.

Format

A hefty 11 pounds, *The Columbia Encyclopedia* measures 9½" × 12" × 3". Due to the size of the volume and its necessarily light-weight paper, the chance for tearing is high. The type is small, but because all the margins are adequate, the pages are clearly legible. The guide words, in bold type, stand out clearly. Subheads are used extensively in the longer essays, but can be difficult to see.

Summary

For other opinions, see the review of the fifth edition in *Library Journal* (Ken Kister), September 15, 1993; *Booklist* (*Reference Books Bulletin,* September 15, 1993; *The New York Times Book Review* (Robert M. Adams), October 31, 1993; and *The Wall Street Journal* (Bret Wallach), March 8, 1994.

The Columbia Encyclopedia is the premier one-volume encyclopedia. It is the most comprehensive, detailed, current, and accurate work of its type. In some cases, it even has entries not found in many larger multivolume encyclopedias. Its nearest competitor, THE RANDOM HOUSE ENCYCLOPEDIA, cannot come close in any of the categories mentioned.

Its many strengths notwithstanding, the encyclopedia also has several weaknesses. There is a dearth of entries in popular culture, and the choices of who or what is included at times seem idiosyncratic. The lack of an index is a major weakness; cross-referencing alone cannot provide the reader with sufficient access points to topics. The map and illustration program is sparse and sometimes inadequate or inappropriate. The lack of paragraphing and choice of italic subheads (with no extra spacing before) makes longer articles dense and difficult to read. Minor factual errors are few, but nonetheless disturbing. Finally, the sheer size of the work makes it unwieldy and the pages can be easily torn because of the paper quality. Nevertheless, the work is so strong compared to its competition that it should be the first choice of libraries, schools, and consumers who want a one-volume encyclopedia. Users of the fourth edition will also want to purchase this new edition.

Compton's Encyclopedia and Fact-Index

Facts at a Glance

Full title: **Compton's Encyclopedia and Fact-Index**
Publisher: Compton's Multimedia Publishing Group
Editor: Dale Good, Director, Compton's Editorial Group
Number of contributors: 500
Edition reviewed: © 1993

Number of volumes: 26
Number of articles: 34,596 (approximately 28,500 of which are brief articles in the Fact-Index)
Number of pages: 10,692
Number of words: 8.5 million
Number of cross-references: 128,700
Number of index entries: 69,083
Number of maps: 1,360
Number of illustrations: more than 22,500 (65 percent in color)
Intended readership: elementary to high school
Trim size: 8½″ × 10″
Binding: hardcover

Price: $495
Sold directly to libraries and schools; also sold by direct mail, in bookstores and other retail outlets, and through catalogs
ISBN 0-85229-572-3
Revised annually; next scheduled revision: 1994 edition currently available; 1995 edition to be available in January 1995

Introduction

The 26-volume 1993 edition of *Compton's Encyclopedia* carries the statement of intent that has guided the work since the first edition was published by F. E. Compton & Co. in 1922: "To inspire ambition, to stimulate the imagination, to provide the inquiring mind with accurate information told in an interesting style, and thus lead into broader fields of knowledge. . . ."

Although *Compton's* is designed primarily for upper elementary, junior high, and secondary school students, it does not use controlled vocabulary and therefore is appropriate for users of all ages.

Authority

First published in 1922 as *Compton's Pictured Encyclopedia* in eight volumes, *Compton's* was notable for having established the innovative policy of continuous revision. The encyclopedia has been issued in annual revisions since its inception. *Compton's* was purchased by Encyclopaedia Britannica, Inc., in 1961, and the word "pictured" was dropped from its title with the 1969 edition. Inadequate updating during the 1970s caused the set to fall behind its competitors, but an extensive, volume-by-volume revision program was begun in 1983 and completed in 1989. The entire set received a major face-lift in 1992, when it was completely redesigned and reset, and the number of four-color illustrations was significantly increased. In July 1993, *Compton's* was purchased by the Tribune Company.

Most of the approximately 500 contributors, consultants, and advisers (who are listed with a brief summary of their credentials in the front of volume 1) are associated with academic institutions or government agencies. A note on the back of the title page of each volume indicates that the encyclopedia is prepared with the editorial advice of the University of Chicago faculty.

Scope

The first 25 volumes of *Compton's* contain the set's approximately 6,096 main articles. Most of these entries are at least one-fourth of a page in length, and the majority are considerably longer. In addition, volume 26, the Fact-Index, not only serves as an index to the encyclopedia proper but also contains about 28,500 brief entries on individuals, concepts, geographical features, and other topics not covered in the main set (for example, **Vladimir Ashkenazy, Black History Month, cult, Madonna,** and **Pepsico, Inc.**). The 34,596 total entries represent all fields of knowledge.

A subject analysis of a randomly selected 50-page sequence in volume 13 (from **leaf** to **library**) revealed that of the 53 entries in this section, 32 percent were related to the social sciences or history, 20.8 percent to the humanities, 20.8 percent to geography, 18.9 percent to the sciences, and 7.5 percent to popular culture. However, the percentages in this small sample belie *Compton's* excellent coverage of topics relating to science and technology, a strength for which it has been noted for many years. Its particularly outstanding treatment of natural history, both in terms of textual and illustrative material, is shown by such entries as **birds, earth, egg, fish, flowers,** and **insects.** The Fact-Index is especially strong in its coverage of contemporary figures, animal and plant species, and geographical entities.

Of the randomly selected 29 entries on pages 212–236 of volume 20 (from **Rhodes, Cecil** to **roads and streets**), only 6 relate directly to the United States and 3 to Great Britain. The others treat broad topics such as **rice** and **river,** geographical features such as **Rhodes** and **Rio de Janeiro, Brazil,** and noted individuals from a variety of countries (for example, the German author **Rainer Maria Rilke,** the French poet **Arthur Rimbaud,** and the Mexican painter **Diego Rivera**). This is not to say, however, that North America does not receive heavy emphasis. For instance, the treatment of Canada's ten provinces is similar to that accorded each of the 50 states of the United States, and the entry **national parks** is divided into sections that describe individual parks in the United States and Canada.

To facilitate comparisons with other encyclopedias, the lengths of some sample articles follow. **Castle** is 2¼ pages, **Mexico** is 24 pages, and **women's rights** is 9 pages. **Nelson Mandela** is accorded 25 lines, while **Elvis Presley** receives 44 lines. **Hamlet** has a 4-line entry in the Fact-Index and brief mentions in **Shakespeare** and **English literature.** Although *Impression-*

Compton's Encyclopedia and Fact-Index

A drawing of Auguste Comte

COMTE, Auguste (1798–1857). The French philosopher who is known as the Father of Sociology is Auguste Comte. Comte advocated a science of society, which he named sociology. He urged the use of natural science techniques in the study of social life. He also originated positivism, a philosophic doctrine that incorporated his views on sociology (*see* Sociology).

Auguste Comte was born in Montpellier, France, on Jan. 19, 1798. His father, Louis, was a tax official. Auguste studied at the École Polytechnique, in Paris, from 1814 to 1816. In 1818 he became secretary to the Comte de St-Simon, a pioneer socialist. Beginning in 1826, Comte delivered private lectures to some of the leading French scholars and scientists of his day. These lectures became the basis of his most famous work, the six-volume 'Course of Positive Philosophy' which was published between 1830 and 1842. In 1827, two years after his marriage to Caroline Massin, Comte suffered a mental breakdown. After his recovery he was on the staff of the École Polytechnique from 1832 to 1842. In his four-volume 'System of Positive Polity' published between 1851 and 1854 Comte formulated a concept called "religion of humanity."

Comte is best known for his "law of the three stages." According to this "law," man's explanations of natural and social processes pass through three stages—the theological, the metaphysical, and the positive. In the first stage, man sees these processes as the work of supernatural powers. In the second, he explains them by means of such abstract ideas as "causes" and "forces."

In the third stage, he accumulates factual data and determines relationships among the observed facts. Comte believed that astronomy, physics, chemistry, and biology had evolved through these stages. He sought to organize sociology along "positive" lines. Comte died in Paris on Sept. 5, 1857.

CONAKRY, Guinea. The capital and largest city of the nation of Guinea is Conakry. The main part of the city is located on the Atlantic island of Tombo, which is connected by a causeway to the mainland of the African continent.

Conakry has one of the best natural deepwater harbors on the west coast of Africa. Its facilities include an alumina-loading dock, from which bauxite and alumina produced by the mining-refining complex at Fria are exported. A railway runs from the plant in Fria to the port. Bauxite from the nearby Los Islands is also shipped from Conakry.

The chief agricultural exports are bananas, coffee, palm kernels, and pineapples. City enterprises include fruit canning, fish packing, printing, automobile assembly, and the manufacture of aluminum utensils and plastics.

The main railroad line connects the capital with Kankan, the second largest city, and provides access to the Niger River. Guinea's only international airport lies 9 miles (14 kilometers) from the city center.

The island is a commercial center and has wide avenues and modern apartment and office buildings. One section is set aside for government administration. On the mainland are the main market, the People's Palace (National Assembly), and residential suburbs. In another area, to the south, is a fishing harbor. Among the city's attractions are beautiful botanical gardens, a large museum and library, a polytechnic institute, and a sports stadium.

Tombo Island was occupied by the French about 1880. Conakry served as the capital of the French Guinea territory before Guinea gained its independence in 1958. Considerable industrial development took place after World War II. (*See also* Guinea.) Population (1980 estimate), 763,000.

CONANT, James Bryant (1893–1978). Over a 50-year span, James Bryant Conant had four careers. He was an outstanding scientist, the president of one of America's major universities, a highly regarded diplomat, and an influential educational reformer.

James Bryant Conant was born in Dorchester, Mass., on March 26, 1893. He was the third child and only son of James Scott Conant and Jennett Orr Bryant. He received a doctorate from Harvard University in 1916. He married Grace Thayer Richards in 1921. They had two sons.

During World War I Conant was a major in the Chemical Warfare Service. He returned to Harvard as an assistant professor in 1919 and became chairman of the chemistry department in 1931. He made important findings on the chemistry of chlorophyll and hemoglobin. In 1933 he became president of Harvard, a position he held for 20 years. During World War II he was chairman of the National Defense Research Committee and played an important advisory role in the development of the atomic bomb. In 1953 he

Page shown at 77% of actual size.

❶ Illustrations include historical as well as current photographs
❷ Caption
❸ Main entry words printed in boldface

❹ Guide word and page number
❺ Locator map provided for each country and city entry

❻ Measurements given in both standard and metric systems
❼ Cross-reference

ism is not accorded its own article, it has 12 references in the Fact-Index. The longest treatment is a 2½-page section (consisting mainly of illustrations) on the French Impressionists within **painting.** *Tyrannosaurus rex* also does not have a separate entry. Instead, the Fact-Index guides the user to one sentence about this dinosaur under **earth.** Surprisingly, considering the age group for which *Compton's* is intended, *dinosaurs* receive only brief mention in several articles (including **animals, prehistoric**) and are not treated in a separate article. In sharp contrast, the WORLD BOOK ENCYCLOPEDIA devotes an 8½-page article to dinosaurs that includes an excellent selection of color photographs, diagrams, and paintings.

Currency

The 1993 edition is remarkably current in most areas. For example, the generously illustrated, four-page article on **Bill Clinton** concludes with his taking office as president on January 20, 1993. The **Persian Gulf War** is treated in a signed, 3-page entry, which is accompanied by two maps. The 18-page article on **Russia** recognizes its status as an independent nation since the breakup of the Soviet Union and refers the reader to the **Union of Soviet Socialist Republics** entry for the history of that earlier period. **Lithuania** is current through the pullout of Soviet troops in February 1992, and **Los Angeles** includes approximately half a column on the 1992 riots. The launching of the *Hubble Space Telescope* and the subsequent problems with its flawed main mirror are covered in several articles, including **observatory, black hole,** and **telescope.**

Many contemporary topics and individuals, including **virtual reality, Ross Perot, R.E.M., radon,** and **Spike Lee,** are covered only in the Fact-Index. The index also contains an 84-word entry on **Frida Kahlo,** the Mexican painter, but makes no reference to the *food pyramid.*

Ironically, the most dated article noted was **reference books.** Signed by the noted authority Louis Shores, who died in 1981, this article refers only briefly to the availability of electronic sources. The paragraph on THE OXFORD ENGLISH DICTIONARY contains no mention of the publication of the second edition or its availability on compact disc. Bibliographies in this article are also dated.

Maps have been revised to reflect the current political situation in Eastern Europe and elsewhere, and photographs are up-to-date.

Purchasers of *Compton's* who wish to maintain the currency of their set have the option of subscribing to *Compton's Yearbook,* which is generally issued in April. Each annual volume covers the events of the previous year and reprints a selection of new and revised articles from the latest edition of the encyclopedia.

Accuracy

Except for the problems mentioned under "Authority" regarding inadequate revisions during the 1970s and early 1980s, *Compton's* has generally been commended for its accuracy. Most of the shortcomings that our content experts noticed in the articles were not factual errors. The specialist who evaluated the section on the *House of Representatives* within **U.S. government** observed that the entry is factually accurate but gives too much attention to "historical oddities or ceremonial functions" and not enough to the law-making process. **Henry VIII** also contains no serious errors, but its treatment tends to be superficial and "out of touch with serious recent scholarship on the subject and the period." In **cancer,** the information regarding incidence and mortality needs updating, and *prostate cancer* should be included. The expert who assessed **oxygen** noted several misleading statements, including the implication that oxygen is present in the upper atmosphere only as ozone, when, in fact, both oxygen and ozone are present. The entry for **comet** is accurate, but brief. It provides a suitable amount of information for a younger audience.

Clarity

Most entries are designed to capture the reader's interest in the first few sentences. The first two paragraphs of the eight-paragraph section on the *Titanic* within **ships, famous** illustrate the interesting style that is characteristic of the set:

> At 2:20 AM on April 15, 1912, the *Titanic,* then the world's largest and most luxurious ocean liner, disappeared into the icy depths of the North Atlantic. With her she took the lives of some 1,500 men, women, and children—more casualties than in any other marine disaster in peacetime history.
>
> After striking a huge iceberg, the 46,500-ton vessel sank in less than three hours. Lloyd's of London, the firm which had insured the *Titanic,* had reasoned that the probability of such an event was one in a million. The ship's specially constructed bulkheads, it was believed, would check the seawater no matter how severely the ship might be damaged. As though fully convinced of the *Titanic's* invulnerability, the White Star Line had provided only enough lifeboats for half the persons aboard.

In biographical articles, a disconcerting tendency to write about living people in the past tense, as though they were deceased, may confuse young readers. For instance, the article on **Jimmy Carter** includes the statement: "In retirement Carter was one of the few modern leaders who did not try to cash in on the presidency." The entry for **Edward Albee** begins: "One of the 20th century's best known American dramatists and theatrical producers was Edward Albee."

Objectivity

Earlier editions of *Compton's* have been criticized for avoiding coverage of controversial issues. However, the 1993 edition includes entries on **AIDS, abortion, bioethics, birth control, Holocaust, homeopathy,** and **sexuality.** In each of the above, the treatment is straightforward, factual, and objective. For example, the one-and-one-third-page article on **AIDS** indicates that 90 percent of new cases diagnosed since 1989 originated from heterosexual sex. The article covers recent treatments and concerns pertaining to infected health-care workers, and it identifies a number of well-known victims, such as Rock Hudson, Magic Johnson, and Arthur Ashe. However, it does not address concerns regarding funding or civil-rights issues. **Abortion** notes the 1992 Supreme Court ruling upholding a Pennsylvania law restricting abortion, and it mentions both the controversy over the use of tissue from aborted fetuses to treat certain diseases and the controversial drug RU-486.

As another example, **Northern Ireland** mentions that the country is politically split according to religion and that civil violence has resulted from this, but it gives no idea of the extent of the violence in terms of lost lives. The *ozone layer* is treated briefly under several entries, including **atmosphere, pollution,** and **science,** each of which notes that there is concern regarding further destruction of the ozone and the resulting exposure of the earth to potentially harmful ultraviolet rays.

Of the dozens of articles sampled during the preparation of this review, **reference books** was found to be the only one containing blatant bias. In the half-column devoted to significant American contributions to encyclopedia publishing, virtually all of the innovations or accomplishments noted pertain to *Compton's.*

Accessibility

With its more than 69,000 entries, the Fact-Index provides excellent and detailed access to the set. It cites volume and page number references not only to the main entry but also to related entries, and includes "see" and "see also" references to other headings in the index. Frequently, the Fact-Index indicates that the reference is to a picture, diagram, table, map, or other illustrative material.

In addition to the 28,500 brief articles mentioned earlier, the Fact-Index includes 140 tables covering such diverse topics as cabinets of U.S. presidents, properties of chemical elements, Nobel Prize winners, and major caves of the world. These tables are indexed in the body of the Fact-Index and in a separate keyword index at the front of the volume.

Throughout *Compton's,* specific articles often are eschewed in place of longer survey articles. For example, the *French language* is treated under **romance languages,** *saxophone* appears under **wind instruments,**

and *Alzheimer's disease* is discussed under **aging.** Moreover, a number of biographical entries appear within longer articles. For instance, Judy Blume, Harper Lee, and Flannery O'Connor are included in the "Notable People" sections of their respective home states rather than being accorded entries of their own. This tendency to bury specific subjects within longer articles makes *Compton's* more cumbersome to use and less effective for quick reference than sets such as the ACADEMIC AMERICAN ENCYCLOPEDIA and the WORLD BOOK ENCYCLOPEDIA.

Arrangement of entries in *Compton's* is letter by letter rather than word by word (for example, **shorthand** comes before **short story**). Numerous "see" and "see also" references are provided within the text of articles, and additional "see" references lead the user from entry terms not used to the proper headings (for example, **self-defense** *see* **martial arts**). Boxed "Fact Finders" guide the user from broad articles, such as **the sciences,** to more specific entries.

Special Features

Each volume begins with two special features designed to stimulate interest and encourage browsing. First, a "Here and There" section organizes a selected group of the volume's articles by broad subject categories such as "Arts," "Living Things," "Technology and Business," and "Potpourri." Second, an illustrated section on "Exploring" the volume poses a variety of interesting questions (for example, "Why did Achilles' heel become famous?") and indicates the pages on which the answers may be found.

The more than 22,500 illustrations in *Compton's* effectively clarify and augment the information contained in the text. For example, the articles on the 50 states contain color photographs, chronological charts, fact boxes and summaries, graphs, and detailed maps. Other striking examples of the high quality of the illustrations are the extensive sections of labeled drawings that accompany the articles on human and frog anatomy.

The glossaries of terms that are provided in a number of articles are particularly useful. For example, **law** includes two pages of legal terms. Bibliographies accompany only a small percentage of the articles. However, those that are provided are quite up-to-date.

Format

Attractively and sturdily bound in dark blue, *Compton's* volumes are appropriately sized for a young readership. The 25 volumes that contain the encyclopedia proper range in length from 296 to 536 pages. At 897 pages, the Fact-Index is significantly larger, but it is easily manageable because it is printed on thinner paper.

The main text is printed in a serif typeface that is attractive and easy to read, and the use of nonjustified right margins and generous spacing between lines not only contributes to an attractive page layout but also facilitates use by younger readers. Entry words and headings at the top of each page are printed in large, bold, uppercase letters, and headings within entries also appear in boldface. Captions for pictures and other graphics are in bold, sans-serif type, a good contrast to the finer serif type used for the text.

Compton's is also available in a CD-ROM version, COMPTON'S INTERACTIVE ENCYCLOPEDIA, reviewed elsewhere in the Buying Guide.

Summary

The *Booklist/Reference Books Bulletin* review of the 1993 edition of *Compton's* concludes: "*Compton's Encyclopedia,* visually appealing, accurate, up-to-date, and easy to use, meets the information needs of students from upper elementary through high school and will be useful in school and public libraries" (September 15, 1993, p. 178). In his review of the 1989 edition of *Compton's* (*American Reference Books Annual,* 1990, entry 48), Bohdan S. Wynar concludes: "In summary, *Compton's* is a very attractive and well-designed encyclopedia. It offers a format that lends itself to browsing and classroom use. It is one of the best school encyclopedias on the market and should be found in most school libraries along with *World Book* and *Merit.* Highly recommended."

The efforts that *Compton's* has made during the past ten years to update both its contents and its appearance have resulted in a substantially improved product. The set's contemporary look is especially attractive, and the text is enjoyable to read. However, it still cannot compare with its closest competitor, the WORLD BOOK ENCYCLOPEDIA, in the areas of ease of use, number of entries, and number and percentage of color photographs. On the other hand, *Compton's* is somewhat less expensive than WORLD BOOK, which makes it a particularly attractive choice for home purchase. Its extensive treatment of curriculum-related topics also makes it a good buy for school and public libraries.

The Concise Columbia Encyclopedia

Facts at a Glance

Full title: **The Concise Columbia Encyclopedia**
Publisher: Columbia University Press
Editors: Barbara A. Chernow; George A. Vallasi
Number of contributors: 59
Edition reviewed: © 1989, second edition

Number of volumes: 1
Number of articles: 15,000
Number of pages: 920

Number of words: 1.5 million (reviewer estimate)
Number of cross-references: more than 50,000
Number of index entries: no index
Number of maps: 24 black and white; 16 color
Number of illustrations: 150 black-and-white line drawings
Intended readership: junior high and up
Trim size: $7^3/_8'' \times 10^1/_2''$
Binding: hardcover

Price: $39.95
Sold directly to libraries and schools; also sold by direct mail and in bookstores
ISBN 0-231-06938-3
No regular revision policy; next scheduled revision: fall 1994

Introduction

The purpose of the second edition of *The Concise Columbia Encyclopedia,* according to the publisher, is to "answer the sorts of questions we believe you are most likely to ask as you sit at your desk at home, at school, or at the office." This 1989 edition updates the 1983 first edition. More than one-third of the original entries were revised and 500 are new to the second edition. A third edition of *The Concise Columbia Encyclopedia* will be published in the fall of 1994.

Authority

The principal editors of the second edition of *The Concise Columbia Encyclopedia* are Barbara A. Chernow and George A. Vallasi, the team who subsequently produced the new fifth edition of THE COLUMBIA ENCYCLOPEDIA. The staff credits list 59 contributors, or writers, without titles or affiliations. All articles are unsigned. A group of 43 subject-area experts served as content advisers. Most of these consultants are on the faculty of Columbia University.

In the first edition of *The Concise Columbia Encyclopedia,* editors Judith S. Levey and Agnes Greenhall acknowledged that much of the information was derived from its renowned parent—the fourth edition of the *New Columbia Encyclopedia* (1975). The front matter of the second edition makes no mention of the larger work, although a comparison of entries reveals many echoes of the COLUMBIA in the *Concise Columbia.*

Scope

The Concise Columbia Encyclopedia aims to provide "succinct information on a myriad of topics." As the preface states, "Our articles always go beyond the mere definitions you might find in a dictionary. We provide context. On the other hand we stop short of summariz-

The Concise Columbia Encyclopedia

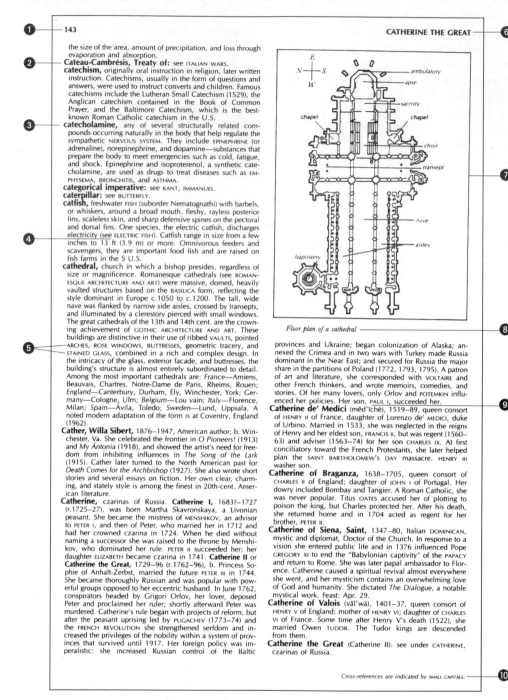

① 143

② CATHERINE THE GREAT ⑥

the size of the area, amount of precipitation, and loss through evaporation and absorption.

② Cateau-Cambrésis, Treaty of: see ITALIAN WARS.

catechism, originally oral instruction in religion, later written instruction. Catechisms, usually in the form of questions and answers, were used to instruct converts and children. Famous catechisms include the Lutheran Small Catechism (1529), the Anglican catechism contained in the Book of Common Prayer, and the Baltimore Catechism, which is the best-known Roman Catholic catechism in the U.S.

③ catecholamine, any of several structurally related compounds occurring naturally in the body that help regulate the sympathetic NERVOUS SYSTEM. They include EPINEPHRINE (or adrenaline), norepinephrine, and dopamine—substances that prepare the body to meet emergencies such as cold, fatigue, and shock. Epinephrine and isoproterenol, a synthetic catecholamine, are used as drugs to treat diseases such as EMPHYSEMA, BRONCHITIS, and ASTHMA.

categorical imperative: see KANT, IMMANUEL.

caterpillar: see BUTTERFLY.

catfish, freshwater FISH (suborder Nematognathi) with barbels, or whiskers, around a broad mouth, fleshy, rayless posterior fins, scaleless skin, and sharp defensive spines on the pectoral and dorsal fins. One species, the electric catfish, discharges **④** electricity (see ELECTRIC FISH). Catfish range in size from a few inches to 13 ft (3.9 m) or more. Omnivorous feeders and scavengers, they are important food fish and are raised on fish farms in the S U.S.

cathedral, church in which a bishop presides, regardless of size or magnificence. Romanesque cathedrals (see ROMANESQUE ARCHITECTURE AND ART) were massive, domed, heavily vaulted structures based on the BASILICA form, reflecting the style dominant in Europe c.1050 to c.1200. The tall, wide nave was flanked by narrow side aisles, crossed by transepts, and illuminated by a clerestory pierced with small windows. The great cathedrals of the 13th and 14th cent. are the crowning achievement of GOTHIC ARCHITECTURE AND ART. These buildings are distinctive in their use of ribbed VAULTS, pointed **⑤** ARCHES, ROSE WINDOWS, BUTTRESSES, geometric tracery, and STAINED GLASS, combined in a rich and complex design. In the intricacy of the glass, exterior facade, and buttresses, the building's structure is almost entirely subordinated to detail. Among the most important cathedrals are: *France*—Amiens, Beauvais, Chartres, Notre-Dame de Paris, Rheims, Rouen; *England*—Canterbury, Durham, Ely, Winchester, York; *Germany*—Cologne, Ulm; *Belgium*—Lou vain; *Italy*—Florence, Milan; *Spain*—Ávila, Toledo; *Sweden*—Lund, Uppsala. A noted modern adaptation of the form is at Coventry, England (1962).

Cather, Willa Sibert, 1876–1947, American author; b. Winchester, Va. She celebrated the frontier in *O Pioneers!* (1913) and *My Ántonia* (1918), and showed the artist's need for freedom from inhibiting influences in *The Song of the Lark* (1915). Cather later turned to the North American past for *Death Comes for the Archbishop* (1927). She also wrote short stories and several essays on fiction. Her own clear, charming, and stately style is among the finest in 20th-cent. American literature.

Catherine, czarinas of Russia. **Catherine I,** 1683?–1727 (r.1725–27), was born Martha Skavronskaya, a Livonian peasant. She became the mistress of MENSHIKOV, an advisor to PETER I, and then of Peter, who married her in 1712 and had her crowned czarina in 1724. When he died without naming a successor she was raised to the throne by Menshikov, who dominated her rule. PETER II succeeded her; her daughter ELIZABETH became czarina in 1741. **Catherine II** or **Catherine the Great,** 1729–96 (r.1762–96), b. Princess Sophie of Anhalt-Zerbst, married the future PETER III in 1744. She became thoroughly Russian and was popular with powerful groups opposed to her eccentric husband. In June 1762, conspirators headed by Grigori Orlov, her lover, deposed Peter and proclaimed her ruler; shortly afterward Peter was murdered. Catherine's rule began with projects of reform, but after the peasant uprising led by PUGACHEV (1773–74) and the FRENCH REVOLUTION she strengthened serfdom and increased the privileges of the nobility within a system of provinces that survived until 1917. Her foreign policy was imperialistic: she increased Russian control of the Baltic

provinces and Ukraine; began colonization of Alaska; annexed the Crimea and in two wars with Turkey made Russia dominant in the Near East; and secured for Russia the major share in the partitions of Poland (1772, 1793, 1795). A patron of art and literature, she corresponded with VOLTAIRE and other French thinkers, and wrote memoirs, comedies, and stories. Of her many lovers, only Orlov and POTEMKIN influenced her policies. Her son, PAUL I, succeeded her.

⑨ Catherine de' Medici (měd'ĭchē), 1519–89, queen consort of HENRY II of France, daughter of Lorenzo de' MEDICI, duke of Urbino. Married in 1533, she was neglected in the reigns of Henry and her eldest son, FRANCIS II, but was regent (1560–63) and adviser (1563–74) for her son CHARLES IX. At first conciliatory toward the French Protestants, she later helped plan the SAINT BARTHOLOMEW'S DAY massacre. HENRY III washer son.

Catherine of Braganza, 1638–1705, queen consort of CHARLES II of England; daughter of JOHN I of Portugal. Her dowry included Bombay and Tangier. A Roman Catholic, she was never popular. Titus OATES accused her of plotting to poison the king, but Charles protected her. After his death, she returned home and in 1704 acted as regent for her brother, PETER II.

Catherine of Siena, Saint, 1347–80, Italian DOMINICAN, mystic and diplomat, Doctor of the Church. In response to a vision she entered public life and in 1376 influenced Pope GREGORY XI to end the "Babylonian captivity" of the PAPACY and return to Rome. She was later papal ambassador to Florence. Catherine caused a spiritual revival almost everywhere she went, and her mysticism contains an overwhelming love of God and humanity. She dictated *The Dialogue*, a notable mystical work. Feast: Apr. 29.

Catherine of Valois (văl'wä), 1401–37, queen consort of HENRY V of England; mother of HENRY VI; daughter of CHARLES VI of France. Some time after Henry V's death (1522), she married Owen TUDOR. The Tudor kings are descended from them.

Catherine the Great (Catherine II): see under CATHERINE, czarinas of Russia.

⑧ *Floor plan of a cathedral* ————

Cross-references are indicated by SMALL CAPITALS. **⑩**

Page shown at 73% of actual size

① Page number
② Cross-reference entry
③ Main entry words printed in boldface
④ Measurements given in both standard and metric systems
⑤ Cross-references indicated by small capitals

⑥ Guide words
⑦ Illustration
⑧ Caption
⑨ Pronunciations given for foreign or unusual entry words
⑩ Running foot repeated on every right-hand page reminds users about

cross references; on the left-hand page, it reminds users about the pronunciation guide in the front matter

ing the very broadest topics." Therefore, the entries are specific. They are linked by numerous cross-references if information is sought for broad topics. For example, the entry **computer** refers the reader to more than 20 other entries.

The work has a heavy biographical emphasis—our reviewers estimate over 44 percent of the entries are biographical. Overall, the coverage of different disciplines is estimated as follows: 58 percent humanities (including history and religion), 17 percent science, 12 percent geography, 8 percent social science, and 5 percent popular culture. Coverage of international topics, with the exceptions of Asia and Africa, is very strong.

Our reviewers estimate the average article length at 75 to 100 words. **Castle,** at 19 lines or 76 words, is a fairly typical entry for the *Concise Columbia*. The comparable entry in THE COLUMBIA ENCYCLOPEDIA is more than 600 words. There is no separate entry for *Hamlet,* but the entry **William Shakespeare** gives information about the play in a condensed version of the table used in THE COLUMBIA ENCYCLOPEDIA. The article on **impressionism** in art is 116 words, and **Nelson Mandela** (who was still in prison at the publication date), receives 108 words; both entries have many cross-references. Finally, in a work that favors the historical and serious over the popular, the entry for **Elvis Presley** is a brief 52 words.

Mexico is typical of the longer entries in this short-entry encyclopedia. At 822 words, it is much longer than the entries in both THE CAMBRIDGE ENCYCLOPEDIA and THE CAMBRIDGE PAPERBACK ENCYCLOPEDIA. The article includes a half-page map showing the major cities, rivers, and mountain ranges.

There is no entry for *tyrannosaurus*. A short entry under **dinosaur** yielded only a mention of the species; more information about it could be found in a dictionary entry.

Currency

Given the length of time between editions, *The Concise Columbia Encyclopedia* is at a disadvantage for currency when compared with encyclopedias that are revised annually. Unfortunately, the second edition was published in 1989—a watershed year in the history of the 20th century. The fall of communism and the sweeping changes in the Soviet Union and Europe are therefore not included. As is to be expected, there are no entries for *Bill Clinton, food pyramid, Gulf War,* or *Hubble Space Telescope*. The entry for the **Union of Soviet Socialist Republics** notes the changes brought on by Mikhail Gorbachev up to the March 1989 elections.

Accuracy

As a work befitting its name, *The Concise Columbia Encyclopedia* conveys accurate information succinctly. While brief, the entries usually tell the most important

parts of the story. For example, while **comet** does not delve into the history or physics of comets, it provides a very clear idea of what a comet is. The accurate and well-written entry **oxygen** includes one of the best discussions of oxidation and reduction in any encyclopedia. **Cancer** and **Congress of the United States** (which discusses the U.S. House of Representatives) are both accurate, although our content experts had minor quibbles with the precision of some of the language. These entries all contain numerous cross-references that lead the reader to more facts on the topics.

As is to be expected, errors do occur. The entry on **Pete Rose,** for example, states that he had 4,191 career hits, when he actually had 4,256. (This was corrected in the 1993 edition of THE COLUMBIA ENCYCLOPEDIA.)

Clarity

The *Concise Columbia* succeeds admirably in addressing the intended audience—the general reader from junior high student to adult. The style is clear and nonacademic and the entries well organized and logical. They begin by answering the most basic question: "What is the significance of this person, place, or thing?" and then proceed to fill in the details. The brief entry for **Titanic,** given in its entirety, exhibits this approach:

> **Titanic,** British liner that sank on the night of Apr. 14–15, 1912, after striking an iceberg in the North Atlantic. The disaster, which occurred on the ship's maiden voyage, claimed the lives of more than 1,500 of the 2,200 people aboard. Many perished because of a shortage of lifeboats. More stringent safety rules for ships and an iceberg patrol were later instituted.

Objectivity

Because of their length, the entries in a one-volume encyclopedia can present only the facts—little room exists for points of view or debates. Discussions of **AIDS, capital punishment, Northern Ireland,** and the **ozone layer** generally ignore whatever controversies may exist for these subjects. The **AIDS** article is particularly terse, which is no doubt partly due to the encyclopedia's 1989 copyright. Entries on **gay rights** and **homosexuality** are unbiased and fairly written. **Northern Ireland** notes that the violence comes from both sides of the struggle. **Ozone** notes the scientific uncertainty concerning the effects of certain pollutants on the ozone layer, although it dates itself by not mentioning chlorofluorocarbons (CFCs). **Surrogate motherhood** gives a factual definition, followed by a brief description of the Baby M legal case. The entry on **Ronald Wilson Reagan** ends: "Despite his economic policy which created the largest federal budget deficit in U.S. history, he made important steps in U.S./Soviet nuclear disarmament negotiations, signing the INF treaty with the USSR."

Accessibility

As a desktop source of quick information, accessibility is a strong point of *The Concise Columbia Encyclopedia*. Although it has no index, the use of short and specific entries means that particular information is easy to look up. The entry words are logical and clear. Further investigation into topic is afforded by a system of more than 50,000 cross-references. As a means of comparison, the CAMBRIDGE PAPERBACK ENCYCLOPEDIA—with 19,000 entries—has only 26,000 cross-references.

Access points to broad topics vary. Some, such as art and literature, have no entries at all; some, such as **modern art,** are "See" entries; and some, such as **religion** and **philosophy,** are defined in full entries. To save space, similarly named rulers are combined into a single article, such as **Henry, kings of England.** This convention is also used for family names such as **Rockefeller.** Titles of foreign works are given in English unless the work is well known under the original title.

Special Features

There are 24 black-and-white maps scattered among the entries. In addition, there is a 16-page insert of Rand McNally color maps of the continents and ocean floors. These are clear and well presented. However, because the maps contain pre-1989 boundaries, several of them are inaccurate and unusable for the 1990s.

Curiously, the front matter lists four color illustrations—"Ecosystems of the World," "The Environment," "Technology," and "The Universe"—which do not appear in the work.

Unlike its parent work, *The Concise Columbia Encyclopedia* contains no bibliographies.

Format

The size of *The Concise Columbia Encyclopedia* is comparable to a desk dictionary; a stand is not necessary to hold the work. The pages spread out nicely when the book is opened and laid on its back. The Smyth binding is durable, and the pages are printed on acid-free paper.

Except for its two-column format, the typography and page design of the *Concise Columbia* is identical to THE COLUMBIA ENCYCLOPEDIA (see review).

According to *Popular Science* (September 1991), a pocket-sized electronic version of the *Concise Columbia* has been produced by Franklin Electronic Publishers. The 12-ounce machine contains 15,000 entries and costs $400. It also includes spell-checking and thesaurus functions.

Summary

For other opinions, see *Booklist (Reference Books Bulletin)*, January 1, 1990, page 944, and *Recommended Reference Books for Small and Medium-Sized Libraries and Media Centers 1990* (Bohdan S. Wynar, ed.), page 12.

The Concise Columbia Encyclopedia, second edition, is a handy source of information. Its accessibility, compact size, and affordable price would make it a very attractive purchase. However, the 1989 publication date renders much of the geopolitical and historical information out-of-date. It is hoped that the third edition, expected in late 1994, will remedy the second edition's problems with currency while retaining the commendable features of its predecessors. In the meantime, users needing a compact one-volume reference may want to consider THE CAMBRIDGE PAPERBACK ENCYCLOPEDIA or WEBSTER'S NEW WORLD ENCYCLOPEDIA, POCKET EDITION, both printed in 1993.

The Encyclopedia Americana

Facts at a Glance

Full title: **The Encyclopedia Americana**
Publisher: Grolier
Editors: Lawrence T. Lorimer, Editorial Director; Mark Cummings, Editor-in-Chief
Number of contributors: 6,500
Edition reviewed: © 1993

Number of volumes: 30
Number of articles: 52,000
Number of pages: 26,740
Number of words: 30.8 million
Number of cross-references: 42,500
Number of index entries: 353,000
Number of maps: 1,300
Number of illustrations: 4,600 four-color; 18,400 black and white
Intended readership: high school to adult
Trim size: 7¼″ × 10″
Binding: hardcover

Price: $1,168
Sold directly to libraries; also sold door-to-door
ISBN 0-7172-0124-4
Revised annually
Next scheduled revision: March 1994

Introduction

Encyclopedia Americana is a 30-volume standard general reference work that, according to the editors' preface in volume 1, is "reliable, readable, and relevant to today's needs." Many articles were prepared by specialists who were asked to write "in a direct style" and "in an orderly way" that will enable readers—from "young students" to "teachers, librarians, and adults in general"—to find and understand the information they

The Encyclopedia Americana

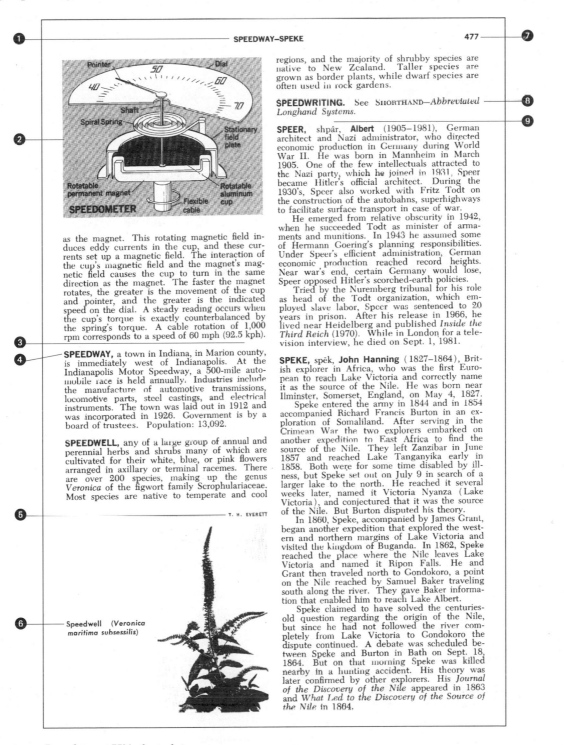

as the magnet. This rotating magnetic field induces eddy currents in the cup, and these currents set up a magnetic field. The interaction of the cup's magnetic field and the magnet's magnetic field causes the cup to turn in the same direction as the magnet. The faster the magnet rotates, the greater is the movement of the cup and pointer, and the greater is the indicated speed on the dial. A steady reading occurs when the cup's torque is exactly counterbalanced by the spring's torque. A cable rotation of 1,000 rpm corresponds to a speed of 60 mph (92.5 kph).

SPEEDWAY, a town in Indiana, in Marion county, is immediately west of Indianapolis. At the Indianapolis Motor Speedway, a 500-mile automobile race is held annually. Industries include the manufacture of automotive transmissions, locomotive parts, steel castings, and electrical instruments. The town was laid out in 1912 and was incorporated in 1926. Government is by a board of trustees. Population: 13,092.

SPEEDWELL, any of a large group of annual and perennial herbs and shrubs many of which are cultivated for their white, blue, or pink flowers arranged in axillary or terminal racemes. There are over 200 species, making up the genus *Veronica* of the figwort family Scrophulariaceae. Most species are native to temperate and cool

T. H. EVERETT

Speedwell (*Veronica maritima subsessilis*)

regions, and the majority of shrubby species are native to New Zealand. Taller species are grown as border plants, while dwarf species are often used in rock gardens.

SPEEDWRITING. See SHORTHAND—*Abbreviated Longhand Systems.*

SPEER, shpâr, **Albert** (1905–1981), German architect and Nazi administrator, who directed economic production in Germany during World War II. He was born in Mannheim in March 1905. One of the few intellectuals attracted to the Nazi party, which he joined in 1931, Speer became Hitler's official architect. During the 1930's, Speer also worked with Fritz Todt on the construction of the autobahns, superhighways to facilitate surface transport in case of war.

He emerged from relative obscurity in 1942, when he succeeded Todt as minister of armaments and munitions. In 1943 he assumed some of Hermann Goering's planning responsibilities. Under Speer's efficient administration, German economic production reached record heights. Near war's end, certain Germany would lose, Speer opposed Hitler's scorched-earth policies.

Tried by the Nuremberg tribunal for his role as head of the Todt organization, which employed slave labor, Speer was sentenced to 20 years in prison. After his release in 1966, he lived near Heidelberg and published *Inside the Third Reich* (1970). While in London for a television interview, he died on Sept. 1, 1981.

SPEKE, spēk, **John Hanning** (1827–1864), British explorer in Africa, who was the first European to reach Lake Victoria and correctly name it as the source of the Nile. He was born near Ilminster, Somerset, England, on May 4, 1827.

Speke entered the army in 1844 and in 1854 accompanied Richard Francis Burton in an exploration of Somaliland. After serving in the Crimean War the two explorers embarked on another expedition to East Africa to find the source of the Nile. They left Zanzibar in June 1857 and reached Lake Tanganyika early in 1858. Both were for some time disabled by illness, but Speke set out on July 9 in search of a larger lake to the north. He reached it several weeks later, named it Victoria Nyanza (Lake Victoria), and conjectured that it was the source of the Nile. But Burton disputed his theory.

In 1860, Speke, accompanied by James Grant, began another expedition that explored the western and northern margins of Lake Victoria and visited the kingdom of Buganda. In 1862, Speke reached the place where the Nile leaves Lake Victoria and named it Ripon Falls. He and Grant then traveled north to Gondokoro, a point on the Nile reached by Samuel Baker traveling south along the river. They gave Baker information that enabled him to reach Lake Albert.

Speke claimed to have solved the centuries-old question regarding the origin of the Nile, but since he had not followed the river completely from Lake Victoria to Gondokoro the dispute continued. A debate was scheduled between Speke and Burton in Bath on Sept. 18, 1864. But on that morning Speke was killed nearby in a hunting accident. His theory was later confirmed by other explorers. His *Journal of the Discovery of the Nile* appeared in 1863 and *What Led to the Discovery of the Source of the Nile* in 1864.

Page shown at 77% of actual size.

① Guide words indicate the first and last entries on the page

② Illustrations include both photographs and drawings with callouts

③ Measurements given in both standard and metric systems

④ Main entry words printed in capitals in boldface

⑤ Contributor's credit

⑥ Caption: scientific name in parentheses

⑦ Page number

⑧ Cross-reference entry

⑨ Pronunciations given for foreign or unusual entry words

seek. The editors' purpose is to build on the firm foundation provided by earlier editions to provide "an accurate and comprehensive picture of past and present times" through a policy of "constant rebuilding and updating." *Encyclopedia Americana*'s main competitors are THE NEW ENCYCLOPAEDIA BRITANNICA and COLLIER'S ENCYCLOPEDIA.

This review is based on the 1993 edition.

Authority

Encyclopedia Americana appeared in 1829 as the first multivolume general encyclopedia published in the United States. The set is presently published by the reference publisher Grolier, which also produces ACADEMIC AMERICAN ENCYCLOPEDIA and THE NEW BOOK OF KNOWLEDGE.

Encyclopedia Americana has more than 6,000 contributors, 80 of whom are new with this edition. Many of the 52,000 articles are signed, giving the contributor's affiliation. As with NEW BRITANNICA and COLLIER'S, most contributors are academics. The list of contributors in volume 1 is not annotated to indicate that some contributors are deceased, retired, or no longer affiliated with the institutions listed.

In the 1993 edition, new articles have been written by contributors or by staff editors. Some articles have been revised by the original authors or by editors, and others have been emended by staff editors. Articles in the last category have an asterisk after the original contributor's name.

Fifty-one advisory editors, 32 of whom were appointed in 1992, are distinguished scholars (primarily scientists and historians) who assist staff editors in organizing content presentation and in choosing authorities in each field to contribute articles.

Scope

The preface states that the 1993 edition "expands the encyclopedia's strong coverage of science" and its "already outstanding coverage of the history of the peoples of the world, their institutions, and their leaders." Examination of a random 50-page sample (volume 13, pages 651–701) indicates that there is broad coverage of natural science and social science topics along with humanities and geography. A topic that is not well represented is popular culture; the emphasis is on academic and traditional subjects.

Like NEW BRITANNICA and COLLIER'S, *Americana* contains both general survey articles and specific-entry articles. Thousands of short entries present facts "briefly and specifically," according to the preface. In other cases, entries of "almost book length" (for example, a 293-page entry on the **United States**) present information in depth. Sample entries indicate a wide range of lengths: **castles and châteaux,** 9 pages, including 12

photographs and an extensive bibliography; *Hamlet,* 2 pages; **Impressionism,** coverage of which is handled in three separate articles (for art, literature, and music), which total 3 pages and include two examples of the art; **Nelson Mandela,** 33 lines; **Mexico,** 61 pages; **Elvis Presley,** 23 lines; and **Tyrannosaurus,** which is cross-referenced to **dinosaurs,** where it receives 13 lines in a 6½-page entry.

Published for the American reader, the encyclopedia nevertheless covers foreign topics well. Examination of pages 280–305 of volume 9 shows, out of 74 entries, 48 non-American entries (65 percent). They include *Don Quixote,* **Giovanni Battista Donati** (nineteenth-century Italian astronomer), **donatism** (fourth- to fifth-century religious movement in North Africa), **Gaetano Donizetti** (nineteenth-century Italian opera composer), **John Donne, Christian Johann Doppler** (nineteenth-century Austrian physicist), **Dorgon** (seventeenth-century Chinese prince), and **Fyodor Dostoyevsky.** Foreign geographic locations featured in these same pages include **Doncaster** (English borough), **Donegal** (Irish county), **Donetsk** (Ukraine city), **Dongola** (Sudan town), and **Dortmund** (German city).

Currency

Encyclopedia Americana is updated annually according to a policy of "continuous revision." In the 1993 edition, 42 entries are new, 96 existing entries were rewritten and replaced entirely, and 65 have had major revisions. Minor revisions were made to 1,031 entries (including 338 updated bibliographies). This represents an article update rate of 2.5 percent. A slightly higher update rate of about 5 percent results from calculating numbers of reset and revised pages (excluding the index). In addition, 209 new photographs (131 in color) were added, and 60 maps were added or revised.

According to a summary of changes to this edition provided by the publisher, major events covered are the breakups of the U.S.S.R. and Yugoslavia and the U.S. presidential elections. The breakup of the U.S.S.R. is handled by updating the first and last sections of the entry **Union of Soviet Socialist Republics.** Although the impact of the breakup is included in the entry, coverage is sometimes confusing. For instance, the section on the economy does not reflect the new government's commitment to a free-market economy. Also, the use of the present tense in sections that were not revised is disconcerting and affects continuity. Captions, too, are outdated (for example, using "Leningrad" when referring to present-day St. Petersburg).

To complement the changes in the U.S.S.R. entry, each of the entries on former Soviet republics has been revised to show their new independent status. These entries feature new or revised maps.

The upheaval in Yugoslavia is handled with replacement articles on **Bosnia and Hercegovina, Croatia, Slovenia,** and **Macedonia** and with revision of the section "After Tito" in the **Yugoslavia** article. Minor revisions were also made to articles on **Montenegro, Kosovo,** and **Serbia.** However, **Vojvodina** was not updated.

To "increase the pace of revisions in the sciences," the publisher features new entries on **Big Bang theory, unification of forces,** and **fractal geometry;** a replacement entry on **Venus;** and a revision of the **nuclear energy** entry to discuss cold-fusion experiments. Also, several entries on aerospace technology, including **aerodynamics, airplane, jet engine,** and **space shuttle,** have been revised. New or revised biographies featuring people in the sciences and mathematics include **Heinrich Olbers, John Stewart Bell, John Archibald Wheeler, Stephen Hawking,** and **Kurt Gödel.**

To reflect political changes, an entry on **political action committee** has been added and the entry on **unemployment** has been replaced. Biographies of **William Jefferson Clinton** and **Boutros Boutros-Ghali** have been added. However, the **Arkansas** entry still lists Clinton as governor, and the **United Nations** entry fails to mention Boutros-Ghali as the current secretary-general.

Despite the updates, *Americana* does have problems related to currency. For example, the coverage of computers is woefully out-of-date. In the section of the main **computer** entry called "How a Computer Works," several paragraphs are devoted to the obsolete process of keypunching. Discussion of current companies and computers such as Apple and Microsoft occur only in the **spreadsheet** entry, which is the only new computer-related entry in the 1993 edition. Coverage of compact discs is also out-of-date, and the **Hubble Space Telescope**—while it has its own entry—is not mentioned in either the **telescope** or **observatory** entries.

The **nutrition** entry does not provide information on the *food pyramid.* The **cancer** entry contains outdated statistics and information on smoking and health and on screening and self-examination, and MRI is not included as a diagnostic tool.

In addition, many population statistics are seriously out-of-date, such as those for Spain (1974 estimate), Mexico (1980), Finland (1979 estimate), and Pakistan (1981). Many tables, such as those of world crude oil production (1981), average monthly Social Security benefits (1982), and air pollutant data (1977), are also outdated.

Most relevant maps reflect the unification of Germany and of Yemen and the breakups of the Soviet Union and Yugoslavia. Some maps, however, such as the country map in the **Sweden** entry, the maps in the **Arabia** and **Arab civilization** entries, and the map in the **Trans-Siberian Railroad** entry, have not noted these

recent changes. One map in the **Yugoslavia** entry reflects the changes in that area, but a second map, showing regions of Yugoslavia, uses the old national boundaries. The map of Africa in the **yellow fever** entry is more than a decade out-of-date, showing "Upper Volta," "Rhodesia," and "Republic of Congo," among other former country names.

The color photograph program (421 new color photographs in the past three years) vastly improves the currency of illustrations in the encyclopedia. However, the illustrations are still overwhelmingly black and white, and many photographs feature outdated fashions or machinery.

Accuracy

The use by *Americana* of 6,500 scholars and other experts as contributors enhances the encyclopedia's degree of accuracy. However, factual errors do occur. The **cancer** entry is fundamentally sound, but the article contains outdated information (see *Currency*), which affects reliability. The **comet** article, written at college level, is accurate (although dry). However, its organization is weak, going only up to the 1700s in the history section and including later history under other subheads.

The **Henry VIII** entry, written by a noted biographer of the king, presents a balanced and not overly sensational view of the ruler. Henry's international policies are discussed particularly well, but domestic politics, especially Henry's innovative policies, are given less attention. One area of confusion, if not inconsistency, in the domestic arena concerns the issue of popular support in England for the Reformation.

The **House of Representatives** entry, written by a leading scholar of legislatures, is an accurate, thoughtful account of the intricacies of membership and qualifications, the advantages of incumbency, careerism, the discretion given to committees, and the special roles of the "Rules," "Appropriations," and "Ways and Means" committees. However, the statement that the House historically tends to be more conservative than the President or the Senate may be considered highly debatable by specialists. In addition, the issue of the House's influence is underplayed, and gerrymandering is not addressed.

The **oxygen** entry is well written and discusses a wide range of topics. However, technical terms (which a reader unfamiliar with chemistry may not know) are used several times without being defined. In addition, the article contains errors. The word *nearly* should be omitted from the sentence "Either free or chemically bound oxygen is required by nearly all known forms of life." The last sentence of the second paragraph, which refers to the amount of oxygen found in the body, should read ". . . the *element* oxygen *when combined with other elements* makes up about 65% of the human body." The melting point of O_2 in Celsius and the conversions to

Fahrenheit for the melting point and boiling point of ozone are incorrect.

Clarity

According to the publisher, the experts who write articles are "reminded of the need to write for the nonspecialist reader." Writers are also asked to explain any technical terms they use so that anyone from young students to adults in general do not have to lose time "trying to comprehend technicalities for which they have no specialized preparation." This goal is not universally met. In general, the writing style of *Americana* is like that of New Britannica and, to a lesser degree, Collier's—scholarly and academic, with high reading and comprehension levels. Complex scientific topics such as **elementary particle** and **Big Bang theory** are comprehensively presented, but they do presuppose knowledge by the reader. Terms such as *redshifted wavelength, isotropy, cosmic microwave background,* and *critical density* are used in the **Big Bang theory** entry without being defined.

The use of section headings or subheads helps to organize long articles. Glossaries are presented for 40 entries, but some, such as **computer,** that would have benefited from a glossary of specialized terms do not have one. Many articles use an advanced diction that decreases readability for the average student or adult (for example, the use of *malefactor* instead of *criminal* and *suburban satellites* instead of *suburbs*).

Although the comprehension level is not as high in the ***Titanic*** entry as in others, the first two paragraphs have some elements common to many articles in the *Americana:* long, complex sentences and above-average vocabulary.

> Shortly before midnight on April 14, 1912, the 46,328-ton White Star liner *Titanic,* on her maiden voyage from Southampton to New York, collided with an iceberg off the Banks of Newfoundland. The night was clear, but apparently there was some surface haze. Two hours and forty minutes after the impact, the magnificent new liner—the pride of the British merchant service, the largest and most sumptuously appointed vessel which had ever put to sea—went down with a loss of more than 1,500 lives.
>
> The root cause of the appalling catastrophe, which was accounted at the time "the most terrible shipwreck in history," was simply bad seamanship. Despite all the urgent warnings of ice, by radio and signal-lamp, the *Titanic,* in hopes of an early arrival in New York harbor, continually increased speed and drove that night into the ice track at over 22½ knots (41.7 km/hr).

Objectivity

The preface states that the editors "have sought to present information in an objective manner." Objectivity is achieved in different ways. For example, the **AIDS** entry avoids the controversial issues of research funding, treatment availability, and civil rights issues related to testing. The **capital punishment** entry discusses the views of proponents and opponents in a generally evenhanded manner. The **Northern Ireland** entry discusses the history of the Protestant-Catholic conflict, giving the motivation of groups on both sides as well as that of the British government without taking sides. The **ozone** entry discusses the sources of problems associated with the stratospheric ozone layer and ground-level ozone and presents some proposed solutions. When available, the entry gives supporting statistics from research findings and identifies the research group.

Objectivity is not universal in *Americana.* In the "Sexism" section of the **prejudice and discrimination** entry, *sexism* is described as "something that a society must attempt to eliminate." Although one may not dispute that issue, this type of statement, as observed in the previous Buying Guide, uses the opinionated style of an essay or editorial rather than the objective style of an encyclopedia. The **nuclear energy** entry is also far from objective. It presents a very persuasive argument for the safety of nuclear power, minimizes health concerns throughout, and concludes the section on the hazards of nuclear power with a speculative statement that has no place in an encyclopedia: "All of the preceding estimates of health hazards may turn out to be high because . . . many of the deaths will not occur if a cure for cancer is developed."

Accessibility

The first and last entry on each page is listed on the top of the page. The entry words are logical and clear and usually are those that the majority of readers would look under. Entries are arranged alphabetically, word by word, using the order of person, place, and thing when articles have the same heading. When pages are added because of a revision, extra pages are shown with a figure and letter (23a, 23b). When pages have been dropped because of revision, one page is designated by a range of numbers to indicate missing pages (200–210). This approach may confuse users who have little experience with reference works.

Cross-references are used within and at the end of articles and as separate entries. The publisher indicates that there are 42,500 cross-references but does not give a rationale for their use. There often seem to be fewer cross-references than needed, especially for complex scientific entries. For example, readers of the **Big Bang theory** article, which contains no cross-references, would have benefited from references to the basic background articles **cosmology** and **elementary particle.** A useful feature—a table of contents that lists the sections of long entries, usually with page numbers—helps the reader find his or her way through many long articles.

Boxes are used in state and country entries to highlight basic information.

The index contains 353,000 entries: articles are indexed, as are subjects that are discussed but do not have a separate article in the encyclopedia. Some index entries are *see* references. Usually an index entry is followed by a parenthetical description that identifies the entry. Occasionally, *see also* references are included within an article index entry. Within entries, maps and illustrations are indexed.

For the most part, the indexing system is clear. However, when an article index entry has multiple references, volumes are listed in numerical order, with no indication as to which reference is the main article. Therefore, the reader may be directed to a peripheral reference before finding the main explanation.

The index is also available as part of *The Grolier Master Encyclopedia Index* on CD-ROM.

Special Features

The illustration program includes photographs, diagrams, graphs, maps, and charts. The size of the program is substantial. As noted earlier, however, photographs are predominantly black and white and the illustration program is somewhat dated. The set offers almost as many illustrations as NEW BRITANNICA and significantly more than COLLIER'S. Diagrams, which are clear and well labeled, are especially helpful in clarifying difficult technical concepts. Newer photographs introduce women and minorities in nonstereotypical roles.

Maps are generally well executed and clear. Several types are used: physical, political, distribution, and historical. There are some inconsistencies, however. Most political maps have latitude and longitude or projections, but some, such as "Africa" and the "Russian Federation," do not. In some cases (such as those of *Azerbaijan* and *Kirghizstan*) the spelling used in the map differs from that in the article.

Some articles include bibliographies and lists of further readings. Ranging from a few books to several pages of entries, these lists contain, as stated in the preface, "books suitable for the general reader . . . along with more advanced or specialized works." In the 1993 edition, 338 bibliographies were updated. Classic works are included regardless of publication date, and some works may be out of print and therefore difficult to obtain.

Format

The 30 volumes of *Americana* use the split-letter system. They are generally uniform in length; the longest is 976 pages and the shortest is 768. With a smaller trim size than COLLIER'S or NEW BRITANNICA, the volumes are easy to hold. They lie open on a flat surface.

The text is arranged in a double-column format. The type is generally readable but dense, with little white space between lines of text. The use of justified margins also contributes to the density. When subheads are used, they are generally helpful in breaking up the text. However, the typeface makes it difficult to distinguish the level of subhead that is roman from the level that is italic. Additionally, because of the density, articles that contain very long paragraphs and have no subheads are difficult to read.

Some features are presented in an inconsistent format, which may complicate ease of use. For example, some bibliographies use a run-on format, with the name of the author in small capital letters; other bibliographies have each entry on a separate line, with the name of the author in bold type. The editors expect that the new electronic publishing system installed with this edition, which puts the entire encyclopedia in a database and offers an electronic composition system, will help correct some formatting problems and expand the scope of revisions in future editions.

Summary

For other opinions regarding the *Encyclopedia Americana*, see Bohdan S. Wynar's review of the 1992 edition in *ARBA 93* and *Booklist (Reference Books Bulletin)*, September 15, 1993, pages 178–179.

The *Encyclopedia Americana*, a major academic multivolume reference work, is comprehensive, scholarly and, for the most part, accurate. The work presents some problems for its intended audience: young students to adults who have no specialized subject background. Those who would benefit most from this work are users with a high reading level and preferably some background knowledge in a topic they look up. The presence of interpretive statements, which call for critical judgment, and the outdatedness of some entries may also limit the usefulness of the set. COLLIER'S ENCYCLOPEDIA is a better buy at a slightly lower price; those purchasing for younger readers may want to consider the WORLD BOOK ENCYCLOPEDIA, which is significantly less expensive but also less scholarly.

Funk & Wagnalls New Encyclopedia

Facts at a Glance

Full title: **Funk & Wagnalls New Encyclopedia**
Publisher: Funk & Wagnalls
Editors: Leon L. Bram, Vice-President and Editorial Director; Norma H. Dickey, Editor-in-Chief
Number of contributors: 1,056
Edition reviewed: © 1993

Number of volumes: 29
Number of articles: 25,000
Number of pages: 13,056
Number of words: 9 million
Number of cross-references: 88,000
Number of index entries: 130,000
Number of maps: 317
Number of illustrations: 9,250; 46 percent in color
Intended readership: age 10 to adult
Trim size: 6¼" × 9"
Binding: *hardcover*

Price: $170 (perfect bound); $250 (Smythe bound); $299 (leather bound)
Sold directly to schools and libraries by Oxford University Press; also sold in supermarket continuity program (one volume per week), and in bookstores
ISBN 0-8343-0094-X
Revision policy: continuous with each printing—twice a year (January and August)

Introduction

Funk & Wagnalls New Encyclopedia is a 29-volume general encyclopedia for readers age 10 to adult. The publishers aim to produce "a useful, accessible set—intelligible to both students and adults—one that would encompass the broadest range of knowledge, and that all families could afford." Reasonably priced and available in supermarkets and bookstores, this encyclopedia offers "detailed information . . . on an enormous range of subjects, and readers with little or no background on a topic are provided with a maximum amount of enlightening material." This review is based on the 1993 edition.

Authority

The *Funk & Wagnalls Standard Encyclopedia* was first published in 1912. It has been revised, expanded, and renamed over the years. It became the *Funk & Wagnalls New Encyclopedia* in 1972. The set has been updated and given a more modern look with more color illustrations and maps, a comprehensive index, and a bibliography.

A large editorial staff oversees the production of this encyclopedia. Vice-President and Editorial Director Leon L. Bram has been head of the group since 1974. Editor-in-Chief Norma H. Dickey has held this post since 1986. Their staff of 91 editors, writers, and indexers produce two printings each year. A total of 76 consultants and 1,056 contributors assure the accuracy of the contents. Most articles are unsigned, but the longer ones, such as those on countries and broad concepts, are signed. A complete list of consultants and contrib-

utors appears in volume 28. Some contributors are deceased, and the listing indicates this. Avery Brundage, Mircea Eliade, and Lionel Trilling are among the late contributors. Distinguished living authorities writing articles or serving as consultants for this edition include psychologist Jerome Kagan, surgeon Michael E. DeBakey, communications experts Arthur Knight and Magnus Magnusson, and historian Peter Gay. Most contributors are academics teaching at or retired from respected universities.

Scope

Funk & Wagnalls New Encyclopedia is a short-entry encyclopedia. Most entries are one to three paragraphs in length. Articles on broad concepts, countries, and states are several pages long. The amount of space given to selected sample entries provides a sense of the type of coverage accorded to various topics. **Castle** receives three-quarters of a page of text and three illustrations. *Hamlet* receives ten lines in the article **Shakespeare, William.** Various interpretations of the play are briefly discussed. **Impressionism** receives 2¾ pages, including illustrations; the article also discusses impressionism in music. **Nelson Mandela** and **Elvis Presley** each receive a short paragraph. **Mexico** receives 19 pages with illustrations, including a country map and key that spans 4 pages. **Tyrannosaurus rex** receives one paragraph with a *see* reference to the article on the **Cretaceous Period.**

Articles in this encyclopedia cover a wide range of topics, with history, science, and geography predominating. Over half the entries are biographies of people from many cultures and fields. A random 50-page sample (volume 13, *Heat–India,* pages 50–100) contains 174 entries, 96 of which are biographies. These include **Katharine Hepburn** and the many European monarchs named **Henry.** The publisher does not provide information about its relative coverage of different disciplines. Our reviewers estimate the following breakdown (with examples drawn from the above sample): humanities and the arts (including history and religion), 55 percent (**Hepplewhite Style, heraldry, heresy**); science and technology, 20 percent (**hemophilia, hemp, herpetology**); geography, 17 percent (**Hempstead** [New York], **Highlands** [Scotland], **Higashiosaka** [Japan]); social sciences, 5 percent (**hermit, Hidatsa** [Native American people], **hieroglyphs**); popular culture, 3 percent (**Henley Regatta, Highland Games**).

The sample does not adequately convey the breadth of subjects that one can find in this encyclopedia. Modern technology is well represented (**computer, telemetry, video recording**), as are mythology (**Hera, Hercules, Zeus**) and sports (**lacrosse, soccer, football**). There are articles on plant and animal species (**huckleberry, Howler monkey, hummingbird**), broad subject areas (**human evolution, monopoly, totalitarianism**),

Funk & Wagnalls New Encyclopedia

BASS

to the Appalachian region; they reach a maximum weight of about 2.3 kg (about 5 lb). *See also* CRAPPIE.

Although some are freshwater fishes, the Serranidae are called sea bass (q.v.). *Contropristes striata*, commonly called black sea bass or blackfish, is found on the Atlantic coast of the U.S. and is usually 30 to 45 cm (12 to 18 in) long. *Paralabrax clathratus*, a saltwater rockfish of California in the same family, is also called kelp bass. The temperate basses, family Percichthyidae, include *Morone saxatilis*, the striped bass, sometimes called rock bass, or rockfish, of the U.S. Atlantic coast. Occasional specimens reach a weight of 45 kg (100 lb). *M. chrysops*, the white bass of the Great Lakes and upper Mississippi Valley, and *M. mississippiensis*, the yellow bass of the lower Mississippi region, are also in this family; both reach a maximum size of 45 cm (18 in) and a maximum weight of 2.3 kg (5 lb).

The family Sciaenidae, the croakers, includes the red drum (*see* DRUM) or channel bass.

— *For further information on this topic, see the Bibliography in volume 28, section 468.*

BASS, Sam (1851–78), American bandit leader, born near Mitchell, Ind. He moved to Texas about 1870 and was a mill hand, cowboy, and deputy sheriff until 1875, when he became an outlaw. In the Black Hills town of Deadwood, S.Dak., Bass formed a gang to rob stagecoaches, and in 1877 the gang held up a Union Pacific train at Big Springs, Nebr., stealing $65,000. Bass, pursued by lawmen, organized a new gang in Denton Co., Tex., and robbed several trains in 1878. One of his followers became an informer for the Texas Rangers, and Bass was shot to death in an ambush during an attempted bank robbery.

BASSANO, family of Venetian painters. The most important member, Jacopo da Ponte, called Jacopo Bassano (1510–92), born in Bassano del Grappa, painted portraits and biblical and mythological scenes. His early Mannerist works used elongated figures and brilliant color. Later work, influenced by Titian and Tintoretto, was darker and more dramatic, as in the *Crucifixion* (1592, Museo Civico, Treviso). His sons Francesco (1549–92) and Leandro (1558–1622) were genre painters.

BASSEIN, city, S Burma, capital of Irrawaddy Division and of the district of Bassein. The city is situated on the Bassein R., one of the mouths of the Irrawaddy R., and is accessible to ocean-going ships. Inland water and rail connections enhance its importance as a commercial center. The principal trade is in rice. The town was captured by the British during the Second Burmese War in 1853 and by the Japanese during World War II. Pop. (1983) 144,092.

336

BASSE-TERRE, town, capital of Guadeloupe (an overseas department of France), SW Basse-Terre Island, a port on the Caribbean Sea. Tourism and the shipping of locally produced coffee, cacao, and vanilla are leading industries. Nearby points of interest include La Soufriére, a dormant volcano situated in a large national park. Basse-Terre was founded by the French in 1643. It declined in the late 18th century, when Point-à-Pitre became the main economic center. Basse-Terre retains the atmosphere and appearance of an old colonial settlement. Pop. (1982) 13,796.

BASSETERRE, town, capital of Saint Christopher and Nevis (also known as Saint Kitts-Nevis), in the West Indies, SE of Puerto Rico. Located on the SW coast of the island of St. Kitts, it is an important seaport of the Leeward Islands. Sugar, molasses, salt, cotton, and copra are principal exports. The leading industries are sugar refining and salt extraction. Founded by the French in 1627, Basseterre came under definitive British colonial possession in 1783. It became the capital of independent St. Christopher and Nevis in 1983. Pop. (1983 est.) 14,725.

BASSET HORN. *See* CLARINET.

BASSET HOUND, sporting dog originally bred in France from the French bloodhound and the Saint Hubert hound. The basset was popular in France, Belgium, and other European countries for hundreds of years before being exhibited for the first time at an English dog show in 1875. After 1880 it gained rapidly in popularity in Great Britain. Standing 28 to 38 cm (11 to 15 in) high at the shoulder, the basset has a long body and heavy bones and weighs 11 to 18 kg (25 to 40 lb). The English basset has deep-set eyes; long, soft, hanging ears; a long head; and a well-developed black nose. Smaller than the English type, the French basset is more agile. The type of basset

Basset hound   © Frédéric Jacana–Photo Researchers, Inc.

Page shown at 77% of actual size.

① Guide word
② Measurements given in both metric and standard systems
③ Cross-references indicated in several ways, including the initials *q.v.* in parentheses, or the words "see" or "see also"
④ Bibliography reference: many entries keyed to the encyclopedia's bibliography
⑤ Main entry words printed in capitals in boldface
⑥ Page number
⑦ Cross-reference entry
⑧ Caption
⑨ Illustration

and assorted subjects of interest to both students and general readers (**short story, plate tectonics,** and **microprocessor**).

Although this encyclopedia is aimed at American and Canadian users, other cultures are well represented. There are comprehensive articles on **Hinduism** and **Islam,** although they are not as extensive as the entry for **Christianity** and its related articles. As an example, pages 100–125 of volume 26, *Transport–Vermeer,* contain 31 articles. Thirteen are not related to the United States, Canada, or Great Britain; these include Spanish composer **Joaquín Turina, Lake Turkana** (in Africa), **Turkestan, Turkey, Turku** (in Finland), **Tuticorin** (in India) and **Desmond Tutu.** Articles on art, architecture, music, and dance cover many cultures, such as **Chinese Art and Architecture, African Music and Dance,** and **Latin American Music.** Biographies include people from diverse backgrounds: **Langston Hughes, Victoriano Huerta, Akira Kurosawa, Huayna Capac,** and **Hua Guofeng.**

Currency

The editors of *Funk & Wagnalls New Encyclopedia* explain their revision policy in an introductory essay in volume 1 called "Information and the Future": "Updates, additions, and revisions are made at every printing of the encyclopedia. Not only are specific facts within articles, or entire articles, subject to change, but so are major systems." The editors also identify the need to keep the illustrations and design up-to-date and to ensure that the language and approach reflect contemporary standards.

The editors do not give specific information as to the extent of the revision for the 1993 edition. However, current events are generally well represented. The entry on **Bill Clinton** includes a photograph and coverage of the 1992 election. Hurricanes Andrew and Iniki are mentioned in several entries, as are the riots in South Central Los Angeles. The 1992 Olympic results are recorded. There are short entries on **Boutros Boutros Ghali** and **Clarence Thomas.** On the other hand, there is no entry for Ross Perot. And there are relatively few entries on figures in contemporary popular culture.

The manner in which current information and events are conveyed is sometimes uneven. The entry for the **Persian Gulf War** is a straightforward account of events, but it gives the impression that the war was a total triumph for the United States. Protests, malfunctioning Patriot missiles, and casualties from friendly fire are not mentioned. The Hubble Space Telescope receives two sentences in **Telescope;** the mechanical problems and pending (at the time of publication) repairs are discussed. The article **Nutrition, Human** discusses food groups but offers no guidelines for servings and makes no mention of the food pyramid.

Coverage of the rapid political changes in the world is adequate but somewhat awkward. Three articles deal with Germany: **Germany; Germany, East;** and **Germany, West.** The first is a historical overview up to 1949; all three mention the reunification. Merging the articles would be helpful. Yemen receives similar treatment in the three articles **Yemen, Peoples Democratic Republic of; Yemen, Republic of;** and **Yemen Arab Republic.** Again, all include information on the unification of the country, but these articles should be combined, too. The article on **Yugoslavia** notes the breakup of the country and refers readers to separate articles on the new countries, but uses old statistics from the former nation. The map has been updated. The entry for **Czechoslovakia** is current to 1992 and mentions the impending division of the country. The article on the **Union of Soviet Socialist Republics** covers the breakup of this country. The map is labeled "Russia and Neighboring Countries," but it does not include the names of the new republics; moreover, readers are referred to this map in the articles on the individual former republics, such as **Lithuania** and **Uzbekistan.**

U.S. statistics are from the 1990 census. Those from other countries include date and source. Photographs and maps are reasonably up-to-date.

Accuracy

Despite the brevity of its articles, the *Funk & Wagnalls New Encyclopedia* offers accurate information on a broad range of subjects. **Cancer** provides a good overview of the subject, although some parts need revision. Cancer statistics, information on smoking and health, and recommendations for screening and self-examination, for example, are out-of-date. And although new information about the experimental use of monoclonal antibodies in cancer treatment is included, there is nothing about magnetic resonance imaging, now used routinely as a diagnostic tool. **Comet** contains basic information, but the overall presentation is poorly organized and confusing. **Henry VIII** covers his marriages and the resulting break with the Catholic Church as well as his role in international politics. However, there are a few unsupported statements that would mean little to an uninformed reader. The U.S. House of Representatives is covered in **Congress of the United States.** While technically accurate, this article seems dated in approach. Several of the examples drawn upon date to the 1940s. It emphasizes historical and constitutional facts rather than explaining the lawmaking process. The writing, moreover, may be too difficult for the intended reader. The article on **Oxygen** is a factually correct and up-to-date summary of its properties and uses, but it is not particularly well written. The entry on **Virus** is a good overview, but the illustrations are poor; in general, it is not as accessible as the one in WORLD BOOK.

Clarity

The writing in *Funk & Wagnalls New Encyclopedia* is often ponderous. Users in elementary school or those with poor reading skills will have trouble understanding the articles because the vocabulary is rather advanced. The use of long, complicated sentences crammed with facts is common. Entries on scientific and technical subjects are the most difficult to understand since they deal with complex ideas. Articles on broad concepts could also be edited for language level and clarity. In **Judaism,** for example, the author spends too much time on philosophical details, obscuring the simple tenets of the faith: "Undergirding this monotheism is the teleological conviction that the world is both intelligible and purposive, because a single divine intelligence stands behind it." WORLD BOOK and NEW STANDARD ENCYCLOPEDIA are much more accessible to users.

This extract from *Titanic* **Disaster** is a good example of the encyclopedia's overall style:

> **TITANIC DISASTER,** one of the worst maritime disasters in history. The British luxury liner *Titanic* (46,000 gross tons) of the White Star Line, on its maiden voyage from Southampton to New York City, struck an iceberg about 153 km (about 95 mi) south of the Grand Banks of Newfoundland just before midnight on April 14, 1912. Of the more than 2220 persons aboard about 1513 died, including the American millionaires John Jacob Astor (1864–1912), Benjamin Guggenheim (1865–1912), and Isidor Straus.
>
> The ship had been proclaimed unsinkable because of its 16 watertight compartments, but the iceberg punctured five of them, one more than had been considered possible in any accident, and the *Titanic* sank in less than three hours. Subsequent investigations found that the ship had been steaming too fast in dangerous waters, that lifeboat space had been provided for only about three-fourths of the passengers and crew, and that the *Californian,* close to the scene, had not come to the rescue because the radio operator was off duty and asleep.

Objectivity

Funk & Wagnalls New Encyclopedia presents balanced coverage of controversial issues. For the most part, articles present both sides without bias. **Acquired immune deficiency syndrome** offers a good overview of the medical aspects and history of this disease. Although it does not discuss the ethical issues related to testing, discrimination, and confidentiality that AIDS patients face, it does mention these points, which many encyclopedias fail to do. **Capital punishment** summarizes the history and arguments for and against the practice without commentary. The article on **Northern Ireland** offers balanced coverage of this country's troubled history through 1990. The two paragraphs on the **ozone layer** discuss the effects of aerosols and the loss of ozone from the atmosphere, but not the opposing views of those scientists who do not feel that this is a serious problem. The entry on **abortion** presents the medical and legal issues but does not discuss the current impact of pro-life and pro-choice advocates on American politics.

Accessibility

This encyclopedia is easy to use. Guide words indicate the first and last entries on a spread. Alphabetization is letter by letter. Names beginning with *Mac* and *Mc* are alphabetized as *Mac,* and those beginning with *St.* are treated as if *Saint* were spelled out. Persons are entered under the name by which they are popularly known with the full or real name following: **Eliot, T(homas) S(tearns)** and **Eliot, George, pseudonym of Mary Ann Evans** are two examples. Important families (for example, **Amati**) receive collective entries that discuss each member. Entries with shared keywords include a qualifier—**meter, in mathematics; meter, in music; meter, in poetry.**

There are several types of cross-references. In addition to the usual *See* and *See also, Funk & Wagnalls* employs the arcane (*q.v.*) after a word within an article that is also the entry heading of another article. It is the only encyclopedia still using this device, which will be unfamiliar to most readers. The cross-references are generally helpful, but they can be hard to distinguish from the rest of the text because of the typography. WORLD BOOK's system is more effective.

The index in volume 29, containing 130,000 entries, is comprehensive. Terms that are entry headings appear in capital letters in boldface. Important terms that are not main entry headings appear in roman capitals. Maps are indexed, but illustrations are not. Many index entries contain extensive lists of subheads, which in themselves provide useful overviews of subjects.

Special Features

Funk & Wagnalls New Encyclopedia has a number of special features. The front matter contains a dense essay, "The Course of Human Society," on the evolution of civilization. It has no relationship to the text and will intimidate users who know nothing about anthropology. This is followed by an illustrated time line of history that refers readers to related entries in the encyclopedia. Volume 1 contains detailed instructions on using the encyclopedia. A condensed version of these instructions appears at the front of each volume.

The set contains 9,250 illustrations and 317 Hammond maps. Because of the small trim size, most of the maps span two-page spreads, making them difficult to read. Illustrations include charts, diagrams, photographs, and art reproductions. The quality of the illustrations is mediocre, and they are poorly reproduced. The illustration program cannot compete with WORLD

BOOK, but it is reasonably current. Articles on states and Canadian provinces contain two-page spreads featuring basic facts and statistics.

This encyclopedia also has brief essays on using the library and writing term papers. They are of limited use because of their brevity, but they can serve as starting points. A 250-page bibliography in volume 28 contains 9,600 entries; the entries contain brief annotations. The bibliography is divided into 1,255 separate reading lists, which are organized by subject using a unique numerical classification. Users are directed to the section number by references at the end of articles. The use of subject headings within the bibliography itself would be helpful. Although overall the bibliography contains a fair number of titles from the 1980s and 1990s, many of the items in the health and medical areas are not current. WORLD BOOK's bibliographies and study guides are superior.

Format

Each volume contains a segment of the alphabet (for example, *A–American* and *Worm–Zy*). The length of each volume is approximately 480 pages. The books are easy to hold and lie flat when opened. There are two columns per page. The margins are small but adequate and are justified on both sides of each column. Guide words in large capitals are clear. Each page is numbered and pagination is separate for each volume. Subheads in boldface divide long articles into sections.

The type is small and light on the page, making the text difficult to read. Those with poor vision will have problems with this set. The paper is adequate, although many of the color photographs are blurred by the printing process. The layout, too, is adequate, though not as inviting as some of the set's more colorful competitors. The library binding is sturdy black cloth with red and gold stamping and page tops edged in gold. Leather binding is also available. The mass-market edition is perfect bound, making it less sturdy.

Funk & Wagnalls New Encyclopedia is also the basis for Microsoft's ENCARTA CD-ROM encyclopedia.

Summary

Funk & Wagnalls New Encyclopedia offers good value. It provides a great deal of current information at a reasonable price. Although it lacks the depth of the NEW BRITANNICA or the ENCYCLOPEDIA AMERICANA and the clarity and fine illustrations of WORLD BOOK, *Funk & Wagnalls* is adequate as a reference source for the home, school, or office, and even as a library ready-reference tool if budget is a factor.

For another opinion regarding *Funk & Wagnalls New Encyclopedia*, see *Booklist*, September 15, 1993, page 180.

Grolier Encyclopedia of Knowledge

Facts at a Glance

Full title: **Grolier Encyclopedia of Knowledge**
Publisher: Grolier
Editors: Jeffrey H. Hacker, Editor-in-Chief; Lawrence T. Lorimer, Editorial Director
Number of contributors: 2,000
Edition reviewed: © 1991

Number of volumes: 20
Number of articles: 22,000
Number of pages: 8,320
Number of words: 6.5 million
Number of cross-references: 60,000 (reviewer estimate)
Number of index entries: 90,000
Number of maps: 1,000
Number of illustrations: 13,000 (including maps), approximately 85 percent in color (reviewer estimate)
Intended readership: elementary school to college and adults
Trim size: 7½″ × 9¼″
Binding: hardcover

Price: contact publisher for price information
Sold in supermarkets
ISBN 0-7172-5300-7
Revised annually

Introduction

The *Grolier Encyclopedia of Knowledge* is a 20-volume general encyclopedia especially created for home use. The publisher states that it is for students from elementary school through college and adults, but the reading level is more appropriate for middle school students and those above that age. The text is an abridged version of Grolier's ACADEMIC AMERICAN ENCYCLOPEDIA, a well-regarded general encyclopedia for libraries. *Grolier Encyclopedia of Knowledge* is sold in supermarkets, one volume at a time, over a period of months. Although the publisher states that the encyclopedia is revised annually, this review is based on the 1991 printing.

Authority

This encyclopedia is relatively new to the market. ACADEMIC AMERICAN, the basis for the *Grolier Encyclopedia of Knowledge,* has been published by Grolier since 1982. Grolier is a respected reference publisher that also produces ENCYCLOPEDIA AMERICANA and THE NEW BOOK OF KNOWLEDGE.

Jeffrey H. Hacker, Editor-in-Chief, heads a staff of more than 50 people who produce the encyclopedia. According to the publisher, 90 percent of the articles are written by outside authorities. The 2,000 contributors and their credentials are listed in the front matter of vol-

Grolier Encyclopedia of Knowledge

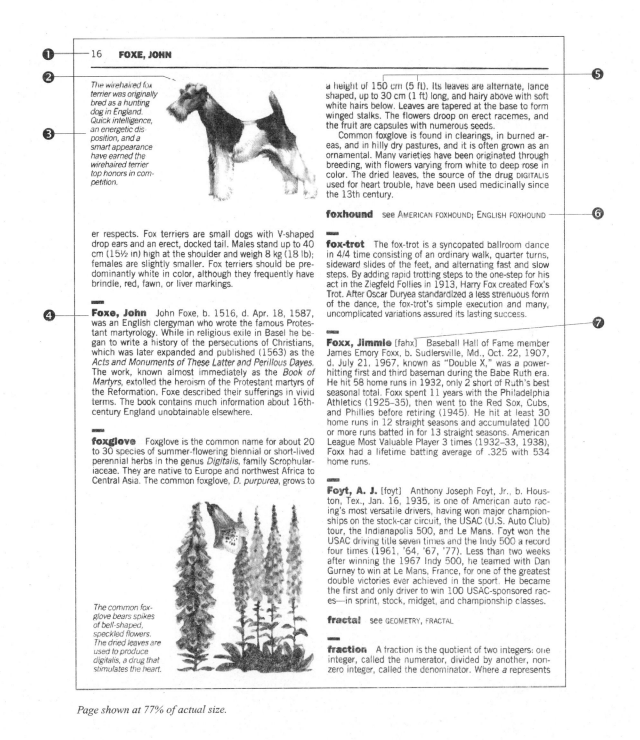

1 16   **FOXE, JOHN**

The wirehaired fox terrier was originally bred as a hunting dog in England. Quick intelligence, an energetic disposition, and a smart appearance have earned the wirehaired terrier top honors in competition.

er respects. Fox terriers are small dogs with V-shaped drop ears and an erect, docked tail. Males stand up to 40 cm (15½ in) high at the shoulder and weigh 8 kg (18 lb); females are slightly smaller. Fox terriers should be predominantly white in color, although they frequently have brindle, red, fawn, or liver markings.

Foxe, John   John Foxe, b. 1516, d. Apr. 18, 1587, was an English clergyman who wrote the famous Protestant martyrology. While in religious exile in Basel he began to write a history of the persecutions of Christians, which was later expanded and published (1563) as the *Acts and Monuments of These Latter and Perillous Dayes.* The work, known almost immediately as the *Book of Martyrs,* extolled the heroism of the Protestant martyrs of the Reformation. Foxe described their sufferings in vivid terms. The book contains much information about 16th-century England unobtainable elsewhere.

foxglove   Foxglove is the common name for about 20 to 30 species of summer-flowering biennial or short-lived perennial herbs in the genus *Digitalis,* family Scrophulariaceae. They are native to Europe and northwest Africa to Central Asia. The common foxglove, *D. purpurea,* grows to

The common foxglove bears spikes of bell-shaped, speckled flowers. The dried leaves are used to produce digitalis, a drug that stimulates the heart.

a height of 150 cm (5 ft). Its leaves are alternate, lance shaped, up to 30 cm (1 ft) long, and hairy above with soft white hairs below. Leaves are tapered at the base to form winged stalks. The flowers droop on erect racemes, and the fruit are capsules with numerous seeds.

Common foxglove is found in clearings, in burned areas, and in hilly dry pastures, and it is often grown as an ornamental. Many varieties have been originated through breeding, with flowers varying from white to deep rose in color. The dried leaves, the source of the drug DIGITALIS used for heart trouble, have been used medicinally since the 13th century.

foxhound   see AMERICAN FOXHOUND; ENGLISH FOXHOUND

fox-trot   The fox-trot is a syncopated ballroom dance in 4/4 time consisting of an ordinary walk, quarter turns, sideward slides of the feet, and alternating fast and slow steps. By adding rapid trotting steps to the one-step for his act in the Ziegfeld Follies in 1913, Harry Fox created Fox's Trot. After Oscar Duryea standardized a less strenuous form of the dance, the fox-trot's simple execution and many, uncomplicated variations assured its lasting success.

Foxx, Jimmie [fahx]   Baseball Hall of Fame member James Emory Foxx, b. Sudlersville, Md., Oct. 22, 1907, d. July 21, 1967, known as "Double X," was a power-hitting first and third baseman during the Babe Ruth era. He hit 58 home runs in 1932, only 2 short of Ruth's best seasonal total. Foxx spent 11 years with the Philadelphia Athletics (1925–35), then went to the Red Sox, Cubs, and Phillies before retiring (1945). He hit at least 30 home runs in 12 straight seasons and accumulated 100 or more runs batted in for 13 straight seasons. American League Most Valuable Player 3 times (1932–33, 1938), Foxx had a lifetime batting average of .325 with 534 home runs.

Foyt, A. J. [foyt]   Anthony Joseph Foyt, Jr., b. Houston, Tex., Jan. 16, 1935, is one of American auto racing's most versatile drivers, having won major championships on the stock-car circuit, the USAC (U.S. Auto Club) tour, the Indianapolis 500, and Le Mans. Foyt won the USAC driving title seven times and the Indy 500 a record four times (1961, '64, '67, '77). Less than two weeks after winning the 1967 Indy 500, he teamed with Dan Gurney to win at Le Mans, France, in one of the greatest double victories ever achieved in the sport. He became the first and only driver to win 100 USAC-sponsored races—in sprint, stock, midget, and championship classes.

fractal   see GEOMETRY, FRACTAL

fraction   A fraction is the quotient of two integers: one integer, called the numerator, divided by another, nonzero integer, called the denominator. Where *a* represents

Page shown at 77% of actual size.

1 Page number and guide words
2 Illustrations include both photographs and drawings
3 Captions often add to the information presented in the text
4 Main entry words printed in boldface
5 Measurements given in both metric and standard systems
6 Cross-reference entry
7 Pronunciations given for foreign or unusual entry words

ume 1; the list is essentially identical to that in ACADEMIC AMERICAN. Most contributors are academics. Among the distinguished experts are anthropologist Ashley Montagu, botanist Richard Evans Schultes, and English professor Hugh Kenner. Unlike ACADEMIC AMERICAN, the articles are unsigned, presumably because they have been abridged.

Scope

The Grolier Encyclopedia of Knowledge provides broad coverage of contemporary events, popular culture, international affairs, and current technology. The publisher claims to cover all significant aspects of a subject and to present important events and ideas in their historical or cultural context. This is a short-entry set: more than half of the articles contain fewer than 500 words.

The amount of space devoted to these sample entries demonstrates the brief coverage given to most topics. Four illustrated pages, one of which is a map, cover **Mexico,** although there is also a separate four-page entry on **Mexico, history of. Impressionism** receives three pages of illustrations and three paragraphs of text; there is also a separate short entry for impressionism in music. **Castle** receives one and a half pages, one of which is devoted to illustrations. The entry for **Hamlet,** two paragraphs, discusses themes and sources, rather than the plot of the play. **Tyrannosaurus** is treated in two paragraphs plus an illustration. **Elvis Presley** receives two paragraphs and a photograph. **Nelson Mandela** receives one paragraph.

This encyclopedia reflects the curriculum in American schools and colleges, but its scope also extends beyond this into areas of contemporary popular interest. **Cable television, compact disc, video,** and various aspects of computers and their applications are among the technical subjects covered. Popular culture is reflected in biographies of film greats from **Paul Muni** and **F. W. Murnau** to **Woody Allen,** as well as articles on **rock music** and **Muppets.**

The publisher does not provide information about the set's relative coverage of different disciplines. Our reviewers estimate the following breakdown, based on a 50-page sample (volume 13, *Mod–Nuc,* pages 125–175): humanities and the arts (including history and religion), 39 percent; science and technology, 24 percent; geography, 15 percent; social sciences, 9 percent; popular culture, 13 percent. Biographical entries comprise about 35 percent of the text.

These numbers underscore the contemporary orientation of the *Grolier Encyclopedia of Knowledge.* Among the biographies in the sampled pages are **Lewis Mumford, Charles Munch, Edvard Munch, Shikibu Murasaki,** and **Rupert Murdoch.** The geography entries include places such as **Munich, Murcia,** and the **Murrumbidgee River;** scientific subjects include **mul-**

tiple myeloma, multiplexer, muntjac, mushroom, and **muscle;** topics in the humanities include **mural painting, muses, art museums,** and **music.**

Although the major focus of this encyclopedia is Western civilization, other cultures are covered. Articles on **dance** and **music** include sections on diverse cultures, and there are articles on **Buddhism, Hinduism,** and **Islam.** Pages 25–50 of volume 6 (*Dan–Ele*), for example, contain entries for **Davao,** a Philippine city, and **Osamu Dazai,** a Japanese novelist. Entries for African Americans **Benjamin O. Davis, Miles Davis,** and **Ossie Davis** and former Mexican president **Miguel de la Madrid Hurtado** also appear.

Currency

The publisher states that the *Grolier Encyclopedia of Knowledge* is revised annually but supplies no information about the extent of the revision. Since this review is based on the 1991 printing, currency cannot be fully assessed or adequately compared to more recent encyclopedias reviewed in this Buying Guide. However, if currency standards can be inferred from this printing, it appears quite up-to-date for a 1991 copyright and even includes events that occurred in that year.

There is an entry for **Gulf war,** a half-page summary of events. The **space telescope** article includes two paragraphs about the Hubble Space Telescope and mentions the mirror flaw. **Lithuania, Latvia,** and **Estonia** have their own articles as independent republics, but **Russia** is still listed as a Soviet republic. The separate article **Russia/USSR, history of** is current through 1991. It mentions the August 1991 coup attempt against Mikhail Gorbachev. The coup attempt is also mentioned in an entry for **Boris Yeltsin.** The article on **Yugoslavia** describes the country as being on the verge of breakup in mid-1991.

As is to be expected, Bill Clinton is listed as the governor of Arkansas. The food pyramid does not appear in the article **nutrition, human.** There is no entry for Frida Kahlo.

Population information for the states and cities of the United States is from the 1990 census. Figures for foreign countries are given as estimates with dates, but no sources are cited. Most are for the 1980s. Most maps are current to 1991. Germany and Yemen are shown as united countries. The illustrations are generally up-to-date. Most are chosen to avoid issues of currency.

Accuracy

As an abridgment of ACADEMIC AMERICAN, one finds the same high degree of accuracy in the *Grolier Encyclopedia of Knowledge.* (See the ACADEMIC AMERICAN review for a discussion of its accuracy.) However, the brevity of the entries makes the coverage of many subjects superficial. Typically eliminated are details and examples that help support and explain the points.

Oxygen and **House of Representatives of the United States** are virtually identical to the corresponding entries in ACADEMIC AMERICAN, and **Henry VIII** is shortened only slightly. **Cancer** and **comet** are abridged by about one-third; while still basically accurate, they do not provide enough detail for comprehension of these complex subjects.

The coverage of the **Holocaust** is brief but comprehensive. The article includes information on Jewish resistance and mentions the fact that other countries did nothing to help the Jews. It fails, however, to note that blacks, Gypsies, homosexuals, and the mentally ill and retarded were also Hitler's victims. The entry for **Judaism** also is quite good. It explains the basic beliefs and practices and clarifies the phrase "Chosen People," meaning "chosen to bring God's message" rather than "privileged." (This misconception is often a basis for anti-Semitism.) The article does, however, state that the Mishnah and Talmud are separate works, which is not the case. The individual articles **Mishnah** and **Talmud** do, however, clarify this.

Clarity

Entries in this encyclopedia are clear and concise. They explain the basic facts about a subject in a straightforward manner. The article on **acupuncture,** for example, makes this traditional medical practice intelligible to lay readers. There is no attempt at stylistic elegance, since a great deal of information must be provided in a small amount of space. Diagrams and charts are helpful in explaining scientific and technical concepts.

The entry **Titanic** in the *Grolier Encyclopedia of Knowledge* is the same as that in ACADEMIC AMERICAN, except for a phrase or two cut for space. See the **Titanic** extract in the ACADEMIC AMERICAN review for an example of the writing style in the *Grolier Encyclopedia of Knowledge.*

Objectivity

The preface (volume 1) states that the editors try to present all points of view on controversial issues. However, the brevity of the entries usually limits them to providing events or facts without explaining their ethical and political ramifications. The entry **abortion,** for example, offers a good summary of the medical techniques, including RU-486, and a summary of American legal history. It mentions the pro-choice and pro-life views on abortion, but fails to discuss the issue of privacy rights or the enormous political impact of the abortion debate. **AIDS** is also largely limited to medical information about the etiology, transmission, symptoms, and treatment of the disease. It ignores the social and ethical issues concerning funding of research and health care,

and discrimination in housing and employment. It does mention HIV testing and the controversy over FDA approval for new drugs. The entry also gives the misleading impression that treatment and even a possible cure are in sight.

The entries **AIDS, ozone layer,** and **Northern Ireland** are essentially the same as those in the 1993 ACADEMIC AMERICAN (see that review). The abridged **capital punishment** covers the history and relevant legal cases, but does not address ethical and philosophical issues.

Accessibility

The *Grolier Encyclopedia of Knowledge* is easy to use. Guide words in bold type in the upper outer corner of every page show the first and last entries on each spread. Entries are alphabetized word by word, so that **New York** appears before **Newfoundland** and **Radio Free Europe** precedes **radioactivity.** Headings containing foreign or unfamiliar words include pronunciation guides. The Pinyin system is used for Chinese terms with the Wade-Giles spelling provided in parentheses—for example, **Beijing** (Peking). Entries with a shared keyword include a qualifier in parentheses: **mass** (liturgy); **mass** (musical setting); **mass** (physics).

There are three kinds of cross-references in this encyclopedia. *See* references refer users from an unused heading to the term used in this source—**Abyssinia** *see* **Ethiopia.** *See also* references appear at the end of an entry to refer users to related material on the subject. The article on **abstract expressionism** directs readers to entries for **abstract art, art, modern art,** and **painting.** In addition to these traditional references, there are internal cross-references within the text of the articles. Words used in articles that have their own entries appear in small capitals within the text. The entry for **albatross** contains internal cross-references for **petrels** and **shearwaters.** Unfortunately, the typography makes these references difficult to see.

The index in volume 20 contains 90,000 entries. Illustrations and maps are indexed. Clear instructions for using the index appear before the index itself. Entry headings in bold type in capital letters indicate that there is an article with that title in the encyclopedia. Subject headings that are not article titles appear in capitals in roman typeface. Related material appears in subheadings under the main entries. Italicized page numbers indicate illustrations. The index provides a convenient overview of the way that various subjects are treated in the encyclopedia. Since most of the entries are brief, the index is crucial for locating all relevant material.

Special Features

The *Grolier Encyclopedia of Knowledge* has an excellent illustration program with 13,000 illustrations, including photographs, drawings, art reproductions, graphs, diagrams, and charts. Approximately 85 percent are in color. There are also 1,000 maps created by Rand McNally, Donnelley Cartographic, and Lothar Ross Associates. The photographs are a mixture of contemporary and historical subjects. Drawings include various species of animals, aircraft, ships, and cross sections of machinery and devices.

Fact boxes with the heading "At a Glance" summarize basic information about continents, countries, U.S. states, and Canadian provinces. These include a map, flag, and information about the area, population, government, and economy. Those for states also include the seal, flower, and bird.

A major weakness of this encyclopedia is that it contains no bibliography or other study aids. Given the brevity of the articles, readers doing research will need further information, and this source offers none. Most other general sets include bibliographies, study guides, or both.

Format

Each volume covers a segment of the alphabet, such as *A–Ann* and *Wor–Zyg*. Volumes are approximately 415 pages, and pagination is independent for each volume. The books are easy to hold and lie flat when opened and placed on a surface. The pages are arranged with two columns of text and ample margins between the columns and around the edge of the page. Both left and right margins are justified to create a precise, neat appearance. A thin rule across the top of the page separates the guide words and page numbers from the text. Article headings are in boldface and are marked by a short, thick rule.

The sans serif type can be a bit difficult to read. As noted, it makes the internal cross references hard to spot. The relatively small print size may be a drawback for those with vision problems, but the overall layout is attractive and suitable for young adult and adult readers. The sturdy binding, an attractive navy and red with white and gold stamped letters, will withstand heavy use.

Pictures and maps are well placed so that they do not break up the text. The overall quality of the illustrations is good, but *Grolier Encyclopedia of Knowledge* does not begin to approach WORLD BOOK in this area. Illustrations occupy about one-third of the encyclopedia's space.

Summary

The *Grolier Encyclopedia of Knowledge* will well serve home users who need basic information. Its brief, superficial coverage of subjects and lack of bibliographies make this encyclopedia inadequate for research. Libraries, schools, and those in need of in-depth information should consider more comprehensive works such as WORLD BOOK.

The New Book of Knowledge

Facts at a Glance

Full title: **The New Book of Knowledge**
Publisher: Grolier
Editors: Lawrence T. Lorrimer, Editorial Director; Gerry Gabianelli, Editor-in-Chief
Number of contributors: 1,813
Edition reviewed: © 1993

Number of volumes: 21
Number of pages: 10,576
Number of words: approximately 6,850,000
Number of cross-references: 4,800
Number of index entries: 85,000
Number of maps: 1,193
Number of illustrations: 24,600, 92 percent in color
Intended readership: ages 7 to 14
Trim size: $7^3/_8'' \times 10''$
Binding: hardcover

Price: $758
Sold directly to schools and libraries; also sold by Discover Toys and door-to-door by non-Grolier distributors
ISBN 0-7172-0524-X
Revision policy: annual updates of 10–15 percent plus major revisions; next major revision: 1997

Introduction

The New Book of Knowledge is a 21-volume encyclopedia designed for children ages 7 to 14. The contents are geared to the school curriculum and to outside interests of this age group. This alphabetically arranged general encyclopedia covers a broad range of subjects and makes them appealing and understandable to young people. This review is based on the 1993 printing of the work; the 1994 printing was not available at the time of the review.

Authority

The New Book of Knowledge has been published by Grolier since 1966. Its predecessor, *The Book of Knowledge* (also published by Grolier), was a topically arranged children's encyclopedia published from 1910 through 1965. Grolier is a well-known, respected publisher of reference works, including THE ENCYCLOPEDIA AMERICANA and the ACADEMIC AMERICAN ENCYCLOPEDIA.

A list of more than 1,800 contributors and reviewers appears in volume 20. Most are academics actively involved in their fields. Among the distinguished contributors are Sally K. Ride, professor of physics at the University of California, San Diego (**astronauts**); Mervyn F. Silverman, M.D., of the American Founda-

The New Book of Knowledge

❶ JET LAG. See Biological Clock.

❷ JET PROPULSION

Jet engines power today's fastest airplanes and missiles. They can move an airplane faster than any other type of engine because of the principle on which they work.

❸ ▶ THE JET PRINCIPLE

Jets are a fairly new development in aviation. They have been widely used only since the 1950's. But the principle on which they work has been known for hundreds of years. It can be stated in this way: For every force in one direction, there is an equal force in the opposite direction. This is known as the reaction principle. A rotating lawn sprinkler, which shoots streams of water from its nozzles, shows the way this principle works. The stream of water shooting out exerts a force in one direction. According to the principle, there is also an equal force in the other direction. Therefore, the sprinkler rotates in the opposite direction. The same kind of reaction force pushes an aircraft forward when the jet exhaust shoots out of the rear of a jet engine. It should be clearly understood that the forward motion of the plane is not provided by the force of the jet exhaust against the air in the rear. The forward motion of the plane is provided by the reaction force inside the engine.

Structure of the Jet Engine

Aircraft jet engines are usually shaped like long, hollow tubes. The engine has four basic parts. They are the compressor, the burner, the turbine, and the jet, or exhaust, nozzle. The compressor is a fan or pump that operates

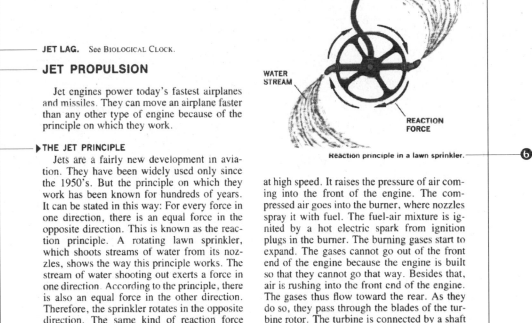

WATER STREAM

REACTION FORCE

❻ Reaction principle in a lawn sprinkler.

at high speed. It raises the pressure of air coming into the front of the engine. The compressed air goes into the burner, where nozzles spray it with fuel. The fuel-air mixture is ignited by a hot electric spark from ignition plugs in the burner. The burning gases start to expand. The gases cannot go out of the front end of the engine because the engine is built so that they cannot go that way. Besides that, air is rushing into the front end of the engine. The gases thus flow toward the rear. As they do so, they pass through the blades of the turbine rotor. The turbine is connected by a shaft to the air compressor in the front of the engine. As the gases flow past, they make the turbine wheel turn. As the wheel turns, its shaft turns the compressor. After the gases leave the turbine, they pass out of the jet nozzle at the rear at high speed. The gases exert tremendous force toward the rear. According to the reaction principle, the force exerted in the other direction is just as strong. This force drives the aircraft forward.

The amount of reaction force created by the engine depends on the speed and weight of the gases coming out of the jet nozzle. The speed of the aircraft may be changed by increasing

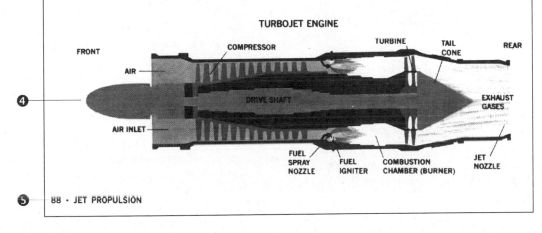

TURBOJET ENGINE

FRONT — COMPRESSOR — TURBINE — TAIL CONE — REAR

AIR

❹ DRIVE SHAFT

AIR INLET

EXHAUST GASES

FUEL SPRAY NOZZLE — FUEL IGNITER — COMBUSTION CHAMBER (BURNER) — JET NOZZLE

❺ 88 · JET PROPULSION

Page shown at 77% of actual size.

❶ Cross-reference entries indicated by small capitals

❷ Main entry words printed in boldface

❸ Article subhead

❹ Illustrations include diagrams with callouts

❺ Page number and guide words

❻ Caption

tion for AIDS Research (**AIDS**); and Richard Berry, former Editor-in-Chief of *Astronomy* magazine (**Milky Way**).

Most articles in *The New Book of Knowledge* are signed by the contributors or reviewers; many are signed by both. The credentials of these people are provided with their names. In addition to the consultants and reviewers, 36 advisers and consultants—most of them academics—were involved with this edition and are listed in volume 1.

Scope

The New Book of Knowledge contains a mixture of long articles (2–15 pages) on broad subject areas such as states and countries, and short entries (½–1 page) for more narrowly focused subjects such as biographies. There are also brief dictionary entries at the back of each volume on subjects not included in the main body of the encyclopedia. The articles cover all major academic subject areas, with an emphasis on those in the North American school curriculum. Although all cultures are represented, American and European topics receive more extensive coverage. **Islam** has a seven-page entry and **Hinduism** a two-page entry, while **Christianity** receives ten pages.

A randomly selected 50-page sample (volume 10, pages 125–175) containing 28 articles suggested the following coverage of different disciplines: humanities and the arts (including history and religion), 36 percent; geography, 25 percent; social sciences and popular culture, 14 percent each; science and technology, 11 percent. About 37 percent of the articles in the sample are biographies.

The New Book of Knowledge gives good coverage of world topics. In a randomly selected 25-page sample (volume 12, pages 400–425), 10 of the 13 articles concern topics not related to the United States, Canada, or Great Britain. These include **Modigliani, Mohammed, Moldova, Monaco, Monet,** and **Mongolia.**

The range of article lengths is illustrated by the sample entries. **Castle** receives two pages with illustrations, while *Hamlet* has a 25-line plot summary and five lines of quotations in the article **Shakespeare, William. Impressionism** is given four pages with illustrations. **Nelson Mandela** receives a 15-line dictionary entry (**Winnie Mandela** has a 10-line dictionary entry) and **Elvis Presley** gets a 7-line dictionary entry. *Tyrannosaurus Rex* receives two paragraphs and an illustration within the 12-page article on **dinosaurs.** The entry for **Mexico** covers 12 pages and includes a map and nine photographs.

The New Book of Knowledge covers science and technology well. There are articles on **computers, compact discs,** and **planets,** for example. Popular culture is reflected in articles on sports (**baseball, football**), handicrafts (**finger painting, origami, weaving**), and assorted subjects of interest to children (**numbers and number systems, folklore**).

Currency

According to the publisher, *The New Book of Knowledge* undergoes an annual 10 to 15 percent update plus periodic major revisions. A major revision is in progress for the 1997 edition. For the 1993 printing, 91 new articles have been added, 21 have been replaced, and 365 have been revised. New and revised articles related to recent world events include **Commonwealth of Independent States, Communism, USSR, Boris Yeltsin,** and **Yugoslavia.** Among the other new or revised articles are **racism, research,** and **women's rights movement.** In addition to the new and revised content, this edition has more than 1,000 new photographs, illustrations, and maps.

Current events, including the South African government's decision to end white minority rule and Bill Clinton's campaign and election to the presidency, are reflected in this edition of *The New Book of Knowledge.* The article on **nutrition** covers the four basic food groups, but does not show the food pyramid or provide information about recommended daily servings. There is no separate article for the Persian Gulf War, but it is mentioned in the articles **Arabs; Iraq; Egypt; Israel; Kuwait; Middle East; United States, Armed Forces of the;** and **United States, history of the.** The Hubble Space Telescope appears in the articles **astronomy, observatories, space exploration and travel, space telescopes** (where it has its own subhead and one and a quarter pages of text), and **telescopes. Lithuania** and **Russia** each have three-page articles. There are also separate articles on **Russia, art and architecture of; Russia, language and literature of;** and **Russia, music of.** The article on the **Union of Soviet Socialist Republics** is historical. There is no entry for *Frida Kahlo.* Most maps and photographs are current. Germany and Yemen are united. Yugoslavia and the former Union of Soviet Socialist Republics are divided, but Czechoslovakia still appears as one nation. The entry for this country does mention the plan to divide into two nations.

Many articles in this encyclopedia, especially those on countries and states, are written so that they will appear to be current for long periods of time. Government officials' names are not given; only office titles are provided. No sources or dates are given for statistics, although the 1990 census is cited for some United States figures. This is a drawback for users needing specific names and statistics with dates.

Accuracy

The New Book of Knowledge receives mixed reviews from the Buying Guide's content experts. The **cancer** article is sound but requires updating, especially the section on "Current Research." It is faulted, too, for referring to smokeless tobacco as "chew"—a term that is not widely used and that overlooks the use of smokeless tobacco as snuff. **Oxygen and oxidation** is well written and factually correct, and discusses the subjects that a student needs to know in sufficient detail. In the discussion of ozone, the author fails to mention ozone pollution, but this is a minor criticism.

Coverage of the House of Representatives within the article **United States, Congress of the** is factually solid and manages to incorporate a good amount of scholarly knowledge in the field into an appropriate reading level. The article stresses the relationship between the House's organization and its legislative procedures, and the sidebars that profile famous House members provide useful color.

The **comets, meteors, and asteroids** article is disappointing. It fails to show the relationships between these bodies, and includes no really hard information. **Henry VIII,** though written by a recognized authority on the subject, covers only the standard material, and the closing paragraph oversimplifies Henry's achievements with statements like "Henry made England an important power."

Clarity

Entries in this encyclopedia are written in simple, clear sentences that convey relevant facts efficiently. Longer articles use up to two levels of subheads to divide major concepts. This extract from the entry **telecommunications** is typical of *The New Book of Knowledge*'s style:

> Without moving from the work station, a nurse can keep track of the condition of several patients in different rooms in the hospital. In their homes, millions of people around the world watch as an astronaut walks on the moon. You dial a number on your telephone, and speak to a friend far away. The nurse, the astronaut, and you are using modern methods of communication. These methods of using electronic equipment to send and receive messages are called telecommunications. The term comes from the Greek work *tele,* meaning "far."
>
> The most familiar telecommunication devices in our lives today are the telephone, radio, and television. The telegraph, too, was once an important telecommunication device. Since their invention, each of these devices has been improved on in a variety of ways. . . .

Dictionary entries in the back of each volume present brief information on topics not found in the main body of the encyclopedia. Unlike some other encyclopedias, *The New Book of Knowledge* treats **Titanic** only in a brief dictionary format:

> **Titanic** (ty-TAN-ic), British steamship, largest and fastest of its time, that sank on its first voyage after colliding with an iceberg in the Atlantic Ocean (1912). Of 2208 passengers and crew, 1503 perished. Later investigation revealed

that warnings to reduce speed had not been heeded, too few lifeboats were aboard, and nearby ships did not react immediately to signals for help. The tragedy helped dispel overconfidence and led to adoption of sea safety rules. In 1985 a U.S.-French oceanographic research team found the sunken wreck of the *Titanic* upright and largely intact about 400 mi (650 km) south of Newfoundland.

Objectivity

There are no obvious biases in this encyclopedia. *The New Book of Knowledge* tends to avoid controversial issues. Those that are included receive minimal coverage. Abortion is discussed in the article on **ethics,** where the basic issues are stated, but the influence of religion and the role of the pro- and anti-choice movements in politics are ignored. No medical information about the procedure appears anywhere in the text. The article on **birth control** covers the history of contraception and explains current available methods, but does not discuss the religious issues related to this subject or mention abortion. The entry for **AIDS** offers a simple explanation of the etiology and transmission of the disease and mentions which countries have the highest rates of infection. It says nothing about the demographics (**homosexuality** receives only a brief definition in a dictionary entry), treatment, funding of research, or civil rights issues related to HIV testing, health insurance, and discrimination in housing and the workplace. **Capital punishment** has a one-paragraph dictionary entry explaining the term and discussing the legal issues. It states that some feel that it is cruel and unusual punishment, while others think that it deters crime. The methods used in the United States and the fact that many countries have banned capital punishment are mentioned, but religious and ethical issues are not covered. **Northern Ireland** presents the history of the country—though only through 1988—covering the religious divisions and Irish Republican Army terrorism, but does not mention that both sides are responsible for the continuing violence. The ozone layer receives two sentences in the article on **oxygen and oxidation** explaining its existence and function. Overall, WORLD BOOK does a superior job of presenting controversial issues in a balanced, accessible manner.

Accessibility

The New Book of Knowledge is easy to use. Entries are arranged alphabetically letter by letter (so that **Newfoundland** precedes **New Guinea**), to the comma if one is included in the heading. Names beginning with *Mc* and *Mac* are interfiled as they are spelled. Names beginning with *St.* are inserted as though the abbreviation were spelled out. Guide words appear at the bottom of each page next to the page number. This is an unusual format, but it should not affect accessibility. Entries with a shared keyword include a qualifier in parentheses: **mass** (in music), **mass** (in physics), **mass** (in Roman Catholic Church).

Article headings appear in bold type in large capitals; main subheads are in bold type in small capitals preceded by an arrowhead; minor subheads are in bold type. There are two kinds of cross-references. *See* references refer users from an unused heading to the term used in this source: **New Delhi.** *See* **Delhi.** *See also* references appear at the end of an entry to refer users to related material on the subject. The article on **Newton, Isaac** directs readers to entries for **gravity and gravitation; light;** and **motion, Newton's laws of.** Both types of cross-references appear in small print at the ends of articles and can be easily overlooked. WORLD BOOK's cross-reference system is more effective.

Indexing is thorough. Each volume has its own index on blue-colored pages at the end of the text. Instructions for using the index appear in volume 1. Some index entries have a pronunciation guide and some have a brief identification. Individual volume indexes include subentries that refer users to related material in other volumes. In addition to the individual volume indexes, volume 21 is a master index to the whole encyclopedia set. Illustrations are indexed only if they appear on a different page from the main entry. Maps are not indexed, but end-of-volume dictionary entries are. *See* and *See also* references appear as needed. People with more than one name are indexed under the best-known name: **Clemens, Samuel Langhorne,** *See* **Twain, Mark.** Stories that are told in full in entries are indexed under **stories. Experiments and other science activities, hobbies,** and **how to** are also index headings, making it easy for users to find project ideas.

Special Features

The New Book of Knowledge is profusely illustrated. More than 90 percent of the illustrations are in color and most are up-to-date. Ethnic diversity is apparent in the photographs and there are also attempts to break down gender-role stereotypes (for example, a male nurse in the article on **nursing,** an African American woman dentist in the article on **dentistry**). In addition to photographs, the encyclopedia contains many maps, fact boxes, charts, and diagrams.

Another special feature of this set is the inclusion of literary excerpts in the articles about authors. There is a selection from *Little Women* in the article on **Louisa May Alcott** and part of *The Adventures of Tom Sawyer* and "The Celebrated Jumping Frog of Calaveras County" appear in the **Mark Twain** entry. The entry for **folk music** contains musical notation for many songs and the articles on foreign languages usually contain lists of common words and charts of non-Roman alphabets.

The encyclopedia offers many learning activities. Projects include growing *Penicillium* molds in the article on **antibiotics,** building a kaleidoscope (**kaleidoscope**), and making paper animals (**origami**). "Wonder Questions," highlighted in special boxes, present interesting facts in answer to questions such as "Why are astronauts weightless?" (**astronauts**) or "How do astronomers measure distance in space?" (**astronomy**).

A 208-page paperback book, *Home and School Reading and Study Guides,* accompanies *The New Book of Knowledge.* Part I, "The Reading Guide," offers bibliographies keyed to the main entries in the encyclopedia. The bibliographies are not annotated. Most of the books listed were published in the 1980s, although a few were considerably older. Part II, "The Study Guide," provides short articles on the school curriculum for various grade levels, as well as suggested learning activities. It is aimed primarily at parents who want to help their children make good use of the encyclopedia.

Format

Most of the 21 volumes are devoted to a single letter, but some combine letters. The volumes contain between 300 and 650 pages. Each has its own pagination. The books are easy to hold and lie open when placed on a surface. The text is arranged in a two-column format and margins are ample. Unfortunately, however, some of the illustrations are allowed to bleed into the center gutter, with a resultant loss of some detail and possible problems when photocopying.

The type is easy to read and the headings, in boldface, stand out well. Page layouts are attractively varied and the overall appearance is of a colorful, lively set. Paper quality is good, with minimal show-through. The binding is sturdy and will stand up to heavy use.

Summary

For another opinion on the 1993 edition of *The New Book of Knowledge,* refer to *Booklist (Reference Books Bulletin),* September 15, 1993.

The New Book of Knowledge is an attractive resource for elementary school students. Its comprehensive coverage, colorful illustrations, and learning activities will appeal to children's natural curiosity. This encyclopedia is the only multivolume work that uses main entries and dictionary entries; this may confuse users who would not think of referring to the dictionary section. Also, having the bibliographies in a separate book will be a drawback for users who don't become fully familiar with the whole package. Overall, though, *The New Book of Knowledge* is a high-quality children's encyclopedia, suitable for home and classroom use. It is more expensive than WORLD BOOK, one of its main competitors, but its range of topics, including many high-interest ones, would probably be more attractive to younger readers.

The New Encyclopaedia Britannica

Facts at a Glance

Full title: **The New Encyclopaedia Britannica**
Publisher: Encyclopaedia Britannica
Editor: Robert D. McHenry, Editor-in-Chief
Number of contributors: more than 6,800
Edition reviewed: © 1993

Number of volumes: 32
Number of articles: "Micropaedia," 64,128; "Macropaedia," 672
Number of pages: 31,919
Number of words: 44 million
Number of cross-references: 33,700
Number of index entries: 228,274
Number of maps: 1,283
Number of illustrations: 23,835 (30 percent in four-color)
Intended readership: intelligent layperson, student to adult
Trim size: $8^{7}/_{16}'' \times 10^{7}/_{8}''$
Binding: hardcover

Price: $1,599 (starting price)
Sold directly to libraries and schools; also sold to individuals by direct mail, in retail outlets, and via in-home demonstrations set up in response to media advertising (no door-to-door)
ISBN 0-85229-571-5
Revised annually
Next scheduled revision: February 1994

Introduction

The New Encyclopaedia Britannica's organization is unique among the major scholarly encyclopedias on the market (its main competitors are COLLIER'S ENCYCLOPEDIA and ENCYCLOPEDIA AMERICANA). *New Britannica* is divided into three parts. A one-volume "Propaedia," or "Outline of Knowledge," serves, in the words of the publisher, "as a topical guide to the contents of the *Encyclopaedia Britannica*," allowing the user "to carry out an orderly plan of reading in any field of knowledge or learning chosen for study in some depth." (See *Special Features* for more on the "Propaedia.") The second part (volumes 1–12), called the "Micropaedia," or "Ready Reference," contains short articles on specific topics. It is, according to the publisher, "best suited for the reader who wishes to browse among the countless subjects in all fields of human learning and history in all times and places." The third part (volumes 13–29) is the "Macropaedia," or "Knowledge in Depth," which contains longer articles that allow the reader, as the user's guide that comes with the set states, to "study [a] subject thoroughly." The set also has a two-volume index.

The purpose of the set, according to a statement by the editors of an earlier (eleventh) edition, is to enable readers to "make a complete study of a given topic" and "a systematic survey of all departments of knowledge."

This review is based on the 1993 printing.

Authority

The Encyclopaedia Britannica is the oldest and largest English-language general reference encyclopedia on the market. The first edition was published in Edinburgh, Scotland (1768–1771). It has been published in the United States since 1901. The three-part organization (described above) was introduced with the publication of the fifteenth edition in 1974. Every article was newly written, and the word *New* was added to the title of the set. The new structure was criticized for, among other things, its lack of an index. An index was added in 1985 as part of major restructuring that included redistributing the number of volumes and entries between the "Micropaedia" and "Macropaedia."

New Britannica, like AMERICANA and COLLIER'S, has a roster of scholars and experts, who are listed at the end of the "Propaedia." It includes a board of editors; three advisory groups (a group of committees of academics from the world's leading universities, a library advisory committee, and a group of advisers on and contributors to the "Propaedia"); and more than 6,800 contributors to and authorities for the "Micropaedia" and "Macropaedia," who include leading academics and writers in science, history, humanities, and social sciences. The initials of contributors, found at the end of articles or sections of articles in the "Macropaedia," are keyed to the credits list in the "Propaedia." Most "Micropaedia" articles are unsigned.

Scope

The "Micropaedia," in a three-column-per-page format, contains 64,128 articles that average 300–400 words. The "Macropaedia," which uses a two-column format, contains 672 articles that run from 2 pages (**Beirut**) to 309 pages (**United States of America**).

The "Micropaedia" volumes serve as the specific-entry part of *New Britannica,* and the "Macropaedia" volumes serve as the broad-entry part. To indicate the allocation of space among topics in these two parts of the set, the **castle** article has 1½ columns in the "Micropaedia," including one photograph (**château** is a separate one-column "Micropaedia" entry that includes one photograph); **Impressionism** is a "Micropaedia" article two columns long, including one illustration; **Nelson Mandela** is covered in one column in the "Micropaedia," including a photograph; and **Elvis Presley** has slightly over one column in the "Micropaedia," including one photograph.

The New Encyclopaedia Britannica

ened paraffin that had itself outmoded the less refined spruce resin for chewing.

To begin the gum manufacturing process, blocks of gathered, hardened chicle are broken up, then screened and strained before mixed with other gum bases, sweeteners, and flavourings during cooking. The blended mass is passed between rollers onto a belt for cooling, after which it is sugared, cut, wrapped, and packaged.

After World War II various waxes, plastics, and synthetic rubber virtually replaced chicle in chewing gum manufacture. Artificially sweetened chewing gum found a wide market in the United States in the late 20th century, while mint remained the favourite among a wide variety of flavours.

chewing louse, also called BITING LOUSE, any of about 2,900 species of small (one to five millimetres), wingless insects of the suborder Mallophaga (sometimes considered an order) having chewing mouthparts, a flattened body, and shortened front legs used to transport food to the mouth. Chewing lice are worldwide in distribution. Colour ranges from white to black. The life cycle is spent on the feathers or hair of the host, though one genus lives in the throat pouches of pelicans and cormorants.

Chewing lice attack mainly birds (*see* bird louse) and some mammals (as Bovicola on cattle); they are not human parasites. Many species are host specific. One dog louse is the intermediate host of the dog tapeworm, and one rat louse transmits murine typhus among rats. Chewing lice that are parasitic on mammals feed on skin secretions, dried blood, fur, and skin debris. Although they are not blood suckers, chewing lice can cause serious discomfort. Symptoms of infestation include itching, loss of appetite, and lowered egg production in fowl. Infested animals are usually treated with a dust or dip.

chewing tobacco, tobacco used for chewing and appearing in a variety of forms, notably (1) "flat plug," a compressed rectangular cake of bright tobacco, sweetened lightly or not at all, (2) "navy," a flat rectangular cake of barley tobacco, highly flavoured with either licorice, rum, cinnamon, nutmeg, sugar, honey, or some other spice or sweetener, (3) "twist," tough, dark tobacco rolled and braided into ropes, (4) "fine-cut," shredded, stripped leaf, not compressed, of expensive blend, and (5) "scrap," cigar by-products consisting of loose leaf ends and clippings.

Tobacco chewing was common among certain American Indian groups. After 1815 it became almost a distinctive mode of tobacco usage in the United States, replacing pipe smoking. Partly the switch was a chauvinistic reaction against European snuff-taking and pipe-smoking; partly it was a matter of convenience for pioneering Americans on the move, since chewing was easier than lighting up a cumbersome pipe. The symbol of the change was the spittoon or cuspidor, which became a necessity of 19th-century America. Manufacturing statistics are revealing: of 348 tobacco factories listed by the 1860 census for Virginia and North Carolina, 335 concentrated wholly on chewing tobacco, and only 6 others even bothered with smoking tobacco as a sideline, using scraps from plug production.

The rising popularity of manufactured cigarettes by the beginning of the 20th century spelled the decline of chewing tobacco. After World War I, plug-taking fell off abruptly.

chewink, bird species also known as the rufous-sided towhee. *See* towhee.

Chewtonian Stage, division of time within the Ordovician Period in Australia and New Zealand (the Ordovician Period began about 505 million years ago and lasted about 67 million years). The Chewtonian Stage follows the Bendigonian Stage and precedes the Castlemainian Stage. Several zones, shorter spans of time, are recognized within the Chewtonian Stage and are based upon the vertical ranges of several species of fossil graptolites of the genera *Didymograptus* and *Tetragraptus.* These forms allow correlations to be made with rocks in North America and Europe.

Cheyenne, North American Plains Indian people of Algonkian stock who inhabited the regions around the Platte and Arkansas rivers during the 19th century. Before 1700 the home of the Cheyenne was in central Minnesota, where they farmed, hunted, gathered wild rice, and made pottery. They later occupied a village of earth lodges on the Cheyenne River in North Dakota; it was probably during this period that they acquired horses and be-

Wolf Robe, Southern Cheyenne Indian, photographed by De Lancey Gill, 1909
By courtesy of the Smithsonian Institution, National Anthropological Archives, Washington, D.C.

came more dependent on the buffalo for food. After the town was destroyed by the Ojibwa (Chippewa), the Cheyenne settled along the Missouri River near the Mandan and Arikara Indians. Toward the close of the 18th century, smallpox and the aggression of the Dakota decimated the village tribes at the same time that the horse and gun were becoming generally available in the northeastern plains. The Cheyenne moved farther west to the area of the Black Hills, where they developed their unique version of the tepee-dwelling nomadic Plains culture and gave up agriculture and pottery. During the early 19th century, they migrated to the headwaters of the Platte River. In 1832 a large segment of the tribe established itself along the Arkansas River, thus dividing the tribe into northern and southern branches. This division was made permanent in the First Treaty of Ft. Laramie with the U.S. in 1851.

Cheyenne religion recognized two principal deities, the Wise One Above and a god who lived beneath the ground. In addition four spirits lived at the points of the compass. The Cheyenne were among the Plains tribes who performed the sun dance in its most elaborate form. They placed heavy emphasis on visions in which an animal spirit adopted the individual and bestowed special powers upon him so long as he observed some prescribed law or practice. Their most venerated objects, contained in a sacred bundle, were a hat made from the skin and hair of a buffalo cow and four arrows—two painted for hunting and two for battle. These objects were carried in war to insure success over the enemy.

The Cheyenne were organized in 10 major bands governed by a council of 44 chiefs and 7 military societies, of which the Dog Soldiers society was the most powerful and aggressive. There were also social, dance, medicine, and shamanistic societies.

The Cheyenne fought constantly with the Kiowa until 1840, when a lasting peace was established between them. From 1857 to 1879 the Cheyenne were embroiled in raids and wars with the whites. They began raiding white settlements and posts on a wide front after Black Kettle's peaceful village was massacred on Sand Creek. In the Treaty of Medicine Lodge (1867), the southern Cheyenne were assigned a reservation in Oklahoma but settled there only after 1875. After Custer's attack on the Washita River village in 1868, the southern Cheyenne were fairly peaceful until 1874–75, when they joined in the general uprisings of the southern Plains tribes. The northern Cheyenne joined the Dakota in the Battle of the Little Bighorn in 1876. In the late 20th century there were about 2,000 northern Cheyenne on the Tongue River Indian Reservation in southeastern Montana and more than 3,000 intermingled among southern Cheyenne and Arapaho in Oklahoma.

Cheyenne, capital (since 1869) and largest city of Wyoming, U.S., and seat of Laramie county, in the southeastern corner of the state, on Crow Creek, 49 mi (79 km) east of Laramie city; it sprawls over high prairie that slopes westward to the Laramie Mountains. Squatters arriving in 1867 just ahead of the Union Pacific Railroad named the place for the Cheyenne Indians; they were removed from the railroad's land grant by federal troops. In the 1870s the town became an outfitting point for the Black Hills goldfields to the northeast and a major shipping point for cattle from Texas. Its own grazing lands became famed for Hereford herds and wealthy cattle barons. Peopled by gunmen, gamblers, and transients, Cheyenne's reputation worsened during the days of the Vigilantes and the war between cattlemen and sheepmen.

Now a trade and distribution centre for the middle Rocky Mountain region, its major economic activities include transportation, oil, timber, livestock interests, chemicals, plastics,

State Capitol, Cheyenne, Wyo.
Milt and Joan Mann from CameraMann

tourism, and governmental activities. Ft. D.A. Russell (1867) became Ft. Francis E. Warren in 1930 and as an Air Force base was designated (1957) as headquarters for the nation's first Atlas intercontinental ballistic missile base. The State Capitol with its lantern-type cupola atop a 145-ft (44-m) dome displays Western murals within. The Supreme Court Building houses the state museum. Laramie County Community College was opened (1968) in Cheyenne. Frontier Days, featuring one of America's oldest and largest rodeos, is a six-day celebration held each July, recalling the spirit of the Wild West and the cattle kingdom days. Inc. 1867. Pop. (1990) city, 50,008; Cheyenne MSA, 73,-142.

Cheyenne River, river, formed by the confluence of South Fork and Beaver Creek in Fall River County, South Dakota, U.S., flowing northeast across the state to join the Missouri River at the Cheyenne River Indian Reservation, north of Pierre. The 527-mi (848-km) river drains 25,000 sq mi (64,750 sq km). Angostura Dam, begun in 1946 as part of the

① Main entry words printed in boldface

② Cross-reference

③ Illustrations include historical and current photographs

④ Caption

⑤ Cross-reference entry

⑥ Page number and guide words

⑦ Measurements given in both standard and metric systems

Hamlet, the play, which is not an article in the "Micropaedia," has its major reference in the 19½-page **Shakespeare** article in the "Macropaedia," where it is given almost one column. **Mexico** has almost 2 pages in the "Micropaedia," including one map; the "Macropaedia" **Mexico** article is 24 pages long, including two maps and one photograph. The **tyrannosaur** "Micropaedia" article is 36 lines plus a photograph, and the topic is discussed in the 16-page **dinosaurs** article in the "Macropaedia," where it is given 6 lines and other intermittent mentions.

The short-entry format of the "Micropaedia" allows *New Britannica* to contain articles on many topics that are not articles in AMERICANA or COLLIER'S. However, some "Micropaedia" articles are too sketchy to be helpful without reading a related "Macropaedia" article, and the reader may need to read more than one "Macropaedia" article to get the total picture of a topic. Also, in many cases, there is overlap between related "Micropaedia" and "Macropaedia" articles.

Examination of a random 50-page sample of the "Micropaedia" (volume 7, pages 290–340), which included 294 entries, indicates that *New Britannica* has broad coverage of the humanities (including history) (40 percent of the entries), geography (25 percent), science (18 percent), and social sciences (17 percent). Of these, 42 percent were biographies. The articles in this sample show good coverage of both historical and modern-day topics and people. *New Britannica*'s coverage of important women from all eras, from Li Ch'ing-chao (twelfth century) to Rita Levi-Montalcini (twentieth century), is also noteworthy.

Although published in the United States since 1901, *New Britannica* has broad coverage of international topics. Of 130 articles in a 25-page sample ("Micropaedia," volume 3, pages 440–465), 74 (57 percent) were non-American. A distinctly British flair is noted in the high percentage of British topics (20 percent) in the sample. A British bias is also shown by the use of British spellings such as *behaviour* and *colour;* in addition, such items as tables of prime ministers of Great Britain, Canada, and Australia are included, whereas tables of governors of American states (a feature in both AMERICANA and COLLIER'S) are omitted.

Currency

New Britannica is updated annually. According to the publisher, more than 10 percent of the pages are opened up for revision each year. The **Union of the Soviet Socialist Republics** articles (in both the "Macropaedia" and "Micropaedia") are updated to the breakup of the Soviet Union in December 1991, as are discussions of the former constituent republics. The effects of the breakup on the economy, government, and so on are well integrated within those articles. Related articles such as "Micropaedia" articles on **Mikhail Gorbachev** and **Boris Yeltsin** also have been updated to include the breakup. Occasionally, however, references to the Soviet Union and to West Germany appear in articles unrelated to the current political situations.

The upheaval in Yugoslavia and realignment of its borders are covered through April 1992, and the independence of the country's former republics is noted in their respective articles or sections of articles in which they are discussed. The 1990–1991 Persian Gulf War is covered in the **international relations** "Macropaedia" article and has its own "Micropaedia" article of about one column; both articles include discussion of the war's aftermath.

Many articles, however, are updated only to the mid-1980s, and many bibliographies feature entries no later than the mid-1980s. Sometimes, in articles in both the "Micropaedia" and "Macropaedia," particularly biographies and articles on countries and sports, the reader is referred to the *Britannica World Data Annual* for up-to-date coverage. Such references will be unhelpful when they refer to the "Book of the Year" section of a previous year's annual that does not accompany the 1993 printing.

The currency of the set is sometimes inconsistent in related articles. For example, the **Bill Clinton** "Micropaedia" article indicates that he is president of the United States, but the **United States of America** "Macropaedia" article stops with the Bush administration, as does the **international relations** "Macropaedia" article. The latter article also stops before the disintegration of the U.S.S.R. The **exploration** article in the "Macropaedia" mentions the Magellan space probe launched in 1989 only as the "Venus Radar Mapper" that is being constructed, whereas in the **solar system** "Macropaedia" article it is given its current name and explained. The focusing problems experienced by the Hubble Space Telescope are mentioned in the **telescopes** "Macropaedia" article but not in the **exploration** article. The Norplant contraceptive technique is mentioned in the **contraception** article in the "Micropaedia" but not in the outdated "Macropaedia" **birth control** article.

Accuracy

New Britannica has long been respected as an accurate source of information. The use of more than 6,800 learned experts to write articles throughout the work's history contributes to that reputation. The **cancer** article is well written, with clear definitions and extensive descriptions of processes and outcomes. The only flaw is one of currency: the sections on statistics, causes, and therapies need updating.

The **Henry VIII** "Micropaedia" article, written in part by the greatest living Tudor political historian, is comprehensible, comprehensive, vivid, and witty. The author presents a serious, well-balanced view of both international and domestic policies that is central to recent study by professional historians.

The **House of Representatives** "Micropaedia" article contains more important facts than do much longer entries in other multivolume encyclopedias. It is factually accurate, and the few interpretive statements are supported by scholarly research. Not covered, however, in a discussion of partisanship are the notable long-term historical patterns of waxing and waning party strength.

The **oxygen** article in the "Micropaedia" is accurate, well written, and comprehensive. The **comet** "Macropaedia" article is a most comprehensive source, more complete and inclusive than some treatises devoted solely to the topic.

Clarity

The tone of the *New Britannica* is scholarly, and the reading level is generally high, suited to college and graduate students and well-educated general readers. To grasp most topics, the reader would need to possess some familiarity with the subject because technical and specialized terms are usually not defined. The idiosyncratic writing styles, particularly of some "Macropaedia" articles, may challenge a reader's comprehension.

The first two paragraphs from the "Micropaedia" article *Titanic* indicate the high reading level, detailed content, and engaging style typical of *New Britannica*. It should be noted, however, that because of the nontechnical nature of this topic, the article is not as difficult to comprehend as others in the set.

> **Titanic,** British luxury passenger liner that sank on April 14–15, 1912, en route to New York City from Southampton, Eng., during its maiden voyage. The vessel sank with a loss of about 1,515 lives at a point about 400 miles (640 km) south of Newfoundland.
>
> The great ship, at that time the largest and most luxurious afloat, had a double-bottomed hull that was divided into 16 watertight compartments. Because four of these could be flooded without endangering the liner's buoyancy, it was considered unsinkable. Shortly before midnight on April 14, the ship collided with an iceberg; five of its watertight compartments were ruptured, causing the ship to sink at 2:20 AM April 15. Inquiries held in the United States and Great Britain alleged that the Leyland liner *Californian,* which was less than 20 miles (32 km) away all night, could have aided the stricken vessel had its radio operator been on duty and thereby received the *Titanic*'s distress signals. Only the arrival of the Cunard liner *Carpathia* 1 hour and 20 minutes after the *Titanic* went down prevented further loss of life in the icy waters.

Objectivity

Overall, *Britannica* "Micropaedia" articles present facts in a straightforward way, usually noting when theory or opinion is being presented. In the "Macropaedia," where articles are written in essay format, contributors often state opinions. However, these opinions are usually supported by scholarly investigation and thought. The reader should be aware of the "Macropaedia" style, however, in order to discern fact from opinion.

The **AIDS** article in the "Micropaedia" and the discussion of AIDS in the "Macropaedia" under **infectious diseases** both mention the need for education and behavior changes to lower incidence rates. Not discussed are issues of privacy, treatment availability, or funding. The **capital punishment** "Micropaedia" article lists without comment the reasoning of both those who favor and those who oppose the death penalty. The **crime and punishment** "Macropaedia" article discusses only the history of capital punishment, not the pros and cons.

The **Northern Ireland** "Micropaedia" article discusses problems between Catholics and Protestants without comment. The "Micropaedia" coverage (in the **United Kingdom** article) is evenhanded for the most part: only mentions of the Protestants as "intrusive" and of the "glaring inequities" imposed on Catholics hint at the contributor's possible leaning.

The problems caused by the breakdown of the ozone layer and possible solutions are discussed in the **ozonosphere** and **chlorofluorocarbon** "Micropaedia" articles. The **atmosphere** article in the "Macropaedia" presents a detailed discussion of research on the effects of different gases on stratospheric ozone and concludes with the caution that the annual drop in the level of ozone in Antarctica "serves as a powerful warning that current scientific understanding of the stratosphere is still rudimentary."

The treatment of the topic of nuclear reactors in the **energy conversion** "Macropaedia" article is perhaps the least evenhanded of the articles reviewed for objectivity. The contributor, who coauthored *Nuclear Energy: A Sensible Alternative,* leaves the reader with the impression that he believes nuclear power is safe, yet concrete proof of that is elusive in the article.

Accessibility

The unique three-part organization of *New Britannica* may impede accessibility because it does not have the familiar configuration of AMERICANA, COLLIER'S, or other traditional sets. In addition, no instruction is given within the set on how to use the "Macropaedia." For example, unless the user hunts for or stumbles across the list of advisers and contributors at the back of the "Propaedia," he or she would not know what the initials after articles refer to.

The user may be further frustrated because some "Micropaedia" articles such as **computer** and **spacecraft** are so brief as to be unhelpful, whereas some "Macropaedia" articles offer the greatest benefit when read in their entirety. These in-depth articles contain few charts, tables, or other visual aids to help the reader see facts quickly.

The "Micropaedia" and the "Macropaedia" are both alphabetized according to the word-by-word principle. The order of person, place, and thing is used when spellings are identical. Guide words indicate the first and last entry on each two-page spread. The entry words in the "Micropaedia" are logical and usually those that would be chosen by the majority of readers. Entry names in the "Macropaedia" are very often so broad (for example, **philosophies of the branches of knowledge** and **European history and culture**) that they would not be typically chosen. For this reason, the index is indispensable (see below).

Entry titles in the "Micropaedia" are printed in boldface type. Some "Micropaedia" articles have subheads in italic type. These are difficult to locate because they are set in the same type size as the main text. "Macropaedia" articles, each of which begins on a new page, start with an overview and an outline of the contents of the article. "Macropaedia" articles have section heads and several levels of subheads. A helpful feature in "Macropaedia" articles is the use of marginal phrases keyed to the topic discussed in a paragraph or section.

In the "Micropaedia," 16,766 cross-references are used within entries and as separate entries. They refer the reader to other entries in the "Micropaedia," to articles in the "Macropaedia," and to sections in the "Propaedia" that contain lists of related articles. The "Macropaedia" has 16,934 cross-references. These include references to sections in the "Propaedia" and to other "Macropaedia" articles. The cross-references in both the "Micropaedia" and "Macropaedia" amount to about one per page, another reason why the index is indispensable.

The two-volume index contains 228,274 boldface entries and 474,675 subentries. Some index entries are *see* and *see also* references. Index entries are identified by volume number, page number, and column number. Columns are identified by an *a* (top) or *b* (bottom). Index entries are annotated in parentheses. When an entry has its own "Micropaedia" article and its own "Macropaedia" article or main section of article, the pages for each are identified. Illustrations and maps (and occasionally tables), as well as "Propaedia" sections, are indexed also.

Special Features

A special feature of *New Britannica* is the "Propaedia" volume, which is provided as a "comprehensive and detailed study guide" for the encyclopedia's users. It is a general and systematic topical, rather than alphabetical, presentation of subjects covered in the set. Subject categories are presented in outline form. At the end of each section of the outline, there are lists of related articles in the "Micropaedia" and "Macropaedia." Biographies related to each section are also listed. The "Propaedia" is meant to complement the alphabetically organized "Micropaedia," "Macropaedia," and index, but it will probably be used only by readers who wish to study a field in depth and who want to take the time to learn to use the volume.

The illustration program includes photographs, maps, diagrams, charts, graphs, and tables. Illustrations in the "Micropaedia," many of which are uninteresting head shots, are usually small; photographs of items such as paintings, flora and fauna, and oriental rugs particularly suffer as they are usually very small and often in black and white; maps in this part are often just small locator maps. Illustrations in the "Macropaedia" are larger and include color plates. In general, the color reproduction is of high quality. Diagrams, charts, and graphs are easy to read. Maps, even those in black and white, are beautifully executed; the color maps are especially clear, easy to read, and informative. However, *New Britannica*, which is larger than both AMERICANA and COLLIER'S, has fewer maps than either of those sets.

New Britannica presents annotated bibliographies after all "Macropaedia" articles and after a few "Micropaedia" articles. They are presented in paragraph form and are sometimes divided by topic. The references are not organized in an easy-to-access way (for example, by year or in alphabetical order). This makes it necessary to read the whole list, and some of the references are very long. The bibliographies are geared to the educated user and include foreign-language titles. For the most part, the bibliographies contain very few recent titles: a spot check revealed no titles published after 1980.

Format

New Britannica is a 32-volume encyclopedia that, like AMERICANA and COLLIER'S, uses the split-letter system. The "Propaedia" and the index are unnumbered volumes. Volumes range in length from 800 to 1,224 pages. The "Micropaedia" is in a three-column format, and the "Macropaedia" is arranged in two columns per page. Although the typeface is relatively small and (especially in the "Macropaedia") text may run unbroken for several pages, the text is easy to read.

Summary

For another opinion regarding the 1993 printing of *The New Encyclopaedia Britannica,* see *Booklist (Reference Books Bulletin),* September 15, 1993, page 182.

The New Encyclopaedia Britannica is the most scholarly and comprehensive general reference encyclopedia on the market. With its high reading and comprehension levels, the set will appeal to well-educated readers who wish to study a topic in depth and comprehensively and who do not need to locate a precise fact at a glance. The *New Britannica*'s treatment of some topics, such as British history, is unparalleled. Articles are sometimes written by the foremost experts in their fields, and the information is exceptionally thorough, well presented, and international in scope.

The New Encyclopaedia Britannica's chief weaknesses lie in its presentation and currency. The three-part format ("Propaedia," "Micropaedia," and "Macropaedia") makes fact-finding difficult and often requires readers to retrieve several volumes to obtain complete coverage of a topic. The indispensable index, fortunately, is thorough and reliable.

Illustrations in the "Micropaedia" are small, mostly black and white, and of limited value. *The New Encyclopaedia Britannica* can be intimidating: pages are dense with text, and the level of writing, especially in the science- and technology-related articles of the "Macropaedia," is often beyond the average reader's comprehension level. In addition, parts of *The New Encyclopaedia Britannica,* particularly the bibliographies, are current only to the early 1980s.

Despite its shortcomings, this work should be one of the cornerstones of any academic or large public library reference collection. High schools may want to select an encyclopedia set with a more accessible writing style, such as COLLIER'S ENCYCLOPEDIA or the ENCYCLOPEDIA AMERICANA. Libraries owning earlier editions of *New Britannica* should at the very least ensure that each year's annual supplement is available with the set. They should also keep in mind that a substantial number of the entries in *New Britannica* are updated annually, making periodic replacement of the set a necessity.

New Standard Encyclopedia

Facts at a Glance

Full title: **New Standard Encyclopedia**
Publisher: Standard Educational Corporation
Editor: Douglas W. Downey, Editor-in-Chief
Number of contributors: 630
Edition reviewed: © 1993

Number of volumes: 20
Number of articles: 17,456
Number of pages: 10,292
Number of words: 6.4 million
Number of cross-references: 40,000
Number of index entries: 103,000
Number of maps: 636
Number of illustrations: 12,000
Intended readership: middle school to adult
Trim size: 6½" × 9¼"
Binding: hardcover

Price: $549.99 plus $20 shipping for libraries and schools; home prices are determined by individual distributors
Sold directly to libraries and schools; sold to individuals by direct mail and door-to-door
ISBN 0-87392-198-4
Revised annually

Introduction

The *New Standard Encyclopedia* is a 20-volume work designed, according to the editor's foreword, "to provide as much information of interest to the general reader as is possible within an illustrated set selling for a moderate price. . . . For advanced students and for adults who need detailed information, this encyclopedia serves as a general source to consult before seeking out more specialized and advanced works." In short, *New Standard* is conceived as a general reference work for the layperson whose interests may be wide-ranging but not necessarily scholarly. This review is based on the 1993 printing of the work, the version current at the time of the review.

Authority

The Standard Educational Corporation (formerly the Standard Educational Society) has published *New Standard* since 1930. The set originated from the 5-volume *Aiton's Encyclopedia,* which appeared in 1910. *New Standard* reached its present 20 volumes in 1989, adding for the first time a separate index. The Standard Educational Corporation also publishes a 10-volume set for children called *Child Horizons* and an annual supplement to *New Standard* called *World Progress Yearbook.*

Most of the articles are written and edited by an in-house editorial staff, who, according to the foreword, "are qualified in their fields by education and experience and are trained in the techniques of encyclopedia writing." This staff works under the experienced direction of Douglas W. Downey, the editor-in-chief since 1964. A five-member editorial advisory board of educators and librarians develops policies concerning the encyclopedia's overall content, style, and approach.

The foreword notes that each article is reviewed by five or more persons, at least one of whom is a "recognized authority in the field being covered." Volume 1 lists 630 "contributors, consultants, advisers, and authenticators" ("authenticator" describes the subject specialist who is responsible for an article's accuracy) along with their credentials and affiliations and the article titles or general subject areas to which they contributed. The list is not particularly strong. Many of these people are employed by corporate public relations departments, professional organizations, or government agencies. Only a very small number of the consultants (such as former astronaut Neil Armstrong and linguist Mario Pei) have achieved wide recognition outside their fields of specialization. Moreover, a number of these individuals (for example, J. Edgar Hoover, Louis Leakey) are deceased. About 75 percent of the consultants are men.

Apart from the subject notations given in the list of consultants, it is difficult to trace responsibility for individual articles. As the publisher notes, "Since each article is the work of several persons, the articles are not signed."

New Standard Encyclopedia

NIGHT — NIGHTHAWK

Babangida became president and promised a return to civilian rule. Attempts to establish a new democratic constitution in 1989 foundered due to conflict between Moslems and Christians, and because of violent clashes between the two groups during 1991-92, Babangida maintained firm military rule.

See also FLAG (color page); IBADAN; LAGOS; MONEY (table); NIGER RIVER.

Books about Nigeria
Decalo, Samuel. *Historical Dictionary of Nigeria*, 2nd edition (Scarecrow Press, 1989).
Isichei, E. A. *A History of Nigeria* (Longman, 1983).
Shaw, T. M., and J. O. Ihonvbere. *Nigeria: the Illusions of Power* (Westview Press, 1992).
For Younger Readers
Bailey, Donna, and Anna Sproule. *Nigeria* (Steck-Vaughn, 1990).
Schultz, J. F. *Nigeria in Pictures* (Lerner, 1988).

Night, the period of darkness caused by the disappearance of the sun below the horizon. The limits of night are not firmly defined. Night can be considered as the period from sunset to sunrise, or as the period from the end of evening twilight to the beginning of morning twilight. (For the duration of twilight, see TWILIGHT.) The length of night in most parts of the world changes with the seasons. (See SEASONS.)

For humans, night is a period of natural rest, but many other animals are more active by night than by day. Many insects, fishes, reptiles, birds, and mammals have eyes that are adapted to faint night light.

See also DAY.

Night Blindness, or **Nyctalopia,** nĭk′-tȧ-lō′pĭ-ȧ, the inability to see normally in dim light. It may be caused by disease or a congenital defect, but more often is caused by lack of sufficient vitamin A in the diet. Night blindness due to lack of vitamin A may be corrected by taking cod-liver oil or other fish oils high in vitamin A content.

Night Crawler. See EARTHWORM.

Night Heron, hĕr′ŭn, a heron that feeds at dusk and at night, remaining hidden during the day. Night herons are about 24 inches (60 cm) long. They have stockier bodies than other herons, and shorter necks and legs. The *black-crowned night heron* is found in temperate and tropical regions throughout the world. It is blackish green on top of its head and on its back. It has gray wings and tail, and a white breast. There are two long white plumes on its nape. The

Leonard Lee Rue III/Tom Stack & Assoc.
Yellow-crowned Night Heron

yellow-crowned night heron breeds in the central and eastern United States and winters south to northern South America. It is bluish gray, with yellowish-white crown and plumes.

Night herons belong to the family Ardeidae. The black-crowned night heron is *Nycticorax nycticorax;* the yellow-crowned, *Nyctanassa violacea.*

Night-blooming Cereus. See CACTUS, subtitle *Kinds and Uses of Cactus.*

Nighthawk, an American bird of the goatsucker, or nightjar, family. Despite the name, it is not a true hawk. Nighthawks are mottled grayish-brown, with white bands across their long, pointed wings. Their tails are slightly forked. They feed on insects, usually flying after their prey at dusk. The female lays two brown-speckled white eggs on the bare ground or on a flat roof.

Male Common Nighthawk
Dr. E. R. Degginger

N-317

Page shown at 77% of actual size

❶ Guide words indicate the first and last entries on the page
❷ Cross-references
❸ Bibliography
❹ Main entry words printed in boldface
❺ Pronunciations given for foreign or unusual entry words
❻ Cross-reference entry
❼ Measurements given in both standard and metric systems
❽ Italics indicate that a term is defined in context
❾ Illustration
❿ Caption
⓫ Endnotes to articles on flora and fauna give scientific classifications

Scope

The *New Standard Encyclopedia* contains 17,456 articles, in addition to some 13,600 "See" entries that serve solely as cross-references. The average article length is about 370 words, though actual article length varies considerably. As a rule, however, the majority of articles are shorter than the 370-word average.

As an indication of how space is apportioned among different subjects, **Mexico** receives 17 pages, including maps, photographs, charts, and bibliography. **Castle** receives over a page, including a photograph and two diagrams. **Hamlet** is over one-half page. The biographical entries tend to be shorter: **Nelson Mandela** receives 23 lines and **Elvis Presley** 19 lines. The brief coverage of *tyrannosaurus* is the only surprise: the topic is discussed in 8 lines of the **dinosaur** article, which itself totals four pages (including illustrations and bibliography).

New Standard covers a wide range of basic topics in all disciplines. The encyclopedia is strongest in traditional curriculum areas. It is also solid in the realm of general and practical knowledge—about household pets, using a library, or how a telescope works, for example. *New Standard* is weakest in the social sciences, including social history, contemporary society and social trends, world cultures, and psychology. In general, the work leans more toward historical and traditional subjects and away from contemporary issues.

The publisher does not provide information about its relative coverage of different disciplines. After reviewing a randomly selected 50-page sample, we estimate the following breakdown: humanities and the arts (including history and religion), 39 percent; science and technology, 23 percent; geography, 20 percent; social sciences, 11 percent; popular culture, 7 percent. About 30 percent of the articles are biographical.

The *New Standard Encyclopedia* covers international topics reasonably well, although overall the work is weighted toward North America and Western culture. Entries on non-U.S. topics in a randomly selected 25-page sample (pages R-165–R-190) include **Rennes** (France), film director **Jean Renoir,** painter **Pierre Auguste Renoir, war reparations,** Italian composer **Ottorino Respighi,** the **Restigouche River** (in Canada), **Restoration** (in English and French history), **Réunion** (island possession of France), **Baron von Reuter,** and the **Reuters** news agency.

A deliberate focus on U.S. states and Canadian provinces tilts coverage in that direction, so that the entry **Kentucky,** at 14 pages, is almost twice as long as that for **Korea.** The treatment of major nations (for example, **France, Germany, Russia, China,** and **India**) may exceed 20 pages; **Brazil** receives about 12 pages, and the entries **Indonesia, Nigeria,** and **Zaire** range from 4 to 6 pages.

Coverage of ways of life around the world (not a strong point in many general encyclopedias) is largely absent from *New Standard.* This is not the work to consult, for example, to learn what people eat in Morocco or how the Indians in Ecuador live. General survey articles vary as to their multicultural perspective. Whereas **dance** encompasses dance forms from around the world, the discussions in **painting** and **music** are limited mainly to Western forms. This is also the case with **literature** and **philosophy,** but these topics are supplemented by specific entries such as **literature, African** and **Oriental philosophy.**

Currency

The *New Standard Encyclopedia* is revised annually; according to the publisher, 20 to 30 percent of the pages are updated in some way. The foreword notes that the revision policy involves three simultaneous approaches. First, "Maps, tables, and articles on contemporary subjects . . . are revised whenever significant new information becomes available. Graphs, bibliographies, and statistics are reviewed for revision at least once every four or five years." Second, major sections within volumes are reviewed annually and the articles revised as necessary to "assure a contemporary approach." Third, groups of related articles are reviewed periodically as a unit.

The 1993 printing appears to reflect this policy; consequently, spot checks reveal some areas to be more current than others. Although several articles are new or were fully revised for this edition, most updating seems to be in the form of new figures (for example, recent death dates), names and dates added to tables (for example, Academy Award winners), and a sentence or two added to the ends of articles.

Major contemporary events receive the most thorough attention and the most up-to-date facts. The entry on **Bill Clinton** describes his background and the 1992 election. **Lithuania** and **Russia** are both very current, the latter including events up to the signing of a new union treaty in 1992. The entry **Czechoslovakia** mentions the agreement (in April 1992) to dissolve the federation, although the map does not show the boundaries of the two republics.

The treatment of a more difficult topic—the former Yugoslavia—is uneven and sometimes confusing. **Yugoslavia,** as the entry itself notes, describes the country as it existed before the civil war; revisions reflecting the present situation have been made only at the beginning and end of the article. The map, too, has not been updated (nor has the one in **Balkan states**); the small inset showing the constituent republics is unhelpful. Entries for the individual republics—with the exception of **Montenegro**—have been updated. Several articles note that Macedonia's declaration of independence in

1991 was not recognized internationally, but nowhere does the set explain why.

Many other contemporary subjects are current to the 1990s. **Persian Gulf War** covers events of the war and its immediate aftermath, mentioning the Kuwait oil-well fires and the uprisings of Kurds and Shiites in Iraq. The entry **telescope** describes the Hubble telescope and its problems and notes that, although it is still useful, the optical system will have to be corrected to be fully functional. On the other hand, **Mexico** makes no mention of the 1991 elections, NAFTA, or *maquiladoras.*

Scattered throughout the set are articles that are basically factual but lack the latest perspectives and a fresh approach. Typical of this is **food and nutrition,** which, while not inaccurate, does not mention the food pyramid nor changes in recommended servings in the text and accompanying "Daily Food Guide" table, although the table "Recommended Daily Dietary Allowances" does list the most current guidance on vitamins and minerals.

The editorial policy on population figures warrants some comment. The foreword indicates that statistics come from "primary sources or from government or United Nations agencies." An appendix in volume 19 lists the year and source of the population data used in the encyclopedia. Even when the official data is over a decade old—which is true for a significant number of countries on the list—the entries on individual countries and cities do not provide recent population estimates. The entries for each continent, however, give 1990 population estimates in chart form for most of their constituent countries. In the cases of nations experiencing rapid population growth (such as Iran and Mexico), the disparity is glaring.

Except for the few previously noted, the maps in *New Standard* are up-to-date. The proportion of color photographs (40 percent in the 1993 printing) continues to rise, giving the set an increasingly contemporary look. However, the currency of the photographs generally lags behind that of the text. Even excluding the numerous pictures of historical and biographical subjects, a noticeable number of the black-and-white photographs appear dated. This is especially true for somewhat obscure subjects (for example, **civil service, merchant marine, power shovel**), but examples can be found throughout.

Accuracy

As a basic reference, the *New Standard Encyclopedia* is reasonably accurate and reliable, a demonstration of careful writing, editing, and fact checking. The usually brief articles give a lucid overview of their subjects but often provide little more than the most rudimentary information. The main criticisms concerning accuracy, therefore, relate less to particular facts and figures than to matters of emphasis and omission.

The entry on **oxygen** is informative, carefully written, and essentially correct. **Comet** is also factually correct, but the range of this entry is limited. **Cancer** is brief but essentially sound; however, the statistics on cancer and the discussion of suspected causes and prevention require updating.

Henry VIII is well written, reliable, and accessible. Although it sticks mainly to the standard topics—Henry's marriages and the Reformation—the way the information is presented reveals a relatively sophisticated understanding of the subject. **Congress** provides an adequate, accurate account of the House of Representatives. For the law-making process, readers are referred to a section of the entry **Law;** perhaps for this reason, the article on Congress is short on congressional behavior and process and long on official constitutional provisions and rules.

Clarity

The clarity of its writing has always been a major strength of *New Standard.* The smooth, almost transparent, style and organization exemplify an expository prose particularly suited to the general reader. Younger readers will find the language accessible, although the set does not talk down to them. Specialized terms are defined as they occur in the text.

The **Titanic** entry, quoted here in its entirety, illustrates the style of a short entry:

> *Titanic,* a British ocean liner that sank on its maiden voyage in 1912, with a loss of at least 1,500 lives. The 882½-foot (269-m) *Titanic,* owned by the White Star Line, was the world's largest ship at that time and was considered unsinkable. It was speeding from England to New York with more than 2,200 people aboard, including many prominent persons, when on the night of April 14 it collided with an iceberg. The ship sank within three hours, about 400 miles (640 km) south of Newfoundland. (The ship was found at that location at a depth of some 13,000 feet [3,960 m] by a scientific expedition in 1985.)
>
> The *Titanic's* lifeboat capacity was slightly less than 1,200 (which, however, was more than regulations required) and in the confusion many boats were lowered half-filled. The liner's distress call was not picked up by the nearby *Californian,* whose wireless operator was asleep. The *Carpathia* heard the call, arrived shortly after the *Titanic* went down, and rescued more than 700 persons. Investigations led to strict rules for safety at sea and to iceberg patrols.

Objectivity

New Standard's writers are careful to avoid partiality. Typically they express controvertible assertions or viewpoints as the conclusions or opinions of abstract "authorities" or "experts." On the other hand, the writers draw conclusions or make assessments about historical events and personalities. The insightful summaries that begin longer historical entries are generally quite informative.

Controversial issues are often skimmed over or ignored. The space limitations inherent in a general encyclopedia and the traditional approach to topics are certainly factors. But the tendency may also reflect the facts that few of the consultants are academics (who may be abreast of the latest issues and perspectives) and that many are directly involved in the subject of their review. (See *Authority.*)

Whenever *New Standard* does confront controversial political and social issues, it does so evenhandedly and briefly, identifying the considerations on both sides but rarely exploring the reasoning or feelings behind them. **Capital punishment** is typical of this brief and factual treatment. The balanced, informative overview in **Ireland, Northern** is an example of a deeper approach. The brief discussion of the ozone layer in **Ozone** simply notes the effects of CFCs and the scientific studies revealing weakening spots in the layer.

The failure of the **AIDS** article to address the social complexities involved renders the entry superficial. It relates nothing about treatment availability, funding, or civil rights issues. The single statement on demographics reads, "AIDS occurs most frequently in male homosexuals, and also in intravenous drug users and hemophiliacs." While this statement may be true (ignoring current trends), it leaves a dated and dangerous impression.

Accessibility

An article in the front matter, "Suggestions on How to Use *New Standard Encyclopedia,*" with a section on "Finding What You Want Quickly," explains the arrangement of entries clearly and simply. Entries follow a word-by-word alphabetical arrangement. When several items have the same heading, they are arranged in order of persons, places, and things or ideas.

Entry headings are printed in boldface type. Guide words at the top of each page indicate the first and last entries on that page. Pagination starts over at page one with each new letter, not each volume. For example, pages D-50 and E-50 are both in volume 6 (*DE*), whereas page S-50 is in volume 15 (*S–Slu*) and page S-550 in volume 16 (*Sma–Sz*). This system may be confusing to some users.

The most significant change to the *New Standard Encyclopedia* since it was last reviewed in the first edition of this Buying Guide is the addition of a comprehensive index (volume 20), which contains 103,000 entries. Before the set was indexed, accessibility depended on an extensive network of 40,000 cross-references and 13,600 "See" entries. While these cross-references are still in place, the addition of an index makes the information in the set more accessible to the user.

The index is generally useful and reliable. Its opening pages explain how to use it, aided by a facsimile of sample entries. Illustrations are indexed, and the presence of bibliographies, maps, lists of related articles, and other features also is indicated. Identifiers are given for identical or unfamiliar entries.

Special Features

New Standard includes 993 bibliographies, located conveniently at the ends of the relevant articles. Many of these include a separate listing of materials aimed at readers in grades 4 to 8, a valuable feature. Although necessarily limited and selective, the bibliographies mostly include titles published in the 1980s and 1990s.

New Standard's illustrations are of varying quality. As noted in *Currency,* some of the black-and-white images are dated. These older photographs also tend to overrepresent white males as scientists or workers. The color photographs are much more balanced and appealing. The set's numerous drawings and diagrams, a mixture of two- and full-color, are clear and well thought out. The article **hologram** is illustrated with an actual hologram.

The quality of the 636 maps is also uneven, which may reflect an ongoing renovation of the map program. U.S. states have one- or two-page, full-color political maps, as do some nations. Articles on continents include political, physical, climate, vegetation, and population maps in color. Most maps, however, are two-color and often show little detail. The linework, combined with the limited use of color, can make it difficult to distinguish boundaries.

Format

The volumes of *New Standard* are organized by whole letters (the system also used by Academic American and World Book). Most volumes contain one or two letters, although *W–Z* are included in one volume, and *A, C,* and *S* are each split into two. Length of volumes ranges from 314 to 716 pages. The set is sturdily bound with bright red covers, and the books lie flat when opened on a desk.

The set's interior design is functional, and the printing and paper are of high quality. The text type, entry words, and subheads stand out clearly. The illustrations also reproduce well.

Summary

For other opinions, see D. A. Rothschild's review of the 1992 edition in *ARBA 93* and *Booklist (Reference Books Bulletin),* September 15, 1993, pages 182–183.

While the *New Standard Encyclopedia* is generally well written, its articles easy to comprehend, and its format easy to use, prospective purchasers should carefully consider its deficiencies in scope and currency. Families requiring a straightforward source of practical information may be satisfied with this set. On the other hand, they may find that such competing sets as FUNK & WAGNALLS (at a fraction of the cost) and WORLD BOOK (which costs more) will provide them with a somewhat more balanced and comprehensive overview of the same information.

Oxford Illustrated Encyclopedia

Facts at a Glance

Full title: **Oxford Illustrated Encyclopedia**
Publisher: Oxford University Press
Editors: Harry Judge, Series Editor; Anthony Toyne, Executive Editor
Number of contributors: more than 400
Edition reviewed: © 1993

Number of volumes: 9
Number of articles: 20,000
Number of pages: 3,376
Number of words: 2.4 million
Number of cross-references: 100,000 (reviewer estimate)
Number of index entries: 54,000 (reviewer estimate)
Number of illustrations: 2,800 (including maps); 50 percent in full-color
Intended readership: general audience, from student to adult
Trim size: 8½″ × 11″
Binding: hardcover

Price: $265
Sold directly to schools and libraries; also sold in bookstores
ISBN 0-19-869223-4
No stated revision policy

Introduction

The *Oxford Illustrated Encyclopedia* is a nine-volume, 3,376-page reference intended for a general audience. Each of the first eight volumes is arranged alphabetically around a broad subject, such as "The Arts" or "Invention and Technology"; the ninth volume contains the index to the entire set.

In the general preface, Series Editor Harry Judge states that the work

> is designed to be useful and to give pleasure to readers throughout the world. . . . Each volume has a clearly defined theme made plain in its title. . . . Nevertheless, taken together, the eight thematic volumes . . . provide a complete and reliable survey of human knowledge and achievement.

Authority

Unlike other multivolume encyclopedias reviewed in the Buying Guide, the *Oxford Illustrated Encyclopedia* was first published volume-by-volume over a period of several years. Volumes 1 and 2 of the work were first published in 1985, with successive volumes following in 1988 (volumes 3 and 4), 1990 (volume 5), 1992 (volumes 6, 7, and 8), and 1993 (volume 9). The work was revised, and all nine volumes were sold as a complete boxed set for the first time in 1993. Oxford University Press, the publisher of this work, has an excellent reputation worldwide for producing authoritative reference books, most notably the OXFORD ENGLISH DICTIONARY.

Each volume of this encyclopedia was developed under the supervision of an internationally known scholar. For example, geologist and Antarctic explorer Sir Vivian Fuchs serves as volume editor for volume 1, "The Physical World." Each volume editor in turn heads a team of expert contributors, who ensure that the articles are accurate, up-to-date, and accessible to a general audience. Although individual articles are not signed, the contributors for each volume are listed on the page opposite that volume's foreword. No mention is made, however, of their areas of specialization or the institutions with which they are affiliated.

Scope

The eight thematic volumes of this work cover the following areas of knowledge: Volume 1, "The Physical World"; Volume 2, "The Natural World"; Volume 3, "World History to 1800"; Volume 4, "World History from 1800 to the Present"; Volume 5, "The Arts"; Volume 6, "Invention and Technology"; Volume 7, "Peoples and Cultures"; and Volume 8, "The Universe." Volume 9, "Index and Ready Reference," contains a 44-page section of alphabetical entries covering important figures in religion and mythology; a 30-page ready-reference section containing tables on a variety of topics, such as chemical elements, world capitals, and British hallmarks; and a comprehensive index to all nine volumes.

By classifying the volumes by their general topics, it is possible to determine the weight the encyclopedia gives to various disciplines. Science and history receive the most coverage, with 32 percent and 26 percent of the pages in the encyclopedia, respectively. The rest of the work is devoted to the arts (16 percent), social sciences (13 percent), geography (12 percent), and religion and mythology (1 percent).

The series editor states in the general preface that efforts were made to "present a balanced picture of the forces that influence people in all corners of the globe." An examination of a randomly selected 25-page sample (pages 323–348, **notation** through **Picturesque** in Volume 5, "The Arts") revealed that the coverage was in-

142 *Encyclopedias, Atlases & Dictionaries*

Oxford Illustrated Encyclopedia

full-scale war, and assistance from Europe was thwarted. The war was ended by the Treaty of Ryswick (1697) and a truce in Maine (1699).

knighthood, the special honour bestowed upon a man by dubbing (when he is invested with the right to bear arms) or by admission to one of the orders of chivalry. In England the emergence of knighthood was slow (the Anglo-Saxon word *cniht* means 'servant'). In the late 11th and early 12th centuries, knights were the lowest tier of those who held land in return for military service. During the 12th century their economic and social status improved, as society became more complex, and the market in free land developed. They became involved in local administration, and the new orders of knights which emerged in Europe in the aftermath of the *Crusades helped to give them a distinct identity. First to appear were the military orders of the *Knights Hospitallers (c.1070), the Knights of the Sepulchre (1113), and the *Knights Templars (1118). Their potential for military colonization was best realized by the German Order of

The investiture of a **Knight Hospitaller**, a woodcut illustration from a history of the order published in Germany in 1496. Here the new knight kneels before the Grand Master. (Order of St John)

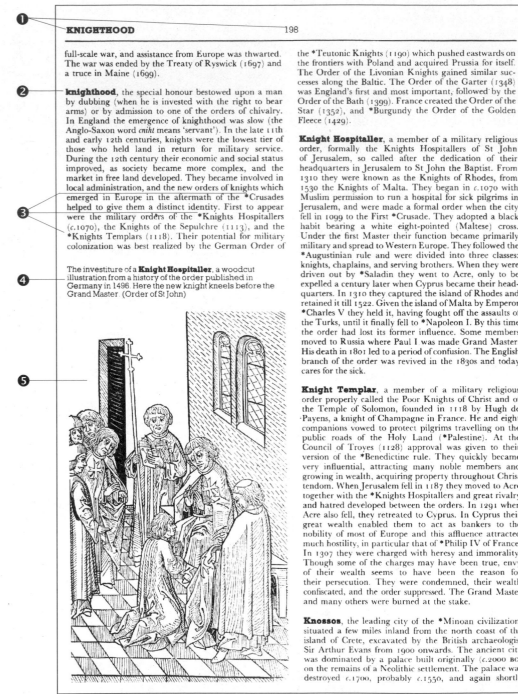

the *Teutonic Knights (1190) which pushed eastwards on the frontiers with Poland and acquired Prussia for itself. The Order of the Livonian Knights gained similar successes along the Baltic. The Order of the Garter (1348) was England's first and most important, followed by the Order of the Bath (1399). France created the Order of the Star (1352), and *Burgundy the Order of the Golden Fleece (1429).

Knight Hospitaller, a member of a military religious order, formally the Knights Hospitallers of St John of Jerusalem, so called after the dedication of their headquarters in Jerusalem to St John the Baptist. From 1310 they were known as the Knights of Rhodes, from 1530 the Knights of Malta. They began in c.1070 with Muslim permission to run a hospital for sick pilgrims in Jerusalem, and were made a formal order when the city fell in 1099 to the First *Crusade. They adopted a black habit bearing a white eight-pointed (Maltese) cross. Under the first Master their function became primarily military and spread to Western Europe. They followed the *Augustinian rule and were divided into three classes: knights, chaplains, and serving brothers. When they were driven out by *Saladin they went to Acre, only to be expelled a century later when Cyprus became their headquarters. In 1310 they captured the island of Rhodes and retained it till 1522. Given the island of Malta by Emperor *Charles V they held it, having fought off the assaults of the Turks, until it finally fell to *Napoleon I. By this time the order had lost its former influence. Some members moved to Russia where Paul I was made Grand Master. His death in 1801 led to a period of confusion. The English branch of the order was revived in the 1830s and today cares for the sick.

Knight Templar, a member of a military religious order properly called the Poor Knights of Christ and of the Temple of Solomon, founded in 1118 by Hugh de Payens, a knight of Champagne in France. He and eight companions vowed to protect pilgrims travelling on the public roads of the Holy Land (*Palestine). At the Council of Troyes (1128) approval was given to their version of the *Benedictine rule. They quickly became very influential, attracting many noble members and growing in wealth, acquiring property throughout Christendom. When Jerusalem fell in 1187 they moved to Acre together with the *Knights Hospitallers and great rivalry and hatred developed between the orders. In 1291 when Acre also fell, they retreated to Cyprus. In Cyprus their great wealth enabled them to act as bankers to the nobility of most of Europe and this affluence attracted much hostility, in particular that of *Philip IV of France. In 1307 they were charged with heresy and immorality. Though some of the charges may have been true, envy of their wealth seems to have been the reason for their persecution. They were condemned, their wealth confiscated, and the order suppressed. The Grand Master and many others were burned at the stake.

Knossos, the leading city of the *Minoan civilization, situated a few miles inland from the north coast of the island of Crete, excavated by the British archaeologist Sir Arthur Evans from 1900 onwards. The ancient city was dominated by a palace built originally (c.2000 BC) on the remains of a Neolithic settlement. The palace was destroyed c.1700, probably c.1550, and again shortly

Page shown at 68% of actual size.

❶ Guide word and page number
❷ Boldface main entry word
❸ Cross-references indicated by asterisks

❹ Caption mentions relevant entry in boldface type
❺ Black-and-white illustration

deed international. Of the 173 articles in the samples, 98 articles (nearly 57 percent) comprised subjects from areas of the world other than the United States, Great Britain, or Canada. Some of these articles include the Russian ballet dancer **Rudolf Nureyev; nyckelharpa,** a Swedish keyed fiddle; German-born French composer **Jacques Offenbach;** Greek **Orders of architecture;** Polish novelist **Eliza Orzeszkowa;** contemporary Senegalese novelist and film director **Sembène Ousmane;** the Indian beast-fables **Pañcatantra;** nineteenth-century Hungarian poet **Sándor Petöfi;** Spanish artist **Pablo Picasso;** and survey articles on **Oceanic music, Olmec art, Ottoman art, Pali literature, Persian literature,** and **Phoenician art.**

In the above 25-page sample, 72 entries (42 percent) are biographies, which places *Oxford* slightly higher in this area than most other multivolume encyclopedias.

The *Oxford Illustrated Encyclopedia* is a short-entry encyclopedia; according to the general preface, articles vary in length from 50 to 1,000 words. The brevity of the entries is apparent in the following standard set of entries: **castle** receives 40 lines of text plus a full page of illustrations; **Impressionism** receives 63 lines of text, a quarter-page illustration, and a 9-line caption; **Nelson Mandela** receives 31 lines of text; and **tyrannosaurus** receives 5 lines of text. *Hamlet* does not appear in the index; however, the play is mentioned in the **tragedy** article. Similarly, **Elvis Presley** does not merit an article, but the singer is mentioned under **rock music. Mexico,** which is given 3 different main articles and a tabular entry, receives 25 lines of text in volume 1 (geography), 21 lines in volume 3 (early history), 46 lines in volume 4 (later history), and over one-quarter page in the "Countries of the World" section in volume 7. In addition, many more specific articles such as **Central American and Mexican art** and **Mexican Revolution** can be found. These scattered articles exemplify the inherent weakness of the work's topical organization; the widespread entries force the reader to consult more than one volume in order to gain a general understanding of a topic.

Currency

As was discussed under the *Authority* section of this review, the *Oxford Illustrated Encyclopedia* was originally published volume-by-volume over a span of eight years, from 1985 to 1993. The earlier volumes were revised, with many current articles added and others updated to reflect recent world events, and the work was offered as a complete nine-volume boxed set in 1993. Unfortunately, the publisher does not have a stated revision policy for this work.

The 1993 boxed set, reviewed here, is very up-to-date. New articles include **Bill Clinton** and **Gulf War** in volume 4. The entry for the **Hubble space telescope** in volume 8 describes Hubble's post-launch problems and

is accompanied by a full-page color illustration. No entries were found, however, for *food pyramid* or *Frida Kahlo.*

The main articles on **Germany,** as well as related entries, have been updated to reflect the country's unification. The articles on **Yemen** have been similarly revised. The many articles on **Russia** and its neighboring countries in volume 1 (geography), volume 4 (current history), and volume 7 (peoples and cultures) also contain current information and statistics. Other recent world events are noted in the articles on **Czechoslovakia** and **Yugoslavia,** which describe the breakups of these countries.

Many of the maps and photographs in the work are historical, thereby avoided the issue of datedness. The more recent photographs do have a contemporary look, however. The illustration for **motor car** includes a drawing of a modern car with a caption that describes the new *crumple zones.*

Accuracy

Our subject consultants found varying degrees of accuracy in the *Oxford Illustrated Encyclopedia.* The astronomy expert ranked the entry on **comet** as one of the best among adult encyclopedias. The entry is accurate, informative, and clearly written, with an excellent illustration. Likewise, **House of Representatives** is thorough and accurate, discussing both the formal constitutional provisions for the House and its internal organizational structure. The article manages to note that committees "often display striking autonomy in their decisions," a useful observation that is missing from some multivolume references. The two articles on **oxygen** (and the related articles **oxidation number, oxidation state, oxides, oxidizing agents,** and **ozone**) were technically accurate. The only error was a statement in both **oxygen** articles that oxygen is the most abundant element on earth; in fact, it is the most abundant element in the earth's crust.

Our history consultant had mixed opinions about the **Henry VIII** entry. It shows a grasp of the larger political and international issues, and the passages on the annulment of his marriage to Catherine of Aragon and the establishment of the English church manage to convey an accurate picture without distortion in a short space. However, the author occasionally makes statements that might confuse a reader without background information; for example, "he remained conservative in doctrine, believing in Catholicism without the pope." In addition, there are no cross-references from the article about **Henry VIII** (page 163) to the genealogical table that lists the descent of the Tudors (page 362); nor does the **Henry VIII** article even mention the name *Tudor.*

The **cancer and cancer therapy** articles tend to focus on minute details and miss the big picture. The first paragraph of the first article, for example, should be made more general and ascribe cancer to alterations in cellular functioning. The second article suggests that the molecular biology of cancer is not understood, when in fact the molecular biology of cancers is a focus of study that is providing better understanding of the disease and its control.

Clarity

The series editor states in the general preface that the *Oxford Illustrated Encyclopedia* was designed so that its entries "can be understood by any interested person who has no previous detailed knowledge of the subject." Because most articles are brief, no subheads are used in any of the entries. Articles are well organized, following a logical train of thought.

The reading level of most articles seems high, considering the work's intended audience of the average lay reader. Some specialized terms are defined in context, but a great deal more are left unexplained. In **cancer and cancer therapy,** for example, the term *cachexia* is defined as "very profound weight loss." In the same entry, however, the following sentence might give many readers difficulty: "Therapy is directed at reducing the primary tumour, for example by surgical excision where this is practicable; this may be supplemented by treatment to limit the growth of metastatic tumours, and to destroy any stray cells left behind after the surgery."

Oddly, the *Oxford Illustrated Encyclopedia* contains no article on the *Titanic* (the Buying Guide's standard entry to illustrate an encyclopedia's writing style), nor is the ship mentioned anywhere in the work. The following article on the **Lusitania,** reprinted in its entirety, is an example of the way information is presented:

> **Lusitania,** British transatlantic liner, torpedoed (7 May 1915) off the Irish coast without warning by a German submarine, with the loss of 1,195 lives. The sinking, which took 128 US lives, created intense indignation throughout the USA, which until then had accepted Woodrow *Wilson's policy of neutrality. Germany refused to accept responsibility for the act, and no reparations settlement was reached. Two years later (1917), following Germany's resumption of unrestricted submarine warfare, the USA severed diplomatic relations and entered the war on the side of the Allies.

Objectivity

The concise nature of the articles in this encyclopedia does not allow for much discussion of differing points of view. When controversies are mentioned, care is usually taken to present opposing viewpoints. **Capital punishment,** for example, briefly states the positions of proponents and opponents of the issue. The entry ends by stating "a careful review of the research evidence suggests that capital punishment has no greater deterrent effect than life imprisonment."

While the articles on **AIDS** provide accurate, up-to-date information, neither discrimination or civil rights issues are discussed. The entries on **ozone** and **ozone depletion** are mostly factual, but one entry in volume 6 ends by stating, "scientists and environmentalists argue that a total ban [on CFCs] is needed now to prevent irreparable damage," thereby dismissing scientists who hold different views. The entries on **Northern Ireland** in volumes 3 and 4 are balanced.

Accessibility

The thematic organization of the *Oxford Illustrated Encyclopedia* may present a challenge to users who are more familiar with conventional works that are organized alphabetically. The editors rely on a system of cross-references, indicated by an asterisk (*), to help guide the user to related entries within each self-contained volume. The lack of cross-references to entries in other volumes is a weakness of this work. According to the user's guide (one of which is located in the front of each volume), cross-references "are not given automatically in all cases where a separate entry can be found." The user is encouraged to look for names and terms in their alphabetical location, and to check the index in volume 9 for entries located in other volumes.

The short-entry system makes it convenient to find specific facts under narrow topics. Conducting research on larger subjects is a different matter, however. Although a user can expand his or her comprehension of a topic by reading related entries, this process can prove time-consuming and frustrating. For example, the history of each country before 1800 is contained in volume 3; events occurring after 1800 are covered in volume 4; cultural aspects of a country are found in volume 5; and an additional entry that very briefly covers the country's political, economic, and social aspects is located in the "Countries of the World" section in volume 7.

The index, located in volume 9, contains a one-page guide to its use. This guide points out a potential problem with the index.

> The page references to volumes 1, 2, and 4 in the index apply to the revised and updated volumes in the boxed-set edition. Earlier editions of these volumes follow a slightly different pagination.

Thus, while the index works well with the 1993 boxed set reviewed here, it will be less helpful for libraries and consumers who purchased the individual volumes over time. Long index entries are broken down into subentries, which are arranged alphabetically. Index references to main entries are indicated by italics. Illustrations, maps, and other special features are not indexed.

Special Features

The illustration program of this work is one of its most outstanding features. The encyclopedia contains 2,800 illustrations, with half of them in full-color. These include photographs, reproductions of artwork, diagrams, anatomical drawings, charts, graphs, tables, and maps. Captions add information not found in the text. The charts and graphs are well executed.

Ready-reference sections in volumes 7, 8, and 9 provide quick access to facts and figures and are printed on yellow paper to differentiate them from the main text. Volume 7 contains the aforementioned "Countries of the World" section, with a small locator map, statistical information, and a brief summary of each country. Volume 8 contains a ready-reference section on the stars and planets, with 8 general tables and 17 tables related to specific text entries. The ready-reference section in volume 9 has a wide variety of items, including tables of world leaders, chemical elements, electronic symbols, and alphabets.

Each volume contains the same general preface, written by the series editor; a foreword written by the volume editor; and a user's guide specific to that volume. The endpapers of each volume contain additional information, mostly in the form of time charts and world maps. For example, volume 5 contains a cultural time line from prehistoric times to 1989. The endpapers are colorful and visually appealing; they are also a handy ready reference.

The encyclopedia does not contain any bibliographies, which will hinder the reader using the set as a first step in serious research.

Format

The large 8½″ × 11″ trim size makes the volume in this set a bit more cumbersome than other multivolume encyclopedias. The volumes are extremely attractive, with heavy, glossy paper and sturdy bindings. Variations in type styles are used to create variety on the page and to differentiate elements such as text and captions. Entry words and guide words appear in boldface, as do appropriate entry words located in captions.

Summary

The *Oxford Illustrated Encyclopedia,* with its short-entry format and thematic arrangement of volumes, serves as a ready reference in a number of fields. Although not as comprehensive as ACADEMIC AMERICAN ENCYCLOPEDIA, ENCYCLOPEDIA AMERICANA, or WORLD BOOK ENCYCLOPEDIA, its organization makes it interesting to browse. The overall attractiveness of the illustrations and the books themselves, as well as the price ($265 for the 1993 boxed set), add to its appeal.

Potential buyers should note, however, that the topical organization of the encyclopedia makes it ill-suited for in-depth research. The set has about half as many volumes and the fewest entries, except for WORLD BOOK, of any other multivolume encyclopedia. Furthermore, the short-entry format can make finding information a time-consuming chore involving flipping through many volumes.

Although the articles are well written, the reading level is markedly higher and the vocabulary more technical than most works geared to a general audience. The absence of bibliographies is another drawback.

The newest edition of the *Oxford Illustrated Encyclopedia* would complement many academic and public library collections; however, it should probably not replace more basic works such as ENCYCLOPEDIA AMERICANA, WORLD BOOK, or THE NEW ENCYCLOPAEDIA BRITANNICA.

The Random House Encyclopedia

Facts at a Glance

Full title: **The Random House Encyclopedia: New Revised Third Edition**
Publisher: Random House
Editors: James Mitchell, Editor-in-Chief; Jess Stein, Editorial Director
Edition reviewed: © 1990

Number of volumes: 1
Number of articles: 25,000
Number of pages: 2,912
Number of words: 3 million
Number of cross-references: 35,000
Number of index entries: not applicable
Number of maps: approximately 300, including 46 in atlas (reviewer estimate)
Number of illustrations: 13,800 (11,325 in color)
Intended readership: high school to adult
Trim size: 8½″ × 11″
Binding: hardcover

Price: $129.95
ISBN 0-394-58450-3
Revision policy: first published in 1977; revised in 1983 and 1990
Next scheduled revision: none planned

Introduction

The Random House Encyclopedia, now in its third edition, was "conceived as a 'family bible' of knowledge for our times," according to the publisher's preface. Issued as a two-volume work when it first appeared in 1977, *The Random House Encyclopedia* is now a 2,912-page, 3 million–word, 25,000-entry, one-volume encyclopedia. Its division into two main sections reflects the editors'

The Random House Encyclopedia

American Federation of Labor — ⑥

Alyssum

Amberfish

Amboise, France — ⑦

① *Alyssum*

position, and acquired a reputation for administrative skill and eloquence. Augustine mentions Ambrose as instrumental in his own conversion. He was also the author of works on theology and ethics that greatly influenced the thought of the Western Church. △1029, 1101, 1839.

Ambrosia, in Greek and Roman mythology, magical substance eaten by gods. The gods kept their immortality by bathing in it or rubbing it into their skin. Without ambrosia a god became weak. A mortal who ate it became strong and immortal. Sometimes it was mixed with nectar as a drink.

Ambulatory Church Layout. △1081, *1093*.

Ambystoma, North American mole salamander. Most hide underground except for breeding. Used in laboratories, they have a sturdy build and broad head. Length: to 13in (33cm). Best known of about 25 species are the marbled, spotted, and tiger salamanders. Family Ambystomidae. *See also* Salamander.

Amchitka Island, Aleutian island 69mi (111km) SE of Kiska Island off Alaska coast; site of underground nuclear testing in 1971. Length: 40mi (64km); width 2–5mi (3.6–8km).

AMC Motorcycles. △1693.

Ameba, rhizopod protozoan that has constantly changing, irregular shape. Found in ponds, damp soil, or animal intestinal tracts, it consists of a thin unit membrane covering, large nucleus, food and contractile vacuoles, and fat globules. It is almost transparent; reproduction is by fission. Length: to 0.1in (3mm). Class Rhizopoda (Sarcodina); species include common *Ameba proteus* and *Entameba histolytica*, which causes amebic dysentery. △458, 460.

Amebic Dysentery. *See* Dysentery. △711.

Ameboid Motion, method of locomotion of amebas, other protozoa, and other animal cells, including white blood cells. When a cell area is stimulated, the outer tube of "gel" protoplasm extends outward in one direction forming a false foot, or pseudopod, and the inner liquid "sol" flows in that direction, carrying the whole cell with it.

Amelia. △1189.

Amendment, Constitutional, procedure to change or modify the US Constitution according to Article V of the document. Upon the recommendation of two-thirds of both houses of Congress, a proposed amendment may be submitted to the legislatures of the states or to special state conventions. Three-fourths of the states must approve in order for the amendment to be approved. *See also* Constitution, U.S.

Amenemhat, four kings of ancient Egypt. In 2000 BC **Amenemhat I** (died *c*.1960 BC) overthrew the nomarchs, centralized government, and founded the XII dynasty. His co-regent, Senusret I, succeeded. **Amenemhat II** (died 1903 BC) co-ruled with Senusret I (1938–35 BC); was king (1935–06 BC), and co-ruled with his son and successor, Senusret II. **Amenemhat III** (died 1801 BC) succeeded Senusret III, set up the first Nilometer, irrigated thousands of acres in the Faiyūm, but his successor, **Amenemhat IV** (died 1792 BC), let the dynasty decline. △960, 1830.

Amenhotep I, ancient Egyptian king of the XVIII dynasty (r. 1557–40 BC), successor of his father, Amasis I. He campaigned in Syria to the Euphrates and pushed

the southern boundary to the second cataract. Thutmose I succeeded.

Amenhotep II, ancient Egyptian king (1448–20 BC), co-regent (1446–48 BC), son and successor of Thutmose III. He crushed an uprising in Syria, defended the frontier as far as the Euphrates, invaded Nubia, and erected temples to Amon at Karnak. Thutmose IV succeeded.

Amenhotep III, ancient Egyptian king (1417–1379 BC), and successor of his father, Thutmose IV. The XVIII dynasty peaked in his reign. Despite raids from the Bedouins and Hittites, he maintained peace throughout the empire. He built the 623-ft (190-m)-long Temple of Luxor, concluded the 1000-ft (305-m)-long Great Temple of Amon, promoted sculpture, and celebrated games. His wife, Queen Tiy, helped with state affairs. Akhenaton succeeded him. △972, 1831.

Amenhotep IV. *See* Akhenaton.

Amenorrhea, absence of menstruation. Abnormal in a nonpregnant, nonlactating woman between the ages of puberty and menopause.

America (song). △1428.

America, Prehistoric. △1828, 1830–31.

American Academy and Institute of Arts And Letters, association formed by the merger (1977) of the National Institute of Arts and Letters and the American Academy of Arts and Letters. The association now has 250 members of literary, musical, and artistic achievement. Awards are given annually for distinguished and creative work in painting, sculpture, novel, poetry, and drama.

American Anti-Slavery Society, abolitionist group founded in Philadelphia (1833). The society was active in US politics and social life, sending ministers and printed material throughout the country to recruit members for the society and organize local groups. Influential figures in the group were William Lloyd Garrison and Arthur and Lewis Tappan.

American Association for the Advancement of Science. △825.

American Bald Eagle. *See* Bald Eagle.

American Ballet, School of. △1431.

American Ballet Theatre. △1369.

American Bar Association, organization whose members are attorneys admitted to the bar of any state in the United States. The association maintains a library and specialized committees varying from maritime law to "Education About Communism and Its Contrast with Liberty Under Law." Founded 1878. Members: about 160,000.

American Blue. *See* Russian Blue Cat.

American Board of Commissioners for Foreign Missions. △1265.

American Broadcasting Company (ABC). △1424.

American Buffalo. *See* Bison.

American Civil Liberties Union (ACLU), organization dedicated to defending "the rights of man set forth in the Declaration of Independence and the Constitu-

tion." Its activities vary from test court cases and opposition to repressive legislation to public protest on inroads of rights. It has defended people and organizations throughout the political spectrum, which has often made its activities controversial. The ACLU maintains a library and specialized committees, and its publications include *Civil Liberties*. Members: about 200,000. Founded 1920.

American Colonization Society, group founded by Robert Finley in 1817 to return free blacks to Africa for settlement. More than 11,000 blacks were transported to Sierra Leone and, after 1821, Monrovia, which became the Republic of Liberia (1847.) Leading forces of the society included James Monroe, James Madison, and John Marshall. △1861.

American Dance Theater. △1431.

American Dictionary of the English Language. △1781.

American Expeditionary Force (A.E.F.), World War I US army contingent sent to Europe (1918) under command of Maj. Gen. John J. Pershing. He preserved its identity and integrity when Allied field commanders wanted to integrate the US troops into the existing defense structure. The A.E.F. was a conscripted army led by professional soldiers.

American Farm Bureau Federation, agricultural organization, represented in 49 states of the United States and Puerto Rico with membership on a family basis. Its purpose is to analyze problems and formulate action to achieve educational improvement, economic opportunity, and social advancement for its members. Its publications include *Farm Bureau News* and *American Farmer*. Members: about 3,000,000. Founded 1919.

American Federation of Labor (AFL), US labor organization. It was founded of craft unions (skilled workers) consolidated into a single federation while each union maintained its autonomy. The AFL was organized in 1886 at a trades union convention in Columbus, Ohio. Samuel Gompers, its first president, served for 37 years (1886–1924). The AFL advocated strikes to gain goals of fair wages and hours, collective bargaining with employer and written contract. With decline of Knights of Labor, AFL grew into leading US union organization. It merged with the CIO in 1955. *See also* Gompers, Samuel. △1279, 1867, 1872.

American Federation of Labor and Congress of Industrial Organizations, The (AFL–CIO), US labor organization. It is a federation of over 125 national and international labor unions, combining both craft and industrial workers. Established in 1955, it combined in a merger the American Federation of Labor (AFL) and Congress of Industrial Organizations (CIO). The merger healed a 20-year breach between the two unions. George Meany was elected president and continued in office until his retirement (1979), when he was succeeded by Lane Kirkland. During the 1970s public employee and service industry unions became a major element in the organization's membership. In 1987 the Teamsters, the largest US union, rejoined the AFL-CIO. Although each union within the federation is fully autonomous, the ultimate governing body of the AFL-CIO is an Executive Council made up of the president, vice presidents, and secretary-treasurer, elected at its convention held every two years. *See also* American Federation of Labor; Congress of Industrial Organizations. △1872.

1905 — ⑧

Page shown at 66% of actual size

① Illustrations include drawings and photographs

② Main entry words printed in boldface

③ Cross-reference entry: triangle symbol indicates page references to the *Colorpedia*

④ Measurements given in both standard and metric systems

⑤ Cross-reference

⑥ Guide words

⑦ Captions

⑧ Page number

desire to achieve the two main purposes of an encyclopedia. The "Alphapedia" section stands as a "comprehensive fact-book," a source of ready-reference information. The "Colorpedia" section offers highly illustrated discussions (called "treatises") of all subjects. The editors at Random House have joined these two traditional sections to create a uniquely arranged one-volume source—and the most heavily illustrated one-volume encyclopedia around.

Authority

Random House, although not traditionally an encyclopedia publisher, enjoys a good reputation overall for its works, including dictionaries. The seven sections of the "Colorpedia" are each introduced by signed essays written by such distinguished scholars as astronomer Sir Bernard Lovell, anthropologist Loren Eiseley, and historian of science I. Bernard Cohen. The remainder of *The Random House Encyclopedia*'s alphabetical entries were written by an international group of contributors and consultants from various institutions and journals. Articles are unsigned, but major contributors and consultants are listed in the book's front matter. A significant number come from British institutions.

Scope

The Random House Encyclopedia is divided into four main sections. The "Colorpedia," which at 1,792 pages comprises more than half of the work, consists of a series of highly illustrated explorations of seven key topics: the universe, the earth, life on earth, humankind, history and culture, science, and technology. Topics are covered in two-page spreads and are arranged thematically. The "Colorpedia" is followed by a 52-page time line of world history, after which comes the second major section, the "Alphapedia." This 885-page section offers brief definitions or descriptions of terms, concepts, people, and places, supplemented by cross-references to mentions in the "Colorpedia" and a bibliography containing over 1,500 citations of suggested further readings. Closing the book is a 130-page atlas with its own complete index.

In the "Alphapedia," biographies comprise 28 percent of the entries surveyed. Geographical entries comprise about 25 percent, followed by science (19 percent), social science (17 percent), humanities (10 percent), and popular culture (1 percent).

The editors remark in their preface that from the start *The Random House Encyclopedia* was conceived of as an international work—"an encyclopedia for the world." The entries reflect this approach. Almost one-third of the entries surveyed related to Africa and Asia, followed by entries related to the United States and Europe (28 percent each) and Latin America and Oceania (14 percent).

Lengths of the sample entries range from 55 words for **Tyrannosaurus** to 510 for **Mexico**. *Hamlet*'s 210 words include some performance information and a brief synopsis, as is typical of entries on literary works. The editors do not cite average word length, but it seems to range from 100 to 125. **Castle** is within this range, but it is supplemented by a brief entry called **castle architecture.** Similarly, the entry on **impressionism** is enhanced by related entries, including two pages of reproductions and text on the Impressionist movement in the "Colorpedia." The biographical entries for **Elvis Presley** and **Nelson Mandela** contain 60 and 100 words, respectively. The **Nelson Mandela** entry is followed by a brief entry on his wife, **Winnie Mandela,** unique among one-volume encyclopedias. The longest entry, **Mexico,** is divided into four sections ("Land and Economy," "People," "Government," and "History") and is fairly typical of geographical articles in the "Alphapedia." Also included for each major geographical entry is a statistical profile of the area. The usefulness of this data is questionable, however, as no dates or sources are cited.

What makes *The Random House Encyclopedia* unique is the "Colorpedia," which provides more discursive exploration of themes and concepts. Titles from a few spreads convey a sense of how the information is divided. The section on the earth, for instance, begins by exploring the structure of the earth and plate tectonics; it then reviews each continent and provides material on resources and agriculture. Spreads in this section include "History of agriculture," "The small farm," "The farming corporation," "Farm machinery and buildings," and "The living soil." Illustrations with detailed captions occupy half or more of each spread; the remainder is text. Each spread also contains a box showing related topics.

Currency

The third edition of *The Random House Encyclopedia* just missed the enormous changes occurring in Eastern Europe and the Soviet Union in 1990. Thus, entries for **Russia** and **Lithuania** still show them as republics within the Soviet Union. Maps also reflect the situation before the recent major changes. Germany and Yemen are divided; the U.S.S.R., Yugoslavia, and Czechoslovakia are united.

The publisher states that 30 percent of the entries in the third edition are new or revised. There are approximately 200 new entries in the "Alphapedia" but, as the length of this section has not increased, an equal number must have been cut. Revisions seem to have been added at the end with little revised within the body of the text. Because of the 1990 publication date, there is no information on *Bill Clinton, the food pyramid, the Gulf War, Frida Kahlo,* or the *Hubble Space Telescope.*

Accuracy

Our content experts found the entries to be quite accurate. The entry for **comets** is factually accurate but tentative about some commonly accepted theories, such as the tails of comets resulting from solar wind. The short paragraph on **oxygen** is technically correct, as is the entry for **House of Representatives.** Information on **Henry VIII** is accurate and unusually balanced and multifaceted for an encyclopedia entry of its scope.

Only the information about **cancer** contains some inaccuracies: a mention of "cancer genes in cells" would be more accurate if it described gene mutation and its causes as one of the greatest mysteries surrounding cancer today. The statement that "research has centered on viruses" neglects studies of chemical and other environmental causes of cancer, and the implication that the risk of cervical cancer in women is reduced by the circumcision of their sexual partners is unsupported by research.

Clarity

The Random House Encyclopedia is aimed at a teenage or adult general reader. The editors' emphasis is on simplicity—getting to the "heart of things." Articles are generally clearly written in an informal style.

The entry for **Titanic** exemplifies the editors' goal. The article is short but answers the basic questions of who, what, where, when, and why. Unfortunately, it was not updated to reflect the attempts to bring the ship to the surface in 1985.

> Titanic, British luxury passenger ship, considered unsinkable, that sank (April 14–15, 1912) on its maiden voyage. The disaster occurred after the liner collided with an iceberg in the North Atlantic. Out of 2,224 people on board, many of them US and British notables, 1,513 were drowned. This disaster led to the first International Convention for Safety of Life at Sea (1913).

Objectivity

The Random House Encyclopedia is generally evenhanded. There are no identifiable biases from the contributors, nor do any of the entries reflect a strong point of view. Controversial topics are handled in a balanced way, but some problems can be noted.

Discussion of AIDS is found in the entry **autoimmune disease;** the problem here is not a lack of objectivity, but lack of information: there are only three sentences on AIDS, a miserably poor total. The entry for **capital punishment** vaguely states that "US opposition to capital punishment remains strong," confusing the reader as to whether the opposition is governmental or from citizens. The entry for **Ozone** mentions the harmful effects of aerosol sprays and freon on the ozone layer. "Pollution of the air" in the "Colorpedia" expands

on this form of pollution and subsequent greenhouse warming, though there is no mention in either article of some scientific doubt on global warming.

On the other hand, the entry for **Northern Ireland** is quite balanced, with extremely well-written sections on religious strife. The "Colorpedia" has a two-page essay entitled "Ireland and Independence" that includes several interesting illustrations showing economic disparity between Ireland and Northern Ireland and a small map demonstrating the religious segregation of the city of Belfast.

Accessibility

Topics covered in the "Colorpedia" can be located in one of two ways. Each "Colorpedia" section has its own table of contents with the topics listed, and the "Alphapedia" contains about 35,000 cross-references. Although these cross-references are useful, the "Colorpedia" pages are so dense with text and art that it is at times difficult to find the cited reference. A device to more specifically locate mention of a word on these spreads would be helpful. There are no cross-references from the "Colorpedia" to the "Alphapedia."

The choice of entry words in the "Alphapedia" is usually logical and very specific, allowing quick access to the information. Guide words at the tops of the pages help the user locate a term. No such device appears in the "Colorpedia," but there is no need for it because topics are always covered in a spread. The "Alphapedia" also makes cross-references to the time line.

Special Features

The illustration program is the unquestioned strength of *The Random House Encyclopedia.* The third edition contains 13,800 illustrations; 11,325 of these are color plates in the "Colorpedia." These illustrations—a range of drawings, charts, graphs, and photographs—provide fascinating visual bits of information. Gender and racial examples are balanced in the illustrations. While the color illustrations are prominent and informative, the color itself is sometimes quite dull and the paper does not show the color to advantage.

The captions that accompany illustrations are an integral part of the work's effort to deliver information. Captions generally do not repeat material in the main text, but offer different information.

Illustrations are not restricted to the "Colorpedia." "Alphapedia" pages generally have three black-and-white illustrations; the time line has a panel of illustrations on each page.

Another special feature is the extensive atlas, which provides excellent, attractive maps produced by Rand McNally. These maps show political boundaries, relief features, major cities, and major roads. Unfortunately, because of the edition's 1990 publication date, these maps do not record the immense boundary changes that have occurred in recent years.

The 46-page time line begins in 4000 B.C. and ends in 1989, highlighting milestones in politics, religion, philosophy, music, literature, art and architecture, and science and technology. The editors suggest that it may be used with the essays in the "Colorpedia" to recognize historical parallels in other fields or discover the context of an event in the world.

The 1,500-item bibliography is arranged to correspond to the sections of the "Colorpedia." Certain items have been updated, but some of the sections show outdated entries. For example, the most recent entry for space exploration is 1982, and in the section on computers, all but two titles are from the 1970s.

Format

The trim size of this volume is 8½" × 11", which makes it a convenient size for shelving. The work's sheer bulk, however, calls for a dictionary stand, even though the sturdy binding should hold up to repeated use. Spread titles in the "Colorpedia" are bold and stand out; entry words in the "Alphapedia" are equally visible. The text is legible and easy to read, although it is sometimes difficult to locate which caption belongs to which illustration in the "Colorpedia." The work is printed on recycled paper, but the stock chosen seems not to show the color to advantage.

Microlytics also produces the "Alphapedia" and time line sections of *The Random House Encyclopedia* in floppy disk format (see the review in Chapter 15).

Summary

For other opinions about *The Random House Encyclopedia,* see *ARBA 91,* pp. 16–17; and *Booklist (Reference Books Bulletin),* January 1, 1991, pp. 946–47.

Since the publication of *The Random House Encyclopedia* in 1990, the newly revised and long-awaited fifth edition of THE COLUMBIA ENCYCLOPEDIA was issued in 1993. Comparable only in terms of price and bulk, *The Random House Encyclopedia* and COLUMBIA are quite different in other respects. *The Random House Encyclopedia* has half the number of articles (25,000, compared with 50,000), half the words (3 million, compared with 6 million), and just over half the cross-references (35,000, compared with 65,000). On the other hand, *The Random House Encyclopedia* boasts far more illustrations than COLUMBIA (13,800, of which 11,325 are in color, compared with 500, in black and white, in COLUMBIA), and its "Colorpedia" provides a chance to explore knowledge far more fully than any other one-volume encyclopedia. Both contain the same number of maps, although COLUMBIA's are of course more up-to-date. A lavishly illustrated one-volume encyclopedia, perfect for browsing, *The Random House Encyclopedia* is an excel-

lent choice for home use, especially for the adolescent to adult reader. It is unfortunate, however, that there are no present plans to update *The Random House Encyclopedia.* Someone who wants an up-to-date ready-reference research tool to locate information, obtain statistics, or discover the links between facts should probably turn to THE COLUMBIA ENCYCLOPEDIA.

Webster's New World Encyclopedia

Facts at a Glance

Full title: **Webster's New World Encyclopedia**
Publisher: Prentice Hall
Editors: Stephen P. Elliot; Martha Goldstein; Michael Upshall
Edition reviewed: © 1992

Number of volumes: 1
Number of articles: more than 25,000
Number of pages: 1,248
Number of cross-references: 14,000 (reviewer estimate)
Number of index entries: none
Number of maps: more than 300 (reviewer estimate)
Number of illustrations: more than 2,500 (more than 1,875 in color)
Intended readership: high school to adult
Trim size: 8½" × 10¾"
Binding: hardcover

Price: $75
ISBN 0-13-947482-X
No stated revision policy

Introduction

Webster's New World Encyclopedia was first published in 1992; it is a revised and updated version of the 1990 ninth edition of the British *Hutchinson Encyclopedia.* More than half of the entries have been updated and rewritten for an American audience for this first edition. The work contains more than 25,000 entries and over 2,500 illustrations (more than 75 percent of which are in color) in its 1,248 pages.

Authority

Hutchinson's Encyclopedia has enjoyed a regular publishing history in Great Britain since it first appeared in 1948. No extensive information is provided in this volume about the contributors: 61 are listed, 39 of whom hold advanced degrees. No university affiliations are listed, and 14 of the contributors have no stated degrees, academic affiliations, or areas of expertise. Prentice Hall is best known for its reputable WEBSTER'S NEW WORLD DICTIONARY.

Webster's New World Encyclopedia

barley

grain

cross
section of
a grain

est military engagements of the Afghan war during Soviet occupation.

Barisal river port and capital city of Barisal region, S Bangladesh; population (1981) 142,000. It trades in jute, rice, fish, and oilseed.

barium soft, silver-white, metallic element, symbol Ba, atomic number 56, atomic weight 137.33. It is one of the alkaline-earth metals, found in nature as barium carbonate and barium sulfate. As the sulfate it is used in medicine; taken in solution (a "barium meal"), its progress is followed by using X-rays to reveal abnormalities of the alimentary canal. Barium is also used in alloys, pigments, and safety matches and, with strontium, forms the emissive surface in cathode-ray tubes. The name comes from the Greek *barytes*, for "heavy," since it was first discovered in heavy spar.

bark the protective outer layer on the stems and roots of woody plants, composed mainly of dead cells. To allow for expansion of the stem, the bark is continually added to from within, and the outer surface often becomes fissured or is shed as scales. The bark from the cork oak *Quercus suber* is economically important and harvested commercially. The spice ◊cinnamon and the drugs cascara (used as a laxative and stimulant) and ◊quinine all come from bark.

Bark technically includes all the tissues external to the vascular ◊cambium (the ◊phloem, cortex, and periderm), and its thickness may vary from 0.1 in/2.5 mm to 12 in/30 cm or more, as in the giant redwood *Sequoia* where it forms a thick, spongy layer.

bark painting technique of painting on the inner side of strips of tree bark, practiced by Australian Aborigines. In red, yellow, white, brown, and black pigments, the works were often painted with the fingers as the artist lay inside a low bark-roofed shelter.

Barlach Ernst 1870–1938. German Expressionist sculptor, painter, and poet. His simple, evocative figures carved in wood (for example, those in St Catherine's, Lübeck, 1930–32) often express melancholy.

Barletta industrial port on the Adriatic, Italy; population (1981) 83,800. It produces chemicals and soap; as an agriculture center it trades in wine and fruit. There is a Romanesque cathedral and a castle.

barley cereal belonging to the grass family (Gramineae). Cultivated barley *Hordeum vulgare* comprises three main varieties—six-rowed, four-rowed, and two-rowed. Barley was one of the earliest cereals to be cultivated, about 10,000 years ago in the Near East and Egypt, and no other cereal can thrive in so wide a range of climatic conditions; polar barley is sown and reaped well within the Arctic Circle in Europe. Barley is no longer much used in bread-making, but it is used as a cereal grain, in soups and stews and as a starch. Its high-protein form finds a wide

use for animal feed; and its low-protein form is used in brewing and distilling alcoholic beverages.

Barlow Joel 1754–1812. US poet and diplomat. Born in Redding, Connecticut, Barlow was educated at Yale. As a member of the literary circle known as the "Connecticut Wits," he published an epic entitled *The Vision of Columbus* 1787. Living as an expatriate in Paris and London, Barlow was deeply affected by the philosophical ideals of the Enlightenment and was granted citizenship in revolutionary France.

In 1795–97 he served as US consul in Algiers, gaining the release of American hostages taken by the Barbary pirates. In 1811 he was sent to France on a diplomatic mission and died while accompanying Napoleon in his retreat from Russia.

bar mitzvah (Hebrew "son of the commandment") in Judaism, initiation of a boy, which takes place at the age of 13, into the adult Jewish community; less common is the bat or bas mitzvah for girls aged 12. The child reads a passage from the Torah in the synagogue on the Sabbath, and is subsequently regarded as a full member of the congregation.

barn a farm building traditionally used for the storage and processing of cereal crops and hay. On older farmsteads, the barn is usually the largest building. It is often characterized by ventilation openings rather than windows and has at least one set of big double doors for access. Before mechanization, wheat was threshed by hand on a specially prepared floor inside these doors.

Tithe barns were used in feudal England to store the produce paid as a tax to the parish priest by the local occupants of the land. In the Middle Ages, monasteries often controlled the collection of tithes over a wide area and, as a result, constructed some enormous tithe barns.

Barnabas, St in the New Testament, a "fellow laborer" with St Paul; he went with St Mark on a missionary journey to Cyprus, his birthplace. Feast day June 11.

barnacle marine crustacean of the subclass Cirripedia. The larval form is free-swimming, but when mature, it fixes itself by the head to rock or floating wood. The animal then remains attached, enclosed in a shell through which the cirri (modified legs) protrude to sweep food into the mouth. Barnacles include the stalked goose barnacle *Lepas anatifera* found on ships' bottoms and the acorn barnacles, such as *Balanus balanoides*, common on rocks.

Barnard Christiaan (Neethling) 1922– . South African surgeon who performed the first human heart transplant in 1967 in Cape Town. The patient, 54-year-old Louis Washkansky, lived for 18 days.

Barnard's star second-closest star to the Sun, six light-years away in the constellation Ophiuchus. It is a faint red dwarf of 9th magnitude, visible only through a telescope. It is named after the US astronomer Edward E Barnard (1857–1923), who discovered in 1916 that it has the fastest proper motion of any star, crossing 1 degree of sky every 350 years. Some observations suggest that Barnard's star may be accompanied by planets.

Barnaul industrial city in S Siberia, USSR; population (1987) 596,000.

Barnet, Battle of in the English Wars of the ◊Roses, the defeat of Lancaster by York on April 14, 1471 in Barnet (now in NW London).

Barnsley town in S Yorkshire, England; population (1981) 128,200. It is an industrial town (iron and steel, glass, paper, carpet, clothing) on one of Britain's richest coalfields.

Barnum Phineas T(aylor) 1810–1891. US showman. In 1871, after an adventurous career, he established the "Greatest Show on Earth" which included the midget "Tom Thumb" comprising a circus, a menagerie, and an exhibition of "freaks,' conveyed in 100 rail automobiles. In 1881, it merged with its chief competitor and has con-

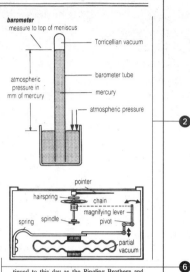

barometer

measure to top of meniscus

Torricellian vacuum

barometer tube

atmospheric
pressure in
mm of mercury

mercury

atmospheric pressure

pointer

hairspring

chain

spring   spindle

magnifying lever

pivot

partial
vacuum

tinued to this day as the Ringling Brothers and Barnum and Bailey Circus.

In 1850, in an attempt to change his image to that of an art promoter, Barnum managed the hugely successful US concert tour of Swedish soprano Jenny Lind, whom he dubbed "The Swedish Nightingale.'

Barocci Federico c. 1535–1612. Italian artist, born and based in Urbino. He painted religious themes in a highly colored, sensitive style that falls between Renaissance and Baroque. The *Madonna del Graffo* (National Gallery, London) shows the influence of Raphael (also from Urbino) and Correggio on his art.

Baroda former name of ◊Vadodara, in Gujarat, India.

barograph device for recording variations in atmospheric pressure. A pen, governed by the movements of an aneroid ◊barometer, makes a continuous line on a paper strip on a cylinder that rotates over a day or week to create a barogram, or permanent record of variations in atmospheric pressure.

Baroja Pio 1872–1956. Spanish novelist of Basque extraction whose works include a trilogy dealing with the Madrid underworld, *La lucha por la vida/ The Struggle for Life* 1904–05, and the multivolume *Memorias de un hombre de acción/Memoirs of a Man of Action* 1913–28.

barometer instrument that measures atmospheric pressure as an indication of weather. Most often used are the mercury barometer and the aneroid barometer.

In a mercury barometer a column of mercury in a glass tube roughly 2.5 ft/0.75 m high (closed at one end, curved upward at the other) is balanced by the pressure of the atmosphere on the open end; any change in the height of the column reflects a change in pressure. An aneroid barometer achieves a similar result by changes in the distance between the faces of a shallow cylindrical metal box which is partly exhausted of air.

baron rank in the ◊peerage of the UK, above a baronet and below a viscount.

Life peers are always of this rank.

baronet hereditary title in the UK below the rank of baron, but above that of knight; the first creations were in 1611 by James I. A baronet does not have

Page shown at 68% of actual size

① Page number and guide word
② Illustration includes callouts
③ Boldface main entry word
④ Cross-references indicated by open arrows
⑤ Scientific classification in italics
⑥ Historical note
⑦ Measurements given in both standard and metric systems

Scope

Webster's New World Encyclopedia emphasizes articles on science and technology, with more than 22 percent of those surveyed relating to such topics. Other subject areas covered are biography (with 16 percent of the encyclopedia's entries), geography (11 percent), social sciences and humanities (8 percent), and popular culture (less than 1 percent).

The publishers sought to gear this new title to an American audience by reworking more than 11,000 entries. American spellings have been used throughout. British and European entries account for 57 percent of the work's entries, with 18.4 percent covering the United States and 11 percent describing African and Asian topics. Other areas of the world, such as Australia, the Caribbean, and South America account for 12.6 percent of the entries. This distribution is similar to that of the other current British one-volume encyclopedia, THE CAMBRIDGE ENCYCLOPEDIA, in which slightly more than 60 percent of the coverage is of British, U.S., and European topics. In that work, however, only about 7 percent of the articles are about American topics.

Article length demonstrates a fair balance between the historical and the contemporary. Country entries are the longest: **Mexico** has an entry of almost 1,000 words, whereas both **Nelson Mandela** and **Elvis Presley** receive about the same amount of coverage (128 and 159 words, respectively). The entry for **castle** is nearly 350 words long, and the entry for **impressionism** is 181 words long, a fairly typical length. Smaller entries (such as **Tyrannosaurus**) run about 75 words. There is no entry under *women's rights,* but a 350-word entry for **women's movement** has five cross-references to its leaders (**Kate Millet, Gloria Steinem, Simone de Beauvoir, Betty Friedan, Germaine Greer**) and one to **suffragist.**

Currency

The copyright for *Webster's New World Encyclopedia* is 1992. Most entries are current through March of that year, although there is some unevenness here. The entry for **Russia** contains only pre-Revolutionary information and refers the reader to the entries for the **Russian Soviet Federal Socialist Republic** and the **Union of Soviet Socialist Republics,** both of which are up-to-date as of December 1991. There is no entry for *Bill Clinton.* **Frida Kahlo** has only a one-sentence statement and her birth and death dates.

There is an entry for the **Gulf War,** described as "hostilities between the United Nations Security Forces and Iraq." A cross-reference is given to the **Iran-Iraq War.** The unifications of **Germany** and **Yemen** are noted. Half of the 500-word essay on **Lithuania** is devoted to events since 1988, including that country's declaration of independence. The separation of **Czechoslovakia** into the Czech Republic and Slovakia is not recognized, nor is the breakup of **Yugoslavia.** No entry is included for the *Hubble Space Telescope,* nor is it mentioned under the entry for Edwin **Hubble,** the astronomer for whom it was named.

Maps for **Yemen** and **Germany** show the new political realities, but those for the **U.S.S.R.** and **Czechoslovakia** do not. Photographs are up-to-date and attractive.

Accuracy

The overall accuracy of *Webster's New World Encyclopedia* is good. The entry for **oxygen** is concise, touching on only a few of the more important aspects of the element, and mostly accurate. However, it says that oxygen does not combine with fluorine, but this is not true; the elements combine to form F_2O and F_2O_2. The entry for **comet** is readable and, according to our subject area reviewer, gives "an excellent mental picture of the object." The brief article on **cancer** cites as fact a controversial and largely unsubstantiated link between psychological stress and the disease. Although the article on **Henry VIII** contains no factual errors, the facts are presented in an awkward order and often without necessary background information. **US House of Representatives** is accurate and more thorough than comparable entries in most of the other concise encyclopedias.

In general, entries in *Webster's New World Encyclopedia* are shorter than those in single-volume works such as THE COLUMBIA ENCYCLOPEDIA or THE RANDOM HOUSE ENCYCLOPEDIA. They are comparable to those in THE CAMBRIDGE ENCYCLOPEDIA.

Clarity

The informal writing style is appropriate for high school students through adults. It is usually clear and nontechnical, as the entry for **Titanic** illustrates:

> British passenger liner, supposedly unsinkable, that struck an iceberg and sank off the Grand Banks of Newfoundland on its first voyage April 14–15, 1912; 1,513 lives were lost. In 1985 it was located by robot submarine 2.5 mi/4 km down in an ocean canyon, preserved by the cold environment. In 1987 salvage operations began.

The information within the longer entries, such as those for countries, is divided into sections, including tables and/or chronologies. Together with the illustrations and straightforward prose, these sections might help make *Webster's New World Encyclopedia* more accessible to younger readers than a more strictly text-oriented work such as THE CAMBRIDGE ENCYCLOPEDIA.

Objectivity

The reporting on controversial topics is straightforward and objective. The article on **AIDS** is well written and clearly explained. Heterosexual transmission—the fastest growing means of transmission—is noted first, other risk groups are mentioned next, followed by transmission information and statistics about the disease's prevalence in the United States. A large color graphic displaying the AIDS virus in cross section and a photograph showing the HIV binding to the inside surface of human T4 cells constitute the best graphical information about the disease provided by any one-volume encyclopedia.

The articles on **capital punishment** and **sexism** are balanced. Limited information on the ozone layer is provided in the entry on **ozone.** A color satellite map showing the ozone hole over Antarctica along with *Dobson units,* which measure ozone, is provided. The cross-reference to **greenhouse effect** leads the reader to an informative but one-sided essay on the warming of the atmosphere; no mention of an alternate or contradictory theory is made. The article on **Northern Ireland** is longer than average for this one-volume encyclopedia. It emphasizes the Protestant discrimination against the Catholic minority, especially in employment, citing the failure of the Fair Employment Act of 1972 to improve conditions. The statistic for this charge, however, is current only to 1987. An appended chronology of recent events ends in 1991; therefore, no mention is made of the renewed talks among all the parties and the Irish government in 1992.

Accessibility

Entries are organized to provide information for quick fact reference. The choice of entry words is specific and logical. Within each entry, there is usually one cross-reference (sometimes two), although these are sometimes omitted from the shorter entries. All entries appear in a single alphabetical listing, including biographical and geographical entries. There is no index.

Special Features

Webster's New World Encyclopedia has more than 2,500 illustrations, including maps, photographs, charts, and tables. They rival those of the excellent RANDOM HOUSE ENCYCLOPEDIA in quality, but not in number. Graphical representations of scientific features (such as **atomic orbitals**) and technological processes (such as **chromatography**) are excellent and are one of the best features of *Webster's New World Encyclopedia.* Sometimes, however, the illustrations are placed two or three pages away from the articles to which they relate, with no cross-references between the article and the illustration.

Except for some of the country maps, most of the maps are small outlines only. A separate section devoted to high-quality, detailed maps would be a valuable addition to this work. Photographs accompanying biographical entries are usually in black and white and are gender- and racially balanced.

Format

The binding is durable and the book lies flat when open. The type is too small to be read from a comfortable distance, but the three-column format of each page makes the small type necessary.

Summary

Webster's New World Encyclopedia has as its chief rivals THE RANDOM HOUSE ENCYCLOPEDIA at $129.95 and THE CAMBRIDGE ENCYCLOPEDIA at $49.95. Priced between these two, *Webster's New World Encyclopedia* has the currency of THE CAMBRIDGE ENCYCLOPEDIA and high-quality illustrations comparable to those in THE RANDOM HOUSE ENCYCLOPEDIA. Its entry count is similar to both works, but its coverage is generally less comprehensive than that of THE RANDOM HOUSE ENCYCLOPEDIA. It also has fewer photographs. Although the quality of the maps in THE RANDOM HOUSE ENCYCLOPEDIA is far superior to that in this work, its maps are not as current. THE RANDOM HOUSE ENCYCLOPEDIA also groups entries thematically and provides more illustrations for each entry.

If illustrations are of little concern, a slight British slant to the entries doesn't matter, and cost is an overriding factor, then THE CAMBRIDGE ENCYCLOPEDIA is the best choice of the three. If price and currency are not of utmost importance but in-depth coverage is, then THE RANDOM HOUSE ENCYCLOPEDIA is unsurpassed. *Webster's New World Encyclopedia* provides an attractive, affordable alternative to these two works. It has succinct, current coverage and quality illustrations.

For other opinions regarding this work, see *Wilson Library Bulletin,* November 1992, pp. 96–97 and *Booklist,* "Reference Books Bulletin," October 15, 1992, pp. 449–450.

Webster's New World Encyclopedia, Pocket Edition

Facts at a Glance

Full title: **Webster's New World Encyclopedia, Pocket Edition**
Publisher: Prentice Hall
Editors: Stephen P. Elliot; Martha Goldstein; Michael Upshall
Edition reviewed: © 1993

Number of volumes: 1
Number of articles: more than 15,000
Number of pages: 928
Number of words: more than 800,000 (reviewer estimate)
Number of cross-references: 6,750 (reviewer estimate)
Number of index entries: none
Number of maps: none

Number of illustrations: none
Intended readership: high school to adult
Trim size: 5½″ × 8½″
Binding: paperback

Price: $14
ISBN 0-671-85035-0
No stated revision policy

Introduction

Webster's New World Encyclopedia, Pocket Edition was published in 1993 and is an updated and condensed paperback edition of the 1992 hardcover WEBSTER'S NEW WORLD ENCYCLOPEDIA. The *Pocket Edition* contains 320 fewer pages (928) and 10,000 fewer entries (15,000) than its parent volume. The editors state that *Webster's New World, Pocket Edition* is "designed for accessibility and clarity." Its 5½″ × 8½″ trim size makes it a truly compact encyclopedia.

Authority

Webster's New World Encyclopedia, Pocket Edition lists 63 contributors, 37 of whom have academic degrees. No disciplines or university affiliations are listed. The editorial staff is essentially the same as that of the parent volume. Like that work, this version is also based on the ninth edition of the British *Hutchinson Encyclopedia,* which has been published and revised in England since 1948. Prentice Hall is best known for its reputable WEBSTER'S NEW WORLD DICTIONARY.

Scope

Webster's New World Encyclopedia, Pocket Edition has a strong emphasis on science and technology, with more than 30 percent of the entries surveyed relating to those topics. All cultures and countries are fairly represented, except perhaps for Canada, which has only less than 1 percent of the entries surveyed. Although based on a British publication, *Webster's New World, Pocket Edition* is appropriate for the American market.

Nelson Mandela and **Elvis Presley** receive about the same amount of coverage (126 versus 162 words), and country entries such as **Mexico** are usually over 300 words long. The entry for **castle** has about 170 words, while the entry for **women's movement** contains about 130 words. **Tyrannosaurus,** at 54 words, has a fairly typical length. The 50 entries from John **Bunyan** to **bushranger** reveal how the pocket edition was cut down from its parent volume. The same range of entries in WEBSTER'S NEW WORLD ENCYCLOPEDIA contains 69 entries, including many more geographical and biographical words. Entries such as Jacob and Johann Ludwig **Burckhardt, Burgas** (a Bulgarian port city), German

poet Gottfried **Bürger,** U.S. Supreme Court Justice Warren Earl **Burger,** and the English towns of **Burnley** and **Burton upon Trent** are all missing from the pocket edition.

The work's 15,000 entries make it one of the most limited adult encyclopedias available, placing it alongside BARRON'S NEW STUDENT'S CONCISE ENCYCLOPEDIA, THE CONCISE COLUMBIA ENCYCLOPEDIA, and THE CAMBRIDGE PAPERBACK ENCYCLOPEDIA in scope.

Currency

The edition reviewed has a 1993 copyright, and most entries are very current. The entry for **Bill Clinton** is current through the U.S. presidential elections of November 1992. Coverage of the *Gulf War* can be found under **Iraq** and includes a reference to the no-fly zone that the United Nations imposed on Iraq in 1992 to protect the Iraqi Shiites. All of the recent changes in government in Eastern Europe are recorded.

Accuracy

The accuracy of the entries is generally very good, although they are sometimes too brief to be very useful. The entry for **comet** is easy to read and accessible to most readers. The entry for **oxygen** is technically correct and well written. The **House of Representatives** entry is too brief and would be inadequate for a typical student or adult in search of a fact or overview. More information can be found in the entry on **Congress.** The entry for **cancer** fails to mention that cancer cells inhibit the function of other cells, organs, and organ systems. The entry for **Henry VIII** takes an unusually mature and nonsensationalist approach to the monarch's reign, but the article's brevity severely limits the amount of information presented.

Clarity

The informal writing style is appropriate for high school students through adults. It is usually clear and nontechnical, and many entries (such as the one for **Titanic**) have been taken verbatim from WEBSTER'S NEW WORLD ENCYCLOPEDIA.

Objectivity

The reporting on controversial topics seems to be straightforward and objective. The article on **AIDS** does not mention at-risk groups but does discuss how the disease is spread and gives statistics of its prevalence in the United States. The articles on **capital punishment** and **sexism** are balanced. The article on **Northern Ireland** is longer than average for this one-volume encyclopedia and emphasizes the Protestant discrimination against the Catholic minority. No mention is made of the renewed talks among all the parties and the Irish government in

Webster's New World Encyclopedia, Pocket Edition

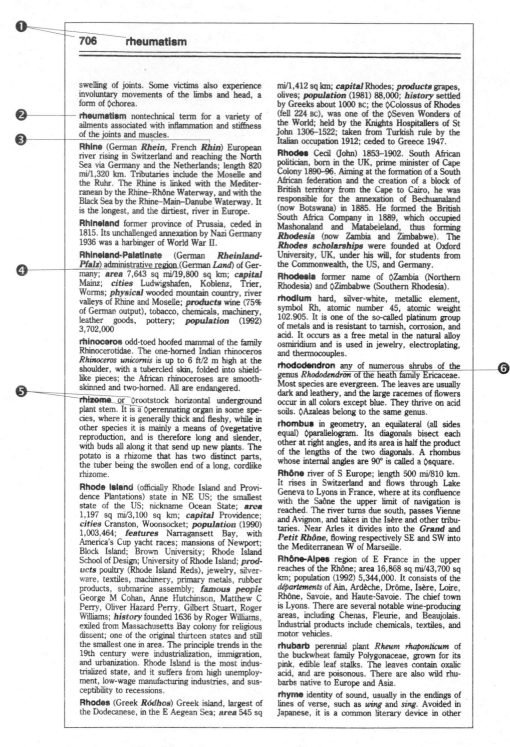

706   **rheumatism**

swelling of joints. Some victims also experience involuntary movements of the limbs and head, a form of ◊chorea.

rheumatism nontechnical term for a variety of ailments associated with inflammation and stiffness of the joints and muscles.

Rhine (German *Rhein*, French *Rhin*) European river rising in Switzerland and reaching the North Sea via Germany and the Netherlands; length 820 mi/1,320 km. Tributaries include the Moselle and the Ruhr. The Rhine is linked with the Mediterranean by the Rhine–Rhône Waterway, and with the Black Sea by the Rhine–Main–Danube Waterway. It is the longest, and the dirtiest, river in Europe.

Rhineland former province of Prussia, ceded in 1815. Its unchallenged annexation by Nazi Germany 1936 was a harbinger of World War II.

Rhineland-Palatinate (German *Rheinland-Pfalz*) administrative region (German *Land*) of Germany; *area* 7,643 sq mi/19,800 sq km; *capital* Mainz; *cities* Ludwigshafen, Koblenz, Trier, Worms; *physical* wooded mountain country, river valleys of Rhine and Moselle; *products* wine (75% of German output), tobacco, chemicals, machinery, leather goods, pottery; *population* (1992) 3,702,000

rhinoceros odd-toed hoofed mammal of the family Rhinocerotidae. The one-horned Indian rhinoceros *Rhinoceros unicornis* is up to 6 ft/2 m high at the shoulder, with a tubercled skin, folded into shield-like pieces; the African rhinoceroses are smooth-skinned and two-horned. All are endangered.

rhizome or ◊rootstock horizontal underground plant stem. It is a ◊perennating organ in some species, where it is generally thick and fleshy, while in other species it is mainly a means of ◊vegetative reproduction, and is therefore long and slender, with buds all along it that send up new plants. The potato is a rhizome that has two distinct parts, the tuber being the swollen end of a long, cordlike rhizome.

Rhode Island (officially Rhode Island and Providence Plantations) state in NE US; the smallest state of the US; nickname Ocean State; *area* 1,197 sq mi/3,100 sq km; *capital* Providence; *cities* Cranston, Woonsocket; *population* (1990) 1,003,464; *features* Narragansett Bay, with America's Cup yacht races; mansions of Newport; Block Island; Brown University; Rhode Island School of Design; University of Rhode Island; *products* poultry (Rhode Island Reds), jewelry, silverware, textiles, machinery, primary metals, rubber products, submarine assembly; *famous people* George M Cohan, Anne Hutchinson, Matthew C Perry, Oliver Hazard Perry, Gilbert Stuart, Roger Williams; *history* founded 1636 by Roger Williams, exiled from Massachusetts Bay colony for religious dissent; one of the original thirteen states and still the smallest one in area. The principle trends in the 19th century were industrialization, immigration, and urbanization. Rhode Island is the most industrialized state, and it suffers from high unemployment, low-wage manufacturing industries, and susceptibility to recessions.

Rhodes (Greek *Ródhos*) Greek island, largest of the Dodecanese, in the E Aegean Sea; *area* 545 sq mi/1,412 sq km; *capital* Rhodes; *products* grapes, olives; *population* (1981) 88,000; *history* settled by Greeks about 1000 BC; the ◊Colossus of Rhodes (fell 224 BC), was one of the ◊Seven Wonders of the World; held by the Knights Hospitallers of St John 1306–1522; taken from Turkish rule by the Italian occupation 1912; ceded to Greece 1947.

Rhodes Cecil (John) 1853–1902. South African politician, born in the UK, prime minister of Cape Colony 1890–96. Aiming at the formation of a South African federation and the creation of a block of British territory from the Cape to Cairo, he was responsible for the annexation of Bechuanaland (now Botswana) in 1885. He formed the British South Africa Company in 1889, which occupied Mashonaland and Matabeleland, thus forming *Rhodesia* (now Zambia and Zimbabwe). The *Rhodes scholarships* were founded at Oxford University, UK, under his will, for students from the Commonwealth, the US, and Germany.

Rhodesia former name of ◊Zambia (Northern Rhodesia) and ◊Zimbabwe (Southern Rhodesia).

rhodium hard, silver-white, metallic element, symbol Rh, atomic number 45, atomic weight 102.905. It is one of the so-called platinum group of metals and is resistant to tarnish, corrosion, and acid. It occurs as a free metal in the natural alloy osmiridium and is used in jewelry, electroplating, and thermocouples.

rhododendron any of numerous shrubs of the genus *Rhododendron* of the heath family Ericaceae. Most species are evergreen. The leaves are usually dark and leathery, and the large racemes of flowers occur in all colors except blue. They thrive on acid soils. ◊Azaleas belong to the same genus.

rhombus in geometry, an equilateral (all sides equal) ◊parallelogram. Its diagonals bisect each other at right angles, and its area is half the product of the lengths of the two diagonals. A rhombus whose internal angles are 90° is called a ◊square.

Rhône river of S Europe; length 500 mi/810 km. It rises in Switzerland and flows through Lake Geneva to Lyons in France, where at its confluence with the Saône the upper limit of navigation is reached. The river turns due south, passes Vienne and Avignon, and takes in the Isère and other tributaries. Near Arles it divides into the *Grand* and *Petit Rhône*, flowing respectively SE and SW into the Mediterranean W of Marseille.

Rhône-Alpes region of E France in the upper reaches of the Rhône; area 16,868 sq mi/43,700 sq km; population (1992) 5,344,000. It consists of the *départements* of Ain, Ardèche, Drôme, Isère, Loire, Rhône, Savoie, and Haute-Savoie. The chief town is Lyons. There are several notable wine-producing areas, including Chenas, Fleurie, and Beaujolais. Industrial products include chemicals, textiles, and motor vehicles.

rhubarb perennial plant *Rheum rhaponticum* of the buckwheat family Polygonaceae, grown for its pink, edible leaf stalks. The leaves contain oxalic acid, and are poisonous. There are also wild rhubarbs native to Europe and Asia.

rhyme identity of sound, usually in the endings of lines of verse, such as *wing* and *sing*. Avoided in Japanese, it is a common literary device in other

Page shown at 92% of actual size.

❶ Page number and guide word

❷ Boldface main entry word

❸ Foreign spellings in bold italics

❹ Measurements given in both standard and metric systems

❺ Cross-references indicated by open arrows

❻ Scientific classification in italics

1992. In this article and in the inclusion of some lesser-known British towns and political figures, one detects a British bias in the work.

Accessibility

Entries within *Webster's New World Encyclopedia, Pocket Edition* are short and organized for quick fact reference. The choice of entry words is specific and logical. There is an average of one cross-reference for every three entries, but they tend to be grouped together with many entries having none.

Format

There are no illustrations, maps, charts, tables, or bibliographies in *Webster's New World Encyclopedia, Pocket Edition.* The type is small but very legible. The work's compact size (slightly larger than a paperback dictionary) makes it easily portable.

Summary

Webster's New World Encyclopedia, Pocket Edition is a paperback, one-volume quick-reference tool that would be of use primarily to home purchasers and students. Its limited scope (15,000 short entries) makes it no match for the more comprehensive (albeit more costly) hardcover single-volume encyclopedias available.

Its chief rival is THE CAMBRIDGE PAPERBACK ENCYCLOPEDIA. Both were published in 1993, are of British origin, and cost approximately the same amount. THE CAMBRIDGE PAPERBACK ENCYCLOPEDIA has a slightly larger format, more entries, and a supplemental section of special features including lists of countries, weights, and measurements. It also has more than 570 maps and over 600 line drawings, whereas *Webster's* has none. Although *Webster's New World Encyclopedia, Pocket Edition* has less of a British bias than THE CAMBRIDGE PAPERBACK ENCYCLOPEDIA, it is recommended for purchase only if THE CAMBRIDGE PAPERBACK ENCYCLOPEDIA is unavailable.

World Book Encyclopedia

Facts at a Glance

Full title: **The World Book Encyclopedia**
Publisher: World Book
Editors: William H. Nault, Publisher; A. Richard Harmet, Editorial Director
Number of contributors: more than 3,000
Edition reviewed: © 1993

Number of volumes: 22
Number of articles: more than 17,000
Number of pages: more than 14,000
Number of words: 10 million
Number of cross-references: 78,000

Number of index entries: more than 150,000
Number of maps: more than 2,300
Number of illustrations: more than 29,000; more than 80 percent in color
Intended readership: elementary to adult
Trim size: 7¼″ × 9¾″
Binding: hardcover

Price: $899 (Imperial); $699 (Majestic); $649 (Diplomat); $599 (Traditional); discount available to schools and libraries
Sold directly to schools and libraries; also sold door-to-door
ISBN 0-7166-0093-5
Revised annually; next scheduled revision: December 1994 (for © 1995)

Introduction

The World Book Encyclopedia is a 22-volume general encyclopedia containing more than 17,000 articles. In its scope and coverage it is most comparable to the ACADEMIC AMERICAN ENCYCLOPEDIA and COMPTON'S ENCYCLOPEDIA AND FACT INDEX. According to the preface, *World Book* is intended both "to meet the reference and study needs of students in elementary school, junior high school, and high school" and to serve as a general reference for "librarians, teachers, and business and professional men and women." This review is based on the 1993 printing of *World Book,* the most recent one available at the time of writing the Buying Guide.

Authority

World Book has had a long and distinguished history since it first appeared as an eight-volume set in 1917. Its first editor, Michael Vincent O'Shea, founded the work with a commitment to the qualities of accuracy, accessibility, and clarity that have become the encyclopedia's hallmarks. When John Morris Jones became editor in the 1940s, he continued to shape the work. Dr. William H. Nault took over in 1962 as publisher and general chairman of the editorial advisory boards; he continues to hold these positions and to serve as the guiding force behind the work.

According to the preface, the eight-person advisory board is "directly involved in the planning, production, and ongoing evaluation of *World Book.*" Six consultant committees (composed of scholars and specialists in area studies, biological sciences, humanities, library science and services, physical sciences, and social sciences) work with the editorial staff to ensure that *World Book* reflects recent research in the various disciplines.

More than 3,000 contributors, most of whom are academic scholars, serve as authors, authenticators, consultants, illustrators, and reviewers. Their names and

World Book Encyclopedia

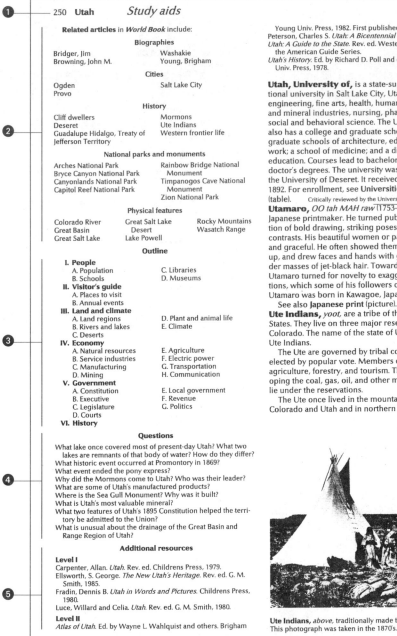

1 250   **Utah**   *Study aids*

Related articles in *World Book* include:

Biographies

Bridger, Jim	Washakie
Browning, John M.	Young, Brigham

Cities

Ogden	Salt Lake City
Provo	

History

Cliff dwellers	Mormons
Deseret	Ute Indians
Guadalupe Hidalgo, Treaty of	Western frontier life
Jefferson Territory	

National parks and monuments

Arches National Park	Rainbow Bridge National
Bryce Canyon National Park	Monument
Canyonlands National Park	Timpanogos Cave National
Capitol Reef National Park	Monument
	Zion National Park

Physical features

Colorado River	Great Salt Lake	Rocky Mountains
Great Basin	Desert	Wasatch Range
Great Salt Lake	Lake Powell	

Outline

I. **People**
  A. Population   C. Libraries
  B. Schools   D. Museums
II. **Visitor's guide**
  A. Places to visit
  B. Annual events
III. **Land and climate**
  A. Land regions   D. Plant and animal life
  B. Rivers and lakes   E. Climate
  C. Deserts
IV. **Economy**
  A. Natural resources   E. Agriculture
  B. Service industries   F. Electric power
  C. Manufacturing   G. Transportation
  D. Mining   H. Communication
V. **Government**
  A. Constitution   E. Local government
  B. Executive   F. Revenue
  C. Legislature   G. Politics
  D. Courts
VI. **History**

Questions

What lake once covered most of present-day Utah? What two
  lakes are remnants of that body of water? How do they differ?
What historic event occurred at Promontory in 1869?
What event ended the pony express?
Why did the Mormons come to Utah? Who was their leader?
What are some of Utah's manufactured products?
Where is the Sea Gull Monument? Why was it built?
What is Utah's most valuable mineral?
What two features of Utah's 1895 Constitution helped the terri-
  tory be admitted to the Union?
What is unusual about the drainage of the Great Basin and
  Range Region of Utah?

Additional resources

Level I
Carpenter, Allan. *Utah.* Rev. ed. Childrens Press, 1979.
Ellsworth, S. George. *The New Utah's Heritage.* Rev. ed. G. M.
  Smith, 1985.
Fradin, Dennis B. *Utah in Words and Pictures.* Childrens Press,
  1980.
Luce, Willard and Celia. *Utah.* Rev. ed. G. M. Smith, 1980.

Level II
Atlas of Utah. Ed. by Wayne L. Wahlquist and others. Brigham

Young Univ. Press, 1982. First published in 1980.
Peterson, Charles S. *Utah: A Bicentennial History.* Norton, 1977.
Utah: A Guide to the State. Rev. ed. Western Epics, 1982. From
  the American Guide Series.
Utah's History. Ed. by Richard D. Poll and others. Brigham Young
  Univ. Press, 1978.

Utah, University of, is a state-supported coeduca-
tional university in Salt Lake City, Utah. It has colleges of
engineering, fine arts, health, humanities, law, mines
and mineral industries, nursing, pharmacy, science, and
social and behavioral science. The University of Utah
also has a college and graduate school of business;
graduate schools of architecture, education, and social
work; a school of medicine; and a division of continuing
education. Courses lead to bachelor's, master's, and
doctor's degrees. The university was founded in 1850 as
the University of Deseret. It received its present name in
1892. For enrollment, see **Universities and colleges**
(table).   Critically reviewed by the University of Utah

Utamaro, *OO tah MAH raw* (1753-1806), was a leading
Japanese printmaker. He turned public taste in the direction of bold drawing, striking poses, and unusual color
contrasts. His beautiful women or pairs of lovers are tall
and graceful. He often showed them only from the waist
up, and drew faces and hands with great elegance under masses of jet-black hair. Toward the end of his life,
Utamaro turned for novelty to exaggerations and distortions, which some of his followers carried even further.
Utamaro was born in Kawagoe, Japan.   Robert A. Rorex
  See also **Japanese print** (picture).

Ute Indians, *yoot,* are a tribe of the Western United
States. They live on three major reservations in Utah and
Colorado. The name of the state of Utah comes from the
Ute Indians.
  The Ute are governed by tribal councils that are
elected by popular vote. Members of the tribe work in
agriculture, forestry, and tourism. They are also devel-
oping the coal, gas, oil, and other mineral deposits that
lie under the reservations.
  The Ute once lived in the mountains and plains of
Colorado and Utah and in northern New Mexico. They

Utah State Historical Society

Ute Indians, *above,* traditionally made tepees of buffalo skins.
This photograph was taken in the 1870's.

Page shown at 72% of actual size

---

1 Page number and guide word
2 "Related articles" cross reference
3 Outline of preceding article
4 Questions
5 Bibliography completes the study guide
6 Main entry words printed in boldface
7 Cross-reference printed in boldface
8 Pronounciations given for foreign or unusual entry words
9 Contributor's credit: most articles are signed
10 Illustrations include historical photographs
11 Caption

affiliations are listed at the beginning of volume 1, and most articles are signed by the contributor(s).

Scope

World Book uses a combination of brief, specialized articles and longer survey entries. For example, a reader looking up specific facts about **Hollywood** would find a half-page article under that heading, as well as broader information on Hollywood in the more comprehensive, 28½-page **motion picture** article.

The wide range of article lengths is reflected by the sample entries. **Nelson Mandela** and **Elvis Presley** each receive two-thirds of a page. Although there is no entry for *Hamlet,* the reader will find a cross-reference to **Shakespeare, William (Shakespeare's plays),** where the play is given three-quarters of a page. **Castle** receives 2 pages. **Mexico,** which is given 28 pages, is representative of *World Book*'s coverage of most countries, the 50 states, and Canadian provinces. **Impressionism** gets 1¼ pages, including one photograph. In addition, the 64-page **painting** article discusses Impressionism. A few topics do not receive as much space as they might. **Tyrannosaurus rex** is cross-referenced to **dinosaurs,** where it receives only 12 lines.

The publisher does not provide an estimate of the percentage of articles from different subject areas. Our reviewers found the following proportions in a randomly selected 50-page sample (volume 12, pages 174–225): humanities and the arts, 50 percent; science and technology, 25 percent; geography, 12 percent; social sciences, 8 percent; and popular culture, 5 percent. A large proportion (54 percent) of the articles in the sample are biographies.

Although the work is intended mainly for the American and Canadian markets, fair coverage is given to topics relating to other countries. In a randomly selected 25-page sample (volume 9, pages 197–222), about 31 percent of the entries were related to countries other than the United States, Canada, or Great Britain. These include **Johann Friedrich Herbart** (German philosopher and educator), **Herculaneum** (ancient Roman city), **Hercules, Herod, Herodotus, Tomás Herrera** (19th-century Panamanian soldier and statesman), German physicists **Gustav Hertz** and **Heinrich Rudolph Hertz, Alexander Ivanovich Herzen** (Russian journalist), **Rudolph Hess, Hermann Hesse, Hestia** (Greek goddess of the hearth), Norwegian ethnologist and author **Thor Heyerdahl,** and **Hezekiah,** king of ancient Judah.

According to the publisher, the selection and emphasis of entries in *World Book* are geared to school curricula. The Nault-Caswell-Brain Curriculum Analysis, a 61-volume study of schools in the United States and Canada, is one method the editors use to gear the reference work toward students. Another method is the Classroom Research Project, in which students in over 400 classrooms fill out cards describing what topic they look up each time they use *World Book.* Editors then review the usage patterns of students in different grades.

Currency

World Book is revised annually. According to the publisher, "*World Book* makes revisions in every field of knowledge or activity whenever developments make it appropriate to do so." The 1993 edition contains 73 new articles, more than 400 extensively revised articles, and more than 2,600 partially revised articles. This shows an article update rate of 18 percent, which is much higher than Encyclopedia Americana's rate of 2.5 percent. The publishers add that the 1993 printing offers more than 550 new photographs, diagrams, and illustrations. In addition, about 240 maps are new or revised.

World Book's revisions do an excellent job of keeping pace with world events. The **Union of Soviet Socialist Republics** article was completely revised for 1993. A new article on the **Commonwealth of Independent States** was added, and separate entries exist for each of the independent nations formed from the former U.S.S.R. According to the publishers, over 500 articles were revised to reflect the breakup of the Soviet Union. A check of related topics, such as **flags, Russian literature,** and **Black Sea** found no flaws in currency. The **Russia** article contains information throughout the entry on the breakup and the move toward a free-market economy.

Similar thorough revisions may be found in the **Yugoslavia** article. Recent changes are reflected in the article's introduction, as well as in the sections on "Government," "Economy," and "History (Recent Developments)." New entries include **Bosnia and Herce-govina, Croatia, Macedonia,** and **Slovenia;** significant revisions were made to **Montenegro** and **Serbia.** No out-of-date facts regarding the former Yugoslavia could be found.

The **Persian Gulf War** and its effects are thoroughly discussed in a three-and-a-half–page entry. A new article on **Boutros Boutros-Ghali** and major revisions to the **United Nations** article reflect the increasing importance of the United Nations in world peacekeeping missions.

A new entry on **William Jefferson Clinton** and revisions to such articles as **Democratic Party, electoral college, Ross Perot,** and **President of the United States** show the outcome of the 1992 presidential elections. However, a table in the **Arkansas** entry lists Clinton as the current governor.

New and revised entries in the areas of science and technology include **AIDS; artificial heart; Graves' disease; holography; interferon; satellite, artificial; scanning probe microscope; sexually transmitted diseases** (replaces *venereal disease*); **space exploration** (replaces *space travel*); **wind shear;** and **word process-**

ing. A revised entry on **telephone** includes discussions and photographs of fax machines, cellular phones, and video phones, along with information about computer-related online applications such as electronic mail and bulletin board services. **Hubble Space Telescope** is briefly covered in a half-page article, and is mentioned in the **astronomy** and **telescope** articles.

All maps checked were current through the end of 1992. Maps of Czechoslovakia show the Czech and Slovak republics as constituent parts of the larger country, not as independent nations.

A few flaws in currency do exist. The *food pyramid* is not mentioned anywhere in the set; nor is there an entry for *Frida Kahlo*. A listing of **Nobel Prizes** includes awards given only through 1991.

Population statistics are usually quite current, even for developing nations. For instance, 1987 census figures are given for Somalia, along with an estimate of the 1993 population and a projection of the population in 1998. ENCYCLOPEDIA AMERICANA lists a 1981 population estimate for Somalia.

Photographs, although not as up-to-date as those found in ACADEMIC AMERICAN ENCYCLOPEDIA, are generally contemporary in look.

Accuracy

World Book receives mixed reviews for accuracy from the Buying Guide's content experts. The **cancer** article, which was updated for the 1993 printing, is excellent—clearly written, logical, and very informative. The **oxygen** article is also very well done and covers the subject thoroughly, with no factual errors. The political science consultant noted that *World Book*'s **House of Representatives** article is among the most detailed treatments in any encyclopedia, addressing virtually all significant topics about the House. The article also includes comparisons of the U.S. House of Representatives with the lower houses of other countries' legislatures.

The other content experts had lower opinions of the encyclopedia. The **comet** article suffers from too little information, much of it out-of-date. Modern researchers such as Whipple and Oort are not mentioned, nor is the 1986 encounter of Halley's comet by the Giotto satellite. However, the facts that *are* given are correct and appropriate for users with a sixth- to eighth-grade reading level. The **Henry VIII** article concentrates on his marriages and on the Reformation, omitting important information on domestic politics and international affairs of the time. Although the article contains no factual errors, it is not balanced.

Clarity

One of *World Book*'s best qualities is its ability to explain complicated subjects to a wide variety of audiences. Articles are well organized and easy to follow,

and the writing style is consistently clear and logical. Longer major articles are broken down into "topical units" that fit within the context of the article.

The editor of each article checks its vocabulary against a 44,000-word list developed for *World Book* by its readability consultants at Ohio State University. All technical terms are italicized and defined, either parenthetically after the term or within the context of the sentence.

Entries are written at a variety of reading levels, depending on the complexity of the topic and the intended audience. For example, **tiger** is written in a short-sentence, basic-vocabulary style that would be comprehensible to young children. A more difficult topic like **trigonometry** is written at an overall higher reading level. Most entries are written in a journalistic "inverted pyramid" style. The article begins with the most basic information, presented at a low reading level. The information becomes more specific, the concepts become more sophisticated, and the reading level increases as the article progresses.

To demonstrate *World Book*'s writing style, the **Titanic** article follows:

> **Titanic,** *ty TAN ihk,* was a British steamer. On the night of April 14–15, 1912, during its first trip from England to New York City, it struck an iceberg and sank. Experts had considered the ship unsinkable.
>
> The *Titanic* sighted the iceberg just before the crash, but too late to avoid it. The collision tore a 300-foot (91-meter) gash in its hull. The lifeboats held less than half of the approximately 2,200 persons, and took on mostly women and children. The ship sank in about 2½ hours. The liner *Carpathia* picked up 705 survivors.
>
> The *Titanic* had been the largest ship in the world. It was 882.5 feet (269 meters) long, with a gross tonnage of 46,328. Death reports varied. A British inquiry reported 1,490 dead, the British Board of Trade, 1,503, and a U.S. Senate investigating committee, 1,517.
>
> In 1985, researchers from France and the United States found the wreckage of the *Titanic.* The team refused to give the exact location of the ship, but reports indicated it was about 500 miles (800 kilometers) southeast of Newfoundland.

The passage makes no mention of either the *Californian,* a nearby ship that could have saved some of the *Titanic*'s passengers had her radio operator been on duty, or the new regulations concerning lifeboats and ship safety that were implemented as a result of the disaster. Nonetheless, this entry gives a number of details about the ship itself not found in many other encyclopedias.

In general, the tone of *World Book*'s writing is less academic than ENCYCLOPEDIA AMERICANA, COLLIER'S, or NEW BRITANNICA, making it a useful resource for many types of readers. Those who need more in-depth or scholarly information, however, would probably prefer one of these three higher-level encyclopedias.

Objectivity

Controversial topics are handled in a balanced manner. The majority of articles in *World Book* are written by academics, rather than by industry groups, and this encourages impartial treatment. Occasionally, articles are critically reviewed by organizations (for example, **National Wildlife Federation** is reviewed by that group), but this does not seem to affect the objectivity of those entries.

World Book's **AIDS** entry is an example of its evenhanded treatment. The section entitled "Social Issues" discusses the conflicts over condom distribution in schools, health and sex education programs, and needle exchange programs for IV drug users. Various forms of discrimination against people with AIDS and HIV are also covered. The article does not limit the group of infected individuals to gay men, but addresses the spread of AIDS among IV drug users, heterosexual men and women, and the children of HIV-infected women.

The first paragraph of the **capital punishment** entry states, "People disagree about whether capital punishment is moral or is effective in discouraging crime." The debate over capital punishment is discussed in the penultimate paragraph, which ends:

> But criminologists have never found a direct link between the death penalty and the murder rate. Studies have shown no unusual increase in murders when the penalty is abolished.

World Book covers the conflicts in **Northern Ireland** more thoroughly than ACADEMIC AMERICAN ENCYCLOPEDIA, especially in the "History" section. Without seeming partial to either side, *World Book* discusses the division of Ireland by Great Britain in 1920, the problems stemming from the division, and the civil rights movement that began in 1967.

The **ozone** entry, however, does not delve deeply into the issue of ozone depletion. One sentence mentions the possible ramifications of the ozone hole, but the scientific and public debate over the issue is left out: "Some experts fear that the ozone layer may eventually thin over more populated areas, endangering human health and harming many plants and animals."

Accessibility

Entries are arranged alphabetically, word by word. Thus, **Sales tax** comes before **Salesmanship** and **New Zealand** comes before **Newark**. Guide words at the top of each page show the first and last entries on each two-page spread.

The encyclopedia contains more than 78,000 cross-references. Four types of cross-references are used in *World Book*. Entries that may be consulted under a variant form are cross-referenced to the correct article: "**Sea Parrot** See **Puffin**." *See* references within the entry use boldface type to guide the reader to related articles. *See also* references at the end of the entry list two or more related articles, also in boldface. Longer entries are often followed by an alphabetical list of related *World Book* articles; these are subdivided as necessary (those following the **Greece** entry are categorized by biographies, cities, physical features, and other related articles). Cross-references are extensive and help the reader make important connections among a wide variety of topics.

The index in volume 22 contains more than 150,000 entries. Articles and topics that are mentioned but do not have separate articles are indexed. Annotations and labels accompany most index entries, clarifying their context to the user. Maps, tables, diagrams, illustrations, and bibliographies are also indexed, and are labeled appropriately. *See also* references appear in the index (for example, "**Cornflower** [plant] *See* Bachelor's Button; Bluebonnet *in this index*"). *World Book*'s index is comprehensive, easy to use, and accurate.

Special Features

With more than 29,000 illustrations, 80 percent of which are in color, *World Book* has the most of any major encyclopedia. Photographs, drawings, diagrams, maps, tables, charts, and graphs are used throughout the work. For the most part, the illustrations are appealing and informative; however, some photographs are of poor quality. It is hoped that in future revisions these fuzzy photos can be replaced as needed.

According to the publisher, about 10 percent of the entries are accompanied by bibliographies (called "Additional Resources"). When necessary, bibliographies are broken down into "Level 1" (elementary through middle school) and "Level 2" (high school through adult) categories. Bibliographies are usually current.

A useful feature for students is the inclusion of an outline and study questions at the end of major entries. The outline is especially helpful, both as a navigational tool for long entries and as an overview.

Volume 22, the "Research Guide and Index," contains more than 200 "Reading and Study Guides" to be used by students and researchers who are studying a variety of broad topics (for example, the cold war, oceans, and William Shakespeare). These guides are arranged alphabetically throughout the index and contain topics for study, lists of books to read (like the "Additional Readings" in the rest of the encyclopedia, these are categorized into easier "Level 1" and more advanced "Level 2" books), and other sources of information.

Finally, volume 22 contains a 34-page "Student Guide to Better Writing, Speaking, and Research Skills." This extremely well-written and organized section should be valuable for students preparing a wide variety of classroom assignments, and serves as a solid introduction to research techniques.

Format

The 22 volumes of *World Book* use a modified unit-letter arrangement: all entries that begin with the letter *A* are found in that volume. In a few cases, articles beginning with the same letter are divided into two volumes (*C–Ch* and *Ci–Cz*); five volumes contain more than one letter. The relatively small trim size of the volumes makes them easy to handle, even for younger readers. The volumes lie flat when opened.

The text is arranged in a two-column format, with adequate margins and white space. The high-quality, slightly glossy paper prevents show-through. The typeface is legible and headings and subheadings in boldface allow the user to locate information easily. *World Book's* overall clean, attractive design and its use of color throughout will encourage browsing for readers of all ages.

Summary

Over the years, *World Book* has earned an excellent reputation among parents and librarians as one of the best resources for students in elementary grades through high school. In addition, many adults and librarians find it a user-friendly ready-reference encyclopedia. The publisher's comprehensive annual revisions, especially those of the past five years, allow *World Book* to seriously compete with the Academic American Encyclopedia.

When compared with competing encyclopedias such as New Standard Encyclopedia and Funk & Wagnalls New Encyclopedia, *World Book* shines. It is much more accessible, accurate, and contemporary than either of those works. *World Book* is highly recommended for purchase by consumers as well as by school and public libraries.

For other opinions regarding the 1993 edition of *World Book,* see *Booklist (Reference Books Bulletin),* September 15, 1993, page 183.

PART THREE
Atlases

Chapter 6
What to Look for in Atlases

Atlases, like encyclopedias and dictionaries, are essential assets to library reference collections. This part of the Buying Guide provides information that will enable reference librarians to make informed decisions when adding atlases to an existing collection. It also gives individuals important information about choosing an atlas for home or office use.

A number of changes have occurred in the world of atlases since the last publication of this Buying Guide. Librarians have always been concerned with including authoritative, reliable, and current atlases in their collections to answer the geographical questions of a variety of patrons. With the recent dramatic changes in national boundaries, especially in Europe and Central Asia, the acquisition of up-to-date atlases becomes even more important. In response to this need, the major atlas publishers have issued a number of new editions. The reviews in this part of the Buying Guide will help librarians and patrons evaluate the success of those efforts.

Another change is the increasing use by cartographic firms of computers to create maps. Computer-based cartography is becoming the norm, rather than the exception. Ease of revision, which should help publishers keep their atlases up-to-date when future changes affect the world, is therefore facilitated.

A final change is an increase in the number of atlases available in computer format, whether on floppy disks or CD-ROM. Five computerized atlases are reviewed in Chapter 16 of the Buying Guide. Anyone contemplating the purchase of an atlas will wish to consult these reviews, as well as those of the print atlases in the next two chapters, before making a final purchase decision.

Characteristics of Atlases

The reviews in this guide consider only general world atlases; topical atlases (such as historical atlases) or specialized works (such as atlases of individual countries) are excluded from this work. (Readers interested in reviews of these types of atlases may find them in *Topical Reference Books,* published by R. R. Bowker in 1991.) These general atlases include a mix of information, ranging from general reference maps of a region or country to thematic maps that depict a particular subject or group of related subjects, such as energy resources.

Atlases provide far more than just maps. Many atlases include additional features to supplement the cartographic information. Some offer photographs depicting the landforms of the region mapped or the culture of the people who live there. Some include information about the solar system as well as the earth's geography. Some offer extensive tables of statistics from the countries of the world or charts and graphs indicating climate or economic activity. Children's atlases often include basic information on map-reading skills. Indeed, atlases today are often lavish publications, frequently appearing in large formats with stunning images in smashing color.

All general world atlases offer maps that cover all the regions of the world, but individual atlases can differ greatly from one another in the extent of this additional information. They can also differ in terms of the quality and style of the cartography. Choosing the appropriate atlas for your particular needs, then, is a more complex process than it might at first appear. Each atlas is designed for a particular audience and purpose. The reviews in the Buying Guide attempt to define the appropriate audience for each atlas and evaluate how well the work meets the needs of that audience.

The reviews assume that most readers are not specialists in the fields of geography or cartography. We have made every effort to keep the information clear and as free as possible of confusing technical terms. To assist you in understanding the special issues that arise with atlases—and any terms used in the reviews with which you may not be familiar—we have provided a glossary of atlas terms at the end of this chapter. In addition, the black-and-white maps on pages 165–170 illustrate the kinds of maps typically found in atlases and the technical issues that affect the quality of cartography. Reading through these samples and the glossary may assist you in using the reviews to their best advantage.

Because all the atlases reviewed in this guide are full-color productions, we are unable to print facsimile pages from the reviewed works. The quality of the image that results when a color illustration is transferred to a black-and-white page is not good enough to use as a basis for judgments about the quality of the atlas. Because the cartography is a major factor in judging the appropriateness of an atlas, we urge librarians and consumers to look at the actual maps before making a purchase. The reviews here can provide guidance as to how accurate or current an atlas is or how its coverage and features compare with competitive works. We also can (and do) comment on the work's clarity and legibility. But each purchaser is the best judge of how well the maps and illustrations meet his or her individual needs.

Structure of the Reviews

Following this introductory chapter, this part of the book contains two chapters: one covers children's atlases, aimed at youngsters from preschool to middle school, and the other covers secondary school and adult atlases. Each review follows the same structure, but the issues addressed in each section sometimes differ, as do the standards against which a work must be judged. Accessibility and legibility must be handled differently for a children's atlas than for an adult work. Similarly, the special features appropriate for an adult atlas may differ from those suitable for an atlas aimed at a younger audience. On the pages that follow, we describe the criteria used by our reviewers in analyzing each atlas, highlighting how those concerns differ according to the work's intended audience.

Facts at a Glance. Each evaluation is preceded by a summary of factual information about the atlas. This information includes the full title of the work, the publisher, the editor or editorial staff, the edition reviewed, the copyright date, the number of volumes (if more than one), the number of pages, the number of maps, the number of index entries, the intended readership (by age or grade level), and the trim size and binding of the book. Price is included, as are distribution channels. Any information the publisher supplied regarding revision policy is given. The information in this section was supplied by the publisher and was accurate at the time it was given; price, of course, is subject to change. When the publisher did not supply the information, the information printed here is followed by the notation (reviewer estimate).

A word on the "edition reviewed" line is appropriate. In many cases, there is a discrepancy between the atlas's copyright date and the date of the edition reviewed. An atlas may be revised, with minor errors corrected and even with new maps prepared to reflect political changes, and the publisher may nevertheless deem the changes insufficient to warrant a new copyright. Thus, the READER'S DIGEST ATLAS OF THE WORLD carries a 1990 copyright date even though the edition reviewed—from September 1993—shows world changes that took place after that date. The prospective purchaser should check the work's copyright page when reviewing a copy before purchase, comparing the information there with what is stated in our review. Such a work, although it may reflect the same copyright date as did the work reviewed here, might be a later edition that has corrected a lapse in currency or an error of fact cited in this review.

Introduction, Format, and Authority. This section provides a brief general overview of the atlas reviewed and of its relation to other atlases by the same publisher, and gives a description of the work's purpose and intended readership. Pertinent statements by the editors or publisher about the purposes or content of the work are often cited.

The specific purpose of an atlas has a direct influence on the content, physical organization, and arrangement of its maps; these issues are addressed in the discussion of format. Some atlases contain only general reference maps; others include thematic maps. In some atlases, the maps cover one page, whereas others place maps on two-page spreads. The latter practice allows the cartographer to portray a larger area or to use a larger scale, giving more in-depth treatment of a smaller area. The intended purpose of an atlas also affects its size. Comprehensive atlases are large to provide adequate space for great detail; compact atlases are smaller because their main goal is convenience. When appraising each atlas's format, reviewers evaluate its ease of handling, the relationship of size to the type of maps it contains, and the convenience of its size for particular uses.

The binding of an atlas also affects its usefulness. If the maps appear on double-page spreads, for example, the atlas should lie flat when opened. If it will not lie flat, detail may be lost in the gutter (the adjoining inside margins of the two facing pages), or the spine may break as users force the book to stay open. The durability of the binding is also a significant factor, especially for librarians, who expect heavy use of their reference materials.

This section of the review also identifies the cartographers and consultants employed and their qualifications. A handful of noted cartographic firms dominates the atlas business; it is worth noting that maps prepared by the same firm may appear in the atlases of more than one publisher. The reader should bear in mind, however, that these few companies are by no means the only guarantors of accuracy and currency. A lesser-known cartographic company can produce quality maps.

Authority is one area where children's and adult atlases differ. An atlas meant to sit in the adult reference section to be used by patrons making vacation plans, students doing research, and librarians answering ready-reference questions has greater need for accuracy in the drawing of borders and coastlines than does an atlas meant primarily to introduce the basic concepts of map-making and map reading. This is not to say, of course, that a children's atlas should be inaccurate. Nevertheless, children's atlases are significantly less detailed, and the maps themselves are more often illustrations rather than the products of a trained cartographer's skill. As long as these simplifications do not seriously misrepresent the area being depicted, the audience is still being served and a reduced level of scrutiny on the reviewer's part is appropriate.

Scope and Special Features. In this section, the reviewers outline the structure of the atlas and indicate the page allocations for each section. They also give brief descriptions of the contents of each section.

One important question addressed by the reviewers concerns the adequacy and balance of the atlas's representation of all regions of the world. Some atlases show the United States in great detail while barely representing developing countries; others offer more balanced coverage. This is not to say that an atlas with a marked geographical bias is necessarily bad; it all depends on the work's intended audience. The three Gage atlases all provide heavy coverage of Canada; such coverage is appropriate—indeed, valuable—for these works, which are aimed primarily at the Canadian market. If an atlas gives disproportionate coverage to one or two areas, the reviewer comments on whether this occurs at the expense of other regions.

As noted above, many atlases contain special features. The reviewers describe these special features where they exist and comment on the quality and accuracy of this information. These features also must be assessed in terms of their usefulness. Children's atlases, in particular, need to be examined for the information value of the text and illustrations. The tendency of publishers to provide less, rather than more, information for children combined with their desire to amuse and amaze young readers means that supplementary text about other lands often emphasizes the colorful and fascinating rather than the characteristic and significant. Reviewers thus comment on the relevance of the information presented.

While the maps themselves should probably be the main criterion on which to judge an atlas, these special features should not be dismissed. Because the maps in the majority of the adult atlases reviewed here are produced by a few firms, this additional material is what sets one atlas apart from its competitors. Thus, the kind of information supplied in these features, and the skill and accuracy with which that information is presented, are significant factors in determining the desirability of the atlas.

Currency. With all that has transpired since 1989, currency is clearly a significant issue in judging an atlas. These reviews, prepared in 1994, were based on the most current edition the publisher supplied at that time. Our position is that any atlas worthy of its name should reflect recent border changes in Central and Eastern Europe, the former Soviet Union, and Yemen. Our reviewers downgrade an atlas that does not show a unified Germany or Yemen or the breakup of Czechoslovakia, the Soviet Union, or Yugoslavia.

In addition, reviewers looked at questions of nomenclature. A number of cities and countries have officially changed their names in recent years. These include Cambodia (formerly Kampuchea); Yangon (formerly Rangoon), the chief city of Myanmar (formerly Burma); Dhaka (formerly Dacca, Bangladesh); Nuuk (formerly Godthåb), the chief city of Kalaallit Nunaat (formerly Greenland); St. Petersburg (formerly Leningrad); and Nizhny Novgorod (formerly Gorky), among others. Some atlases provide only the new name; others offer the preferred name followed by the previous, more familiar, term in parentheses.

But the caution mentioned earlier in this chapter must be kept in mind regarding currency. These reviews can only provide a snapshot view of an atlas and must reflect its currency at the time of the edition reviewed. If an atlas is revised subsequent to the publication of the Buying Guide and out-of-date boundaries and place names are updated, any criticism offered here on that score may be considered moot. In that case, the prospective purchaser must consider the other comments in the review to determine whether the now more current edition is worth buying.

Reviewers also evaluated the statistics and other non-map information to assess the currency of the atlas. Are population figures up-to-date? How recent are data about economic factors? Comments on the currency of such information need to be balanced against real-world constraints; some nations do not generate statistical information as frequently as others.

Finally, reviewers looked at the currency of the illustrations (other than maps). Photographs, as well as text, need to be judged in terms of currency.

Accuracy.   Among the criteria used by reviewers in assessing accuracy are two key elements of cartography: scale and projection. In order to depict a given area in sufficient detail and with a minimum of distortion, cartographers must choose the scale and projection of each map carefully. The size of the page is often a limiting factor and must be an important consideration of the publisher.

The ratio between the distance or area on the map and the same distance or area on the ground is called the *map scale.* This relationship can be represented in three ways: (1) as a simple fraction, or ratio, called the *representative fraction, or RF;* (2) as a written statement of map distance in relation to earth distance, or *verbal scale;* and (3) as a graphical representation, or *bar scale.* The representative fraction is usually written as a ratio, such as 1:300,000, where 1 refers to a unit of distance on the map and 300,000 (or any other number to the right of the colon) refers to the number of the same units it takes to cover the same distance on the ground. For example, 1 inch on the map equals 300,000 inches on the ground. The verbal scale expresses the relationship in such terms as "one inch equals 64 miles." The bar scale is usually a line placed on the map that has been subdivided to represent units of miles or kilometers on the map.

Many maps include all three types of scale statements. The first two facilitate comparison of the scales of two or more maps; the third allows the map user to estimate distances on the map itself. See page 169 for an illustrated explanation of map scale to clear up any confusion over the terms *large scale* and *small scale.*

Scale is important because equivalent sizes on the page may suggest to a user equivalent sizes on the ground. With relatively few different scales employed, an atlas presents a more consistent and accurate view of the world; a one-page map of part of Europe portrays the same area as a one-page map of part of Asia. Widely varying scales, on the other hand, mislead the user. Reviewers note both how scale is indicated and the range of scales employed, commenting on whether the practice in a given atlas is misleading or helpful.

A map projection is the method employed to transfer a curved area—a section of the earth—to the flat, two-dimensional plane of the page. All methods of map projection involve some shrinking or stretching of certain portions of the earth. Whatever the projection used, then, a map must distort reality somewhat. (See pages 167–168 for illustrated explanations of different projections.) Cartographers choose projection based on a number of factors, including the purpose of the map, the area

covered, and the ease with which the projection can be rendered. Our reviewers comment when the projections used seem ill-advised.

In addition to evaluating the scales and projections employed on the maps, the reviewers assess the accuracy of the basic cartography, determining whether borders and coastlines are accurately drawn and locations correctly plotted.

The reviewers also analyzed the nonmap material for accuracy, spot-checking statistics against reliable sources, checking the spellings of place names, and confirming the accuracy of dates.

Legibility.   Perhaps no element of a map is so important in evaluating its usefulness as the lettering or typefaces used and how labels are positioned. The recognition of specific named features, the search time needed to find names, and the ease with which lettering can be read are all important. Reviewers analyze legibility, then, by looking at a number of factors.

First is the matter of the visibility of the colors and type labels. Reviewers note whether maps are positioned across two pages. If so, they comment on whether any detail is lost in the gutter between the pages. They also note whether labels adequately clear the top, bottom, and side margins of the page. Cartographers use colors to differentiate between areas, whether those are the areas of different nations (as on a political map), different regions (as on a thematic map of world climates or economic activity), or different elevations (as on a physical map). Another area that requires comment is the density of the labels on the map. Reviewers discuss whether the amount of labeling is appropriate to the level and permits easy reading of each label. Finally, reviewers assess the effectiveness of the color schemes chosen, noting whether the colors are adequately distinguished from each other and whether the type labels show clearly through these color treatments. Some atlases employ the technique called *shaded relief* to indicate high ground, such as mountains. This technique uses gray shading to indicate height, representing the shadow cast by mountains when a light shines on them from the northwest. Sometimes this shading can interfere with the clear legibility of the map's labels.

Type size and treatment can also be used to differentiate between types of geographic information and the relative size and importance of the feature being labeled. For example, blue type is traditionally used to identify all bodies of water. Black type is used for political and other physical features. Within these general principles, a cartographer may choose one type style for all physical features and another for political labels. Larger type may be employed to indicate a feature that covers a greater area. Reviewers comment on whether these type distinctions are clear, consistent, and understandable. An area of frequent failing by cartographers is the type used

Political Maps

General nonthematic maps in an atlas may be either **political** or **physical** maps. Political maps highlight nations as distinct political entities. They also present information about man-made (artificial) entities on the earth, using a variety of symbols. These symbols are described in a map key or legend, which may be located in the front of the atlas as well as, in an abbreviated form, on each map page.

Typically, political maps depict the following features: (1) political boundaries (national, and often state or provincial; disputed boundaries or territories may also be indicated); and (2) cities. Depending upon the level of detail and the map scale, these symbols may distinguish the size of the city. Extremely large or densely populated urban areas may be shown by a mark that indicates the actual extent of the area. Otherwise, dots of different sizes or configurations may be used to distinguish different levels of population. Capital cities are frequently marked by a star or some other recognizable symbol. City symbols are invariably printed in black.

Some political maps also designate elements of the transportation system: major highways, railroads, and international airports. Sea shipping lanes may be indicated as well. On most four-color maps, colors are used to identify different types of routes.

Physical Maps

Equally important in helping the user distinguish among varying features are the typefaces in which the labels appear. Ideally, different typefaces and type sizes are used to identify nations, provinces, and cities or other populated areas.

Political maps often show limited physical features as well—primarily, important bodies of water such as lakes, rivers, and oceans. The presence of extensive landforms such as deserts and mountain ranges is sometimes designed by name labels, but political maps rarely indicate the actual natural boundaries of such areas.

For these, readers turn to physical maps. Some physical maps use color, shades of color, or relief to indicate altitude. Others use color or shading to depict actual land types such as forest, desert, or tundra. The physical map shown here uses a common technique called layered relief to indicate the level of the land.

Few maps are purely political or purely physical. Physical maps, for example, may show national borders. Like political maps, they may show roads and cities and distinguish among population centers. As a rule, physical maps are more complex than their political counterparts: they endeavor to interpret the relationship between society and environment.

Projection Types—World Maps

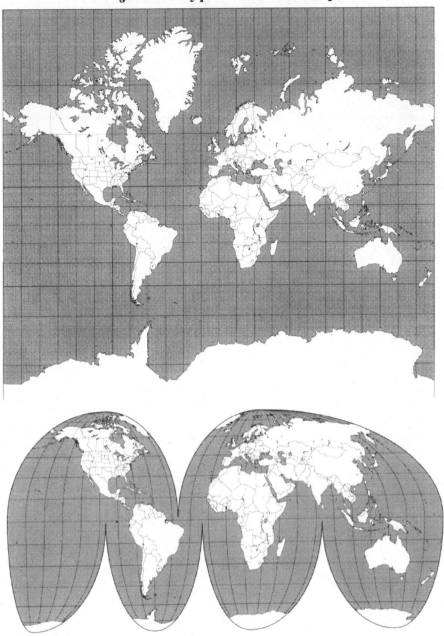

The maps on this page illustrate two types of projections (Mercator and Mollweide Interrupted) and the kinds of distortions that can occur on world maps. Note that virtually all world maps are made from some type of cylindrical projection.

The Mercator projection shows the correct shape of land masses, but distorts their area (that is, their size). This distortion is minimal in equatorial regions, but increases near the poles. As a result, Greenland appears larger than South America. In fact, Greenland's area is only 840,000 square miles, whereas that of South America is 7 million square miles. The Mercator projection is used for ocean navigation because a line drawn between any two points on this map gives the true compass direction from one point to the other. Many readers will be familiar with the Mercator projection from wall maps of the world. It is one of the cheapest and easiest projections for cartographers to use, and it results in a rectangular map.

A more complex projection for world maps found in a number of atlases is the Mollweide Interrupted Homolographic projection. While it allows fairly faithful representation of both the shape and size of large land masses, its major distortions—the interruptions—occur in ocean areas. Mollweide's Homolographic projection is useful for population distribution and other thematic world maps as well as for political and physical world maps.

Projection Type—Regional Map

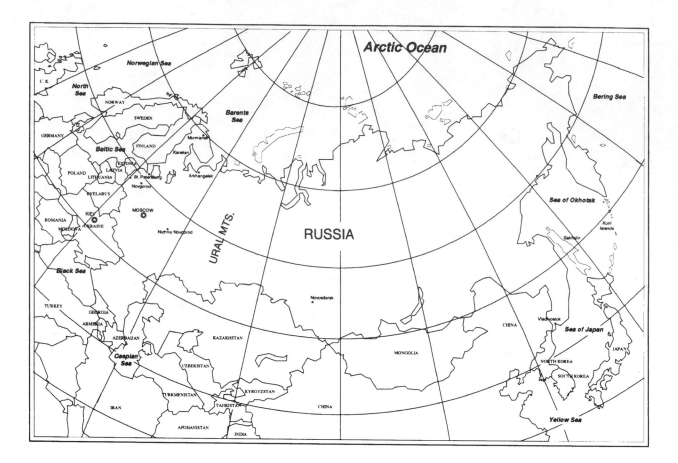

The larger the area covered in a map, the greater the distortion will be, regardless of the type of projection used. Thus, while distortions on a map of a continent are not as severe as on a map of the entire world, the choice of projection still affects the accuracy of size, shape, or direction. To produce national and continental maps, cartographers can use conic or plane as well as cylin-drical projections. Their preference depends largely on the size, shape, and location of the nation or continent.

The projection shown above depicts Russia in the Miller projection, a cylindrical projection similar to the Mercator projection. It shows shapes less accurately than does the Mercator projection, but it also distorts sizes less severely.

Large Scale and Small Scale Maps

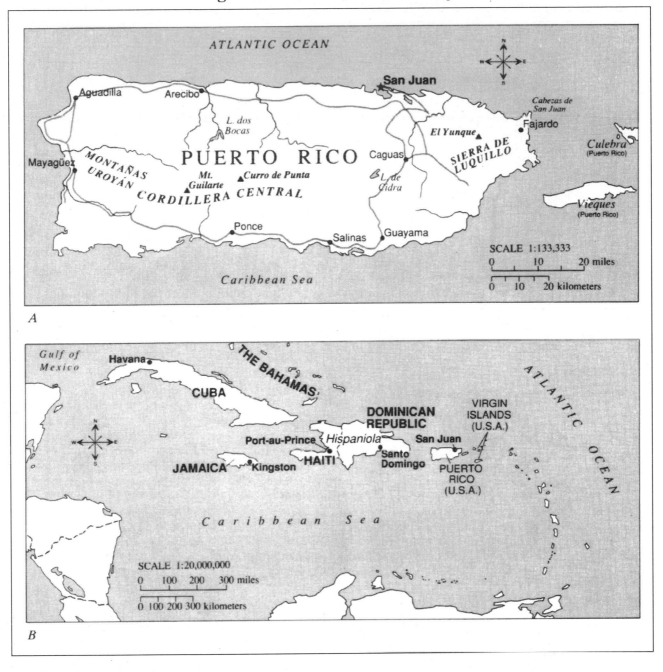

A

B

Readers are often confused by the terms **large scale** and **small scale**. *These expressions do not refer to the size of a map, but rather to the size of the area that the map covers. The larger the scale, the smaller the area that the map can cover, but the greater the amount of detail that it can include about that area. Different scales are used for different purposes. Each has its advantages and its disadvantages.*

The two maps on this page are both the same size, but each is drawn to a different scale. Map A (Puerto Rico) has a scale of 1:333,333, a larger scale than that used for

Map B (the Caribbean Sea), which is drawn to a scale of 1:20,000,000.

Map A depicts major towns, roads, and rivers in Puerto Rico, and is therefore useful for anyone needing detailed information about the features of this island only. Map B covers a substantially larger area, allowing the reader to compare the size of Puerto Rico to that of its neighbors and to see the island's location in the Caribbean chain. At the same time, however, it does not render the features of Puerto Rico in as much detail as is possible in the larger-scale map.

Thematic Maps

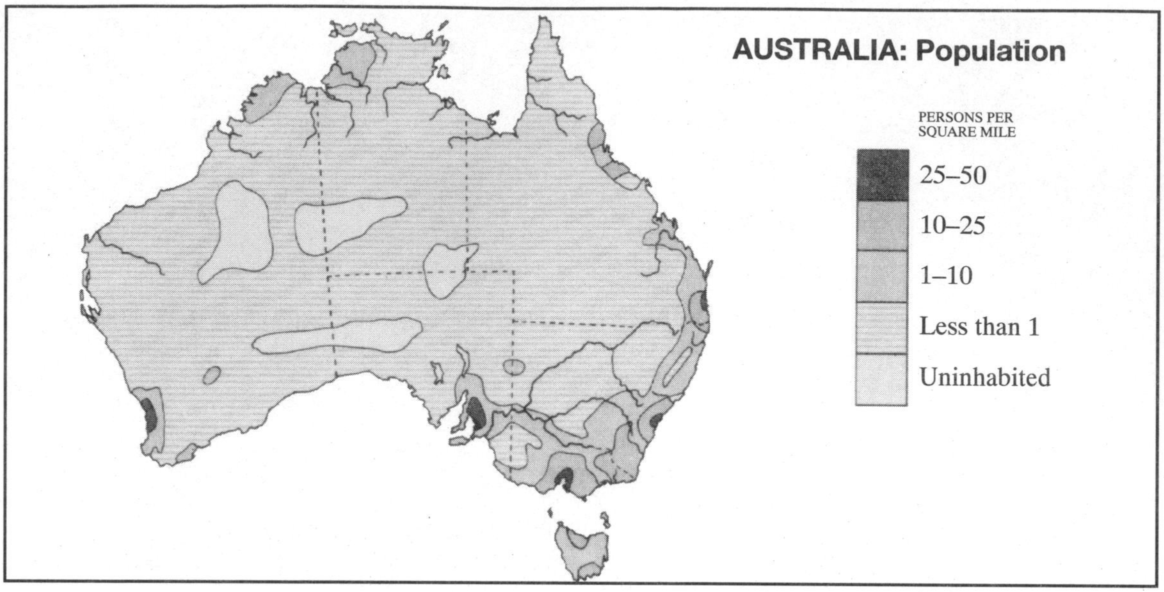

AUSTRALIA: Population

PERSONS PER
SQUARE MILE

25–50

10–25

1–10

Less than 1

Uninhabited

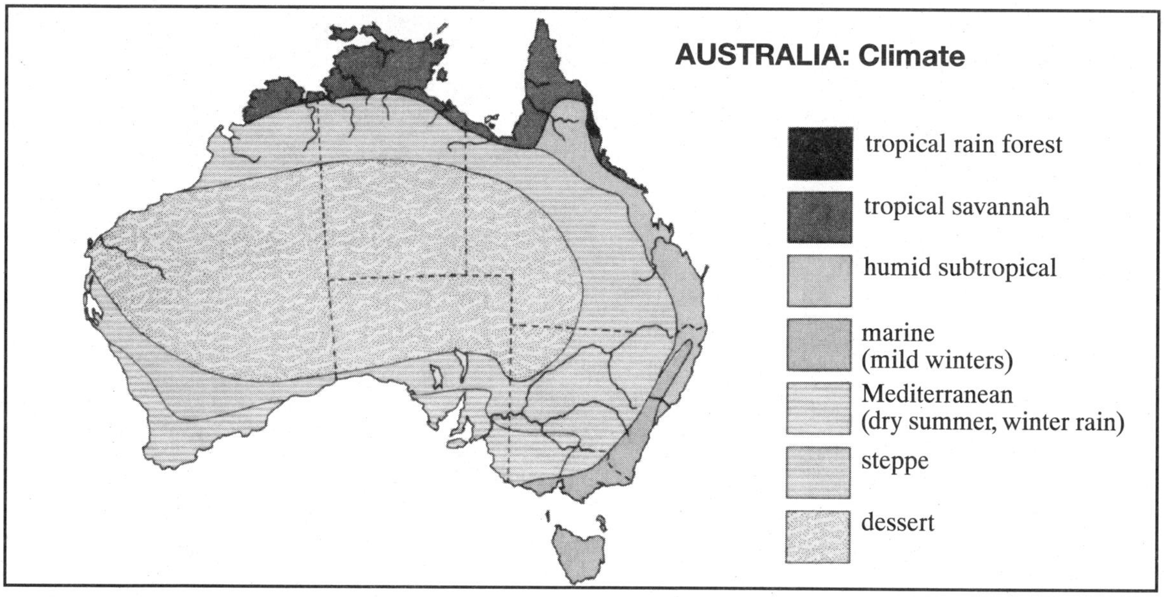

AUSTRALIA: Climate

tropical rain forest

tropical savannah

humid subtropical

marine
(mild winters)

Mediterranean
(dry summer, winter rain)

steppe

dessert

Thematic maps present information about particular aspects of geography, the environment, or society. Thematic maps can be used to show agricultural patterns, industry, income, life expectancy, geological structure, military alliances, or a myriad of other topics. An atlas that includes a broad selection of good thematic maps can be a valuable asset to any reference collection.

The two thematic maps on this page are typical of climate and population maps found in many atlases. Generally, such maps are in color, with different colors and patterns representing different features. These black-and-white maps follow the same principles used in color maps, with different types of shading standing for colors.

It is important to remember that, whereas political and physical maps show specific features in exact locations, thematic maps show prevailing characteristics in less specifically defined areas. In other words, thematic maps generalize about the types of features found in a given area, and present this information in a form that can be readily interpreted by the ordinary reader. By comparing different thematic maps of the same region, the reader can assemble a mental image of the conditions in that region and draw conclusions about the interrelation of various factors, such as climate and population.

for city names. Typically, larger or bolder type is used for larger cities, with labels decreasing in size and weight as the population of the labeled entity decreases. Reviewers note whether these treatments are consistent with the actual populations of the units mapped.

Accessibility. An atlas is only as good as the ease with which a user can access its information. Reviewers evaluate the accessibility of each atlas by looking at three factors.

First is the general question of how easy it is for readers to move from page to page. An atlas is most effective if it is organized logically, with, for example, North America and South America in close proximity. The overall layout of an atlas, including the number of one-page and two-page maps, affects this organization, and the atlas that organizes its map coverage logically aids the reader greatly in moving from area to area.

Some atlases, especially the more comprehensive ones, offer additional aids to users. They may reprint an outline map of the world on the front or back endpapers of the book showing, by use of rectangles and numbers, the different areas depicted in the book and the pages on which each area appears. These are called *index maps.* Another technique is to place arrows, accompanied by page numbers, at the edges of maps to show the page on which the contiguous area is covered in the atlas.

A second issue of accessibility is where the legend to the maps is printed. Most atlases place the legend on the last page before the main map stock appears. This location offers the user a handy explanation of the maps' various symbols and type distinctions and can generally be located easily by the user. A legend that is buried deep in the atlas's introductory material is less useful; conversely, an atlas that includes the main points of the legend on each map provides greater ease of use.

The final criterion for judging accessibility is the quality and comprehensiveness of the map index. The best index is one that, at a minimum, lists every name that appears on all the general reference maps. Ideally, there should also be cross-references to popular or variant name spellings, which is especially useful nowadays because so many place names have changed. Most atlas compilers index names to the largest-scale map on which they appear.

After each name and page number in an index, either an alphanumeric grid coordinate or a latitude/longitude reference is used to indicate the location of the label on the map. The most accurate is the latitude/longitude figure, which allows the user to locate the information easily and offers the added benefit of providing accurate geographical information, as found in a gazetteer. The grid coordinate system is often used in less comprehensive atlases and is appropriate for less experienced atlas users. An atlas that lists only page numbers, however, serves its audience poorly. A word of caution on lati-

tude/longitude figures in indexes: due to production limitations, latitude and longitude are often expressed as a decimal, such as "103.50," which actually means "103 degrees 50 minutes" (60 minutes = 1 degree). This can be confusing to the user.

Reviewers comment on these features of the index, also noting whether the information outside the general reference maps is indexed. Reviewers also assess the clarity with which the indexing system itself is explained and the accuracy of index information.

Summary. Every user certainly wants to get the best value possible when purchasing an atlas, but content alone is not necessarily a basis for deciding whether an atlas is priced fairly. Overall quality is of equal importance. Whenever possible, the reviewers make broad comparisons between the atlas being reviewed and competing works. They weigh the merits and drawbacks of the atlas and give an overview that can help the reader make a purchasing decision.

Derived Works. Some atlases are derived from longer works, employing the same map stock, but arranging it in a different manner or perhaps omitting some of the main work's special features. Reviews of these atlases are shorter and are organized as follows:

Facts at a Glance
Introduction, Format, and Authority
Scope and Special Features
Summary

These reviews refer the reader to the review of the main work for a full discussion of such issues as currency, accuracy, legibility, and accessibility, noting only any differences between the derived and main works on those points. The main thrust of these derived reviews is the "Scope and Special Features" section, in which the reviewer explains the content of the atlas and assesses its appropriateness for the target audience.

Glossary

In the event that the readers of this guide are unfamiliar with the cartographic terms employed in these reviews, a glossary of terms is provided below:

bar scale A subdivided line that shows the lengths of units of earth distance as represented on a map.

cartogram A map that deliberately distorts size or shape to indicate the value of a mapped variable associated with the area depicted; used for thematic maps as a method of portraying by size (often in conjunction with color) such factors as the extent of a given resource associated with each area of the world.

conic projection Any **map projection** in which the parallels of latitude or meridians of longitude appear as they would if a cone were laid over a globe, touching it along one or two parallels.

contour A line joining points of equal elevation on a surface.

contour interval The numerical value attached to the difference between adjacent contour lines.

contour map A map that uses contour lines to portray **relief.**

cylindrical projection Any **map projection** in which the parallels of longitude and meridians of latitude appear as they would if a cylinder were wrapped around the globe, touching it at the equator.

dot distribution map A map in which each discrete dot represents a set number of objects, the distribution of which are portrayed on the map. Used to show the distribution of population or resources.

elevation The height of a geographical feature in relation to sea level; see also **relief.**

equal-area projection Any **plane projection** that shows land areas in their correct proportions.

gazetteer A list of geographic names, together with descriptive information or references to their geographic location.

geographic coordinates A system that expresses the position of geographical features in terms of **latitude** and **longitude.**

Goode's interrupted homolosine projection An **equal-area projection** that produces an oval-shaped map, often used for world distribution maps.

grid A network of two sets of uniformly spaced parallel lines that intersect at right angles; used instead of latitude and longitude to indicate the location of features on a map.

grid coordinate The position of a geographical feature in terms of an atlas's letter-and-number grid system, used instead of latitude and longitude.

index map A graphical index, usually based on an outline map of the entire area covered by an atlas, that shows the layout and numbering system of map sheets that cover the area.

inset map A separate map positioned within the **neat line** of a larger map to show related areas.

Lambert azimuthal equal-area projection An **equal-area projection** that uses two standard parallels instead of the single parallel used in most conic projections. Because distortions of shape and size are minimal, this projection is useful for mapping regions in middle latitudes with extended east-west areas, such as the United States or Asia.

latitude Angular distance on a meridian measured north or south of the equator; see also **longitude.**

layered relief map A map on which relief is represented by layers associated with different values.

locator map A small-scale map inset in, or placed in the margin of, a map of larger scale to show the location of the area represented by the larger-scale map.

longitude The angular distance east or west of a reference meridian, usually the **prime meridian;** see also **latitude.**

map projection Any systematic arrangement of meridians and parallels used to portray the curved surface of the earth upon a two-dimensional surface.

Mercator projection A **cylindrical projection** that shows correct land shapes but distorts land areas, especially in higher latitudes. Frequently used for world maps. Meridians and parallels always meet at right angles, preserving the accuracy of relative direction.

meridian A great circle arc of 180 degrees terminated by the geographic poles used to indicate **longitude;** see also **parallel.**

Miller cylindrical projection A **cylindrical projection** used for showing the world. As in the **Mercator projection,** distortion increases in higher latitudes.

Mollweide homolographic projection An **equal-area projection** that produces an oval-shaped map, often used for world distribution maps.

neat line The line that encloses the detail of a map.

outline map A map that presents the borders of geographic areas but no detail within.

parallel Any line of **latitude** running parallel to the equator in an east-west direction. See also **meridian.**

plane projection Any **map projection** in which the parallels and meridians appear as if the surface of a globe were projected onto a flat surface (a plane) touching the globe at a single point.

prime meridian The meridian on the earth's surface from which longitude is measured. Since 1884, the meridian passing through Greenwich, England, has been recognized as the prime meridian, 0° longitude.

relief The height of a geographical feature in relation to sea level; see also **elevation.**

relief map A map produced primarily to represent the physical configuration of the landscape.

representative fraction (RF) The scale of a map expressed as a fraction or ratio that relates a unit of distance on the map to distance, measured in the same units, on the ground.

scale The ratio of distances on a map to the actual distances they represent. *Large scale* is used for more detailed mapping of a smaller area; *small scale* is used for less detailed presentation of a larger area of the earth.

schematic map A map representing features in a much simplified or diagrammatic form.

shaded relief A cartographic technique that provides an apparent three-dimensional configuration of the terrain on maps by the use of graded shadows that would be cast by high ground if light were shining from the northwest.

thematic map A map portraying information on a specific topic, such as geology, agriculture, or demography, rather than general geographic distributions.

topographic map A map designed to portray and identify the features of the earth's surface as precisely as possible within the limitations imposed by scale.

verbal scale The relationship that a small distance on a map bears to the corresponding distance on the earth, expressed as an equivalence (such as 1 inch on the map equals 64 miles on the ground).

Chapter 7
Evaluations of Children's Atlases

Discovering Maps: A Children's World Atlas

Facts at a Glance

Full title: **Discovering Maps: A Children's World Atlas**
Publisher: Hammond
Editors: Alma Graham, Project Educational Editor;
　Robert Thomas, Hammond Cartographic Editor
Edition reviewed: © 1993

Number of pages: 80
Number of maps: 75
Number of index entries: 217
Intended readership: ages 8 to 12
Trim size: 8½" × 11"
Binding: hardcover

Price: $11.95; discount available to schools and
　libraries
ISBN 0-8437-3412-4
Revised periodically; next revision scheduled for Sep-
　tember 1994

Introduction, Format, and Authority

Discovering Maps: A Children's World Atlas was published by Hammond in 1993 and is a revision of the
1991 edition, published under the title *Discovering
Maps: A Young Person's Atlas.* The 75 maps are found in
a one-volume, 80-page, 8½" × 11" format. Most of the
maps appear on one page, with smaller maps occurring
two to a page. According to the introduction, "This book
was written to teach you the basic code of maps." This
work is aimed at children ages 8 to 12, according to the
editors, but would probably be most suitable for the
younger end of that spectrum due to the elementary nature of some of the material.

The size of the work is appropriate for children, and
the durable cover will make it useful for schools and libraries.

Hammond is one of the leaders in the field of atlas
production and cartography and has a long history of
publishing excellent atlases.

Scope and Special Features

Since this is more of an instructional tool than a true atlas,
almost half of the work is devoted to teaching students
how to read various kinds of maps. Thirteen two-page
sections deal with map-reading skills such as direction,
distances, longitude and latitude, time zones, and the various kinds of maps. The introductory sections include
questions in several "Think about It" sections. An answer
key is included on the final two pages of the atlas.

The actual atlas section begins with a map of the
world on page 34. This is followed by sections covering
each continent. The first page of each section presents
brief descriptive text with a population distribution map
of the continent. This is followed by a full-page physical
map, two small maps showing vegetation and leading
products (accompanied by more text and a fact box),
and a full-page political map.

A ten-page table highlights some facts about each
continent, such as highest and lowest places, climate extremes, rivers, volcanoes, and plant and animal life.

There seems to be an awkward fit between the sections intended to teach map-reading skills and the actual atlas. The first 30 pages lay out lesson plans for geography teachers and attempt to cover every conceivable kind of map-reading skill. This section includes study questions, activities, and boxed features. The book seems more appropriate as a classroom tool than as a library resource.

Currency

This new edition recognizes recent political changes in the world, such as a unified Germany and unified Yemen and the divisions of Czechoslovakia, Yugoslavia, and the former Soviet Union.

Preferred place names are less current. (Future revision is planned for September 1994.) The map of Asia still shows Burma instead of Myanmar, and Greenland's new name is not recognized.

Very little statistical information is provided. The only population data presented covers the continents and uses rounded figures.

Accuracy

Scales are provided on most of the maps in this atlas, and there is a chapter on how to read them. Scales are shown in both miles and kilometers. Unfortunately, scale varies widely from map to map. Since all continental maps are accorded one page, scale differences are confusing and give a distorted picture of the relative size of the continents.

Borders, place names, and major geographical features are accurately shown, but very little detail is provided. The United States, Canada, and Mexico are the only countries with full-page maps.

Legibility

The maps are clear, with no detail lost because of crowding. The political maps use color to highlight countries and bold outlines for borders. Type size is appropriate for the intended age group.

Accessibility

This work cannot be thought of or used in the same way as a traditional atlas. Although most children's atlases include some introductory material with an instructional intent, it is usually less didactic in nature. The introduction in the RAND MCNALLY CHILDREN'S WORLD ATLAS, for example, gives an overview of various aspects of the world, such as landforms, population distribution, and climate. *Discovering Maps* shows that, by attempting to combine the attributes of a geography textbook and an atlas, some of the best features of both are lost.

This is not a work that lends itself to finding particular countries, cities, or physical features of the world. The one-page index is quite selective in its coverage. It includes some large cities of the world, but these tend to be heavily weighted toward North America. For example, neither Madrid nor Tehran is indexed, although these cities appear on the maps. Kazakhstan is included in the index, but not Armenia, Ukraine, or Azerbaijan. Page numbers and coordinates are given for each entry.

Summary

Discovering Maps could be useful for younger children who are being introduced to map-reading skills. Even students in fourth or fifth grade, however, will probably be more interested in atlases that contain more detail, especially about particular countries. Since it functions more like a textbook than an atlas, this work should probably be used in a classroom setting.

The RAND MCNALLY CHILDREN'S WORLD ATLAS would be a better choice for libraries, even though its political maps are not as current.

The Doubleday Children's Atlas

Facts at a Glance

Full title: **The Doubleday Children's Atlas**
Publisher: Delacorte Press
Editor: Jane Olliver
Edition reviewed: © 1987

Number of pages: 93
Number of maps: 37
Number of index entries: 1,480 (reviewer estimate)
Intended readership: kindergarten to grade 6 (reviewer estimate)
Trim size: 9″ × 12″
Binding: hardcover

Price: $14
ISBN 0-385-23760-X
No stated revision policy

Introduction, Format, and Authority

The Doubleday Children's Atlas, edited by Jane Olliver, was published in 1987 by Delacorte Press. This edition contains 37 maps and 100 color photographs, plus charts and illustrations. It is similar in appearance to the KINGFISHER REFERENCE ATLAS, although its coverage is much more limited, making it suitable for children in elementary grades.

Most maps are full-page treatments and contain two or more countries. A few European countries, such as

Germany and France, receive an entire map. The 9″ × 12″ size makes it fairly easy to handle.

Scope and Special Features

Arrangement is by region and by country within regions. The atlas begins with Europe and, in fact, devotes 30 pages to this continent. This compares with eight pages for Asia and six for Africa.

A seven-page introductory section briefly explains map-reading skills, map projections, facts and figures about the planet, and an overview of countries and continents. While the information is useful, this section is not nearly as comprehensive as in other atlases.

Brief text is provided with each map, explaining something about the history, climate, and products of each identified area or country.

Color reproductions of each country's flag are provided, as well as color photographs and illustrations of some of the more well-known sites and scenery.

An appendix listing each continent and its countries in tabular form shows area in square miles, population, capital city, official language, currency, and major products.

Currency

This atlas is uneven regarding currency. It incorporates more recent changes than THE DOUBLEDAY PICTURE ATLAS, but it is not as up-to-date as DISCOVERING MAPS or THE READER'S DIGEST CHILDREN'S WORLD ATLAS. Although the date of publication is listed as 1987, more recent events, such as the unification of Germany, are recognized. On the map titled "The Balkans and Romania," Slovenia, Croatia, and former Yugoslavia are labeled. Bosnia-Hercegovina, Montenegro, Serbia, and Macedonia are labeled as regions of former Yugoslavia. A note on the map explains:

> At the time of printing, the borders of the former republics of Yugoslavia were uncertain. Bosnia-Hercegovina and Macedonia had recently declared independence. Montenegro had voted to remain with Serbia as part of the new Yugoslavia.

Czechoslovakia is not shown as split into two countries. All of the new countries carved out of the former Soviet Union are shown in the section titled "Russia and Its Neighbors," but outdated city names like Gorki and Leningrad are still used. Myanmar is identified by its new name, but Greenland is not.

The population statistics are given in round figures and in most cases do not match the 1992 estimates that can be found in a world almanac.

Accuracy

All of the maps are drawn to scale, but this scale varies as widely as 1 inch equaling about 20 miles in the map of the Benelux countries and 1 inch equaling about 500 miles in the map of Russia and its neighbors. This variation occurs from map to map, with no explanation. The relative size of countries or regions would be particularly confusing to the reader.

Places are accurately plotted. This is also true of borders and major geographical features.

Legibility

The maps are clearly labeled and uncluttered. Borders are drawn in bold blue lines and the typeface on the maps is excellent. As with many other atlases intended for this age group, only major cities are identified on these maps.

The atlas lies flat when open, and maps that are positioned across two pages are easy to read, with no information lost in the gutter. This aspect is often flawed even in otherwise noteworthy children's atlases, such as the RAND MCNALLY CHILDREN'S WORLD ATLAS.

Accessibility

The table of contents lists the areas treated by continent and, to a certain extent, by country within those continents. Most, but not all, European countries are identified by name in the contents, but the only Asian countries identified are India, China, and Japan. African countries are not listed at all in the table of contents.

The index gives page numbers but no map coordinates, since the maps are not set up to show coordinates. Multiple page numbers are given for places that appear on more than one map. The index is quite comprehensive for an atlas of this size. For example, it lists several cities in Mexico, unlike the index of the RAND MCNALLY CHILDREN'S WORLD ATLAS, which has more detailed maps but a less comprehensive index.

Summary

The Doubleday Children's Atlas has a lot to recommend it. The excellent, uncluttered maps make it a good choice for elementary school and public libraries. The cartography and overall design make it appropriate for young children as well as older elementary students.

Purchasers, however, should take note of this atlas's flaws. Its lack of currency causes it to fall short of more recently revised works like THE READER'S DIGEST CHILDREN'S WORLD ATLAS. The atlas also suffers from a regional bias. Detailed coverage of Europe (and to a lesser extent, North America) comes at the expense of other regions of the world. A final drawback is the lack of any geographic or grid coordinates. Potential buyers should take these shortcomings into account and compare this work with its competitors.

The Doubleday Picture Atlas

Facts at a Glance

Full title: **The Doubleday Picture Atlas**
Publisher: Doubleday
Author: Wendy Roebuck
Edition reviewed: © 1988

Number of pages: 63
Number of maps: 26
Number of index entries: 570 (reviewer estimate)
Intended readership: grades 2 to 5
Trim size: 8½″ × 10¼″
Binding: hardcover

Price: $11.99
ISBN 0-385-24818-0
No stated revision policy

Introduction, Format, and Authority

The Doubleday Picture Atlas, written by Wendy Roebuck, was published in 1988 by Doubleday. The atlas contains about 26 maps, as well as color photographs and illustrations.

This atlas will be most suitable for children in the early to middle elementary grades. According to the introduction, it is intended to "introduce young readers to the world." The atlas takes a hybrid approach to its map selection, showing neither entire continents, nor, in most cases, individual countries. Instead, the maps cover large regions, such as Southeast Asia, or Canada and Greenland.

The atlas is sturdily bound and is conveniently sized for young readers.

Scope and Special Features

The 12 pages of introductory material are divided into one- or two-page sections on map-reading skills such as scale, the use of different types of maps, and projections. An explanation is given of direction as used by mapmakers, but none for more sophisticated concepts such as longitude and latitude. These pages provide a clear introduction to beginning map skills for young readers.

The body of the atlas is made up of two-page sections covering various regions, beginning with northern Europe (defined as Denmark, Norway, Finland, Iceland, and Sweden). Japan, the United States, and the former Soviet Union rate their own sections, but are the only countries that do.

The very brief text accompanying the maps does not supply any meaningful information, especially compared with the well-written text in the RAND MCNALLY PICTURE ATLAS OF THE WORLD. The color photographs are standard and even clichéd: a fjord in Norway; Chinese farmers in a rice field.

A table at the bottom of each section contains the names of each country in the section, the capital city, the major language, the currency, and the population.

Currency

This atlas is virtually obsolete. The breakups of the former Soviet Union, Czechoslovakia, and Yugoslavia are not recognized, nor are the unifications of Germany and Yemen. Cambodia is still called Kampuchea but, strangely enough, Greenland is noted with its new name in parentheses.

The only statistics provided are population figures for countries. These are rounded off and do not reflect the most current estimates.

Accuracy

All of the maps are drawn to scale, but the scales vary widely. This could create considerable confusion for children who do not have a background in map reading. For example, the scale on the map of Japan is 1 inch to 125 miles, while that on the map of the United States is 1 inch to 235 miles.

None of the maps contain a great deal of detail, but the borders, place names, and geographical features that do appear are accurate. One major omission is that Alaska is not found on either map of the United States, even as an inset (as Hawaii is treated). Instead, it is included with Canada and Greenland.

Most of the small European countries are included on the maps and in the statistics; however, Vatican City, while it appears on the table, is not shown on the map.

The names given to particular regions are sometimes misleading. For example, "Western Europe" includes the Netherlands, Belgium, Germany, Switzerland, and Austria. Portugal, Spain, France, and Italy are identified as "France and Southern Europe."

Legibility

The illustrated maps are drawn in green and brown, with little attempt to show relief other than in drawings of mountain ranges. Borders are shown in a bright, contrasting red.

Most maps of countries show only the capital city, or perhaps a few of the larger cities. Capital cities are marked by a black square, which differs little from the black circle denoting other cities.

The large bold print of the text is easy to read. However, the pages appear crowded in their attempt to show the map, photographs, illustrations, and tables.

Accessibility

The index indicates countries in capital letters, which will be helpful for students looking for particular nations. No grid system or geographical coordinates are provided, however. Only page numbers are given, which sharply lessens the value of the index for students.

While there is a definite European and North American bias, even these regions are not well defined. Any student hoping to find information about any of the newer countries of the world (for example, Ukraine, Kazakhstan, or a united Germany or Yemen) will have to look elsewhere.

Smaller countries, such as Bahrain, are listed in the index, but are sometimes not readily identifiable on the map. There is virtually no coverage of small island nations in the Pacific or Indian oceans or Caribbean Sea. Some are not listed in the accompanying tables, and their locations may or may not be found on the maps.

Summary

This atlas does not differ substantially from several other children's atlases in its treatment of the world by regions; however, its maps and information are woefully outdated.

Students looking for information about a particular country will find little to help them here. However, the introductory material on map-reading skills may be helpful for very young students.

The Facts On File Children's Atlas

Facts at a Glance

Full title: **The Facts On File Children's Atlas**
Publisher: Facts On File
Editors: David Wright; Jill Wright
Edition reviewed: © 1993

Number of pages: 96
Number of maps: 56
Number of index entries: 2,000 (reviewer estimate)
Intended readership: elementary school
Trim size: 9½″ × 11½″
Binding: hardcover

Price: $15.95
ISBN 0-8160-2925-3
No stated revision policy

Introduction, Format, and Authority

This 9½″ × 11½″ atlas contains 56 maps and many color illustrations and photographs. This work was originally published in 1987, revised in 1991, and revised again for this 1993 edition.

Colorful maps, illustrations, and photographs add to the eye appeal of this work and its size should make it easy for children to handle.

Facts On File is a highly respected firm that publishes yearbooks and topical reference books on a variety of subjects. The maps were prepared by George Philip Limited, a respected British cartographic firm.

Scope and Special Features

All of the regions of the world are covered. Larger countries such as the United States, India, and China are each given a separate two-page spread, while most African, Asian, and Latin American countries are grouped together with several other surrounding nations.

The first two-page spread, entitled "Our Planet Earth," discusses the planet and its relationship to the solar system and the rest of the universe. Subsequent sections treat population distribution, physical features of the earth, political divisions, and climate. These sections are followed by a guide to map-reading skills and to using the atlas. The helpful guide includes a description of scale and of the colors used to indicate topography.

The work includes excellent color photographs and illustrations. Captions to the illustrations and fact boxes provide a great deal of information not found in the main text sections. "Puzzle Pictures," which ask readers to identify photographs, and numerous text questions engage students' curiosity. The answers to all questions and puzzles are found in the back of the book.

One unique feature of this atlas is the use of postage stamps from around the world to illustrate interesting facts about various countries. The color reproductions of stamps are accompanied by text describing them and their relevance.

A two-page quiz and activity section comes just before the index. Readers are encouraged to name various islands and countries, solve a mystery message, answer trivia questions about the United States, and start a stamp or coin collection. Answers to all of the quiz questions are found at the end of the book.

Currency

This 1993 edition is very current. The Czech Republic and Slovakia are included, as are the individual republics that constitute the former Yugoslavia. The new countries formed from the former Soviet Union are recognized on the map of the world; these are also discussed in the section on Russia and its neighbors. However, some counties are still identified by their former names, including Burma and Greenland, and the older Wade-Giles system of romanization for Chinese names is used. Despite this, the work as a whole is one of the most current children's atlases available.

Accuracy

Although scales vary from 1:45,000,000 on the map of Russia and its neighbors to 1:2,000,000 on the map of the Benelux countries, similar scales are used consistently for like-sized areas. Scale is clearly identified on each map by ratio and by a bar scale of distances in miles and kilometers.

Place names, borders, and major geographical features are accurately identified. A red square designates the largest cities (those with a population of more than 1 million). Two sizes of red dots indicate other cities (one for "middle-sized cities" and one for "smaller cities"); unfortunately, the dots are not keyed to specific population information.

Legibility

Except for the maps of the entire world, each map is confined to one page. Labels and cartographic details are clear and the maps are uncluttered.

The use of color is one of the best features of this atlas. Topography is shown using colors ranging from dark brown to green to white. The shading is easy to understand and every map contains an altitude key. Elementary school children should have no difficulty comprehending these distinctions.

Accessibility

The Facts On File Children's Atlas is organized by region, a traditional approach for atlases. Students should be able to locate countries, geographical features, and cities.

The index is excellent for an atlas of this size and scope. All index entries include page numbers and coordinates. A spot check of the index found no inaccuracies or blind references. The explanation of how to use the index will be helpful to students.

Locator maps and legends explaining topography and scale appear on each map. These are unobtrusive and easy to understand.

Summary

Many other recent atlases intended for this age level, including THE KINGFISHER REFERENCE ATLAS, contain more comprehensive information about countries. *The Facts On File Children's Atlas* will be useful for students just beginning a study of world geography and is appropriate for elementary schools and libraries. The excellent, visually appealing maps are its greatest strength, along with its modest price. The mixture of maps with lively illustrations, quiz questions, activities, and interesting facts makes this work a solid and entertaining introduction to maps and geography.

Gage Atlas of the World

Facts at a Glance

Full title: **Gage Atlas of the World**
Publisher: Gage Educational Publishing Company
Edition reviewed: © 1985

Number of pages: 192
Number of maps: 170
Number of index entries: 10,500
Intended readership: grades 7 to 12
Trim size: 8½″ × 11″
Binding: hardcover

Price: $19.35
ISBN 0-7715-8162-9
Currently under evaluation for revision or replacement in 1997–1998

Introduction, Format, and Authority

The *Gage Atlas of the World,* unrevised since this 1985 edition, is intended for Canadian high school students. It is divided into three sections. The first section focuses on both physical and human patterns in the world, including the solar system, population density, occupations, and food resources. Continental and regional studies comprise the second section, which features a variety of political, topographical, and thematic maps. Tables of meteorological statistics for the countries of the world follow the map section of the atlas. A major portion of this third and final section profiles Canada's economic and social features.

The maps and index were prepared by George Philip and Son Limited, a London cartographic service. Founded in 1834, George Philip is well known in Europe as a producer of quality map products. The Gage Educational Publishing Company, which issues this book in North America, also publishes the GLOBAL ATLAS and THE MACMILLAN SCHOOL ATLAS.

Scope and Special Features

The atlas contains a wide variety of maps. Separate physical and political maps accompany sections on the world, North America, Central and South America, Europe, Africa, Asia, and Australasia; except for those on the world and Australasia, the sections also include an economic map. Each of these major maps occupies one page.

Regional political/physical maps, both one- and two-page spreads, supplement the continental cartography. These sections also feature a variety of smaller thematic maps on climate, vegetation, population, and trade. Each regional section also contains an economic map. In addition, special features on Canada provide detailed maps with data concerning the nation's geology, landforms, vegetation and soils, agriculture, fisheries, energy, trade, and specific provinces and cities.

All maps include a bar scale and note the projection used. Map scales are usually reasonable for the size of the area being represented. The atlas uses a variety of scales expressed in kilometers. Physical maps include a color code for the elevations portrayed. A master legend for physical and political maps appears in the front of the book; thematic maps have their own legend.

The back of the atlas contains statistical tables and two indexes. The tables, which provide pertinent data on both the world and Canada, lend themselves well to graph making and other classroom activities.

The atlas has a deliberate Canadian bias. Cartography of Canada, its provinces, and its cities occupies nearly one-fourth of the book. Likewise, a majority of the statistical data in the back of the atlas is devoted to information about Canada.

An important strength of this atlas is its special features. In addition to the master key, the introductory material includes diagrams of map projections, an illustrated explanation of the solar system, and a two-page spread on time and distance. A 27-page section containing statistics on the world and Canada completes the introduction.

Currency

Because of its 1985 publication date, the *Gage Atlas* does not reflect recent political changes such as the breakups of the Soviet Union, Yugoslavia, and Czechoslovakia; nor does it include the reunification of Germany. Statistics are also out-of-date.

The atlas uses very few photographs. Although contemporary, they are disappointingly small and the captions furnish minimal information.

Accuracy

Place names are spelled correctly. The atlas uses generic rather than official political names. However, place names are not always used consistently. For example, "United Kingdom" appears as the title on the political map of Europe, but "British Isles" is the title used on the subregional map. Although both headings appear in the index, only the United Kingdom is listed on the statistical table of principal countries of the world.

One notable omission is the state of Alaska from the map of the United States. Although this map includes an inset of Hawaii, Alaska is shown only on the political map of North America.

Legibility

Legibility is not one of this atlas's strong features. The type is often too thin to read easily. For example, state names on regional maps of the United States are hard to locate and read. Likewise, the names of physical features are not always easy to distinguish. Boundary lines are another weak feature. International boundaries, internal boundaries, freeways, and roads are all printed in red, making them hard to differentiate.

Accessibility

The *Gage Atlas* has two indexes, one for Canada and a second for the rest of the world. Since a large segment of cartography is devoted to Canada, the decision to provide two indexes has the advantage of ease of access.

A two-page introduction precedes the indexes. One page explains how to use the index and what abbreviations are used. The second page provides a diagrammed explanation of latitude and longitude.

Summary

The *Gage Atlas of the World* ably fulfills its stated purposes. The imaginative teacher will find that it offers a wealth of information for drawing conclusions about people, their environment, and how their interaction has produced a variety of world problems. However, while the *Gage Atlas* has many worthwhile features and finely executed maps, this edition is now a decade old. Special maps and features are based on statistics dating back as early as 1980. This serious lack of currency means that it cannot be recommended.

Giant Atlas of the World

Facts at a Glance

Full title: **Giant Atlas of the World**
Publisher: Rand McNally
Illustrator: Stuart Brendon
Edition reviewed: © 1993

Number of pages: 13
Number of maps: 12
Number of index entries: none
Intended readership: ages 2 to 7
Trim size: 15" × 21"
Binding: heavy cardboard

Price: $27.95
Sold in bookstores
ISBN 0-528-83589-0
No stated revision policy

Introduction, Format, and Authority

The *Giant Atlas of the World,* illustrated by Stuart Brendon, was published in 1993 by Rand McNally in association with Grandreams Limited of London. The large-format heavy cardboard children's atlas consists of 12 illustrated maps of continents or large areas of the world. According to the explanation on the back cover, each map is "accompanied by a fact panel that young readers will find easy to understand." Although the work is published by Rand McNally, the highly stylized maps are not attributed to that company's cartography staff. Their cartoonlike colors lead one to believe that they were drawn by the book's illustrator.

Scope and Special Features

The first two-page spread contains a large map of the world with a compass rose. Whimsical drawings of major geographical features and representative plant and animal life cover the map's surface. Three smaller maps show the Arctic Circle, Antarctica, and the outlines of the continents with their names labeled.

Maps of each continent follow, beginning with Europe, followed by Africa, North and South America, Asia, and Russia, and ending with Australia and New Zealand on the back cover. The countries on each map are labeled and the capital cities are identified. Cartoon illustrations cover each map, and are intended to give readers an idea of the vegetation, animal life, and in some cases, the industries and activities of a region's people. For example, a film crew is shown in southern California, and a bicycle rider appears in France. Except for some crude representations of mountains, the maps give very little information about geographical features.

A table accompanying each map provides an alphabetical list of the countries depicted, the area of each in square miles and kilometers, the 1993 population of each, and each country's capital city and its population. The statistics given in these charts seem directed at an older reader than the maps themselves are. The maps will be of interest only to very young, picture-oriented children.

A small hole has been drilled through the top of each page so that the book can be hung from a wall or bulletin board.

Currency

Most of the recent changes in the world, such as the reunification of Germany, the separation of Yugoslavia into several new countries, and the breakup of the Soviet Union, are depicted. The statistical information provided is identified as 1993 data. A check against the 1994 *World Almanac and Book of Facts* shows the numbers to be up-to-date. No information is provided about possible revisions of this 1993 publication.

Accuracy

Since the maps are illustrative rather than truly geographical, this atlas cannot be used to help students get an idea of the physical or political features of any country. Borders are only approximate and no scale is pro-

vided. Only capital cities are identified, with the exception of a few large cities in the United States and Canada. North and South America are shown side by side on facing pages, a potentially confusing arrangement.

The illustrations portray the most obvious and clichéd national stereotypes, such as a serape-clad peasant with a burro in Mexico and an Eskimo in a kayak for Alaska. Amazingly, no native Africans appear in the cartoons illustrating South Africa. Instead, well-dressed people of European descent are shown digging for diamonds. These illustrations are misleading, and they also reinforce cultural stereotypes. They provide very little accurate or current information about a country or region and are educationally inappropriate for children.

Country information in the tables is accurate, except that Alaska is listed as a country in the table on the "North America" map. Smaller island nations, such as those in the Indian Ocean or the southwestern Pacific, do not appear in either the maps or in the tables.

Legibility

The maps are large and colorful, but the names of countries are often squeezed into small spaces between the illustrations, making them hard to locate in some cases. Boundaries are sometimes obscured by the illustrations or not identified with clearly marked lines. Countries are color coded using green, yellow, brown, orange, and pink.

The charts are reproduced in rather small print compared with the size of the maps. If these maps are used as a wall chart, as suggested by the publisher, they would have to be viewed from very close range.

Accessibility

The countries listed in the tables are in alphabetical order, but there is no comprehensive index listing of all of the countries in one place. As a result, there is no easy way to locate a particular country. Countries such as the Maldives, Fiji, Tonga, and many other island nations are left out entirely. No map includes the islands of Oceania.

The last spread of the atlas contains three paragraphs of explanatory material about Russia, the northeastern part of which is shown in the large map on those pages. Although accurate and current, the information is anomalous, as no other map has similar descriptive writing. The spread also contains a small outline map of the continents and two paragraphs explaining the division of the earth's land area into continents and the populations of each. These paragraphs seem out of place at the back of the book.

Summary

The maps of this atlas provide almost no useful geographical information, especially compared with those of THE DOUBLEDAY PICTURE ATLAS, reviewed elsewhere in this guide. Although that work is not as up-to-date as this one, it has more clearly defined mountain ranges, national boundaries, lakes, and rivers. It also has useful and interesting information about cartography and the nations of the world, written at a level suitable for young children. Population information and statistics in the *Giant Atlas of the World,* although accurate, seem aimed at an older reader than the maps themselves.

The large size of this book and the bright cartoon illustrations will undoubtedly appeal to young children. The illustrations, however, are stereotypical and even misleading: the drawing of Mount Rushmore, for example, is located due north of the drawing of Old Faithful. Purchasers should buy this book only for its entertainment value; at $27.95, it is hardly a bargain even for that purpose.

Global Atlas

Facts at a Glance

Full title: **Global Atlas**
Publisher: Gage Educational Publishing Company
Editor: Graham Draper
Edition reviewed: © 1993

Number of pages: 100
Number of maps: 150
Number of index entries: 2,660
Intended readership: grades 7 to 10
Trim size. 15¼″ × 11″
Binding: paperback with spiral binding

Price: $24.20 (U.S.); $32.50 (Canadian)
Sold directly to schools and libraries; also sold in bookstores
ISBN 0-7715-8170-X
No stated revision policy

Introduction, Format, and Authority

Containing 300 color illustrations and 150 maps, this spiral-bound, 15¼″ × 11″ atlas was published in 1993. Intended for older students in grades 7 through 10, the atlas is designed to "help you investigate the world around you . . . even parts of the world that you may never have seen."

The spiral-bound format allows the atlas to lie flat, but also makes it less durable than other atlases. Maps vary greatly in size, with as many as eight to a page and as few as one.

Gage Educational Publishing Company is a division of Canada Publishing Company. The cartography is by George Philip Limited of London, a respected cartographic firm.

Scope and Special Features

The atlas is arranged thematically, beginning with three pages of introductory material that explain basic map skills such as longitude and latitude, scale, and color contours. The introduction also explains the various kinds of graphs and charts used in the atlas and how to interpret them.

The next section focuses on worldwide information: the earth's relationship to other planets, environment and resources, and economic activity. Thirty pages are devoted to everything from forestry to energy resources to tourism. Next come 31 pages that treat the world by regions or continents (for example, one page is devoted to the Middle East and two to Africa). Seventeen of these pages are devoted to Canada, making this atlas perhaps most suitable for students in that country.

Currency

Copyrighted first in 1991, this 1993 edition states no policy concerning future revisions.

The unifications of Germany and Yemen are recognized, Myanmar and Cambodia are given their proper names, and the new countries that resulted from the breakups of Yugoslavia and Czechoslovakia are all here. A section, however, is still devoted to the nonexistent U.S.S.R. The various new republics appear on the map, along with an explanation of the changes taking place and the change to the Commonwealth of Independent States. The new republics do not get separate treatment in statistical breakdowns, however.

Statistical data on the many graphs and charts is dated. Life expectancy and birthrate data for China are from 1985, an energy consumption chart for Canada is dated 1987, and most population statistics are from the 1980s. Many statistical charts or graphs give no date at all.

A special symbol and an asterisk accompany any information that does not reflect current global events. Four pages called "Dealing with Change" at the end of the atlas discuss how atlases and statistical information are revised to keep up with changes.

Accuracy

Map scales are given in centimeters (appropriate for Canada, where metric measures are employed). All of the major maps are drawn to scale, which varies widely from 1 centimeter equaling 25 kilometers on small inset maps (such as that of Israel) to 1 centimeter equaling 800 kilometers on the map of the Pacific Rim. On every map the scale is given in a ratio, a distance equivalent, and a line graph.

Borders, place names, and major geographical features are mostly accurate but, except in the case of Canada, maps show little detail. For example, the map of the Middle East includes 14 countries in a 7″ × 7″ map.

One drawback of this work is the inconsistent treatment of different countries or regions. An inset map of Australia shows rainfall, while one of Russia treats energy resources, and one of Italy displays population density by provinces.

Legibility

The use of color in this atlas is one of its truly outstanding features. Bold colors, clean design, and striking contrast make the political and physical feature maps easy to read. Graphs and charts are also enhanced by bright colors. Full-color photographs throughout the atlas are also a plus.

All of the maps are uncluttered and graced by bold and easily readable type. The vast majority of maps are given half a page or less, so detail must be sacrificed to maintain the high level of legibility. Pages that include graphs, charts, and photographs make good use of white space for a pleasing, uncluttered look.

Accessibility

The short topical index that precedes the main index will be helpful in locating some of the information in the introductory sections. These sections, however, contain such an eclectic variety of material that users may prefer browsing.

The main atlas section proceeds from oceans and polar regions to continents and regions, but in no discernible pattern. The comprehensive index will be helpful in finding specific places. The index gives a page number, grid location, and the longitude and latitude for each entry.

Summary

The *Global Atlas* will be of most value to Canadian schools and libraries. It is a good introduction to the use of maps and data for middle school and high school students, and an effective tool for geography and social studies classes. The large amount of data and information included could be useful in a classroom or library setting, but is more suitable for browsing than for locating specific facts. The excellent maps and appealing design make it a good purchase for homes, schools, and libraries.

The Kingfisher Reference Atlas

Facts at a Glance

Full title: **The Kingfisher Reference Atlas: An A to Z Guide to Countries of the World**
Publisher: Kingfisher Books
Author: Brian Williams
Edition reviewed: © 1993

Number of pages: 216
Number of maps: over 500 color maps, graphs, charts, and diagrams
Number of index entries: 8,300 (reviewer estimate)
Intended readership: all ages
Trim size: 10¼″ × 8¼″
Binding: hardcover

Price: $19.95
Sold directly to libraries and schools; also sold in bookstores and other retail outlets
ISBN 1-85697-838-9
No stated revision policy

Introduction, Format, and Authority

The *Kingfisher Atlas,* written by Brian Williams, was published in 1992 by Kingfisher Books in the United Kingdom. Kingfisher is a respected publisher of children's books, including THE KINGFISHER CHILDREN'S ENCYCLOPEDIA. This first American edition (released in 1993) contains over 500 maps, graphs, charts, and diagrams in a 10¼″ × 8¼″ format. It is intended to serve all ages but will be most useful to younger students. According to the introductory material, this atlas "combines all the ingredients of an atlas, gazetteer and an almanac."

The wide format may make it difficult for younger children to handle easily, but since the book lies fairly flat when opened, this should not present a problem for most readers. The maps, graphs, and text in this durable hardcover edition take up one full page per country, with some countries (China, Germany, and South Africa) allotted two pages.

Scope and Special Features

After a brief introduction that points out some of the book's features, the maps of each country, continent, or, occasionally, regional group, are arranged alphabetically.

The basic format of each entry includes a statistical box, followed by brief text describing some of the geography and history of the country. A separate sidebar details the country's main economic activities. Imports and exports are shown in a bar graph and age distribution of the population in a pie chart. Additional graphs present population growth from 1940 projected up to the year 2000 and month-by-month rainfall and temperature for the capital city of the country.

A main map of the country shows major cities, roads, railroads, and physical features. These maps are small, averaging about 4″ × 6″, which means that very little detail can be included. Even smaller are the locator and elevation maps for each country. While the size is adequate for the locator maps, the elevation maps are often difficult to read.

Currency

This atlas was first published in Great Britain in 1992. The American edition appeared in 1993. No policy for future revisions is stated.

The unifications of Germany and Yemen are reflected in this edition, but a publisher's note at the beginning addresses the difficulties encountered dealing with Yugoslavia and Czechoslovakia. The entry for Yugoslavia is entitled "Former Yugoslavia" and recognizes that there are now six republics (albeit in a state of flux), but the statistical breakdown still treats them as one country. The publisher's note points out that, at press time, Czechoslovakia had split into its now existing two states, and the text of the entry mentions this. Again, however, the statistical breakdown and related information treat it as one country.

An even more serious problem exists in the treatment of the former Soviet Union. All 12 countries are combined under one entry entitled "Russia and Its Neighbors." Again, there is no statistical breakdown for each country. Anyone wanting to look up Ukraine or Kazakhstan must go to the index because these countries are not placed in correct alphabetical order.

Place names are current in some cases, not in others. The reversion to Cambodia from Kampuchea is recognized, but Greenland's new name is not mentioned, nor is the new name of its capital city.

Statistical data is fairly current. The U.S. population figure, for example, reflects the updated estimate since the 1990 census.

Accuracy

All maps are drawn to scale and the scale is shown in both kilometers and miles. The scale varies from 1 inch equaling 100 miles to as much as 500 miles, depending on the country in question. Since all maps for all countries are accorded approximately the same amount of space, scale could be quite confusing. The small inset locator maps help only minimally in giving the reader a sense of the relative size of a country.

Borders, place names, and major geographical features are accurately portrayed insofar as possible on such small maps. Occasionally one finds the name of a smaller city without an accompanying dot to locate it, as in the case of Santiago de Compostela in Spain. Where major cities cluster together (for example, San Francisco, Oakland, and San Jose), it is difficult to ascertain their accurate relative positions, again due to the small size of the maps. States and provinces are, in the majority of cases, entirely left out due to space considerations. This is not true in the case of the United States, where all the states are identified on the map of the United States; their individual areas and populations are even given in a special table.

Legibility

Although the maps are small, they are clearly labeled and easy to read in most cases. Country boundaries are outlined in red and the labels are in dark bold type. Care has been taken not to crowd the maps with too many labels. This makes for easy legibility but sacrifices detail.

Reading the inset graphs and charts will be difficult for some users because of the extremely small typeface employed. This is especially true in the case of the "imports and exports" graph that accompanies most maps.

Accessibility

The straightforward alphabetical scheme is used, but, unfortunately, not in all cases. As previously mentioned, the republics of the former Soviet Union are not each given a separate entry but are on the page entitled "Russia and Its Neighbors." These can be located in the atlas by using the index, but this seems a cumbersome way to proceed. Similarly, anyone looking for the Maldive Islands, Seychelles, or Comoro Islands (all in the Indian Ocean) will have to look in the index to find that they are listed on the page labeled "Indian Ocean." Similar treatment is accorded other small nations.

The index is complete and thorough. Virtually all of the places marked can be found, including the mountain ranges, rivers, and other physical features. "See" references for countries that have recently changed their name (for example, Burma to Myanmar, Kampuchea to Cambodia) would have been a helpful addition to the index. Country and continent names in the index are in boldface. Index entries are followed by a page number and coordinates.

Summary

The *Kingfisher Reference Atlas,* although promoted by the publisher for "all ages," will be most useful for elementary school students. The maps, while clear and uncluttered, do not provide much detail about the countries. The information in the text and charts is concise and up-to-date, and will help with short research reports that do not require in-depth information.

School and public libraries needing a supplementary atlas may find their needs met by this one, with the caveats that it has not treated the recent changes in the world as thoroughly or accurately as it could have, that maps have very little detail, and that smaller countries are not, in some cases, given equal treatment. THE NATIONAL GEOGRAPHIC PICTURE ATLAS OF OUR WORLD surpasses the *Kingfisher Reference Atlas* in these respects.

The Macmillan First Atlas

Facts at a Glance

Full title: **The Macmillan First Atlas**
Publisher: Macmillan
Writers and designers: Nicola Wright; Tony Potter;
   Dee Turner; Christine Wilson
Edition reviewed: © 1991

Number of pages: 40
Number of maps: 17
Number of index entries: 182
Intended readership: ages 4 to 7
Trim size: 10¼″ × 13″
Binding: hardcover

Price: $12.95
Sold directly to schools and libraries; also sold in
   bookstores and other retail outlets
ISBN 0-02-774920-7
No stated revision policy

Introduction, Format, and Authority

Intended for very young children, this 1991 publication contains 40 full-color pages with 17 maps, color drawings of flags, and inset fact files. All of the maps are of the illustration type, rather than formal cartographic productions. The Sussex University Map Library is listed as a map consultant, and Diane Snowdon served as a geography consultant. Macmillan is a major publisher of reference works.

Scope and Special Features

A two-page introduction entitled "All About Maps" introduces some basic map-reading concepts, including legends, scale, and direction. This is followed by a two-page world map. An eight-page section on the United States includes a map, drawings of the state flags, and regional information.

There are no separate maps for other countries; treatment, as in many similar children's atlases, is by region or continent. Each of these sections contains an insert box entitled "Fact File," which contains five or six facts about the area, such as the highest mountain or the population.

Cartoon illustrations of people or animals (similar to the drawings in MY FIRST ATLAS) are found on every page, and many of these are shown with a balloon relating facts about an area or country.

Currency

The atlas does not recognize the breakup of the former Soviet Union, Yugoslavia, or Czechoslovakia. A unified Germany is shown, but Yemen is still on the map as two countries. The new names of Burma and Greenland are not given. No date has been set for a future revision of this 1991 publication.

Accuracy

The illustrated maps in this atlas do not lend themselves to much detail. The only map of the United States that shows all 50 states positions some capital cities in a very approximate manner.

Scale is indicated by a bar graph running along the bottom of each two-page spread. While it shows both kilometers and miles, no explanation of the metric system is given, lessening its effectiveness for teaching very young children.

Facts and statistics, while minimal, are often approximate. All population figures are estimates, and statements about the weather in various regions are too generalized to be useful. For example, the "Fact File" on the Middle East states that "these countries have hot summers and cold winters."

Another problem with accuracy is the sometimes condescending and often misleading information provided in the brief sentences of text that accompany the maps. For instance, three pieces of information provided about Spain are: "Bullfighting is the national sport of Spain"; "Eagles and vultures live in the Pyrenees"; and "Monkeys live on the Rock of Gibraltar." These statements do not convey useful information about Spain and are typical of the kind of comments found throughout the book.

Legibility

While the pages are not as crowded with text and illustrations as those in THE DOUBLEDAY PICTURE ATLAS, more white space would make this work more appealing and comprehensible to very young children. Except for the labels used for lakes and rivers, the print is large and suitable for young children.

The maps feature bright and attractive colors, but lack detail. Although the section on U.S. state flags portrays every flag, the illustrations lack sharpness. This makes it hard to pick out detail, especially on the state seals that appear on the flags.

Accessibility

Countries can be located using the index, but cities, bodies of water, and landforms are not included. For some reason, the Falkland Islands and Galapagos Islands appear in the index, although they are shown with no detail at all on the maps. The Japanese island of Hokkaido rates an entry because it is labeled, but that label may lead a young reader to think that Hokkaido is a separate country. Index entries are followed by a page number. There is no grid system of coordinates in this atlas and the concepts of longitude and latitude are not addressed.

The table of contents lists the continent and regional map sections.

Summary

A good children's encyclopedia such as the WORLD BOOK ENCYCLOPEDIA or COMPTON'S ENCYCLOPEDIA will have much better maps and flag representations than this atlas. The fact that this atlas is intended for very young children does not mean that the information should be misleading or overly simplistic, as it often is here. A better, albeit briefer, introduction to map skills can be found in the RAND MCNALLY CHILDREN'S WORLD ATLAS. Finally, no library, school, or home should purchase an atlas that is out-of-date regarding recent changes in the world.

The Macmillan School Atlas

Facts at a Glance

Full title: **The Macmillan School Atlas**
Publisher: Gage Educational Publishing Company
Editor: Ronald C. Daly
Edition reviewed: third edition, © 1993, 1992

Number of pages: 140
Number of maps: 96
Number of index entries: about 950 for the index of
    Canada; about 1,400 for the rest of the world
Intended readership: grades 4 to 6
Trim size: 10½″ × 13″
Binding: hardcover

Price: $19.35 (U.S.); $26 (Canadian)
Sold in bookstores and other retail outlets; also sold
    directly to schools and libraries
ISBN 0-7715-8269-2
Revised every 7 to 10 years, or as required by global
    events; next revision planned for the year 2000

Introduction, Format, and Authority

The Macmillan School Atlas contains 96 maps in a one-volume, 140-page format. The work is intended primarily for use by Canadian students in grades 4 through 6. This hardcover atlas is attractively designed and sturdily bound. According to its "Introduction to Maps," students are invited to use the atlas to "find interesting and important information about places and people."

The 1993 *Macmillan School Atlas* is the third edition of this work. John Waller and Joe Stevens are the map illustrators. The Gage Educational Publishing Company also produces several other atlases for young people.

Scope and Special Features

The atlas is divided into six sections. The first, an introduction to maps and mapping, presents concepts of hemisphere, latitude, longitude, time, and map projections. This section is well written, with excellent explanations of map skills.

The second section contains maps of the world, the hemispheres, and North America. The world maps show vegetation and landforms, and those of the hemispheres show countries. The maps of North America show landforms, winter and summer temperatures, annual rainfall, and vegetation. One map shows political divisions.

The third and largest part of the atlas features Canada and its provinces. There are eight full-page maps of Canada featuring political divisions, landforms, vegetation, settled areas, lakes and rivers, transportation, and natural resources. Thirty-five maps of the provinces and territories follow; these include relief maps of landforms and thematic maps on vegetation, farming, and industry.

The fourth section covers the rest of the world, with political and physical maps for each continent, as well as maps of the South American rain forest, the Pacific Rim, and the Arctic. The fifth section, entitled "World Exploration," contains 17 maps showing the routes of various world explorers. The final section is a two-part gazetteer. The first part contains about 950 Canadian place names; the second has about 1,400 place names for the rest of the world.

This atlas is heavily weighted toward North American countries, especially Canada. This coverage makes the work particularly valuable for Canadian libraries.

The atlas includes several special features. Map and fact boxes for Canada appear on the inside front cover, with the world treated in a similar way on the inside back cover. Color photographs of various places around the world are scattered throughout the book. A two-page spread entitled "Canada: A Multicultural Society" shows the country's ethnic diversity through photographs, charts, and graphs.

Currency

This edition was updated in June 1993, and reflects the unifications of Germany and Yemen, the independent states of the former Soviet Union, and the splitting of Czechoslovakia into the Czech Republic and Slovakia. The republics of the former Yugoslavia are labeled, but are unified by the use of a single color for all of them and the word "Yugoslavia" across them. While the atlas uses the names St. Petersburg, Yangon, and Myanmar, it also has many outdated names, such as Gorki, Kampuchea, Christmas Island, Dacca, Greenland, and Godthåb. Nevertheless, the currency of this atlas compares favorably with other 1993 works, such as THE READER'S DIGEST CHILDREN'S WORLD ATLAS.

Accuracy

The maps appear to be accurately drawn when compared against the NATIONAL GEOGRAPHIC ATLAS OF THE WORLD. The scales are consistent and easy to use; as befitting a Canadian atlas, kilometers are used.

There is some confusion over the treatment of city size. Different symbols and type treatments are used for larger and smaller cities, and no criteria are stated for the distinction. San Antonio and San Diego, for instance, are given the symbol for a larger city but the lighter typeface used for smaller cities.

The political world map shows the peninsula of Korea as having two nation-states, one appearing in orange and the other in green. The name "Korea" is printed along the peninsula, however, blurring any distinction between the two countries.

Legibility

The maps are generally clear and easy to read, with effective use of color, symbols, and typefaces. Only about six of the maps appear on two-page spreads, but, unfortunately, information on most of these is lost in the gutter.

Accessibility

Maps are arranged in a logical sequence. The atlas gives a good explanation of a map legend, with examples. Locator maps throughout the atlas help users place provinces and continents within a larger context.

The two-part gazetteer contains both political and physical features, with abbreviated labels describing the latter. The page number and a letter-number grid coordinate follow each gazetteer entry. A spot check found no inaccuracies in the gazetteer.

Summary

Overall, *The Macmillan School Atlas* does a good job of introducing students to North America (particularly Canada), with clear maps on many different topics. The text is written in a lively style and is well suited for the intended grade level of the work. Given its limitations as a world atlas, this would be an excellent complement to an atlas like THE READER'S DIGEST CHILDREN'S WORLD ATLAS or the RAND MCNALLY CHILDREN'S WORLD ATLAS.

My First Atlas

Facts at a Glance

Full title: **My First Atlas**
Publisher: Troll Associates
Illustrator: Alan Snow
Edition reviewed: © 1992

Number of pages: 30
Number of maps: 13
Number of index entries: 240 (reviewer estimate)
Intended readership: kindergarten through third grade
Trim size: 7½″ × 10″
Binding: hardcover; paperback

Price: $12.79 (hardcover); $4.95 (paperback)
Sold in bookstores and other retail outlets
ISBN 0-8167-2518-7
No stated revision policy

Introduction, Format, and Authority

A very brief (30-page) picture-book format is the hallmark of *My First Atlas,* which was published in 1992. Each two-page spread contains an illustrated map of a large landmass, such as North America, South America, or Asia. The text presents very brief and general facts (usually included as captions to illustrations) such as, "Wheat is an important crop in the USA and Canada." The cartoon style of the maps and the overall format are similar to the MACMILLAN FIRST ATLAS.

Because the publisher did not supply a hardcover copy for review, we cannot comment on the book's durability. The purpose of the work is to introduce young children to atlases and some of the elementary concepts of their use, although this purpose is not explicitly stated.

Troll Associates also publishes other reference works for children, including the STUDENT ATLAS.

Scope and Special Features

Only the major landmasses are treated in this atlas, beginning with the Western Hemisphere and proceeding to the polar regions. Each two-page spread contains a color map, a key to the colors indicating vegetation, cartoon illustrations, and some brief factual text.

The final section, entitled "Atlas Fun," contains three pages of questions and games intended to test the knowledge gained by using the atlas.

Currency

The atlas's treatment of the breakup of the former Soviet Union reflects its publication during the transitional phase. The map entitled "USSR" includes text hinting that the Soviet Union began changing in 1991. Ukraine, Estonia, Latvia, and Lithuania are labeled in roman type, indicating their independence. However, other now independent republics such as Georgia, Russia, and Armenia are labeled in italic type. Throughout the two-page spread, the Soviet Union is treated as a unified entity.

The republics of the former Yugoslavia appear, but, as with the former Soviet Union, they are treated as parts of a larger whole. While a unified Germany is shown, the atlas does not reflect the splitting of Czechoslovakia. Myanmar is correctly labeled, but the names Kampuchea and Greenland are still used.

Accuracy

Since these maps are merely color illustrations, no attempt is made to indicate scale or even proportion. The map of the United States shows individual states, but their actual shapes and borders are quite distorted.

Countries are labeled, but very few cities or other place names appear on the maps. Because of the cartoon nature of the maps themselves, it would be difficult for a child to determine accurate locations of the mountain ranges, rivers, and other physical features.

The color key indicating vegetation has two problems. First, no distinct difference indicates, for example, different kinds of forest. Coniferous, evergreen, and broadleaf forests are all shown in various similar shades of green. Second, the accuracy of the vegetation designations is often questionable. The maps mistakenly show a wide band of broadleaf forest running through western South Dakota and an area of desert landscape in southwestern France.

Legibility

The maps in this atlas are not cluttered, but neither do they contain any significant amount of detail. As previously mentioned, the color keys are confusing, especially on the maps of continents, such as South America, that include a variety of terrain and vegetation. Country borders are indicated by gray lines that are often hard to see.

The two-page spreads of each major landmass are crowded with more information than seems necessary. A simpler overall design would help young children to use the atlas.

Accessibility

The maps seem to appear in a logical order. There is a table of contents and an index, which is flawed. The few rivers, oceans, mountain ranges, and other physical features that are labeled on the maps are rarely found in the index.

This atlas will not be very useful to a child wishing to find details about a particular country. Most countries get no treatment in the text at all; even one as significant as Japan gets only two paragraphs.

Summary

Although it is inexpensive, *My First Atlas* is poorly designed and executed. Even very young children can be introduced to maps using the kind of representations found in more advanced atlases. In addition, factual data can be presented with more detail and without the kind of condescension found here. This atlas is not recommended. Parents and librarians seeking an atlas for young children would do well to invest in a high-quality work such as the NATIONAL GEOGRAPHIC PICTURE ATLAS OF OUR WORLD.

National Geographic Picture Atlas of Our World

Facts at a Glance

Full title: **National Geographic Picture Atlas of Our World**
Publisher: National Geographic Society
Editor: Mary B. Dickinson
Edition reviewed: © 1993

Number of pages: 276
Number of maps: 130
Number of index entries: 3,200 (reviewer estimate)
Intended readership: all ages
Trim size: 10½″ × 10½″
Binding: hardcover

Price: $21.95 for members of the National Geographic Society; $27.50 for nonmembers
Sold directly to schools and libraries; also sold by direct mail
ISBN 0-87044-960-5
No stated revision policy

Introduction, Format, and Authority

This atlas, which contains several hundred large, striking color photographs, was published by the National Geographic Society in 1993.

Readers of all ages can find something useful in this work, either in its maps, statistical information, or text. The National Geographic Society is one of the premier publishers of maps in the world. This 1993 revision is an update of the first edition, which appeared in 1990. The atlas divides the world by continents and then by countries or groups of countries. The introduction states that every effort has been made to "meet the National Geographic Society's educational mission . . . and present accurate information about the world, parts of which are still remote or in turmoil."

This handsome atlas is sturdily bound. Its small size makes it easy to handle, even for young children.

Scope and Special Features

Included in the introductory material are sections that explain the uses of longitude and latitude, various map projections, time zones, seasons, vulcanism, and plate tectonics. The introduction also includes a brief glossary of geographical terms and a page explaining the various symbols used on the maps.

Each continent is introduced with a page of text and a full-page color map showing relief and other physical features. This is followed by maps showing countries or groups of countries.

Following these maps are pages of text in which each country is discussed in a few paragraphs, including basic statistics such as area, population, language, and chief economic activities. This information is followed by two or three pages of color photographs, some taking up a full page.

No particular regional bias is demonstrated in this atlas. Small African countries are treated equally with Europe and North America. Even very small countries are easily identified on the maps. The map of Asia, for example, clearly points out Bhutan, Kyrgyzstan, and Armenia. Readers looking for individual maps of the U.S. states will have to find them in other atlases.

Current problems of, and prospects for, each country are written about in an honest and forthright manner, making this an excellent source of information for people of all ages. The many conflicts that have erupted in and between the former Soviet republics, for example, are treated fairly.

A one-page section labeled "Facts at Your Fingertips" appears after the maps and supplies such information as the highest mountain, largest lake, and longest river. The atlas also has a glossary, which defines more than 160 terms used in the book.

Currency

Every effort has been made to produce up-to-date maps and information. All of the new countries created by the breakups of the former Soviet Union and Yugoslavia are not only clearly shown on the maps, but are also given separate entries in the text. Kalaallit Nunaat (Greenland), Myanmar (Burma), and Cambodia (Kampuchea) are recognized with their current names.

Statistical information, though sparse, reflects the most recent data available. Even very current events relating to a particular country are recognized, such as Malta's 1992 entry into the United Nations and the Italian elections of 1993.

The numerous color photographs avoid the clichés of many other atlases. Both modern and traditional ways of life are portrayed in original shots unlike those found in other sources.

Accuracy

Most of the maps are drawn to scale, with some variation, but not so much as to make the relative size of various countries too confusing.

Borders are not shown with any kind of lines, but are easy to interpret because of the contrasting colors used

for countries. Borders, placements of cities, and important physical features are accurately portrayed.

Even small European nations and the island countries of the Indian and Pacific oceans are shown in accurate, though small, maps.

Legibility

One of the most attractive features of this atlas is the stunning use of color. The maps, reproduced in various contrasting and complementary shades of blue, green, red, pink, orange, yellow, and brown, are easy on the eye and make country locations and relative positions obvious.

All of the maps have a graceful and uncluttered appearance. As a trade-off for this, some detail must be sacrificed and relief is less obvious than on more traditional maps. Also, lines of latitude and longitude are not shown on the main maps.

The contrast of dark print against the colorful background of the maps provides an effective mechanism for locating important places. The text describing the countries is small and dense, but because it is well written and packed with useful, up-to-date information, this is a minor flaw.

Accessibility

A thorough index containing some 3,200 entries gives page numbers and grid locations. Each map uses a grid coordinate system, although the lack of lines can make this somewhat difficult to use.

Summary

The *National Geographic Picture Atlas of Our World* is highly recommended for home and library purchase. The maps are excellent, if somewhat small and lacking in detail, but the true worth of this work is in the honest and up-to-date information provided about countries and regions of the world. All countries—even small ones—are given excellent coverage. As seems natural in a work by the publishers of *National Geographic Magazine,* the color photographs are visually stunning and original. Overall, the *National Geographic Picture Atlas of Our World* is an excellent introduction to maps and geography for children and students, and a useful ready-reference tool for older users.

Rand McNally Children's World Atlas

Facts at a Glance

Full title: **Rand McNally Children's World Atlas**
Publisher: Rand McNally
Editor: Elizabeth Fagan Adelman
Edition reviewed: © 1992, 1991

Number of pages: 93
Number of maps: 60
Number of index entries: 480 (reviewer estimate)
Intended readership: elementary school children
Trim size: 8½″ × 10⅝″
Binding: hardcover

Price: $14.95
ISBN 0-528-83455-X
No stated revision policy

Introduction, Format, and Authority

This atlas is a revision of the 1985 edition and was published in 1992 by Rand McNally, a leading publisher of atlases. Its intended audience is elementary school children, but it also could be a useful reference for older readers.

The basic aims of this atlas are to present maps of all parts of the world and to teach children some of the basic skills needed to interpret maps. The size and format are similar to many other children's atlases and should be easy for children to use and understand. The binding seems durable. The color maps vary in size and often cover two pages.

After a general introduction entitled "Our Planet Earth" and a section called "Using the Atlas," maps are arranged by continent, beginning with Europe.

Scope and Special Features

The introductory "Our Planet Earth" section includes thematic world maps on terrain, climate, economic activity, population, and countries. These consist of two-page sections with a color-coded map of the world and brief accompanying text.

In the four-page "Using the Atlas" section, readers are introduced to the concepts of scale, longitude, and latitude; various kinds of maps (physical and political); and map symbols and legends. This illustrated section is clearly written and includes exercises to help children test their map skills.

Coverage is extremely balanced. Each continent is given five two-page spreads. These contain maps and photographs or illustrations showing terrain, animal life, economic activity, and, on two maps, political divisions. One of these political maps includes relief and major physical features.

A one-page appendix entitled "World Facts and Comparisons" contains charts of islands, lakes, oceans and seas, mountains, and rivers.

Currency

Since this is an update of the 1985 publication, one would hope that currency would be a major improvement over the previous edition. Unfortunately, the result is uneven. The world political map, for example, does recognize the breakup of the former Soviet Union, but not that of Czechoslovakia. Germany is shown as unified, as is Yemen, but the new name of Greenland is not recognized. Fortunately, the new republics that grew out of Yugoslavia are all shown and labeled.

The only statistics that might be subject to change are the population statistics given for each continent. These are the most current available.

Accuracy

The large major maps of continents or sections of continents are consistently scaled at 1 inch to 265 miles. Scale on the inset maps sometimes varies. Scale is only shown on the maps that contain both political and physical features, which are larger and more detailed than the other maps.

Borders, place names, and major geographical features are accurately placed. Quite a bit of detail must be sacrificed on the maps showing the terrain of each continent, however, because of their small size.

Legibility

All of the maps are clearly labeled, uncluttered, and easy to read. The main large maps, which consist of political and physical features, use five distinct colors to indicate countries. The smaller, purely political maps use color less effectively, employing greens, yellows, and browns that are similar in appearance.

The typeface is clear, although often too small for young children to read, and white space is used effectively around the text and maps. The animal life and economic activity maps have less precise continental outlines and the illustrations on the maps themselves are somewhat crowded.

Accessibility

Since continents are the focus of each section, the reader must look up particular countries, cities, or places in the index. The index indicates page numbers and grid coordinates. The coordinates fall between lines of latitude and longitude.

The index is flawed. Only the largest cities and the most well-known physical features will be found there. For example, the Nile River can be found in the index, but not the Niger, even though both rivers appear on the map. The only Mexican city in the index is Mexico City, while the map of Mexico clearly locates several other large population centers.

Summary

The *Rand McNally Children's World Atlas* contains many features that would make it a good choice for school and library use. The major maps, while not providing the same amount of detail for particular countries as, for example, the Doubleday Children's Atlas or the Kingfisher Reference Atlas, are certainly well laid out, colorful, and accurate. While this is a reasonable introductory atlas for elementary school students, it is not as visually appealing as the Kingfisher work or the National Geographic Picture Atlas of Our World, and its faulty index is a serious drawback.

Rand McNally Picture Atlas of the World

Facts at a Glance

Full title: **Rand McNally Picture Atlas of the World**
Publisher: Rand McNally
Editor: Emma Johnson, Senior Editor
Edition reviewed: 1993 revised edition; © 1991, 1992

Number of pages: 80
Number of maps: 50
Number of index entries: 1,850 (reviewer estimate)
Intended readership: ages 8 to 12
Trim size: 10¼″ × 13¾″
Binding: hardcover

Price: $19.95
ISBN 0-528-83564-5
No stated revision policy

Introduction, Format, and Authority

The *Rand McNally Picture Atlas of the World,* first published in the United Kingdom in 1991 by Dorling Kindersley Limited, was revised and published in the United States in 1993. The atlas is intended for students ages 8 to 12, but will be of interest to younger readers as well.

Although the oversized, 10¼″ × 13¾″ format may be slightly cumbersome for younger users, it allows a great deal of space for presenting the maps. The book is sturdily bound and lies flat when open.

Dorling Kindersley is well-known for its lavishly illustrated nonfiction and reference books for children, including My First Dictionary and My First Encyclopedia. Rand McNally is one of the foremost publishers of children's and adult atlases. The political maps were prepared by Luciano Corbella; Keith Lye served as consultant.

Scope and Special Features

The atlas begins with nine pages of illustrated introductory material, which includes topics such as the planet and solar system, climate, a world political map, the largest water and landforms on earth, and world population. A one-page explanation entitled "How to

Use This Atlas" follows, and includes a key to the maps. This guide is clear, showing sample pages with callouts describing the atlas's features, but perhaps could have been expanded considering the intended young audience.

Map sections are arranged by continent. Each continent section opens with a few paragraphs of text, a quarter-page political map, a box containing facts about the continent, and a one-page physical map that displays the continent in the context of its hemisphere. (The use of this technique is a helpful orientation tool, but physical features are unclear because of the map's small scale.)

After each section opener, countries or regions within the continent are covered, usually on two-page spreads. These maps combine political and physical features (although the colors and shadings of landforms and vegetation are not explained); the maps are also covered with tiny, detailed, labeled illustrations of plants, animals, products, people, and natural and man-made landmarks. Other features on these pages include a locator map, well-written text material, the flags for each country on the main map, small photographs, special feature boxes on topics such as the Amazon rain forest and China's Forbidden City, and a "Facts and Figures" sidebar.

Continents are given the following page allotments: the Arctic and Antarctica, 2 pages; North America, 12 pages; South America, 6 pages; Europe, 18 pages; Asia, 14 pages; Africa, 6 pages; Oceania, 2 pages; and Australia and New Zealand, 2 pages. The amount of space given to North America, Europe, and Asia is especially generous compared with many other children's atlases; unfortunately, South America and Africa receive much less attention.

Currency

The recent revision of this work reflects recent political changes. The unifications of Germany and Yemen are present, as are the divisions of Czechoslovakia, Yugoslavia, and the former Soviet Union. Most place names are current: Cambodia, St. Petersburg, and Dhaka are used. Burma is labeled as such, with Myanmar in parentheses. Like many other recent atlases, however, the work does not reflect the new name of Greenland or its capital city.

Statistical data is minimal, but includes populations for most countries (although these are generally rounded off). The figures represent the most current data available.

Accuracy

Only the illustrated region/country maps provide bar scales, and these vary widely. The scale on the map of northern Eurasia is 1 inch to about 650 kilometers and that on the map of the Benelux countries is 1 inch to 32 kilometers.

Borders, place names, geographical features, and statistics are accurate. One troublesome omission is the lack of population statistics, or even area, for the countries of Africa. This omission is not explained.

Legibility

The maps are beautifully drawn, with an eye to detail. The typefaces employed are easy to read; users should have no trouble identifying the various labeled features. Maps do not contain lines of latitude or longitude, but a grid system (appropriate for a younger audience) is used. Skillful use of color, both in the maps and in the special features, adds to the beauty of this work. Although much information fills each two-page spread, the book's clean design creates a unified, uncluttered look.

It is possible, however, that the small illustrations covering each region/country map may confuse young children, especially those who have little experience using atlases. While meticulously drawn and fascinating to look at, the drawings tend to obscure the faint, dotted borders and physical features on the maps.

Young children may also have trouble with the microscopic typeface employed in the "Facts and Figures" boxes, as well as the small photographs (each is less than 1″ × 2″).

Accessibility

The main continent sections follow a typical arrangement, beginning with North America and moving east. One of the work's best features is its index—with over 1,800 entries, it is superior to most children's atlases. All cities, landforms, and islands that appear on the maps are indexed, followed by page numbers and grid coordinates. If places or features are found on more than one map, multiple listings are included. Index entries are distinguished by the country or continent location, and, where appropriate, by parenthetical labels (for example, **La Plata** (City) Argentina, **32** M11; **La Plata, Rio de** (River) Argentina-Uruguay, **29** K17, **32** N11).

Summary

The *Rand McNally Picture Atlas of the World* is designed to spark children's curiosity about faraway places. The illustrated maps and special features encourage browsing, and the outstanding text (usually the most lackluster feature in a children's atlas) is educational and lively. The focus is on exploring other cultures, not on map skills. Because of this, the book functions less as a reference work than as a worthwhile supplement to beginning atlases like THE READER'S DIGEST CHILDREN'S WORLD ATLAS and the RAND MCNALLY CHILDREN'S WORLD ATLAS.

The Reader's Digest Children's World Atlas

Facts at a Glance

Full title: **The Reader's Digest Children's World Atlas**
Publisher: Reader's Digest Association
Editors: Nicolas Barber; Nicholas Harris
Edition reviewed: © 1991, 1993 printing

Number of pages: 128
Number of maps: 61
Number of index entries: 3,795 (reviewer estimate)
Intended readership: ages 7 to 12
Trim size: 9″ × 12″
Binding: hardcover

Price: $20
Sold in bookstores, by direct mail, and to libraries and schools
ISBN 0-89577-500-X
No stated revision policy

Introduction, Format, and Authority

Published by the Reader's Digest Association, *The Reader's Digest Children's World Atlas* (revised edition) contains 61 maps, 300 drawings, and 100 color photographs in a 128-page volume. This reference tool is intended primarily for ages 7 to 12.

The atlas's 9″ × 12″ size, bold headings, and attractive format make it easy to hold and use. The maps are large and often run across two pages. The atlas appears to be of sturdy quality, which will help it withstand the wear and tear of heavy use.

The reference work is divided into nine sections: an introductory "How to Use This Atlas" section; a section entitled "Planet Earth"; six sections devoted to the continents of North America, South America, Europe, Asia, Africa, and Oceania; and a final section containing two indexes.

The 1991 edition of *The Reader's Digest Children's World Atlas* is based on *The Children's World Atlas,* a work published by Reader's Digest of Australia. Reader's Digest publishes two well-known atlases for adults: READER'S DIGEST ATLAS OF THE WORLD and READER'S DIGEST BARTHOLOMEW ILLUSTRATED ATLAS OF THE WORLD (both revised in 1992).

Scope and Special Features

The "Planet Earth" section opens with general information about our planet, including its position in the solar system. A physical map follows, illustrating the world's surface with its lakes, deserts, and other geological features. Next come thematic world maps showing climate and vegetation, animals, population, languages and religions, land use and agriculture, and minerals and industry. Color drawings, text, charts, tables, and graphs provide additional information.

Each of the next six continent sections begins with a locator map and a political map showing the countries making up each continent. Accompanying these introductory sections are photographs, a few paragraphs describing the continent and its regions, and a chart for each country on the political map. Each chart contains a picture of that country's flag and facts and figures, such as area, population, capital, largest cities, currency, official languages, chief products, exports, and imports. The amount of information provided in the charts varies according to the size of the country in question.

Following each opening section are two-page spreads featuring physical environment maps for each country in the continent. These maps, which are one-half to one page in size, show landforms, major cities, and major bodies of water. In addition, a locator map, full-color photographs, line drawings, and text provide a well-rounded depiction of each country.

There is considerable variation in the amount of space devoted to each continent and region. The chapters on North America and Asia, for example, have 22 and 18 pages respectively, while those for South America and Africa have 6 and 8 pages. This proportion is similar to other atlases for this age group, such as the RAND MCNALLY PICTURE ATLAS OF THE WORLD.

Currency

The atlas was first published in 1991 and was updated in 1993. The publisher has made an effort to be as current as possible by reflecting many recent political and name changes. For example, Myanmar, St. Petersburg, and Dhaka replace Burma, Leningrad, and Dacca. The atlas reflects the unifications of Germany and Yemen as well as the individual states of the former Soviet Union. In addition, the breakup of Yugoslavia into separate republics and the division of Czechoslovakia into Slovakia and the Czech Republic are reflected in the maps, making it one of the most current atlases for children on the market. The photographs appear current and reflect contemporary images.

Accuracy

This atlas gets mixed reviews for accuracy. The maps appear to be accurately drawn, as are the positions of cities, rivers, borders, and coastlines. Young readers, however, wanting to find accurate measurements for distances or for the size and shape of places on the map might be confused by the atlas's lack of consistent explanatory notes. With no reason given for why or how distortions occur on the maps, readers might get a false sense of the world's perspective. The atlas does include bar scales in miles and kilometers, but these do not appear with maps opening the continent sections. Further,

the scales for maps vary widely: 1 inch equals 300 miles on the map of Canada, 100 miles on the map of Central Europe, and 800 miles on those of Northern Africa.

The symbols can be misleading. For example, three different symbols are used to designate capitals, cities with populations over 1 million, and cities with populations under 1 million. Users cannot gauge the relative size of capital cities, since only the capital symbol is provided. In addition, different symbols are used for "river" and "seasonal river" and for "lake" and "seasonal lake," but these distinctions are not explained.

Legibility

The maps and labels are, for the most part, clear and readable. National boundaries are identified by heavy red lines, states and provinces by narrower red lines. Labels of countries, cities, landforms, and bodies of water are generally well placed. Maps are large and easy to read, but the few that are spread over two pages lose some information in the gutter. Attractive colors and page layouts contribute to the overall readability of the atlas.

Accessibility

The maps are organized in a logical sequence within sections and the reader should be able to move easily from one to another. The legend appears in the "How to Use This Atlas" section so the user can become familiar with the symbols from the start.

One of the atlas's two indexes, the general index, is keyed to the facts given on map pages. The other one, an index to places, is less useful, however. This map index lists countries and cities with page numbers only. The indexes do not note the longitude and latitude, and this limits the atlas's suitability for older students in the age group for which it is intended. A spot check of the index indicates a high level of accuracy.

Summary

Overall, this atlas should be useful to students, ages 7 to 12, who are trying to understand the world around them. The atlas is inexpensive and its format is attractive and well organized. The maps are plentiful, readable, up-to-date, and generally accurate, as is the index. An abundance of facts and figures (in the form of charts, tables, and graphs) and cultural geography (in the form of photographs and accompanying text) supplement the maps. The work's main drawback is its lack of explanatory material. This deficiency seems to occur in most recent children's atlases, however, including such favorably reviewed ones as the RAND MCNALLY PICTURE ATLAS OF THE WORLD. *The Reader's Digest Children's World Atlas* is recommended for library and home purchase.

Student Atlas

Facts at a Glance

Full title: **Student Atlas**
Publisher: Troll Associates
Author: Michael Dempsey
Edition reviewed: © 1991

Number of pages: 128
Number of maps: 30
Number of index entries: about 3,500
Intended readership: grades 1 through 8
Trim size: 8½″ × 11″
Binding: hardcover and paperback

Price: $14.95 (hardcover); $9.95 (paperback)
Sold in bookstores and other retail outlets; also sold directly to libraries and schools
ISBN 0-8167-2254-4
No stated revision policy

Introduction, Format, and Authority

The *Student Atlas* was published by Troll Associates in 1991. It contains 30 maps in a one-volume, 128-page, 8½″ × 11″ format, and is intended primarily for students in grades 1 through 8. Because the publisher provided only a paperback copy of the *Student Atlas* for review, we cannot comment on the durability of the hardcover version.

Scope and Special Features

The atlas is divided into five sections. The first and longest section is an "A–Z Gazetteer of World Place Names," which includes text and one or two full-color photographs on each page. The entries provide capital, area, climate, industry and resources, tourist attractions, and interesting facts about approximately 1,000 countries, cities, landforms, and bodies of water.

The second and third sections, entitled "United States of America" and "Our World," outline basic principles of geology, climate, and demography. While these sections are clear and informative, they do not cover topics especially pertinent to atlases: how to read a map, what scale and projection mean, or how different maps are used.

The fourth section contains 24 maps, a small number compared with THE READER'S DIGEST CHILDREN'S WORLD ATLAS (containing 61 maps) and THE MACMILLAN SCHOOL ATLAS (containing 96 maps). The map section in the *Student Atlas* begins with a political map of the world spread across two pages. The maps that follow all combine political and physical features, and most are two-page spreads. Types of vegetation are shown using different colors. Elevation is indicated by shading

mountainous areas and by labeling the height of selected peaks.

The atlas's coverage is heavily weighted toward European countries. There are nine maps of Europe and its countries, five maps of Asia, one of Africa, two of North America, two of South America, two of Australasia, and two of polar regions.

The final section is an index; this is discussed in more detail under **Accessibility.**

Currency

The atlas was published for the first time in 1991 and compares unfavorably with more recent atlases, such as THE READER'S DIGEST CHILDREN'S WORLD ATLAS and THE MACMILLAN SCHOOL ATLAS, both revised in 1993. The Troll atlas does reflect a unified Germany and a unified Yemen, but does not show the independent states of the former Soviet Union, the splitting of Czechoslovakia, or the breakup of Yugoslavia.

Also missing from the *Student Atlas* are recent changes in place names: the work employs the outmoded names Burma, Christmas Island, Godthaab, Greenland, Kampuchea, Leningrad, and Rangoon. The gazetteer, however, does mention under Christmas Island that it is also called the Kiritimati Atoll, and uses the preferred Dhaka as the capital of Bangladesh.

Accuracy

No ratios are given for scale, but a bar scale in miles and kilometers appears at the bottom of every map except the map of the world. Scale varies widely, from 1 inch equaling about 32 miles in the map of England and Wales, to 1 inch equaling about 800 miles for maps of the polar regions. Australia and New Zealand are shown on the same spread at different scales, which leads to confusion by making New Zealand seem much larger than it is.

The maps are accurately drawn. Most cities are placed correctly, with the exception of some coastal cities (such as San Diego and Genoa) that appear farther inland than they actually are.

Legibility

The maps and labels are generally clear and easy to read. National boundaries are indicated by heavy red lines; states and provinces are separated by narrower red lines. Borders contrast well against the green and tan colors that show elevation.

The lack of white space along the inner margins is a major problem, since most of the maps are two-page spreads. A great deal of information is lost in the gutters; some cities (for example, Sarajevo and Manila) are swallowed completely.

Accessibility

Maps are arranged in a logical sequence within the atlas section, although it might have been more convenient to place the maps before the first three sections. The very brief legend appears on the same page as the table of contents and "How to Use This Atlas." Unfortunately, the star symbol used on the maps to show state capitals is not included in the legend.

Although it includes about 3,500 place names, the index is not comprehensive. Many places marked on the maps do not appear in the index—Cape Canaveral, Florida; Roseau, Dominica; and Suva, Fiji are only a few examples. Furthermore, no identification is given in the index for entries that are not countries (such as mountains or rivers), nor is there a label naming the country where cities are located. Despite the statement in "How to Use this Atlas," which says "To find a particular place, first look in the map index for the page number," index entries are followed by the *map* number and a grid coordinate. Coordinates generally seem accurate.

Summary

The *Student Atlas* appears to be of limited use to students, and is not recommended for either library or home purchase. The datedness of the maps and gazetteer, the small number of maps as a whole, the loss of information in the gutters, the lack of explanatory material, and the faulty index are serious liabilities. While the maps for the most part are accurate and legible, they would prove far too complex for first graders and too simple for eighth graders. Purchasers would do better to invest in a more up-to-date and usable work such as THE READER'S DIGEST CHILDREN'S WORLD ATLAS.

Chapter 8
Evaluations of
Secondary and Adult Atlases

Atlas of the World

Facts at a Glance

Full title: **Atlas of the World**
Publisher: Oxford University Press; Reed International
  Books
Edition reviewed: © 1993, second edition

Number of pages: 400 (reviewer estimate)
Number of maps: 160 (reviewer estimate), all in color
Number of index entries: 75,000
Intended readership: junior high school to adult
Trim size: 11″ × 14½″
Binding: hardcover

Price: $65
ISBN 0-19-521025-5
No stated revision policy

Introduction, Format, and Authority

The *Atlas of the World* is a large-format (11″ × 14½″),
medium-priced world atlas aimed at the general reader.
It is published in the United States by Oxford University
Press (OUP) and copyrighted by Reed International
Books. The 1993 second edition updates a work originally published in 1992. The 160 reference maps and 23
topical features in the atlas were produced by the well-
known British cartographic firm George Philip & Son.
The reference maps, which use up to 14 shades of color,

are very attractive, readable, and generally reliable. The
durable hard binding is flexible enough to allow the
book to lie flat when opened, making the work easy to
read and use.

Scope and Special Features

The *Atlas of the World* is divided into four sections:
"World Statistics," "Introduction to World Geography,"
"City Maps" (and index), and "World Maps" (and index). The "World Maps" section—the base atlas—contains 160 pages and its index 128 pages.

"World Statistics" (six pages) includes five tables: 1)
a fact chart of all countries and territories of the world
(including per capita GNP in U.S. dollars); 2) the populations of world cities with more than 500,000 inhabitants; 3) the air distances between 30 major cities; 4) the
average monthly temperature and rainfall of over 70
world cities; and 5) physical dimensions of the world's
major features (for example, continents, oceans, seas).
Most measurements are given in both the metric and
English systems.

"Introduction to World Geography" (48 pages) provides an overview of 23 topics such as the earth's geology, atmosphere, demography, agriculture, energy,
minerals, manufacturing, health, and environment.
Handsomely illustrated with colorful thematic maps,
charts, graphs, diagrams, and schematic drawings, each
topic occupies a two-page spread and includes a brief introductory essay. This section serves as an interesting in-

troduction to geography and provides a context for the remainder of the atlas. While informative, the authority of these features is difficult to gauge, since specific sources or contributors are not noted.

"City Maps," the third section of the *Atlas of the World,* is a collection of 66 maps of major cities from each region of the world, showing such landmarks as rivers, canals, roads, railroads, airports, parks, and woodland. These maps are drawn to the same scale (1:200,000) and range from one-quarter page (for Madrid, Barcelona, Hamburg, and others) to a two-page spread (for New York City and its environs). For the most part, the cities included are the largest in each region, although this criterion is not applied consistently (for example, the inclusion of Boston and Baltimore instead of Dallas or Houston, Johannesburg instead of Kinshasa, and Helsinki instead of Amsterdam). This section also includes a 16-page place-name index that provides both grid and geographic coordinates for place names.

The core of the atlas is the "World Maps" section, which contains 160 pages of colorful and detailed maps. The section opens with physical and political maps of the world on two-page spreads, followed by maps of Antarctica and the Arctic and Atlantic oceans (maps of the Indian and Pacific oceans follow later). Each continent is then treated separately, introduced by physical and political maps followed by regional maps that combine both physical and political features. The coverage of Europe is more comprehensive than that of other continents, with some maps covering an entire country or a portion of it (such as western Spain and Portugal) and others a somewhat broader area (Scandinavia and the Baltic nations). About 30 percent of the maps represent Europe, 25 percent Asia, 12 percent Africa, 8 percent Australia and Oceania, 17 percent North America, and 8 percent South America. Except for the continental political maps, all maps in this section use both shaded relief and layered colors to show elevations.

A comprehensive index (more than 75,000 entries) contains the names of the principal places and features shown on the maps. A one-page introduction to the index contains an explanation of its features, its use of symbols and grid and geographic coordinates, and a table of abbreviations.

Currency

First published in 1992, and revised in 1993, the *Atlas of the World* reflects most recent changes in the world, including the unification of Germany and of Yemen, the breakup of the Soviet Union and Yugoslavia, the splitting of Czechoslovakia into two nations, and the independence of Eritrea from Ethiopia. Some place names have been changed to reflect current national preferences, but others have not. Updated names include St. Petersburg, Nizhny Novgorod, Namibia, Cambodia, Myanmar (Burma is also used), Dhaka, and Kiritimati.

Place names for Greenland, Rangoon, Godthåb, Denali, and Formosa Strait have not been updated.

The atlas uses both English and local place names (the English names are in parentheses after the local names where appropriate) except on smaller-scale continental maps, which use only English names. For China, the Pinyin system is used, although some widely used forms (such as Peking) also appear in parentheses. Both English and local names appear in the index; the English forms are cross-referenced to the local form.

In the "Introduction to World Geography" section, the data and statistics are somewhat dated, although most information is from the last three to six years. In some instances, this should not be regarded as a failure of the atlas, for certain data is not available on an annual basis. Other times, however, more recent statistics could have been cited (as in the case of population data). One weakness of this section is that, although the years of the statistics are provided, their sources are not.

Accuracy

The maps for the *Atlas of the World* were done by George Philip & Son, one of Europe's finest cartographers. As a result, the maps are accurate and well done. All maps, with the exception of those in the "Introduction to World Geography" section, have both a ratio scale of representative fractions and a bar scale displaying both miles and kilometers. These scales are prominently displayed at the top of each page. Scales are used consistently throughout the atlas, and the same scale generally is used for comparable areas. Map projections are also given for all maps in the "World Maps" section.

Borders, rivers, and other features are accurately drawn and cities are located correctly. However, the system used for distinguishing cities and towns of different sizes is somewhat confusing. The atlas employs eight different types of settlement symbols and lettering styles, and states that these vary according to the scale of each map and the importance of the site (rather than population). Herein lies the problem. First, the atlas does not indicate what factors are used to judge a place's "importance." Moreover, changing the symbol and lettering for a particular city from map to map is confusing. For example, Beirut is indicated by three different symbols and lettering styles on three different maps. More objective criteria and a consistent application would seem to have been a better approach.

Legibility

The maps in the *Atlas of the World* are quite legible. Place names are not overcrowded, and there is adequate marginal space for titles, scales, and grid markings. The majority of maps in the "World Maps" section are two-page spreads. The use of white marginal space in the gutters and the fact that the book lies flat when opened ensures that information on these maps is not lost.

Elevation scales accompany each map in the "World Maps" section (except for the continental political maps). The color gradations used in these scales are subtle and attractive, yet easily differentiated. The type used for place names is neat and generally easy to read, although some legibility is lost when lighter typefaces are used over dark colors or in areas of heavy relief shading. International boundary lines are easy to see. Other administrative borders, however, are sometimes less legible and may be confused with highways and roads (this is especially true with some of the large-scale maps).

Accessibility

The *Atlas of the World* contains a one-page overview of its basic features, including its organization; map presentation; use of symbols, scales, and projections; latitude and longitude markings; and use of English and local place names. This clearly written overview provides a handy and useful explanation of the atlas and its structure.

The table of contents contains a very interesting feature—a series of small locator maps showing the areas covered by each of the maps in the "World Maps" section. These locator maps are repeated again on each of the map pages. An "at-a-glance" country index is found in the front endpapers. The front endpapers also include continent-by-continent index maps, and the back endpapers have a world index map. These various finding aids help to make the atlas very accessible and easy to use.

The maps in the "World Maps" section are arranged in a logical order beginning with Europe and proceeding through Asia, Africa, Australia and Oceania, North America, and South America. The maps in the "City Maps" section follow this same order. The placement of maps within each continent is less orderly, however, especially in Europe, where maps sometimes jump from one part of the continent to another. One particular oddity is the inclusion of an inset map of Alaska with the map of Canada, yet Alaska does not appear with any of the maps of the United States.

Clear, concise, and well-organized map legends appear at the beginning of the "City Maps" and "World Maps" sections. Compared with comprehensive map legends like those in THE TIMES ATLAS OF THE WORLD, these contain relatively few symbols. Although probably not sufficient for map aficionados, they are certainly adequate for the general user. Certain abbreviations are used on the maps (for example, "L." for lake, "W." for wadi), but these are not found with the map legends. Instead, all abbreviations are listed on the first page of the indexes.

The indexes for the *Atlas of the World* are fairly comprehensive and detailed. A spot check of the "City Maps" index revealed no missing entries. In the "World Maps" index, place names are indexed by local spellings and cross-referenced at their English spelling. If a particular place is found on more than one map, the index generally references the largest-scale map on which it appears. Accurate locator references use both a letter-number grid system and latitude and longitude, which provides flexibility in locating a place and makes the atlas useful to both novices and experienced users. The "World Maps" index claims to contain the names of all the principal places and features shown on the maps, and spot checks revealed this to be true. However, some more obscure places of similar "weight" or importance were included and others were not. This inconsistency makes one question the criteria for inclusion.

Summary

The *Atlas of the World* is an excellent atlas for the price ($65) and would be a valuable addition to any collection. Its few weaknesses pale in comparison with its strengths: it has accurate and attractive maps, is interesting and easy to use, is very up-to-date, and is quite comprehensive. An outstanding feature is the collection of 66 city maps, a range found only in the most comprehensive atlases. While not as all-encompassing and authoritative as THE NEW INTERNATIONAL ATLAS and THE TIMES ATLAS OF THE WORLD, budget-minded librarians and individuals may be satisfied with this work at the top of their collection.

In scope and format, the *Atlas of the World* invites comparison with another newly published atlas, HAMMOND ATLAS OF THE WORLD. Both are worthy atlases and offer different special features—the OUP atlas its city maps and topical articles, and the Hammond atlas its world physical maps and index. The OUP work also focuses more on Europe and the Hammond on North America. In the end, the choice may come down to personal preference in the appearance and quality of the maps.

Bartholomew Mini Atlas World

Facts at a Glance

Full title: **Bartholomew Mini Atlas World**
Publisher: Bartholomew
Edition reviewed: © 1993

Number of pages: 192
Number of maps: 112
Number of index entries: 20,000
Intended readership: high school to adult
Trim size: 4½″ × 6¼″
Binding: hardcover

Price: $15.95
Sold by direct mail; also sold in bookstores and other retail outlets
ISBN 0-7028-2375-9
Revised as needed; most recent revision completed September 1993

Introduction, Format, and Authority

The *Bartholomew Mini Atlas World* is a pocket-sized (4½″ × 6¼″) atlas for student or adult general reference. The atlas is a smaller, more compact version of THE RANDOM HOUSE COMPACT WORLD ATLAS, which is described on pages 227–228 of this Buying Guide. The *Bartholomew Mini* is sturdily bound in a padded, blue, simulated-leather cover with gold-edged pages.

The maps were compiled by Bartholomew, the respected Edinburgh-based cartographic firm. Originally published in 1984 (with the more logical title *Bartholomew Mini World Atlas*), a revised edition was produced in 1991. The 1993 copyright edition was examined for this review. As it is a more recent version than the RANDOM HOUSE COMPACT reviewed, it reflects several updates, including the separated Czech Republic and Slovakia and an independent Macedonia. But it is still somewhat behind the times in minor place-name changes.

The degree of accuracy is the same as in the RANDOM HOUSE COMPACT—acceptable on the whole, particularly for an atlas this small. The place names are legible, and the various typefaces and borders are easily distinguished. However, the page format creates some legibility problems, as noted in *Scope and Special Features* below.

Scope and Special Features

Page for page, the atlas is the same as THE RANDOM HOUSE COMPACT WORLD ATLAS except for a major difference in map style: maps that are physical-political maps in the RANDOM HOUSE COMPACT are rendered here as simple political maps. The size of the *Bartholomew Mini* is also about one-third smaller than the RANDOM HOUSE COMPACT, so everything is on a reduced scale. As a result, some content (such as roads and maritime boundaries) is eliminated. Shaded relief is not shown. Scales are presented only in bar scale form (showing miles and kilometers).

Unlike the maps in the RANDOM HOUSE COMPACT, which are enclosed in neat lines, the *Bartholomew Mini* maps bleed off the bottom and sides of the page and into the gutter. Symbols and labels generally stay well clear of the outer edges, but quite a few disappear into the gutter. The lack of a gutter margin can cause confusion when two different views are shown on facing pages—the maps literally run into one another.

A few place names that appear in the RANDOM HOUSE COMPACT are omitted here, although these tend to be located at the page edges. Papua New Guinea, for example, loses several towns on its eastern coast. This would not be a significant problem except that the indexes for both books contain the same entries, resulting in some blind index references in the *Bartholomew Mini*. The town of Finschhafen in Papua New Guinea, for instance, is listed in both indexes but appears on the indicated map only in the RANDOM HOUSE COMPACT.

The special features of the *Bartholomew Mini* are essentially the same as those in the RANDOM HOUSE COMPACT. The table of contents, however, lacks the useful index maps found in the RANDOM HOUSE COMPACT.

Summary

The *Bartholomew Mini Atlas World* is an attractive and durable volume, but its flaws make it a poor choice for either library or personal collections. Although its compact size could be useful for basic reference and for easy storage in a desk drawer, the RANDOM HOUSE COMPACT is not much bigger, is cheaper, and is much more useful. The *Bartholomew Mini* is also similar in size and price to the HAMMOND WORLD ATLAS, COLLECTORS EDITION. *Bartholomew* contains more and better world maps but fewer special features than the Hammond atlas. However, while some of the Hammond work's features (such as mileage charts) are handy in a pocket atlas, others (such as thematic maps) are of dubious value.

Britannica Atlas

Facts at a Glance

Full title: **Britannica Atlas**
Publisher: Encyclopaedia Britannica
Editor: William A. Cleveland
Edition reviewed: © 1992

Number of pages: 560
Number of maps: 286
Number of index entries: 170,000
Intended readership: general adult
Trim size: 11″ × 14¾″
Binding: hardcover

Price: $99.50
Sold by direct mail; also sold through local representatives
ISBN 0-85229-582-0
Revised approximately every 2 to 3 years

Introduction, Format, and Authority

Originally published in 1970, the *Britannica Atlas* is a joint venture with Rand McNally & Company. The contents, except for the foreword, are taken directly from THE NEW INTERNATIONAL ATLAS, published by Rand McNally. The *Britannica* is a large-size (11″ × 14¾″) general world atlas that compares with flagship atlases such as THE TIMES ATLAS OF THE WORLD and NATIONAL GEOGRAPHIC ATLAS OF THE WORLD. The highly detailed maps are reliable, attractive, and legible. The hard simulated-leather binding will withstand heavy use.

The distinguishing quality of this work is its "internationalism." The planners, advisers, and contributors are distinguished academics, cartographers, and government officials from all over the globe. The maps were produced by the cartographic firms of Rand McNally (Chicago), Mondadori-McNally GmbH (Stuttgart), Cartographia (Budapest), Esselte Map Service (Stockholm), George Philip & Son (London), and Teikoku-Shoin Co. (Tokyo). These are some of the most reputable mapping companies in the world. The thematic maps were produced by cartographer David Burke with the help of a team of contributors from American universities. The atlas texts are printed in five languages—English, German, Spanish, French, and Portuguese. The work is geared to the serious information seeker in a multinational audience.

Scope and Special Features

The *Britannica Atlas* is divided into six sections: introductory material (contents, legend, and index maps); thematic maps ("World Scene"); world and regional maps; glossary and abbreviations; statistical information; and geographic index. The world and regional maps—the base atlas—occupy some 300 pages; the index is 200 pages long.

In scope and coverage, the atlas lives up to its billing of "internationalism." According to the foreword, about two-thirds of the map pages in the base atlas are devoted to Anglo-America, Asia, and Europe, and one-third to Africa, Australia and Oceania, Latin America, and the former Soviet Union. As an example of the allotment, South America is blanketed with 17 pages of maps—more than in any other comparable atlas.

The base atlas opens with two world maps (one political and one physical) at 1:75,000,000, and 14 pages of physical relief maps of the oceans and continents. The regional maps comprising the heart of the atlas consist of three series. Major land regions (continents and subcontinents) are introduced with one or more maps at a scale of 1:12,000,000. The emphasis of these is political, with boundaries highlighted by different colors over a background of shaded relief. The second series of maps, which constitutes about half of the atlas pages, covers regions in more detail: 1:6,000,000 for most of the world and 1:3,000,000 for Europe and the United States. These physical-political maps are alike except for their scale and use both shaded relief and colors to show land elevations and offshore water depths. The third series of maps, at 1:1,000,000, shows densely populated regions or regions of great economic importance, highlighting human activity (municipalities, transportation, cultural sites). The majority of these maps focus on Europe and the United States.

Following the regional maps are detailed (1:300,000) maps of 60 of the world's largest or most important cities and their surrounding areas. Of all the cities in the world with a population of over 5 million, only Bogota, Madras, Karachi, and Tianjin (Tientsin) are excluded. While the NATIONAL GEOGRAPHIC ATLAS OF THE WORLD has more city maps, *Britannica's* are more detailed. This atlas shows the locations of universities and shopping malls, and it names U.S. counties. The competitors do not.

The 24 pages of thematic maps in "World Scene" are excellent and fascinating. They include historical maps as well as those relating to political, cultural, economic, and physical geography. These maps rank above those in THE TIMES ATLAS because of their depth and clarity. For example, on the five mineral resources maps, the locations of principle mining areas are identified by name. Many maps are accompanied by charts and graphs. The fairly high-level text accompanying the maps is informational rather than interpretive.

The seven-page glossary (including abbreviations of geographical terms) is exhaustive. The statistical information section consists of three parts. The "World Information Table" lists each country and other major political units (for example, states and provinces) and significant facts about them, including area, population, and political status. Rather than being grouped by country, all entities are alphabetized together—so that California follows Burundi. This may cause some confusion. The brief "Metropolitan Area Table" lists all the urban areas in the world with a population over 1 million. Because they are grouped by region, the table gives the reader an immediate sense of how the world's cities compare in size. A lengthier chart, "Population of Cities and Towns," gives the population of all urban centers with more than 50,000 inhabitants, grouped by country. Also included are cities that are well known or of historical importance, such as capitals. The largest city of each country is indicated, as is the metropolitan area to which a city might belong.

The helpful index to the *Britannica Atlas* has 170,000 entries, somewhat fewer than THE TIMES ATLAS, but still exhaustive. In addition to listing the page and location (using latitude and longitude coordinates) of each place name, it uses symbols to indicate the type of feature (for example, river, mountain) associated with entries other than inhabited places.

Currency

The *Britannica Atlas* is current up to the beginning of 1992, its copyright year. The unification of Germany and of Yemen and the breakup of both the Soviet Union and Yugoslavia are accounted for; the splitting of Czechoslovakia, of course, is not. (The 1993 NEW INTERNATIONAL ATLAS, *Britannica's* alter ego, includes this change as well as the independence of Eritrea.) Place names are up-to-date and generally in accordance with national preferences. Alternate and historical names are liberally inserted where space permits.

While the data presented in the thematic maps is informative, some is dated. The energy consumption and production maps, for example, are based on 1982 figures. Similarly, the gross national product and international trade maps rely upon 1986 numbers.

The "World Information Table" gives 1992 population estimates by Rand McNally based on figures from the United Nations and other sources. The "Population of Cities and Towns" chart uses national census data or official estimates, with the year of the census or estimate listed so the reader can judge how current the data is. Most are from the 1980s, although they range considerably. For example, the numbers for India are based upon the 1991 national census, while those for Guyana are based upon a 1983 official estimate.

Accuracy

The maps in the *Britannica Atlas* are accurate. All the cartographic firms involved have excellent reputations for their high standards of mapping accuracy. As is appropriate for an authoritative work, every map includes bar and verbal scales in kilometers and miles as well as the representative fraction; the representative fraction is identified by a color bar (each scale of 1:3,000,000 is highlighted in green, for example), which makes comparison among maps easy. Likewise, every map lists its projection. The scales are used uniformly throughout the atlas. The statistical tables in the *Britannica Atlas* are accurate and comprehensive.

Legibility

Legibility is a strong point of the *Britannica Atlas*. The maps are clear and not overcrowded, and important areas are well centered on the page. Nearly all the maps spread across two pages. Because the pages lie flat without breaking the spine, no information is lost in the gutter. The outer margins are ample for the titles, grid labels, and other information they contain.

The colors are well chosen and pleasing to the eye. On the medium-scale regional maps, the range of tints used to indicate land elevation and sea depth differences is logical and natural. The relief shading is distinct and not too heavy. Neither the shading nor the coloring interferes with legibility. The typefaces are neat and legible, but some of the smaller fonts are difficult to see at arm's length. Political boundaries are easy to distinguish; the *Britannica Atlas* is superior to THE TIMES ATLAS in this regard.

Accessibility

Aimed at the serious map reader, the *Britannica Atlas* offers no "how to" guide for using an atlas. But it provides many points of access to the wealth of information on the maps. Introductory notes (in five languages) before each section explain its purpose and content. The introductory section of the atlas contains complete index maps; a summary index map can also be found in the endpapers. This latter feature (which is not found in the otherwise identical NEW INTERNATIONAL ATLAS) makes the atlas extremely easy to use—one does not have to fumble through the book pages to find the map indexes.

The legend, which appears only in the introductory section, is thorough. However, while the five-language approach increases the number of people who can understand the atlas, it makes the legend difficult to use quickly. Typefaces, symbols, and colors are used consistently on all the maps.

The regional maps are arranged in a logical order: Europe, Asia, Australia and Oceania, Africa, North America, and South America. The reader will be able to move easily from one map to the next, aided by marginal indicators to maps of adjoining areas. Consistent with its international outlook, place names are usually given in the local language, with an English alternate if the name is likely to be unfamiliar. Major exceptions are names of countries and large landforms and bodies of water, which are named in English. Each map includes a list of the local-language feature types found on that map (such as "ben" and "loch" in Scotland) with their equivalents in the atlas's five languages.

The 170,000-entry index is quite complete. As on the maps, place names are generally indexed by their local-language spellings except for large features, whose names are given in English. English equivalents for many place names appear as cross-references. References are usually to the largest-scale map on which a place appears.

Index entries give precise degrees of latitude and longitude, rather than the more common letter-number coordinates, to locate a place. Although this system permits experienced atlas users to find places much more accurately, it may hinder novice users.

Summary

The excellent *Britannica Atlas* must be considered a first choice for those looking for a comprehensive and authoritative large-format world atlas. Its innumerable strengths include its geographic balance, accuracy, currency, and excellent index. Overall, the *Britannica* has very few flaws. This atlas receives the highest ranking possible, rivaling, although not surpassing, the larger, more expensive THE TIMES ATLAS OF THE WORLD.

The *Britannica Atlas,* at $99.50, is a much lower-priced version of THE NEW INTERNATIONAL ATLAS, published by Rand McNally. As such, it represents good value for a top-of-the line atlas. Libraries that do not require so comprehensive an atlas, however, might be just as well served by equally authoritative but less expensive atlases such as the NATIONAL GEOGRAPHIC ATLAS OF THE WORLD.

Concise Atlas of the World

Facts at a Glance

Full title: **Concise Atlas of the World**
Publisher: Oxford University Press; Reed International Books
Edition reviewed: © 1993

Number of pages: 264
Number of maps: 80 (reviewer estimate)
Number of index entries: 44,000 (main index)
Intended readership: junior high school to adult
Trim size: 9″ × 12″
Binding: hardcover

Price: $30
Sold in bookstores; also sold by direct mail by the publisher
ISBN 0-19-521024-7
No stated revision policy

Introduction, Format, and Authority

The 1993 edition *Concise Atlas of the World* is a new medium-sized (9″ × 12″) work published by Oxford University Press, derived from its larger, more comprehensive ATLAS OF THE WORLD (also 1993). The maps have been scaled down and the feature material abridged to produce a smaller desk reference for home, school, library, or business use. The base atlas contains fewer maps than the parent work (spanning 96 pages, compared with 160) and the index fewer entries (44,000, compared with 75,000). The world city maps have also been dropped, but a special section of U.S. thematic, regional, and city maps has been added. The atlas comes in a sturdy hardcover binding that is flexible enough to allow the book to lie flat when opened, making the work easy to read and use.

For a detailed discussion of the authority, currency, accuracy, and legibility of the cartography, see the review for ATLAS OF THE WORLD.

Scope and Special Features

The *Concise Atlas of the World* is divided into four sections: "World Statistics and User Guide," "United States Maps," "Introduction to World Geography," and "World Maps." The first section (five pages) includes two statistical tables ("Countries" and "Physical Dimensions") and a user's guide, all adapted from the parent atlas. An informative feature on map projections that is new to this work also appears in this section. The "Introduction to World Geography" section (32 pages) covers 15 topics relating to physical and human geography with thematic maps, graphs, and diagrams. These topics have been condensed from the 23 in the parent work and some information has been rearranged, but the overall approach is similar. In both number and quality, these features set this atlas apart from others in its class. A brief index on the last page of the section lists the main subjects covered.

The addition of the "United States Maps" section to this atlas presumably represents a gesture to increase the book's appeal to American buyers. The section opens with seven thematic maps of North America relating to physical geography (for example, geomorphology, climate, vegetation). These are followed by 16 pages of regional maps, 11 city maps, and an index of about 7,500 entries. The majority of the regional maps are identical to maps found later in the world atlas (in the "North America" section), with the coloring altered to make them primarily political. A few new maps have been inserted, including a map of Chicago and the Midwest, and maps of Alaska, Hawaii, and Puerto Rico and Guam, American Samoa, and Micronesia. But apart from these new maps, the regional maps in this section provide little new information from those found in the base atlas; in fact, they have been slightly simplified by virtue of their political emphasis. The separate index to the section is of some benefit, but most of the entries also appear in the main index (with references to the world maps). However, unlike the main index, the U.S. index gives references only in latitude and longitude coordinates, which makes it more difficult to use.

The U.S. city maps mainly derive from the parent work. The selection of cities does not seem to follow the criterion of size, but rather emphasizes northern urban centers and neglects the Sunbelt: Pittsburgh, for example, is included but Houston, Dallas, and Phoenix are omitted.

The "World Maps" section follows the sequence of the parent work, although regions are covered in much less depth. The scales employed are necessarily smaller; the most typical views are in the range of 1:6,000,000 to 1:8,000,000, although parts of Europe and the United States are shown at 1:2,000,000 or 1:2,500,000. Given the smaller number of maps, the cartographers of the *Concise Atlas* deliberately chose scales to include whole countries or related groups of countries. Compared with the parent work, proportionately fewer pages are devoted to Europe and more to North America, with the rest of the world given about the same proportion of coverage.

The 44,000-entry main index (80 pages) is impressive in size and easy to use; as in the parent work, references use both letter-number grid and geographic coordinates. It is unfortunate that one finding aid, the very useful set of index maps that appears in the endpapers of the parent atlas, is not included in this work; instead, the endpapers of the *Concise Atlas* show flags of the world. They are up-to-date.

Summary

The most prominent selling feature of the *Concise Atlas of the World*—the section of U.S. maps—reflects more style than substance. It might have been better if these pages had been used to provide more extensive global coverage. Nevertheless, this work is a very fine atlas for the price ($30) and would be a valuable quick-reference tool for homes, schools, or libraries. Abridged from an excellent atlas, the cartography is very fine, the thematic features are interesting, and the work overall is easy to use. It does, however, contain fewer world maps than comparable volumes such as HAMMOND CONCISE, READER'S DIGEST ATLAS OF THE WORLD, and WORLD ATLAS OF NATIONS, each of which costs somewhat more.

The Economist Atlas

Facts at a Glance

Full title: **The Economist Atlas**
Publisher: Henry Holt
Edition reviewed: © 1991, 1992 revised second edition

Number of pages: 384
Number of maps: 48 world maps (reviewer estimate)
Number of index entries: 28,500 (reviewer estimate)
Intended readership: high school to adult
Trim size: 7½″ × 10″
Binding: hardcover

Price: $47.50
Sold directly to libraries and schools; also sold by direct mail and in bookstores
ISBN 0-8050-1987-1
No stated revision policy

Introduction, Format, and Authority

The Economist Atlas is a medium-sized geographical reference designed, according to the jacket blurb, "to provide decision-makers and all those who need to be well informed with a lively and authoritative presentation of the modern world." Despite its title, the volume is not strictly a world atlas but a combination atlas and encyclopedia of nations. First published in 1989, the work was produced in Great Britain. This review is based on the 1992 "First American Edition" published in the United States by Henry Holt, which is the same as the revised second edition (1991) published in Britain.

The world maps were produced by the authoritative Swedish cartographic firm of Esselte Map Service. The thematic and encyclopedia maps were created by Lovell Johns of Oxford. The book jacket states that the encyclopedia entries were "written by experts," but no credentials are given for the 30 contributors listed on the copyright page. A page of editorial sources preceding the index lists many highly authoritative works.

Intended for high school and adult readers, *The Economist Atlas* is durable and has an attractive appearance. Its medium size (7½″ × 10″) makes it handy to use as a desk reference.

Scope and Special Features

The overall structure of *The Economist Atlas* is its most significant special feature. The atlas is divided into four sections: "World Maps," "World Comparisons," "World Encyclopedia," and a collection of finding aids. The "World Maps" section, 103 pages long, includes only 35 physical-political reference maps—a small number for a world atlas. The 189-page "World Encyclopedia," which includes 200 country and regional profiles, makes up about half of the book. The other significant feature of the work, as its title suggests, is its editorial focus on economic geography.

The "World Maps" section is divided into standard continental areas (except the Middle East, which is treated with Africa instead of Asia). The colorful general reference maps use shaded relief to show land elevation and a series of colors and textures to depict physical regions such as deciduous forest and savanna. The scales used are small but consistent: all regions are shown at 1:14,000,000, except Europe, which is shown at 1:7,000,000. International coverage is thus evenly balanced, with a slight emphasis on Europe. The maps are surprisingly detailed given their small format, but some of the typefaces are tiny.

"World Comparisons," the thematic section of the atlas, covers 19 topics, including economic strength, foreign debt, trade in manufactures, foreign aid, and living standards. The information is presented on two-page spreads of thematic maps, graphs, diagrams, and statistics, elucidated by brief narratives.

The "World Encyclopedia" is organized into the following regions: The Americas, Europe, Asia, Oceania, The Middle East, and Africa. Within these sections, several pages of material are devoted to the region as a whole, followed by profiles of individual countries. The amount of information presented for each country varies. The United States, Soviet Union, Germany, and other major powers receive longer treatment, while smaller countries, such as those located in the Pacific and Caribbean regions, receive shorter entries. The section on Africa, which receives brief treatment in most atlases, is about 37 pages long—about the same length as the Americas, which includes the United States.

Written at a fairly sophisticated level, the articles emphasize economic geography, putting political events and cultural information in economic perspective. The entries on countries include a list of basic facts (for example, official name, capital, climate, currency) and a depiction of the country's flag. Many entries also include an economic profile that presents the basic economic issues facing the country and includes charts and graphs on such information as imports and exports and gross domestic product. Other maps and illustrations also supplement the text. Overall, the information is clearly presented; the graphs are of high quality and are user friendly.

The end matter includes a glossary of political and economic terms, notes on data and sources, a 3-page general index of topics, and a 69-page map index.

Currency

The Economist Atlas went to press, according to an editorial note, in May 1991—in the midst of sweeping political changes in the world. The maps and text are quite current to that time, although this edition is unfortunately not fully up-to-date to our time. Germany and Yemen are both shown unified on the maps, but so, of course, are the Soviet Union and Yugoslavia. Interestingly, the encyclopedia entry for the Soviet Union includes the August 1991 coup attempt against Mikhail Gorbachev.

Accuracy

Each general reference map is clearly labeled with its scale, which is given as a representative fraction (for example, 1:7,000,000) and a bar scale in kilometers and miles. Generally, maps appear to be accurately drawn, as are the position of cities, rivers, borders, and coastlines. The projection used for the world thematic maps is not noted and creates some unusual distortions, but this presents only a minor distraction.

Legibility

The typefaces used on the general reference maps are clear and readable, although some are very small. The labels of countries, cities, landforms, and bodies of water are generally well placed. The 19 different colors and textures used to indicate physical features occasionally overwhelm the type, as, for example, in the Pamir, Hindu Kush, and Himalaya ranges of Central Asia (page 51). However, the color variations also provide much detailed physical information. Most maps span two pages, but symbols and labels are carefully placed clear of the gutter.

The thematic maps and encyclopedia pages are well designed. Attractive type and page layouts contribute to the overall readability of the atlas.

Accessibility

There is no feature on how to use the atlas or even an introduction to the work as a whole, something that would greatly facilitate use. The brief "Notes on Data" section near the index explains how the information in the atlas is derived and used. A useful glossary helps to explain terms like *tropical climate, OPEC,* and *Warsaw Pact.* With no introduction or explanatory section, however, the reader might be unaware of these useful features. The table of contents is thorough and is supplemented by summary tables of contents before each section.

The sequence of atlas maps is logical to follow and is aided by index maps at the beginning of the section. The legend, which comes after the maps, is clearly presented; the system for denoting the population of cities is particularly well conceived. In the encyclopedia, the individual countries are organized by subregion (rather than alphabetically) within regions, which makes them difficult to access quickly.

The atlas has two indexes—a general index of about 1,140 entries (referring to the thematic maps and encyclopedia) and a map index of about 27,700 entries. But no explanation is given as to when the reader should use each index. Still, the indexes are thorough. A spot check of names indicated no omissions or errors. The map index uses a simple letter-number reference system.

Summary

The Economist Atlas is not strictly a world atlas, but rather a geographical presentation of economic data. It contains well-drawn maps (although few in number) and is loaded with useful information, which is made easy to find by the inclusion of two indexes. The lack of explanatory material detracts somewhat from its accessibility. However, the major drawback of the edition reviewed is its publication date. In many ways, the work is more current than many reference books on the market—in the range of modern issues presented, its international scope, and its fresh design. But given how much Europe has changed in the past few years, *The Economist Atlas* can be recommended for library or home purchase only with reservations. In library collections, it would best serve as a supplement to larger world atlases with a more comprehensive map stock.

The Great World Atlas

Facts at a Glance

Full title: **The Great World Atlas**
Publisher: American Map Corporation
Editor: Vera Benson, Director of Cartography
Edition reviewed: © 1992, third edition

Number of pages: 367
Number of maps: 120 (reviewer estimate)
Number of index entries: 100,000
Intended readership: high school to adult
Trim size: 10¼″ × 13¾″
Binding: hardcover

Price: $49.95
Sold in bookstores; also sold by direct mail and
    directly to libraries
ISBN 0-8416-2004-0
No stated revision policy

Introduction, Format, and Authority

The 1992 copyright of *The Great World Atlas* is the third
edition of a work that first appeared in 1986. According
to the publishers, the atlas aims to combine "the happy
blending of old cartographic skills with the latest technology, which finds its finest expression in the most beautiful and useful satellite photographs ever arranged in a
single atlas." Aimed primarily at the adult audience, *The
Great World Atlas* contains many noncartographic features, including a 32-page section on "The Nature of Our
Planet" and "The Nature of Our Universe" (both new to
this edition) and 32 pages of satellite photographs with
explanatory text. Bound in a simulated-leather hard cover,
this large-format (10¼″ × 13¾″) atlas appears sturdy, and
the flexible binding allows the book to lie open flat. The
maps are well printed on thick, semigloss paper.

Most of the work was created in Germany, and the text
was translated into English for an American audience.
The cartography was executed by the German firm Kar-
tographisches Institut Bertelsmann. The fourth edition of
this work, published in 1994, was not available at the time
of this review. The price for that edition is $59.95.

Scope and Special Features

The contents of *The Great World Atlas* fall into five
main sections: (1) a collection of satellite images of various parts of the earth; (2) the world maps; (3) thematic
and political maps; (4) editorial features on the planet
and the universe; and (5) the index. The section on world
maps and the index are each 128 pages long.

The collection of world maps includes approximately
70 regional maps organized by continent, interspersed
with about 50 close-up maps of major urban areas. The
maps are notable for their use of highly detailed nomenclature to identify a broad variety of geographical features. The physical-political regional maps use a
combination of color and shading to show topographical
relief. The scale of tints used for land elevations is light
enough for the type and symbols on the maps to be
clearly visible, but the differences between colors are
too subtle for the reader to be able to match them up eas-

ily and accurately with the key. Also, the color key is located only on the "Explanation of Symbols" page at the
front of the section, rather than on each map.

Nearly half of the map pages in *The Great World Atlas* are devoted to North and South America. While the
United States and North America receive the most emphasis (36 pages), the 23 pages representing South
America cover that continent more completely than in
any other atlas. The remaining atlas pages are distributed equitably around the rest of the globe: 18 pages
represent Europe, 25 Asia, 7 Australia and Oceania, and
14 Africa. The metropolitan maps are also fairly well
distributed, with a slight bias toward cities in North
America and Europe. These maps, which appear at the
end of each continental section, highlight political, economic, and cultural features.

The world map section begins with an introduction
that provides the reader with a variety of aids for use, including a key to map coverage; a description of map
types, scales, and projections; abbreviations of geographical names and terms; and an explanation of symbols
used. The information is remarkably comprehensive.

The section containing thematic and political maps
includes approximately 35 maps of the world and of
specific regions. The thematic maps focus on topics
such as nutrition, the economy, and population density.
Most are presented on a full page or on a two-page
spread, which gives ample room for the level of detail
shown. In this section, special attention is again given to
the Americas, which are the only regions represented individually in thematic maps.

The truly distinguishing special feature of this atlas is
the 32-page collection of satellite images of selected areas of the world. The section opens with an overview of
satellite photography technology and applications. The
stunning photographic images themselves cover a variety of locales, including the New York metropolitan
area, San Francisco, the Rocky Mountains, and London.
The photographs are accompanied by informative and
lucid explanations that point out specific features (such
as urban areas, bodies of water, and geological formations), keyed by number to each image.

Two sets of editorial features are new to this third edition. The first, "The Nature of Our Planet," explores 19
topics relating to the earth's composition and physical history, including plate tectonics, rock types, erosion, coral
reefs, ice caps, glaciers, and volcanoes. "The Nature of
Our Universe" covers five topics about the solar system
and outer space. These features are well written and amply illustrated with color photographs and drawings.

Currency

Currency is the weakest aspect of *The Great World Atlas*. Although it carries a 1992 copyright, the editors of
the third edition have not incorporated many of the re-

cent major political changes that have swept the world. Although it shows the reunification of Germany, the Soviet Union, Yugoslavia, and Czechoslovakia are all still presented with their former borders. The Russian city of Nizhny Novgorod is called by its former name of Gor'kij (Gorky), although St. Petersburg is labeled with its current name. A number of other name changes, such as Kalaallit Nunaat for Greenland and Kiritimati for Christmas Island, do not appear on the maps.

Accuracy

According to the publisher's introduction, deliberate care was taken in compiling the atlas to use "fewer, chiefly true-to-area projections and fewer scales." Scales are thus relatively standard for similar geographic units. The continents, with the exception of Antarctica, are presented at a scale of 1:13,500,000 (in one to four parts, depending on the area). With the exception of Alaska, the United States is depicted at a scale of 1:3,750,000. The editors note that for Alaska it was necessary to show a scale of 1:4,500,000 in order to be able to depict the mainland on one map. The coverage of the United States makes it possible to see a complete rendering of each individual state on one map (although half of Florida appears in an inset on the "Atlantic States South" map).

Other areas of the world, including Canada, South America, Europe, and South and East Asia, are mapped at 1:4,500,000. There are also a few isolated maps of various regions (for example, New Zealand and East Africa) at 1:6,750,000. These scales were chosen, according to the editor, based on the criteria of population density as well as political, economic, or tourist significance. The metropolitan maps each use the same scale of 1:225,000, which, as the editors note, makes possible "immediate and global comparisons."

Scales are generally presented in fractional, verbal, and bar scale format, the last calibrated in miles and kilometers. Projections are not stated on the maps, but the system of projections used is thoroughly explained at the opening of the maps section. Apart from the currency issue, no major errors in accuracy were discovered.

Legibility

Maps are printed on either single pages or on two-page spreads and use a variety of formats. They are large and easy to read, and although there is no gutter margin, even those maps spread over two pages do not lose information in the gutters. Labels of cities, countries, landforms, and bodies of water are generally properly placed.

One trade-off in the use of consistent scales is that maps cut somewhat arbitrarily across national borders. As is commonly the case in atlases, the maps in *The Great World Atlas* sometimes break out of their neat lines and may bleed off the page in places to include salient borders. However, the editors were not meticulous in clearing the margins of type, so frequently symbols and labels are cut off at page's edge.

Local name spellings are preferred over conventional Anglicized forms, with the latter usually provided in parentheses for major places. Both forms have entries in the index. The main exception is for names of countries and other major features, which appear in English.

A multilingual list of abbreviations of geographical names and terms is grouped by general feature type, such as "Mountains." It would have been helpful if English equivalents were given for all foreign terms that appear on the maps, but only those that have been abbreviated appear on this list.

Accessibility

The detailed explanatory material provided throughout the atlas is one of this work's strongest features. The general introduction summarizes the features and organization of the atlas as a whole, and the description of map types, scales, and projections provides some of the best map-reading information available in any atlas. Finding aids include a lengthy table of contents and index maps. The legend is clear and comprehensive. One inconvenience is that the maps do not indicate the pages of adjoining maps.

The index contains over 100,000 entries, an impressive number for an atlas of this scope. The index is easy to use, with page references indicating letter-number grid coordinates, but not latitude and longitude. A state abbreviation is given for all place names in the United States, although the country of all other place names is not noted unless there are identical names in different countries.

Summary

The Great World Atlas contains sophisticated maps and presents a great deal of information in an interesting and readable format. Despite some occasional shortcomings, the atlas has been thoughtfully organized and prepared to be accessible and easy to use. The satellite images, high-quality cartography, and special features rate very high for a moderately priced general atlas. However, this edition does not reflect the major world changes of the early 1990s, which is probably the single most important consideration for any atlas purchaser today. Were it not for a lack of currency, *The Great World Atlas* would be recommended for library and home collections. Prospective buyers should review the fourth edition (published too late to be reviewed here) to see if it incorporates these changes. Another option would be to consider the slightly more expensive but more current NEW YORK TIMES ATLAS OF THE WORLD, THIRD REVISED CONCISE EDITION.

Hammond Atlas of the World

Facts at a Glance

Full title: **Hammond Atlas of the World**
Publisher: Hammond
Edition reviewed: © 1994, third printing

Number of pages: 304
Number of maps: 230
Number of index entries: 115,000
Intended readership: high school to adult
Trim size: 10¾″ × 14″
Binding: hardcover

Price: $69.95; 15 percent discount to libraries and schools
Sold directly to libraries and schools; also sold in bookstores and other retail outlets
ISBN 0-8437-1175-2
Revised when inventory is depleted—approximately every year

Introduction, Format, and Authority

Introduced in 1992 as Hammond's new top-of-the-line atlas, *Hammond Atlas of the World* is the result of the company's five-year project to develop a computerized map-making system. Based on a huge database of geographical features, computers generated all components of the maps except the topographical relief. This atlas also features a new projection created by Hammond, the Optimal Conformal, which is used for mapping whole continents. The 1994 edition reviewed here is the third printing.

The large format (10¾″ × 14″), heavy paper stock, and cloth spine create a highly durable volume of 230 maps. The design of the atlas is fresh and attractive, and the colors used are appealing. The intended audience is high school students to adults.

Hammond is one of the largest commercial map and atlas makers in the United States. While Hammond is not as renowned as Rand McNally or the National Geographic Society, its maps are reliably accurate and up-to-date.

Scope and Special Features

The *Hammond Atlas of the World* consists of six sections: "Interpreting Maps," "Quick Reference Guide," "Global Relationships," "The Physical World," "Maps of the World," and "Statistical Tables and Index." The "Maps of the World" section, the base atlas, occupies 160 pages.

The *Hammond* has less introductory material and special features than most other atlases its size. The material in "Interpreting Maps" consists of brief articles on cartography and map projections as well as a general overview of the atlas called "Using this Atlas." The articles focus primarily on the selling features of this atlas—computer-assisted mapmaking, the new Hammond database, and the Optimal Conformal projection. The article on projections is particularly good. "Using this Atlas," which includes the atlas legend, contains too much information crammed onto a two-page spread (see *Accessibility*). A three-page "Quick Reference Guide" lists important facts about countries, states, territorial possessions, and other major geographical areas, and gives a page/grid reference for them. The guide is a useful at-a-glance reference.

Sixteen pages of thematic maps ("Global Relationships") cover standard topics in human and physical geography, including environmental concerns. The maps are supplemented by photographs, charts, cartograms, and other illustrations. The spreads are attractively designed and informative—except for the climate map, which is difficult to read (see *Legibility*). Overall, this atlas has fewer thematic maps than most of its competitors.

"The Physical World" is a 16-page collection of relief maps covering the continents and the oceans. While the maps are attractive and accurate, no map has a scale, a major failing of this section. And while the collection is large for a work of this scope, the coverage is varied. Australia is included with the whole Pacific Ocean, Antarctica is completely missing, and there are no individual maps of the Atlantic or Indian oceans. Finally, four maps detail parts of Asia and one focuses on the United States, but no other parts of continents are given detailed coverage.

On the other hand, the "Maps of the World" section—the heart of the *Hammond Atlas of the World*—blankets the globe quite well. Most regional maps are 1:3,000,000 or 1:6,000,000. Some maps, notably those of Europe and the United States, are 1:1,000,000, while close-ups of major cities are 1:500,000. Nearly all of the maps are political-physical with a background of shaded topographical relief. The exceptions are the maps of continents, which are primarily political. A locator map is provided in the top margin for each map.

The maps are grouped by continents. As in most atlases, Europe and North America receive the most coverage—over half of the maps represent these areas. But the *Hammond Atlas of the World* also has the best coverage of Africa of any world atlas and excellent coverage of both Australia and South America. Coverage is not comprehensive, however. Since the maps treat regions rather than specific countries and use overlapping views at various scales, some countries are covered more thoroughly than others. While Spain and Ukraine, for example, can be viewed whole at the medium scale of 1:3,000,000, Italy and Japan cannot.

The "Statistical Tables and Index" section includes tables of statistics on the solar system, dimensions of the earth, oceans and seas, the continents, and major canals, islands, mountains, rivers, and lakes. Where possible, information is given in both English and metric measurements. An additional table gives the population for all cities with over 100,000 inhabitants and all national capitals. The currency of these figures is spotty (see *Currency*).

The 115,000-entry "Index of the World," 87 pages long, includes a table of abbreviations at the beginning of the section. Since the *Hammond* uses simple abbreviations rather than symbols to note geographical features, the index is easy to use. Each entry gives the country of each place name, a feature found in few other atlases. The index uses letter-number grid coordinates; no latitude-longitude coordinates are given.

An additional feature of the *Hammond Atlas of the World* is its overall design, which enhances the look of the atlas and invites browsing. A title page for each section contains a pithy geographical quotation. Each map includes a short blurb of text in the top margin highlighting the subject area's geographical significance. While generally informative, the brief statements are at times cryptic. The text for "Central Pacific Ocean," for example, states that across "this vast area traders moved westward, reaching Fiji by 1300 B.C., and shortly thereafter Tahiti." This unexplained statement raises many more questions than it answers: Who were these traders? Where were they moving westward from? Why did they reach Fiji before Tahiti?

Currency

The main advantage of Hammond's computerized map-making system, according to the publisher, is that updates and changes can be made quickly and accurately. Given its 1994 copyright, the *Hammond* should and does show the recent major political changes—the unification of Germany and of Yemen, and the breakups of the Soviet Union, Yugoslavia, and Czechoslovakia. However, the atlas maps were not updated to show the independence of Eritrea from Ethiopia—although Eritrea is listed as a separate country in the indexes and population chart and is clearly delineated on the index map. The inconsistency seems to contradict the publisher's claim that its map-making system "moves as fast as the world is changing."

The "Using this Atlas" section notes that the main source for place names is the U.S. Board of Geographic Names. When foreign names may be unfamiliar to the general user, Hammond's policy is to translate the names into recognizable English forms. This may appeal to English-speaking users, but it sets the atlas apart from more scholarly works. Local and historical alternatives are given in parentheses—for example, **Greenland (Kalaallit Nunaat), Moscow (Moskva),** and **Ho Chi Minh City (Saigon).**

No dates or sources are given for any of the thematic maps or statistical data. Some of the thematic maps give data for Czechoslovakia as a unified country; this is understandable, though it should be noted and explained. Population figures in the "Quick Reference Guide" are reasonably current. However, several cities (such as Dakar, Senegal; Kinshasa, Zaire; and São Paulo, Brazil) on the "Population of Major Cities" table show population figures vastly below current estimates in other sources. On the maps, the population symbols for these cities agree with the table's low figures.

Accuracy

Generally, the maps in the *Hammond Atlas of the World* are accurate. A minor error was detected on the map of the Great Lakes Region (page 198): two towns in Ohio are labeled "Mt. Vernon."

Every large map in the "Maps of the World" section has a scale statement and bar scale in both miles and kilometers. The projection used is also stated. The inset maps have only a bar scale. This makes it difficult to determine their scale and especially difficult to compare them with other maps. The physical relief maps provide no scale or projection information. Maps of the continents vary greatly in scale.

Except for the problems with population data (see *Currency*), the statistics in this atlas are accurate. However, the *Hammond* should not be considered an authoritative source for statistics since neither dates nor sources are provided.

Legibility

The shaded relief of the *Hammond Atlas of the World* is strikingly realistic. It does, however, tend to overwhelm the print, making some labels hard to read; potential buyers may find this a major drawback. The maps are very pleasing to the eye—far more than those of any of its competitors. The colors used to distinguish areas are well chosen. In general, the typefaces and sizes work well, with the exception of alternate place names, which are often in such tiny type that they are lost.

Most of the maps appear across two pages. There is no gutter margin, but only a minimal amount of information is obscured because the book lies very flat when open. The outer page margins are ample.

The legend is clear. The symbols are not of standard convention—some are unique to this company. This is apt to confuse the first-time reader. Exact elevations are marked by spot heights. The shaded relief merely shows the presence of elevation differences.

Some of the thematic maps are too small and indistinct to be useful. The design of the climate map is a disaster; the stylized pattern used is hard to read and inappropriate for a serious atlas.

Accessibility

"Using this Atlas" outlines most features of the atlas but does not tell the user how to read a map. The "Map Projections" article tells the reader how to use coordinates but does not indicate how to apply this knowledge to maps in the atlas. As noted before, the legend is clear and logical, but it is located only in the "Using this Atlas" section, where it is buried on the page. The reader could easily mistake it for just another diagram. "Using this Atlas" also includes a list of type styles used on the maps (although it is missing at least one—the style used for historical regions such as Normandy and Tibet), but it does not explain what the differing sizes of type indicate.

The index map inside the front cover helps guide the reader easily, as do arrows on the edges of maps showing where connecting maps are located. However, the order in which the continents appear is unusual: Europe; Asia; Australia, Antarctica, and Pacific; Africa; Latin America; United States and Canada. Rather than being placed with North America, the maps for Middle America (including Mexico) are adrift between Africa and South America. While the arrangement of maps takes getting used to, it is also annoying that often maps of parts of countries come before maps of the whole country—for example, Central Scotland comes before the United Kingdom and Budapest comes before Hungary.

The page numbers create another impediment to accessibility. Printed in red and in very small type, and indented from the outer margin, they are very difficult to see when flipping the pages to locate a map. Also, the page numbers appear only on the right page of a two-page map (*164–165,* for example), a device that takes some getting used to. The index, on the other hand, is easy to use. This is by far the largest index for an atlas in this class—only the most comprehensive atlases have more entries.

Summary

The *Hammond Atlas of the World* is a solid work but contains some weaknesses. Some flaws, such as the lack of scales on some maps, are technical; others, such as problems with the legend, legibility problems caused by the heavy shaded relief, and the design of the page numbers, affect its ease of use. As to the issue of currency, only time will tell how "up-to-the-minute" future editions will be. The atlas's strengths include its attractive maps, superior coverage of Africa and South America, and excellent index. In all, *Hammond*'s world map stock is more comprehensive than most other mid-range atlases, including The New Cosmopolitan World Atlas and Readers' Digest Atlas of the World. Its range is similar to Atlas of the World (Oxford University Press), but the *Hammond* reflects a North American bias, while the Oxford atlas favors Europe.

While lacking some attributes of the more authoritative and comprehensive atlases, the *Hammond* is also less expensive than these. It represents a good value for potential buyers who seek good global coverage and accurate maps, but who are willing to sacrifice scholarship and special features.

Hammond Atlas of the World, Concise Edition

Facts at a Glance

Full title: **Hammond Atlas of the World, Concise Edition**
Publisher: Hammond
Edition reviewed: © 1993

Number of pages: 232
Number of maps: 156
Number of index entries: 60,000
Intended readership: high school to adult
Trim size: 9³/₈″ × 12¼″
Binding: hardcover; paperback

Price: $39.95 (hardcover); $24.95 (paperback); 15 percent discount to libraries and schools
Sold directly to schools; also sold in bookstores and other retail outlets
ISBN 0-8437-1181-7
No stated revision policy

Introduction, Format, and Authority

This 1993 edition of the *Hammond Atlas of the World, Concise Edition* is a medium-sized (9³/₈″ × 12¼″), single-volume work derived from the new Hammond Atlas of the World. Most of the maps and feature material in the *Hammond Concise* are taken directly from the larger work. Because of the smaller dimensions of the *Hammond Concise,* the maps are scaled smaller and the editorial features are abridged. The base atlas contains fewer maps than the parent work (spanning 120 pages as opposed to 160), and the index contains about half as many entries.

The overall look of both editions is very similar. However, the background relief of the maps in the *Hammond Concise* is much more subdued than in the larger Hammond. This renders the *Hammond Concise* maps less striking but more legible—more appropriate, perhaps, for general home users and students. The binding is of lower quality, so that the maps on the two-page spreads do not meet as precisely at the gutter. It will also be less durable.

As with the parent work, the maps in this edition are computer generated. Its intended audience is high school students to adults. The smaller format makes it easier to use as a desk reference than the full atlas. In terms of accessibility, the strengths and weaknesses of the HAMMOND ATLAS OF THE WORLD generally carry over to the *Hammond Concise.*

The maps in the *Hammond Concise* are accurate and current to 1993, the year of publication. As in the parent work, however, there are lapses in the currency of the population data. The statistics are basically reliable but not authoritative.

For additional comments on format, authority, currency, accuracy, legibility, and accessibility, see the review for HAMMOND ATLAS OF THE WORLD on pages 208–210.

Scope and Special Features

The overall arrangement of the *Hammond Atlas of the World, Concise Edition* basically follows that of the parent work. The main difference is that the tables of world statistics and population of world cities have been moved from the index into a separate section called "Geographic Comparisons." This section also includes a time-zone map, which appears in the back endpapers of the parent atlas. Both the front and back endpapers of the *Hammond Concise* contain an index map.

The introductory section, "Interpreting Maps," contains abridged versions of the short features in HAMMOND ATLAS OF THE WORLD. The feature called "Using this Atlas" includes the legend for the atlas maps, which is buried on the page. The legend should appear more prominently and nearer the maps. The user's guide provides little information as to how to read the maps; it contains no explanation of the various type styles used for geographical features and type sizes for cities.

The "Quick Reference Guide," an at-a-glance reference and index to major geographical areas, is identical to the one in the parent work. On the other hand, the thematic maps in "Global Relationships" have been significantly abridged. The maps on languages, religions, and vegetation have been cut; in the remaining maps, the explanatory text has been eliminated. The maps do, however, maintain their visual appeal and impact—the climate map here is better than that in the parent work. "The Physical World," the collection of physical relief maps, is essentially lifted from the larger atlas with three maps eliminated. The 60,000-entry "Index of the World," while not comprehensive, is excellent for a work of this scope.

Although its size is reduced by one-quarter from the HAMMOND ATLAS OF THE WORLD, the "Maps of the World" base atlas still blankets the globe quite well. In many cases, the maps in the *Hammond Concise* are picked up directly (and scaled down proportionately) from the larger Hammond work; some areas, most notably the United States, are mapped differently in larger regions.

Several detailed views, particularly of Europe, have been eliminated entirely. Most regional maps are 1:3,500,000 or 1:7,000,000. A few maps of highly urbanized areas are 1:1,170,000, while close-ups of major cities are 1:587,000. The top margin of each map contains a locator map, but the text blurbs found in the larger Hammond atlas do not appear here.

In terms of international coverage, the *Hammond Concise* maintains about the same proportional distribution as the parent work. Although the focus of the atlas is on Europe and North America, it has the best coverage of Africa of any atlas in its class and excellent coverage of both Australia and South America. One significant improvement over the parent work is that the maps of Middle America more logically appear with the rest of North America (instead of with South America).

Summary

Abridged from a very solid work, the *Hammond Atlas of the World, Concise Edition* provides a basic stock of high-quality maps in a manageable format. It would serve as a good map reference for most home or school uses. Although it carries over some of the flaws of its parent work, most of these would not be noticed by the student or general user. The hardcover version, at $39.95, represents a reasonable value; while the paperback version costs much less ($24.95), it may not be as durable. Readers may also want to consult the review in this Buying Guide of the WORLD ATLAS OF NATIONS (Rand McNally), a work similar in scope and price to this one.

Hammond International Atlas of the World

Facts at a Glance

Full title: **Hammond International Atlas of the World**
Publisher: Hammond
Edition reviewed: © 1994

Number of pages: 168
Number of maps: 90
Number of index entries: 45,000
Intended readership: junior high school to adult
Trim size: $9^3/_8" \times 12^1/_4"$
Binding: hardcover; paperback

Price: $27.95 (hardcover); $15.95 (paperback); 15 percent discount to libraries and schools
Sold directly to libraries and schools; also sold in bookstores and other retail outlets
ISBN 0-8437-1183-2
Revised when necessary to reprint

Introduction, Format, and Authority

Published in 1994, the *Hammond International Atlas of the World* is one of the new generation of Hammond computer-generated atlases. The others include the Hammond Atlas of the World, the head of the family, and its derivative Hammond Atlas of the World, Concise Edition. The *Hammond International* is spun off from the same computerized map-making system, and its map stock is essentially an abridged version of the Hammond Concise, with one basic difference—most of the maps are basically political and do not show topographical relief. Other features have also been altered but, overall, the content, configuration, and design of the *Hammond International* reflect the other new Hammond atlases.

The *Hammond International* is clearly intended as a basic, lower-priced atlas for the family and college markets. The core atlas contains 90 pages of world maps (compared with 160 in the Hammond Atlas of the World and 120 in the Hammond Concise). The medium-sized pages ($9^3/_8'' \times 12^1/_4''$) and slimmer format make it easy to handle. But while downsized and simplified, it also has the advantage of being generated by the computer system used to render the accurate higher-end Hammond atlases. The atlas comes in hardcover and paperback editions; only the hardcover version was examined for this review.

For additional comments on format and authority, see the reviews in this guide for the Hammond Atlas of the World and the Hammond Atlas of the World, Concise Edition.

Scope and Special Features

The overall arrangement of the *Hammond International* basically follows that of the Hammond Concise, although many features have been reduced to the bare bones. One new addition is a six-page section called "World Flags and Reference Guide" that shows flags and facts about each nation of the world. The entries include page and grid coordinates for quick reference.

A section called "Interpreting Maps" contains a brief but informative essay on map projections (including Hammond's new Optimal Conformal projection, which is used to map the continents) and a user's guide called "Using this Atlas" that includes the legend for the atlas maps. The guide and legend are barely adequate (see *Legibility* and *Accessibility* in this review). A section called "Global Relationships" includes only three thematic maps—environmental concerns, population, and standards of living; they are identical to those in the Hammond Concise (see that review). "The Physical World" includes just six of Hammond's excellent physical relief maps—the continents of Australia and Antarctica do not receive individual maps. A "Time Zones of the World" map and "World Statistics" table precede the

index; they also are identical to those in the Hammond Concise.

The "Maps of the World" base atlas provides decent, but not particularly in-depth, coverage of the globe. Most regional maps are at the smaller 1:10,500,000 and 1:7,000,000 scales, although most of Europe is covered at 1:3,500,000. The several 1:1,170,000 views of major metropolitan areas focus mainly on the United States and Europe; only two cities, London and Paris, are shown at the largest scale employed, 1:587,000.

As with its two Hammond siblings, just over half of the atlas pages in the *Hammond International* are devoted to Europe and North America. Coverage of Mexico, Central America, and the Caribbean is disappointing, however, as they are treated only on one small-scale map with Western Mexico broken off in an inset. Compared with other atlases in its class, coverage of Africa, Australia, and South America is quite good, although few regions are treated in any particular depth.

Unlike the regional maps, the maps of continents show physical relief, although only a minimal amount. On the regional maps, individual countries, states, and provinces are colored differently to highlight political divisions. A locator map appears in the top margin for each map.

Currency

In the "Acknowledgments" section, the publishers of the *Hammond International Atlas of the World* tout their computerized geographic database as a "map-making system that moves as fast as the world is changing." Indeed, this 1994 edition is as current as an atlas can be. All of the recent global changes are accounted for in the atlas and features—including the independence of Eritrea from Ethiopia, a change that even the 1994 Hammond Atlas of the World does not incorporate. The population statistics are reasonably current. However, it should be noted that this is a first edition with no history of revision behind it.

The "Using this Atlas" section notes that the main source for place names is the U.S. Board of Geographic Names. When foreign names may be unfamiliar to the general user, Hammond's policy is to translate the names into recognizable English forms—an appropriate practice for this level of work. Local and historical alternatives are given in parentheses—for example, **Moscow (Moskva)** and **Ho Chi Minh City (Saigon).**

Accuracy

The base maps in *Hammond International* are virtually the same as those in the Hammond Concise. (See that review and the review for Hammond Atlas of the World.) Overlapping maps covering a particular world region (such as Asia or the United States) are consistent in scale.

Legibility

The designers of the *Hammond International Atlas of the World* have chosen a muted color scheme, which serves to distinguish the countries adequately while also allowing features and labels to stand out quite well. The colors used are consistent from map to map—an attractive feature. Dominated by brownish and greenish tones, the palette will seem either sophisticated or drab, depending on your taste.

The labels stand out clearly on the page and, although some small-scale maps are cluttered with labels, it is easy to link cities with names. This is much less true of other features. A wide variety of typefaces and sizes are used on the maps, but there is no explanation in the legend as to what kinds of features the different styles designate. Also, various sizes of type are used for city names—again with no explanation (although a legend for the city symbols, which designate population, appears on every map). The legend itself is buried in the front matter. These problems unnecessarily limit the effectiveness of the maps.

Most of the maps appear on two pages with no gutter margin. The tight binding prevents the book from lying completely flat when opened, and much information is obscured in the gutter. The maps on the two-page spreads often do not meet precisely at the gutter.

Accessibility

The *Hammond International* offers most of the user aids found in the HAMMOND ATLAS OF THE WORLD and HAMMOND CONCISE (see those reviews). Both the front and back endpapers contain a map index. Adjacent area page numbers on the perimeters of maps guide the reader from map to map—an exceptional feature in an atlas of this scope. However, they often refer to maps of different scales, which could be a source of confusion for some users. The "World Flags and Reference Guide" provides a quick page and location reference for countries. The table of contents is lengthy and useful.

The introductory material is easy to read and outlines the parts of the atlas well. It does not, however, tell the user how to read a map. The legend should be more prominently displayed and appear closer to the maps. The atlas maps are grouped together by continent, although the continents appear in unusual order (as in the other Hammond atlases).

Although the editors state that the index is a "comprehensive listing of the places and geographic features found in the atlas," it is truly comprehensive only for the United States and Canada. Some smaller towns and lesser features in other parts of the world are not indexed. Overall, however, the index is adequate for a work of this scope. It is also particularly easy to use.

The index follows the format and design of the HAMMOND ATLAS OF THE WORLD and HAMMOND CONCISE. For additional comments, see those reviews.

Summary

In the *Hammond International Atlas of the World,* Hammond has produced a basic, economical, family atlas with no sacrifice of map quality and accuracy. As it contains fewer special features than many other family atlases, the focus of the work is on its map stock. These maps are a reliable and straightforward source for basic "Where in the world?" information. The work is also very current, but whether this quality can be applied to future editions depends on the publisher's avowed ability to make changes "as fast as the world is changing."

Although entitled "International," its global scope is not deep. Other factors weighing against the atlas are the binding, which creates legibility problems and may not stand up to heavy use, and the weaknesses in the user's guide and legend. These factors would recommend against purchase by libraries, except where price is a primary consideration, or perhaps for use as a circulating atlas. Individuals buying for family or college use might note that the paperback HAMMOND CONCISE, a more sophisticated atlas, lists for less ($24.95) than the hardcover *International* ($27.95), and the hardcover CONCISE ATLAS OF THE WORLD (Oxford University Press) is only slightly more ($30).

Hammond Nova World Atlas

Facts at a Glance

Full title: **Hammond Nova World Atlas**
Publisher: Hammond
Edition reviewed: © 1991

Number of pages: 176
Number of maps: 174
Number of index entries: same-page indexes (no master index)
Intended readership: junior high school to adult
Trim size: 8½″ × 10⅞″
Binding: paperback

Price: $10.95; 15 percent discount to schools and libraries
Sold directly to libraries and schools; also sold in bookstores and other retail outlets
ISBN 0-8437-1216-3
No scheduled revision

Introduction, Format, and Authority

The *Hammond Nova World Atlas* is an inexpensive, medium-sized (8½″ × 10⅞″), paperback atlas. The edition reviewed carries a 1991 copyright and was last revised by inserting maps of Russia and neighboring countries, the Balkan countries, and the Baltic republics into the section called "Union of Soviet Socialist Republics." No changes were made to existing maps (including several maps of the Soviet Union as well as world and continental maps) to reflect these changes. This fact seriously undermines the value of this atlas, even considering the price.

Scope and Special Features

The arrangement of the *Hammond Nova World Atlas* is unusual for an adult atlas. According to the publisher's introduction, "The guiding principle in organizing the atlas material has been to present separate subjects on *separate* maps. . . . [T]he basic reference map of an area is accompanied on adjacent pages by all supplementary information pertaining to that area." This supplementary information usually includes facts and flags, a topographical map, one or more thematic maps, and a map-specific index (except on U.S. maps). This arrangement may have some advantages, particularly for students, but the lack of a master index presents a major problem with accessibility. The maps of individual U.S. states inexplicably have no indexes, although maps of individual Canadian provinces do. About two-thirds of the atlas pages are devoted to the United States, Canada, and Europe.

The general reference maps are primarily political; subject areas are white with borders clearly highlighted in pastel colors. No distinctions, such as by population or relative importance, are made between cities (except for capitals). Projections are noted, and scales are given with bar scales in miles and kilometers.

The "Introduction to the Maps and Indexes" explains the organization of the atlas and how to use it. Simple legends are located on the individual maps, although these are not always comprehensive, especially considering the relatively few types of symbols employed on the maps. A two-page "Gazetteer—Index of the World" serves as the only general finding aid. It also includes important facts about countries, states, provinces, and so on; however, the list has not been updated to include the new countries of Europe and the former Soviet Union, and the world population figures are not current. On a separate fact chart for the United States, the population figures purport to be from 1990, but they do not correspond to the official 1990 census.

About half of the maps spread across two pages. Symbols and labels are split arbitrarily by the gutter, and the two map pages do not always align precisely. Some place names are therefore difficult, if not impossible, to read.

Summary

Considering the wealth of new or thoroughly revised world atlases on the market today (including several inexpensive products in Hammond's own computer-gener-

ated line), there is little reason to select the patched-up *Hammond Nova World Atlas*. It is not recommended for purchase.

Hammond World Atlas, Collectors Edition

Facts at a Glance

Full title: **Hammond World Atlas, Collectors Edition**
Publisher: Hammond
Edition reviewed: © 1993

Number of pages: 224
Number of maps: 182
Number of index entries: 7,400
Intended readership: adult
Trim size: $4^3/_8'' \times 6^3/_4''$
Binding: hardcover

Price: $15.95; 15 percent discount to libraries
Sold by direct mail; also sold in bookstores and other retail outlets
ISBN 0-8437-1604-5
No stated revision policy

Introduction, Format, and Authority

The *Hammond World Atlas, Collectors Edition* is a pocket-sized world atlas for general adult reference. While small, the volume is sturdily bound in a padded, blue, simulated-leather cover with gold-edged pages.

Scope and Special Features

The *Hammond World Atlas, Collectors Edition* consists of six sections: a quick-reference gazetteer, thematic maps and statistical tables, maps of the world, flags of the world, a "road atlas" of the United States and Canada, and an index. The section containing maps of the world occupies 88 pages, the road atlas 68 pages, and the index 32 pages.

The "Gazetteer—Index of the World" (11 pages) gives the area, population, and page/grid reference for continents, countries, states, and other major political units. This section is followed by four black-and-white world thematic maps (languages, occupations, vegetation, and climates) and a time-zone map, a chart of world air distances, and statistical tables of the world's major features. An additional full-color population map appears at the beginning of the world maps section. While the tables are handy features, the thematic maps are too small and too general to be of any real use. Other special features include the "Flags of the World" (six pages) and a brief U.S. highway mileage table (one page).

The collection of world maps, organized by continent, generally treats whole countries or related groups of countries. The section is heavily weighted toward Europe and the former Soviet Union; coverage of Asia is decent, but Africa and South America receive only two maps each. The maps are primarily political, with subject areas shown in solid pastels and countries or other political units differentiated by color. No roads or railroads are depicted.

A separate section of maps of the United States and Canada is billed as a road atlas, although due to the size of the maps it would only be useful as such in a pinch. Maps are organized alphabetically. Included with the maps of the states and provinces are insets of major metropolitan areas and a map of Mexico.

Currency

The countries and names shown in *Hammond Collectors* are current to its 1993 copyright, including the breakup of Czechoslovakia. However, some of the population figures in the statistical tables, such as those for Iran and Mexico, are very out-of-date.

Accuracy

The accuracy of *Hammond Collectors* is adequate for the most basic purposes. The small scales used limit the precision of the maps, and labels are sometimes difficult to connect with their symbols and frequently break up border markings. Except for capitals, no distinction is made among cities in terms of size or importance. As each map shows one or more whole countries, the scales used vary greatly, making comparisons difficult. Scales are indicated only with a bar—in miles and kilometers on the world maps and in miles only on the road maps. The statistics in the atlas are generally accurate, except for the population figures (as noted above).

Legibility

The small size of the maps and relatively large subject areas they cover make some maps overcrowded and difficult to read. The typefaces on some maps are necessarily very small. On several maps, the type is broken or fuzzy. Most of the world maps and some of the road maps span two pages. Labels and symbols are often broken by the gutter, making that information very difficult to read. The maps bleed off the side and bottom edges of the pages, but as the subject areas are well centered, this in itself does not interfere with legibility.

Accessibility

Accessibility is one of the stronger points of this atlas. It is easy to find the map you want. The gazetteer at the front of the book and the master index at the end are both helpful but not very detailed. The road maps have arrows indicating the maps of connecting areas. No legend is given for the world maps, but the road atlas includes a short list of symbols.

Summary

While outwardly handsome and durable, the *Hammond World Atlas, Collectors Edition* has little inside that would attract the personal or library atlas collector. At $15.95, it is not a particularly good value for the information it contains. Its compact size could make it a handy reference for carrying in a briefcase or book bag or storing in a desk drawer, but THE RANDOM HOUSE COMPACT WORLD ATLAS is less expensive and similarly sized.

National Geographic Atlas of the World

Facts at a Glance

Full title: **National Geographic Atlas of the World**
Publisher: National Geographic Society
Editor: William Graves, Editor; John F. Shupe, Chief Cartographer
Edition reviewed: © 1992, revised sixth edition

Number of pages: 412
Number of maps: approximately 150 world maps and 200 city maps (reviewer estimate)
Number of index entries: 150,000
Intended readership: adult
Trim size: 12½" × 18¼"
Binding: hardcover; paperback

Price: $100 (hardcover); $80 (paperback)
Sold in bookstores; also sold by direct mail by the publisher
ISBN 0-87044-835-8 (hardcover);
  ISBN 0-87044-834-X (paperback)
No scheduled revision

Introduction, Format, and Authority

The oversized (12½" × 18¼") *National Geographic Atlas of the World* is the revised sixth edition (© 1992) of a work that first appeared in 1963. The original sixth edition was published in 1990, but the enormous changes to the world's political landscape that began just months after its release compelled the publisher to generate this revised edition. According to the editor's foreword nearly one out of every three plates in the atlas was altered to keep pace with political events, and thousands of index entries were revised. Twenty new nations are included in the "Nations of the World" country profiles. In addition, the atlas features completely revised essays on Europe and Asia as well as updated thematic maps, including new "environmental stress" maps depicting such threats as deforestation, desertification, and soil salinization.

The National Geographic Society staff compiled the atlas with the help of numerous cartographic and editorial consultants from U.S. and foreign government agencies, American universities, and private and public environmental institutes. Their names appear on the copyright page and on a page of acknowledgments at the back of the book. Most of the textual material is signed by the individual writers. No specific credentials are listed for these contributors, although the list includes such notables as Edward O. Wilson, the eminent Harvard biologist.

The atlas is published in both hardcover and paperback versions; only the paperback version was examined for this review. The cover material is relatively thick and strong, and the sewn binding is flexible enough to be opened flat without breaking. However, the sheer size and weight of the atlas, combined with the pliable soft cover, make it cumbersome to handle.

Scope and Special Features

The most striking feature of the *National Geographic Atlas* is its overall organization and presentation of a variety of geographical information. The table of contents lists 11 main illustrated sections, 8 of which are the maps of each continent and the oceans. This sequence opens with an editorial feature on the earth ("Dynamic Earth") and several world thematic maps ("Habitable Earth"), followed by the continental maps. It closes with a feature on the moon, solar system, and universe ("Worlds Beyond"). The end matter includes country profiles, charts of statistical data, a glossary, and two indexes—the general map index and a moon index. The base atlas occupies 200 pages and includes thematic maps, city maps, and other features related to each continent in addition to the general reference maps. The 150,000-entry main index spans 135 pages.

The brief but informative feature articles are beautifully illustrated with large maps, diagrams, and photographs. Topics covered in "Dynamic Earth" include continental drift and plate tectonics; earthquakes, volcanoes, and geological age; and forces that shape the earth's surface. "Worlds Beyond" begins with a speculative section on the origins of the universe and a stunning satellite photograph of the Andromeda Galaxy, 2.2 million light-years away. This is followed by a map of the moon's surface (whose place-names are indexed in the end matter) and diagrams of the solar system, constellations in the northern and southern skies, and a fascinating and unique graphic representation of the known

universe and the position of our solar system within it. Although many other world atlases have features on outer space, none can match the quality and clarity of what is presented here.

The world thematic maps highlight a range of contemporary topics, including the biosphere, climate, population (including religion and language), food (including famine and infant mortality), minerals, and energy (including greenhouse gases and global warming). While most are straightforward, the satellite-produced biosphere map is a challenge to interpret.

The collection of world reference maps begins with a fold-out page containing an oversized physical relief world map on one side and a political-physical world map on the other. These are excellent features, although they may not long survive heavy library use. The political-physical regional maps are bold and clear. International and internal borders are highlighted in pastel colors. Land elevation is indicated by shaded relief and spot elevation markings; sea depths are indicated with layered tints.

Each continental region of political-physical maps (except that of Antarctica) is preceded by a large satellite image of the continent, several thematic maps, and a physical map. The same themes—population, land use/land cover, resources and industry, transportation, and environmental stress—are covered for each continent, and the maps are interpreted in brief captions. Following each section of maps are two to eight pages of urban regional insets. Numbering about 200, these are not detailed street maps, but they do locate suburbs, outlying towns, and main roads.

The section on the oceans includes a series of physical ocean-bottom maps as well as standard political-physical maps of these areas. Maps of the Pacific islands are located in this section.

This atlas has fairly good geographical balance, although Africa is slighted somewhat. Of the 120 pages of political-physical maps, 42 pages are devoted to North America (28 of these to the United States), 28 to Europe, 26 to Asia, 10 to South America, 8 to Africa, and 6 to Australia, Antarctica, and Oceania.

Following the maps section, "Nations of the World" gives brief profiles of all independent nations (those currently recognized by National Geographic's cartographers), U.S. states, and Canadian provinces. Fact boxes accompany each profile and highlight demographic, geographical, and economic data. Other statistical data in the end matter includes geographical comparisons, airplane flight distances, a time-zone map, metric conversion tables, monthly climate data for more than 300 places in the world, 1990 populations of U.S. cities, and 1992 (estimated) populations of foreign cities. A list of foreign terms, abbreviations, and the map legend are also located here, preceding the index.

Currency

The president and chairman of the National Geographic Society notes in the preface that upon finishing the 1990 edition, the staff "heaved a collective sigh of relief. Despite a flood of dramatic late-minute events—the reuniting of Germany, the fall of Poland's communist regime—we had produced a work that we hoped would last for more than a few years. Clearly, that was not to be." The 1992 revised edition was issued to incorporate the even greater global changes that took place during the intervening two years.

As a result, this atlas is thoroughly current as of its mid-1992 press date. At that time, Czechoslovakia was approaching dissolution, a fact that is annotated on the appropriate map and noted in the country profile. Eritrea is depicted as quasi-independent on the maps (though without annotation), and its then-impending independence is noted in the profile of Ethiopia. Place names are generally up-to-date and in accordance with national preferences.

Accuracy

There is no real standardization in the use of scales and projections. Scales used for the maps vary from 1:2,280,000 to 1:9,900,000. This variety gives a misleading impression of relative size and shape when comparing two areas, although it probably will not hinder the general user. Scales on the regional political-physical maps are expressed in representative fractions and in verbal and bar scale form in both miles and kilometers, and projections are also noted. Scales for the city maps are given only in bar scale form, and they vary, even on the same page.

Names have been placed accurately on the maps. A glossary makes it easy to interpret foreign terms used throughout the atlas. A variety of colored lines designates international boundaries, but the larger the map, the more difficult it is for the reader to distinguish the boundaries. Territorial disputes and other political situations affecting the cartography are annotated in red type on the maps.

Legibility

Legibility is perhaps the strongest point of the *National Geographic Atlas*. The cartography is attractive and the text and labels easy to read. Moreover, labels of cities, countries, landforms, and bodies of water are generally well placed, and there seems to be no distortion despite the variety of scales and projections used. Many maps are spread over two pages, but no information is lost in the gutters.

Accessibility

The 150,000-entry comprehensive index includes 14,000 name changes since the 1990 edition was published. Entries refer to the map that provides the "best presentation" of the place name listed. When cities are also shown on an inset map, the entry references that map as well, and entries for countries, states, and provinces include a page reference to the country profile. All entries give the country (or state or province) of the place name listed. Entries for features other than inhabited places list the type of feature (for example, *lake, river*). The reference system of letter-number coordinates is easy to use. Latitude and longitude are not given. Other finding aids include an index map conveniently printed on the front endpapers and a detailed table of contents.

An introductory "How to Use" section could have made the atlas more accessible. As it is, the atlas is fairly easy to use, although the map legend is hidden in the end matter, seemingly out of place between two statistical charts. The legend itself does not explain what criteria (such as population or relative importance) determine the different sizes of symbols and type used for towns.

Summary

The *National Geographic Atlas of the World* (particularly the paperback version) is difficult to handle because of its size, and its relatively high cost will make it a selective purchase for individuals. On the whole, the general reference maps convey more political than physical information, in contrast to other topflight atlases such as THE NEW INTERNATIONAL and THE TIMES ATLAS. *National Geographic* is also not as comprehensive as these. But these weaknesses are more than offset by this atlas's many strengths. The excellent cartography of the National Geographic Society shines, and the work is packed with useful geographical information. *The National Geographic Atlas of the World* would be a welcome addition to the shelves of all kinds of libraries and research institutes.

The New Cosmopolitan World Atlas

Facts at a Glance

Full title: **The New Cosmopolitan World Atlas**
Publisher: Rand McNally
Edition reviewed: © 1992, 1993 revised edition

Number of pages: 344
Number of maps: 236
Number of index entries: 69,000
Intended readership: adult
Trim size: 11" × 14¾"
Binding: hardcover

Price: $60; discount available to schools and libraries
Sold directly to schools and libraries; also sold by direct mail and in bookstores
ISBN 0-528-83553-X
Revised as necessary to keep up with world events

Introduction, Format, and Authority

The New Cosmopolitan World Atlas, published by Rand McNally, is a large-format world atlas for general adult use. Its world map stock derives from the maps created for Rand McNally's top-of-the-line THE NEW INTERNATIONAL ATLAS, but *The New Cosmopolitan* is neither as large nor as comprehensive as THE NEW INTERNATIONAL. Incorporated into the set of world maps are individual maps for the American states and Canadian provinces, which are adapted from maps that appear in Rand McNally's *Atlas of the United States.*

Originally entitled *Rand McNally Cosmopolitan World Atlas, The New Cosmopolitan,* according to the book jacket, has been "completely redesigned and revised." Indeed, the atlas's overall structure is more unified and its design more consistent than in previous editions. The features at the front of the book have been given a strong environmental focus reflecting current global concerns. The world maps are bigger and more legible. The maps of the United States and Canada have a fresher look. A single index lists places on all the maps. *The New Cosmopolitan* has a 1992 copyright; this review is based on the 1993 "revised edition."

In format and price, *The New Cosmopolitan* compares with mid-range atlases such as ATLAS OF THE WORLD (Oxford University Press) and the HAMMOND ATLAS OF THE WORLD. The large size (11″ × 14¾″), heavy paper stock, and sturdy simulated-leather binding create a physically heavy volume, but one that should prove durable.

Scope and Special Features

The table of contents lists seven sections: "This Fragile Earth" (features and thematic maps), "Using the Atlas," "World Time Zones," "Reference Maps" (the base atlas), "Index to Reference Maps," "World Geographical Tables," and "United States Geographical Tables." The "Reference Maps" section totals 160 pages, with 58 pages of these dedicated to individual maps of U.S. states and Canadian provinces. The index is 96 pages.

The New Cosmopolitan opens with a 32-page feature, "This Fragile Earth," which is divided into three sections: "Earth in Balance," discussing the earth, the biosphere, and human population; "Upsetting the Balance," focusing on environmental problems such as pollution, ozone layer depletion, extinction, and overpopulation; and "Restoring the Balance," a continent-by-continent look at environments, land use, and possible solutions to

environmental problems. The copyright page credits a writer (Jerry M. Sullivan) but gives no credentials. While very general, the feature is well written and easy to comprehend. It is illustrated with fully captioned thematic maps, diagrams, drawings, and photographs, which support and clarify the text. Although relatively few in number, the thematic maps are well presented.

The "Reference Maps" collection is organized into standard continental regions. A world political map opens the section. The state and province maps follow the general maps of their respective countries. Two physical relief maps close the section, one focusing on the Pacific and Indian oceans and the other on the Atlantic Ocean. These two maps and the Antarctica map are the only physical maps in the atlas, a rather small number for a work of this scope. There are no maps of cities outside the United States and Canada.

Because of the large proportion of maps devoted to states and provinces, total coverage is heavily weighted towards the United States and Canada. These maps aside, coverage is fairly evenly spread around the globe, with a slight emphasis on Europe. However, regions are not covered with any particular depth. *The New Cosmopolitan* has fewer than 100 pages of non–U.S. regional maps (compared, for example, with 146 in Oxford's ATLAS OF THE WORLD and 144 in the HAMMOND ATLAS OF THE WORLD). Oceania has been virtually overlooked, appearing only on the small-scale (1:48,000,000) map of the Pacific and Indian oceans.

Since the "Reference Maps" collection is a blend of two sets of maps, the world maps differ somewhat in style and treatment from the state and province maps. The world maps were produced by an international group of cartographers led by Rand McNally. Most views are taken directly from THE NEW INTERNATIONAL ATLAS, although some have been altered in scale. The maps are primarily political and employ a consistent range of projections and scales. Continents are scaled at 1:24,000,000 except for Europe, which is at 1:12,000,000. Most regional maps are 1:12,000,000 and 1:6,000,000, while maps of Europe and East Asia are 1:3,000,000. A few larger-scale maps focus on parts of Europe and the Middle East. The maps are white with a background of shaded relief. Pastel colors clearly highlight international and major internal boundaries.

Derived from a different Rand McNally map stock, the 58 maps of states and provinces employ different typography and symbols. Each state and province occupies a full page, so scales vary greatly, ranging from 1:304,000 to 1:12,000,000 (see *Accuracy*). However, the state and province maps are consistent with the world maps in color and overall appearance. Subject areas are white with a background of shaded relief. External borders and internal boundaries (such as counties) are highlighted in color, and nonsubject areas are in pastels. The maps display most large cities and towns, major roads and railroads, and physical features. Insets show major urban areas in somewhat greater detail.

Additional features in the front of the atlas include a three-page discussion of map-reading skills ("Using the Atlas") and a time-zone map. In the back of the work (after the index) are the "World Geographical Tables" and "United States Geographical Tables." The world tables include a fact chart of world nations and other political units ("World Political Information"), statistical tables of the earth's physical features, and a population table of major cities ("World Populations"). The "World Political Information" and "World Populations" tables are essentially identical to those found in the most authoritative Rand McNally works, the NEW INTERNATIONAL and BRITANNICA atlases. The U.S. tables include lists of geographical and historical facts, a chart of state areas and populations, and a 23-page list of all U.S. counties and more than 15,000 cities and towns with their 1990 populations and zip codes. This last feature is unique for a general world atlas and reflects its U.S. emphasis.

The index contains 69,000 entries, a number comparable to its chief rivals. It includes a helpful introduction and list of abbreviations. Cities are clearly differentiated from other types of features. The index uses letter-number grid references; no latitude/longitude coordinates are given.

Currency

The New Cosmopolitan is current up to its 1993 publication date. All major world changes—including the division of Czechoslovakia into two nations and the independence of Eritrea from Ethiopia—are accounted for on the maps and in the information tables and index. The capital of Nigeria, however, is shown inconsistently on various maps as either Abuja (the new capital), Lagos (the former capital), or both.

The environmental focus of the opening feature essay is very timely, and the thematic maps, photographs, and illustrations it contains are all up-to-date. The "World Political Information" table gives 1993 population estimates by Rand McNally based on information from the United Nations and other sources. The "Population of Cities and Towns" chart uses national census data or official estimates, with the year of the census or estimate listed so the reader can judge how current the data is. Most are from the 1980s. Place names are up-to-date and generally in accordance with national preferences. Alternate and historical names are liberally inserted where space permits.

Accuracy

The individual maps and statistical information in *The New Cosmopolitan World Atlas* are highly accurate. Every map includes a projection statement and gives the scale in three ways: with the representative fraction, a verbal scale, and a bar scale in miles and kilometers.

However, as noted above, there are some inconsistencies in scale. The maps of the United States and Canada do not follow a regular scale pattern, since each state is depicted on a full page. This in itself will have little bearing on the average reader. But since the level of detail does not increase with the scale, Delaware looks as large as California and empty by comparison. This is misleading when trying to compare states.

Legibility

Most of the world maps in *The New Cosmopolitan* span two pages with slim gutter margins. No information is lost, however, since the book lies flat when opened without breaking the spine, and no labels cross over the gutter. The outer page margins are ample.

The world regional maps are attractive, uncluttered, and legible, and the typefaces used are of a good size and pleasing style. The state and province maps, on the other hand, are somewhat cluttered. On the whole, however, labels, features, and boundaries stand out quite clearly over the white background and subtle shaded relief. The state and province maps reflect a great improvement over previous editions in which the subject areas were heavily tinted.

Accessibility

The "Using the Atlas" section discusses the sequence of maps in the atlas and covers skills such as using the index, finding places, measuring direction, and understanding map symbols. The section is comprehensible and well illustrated. The page with the index map and legend appears at the beginning of the "Reference Maps" section, so finding it involves flipping through the pages. The legend is quite clear, although it does not explain the various-sized symbols used for cities. An inset in the legend lists the symbols on the state and province maps.

Every map includes a locator map in the margin indicating which part of a particular region is being shown. While these are helpful, they are not substitutes for arrows or text indicating adjoining maps, which this atlas lacks.

The index is lengthy but not fully comprehensive. Not all of the places shown on the maps of the United States and Canada are listed in the index; for example, small towns and small streams are not included. The index is, however, easy to use. All features except cities are printed in italic type. As an added help, the country (or continent, in the case of large features) of each place name is listed.

Summary

The New Cosmopolitan World Atlas's large format and moderate price ($60) put it in the arena with many other well-made general-purpose atlases, including Oxford's

ATLAS OF THE WORLD. Setting *The New Cosmopolitan* apart from most others is its extensive coverage of U.S. states and Canadian provinces, which aims it especially toward a North American audience. The range of world maps does not match that of the Oxford work, but as the coverage is fairly broad (with a few noted exceptions), the work in a sense represents two atlases in one.

Therefore, for libraries and individuals seeking strong U.S. and Canadian coverage in a general world atlas, *The New Cosmopolitan World Atlas* is a good purchase. In terms of international scope, however, it does not compare with Oxford's ATLAS OF THE WORLD nor with the somewhat higher-priced HAMMOND ATLAS OF THE WORLD, NATIONAL GEOGRAPHIC ATLAS OF THE WORLD, or NEW YORK TIMES ATLAS OF THE WORLD.

The New International Atlas

Facts at a Glance

Full title: **The New International Atlas**
Publisher: Rand McNally
Edition reviewed: © 1993 "Anniversary Edition"

Number of pages: 560
Number of maps: 286
Number of index entries: 170,000
Intended readership: general adult
Trim size: 11″ × 14¾″
Binding: hardcover

Price: $125; volume discount to libraries and schools
Sold directly to libraries and schools; also sold by direct mail and in bookstores and other retail outlets
ISBN 0-528-83548-3
Revised as necessary to keep up with world events

Introduction, Format, and Authority

The New International Atlas, published by Rand McNally, is identical in content to the BRITANNICA ATLAS. The main differences are the *New International*'s heavier paper stock and a higher price of $125. The *New International* also lacks the abridged index map printed in the endpapers of the BRITANNICA—an extra convenience—but it retains the comprehensive index maps within its front matter. Both the *New International* and BRITANNICA are comprehensive world atlases of the highest quality.

The 1993 copyright edition of *The New International Atlas* is up-to-date and fully accounts for the new states of the Czech Republic, Slovakia, and Eritrea. One flaw noted, however, is that Abuja is not indicated as the capital of Nigeria on the maps of Africa.

For a full description of the maps and other features of this atlas, see the review for BRITANNICA ATLAS.

Summary

The New International Atlas can hold pride of place among general reference atlases in any public or academic collection. Less expensive than the excellent, larger TIMES ATLAS OF THE WORLD, published by Times Books, many users will prefer *New International*'s cartography and its more extensive, more modern-looking thematic maps. Although it is more costly than the other major large-format atlases, including THE GREAT WORLD ATLAS, NATIONAL GEOGRAPHIC ATLAS OF THE WORLD, and THE NEW YORK TIMES ATLAS, this price is justified by the *New International*'s greater sophistication and variety of contents. Purchasers may also want to consider the nearly identical BRITANNICA ATLAS, which costs $25 less than the *New International* but is printed on thinner paper stock.

The New York Times Atlas of the World, New Family Edition

Facts at a Glance

Full title: **The New York Times Atlas of the World, New Family Edition**
Publisher: Times Books/Random House
Edition reviewed: © 1992

Number of pages: 224
Number of maps: 84
Number of index entries: 30,000
Intended readership: high school to adult
Trim size: 8¾″ × 12⅛″
Binding: hardcover

Price: $37.50
Sold directly to libraries and schools; also sold by direct mail and in bookstores
ISBN 0-8129-2075-2
No stated revision policy

Introduction and Authority

The New York Times Atlas of the World, New Family Edition is a medium-sized world atlas designed, according to the editor's foreword, "for use in the home, office or school, for those who travel the world and also those, like Francis Bacon, who journey only 'in map and chart.'" The cartography was executed by John Bartholomew & Son, the renowned British cartographic firm—and the source of the other New York Times atlases. The atlas is a convenient size for desk use and will store easily on a shelf. Its binding appears durable.

This atlas is the basis for THE NEW YORK TIMES ATLAS OF THE WORLD, PAPERBACK EDITION, which contains an identical map stock and index but fewer special features. (A full discussion of the cartography can be found in the review for that title.) In turn, some of the special features in the *New Family Edition* (but not the cartography) derive from the head of the New York Times line of atlases, THE NEW YORK TIMES ATLAS OF THE WORLD, THIRD REVISED CONCISE EDITION.

Scope and Special Features

The atlas is divided into four sections: the "Introductory Section" (68 pages), the main body of 54 general reference maps (76 pages), 49 city maps (16 pages), and the index and other user aids (64 pages). The front endpapers contain index maps to the world maps and city maps, and the back index contains a distance table for selected world cities.

The introductory section opens with a 40-page feature that offers facts about the states and territories of the world and a 4-page feature of geographical comparisons. Both are identical to those found in THE NEW YORK TIMES PAPERBACK EDITION (see that review). Both are appropriate and useful components in a family atlas; the feature on geographical comparisons is particularly helpful because it uses outline maps to compare sizes of major physical features, including continents, islands, oceans, and inland bodies of water.

The introductory section continues with seven full color physical maps of each of the continents and surrounding oceans; these are reprinted from maps that appear in THE NEW YORK TIMES THIRD REVISED CONCISE (and also in THE TIMES ATLAS OF THE WORLD). These visually appealing maps are drawn to give the impression of viewing the earth from outer space.

Following the physical maps are two one-page text features on the solar system and the earth; eight half-page thematic maps on topics including earthquakes and volcanoes, minerals, climate, vegetation, and population; and a time-zone map. The text features and thematic maps also derive from the THIRD REVISED CONCISE. They are accurate and well prepared, but their level of complexity may be beyond the reach of younger readers.

The core atlas of 54 physical-political general reference maps follows the introductory section. In scope and geographical balance, accuracy, and overall legibility, this atlas is identical to THE NEW YORK TIMES PAPERBACK EDITION. The *New Family Edition* reviewed here is less up-to-date than THE NEW YORK TIMES PAPERBACK EDITION, since it shows Czechoslovakia as unified, although the atlas is current to its copyright year of 1992.

The third section consists of 49 "city plans" of varying scales and levels of detail, ranging in size from one-sixth of a page to a full page for London, Paris, and New York. (These are not found in THE NEW YORK TIMES PAPERBACK EDITION.) The selection is fairly well balanced geographically, although Africa, which is represented by only two cities, is somewhat slighted. Scales are given only in bar form (in kilometers only), which limits the ease with which the maps may be compared. A separate key and alphabetical list of maps appears at the beginning of the section.

The final section of the atlas, preceding the index, contains additional special features. First is a one-page guide to pronunciation of the common foreign letters and combinations of letters used in the atlas; 19 languages are included. Next comes a six-page geographical dictionary of terms and definitions. Both features are unique to this atlas.

The 56-page index includes about 30,000 place names, significantly less than most other atlases in its class. The index is accompanied by a list of abbreviations used on the maps. This index is identical to that in THE NEW YORK TIMES PAPERBACK EDITION (see that review for a full analysis).

Two characteristics make the *New Family Edition* easier to use than its paperback counterpart. First, the book lies flat when open, so the maps can be more easily viewed. Second, the index maps printed in the front endpapers make the maps more accessible.

Summary

The New York Times Atlas of the World, New Family Edition contains well-drawn maps and a variety of well-presented special features. Like THE NEW YORK TIMES PAPERBACK EDITION, it has some significant flaws, which are enumerated in that review. The 1992 edition reviewed here is also now out-of-date; thus, this atlas would not be recommended for purchase at the time of this writing.

At $37.50, the price is in the range of several other mid-sized family atlases, including the CONCISE ATLAS OF THE WORLD and the HAMMOND ATLAS OF THE WORLD, CONCISE EDITION, as well as larger-format atlases such as READER'S DIGEST ATLAS OF THE WORLD and Rand McNally's WORLD ATLAS OF NATIONS. All of these works are more current than the *New York Times New Family Edition*, and prospective purchasers should compare this atlas's features and flaws with the others before making a selection.

The New York Times Atlas of the World, Paperback Edition

Facts at a Glance

Full title: **The New York Times Atlas of the World, Paperback Edition**
Publisher: Times Books/Random House
Edition reviewed: © 1993

Number of pages: 132
Number of maps: 54
Number of index entries: 30,000
Intended readership: high school to adult
Trim size: 8¾" × 12⅛"
Binding: paperback

Price: $22.50
Sold directly to libraries and schools; also sold by direct mail and in bookstores
ISBN 0-8129-2266-2
No stated revision policy

Introduction, Format, and Authority

A medium-sized world atlas, *The New York Times Atlas of the World, Paperback Edition* is a smaller, paperback companion to the New York Times atlases. The cartography was executed by John Bartholomew & Son, a reputable Scottish cartographic firm—and the source of the other New York Times atlases. (This atlas is very close in coverage to the READER'S DIGEST-BARTHOLOMEW ILLUSTRATED ATLAS OF THE WORLD, and is nearly identical to THE NEW YORK TIMES ATLAS OF THE WORLD, NEW FAMILY EDITION. A full discussion of the cartography can be found in the reviews for these titles.)

Scope and Special Features

The atlas is divided into three sections. The first (45 pages) offers facts about the independent nations of the world (for example, area, population, capital, language, and religion, with a brief write-up on resources and products). The second is the main body of maps, of which there are 54 on 76 pages. The third section is the 56-page index.

The initial section has greater merit than the opening material in the READER'S DIGEST-BARTHOLOMEW ILLUSTRATED ATLAS. In this atlas, all nations are included, and a world map on the center of each two-page spread shows the location of each nation on the spread. Statistics, however, suffer from the same problems as in the Reader's Digest work. No source is given for population figures, and they don't match figures given in the *Statesman's Yearbook* (although at least this atlas shows the correct 1990 census figure for the United States, which the READER'S DIGEST-BARTHOLOMEW atlas does not).

Following the "States and Territories" section are a few pages of world statistics, which use maps to compare the sizes of continents, islands, oceans, and inland bodies of water and use tables to compare the sizes of major metropolitan areas, mountains, and rivers.

The atlas provides less balanced coverage than the READER'S DIGEST-BARTHOLOMEW ILLUSTRATED ATLAS. Coverage of Europe and Asia is comparable, but South America and Africa receive fewer maps. There is only one map of Canada (compared with three in READER'S DIGEST-BARTHOLOMEW), and there are more maps of the United States, although these are regional rather than state-specific.

Published in 1993, the *New York Times, Paperback Edition* is more up-to-date than the READER'S DIGEST-

BARTHOLOMEW ATLAS because it shows both Yugoslavia and Czechoslovakia as divided.

Other than that, the maps are virtually identical to those in READER'S DIGEST-BARTHOLOMEW, although some show different land areas. As in READER'S DIGEST BARTHOLOMEW, the maps are inaccurate regarding the size of communities throughout the world. Maps in this atlas are somewhat more legible than in the other work because the paper is glossier, therefore showing color and type more clearly.

The final section of the atlas is the index, which occupies 56 pages. This index is comprehensive but has some inconsistencies (see the review of the READER'S DIGEST-BARTHOLOMEW ILLUSTRATED ATLAS for a full analysis).

Almost half of the maps are printed on two-page spreads. While no information is lost in the gutter, the book is somewhat more difficult to use than the READER'S DIGEST-BARTHOLOMEW because it does not lie as flat.

Summary

The New York Times Atlas of the World, Paperback Edition contains well-drawn maps that are more up-to-date than those in the READER'S DIGEST-BARTHOLOMEW ILLUSTRATED ATLAS. Its statistical information seems to be of questionable reliability, and the confusion in labeling of world communities is troublesome. It is a reasonable value for home purchase (although the hardcover version at $22 actually costs less), but is not recommended for libraries, where more accuracy is desirable.

The New York Times Atlas of the World, Third Revised Concise Edition

Facts at a Glance

Full title: **The New York Times Atlas of the World, Third Revised Concise Edition**
Publisher: Times Books/Random House
Edition reviewed: © 1993

Number of pages: 288
Number of maps: 146 pages of world reference maps
Number of index entries: 100,000
Intended readership: adult
Trim size: 10¾″ × 14¾″
Binding: hardcover

Price: $75
ISBN 0-8129-2076-7
Revised periodically; fourth edition to be published in late 1994

Introduction, Format, and Authority

The New York Times Atlas of the World is a large-format general world atlas prepared by the British cartographic firm John Bartholomew & Son in association with *The Times* of London. Despite its title, this atlas is connected with *The New York Times* in name only. The publisher is Times Books, a division of Random House. In Britain, the atlas is sold as *The Times Atlas of the World. Concise Edition, Sixth Edition,* a title that highlights the fact that this book is marketed as a "junior" version of the massive TIMES ATLAS OF THE WORLD. The British edition was originally published in 1992; the work reviewed here carries a 1993 copyright. A fourth edition will be published in late 1994.

Although it is large-sized ($10\frac{3}{4}'' \times 14\frac{3}{4}''$), this atlas is relatively thin (1 inch wide) and easy to handle. The binding is excellent, and the simulated-leather cover should withstand heavy use.

Scope and Special Features

The atlas consists of three main sections: special features (40 pages), the collection of full-color general reference maps (146 pages), and the glossary and index (97 pages). The majority of the maps are physical-political, and many are spread over two pages. The cartography is similar to what is found in THE TIMES ATLAS OF THE WORLD (see that review) although many of the views chosen are quite different. For example, THE TIMES ATLAS includes four two-page maps of France, dividing the country into quadrants. *The New York Times Atlas of the World* covers the country in two two-page spreads and a single-page map. The maps employ tinted, layered relief to depict land elevation and sea depths; color keys on each map identify the scale of tints. In addition to the physical-political maps, a few primarily political maps (generally of whole continents) appear, but not in any consistent fashion. The atlas also contains a number of large-scale insets of cities and islands; many of the approximately 60 city maps occupy one-half or a full page.

The general reference maps are organized by continent, beginning with Europe, then moving to Asia, Africa, North America, South America, Australia, and Antarctica. Maps of the oceans and their islands are placed in geographical sequence between the continents they separate. However, the actual sequence of maps within this overall arrangement is idiosyncratic. Traditionally, atlas maps cover each continent in a north-to-south, east-to-west pattern, so that maps of adjacent areas are generally on adjacent pages. In this atlas, however, the maps for the individual regions of the United States are arranged in a geographically counterclockwise order, starting with the northeast and ending with the southeast. In consequence, the map of the southeast United States is 11 plates away from the map of northeast United States. Other peculiarities occur: for

example, the map of Sri Lanka appears on a spread with Africa—seven pages after the map of South India.

As in most atlases, Europe and North America receive the most coverage—well over half of the maps represent these areas. Australia and New Zealand also receive particularly close and detailed attention. The rest of the world is adequately represented. Overall, however, this atlas betrays a greater Anglo-European bias than two of its competitors, Oxford's ATLAS OF THE WORLD and HAMMOND ATLAS OF THE WORLD. The bias is most evident in the choice and scales of city insets, which strongly favor Europe, the United States, Canada, Australia, and New Zealand.

The New York Times Atlas of the World contains several special features, many of which derive (usually in abridged form) from THE TIMES ATLAS. The three statistical features that open the atlas are particularly useful. Leading off is a three-page table of "States and Territories of the World," which gives the name, area, and population of every country as well as of the states and provinces of selected countries (including the United States and Canada). Next is a one-page table listing the populations for over 275 metropolitan areas in the world. Last is a two-page geographical comparison chart of the world's major physical features, in which small outline maps show the relative sizes of the continents, the oceans, and major drainage basins, inland waters, and islands. Major mountain heights and river lengths are given in tabular format. The information in each of these tables is accurate and conveniently presented.

The section of special features also includes large, bold physical maps of each of the continents; three star charts; illustrated encyclopedic features on the universe, solar system, space flight, earth structure, dynamic earth, and map projections; and thematic maps (with explanatory text) on climate, vegetation, minerals, energy, food, and population. The feature on map projections, condensed from a feature that appears in THE TIMES ATLAS, explains the processes by which different projections are achieved and the distortions that they involve.

Written at a fairly high level, these features are accurate and up-to-date. Like those in *The Times Atlas,* however, their authority cannot be gauged because specific sources are not cited. The physical maps unfortunately do not include a legend to identify the types of environments they show.

Currency

The New York Times Atlas is up-to-date to 1993, its copyright year. The atlas maps depict the separate countries of the Czech Republic and Slovakia, although the index reflects the previous political situation (as is duly noted by the editors). The book jacket blurb lists over a dozen categories of changes that were made to this atlas since the previous edition in 1986, including boundary and name changes in the former Soviet Union and Eastern Europe, updates of Canadian railways and European highways, new settlements on the West Bank, and new Antarctic research stations. However, as in the ninth edition of THE TIMES ATLAS, one place was overlooked: The city of Ciudad del Este, Paraguay, is labeled with its former name of Puerto Presidente Stroessner.

Most of the population figures in the "States and Territories of the World" table date from 1990 or after. The information in the encyclopedic features and thematic maps is current to the early 1990s, and the illustrations and photographs are contemporary.

Accuracy

Whether they were originally drawn at different times or for different purposes, there are numerous small variations in style and presentation among the maps in this atlas. Most of these involve the typography and are only minor distractions. However, the level of detail shown can vary among maps at the same scale, which is a more significant concern. For example, the maps of India on pages 74–76 provide much less detail than the maps of Central Siberia and Central Asia on pages 56 and 57, although all are at the scale of 1:6,000,000. (The maps of India also show less detail than maps at the same scale in other atlases.)

Many different scales are used, but each continent is covered at fairly consistent scales. Areas within Europe and North America are mapped at scales of 1:300,000 to 1:5,000,000, with 1:3,000,000 a common standard. For Asia, Africa, and Australasia, the most common scale is 1:6,000,000. However, some areas on these continents are mapped at the smaller scale of 1:12,000,000. The most typical scale of city insets is 1:300,000.

Scales are given as representative fractions and in bar form (in miles and kilometers), and projections are stated. The range of projections used has been selected to minimize distortion and permit distance and size comparisons for all areas on a particular map.

With the exception noted in *Currency,* no major errors were detected on the maps or in the index. For a more detailed discussion of the accuracy of the cartography in general, see the review for THE TIMES ATLAS OF THE WORLD.

Legibility

The maps in this atlas are generally clear and uncluttered. (The maps for the eastern United States, on which labels obscure most other information, are an exception.) The labels are usually well placed. The background colors and physical markings are sharp and easily distinguished but do not interfere with the legibility of the type.

Unlike the maps in THE TIMES ATLAS, which are carefully designed to accommodate the page format, place names in this atlas cut across the gutter in a more haphazard fashion, which reduces legibility. Fortunately, the book lies flat when open, and a very narrow margin in the gutter ensures that no information is completely lost there. However, labels and cartographic details are sometimes cut off at the outside edge of the page.

The map legend (which is identical to that found in THE TIMES ATLAS) clearly lists the large number of symbols and lettering styles used on the maps. However, as noted above, the typefaces used on the maps differ throughout the atlas, so the typefaces on a given map often do not match those shown in the legend. This may present a problem for some users. But since all the map typefaces follow the logic of the legend styles (for example, roman type for political place names and italic for all others), the reader can overcome this problem with varying degrees of effort.

Accessibility

The index of *The New York Times Atlas* is extensive, containing about 100,000 entries. A set of abbreviations is used to identify the feature type for entries other than cities and towns. The country of each place is given, and for places in the United States and Canada, the state or province is also given. Index references use a letter-number grid system only; no latitude and longitude coordinates are given. For the serious geographer, such an omission is a drawback, but it should not affect the layperson's use of this atlas.

The endpapers contain index maps of the world (front) and of the United States and Europe (back). The map pages include marginal arrows that indicate the page number of adjoining maps. Both of these aids, as well as the table of contents, are indispensable because of the often peculiar arrangement of maps. Even so, it is somewhat difficult to move from one page to another in this atlas.

Summary

With its large format, quality cartography, and medium to high price ($75), *The New York Times Atlas of the World* is in a class with two relative newcomers, Oxford's ATLAS OF THE WORLD and the HAMMOND ATLAS OF THE WORLD, as well as with an established veteran, the NATIONAL GEOGRAPHIC ATLAS OF THE WORLD. All have easy-to-read and informative maps, and all are equally up-to-date; NATIONAL GEOGRAPHIC has the oldest (1992) copyright date of the four, but it includes all of the major political changes of the early 1990s. The chief advantages *The New York Times Atlas* has to offer in this lineup are the authority, accuracy, and clarity of Bartholomew's cartography and the extensive index. It is, however, more difficult to use than these other atlases. Also, while the cartography is very good, it does not consistently meet the high standards found in its parent, THE TIMES ATLAS.

Rand McNally Goode's World Atlas

Facts at a Glance

Full title: **Rand McNally Goode's World Atlas**
Publisher: Rand McNally
Editor: Edward B. Espenshade, Jr.
Edition reviewed: © 1990, 18th edition; revised seventh printing, 1993

Number of pages: 384
Number of maps: 422
Number of index entries: 34,000
Intended readership: students to adults
Trim size: 8¾″ × 11″
Binding: hardcover; paperback

Price: $29.95 (hardcover); $14 (paperback)
ISBN 0-528-63004-0
No stated revision policy

Introduction, Format, and Authority

The *Rand McNally Goode's World Atlas* is a medium-sized (8¾″ × 11″) reference atlas. It bears the name of its original compiler, the American cartographer J. Paul Goode, whose first edition appeared in 1922. Now in its 18th edition, the atlas is edited by Edward B. Espenshade, Jr., Professor Emeritus of Geography at Northwestern University; Joel L. Morrison of the U.S. Geological Survey is listed as senior consultant. The front matter also acknowledges several other academic experts and cartographers who have contributed to the atlas over the years. The atlas's publisher, Rand McNally, is one of the foremost commercial mapmakers in the United States. The following review is based on the 1993 revised seventh printing.

The atlas is published in both hardcover and paperback formats. The hardcover version was not examined by reviewers. In the paperback edition, the medium-weight paper stock and sewn binding are of high quality. The size of the atlas makes it easy to handle and convenient to store, but also leads to overcrowding on its maps and elimination of worthwhile detail.

Scope and Special Features

Goode's World Atlas is divided into six sections: "Introduction" (10 pages), "World Thematic Maps" (54 pages), "Regional Maps" (159 pages), "Plate Tectonics and Ocean Floor Maps" (8 pages), "Major Cities Maps" (19 pages), and "Geographical Tables and Indexes" (128 pages). While the "Regional Maps" section appears large at first glance, it actually includes about 47 pages of regional thematic maps. These, taken together with the large section of world thematic maps, set *Goode's* apart as having by far the largest collection of thematic maps of any world atlas. The range of general reference

maps, on the other hand, is adequate but not outstanding.

Evident in the scope and special features of *Goodes' World Atlas* is its emphasis on the study of geography and the broadening of geographical understanding. The introduction contains a basic discussion of maps and mapmaking, including map scales and projections and technologically advanced imagery systems. The text is brief, basic, and good, and is supplemented by many color photographs and illustrations. It is also fairly technical, however, and might be difficult for the layperson to comprehend. The introduction also discusses the five fundamental themes of geography, which are the basis of geographical education.

The "World Thematic Maps" contains maps on a wide variety of subjects, including political and physical features, climate, weather, vegetation, soils, population, health, economics, industry, agriculture, minerals, and transportation. (Absent from this list is the environment, a topic on which many other atlases now focus.) Many of the topics covered—such as the areas of potato and cassava growing, zinc mining, and vegetable oil production—are unique to this atlas. Many of the maps are accompanied by statistical graphs. While these maps are an excellent ready source of basic information, they have not been reconfigured to reflect the global political changes of the late 1980s and early 1990s (see *Currency*). And unlike the thematic maps in most atlases, they are not accompanied by narrative.

The "Regional Maps" section is divided into standard continental areas. A selection of thematic maps precedes the general physical-political maps of each area. Many insets highlight important population centers throughout this section. The general reference maps use both shaded relief and tinted layered relief to show land elevation and water depths. The scales used vary considerably from region to region, but are generally consistent within regions. Most of North America and Europe are covered at 1:4,000,000, a scale that provides a good overall picture, although at the cost of some detail. In contrast, Africa and South America are afforded much less detail, with the largest scales (excepting a few insets) at 1:10,000,000 and 1:16,000,000, respectively.

On the whole, the atlas is heavily weighted toward the United States and Canada. Of the 159 pages in the section, 63 represent North America, 40 Europe, 23 Asia, and 10 Australia and Oceania; only 14 show Africa and 8 South America. The thematic maps, which make up 20 to 30 percent of these page counts, are distributed in about the same proportion; the thematic maps preceding the section on North America are thus far more extensive than those in any other section.

"Plate Tectonics and Ocean Floor Maps" includes text, diagrams, and five physical relief maps of the ocean floors. "Major Cities Maps" includes 62 maps of the world's most populous metropolitan areas, all depicted at the same scale (1:300,000) and in a standardized and comparable format. While weighted towards North America (14 of the 62 maps show U.S. or Canadian cities), the "Major Cities" section is more balanced overall than the regional maps, and several more unusual cities are represented, including Kinshasa, Manila, and Teheran.

The "Geographical Tables and Indexes" section is 127 pages long. The geographical tables include political information, comparisons, principal cities, and foreign geographical terms (all standard in most Rand McNally atlases). The 34,000-entry main index has an unusual feature in an atlas—most of the place names listed include a pronunciation. This helpful guide reports the differences in pronunciation between Newark, Delaware, and Newark, New Jersey, for example, and Lima, Peru, and Lima, Ohio. Following the main index is a one-page index of major topics covered by the thematic maps—a very welcome feature.

Currency

The currency of *Goode's World Atlas* is uneven. The general reference maps show the major world changes up to its 1993 printing date, including the breakup of Czechoslovakia and the independence of Eritrea from Ethiopia. However, the new capital of Nigeria—Abuja—is not located on any map or in the index (but it is mentioned in the political table at the end of the atlas). Recent name changes such as Leningrad to St. Petersburg and Christmas Island to Kiritimati are included, but the names Kalaallit Nunaat (for Greenland) and its chief city Nuuk (for Godthäb) do not appear anywhere.

The currency of the thematic maps is also problematic. Some of the sources noted are quite dated, but given the broad scope and generalized nature of the data presented, the maps in total still provide a unique picture of global geographical concerns. One glaring problem is that very few of the world thematic maps have been altered to reflect the realignments in the Soviet Union and Eastern Europe. This leaves the reader unenlightened about the economic impact of the new world order. Further, the North American thematic maps do not reflect 1990 census data. Most U.S. maps were based on the 1980 census, but some use data from 1960 (population density) and 1970 (life expectancy). Moreover, not all of the thematic maps are dated, particularly those relating to other regions of the world.

The information tables at the end of the book are the most up-to-date part of the atlas. The population figures are Rand McNally's 1993 estimates based on figures from the United Nations or other official sources.

Accuracy

Considerable effort is evident in the positioning of place names in their proper relationship to symbols. Unfortunately, confusion and overcrowding occasionally result

from the small size and large scale of maps, combined with the variety of information the cartographers are trying to include.

Scales are noted with the representative fraction (for example, 1:4,000,000), a verbal statement, and a scale bar in miles and kilometers. Each map also includes a projection statement. The differing scales used from region to region are a drawback in an atlas of this scope, as they make it more difficult for readers to compare regions.

The use of color gradients in combination with shaded relief provides more accurate elevation information than can be found in atlases that show only shaded relief. Each map includes a legend of the relief colors used. Most maps also include a legend of the city and town population symbols.

Legibility

The typefaces used on the maps are legible; however, their size, combined with the range of information portrayed, sometimes results in an overcrowded map that is difficult to read. The use of shaded color gradients enhances the depiction of relief but also hinders the readability of the print. Most maps break out of their neat lines, and quite a few bleed off the edge of the page. Thus, there is often little space left for marginal information such as the map title, scales, and legends. Moreover, place names and symbols are occasionally divided by the gutter, which makes them hard to read. The paperback edition does lie flat when opened, however, so no information is completely lost.

Several of the thematic maps are quite small for the amount of information they contain. Although they are carefully produced, this factor limits the amount of specific information that can be obtained from them.

Accessibility

The *Goode's World Atlas* index is small compared with other mid-range atlases. Through spot checks it appears that all cities and towns are indexed; for other types of features, the index is quite comprehensive for North America but less so for other parts of the world. The index gives latitude and longitude coordinates for locating places, a practice that provides valuable geographical information but also requires some experience in using atlases. A brief explanation of latitude and longitude would have been a welcome addition.

Moving from region to region takes some getting used to with this atlas as there is no index map and because regional thematic maps are inserted throughout. Adjoining maps are noted in the margins in a very small typeface as space permits—but often it does not. An attractive feature of the regional maps is the inclusion of cross-references to the major cities section.

The detailed table of contents is an important and necessary asset, as many insets may appear out of strict geographic order and most thematic maps appear two-or-more to the page. The extended introduction of *Goode's World Atlas* describes the overall organization of the atlas. Legends appear at the beginning of the "Regional Maps" and "Major Cities Maps" sections (the two sections are somewhat different in style). They are well organized and easy to understand.

Summary

The longevity of *Rand McNally Goode's World Atlas* (18 editions since 1922) attests to its position over the years as a standard geographical reference. The thematic maps in particular have made *Goode's* an attractive purchase for public and academic libraries as a useful supplement to larger, more comprehensive atlases such as THE NEW INTERNATIONAL ATLAS and THE TIMES ATLAS OF THE WORLD. However, the current edition can be recommended only with a qualification: Prospective purchasers should consider the currency of the thematic maps, particularly if the atlas is intended to update an old edition. One would hope for a thorough revision of the thematic maps in the near future to bring them more completely up-to-date.

Nevertheless, *Goode's* remains a fine quick-reference source, with particularly helpful features in the thematic maps and pronouncing index. For home users in the market for a medium-sized general atlas, the flaws of *Goode's* may be overshadowed by its low price.

The Random House Compact World Atlas

Facts at a Glance

Full title: **The Random House Compact World Atlas**
Publisher: Random House
Edition reviewed: © 1991; second revised U.S. edition, 1992

Number of pages: 192
Number of maps: 112, all in full color
Number of index entries: 20,000
Intended readership: high school to adult
Trim size: 6″ × 8⅝″
Binding: paperback

Price: $12
ISBN 0-679-74330-8
No stated revision policy

Introduction, Format, and Authority

The Random House Compact World Atlas is a small (6″ × 8⅝″) paperback atlas intended to provide the general reader with basic physical-political maps of the world in a convenient and inexpensive format. The maps were rendered by John Bartholomew & Son, the same respected Edinburgh-based cartographers responsible for THE TIMES ATLAS OF THE WORLD. The atlas was originally published in 1984 and called *The Random House Concise World Atlas;* a revised edition with the current title was published in 1991. This review is based on the "Second Revised U.S. Edition, 1992" (copyright 1991).

The sewn paperback binding is sturdy. The pages are heavy and nonglossy. It should be noted that the BARTHOLOMEW MINI ATLAS, WORLD represents a smaller, deluxe-bound version of this work with somewhat simplified maps.

Scope and Special Features

The world maps (112 pages) and the index (80 pages) encompass all but 16 pages of *The Random House Compact World Atlas.* The base atlas consists predominantly of physical-political maps of regions and countries interspersed with smaller-scale political maps of the continents. The regional maps use layered tints to show land elevation and ocean depths. Unfortunately, the relatively small page size precludes a legend for these tints on each page, so the reader must refer to the master legend, located on the last page of the introductory material.

Maps are organized by continent with one major peculiarity: A medium-scale map called "Middle East" (Southwest Asia and Northeast Africa) appears with Asia, while more detailed maps of Southwest Asian countries (including Turkey and Israel) are in the "Africa" section. Most of the world is well represented, although the western Aleutian Islands and the northeastern portion of Russia are not covered by regional maps. There is better coverage of the United States and Europe than of any other regions, both in terms of scale size and number of maps.

Various scales are used throughout the atlas. In general, densely populated areas have been selected for detailed representation. The slight Anglo-American bias, however, leads to such instances as a two-page map of New Zealand at 1:5,000,000 and a one-page map of the Philippines (larger in both population and land area) at 1:10,000,000. The largest scale used is 1:2,500,000—for Europe, parts of the United States, and Israel and Lebanon. The most typical scales are 1:20,000,000 and 1:7,500,000.

Apart from the map collection, the *Random House Compact* has few special features. Four special-purpose maps ("World Physical," "World Political," "World Time Zones," and "World Environment") complement the general reference maps. The world physical map is too general to be of much use, although it contains a decent diagram of global elevations and shows major air travel routes. While also general, the environment map is more informative. The time-zones map is a desirable feature in an atlas; however, the use of 24-hour clock readings rather than A.M. and P.M. might be a drawback for American readers.

Currency

The *Random House Compact* adequately reflects the world situation as it existed in 1991: Germany and Yemen are both unified and the Soviet Union is split into independent republics. The treatment of the Balkans reflects a time of transition: Slovenia and Croatia are shown as independent entities, whereas Bosnia and Herzegovina, Serbia, Montenegro, and Macedonia are together called Yugoslavia. While generally up-to-date with large changes, many smaller place names do not reflect current preferences. For example, Mt. McKinley is still used for Denali, Formosa Strait for Taiwan Strait, and Puerto Presidente Stroessner for Ciudad del Este. The names Kalaallit Nunaat and Nuuk (for Greenland and Godthåb) do not appear on the maps or in the index.

Accuracy

The linework and plotting of symbols and labels reflect an above average degree of accuracy for maps of this size. An inadvertent error was noted on the map of West Africa: The new Nigerian capital Abuja is plotted (with the symbol for capital) but not labeled. Scales are presented both as representative fractions and as bar scales (kilometers and miles). The capital letter *M* is used after the representative fractions to denote "million," but nowhere is this explained; this might be confusing to American readers. Projections are not stated.

Names of countries appear in their conventional Anglicized forms. Other place names are usually spelled according to the official language(s) of each country. On larger-scale regional maps, English or other alternate spellings are given in parentheses. The use of local spellings raises the level of sophistication of the maps, making them more challenging to less experienced map readers (see also *Accessibility*). Names of physical features often do not include a generic term (such as *desert* or *upland*), although this information can be found in the index.

Legibility

Typefaces on the maps are generally legible, although the lightest typefaces used compete against strong relief tints. The typefaces are sufficiently differentiated to distinguish categories. The level of detail is suited to the size of the maps to avoid a cluttered appearance, although maps of densely populated areas with major elevation (such as Alpine Europe) are somewhat cramped. Nine levels of shading indicating relief above sea level are sharp and easily distinguishable, as are the six tints of sea depth.

Most of the maps are printed on two-page spreads. Unfortunately, the gutter arbitrarily cuts through symbols and labels. An ample gutter margin means that no information is lost completely, although some is very difficult to read. In a few instances (for example, West Africa and Southeast Asia), maps escape their outer-margin neat lines and run off the edge of the page, cutting off parts of labels.

Accessibility

The 20,000-entry index is quite extensive for a work of this scope. While not error free, it is more than adequately helpful. Names in the index are followed by the name or abbreviation of the country in which they are located. The names of physical features are identified by type (such as bay, cape, or lake). The index includes some (but not many) cross-references for historical names and for conventional English spellings of place names that appear in the vernacular on the map (such as "Vienna" for "Wien"). The index indicates place using a letter-number grid system. Latitude and longitude coordinates are not used.

Other finding aids include a good table of contents supplemented by small index maps of each continent. This feature is especially welcome given the unusual order of some of the maps. The legend ("Key to Symbols") is clear and easy to locate.

Summary

Random House Compact World Atlas provides a decent set of high-quality Bartholomew maps at a very reasonable price ($12). While not as meticulously accurate, up-to-date, and geographically balanced as higher-end atlases, these shortcomings should be weighed in relation to its affordable price and convenient format. Of course, some of the problems in currency reflect the atlas's publication date. With these qualifications in mind, the *Random House Compact* is recommended for purchase.

Reader's Digest Atlas of the World

Facts at a Glance

Full title: **Reader's Digest Atlas of the World**
Publisher: Reader's Digest
Editor: Joseph L. Gardner, Project Editor
Edition reviewed: © 1990; tenth printing, September 1993

Number of pages: 240
Number of maps: 86
Number of index entries: 42,000
Intended readership: high school to adult
Trim size: 10½" × 14¾"
Binding: hardcover

Price: $39.95 plus delivery; 30 percent discount to
  schools and libraries
Sold directly to schools and libraries; also sold by di-
  rect mail
ISBN 0-89577-264-7
No stated revision policy

Introduction, Format, and Authority

Originally published in 1987, the 1993 updated version
of the *Reader's Digest Atlas of the World* contains 125
pages of world maps produced by Rand McNally. The
maps were compiled from the maps stock created for
THE NEW INTERNATIONAL ATLAS, Rand McNally's authoritative top-of-the-line atlas. The *Reader's Digest Atlas*
presents a basic selection of maps in large format (10½″
× 14¾″) as a reference tool for the general reader. To the
base atlas have been added 60 pages of geographical articles called "A World of Wonders." The easy-to-use volume is sturdily bound in a hard simulated-leather cover.

Scope and Special Features

The atlas is divided into two main sections. The first
section, entitled "A World of Wonders," contains 60
pages describing the universe, geology, geography, and
the history of the world. The second section, "The World
in Maps" contains a 125-page collection of 86 world
maps, a 4-page world information table, and a 43-page
index.

"World of Wonders" contains 30 two-page articles,
with subjects ranging from the formation of the universe
to earthquakes to the evolution of humans. This section
contains many pictures; most are appropriate and clear.
The photographs of the universe as seen from the earth
and of the planets with their moons are excellent. There
are detailed diagrams of the earth's surface, including
coastlines, rock formations, and mountain ranges. Thematic maps of the modern world occupy only six pages.
The articles are factually accurate and easy to comprehend by the intended general reader, but limited in
scope. For example, the written history of the world is
condensed to six pages.

Although most of the illustrations accompanying the
text are well done, they are occasionally blurry or fuzzy,
and their content is sometimes difficult to interpret. For
example, the graphics describing weather are unclear
and hard to distinguish. A computer-generated map
showing the populations of cities using clusters of shad-
owy peaks to represent their relative size is difficult for
an adult, much less a child, to understand. Finally, in at
least two instances, the progression of images starts in
the upper right corner and proceeds counterclockwise to
the bottom left corner. This scheme is counter-intuitive
and can lead to misinterpretation.

The focus of the base atlas itself is North America,
which is represented by 40 pages of maps. Europe (22
pages), and Asia (28 pages) are also well represented.
The remaining atlas pages are divided among the rest
of the world as follows: eight pages of Africa, eight of
South America, nine of Australia and Oceania, one of
Antarctica, and three of the oceans. Most maps employ
one of three scales—1:12,000,000, 1:6,000,000, or
1:3,000,000; the latter is used exclusively for North
America, Europe, and East Asia. There are three maps
at larger scales—two at 1:1,500,000 (Switzerland; and
Belgium, Netherlands, and Luxembourg), and one at
1:1,000,000 (Israel). There are no city maps.

The maps are organized by continent, opening with
two-page world political and world physical maps. At the
beginning of each continental section is an environment
map displaying features such as croplands, swamps, and
forests. The environment maps have the crisp detail of
computer-generated images. These are by far the most
interesting maps in the atlas.

In general, scales are consistently applied in related
areas. However, coverage is not particularly deep, and
gaps occur. Some countries or related groups of countries cannot be viewed whole except at the largest scale.
In Europe, for example, the former Yugoslavia is shown
on two different spreads, and there is no map of
Ukraine. No special attention is given to the countries of
Germany, Poland, or Greece, yet there is a map devoted
to Switzerland. In the United States, North Carolina, for
example, can be viewed in its entirety but Virginia cannot. Canada lacks a key area—southern Ontario and
southern Quebec. This region can be found on maps of
the United States but nowhere within the set of Canadian maps, which prospective purchasers in Canada will
consider a drawback.

Overall, the coverage of the United States is excellent
for a world atlas. Many small towns can be located. The
map of Central America shows the area from Guatemala
to the Panama Canal in extraordinary detail. This atlas
also does an excellent job with Asia, portraying the continent well. There is a detailed map that shows not only
the Korean Peninsula, but the area of China surrounding
the Yellow Sea, which includes Beijing. Similarly, there
are well-thought-out maps of Japan, northern and southern India, and insets of both Java and Luzon. The map of
the Middle East is appropriate for this work, displaying
the entire area from Egypt to the Gulf of Oman, including a detailed map of Israel.

Africa and South America are covered only mod-
estly—most of the region can be examined only at the
largest scale of 1:12,000,000. There are more detailed
maps of southern Africa and of heavily populated southeastern Brazil and central Argentina and Chile.

The general reference maps use a combination of
shaded relief and layered tints to show land elevation
and sea depths. The combination of these devices pro-

vides more precise elevation information than either alone, and in areas where there are no great elevation differences, it has no drawbacks. But the heavy coloring and shading in mountainous regions make the maps difficult to read as details are lost. For example, in the map of southwestern Canada, it takes a painstaking review to locate the city of Banff in the middle of the Rocky Mountains. In addition, the key to elevation and depth tints is located only on the general legend page; showing the key on every map (a feature found in many large-format atlases) would have been helpful.

Following the world maps are the "World Information Table" and the index. The table is identical to those found in the most authoritative Rand McNally works, the New International and Britannica atlases. It lists every major political unit (country, territory, state, province) in the world and gives the area, population, population density, capital, and political status of each.

The index contains over 40,000 entries—not nearly as many as other atlases of comparable scope. Like Rand McNally's New International Atlas, it uses a set of symbols to indicate the type of feature for place names (other than inhabited places, such as countries and cities). The index includes a helpful introduction, list of abbreviations, and key to symbols.

Currency

Revised in September 1993, the *Reader's Digest Atlas of the World* is current in nearly every respect. It incorporates all the recent major world changes, including the breakup of Czechoslovakia and the independence of Eritrea from Ethiopia. The capital of Nigeria, however, is shown inconsistently on various maps as either Abuja (the new capital), Lagos (the former capital), or both. Place names are up-to-date and generally in accordance with national preferences. Alternate and historical names are liberally inserted where space permits. The "World Information Table" gives 1993 population estimates by Rand McNally based on figures from the United Nations and other sources.

Accuracy

The maps and statistical information in the atlas are accurate, reflecting the authority of Rand McNally and its cartographers. Every map includes a projection statement and gives the scale in three ways: with the representative fraction, a verbal scale, and a bar scale in miles and kilometers. The maps also include useful locator maps showing how the subject area relates to a larger region.

Local official names are used for most place names on the maps and in the index, the major exception being names of countries and large features, which appear in English. The naming system is fully explained in the index.

Legibility

The majority of maps span two pages. Reflecting careful cartography, the gutters are free of clutter—few labels cross from one page to the other. The volume also lies open very flat without breaking the spine. Symbols and labels are also well clear of the outer margins. Overall, the maps are attractive and uncluttered, and the typefaces used are of a good size and pleasing style. As previously noted, however, the shaded and tinted relief tends to overwhelm the type in some places.

Accessibility

There is no introductory section explaining the overall arrangement of the atlas or how to best use it. The opening table of contents lists the "World of Wonders" feature articles in detail, but gives only a short summary of the rest of the atlas. A more detailed listing of maps precedes the world map section, this followed on the next page by index maps and the map legend. The finding aids are helpful, but since they appear in the middle of the book, locating them involves some flipping through the pages. The legend is well organized and clearly explains the more than 60 symbols used on the maps.

The index is comprehensive and accurate. Page references, according to the introduction, are generally to the map that "shows the feature to the best scale." The index gives only letter/number references (no latitude/longitude coordinates), which is appropriate for this level of atlas. The system of place-name symbols is somewhat complex, however.

Summary

The *Reader's Digest Atlas of the World* provides a good set of high-quality Rand McNally maps on a large-page format for a reasonable price. Some readers may find that the shading used to indicate mountainous regions is too dark and obscures other map information. But overall, the work is well organized, easy to use, up-to-date, and represents a good buy for homes, schools, and libraries. However, for libraries that already possess a comprehensive atlas (especially the Rand McNally New International Atlas or its clone, Britannica Atlas), the maps in the *Reader's Digest Atlas* are superfluous. The maps also overlap a great deal with the map stock of The World Atlas of Nations, another Rand McNally product, although they differ in color and presentation.

Reader's Digest–Bartholomew Illustrated Atlas of the World, Revised Edition

Facts at a Glance

Full title: **Reader's Digest–Bartholomew Illustrated Atlas of the World, Revised Edition**
Publisher: Reader's Digest
Edition reviewed: © 1992, revised edition

Number of pages: 176
Number of maps: 90
Number of index entries: 30,000
Intended readership: high school to adult
Trim size: 8¾″ × 12⅛″
Binding: hardcover

Price: $22
Sold directly to libraries and schools; also sold by direct mail and in bookstores
ISBN 0-89577-422-4
No stated revision policy

Introduction, Format, and Authority

A medium-sized world atlas, the *Reader's Digest–Bartholomew Illustrated Atlas of the World* is a 1992 update of a work originally published in 1987 in Great Britain. The maps were created by John Bartholomew & Son, an esteemed Scottish cartographic firm that also supplied the maps in the New York Times atlases reviewed elsewhere in this Buying Guide. (This atlas is very close in coverage to THE NEW YORK TIMES ATLAS OF THE WORLD, NEW FAMILY EDITION and to THE NEW YORK TIMES ATLAS OF THE WORLD, PAPERBACK EDITION.) Reader's Digest publishes this American edition. A second revised edition of the *Reader's Digest–Bartholomew Illustrated Atlas of the World,* published in 1994, was not available at the time of the review. The price for that edition is $24.

The atlas is a convenient size and is easy to use; it lies flat when opened. The binding seems durable.

Scope and Special Features

The atlas is divided into three sections. The first (32 pages) offers maps, tables, photographs, and some text that provide an overview of the earth and continents. The second section contains the main map section, with 64 maps on 80 pages. The third section is the 64-page index.

The initial section is of dubious value. Continent maps are supplemented by some photographs and text about significant features of the areas mapped, but the features chosen are not always the most important. The North America map, for instance, chooses cliff diving in Acapulco as one of only four features. These continental maps are also accompanied by flags of and facts about

selected nations, but the choices are so few (only eight for Africa) and so questionable (Liechtenstein is included, but not Russia), that the feature has little value.

A final part of this initial section—a table of area and population figures for the nations of the world—offers interesting information, but the derivation of population statistics is not explained and only 1 out of 20 randomly chosen statistics that we checked against the *Statesman's Yearbook* matched the figures found there.

The main body of maps eschews detailed studies of U.S. states, focusing on providing balanced coverage of the entire world. There are 16 maps of North America, 5 of South America, 11 of Europe, 17 of Asia, 6 of Africa, 3 of Australasia, and 2 of polar regions. Most maps are small scale (1:10,000,000 and smaller) or medium (1:5,000,000 or 1:7,500,000). The few large-scale maps (1:2,500,000) cover Southern California; the Eastern Seaboard of the United States; the United Kingdom; the area from London to Paris to Bonn; the Alps; and Israel, Lebanon, and Cyprus.

Each continent is introduced by a colorful political map followed by physical-political maps using layered relief to portray various regions of the continent (for example, Africa, North-East; Africa, West; North and West African Coasts; Africa, Central and Southern; and South Africa). There are no specific city maps, and few countries are allocated an entire map. Most nations appear in their entirety on at least one medium-scale map. Exceptions are Russia, India, Indonesia, and Brazil.

Currency

Revised in 1992, this atlas reflects the unification of Germany and of Yemen and the breakup of the Soviet Union. Yugoslavia and Czechoslovakia are both treated as single countries, however, leaving the atlas seriously deficient compared with others, even those in this relatively inexpensive class.

Many recent name changes are incorporated; thus, the Russian Federation includes the cities Sankt Peterburg (formerly Leningrad) and Nizhny Novgorod (formerly Gorky); the Africa maps use Namibia rather than South-West Africa; and the Asia maps employ Cambodia (not Kampuchea), and Dhaka (not Dacca) for the capital of Bangladesh. A number of other name changes (Myanmar for Burma, Yangon for Rangoon, Kalaallit Nunaat for Greenland, and Taiwan Strait for Formosa Strait) do not appear on the maps as the preferred name, although the first three of these are shown parenthetically as alternates.

Accuracy

Bartholomew is a highly reputable cartographic firm, and the linework on the maps in this atlas reflect the care and accuracy that usually accompany the company's work. Each map is clearly labeled with its scale, given in terms of a ratio, and supplemented by a bar scale with kilometers and miles. Projections are not stated.

While the sizes, shapes, and locations shown on the maps seem accurate, the system used to indicate towns and cities is deficient. Maps use symbol and label size to differentiate seven different types of communities from village through major city. While the atlas itself never explains what population levels correspond to each type, it does provide examples from which comparative population levels can be inferred. Québec, for instance, is a large town and Ottawa a small city. Unfortunately, other communities are given symbols inconsistent with these distinctions: Fort Worth and Austin, Texas—both more populous than Ottawa—are labeled as large towns, like Québec; Providence, Rhode Island, with fewer people than Québec, is treated as a city. Examples of these errors abound. These maps should not be considered as reliable guides to the relative size of various world communities.

Legibility

Nineteen of the maps cover two pages; very few are less than a page. The maps are, on the whole, legible. Labels are not too dense to read, and the color divisions for various elevations are clearly distinct from one another. State and provincial boundaries (thin gray lines) are sometimes difficult to make out, especially when printed over the brown and dark brown shades that mark higher elevations. Colors and labels stand out better in The New York Times Atlas of the World, Paperback Edition (using the same map stock) than in this atlas because of that work's glossier paper.

The use of white space around all maps ensures that no type is lost either in the gutter between pages or at the outside edge of any page. Even two-page maps have a thin white margin at the inside edge of both pages so that no details are lost.

Accessibility

The sequence of maps is logical, although maps of the North Central United States and the South Central United States are separated unnecessarily by four pages of maps of the East Coast. Explanatory information for the maps is poorly placed, however. The legend appears between the world map section and the main map section, an unfortunate location because the world maps that precede it employ some of its symbols. The list of abbreviations comes at the end of the second section—*after* all the maps. The table of contents—printed on the front and back endpapers—includes index maps indicating the area and page location of each map. This provides a clear visual reference for each map subject.

The index is detailed and comprehensive, including every small island or village that appears on the maps. Abbreviations indicate whether index entries are moun-

tains, rivers, islands, or other geographical features, and the general location (country, continent, or ocean) of each index entry is given. (The index is inconsistent in regard to indicating the U.S. state or Canadian province to which index entries belong; many entries have these designations, but not all.) These identifiers are followed by a page number and the grid coordinates where the feature may be found. Alternative or former names (for example, Leningrad) appear in the index followed by the correct label.

While comprehensive, the index is frustrating. Most entries refer to smaller-scale maps, which locate sites in the widest context, but this is not true in all cases. Washington, Boston, Baltimore, and New York refer the user to the map of the entire United States; Hartford, Philadelphia, and Providence, though also appearing on that map, are indexed to the map of the Eastern Seaboard. There are many other examples of this inconsistency.

Summary

The *Reader's Digest–Bartholomew Illustrated Atlas of the World* contains well-drawn maps but suffers from some serious deficiencies: the apparent inaccuracy of its statistics, its lack of currency regarding Yugoslavia and Czechoslovakia, the confusion created in town and city labeling, and the inconsistent indexing. It is not recommended for purchase.

Student Atlas of the World

Facts at a Glance

Full title: **Student Atlas of the World**
Publisher: Charles E. Tuttle Company
Edition reviewed: © 1993

Number of pages: 264
Number of maps: 75 (reviewer estimate)
Number of index entries: 40,000
Intended readership: grade 6 and up
Trim size: 9¼″ × 11½″
Binding: hardcover

Price: $30; 25 percent discount to schools and libraries
Sold directly to schools and libraries; also sold door-to-door and in bookstores and other retail outlets
ISBN 0-8048-1980-7
No stated revision policy

Introduction, Format, and Authority

The *Student Atlas of the World* is published, according to the foreword, "with the explicit aim of meeting the need for a convenient and moderately priced reference atlas." Indeed, its medium size (9¼″ × 11½″) and concise format make it convenient to handle and use as a desk reference. In outward appearance, the atlas resembles a textbook, with a glossy four-color cover that matches the book jacket. While not well reinforced, the binding is adequate and is flexible enough to allow the book to be opened flat without breaking the spine.

This work was compiled in Great Britain by Harper-Collins, with maps credited to Collins-Longman Atlases. The 1993 copyright edition is the first to be published in the United States (by Charles E. Tuttle Company), although it apparently revises one or more previous editions, presumably published in Great Britain.

The publisher indicates that this atlas is intended for grades 6 and up. However, the text is at least high school reading level (in fact, it reads more like a college textbook, although with fewer supporting details). The maps also reflect a higher degree of sophistication than one would expect to find in a middle school atlas. Therefore, the *Student Atlas* should be considered primarily an adult reference that could also be used by high school and college students.

Scope and Special Features

The contents of the *Student Atlas* are divided into three main sections: "Geographical Encyclopedia," "World Atlas," and "Geographical Data" (which includes the index). The front matter and "Geographical Encyclopedia" cover 40 pages, the "World Atlas" reference maps occupy 128 pages, and the "Geographical Data" section has 96 pages.

The "Geographical Encyclopedia" consists of highly illustrated two-page text features on such topics as the structure of the earth, earthquakes and volcanoes, atmosphere and climate, vegetation, population, food, minerals, energy, and environmental problems. Within these topics, the focus is on contemporary global concerns such as deforestation, desertification, soil erosion, renewable energy sources, and hazardous waste exports and imports. The brief text passages are illustrated with thematic maps (some of which are too small) and numerous excellent graphs, diagrams, and photographs. While informative, the overall presentation (including the text level, as noted above) is fairly complex. No authorities or sources are cited for the written information or the numerical data presented. This section also includes special features on the history of cartography and how maps are made.

The collection of world maps in the "World Atlas" section is organized by continent, opening with separate world political and world physical maps. Each section begins with a "Global View" political map of the continent, which shows the continent as it appears on a round globe. These maps, according to the publisher, "allow for a realistic area comparison between land areas of each continent."

The regional reference maps are physical-political, using a combination of layered tints and three-dimensional shading to show relief (spot markings are also used to indicate specific land elevations and sea depths). The coloring system is good: the tints can be easily distinguished from one another and yet are light enough not to overwhelm the type. Most maps include a color key, which is a major convenience. The nomenclature on the maps reflects the practice of supplying place names in the local language of the particular country, except for names of countries and major features.

Map coverage in this atlas leans heavily toward Europe, in both the number of pages devoted to the region (40, or nearly one-third of the base atlas) and the scales used (see *Accuracy*). While no other region is treated in as much depth, coverage is fairly evenly spread over the rest of the world: 22 pages represent Asia, 14 Africa, 12 Oceania, 24 North America, and 9 South America. Although atlases in the family or student class usually have heavy coverage of the United States and Canada, this atlas is not particularly strong in these areas. For one thing, it does not specially notate internal capitals (anywhere in the world); capitals of states and provinces are thus not designated, and some capital cities are excluded from some smaller-scale regional maps (for example, Olympia, Washington, on the map of the United States).

The "Geographical Data" section includes comparison data on the world's major physical features (such as continents, rivers, and mountains), major international organizations (such as the Organization of African Unity), and a table on nations of the world. This table gives the area, population, form of government, and other information, but only for independent countries. The end matter also includes a glossary, which is a great help in interpreting the foreign geographical terms shown on the maps.

Currency

The maps in the *Student Atlas of the World* are current to the 1993 copyright date, reflecting all major world changes through the division of Czechoslovakia into the Czech Republic and Slovakia. One minor oversight is that, while Macedonia is shown on the maps as independent, it is not listed in the "Nations of the World" table. Local place names are also current and generally reflect national preferences. Curiously, the local name for Burma is given throughout as *Myanma* rather than *Myanmar,* which is how it usually appears in English.

Dates are not given for the facts and figures in this atlas, although they are reasonably current (see *Accuracy*).

Accuracy

While the authority of the mapmakers is not explicitly stated in the work, the cartography in the *Student Atlas of the World* is good, and the accuracy will adequately serve the general reader. Spot checks of the maps revealed no major errors, although in a few instances (for example, Abuja, Nigeria, on the "West Africa" map and Columbus, Ohio, on the "Northeastern United States" map), city markers are misplaced relative to their surrounding features.

Since, as the publisher notes, each map "has been planned deliberately to cover an entire physical or political unit," the map scales vary; however, they "have been limited in number, as far as possible, in order to facilitate comparison between maps." Except for Europe and a few other areas, scales are relatively small, with 1:7,500,000 and 1:10,000,000 being the most typical. Western Europe is blanketed at scales of 1:2,000,000 and 1:2,500,000, and these are used as well for maps of other "particularly densely populated areas" ("Northeastern United States," "South Central Canada," "Japan," and "The Holy Land"). Scales are presented in fractional and bar scale (miles and kilometers) form, and projections are also stated.

Since neither dates nor sources are given for statistical data, it cannot be considered authoritative, although most data is reasonably accurate. One exception is a population list of 15 world cities: the figures are somewhat inflated, even if they are meant to represent metropolitan area population (which is not stated).

Legibility

The typefaces used are distinct and print clearly and legibly over the background colors. There are several problems with legibility, however. The red line used for international borders is too similar to the thinner one used for roads on certain maps. And while the effort to delineate major internal divisions is commendable in a work of this scope, the linework for these borders is very hard to pick out, and the labeling contributes to overcrowding. It is also impossible to determine the *de facto* jurisdiction of disputed areas such as Kashmir. Finally, the maps of the Indian Ocean and Pacific Ocean, which attempt to show ocean-bottom relief, look instead as though they were pressed against the wet plate of another map.

Maps are printed on either single pages or two-page spreads using a variety of formats. Labels are generally carefully placed clear of the gutter, although this is not always the case. Since the book lies flat when open, however, information is not entirely lost in the gutters.

Accessibility

User support is one of this atlas's stronger points. Aids include a "Guide to the Atlas" that explains the organization of the work and discusses the particulars of map scales, projections, symbols, and place names. Two additional text features discuss mapmaking and mapreading in general. The legend covers all of the major markings and type styles. The opening page of each continental section includes a unique finding aid—an alphabetical list, with page references, of each country in the region. Other finding aids include index maps in the front and back endpapers and marginal locator maps on each map plate.

The 40,000-entry index is impressive, containing more listings than RAND MCNALLY GOODE'S WORLD ATLAS, for example. References are given in latitude and longitude coordinates only, a practice that provides useful geographical information but also makes the index harder to use. Unfortunately, the decimal system used for denoting latitude and longitude is not explained (the feature on mapreading, in fact, uses a different convention). In all other respects, the index is helpful and complete.

Summary

The list price of *Student Atlas of the World* is $30, which is a reasonable value for a hardcover, general purpose desk atlas. Within its class, this atlas rates highly in a majority of categories. However, prospective purchasers should be aware of some peculiar characteristics. First, the reading level of the maps and text are much higher than the "Student" title might suggest. Furthermore, Europe receives disproportionate coverage, and the coverage of North America is weaker than in most comparable atlases. Finally, there are a few legibility problems.

In size and price, this atlas competes directly with Oxford's CONCISE ATLAS OF THE WORLD. Both have strengths and weaknesses, but the Oxford is superior to this atlas in geographical balance and the overall quality of the cartography. Other atlases in this class, including the HAMMOND CONCISE, READER'S DIGEST ATLAS OF THE WORLD, and WORLD ATLAS OF NATIONS, cost from $5 to $10 more than the *Student Atlas* but are more clearly oriented toward a North American audience.

The Times Atlas of the World, Ninth Comprehensive Edition

Facts at a Glance

Full title: **The Times Atlas of the World, Ninth Comprehensive Edition**
Publisher: Times Books/Random House
Edition reviewed: © 1994

Number of pages: 514
Number of maps: 123 map plates
Number of index entries: 210,000
Intended readership: adult
Trim size: 11″ × 17¾″
Binding: hardcover

Price: $175
Sold in bookstores; also sold by direct mail and
   directly to libraries
ISBN 0-8129-2077-5
Revised periodically

Introduction, Format, and Authority

The Times Atlas of the World is an oversized, general world atlas. It is compiled jointly by *The Times* newspaper of London and the Edinburgh-based cartographer John Bartholomew & Son. The first *Times* atlas was published in 1895, with German cartography; the collaboration with Bartholomew began following World War I. The first "Comprehensive Edition"—the work in its current, single-volume format—was published in 1967 and has been revised every year or two since. The edition reviewed for the Buying Guide is a 1994 revised printing of the "Ninth Comprehensive Edition," first published in 1992.

The Times Atlas derives its authority from several dozen cartographers, geographers, scholars, and government agencies around the world. Among the organizations contributing to it are the Academy of Sciences and the National Atlas Committee, Moscow; the American Geographical Society, New York; Esselte Map Service, Stockholm; Institut Géographique National, Paris; the British Meteorological Office; NASA; the National Geographic Society; Rand McNally; the Royal Geographical Society, London; and the U.S. Geological Survey. H. A. G. Lewis and P. J. M. Geelan served as editorial consultants. Needless to say, *The Times Atlas* is one of the most authoritative world atlases available today.

The version sold in the United States (published by Times Books, a division of Random House) is identical to the British edition published by Times Books Limited, London, a division of HarperCollins. Other editions are available in German, Dutch, and French. A "concise" edition is available in the United States under the title THE NEW YORK TIMES ATLAS OF THE WORLD, reviewed in this Buying Guide.

With a trim size of 11″ × 17¾″ and a thickness of nearly 2″, *The Times Atlas* is the largest atlas currently on the market. The volume is quite heavy and unwieldy, but it is very well made. The pages lie flat when open, and there is a narrow interior margin so that no map information is lost in the gutter. The binding is durable, and the book should stand up well to heavy library use.

Scope and Special Features

The contents of the atlas are divided into three main sections: special features (46 pages); 123 plates of general reference maps and several thematic maps (245 pages); and a glossary and index-gazetteer (222 pages). Nearly all of the maps are double-page spreads. Many of the plates contain large-scale insets of cities (totaling about 70), islands, and other important areas.

The atlas contains primarily physical maps of regions and political units. Unlike the maps in virtually every other atlas, which are four-color, the maps in *The Times Atlas* are eight-color, which allows for exceptional subtlety and level of detail. For example, different shades of solid red are used for borders and for roads, so that each is clear and easily distinguished. The maps employ tinted, layered relief to depict land elevation and sea depths. The scale of tints varies somewhat from plate to plate, although this is not a problem because each plate contains an elevation color key. Additional markings are used for spot elevations and to indicate such features as glaciers, ice caps, lava fields, deserts, dunes, marshes, flood areas, and swamps.

The maps are organized by continent, beginning with Australia, then moving to Asia, Europe, Africa, North America, South America, and Antarctica. Maps of the oceans (with insets of midocean islands) are placed in geographical sequence between the continents they separate. Many users may find the order of the continents unusual, and there are several other peculiarities. Most of the continental sections open with a political-physical map of the region, except for the section on North and South America, whose political-physical map is interspersed among the maps of North America. Also, most of the former Soviet Union, including the European states, appears with Asia rather than with Europe. Finally, some islands of Oceania appear at the beginning of the reference maps (Plate 9) and others at the end (Plate 122).

In scope and coverage, *The Times Atlas* leans toward Western Europe and the United States, which are the subjects of more maps at larger scales than other regions. Coverage of Australia and New Zealand is also particularly thorough. However, this coverage does not come at the expense of other areas, which are shown in admirable detail. As an indication of the geographical balance of *The Times Atlas,* Australia and Oceania are covered on 8 plates, Asia on 22, Europe (including Russia) on 40, Africa on 12, North America on 20, and South America on 5. On the other hand, far more city inset maps are devoted to the United States, Europe, and other industrialized areas than to developing areas; for example, ten cities in Australia and New Zealand are shown, compared with only three in Africa (two of which are in South Africa). The atlas includes individual two-page plates of London and Paris.

Although the focus of this atlas is clearly on the general reference maps, the work does include several special features. The three statistical features that open the atlas are particularly useful. Leading off is a five-page table of "States & territories of the world," which gives the name, area, and population of every country. This data is also given for the major internal divisions of several countries, including Brazil, China, and India as well as the United States and Canada. This table gives the map plate number on which each area is represented. Following this table is a two-page chart of geographical comparisons of the world's major physical features. Whereas most atlases give this information in tabular form, *The Times Atlas* portrays the relative sizes of the continents, oceans, drainage basins, inland waters, and islands using outline maps—an attractive feature. The third table gives the population for more than 275 metropolitan areas in the world. The information in each of these tables is accurate and conveniently presented, although its authority is unclear (see *Accuracy*).

The Times Atlas also includes illustrated encyclopedic features on the universe, solar system, space flight, earth science, and map projections, as well as three star charts, seven physical map plates, and eight world thematic map plates. The feature on the solar system includes a map of the earth's moon. The encyclopedic features are detailed and quite sophisticated, although they do not add significantly to the value of the atlas. The double-page physical maps of each of the continents are large and bold, although unfortunately there is no legend identifying the types of environment shown. The thematic maps provide information on climatology and on the world's minerals, climate, vegetation, population, food, energy, and political divisions. The title maps, which span two pages, are quite large and detailed; they are supplemented by several smaller, more general maps (on subtopics such as languages and religion) as well as by statistical charts and graphs. Most contain brief explanatory captions.

Currency

The information contained in *The Times Atlas* is up-to-date to 1994, its copyright year. The maps include the separation of Czechoslovakia into the Czech Republic and Slovakia and the independence of Eritrea from Ethiopia. In both of these cases, the main index reflects the previous political situation; however, a separate index covering the Czech Republic and Slovakia has been inserted before the main index. One error in currency was noted: the city Ciudad del Este, in Paraguay, is labeled with its former name, Puerto Presidente Stroessner.

The majority of population figures in the "States & territories of the world" table date from 1990 or after, although some figures go back to the 1980s. The information in the encyclopedic features is current to the early 1990s, and the illustrations and photographs are contemporary.

Accuracy

As is to be expected in a work of this authority, great consideration is given to such matters as scales, projections, and nomenclature. In the foreword, the editors note that while "aiming at a standard range of scales for the maps in *The Times Atlas,* the publishers have departed from this principle when a special scale best suits a particular area." (This is unlike the other major comprehensive atlas on the market, Rand McNally's New International Atlas, which employs a uniform series of scales.) Given the large trim size of *The Times Atlas,* the scales used are exceptionally large. Most European countries are mapped at scales ranging from 1:500,000 to 1:1,250,000. The largest consistent scale for regions in Australia, Asia, Africa, and South America is 1:5,000,000, although some individual maps are drawn at larger scales, up to 1:200,000. Most island and city insets are at 1:250,000, so their sizes can be accurately compared. London and Paris are each mapped at 1:100,000.

Scales are given as representative fractions and in bar form (in miles and kilometers), and projections are stated. The range of projections used has been selected to minimize distortion and permit distance and size comparisons for all areas on a particular map.

According to the editor's foreword, the spelling of place names is "in accordance with the principles and practice of the British Permanent Committee on Geographical Names." Except for names of countries and large features, place names appear in the official language of the country shown, a standard practice in major international atlases. More familiar English equivalents or historical names are also given in parentheses as space permits. In some cases, the historical versions—such as Siam for Thailand and Persia for Iran—reach well back in history and seem more nostalgic than useful.

With the one exception noted in *Currency,* no errors were detected on the maps or in the index. The statistical tables and features also are accurate, although specific sources for the data are not cited, and the encyclopedic articles are unsigned. In the "States & territories of the world" table, the year of the population figure is given, and it is noted whether the figure relates to an official census. However, in the "Metropolitan area populations" table, no dates are given, and the individual entries do not indicate whether the figure is an estimate or based on census returns.

Legibility

Despite the remarkable range of information they contain, the maps in *The Times Atlas of the World* are clear and not overcrowded. Labels of cities, countries, landforms, and bodies of water are generally well placed; only on maps of heavily populated regions is it difficult to locate the name of an individual town. As was noted previously, the background colors and physical markings are sharp and easily distinguished but do not interfere with the legibility of the type.

The map legend lists the range of lettering styles that are used to distinguish names of various types of political features from those of physical and cultural features. Different styles denote country names, levels of administrative divisions and capitals, historical regions, and physical regions. In practice, however, the type styles used on the maps vary from map to map—and even vary on the same map. On Plate 67 of France, for example, the typefaces used for France do not match those in the legend or those used in the adjoining countries on the same map. While somewhat distracting, these inconsistencies do not seriously hinder use.

To maximize the scales used in the space allotted, the cartographers frequently resort to showing continuations of the main subject area (such as panhandles) in same-scale insets. This has both benefits and drawbacks: the subject area is shown in the greatest possible detail but in somewhat disjointed fashion. Overall, however, *The Times Atlas*'s cartographers achieve a judicious balance between maximized scale and minimized distortion.

Accessibility

Aimed at the serious user, *The Times Atlas* offers no "how to" guide for using the atlas. But the publishers have provided some basic finding aids. The three-page table of contents is thorough and easy to use, listing the subject areas and inset maps contained on each plate. The book's endpapers contain useful index maps of the world (front) and of North America and Europe (back). The map plates include arrows in the margins indicating the plate number of adjoining regions. This is a helpful means of moving from page to page, particularly given the unusual sequence of maps (see *Scope and Special Features*).

A full-page legend of symbols and abbreviations precedes the main map section. In addition, this information is duplicated on a separate, laminated 5½″ × 16″ card for easy reference. This card is not stored in a pocket in the book or attached to the work in any way, which may present a problem for libraries. The legend is thorough and clear.

The most significant point of access to the wealth of information contained on the maps is the 210,000-entry main index, certainly the most comprehensive of any atlas on the market. According to the publisher, the index was completely revised and reset for the ninth edition. Index entries include both letter-number grid location (for ease of use) and latitude/longitude coordinates (for accuracy). According to the foreword, the latitudes and longitudes allow the positions of places to be defined to about 1,000 yards. As far as our reviewers can determine, every name appearing on the maps (with the exception of large-scale city insets) is listed in the index.

Summary

Consistently authoritative, accurate, and up-to-date, *The Times Atlas of the World* has long been considered the most definitive general reference world atlas available.

Perhaps befitting an enduring classic, the atlas has its idiosyncrasies, but it has no major flaws. Like the others that have preceded it, the fully revised ninth edition is an essential reference for the scholar or nonscholar alike who is in need of the most reliable and current geographical information available. Every serious reference collection should include it.

The Times Atlas's chief competitor is Rand McNally's 560-page NEW INTERNATIONAL ATLAS (and its clone, BRITANNICA ATLAS), which rivals *The Times Atlas* in scope, accuracy, authority, and sophistication. Each has its strengths. The maps in *The Times Atlas* convey a greater level of detail at larger scales and on larger pages than do the maps of any other atlas. The main strength of the well-organized NEW INTERNATIONAL lies in its use of overlapping views at uniform scales, which allows the reader to more accurately compare regions of the world. In the end, the works complement each other, and an ideal reference collection would include both.

Today's World

Facts at a Glance

Full title: **Today's World**
Publisher: Rand McNally
Edition reviewed: © 1992, 1993 revised edition

Number of pages: 200
Number of maps: 85
Number of index entries: 52,000
Intended readership: adult
Trim size: 11″ × 14¾″
Binding: hardcover

Price: $29.95; discount available to schools and libraries
Sold directly to schools and libraries; also sold by direct mail and in bookstores and other retail outlets
ISBN 0-528-85300-9
No stated revision policy

Introduction, Format, and Authority

First published in 1992 and revised in 1993, *Today's World* is Rand McNally's most basic atlas. This large-sized (11″ × 14¾″) atlas consists simply of world maps and an index. The set of maps and the index are identical to those found in Rand McNally's WORLD ATLAS OF NATIONS. The volume is similarly well bound in an attractive simulated-leather cover.

For more detailed comments on the format, authority, and quality of the cartography in this atlas, see the review for WORLD ATLAS OF NATIONS.

Scope and Special Features

The only special features in *Today's World* are a three-page essay on maps and map reading called "Using the Atlas" and a time-zone map. Both are picked up from Rand McNally's NEW COSMOPOLITAN WORLD ATLAS. Not found in the WORLD ATLAS OF NATIONS, the "Using the Atlas" feature helps make the high-level maps in *Today's World* more accessible to the average map reader. However, a glossary of terms and a more extensive legend would have been even more helpful.

Summary

At $29.95, *Today's World* is the least expensive hardcover, large-format adult atlas on the market. It presents a basic but geographically balanced set of accurate, current, and legible world maps that will meet a variety of reference needs for students or families. Those looking for a desk reference, however, should note that its large size makes it less convenient to handle than medium-sized or smaller "concise" atlases such as Oxford's CONCISE ATLAS OF THE WORLD. It also does not contain the gazetteer data, thematic maps, and other types of geographical information that distinguish so many other full-size atlases, such as the HAMMOND ATLAS OF THE WORLD or THE TIMES ATLAS OF THE WORLD.

World Atlas of Nations

Facts at a Glance

Full title: **World Atlas of Nations**
Publisher: Rand McNally
Editor: Elizabeth Fagan Adelman
Edition reviewed: © 1993

Number of pages: 256
Number of maps: 85
Number of index entries: 52,000
Intended readership: adult
Trim size: 11″ × 14¾″
Binding: hardcover

Price: $39.95; discount available to schools and libraries
Sold directly to schools and libraries; also sold by direct mail and in bookstores and other retail outlets
ISBN 0-528-83618-8
No stated revision policy

Introduction, Format, and Authority

The 1993 edition of Rand McNally's *World Atlas of Nations* is designed, according to the jacket blurb, as a useful general reference for "home, school, or office use." It consists of a basic set of 85 world reference maps com-bined with a section of fact charts of the world's nations, U.S. states, and Canadian provinces, all presented in a large-page (11″ × 14¾″) format. The handsome simulated-leather cover and binding should prove durable.

The maps in the *World Atlas of Nations* are page-for-page the same as those in Rand McNally's NEW COSMOPOLITAN WORLD ATLAS for all parts of the world except the United States and Canada (NEW COSMOPOLITAN includes individual maps of each state and province, whereas this atlas covers them by region). These maps derive from the stock created for Rand McNally's top-of-the-line NEW INTERNATIONAL ATLAS, adapted to primarily emphasize political information. They are geared to adult readership.

World Atlas of Nations does not include the thematic maps and statistical tables found in THE NEW COSMOPOLITAN, and its index is not as lengthy. Also not included is the helpful "Using this Atlas" feature on maps and map reading. Overall, however, the simple arrangement and inclusion of fewer features adds to its convenience as a basic map reference.

For a detailed discussion of currency, accuracy, and legibility, see the review for THE NEW COSMOPOLITAN WORLD ATLAS.

Scope and Special Features

This atlas consists of three sections: the "World Data" fact charts (59 pages), the "Reference Maps" world maps (128 pages), and the index (64 pages). The "World Data" section is organized by continent (Australia is included in "Oceania and Antarctica"), with individual countries arranged alphabetically therein. Information provided about each country includes the flag, the official name, and data on people, politics, economy, and land. The state and province entries are shorter and include population, population density, area, capital city, largest city, and highest point. This section is illustrated with more than 100 fully captioned color photographs emphasizing the world's physical and cultural diversity.

The "Reference Maps" section leans toward North America, which is represented on 40 pages of maps (28 of these are of the United States). Outside this region, the atlas is very well balanced geographically: 28 pages are devoted to Asia, 20 to Europe, 16 to Africa, 12 to South America, and 6 to Australia and Antarctica. As in THE NEW COSMOPOLITAN, the only significant gap in coverage is for Oceania, which appears only on the small-scale (1:48,000,000) map of the Pacific and Indian oceans.

The high quality of the cartography in this atlas reflects the fact that the maps were originally compiled for a scholarly international atlas. They characteristically show a detailed variety of features and use local languages for most place names (a fact that is not noted in this atlas). However, this atlas does not include many of the aids that help make those maps fully comprehensible—in particular, a glossary of foreign terms and a comprehensive legend. (The legend in *World Atlas of Nations,* identical to that in THE NEW COSMOPOLITAN, is downsized from that in THE NEW INTERNATIONAL.) Thus, interpreting many of the labels on the maps may be challenging for the average intended reader. The index provides some help by giving the generic type for physical features, but it is not fully comprehensive. The inclusion of more, rather than fewer, interpretive aids in a lower-level atlas would seem a better practice.

The 52,000-entry index follows the format of THE NEW COSMOPOLITAN but is somewhat reduced in length. The criteria for including or excluding places are not clear since both indexes apply to about the same number of maps. It appears that all localities in the United States are indexed, although some minor physical features (such as small streams) are not. Outside the United States, places appearing in the smallest type on the maps are generally not indexed.

Summary

World Atlas of Nations presents a basic but geographically balanced set of accurate, current, and legible world maps that will meet a variety of reference needs for students or families. Its major drawback is a lack of interpretive aids to help the general reader reap the full benefit of the high-level maps. It is one of the least expensive hardcover large-format atlases on the market, although it contains fewer special features than most (it has no topical essays or thematic maps, for example).

Overall, this atlas represents a good—but not exceptional—value. The *World Atlas of Nations* is very similar in coverage to the identically priced READER'S DIGEST ATLAS OF THE WORLD: both, in fact, have most of the same Rand McNally maps, although those in the READER'S DIGEST ATLAS are more physical in nature. The READER'S DIGEST ATLAS contains more special features and provides better map-reading information, but it has a smaller index. Also at this price is the smaller-format HAMMOND ATLAS OF THE WORLD, CONCISE EDITION, which is a bit easier to handle and use, although its maps are not as sharp and clear. Finally, Rand McNally's own TODAY'S WORLD atlas offers the identical map stock and index found in *World Atlas of Nations* (without the "World Data" information) for $29.95, an economical purchase.

The World Book Atlas

Facts at a Glance

Full title: **The World Book Atlas**
Publisher: World Book
Editor: William H. Nault, Publisher
Edition reviewed: © 1992, revised printing

Number of pages: 432
Number of maps: 284
Number of index entries: 67,000
Intended readership: elementary school to adult
Trim size: $10^{9}/_{16}'' \times 14\frac{1}{2}''$
Binding: hardcover

Price: $89 (when sold separately); $75 (when sold with THE WORLD BOOK ENCYCLOPEDIA); $79 to schools and libraries
Sold door-to-door; also sold directly to schools and libraries
ISBN 0-7166-2695-0
Revised annually, with additional updates as needed

Introduction, Format, and Authority

The World Book Atlas, a large-sized ($10^{9}/_{16}'' \times 14\frac{1}{2}''$) general world atlas, is a compilation of material from several sources. The collection of world maps were created by Istituto Geografico De Agostini, Italy's top cartographic firm. The individual maps of U.S. states and Canadian provinces were produced by Rand McNally and are essentially the same as those that appear in several Rand McNally products, including THE NEW COSMOPOLITAN WORLD ATLAS. The thematic maps were adapted from Rand McNally's GOODE'S WORLD ATLAS. These three sets of maps have been packaged with several features produced by World Book. The "revised printing" version (copyright 1992) was reviewed.

The intended audience of *The World Book Atlas* is wide ranging—from school-age children to adults. However, not all components of the atlas are geared to the whole audience. The feature material and illustrations, for example, would appeal primarily to children and young adults. The world maps, on the other hand, are quite complex and were designed for more sophisticated users (the legend, in fact, is printed in five languages).

This durably bound volume is intended as companion atlas to THE WORLD BOOK ENCYCLOPEDIA, but it also can be used by itself. As a stand-alone, *The World Book Atlas* presents a wide variety of geographical information; however, it should be noted that it contains fewer world maps than all other atlases of its size and price. Over half of the total number of maps in the atlas are dedicated to the United States and Canada.

Scope and Special Features

The structure of *The World Book Atlas* can be grouped into four parts: features and thematic maps (88 pages), maps of the world (128 pages), maps of the United States and Canada (64 pages), and statistical tables and index (144 pages). The United States and Canada are thus covered twice—in the world maps and in a separate group of maps.

The atlas opens with 26 two-page illustrated articles on physical and cultural geography. The articles fall into three sections: "Looking at the Earth's Features," which focuses on landforms, bodies of water, and climate regions; "Looking at Earth's People and Their Lands," which explores world cultures; and "Looking at Earth as a Planet," which discusses the solar system, atmosphere, and forces shaping the earth. The illustrations include many color photographs, drawings, maps, and diagrams. The texts are factually accurate but very general. The level of the text and the nature of the illustrations are clearly intended to capture the interest of a younger, perhaps junior-high-school age, audience, and on this level they are clear and readable. They are not of much use to the more mature reader in search of in-depth facts. An additional section called "Understanding Maps" includes brief articles on the history of maps and on reading maps.

The World Book Atlas also includes a wide-ranging selection of 30 thematic maps drawn from Rand McNally's GOODE'S WORLD ATLAS. These detailed and complex maps have been supplemented with explanatory text, photographs, and graphs, which makes them more meaningful and easier to understand than those in GOODE'S. Many topics are unique to *World Book* (and GOODE'S), including birth and death rates, air pressure and predominant winds, and shipping routes of specific metals and alloys. Several of the maps need to be redesigned, however, to reflect post–Cold War changes (see *Currency*).

The 128-page "Maps of the World" collection is organized by continent. Each continent begins with separate physical and political maps at the scale of 1:30,000,000, except for Europe, which is shown at 1:15,000,000. The physical maps use shaded relief and colors to show land elevations and offshore water depths; the political maps use solid colors for individual countries. The regional maps are political and physical, with a neutral background of shaded relief and primary boundaries highlighted with color. The scales used on the regional maps differ considerably from one continent to the next: 1:3,000,000 for Europe, 1:9,000,000 for Africa and parts of the former Soviet Union, and 1:12,000,000 for Asia. A handful of larger-scale maps cover northwest Europe and several islands in the Pacific Ocean and Caribbean Sea. There are no maps of major world cities.

Overall, the scope of the world maps section is uneven. The maps themselves are attractive and of a quality comparable to top-of-the-line atlases. Coverage is evenly spread around the globe—with a slight emphasis on Europe. However, regions are not covered with any particular depth. *World Book* has only 100 pages of detailed regional maps, compared with 110 in READER'S DIGEST ATLAS OF THE WORLD and 144 in the HAMMOND ATLAS OF THE WORLD. Notably lacking are detailed maps of

Israel and the Middle East, standard coverage in most atlases because of the area's importance in current events. Coverage of South America is also sparse.

A few areas, on the other hand, are very well represented, especially the former Soviet Union. Three maps (of the Urals, the Tashkent region of Central Asia, and Northeast Asia) found here are not found in any of the competing atlases or even in some comprehensive atlases. With the new republics of the former Soviet Union making headlines daily, these maps are greatly appreciated. Kalaallit Nunaat (Greenland) and Oceania are also well covered; few other works come close to having so many maps of individual islands.

The base atlas is supplemented by 64 full-page maps of individual U.S. states and Canadian provinces. Created by Rand McNally for their *Atlas of the United States,* these maps differ considerably from the world maps in treatment and appearance. Scales vary greatly, ranging from 1:304,000 to 1:12,000,000 (see *Accuracy*). Subject areas are pale orange—a color that is neither helpful nor attractive—and show very light shaded relief. The maps display most large cities and towns, major roads and railroads, and physical features; counties are also noted. Insets show major urban areas in somewhat greater detail. Each map includes an index of cities and towns (with population) in the margin.

Several information tables accompany the index, including a fact chart of world nations and other political units, statistical tables of the earth's physical features, and a population table of major cities. The rest of the end matter relates specifically to the world map collection. It includes a list of sources used to compile the world maps (which offers an interesting glimpse into how maps are compiled); an explanation of the transliteration systems used; and an eight-page glossary. The 114-page index also refers only to the world maps. At 67,000 entries, it compares favorably with most atlases of this size (except the HAMMOND ATLAS OF THE WORLD, which has a considerably larger index).

Currency

The World Book Atlas is basically current to the beginning of 1992, its copyright year—though there are lapses. The unification of Germany and of Yemen and the breakup of both the Soviet Union and Yugoslavia are accounted for. However, the capital of Nigeria is shown as Lagos, although it had officially moved to Abuja in 1991. (An annotation on the West-Central Africa map does note that Abuja is the future federal capital.) Several of the thematic maps, particularly those relating to economic output, still represent data from the Soviet Union and West Germany.

Place names are generally up-to-date and in accordance with national preferences, although there are again exceptions: Ciudad del Este, Paraguay, is still labeled

Puerto Presidente Stroessner and Denali is called Mt. McKinley. The world regional maps use local spellings and may include alternates if more than one official language is used in a particular area. English equivalents are given for major features (countries, major cities, and large physical features). Alternate and historical names are liberally inserted where space permits. Maps of continents give country names in English only.

The population information in the geographical tables is very up-to-date; most comes from the 1992 edition of THE WORLD BOOK ENCYCLOPEDIA and is based on recent census data or official estimates. The year of the census or estimate is given for each figure, so readers can judge currency.

Accuracy

The maps of the *World Book Atlas* are accurate. The two firms responsible for the maps, Istituto Geografico De Agostini and Rand McNally, both have excellent worldwide reputations for accuracy and currency. The statistical and textual information is derived from THE WORLD BOOK ENCYCLOPEDIA and Rand McNally, two reliable sources.

The world maps indicate scale with a bar scale (miles and kilometers) and the representative fraction, but give no verbal scale. Projections vary throughout the section, but this is neither a hindrance nor a distraction. One major exception involves the three world maps (physical, political, and oceans) that open the base atlas section. They are drawn with an unusual-looking projection (rather than the common Robinson projection) that may confuse some readers.

Each of the U.S. and Canadian maps includes a bar scale, verbal scale, and representative fraction and the type of projection used. Since each map fills up a whole page, the scales and projections vary greatly. While the projections have little bearing on the average reader, the scales can be confusing. Rhode Island looks as big as Texas, and so Rhode Island appears sparsely populated in comparison. This could be easily misunderstood.

Legibility

Most of the world maps spread across two pages. The pages lie flat when opened, so little information is lost in the gutter. While a few labels cross over the gutter, most are carefully confined to one page. Ample margins surround each map page.

The legend for the world maps is clear and extensive. The colors used on these maps are good—the international boundaries are particularly easy to distinguish. The typographical detail is appropriate for this level of work, and the type size is readable. The shaded relief does not overwhelm the type.

Accessibility

The World Book Atlas contains no general description or explanation of the atlas as a whole, something that would be very helpful given the variety of its components and the way they are organized. For example, the glossary and index, which refer only to the world maps, are separated from those maps by the section of U.S. and Canadian maps. The index map for the world maps is located just before the maps themselves on pages 100–101, but since it is in the middle of the book, it is difficult to find quickly. Moreover, the index map refers to the maps by plate number, whereas the index at the end of the book refers to them by page number—this of course is very confusing. The world maps include neither locator maps (which show the subject area in context) nor arrow references to adjoining maps (which help the reader move from page to page).

The legend to the world maps is located with the map section and is written in five languages. A note on the legend explains that the languages "permit the interpretation of the maps by a broad readership." Yet no other part of *The World Book Atlas* appears in any language other than English, so the other languages serve little purpose. In spite of this, the legend is well organized and easy to understand.

The index gives both a map grid reference and latitude/longitude coordinates, a feature that makes the index more useful to a broad audience. The index is explained well and is easy to use. A list of symbols used is repeated at the bottom of every index page. The index does not refer to the thematic maps or to the maps of the United States and Canada, although the latter include an index of cities and towns on each map.

The use of local-language spellings will make the maps somewhat difficult for less-experienced atlas readers to use. Ho Chi Minh City, for example, is labeled and indexed as Thanh-Pho Ho Chi Minh and is thus found under *T,* not under *H,* where most English-speaking readers would look for it. (The city is, however, cross-indexed under its former name of Saigon.)

Summary

The World Book Atlas is a good atlas, but at $89 it is not a good buy. Its strong points include a good set of thematic maps and extensive coverage of the United States and Canada. Unfortunately, the overall presentation is disjointed. Given that its price puts it in the range of the most comprehensive atlases (such as BRITANNICA)—which clearly *The World Book Atlas* is not—its relative weaknesses become apparent. Although aimed at a family market, the atlas is not especially easy to use. Most important, *World Book* is comparatively short on world coverage, having far fewer world maps than ATLAS OF THE WORLD (Oxford University

Press) and HAMMOND ATLAS OF THE WORLD. Coverage is similar to Rand McNally's NEW COSMOPOLITAN WORLD ATLAS, but NEW COSMOPOLITAN's presentation and accessibility are superior. All of the atlases named above are less expensive than *World Book*. In short, libraries and individuals seeking a large-format, general-purpose atlas can spend a lot less money and get more than *The World Book Atlas* offers.

PART FOUR

Dictionaries

Chapter 9
What to Look for in Dictionaries

People consult general dictionaries in search of a wide range of information—from definitions or correct spellings to synonyms, word histories, and guidance on pronunciation or usage. If a dictionary is the sole reference source that is owned or habitually used—as is the case in many homes—the inclusion of tables, charts, lists, biographical or geographical names, and other features may become especially important. People also consult dictionaries in a variety of other locations, including library, office, and school.

Because dictionaries meet these wide-ranging needs and are used in these different locations, it should not be surprising that they are far more varied than may be readily apparent. Yet that notion does surprise some. If words have commonly understood meanings, how can one dictionary differ from another? If scholars know the origins of many terms, how can etymologies differ from one another? If language experts agree on how words should be used, how can the usage advice contained in dictionaries differ from one another? As these reviews reveal, there are indeed many ways to approach the English language. We hope that through these reviews, readers can come to appreciate how different dictionaries can be—and to see how at least one dictionary can be found to meet each prospective buyer's needs.

Because of this variety—and the differing needs of dictionary users—the selection of general-purpose dictionaries is a complicated process. The reviews in this Buying Guide attempt to cut through some of that complexity by helping potential purchasers identify their specific needs in a dictionary, determine which of the varied resources available seem appropriate for them,

and focus on one or a few specific titles that seem to offer the best match to meet those needs. This function is especially valuable now, when major dictionary publishers such as Houghton Mifflin and Merriam-Webster have recently released highly publicized new editions of their works.

Characteristics of Dictionaries

The reviews in this Buying Guide consider only general English-language dictionaries. They do not include such other word books as thesauruses, usage manuals, pronouncing dictionaries, or any of the myriad other guides to language that can delight the lover of words. But, then, dictionaries themselves provide variety enough.

This part of the Buying Guide is divided into four chapters, each of which contains reviews of a given type of dictionary. Chapter 10 reviews children's dictionaries, for the range of users from preschool through the elementary grades. Chapter 11 contains reviews of middle school dictionaries, aimed at students in the upper elementary grades through eighth or ninth grade. Chapter 12 presents reviews of high school and adult dictionaries, ranging from compact home dictionaries to that authoritative, multivolume nonpareil, THE OXFORD ENGLISH DICTIONARY (OED). Finally, Chapter 13 offers reviews of what we call "special dictionaries"—works meant for students of English as a second language (ESL) and visual dictionaries.

Some readers may be interested in investigating electronic dictionaries. Chapter 17 reviews these computerized versions of print dictionaries. (Note that the reviews of electronic dictionaries are limited to those works that are true, stand-alone reference products, albeit in computerized form. The chapter does not address the spell-checking, synonym-finding, or usage-checking features that are part of many word-processing programs.)

When determining the scope of this Buying Guide, we decided not to review any work that sold for less than ten dollars. That decision has an impact on this category more than any other—there are scores of dictionaries, at all levels, that sell for less than this amount. We would hardly claim that no such dictionaries have any value; indeed, many paperback dictionaries offer impressive scope along with delightful economy. On the other hand, some inexpensive dictionaries are overpriced for the value offered. A paperback dictionary based on a 20-year-old lexicon and definitions may not be worth even its low price.

We urge any reader who considers buying a low-cost dictionary to take advantage first of the resources in this book by reading this chapter to learn what factors are important in evaluating dictionaries and how different works may be analyzed in light of those factors. This volume can help in another way; reviews of parent works, such as MERRIAM-WEBSTER'S COLLEGIATE DICTIONARY, can be used as a guide to the authority, quality, and currency of inexpensive paperbacks derived from it, such as *Webster's Compact Dictionary*. We offer one other piece of advice to the budget-conscious dictionary shopper: dictionaries are great values for the money. Comprehensive dictionaries offer a wealth of information and features in a durable binding at a cost that may not greatly exceed the price of a smaller, less sturdy, less authoritative paperback. Lowest price is not always the best buy.

Structure of Reviews for Children's Dictionaries

Criteria for judging children's dictionaries differ from those appropriate for adult dictionaries. As a result, we follow two different formats for the works evaluated in this part of the Buying Guide. Here we will explain the criteria used to analyze works meant for young children; in the next section we address the structure of reviews for dictionaries meant for users from middle school through adults.

Children's dictionaries come in three main types. First are the *word books* that are created for the benefit of preschoolers and kindergartners. These books rely on pictures and labels, often grouping together related objects in a scene that would appeal to children, such as a park or a beach. These works help young children prepare to read by learning to associate written words with concepts.

Picture dictionaries are created for students who are beginning to read. These books generally include a limited lexicon, but begin to incorporate more traditional dictionary features. Words are not just listed, but defined—and sometimes multiple definitions are acknowledged. Some of these dictionaries also include usage examples. Illustrations still play an important role in these works, but by moving into the language itself, picture dictionaries can include abstractions that are not available to the object-oriented word books.

The third type consists of bona fide dictionaries, although they may lack many of the lexicographical features of the major adult versions. Still, these children's dictionaries are much larger than the word books and picture dictionaries and provide more detailed information on the entry words. These works differ from one another in amount of detail, but they draw from such common language concerns as parts of speech, multiple definitions, pronunciations, syllabication, etymologies, usage notes, and synonyms and antonyms. Illustrations may still be present, but the main focus of the work is on the words themselves.

While this division of children's dictionaries into three categories makes it seem simple to compare one with another, children's dictionaries do not always neatly conform to these categories. Publishers may not always be clear about which category a given work belongs to. For every clearly labeled title like the ROUND THE WORLD PICTURE WORD BOOK there is a confusing one like MY PICTIONARY (is it a word book or a picture dictionary?). Generally speaking, works entitled *My First Dictionary,* or some variation thereof, are picture dictionaries; those called *Children's Dictionary* belong to the third category outlined above. The reviews themselves often compare one work with another, clarifying which of all the works reviewed here are truly competing works. We next examine the structure of those reviews to see what criteria are used to judge children's dictionaries.

Facts at a Glance. Each review begins with a list of basic factual information, such as the names of the publisher and editor; the number of pages, words, and illustrations; the intended readership; the trim size and binding; and pricing and ordering information. This information was all supplied by the work's publisher and is accurate at the time it was given. When the publisher did not supply the information, the data printed here is followed by the notation (*reviewer estimate*).

Scope and Format. The body of each review begins with a description of the work in general terms, including its size (pages, number of words defined, and illustrations), audience (age or grade levels), and general aims. In many cases these aims are quoted directly from the editor's introduction. This section briefly states how words are defined and whether any traditional lexicographical features (pronunciation, etymologies, or usage notes) are included.

Reviewers also note what edition is reviewed, mentioning the copyright year of the edition and any information regarding printing if that differs from the copyright date.

In this initial section, reviewers also evaluate the work in terms of its format, noting whether the overall look of the book is attractive and appealing to children, whether children can easily manage the size of the book, whether the paper quality is adequate, and whether the binding can withstand heavy use—a particularly important question for this market.

Authority. This section discusses the publisher's reputation for preparing reference works and mentions any other dictionaries published by that firm. Reviewers identify the editor or compiler who prepared the work, noting whether these individuals are specialists or have any other particular qualifications that suit them to the task of making a children's dictionary. They discuss the lexicographical database that forms the basis for the dictionary, as stated by the publisher.

Entries. In this section, reviewers evaluate the work in terms of the scope and quality of the treatment of entries. They comment on whether definitions are limited to one meaning or offer multiple meanings and, if only one meaning is given, whether the sense chosen is the most frequently encountered one. Reviews also comment on the accuracy and clarity of the definitions—key concerns in works aimed at pre-readers and early readers—and the quality and clarity of the other lexicographical features, such as etymologies, pronunciations, or usage notes.

To assess the quality, comprehensiveness, and clarity of the definitions, reviewers checked treatment of the following words in each work: **bird** (which should note that not all birds are able to fly); **family** (which should reflect the legitimacy of nontraditional families); **left** (the direction); **red** (which should reveal how abstractions are defined); and **star** (to see whether multiple definitions are included). Reviewers may also discuss the definitions of other words of their own choosing.

Reviewers also comment in this section on approximately how many words are illustrated.

Illustrations. In this section, reviewers provide detailed assessments of the illustrations themselves. First they note the style of the illustrations—whether they are color or black and white, photographs or drawings, or a mixture. Most important, reviewers comment on whether the illustrations clarify or obscure the meaning of the word being portrayed. This means evaluating the quality of the illustrations, commenting on how appealing the art should be to children at the level of the intended audience. Reviews also note the degree to which illustrations avoid using stereotypes by offering a balance of males and females and a reasonable representation of characters from diverse racial and ethnic groups.

Finally, reviewers assess the currency of the illustrations to ensure that they reflect contemporary situations.

Summary. The final section in each review describes any special features that the dictionary may include; for example, some children's dictionaries include word-related game activities. Reviewers also comment on the appropriateness of these features for the ability level of the work's audience.

The evaluation concludes with a summary that recaps the dictionary's strengths and weaknesses, commenting on whether the work is a reasonable value for the price and assessing its worth in relation to competing works.

Facsimiles. About two-thirds of the children's dictionary reviews are accompanied by a page reproduced from the work in question. These facsimiles, often reduced to fit on the pages of the Buying Guide, give the reader a feel for what the work looks like and allow us to highlight the work's main features. Children's dictionaries are mostly illustrated in color, which does not convert well to our black-and-white format. Thus these facsimiles should not be used to judge the quality or attractiveness of the illustrations, as any conclusions drawn would be unfair. The facsimiles do, however, provide a sense of the layout of the page, the combined use of text and art to explain and illustrate a word's meaning, and the clarity and readability of the text. Although they provide a useful first look at the work, we still urge readers to look at an actual copy of the dictionary in question—whenever possible—before making a final decision.

Structure of Reviews for Dictionaries Aimed at Users from Middle School to Adults

Dictionaries aimed at older students and adult users offer more sophisticated and varied lexicographical features than those intended for beginning readers. The reviews for these works, therefore, are more involved. The sections employed in these reviews are listed and explained below. Describing the criteria that our reviewers used will highlight some of the features of general dictionaries, giving the prospective purchaser a sound basis for making an evaluation of the works reviewed.

In this Buying Guide, the term *special dictionaries* refers to two main kinds of reference works. The first type—ESL dictionaries—is used primarily by ESL teachers and nonnative learners of English of all ages. These dictionaries typically feature a lexicon based on a core vocabulary—the most commonly used words in spoken and written communication. Many also provide detailed usage information and numerous example phrases or sentences.

The second type of special dictionary—visual dictionaries—is often used by nonnative learners of English, as well as by people who want to know the name of a specific item and curious browsers. Visual dictionaries contain detailed illustrations with labels or callouts identifying each part. These books do not include many of the features found in standard dictionaries, such as definitions, pronunciations, part-of-speech labels, synonyms, or usage guides. Instead, the illustrations are used to "define" each word. Because visual dictionaries are so different from standard dictionaries, the formats of these reviews vary according to the features found in each individual visual dictionary.

Facts at a Glance. Each review opens with a listing of basic statistical information about the dictionary—the names of the publisher and editor or compiler; the number of volumes, pages, entries, and illustrations; the age or ability level of the intended readership; the trim size, binding, and price; and ordering information. This information was supplied by the work's publisher and was accurate at the time that it was given. Some of the data—price, for instance—may, of course, change in the future. When the publisher did not supply the information printed here, we include the notation (*reviewer estimate*).

Introduction and Scope. This section provides a brief description of the work's purpose and intended audience and comments on the relation of this work to other general dictionaries by the same publisher. Pertinent statements about the purposes or content from the introduction or preface of the work are included here.

As part of this section, reviewers note the edition of the dictionary reviewed, a point that may cause confusion to some users. Dictionaries are not revised each year, as many general encyclopedias are. Nevertheless, a dictionary copyrighted one year can be updated and revised prior to a subsequent printing without the publisher feeling justified in claiming a new copyright. Thus, a work with a 1987 copyright may have information from 1993 in its biographical section if that portion of the work was revised prior to a new printing in 1994. We have endeavored to state clearly which edition and printing formed the basis of our review (of course, these efforts are limited to the clarity of the information provided by the publisher in the work itself). The user of this Buying Guide, similarly, should check *current* editions at the time of considering a purchase to see if errors or omissions noted in a review here have been rectified in a subsequent printing.

Authority. This section briefly summarizes the history of the work, including its previous editions and general reputation, as well as the publisher's involvement with dictionaries (as that affects the authority of the work being reviewed). Reviewers comment on the credentials of the editor or editors and of other individuals (for example, a panel of usage experts) on whose reputation the dictionary relies for authority. They also comment on the lexicographical database that forms the basis for the definitions, plus any research that the publisher states was used to develop the word list. Many publishers mention the extent and origin of their citation files; such information is presented here.

This assessment of the authority of a dictionary gives buyers some basis on which to judge its contents. Buyers should keep in mind, however, that some dictionaries that originated with well-researched word lists prepared by experienced lexicographers have now fallen into the hands of less-skilled editors or publishers whose main concern is to keep a database that is inexpensive to maintain and lucrative to foist on an unsuspecting public. Thus, a reputation for authority can guide the buyer in the initial selection of a work, but cannot be substituted for a thorough assessment of the work's contents.

Comprehensiveness of Entries. In these reviews, comprehensiveness is viewed from a few perspectives. First is the size of the lexicon and how that size compares with the scope of competing works. Reviewers base their analysis on the publisher's representations.

Second is the character of the lexicon. Reviewers analyzed a random sample of 50 words (that do not share a common prefix), counting the number of scientific and technical terms included, as a way of determining the technical or general nature of the work. Reviewers also comment on whether the work includes vulgarisms (the presence of which may be undesirable to some users) and whether it shows evidence of Britishisms in entry words, spellings, or definitions.

Third is the presence or absence of such lexicographical features as etymologies, synonym or antonym guides, usage labels and usage notes, and citations or quoted examples. Reviewers comment on the accuracy and usefulness of these elements, quoting from actual reviews to indicate any of these features found to be either outstanding or deficient. Reviewers also note whether quoted examples are real quotations or invented phrases and how effectively the example illustrates the sense of the word to which it is linked.

Reviewers of ESL dictionaries, in particular, comment on these features because synonym studies, usage notes, and quoted examples can help make the language come alive for the new learner of English.

Reviewers are careful to make judgments on these special features appropriate to the editorial aims of the work in question. Every dictionary cannot have the extensive quotation files of the OED (nor should every dictionary have them), and some dictionaries choose to eschew etymologies. There is nothing wrong with such a decision—many dictionary buyers have no desire for more extensive studies of word origins. Our purpose is to describe the scope of the work, leaving it to the reader to determine if the practices of one work or another are suitable to his or her needs.

The fourth area that forms part of the evaluation of a dictionary's comprehensiveness is whether biographical or geographical entries are included and, if so, whether they are found within the main lexicon or placed in separate sections. To have a sense of the scope and currency of such entries (if a dictionary does indeed contain such entries), reviewers looked for inclusion of the following people and places: **Violeta Chamorro; Germany** as a unified country; **Michael Jackson; Lithuania; Ukraine;** and **Boris Yeltsin.**

Quality and Currency of Entries. This section characterizes the entries and the definitions included in a dictionary—their extent, quality, variety, and usefulness. The reviewers also assess whether or not the entries will meet the needs of the intended users.

Reviewers comment on whether definitions are accurate and to the point, whether they are adequate (within the context of the dictionary's scope) or too brief, whether meanings are carefully discriminated, and whether special senses are labeled. They also note, drawing on the publisher's information, whether definitions are ordered in terms of chronology of meaning or frequency of use. They discuss the clarity of the definitions by noting the reading or understanding level that would be required to comprehend a definition.

Reviews describe the general sequence of information in the entries (for example, main word, pronunciations, part-of-speech labels, etymologies) and note how senses and homographs (two words spelled alike but with different meanings) are ordered. In part, the sequence of information presented in dictionaries depends on custom: a bold main entry word is usually followed by its respelled pronunciation. Thereafter, the sequence varies considerably. Buyers will want to look at the sequence of information of each work to determine if such items as the part of speech, field label, or etymology can be located easily. Buyers should also check on the discriminated senses of words to note whether they are numbered within entries or otherwise clearly differentiated.

Entries for a given word differ markedly from one dictionary to the next. To help identify those differences, reviewers reprint a sample entry from each work. These samples show the structure of the dictionary's entries and provide some sense of the flavor of its definitions. Facsimiles, when they are included, also provide a chance to glimpse the work's treatment of entries.

To assess the currency of the dictionary, reviewers looked for the following entries: **bungee jumping, dis, fax, HDTV, intifada, maquiladora, rap** (as a kind of music), **retrovirus,** and **virtual reality.**

Syllabication and Pronunciation. This section briefly discusses how the main entry words are divided into syllables, and how pronunciation information is conveyed. Syllabication is covered by describing how word breaks are shown and indicating whether they are given only for main entry words or also for inflected forms. Reviewers indicate whether the work's pronunciations are based on the International Phonetic Alphabet (IPA) or some other system. They also point out the location of the pronunciation key (this is usually somewhere in the front matter of the dictionary) and whether condensed versions appear within the body of the work.

The reviews also explain a dictionary's method of indicating acceptable alternate pronunciations and whether the work includes regional variations.

Accessibility. Accessibility means the ease with which a reader can locate the required information within a dictionary. The reviews describe how information is placed on a dictionary's pages and point out the specific finding aids—such as guide words and thumb indexes—that assist the dictionary user in locating information in the lexicon or elsewhere in the work. Among the topics addressed here are the alphabetization of entries, including how abbreviations are treated.

Each review includes a description of any introductory material or guides to using the contents of a dictionary. These important sections should have clear headings and specific instructions with examples. This is especially true of dictionaries intended for students. Reviewers comment on the comprehensiveness, clarity, and overall usefulness of these sections.

Special Features. In this section, reviewers describe and comment on any special sections that are included in the dictionary. The purpose of this section is to point out the kinds of additional information provided and to assess their quality, currency, and usefulness. Reviews note when these features seem to be merely tacked onto a dictionary or when they do not match the standards of the main vocabulary.

Readers' needs for such additional material will vary. In general, biographical and geographical lists are useful for quick checking of unfamiliar names or places, although readers should not rely on the dates in these sections—dictionaries are generally updated less frequently than almanacs or encyclopedias. Full, up-to-date lists of abbreviations are valuable features in a dictionary because abbreviations and acronyms are used with such frequency. Student dictionaries often include extended sections of background information on language and writing, which can be useful reminders of principles that students are taught in their writing classes.

Graphics and Format. The illustrations, general appearance, and physical format are important features of any dictionary. Because a dictionary must stand up to frequent use, a sturdy binding and paper of good quality, preferably with a minimum of show-through from one page to another, are necessary. Durability is especially important for any dictionary that many people will use, as in a library or office—or even in the home. This section assesses all these features, as well as the suitability of the format to the work's contents and purpose.

Reviewers also comment on illustrations, captions, tables, and charts as they relate to definitions. They note whether these elements clarify the meaning of definitions or obscure them and whether the illustrations themselves are clear and of adequate size to be understood.

The reviews describe the general appearance of entry words and other features, noting whether the type size is adequate for reading, the margins are ample enough for clarity, and the key words (entry words and guide words) are sufficiently distinguished typographically to stand out.

Summary. The summary of each dictionary's evaluation coordinates the main points made in each section of the review to provide an overall evaluation of the work's merit, often making brief comparisons with similar works. The strengths and weaknesses of the volume are balanced and a general judgment as to its overall quality and specific usefulness given.

Facsimiles. As with the reviews of children's dictionaries, about two-thirds of the reviews of adult dictionaries are accompanied by the reproduction of parts of pages from the original work. These facsimiles are often *not* reductions from the original, unlike the case for other facsimiles in this book, so they provide a good sense of the size and readability of the type. (If a facsimile is a reduction, the percentage by which the page is reduced is mentioned beneath the facsimile.)

Derived Works. Some dictionaries are derived from longer works, employing the same format for presenting words and definitions but condensing the lexicon or eliminating certain special features. Reviews of these works are shorter and are organized as follows:

Facts at a Glance
Introduction and Scope
Special Features
Graphics and Format
Summary

These reviews refer the reader to the review of the main work for a full discussion of such issues as the quality of the definitions and other lexicographical concerns. The review of the derived work focuses on differences between it and the parent work in terms of the size of the word list and the comprehensiveness of the information supplied.

Derived reviews are *not* used for some works—such as THE AMERICAN HERITAGE COLLEGE DICTIONARY—that are derived from unabridged dictionaries (in this case, THE AMERICAN HERITAGE DICTIONARY OF THE ENGLISH LANGUAGE) but are major works in their own right.

Glossary

For users of this guide who are unfamiliar with some of the terms employed in these reviews, the following glossary is provided:

abridged (dictionary). Any adult dictionary that is not **unabridged;** a dictionary of about 50,000 to 300,000 entries condensed, shortened, or reduced from a larger or longer work.

antonym. A word that has an opposite or nearly opposite meaning to another. See **synonym.**

citation(s). The source(s) of definitions; quotations in the context of actual usage used to provide a basis for defining new words and new meanings or senses of established words.

citation file. A collection of illustrative quotations, usually from newspapers, magazines, or books with a wide reading public, in the context of actual usage that is kept by the publisher and used to develop lexical matter.

college (dictionary). A category of dictionary usually containing from 130,000 to 170,000 entries, desk-sized and directed toward the vocabulary needs of the college community.

concise (dictionary). A dictionary that is abridged or condensed; one with little detail.

condensed (dictionary). A dictionary with shortened definitions or an abbreviated lexicon; sometimes called *compact.*

cross-reference. A key word or phrase directing the reader from one entry or word in the dictionary to another.

definition. The meaning of a word (most effective if it avoids circularity) or the defining of a word using the same word or a variant form.

desk (dictionary). A dictionary with from 50,000 to 100,000 words, conveniently sized for home or office use.

D'Nealian® Alphabet. Oval, slanted letters, introduced in 1978 into the elementary schools, that are more like cursive writing than traditional print letters. Intended to make cursive easier for children to learn.

discriminated. Meanings and usages of words that are carefully distinguished to identify the subtle shades of meaning.

entry. A word or phrase identified to be defined. Also called a *main entry.* See also **run-on entry.**

ESL. An acronym standing for English as a Second Language, referring to those students who are nonnative speakers of English, whether they are children or adults. Also referred to as ELT (English language teaching).

etymology. The study of word origins.

field label. A qualifying term that restricts a word's meaning to its use in a specific area in the sciences or technical field. Used to identify a specialized definition.

finding aid. Any device that helps a reader find information in a reference work, such as **guide words** and **cross-references.**

guide word(s). A term at the head of a column or page that repeats the first or last entry on that page.

homograph(s). Words that are spelled the same way but are often pronounced differently and have different meanings (for example, a *lead* pencil and to *lead* the way).

homonym(s). Words that are spelled and pronounced the same way but have different meanings (for example, a polar *bear* and to *bear* arms).

homophone(s). Words that are spelled differently and have different meanings but sound alike (for example, *to, two,* and *too*).

idiom. A phrase whose meaning cannot be understood from the definitions of its separate parts; an expression that functions as a single unit that conveys distinctive meanings in a particular language.

inflected form. Any word that reflects an alteration (as of number, tense, or person).

IPA. International Phonetic Association; also International Phonetic Alphabet. IPA designates a phonetic pronunciation system.

lexicon. A dictionary; also, the dictionary's main vocabulary or word list.

nonstandard. A label used in some dictionaries to indicate words or usages not considered acceptable in all circumstances.

phonetic. Notation of actual speech sounds with a distinct set of symbols, each representing a particular sound or articulation. American English has about 45 distinct speech sounds.

run-on entry. A word added to the end of an entry that is related to the entry, formed by adding or dropping suffixes or prefixes, and easily understood in terms of the meaning of the main entry.

semi-abridged (dictionary). A category of dictionary intermediate in size between **college** and **unabridged,** with 200,000 or slightly more entries.

standard. A term that refers to words or usage generally recognized and accepted as correct by all native speakers of the language.

synonym. A word that can be substituted for another word that is close in meaning; see also **antonym.**

synonym study. A longer descriptive paragraph in a dictionary that lists and distinguishes among a variety of synonyms.

unabridged (dictionary). A dictionary that is not condensed; a category that includes works with over 300,000 and up to 600,000 entries that provides full coverage of the vocabulary of a language that is in general use. Quotations are generally provided to support definitions and illustrate context and varieties of usage.

usage label. Information given in a dictionary to identify restrictive or special usage of a particular word or phrase.

usage note. Information given in a dictionary that discusses the standard and other uses of a given word.

variant. A slight difference in the form of a word such as an alternate acceptable spelling or pronunciation.

WNI rule. The principle that all words used in a definition should appear in the dictionary; the initials come from the phrase *words not in.*

word history. A term used in some dictionaries for short studies of a word's etymology.

Chapter 10
Evaluations of Children's Dictionaries

The American Heritage Children's Dictionary

Facts at a Glance

Full title: **The American Heritage Children's Dictionary**

Publisher: Houghton Mifflin

Editors: staff of the American Heritage dictionaries

Edition reviewed: © 1994

Number of pages: 864

Number of entries: 37,000

Number of illustrations: more than 800, all in full color

Intended readership: grades 3 to 6

Trim size: 8″ × 10″

Binding: hardcover

Price: $14.95

ISBN 0-395-69191-5

No stated revision policy

Scope and Format

The 1994 edition of *The American Heritage Children's Dictionary* is an 864-page work with 37,000 entries and more than 800 full-color photographs and drawings. The book is aimed at children in grades 3 to 6 who have advanced beyond beginning dictionaries and are ready for a more comprehensive reference work.

The dictionary provides the lexicographic features that are appropriate for this age level, including defini-tions, pronunciations, and parts of speech for all words and example sentences for many words. In addition, homophones and idioms are sprinkled throughout. Other features, including synonyms, etymologies, and prefixes and suffixes, appear in color-coded boxes adjacent to the corresponding entry word. The dictionary does not, however, include biographical or geographical entries.

At the front of the work, a 17-page "How to Use This Dictionary" section explains how to find information in the dictionary and describes the many parts of the book. This section includes a full pronunciation key and a one-page "Preview of the Dictionary," which is a sample page with labels. This user's guide is detailed and com-prehensive, but it is written using language that children at this level will understand.

At 8″ × 10″, the book is a standard size for this age level. As with the other dictionaries in the American Heritage series, this volume is sturdily bound and should withstand years of use.

Authority

Houghton Mifflin is the publisher of the highly regarded American Heritage dictionaries, which include refer-ence works for both children and adults. *The American Heritage Children's Dictionary* was previously pub-lished in 1986. According to the promotional material for the book, it has been "thoroughly revised and ex-panded for the 1990s. . . ."

The American Heritage Children's Dictionary is the third in a series of four dictionaries for children. The se-ries also includes THE AMERICAN HERITAGE PICTURE DIC-

TIONARY, THE AMERICAN HERITAGE FIRST DICTIONARY, and THE AMERICAN HERITAGE STUDENT'S DICTIONARY.

As with the other books in this series, *The American Heritage Children's Dictionary* was created by Houghton Mifflin's staff of professional dictionary editors. In addition, a list of consultants, which includes advisory boards for science and mathematics and for language arts, is provided at the front of the book. The names listed include many childhood educators and specialists from schools across the United States. The publisher does not indicate how the dictionary's word list was chosen.

Entries

Similar to WEBSTER'S NEW WORLD CHILDREN'S DICTIONARY, *The American Heritage Children's Dictionary* introduces each letter of the alphabet with a history of the letter's evolution. Accompanying this history is a watercolor illustration of an animal whose name begins with the letter being introduced. On the pages that follow, the focus letter appears in white on a magenta-colored block on each right-hand page. Guide words are shown in the top corner of each page in a strip of the same color.

Entry words are shown in bold type and overhang the text. Each entry word is followed by the part of speech and the definition. Multiple definitions are provided and numbered. Example sentences, shown in italics and preceded by a colon, are provided for many entry words. (One slightly negative aspect of these example sentences is that the entry word is not highlighted.) The pronunciation of the entry word appears at the end of the entry instead of at the beginning. It is shown with the inflected forms of the word and is not readily visible.

Definitions are clear, accurate, and comprehensive and use words that will be understood by the book's intended audience of 8- to 11-year-old children. The following is a typical entry:

> **pair** *noun* **1.** A set of two identical or matched things that are usually used together: *I lost a pair of shoes.* **2.** One thing that is made up of two connected parts: *I used a pair of scissors to cut the fabric.* **3.** Two persons or animals; couple: *A pair of dancers circled the ballroom floor.*
> ◊*verb* To arrange in or form pairs.
> **pair** (pâr) ◊*noun, plural* **pairs** ◊*verb* **paired, pairing** ||*These sound alike:* **pair, pare, pear**

Definitions are also current, reflecting contemporary themes and situations. The entry for **family,** for example, contains six numbered definitions, including one that allows for alternative lifestyles: "All the members of a household who live under one roof."

Illustrations

The book's pages have a crisp, contemporary look. Approximately 75 percent of the 800 full-color illustrations are photographs, and 25 percent are drawings. The sharp, colorful photographs are a highlight of the book and will most certainly appeal to the intended audience. Illustrations appear near the entry word to which they refer and are labeled with the entry word. Occasionally, a phrase or sentence has been included to provide additional information or clarification. For example, under the illustration and label for **mollusk** is the following: "Clams and snails are kinds of mollusks."

Most of the illustrations are quite current. A photograph of a contemporary **computer** is shown, and the illustration for **disk** shows three different types of computer disks. The entry for **inauguration** is illustrated with a photograph of Bill Clinton being sworn in as president. The illustrations depict an equal number of men and women and avoid gender stereotypes. Women are shown wearing construction and baseball **helmets,** throwing a **discus,** and using a **microscope.** In addition, ethnic and racial groups are well represented in the illustrations.

Special Features

Many special features appear throughout the book in the form of highlighted boxes. These color-coded boxes contain synonym guides (some of which also include antonyms), word histories, and "Vocabulary Builders," which give examples of how to use prefixes and suffixes. "Language Detective" boxes, a unique feature of this dictionary, describe regional variations in vocabulary. In addition to these features, a short thesaurus appears at the back of the book. It contains synonyms and example sentences that are appropriate for the intended audience.

Summary

The American Heritage Children's Dictionary compares favorably with WEBSTER'S NEW WORLD CHILDREN'S DICTIONARY. Both works have clear, age-appropriate definitions, though the former has about 4,000 more entries than the latter. Both works also have beautiful, contemporary illustrations, which are superior to those found in THORNDIKE-BARNHART CHILDREN'S DICTIONARY. WEBSTER'S NEW WORLD CHILDREN'S DICTIONARY does have an advantage over *The American Heritage Children's Dictionary,* however, because it includes biographical and geographical entries, neither of which are found in the other work. Nonetheless, *The American Heritage Children's Dictionary* is a valuable reference tool for elementary school students and would be an excellent addition to a home, school, or library.

The American Heritage First Dictionary

Facts at a Glance

Full title: **The American Heritage First Dictionary**
Publisher: Houghton Mifflin
Editors: Kaethe Ellis, Senior Coordinating Editor;
   David M. Weeks, Senior Editor
Edition reviewed: © 1994

Number of pages: 368
Number of entries: 1,800
Number of illustrations: more than 650, all in full color
Intended readership: grades 1 to 2
Trim size: 8″ × 10″
Binding: hardcover

Price: $13.95
ISBN 0-395-67289-9
No stated revision policy

Scope and Format

The 1994 edition of *The American Heritage First Dictionary* contains 368 pages filled with 1,800 entries and more than 650 full-color illustrations. The book is intended for children in first and second grade who are starting to learn how to read and write.

Each definition in this dictionary consists of a few short sentences, and variant forms of words are provided. As with other dictionaries for this level, pronunciations, parts of speech, and usage notes are not included.

The book's trim size is similar to that of other dictionaries for this age group. The hardcover binding should withstand years of use in the home, school, or library.

Authority

Houghton Mifflin publishes many school and reference books, including a series of children's dictionaries. According to the book's back cover, these American Heritage dictionaries were developed by Houghton Mifflin's "staff of professional dictionary editors supported by expert educational consultants." Unlike THE AMERICAN HERITAGE PICTURE DICTIONARY, which describes the research involved in the selection of the book's word list, *The American Heritage First Dictionary* does not state the criteria on which its vocabulary selection was based. The 1994 edition of *The American Heritage First Dictionary* has been completely updated and redesigned since the 1986 edition.

Entries

The American Heritage First Dictionary begins with a four-page section called "How to Use Your Dictionary," which is directed toward the young reader. This section uses examples from within the book to explain how to look up words and to show what types of information are provided in the dictionary.

At the top corner of each page in the book, the focus letter is displayed in uppercase in a green square, and the lowercase letter appears beneath it in an orange diamond. Guide words are also provided at the top of each page.

Entry words are presented in large blue type, which matches the type in the letters and guide words at the top of the pages. As in the MACMILLAN FIRST DICTIONARY, definitions are written in complete sentences for easier comprehension. Two or more sentences are given for each entry word. Many entries include example sentences and variant forms of words. Every time the entry word—or a variant form of the word—appears, it is shown in bold type. For instance, the entry for **carry** reads:

> To **carry** means to hold something and take it somewhere. Lindsay **carries** her lunch in a bag.—**carries, carried**

The definitions are clear and accurate and use language that is accessible to children in first and second grades. The information provided illustrates the word and clarifies its meaning. The definition for **bird** is a good example:

> A **bird** is a kind of animal. It has two wings and is covered with feathers. Robins, chickens, eagles, and ostriches are all **birds.** Most **birds** can fly.

Multiple definitions are sometimes provided and are numbered. When homonyms are given, they are shown as separate entries with superscripts.

Illustrations

A creative mixture of photographs and drawings introduces each letter of the alphabet. Colorful drawings of the letter (in both uppercase and lowercase) are combined with photographs of one or more children "playing" with the letters. For example, a young boy is shown "pulling" a drawing of an *M* and "carrying" an *m*. The bright and cheerful colors and playful approach are inviting. Underneath this illustration, the entire alphabet is displayed in both uppercase and lowercase, with the focus letter highlighted.

The illustrations in *The American Heritage First Dictionary* are colorful, vivid, and lively. About two-thirds of the illustrations are full-color photographs, and the other one-third are full-color drawings. Most pages contain between one and three illustrations, which appear adjacent to the words they represent.

Simple, one-word labels accompany the illustrations. Most illustrations are self-explanatory. For others, however, it is necessary to read the definition to understand what is being illustrated. For example, the illustration for **both** shows a girl eating a sandwich. The definition reads, "**Both** means two together. Naomi uses **both** hands to eat a sandwich." This may be confusing for children who are merely browsing through the dictionary, looking at the pictures and not necessarily reading every definition. In other cases, the illustration may be somewhat misleading. For example, the illustrations for **cheek, lip, mouth,** and **smile** are virtually the same—head-and-shoulders photographs of children. No indication is given as to which part of the illustration represents the entry word. An additional cause for confusion is that the labels provided beneath the illustrations always show the singular form of the word, even though the illustrations sometimes depict the plural form.

The book avoids the use of stereotypes: a male **nurse** is shown helping a patient, and men are shown doing the **laundry** and using the **oven** and the **stove;** women are presented in the illustrations for **doctor** and **scientist.** The illustrations show a balance of males and females, and various ethnic and racial groups are represented. In addition, the photographs appear quite contemporary. The computers and printer shown in the photographs for **computer** and **machine** look current, and the clothing worn by the people in the photographs is not dated.

Summary

The definitions in *The American Heritage First Dictionary* are exceptionally clear and easily accessible to the intended audience of children in first and second grade. The colorful illustrations are lively and inviting and give the work a contemporary look. In some cases, however, the connection of the illustration to the entry word cannot be understood without first reading the entry. Despite this fact, the work compares favorably with other dictionaries for this age group, such as the MACMILLAN FIRST DICTIONARY. *The American Heritage First Dictionary* serves as a good beginning dictionary for children who are learning how to read and write. It would be a good choice for home, school, or library purchase.

The American Heritage Picture Dictionary

Facts at a Glance

Full title: **The American Heritage Picture Dictionary**
Publisher: Houghton Mifflin
Compiler: Robert L. Hillerich
Illustrator: Maggie Swanson
Edition reviewed: © 1989, 1994 printing

Number of pages: 144
Number of entries: 900
Number of illustrations: 650, all in full color
Intended readership: kindergarten to grade 1
Trim size: 8½″ × 11″
Binding: hardcover

Price: $10.95
ISBN 0-395-69585-6
No stated revision policy

Scope and Format

The 1994 printing of the 1989 edition of *The American Heritage Picture Dictionary* is a 144-page book containing 900 entries and 650 full-color illustrations. Although this work is called a picture dictionary, it actually falls between the categories of picture word book and picture dictionary. Unlike many picture dictionaries, this book does not provide definitions. However, because example sentences are included for about half of the entries, this work provides more information than a standard picture word book.

This dictionary is intended for use by children in kindergarten and first grade. According to the book's preface

> The *American Heritage Picture Dictionary* is designed to provide the help and encouragement young children need now, in the preschool and early primary years, as well as to provide the readiness that will be needed in the future for more advanced levels of dictionary use.

At 8½″ × 11″, this work is the size of a standard notebook. The hardcover binding appears to be sturdy and durable.

Authority

Houghton Mifflin is the publisher of the highly respected family of American Heritage dictionaries. *The American Heritage Picture Dictionary* is the first in the publisher's series of children's dictionaries, which also includes THE AMERICAN HERITAGE FIRST DICTIONARY (for grades 1 and 2), THE AMERICAN HERITAGE CHILDREN'S DICTIONARY (for grades 3 to 6), and THE AMERICAN HERITAGE STUDENT'S DICTIONARY (for grades 6 to 9). *The American Heritage Picture Dictionary* was first published in 1986, revised in 1989, and reprinted in 1994. A comparison of the current edition with the 1986 edition revealed that few changes appear to have been made.

The book's preface indicates that the words included in this dictionary "have been carefully chosen from studies of children's reading, speaking, and writing vocabularies." The preface details the extensive research involved in the compilation of the word list "from an analysis of ten different word counts." The book's compiler, Robert L. Hillerich, has published several well-known pedagogical works.

Entries

The American Heritage Picture Dictionary begins with a preface directed at teachers and parents. This is followed by two pages for children—simple directions on how to use the dictionary and basic activities to help children become familiar with the book.

The book employs two formats to display the entries. The first (and most prevalent in the book) shows the entry word in blue type with the accompanying illustration beneath it. Entry words are listed in alphabetical order, and all entry words are illustrated. Example sentences, which are provided for roughly half of the entry words, are shown between the entry word and the illustration. The sentences are in black type, with the entry word appearing in blue. Example sentences are provided for words, including verbs and adjectives, whose meaning would be better understood when shown in the context of a sentence. For example, the illustration for **same** shows two identical puppies accompanied by the sentence, "Alex and Buster are the **same.**" Example sentences are not provided for those entry words whose illustration makes the word's meaning self-explanatory. Examples of entries without sentences include nouns such as **house, kitten,** and **umbrella.**

The second format used is more like that found in picture word books. Nine topics are illustrated on single pages or two-page spreads at the back of the book: "Astronaut," "Body," "Classroom," "Dinosaur," "Farm," "Games and Fun," "Supermarket," "Word," and "Zoo." On these pages, various scenes are depicted, and the objects within the scene are labeled. For example, the two-page spread entitled "Supermarket" displays aisles with shoppers and food. The labels include **bananas, carrots, cashier, eggs, juices, milk, paper bag, potatoes, register, scanner,** and **shopping cart.**

The dictionary uses a cross-referencing system to tie in the topics illustrated at the end of the book with the entry words given in the first part of the book. The topic words are listed within the main text in their proper alphabetical order and appear in a band of color. The word's color is cross-referenced in the border surrounding the illustration in the back of the book and thus to the related words. The explanation for this system is provided in the preface and in the "How to Use Your Dictionary" section. However, without the explanation, this technique is not immediately obvious. Without adult interpretation, it will be lost on many young readers.

Illustrations

All of the illustrations in *The American Heritage Picture Dictionary* are full-color drawings by Maggie Swanson. Many of the illustrations show people participating in various activities. Throughout the work, illustrations use many of the same characters, who are given proper names. This technique creates a sense of consistency, if not excitement. The book's preface suggests that, over time, children will become familiar with these characters. So many different characters are

illustrated, however, that this premise seems somewhat unlikely.

The illustrations in *The American Heritage Picture Dictionary* show a balance of males and females and an excellent representation of minority groups, including people who are physically challenged. The book avoids stereotypes, showing illustrations of females in such nontraditional roles as **doctor, pitcher,** and **police.** Illustrations also depict a man who likes to **cook** and a male **teacher.** The people shown in the illustrations look fairly contemporary.

Summary

The word list for *The American Heritage Picture Dictionary* has been thoroughly researched and is appropriate for the intended audience of children in kindergarten and first grade. In addition, the number of words in the word list is comparable to that of other picture dictionaries for this age group. The book's simple full-color illustrations help enhance the meanings of the entry words and would be appealing to children in this age group. The use of one illustrator for all of the illustrations creates a sense of consistency in visual style but a lack of variety. Prospective buyers looking for a picture word book with more lively and varied illustrations should consider Scott, Foresman's MY PICTIONARY or Dorling Kindersley's MY FIRST DICTIONARY. Nonetheless, *The American Heritage Picture Dictionary* serves as a good introduction to teach beginning readers the skills needed to start using "real" dictionaries, and it would be a good choice for home, school, or library use.

Beginning Dictionary

Facts at a Glance

Full title: **Beginning Dictionary**
Publisher: Macmillan
Editors: William D. Halsey, Editorial Director; Phyllis R. Winant, Supervising Editor
Edition reviewed: © 1987

Number of pages: 816
Number of entries: 30,000
Number of illustrations: 1,200, all in full color
Intended readership: grade 2 and up
Trim size: 8" × 10"
Binding: hardcover

Price: $35.16; $26.37 to schools
Sold directly to schools
ISBN 0-02-195370-8
No stated revision policy

Beginning Dictionary

❶ Example sentences show the entry word in context, sometimes using inflected forms

❷ Pronunciation, parts of speech, and inflections set off at end of an entry

❸ Informal etymologies or language notes are marked with a small solid blue triangle, and set apart from the text by blue rules above and below the paragraph

❹ Four-color illustration of meaning **1**

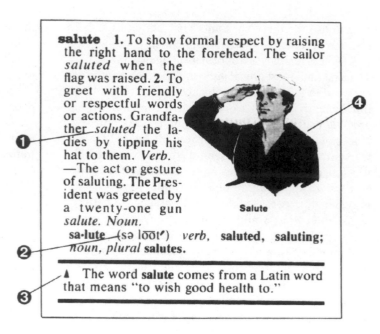

salute **1.** To show formal respect by raising the right hand to the forehead. The sailor *saluted* when the flag was raised. **2.** To greet with friendly or respectful words or actions. Grandfather *saluted* the ladies by tipping his hat to them. *Verb.* —The act or gesture of saluting. The President was greeted by a twenty-one gun *salute. Noun.*
sa·lute (sə lōōt′) *verb,* **saluted, saluting;** *noun, plural* **salutes.**

▲ The word **salute** comes from a Latin word that means "to wish good health to."

Salute

Scope and Format

Macmillan's *Beginning Dictionary* identically reproduces the 724-page word list and the pronunciation key found in the 1987 edition of the MACMILLAN DICTIONARY FOR CHILDREN. Although the latter work was revised in 1989, the *Beginning Dictionary* has not been revised since 1987. The *Beginning Dictionary* contains 30,000 entries and 1,200 full-color illustrations. It is intended for use by elementary school children in grade 2 and above.

The *Beginning Dictionary* opens with a full listing of the volume's contents. The preface, which is directed to adults, especially teachers, defines the book specifically as a *school* dictionary "intended to be the first real dictionary that students use in the classroom." After the preface, an expanded "Guide to the Dictionary" begins with a useful sample page keyed to the guide. The guide uses text, illustrations, and examples to lead students through the process of finding a word and to introduce the many kinds of information—such as spelling, pronunciation, and usage—available in the dictionary.

The *Beginning Dictionary* is sturdily bound and will hold up well to steady use in the home, classroom, or library.

Authority

Macmillan is a well-known publisher of reference books and publishes a line of children's dictionaries. Phyllis R. Winant, the supervising editor of this work, was assisted by a staff of editors, consultants, and artists.

The vocabulary selection for this dictionary was "based on a careful and systematic study of the words actually encountered by students, both in and out of the classroom."

Entries

Entry words are arranged alphabetically, letter by letter. A unique and useful feature of this dictionary, for younger readers, is that entry words appear as they are seen in any other printed source, *not* divided into syllables. As in other Macmillan dictionaries, definitions are grouped according to part of speech and are numbered consecutively. In the case of multiple meanings, the one most commonly used is placed first. Parts of speech are not abbreviated, which will be helpful to young readers. The print is large, and the definitions, which follow the entry words, are stated simply and adequately. For example, the definition of **complacent** is "pleased with oneself; satisfied."

Many illustrative sentences are used to explain a word both in its multiple meanings and in its various parts of speech. These illustrative examples are not set off in any way and could be confused with the definitions themselves, although the entry word within them is italicized. Most entries have only one or two definitions.

Most of the definitions are quite acceptable for the intended age group, but a few are questionable. For example, the second definition given for **colored** is "**2.** Of the Negro race." There is no usage note to indicate that **colored** is not an acceptable substitute for the word *Black*. Nor is the term **black** as clearly defined as it might be in terms of current racial usage. The dictionary merely states in a second definition that a black is "A member of one of the major divisions of the human race." **Indian, Jew,** and **Oriental** with capital first letters are included. *Black* with a capital *B* is not.

The dictionary does not contain any biographical entries, foreign words or phrases, or slang terms. The book's geographical listings include U.S. states (with location and state capital given), major countries of the world (with location and capital given), and continents (with location and, in some cases, relative size given). Due to the book's 1987 publication date, of course, some of the geographical information is outdated. Contractions, prefixes, and suffixes are included as main entries.

Homophones are signaled by a solid black triangle and prefaced with the statement, "Another word that sounds like this is. . . ." The history of words is indicated for some entries. These are attractively presented, varied in their focus, and likely to interest students. Called "Word Stories," they are set apart from the definition by bright blue borders that are signaled by a solid blue triangle. The dictionary does not list synonyms or antonyms, and very few usage notes are provided.

Because the dictionary has not been revised since 1987, the word list is outdated. For example, computer terms are not defined within the text, although a glossary of computer terms (which is also outdated) was added to the back of the book. This practice may not be helpful for young readers who may not know that the word they are seeking is a computer term. Further, not all of these definitions are geared to the dictionary's intended audience.

Illustrations

This dictionary is very attractive and has eye appeal. Each double-column page has from one to three full-color drawings captioned with main entry words. Drawings are two to three inches in size and located immediately above or below the word they help to define. Minority groups are well represented in the drawings. The history of each letter of the alphabet is described and brightly illustrated at the beginning of every letter section.

Special Features

A particularly valuable feature for classroom use is the inclusion of "Try This" exercise sections within the "Guide to the Dictionary": these allow students to practice such skills as alphabetizing, forming words with suffixes and prefixes, and selecting correct verb forms. The *Beginning Dictionary* also contains a useful "Table of English Spellings," enabling students to locate words that they know how to pronounce but not spell.

A number of special features also appear in the back of the dictionary. One is an illustrated listing of events in U.S. history through 1976. Portraits of U.S. presidents through Ronald Reagan appear, along with their dates in office. A glossary of computer terms (discussed above) and tables of measure are included. Geographic information is limited to a map of the United States on a double-page spread and one of the world which, due to the book's 1987 publication date, is very outdated. The dictionary includes an additional feature that would be useful for its intended readers: a 29-page supplement, "Practice Pages," exercises that further reinforce information and skills presented in the guide.

Summary

The *Beginning Dictionary* presents words in the way that they are normally seen in print. This practice makes it easier for children to locate words, but may not prepare them well for other dictionary use as they grow older. It also provides simple, clear definitions of words and uses the words in many illustrative sentences. In addition, it contains numerous colorful pictures, and the large type and layout make it easy for elementary school children to use.

The expanded "Guide to the Dictionary" and practice exercises make it especially appropriate for use in the classroom. However, the book's 1987 copyright date makes works such as WEBSTER'S NEW WORLD CHILDREN'S DICTIONARY or the revised MACMILLAN DICTIONARY FOR CHILDREN more attractive purchases.

The Doubleday Children's Dictionary

Facts at a Glance

Full title: **The Doubleday Children's Dictionary**
Publisher: Doubleday
Compiler: John Grisewood
Edition reviewed: © 1989

Number of pages: 319
Number of entries: over 8,000
Number of illustrations: over 500, most in color
Intended readership: grades 2 to 6 (reviewer estimate)
Trim size: 7½″ × 10″
Binding: hardcover

Price: $14.95
ISBN 0-385-26356-2
No stated revision policy

Scope and Format

The 1989 edition of *The Doubleday Children's Dictionary* has 319 pages with about 8,000 words and definitions and more than 500 illustrations. This work falls into the category of children's dictionaries; however, with only 8,000 word entries, it is substantially smaller than most other dictionaries in this category, including THORNDIKE-BARNHART CHILDREN'S DICTIONARY (28,000 entries) and WEBSTER'S NEW WORLD CHILDREN'S DICTIONARY (33,000 entries).

Each entry in *The Doubleday Children's Dictionary* includes the part of speech and one or more definitions. Pronunciations are given for some words, and sample sentences are sometimes provided. Throughout the book, illustrations appear with captions. In addition, a list of abbreviations used in the dictionary is given in the front of the book.

Although the publisher does not provide the ages of the dictionary's intended audience, the book jacket states, "Children can use the dictionary on their own or side by side with adults; readers of all ages will find something new to learn on every page."

The book has a standard trim size for a children's dictionary. The hardcover binding seems sturdy and durable.

Authority

The Doubleday Children's Dictionary was first published in Hong Kong in 1984. This 1989 edition is the first U.S. edition. Doubleday is a well-known publisher of children's reference books, including THE DOUBLEDAY CHILDREN'S PICTURE DICTIONARY and THE DOUBLEDAY CHILDREN'S ATLAS. The publisher does not describe the method used for developing the word list for this dictionary.

John Grisewood, the compiler of this dictionary, is a graduate in English from Oxford University. When the dictionary was published, he was head of the reference division at Kingfisher Books in London.

Entries

At the top of each page in the dictionary, the focus letter appears in boldface type on a colored block, and a guide word is shown next to it. Each entry word appears in boldface type and is followed by a label indicating the part of speech and then the definition. Multiple definitions are numbered. The number of entry words on each page varies greatly—from roughly 20 to 35—depending on the number and size of the illustrations on the page.

The definitions in this work are an uneven mix. Some definitions are clear and at a suitable level for children in grades 2 through 6. Other definitions, however, are overly complex and contain many words that would be unfamiliar to children in this age group. The following is an example of the second type:

> **nickel** 1. *n.* a tough, hard, silvery-white metal element widely used in the form of plating and in alloys. It is electroplated onto metals such as steel to protect them from corrosion, and is added, with chromium, to steel to make it stainless. 2. *n.* a U.S. coin worth five cents.

The unevenness in this dictionary extends beyond the definitions to the seemingly random inclusion of pro-nunciations and sample sentences. Pronunciations are provided for select word entries, but they are not included for many difficult words. For instance, the pronunciation is provided for **earache** but not for **ecclesiastical.** Similarly, sample sentences are given for **enough** and **ensure** but not for **endeavor** or **endure.**

Interestingly, a significant number of the mere 8,000 entries in *The Doubleday Children's Dictionary* are not found in most other children's dictionaries. Examples of these entries include **balalaika, circumcision, contraception, dyspepsia, farrago, kittiwake, naphtha, portcullis, rape,** and **wadi.** These words are too difficult or inappropriate for children at this level.

Entry words in this dictionary also include several British terms, such as **bonny, lorry,** and **kipper.** In addition, certain entry words with multiple meanings, such as **pound, stone,** and **cracker,** include British usages. These terms and usages reflect the British origins of the work but would most likely confuse American children.

Illustrations

Most of the illustrations in *The Doubleday Children's Dictionary* are full-color drawings. A few of the drawings are in black and white, and a very small number of photographs are included. Most pages have one or two drawings, and in general, the illustrations are well drawn and realistic. The drawings are usually on the same page as the entry words being illustrated, but they are not necessarily adjacent to the words.

Many of the illustrations in the book are historical. Historical drawings are sometimes used when contemporary illustrations would have been more accessible to young readers. For example, the illustration for **actor** is an actor on an Elizabethan stage. The entry for **oar** is illustrated with a Greek trireme.

The book also contains many scientific illustrations with labels. In some cases, these illustrations add noteworthy information and help to clarify difficult concepts. Often, however, the drawings make the concept unnecessarily complicated, and the labels use complex scientific terms. For instance, the illustration for **hair** includes a diagram of skin and a hair follicle, with the labels *hair shaft, erector muscle, sebaceous gland,* and *hair follicle.* None of these terms are defined in this dictionary.

Captions are provided for all of the illustrations in the book. Some captions consist of phrases, while others are complete sentences. Many of the captions provide additional information about the entry word that was not included in the definition. Sometimes, this is a worthwhile tool to help children learn about the word or expand their knowledge. For example, the caption for the illustration of **penguin** reads: "*Penguins use their wings as flippers to swim.*"

In other cases, however, the caption contains high-level words and concepts and would only confuse children at this level. For instance, the illustration for **mermaid** shows dugongs, and the caption reads: "*The legend of the mermaid may have arisen from sailors mistaking the dugong for a human.*" The word *dugong* is not an entry in this dictionary.

An additional problem with the captions in this book is that the entry words are not highlighted. Because the illustrations may appear anywhere on the page with the entry word, it is not always clear which word is being illustrated. Worse yet, sometimes the entry word does not even appear in the caption. For example, the caption for the illustration of **banner** reads: "*Flags of the 16th century.*" The caption under the drawing for **muscle** is: "*To bend your forearm, the biceps contract.*"

Summary

Although *The Doubleday Children's Dictionary* has far fewer entries than other children's dictionaries, the book contains many words that are too difficult or that are inappropriate for its intended audience. The book attempts to go beyond the scope of a standard dictionary by providing children with more information about words than just definitions—an admirable goal. However, the book fails to accomplish this goal because its use of complex terms and concepts makes the work inaccessible to children.

The Doubleday Children's Dictionary also would be visually unappealing to children because of its overuse of historical and scientific illustrations. Several other dictionaries, including AMERICAN HERITAGE CHILDREN'S DICTIONARY and WEBSTER'S NEW WORLD CHILDREN'S DICTIONARY, are much more suitable and inviting to children at this level.

The Doubleday Children's Picture Dictionary

Facts at a Glance

Full title: **The Doubleday Children's Picture Dictionary**
Publisher: Doubleday
Compiler: Felicia Law
Illustrator: Carol Holmes
Edition reviewed: © 1986

Number of pages: 199
Number of entries: over 1, 500
Number of illustrations: 199 pages in full color
Number of maps: 6 in full color
Trim size: 9" × 10¾"
Binding: laminated paper over boards

Price: $16
Intended readership: early elementary grades
Sold in bookstores and other outlets; and also sold to libraries and schools
ISBN 0-385-23711-1
No stated revision policy

Scope and Format

The Doubleday Children's Picture Dictionary, unrevised since it was first published in 1986, is an illustrated dictionary of over 1,500 words. The language used in the definitions is comprehensible by children in the primary grades. This book advances beyond the word-picture identification dictionaries in that there is an average of nine definitions per page and only one or two illustrations to a page.

Originally published in the United Kingdom under the title *Kingfisher First Dictionary*, the book provides, in its introduction, a global view of the English language. According to the introduction, "In ordinary life few people use more than 1,500 to 3,000 words. . . . [This dictionary] will tell you about 1,500 of these English words."

Arrangement of the entry words is alphabetical with two guide words at the top of each page that indicate the first and last words defined on it. Big bold black roman type identifies the entry word on the line above the definition. When the word or a form of it is repeated in the definition, it is also highlighted with a heavier type than the rest of the sentence. When more than one definition is provided, the meanings are numbered. Because of the clear graphic layout, access is quite easy. Each page is divided into two columns with wide margins. Definitions are distinctly set apart with white space. The letters of the alphabet are introduced on the appropriate page in 1¾" upper and lowercase blue letters.

Authority

Although the introduction implies that the words included in the dictionary constitute approximately half of the most commonly used English words, no authority for the selection is cited. The compiler's credentials are not listed.

Entries

Many of the definitions are inadequate, inconsistent, or in need of a clarifying illustration. For example: "A is used a lot in talking and writing. It is often used before the name of a thing. We say, '**a** ball can bounce,' or 'I saw **a** bird fly.' The word *a* is used five times in the entry, yet it has not been defined, only talked about. Of the numbers zero (0) through ten (10), only eight are iden-

The Doubleday
Children's Picture Dictionary

❶ Entry word in boldface, with senses numbered
❷ The entry's plural form, in boldface, used in a sentence
❸ Four-color illustration aids in understanding meaning of the entry word
❹ Entry word in boldface in definition
❺ Illustrative sentences explain meaning

Lucy **likes** playing with her toys.

like

1. I **like** all my toys. I enjoy playing with them. I **like** people I enjoy spending time with.
2. If one thing is **like** another, they are similar. Tom is just **like** his twin sister.

tified in the text as numbers; three (3) is defined as "a small number."

There are also errors in the definitions that will prove confusing to young readers. For example, under the entry word **quick,** not the adjective but the related adverb is defined: "Things done **quickly** take only a short time. We ran **quickly.**"

Pronunciation is given for some words. However, the selection is erratic and without an apparent rationale: it will certainly leave the young reader with inadequate information. For example, pronunciation is provided for **captain, cough, gnome,** the *kn* words, and for **listen, loose,** and **lose,** but not for **champion, couple, dwarf, leopard, restaurant,** or **soldier.** Parts of speech, syllabication and etymology are not given for any words. Although this may be appropriate for the youngest intended users, the complete omission of information in these categories renders the book inadequate for even a slightly older audience.

Illustrations

The full-color illustrations are pleasing and add to the graphic design. Unfortunately, some words whose defi-

nitions should have been reinforced visually were not, and words not especially in need of such clarification are sometimes illustrated. For example, on the page containing the entry **lasso,** no illustration is provided for that word, but an illustration depicting three men in a boat is provided to amplify definitions of **large, lake,** and **land.** On the other hand, the drawings manifest good minority representation, and illustrator Carol Holmes added interest to the pictures by using a variety of artistic styles and by often working an interpretation of two or more words into a single scene.

Special Features

A special feature of the dictionary is a spelling list of 3,000 words, almost half of which are not defined in the volume. The copy on the back cover calls this a "300-word 'speller,'" an obvious numerical typographical error. Words that are considered difficult to spell are in bold print.

A second special feature is a map section at the end of the volume, which begins with a map of the world. Following this are maps of the world's English-speaking countries: the British Isles, the United States, Canada,

Australia, and New Zealand. Because this book has not been revised since 1986, however, these maps are obviously quite dated.

Summary

The Doubleday Children's Picture Dictionary falls below standard. It is inconsistent and suffers from poor editing; it will not adequately serve the needs of young dictionary users. Home, public, and school libraries would do well to pass this one up.

The First Thousand Words: A Picture Word Book

Facts at a Glance

Full title: **The First Thousand Words: A Picture Word Book**
Publisher: EDC Publishing
Compiler: Heather Amery
Illustrator: Stephen Cartwright
Edition reviewed: © 1989

Number of pages: 63
Number of entries: more than 1,000
Number of illustrations: 1,080 in full color
Intended readership: ages 2 to 12
Trim size: $9^{1}/_{8}'' \times 12''$
Binding: hardcover

Price: $11.95
Sold in bookstores; also sold through vendors
ISBN 0-86020-266-6
No stated revision policy

Scope and Format

The First Thousand Words is a picture word book, not a dictionary. Like ROUND THE WORLD PICTURE WORD BOOK, it is intended to help beginning readers increase their vocabularies through the use of lively, humorous illustrations.

More than 1,000 words are grouped under 35 subject headings, ranging from **The yard** to **The hospital** to **Storybook words.** No criteria for the selection of words are given; however, the words and subjects chosen seem to be those with which many young children would be familiar.

According to the publisher, the book is intended for children ages 2 to 12, with older readers using it as a source for story ideas and correct spellings. However, the simple format of the book will probably appeal only to children in preschool through second grade.

This book was originally published in England in 1979; the text was adapted for American audiences in 1983. Foreign-language editions are available in French, German, Spanish, Italian, Russian, and Hebrew. The 1989 edition differs from the 1983 edition only in minor changes to the cover: since 1983, Britishisms like **aeroplane, pram,** and **ices** have been replaced by the American usages **airplane, baby carriage,** and **ice cream cones.**

Authority

The First Thousand Words was created by the British firm Usborne Publishing and published in the United States by EDC Publishing. The work was compiled by Heather Amery and illustrated by Stephen Cartwright, neither of whose credentials are listed in the book. Betty Root, a consultant on the teaching of reading and language in the United Kingdom, served as the consultant for this book and for ROUND THE WORLD PICTURE WORD BOOK. Root's additional experience includes writing Dorling Kindersley's MY FIRST DICTIONARY.

Entries

Two methods are used to present the words. The first method uses a two-page spread to display a scene. In the outer margins surrounding the scene, individual items are redrawn and labeled. This method allows a child to hunt for labeled objects within the scene. The book contains 15 two-page spreads. For example, in the illustration of **The yard,** a family is shown working outside. Various items from the scene are drawn and labeled in the margins, including a **wheelbarrow,** a **trashcan,** a **caterpillar,** a **ladder, flowers,** a **hedge,** a **bird's nest,** and a **lawn mower.** Although the objects in the margins are not identical to the ones in the scene, they are easy to find.

The second method displays related objects or actions against a white background. The words in these pages are grouped into such categories as **Pets, Seasons,** and **Doing things.** The categories are arranged in no particular order; rather, children may find groups of related words by browsing.

A seven-page index, called "Words in order," is included in the book. A brief explanation accompanies it. In general, the index is a useful tool for finding an individual word. The words that head each category (such as **Seasons** or **Storybook words**) are included in the index but are not typographically distinguished from the rest of the entries. Each letter of the alphabet is shown in oversized, lowercase form and is accompanied by a cartoon of an object that begins with that letter (*n* shows a man reading a newspaper). Index entries are followed by a page number. A spot check found several incorrect page numbers in the index. Although British words have been changed to American usage in the rest of the book, some Britishisms remain in the index. For example, "bonnet (of car)" leads the reader to page 21, where a **hood** is labeled. In addition, the drawing next to the letter *v* shows a girl displaying her undershirt (or *vest* in British usage).

A one-page list of "Words without pictures" precedes the index. This alphabetical list has "lots of words to read, say and spell," including many prepositions, conjunctions, pronouns, days of the week, and months of the year. The words in this list do not appear elsewhere in the book.

Illustrations

Illustrator Stephen Cartwright's drawings are colorful and appealing. Cartwright, who is a well-known and popular illustrator for the "young set," uses two types of graphic design for the two methods of presenting words. In the larger two-page spreads, his scenes are full of people, activity, detail, and humor. These scenes are edged by bold, black lines with wide margins for the labeled objects. His other technique involves many smaller drawings of single objects or miniature scenes, arranged in an orderly way.

Like the dog in Round the World Picture Word Book, a small yellow duck hides somewhere on each two-page spread. (This is explained on the inside back cover.)

One disconcerting element of this book is its portrayal of men and women in sexist roles. For instance, out of 28 occupations shown under **People,** only two (**singer** and **dancer**) portray women. While men work and children play in **The yard** scene, a woman wearing an apron scolds from the door of the house. In **The hospital,** all the doctors are male and all the nurses are female. In addition to its sexist stereotyping, *The First Thousand Words* shows very few people of color. These factors make it a less than ideal book for impressionable young children.

Summary

Although the publisher states that the intended audience for *The First Thousand Words* is children ages 2 to 12, children above the second-grade reading level would probably have little interest in this book. *The First Thousand Words* would function best as a read-aloud book for adults and preschoolers. However, the drawings' lack of ethnic diversity and the stereotypical representation of women and men seriously limit the book's appeal. A better choice for a picture word book would be Scott, Foresman's My Pictionary.

Macmillan Dictionary for Children

Facts at a Glance

Full title: **Macmillan Dictionary for Children**
Publisher: Macmillan
Editor: Judith S. Levey
Edition reviewed: © 1989

Number of pages: 896
Number of entries: 35,000
Number of illustrations: 1,100 in full color
Intended readership: ages 8 to 12
Trim size: 8″ × 10″
Binding: hardcover

Price: $14.95
Sold in bookstores; also sold to libraries and schools
ISBN 0-02-761561-8
No stated revision policy

Scope and Format

This 1989 edition is a revision of a work originally published in 1975, with previous revisions in 1982 and 1987. Considerably expanded since the last edition, the current one contains 35,000 entries, 1,100 full-color photographs, 832 pages of word definitions, and 64 pages of introductory and appended material. The lavish use of bright colors, as well as the simple format, numerous illustrations, and inviting introductory pages are designed to lure young readers into the book. The text portion is published as the *Macmillan School Dictionary 1,* which is intended for classroom use.

Authority

The editor-in-chief of this work is Judith S. Levey, who is also the editor of the Macmillan First Dictionary. Sidney I. Landau served as the lexicographic consultant. The *Macmillan Dictionary for Children* has been highly regarded ever since it first appeared in 1975. With each subsequent edition, the editors have taken great care to ensure that the work provides clear, accurate definitions appropriate to its audience.

Entries

The volume includes a basic vocabulary of words and easily understood definitions for young readers. Some entries contain as many as three or four definitions for different meanings of a word. Most entries are brief, containing no more than two or three definitions. One of the exceptions to this rule is the definition of **so long,** which has six adverb meanings, one adjective, one conjunction,

Macmillan Dictionary for Children

❶ Main entry words in boldface

❷ Definitions grouped according to the part of speech, with the most commonly used meaning placed first

❸ Triangle symbol indicates homophone

❹ Parts of speech spelled out, in italic; noun plurals and other forms in boldface

❺ Full-color captioned illustration

❻ Syllabication, in boldface, precedes pronunciation in parentheses

❼ Illustrative sentences provided, with the entry word italicized

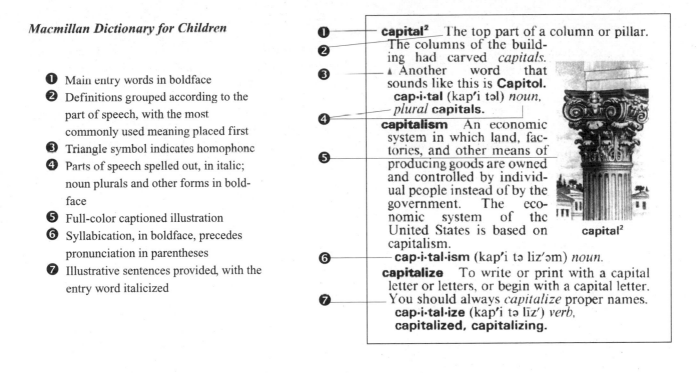

two pronouns, one interjection, two homophones, and two compounds. Biographies are not included, but major geographical locations are. These geographical entries cover countries, but not capitals. The alternate spelling for **Cambodia, Kampuchea,** is given. Individual states within the United States are entered.

No foreign words, slang, or mentions of sex or sexually transmitted diseases appear. Children may wonder why such familiar words as *rap* (music) or *fax* are missing. Other terms that are not included, such as *AIDS,* will be part of their vocabulary and perhaps should be recognized. Mythological figures are not represented; however, names of planets are.

Occasional idioms such as *under one's nose* and *to iron out* are identified at the end of appropriate entries. Compound words like **cave man** are included. There are entries for contractions, suffixes, and prefixes. Homophones, homographs, inflections, plurals, verb forms, and parts of speech are included; however, synonyms and antonyms are not.

Helpful word histories are set apart in brightly colored red boxes scattered throughout the text:

The word **doughnut** developed from an earlier form of the word *doughnought,* a "dough circle." *Nought* is an old-fashioned word for "zero."

Usage notes are less frequent but punctuate the text in bright blue boxes, adding color and instruction in a creative and unobtrusive way.

Proper names of major religious figures and highly visible holidays such as **Christmas** and **Easter** are included. *Kwanzaa* and *Ramadan* are not. There are entries for selected ethnic groups such as **African-American** and **Chicano,** but *Asian-Americans* are not identified. This edition offers an advance over the 1987 edition: **colored** is now identified as the past tense of the verb "to color" and not as a substitute for the term "black."

The word arrangement is alphabetical, letter by letter. Each word is clearly presented without diacritical marks or syllable divisions. Numbered definitions follow, with the most common meaning first. Definitions are simple and straightforward. If the word is used as more than one part of speech, renumbering occurs within the entry. An example follows each definition, with the entry word italicized. A small blue triangle identifies homophones and a small black dot sets off idiomatic use of a word. Homographs receive separate entries and are signaled with superscript: **ash[1], ash[2].**

Syllabication is given at the end of the entry followed by pronunciation in parentheses, italicized parts of speech, and the plural form of verbs. Unusual plural forms and past participles receive separate entries: "**mown,** Past participle of **mow.**" The juxtaposition of italicized words after the pronunciation is slightly distracting: "**jet (jet)** *noun, plural* **jets;** *verb,* **jetted, jetting.**"

Terminology is reasonably current. *Bungee jumping* is not included, but **hang glider** is. Computer terms have been incorporated since the last revision. **LOGO** and **BASIC** are defined. **Software** is included and a third definition of **monitor** relates to computers. **Disk** is defined two ways and refers to the alternate spelling **disc,** for which there is a separate entry.

A typical entry follows:

kennel 1. A building where dogs are kept. **2.** A place where dogs are raised and trained or cared for while an owner is away.
ken·nel (ken′əl) *noun, plural* **kennels**

Syllabication occurs at the end of each entry in bold-face type followed by pronunciation in parentheses: "**pen·guin (pen′gwin** or **peng′gwin) noun, plural penguins.**" Pronunciations are provided for words used as alternate parts of speech ("es′tə mit *for noun;* es′tə māt *for verb*").

The volume is not thumb indexed, but bands of color along the edge of each page divide the work into thirds—*A* to *F* in blue, *G* to *P* in red, and *Q* to *Z* in green. Section letters are white against these colors on the right margin. First and last words appear at the top of each page against a bright yellow bar. A pronunciation guide, also in yellow, is placed at the bottom right-hand corner of odd-numbered pages. One improvement over the previous edition is a table of contents that lists all parts of the volume.

Illustrations

Full-color photographs and drawings appear on every page and include a fair mixture of races, ethnicities, and age groups. Illustrations are well placed, adjacent to appropriate entries. Color is the key to this volume, especially in the supplementary pages, and although no cartoons are used as illustrations, humor is present in the introductory graphics. Good graphics accompany the units of weights and measures. For example, a liter of strawberries next to a quart of the fruit helps the student visualize the conversion.

Boldface type and italics are used to highlight parts of each entry. The binding is sturdy. The cover is plastic and durable.

Special Features

A well-written section in the introductory pages, entitled "How to Use Your Dictionary," is carried over from previous editions. In addition to "How to Use Your Dictionary," the introductory section has handsomely illustrated pages covering word meanings and the history of the English language, a table of words derived from other languages, and a pronunciation key.

A "Reference Section" at the end of the book includes portraits of all the presidents of the United States through George Bush, a time line of U.S. history, maps (which were current in 1989), and sections entitled "Flags of the World," "Time Line of World History," and "Tables of Weights and Measures."

Summary

The *Macmillan Dictionary for Children* is a valuable reference source for the intended audience of 8- to 12-year-old children. The bold use of color is appealing. Presentation of words in context as a child sees them is a unique feature not found in other standard elementary dictionaries such as Webster's New World Children's Dictionary. This feature makes the volume useful in the classroom, where preparation for more advanced sources is taught. The supplementary materials are graphically sound and the price is comparable to that of its competitors. The *Macmillan Dictionary for Children* would be a good choice for home, school, or library purchase.

Macmillan First Dictionary

Facts at a Glance

Full title: **Macmillan First Dictionary**
Publisher: Macmillan
Editor: Judith S. Levey
Edition reviewed: © 1990

Number of pages: 416
Number of entries: 2,200
Number of illustrations: 550 in full color
Intended readership: ages 5 to 9
Trim size: 8½″ × 11″
Binding: hardcover

Price: $12.95
Sold in bookstores; also sold to libraries and schools
ISBN 0-02-761731-0
No stated revision policy

Scope and Format

The *Macmillan First Dictionary* is a completely revised and expanded edition of the *Macmillan Very First Dictionary,* which was originally published in 1977 and went through subsequent revisions. This 1990 edition of the *Macmillan First Dictionary* is designed for the preschool and primary-grade children who have progressed beyond picture word books and are ready for a simple dictionary. The text and most of the appended matter are also published as the *Macmillan McGraw-Hill Primary Dictionary,* a classroom edition. The *Macmillan First Dictionary* contains almost 2,200 of the most common words in the English language and 550 color photographs and illustrations. Simple word definitions are followed by example sentences.

This eye-appealing work is 8½″ × 11″, the size of a standard notebook. It combines the visual appeal of a

Macmillan First Dictionary

❶ step

❷ 1. Step means to raise your foot from one place and put it down somewhere else. Be careful not to **step** in the puddle. ▲ **stepped, stepping.**

❸ 2. Step also means a place to put your foot when you are going up or down. Someone left a toy on the top **step.** We sat on the front **steps** of our house. ▲ **steps.**

❺

The **step** is a little high. ── ❻

❶ Entry word in large bold type is on a line by itself, making it easier to find

❷ When more than one meaning is given, each entry is numbered

❸ Triangle symbol indicates other forms of the entry word

❹ Example sentence shows the entry word in context

❺ Four-color illustration depicts both meanings

❻ Caption also an example sentence

picture book with the solid reference features of a dictionary.

Authority

Judith S. Levey, editor-in-chief of this volume, has edited other successful dictionaries for Macmillan, including the highly praised MACMILLAN DICTIONARY FOR CHILDREN for upper elementary school children. The Macmillan series of dictionaries includes text and trade editions that have been highly successful in schools, libraries, and homes.

The method for choosing the words is not described as it is in the Scott, Foresman series of children's dictionaries, for which words are selected from word lists; however, the vocabulary is designed to be familiar to children of this age group, and, as stated in the introduction, consists of the "most common words in the English language."

Entries

Entry words appear in boldface type in alphabetical order. The definitions are designed to answer a child's question "What does _____ mean?" or "What's a

_____?"—an interesting approach. The use of this method leads the editors to construct the definition as a sentence: "A **skyscraper** is a very tall building." Multiple definitions are numbered. One or more example sentences accompany each definition; the entry word appears in bold type in these examples:

smile
1. When you **smile,** the corners of your mouth turn up. You **smile** when you are happy. Everyone **smiled** when we had our picture taken. **smiled, smiling.**
2. When you **smile,** you have a **smile** on your face. The winning team had **smiles** on their faces. **smiles.**

The illustration for **smile,** which depicts a smiling boy receiving a trophy as a prize, is adjacent to the entry.

As shown in the example above, noun and verb forms are used in illustrative sentences but not identified as such. Inflected forms and plurals appear at the end of entries preceded by a blue triangle. This convention is used in other Macmillan dictionaries for children and will be recognized by them as they graduate through the series.

Subentries expand the child's understanding of the relationship of the word to other words: "Another word for **autumn** is **fall.**" Homographs receive separate numbered entries, with the most commonly used word entered first. An appendix called "Words That May Confuse You" introduces the concept of homophones—a nice feature not commonly found in dictionaries at this age level. A few proper names, such as those for holidays, are included. The editors have provided an alternate spelling for **Hanukkah (Chanukah),** which demonstrates an interest in important detail. Terms and situations familiar to children are included in the list. Words such as **seatbelt** and **escalator** illustrate this fact. The vocabulary is reasonably current; words such as **computer, disk,** and **keyboard** are represented. Definitions are clear: "A **photograph** is a picture you take with a camera."

Illustrations

The colorful, eye-appealing illustrations are an outstanding feature of this volume. They are varied, mixing drawings and photographs. They are placed adjacent to the words they illustrate and each caption has a full sentence with the defined word in boldface. This furnishes the opportunity to add action to the definition and to further define a word by using inflected forms and plurals. Each letter of the alphabet is introduced with pictures of animal cutouts performing childlike humorous antics (for example, the "D" section shows "Dancing Dogs").

The illustrations are superior to those in Scott, Foresman's MY FIRST DICTIONARY. WORDS FOR NEW READERS, designed for children in kindergarten and first grade, incorporates fine art mixed with drawings, photographs, and cartoons. In this respect, it is the most cleverly illustrated of the group. The Macmillan work's pages have a glossy quality that the above-mentioned volumes do not have, giving it a more expensive look at a comparable price.

Differently abled children and diverse ethnic populations are well represented in the illustrations. A child in a wheelchair joins a group of stargazers near the definition for **star.** Men and women are depicted in nonstereotypical roles. A **doctor** is depicted as a woman; father and son **cook** spaghetti together. The elderly are included in healthy roles playing **checkers,** being **close,** and helping **celebrate.**

Special Features

The color and vibrancy of the text illustrations is carried over into the supplementary materials. "How to Help a Child Use This Book" and the "Sample Page" are followed by illustrated essays on language, material that offers an opportunity for parents to share information about words with their children. The pictures are delightful.

In one appendix the homophones **pear** and **pair** are treated with a large illustration of each and seven practice sentences. Other material on these pages includes information on a calendar, numbers, weights and measures, and money.

In contrast to this work, the Scott, Foresman MY FIRST DICTIONARY does not include the lengthy introductory material but does include a good computer section plus pages on environmental issues, nutrition, time, holidays, parts of a letter, the D'Nealian® Alphabet, and two pages of activities. Both dictionaries include maps of the United States and the world. The *Macmillan First Dictionary* maps are larger and the United States map includes state capitals.

Summary

The entry words in the *Macmillan First Dictionary* are larger and bolder than those in the Scott, Foresman MY FIRST DICTIONARY, making it more accessible to a slightly younger reader. The books are comparable in size, but the latter treats almost twice as many words and illustrations and its lexicon was chosen from word lists and reading materials for children, which lends more authority to the choice of words. However, the *Macmillan First Dictionary* brings its words to life in a vibrant, visually attractive way and is an excellent choice for a first dictionary. It is priced competitively and is sturdy enough to withstand use in the home, library, or school.

My Big Dictionary

Facts at a Glance

Full title: **My Big Dictionary**
Publisher: Houghton Mifflin
Editors: staff of the American Heritage dictionaries
Illustrator: Pamela Cote
Edition reviewed: © 1994

Number of pages: 40
Number of words: 170
Number of illustrations: 170 plus 10 full-page vignettes, all in full color
Intended readership: ages 2 to 5
Trim size: $15^7/_8'' \times 19^3/_8''$
Binding: paperback

Price: $18.95
ISBN 0-395-66377-6
No stated revision policy

Scope and Format

The 1994 edition of Houghton Mifflin's *My Big Dictionary* contains 40 pages filled with more than 170 words and illustrations in an oversized format. Although the words are listed in alphabetical order, this work resembles a picture word book more than a picture dictionary because no definitions or other dictionary features are provided. The book is aimed at two- to five-year-old children and, according to the introductory note, it "will help develop and expand a child's vocabulary and kindle an interest in letters, sounds, and words and a love of reading and writing."

With an unusually large trim size ($15\,7/8'' \times 19\,3/8''$), *My Big Dictionary* is the first oversized dictionary available for preschoolers, according to the book's promotional material. The publisher states that children "gain *autonomy* through being able to manipulate the large sturdy pages on their own." It seems that the book is intended for more than one child to use at a time—most likely in a home with several young children or in a classroom. The publisher states, "The oversize format has been classroom-tested and proven an irresistible introduction for the littlest dictionary 'readers.'" The large format, however, makes the book quite cumbersome. In order to use *My Big Dictionary,* a large surface area, such as a table or floor, is needed. The book is also difficult to carry or store—it will not fit on a standard bookshelf—and therefore seems somewhat impractical for a library. Although the paper stock used for the pages within the book is of a high quality, the book's paperback binding creases easily and may not withstand heavy use.

Authority

Houghton Mifflin publishes the highly regarded family of American Heritage dictionaries, including a series of children's dictionaries also reviewed in the Buying Guide. *My Big Dictionary,* first published in 1994, was developed by the editors of the American Heritage dictionaries and illustrated by Pamela Cote. According to the publisher, the words included in the book "were carefully selected from children's speaking, reading, and writing vocabularies." Moreover, "The vocabulary list was developed in close consultation with Houghton Mifflin's renowned school division. . . ."

Entries

My Big Dictionary opens with a note "To Parents and Teachers," which includes ten simple activities to introduce children to the book. The words and illustrations in the dictionary are presented in alphabetical order, and the book is organized into 29 "alphabet pages" and ten "alphabet scenes." On alphabet pages, the letter of the alphabet being addressed is shown in large uppercase and lowercase letters on a colored block at the top of the page. Each word that begins with that letter is printed in large, bold black type and accompanied by an illustration. Most letters take up a single page that contains six words and illustrations. For example, the page for *K* contains words and drawings for **kangaroo, kick, kite, king, knock,** and **koala.** A few common letters (*B, C, P,* and *S*) take up two or three pages and some less-common letters (*I, J, U, V, X, Y,* and *Z*) only one-half or one-third of a page.

Ten pages contain an alphabet scene—one for each of ten different letters. Each alphabet scene is packed with animals, objects, and actions that begin with one letter of the alphabet. For example, the alphabet scene for the letter *B* shows Ben's bedroom. Ben's toy chest is filled with items such as a baseball bat, basketball, book, bus, and bank. Ben, asleep in his bed, is dreaming of bears taking a bubble bath, riding a bicycle, and sitting in a boat. A beaver plays with building blocks, and a buffalo wears a beret.

Almost every object in an alphabet scene begins with the same letter, and these scenes are so filled that children will find new items every time they look at the page. Unlike other picture word books such as My Pictionary and The First Thousand Words, however, the objects in the scenes are not labeled. An index at the end of the book lists the words depicted in alphabet scenes as well as those words on alphabet pages and their corresponding page numbers. Preschoolers and kindergartners will certainly be able to identify many of the words illustrated in the alphabet scenes, but without the help of an adult, they will not be able to identify all of them.

Illustrations

The delightful full-color drawings by Pamela Cote will most certainly appeal to the book's intended audience of preschoolers and kindergartners. The illustrations are colorful, lively, and full of fun. On the alphabet pages, the drawings are large and detailed. The alphabet scenes are filled with activity and, consequently, the objects depicted are much smaller. Because the pages are so large, however, the objects are still clearly visible. A "mascot character"—a cartoon animal wearing goggles and a scarf—appears in the alphabet scenes throughout the work and adds a sense of continuity. Children will enjoy "finding" this character in the book's busy pages.

Because most of the drawings depict animals instead of people, the need to avoid stereotypes and to show a mix of ethnic and racial groups has been minimized. Of the very small number of people who are depicted, however, an equal number of males and females are shown.

Summary

My Big Dictionary is a fun and fanciful introduction to words and dictionaries for children ages two to five. They will be encouraged to browse through the pages on their own or, with the help of an adult, to locate and identify the many objects and actions depicted in the appealing illustrations. Because many of the objects are not labeled, however, My Pictionary is a better choice for beginning readers in kindergarten and first grade because all of the objects in that work are identified.

My Big Dictionary's unique oversized format is best suited to preschool classrooms, where the book can be set on the floor and several children can peruse the large pages at the same time. The large format may also be appropriate for homes with more than one young child, but it seems impractical for library use. With a price of $18.95, this book is more expensive than most other works for this age group. In addition, buyers should beware of the paperback binding that will crease over time.

My First Dictionary

Facts at a Glance

Full title: **My First Dictionary**
Publisher: Dorling Kindersley
Compiler: Betty Root
Editors: Elizabeth Wilkinson; B. Alison Weir (U.S. editor)
Edition reviewed: © 1993

Number of pages: 96
Number of entries: 1,000
Number of illustrations: 1,000 in full color
Intended readership: ages 5 and up
Trim size: 10″ × 13″
Binding: hardcover

Price: $16.95; discount available to libraries
Sold in bookstores and through wholesalers; also sold to libraries
ISBN 1-56458-277-9
No stated revision policy

Scope and Format

Dorling Kindersley's *My First Dictionary* was developed in Great Britain and first published in the United States in 1993. It is a 96-page book containing 1,000 words, definitions, and illustrations. Although it is intended mainly for children age five and older, preschoolers would be drawn to the colorful and appealing illustrations. According to the introductory "Note to parents and teachers," *My First Dictionary* "is designed to encourage children to practice using a dictionary, and to learn more about the language they use every day."

Entries are shown in alphabetical order, and about 24 entries appear on each two-page spread. Large, boldface entry words are defined in one to three sentences. No pronunciations, etymologies, or syllabications are included, as is appropriate for this age level. Each entry is illustrated with a full-color photograph or drawing, which appears directly adjacent to the entry.

The large trim size of the book might make it difficult for very young hands to manipulate without resting it on a table or other surface; however, the pages lie flat when the book is open. The cover and binding seem sturdy enough to withstand years of use.

Authority

The British publisher Dorling Kindersley is well known for its high-quality, lavishly illustrated reference books for children, mainly in the areas of nature and science. *My First Dictionary* (part of a series of books that includes MY FIRST ENCYCLOPEDIA) is written by Betty Root, a consultant on the teaching of reading and language in the United Kingdom. William E. Nagy, Ph.D., a professor at the Center for the Study of Reading at the University of Illinois, served as U.S. consultant.

Root's "Note to parents and teachers" states that each of the words in *My First Dictionary* "has been carefully selected from words commonly used by young children." The publisher states that the dictionary was tested in schools to ensure that the photographs and illustrations accurately depict the words, though no details are given about these tests or their results.

Entries

Words are listed in alphabetical order, and a variety of words are defined, including such topics as numbers, colors, shapes, animals, plants, places, everyday items, machines, parts of the body, food, occupations, musical instruments, sports, and imaginary creatures. Definitions are included for words not ordinarily found in beginning dictionaries, such as **chopsticks, compact disc, hearing aid, optometrist,** and **synagogue.**

Each entry word is presented in large, boldface type. Underneath, a one- to three-sentence definition appears. For the most part, definitions are limited to one meaning, but occasionally two separate entries are given for homographs:

> **bat** A **bat** is a kind of stick that is used to hit a ball.
> **bat** A **bat** is a small, furry animal with wings. Bats hang upside down to sleep during the day. They hunt for food at night.

Each of these meanings is accompanied by a photograph.

Definitions generally are appropriate for the age level, giving a clear description of the word in simple language, as in the following definition for **family:**

> A **family** is a group of people who are related to each other. A **mother,** a **father,** a **brother,** and a **sister** are just one kind of family.

Some entries, however, include words that would be too difficult for young children. For example, the definition for **race** reads "A **race** is a competition to find out who is the fastest."

The format of including an illustration with each entry allows *My First Dictionary* to better define abstract

My First Dictionary (Dorling Kindersley)

camp

To **camp** is to live outside. A **campsite** is a place where you set up your outdoor equipment.

❶ Entry word in large bold type is on a line by itself, making it easy to find

❷ Derivative given for more information

❸ Four-color illustration

concepts, such as colors, that are inadequately defined (or not included) in such dictionaries as Troll's YOUNG PEOPLE'S DICTIONARY.

Illustrations

The beautiful illustrations in *My First Dictionary* place it far ahead of other works for this age level. About 75 percent of the illustrations are photographs, and 25 percent are drawn art. The photographs are crisp and saturated with color. The drawn art shows a good amount of interesting detail and activity, without appearing cluttered.

The illustrations are well matched to the words they explain. In the entry for **transparent,** for example, a girl holds a clear glass pitcher in front of her face. Frequently, illustrations provide valuable information that is not included in the definitions.

The illustrations portray a variety of children and adults from many ethnic and racial groups, as well as a balance of males and females in a variety of nontraditional roles. Entries and illustrations appear not only for **church,** but also for **mosque, synagogue,** and **temple.**

Illustrations reflect contemporary situations, including a drawing of the space shuttle under **astronaut** and an up-to-date photograph of a **computer.**

Special Features

At the end of the book, a four-page section of "Dictionary Games" provides activities aimed at strengthening alphabet, spelling, and dictionary skills through play.

Also included in the end matter is an "Index of Additional Words" listing page numbers for over 150 words that are printed in boldface type within entries, many of them variants of entry words.

Summary

With only 1,000 words, *My First Dictionary* has less than half the number of entries as the MACMILLAN FIRST DICTIONARY. With an illustration for every entry, however, *My First Dictionary* has nearly twice as many illustrations as the Macmillan work. The two books have completely different graphical styles: MACMILLAN FIRST DICTIONARY has a standard dictionary format, while *My First Dictionary* has a bold, magazinelike look that is very contemporary. The Macmillan work is best suited for beginning readers who want to look up words and definitions. *My First Dictionary* introduces an element of fun that will invite children in preschool and kindergarten to browse through the book and discover the world of language.

My First Dictionary

Facts at a Glance

Full title: **My First Dictionary**
Publisher: Scott, Foresman; distributed by HarperCollins
Edition reviewed: © 1990, 1991 printing

Number of pages: 448
Number of entries: 4,000
Number of illustrations: over 1,000 in full color
Intended readership: grade 2
Trim size: $8\frac{1}{8}'' \times 10\frac{1}{4}''$
Binding: hardcover

Price: $12.95
Sold in bookstores; also sold to libraries and schools
ISBN 0-06-275001-1
No stated revision policy

Scope and Format

The 1990 edition of *My First Dictionary* is one of a series of Scott, Foresman picture dictionaries and is designed for children who are reading, able to alphabetize, and ready for a true dictionary. It is the publisher's trade edition of the classroom title MY SECOND PICTURE DICTIONARY, which is designed for second graders who have progressed beyond WORDS FOR NEW READERS (and its text edition MY FIRST PICTURE DICTIONARY). Over 4,000 words were chosen by a panel of experts from reading materials meant for primary school students. Over 1,000 illustrations accompany the words. Clear definitions and example sentences show multiple meanings of words. Smaller in size than other primary dictionaries, this is a sturdy, hardcover volume. At only $8\frac{1}{8}'' \times 10\frac{1}{4}''$, it has somewhat less of a picture-book quality than works such as the MACMILLAN FIRST DICTIONARY or WORDS FOR NEW READERS. It appears to be aimed at a slightly older age group than the Macmillan work, although both are advertised for the same audience.

Authority

Scott, Foresman has published children's dictionaries for more than 50 years. An advisory panel of primary school teachers helped choose vocabulary from "novels, poems, plays, and books of nonfiction" as well as "textbooks in reading, language arts, science, health, math, and social studies" (Introduction). Words that describe things familiar to children were also chosen.

Entries

Entry words are arranged alphabetically. Each entry word is printed in boldface type, and multiple meanings are numbered. An attractive feature is a colon separating the definition from an italicized sentence to show how each meaning is used. Noun plurals, verb forms, and comparative adjective forms are printed at the end of entries, where appropriate, in boldface type; however, the parts of speech are not identified. This is a customary omission in dictionaries for this age group. There are separate word entries in this vol-

ume for the parts of speech themselves (**adjective, adverb, noun,** and so on)—a unique feature. No pronunciation or syllabication is present. Prepositions such as **after** are handled with example sentences but no definition.

Homographs are treated in the standard manner, with superscript numbers on successive entry words with the same spelling. Most frequently used meanings appear first. There are entries for compound words such as **polar bear.** Verb definitions begin with the infinitive form (**bloom,** "to have flowers"), which represents a step toward a standard dictionary format. Both noun and verb forms of a word are defined. Only a few proper nouns—including names of holidays, months, and states—appear. Contractions receive separate entries.

The words are familiar and reasonably current, with entries for **computer, video,** and **microwave.** A few terms children encounter in everyday life do not appear, such as *joystick* and *skateboard.* The entries adhere to a traditional set of values and make no attempt to recognize alternative lifestyles. Families are defined as mothers, fathers, and close relatives. The volume does, however, address the problem of abstractions creatively:

> **blue**
> **1.** the color of the clear sky during the day. **2.** having this color: *The water in the lake looks very blue.* **blues; bluer, bluest.**

Illustrations

A wide variety of color drawings, photographs, and cartoons illustrates 25 percent of the words. Captions accompany all illustrations. These may be one word (the entry) or a full sentence, with the entry word highlighted in boldface type. A unique feature is the practice of identifying which definition of a particular word is illustrated. Example sentences are once again italicized in the caption to set them apart. Illustrations appear mainly in the margins, and, in most cases, are less intrusive than those in primary dictionaries such as WORDS FOR NEW READERS. They are placed close to the words they illustrate and depict familiar objects and activities in a child's life. The colors are more subdued than those in works for younger children, except for those in the appendixes (see "Special Features").

A good mixture of ethnicity is represented. There are no illustrations for words like **doctor, firefighter,** and **teacher,** skirting the issue of gender stereotypes; however, there is a picture of a female doctor beside **checkup.** Cartoons add humor. Some pictures use balloons to show thoughts and conversations of the various characters. Illustrations are current. A student operates a computer and views the screen at a **terminal,** and an **as-**

My First Dictionary (Scott, Foresman; dist. by HarperCollins)

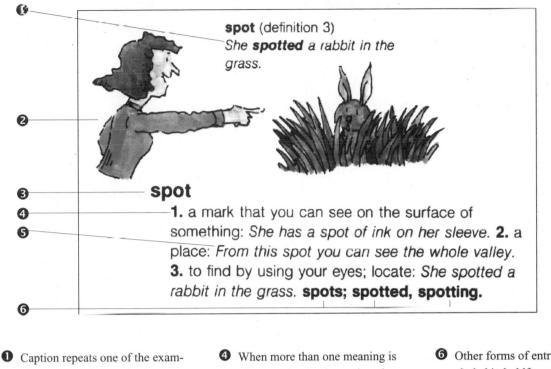

spot (definition 3)
*She **spotted** a rabbit in the grass.*

spot

1. a mark that you can see on the surface of something: *She has a spot of ink on her sleeve.* **2.** a place: *From this spot you can see the whole valley.* **3.** to find by using your eyes; locate: *She spotted a rabbit in the grass.* **spots; spotted, spotting.**

❶ Caption repeats one of the example sentences for emphasis

❷ Four-color illustration

❸ Main entry word in boldface

❹ When more than one meaning is given, each entry is numbered

❺ Italicized example sentences help clarify different meanings

❻ Other forms of entry words included in boldface at the end of the entry

tronaut walks in space. Overall, the illustrations are good but not as eye-catching as those in the Macmillan series. Emphasis is on the words themselves.

Special Features

In contrast to Macmillan dictionaries, few special features are included at the beginning of *My First Dictionary*. There is an introduction for the parent and a useful sample page on how to read an entry. The appendixes, however, contain several added features that are outstanding. Important parts of a computer (including a disk drive, mouse, and different-sized floppy disks) are labeled in a full-page picture of boys and girls at a workstation. Color maps of the United States and the world are included; as in other dictionaries for this age group, only continents and oceans are named. The maps are followed by a page about landforms such as rivers, mountains, and forests. A page on tips for protecting the environment is included. Children and animals illustrate nutrition and healthy snacks. A page on time shows various types of clocks in a clock shop. Pages on weights and measures, calendars, and holi-

days precede a page on the D'Nealian® Alphabet. A unique feature is the activity section inside the back cover, which contains exercises children can perform to learn alphabetizing and to lead them into examining words in the dictionary.

Summary

My First Dictionary is especially strong in its mature approach to presentation of dictionary elements for young readers who have advanced beyond picture dictionaries and word books. The entries begin to emphasize the words more than the illustrations. Compared with 2,200 words in the MACMILLAN FIRST DICTIONARY, *My First Dictionary* contains nearly twice as many entries. Both of these works have a four-to-one ratio of words to illustrations, but the illustrations in the MACMILLAN FIRST DICTIONARY are larger and more eye appealing. Although both of these works would be good choices for a beginning dictionary, the Macmillan work is probably best suited to children in kindergarten and first grade and *My First Dictionary* is more appropriate for children in second and third grades.

My First Dictionary

Facts at a Glance

Full title: **My First Dictionary**
Publisher: Troll Associates
Illustrator: Alan Snow
Edition reviewed: © 1992

Number of pages: 32
Number of entries: 350
Number of illustrations: about 350 in full color
Intended readership: kindergarten to grade 3
Trim size: 8¾″ × 11¼″ (hardcover); 8½″ × 11″ (paperback)
Binding: hardcover; paperback

Price: $12.79 (hardcover); $4.95 (paperback)
Sold in bookstores and through wholesalers; also sold to libraries
ISBN 0-8167-2515-2 (hardcover);
ISBN 0-8167-2516-0 (paperback)
No stated revision policy

Scope and Format

My First Dictionary, with illustrations by Alan Snow, is a 32-page book containing about 350 words, definitions, and illustrations. The publisher states that the book's intended audience is children in kindergarten through third grade. Because of the limited vocabulary, however, this source is geared more to preschoolers, kindergartners, and first-grade students. Inherent in the work's conceptualization is the reading-readiness mode in early childhood education, which prepares children for reading by introducing letters and basic reading skills.

About 16 to 19 entries are included on each page. The letter appears at the top of the page in capital and lowercase form on a strip of bright color. Entry words are shown in boldface type, followed by one or more illustrations, followed by a one- or two-sentence definition that uses the entry word. No pronunciations, etymologies, or syllabications are included, as is appropriate for this age level.

This work is the size of the average magazine. Young children would have no problem manipulating and handling the book. The paperback edition was reviewed. The publisher also has a hardcover version, which prospective buyers should examine for durability, especially if the work is being obtained for a library.

Authority

Troll Associates is a subsidiary of Educational Reading Services, located in New Jersey. The organization was founded in 1969 with a special focus on juvenile publications. The illustrator, Alan Snow, has a history of working with books that are designed for preschool-age and beginning readers.

This book does not open with a "Note to parents and teachers," nor is there a goal statement. How the vocabulary of 350 words was defined for inclusion is not explained.

Entries

Several different types of words are defined, including animals, everyday items, feelings, and actions. The number of entries for each of the letters varies: there are 11 for *A,* 36 for *B,* 27 for *C,* and so on. With a total of only 350 entries, however, the vocabulary is quite limited. For example, entries are provided for the words **color** and **number,** but entries do not exist for any colors or numbers. Also surprising is the omission of an entry for *family.*

Each entry word is presented in boldface type, followed by at least one illustration and a sentence definition of the term. For example, **angry** has two characters facing each other with one showing displeasure on his face. The definition of the term reads: "If you are **angry,** you are mad at someone or something." Homographs, such as **bark,** are reflected wherever they appear in the dictionary. It first states, "The **bark** of a tree is its skin"; then, "The loud noise that a dog makes is its **bark.**"

Definitions generally are appropriate for the age level, providing a clear description of the word in simple language. For example, **man** is defined in this way: "A **man** is an adult male person. A boy grows up to be a **man.**" The definitions do not tend to overgeneralize, despite the simple reading level.

The format of including an illustration with each entry enhances the explanation for abstract concepts.

> **Soft** If something is **soft,** you can push your fingers into it easily.

The accompanying illustration shows a finger poking into a teddy bear.

Illustrations

The humorous, colorful illustrations in *My First Dictionary* have child appeal, reflecting pleasant facial expressions wherever possible. A wide range of ethnic and racial groups is apparent throughout the work. Many of the illustrations are mounted on blocks of color that enhance their presentation. Some concepts, such as **neat, week,** and **word,** lack an illustration.

Special Features

The work opens with an informative essay entitled "How Words Came to Be" and a brief note called "How to Use This Dictionary." Four pages at the back of the book are devoted to a variety of activities under the

My First Dictionary (Troll Associates)

❶ Main entry word in boldface on a line by itself, making it easier to find

❷ Four-color illustration

❸ All definitions given in complete sentences, with entry word in boldface

❹ When more than one meaning is given, each entry is numbered

❺ Example sentence shows entry word in context

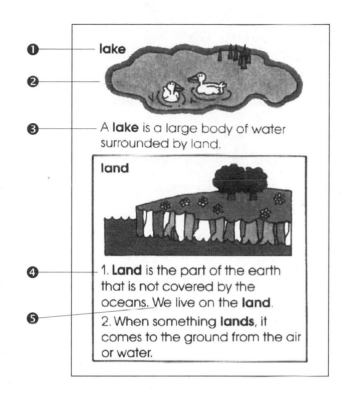

theme "Word Fun," including identification, concepts, riddles, matching exercises, and a short story. "Word Fun" allows children to practice dictionary skills.

Summary

On the whole, *My First Dictionary* adheres to the concept of presenting only "basic words." When compared with other beginning dictionaries, such as Dorling Kindersley's MY FIRST DICTIONARY (1,000 entries) and Scott, Foresman's WORDS FOR NEW READERS (1,500 entries), the Troll work has a very limited vocabulary. The words that are included in the book, however, are clearly defined and at the appropriate level. The appealing illustrations in Troll's *My First Dictionary* create a sense of fun that will invite preschoolers and kindergartners to start learning about words and about how to use a dictionary.

Price: $13.95 (hardcover); $10.95 (paperback)
Sold directly to schools; also sold in bookstores
ISBN 0-673-12489-4 (hardcover);
    ISBN 0-673-28452-2 (paperback)
No stated revision policy

Scope and Format

Scott, Foresman's *My First Picture Dictionary* is the school edition of WORDS FOR NEW READERS (distributed by HarperCollins), and it is identical to that work except that it does not include a two-page activity section that appears inside the back cover of WORDS FOR NEW READERS. For a full description and evaluation, see the review of WORDS FOR NEW READERS elsewhere in this Buying Guide.

My First Picture Dictionary

Facts at a Glance

Full title: **My First Picture Dictionary**
Publisher: Scott, Foresman
Edition reviewed: © 1990

Number of pages: 312
Number of entries: 1,500
Number of illustrations: 1,100 in full color
Intended readership: grade 1
Trim size: 8⅝″ × 11⅛″
Binding: hardcover; paperback

My Pictionary

Facts at a Glance

Full title: **My Pictionary**
Publisher: Scott, Foresman
Edition reviewed: © 1990

Number of pages: 144
Number of words: 850
Number of illustrations: 850, all in full color
Intended readership: kindergarten to grade 1
Trim size: 8¾″ × 11⅛″
Binding: hardcover

Price: $11.95
Sold directly to schools and bookstores
ISBN 0-673-12488-6
No stated revision policy

Scope and Format

My Pictionary was first published in 1970 and was most recently revised in 1990. The work is a 144-page picture word book filled with 850 words, each one accompanied by a full-color illustration. As is standard with picture word books, no definitions or pronunciations are included.

The introduction to *My Pictionary* states that the volume "is designed as a source book of words for children who are just learning to read and write." Although the book is geared to children in kindergarten and first grade, preschoolers might also enjoy the colorful and lively illustrations.

The words in the book are arranged according to categories of meanings. The table of contents lists these categories and the page number on which they begin. Following the table of contents is a two-page spread showing the letters of the alphabet. Each letter is accompanied by an imaginative drawing with objects that begin with that letter. For example, the letter *B* is illustrated by a bear in a bathtub with a boat and a balloon. A complete index at the end of the book provides an alphabetical listing of every word "defined" in the book and the page number on which the word is found.

The book is a standard-sized format for children at this level. The sturdy hardcover binding should withstand years of use.

Authority

Scott, Foresman is a highly regarded publisher of schoolbooks. Other books published by the firm include the THORNDIKE-BARNHART dictionaries. According to the book's introduction

> An experienced team of editors, designers, illustrators, and teacher consultants have examined every element of *My Pictionary* to make sure it will stimulate beginning readers to read, to write, to talk, to think, and to learn.

The introduction also states that the words chosen for inclusion in this book were selected from a list "made up of words, images, and concepts that children will encounter in kindergarten." The list was compiled after examining current books and other materials that kindergartners would use. Words for common home and school items were also included in the book.

Entries

The entries in *My Pictionary* are divided into 15 categories. At the top of each page, the category is identified in a large color-coded strip, which corresponds to a colored strip in the table of contents. Categories include "People," "Things," "What We Do," "Opposites," "Helping Words," "Colors," "Numbers," and "Seasons." Some of these categories are further divided into subcategories. For example, "Animals" contains subcategories for "Pets," "Farm Animals," "Wild Animals," "Birds," "Insects / Bugs," and "Dinosaurs."

The book employs two techniques to present the words. One technique is to depict a scene and label the items within the scene. For example, in "Classroom Things," boys and girls in a classroom are shown using **paint, paste, crayons, scissors,** and **paper.** The other technique displays groups of related objects, which are labeled and appear on a white background. This technique is used to show such categories as "Clothes / Clothing" and "Musical Instruments."

The words depicted in the book are printed in large type and are shown next to or on top of the related illustration. The words appear in an oval, which sets them off so that they are easily noticed. In several instances, more than one word is provided with an illustration. For example, in the illustration for "Family," the woman seated at one end of the table has three labels: **mother, mom,** and **mama.** A young child in this picture is labeled **son** and **boy.** These related labels are connected by a short line. In some cases, additional parts of the drawing are identified by a label in smaller type. For instance, the illustration for **fish** also labels the **tail, fin,** and **scales.** These additional labels should help children increase their vocabulary.

Illustrations

The illustrations in *My Pictionary* are the key element of the work. They are filled with color, beautifully rendered, and visually appealing. The illustrations are large and exceptionally clear, and they accurately represent the words to which they refer.

Many artists employing a wide variety of media contributed to this work. The result is a diverse and exciting mix of illustrations. The combination of artwork does not appear haphazard, however, because a distinct medium has been used for each category within the book. For example, the section on "Animals" is illustrated with stunning full-color photographs; cartoonlike drawings are used to depict the scenes in "Places"; the illustrations for "Colors" and "Shapes" are done in watercolors; and paper cutouts illustrate "Months of the Year and Holidays."

The illustrations are current and give the book a contemporary look. In "Things Around the House," drawings of a **computer, VCR,** and **microwave** are shown. The illustrations present a balanced treatment of males and females and a good representation of minority groups. The illustrations also avoid the use of stereotypes. Women are depicted in several nontraditional roles such as **doctor, lawyer,** and **police officer.**

Summary

My Pictionary is a highly appealing picture word book, presenting familiar words in a visually inviting way. The book's illustrations are bold, creative, and lively. The diversity of artists and techniques used creates a sense of variety that will hold children's interest. The book is much more contemporary and suitable for children in kindergarten and first grade than either THE FIRST THOUSAND WORDS or ROUND THE WORLD PICTURE WORD BOOK. *My Pictionary* is highly recommended for home, school, and library purchase.

My Second Picture Dictionary

Facts at a Glance

Full title: **My Second Picture Dictionary**
Publisher: Scott, Foresman
Edition reviewed: © 1990

Number of pages: 448
Number of entries: 4,000
Number of illustrations: over 1,000 in full color
Intended readership: grade 2
Trim size: 8⅛″ × 10¼″
Binding: hardcover; paperback

Price: $15.95 (hardcover); $12.95 (paperback)
Sold directly to schools; also sold in bookstores
ISBN 0-673-12490-8 (hardcover);
   ISBN 0-673-28453-0 (paperback)
No stated revision policy

Scope and Format

Scott, Foresman's *My Second Picture Dictionary* is the school edition of MY FIRST DICTIONARY (distributed by HarperCollins), and it is identical to that work except that it does not include a two-page activity section that appears inside the back cover of MY FIRST DICTIONARY. For a full description and evaluation, see the review of MY FIRST DICTIONARY elsewhere in this Buying Guide.

Round the World Picture Word Book

Facts at a Glance

Full title: **Round the World Picture Word Book**
Publisher: EDC Publishing
Compiler: Carol Watson
Illustrator: David Mostyn
Edition reviewed: © 1980

Number of pages: 47
Number of entries: approximately 600
Number of illustrations: 586 in full color
Intended readership: ages 2 to 12
Trim size: 9⅛″ × 12″
Binding: hardcover

Price: $11.95
Sold in bookstores and through wholesalers; also sold to libraries
ISBN 0-86020-485-5
No stated revision policy

Scope and Format

Round the World Picture Word Book is a 47-page book published in England in 1980. Because it is a picture word book and not a dictionary, it does not contain definitions, pronunciations, and so forth. This volume serves strictly as a resource for concept and vocabulary development. The introduction states that the book was created to give children "an exciting look at far-away places and introduce them to peoples and unfamiliar things in an interesting and lighthearted way."

The words in the book are arranged under 18 subjects, including **In the desert, Under the sea,** and **Houses and homes.** The subjects and words chosen center on the theme of cultural diversity around the world. A world map and an index of all the words used in the book appear at the end of the work.

The publisher states that the book's intended audience is 2- to 12-year-old children, but the true age range for this book seems to be 3- to 8-year-old children. Children at that level could use the book to match words with pictures and learn new concepts. Children over 8 years old, however, would probably not be stimulated by the simple format of a picture word book. To manipulate this oversized book, young readers will need some type of physical support, such as the lap of an adult, a desk, or a table. The book's cover and binding seem durable.

Foreign-language editions in the *Round the World* series are available in French, German, Spanish, and Italian. These editions include a foreign-language/English dictionary, which provides meanings and a pronunciation guide.

Authority

This work was created by Usborne Publishing, a British firm, and published in the United States by EDC Publishing. Betty Root, affiliated with the Centre for the Teaching of Reading at the University of Reading in England, served as the consultant. Root's experience with children's dictionaries includes writing Dorling Kindersley's MY FIRST DICTIONARY.

Round the World Picture Word Book

① Words organized by a theme under a subject heading in boldface

② Many subject headings defined by a

four-color, two-page, humorous illustration

③ Words related to the subject heading

labeled and redrawn around the outer margins

Entries

The book is organized into 18 two-page spreads. Like EDC Publishing's THE FIRST THOUSAND WORDS, two types of displays are used to present the words. In the first type, a scene is depicted. These scenes, such as **Cold lands,** show various types of climates and environments from around the world. From these scenes, selected items are redrawn, labeled, and shown in the border around the scene. For example, in the illustration of the desert, pictures of a **nomad, camel, dune, tent, oasis, lizard,** and **palm tree,** among others, are redrawn and labeled in the border. The pictures that were redrawn are identical or very similar to their counterparts within the scene. These pages are quite busy, however, and preschoolers may have difficulty locating the objects within the scene.

The second type of display used in this book shows groups of similar objects or actions from different places in the world. Examples of subjects include **Houses and homes, Dangers,** and **Growing things.** These displays emphasize the book's theme of cultural diversity and reflect the idea that all the world's people share common traits and qualities.

One drawback to the word entries in the book is the common use of British terms, such as **lorry, flyover,**

flats, and **petrol tanker.** Use of these terms reflects the British origins of the work and suggests that the book has not been adapted for an American audience. These British terms are liable to confuse young American children.

A six-page index, containing all the words used in the pictures, appears at the end of the book. The letters of the alphabet are shown in large, bold type. Next to each letter is a drawing of an object that starts with that letter (for example, a drawing of a guitar accompanies the letter *g*). The page number on which the word can be found follows each index entry.

Illustrations

Illustrator David Mostyn's cartoonlike drawings are colorful and humorous and appeal to children. The whole work conveys an atmosphere that is pleasant and fun. In general, the illustrations are positive in their portrayal of diverse cultures.

Some negative elements of the book mar its appeal, however. One such element is the obvious lack of a balanced representation of women and men in several of the scenes. For example, **In the jungle, Up the mountains,** and **In the harbour** are scenes that show many people but few, if any, women. The scene **In the jungle** contains another disturbing element. This illustration seems to promote racial stereotypes of great white hunters and noble savages. This scene detracts greatly from the work.

Special Features

The final display at the back of the book is **Famous buildings and places,** which includes such well-known sites as **The Statue of Liberty—USA, The Eiffel Tower—France,** and **The Taj Mahal—India.** These buildings and places are labeled and numbered. An activity is provided in which these numbers correspond to numbers found on the map of the world on the two pages that follow this display. Children are asked to match the two sets of numbers to determine where these famous places are in the world.

Another activity features a small spotted dog that is hidden in each of the scenes throughout the book. This is explained on the inside front cover, and children are asked to locate the dog in each picture. This activity was also used (with a duck) in EDC Publishing's THE FIRST THOUSAND WORDS.

The title page states that an "easy pronunciation guide" is included in the work. However, no such guide exists in this English-language edition.

Summary

Round the World Picture Word Book has a unique configuration for a picture word book. The book's universal approach is timely, especially given the desire for works that reflect cultural diversity. Respecting people and cultures should be an underlying objective of this type of publication. Unfortunately, the jungle scene seriously undermines this goal. In addition, the book shows an unbalanced representation of men and women in illustrations and includes many British terms. For these reasons, *Round the World Picture Word Book* is not recommended for purchase. Instead, prospective buyers should consider Scott, Foresman's MY PICTIONARY—an excellent picture word book.

Scott, Foresman Beginning Dictionary

Facts at a Glance

Full title: **Scott, Foresman Beginning Dictionary**
Publisher: Scott, Foresman
Editors: E. L. Thorndike; Clarence L. Barnhart
Edition reviewed: © 1993

Number of pages: 832
Number of entries: 28,000
Number of illustrations: 1,075, 80 percent in color

Intended readership: grades 3 to 5
Trim size: 8⅛" × 10¼"
Binding: hardcover

Price: $17.95
Sold in bookstores; also sold directly to schools
ISBN 0-673-12383-9
No stated revision policy

Scope and Format

The *Scott, Foresman Beginning Dictionary* is the school edition of the 1988 THORNDIKE-BARNHART CHILDREN'S DICTIONARY (distributed by HarperCollins). It is identical to that work except that some of the end matter, including the world map and information about U.S. presidents, has been updated in this 1993 edition of the *Beginning Dictionary.* For a full description and evaluation, see the review of the THORNDIKE-BARNHART CHILDREN'S DICTIONARY elsewhere in this Buying Guide.

The Sesame Street Dictionary

Facts at a Glance

Full title: **The Sesame Street Dictionary**
Publisher: Random House
Compiler: Linda Hayward
Illustrator: Joe Mathieu
Editors: Sharon Lerner, Editor-in-Chief; Janet Schulman
Edition reviewed: © 1980

Number of pages: 253
Number of entries: over 1,300
Number of illustrations: full color throughout
Intended readership: ages 3 to 8; preschoolers and up
Trim size: 8½" × 11"
Binding: laminated paper over boards

Price: $15.95
Sold in bookstores
ISBN 0-394-84007-0
No stated revision policy

Scope and Format

The exuberance of the Sesame Street television show has been translated into a comic-strip style book format in *The Sesame Street Dictionary.* Bert, Ernie, Big Bird, Cookie Monster, Oscar the Grouch, and other familiar characters are here. The Muppets maintain their well-known personalities and continue to teach children in this book of over 1,300 words. According to its preface, the book is designed for children ages three to eight and can be used in three stages: "as a word book and vocabulary builder, as a reading-readiness storybook, [and] as a first dictionary." The word selection was based, the preface states, on "several current vocabulary lists compiled by well-known educators," but these are not identified. Most of the words used are those found in beginning readers and in the everyday language of young children, but others such as **rocket, dinosaur,** and **skeleton,** were chosen because "they fascinate young children," the preface notes.

This book is hardbound; however, the sheets are glued, not sewn, and the endpapers began to tear as the book was being looked at for review. Long-term durability in the hands of young children, therefore, seems unlikely.

Authority

The dictionary, which is published by Random House, is copyrighted by Children's Television Workshop, the producers of several television series that have been innovative and creative in educating the very young.

Entries

The definitions are accurate as far as they go and the vocabulary is geared to very young children and beginning readers. Each word is "defined" by an illustration with a caption—usually a statement by a Muppet—and used in one or two sentences to show context. For example:

> **have** When you have something, it belongs to you.
> **have** Have also means to be holding or keeping something for someone else.

A picture of Big Bird and Little Bird has two comic-book speech balloons:

> I think I **have** your scarf, Big Bird.
> I think I **have** yours, Little Bird.

The main entry words and definitions are in bold lowercase serif type; and the Muppets' speech is always in sans-serif type in the balloons. Many of the interpretations are funnier if the reader is familiar with the individual personalities of the Muppets, but knowledge of the characters is not necessary to enjoy them. For example, **not** is defined with the sentence "Not means in no way." Oscar, shown sitting in his garbage can with odors wafting up from the surrounding plants, says, "I love stinkweed. Stinkweed does **not** smell nice. It smells terrible. That is why I love it." **Silent** is defined by "Silent means without any sound." A huge creature is snoring under a blanket while Big Bird says, "Shhhh! we must be **silent** while Mr. Snuffle-upagus takes his nap!"

The lively interpretations and all their surrounding activity tempt the child to study everything carefully before moving on to the next word. The Amazing Mumford, who appears throughout the book, is the only one who introduces homonyms. Computer words are not defined, and parts of speech, syllabication, pronunciation, and etymology are not given. This is not a flaw, as these are seldom found and would be fairly meaningless in a volume directed toward this very young age level.

Words are in alphabetical order. Each letter of the alphabet is boisterously announced on the appropriate page: an airplane piloted by Grover flies by trailing a banner with the letter *A* in upper- and lowercase; pigs and Oscar romp around *P*; a train brings in *T*. Guide words are used inconsistently at the tops of pages. They appear only when the art does not bleed off the page.

The entry words are in bold type with the definition or descriptive sentence following on the same line. When more than one definition is given, the entry word is treated as another main entry, and occasionally the definition states that it can also mean the other definition. Access is not as easy as in other dictionaries. The irregular layout often makes it difficult to locate and separate entry words.

Illustrations

The illustrations, which feature extensive use of primary colors, are so eye-catching that one tends to look at them and forget the word being sought. The upper- and lowercase letters that begin a new letter section appear above a horizontal band of color containing all the letters of the alphabet, with the proper letter dropped out in white or printed in another color for emphasis. The color of the band is repeated in horizontal rules separating entries throughout the pages assigned to that letter. However, these are often not readily visible, and sometimes the art almost covers them, so that there is inconsistent visual separation of the boxes in which the entries appear, even though a vertical black rule consistently divides each page into two columns. Jokes, riddles, and stories abound in the brightly colored illustrations. Activity prevails in these drawings; the characters are shown *doing* things rather than thinking about them.

Special Features

The book abounds with jokes, as well as games and activities—naming the parts of the body, counting, or matching shapes. These features encourage young readers to think about the words and to practice dictionary and other skills.

Summary

The Sesame Street Dictionary is vibrant and is sure to attract a readership because it stars the Muppets. The definitions can be read by the beginning reader and, for those too young to read, the illustrations suggest stories. Even very young children will enjoy browsing through the book and telling in their own words what they see happening. This may be a worthwhile purchase for home use and for public and school libraries because it does indeed make learning fun. However, it should be noted that any newer characters introduced on the show since 1980 are not included in this book. In addition, buyers should beware of the weak binding; illustrations are printed close to the center margins so the book cannot be rebound easily.

Thorndike-Barnhart Children's Dictionary

Facts at a Glance

Full title: **Thorndike-Barnhart Children's Dictionary**
Publisher: Scott, Foresman; distributed by HarperCollins
Editors: E. L. Thorndike; Clarence L. Barnhart
Edition reviewed: © 1988, 1991 printing

Number of pages: 832
Number of entries: 28,000
Number of illustrations: 1,075, 80 percent in color
Intended readership: grades 3 to 5
Trim size: 8⅛″ × 10¼″
Binding: hardcover

Price: $14.95
Sold in bookstores and other retail outlets; also sold to libraries and schools
ISBN 0-06-275006-2
No stated revision policy

Scope and Format

The introduction for this work best sums up its philosophy:

> Children love using words, both in their conversation and in their writing activities, and they have a natural interest in learning about words. This dictionary endeavors to encourage this interest.

The *Thorndike-Barnhart Children's Dictionary* succeeds admirably in this task, combining lucid definitions with a large number of illustrations (mostly color), along with added features such as word-history and word-source boxes. All features are well explained in a detailed section on using the dictionary. The work concludes with a useful "Student's Reference Section" of appendixes typical of dictionaries for this age group. The work is also published in a classroom edition as the SCOTT, FORESMAN BEGINNING DICTIONARY.

Authority

The *Thorndike-Barnhart Children's Dictionary* comes from the same publisher as the THORNDIKE-BARNHART STUDENT DICTIONARY. Scott, Foresman began publishing the Thorndike-Barnhart series in 1929, and these works bear the names of two of the preeminent dictionary makers in the business. Although this book's title page still credits E. L. Thorndike, who died in 1949, and Clarence L. Barnhart with creating the work, Barnhart's preface makes clear that Thorndike's philosophy remains firmly ingrained in the work. The introduction adds that "every effort has been made to carry out the original precept of Dr. Thorndike." The introduction also discusses the basis for the word list:

> A wide variety of contemporary children's textbooks and other literature was read to check for new words and new meanings. Current word frequency counts were reviewed to ensure that the dictionary contains the words and meanings most likely to be encountered by its users. This reading is backed by Scott, Foresman's citation files. . . .

Entries

The *Thorndike-Barnhart Children's Dictionary* features slightly fewer entries (approximately 28,000) than some of its somewhat more up-to-date competitors—including WEBSTER'S NEW WORLD CHILDREN'S DICTIONARY and MACMILLAN DICTIONARY FOR CHILDREN. Still, this does not detract from the generally excellent coverage of words, including a fair number of scientific and technical entries. Despite its publication date, however, the dictionary is somewhat behind in its coverage of computer technology, including an entry for **floppy disk** and for **RAM** but not for *hard disk* or *compact disc.*

The first and last entries on a page are given in large, boldface type at the outside corners of each page. In addition, vertical color bars appear on the outer margins of the right-hand pages with the relevant letter of the alphabet in white. Different colors are used for a third of the entries: red for the letters *A* through *F,* blue for *G* through *P,* and green for *Q* through *Z.*

Main entries are shown as syllabicated words in boldface type. Following the main entry are the pronunciation (in parentheses) and numbered definitions. The following entry is typical:

> **blame** (blām), **1** to hold responsible for something bad or wrong: *The driver blamed the fog for the accident.* **2** responsibility for something bad or wrong: *I won't take the blame for something I didn't do.* **3** to find fault with: *I don't blame her for wanting a better bicycle.* 1,3 *verb,* **blames, blamed, blam·ing;** 2 *noun.*

Definitions are written in easily understood language, long a criterion for *Thorndike-Barnhart* works. Although no statement is made regarding how the definitions are ordered, frequency of usage seems to be the criterion.

Although there are no specially marked usage notes within definitions, the editors advise the reader on the use of the word within the definition itself. The entry on **ain't,** for example, concludes: "Careful speakers and

Thorndike-Barnhart Children's Dictionary

❶ Pronunciation key on each right-hand page

❷ Main entry word in boldface, divided into syllables, followed by pronunciation guide in parentheses

❸ When more than one meaning is given, each entry is numbered

❹ Part-of-speech label

❺ Word history

❻ Illustrations include diagrams with callouts and captions

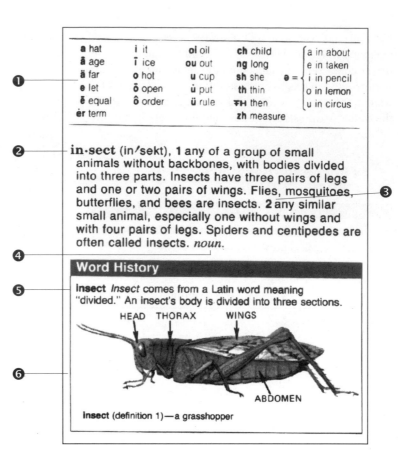

a hat	i it	oi oil	ch child	ə = {	a in about
ā age	ī ice	ou out	ng long		e in taken
ä far	o hot	u cup	sh she		i in pencil
e let	ō open	u̇ put	th thin		o in lemon
ē equal	ô order	ü rule	ᵀʜ then		u in circus
ėr term			zh measure		

in·sect (in′sekt), **1** any of a group of small animals without backbones, with bodies divided into three parts. Insects have three pairs of legs and one or two pairs of wings. Flies, mosquitoes, butterflies, and bees are insects. **2** any similar small animal, especially one without wings and with four pairs of legs. Spiders and centipedes are often called insects. *noun*.

Word History

insect *Insect* comes from a Latin word meaning "divided." An insect's body is divided into three sections.

HEAD　THORAX　WINGS

ABDOMEN

insect (definition 1)—a grasshopper

writers do not use *ain't.*" Parts of speech are noted at the end of the entry, with definition numbers given before each label; **jolt,** for example, concludes: "1,4 *verb,* 2,3 *noun.*" These labels do not use abbreviations, which is helpful for the young user.

Children's dictionaries must feature sufficient examples of the word for their meanings to be clear to its readers. *Thorndike-Barnhart* uses invented—rather than real—quotations, as is appropriate for a work at this level. The vast majority of entries feature these illustrative sentences, which appear in italics. The entry **set,** for example, which features 17 numbered definitions, has illustrative sentences or phrases for 15 of them.

A complete 41-symbol pronunciation key is given opposite the front and back covers of the dictionary. An abbreviated 23-symbol key is on the upper right-hand side of every right-hand page. In addition, six pages of the user's guide are devoted to explaining the symbols used. Variant pronunciations are included; if the pronunciation changes depending on the meaning of the word, this is indicated with definition numbers: **per·mit** (pər mit′ *for 1;* pėr′mit *for 2*).

Any children's dictionary must have an adequate user's guide, and the one in *Thorndike-Barnhart* is exemplary. The 39-page "How to Use This Dictionary" is a self-teaching guide to using the work with numerous examples and illustrations. Prepared with classroom teachers as consultants, the guide has useful exercises that build familiarity with the dictionary.

Illustrations

With about 80 percent of its 1,075 illustrations in color, *Thorndike-Barnhart* is a visually appealing dictionary. The vast majority of the illustrations are photographs. Unique are illustrations depicting feelings, ideas, or actions. **Headlong,** for example, shows a drawing of an elephant bumping into a tree, with the caption "The elephant ran **headlong** into a tree." One complaint is that some illustrations present a confusing pastiche of objects; **column** and **spring,** for example, attempt to show, respectively, four and five different definitions of the word within one illustration. Another complaint is that some of the photographs look a bit dated.

The work is well bound and attractively designed. It will be inviting to those for whom the work is intended.

Special Features

Thorndike-Barnhart features a 34-page "Student's Reference Section" that is a potpourri of material including a map of the United States and a now-outdated world map, facts about the 50 states, pictures and brief biographies of the presidents of the United States (Ronald Reagan being the most recent), a time line, lists of words borrowed from other languages, and metric measurements. Some of the material in this section, including the world map and biographies of the presidents, was updated for the 1993 edition of the SCOTT, FORESMAN BEGINNING DICTIONARY.

Another special feature is the inclusion of word histories sprinkled throughout the book. These appear in blue type at the end of a word entry or as separate "Word History" boxes along with an illustration. Such word histories also appear at the end of every entry for a state, and for many words that originated from someone's name, such as **forsythia, nicotine,** and **volt.** Word histories that the user's guide states are "especially interesting" are featured in a blue frame with a picture.

Summary

Although it has fewer entries and is somewhat less up-to-date than the MACMILLAN DICTIONARY FOR CHILDREN, one cannot help but be favorably impressed by the *Thorndike-Barnhart Children's Dictionary.* Its understandable definitions, good illustrations, and excellent illustrative sentences more than offset any drawbacks the work may have. This work is a valuable reference tool for children in grades 3 to 5 and is a recommended purchase for home, school, or library use.

Webster's Elementary Dictionary

Facts at a Glance

Full title: **Webster's Elementary Dictionary**
Publisher: Merriam-Webster
Edition reviewed: © 1986

Number of pages: 600
Number of entries: 32,000
Number of illustrations: 600 in full color
Intended readership: elementary school students
Trim size: 8″ × 10″
Binding: cloth

Price: $14.95
Sold in bookstores and other outlets; also sold to libraries and schools
ISBN 0-87779-475-8.
Revision scheduled for 1994

Scope and Format

Webster's Elementary Dictionary, (formerly called *Webster's Beginning Dictionary*), suitable for grades 4 to 6, is part of a series of three titles published by Merriam-Webster including WEBSTER'S INTERMEDIATE DICTIONARY and WEBSTER'S SCHOOL DICTIONARY. Originally published in 1980 and revised in 1986, the dictionary contains 32,000 entries and 600 illustrations in color. The preface to the dictionary states that words were chosen based on the frequency with which they appeared in school textbooks, in other materials that a student would normally read (these are not identified), and in everyday language use. A revision of this work is expected to appear in 1994, with the new title *Merriam-Webster's Elementary Dictionary.*

Authority

Merriam-Webster has been producing dictionaries since 1847 and is one of the most respected names in dictionary publishing. The preface states that the Merriam-Webster staff made use of the same information for this young readers' dictionary that is on file for the *Webster's Third New International* and *Webster's Ninth New Collegiate* dictionaries, and that the *Elementary Dictionary* might be viewed as a "little brother or sister to those larger books." MERRIAM-WEBSTER'S COLLEGIATE DICTIONARY, tenth edition, has since been published and is reviewed elsewhere in this Buying Guide.

Entries

With its 32,000 words and phrases, this dictionary includes those words most students will ordinarily encounter. Synonyms are included and identified, but antonyms are not. There are separate entries for prefixes and suffixes: run-on entries follow the end of the entry for the base word and are preceded by a dash:—**hang on to** under the entry word **hang.** Run-in entries are also noted in boldface type and appear in parentheses in the middle of the definition, such as **summer solstice** under the entry word **solstice.** Some words are defined by a synonym.

This dictionary also includes usage notes, homographs, and word histories. Usage notes follow the definition and are separated from it by a dash. Homographs are given separate entries; homophones such as **bare** and **bear,** are given no special notation.

There are a substantial number of word history paragraphs in the dictionary. These are indented under the main entry, labeled **"Word History,"** and printed in bright blue type. They are written in a style appropriate for children and are accurate and informative.

Few abbreviations are to be found in the dictionary. Some exceptions include **Mr., Mrs., TNT,** and **DNA.** Unfortunately, neither **TNT** nor **DNA** is spelled out, although they are defined. There are, in general, very few scientific terms included.

Even though this reference work is intended for elementary school, the publisher did not avoid the inclusion of sex organs, although such terms as *homosexual,*

Webster's Elementary Dictionary

❶ Pronunciation, within slashes, followed by the abbreviated part of speech, in italics

❷ Examples of usage appear in angle brackets

❸ Inflected forms, in boldface, show syllable divisions with centered dots

❹ Synonyms in small capital letters, cross-referenced to main entry words, follow some definitions

❺ Word History paragraph set off in blue type provides informal anecdotes that explain word origins

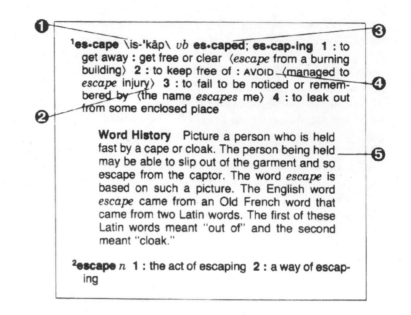

¹**es·cape** \is-'kāp\ *vb* **es·caped; es·cap·ing** **1** : to get away : get free or clear ⟨*escape* from a burning building⟩ **2** : to keep free of : AVOID ⟨managed to *escape* injury⟩ **3** : to fail to be noticed or remembered by ⟨the name *escapes* me⟩ **4** : to leak out from some enclosed place

Word History Picture a person who is held fast by a cape or cloak. The person being held may be able to slip out of the garment and so escape from the captor. The word *escape* is based on such a picture. The English word *escape* came from an Old French word that came from two Latin words. The first of these Latin words meant "out of" and the second meant "cloak."

²**escape** *n* **1** : the act of escaping **2** : a way of escaping

---

lesbian, and the definition of *gay* as homosexual are absent. Computer terms such as *bit* and *byte* are also not included, nor are *VCR* and *videocassette.* Biographical and geographic names are not included in the main alphabet, but a separate pronouncing glossary for place names is appended to the back of the dictionary.

Main entry words are in boldface type overhanging the text. A typical order for entries is: main word, pronunciation, abbreviated part of speech, and definition(s), numbered and occasionally cross-referenced to other entries. For example:

> **cor·rec·tion** │kə-'rek-shən'n **1** : the act of correcting **2** : a change that makes something right **3** : PUNISHMENT.

Definitions are clearly and simply stated and are very adequate. Several senses are given for many words and are listed in historical order. Separate, numbered entries are given for the various parts of speech, which are identified with abbreviations. Examples are used to help define difficult words and appear in angle brackets to separate them from the definitions:

> ¹**cor·rect** . . . *vb* **1** : to make or set right ⟨*correct* a misspelled word⟩ . . . .

Most verbal illustrations, as in this example, are in the form of phrases or modifiers rather than complete sentences. In *Webster's Elementary* not nearly as many definitions have verbal illustrations as in the MACMILLAN DICTIONARY FOR CHILDREN, which consistently uses sentences. However, more senses of a word are given in the Merriam-Webster work than in the Macmillan one. Both syllabication and pronunciation are indicated. Entry words are given in syllables separated by bold, centered dots. Pronunciation follows and appears between back slashes: **prize·fight·er** \'prīz-fīt-ər'\. Forty-three symbols, with diacritical marks, are used in the pronuncia-

tion key, which appears on the page preceding the main body of the dictionary; accent marks indicate primary or secondary stress. There is also a useful short key to 25 of the most frequent symbols on the lower right-hand corner of each right-hand page. The key provides a quick reference for students. Variant pronunciations ("used by large numbers of educated people") are indicated, which is not always the case in children's dictionaries. Such accuracy is admirable in a children's dictionary, and although it may be confusing to some students, it will also help to explain to students the frequent inconsistencies heard in everyday speech.

Illustrations

The dictionary has 582 pages plus 18 pages of prefatory matter. There are 600 illustrations in full color. They are less cartoonlike in style and more artistically rendered than most pictures in elementary dictionaries.

Most of the illustrations depict objects rather than people; care has been taken, however, to include a variety of ethnic groups among those people illustrated. Most of the illustrations appear immediately above or below the entry word that they help to define, and all are clearly captioned. A few are placed in a different column or even on a different page, which makes them less useful to a reader.

The overall layout of the pages is pleasing and the text easy to read. The illustrations and the bright blue word histories help to break up the pages of type.

Special Features

The features in this dictionary include the guide and the key to pronunciation in the front, and several appendixes in the back. The guide makes use of color blocks to emphasize examples in its explanation of the parts of the dictionary. This will help young readers to understand how to use the dictionary. The appendixes are: a list of abbreviations, which includes the two-letter postal abbreviations for the states; a chart of signs and symbols; separate chronological lists for U.S. presidents and vice presidents that indicate pronunciation of name, birth and death dates, birthplace, and terms of office (Ronald Reagan and George Bush are the most recent ones included); and a list of geographic names that includes U.S. states, Canadian provinces and territories, nations of the world and their capitals (many of which are out of date because of the age of this work) and continents and oceans. Each geographic name is given a pronunciation. Entries are in letter-by-letter alphabetical order, including abbreviations and disregarding spaces and hyphens. There are guide words at the top of each double-column page, but no thumb guides. Words beginning with capital letters are included as appropriate and variant spellings of words are given.

Summary

If it is possible to put together a "scholarly" children's dictionary, then Merriam-Webster has succeeded with the *Webster's Elementary Dictionary*. Admirably, the publisher has attempted not to compromise quality for the sake of simplicity. The problem is that this is not an easy dictionary for children to use without assistance. The guide to the dictionary's use may be especially difficult to understand because of its large amount of explanatory (although excellent) text. Children may need a teacher's or parents guidance to understand the information. In comparison, the MACMILLAN DICTIONARY FOR CHILDREN has more eye appeal and is far easier to use. The Macmillan work does, however, sacrifice the detail and, sometimes, the accuracy that Merriam-Webster has tried to maintain. *Webster's Elementary Dictionary* should be available for bright students in the upper elementary grades, but even they will need assistance in understanding the finer points of its use. The work is also a possible choice for older students (junior high and high school) who need a simpler dictionary and also for those whose first language is not English. WEBSTER'S BASIC ENGLISH DICTIONARY, which contains the same word list as *Webster's Elementary Dictionary*, is sold as an ESL title. Especially useful would be the multiple senses given under an entry such as **bug,** including both flaw and an enthusiast. *Webster's Elementary Dictionary* is an excellent dictionary with much to recommend it, even though it will not be especially easy for elementary students to read. However, those who do learn its intricacies will be well prepared to go on to more adult dictionaries. One final note: Prospective buyers would be well advised to wait for the publication of the 1994 edition of this work.

Webster's New World Children's Dictionary

Facts at a Glance

Full title: **Webster's New World Children's Dictionary**
Publisher: Prentice Hall
Editors: Victoria Neufeldt, Editor-in-Chief; Fernando de Mello Vianna, Project Editor
Edition reviewed: © 1991

Number of pages: 896
Number of entries: more than 33,000
Number of illustrations: approximately 700, all in full color
Intended readership: ages 8 to 11
Trim size: 8⅛″ × 10¼″
Binding: hardcover

Price: $16
ISBN 0-13-945726-7
No stated revision policy

Scope and Format

Webster's New World Children's Dictionary, first published in 1991, is an 896-page work designed for 8- to 11-year-old children. The book is filled with more than 33,000 entry words and definitions and nearly 700 full-color illustrations. As stated in the book's foreword, special care was taken during the preparation of this work "because a good dictionary can play a significant role in the development of the language skills that are so important to the progress of all other learning."

All entries in the dictionary include the pronunciation and parts of speech. Example sentences are provided for many entries, and usage notes, idioms, and homonyms are included where appropriate. Many geographical and biographical names are included as entries. The book contains several special features, including word histories and synonyms that are highlighted in feature boxes throughout the book, as well as an atlas and albums of presidents and states at the back of the book.

This book features an 11-page introduction called "How To Use This Dictionary," which describes how to find words in the dictionary and explains all of the parts of the book, including the special features. This section is addressed to children and is written clearly, using terms that young readers will understand.

The book is a standard size for a children's dictionary. The hardcover binding is sturdy and should withstand years of use.

Authority

This book was "written and produced by the same highly skilled lexicographical staff that prepared *Webster's New World Dictionary*®, Third College Edition."

In addition, two groups of educators—an advisory board of five specialists in childhood education and seven consultants from school districts around the country—helped during the book's development.

In reference to the creation of the word list for this dictionary, the book's foreword states:

> Current and classic children's literature, current school texts, and children's own compositions were examined to ensure that the vocabulary coverage in this dictionary was appropriate.

Entries

In *Webster's New World Children's Dictionary,* each letter of the alphabet is introduced with a history of the evolution of the letter's shape, showing the Phoenician, Greek, Roman, and medieval forms. This introduction is accompanied by a photograph of a historical building or object on which the letter appears. On subsequent pages, the letter being addressed is presented in a colored block on the right-hand pages, and guide words are shown at the top of each page in a block of a lighter shade of the same color.

Each entry word appears in bold type and is followed by the pronunciation, part of speech, and definition. Multiple definitions are presented and numbered. Example sentences or phrases are provided for many of the entry words. They appear within brackets, and the entry word is shown in italics, making it easy to locate. The number of entries per page ranges from about 12 to 20.

The definitions in this dictionary are exceptionally clear, accurate, and accessible to children. The words used in the definitions would be familiar to children ages 8 to 11—the book's intended audience. The following example of an entry is typical:

> **bitter** (bit′ər) *adj.* **1** having a strong, often unpleasant taste [*The seed in a peach pit is bitter.]* **2** full of sorrow or pain [*Poor people often suffer bitter hardships.]* **3** with strong feelings of hatred [*bitter enemies].*
> **bit·ter** *adj.*

Where appropriate, usage notes are included at the end of entries. For example, within the entry for **needle** is the following: "**v.** [*an informal use*] to tease or annoy [*Don't needle your brother.]*" Idiomatic expressions are also provided, as in the following example within the entry for **neck:** "—**neck and neck** very close or even in a race or contest."

Illustrations

Webster's New World Children's Dictionary is a beautifully illustrated work, incorporating both drawings and photographs in full color. The illustrations are clear and appealing, accurately portraying the meaning of the entry word to which they refer. Illustrations appear adjacent to the entry word and are clearly labeled.

The illustrations show a balance of males and females and an adequate representation from various ethnic and racial groups. The book avoids the use of stereotypes, mostly because topics such as occupations are not illustrated.

The photographs in this book are more contemporary than those in the THORNDIKE-BARNHART CHILDREN'S DICTIONARY. Up-to-date photographs of a **computer, joystick, mouse,** and **printer** are shown. The entry word **hatchback** is illustrated with a photograph of a late-model four-wheel-drive vehicle. In addition, clothes worn by the people in the photographs do not appear dated.

One special illustration feature of this dictionary is the inclusion of U.S. maps. At the entry for each of the 50 states, an outline map of the United States is shown, with the appropriate state highlighted and labeled.

The only complaint—a relatively minor one—that might be made about the illustrations is that the use of labels only instead of caption sentences limits their usefulness. Some other dictionaries for this level, including the THORNDIKE-BARNHART CHILDREN'S DICTIONARY, use caption sentences with the illustrations to help convey the meaning of abstract concepts, such as emotions.

Special Features

Webster's New World Children's Dictionary contains many special features, some of which appear as highlighted boxes within the text and others that are found at the end of the book. Categories for feature boxes include "Word History" (etymologies), "Word Choices" (synonyms), "Word Maker" (words formed with prefixes and suffixes), and "Spelling Tip." An example of a spelling tip in the book is: "Use this memory aid to spell **lesson.** Dad taught his *son* a les-*son.*" In addition, homonyms and their sample sentences appear throughout the book and are highlighted with a blue dot.

The special features at the back of the book include an atlas with a U.S. time-zone map and political maps of the United States, Canada, Mexico, Central and South America, and the world. (These maps were current as of the book's 1991 printing date.) Also at the back of the dictionary are an album of presidents (ending with George Bush), an album of the states, illustrations of state birds and state flowers, and two pages on weights and measures.

Summary

Webster's New World Children's Dictionary compares favorably with other dictionaries for this age group of 8- to 11-year-old children. The word list is much more comprehensive and accessible than that of THE

DOUBLEDAY CHILDREN'S DICTIONARY, and the book's up-to-date photographs give it a more contemporary and appealing look than the THORNDIKE-BARNHART CHILDREN'S DICTIONARY. Moreover, the inclusion of biographical and geographical entries makes *Webster's New World Children's Dictionary* especially useful for elementary school students and gives it a slight advantage over THE AMERICAN HERITAGE CHILDREN'S DICTIONARY. *Webster's New World Children's Dictionary* would be an excellent choice for home, school, or library purchase.

Words for New Readers

Facts at a Glance

Full title: **Words for New Readers**
Publisher: Scott, Foresman; distributed by HarperCollins
Edition reviewed: © 1990, 1991 printing

Number of pages: 312
Number of entries: 1,500
Number of illustrations: 1,100 in full color
Intended readership: grade 1
Trim size: $8\,5/8'' \times 11\,1/8''$
Binding: hardcover

Price: $10.95
Sold in bookstores; also sold to libraries and schools
ISBN 0-06-275-008-9
No stated revision policy

Scope and Format

The 1991 printing of *Words for New Readers* is published for "children who have advanced beyond the picturebook level" and it strives to introduce young readers to the "idea of using a reference book. . . . It prepares them for actual dictionary use by familiarizing them with simple dictionary skills." (Introduction) It is the trade edition of MY FIRST PICTURE DICTIONARY (published by Scott, Foresman), which is used in kindergarten and first-grade classrooms, and is intended for beginning readers and writers in the 4- to 6-year age range.

Words for New Readers falls between simple picture word books and the more advanced MY FIRST DICTIONARY (also published by Scott, Foresman). It is intended for children who are familiar with the alphabet and have some experience alphabetizing letters and words. Words are defined in clear, simple sentences with one or more examples. Extensive introductory material is avoided, but strong appendixes add value to this dictionary. The trim size is similar to many picture books.

There are 1,500 entries, alphabetically arranged in 312 pages. Over 1,100 illustrations form a colorful and important part of this transitional reference work. Young readers will find it a friendly and sturdily bound volume. Librarians will find it likely to withstand frequent use.

Authority

For over 50 years, the Scott, Foresman series of children's dictionaries has included reference works for trade publication and text editions for classroom use. The entry words in *Words for New Readers* were chosen from a list of words that children use in school and at home. Primary school teachers assisted in development of the word list. The individual editors are not named.

Entries

Each letter section begins with a capital letter and a small letter, which are reproduced at the top of each page in that section. This is an appropriate convention for young readers. (Scott, Foresman's MY FIRST DICTIONARY and other middle-level primary dictionaries often use the first and last words on a page as headers for quick reference.) Each entry word is printed in large boldface type. Entries are brief. Within the entry, the entry word appears only slightly darker than the other words in the definition and in the example sentence that follows. Multiple meanings are numbered clearly. The most familiar meanings are the ones included. Unlike more advanced dictionaries, no more than two meanings appear. Inflected and plural forms are given in boldface at the end of each entry. These are kept simple and reflect the vocabulary with which the child is familiar. Comparative and superlative forms are also given ("**drier, driest**"). Nouns and verbs are treated with separate meanings and sample sentences; however, these sentences are not distinguished typographically from the definition—a potential cause for confusion to young readers. For example:

> **slide** 1. A **slide** is something to play on at a playground. You can slip down a slide or climb up it. **slides.**
> 2. **Slide** also means to move over something easily. Rose **slides** down the hill on her sled. **slid, sliding.**

Proper nouns are not included in the lexicon. Holidays such as Halloween, Hanukkah, Easter, and Martin Luther King Day do appear in the "Special Features" pages at the end of the volume. Abstractions are handled as examples. "**Red** is a color. Strawberries are **red.**" Homographs are numbered in superscript and occupy separate entries.

Five to six entries appear on each page, allowing ample room for illustrations. Most of the definitions are well chosen, accurate, and meaningful for the intended readership. Occasionally a second meaning would have

Words for New Readers

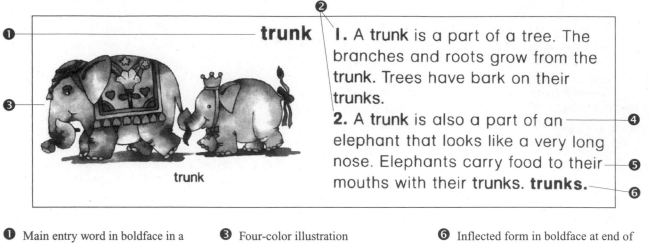

trunk

I. A trunk is a part of a tree. The branches and roots grow from the trunk. Trees have bark on their trunks.

2. A trunk is also a part of an elephant that looks like a very long nose. Elephants carry food to their mouths with their trunks. **trunks.**

trunk

❶ Main entry word in boldface in a separate column, making it easy to find

❷ When more than one meaning is given, each entry is numbered

❸ Four-color illustration

❹ All definitions given in complete sentences

❺ Example sentence shows the entry word in context

❻ Inflected form in boldface at end of entry

been helpful, as in the entry for **pad.** The definition—"A **pad** is a large, floating leaf"—is accompanied by a very large illustration of a frog sitting on a lily pad. This relates to storybooks about frogs and will seem familiar to a child, but it leaves out other types of pads such as writing pads, nap-taking pads, exercise pads, and knee pads. This definition demonstrates the fact that words have been chosen from the literature of childhood and not entirely from the experience of childhood.

Illustrations

Illustrations consist of drawings, some photographs, and cartoons. Most use good, strong colors. Each illustration is accompanied by a caption, which is the entry word. The size of the illustrations varies, from a small **puppy** to a large **zebra** (which occupies almost an entire page). This lends texture and variety, and it bridges the gap between the "pictionary" style of reference book and a beginning dictionary.

The illustrations are full of situations and activities appropriate for young readers. The first illustration in the book shows a child performing a handstand in front of a picket fence with flowers blooming along the bottom. It illustrates the word **able** and provides a positive, lively introduction. Different forms of original art are used: a Grandma Moses–style picnic illustrates **ate;** a Currier and Ives–style skating scene accompanies the word **ice.**

Many of the illustrations also demonstrate currency. Examples are a portable **radio** that resembles a "boom box," an **astronaut** walking outside his spaceship, and

a **computer** operated by a real mouse. The latter demonstrates the subtle humor in many of the pictures. A good mixture of ethnicities is included; however, gender and family roles tend to be traditional. Although there are a few exceptions (a female **scientist,** a man in a **kitchen**), men are portrayed as doctors and airline pilots, women as teachers, librarians, and nurses.

Special Features

A section called "Find Out the Facts!" includes illustrated pages on shapes, numbers and measurement, clocks and time, parts of the body, healthy snacks, maps of the United States and the world, days of the week and months, holidays throughout the year, opposites, and colors. These pages are colorful, with clearly drawn figures and easily understood messages. This section shows the objects that words represent in a conceptual framework, just as picture word books like THE FIRST THOUSAND WORDS do, providing another link between word books and beginning dictionaries.

Like Scott, Foresman's MY FIRST DICTIONARY, the inside back cover contains black-and-white drawings and activities geared to the intended audience. "Not meant to be completed in one sitting," these are intended to help children learn "to categorize, to compare and contrast, and to draw conclusions." Adults may assist with these activities but children may complete them on their own or with friends. There is a D'Nealian® Alphabet chart with capital and lowercase letters and numbers 1 through 10. This may appeal to parents more than to children, but it is a useful guide.

Summary

Words for New Readers is a well-illustrated beginning dictionary for young readers who are not yet ready for advanced primary school reference works such as Scott, Foresman's MY FIRST DICTIONARY. Pages are strikingly balanced between text and visual material and varied enough to keep an eager reader moving along. It compares favorably with other primary dictionaries such as the MACMILLAN FIRST DICTIONARY, which also contains excellent illustrations. The latter is designed to cover a much broader age range (5 to 9), but appears to overlap with *Words for New Readers* for the younger readers and with MY FIRST DICTIONARY for the older readers. All of these dictionaries are good choices for primary school students. The format of *Words for New Readers* is comparable to other dictionaries in its class and the price is very competitive, making it a worthwhile purchase for librarians and parents.

Young People's Dictionary

Facts at a Glance

Full title: **Young People's Dictionary**
Publisher: Troll Associates
Compilers: David Smith; Derek Newton
Edition reviewed: © 1991

Number of pages: 128
Number of words: 1,248
Number of illustrations: approximately 250 in full color
Intended readership: grades 1 to 4
Trim size: 8¾″ × 11¼″ (hardcover); 8½″ × 10⅞″ (paperback)
Binding: hardcover; paperback

Price: $14.89 (hardcover); $9.95 (paperback)
Sold through vendors and direct to libraries and schools
ISBN 0-8167-2255-2 (hardcover);
    ISBN 0-8167-2256-0 (paperback)
No stated revision policy

Scope and Format

Young People's Dictionary was published by Troll Associates in 1991 and is designed for primary school children. This volume contains 128 pages of words, definitions, pronunciations, and illustrations.

The publisher does not provide the criteria on which the words were chosen. For each of the dictionary's 1,248 words, a pronunciation and one or more definitions are provided. Some of the words are illustrated, and some include sample sentences.

The paperback edition of this book was reviewed. The publisher also has a hardcover version, which prospective buyers should examine for durability, especially if the work is being obtained for a library.

Authority

Troll Associates is a publisher of juvenile books. The firm also publishes MY FIRST DICTIONARY, STUDENT ENCYCLOPEDIA, and STUDENT ATLAS. *Young People's Dictionary* was compiled by David Smith and Derek Newton.

Entries

Young People's Dictionary contains definitions of many words that should be part of primary school children's vocabulary. Topics include animals, clothing, food, shapes, months, modes of transportation, emotions, and parts of the body.

At the top of each page of *Young People's Dictionary,* the letter being addressed is displayed in large boldface type on a square, colored grid. Each page of the dictionary contains about ten entry words, which appear in boldface type. Next to each entry word is the pronunciation. (Pronunciations are not usually included in dictionaries for this age group.) The definition appears underneath the entry word and pronunciation and, where appropriate, multiple definitions are provided and numbered. Occasionally, sample sentences are given; they appear in italics, but the entry words are not highlighted.

The definitions in the book are simple, which is generally appropriate for this age level. Sometimes, however, the definitions are inadequate and do not provide enough information for full comprehension. For example, the definition for **left** is "the opposite side of right," and the corresponding definition for **right** is "the opposite of left." **Bird** is simply defined as "an animal that has wings and feathers."

In addition to this lack of information, omissions of important entry words and their definitions will most likely cause confusion for young readers. For instance, words used in definitions are not always included as entry words. **Car** is defined as "an automobile," but *automobile* is not an entry word. The second definition of **patient** is "a person who is being helped by a doctor, dentist, or nurse." However, the words *doctor, dentist,* and *nurse* are not defined. Similarly, the sample sentence for **rainbow** includes the seven colors in a rainbow, but this dictionary provides no definitions of colors.

Illustrations

The illustrations in *Young People's Dictionary* are all full-color drawings, which are labeled and located in the right-hand margins next to the related entries. The illus-

Young People's Dictionary

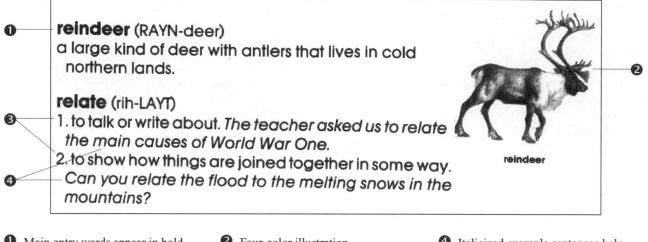

❶ reindeer (RAYN-deer)
a large kind of deer with antlers that lives in cold
    northern lands.

❸ relate (rih-LAYT)
❸ 1. to talk or write about. *The teacher asked us to relate
    the main causes of World War One.*
2. to show how things are joined together in some way.
❹ *Can you relate the flood to the melting snows in the
    mountains?*

reindeer

❶ Main entry words appear in boldface, followed by pronunciation
   guide in parentheses

❷ Four-color illustration
❸ When more than one meaning is
   given, each entry is numbered

❹ Italicized example sentences help
   clarify different meanings

trations are finely detailed and fairly realistic, but the number of illustrations is limited. With approximately 1,250 word entries and 250 drawings, only about 20 percent of the words in the book are illustrated. A greater number of illustrations would have enhanced the appeal of a dictionary for this age level.

In most cases, the illustrations match the entries to which they refer. Occasionally, the elaborate detail of the illustrations detracts from the understanding of the term. For example, the illustration for **west** shows a covered wagon, mountains, a cactus, and a very small signpost, located off to one side of the scene, containing the word *west.*

Compared with MACMILLAN FIRST DICTIONARY, the illustrations in *Young People's Dictionary* are somewhat small, which may cause confusion at times. For instance, the illustration for **price** shows a car with a price sticker on the windshield. The sticker is so small, however, that its relevance may be unclear to young readers.

Many of the illustrations in this dictionary are also quite static. Few people are depicted. For example, the illustration for **bicycle** does not include a rider, and the drawing for **hat** does not show a head. Even illustrations for action words, such as **melt, pour,** and **sew,** do not show people participating in the actions. In addition, very few of the people who are depicted in the illustrations are people of color.

Summary

The illustrations in *Young People's Dictionary* are limited in number and lack activity. Compared with other works, such as Dorling Kindersley's MY FIRST DICTIONARY and MACMILLAN FIRST DICTIONARY, the illustrations in this book would not be as appealing to young children. In addition, the very simple definitions in *Young People's Dictionary* can be confusing and do not always supply enough information for adequate understanding. In comparable works, such as the AMERICAN HERITAGE FIRST DICTIONARY, the definitions have a degree of simplicity but are enhanced by the necessary details. *Young People's Dictionary* also omits entries for important words and topics, such as colors, numbers, and occupations. For these reasons, *Young People's Dictionary* is an incomplete work for children at this level and is not recommended for purchase.

Chapter 11
Evaluations of
Middle School Dictionaries

The American Heritage
Student's Dictionary

Facts at a Glance

Full title: **The American Heritage Student's Dictionary**
Publisher: Houghton Mifflin
Editors: Peter Davies, Editor-in-Chief; Barry
  Richman, Executive Editor: Fernando de Mello
  Vianna, Managing Editor
Edition reviewed: © 1986

Number of pages: 992
Number of entries: more than 70,000
Number of illustrations: 2,000 all in black and white
Intended readership: grades 7 to 10; ages 12 to 15
Trim size: 7½" × 9¼"
Binding: laminated paper over boards

Price: $16.95
Sold in bookstores; also sold to libraries and schools.
ISBN 0-395-40417-7
Revised edition published in 1994

Introduction and Scope

The American Heritage Student's Dictionary is the
most advanced in a series of four dictionaries from
Houghton Mifflin intended for children from preschool
through ninth or tenth grades. The earlier volumes are
THE AMERICAN HERITAGE PICTURE DICTIONARY, THE AMER-
ICAN HERITAGE FIRST DICTIONARY, and THE AMERICAN
HERITAGE CHILDREN'S DICTIONARY. There are 35,000
main entries, and about 70,000 separately defined
meanings and uses.

The work's introduction states that the dictionary is
"intended for use in American schools in grades 6
through 9," although a sales sticker on the front notes:
"Revised! For students ages 12–15 in grades 7–10." This
dictionary's lexicon is much simpler than that of the
AMERICAN HERITAGE HIGH SCHOOL DICTIONARY, introduced
in 1993.

Authority

The American Heritage dictionaries are well known for
their readable definitions and attractive design. The editors of the *Student's Dictionary* are members of the
publisher's permanent lexicographic staff. The members
of the advisory board and the consultants are experts in
the fields of education, psychology, mathematics, the
environment, and language arts. Words were selected by
computerized research and were based on "textbooks,
magazines, encyclopedias, workbooks, and other printed
materials that are used in schools," according to the editors; thus, the dictionary will harmonize well with junior high students' overall academic experience.

Comprehensiveness of Entries

The 35,000 entry words are likely to be familiar, through the printed word, to sixth- through ninth-grade students. Not all of the words are common; some are, as the introduction points out, "important [in] specialized ways—in science or mathematics, for example." So, while students will be familiar with many of the words, there are still many new ones to learn.

Geographic and biographical entries are incorporated in the main alphabetical vocabulary. This feature is especially helpful because student users often will not know that the word they are seeking is the name of a person or a place and might not search for it in a separate listing. Phrases, as well as words, are included as main entries; for example, **first base, petty larceny,** and **square root** are main entries.

Not surprisingly for a work published in 1986, this dictionary contains none of the words used by the Buying Guide to assess currency. Houghton Mifflin has since revised this work, which was renamed *The American Heritage Student Dictionary*, but the new 1994 edition was issued too late to be reviewed here.

Quality and Currency of Entries

The definitions are accurate, clear, and appropriate in their level of complexity for the intended audience. For example, the first meaning given for the word **definition** is

> a statement of the precise meaning or meanings of a word, phrase, etc.

In the margin, where, in italicized passages, meanings sometimes receive more elaboration, we find

> **Definitions** in dictionaries cannot be truly precise. Meaning is still mysterious, and every word is unique. Most dictionaries, including this one, define a word by a phrase or another word that seems to mean the same thing. But a phrase cannot have exactly the same meaning as a single word. . . .

This is an impressively clear statement of the complex nature of meaning, well suited to the intended student audience.

The definitions are brief, in general, with the most common meaning given first. Illustrative sentences are frequently used to put the word in context, and occasional black-and-white illustrations and photographs in the margin give visual meaning to the entry words. Synonyms are not given as such, although they may be derived in many cases from the statements of definition. The definitions also include parts of speech, modifiers, run-on entries, phrasal verbs, inflected forms, variants, and homophones, providing students with information that will complement their increasing knowledge of English grammar and, to some extent, their foreign language studies.

Syllabication and Pronunciation

Syllabication is provided for every word of two or more syllables. Pronunciation is included for every word or abbreviation that is part of the spoken language. For example, the dictionary gives **PG** │pē′jē′│ for the PG rating of the film industry, but **Cl,** the symbol for the element chlorine, receives no pronunciation. Alternative pronunciations are provided following standard American English pronunciation. A full pronunciation guide is given in the "How to Use Your Dictionary" section and repeated on the right side of the front endpapers, seen when the front cover is opened. For quick reference, an abbreviated pronunciation guide, focused primarily on vowels, is also given at the lower left corner of each double spread. Diacritical marks and phonetic spellings are effectively used.

Accessibility

Access to the information is strictly alphabetical. No thumb index is provided. Two guide words, such as **boll weevil** │ **bonehead,** appear at the top of each page, giving the first and last words defined on the page. The sequence of information under each main entry, beginning with pronunciation and part of speech, is clear and easy to follow.

Alternative spellings are included in bold type after main entries, and distinguished according to relative frequency or preference. Examples are **cat·a·log** or **cat·a·logue** (words occurring with the same degree of frequency) and **lunch·room,** also **lunch-room** (first form preferred). The dictionary's special features are listed in the contents and therefore are easily found.

Special Features

Two special features written for student readers precede the dictionary. One is an excellent comprehensive introduction to the use of the dictionary where each part of the entry is carefully and clearly described. There is also a "Style Guide" that shows uses of punctuation, capitalization, and italics. Within the dictionary, in the outer margins of the pages, usage notes, etymology, and additional information are provided for some words. At the end of the volume are also charts on weights and measures and the metric system, valuable adjuncts to students' math and science studies.

Graphics and Format

The text is printed in two columns; the entry word in bold sans serif type overhangs the text; the definition is in roman, the part of speech and illustrative sentences in italic, and word variants in small bold sans serif. These typefaces are all easy to read, and their variety will enable students to pick out the information in which they are particularly interested.

Two thousand drawings, all placed in the outside margins of the pages, and all in black and white, serve to increase knowledge of a word and to encourage the student reader to browse. (The same device is used effectively in the parent dictionary.) There are, however, no maps. The attention to detail in graphics can be seen in the photograph illustrating **handlebar:** the man riding a bike, holding onto the handlebars, has a handlebar mustache.

The book is sturdily bound and will withstand heavy use.

Summary

The American Heritage Student's Dictionary is a well-crafted dictionary, designed so that students who learn to use it will be prepared to understand the layout of THE AMERICAN HERITAGE HIGH SCHOOL DICTIONARY and THE AMERICAN HERITAGE COLLEGE DICTIONARY. Although the 1986 edition is now dated, the work's general quality should continue to be apparent in the 1994 revision. This dictionary is highly recommended for students needing a simpler lexicon than that offered by the publisher's more advanced dictionaries. Prospective purchasers should review the 1994 revision for currency, however.

The Christian Student Dictionary

Facts at a Glance

Full title: **The Christian Student Dictionary**
Publisher: Bob Jones University Press
Editor: Grace C. Collins
Edition reviewed: © 1982

Number of pages: 864
Number of entries: 13,000
Number of illustrations: 1,400 (700 full-color; 700 black and white)
Intended readership: grades 2 to 5
Trim size: 8″ × 10″
Binding: laminated paper over boards

Price: $19.95
Sold in bookstores and other outlets; also sold to schools and libraries and by direct mail
ISBN 0-89084-172-1
No stated revision policy

Introduction and Scope

This work, unrevised since it was first published in 1982, is described by its publishers as "a *complete* up-to-date dictionary reflecting a Christian world view." It is designed to be used for school and home reference by students in elementary school.

The goal of the dictionary is to fill a void left by "the most highly regarded student dictionaries," none of which could be whole-heartedly recommended for use by Christian young people. Many key definitions reflected a skeptical or humanistic bias about the existence of God, about the life and redemptive work of Jesus Christ, and about the important doctrines of the Christian faith. Illustrative sentences . . . presented examples of dishonesty, disrespect for authority, disregard for Sunday as the Lord's day, humanism, role reversal in the home, magic and the occult, and objectionable activities.

The stated purpose of the dictionary is to replace these "objectionable features" with entries that reflect a biblical perspective. While the preface takes a doctrinaire fundamentalist position, much of the text is not couched in religious terms. The "Guide to the Dictionary," for example, includes no religious content, and most of the entries within the word list are comparable to those of other children's dictionaries. However, selected entries within the word list *are* dominated by a fundamentalist view. In some instances, the text's emphasis on a specific sectarian Christian usage of a term obscures its other meanings. For example, **justification** is defined first as "In the Bible, the act of God by which He declares righteous those who put their faith in Jesus Christ," and second as "The act of showing or proving that one's actions are just, fair, and right." Adult dictionary buyers *outside* the specific, sectarian group for which this work is intended would find it limited and clearly biased, Elementary readers would not be capable of distinguishing the bias.

Authority

The Christian Student Dictionary's word list is based on the lexical database of the 1981 Houghton Mifflin *Children's Dictionary.* The choice of words is based on their inclusion in *The American Heritage Word Frequency Book* (Houghton Mifflin, 1971)—a compilation of the words most frequently used in books and periodicals for students of different ages—and *The Living Word Vocabulary,* by Edgar Dale and Joseph O'Rourke (Field Enterprises Educational Corp., 1976), a vocabulary inventory reflecting word recognition at various age levels. Both these sources are reliable, but extremely dated.

To ensure the dictionary's comprehensive inclusion of religious terms, its compilers included words related to biblical Christianity regardless of whether or not they appeared in word frequency listings. Sources consulted for the selection of these terms included, according to the publishers, "Bible glossaries, Bible dictionaries, and basic word lists for Bible study."

Bob Jones University Press is affiliated with Bob Jones University in Greenville, South Carolina. Founded

The Christian Student Dictionary

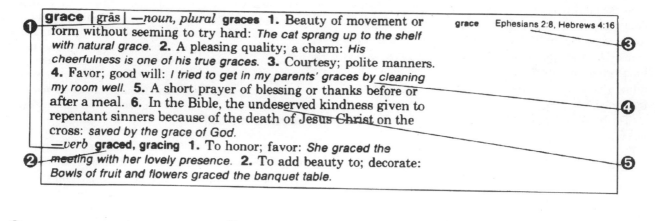

❶ Part of speech is set off by a dash, spelled out in italics, and listed with its separate numbered definitions

❷ Inflected forms follow the part-of-speech label

❸ Brief cross-references from an entry word to scriptural passages appear in the margins

❹ Illustrative sentences follow some definitions

❺ Some meanings are specific to fundamentalist Christian doctrine

by evangelist Bob Jones in 1927, the accredited university has an enrollment of over 5,000 and also runs schools for grades K through 12. Grace Collins, the dictionary's editor and consultant for lexicography and linguistics, chairs the university's Department of Linguistics.

Comprehensiveness of Entries

The Christian Student Dictionary includes most words that students in grades 2 through 5 might encounter in school and private reading; main entry words are comparable to those found in such standard student dictionaries as WEBSTER'S ELEMENTARY DICTIONARY and the MACMILLAN DICTIONARY FOR CHILDREN. While scientific terms such as **gene** and **chlorophyll** are included, those for most scientific processes—such as *mitosis* and *photosynthesis*—are not. Although some words from the field of space technology are included (for example, **astronaut, lunar module, space walk**), the work excludes computer science terms—such as *floppy disk* and the computer-related meanings of *disk, file,* and *terminal*—that would be appropriately included in a dictionary for this age group and are included, for example, in the MACMILLAN DICTIONARY FOR CHILDREN. The 50 entries from **paddle** to **paper** include **paddock, pagan, pagoda, painstaking, palate, palisades, palmetto, pancreas, panorama,** and **papaya**. Names for human sexual and reproductive organs are omitted.

Etymologies for some words appear as boxed items in the wide outer margin of the page. They often present the history of more than one sense of a word. They are

written at an appropriate age level, sometimes at the expense of substance:

> **Calf**[1] comes from an old English word that meant the same thing it does today. That word came from Germanic. **Calf**[2] comes from a word used a very long time ago by people who lived in Scandinavia. Its meaning has always been the same.

Also included are homophones, homographs, verb forms, phrasal verbs, illustrative phrases and sentences, and—in the margins—biblical references for selected words. Biographical entries are excluded, but brief geographical entries appear, including U.S. states, with location and capital, and major foreign countries.

Quality and Currency of Entries

Entries are generally clearly written at an appropriate reading level for the intended audience. The publishers' avowed objectives, however, result in a number of definitions that will be unacceptable to a nonfundamentalist reader. For example, the second meaning listed for **evolution** is

> The imagined processes by which living things supposedly formed by themselves without a Creator and then somehow kept improving by themselves.

The editors' disbelief also appears in the third definition provided for **evolve:** "To undergo the imagined evolution of living things: *How could birds evolve from reptiles?*"

The use of "imagined" in these definitions violates a basic principle of good lexicography: to describe what a word means, not to characterize its concept—especially from a limited point of view and for children at a formative stage of intellectual development.

Definitions of other words are also influenced by fundamentalist authoritarian thought as well as questionable lexicography. For example, **definition** is defined as "An explanation of the exact meaning or meanings of a word or phrase." Definitions in comparable dictionaries avoid such terms as "exact." The word **fate** bears this unwieldy first definition:

> The supposed power or force that some people believe in instead of God. They believe that this force decides everything that happens to a person in this life. Other people use the word without thinking what it means: *Fate dealt him a cruel blow.*

In some instances, especially in the case of words with religious usages, some important senses of the word are not defined. For example, **heaven** is defined as

> 1. Often **heavens** The sky or universe as seen from the earth. 2. The eternal place of God, the angels, and those who are saved; the place of complete happiness.

This definition does not indicate that *many* world religions share a belief in an "eternal" heaven, nor does it reflect the metaphorical, nonreligious use of the word to mean "a pleasant place."

Syllabication and Pronunciation

Syllabication is indicated by centered bold dots within the main entry word. Pronunciation is given for each word, following the main entry word. Stressed syllables are indicated by boldface type and accent marks, and phonetic spelling and diacritical marks indicate pronunciation. A full pronunciation key appears at the front of the volume; an abbreviated key, for quick reference, appears at the bottom left of each double spread. Variant pronunciations are rare—for example, **creek** |krēk| or |krĭk|—but the choices are appropriate for use at this level.

Accessibility

Entry words are alphabetized letter by letter. Some alternative spellings are provided, with the most common American spelling given first, as for **catalog** or **catalogue.** Occasionally the variant spelling is given in bold type at the end of the entry; for example, the conclusion of the entry for **Chanukah** (which provides an accurate but sketchy definition) reads "Another form of this word is **Hanukkah.**" The words shown with variant spellings are primarily those borrowed from other languages and those British spellings that are acceptable in the United States.

The book is not thumb indexed, but colored bars, with the letter appearing in white, are printed near the top of each page. All of the bars are in the same color and are located at the same spot on pages. Because there is no clear demarcation between sections, this feature will be of limited use to novice dictionary users. More helpful are the pairs of guide words at the top of each page that enable a reader to narrow the search for a word. A table of contents at the beginning of the volume lists the work's special features, ensuring that they will not be overlooked.

Special Features

Special features within the word list include a brief visual history, heading each section, of the letter of the alphabet, as well as the boxed etymologies and the scriptural references already discussed. The work also includes a detailed "Guide to the Dictionary," clearly written for children, that introduces them to the information found in the dictionary and the skills required to locate it. Exercises, suitable for individual or classroom use, are interspersed within the guide and are well designed to give children practice with dictionary skills. A "Spelling Table" presents the varied ways in which sounds are spelled in English and enables students to look up words they know how to pronounce but not how to spell.

Graphics and Format

The Christian Student Dictionary is profusely illustrated in color and has line drawings and photographs, both black and white and toned. The line drawings and some of the photographs have a dated appearance. Illustrations appear next to their entries and are captioned with the main entry word and sometimes a brief phrase of further clarification. A good ethnic balance is evident in the illustrations. However, in keeping with its stated opposition to "role reversal in the home," the dictionary depicts men and women *exclusively* in traditional roles. Illustrations are attractive and generally helpful adjuncts to the verbal definitions. Some drawings, however, such as the anatomical diagrams illustrating body organs, are sketchy; the drawings of plants and animals are more detailed.

The pages are attractively laid out, with bright blue rules guiding the eye to the two-thirds width of each page devoted to text. The remaining one-third serves as a wide margin, providing uncrowded space for illustrations, etymology boxes, scriptural references, and brief pronunciation keys. Main entry words appear in boldface type overhanging the text. Also in boldface are variant and derived forms; part-of-speech labels and illustrative sentences are italicized. The print is of appropriate size for a work at this level, and variations in typeface help a student reader to locate information. The paper is bright white and of high quality with minimal show-through. The laminated washable cover is sturdy, and the pages are securely bound.

Summary

In those private school and home settings where conservative Christian fundamentalism is the ruling world view, this dictionary will serve to teach children new words, show them how to use words in context, and provide practice with dictionary skills. Public schools will find *The Christian Student Dictionary* out-of-date and unsuited to the typical reference needs of students; the clientele of some public libraries, however, may include patrons who would elect to use just such a work.

HBJ School Dictionary

Facts at a Glance

Full title: **HBJ School Dictionary**
Publisher: Harcourt Brace Jovanovich
Edition reviewed: © 1990

Number of pages: 1,088
Number of entries: 60,000
Number of illustrations: 1,600 (reviewer estimate)
Intended readership: grades 4 to 8
Trim size: 8⅛″ × 10¼″
Binding: hardcover

Price: $24.99
Sold directly to schools
ISBN 0-15-321132-6
No stated revision policy

Introduction and Scope

The *HBJ School Dictionary,* revised in 1990, is a 1,088-page work intended for students in grades 4 to 8. In the book's preface to teachers and parents, the editors of the dictionary state that "An elementary school dictionary should be both a useful reference book and a textbook." In an effort to achieve this goal, they have assembled a volume that includes not only 60,000 word entries but also a plethora of supplementary materials.

Authority

The *HBJ School Dictionary* has been in existence since 1968, with revisions in 1972, 1977, 1985, and, currently, 1990. The first edition was edited by the venerable Sidney Landau, but the current edition bears no editors' names. Instead, an advisory board of seven scholars is listed.

Harcourt Brace Jovanovich is an experienced publisher of dictionaries, including THE LINCOLN WRITING DICTIONARY. According to the note for teachers and par-

ents, the sources for words in the *HBJ School Dictionary* include textbooks, juvenile literature, magazines, and newspapers.

Comprehensiveness of Entries

At 60,000 entries, the *HBJ School Dictionary* is somewhat smaller than the older WEBSTER'S INTERMEDIATE DICTIONARY and the well-regarded SCOTT, FORESMAN INTERMEDIATE DICTIONARY. Entries such as **CD** (for compact disc), **disk drive,** and computer-related definitions for **file** and **mouse** all point toward a reasonably up-to-date dictionary, as does the inclusion of **Kwanza** or **Kwanzaa.** The entries from **dust** to **dysphasia** include words such as **dust bowl, D.V.M., dwarf star, dybbuk, dynamometer, dyne, dysentery, dysgenic,** and **dyslexia.** The work includes no vulgarisms. Britishisms are evident (as within definitions for **lift** and **lorry**), though scattered in main entries. There is, for example, a main entry for **cheque** but not for *colour.*

There are no synonym or antonym guides in this work. Oddly, both etymologies and usage notes are preceded by the same symbol—a colored diamond. As in the previous edition, the etymologies do not provide the original word but rather describe the word's origin. For example, the etymology for **democracy** reads: "*Democracy* comes from a Greek word meaning *rule of the people.*"

Usage notes vary from describing correct grammatical usage to explaining the difference between similar words. The entry for **I,** for example, has the following grammatical usage note: "*I* is often used incorrectly as part of an object (as in "a great day for Tom and I"). Use *me* instead." The usage note for **serious,** on the other hand, explains the different ways in which the words *serious, earnest,* and *sober* can be used to describe people. The entries for **earnest** and **sober** both bear "see" references directing the reader to **serious** for a usage note.

All illustrative phrases and sentences are invented. These sentences are often difficult to distinguish from the definition proper because they are merely preceded by a colon, with only the target word in italics. In most other dictionaries, the entire sentence is italicized, making it easier to differentiate it from the definition.

Biographical and geographical entries do not appear within the main lexicon but rather as two separate sections at the back of the book. Here, the work shows its age. **Germany** is listed as a divided country, and **Lithuania** and **Ukraine** are each listed as a "constituent republic" of the Soviet Union. There are no entries for *Violeta Chamorro, Michael Jackson,* or *Boris Yeltsin.*

Quality and Currency of Entries

Main entries are syllabicated words in bold type, followed by the pronunciation in brackets. The part-of-speech and usage labels appear next, followed by any inflectional forms. Next come the numbered definitions,

HBJ School Dictionary

❶ Boldface main entry word divided into syllables by centered dots

❷ Pronunciation appears in brackets

❸ Italicized abbreviated part-of-speech label is followed by inflected forms in boldface type

❹ Two-color illustration includes both callouts and caption

❺ Illustrative sentence shows how entry word is used in context

fo·cus [fō′kəs] *n., pl.* **fo·cus·es** or **fo·ci** [fō′sī′], *v.* **fo·cused** or **fo·cussed**, **fo·cus·ing** or **fo·cus·sing** **1** *n.* In physics, a point at which light rays, sound waves, or radio waves come together after passing through something that bends them, as a lens, or after bouncing off a curved reflector. **2** *v.* To bring something, as light rays or sound waves, to a focus. **3** *n.* Focal distance. **4** *n.* An adjustment, as of the eye or a lens, that produces a clear image: to bring binoculars into *focus*. **5** *v.* To adjust the focus of (as the eye or a lens) to receive a clear image. **6** *n.* The place where a visual image is clearly formed, as in a camera. **7** *v.* To become focused: Our eyes *focused* on the door. **8** *n.* Any central point, as of interest or importance: The mysterious package was the *focus* of attention. **9** *v.* To fix; concentrate: to *focus* one's mind on a problem. **10** *n., pl.* **fo·ci** Either of two points inside an ellipse, the sum of whose distances to any point on the curve is always the same.

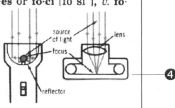

Foci in flashlight and camera

---

with any illustrative phrases or sentences within the definitions. Any idioms, usage notes, and run-on entries conclude the entry. When there is more than one definition for a word, that which "is used most often is listed first," according to the user's guide. The clarity of the definitions is quite good. The following is a typical entry:

> **cun·ning** [kun′ing] **1** *adj.* Clever or tricky. **2** *n.* Slyness or cleverness in getting something wanted: Cats use great *cunning* to catch their prey. **3** *adj. U.S.* Cute and appealing: a *cunning* toy. —**cun′ning·ly** *adv.*
>
> ♦ If you called someone *cunning* today, it would not be appreciated, but in former times it would have been taken as a compliment. A *cunning* craftsman was very skillful.

The book's word list is relatively up-to-date, although none of the following are included: *bungee jumping, dis, HDTV, intifada, maquiladora, retrovirus,* or *virtual reality.* The entry for **rap** does include a definition for music, however. **FAX** also has an entry, although the all-capitals spelling is rarely used anymore.

Syllabication and Pronunciation

Primary and secondary stress are shown in the pronunciation with accent marks in boldface and roman, respectively. Syllable divisions and stress are given for inflections as well as for run-on entries. Pronunciation is given for inflections when the inflected form is significantly different from the main entry. Variant pronunciations are shown in two ways. The first shows the two forms simply separated by the word *or* (for example, **tomato** [tə·mā′tō *or* tə·mä′tō]). The second shows the differing sound within parentheses in the pronunciation

of the word (for example, **dubious** [d(y)oo′bē·əs]). This latter technique may be confusing to young readers.

The full pronunciation key, which features 43 symbols, is somewhat hidden in the middle of the user's guide at the front of the dictionary. An abbreviated version (containing 23 symbols) appears in the lower right-hand corner of every odd-numbered page.

Accessibility

Entries are arranged in letter-by-letter order: **plywood, p.m., Pm, P.M., pneumatic.** Entries for alternate spellings contain the phrase "another spelling of. . . ." Guide words in the *HBJ School Dictionary* have an unusual placement, with the first word at the top of the page flush with the left margin and the last word flush with the right margin. (The standard practice is to show pairs of guide words at the outside corner of each page.) Tab letters also appear on the outside margins of every right-hand page.

A strong point of the *HBJ School Dictionary* is its extensive user's guide. The 54-page explanation of all of the parts of the dictionary is accompanied by exercises designed to entice readers to try the book and to teach them how to use it. A two-page spread of sample entries opens the user's guide and includes every possible aspect of an entry.

Special Features

The extensive appendix to this work comprises 143 pages. Included in this section are lists of the U.S. presidents (through George Bush), weights and measures, and 20th-century political leaders. The appendix also contains items less commonly found in dictionaries, such as the texts of the Declaration of Independence and the Bill of Rights, and lists of chief justices of the Supreme Court and winners of the Nobel Prize for Peace through 1988. The biographical section has an excellent representation of women from many countries, including U.S. author **Maya Angelou,** Japanese mountain climber **Junko Tabei,** and Russian cosmonaut **Valentina Tereshkova.** The geographical section features beautiful full-color photographs—the only color photographs in the entire dictionary. The dictionary concludes with a 14-page section of maps, many of which are outdated.

Graphics and Format

The quality of the illustrations is an area in which the *HBJ School Dictionary* sorely needs an overhaul. Drawings outnumber photographs by a margin of almost four to one, and the few photographs that do exist are of poor quality black and white, often drab or dark. One can barely discern the picture of the **orangutan,** for example.

The drawings, which are usually two-tone, look as if they have not been changed since the original 1968 edition of this dictionary. They seem very old-fashioned and often depict dated material. The drawing illustrating **compact,** for example, compares two cars—a large, very old-looking sedan and a Volkswagen Beetle.

It is a shame that the drab appearance of this work detracts from the fine definitions. The editors would have done well to emulate the excellent graphical quality of THE LINCOLN WRITING DICTIONARY, their other publication for this market.

The *HBJ School Dictionary* is sturdily bound, but the margins are somewhat narrow.

Summary

The *HBJ School Dictionary* features quality definitions and a fairly up-to-date word list. The user's guide is extensive, and the amount of supplementary material is much greater than that found in most other comparable dictionaries. However, the dull and outdated illustrations in this dictionary detract considerably from the book's appeal. A better choice for this age group would be the 1993 SCOTT, FORESMAN INTERMEDIATE DICTIONARY, which features color illustrations and more definitions.

The Lincoln Writing Dictionary

Facts at a Glance

Full title: **The Lincoln Writing Dictionary**
Publisher: Harcourt Brace Jovanovich
Editor: Christopher Morris, Editor-in-Chief
Edition reviewed: © 1989

Number of pages: 934
Number of entries: 35,000
Number of illustrations: 700
Intended readership: grades 3 to 8
Trim size: 8¼″ × 10¼″
Binding: hardcover

Price: $28.26
Sold directly to schools
ISBN 0-15-321130-X
No stated revision policy

Introduction and Scope

The 1989 edition of *The Lincoln Writing Dictionary* contains 934 pages, filled with 35,000 word entries and 700 illustrations, most in full color. According to the book's introduction, the editors have attempted to create a dictionary like that from Abraham Lincoln's era, when people not only looked up words in the dictionary but actually *read* the dictionary. To achieve this goal, three "lost features" of these older dictionaries have been restored in *The Lincoln Writing Dictionary:* quotations from famous authors, essays on the many facets of language, and usage notes.

As the book's title suggests, *The Lincoln Writing Dictionary* is intended to serve not only as a standard dictionary but also "as a guide to help you become an effective writer." It attempts to achieve this goal by providing "writing articles" throughout the main text and a "Writer's Resource Guide" that appears at the end of the book.

The publisher states that the book is intended for children in grades 3 to 8—a wide age range. Although the scope of the lexicon is comparable to that of several children's dictionaries, the "writing articles" (on topics such as "irony," "mood," and "research papers") seem aimed at older students.

Authority

The Lincoln Writing Dictionary was first published in 1989 by Harcourt Brace Jovanovich (HBJ). HBJ is a well-known publisher of textbooks and reference books, including the HBJ SCHOOL DICTIONARY. According to the introduction, the selection of the dictionary's lexicon was "based on a computerized survey of more than 10,000,000 words of running text." About 2,000 documents—including textbooks, novels, magazines, and newspapers—were surveyed.

Comprehensiveness of Entries

With 35,000 entries, *The Lincoln Writing Dictionary* compares favorably with most others in the category of children's dictionaries, including the MACMILLAN

The Lincoln Writing Dictionary

❶ Boldface main entry word divided into syllables by centered dots

❷ Pronunciation enclosed in brackets

❸ Part-of-speech label followed by inflected forms in boldface type

❹ Illustrative sentence shows entry word used in context

❺ Idiom, in boldface type, is placed after the definition of the main entry word

❻ Usage note, identified by a diamond symbol, gives information about the entry word or a related word

❼ "Writing article" provides information about an aspect of writing

ques•tion [kwes′chən] *noun, plural* **questions.**
1. something that is said or written to get an answer, to find something out, or to test what a person knows. **2.** a matter to be thought about, discussed, or settled; an issue or problem: At tonight's meeting the school board will take up the *question* of whether Midland Avenue School should be closed. **3.** the fact of being uncertain or in doubt: Cindy didn't do very well on that test, but there's no *question* she's a good student. **4. out of the question.** not to be considered. *—verb,* **questioned, questioning.**
1. to ask a question or questions. **2.** to have or show doubts about: I'm not *questioning* his judgment, but I think we need more information to decide. ♦ Something that is **questionable** is uncertain or open to question: Quitting his job like that was a *questionable* decision.

questions English has two kinds of questions. One is called a *yes/no question*, because it asks for that kind of answer: "Is that your brother?" The other is an *information question*; it asks for some kind of information, rather than just *yes* or *no*: "*Who* was that on the phone?" "*Why* did Jimmy leave early?" A yes/no question can also be presented as a *tag question*—an extra phrase "tags along" at the end. We use this to invite the listener to respond, and also to soften the question: "You don't mind if I borrow your pen for a minute, *do you?*" A question normally has a question mark at the end, rather than a period. But an *indirect question* uses a period. "Jerry asked, 'Why was the talent show called off?'" BUT: "Jerry asked me why the talent show was called off." (Note the period.)

DICTIONARY FOR CHILDREN (35,000 entries) and the newer AMERICAN HERITAGE CHILDREN'S DICTIONARY (37,000 entries). However, *The Lincoln Writing Dictionary* falls considerably short when compared with those in the category of intermediate dictionaries, such as the HBJ SCHOOL DICTIONARY (60,000 entries) and the SCOTT, FORESMAN INTERMEDIATE DICTIONARY (68,000 entries).

The sequence of words from **crag** to **crevice** includes **Crane, Stephen; crater; crayfish; Crazy Horse; creationism; credit card;** and **crepe.** Several technical terms (such as **floppy disk, hard disk, quasar,** and **Richter scale**) are included, although there is no entry for *compact disk.* The dictionary contains neither vulgarisms nor Britishisms.

The book employs a great many usage labels, usage notes, and quoted examples to guide users. Usage notes within an entry are noted with a ♦ and can contain grammatical information or other information on how the word is used. The work does not include synonym or antonym guides.

A unique aspect of this work is the use of 4,000 real quotations in addition to the more standard invented illustrative quotations within definitions. The diverse group of about 500 authors quoted in this dictionary includes many who are frequently quoted, such as Charles Dickens, Ernest Hemingway, and James Joyce, as well as contemporary authors, such as Judy Blume, Stephen King, and Joseph Wambaugh. Unfortunately, illustrative quotations are not set off by type style from the definition, except for a colon preceding the quote.

Biographical and geographical entries are included within the main text, though these entries are out-of-date by today's standards. The entry for **Germany,** for example, notes that it is a divided country, and none of the following appear at all: *Violeta Chamorro, Michael Jackson, Lithuania, Ukraine,* or *Boris Yeltsin.*

Quality and Currency of Entries

Main entries appear as syllabicated words in bold type, followed by the pronunciation (in brackets), part of speech label, inflected forms or variant spellings (in bold type), and the numbered definitions with any illustrative quotations. Any idioms will appear last. Usage notes appear in the entry after the definition for which the note is intended, though the majority are placed at the conclusion of the entry.

Definitions are arranged in order of frequency of use. The definitions are clearly worded, with the usage notes often providing additional information. The following is a typical entry:

> **pro·voke** [prəvōk′] *verb,* **provoked, provoking. 1.** to cause to happen; bring about: ". . . do nothing that might *provoke* any public outbreak." (T.S. Eliot) **2.** to excite or stir up: The British tax on tea *provoked* the American colonists to hold the protest known as the Boston Tea Party. ◆ Something that provokes is a **provocation** [prä′vəkā′shən].

In places, the work shows its age. The illustration for **computer** calls the extinct Apple II "a popular modern computer," and none of the following words are included in the work: *bungee jumping, dis, fax, HDTV, intifada, maquiladora, rap, retrovirus,* or *virtual reality.*

Syllabication and Pronunciation

Main entry words are divided into syllables, shown by centered dots. Primary and secondary stress is shown using accent marks in boldface and roman, respectively. Syllable divisions are given only for main entry words and not for inflections, unless a new form is introduced in a usage note that has a different pronunciation from the main entry.

The work employs an easy-to-use pronunciation system and offers alternate pronunciations. The placement of the pronunciation keys, however, is perhaps the weakest aspect of this otherwise user-friendly work. The only full pronunciation key appears on the last page of the user's guide within the front matter. Rather than the usual abbreviated pronunciation key shown throughout the work, the editors have chosen to repeat the entire pronunciation key—ten symbols at a time—on the lower right-hand corner of every odd-numbered page. Thus, for example, page 3 contains the pronunciation key for *A–F,* page 5 for *G–N,* and so forth. The entire key takes six pages to get through—an inconvenience for users who may have to leaf back and forth to find the pronunciation for a word.

Accessibility

Entries are arranged in strict letter-by-letter order: **newt; New Testament; Newton, Sir Isaac; New World.** Abbreviations are interspersed with other entries: **usher, U.S.S.R., usual.** Alternate spellings include the phrase "another spelling of."

Although the "How to Use the Dictionary" section is relatively brief for this age group, the explanations are clear and all aspects of an entry are covered. The first and last entry words on each page appear as boldface guide words in the upper outside corner of each page, and a tab letter is printed in the outside margin of each page.

Special Features

Special features in *The Lincoln Writing Dictionary* include 600 "writing articles," paragraph-long passages that "provide interesting information about all aspects of writing." These passages appear in alphabetical order within the text and are highlighted in a colored box. The wide range of topics includes punctuation (**apostrophe, semicolons**), grammar (**modifiers, present tense**), usage (**complement/compliment, farther/further**), etymologies, and literary issues (**inventing characters, poems**). They cite many published authors and are very clear and well written. Their depth and scope, however, make them much more appropriate for a high school, or even an adult, readership.

In addition to the writing articles, a 38-page "Writer's Resource Guide" appears at the back of the book. According to the introduction to this section, "This guide provides not only models and tips for writing different types of compositions, but it also lists ways to use the dictionary as you write." The first section of the guide is called "The Writing Process"; it is followed by 13 writing models, including "Writing a Descriptive Paragraph" and "Writing a Story."

Graphics and Format

The 700 illustrations in *The Lincoln Writing Dictionary* greatly enhance this work. An equal number of photographs and drawings are included, nearly all of which are in full color. The illustrations are crisp and clear and do not appear dated.

All of the illustrations are labeled with the entry word in bold type, and most include a one- or two-sentence caption. Many of the captions provide additional information. For example, the caption for **penguin** reads: "The male of the emperor penguin hatches the egg. He keeps the egg warm on top of his feet, covering it with his belly."

The work has a contemporary, eye-appealing look. The book has a sturdy binding and adequate margins, and it lies flat when opened.

Summary

The Lincoln Writing Dictionary is a very attractive work with a bit of an "identity crisis." The book's beautiful color illustrations will appeal to students of all ages, and the number of entries should prove adequate for most younger readers. The informative and often fascinating advice provided in the "writing articles," however, is aimed at a much older reader and will be of little use to elementary school students. Although the lexicon contains clear definitions and helpful usage notes, older readers may prefer a more comprehensive work, such as the Scott, Foresman Intermediate Dictionary.

Macmillan Dictionary

Facts at a Glance

Full title: **Macmillan Dictionary**
Publisher: Macmillan
Editor: William D. Halsey
Edition reviewed: © 1987

Number of pages: 1,232
Number of entries: 95,000
Number of illustrations: 1,800 black-and-white; some
    with one added color
Intended readership: grade 7 and up
Trim size: 8″ × 10″
Binding: hardcover

Price: $36.16; $27.12 with school discount
Sold directly to schools
ISBN 0-02-195390-2
No stated revision policy

Introduction and Scope

The *Macmillan Dictionary* is intended for home, class-room, or library use by students in grades 7 and above. An abridged dictionary, its 120,000 definitions "reflect current American usage." The volume also contains special features that enhance its value as a reference source for students. The *Macmillan Dictionary* is the most advanced of a series of four Macmillan dictionaries for students; the series also comprises the MACMILLAN DICTIONARY FOR CHILDREN, MACMILLAN SCHOOL DICTIONARY, and MACMILLAN DICTIONARY FOR STUDENTS.

Authority

The *Macmillan Dictionary* was first published in 1981. Macmillan is well known for its reference materials and educational books. William D. Halsey, the series' editorial director has served as the editorial director of the *Merit Students Encyclopedia* and *Collier's Encyclopedia*. The dictionary's front matter lists 12 consultants. Only one, the etymology consultant Ralph L. Ward, Professor of Classics at Hunter College, is listed as being affiliated with a university. According to the editors, words included in the dictionary have been drawn from "two primary sources: (1) the language of literature, history, and science that you study in school; and (2) the language of everyday speech and conversation."

Comprehensiveness of Entries

A glossary of computer terms is included among the special features at the end of the volume. Biological terms for sexual and reproductive organs are included in the dictionary, as are the words **homosexual** and **lesbian.** Etymological notes appear in brackets at the end of the entry. Although etymological information is not provided for *all* entries, the amount and selection appear adequate for the dictionary's intended audience and purpose. Synonyms, included for some entries, are introduced by the abbreviation *Syn.* and appear in a separate paragraph at the end of the entry. Extensive usage notes, marked by a boldface triangle, appear in many entries. Also included in the dictionary are abbreviations; biographical and geographic entries; combining forms; prefixes and suffixes; inflected forms of verbs, nouns, and adjectives; and irregular noun plurals.

Quality and Currency of Entries

Definitions are accurate and concise, with a reading level appropriate for the intended audience. Illustrative phrases and sentences that help to clarify definitions are extensively used. Some are quotations from literature, including Shakespeare and the Bible, with sources given; others are created by the lexicographers. Scientific and technical terms are made accessible to the general reader. Unfortunately, the *Macmillan Dictionary* is quite out-of-date. Even commonly used words that should appear in a 1987 dictionary, such as *aerobics*, *compact disc*, and *videocassette*, do not appear.

Grouped according to part of speech, definitions are numbered consecutively in bold type. The most commonly used meaning is placed first. Appropriate designations signal informal use, slang, archaic forms, and British usage. Homographs are given separate entries.

Geographical entries are dated. An entry appears for the **Soviet Union**, and **East Germany** is defined as a "communist country in north-central Europe." A spot check indicated that many of the population figures in the geographic entries are estimates dating from the late 1960s and early 1970s. Updating these numbers would make the valuable geographic feature more helpful for today's students. Biographical entries, although often very brief, will also prove useful to students.

Syllabication and Pronunciation

Dots are used to divide words into syllables, and dashes mark a hyphenated entry. Accent marks indicate stressed syllables; phonetic respelling and simple diacritical marks represent pronunciation. The system is explained in the "Guide to the Dictionary" and in the "Pronunciation Key" at the front of the volume. An abbreviated pronunciation key is also provided at the bottom of every page.

Accessibility

Guide words indicate the first and last words defined on each page. The book is not thumb indexed, but there are black thumb tabs printed on the far right-hand margin of every double spread with the letter designation in white. Under words for which a full entry is not given, cross-references direct the user to appropriate main entries and definition numbers.

Special Features

One of the outstanding special features of this work is its introductory "Guide to the Dictionary." It is preceded by a well-marked sample page, which is numerically coded and keyed to sections in the guide. A "List of Abbreviations Used in This Dictionary," a "Table of English Spellings," and the pronunciation follow the guide.

At the back of the book the student will find 13 pages of full-color maps. A one-page chart lists U.S. states with their postal abbreviations, capitals, dates admitted to the Union, and state mottoes. This is followed by a chart depicting the interrelationships among the Indo-European languages and a very brief history of the English language. Next come four pages of portraits of U.S. presidents (through Ronald Reagan) with their dates of office and names of vice presidents. A chronology of historical events in the United States through 1981 is followed by tables of measure and chemical elements.

Perhaps the finest special feature in the dictionary is the supplement that provides follow-up activities for students to reinforce the guide material. The supplement is not well titled, however, and is listed in the dictionary's main contents only as "Practice Pages."

Graphics and Format

The *Macmillan Dictionary* is sturdy and attractive, with bright wipe-clean board covers. The volume lies flat when opened. The paper used is heavy and allows for minimal show-through of text and pictures. The double-column pages have ample margins; main entry words, in bold type, overhang the text. Typefaces are appropriately sized and easy to read. Illustrations are black line drawings, in some instances enhanced with brown or green.

Summary

Although the *Macmillan Dictionary* is dated, the book includes a strong "Guide to the Dictionary" and an accompanying section of follow-up activities. The comprehensiveness of the entries, especially the extensive usage notes and illustrative phrases and sentences, is noteworthy, as is the inclusion of biographical and geographical information. The *Macmillan Dictionary* is a high-quality reference tool, but schools and libraries may want to consider more current dictionaries such as the 1993 WORLD BOOK DICTIONARY.

Macmillan Dictionary for Students

Facts at a Glance

Full title: **Macmillan Dictionary for Students**
Publisher: Macmillan
Editor: William D. Halsey
Edition reviewed: © 1984

Number of pages: 1,190
Number of entries: 90,000
Number of illustrations: 1,800
Intended readership: ages 11 and up
Trim size: 8″ × 10″
Binding: hardcover

Price: $16.95
Sold in bookstores and other outlets; also sold directly to schools and libraries
ISBN 0-02-761560-X
No stated revision policy

Introduction and Scope

The *Macmillan Dictionary for Students,* a comprehensive reference source for junior and senior high school students, is in most respects identical to the MACMILLAN DICTIONARY, reviewed in this guide. While the MACMILLAN DICTIONARY carries a copyright date of 1987 (earlier edition © 1981), the most recent copyright date for the *Macmillan Dictionary for Students* is 1984 (earlier editions © 1981, 1979, and 1973). This unfortunately gives the dictionary the same problems with datedness mentioned in the review of the MACMILLAN DICTIONARY.

Differences between the two books appear in the dictionaries' special features. The "Sample Page," "Guide to the Dictionary," "Abbreviations Used in This Dictionary," "Table of English Spellings," and "Pronunciation Key," are located at the front of both volumes. At the back, both contain a chart of the Indo-European languages; a history of the English language; information on U.S. presidents (through President Reagan); a listing of important events in U.S. history (with minor variations between the lists in the different editions); and a "Glossary of Computer Terms." Included in the MACMILLAN DICTIONARY, but not in the *Macmillan Dictionary for Students,* are a 13-page atlas, facts about U.S. states and territories, portraits of the presidents, tables of measure and chemical elements, and a supplement of follow-up activities to accompany the Guide.

Two features in the *Macmillan Dictionary for Students* do not appear in the MACMILLAN DICTIONARY: a handbook of style (punctuation, capitalization, and numbers) and a seven-page article, "The World of Computers." These features enhance the book's usefulness to the intended student audience; however, this volume's

Macmillan Dictionary for Students

① hear (hĕr) heard.(hurd), hear·ing. *v.t.* **1.** to be able to perceive (sound) by means of the ear. **2.** to pay attention to; listen. *We heard both sides of the argument before we made a decision.* **3.** to be informed of: *We heard the news on the radio.* **4.** to give a formal, official, or legal hearing to: *The judge heard the testimony of all the witnesses.* **5.** to listen to with compliance; accede to; grant: *His prayers were heard.* **6.** to attend and listen to as part of an audience. **7. to hear out.** to listen to until the end: *Hear me out before you decide.* —*v.i.* **1.** to perceive or be able to perceive sound by means of the ear. **2.** to receive information; be told; learn (with *of, about,* or *from*): *What have you heard about the situation? Have you ever heard of him?* **3. to hear of.** to allow, consider, or agree to: *I will not hear of your leaving.* **4.** usually with the negative. **4. to hear tell.** *Informal.* to learn: *I hear tell you're getting married* —*interj.* **hear, hear.** well done or well spoken. [Old English *hēran* to perceive sound, listen.] —**hear'er,** *n.*
Syn. *v.i.* **1. Hear, listen** mean to perceive sound by the ear. **Hear** suggests the physical act of perceiving sound: *Deaf men cannot hear.* **Listen** implies giving heed or paying attention to what is heard. *The audience listened very carefully to the president's speech.*

① Inflected forms, in boldface type, follow the main entry and are given pronunciations where necessary

② Sentences illustrating the various discriminated meanings of the main entry word are set in italics; these sentences occasionally use the inflected form of a main entry word

③ Idiomatic phrases or common expressions are printed in boldface type so they can be seen easily; the idioms are given definitions and are used in sentences in italic type

④ A bold upright triangle precedes a usage note that applies to a previous illustrative sentence

⑤ The etymology is presented in square brackets at the end of an entry paragraph and includes meanings for the root or source word

⑥ A synonym study indicated by **Syn.** briefly defines the given synonyms, explains nuances of the meanings, and gives precise illustrative sentences

omission of features contained in the other dictionary, especially the tables and follow-up activities, may limit its use for classroom applications.

The final difference between the dictionaries is price: the MACMILLAN DICTIONARY lists at $36.16, with a school price of $27.12; the *Macmillan Dictionary for Students,* at $16.95, is certainly a better buy for home use, while variations in the special features may determine the selection of either version for schools and libraries, purchasers should consider the publication dates of these dictionaries before buying.

Macmillan School Dictionary

Facts at a Glance

Full title: **Macmillan School Dictionary**
Publisher: Macmillan
Editor: William D. Halsey
Edition reviewed: © 1987

Number of pages: 1,136
Number of entries: 65,000
Number of illustrations: 1,500, most in two colors
Intended readership: grades 4 and above
Trim size: 8″ × 10″
Binding: hardcover

Prices: $35.28; $26.46 to schools
Sold directly to schools
ISBN 0-02-195380-5
No stated revision policy

Introduction and Scope

The *Macmillan School Dictionary* (originally copyrighted in 1981) is a companion to the MACMILLAN DICTIONARY and is intended for use by upper elementary students. In addition to its 65,000 entries, the dictionary contains special features that expand its usefulness as both a reference source and a manual of practical skills.

Authority

Macmillan publishes a complete range of school dictionaries. The firm's reference works have been highly regarded by teachers and librarians for many years.

According to the editors, the lexicon is based on four sources, the most important of which is textbooks: "The editors studied and selected vocabulary found in the current textbooks of all major publishers." Other sources for words included are literature, current periodicals, and conversational American English.

Macmillan School Dictionary

❶ Homographs indicated by super-script numbers

❷ Illustrative sentence or phrase provided in italics

❸ Homograph has an etymology with definitions provided within square brackets

❹ Usage labels provided in italics

❺ Labeled illustration of first homograph's second meaning (with superscript and definition numbers)

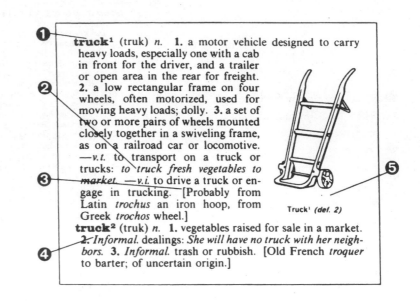

❶ **truck**¹ (truk) *n.* **1.** a motor vehicle designed to carry heavy loads, especially one with a cab in front for the driver, and a trailer or open area in the rear for freight. **2.** a low rectangular frame on four wheels, often motorized, used for moving heavy loads; dolly. **3.** a set of two or more pairs of wheels mounted closely together in a swiveling frame, as on a railroad car or locomotive. —*v.t.* to transport on a truck or trucks: *to truck fresh vegetables to market.* —*v.i.* to drive a truck or engage in trucking. [Probably from Latin *trochus* an iron hoop, from Greek *trochos* wheel.]
truck² (truk) *n.* **1.** vegetables raised for sale in a market. **2.** *Informal.* dealings: *She will have no truck with her neighbors.* **3.** *Informal.* trash or rubbish. [Old French *troquer* to barter; of uncertain origin.]

Truck¹ *(def. 2)*

Comprehensiveness of Entries

For its size and scope the *Macmillan School Dictionary* is comprehensive. In addition to conventional definitions and part-of-speech labels, it provides 37,000 examples of words in context—that is, sentences illustrating how the word is used. For example, to explain the usage of **file** as a transitive verb, the following is given:

> *v.t.* **1.** to keep (papers or similar items) arranged in order. **2.** to place in a file: *The clerk filed the letter in its proper alphabetical place.* **3.** to hand in legally or officially; enter on a record: *to file a report, to file one's income tax return.*

While synonyms and antonyms are excluded, many entries include usage labels, usage notes, quotations, variants, and etymological notes. When the etymology is given, it appears in brackets at the end of the entry and in some instances contains anecdotal information. For example, the definition of **decimate** is followed by

> [Latin *decimātus*, the past participle of *decimāre* to select every tenth man for punishment. In ancient Rome an army revolt was punished by taking every tenth soldier and executing him.]

Under **teddy bear** appears

> [From *Teddy*, a nickname of President Theodore Roosevelt; from a cartoon in which he was shown sparing the life of a bear cub while hunting.]

Included in the word list are geographic and biographical entries. Geographic entries include, as appropriate, such information as location, capital, area, and population. Population figures for U.S. states are based on 1970 estimates, despite the existence of more recent census figures; those for countries of the world range

from the early 1970s to the early 1980s. Biographical entries include dates and a concise, informative phrase of identification.

Computer terms are included—not, however, in the main word list, but in an appended glossary, where they may be overlooked. Many recent additions to the language are omitted: while **video tape** appears as a main entry, *videocassette* and *compact disc* do not. Appropriate to the intended audience are the exclusions of most archaic word meanings and of the scientific terms for plants and animals.

Quality and Currency of Entries

Definitions are straightforward and easily understood. Within entries, definitions are grouped according to part of speech and are numbered consecutively. The most commonly used meaning appears first. One of this dictionary's strengths is its frequent use of words in illustrative phrases and sentences; one of its weaknesses, however, is a tendency to oversimplify difficult words.

Syllabication and Pronunciation

Black dots divide words into syllables, and dashes mark a hyphenated entry. Pronunciation for each word is given in parentheses immediately following the main entry word. Alternative pronunciations are provided, with the most common appearing first. Accent marks indicate stressed syllables, while phonetic respelling and diacritical marks clarify pronunciation. A full pronunciation key appears at the front of the volume, and a shorter key, for quick reference, is located in a color block at the bottom of the right-hand column on all right-hand pages.

Accessibility

The *Macmillan School Dictionary* is not thumb indexed, but there are useful black-and-white thumb-shaped markings on the far right-hand margin of every double-page spread. Guide words appear at the top of each page, and a table of contents at the front of the volume facilitates access to special features.

Special Features

Among the dictionary's special features are those designed to teach dictionary skills. A "Guide to the Dictionary" clearly explains what information appears in the dictionary and how it may be located. "Try This" practice exercises are well designed and useful; however, their placement, interspersed throughout the guide, makes the guide more difficult to use. Supplementary dictionary exercises also appear in a section called "Practice Pages" at the back of the volume. The "Practice Pages" supplement is a clear and thorough follow-up to information and skills imparted in the guide.

Following the guide are three more features designed to help the student use the dictionary. In addition to a list of abbreviations used in the dictionary and the full pronunciation key is a "Table of English Spellings," designed to help students locate words they know how to pronounce but not how to spell.

The reference section appended to the back of the volume includes a 13-page atlas, as well as additional geographic, historical, linguistic, and scientific information.

Graphics and Format

The *Macmillan School Dictionary* has the same layout, paper weight, and illustrations as the MACMILLAN DICTIONARY. Each two-column page has adequate margins, and the good-quality paper allows for minimal show-through of text. The type size is, appropriately, larger than that found in the MACMILLAN DICTIONARY.

There are generally one to three illustrations on a page—line drawings, some of which have added brown or green coloring. They appear next to the words they clarify and are captioned with main entry words. They are acceptable for this age group and serve to amplify definitions.

The book is sturdily bound in an attractive bright orange and yellow-green cover that does not look drably institutional.

Summary

The strengths of the *Macmillan School Dictionary* lie in its attractive format, sturdy binding, and concise, simply stated, well-illustrated definitions. The learning activities are well designed and make the work

useful in the classroom as well as the library. Unfortunately, the dictionary's 1987 publishing date does not compare favorably with that of the similar HBJ SCHOOL DICTIONARY (1990) and the SCOTT, FORESMAN INTERMEDIATE DICTIONARY (1993). Even with a school discount, the *Macmillan School Dictionary* is still the most expensive of the three; those with limited budgets will probably want to purchase a more current dictionary at a better price.

Scott, Foresman Advanced Dictionary

Facts at a Glance

Full title: **Scott, Foresman Advanced Dictionary**
Publisher: Scott, Foresman
Editors: E. L. Thorndike; Clarence L. Barnhart
Edition reviewed: © 1993

Number of pages: 1,328
Number of entries: 100,000
Number of illustrations: 1,500, most black and white
Intended readership: grades 7 to 12
Trim size: $7\frac{1}{2}'' \times 9\frac{1}{8}''$
Binding: hardcover

Price: $17.95
Sold directly to schools; also sold in bookstores
ISBN 0-673-12377-4
No stated revision policy

Introduction and Scope

The *Scott, Foresman Advanced Dictionary* is the school edition of the THORNDIKE-BARNHART STUDENT DICTIONARY by HarperCollins. It is nearly identical to that work; practice exercises for students appear in the Scott, Foresman version's user's guide. For a full description and evaluation, see the review of the THORNDIKE-BARNHART STUDENT DICTIONARY elsewhere in the Buying Guide. Although the added exercises in this version might prove useful to teachers planning a lesson on dictionary skills, most buyers will not find their presence worth the extra dollar that this work costs.

Scott, Foresman Intermediate Dictionary

Facts at a Glance

Full title: **Scott, Foresman Intermediate Dictionary**
Publisher: Scott, Foresman
Editors: E. L. Thorndike; Clarence L. Barnhart
Edition reviewed: © 1993

Number of pages: 1,098
Number of entries: 68,000
Number of illustrations: 1,240; black-and-white pho-
   tographs, single-color line drawings
Intended readership: grades 5 to 8
Trim size: 8″ × 10″
Binding: hardcover

Price: $17.95
Sold directly to schools
ISBN 0-673-12376-6
No stated revision policy

Introduction and Scope

One of several dictionaries published by Scott, Foresman that bears the Thorndike and Barnhart names, this
volume, according to the preface,

> is designed specifically for use in schools and for study at
> home by young people who are passing from the simple
> curriculum of the lower elementary grades to the more
> complex studies of high school.

E. L. Thorndike (now dead) and Clarence Barnhart
(now over 90 years old) met at Scott, Foresman in the
1930s and edited several noted school dictionaries.
This volume is a direct descendant of those works. The
present-day editors have chosen to follow lexicographical practices that the two men established, including
writing definitions in language simpler than the entry
word, sequencing them in order of frequency of use,
grouping related meanings together, and providing a
single alphabetical lexicon. The *Scott, Foresman Intermediate Dictionary* has a very recent publication date
and a high number of entries compared with its principal competitors.

Authority

The *Scott, Foresman Intermediate Dictionary,* first pub-
lished under that name in 1971, belongs to a series of
Thorndike-Barnhart works, including the Scott,
Foresman Beginning Dictionary (also published as the
Thorndike-Barnhart Children's Dictionary) and the
Scott, Foresman Advanced Dictionary (also published
as the Thorndike-Barnhart Student Dictionary). The
Intermediate Dictionary's intended readership (grades
5–8) and number of entries (68,000) places it between
the other two works.

According to the preface, "the selection of words
and meanings in this dictionary was checked against
current word frequency counts." New words and
meanings have also been gleaned from contemporary
textbooks, newspapers, magazines, books, and other
publications.

Comprehensiveness of Entries

The *Scott, Foresman Intermediate Dictionary*'s 68,000
entries make it about average for this level of dictionary.
Its recent publication date ensures a reasonable number
of current entries such as **floppy disk** (although there is
no entry for *hard disk* or *CD-ROM*) and **Health Main-
tenance Organization.** The sequence of words from
gas to **gazpacho** includes **gas guzzler, gasohol, gastro-
pod, gaucho, gauss, gavotte,** and **gazetteer,** which is in-
dicative of the fine, general coverage of all fields of
knowledge in this work.

Typical of dictionaries for this age range, vulgarities
are not included. The work also steers clear of sexually
connotative definitions for other words, such as **gay.**
Britishisms are evident in some main entries such as
lorry and **petrol,** though **lift** and **bonnet** do not have the
British meanings among their definitions.

Somewhat surprisingly for a student dictionary, the
work does not include any synonym studies or usage
notes. It does feature about 1,800 etymologies, many of
which are set off from the text in colored frames with
the label "Word History." For example, the following is
included for **rival:**

> *Rival* is from Latin *rivalis,* meaning "one who uses the
> same stream as another," which comes from *rivus,* meaning
> "stream."

Other etymologies appear at the end of entries within
brackets. Though brief, they admirably avoid abbreviations, which could confuse young users.

The work also features about 60 "Word Family"
boxes, each set off from the text and enclosing a list of
words derived from a common root. Standard usage labels appear and are always spelled out, rather than abbreviated.

Like other Thorndike-Barnhart works, this volume
contains excellent illustrative sentences, all of which
were written by the editors. Biographical and geographical entries are integrated within the main alphabet, and
include **Germany** as a unified country, **Lithuania** and
Ukraine as independent republics, and **Boris Yeltsin** as
president of Russia. Not included are entries for *Violeta
Chamorro* or *Michael Jackson.*

Quality and Currency of Entries

Main entries are shown as syllabicated words in bold
type. Following the main entry are the pronunciation
(in parentheses) and numbered definitions, ordered by
frequency of use. Illustrative sentences within the definitions are italicized. As in other Thorndike-Barnhart
works, the part-of-speech label appears at the end of
the definition entirely, rather than within the definition
itself. Next appear any inflected forms, followed by the
bracketed etymology (if any) and run-on entries. Any
idioms appear after the entry proper, each in bold type

beginning on a separate line. The following is a typical entry:

> **prom·ise** (prom′is), **1** words said or written, binding a person to do or not do something: *You can count on her to keep her promise.* **2** give one's word; make a promise: *They promised to stay till we came.* **3** make a promise of: *to promise help.* **4** indication of what may be expected: *The clouds give promise of rain.* **5** that which gives hope of success: *a young scholar who shows promise.* **6** give hope; give hope of: *The rainbow promises fair weather.* **1,4,5** *n.,* **2,3,6** *v.,* **prom ised, prom is ing. –prom′is er,** *n.*

Despite the dictionary's recent publication date, none of the following words has an entry: *bungee jumping, dis, fax, HDTV, intifada, maquiladora, rap, retrovirus,* or *virtual reality.*

Syllabication and Pronunciation

Syllabication is indicated in the main entry word by spaces between syllables, rather than the centered dots typical of other works. Primary and secondary stresses are noted in the pronunciation by boldface and roman stress marks. Syllable divisions are given for both inflected forms and run-on entries, though—as the above example shows—stress is only given for run-on entries.

The 41-symbol pronunciation key conveniently appears opposite the front and back covers of the volume, with a shorter key appearing at the upper outside corner of every right-hand page. Variant pronunciations are given. The following are typical entries: **a·bout** (ə bout′), **Eng·lish** (ing′glish), **o·bey** (ō bā′), and **rhythm** (riŦH′əm).

Accessibility

Entries are arranged in strict letter-by-letter order: **pneumonia, Po, P.O., poach.** A 34-page user's guide features student exercises and easy-to-read explanations of each part of an entry; an answer key for the exercises appears at the conclusion of the work. Guide words are given at the upper outside corner of every page.

Special Features

A 32-page "Student's Reference Section" concludes the work. This section includes world maps, a picture of and information about each U.S. president (through President Clinton), a two-page spread on "English Words from Other Languages," a table of "Words That Are Often Misspelled," and other features.

Graphics and Format

The attractive illustrations include a roughly equal number of drawings and photographs. The preface points out that "words that express feelings, qualities, ideas, and actions" are illustrated, in keeping with a Thorndike-Barnhart tradition. Thus, users will find illustrations demonstrating **grief, irascible, jubilation, tantrum,** and other concepts. Illustrations of animals include height or length in both standard and metric measurements. Illustrative examples of grammatical terms and literary devices also appear: **alliteration, couplet, epigram, limerick,** and **pun,** for example, are accompanied by a colored box demonstrating them.

The work is sturdily bound and has adequate margins all around.

Summary

Although its failure to include some contemporary terms is a matter of concern, the *Scott, Foresman Intermediate Dictionary* will more than adequately serve the needs of students. It is more up-to-date than two of its competitors, the MACMILLAN DICTIONARY FOR STUDENTS and the HBJ SCHOOL DICTIONARY. The former work has a larger lexicon, but this volume's excellent definitions, illustrative sentences, and overall appearance will appeal to all users. These features make the *Scott, Foresman Intermediate Dictionary* an exceptional purchase for both homes and libraries.

Thorndike-Barnhart Student Dictionary

Facts at a Glance

Full title: **Thorndike-Barnhart Student Dictionary**
Publisher: HarperCollins
Editors: E. L. Thorndike; Clarence L. Barnhart
Edition reviewed: © 1993

Number of pages: 1,302
Number of entries: 100,000
Number of illustrations: 1,500; black-and-white photographs, single-color line drawings
Intended readership: junior high to high school
Trim size: 7½″ × 9⅛″
Binding: hardcover

Price: $16.95
Sold in bookstores and other retail outlets; also sold to libraries and schools
ISBN 0-06-275011-9
No stated revision policy

Introduction and Scope

According to the preface, the latest edition of this dictionary continues its tradition of supplying "to high-school and mature junior-high students the essential information about English vocabulary." A very up-to-

Thorndike-Barnhart Student Dictionary

❶ Boldface entry word divided into syllables

❷ Superscript indicates separate homograph entries

❸ Part-of-speech label followed by inflected forms in boldface type

❹ Labeled illustration of first homograph's second meaning includes superscript and definition numbers

❺ Etymology, in brackets, traces the development of the entry word, with recent sources first

❻ Restrictive label, in small capitals, shows how the word is used in particular circumstances

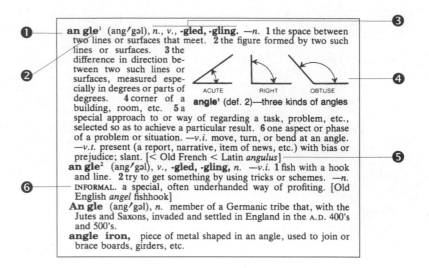

an gle¹ (ang′gəl), *n., v.,* **-gled, -gling.** —*n.* 1 the space between two lines or surfaces that meet. 2 the figure formed by two such lines or surfaces. 3 the difference in direction between two such lines or surfaces, measured especially in degrees or parts of degrees. 4 corner of a building, room, etc. 5 a special approach to or way of regarding a task, problem, etc., selected so as to achieve a particular result. 6 one aspect or phase of a problem or situation. —*v.i.* move, turn, or bend at an angle. —*v.t.* present (a report, narrative, item of news, etc.) with bias or prejudice; slant. [< Old French < Latin *angulus*]
an gle² (ang′gəl), *v.,* **-gled, -gling,** *n.* —*v.i.* 1 fish with a hook and line. 2 try to get something by using tricks or schemes. —*n.* INFORMAL. a special, often underhanded way of profiting. [Old English *angel* fishhook]
An gle (ang′gəl), *n.* member of a Germanic tribe that, with the Jutes and Saxons, invaded and settled in England in the A.D. 400's and 500's.
angle iron, piece of metal shaped in an angle, used to join or brace boards, girders, etc.

angle¹ (def. 2)—three kinds of angles

ACUTE   RIGHT   OBTUSE

date work with a fine, almost tutorial user's guide, the *Thorndike-Barnhart Student Dictionary* skillfully blends readable definitions, pertinent illustrations, and an attractive, crisp layout into one of the best student dictionaries available.

Besides a top-notch lexicon, *Thorndike-Barnhart* includes additional features such as "Word Source" tables that list frequently used words borrowed from a given language; "Word Families" (lists of words related to a common root word); and several usage notes. The work concludes with "Basic Style Rules for Writers" and a metric conversion table.

Authority

Also published as the SCOTT, FORESMAN ADVANCED DICTIONARY, the *Thorndike-Barnhart Student Dictionary* comes from the same publisher as the THORNDIKE-BARNHART CHILDREN'S DICTIONARY. E. L. Thorndike and Clarence Barnhart were noted lexicographers who developed student dictionaries in the 1930s and 1940s on which these works are based. (See the review of the SCOTT, FORESMAN INTERMEDIATE DICTIONARY for more information about the two men and their ideas.) Although Thorndike and Barnhart did not directly participate in the production of the present edition of the *Thorndike-Barnhart Student Dictionary,* their names remain on its title page and many of their lexicographical innovations have been retained in the text. According to the preface, sources for the words in the work include current textbooks and "other literature most apt to be read by the dictionary's users."

Comprehensiveness of Entries

At 100,000 entries, the *Thorndike-Barnhart Student Dictionary* is one of the most comprehensive dictionaries for its age group, ranking just above the somewhat dated MACMILLAN DICTIONARY FOR STUDENTS. All fields of study are well represented in the work. The sequence of words from **ribbon** to **Riff** includes **riboflavin, ribose, Richter scale, rickettsia,** and **riel** (the Cambodian monetary unit). Current science- and technology-related entries include the AIDS drug **azidothymidine** (better known as **AZT**), **Hubble Space Telescope, parthenogenesis,** and **recombinant DNA.** Vulgarisms and vulgar slang meanings of words are not included. Britishisms (such as **colour** and **petrol**) are included as entry words as well as within definitions, as for the entry **lift.**

According to the preface, etymologies are given for 18,000 root words. Synonym studies are also present for many entries (although antonyms are not given), as are usage labels. Usage notes (indicated by →) address formal and informal use, grammatical and rhetorical terms, questions of pronunciation or spelling, and words often confused.

Forty-three "Word Source" tables, set off from the lexicon, list words traceable to a common language. The entry **Spanish,** for example, features a list of 60 words that entered the English language through Spanish, including **armada, cigar, patio,** and **tango.** In addition, 70 "Word Family" tables list words derived from the same root. The entry **logic** features a list of 60 words that came from the Greek word *logos* or *legein,* including **analogous, epilogue, monologue,** and **trilogy.** Such entries will help students appreciate the diverse origins of the English language.

Quality and Currency of Entries

Main entries are presented as syllabicated words in bold type. After the main entry come the pronunciation within parentheses, the part-of-speech label in italics, and inflected forms. Definitions follow, with numbers in boldface for each meaning. Illustrative sentences (all of which were written by the editors) are italicized. The etymology is at the end of the entry, in brackets, followed by run-on entries. Synonym studies and usage notes, if any, appear last.

Definitions are arranged by frequency of use within each part-of-speech group. One continuing Thorndike-Barnhart hallmark is mentioned in the preface: "Definitions are written, insofar as possible, in simpler language than the main entry being defined." The following entry is typical:

> **fea si ble** (fē'zə bəl), *adj.* **1** that can be done or carried out easily; possible without difficulty or damage; practicable: *The committee selected the plan that seemed most feasible.* See **possible** for synonym study. **2** likely; probable: *The witness's explanation of the accident sounded feasible.* **3** suitable; convenient: *a feasible construction site.* [<Old French *faisable*, ultimately < Latin *facere* do] **–fea'si bil'i ty,** *n.* **–fea'si ble ness,** *n.* **–fea'si bly,** *adv.*

Biographical and geographical entries are included within the main lexicon and are quite current. Although the work fails to include either *Violeta Chamorro* or *Michael Jackson,* it does include **Germany** as a unified country, **Lithuania** and **Ukraine** as independent republics, and **Boris Yeltsin** as president of Russia. Currently popular words such as *bungee jumping, dis, fax, HDTV, maquiladora,* and *rap* are not included in the dictionary, although there are entries for **retrovirus** and **virtual reality.**

Syllabication and Pronunciation

Unlike other dictionaries that use a dot between each syllable in the main entry, *Thorndike-Barnhart* simply uses a space. This practice may lead some students to believe that an unfamiliar compound word should be written as two words. The entry for *freeway,* for example, appears as **free way.** Although two-word main entries (such as **free verse**) appear with two spaces between the words instead of one, the distinction is not as clear as it is in dictionaries that use space markers such as dots between syllables.

Syllabication is given for inflected forms when they differ from the main entry. Primary and secondary stresses are indicated for main entry words by boldface and roman stress marks within the pronunciation. The 41-symbol pronunciation key appears inside the front and back covers of the volume; a shorter version is located in the upper outside corner of every right-hand page. Variant pronunciations (as for **tomato**) are noted, as are regional variations.

Accessibility

Thorndike-Barnhart features an excellent 18-page guide called "Using This Dictionary," which includes several "Teach Yourself" exercises for students. Two crossword puzzles provide practice with pronunciation and etymologies, and the section illustrating the various sounds of the English language is particularly well done.

Entries are arranged alphabetically in strict letter-by-letter order: **ETA, et al., etc., et cetera, etch.** Alternate spellings simply note the preferred spelling but do not provide an explicit cross-reference to that entry:

> **es thet ic** (es thet'ik), *adj.* aesthetic.
> **mous tache** (mus'tash, mə stash'), *n.* mustache.

Guide words are given in bold type at the outside corners of each page.

Special Features

Apart from the excellent user's guide, *Thorndike-Barnhart* has little appended material except for a 16-page "Basic Style Rules for Writers" and a 1-page "Metric Conversion Table" that conclude the work. The most noteworthy embellishments are those within the lexicon itself: the "Word Source" and "Word Family" tables. Several other well-done charts and tables within the lexicon accompany entries such as **decibel** and **Richter Scale.** Full pages are devoted to "Geological Time," "Indo-European and Other Language Families," and "Measures and Weights." A "Periodic Table of the Elements" appears on a two-page spread.

Graphics and Format

A sturdily bound work, the *Thorndike-Barnhart Student Dictionary* lies flat when opened and has adequate margins all around. Illustrations are an even mixture of well-labeled line drawings and photographs. The illustrations of literary devices are particularly creative. At the entry **eye rhyme,** for example, a large-type rhyme is given demonstrating the principle. Excellent examples also appear at entries such as **internal rhyme** and **trochee.** Photographs are generally good and provide adequate contrast so the user can clearly see what is being depicted.

Summary

The *Thorndike-Barnhart Student Dictionary* is one of the best buys available for high school and junior high school students. One could quibble about its somewhat limited selection of contemporary words, but the dictionary's fine instructional material and unique etymological features more than compensate for that slight shortcoming. It has one of the largest lexicons of the student dictionaries, and is more current than major competitors such as the MACMILLAN DICTIONARY FOR STUDENTS. This attractive work is highly recommended for purchase by librarians, parents, and schools.

Webster's Intermediate Dictionary

Facts at a Glance

Full title: **Webster's Intermediate Dictionary**
Publisher: Merriam-Webster
Editors: Merriam-Webster editorial staff
Edition reviewed: © 1986

Number of pages: 960
Number of entries: more than 65,000
Number of illustrations: 1,000 black and white
Intended readership: grades 5 to 8
Trim size: $7\frac{1}{8}'' \times 9\frac{1}{4}''$
Binding: cloth

Price: $13.95
Sold in bookstores and other outlets; also sold to libraries and schools
ISBN 0-87779-379-4
Revised edition to be published in 1994

Introduction and Scope

Webster's Intermediate Dictionary is the middle volume in a series of three school dictionaries published by Merriam-Webster. According to the preface, it is intended for middle and junior high school students: "The range of vocabulary covered is suited to the needs of older students, but the definitions have been written in everyday language that young students will find clear." The dictionary focuses on words that students will encounter in curricular materials. This 1986 work is a first edition, although a similar dictionary, intended for junior high and high school students, was published in 1977 under the title *Webster's New Student's Dictionary*. A revision of this work was published in 1994, although too late for review in this volume.

Authority

The dictionary was compiled by Merriam-Webster's permanent staff of trained, experienced lexicographers. Entries were selected primarily on the basis of their occurrence in textbooks and other materials used in schools. In addition, the editors have consulted Merriam-Webster's extensive citation files (the files that underlie *Webster's Third New International Dictionary* and other Webster dictionaries).

Comprehensiveness of Entries

Webster's Intermediate Dictionary is comprehensive for its size and intended audience. Words are included from such fields as computer science (**byte, COBOL, floppy disk**) and video technology (**videocassette recorder,** cross-referenced to **VCR**), but those popularized after 1986 (for example, *fax, mouse* as a computer term, and *rap* as a form of music) are not included. Terms for sexual and reproductive organs are included, with clear, brief definitions. Included are the words **homosexual** and **lesbian;** unusual, but appropriate is a synonymous cross-reference from **gay** to **homosexual.** Abbreviations and biographical and geographic entries appear in separate appended lists that are among the dictionary's special features.

The dictionary also includes irregularly formed plurals and inflected verbs; usage labels and notes; illustrative phrases for many common words; synonym paragraphs; etymologies; and anecdotal word histories. Etymologies for main entry words provide the root word with its language and meaning and, in some cases, cross-references to related words. Historical language periods are distinguished only for English. Word history paragraphs are interestingly written and amplify the origins of words. For example, the origin of **sideburns** is explained in the following paragraph, which appears between the definition and the etymology:

> During the American Civil War, the Union general Ambrose Everett Burnside became known for the long bushy whiskers he wore on the sides of his face. Burnside was a popular figure in the city of Washington during the early days of the war. His unusual appearance caught the public eye. and other men soon began growing long whiskers like his. Such whiskers, which became the fashion throughout America, were originally called *burnsides* after the general. The modern word *sideburns* was formed by rearranging the letters of the older word *burnsides.*

The length and narrative quality of these paragraphs will encourage students to browse through the volume.

Quality and Currency of Entries

Definitions are clearly stated. When an entry contains multiple definitions, they are numbered in order of frequency of use with separate senses identified by lowercase letters. Although the illustrative phrases (provided in angle brackets) are helpful, they are less useful for students than the *full* sentences provided in other dictionaries, such as the MACMILLAN SCHOOL DICTIONARY.

Webster's Intermediate Dictionary

❶ Boldface entry word, divided into syllables, followed by pronunciation within slashes

❷ Cross-reference to synonym (in small capital letters) preceded by a colon

❸ A "Word History" introduces related words

❹ Etymology, within square brackets, spells out the names of languages

❺ Labeled illustration of first definition

❻ Brief illustration of use appears in angle brackets

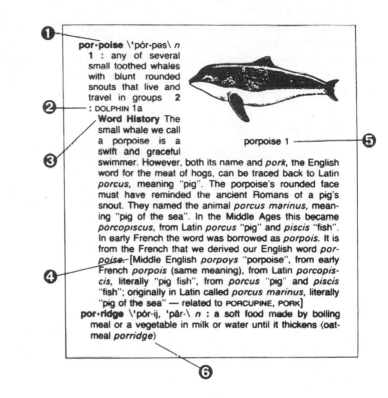

por·poise \\'pȯr-pǝs\ *n*
1 : any of several small toothed whales with blunt rounded snouts that live and travel in groups **2** : DOLPHIN 1a
Word History The small whale we call a porpoise is a swift and graceful swimmer. However, both its name and *pork*, the English word for the meat of hogs, can be traced back to Latin *porcus*, meaning "pig". The porpoise's rounded face must have reminded the ancient Romans of a pig's snout. They named the animal *porcus marinus*, meaning "pig of the sea". In the Middle Ages this became *porcopiscus*, from Latin *porcus* "pig" and *piscis* "fish". In early French the word was borrowed as *porpois*. It is from the French that we derived our English word *porpoise*. [Middle English *porpoys* "porpoise", from early French *porpois* (same meaning), from Latin *porcopiscis*, literally "pig fish", from *porcus* "pig" and *piscis* "fish"; originally in Latin called *porcus marinus*, literally "pig of the sea" — related to PORCUPINE, PORK]
por·ridge \\'pȯr-ij, 'pär-\ *n* : a soft food made by boiling meal or a vegetable in milk or water until it thickens (oatmeal *porridge*)

porpoise 1

Some useful adjuncts to definitions are provided. Under **bell,** for example, there is a table of a ship's bells indicating how many are tolled for each hour of the day. Under **Bible** appears a list of Old and New Testament biblical books. A table under **element** provides symbol, atomic number, and atomic weight of chemical elements.

Syllabication and Pronunciation

Syllabication is indicated by centered boldface dots. Pronunciation, following the main entry word, is provided for all words. Variant pronunciations are given in order of frequency. The dictionary uses a pronunciation system consisting of 44 symbols and five diacritical marks. A full key appears opposite the first page of the word list; abbreviated keys are found at the lower outside corner of each right-hand page. Accessible sample words in both versions of the key will make it easy for young students to use.

Accessibility

Alphabetization is letter by letter. Variant spellings are offered according to a complex system. Equal variants—that is, two spellings that are equally acceptable in current English—are separated by the word *or.* If one of them occurs with slightly greater frequency, it is listed first; for example, "**di·a·logue** *or* **di·a·log**." Unequal variants are separated by *also;* the one listed first is significantly more common. When three or more variants are presented, both *or* and *also* may be used. An acceptable

variant is given its own entry, with a cross-reference, when it appears one column away or farther from the main entry. Restricted variants, such as British spellings, appear only at their own main entry. This system may be cumbersome for young readers.

The volume has no thumb index or thumb guides. Guide words, however, appear at the top of each page indicating the first and last word defined on the page. A table of contents at the front of the book lists special features, making them easy to locate.

Special Features

Websters Intermediate Dictionary begins with an eight page guide, "Using Your Dictionary." The guide is thorough and written in a style appropriate for the intended audience.

Four additional reference sections appear at the back of the volume: abbreviations and symbols for chemical elements; biographical, biblical, and mythological names; geographical names; and signs and symbols. The biographical and geographical entries are dated by today's standards, though they would have been current in 1986 when the dictionary was first published. *George Bush* does not appear, nor does *Gorbachev* or *Yeltsin.* **Germany** is listed as a divided country, and **Lithuania** and **Ukraine** are both listed as Soviet republics. The signs and symbols list includes those used in a number of fields, including astronomy, business, and music. Although many student dictionaries, such as the SCOTT, FORESMAN and THORNDIKE-BARNHART works, incorporate biographical and geographical information into the main lexicon for easier access, the presence of these appended lists enhances the usefulness of *Webster's Intermediate.*

Graphics and Format

Webster's Intermediate Dictionary is illustrated with small black-and-white line drawings. Illustrations are not provided for many words whose meanings could be well clarified visually, such as **castanet** and **catamaran;** however, those illustrations that appear are well chosen and helpful. They are captioned with main entry words and, when applicable, definition numerals; occasionally a phrase of clarification is added to the caption.

The sans-serif typeface is medium-sized and easy to read. Text is printed in two columns on each page, with ample margins. Main entry words, in boldface, overhang the text. Boldface is also used for inflected forms. Synonyms appear in small capitals. Italics are used for part-of-speech abbreviations, entry words recurring within illustrative phrases, and non-English words in etymologies. These variations facilitate the location of information; however, illustrative phrases, although they are enclosed within angle brackets, do not stand out as sharply as they would if entirely italicized, as in the MACMILLAN SCHOOL DICTIONARY. The text is printed on non-glare paper with minimal show-through. The volume lies flat when opened. Sturdily bound with an easily cleaned cover, it will hold up to heavy use.

Summary

Webster's Intermediate Dictionary is a straightforward, inexpensive dictionary. Its clear definitions are accessible to middle and junior high school students, although some younger readers may find the discrimination of meaning formidable. Anecdotal etymologies add interest to the volume and encourage students to browse. The appearance of the dictionary is very sober. No color is used in the illustrations, and although the guide to the dictionary is clear, it does not invite students' interest. Furthermore, its lack of currency may be a drawback for many users. Prospective buyers should review the revised edition of this work, when it becomes available, to see if these problems have been corrected.

The dictionary is comparable to the MACMILLAN SCHOOL DICTIONARY, which has about the same number of entries, but which uses color, illustrations, and larger type advantageously. Although the Macmillan dictionary is slightly more expensive, it may be more attractive to many younger students and more easily used without adult assistance.

Webster's New World Dictionary for Young Adults

Facts at a Glance

Full title: **Webster's New World Dictionary for Young Adults**
Publisher: Prentice Hall
Editors: Jonathan L. Goldman, Project Editor; Andrew N. Sparks, Senior Editor
Edition reviewed: © 1992

Number of pages: 1,040
Number of entries: 47,500
Number of illustrations: more than 600
Intended readership: grades 5 to 8
Trim size: 8⅛″ × 10¼″
Binding: hardcover

Price: $18
ISBN 0-13-945734-8
No stated revision policy

Introduction and Scope

The 1992 edition of *Webster's New World Dictionary for Young Adults* is a 1,040-page volume containing 47,500 word entries. The dictionary is aimed at young adults in grades 5 to 8 and, according to the user's guide, is "intended to serve as a guidebook on the meanings and uses of all the words you are most likely to hear, read, and use."

Authority

Prior to its 1992 revision, this work was published under the title *Webster's New World Dictionary for Young Readers.* It is part of the *Webster's New World* family, which includes the third college edition of the WEBSTER'S NEW WORLD DICTIONARY. In fact, the same lexicographers who worked on the college dictionary worked on the *Dictionary for Young Adults,* along with an advisory board of five educators and four "multicultural consultants." These consultants include Dr. Andrea B. Bermúdez, Professor of ESL/Multicultural Education at the University of Houston; Carl A. Grant, Professor of Curriculum and Instruction at the University of Wisconsin at Madison; Judith Elaine Towne-Hankes, Education Consultant with the Wisconsin Chippewa Indians; and Dr. Wendy D. Walker, of the University of California at Berkeley.

The vocabulary words included were "chosen to meet the needs of the intended audience," according to the foreword. In an interesting twist on the usual literature survey, the editors reveal that

A computerized database of vocabulary from approximately 16,000 compositions recently written by children in schools across the country served as a valuable check to ensure adequate coverage of the active vocabulary of today's young adults.

Comprehensiveness of Entries

This work contains 47,500 entries—a relatively low number when compared with its competitors. The SCOTT, FORESMAN INTERMEDIATE DICTIONARY, for example, has 68,000 entries, and the HBJ SCHOOL DICTIONARY has 60,000. Nevertheless, a major advantage of *Webster's New World Dictionary for Young Adults* over its competition is its recency. Terms such as **CD** (as a short form for compact disc) and **nacho,** for example, are in the work. The entries from **hesitation** to **high-handed** include terms such as **heterosexual, hiatus, hibachi, hieroglyphic,** and **highbrow.** The dictionary does not include vulgarisms. Britishisms are evident both in entry words (**colour, petrol**) and within definitions (**lift, lorry**).

Webster's New World Dictionary for Young Adults is full of eye-catching features that will interest its young readers. For example, 700 words are shown in synonym notes. The synonym notes are set off as boxed entries within the text and are cross-referenced from other dictionary entries. Rather than simply listing a variety of synonyms for a word, the synonym notes tend to concentrate on a relatively few number of words but provide lengthy explanations. Here, for example, is the synonym note for **consider:**

> To **consider** is to think over something in order to understand it or make a decision *[Please consider my poem for publication.]* To **weigh** is to balance in the mind facts or opinions that conflict with each other *[The jury will weigh the defendant's story against that of her accuser.]* To **reflect** is to think about something in a quiet, serious way *[Reading philosophy makes us reflect on ideas of love and truth.]*

Etymologies appear in one of two ways: as one of about 200 "Word History" boxes, or as one of 1,100 additional etymologies appearing in double brackets at the end of an entry, as for **angle:**

> [[This word comes to us, through Old French, from Latin *angulus,* meaning "a corner." *Angulus* goes back to the ancient Greek adjective *ankylos,* meaning "bent."]]

Usage labels and usage notes are also present. Longer usage notes are preceded by a colored ■ symbol at the end of an entry. Shorter ones are simply preceded by a colon as part of a numbered definition. All illustrative sentences and phrases within definitions are invented and appear within italicized brackets, with the entry word also italicized in the sentence.

The dictionary, according to its back cover, contains over 1,100 geographical entries and over 400 biographical entries within the main text. Here, too, the recent date of publication is advantageous, as there are entries for **Lithuania** and **Ukraine** as separate countries, **Ger-**

many as a unified country, and **Boris Yeltsin** as president of Russia.

Quality and Currency of Entries

Main entries are syllabicated words in bold type, followed by the pronunciation in parentheses, the part of speech and usage labels, and numbered definitions. Illustrative sentences or phrases are in brackets within definitions. Following are inflected forms for that particular part of speech. Usage notes follow, then idioms and run-on entries (called "derived forms" in the user's guide). The entry concludes with a word history (if provided). If a word has more than one definition, the "basic or most common one" is given first. If a word has more than one part of speech label, the second always begins on a separate line, which greatly increases the readability of the entry. Definitions are clear and accurate and use terms that are appropriate for the book's intended audience. The following entry for **damage** is typical:

> **dam·age** (dam′ij) *n.* **1** injury or harm to a person or thing that results in a loss of health, value, etc. *[A poor diet can cause damage to the heart. The storm caused some damage to the barn.]* **2 damages** money asked or paid to make up for harm or damage done *[The victim of the accident sued for $10,000 in damages.]*
> *v.* to do damage to *[The frost damaged the crops.]* **–aged, –ag·ing**
> ● See the synonym note at INJURE

Despite its 1992 date, the dictionary does not have definitions for *bungee jumping, dis, fax, HDTV, intifada, maquiladora, retrovirus,* or *virtual reality.* It does, however, have a definition for **rap** music.

Syllabication and Pronunciation

Primary and secondary stress is shown using accent marks in boldface and roman, respectively, in the pronunciation. Syllable divisions as well as stress are given for inflections and for derived forms, though inflections are not always spelled out in their entirety. Variant pronunciation is given when needed. A 41-symbol full pronunciation key is conveniently located opposite the inside front cover. An abbreviated pronunciation key appears in the lower right-hand corner of every left-hand page. Although these are located in an unusual position, the dictionary's ample gutter margins allow them to be read easily. A "Word Finder Table" for students who have a pronunciation but no spelling appears on the inside back cover.

Accessibility

Entries are arranged in strict letter-by-letter order: **étude, ETV, etymology, Eu, eucalyptus.** Word entries for alternate spellings include the italicized phrase "another spelling of. . . ." Guide words appear at the upper outside corner of every page and are clearly separated from the main text by a colored line. Tab letters are printed on the outside margin of every right-hand page.

Given its intended audience, the "Guide to the Use of the Dictionary" in *Webster's New World Dictionary for Young Adults* is remarkably brief (11 pages). Without any illustrations or exercises, this section lacks the inviting look that many other dictionaries employ to entice their young readers to use the guide.

Graphics and Format

The "over 600" illustrations advertised on the back cover of this work seems to be a rather low number for a dictionary appealing to a young audience, particularly since there are no color illustrations. According to the foreward, "all but a handful" of the drawings were done by one artist—Anita Rogoff—which gives the volume a certain consistency. All illustrations are set into the column of text adjacent to the entry word they depict. The drawings are very clear, as are the black-and-white photographs, which comprise just under half of the illustrations. Captions, however, are used inconsistently. The drawing for **camel,** for example, depicts a dromedary as well as a Bactrian camel, yet the caption merely reads "camels." On the other hand, the drawing at **elephant** depicts both an African and Indian elephant and identifies them as such.

Despite these criticisms—and the lack of color illustrations—the work has a remarkably bright, crisp look that is inviting. The typeface is slightly larger than normal, the margins more than adequate, and the binding sturdy.

Summary

The *Webster's New World Dictionary for Young Adults* is a well-constructed work that—despite the relatively low number of entries—features an attractive appearance with an up-to-date vocabulary. Users looking for a larger, more illustrated work may still want to turn to the SCOTT, FORESMAN INTERMEDIATE DICTIONARY, but *Webster's New World Dictionary for Young Adults* will certainly not disappoint the reader. Its relatively low price tag (as compared with Macmillan's and HBJ's student dictionaries) may appeal to librarians or educators with limited budgets.

The World Book Student Dictionary

Facts at a Glance

Full title: **The World Book Student Dictionary**
Publisher: World Book
Editors: William H. Nault, Publisher; Dominic J. Miccolis, Vice President and Executive Editor
Edition reviewed: © 1993

Number of pages: 900
Number of entries: 30,000
Number of illustrations: more than 1,000; 100 percent in color
Intended readership: upper elementary and middle school students
Trim size: 8″ × 10″
Binding: hardcover

Price: $23
Sold directly to schools and libraries; also sold door-to-door
ISBN 0-7166-1593-2
Revised annually

Introduction and Scope

The World Book Student Dictionary is a one-volume work intended for upper elementary and middle school students. It emphasizes vocabulary development and contains exercises that teach students to use the dictionary and master basic language skills. The same work without these exercises is published under the title *Childcraft Dictionary* and sold with CHILDCRAFT: THE HOW AND WHY LIBRARY. Both are revised annually.

Authority

The World Book Student Dictionary is published by World Book, whose reference books include not only the two-volume WORLD BOOK DICTIONARY and the *Childcraft Dictionary* but also the WORLD BOOK ENCYCLOPEDIA and CHILDCRAFT: THE HOW AND WHY LIBRARY. The large staff includes executive editor Dominic J. Miccolis, editor Suzanne Stone Brooks, and publisher William H. Nault. They have produced a dictionary based on *The Living Vocabulary: A National Vocabulary Inventory* by Edgar Dale and Joseph O'Rourke. This well-known and widely used document contains the results of a 25-year study on word recognition by students of varying grade levels. Although somewhat dated, the guide allowed the editorial staff to create definitions appropriate for the grade level of the dictionary's users.

Comprehensiveness of Entries

The World Book Student Dictionary contains more than 30,000 entries, a number comparable to other dictionaries in its age range. The AMERICAN HERITAGE CHILDREN'S DICTIONARY has 36,000 entries; the THORNDIKE-BARNHART CHILDREN'S DICTIONARY has 28,000. Its scope is suited to students in grades 3 to 6 and includes many words from the fields of history, science, technology, religion, and world cultures. No slang terms or vulgarisms appear. A particular strength is the number of illustrated entries for animals, including specific breeds of dogs and cats. A sequence of entries from **computer** to **congratulations**

The World Book Student Dictionary

❶ Italicized sample sentence shows the entry word in context

❷ Syllabication of the entry word appears after the definitions and is shown by a vertical rule

❸ Part-of-speech label appears in italics and is followed by inflected form in boldface type

❹ Entry word abbreviation appears on a separate line

❺ Idiom indicated by black square

❻ Labeled diagrams illustrate definitions 1 and 4

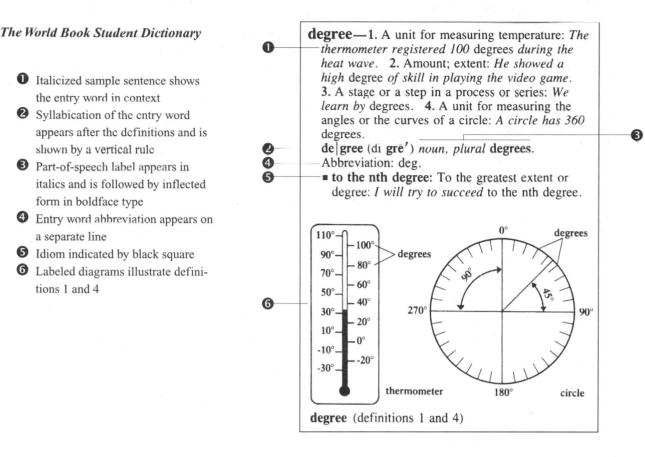

degree (definitions 1 and 4)

includes the following terms: **comrade, concave, conceal, conceited, concentrate, condor, cone** (mathematics and botany), **confederacy** (as a general term and in American history), **confession, confetti, confirmation,** and **confusion.**

The publisher states that this dictionary emphasizes vocabulary development. It succeeds well in this area. Most pages have at least one special inset bordered in blue, containing information labeled "Word History," "Word Power," or "Language Fact." These provide information on etymology, using prefixes and suffixes to build words, and correct usage.

The entries are clear and easy to understand. Labels indicate parts of speech and most entries include sentences that illustrate the definition and usage. Synonyms and antonyms are listed at the end of the entry, marked by a blue dot. A red square at the end of an entry indicates examples of idiomatic usage.

The biographical and geographical information in this work is limited. Lists of presidents of the United States and prime ministers of Canada with birth and death dates are the only biographical facts. These lists precede the latest elections in both countries and end with George Bush and Brian Mulroney, respectively. The geographical information consists of lists of the 50 states, and provinces and territories of Canada, with their capitals; independent countries of the world and their capitals; continents; oceans and seas; and longest rivers. The list of countries includes **Germany** as a unified country and reflects the breakup of the U.S.S.R. into independent states. Country names are very current.

Quality and Currency of Entries

Main entries in this dictionary are arranged in the following manner: the word in boldface overhanging the text; the definitions preceded by numerals in boldface and followed by illustrative phrases in italics; the syllabicated word; the pronunciation with alternates in parentheses; the part-of-speech label in italics; the plural in boldface; and the synonyms and antonyms in boldface preceded by a blue dot. Here is the entire entry for the word **entertainment**:

> **entertainment—1.** An activity that gives pleasure; amusement: *The* entertainment *at the party was a live disk jockey.* **2.** Pleasure; fun; relaxation: *He told jokes for our* entertainment *while we waited.* **en│ter│tain│ment** (en′ tər tān′ mənt) *noun. plural* **entertainments.**
> • Synonyms: **game, pastime, play, recreation, sport,** for **1.**
> Antonyms: **chore, duty, task, work,** for **1.**

The definitions in this dictionary are brief, clear, and well suited to its users. Illustrative phrases are always specially written sentences rather than quotations from established authors. This allows the editors to ensure that the examples reflect the basic meanings being given.

Although it is quite up-to-date, there are no entries for *bungee jumping, HDTV, intifada, maquiladora, retrovirus,* and *virtual reality.* **Dis-** is included only as a prefix and **rap** is not defined to include the musical style. Other contemporary terms such as **AIDS, CD, fax,** and **VCR** are included. The entry for **AIDS** briefly describes the disease without explaining that the term is an abbreviation of *acquired immune deficiency syndrome.* The entries for **CD** and **VCR** refer the user to those for **compact disc** and **videocassette recorder,** respectively.

Syllabication and Pronunciation

The World Book Student Dictionary indicates syllabication in main entries using vertical lines. Entries for open compounds such as **flying fish** are also syllabified. Syllabication of pronunciation follows phonetic rules and sometimes differs from that of the main entry, as in **Jef|fer|son Da|vis's Birth|day (jef′ ər sən dā′ vis iz burth′ dā).** Syllabication is provided after the definition. The main entry heading is printed in undivided form.

Pronunciations are given at the end of the entry after the syllabication. Both standard and alternative pronunciations are given when necessary (for example, **envelope**). The International Phonetic Alphabet (IPA) is the basis for pronunciations. The introductory section of the book contains a detailed explanation of pronunciation and a full pronunciation key. An abbreviated pronunciation key appears at the bottom of the outside column of each left-hand page. Stress is indicated with a combination of bold type and stress marks. These examples illustrate *World Book*'s use of syllabication and pronunciation: **a|bout (ə bout′), Eng|lish (ing′ glish), o|bey (ō bā′), rhythm (rith′ əm).**

Accessibility

The World Book Student Dictionary is easy to use. A 19-page section entitled "How to Use Your Dictionary" explains the organization in detail. Sixteen pages of "Student Exercises" offer practice and build confidence in dictionary use. Entries are in strict alphabetical order, letter by letter: **cavern, cavity, caw, CD, cease, cedar.**

Each page has guide words in the upper outer corner indicating the first and last entries for that page. Alternate spellings of a word have their own entries with a "see" reference to the standard spelling. The entry for the standard spelling also notes the variant form. For example, the entry "**moustache**—*see* **mustache**" refers the reader to "**mustache**—Hair that grows on the upper lip of a man. . . . This word is also spelled **moustache.**"

Special Features

In addition to the introductory material and student exercises, this dictionary has a reference section. It includes "Word Power Exercises" with answer keys that offer vocabulary building at the third-, fourth-, fifth-, and sixth-grade levels. A section called "The Magic of Words" contains word games, riddles, tongue twisters, palindromes, and basic information on the meaning of names and the etymology of common words.

Graphics and Format

Like all World Book publications, this dictionary is attractive and well printed. The layout facilitates use with clear guide words and bold type separating the entry headings from the definitions. The margins are adequate. Blue stripes and headings effectively set off the language facts and word histories, as do the red stripes that mark the pronunciation guides. The smooth white paper minimizes show-through. The binding is sturdy enough to withstand heavy use.

Over 1,000 color illustrations bring the definitions to life. They are clear and compare favorably to those in other advanced children's dictionaries. Pictures of animals, tools, and plants predominate, but there are also illustrations of a thermometer and a circle to explain **degree** and jumping cheerleaders to demonstrate **enthusiastic.** Illustrations and a brief history of the evolution of each letter of the alphabet begin every section of the dictionary.

Summary

The World Book Student Dictionary is an excellent source for upper elementary and middle school students. It is easy to use and contains exercises that help students master language skills. It is well illustrated and more up-to-date than the MACMILLAN DICTIONARY FOR CHILDREN (1989), which is similar in size and scope. Purchasers may want to consider, however, that this dictionary is expensive. At $23, it is well outside the $13–$18 price range of its closest competitors. Annual revision maintains currency and the sturdy binding assures good wear in the library and classroom.

Chapter 12
Evaluations of Secondary and Adult Dictionaries

The American Heritage College Dictionary

Facts at a Glance

Full title: **The American Heritage College Dictionary**
Publisher: Houghton Mifflin
Editor: Robert B. Costello
Edition reviewed: © 1993, third edition

Number of pages: 1,630
Number of entries: 200,000 (reviewer estimate)
Number of illustrations: 2,500, all in black and white
Intended readership: college to adult
Trim size: 7″ × 9½″
Binding: hardcover

Price: $19.95 (cloth); $24.95 (deluxe)
Sold in bookstores; also sold to libraries and
    educational institutions
ISBN 0-395-66917-0 (plain edge);
    ISBN 0-395-44638-4 (cloth, thumb indexed);
    ISBN 0-395-66918-9 (deluxe)
No stated revision policy

Introduction and Scope

The third edition of *The American Heritage College Dictionary,* 1993, is the offspring of THE AMERICAN HERITAGE DICTIONARY OF THE ENGLISH LANGUAGE (AHD), third edition, which was published in 1992 by Houghton Mifflin. It offers 200,000 entries and 1,630 pages in contrast to the 350,000 entries and 2,140 pages of the parent volume. The college edition, which draws its vocabulary from the same database as the AHD, may be considered an abridged edition. Its compact size is typical for desktop dictionaries. The 2,500 illustrations, which are in the page margins, were picked up from the AHD. There are approximately 30,500 etymologies, 12,000 new words and meanings, and 400 usage notes.

Authority

Houghton Mifflin has a reputation for producing high-quality dictionaries that are popular with both librarians and students. Nearly 70 well-known writers, scholars, and experts in a variety of fields contributed to the third edition of this college dictionary. In addition, Houghton Mifflin retains a usage panel, the members of which are periodically polled by the publisher regarding questions of disputed word usage. The 173 members listed in the front matter include noted writers such as Margaret Atwood, Jacques Barzun, Annie Dillard, Paul Theroux, and Eudora Welty; economist John Kenneth Galbraith; U.S. Senators Bill Bradley and Mark Hatfield; and other luminaries such as Carl Sagan, Arthur Schlesinger, and Tony Randall. Panel members are chosen because they "use the English language regularly and publicly and are noted for their command of it." The dictionary's front

The American Heritage College Dictionary

❶ Syllabication shown by centered dots

❷ Italicized part-of-speech label appears before the definition or definitions to which it applies

❸ Captioned drawing illustrates definition **6a**

❹ Subject label indicates restricted meaning

❺ Plural form entered separately, in boldface type

❻ Inflected forms follow part-of-speech label

❼ Etymology appears in brackets at the end of the entry

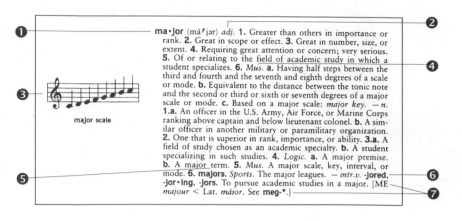

ma•jor (mā′jər) *adj.* **1.** Greater than others in importance or rank. **2.** Great in scope or effect. **3.** Great in number, size, or extent. **4.** Requiring great attention or concern; very serious. **5.** Of or relating to the field of academic study in which a student specializes. **6.** *Mus.* **a.** Having half steps between the third and fourth and the seventh and eighth degrees of a scale or mode. **b.** Equivalent to the distance between the tonic note and the second or third or sixth or seventh degrees of a major scale or mode. **c.** Based on a major scale: *major key.* — *n.* **1.a.** An officer in the U.S. Army, Air Force, or Marine Corps ranking above captain and below lieutenant colonel. **b.** A similar officer in another military or paramilitary organization. **2.** One that is superior in rank, importance, or ability. **3.a.** A field of study chosen as an academic specialty. **b.** A student specializing in such studies. **4.** *Logic.* **a.** A major premise. **b.** A major term. **5.** *Mus.* A major scale, key, interval, or mode. **6. majors.** *Sports.* The major leagues. — *intr.v.* **-jored, -jor•ing, -jors.** To pursue academic studies in a major. [ME *majour* < Lat. *māior.* See **meg-*.**]

major scale

---

matter cautions that the usage panel "should not be thought of as an Academy, charged with ruling on all questions of disputed usage," and stresses that controversy and "split decisions" about usage are frequent among its members. Nonetheless, the opinions of these prominent language users lend authority and authenticity to the work.

Comprehensiveness of Entries

The number of entries—close to 200,000—compares favorably with other desktop competitors. RANDOM HOUSE WEBSTER'S COLLEGE DICTIONARY, 1992, features 180,000 entries; WEBSTER'S NEW WORLD DICTIONARY OF THE AMERICAN LANGUAGE: THIRD COLLEGE EDITION, 1991, contains 170,000; and MERRIAM-WEBSTER'S COLLEGIATE DICTIONARY, tenth edition, 1993, claims 185,000 words.

A randomly selected sample of the 50 entries from **Cleisthenes** to **cliff brake** illustrates how diverse the topics are in this work. In addition to 15 botanical and technical terms (**cleistogamous, clematis, clepsydra, clevis,** and others) the sample contains one Greek theologian (**Clemont of Alexandria**), one French politician (**Georges Clemenceau**), the American pianist **Van Cliburn, Samuel Clemens,** three Popes, and **clerihew,** a type of short poem. Geographical entries include two American and two French cities. One entry (**clew**) is labeled *Chiefly British.* Although there are no vulgarisms or slang words in this sample, they can be found throughout the dictionary with status labels that include *Non-Standard, Offensive, Vulgar, Obscene, Slang,* and *Informal.*

Etymologies are designed for clarity. They employ standard abbreviations and symbols to identify root languages, and often contain cross-references to other entries:

bat³ (băt) *tr. v.* **bat•ted, bat•ting, bats.** To wink or flutter; *bat one's eyelashes.* [Prob. a var. of BATE².]

Indo-European roots of words are set in boldface type, identified with an asterisk, and cross-referenced to the "Indo-European Roots" appendix. For example, the etymology for **regress** instructs the reader to "see **ghredh-*.**"

Synonyms are introduced at the end of entries. One difference between the college edition and the AHD is the abbreviation of labels such as **Syns** (synonyms) and **Ants** (antonyms) that are spelled out in the parent volume.

The "Usage Note" category is one of the most significant features of this dictionary. The notes vary in content and length. Some deal with technical points, such as the difference between **flotsam** and **jetsam;** others treat matters of grammatical, social, or critical concern. The following example illustrates the thoroughness of the notes and the role of the usage panel:

> **Usage Note:** *Decimate* originally referred to the killing of every tenth person, a punishment used in the Roman army for mutinous legions. Today this meaning is commonly extended to include the killing of any large proportion of a group. Sixty-six percent of the Usage Panel accepts this extension in the sentence *The Jewish population of Germany was decimated by the war,* even though it is common knowledge that the number of Jews killed was much greater than a tenth of the original population. However, when large-scale destruction other than killing is meant, as in *The supply of fresh produce was decimated by the accident at Chernobyl,* the usage is accepted by only 26 percent of the Panel.

Illustrative phrases and sentences appear often in the usage notes and synonym studies but less frequently within the main entries. Some are quotations from literary works and public figures (such as Jesse Jackson, H. G. Wells, and Sir Walter Scott); most have been devised by the editors themselves.

Dialectal usage of a word is treated under the heading "Regional Note." For example, the note at the **dragonfly** entry locates various regional terms used to identify the insect such as *darning needle, ear sewer, mosquito hawk,* and *snake doctor.* "Word History" notes, which occasionally appear at the end of entries, expand on etymologies.

Biographical and geographical entries, which were treated in a separate section in the second college edition, are now included in the main lexicon. Proper names follow common nouns of the same spelling.

On the whole, entries are current. **Lithuania** and **Ukraine** appear as independent republics. Entries for **Germany** and **Boris Yeltsin** are up-to-date. *Violeta Chamorro* and *Michael Jackson* do not appear in this dictionary.

Quality and Currency of Entries

The entries in *The American Heritage College Dictionary* are well written, and their format is logically ordered. Each entry begins with the syllabicated boldface term overhanging the text. Entry words are followed by the pronunciation in parentheses, the abbreviation of its part of speech, any inflected forms in boldface, and numbered definitions. Illustrative examples are set in italics. If the word may be used in more than one grammatical function, a dash introduces the syllabicated alternative form and its pronunciation and definition(s). When applicable, the entry may end with idioms, synonyms, antonyms, or a bracketed etymology. The following entry shows many of these elements:

> **com·pli·ment** (kom′ plə-mənt) *n.* **1.** An expression of praise, admiration, or congratulation. **2.** A formal act of civility, courtesy, or respect. **3. compliments.** Good wishes; regards. See Usage Note at **complement. —***tr.v.* **-ment·ed, -ment·ing, -ments. 1.** To pay a compliment to. **2.** To show fondness, regard, or respect for by giving a gift or performing a favor. [Fr. <Ital. *complimento* < Sp. *cumplimiento* < *cumplir,* to complete < Lat. *complēre,* to fill up : *com-,* com- + *plēre,* to fill; see **pelə–**[1*].]

According to the dictionary's user's guide, the "central and often the most commonly sought" meanings are given first. Definitions are clear and easy to understand. They are usually phrases, similar in content to the full sentences used in AHD. Entries are free of distracting symbols and grammatical jargon, except for the standard etymological notations. Terms may be labeled *archaic* or *obsolete,* and subject labels such as *Comp. Sci.* or *Biol.* are used where appropriate.

Many current terms, including **fax, HDTV, maquiladora, rap, retrovirus,** and **virtual reality** are defined in this edition. There are, however, no entries for *bungee jumping, dis,* or *intifada.*

Syllabication and Pronunciation

Entries are clearly marked for syllabication and pronunciation. Entry words, as well as inflected and derived forms, are divided into syllables by centered dots: **a·bout, Eng·lish, o·bey,** and **rhythm.** Words that are part of an open compound, such as **laser printer,** are syllabicated at the entry for each individual word. Phrasal verbs, such as **rejoice in,** are set in boldface but are not divided by syllables.

The boldface entry is followed by the pronunciation or pronunciations in parentheses, with the most common occurring first. Both primary and secondary stresses are marked. The pronunciation guide in the front matter explains the symbols used, and examples are provided in a table. A condensed pronunciation guide appears in the lower outside corner of one of the pages in each two-page spread.

Accessibility

Users will find it relatively easy to locate information in this dictionary. All words, including abbreviations and biographical and geographical names, are listed alphabetically, letter by letter. People with the same last name but different first names appear as separate entries, unlike in WEBSTER'S NEW WORLD DICTIONARY, where persons with the same last name are treated in one entry.

The seven-page "Guide to the Dictionary" contains extensive material on how to find and understand information in the entries. The guide is well written, and the heads and subheads make finding specific topics quick and easy. An additional 15-page booklet of exercises to help students understand the dictionary's guide is included with copies of the work that are sold to schools.

Pairs of guide words appear in the upper outside corners of each page. The dictionary uses cross-references extensively to refer readers to the "Indo-European Roots" appendix; in entries representing variant forms such as Britishisms; and for the sake of brevity, as in the following example: **country and western** *n.* See **country music.**

Special Features

A number of special features contribute to this work's value as a reference tool. Introductory materials include an essay by noted linguist Geoffrey Nunberg on "Usage in the American Heritage Dictionary: The Place of Criticism," which also appears in the AHD. Unique to the college edition is a guide to abbreviations and labels, a "Table of Alphabets," and a chart entitled "Development of the Alphabet."

The appended materials are almost exactly the same as those in the parent volume: "A Guide to the Appendix," "Indo-European Sound Correspondences," and the lengthy "Indo-European Roots" section to which there are cross-references throughout the dictionary. The college edition also includes an essay (slightly altered) from the parent work entitled "Indo-European and the Indo-Europeans" by Calvert Watkins.

An elaborate diagram of the Indo-European languages has replaced the index that was located on the inside back cover of the previous college edition. The list of four-year and two-year colleges and universities has also been dropped. The "Style Manual" now appears in THE AMERICAN HERITAGE HIGH SCHOOL DICTIONARY, third edition, instead of in the college edition.

Graphics and Format

The layout and use of illustrations in the outside margins of each page make this a very attractive dictionary. The editors used 2,500 of the 4,000 illustrations in the AHD. Although the black-and-white photographs have been reduced in size, they are still generally clear and informative. The line drawings are clear and well executed; however, many do not appear adjacent to the word they define. Illustrations are reasonably current and include portraits of well-known personalities, such as President Clinton and First Lady Hillary Rodham Clinton.

The volume is sturdy. However, the pages are thinner than those of the AHD, the point size of the text is reduced, and the typeface is less bold. Because the college edition is an easy size to handle, however, it meets the requirements of a desktop dictionary better than the parent volume.

Summary

The college edition is a smaller version of the AMERICAN HERITAGE DICTIONARY OF THE ENGLISH LANGUAGE, third edition; it is compact, easy to handle, and visually appealing. With the exceptions of special features and the treatment of vulgarities, it is identical to the high school version. The definitions are clear and relate to subjects that interest students in this age group. It is intentionally different from dictionaries, like the RANDOM HOUSE WEBSTER'S COLLEGE DICTIONARY, that tend to resemble standard unabridged dictionaries in style and content. The American Heritage series also differs from other dictionaries, including those by Merriam-Webster, in that it offers a more "prescriptive" approach to usage advice rather than a "descriptive" approach.

The American Heritage College Dictionary contains much more information on Indo-European languages than dictionaries such as WEBSTER'S NEW WORLD and MERRIAM-WEBSTER'S COLLEGIATE DICTIONARY, tenth edition. Those works, however, contain more useful information on editorial style, special abbreviations, signs, and symbols.

Although the college edition lacks a broad range of technical terms and is slightly less up-to-date than RANDOM HOUSE, it presents information in a visually un-cluttered, balanced format that makes using it a pleasant experience. Since most libraries will collect several dictionaries, this competitively priced college edition should be among them.

The American Heritage Desk Dictionary

Facts at a Glance

Full title: **The American Heritage Desk Dictionary**
Publisher: Houghton Mifflin
Editor: Fernando de Mello Vianna, Editor-in-Chief
Edition reviewed: © 1981

Number of pages: 1,184
Number of entries: more than 100,000
Number of illustrations: more than 1,500 black-and-white photographs and line drawings
Intended readership: adult
Trim size: 6¾" × 9⁹⁄₁₆"
Binding: cloth

Price: $12.95
Sold in bookstores and other retail outlets; also sold to libraries and other educational institutions
ISBN 0-395-31256-6
No stated revision policy

Introduction and Scope

The American Heritage Desk Dictionary contains more than 100,000 entries, plus 2,500 biographical and geographical entries. The *Desk Dictionary* is based on the larger AMERICAN HERITAGE DICTIONARY. While a new, third edition of that work was published in 1993, the *Desk Dictionary* has not been updated since 1981.

Authority

This volume was prepared under the guidance of Fernando de Mello Vianna, who was also the editor-in-chief of the publisher's respected *Roget's II: The New Thesaurus.* The American Heritage family of dictionaries not only is well known but has also generally received excellent reviews.

The American Heritage Desk Dictionary has a contemporary, accessible design; the many photographs are generally appropriate for the entries, placed as close to them as possible, and provided with a clear caption in boldface.

Comprehensiveness of Entries

For an abridged work, *The American Heritage Desk Dictionary* is sufficiently comprehensive for most users as a general, everyday reference. Unfortunately, given

The American Heritage Desk Dictionary

❶ Pronunciations enclosed in parentheses

❷ Inflected forms, abbreviated where possible, set in boldface type

❸ Idiomatic expressions, set in small boldface type and preceded by the boldface italic subhead—*idioms,* are defined after the main entry

❹ Usage labels italicized

❺ Synonyms discussed in a separate note headed by a boldface italic *syns*

❻ Cross-references set in boldface type

❼ Etymologies enclosed in brackets

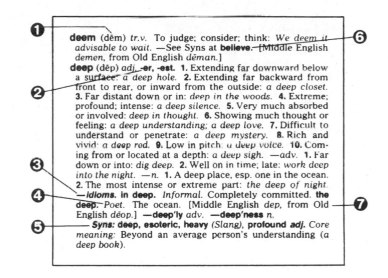

deem (dēm) *tr.v.* To judge; consider; think: *We deem it advisable to wait.* —See Syns at **believe.** [Middle English *demen,* from Old English *dēman.*]
deep (dēp) *adj.* **-er, -est. 1.** Extending far downward below a surface: *a deep hole.* **2.** Extending far backward from front to rear, or inward from the outside: *a deep closet.* **3.** Far distant down or in: *deep in the woods.* **4.** Extreme; profound; intense: *a deep silence.* **5.** Very much absorbed or involved: *deep in thought.* **6.** Showing much thought or feeling: *a deep understanding; a deep love.* **7.** Difficult to understand or penetrate: *a deep mystery.* **8.** Rich and vivid: *a deep red.* **9.** Low in pitch: *a deep voice.* **10.** Coming from or located at a depth: *a deep sigh.* —*adv.* **1.** Far down or into: *dig deep.* **2.** Well on in time; late: *work deep into the night.* —*n.* **1.** A deep place, esp. one in the ocean. **2.** The most intense or extreme part: *the deep of night.* —**idioms. in deep.** *Informal.* Completely committed. **the deep.** *Poet.* The ocean. [Middle English *dep,* from Old English *dēop.*] —**deep'ly** *adv.* —**deep'ness** *n.*
— **Syns: deep, esoteric, heavy** (*Slang*), **profound** *adj. Core meaning:* Beyond an average person's understanding (*a deep book*).

its 1981 publication date, the work is becoming outdated, especially in its lack of current scientific and technical terms. A comparison of a representative segment of entries from **paprika** to **parachute** shows that THE AMERICAN HERITAGE COLLEGE DICTIONARY, third edition, includes 24 separate entry words, while the *Desk Dictionary* has 9. The following entries between **paprika** and **parachute** can be found in the third college edition but not in the *Desk Dictionary:* **Papuan** *n.,* **papule, papyrology, para-aminobenzoic acid, parabiosis, parablast,** and **paraboloid.** Students requiring specialized vocabulary in the sciences and technology will be better served by a textbook, special glossary, or a more comprehensive and up-to-date dictionary such as THE AMERICAN HERITAGE COLLEGE DICTIONARY, third edition. In addition, the *Desk Dictionary*'s 1981 publishing date precludes entries for many words now in frequent use, such as *videocassette* and *aerobics.*

Quality and Currency of Entries

A typical entry includes the following information: boldface syllabication, pronunciation with abbreviated variations given in parentheses, italicized abbreviation of the part of speech, definitions, variant word forms with the parts of speech indicated, usage information for some entries, and etymology or source.

In general, definitions are concise and easy to understand. Frequent italicized short examples (phrases or brief sentences) follow immediately after many of the meanings. The order of defined meanings tends to present the most widely used meaning first. Synonyms are listed after the appropriate meaning or cross-referenced.

Several other features are especially helpful, including the identification of homographs, listing of prefixes and suffixes, and listing of plural forms of verbs. Idiomatic usage is clearly labeled and defined, with multiple meanings when necessary. The usage notes following many definitions seem up-to-date and useful.

Syllabication and Pronunciation

As in other American Heritage dictionaries, bold centered dots divide syllables in all main entries: **mor·a·to·ri·um.**

Pronunciation symbols are given for all main entries and for other forms as required. The pronunciation key appears in a large chart with a good explanation at the front of the dictionary. A shortened form of the key is printed at the bottom of each page of the dictionary for quick reference. The system of symbols is common to all American Heritage dictionaries. If more than one pronunciation is listed for a word, the first is assumed to be more common. Primary and secondary stress is indicated with boldface and roman stress marks.

Accessibility

All entries, including compound words, are arranged in strict letter-by-letter alphabetical order. The two-column format with boldface main entries makes this dictionary easy to access. Inflected forms of a word, numbers preceding definitions with an entry, cross-referenced words, and labels for phrasal, modifying, and idiomatic examples are printed in sans-serif bold type and are easily found within entries. Synonym lists are placed in separate paragraphs following the main body of an entry.

A special effort has been made in the "How to Use the Dictionary" section to define what a dictionary is and to explain what its various parts are intended to do—both in general and in this desk version.

Special Features

Tables located after the lexicon include a "Guide to the Metric System," "Periodic Tables of Elements," proofreaders' marks, symbols and signs, and alphabets.

Following the tables are separate sections of approximately 2,500 very brief biographical and geographical entries for quick reference. Neither section is current for dates, population figures, or geographical changes after the early 1980s. Thus, for example, state leaders Gorbachev, Kohl, and Mulroney are excluded, and artist Andy Warhol and writer Saul Bellow suffer a similar fate.

A brief list of standard abbreviations is included at the end of the book. In addition, there is an extensive, separate listing of abbreviations used in the dictionary's entries, including field labels, abbreviations used in the etymologies, and those used in the biographical and geographical entries. This gathering together in one place of all abbreviations used in the dictionary is an excellent idea, providing users with an easily accessible reference page.

Other special features include "Synonym Studies," "Usage Notes," and "Alphabet Letter Histories." An eight-page "Manual of Style" includes sections on punctuation, capitalization, use of italics, and business letters.

Graphics and Format

The overall design of the dictionary is attractive. While the quality varies among the more than 1,500 captioned illustrations, most pictures are clear and useful. Schematic drawings of human anatomy are clear; line drawings of flowers and birds are exceptionally detailed. There are no portraits in the biographical section and no maps in the geographical section.

Summary

Although somewhat dated, the *American Heritage Desk Dictionary* remains a useful reference for those who may not require the additional special features or the more updated technical and scientific vocabulary of the larger, more recent AMERICAN HERITAGE COLLEGE DICTIONARY, third edition. The typeface is readable, access is easy, the paper quality is good, and the binding is sturdy. The simplified definitions are clear and well written. The illustrations give the pages an open and more accessible look than those of a typical desk dictionary such as MERRIAM-WEBSTER'S COLLEGIATE DICTIONARY, tenth edition. That work, although it costs nearly twice as much as *The American Heritage Desk Dictionary,* has a much more comprehensive and up-to-date lexicon than the desk dictionary's, and would make a better purchase for those who use a more technical or specialized vocabulary.

The American Heritage Dictionary of the English Language

Facts at a Glance

Full title: **The American Heritage Dictionary of the English Language**
Publisher: Houghton Mifflin
Editor: Anne H. Soukhanov, Executive Editor
Edition reviewed: © 1992, third edition

Number of pages: 2,140
Number of entries: 350,000
Number of illustrations: 4,000, all in black and white
Intended readership: adults and all ages (reviewer estimate)
Trim size: 8½″ × 11″
Binding: hardcover

Price: $45
ISBN 0-395-44895-6
No stated revision policy

Introduction and Scope

The new *American Heritage Dictionary of the English Language (AHD),* third edition, 1992, is the progenitor of two smaller, more compact 1993 editions, THE AMERICAN HERITAGE COLLEGE DICTIONARY, third edition, and THE AMERICAN HERITAGE HIGH SCHOOL DICTIONARY. The parent volume contains 350,000 entries and more than 4,000 illustrations. There are 16,000 new words and meanings in this edition. They relate to social patterns, health, medicine, genetics, ecology, physics, astronomy, electronics, computers, and technology. Many of these words have been retained in the 200,000 entries of the smaller dictionaries.

The stated aim of this edition is to meet the "needs of the contemporary user." The emphasis is on the word *contemporary.* The goals of readability and clarity of terms and abbreviations have been admirably met. The most frequently sought meanings of words are presented, leaving specialized terms and definitions to specialized dictionaries and much larger unabridged ones.

The intermediate size (8½″ × 11″) and generous content make it more portable and useful in libraries where location and space are problems. The introduction states that, unlike previous editions, this dictionary was generated from a "complex, highly versatile structured database." The nature and origin of this database is never explained, but references are made in the "Guide to the Dictionary" to methods for ascertaining first and subsequent definitions by searching for occurrences of words in context. There is also mention of electronic and print citation files.

Although this edition moves away from a prescriptive philosophy and toward a descriptive one, the dictionary

The American Heritage Dictionary of the English Language

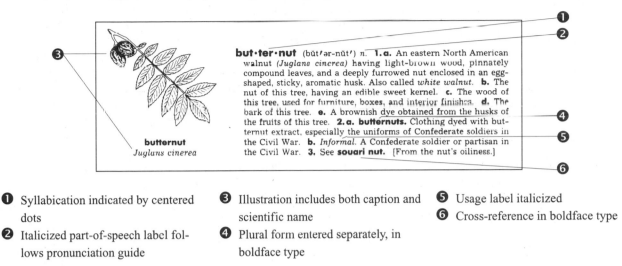

butternut
Juglans cinerea

❶ Syllabication indicated by centered dots

❷ Italicized part-of-speech label follows pronunciation guide

❸ Illustration includes both caption and scientific name

❹ Plural form entered separately, in boldface type

❺ Usage label italicized

❻ Cross-reference in boldface type

still leans toward guidance, while recognizing strong contemporary influences on language.

Authority

The first *American Heritage Dictionary of the English Language* was published in 1969 under the editorial leadership of the highly respected William Morris. He wanted to publish a dictionary that would be prescriptive rather than descriptive. The aim was to prescribe usage rather than merely to describe it, something he felt WEBSTER'S THIRD NEW INTERNATIONAL DICTIONARY and others were doing. He wanted to change the image of the dictionary. He was the first to write out symbols and abbreviations to free entries from obscure jargon. The dictionary of 155,000 entries that he produced met with popular success and good reviews. The 1982 edition, which was smaller, became the forerunner of THE AMERICAN HERITAGE COLLEGE DICTIONARY, third edition.

The dictionary discussed here, the third edition of the *AHD*, features an editorial and production staff headed by Anne H. Soukhanov, who has been associated with other successful American Heritage dictionaries such as WEBSTER'S II NEW RIVERSIDE UNIVERSITY DICTIONARY. Kaethe Ellis and Anne D. Steinhardt were editors on the *AHD*'s first and second editions. Although no credentials are listed for the 50 editorial staff members, the impressive list of 69 special contributors and consultants represents language and etymology experts from major universities and research centers. Included is Geoffrey Nunberg, Department of Linguistics, Stanford University, who is chair of the usage panel.

The usage panel consists of 173 members, 75 of whom are new to this edition. The panel is made up of writers, editors, scholars, and representatives in the fields of law, diplomacy, government, business, science and technology, medicine, and the arts. Eighteen members are Pulitzer Prize winners. The panel's role was to respond to usage questions, many of which are included in the usage notes that follow entries' definitions.

Comprehensiveness of Entries

The sheer number of entries—350,000—in this work compares favorably with other desktop dictionaries that average 170,000 to 200,000 words. Because of the larger format, more technical terms such as **microdensitometer** are included. Entries cover all aspects of contemporary language; there are also occasional entries on archaic language.

Vocabulary is presented in a clear, concise manner. However, some definitions are quite lengthy. For example, the word **turn** has 27 definitions of the transitive verb (including one slang definition), 21 definitions for the intransitive verb, and 23 definitions for the noun, followed by numerous phrasal verbs and idioms in alphabetical order.

The diversity of entries is evident in the random sample from **hockey** to **Hohokam.** This 50-entry sample contains not only five scientists, two diseases (**Hodgkin's** and **hog cholera**), four technical terms (**hod, hoe, hogan, hogback**), and one unit of measure (**hogshead**), but also seven artists and writers, three famous German families, two slang terms, and two sports terms.

Vulgarisms, slang, informal usages, and Britishisms are italicized within the entries. There are language and dialect labels, and subject labels such as "Chemistry." In addition to "Vulgar," "Slang," and "Informal," other status labels include "Non-Standard," "Usage Problem," "Offensive," and "Obscene." Special symbols, abbreviations, and technical vocabulary are minimal. Labels such as "Middle English" are spelled out.

Etymologies have been revised and expanded in this edition. Many trace words back to their Indo-European roots with cross-references to the "Indo-European Roots" appendix. For example, the root for **secret** is **krei-**. In the appendix, the reader learns that a number of other English words are derived from that same root, including *riddle* and *garble*.

Nine hundred entries contain synonym notes. They are easy to locate because the word *synonyms* appears in boldface capital letters. When appropriate, antonyms follow the synonyms. The length of the synonym notes varies widely from a few lines to more than 15.

"Usage Notes," unique to this dictionary, were resurveyed for the third edition to address gender, ethnicity, and sexual preferences. The notes may be short and succinct, or long and detailed. For example, **infinite** is followed by a 13-line usage note that ends with a cross-reference: "See Usage Note at **unique.**" The usage note at **aggravate,** which traces the use of the word back to the seventeenth century, reveals that 68 percent of the usage panel accepts "to irritate" as a definition and further discusses the way that Charles Dickens used the word in *Nicholas Nickleby.*

Geographical and biographical entries appear within the main lexicon. Due to the book's 1992 publication date, some recent political developments, such as Ukraine's independence, are not included. However, the reunification of Germany and the independence of Lithuania are included.

Quality and Currency of Entries

On the whole, definitions are clear and accurate, and cover the necessary range of meanings. There are some cases, however, in which definitions are too brief, as in the entry **whom,** which is merely defined as "The objective case of **who.**" Other definitions may be too circular, as in **black comedy,** which reads "Comedy that uses **black humor.**"

Words are divided by syllable, followed by the pronunciation in parentheses and the italicized part of speech. Definitions are numbered, with the most frequently sought meaning first. If the word is used as more than one part of speech, definitions follow each one. Inflected forms are in boldface. The etymology follows the definitions. A reference to the "Indo-European Roots" appendix may be included, as in the following example:

> **glow·er** (glou′ŭr) *intr.v.* **-ered, -er·ing, ers.** To look or stare angrily or sullenly. See Synonyms at **frown. -glower** *n.* An angry or sullen look or stare. [Middle English *gloren,* probably of Scandinavian origin. See **ghel-²** in Appendix.] -**glow′er·ing·ly** *adv.*

The various types of notes follow the entries.

Definitions are current, reflecting the editorial effort to bring contemporary usage to the lexical table. **Nerd,** for example, is labeled slang, but offers more than one definition and a lengthy word history that traces the

word to Dr. Seuss. Phrasal verbs are treated at the end of entries, such as in the entry **take,** which requires two full columns to define **take to the cleaners,** a slang term.

Information in the dictionary appears to be current through the fall of 1991. Entries for **fax, maquiladora, rap,** and **retrovirus** are included. The entry for **HDTV** spells out the term but does not define it. **Bungee** is defined, but there is no mention of jumping. There are no entries for *dis, intifada,* and *virtual reality.*

Syllabication and Pronunciation

This dictionary's style of syllabication and pronunciation is easily understood. Entry words, derived and inflected forms, are divided into syllables with boldface centered dots, such as **bu·reauc·racy.** When the entry consists of two or more words, such as **burden of proof,** syllabication occurs at the entry for each individual word.

The pronunciation of a word is enclosed in parentheses following the boldface entry. Primary stress and secondary stress are marked.

A "Pronunciation Key" appears in the introductory pages of the book. Examples of pronunciations, the *American Heritage Dictionary* pronunciation symbols, and the comparative International Phonetic Alphabet (IPA) symbols are shown in a table. There is a simplified pronunciation key at the bottom of every right-hand page of the dictionary. When more than one pronunciation is given, the first is considered to be the most common. An inflected form, or the parts of the word that are changed, receives a pronunciation key if it differs from that of the entry word.

Accessibility

Readers of this dictionary can easily locate the information they are seeking. The volume is thumb-indexed, and the first and last words on a page serve as guide words above each column. Each guide word appears in boldface above a heavy line.

Entries are in alphabetical order, letter by letter, including abbreviations and acronyms: **tuz·zy-muz·zy, TV, TVA, TV dinner, twa.** Abbreviations are not defined; only the full name is given. Therefore, **TVA** is followed only by Tennessee Valley Authority. Because this is a mid-sized volume, readers must consult encyclopedias and unabridged works for more detailed definitions. Some scientific terms, such as **TEPP,** a crystalline compound, are included and fully defined. Inclusion of abbreviations appears to be arbitrary. For example, **UNIX** is included, but *IBM* is not.

Alternate spellings of words are treated as variants. The word *or* signals that both forms occur with equal frequency in the electronic and print citations used by the editorial staff (for example, **ar·chae·ol·o·gy** or **ar·che·ol·o·gy**). The word *also* is used to denote less frequently used variant forms. Words that would not appear adjacent to each other due to their spellings occupy separate entries. For example, British variants have separate entries and are labeled "Chiefly British."

Cross-references are used in the notes sections, especially those that refer readers to the "Indo-European Roots" appendix. Some cross-references to variant spellings and Britishisms are included. Although there is no mention of **behaviour** at the entry for **behavior,** there is a note at the British spelling that it is a variant of the other word.

An excellent ten-page "Guide to the Dictionary" precedes the entries; it is included in a slightly abbreviated form in the 1993 college and high school editions. Each element of the dictionary is clearly and completely described in the guide, and examples are drawn from the text.

Special Features

Many special features of this work have already been discussed, including the usage panel, notes, and appendix. Another feature that makes this work outstanding is the collection of scholarly essays. In the first of four essays in the introductory material, Lee Pederson, Department of English, Emory University, discusses "A Natural History of English: Language, Culture, and the American Heritage." He traces the history of American English and pinpoints the importance of the Indo-European influences on English.

Calvert Watkins, Professor of Linguistics and the Classics, Harvard University, follows with an essay on "The Indo-European Origin of English," stressing the American Heritage theme. "Usage in the American Heritage Dictionary: The Place of Criticism," written by Geoffrey Nunberg, chair of the usage panel, is the only essay retained in both the college and high school editions. In it, Nunberg proudly defends the concept of a usage panel. Henry Kučera, Department of Linguistics, Brown University, analyzes the structure of language and how it relates to the advent of the computer in "The Mathematics of Language." Calvert Watkins supplies the volume with another essay, "Indo-European and the Indo-Europeans," at the end of the dictionary.

Several other special features also appear at the end of the volume, including a "Guide to the Appendix," a table of "Indo-European Sound Correspondence," and the "Indo-European Roots" appendix to which cross-references in the text refer. The latter covers 41 pages of roots and their derivatives followed by etymologies. Each section of an entry begins with a list of words derived from a form of the root. There are cross-references between etymologies. The last page and the inside back cover feature an elaborate fan-shaped diagram of the "Indo-European Family of Languages," which is also included in the college and high school editions.

This dictionary places a heavy emphasis on these scholarly features. Anyone who is interested in the development of modern English will enjoy these materials. However, readers who merely want to look up a word in a desktop dictionary may not appreciate the weight and extra cost that these features add.

Graphics and Format

The graphic elements and format of this dictionary contribute to its overall appeal. The binding is sturdy and the paper does not crease or tear easily. Show-through from one page to another is minimal, considering the number of illustrations on each page.

Black-and-white photographs and line drawings enhance this work's value as a reference source. The volume's 4,000 illustrations can be found in the outside margins of most pages. There are portraits of famous people, such as Elvis Presley, Langston Hughes, and Sandra Day O'Connor. Photographs depict pieces of art along with everyday objects, historical sites, activities, and living things. Line drawings include maps, floor plans of buildings, musical notations, and tables of information in addition to the standard illustrations that accompany definitions. Illustrations are located reasonably close to the relevant entries and are clearly labeled. Some captions provide additional information. Throughout the volume, the photographs and line drawings are fairly current and represent a multicultural cross-section. The quality, number, variety, and usefulness of the illustrations greatly add to the dictionary's value.

The format of this dictionary is clean and devoid of clutter. Entry words are in boldface and set slightly to the left of the definition paragraph. The guide words are printed in a larger boldface type at the top of each column. The text, which is printed in a two-column format, has sufficient white space in the margins and between the lines for readability.

Summary

The American Heritage Dictionary of the English Language fulfills its stated intentions. It is visually appealing and easy to use. It provides solid definitions for contemporary terms as well as valuable advice on word usage through the notes and the opinions of the usage panel. Essays and appendixes contribute to the prescriptive approach, and the special emphasis on Indo-European roots is a unique characteristic of this dictionary.

Readers who want a more descriptive approach or a more standard-sized package may find MERRIAM-WEBSTER'S COLLEGIATE, tenth edition, or RANDOM HOUSE WEBSTER'S more appealing. Those who need or want a large, unabridged dictionary may prefer WEBSTER'S THIRD NEW INTERNATIONAL. However, librarians and readers will find that the *AHD* occupies an important niche between cumbersome unabridged works and more limited college dictionaries.

The American Heritage High School Dictionary

Facts at a Glance

Full title: **The American Heritage High School Dictionary**

Publisher: Houghton Mifflin

Editor: Robert B. Costello

Edition reviewed: © 1993, third edition

Number of pages: 1,630

Number of entries: 200,000 (reviewer estimate)

Number of illustrations: 2,500 (reviewer estimate), all in black and white

Intended readership: high school students

Trim size: 7″ × 9½″

Binding: hardcover

Price: $21.95

Sold in bookstores; also sold to libraries and educational institutions

ISBN 0-395-67148-5

No stated revision policy

Introduction and Scope

The 1993 edition of *The American Heritage High School Dictionary* is designed, according to the preface, for high school students to keep in their "classroom, locker, desk, or backpack." Except for changes in the front matter and the deletion of vulgarisms, the text is identical to THE AMERICAN HERITAGE COLLEGE DICTIONARY. Both volumes are direct descendants of THE AMERICAN HERITAGE DICTIONARY OF THE ENGLISH LANGUAGE, third edition, published by Houghton Mifflin in 1992.

The editorial and production staff, contributors, consultants, and usage panel are the same in both the college and high school editions. Many of the editorial and production staff from both editions are associated with THE AMERICAN HERITAGE DICTIONARY OF THE ENGLISH LANGUAGE. The contributors and consultants are the same as those in THE AMERICAN HERITAGE DICTIONARY OF THE ENGLISH LANGUAGE, with one name added to the law section in the high school and college editions. The 173 members of the usage panel are the same in all three volumes.

Special Features

The introductory materials in *The American Heritage High School Dictionary* are significantly different from those in the parent volume and the college edition.

"Welcome to the Dictionary" is a brief and upbeat preface targeted at high school students. It introduces the organization of the dictionary as well as features such as the word histories, regional notes, usage notes, and synonym paragraphs.

The scholarly essays on language in THE AMERICAN HERITAGE DICTIONARY OF THE ENGLISH LANGUAGE and the college edition have been replaced in the *High School Dictionary* by a section entitled "Capitalization, Punctuation, and Style Guide." It purports to set forth "the basic points of style used in written and printed American English." Example phrases and sentences are used to illustrate each rule. Rules governing the use of punctuation, numbers, and italics are adequate; however, the guide to organizing a bibliography is minimal and does not include a footnote or citation form for multimedia and electronic sources. Students will need to refer to other style guides for this material.

The "Guide to the Dictionary" is identical to the one in the college edition, which is an abbreviated version of the one in THE AMERICAN HERITAGE DICTIONARY OF THE ENGLISH LANGUAGE. "Abbreviations and Labels Used in This Dictionary," "Pronunciation," "Table of Alphabets," and the "Development of the Alphabet" are included in both the college and high school editions.

As noted previously, vulgar entry words and definitions from the college edition have been replaced in this version with either new entries or extensions to existing entries. Included, for example, is an entry for **shittim-wood** and a lengthier **Regional Note** for **shivaree** in place of the college version's **shit** and **shit list.** Offensive words and meanings, labeled as such, remain.

Graphics and Format

This volume's appealing graphic design is identical to that of the college edition. The 2,500 black-and-white illustrations are a mix of portraits of well-known people and line drawings that will enrich classroom studies. Most pages have at least one illustration; the majority have two or more. The placement of the illustrations in the margins adds a decorative, pleasing quality to the text.

The tables, one of the advertised features of the volume, are not always clearly referenced in the text. For example, although a two-page "Periodic Table of the Elements" appears on the spread following the entry for **element,** no reference to the table is made within the entry.

The binding is sturdy and should hold up well, even in a locker or backpack. Like the college edition, the pages are thinner and all elements are more compact than those in the parent AMERICAN HERITAGE DICTIONARY OF THE ENGLISH LANGUAGE. The print is still large enough and the format clear enough, however, that readers will have no trouble using this dictionary.

Summary

The *American Heritage High School Dictionary* is so similar to the college edition that they are nearly interchangeable. Because of the punctuation and style guide, the high school volume might be the more helpful of the two for students and adults who do not have other style books available.

The content of the dictionary itself is appropriate for academic use at the secondary or college level. The number and quality of the entries place this work well ahead of most "high school" dictionaries such as the FEARON NEW SCHOOL DICTIONARY or the WEBSTER'S SCHOOL DICTIONARY; schoolteachers and librarians may prefer this work over college dictionaries (which it most nearly resembles) because of its features and the omission of vulgarities. The volume is competitively priced at $21.95 and is an excellent purchase for schools and students; public libraries should select the college version or THE AMERICAN HERITAGE DICTIONARY OF THE ENGLISH LANGUAGE.

Cassell Giant Paperback Dictionary

Facts at a Glance

Full title: **Cassell Giant Paperback Dictionary**
Publisher: **Cassell; distributed by Sterling**
Editor: **Betty Kirkpatrick**
Edition reviewed: © 1993

Number of pages: 1,600
Number of entries: 160,000 definitions
Number of illustrations: none
Intended readership: adult and general public
Trim size: 6″ × 9⅛″
Binding: paperback

Price: $16.95; discount available to schools and
    libraries
Sold directly to bookstores, libraries, schools, and re-
    tail stores; also sold by direct mail
ISBN 0-304-34288-2
No stated revision policy

Introduction and Scope

The 1993 edition of the *Cassell Giant Paperback Dictionary* contains 1,600 pages packed with 160,000 definitions. No illustrations accompany the text, which attempts to deal with as many words as possible in the least amount of space. The work provides not only lexical information but also appendixes of facts, figures, games, and tables. This dictionary was published in Great Britain and has a decidedly British flavor; North America is the secondary market for the book.

Authority

The Cassell name has been associated with dictionary publishing in Great Britain since 1891. According to this book's cover flap, new technologies have allowed the Cassell lexicographers "to create a flexible database for a range of English reference works." The *Cassell Giant Paperback Dictionary* contains the same information found in the *Cassell Concise English Dictionary*. The CASSELL STUDENT ENGLISH DICTIONARY, also a 1993 publication, is a smaller version of this "giant" paperback edition. Betty Kirkpatrick, the editor of both dictionaries, was assisted by a team of lexicographers and consultants.

Comprehensiveness of Entries

With 160,000 definitions, the *Cassell Giant Paperback Dictionary* is undoubtedly comprehensive. It treats a broad range of words, including a fair sampling of scientific and technical terms.

The choice of vocabulary in this book is British. For example, entries at **O** describe the **O-grade** and **O-level** examinations, which are not included in North American dictionaries. In addition, British spellings (**colour, manoeuvre, oesophagus**) and definitions (**cracker, flat, lift**) are used throughout the book.

The dictionary includes etymologies, which are brief compared with the detailed ones found in works such as MERRIAM-WEBSTER'S COLLEGIATE DICTIONARY. Synonyms and antonyms are not identified or labeled, but numerous usage labels are provided. Vulgarisms are included and are labeled "(*taboo*)," and offensive language is labeled as such. Quotations are used only in the "Register of New Words," which appears in an appendix. In most cases, these quotes are taken from publications such as *The Times, Scotsman, Independent,* and *Newsweek.*

This dictionary does not include biographical entries. Geographical entries appear in the gazetteer, which is at the back of the book. The gazetteer is quite up-to-date, listing **Germany** as a unified country and the former Soviet states of **Lithuania** and **Ukraine** as independent republics. Violeta Chamorro and Boris Yeltsin are correctly included as presidents of **Nicaragua** and **Russia,** respectively.

Quality and Currency of Entries

Entry words appear in boldface type and are followed by the pronunciation, part of speech, and definition. Multiple definitions are not numbered but are merely separated by a semicolon. Usage labels appear in parentheses, and etymologies are shown in brackets at the end of the entry. Homographs receive separate entries, marked with superscripts.

According to the user's guide, "Many words and expressions which are derived from the same root have been grouped or 'nested' together. . . ." Where applicable, these receive part of speech and definition. The entry for **profess,** for example, contains the parts of speech and definitions for **profession, professional,** and other variations that do not have separate entries. Readers who are unaccustomed to this format may find it confusing.

The definitions seem to be ordered in terms of frequency of use, although no explanation of this is provided in the user's guide. The definitions are fairly accurate and complete, but the preponderance of British spellings and definitions will be disconcerting to American readers. The following is a typical entry:

> **oedema,** (*esp. N Am.*) **edema** (idē′mə), *n.* (*Path.*) swelling due to accumulation of serous fluid in the cellular tissue; dropsy; in plants, swelling due to water accumulation in the tissues. **oedematose** (-tōs), **-tous, edematose, -tous,** *a.* **oedematously,** *adv.* [Gr. *oidēma -matos,* from *oideein,* to swell]

The entry for **edema** provides the pronunciation and the cross-reference OEDEMA.

Entries in the main lexicon are fairly current, including definitions for **fax, intifada, rap** (music), and **retrovirus.** In addition, very contemporary vocabulary is listed in the "Register of New Words" appendix, which contains entries for **bungee jumping, diss, HDTV,** and **virtual reality.** Unfortunately, not all readers will know that a word they are looking for is considered a "new word" or even that this list exists.

Syllabication and Pronunciation

Entry words are not divided into syllables. Partial syllabication—where the main stress is indicated— appears in the pronunciation. The main stress is noted with an accent mark *after* the syllable rather than before it, and secondary stress is not shown. A full pronunciation key is shown in the front matter, and a shortened key appears across the bottom of each two-page spread. According to the pronunciation guide, to make comprehension easier, only a few special symbols and accent marks were used. In the case of derived words, pronunciation is provided only for the part of the word that differs from the main entry word. For example, the pronunciation for **mobocracy,** which is nested with the entry for **mob,** is shown as "(-ok′-)." This device requires the reader to refer back to the pronunciation for the main entry word and also assumes prior knowledge of the pronunciation of prefixes and suffixes.

Accessibility

Entries are sequenced in letter-by-letter order. The space-saving device of nesting related words in an entry creates many deviations in alphabetical order and often makes it difficult to locate a word. For example,

although **virtual** precedes **virtue** in alphabetical order, **virtual** is nested within the entry for **virtue** and therefore appears after **virtue** in this dictionary.

A simple one-page user's guide provides only the most basic information about using the dictionary. In addition to this guide, the front matter includes a list of abbreviations, a pronunciation guide, and a list of symbols. Guide words in boldface type appear at the top left and right side of each page, with the page number between them. Thumb indexing is not provided. Entries for alternate spellings show the pronunciation and the cross-referenced word in small capital letters.

Special Features

The special features in this dictionary appear in the appendixes. The "Register of New Words" includes current technical terms, acronyms, and colloquial expressions. A "Compendium of Word Games," devised by a team of MENSA experts, adds a light note to the book, though it seems somewhat out of place. The gazetteer contains information on the head of state, population, area, capital, language, and currency of every country. Much of the information in the "Politics" appendix pertains to the British government, including lists of British royalty and prime ministers of countries in the United Kingdom, a breakdown of the Houses of Parliament, and a list of office holders in the current government. Tables of weights and measures, temperatures, and chemical elements, as well as lists of various signs and symbols, complete the volume.

Graphics and Format

The dictionary contains no illustrations. The work is compact, with narrow margins and two columns of text per page. The boldface entry words overhang the text and stand out clearly from the definitions. Nested words are also in boldface.

The paper stock is of a reasonable quality. Because the work is thick, the paper cover tends to pull away from the contents. However, the book's small trim size makes the work easily portable.

Summary

The entire work emphasizes volume of words and compact presentation. Unfortunately, the space-saving techniques used—especially the device of nesting related words within entries—create confusion and make the book difficult to use. In addition, the entirely British nature of the work, including British vocabulary, spellings, and definitions, makes the *Cassell Giant Paperback Dictionary* of little value for most American users. American users who need a British dictionary for reference should consider THE CONCISE OXFORD DICTIONARY.

Cassell Student English Dictionary

Facts at a Glance

Full title: **Cassell Student English Dictionary**
Publisher: Cassell; distributed by Sterling
Editor: Betty Kirkpatrick
Edition reviewed: © 1993

Number of pages: 1,024
Number of entries: 110,000 definitions
Number of illustrations: none
Intended readership: high school to college
Trim size: 5¼" × 8½"
Binding: hardcover

Price: $14.95; discount available to schools and
  libraries
Sold directly to bookstores, libraries, schools, and re-
  tail stores; also sold by direct mail
ISBN 0-304-34290-4
No stated revision policy

Introduction and Scope

The *Cassell Student English Dictionary* is a condensed
version of the CASSELL GIANT PAPERBACK DICTIONARY. Following is a description of the major similarities and differences between the two works. For a full description
and evaluation of the quality of the definitions and other
lexicographical issues, see the review of the CASSELL GI-
ANT PAPERBACK DICTIONARY elsewhere in this Buying
Guide.

The *Cassell Student English Dictionary* has 110,000
definitions, compared with 160,000 in the parent volume. The definitions that remain are identical; however,
within some entries, a few definitions and derived words
have been dropped to save space. In addition, etymologies have been omitted, and obsolete and archaic words
are not identified. Obscure terminology, less adapted to
students, has been excluded. Scientific terms are retained, but the number of definitions is reduced and
fewer derivatives are included. The front matter in the
parent volume and the student edition is virtually identical.

Special Features

As with the CASSELL GIANT PAPERBACK DICTIONARY, this
student edition contains supplementary information
found within several appendixes. Most of the information in the appendixes from the parent volume has been
retained in this work, including the "Register of New
Words," the gazetteer, information about the British government, and various scientific charts and tables. In the
student edition, however, much of this supplementary information has been rearranged into categories geared
more toward students, such as "The Arts," "History," and
"Geography." The only major part of the appendixes in
the parent work but not in this volume is the "Compendium of Word Games." New information added to the
appendixes in the student edition includes lists of Nobel
Prize winners from 1985 to 1992, Shakespeare's plays,
winners of the Booker Prize (a major British literary
award) from 1969 to 1992, books of the Bible, and world
facts and figures.

Graphics and Format

This compact dictionary contains no illustrations. The
page format is identical to that of the parent volume, but
the type size has been reduced considerably. The letters
in the boldface entry words bleed together, making the

Cassell Student English Dictionary

❶ Italicized part-of-speech label precedes each definition or definitions
  to which it applies

❷ Field label indicates scientific classification

❸ Compound entries follow main entry word

❹ Usage label

❺ Cross-reference, in small capitals,
  has superscript that indicates which
  meaning to look up

❻ Direct derivatives placed after the
  last meaning of the last compound
  entry

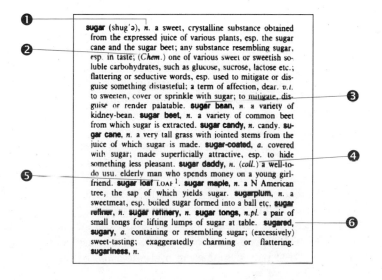

words nearly illegible. The typeface used in the definitions is so small that it is extremely difficult to read. The pages have minimal bleed-through, but they pull away from the hardcover binding quite easily.

Summary

The *Cassell Student English Dictionary* suffers from all of the same problems as the Cassell Giant Paperback Dictionary. In addition, it is much less readable because of the extremely small type size. As with the parent volume, the *Cassell Student English Dictionary* is not recommended for purchase.

The Compact Oxford English Dictionary

Facts at a Glance

Full title: **The Compact Oxford English Dictionary**
Publisher: Oxford University Press
Editors: John Simpson; Edmund Weiner
Edition reviewed: © 1991, 1992 printing

Number of pages: 2,416
Number of entries: 290,500
Number of illustrations: none
Intended readership: adult
Trim size: 10¼″ × 14¼″
Binding: hardcover

Price: $325
Sold in bookstores; also sold by direct mail
ISBN 0-19-861258-3
No stated revision policy; *OED Additions Series* currently being published

Introduction and Scope

The Compact Oxford English Dictionary is a single-volume photoreduction of the 20-volume Oxford English Dictionary, Second Edition (OED). The intent of the OED is to provide illustration, through the use of quoted passages from published literature, of how each word in the English language has been used throughout its history. The dictionary includes some 2.4 million illustrative quotations, including each word's first appearance in print. Many obsolete words and definitions are included also. The OED is intended to be a tool for historical research; as such, it does not include many features of a standard desk dictionary such as syllabication, usage notes, or synonym references. It also has a distinctly British bias, apparent in the pronunciations and certain definitions.

The text of the *Compact OED* is identical to that of the OED, but it has been photographically reduced so that nine OED pages appear on a single page of the

Compact OED. This reduction makes the immense and expensive dictionary affordable for a home user, but necessitates the use of a magnifying lens (included with the dictionary) to make the text readable. The previous edition of the *Compact OED* consisted of two volumes plus a supplement. This new edition, because it is based on the 1989 second edition of the OED, is now contained in a single volume. The work includes all 290,500 main entries in 2,416 pages, rather than the 22,000 pages of the parent OED.

Special Features

The dictionary includes a cardboard slipcase, a magnifying lens, and a 71-page booklet entitled "A User's Guide to the Oxford English Dictionary." The high-quality solid-glass circular lens measures approximately 1″ × 3″ and lies flat on the page. It magnifies the text to a size that, while comfortable to read, is not quite as large as the text of the 20-volume edition. The user's guide, by Donna Berg, is clear and thorough. Written in an engaging style, it includes entertaining and informative examples of each of the dictionary's features.

Graphics and Format

The Compact Oxford English Dictionary is a very large and attractive volume. Its 10¼″ × 14¼″ trim size enables it to lie flat when open (essential for the use of the magnifying lens) and to provide ample white space surrounding each of the nine OED pages located on one *Compact OED* page. Each *Compact OED* page has guide words at the top that encompass the span of the nine OED pages on that page: for example, the **Gainable** to **Galimatias** page encompasses the OED pages **gainable** to **gainless, gainly** to **gainstand, gainstrive** to **gaiterless,** etc. . . . The guide words on the OED pages (which were printed in the 20-volume version in a larger typeface than the text) are readable in photoreduced form, so the user will have little difficulty locating entries in this compact version.

Summary

The *Compact OED* is the most affordable version of the complete text of the Oxford English Dictionary. It contains all of the features of the original work in photoreduced form, including the 2.4 million illustrative quotations showing each word's use throughout the history of the language. The convenience of having the 20 volumes of the OED in a single volume is mitigated by the fact that one must use a magnifying lens to read the tiny print.

At $325, the *Compact OED* is a costly work. It is not intended to be used as a desktop dictionary for quick reference; only serious language lovers or scholars will find it a worthwhile purchase for home use. Most libraries will prefer the full 20-volume set as an essential reference tool, but those that receive only limited requests for the dictionary's use might consider buying this volume at a considerable savings in cost. Institutions that have the proper equipment should consider the very accessible CD-ROM version of the dictionary, which lists for $895.

The Concise Oxford Dictionary of Current English

Facts at a Glance

Full title: **The Concise Oxford Dictionary of Current English**
Publisher: Oxford University Press
Editor: R. E. Allen
Edition reviewed: © 1990, eighth edition; 1991 printing

Number of pages: 1,504
Number of entries: 120,000
Number of illustrations: none
Intended readership: adults
Trim size: 7" × 9¾"
Binding: hardcover

Price: $27.50 (plain); $29.95 (thumb indexed)
ISBN 0-19-861200-1 (plain); ISBN 0-19-861243-5 (thumb indexed)
No stated revision policy

Introduction and Scope

The well-known *Concise Oxford Dictionary* is the principal entry of the Oxford University Press (OUP) into the desk-reference market. It is primarily a dictionary of English as it is used in Great Britain, although American spellings, definitions, idioms, and usages are also present. The single-volume *Concise Oxford Dictionary* has 120,000 entries in 1,504 pages.

Authority

The *Concise Oxford Dictionary* enjoys a history almost as long as that of the OXFORD ENGLISH DICTIONARY (OED). It was first published as a companion to that work in 1911 by H. W. and F. G. Fowler, brothers noted for their grammar manual *The King's English.* Editor R. E. Allen acknowledges the help of many well-respected OUP employees in the preparation of the current edition, including Dr. R. W. Burchfield, the former chief editor of the Oxford English Dictionaries.

Comprehensiveness of Entries

Several rival desk dictionaries such as MERRIAM-WEBSTER'S COLLEGIATE DICTIONARY (with 160,000 entries), THE AMERICAN HERITAGE COLLEGE DICTIONARY (200,000 en-

tries), and the RANDOM HOUSE WEBSTER'S COLLEGE DICTIONARY (180,000 entries) are more comprehensive than the *Concise Oxford* (120,000 entries). A randomly selected sample of the 50 entries from **languid** to **largely** reveals adequate coverage of scientific and technical terms. The sample includes **langur,** a species of long-tailed monkey; **lantana,** an evergreen shrub; **lanthanum,** the chemical element; **laparoscope,** the surgical tool; the Latin expressions **lapsus calami** and **lapsus linguae,** and **laptop,** which is defined as: "(of a microcomputer) portable and suitable for use while travelling."

Potential purchasers should be aware that this dictionary best reflects contemporary *British* English. Entries such as **Godwottery** (*"joc.* affected, archaic, or excessively elaborate speech or writing, esp. regarding gardens") and **Fanny Adams** (*"Brit. sl.* . . . also **sweet Fanny Adams** . . . nothing at all."), while interesting, betray the volume's strong British bias. The entry **theatre** includes "(US **theater**)"; **mustache** and **esthetic** are listed as US variants of MOUSTACHE and AESTHETIC. Vulgarisms are present, both as main entry words and as definitions of words with other meanings. They are labeled *offens.*

Etymologies appear at the end of most entries; they are clear and avoid many abbreviations. The work does not include synonym/antonym guides. Usage labels and usage notes (indicated by the symbol ¶) are both present. Biographical and geographical entries are not included, unless they or their derivatives have entered the general vocabulary: **Morris chair, Pakistani,** and **Paisley** (from the Scottish town near Glasgow) all appear.

Quality and Currency of Entries

The clear definitions, ordered by frequency of use, generally avoid abbreviations and what the editor refers to in his preface as "dictionary 'telegraphese.'" Illustrative phrases, written by the editors, are set in italics and set off by parentheses. Phrases and idioms are preceded by □, derivatives by □□. A typical entry follows:

> **hedgehog. . .** *n.* **1** any small nocturnal insect-eating mammal of the genus *Erinaceus,* esp. *E. europaeus,* having a piglike snout and a coat of spines, and rolling itself up into a ball for defence. **2** a porcupine or other animal similarly covered with spines. □□**hedgehoggy** *adj.* [ME f. HEDGE (from its habitat) + HOG (from its snout)]

Entries are quite current. **Factoid, fax, PIN, rap,** (as music) and **retrovirus** appear, though *bungee jumping, dis, HDTV, intifada, maquiladora,* and *virtual reality* do not.

Syllabication and Pronunciation

As in the OED, entry words are not syllabicated. Primary and secondary stress marks are indicated in the pronunciations, but syllabication therein is often unclear.

According to the dictionary's user's guide, pronunciations use the International Phonetic Alphabet (IPA) and are based on "the pronunciation associated especially with southern England." Pronunciation keys appear in the guide and on the inside of the book's back cover.

Accessibility

Entries are arranged alphabetically in strict letter-by-letter order, including abbreviations. The user's guide is straightforward and thorough: topics such as "Headwords" and "Etymologies" are covered under 15 numbered headings. Thumb indexing costs extra—a slightly more expensive edition has that feature. Guide words appear at the upper corners of every page.

Special Features

The dictionary's front matter includes an ambitious nine-page essay entitled "English over Fifteen Centuries" and a shorter description of the history of the *Concise Oxford Dictionary* itself. Appendixes include "Countries of the World" (Germany appears as a united country but so does the U.S.S.R), "Major Divisions of Geological Time," "The Chemical Elements," "Weights and Measures" (both British and American), "Counties of the United Kingdom," "States of the USA," "Books of the Bible," "Punctuation Marks," and "The Greek and Russian Alphabets."

Graphics and Format

No illustrations are included. The typeface is easy to read, and the text is set in two columns. Although the sturdily bound book lies flat when opened, the gutter margin is somewhat inadequate, making the center columns of each spread difficult to read.

Summary

The *Concise Oxford Dictionary*'s strengths include its up-to-date lexicon and clear, well-written definitions. The work's British bias, however, will disappoint users needing thorough coverage of contemporary American English. Home users seeking a desk-reference tool might prefer college dictionaries by Merriam-Webster, Random House, or Houghton Mifflin. Libraries should consider purchasing this volume only as a quality guide to "the King's English."

Fearon New School Dictionary

Facts at a Glance

Full title: **Fearon New School Dictionary**
Publisher: Janus
Editors: Alvin Granowsky; Ken Weber
Edition reviewed: © 1987

Number of pages: 1,267
Number of entries: approximately 70,000
Intended readership: junior high to high school
Trim size: 4¼" × 7"
Binding: cloth

Price: $17.90
Sold in bookstores and other outlets; also sold to libraries and schools
ISBN 0-8224-3049-5.
No stated revision policy

Introduction and Scope

The *Fearon New School Dictionary* was created for use "in school, at the office, and at home. . . . Sophisticated enough for all but the most scholarly use, yet friendly enough to be a constant companion." According to the publisher, the dictionary contains 70,000 entries; however, an informal count by our reviewers produced less than half that figure. This suggests that the publisher's count includes variant forms.

Authority

The editorial staff is identified by name, but their credentials are not included. A quick search through standard biographical reference sources yielded no information. No consultants are identified, and there is no mention of a citation file or of the books, periodicals, or media used in drawing up the volume's word list. This edition appears to be drawn from 1976 and 1978 volumes published by Heinemann Educational Australia and a 1984 edition from Globe Modern Curriculum Press. However, the authorities and sources for these preceding dictionaries and their relationship to the current *Fearon New School Dictionary* is not made clear in its brief preface. Therefore, it is impossible to determine whether or not this dictionary was compiled according to reliable and acceptable standards.

Comprehensiveness of Entries

This relatively short dictionary adequately covers current American English as it is used in popular media and speech. Although some important new words such as *AIDS, sonogram,* and *fax* are omitted, many other words, such as **terrorist, floppy disc,** and **byte** are included.

This dictionary also includes a number of slang and informal words, related phrases, and idiomatic expressions. Words and phrases such as **busman's holiday, burnout, hang-up, under the hammer, hand in glove, deck out, cut in,** and **take to heart** are included. Furthermore, this dictionary is not as sanitized as many other school dictionaries. Words such as **penis, vagina, pornography,** and **syphilis** are included.

Fearon New School Dictionary

❶ Boldface entry word, on a line by itself, followed by italicized part-of-speech label, which is spelled out

❷ Subject label in italics

❸ Cross-reference in small capitals

❹ Idioms, in boldface type, follow the main entry

❺ Run-on entry, in boldface type, appears at the end under the italicized heading "Word Family"

❻ Usage label in parentheses

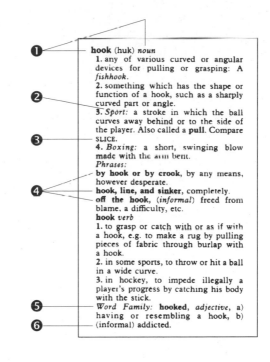

Etymologies are not consistently provided and are very simple and informal, providing almost no scholarly apparatus. Words with complicated histories are explained in more detail.

The word "synonym" is used neither in the prefatory remarks nor the user key. Nevertheless, alternative words are used to describe entries and convey meaning. Inconsistencies in etymological presentation and the lack of a clear explanation of synonyms tend to make this dictionary insufficient for youngsters in their preparation of many school assignments.

Quality and Currency of Entries

In general, definitions are short and uneven. Several different parts of speech may be included in an entry, but they are not always defined. No information on plural spellings is provided, although some irregular forms are given under the main entry, such as **tomatoes,** plural of **tomato,** and **sheep,** plural of **sheep.** This means that readers must remember rules such as changing *y* to *i* before adding *es* (babies). Readers also have to remember exceptions, such as *hellos.* Dictionaries should provide this type of information; readers—especially students—should not be presumed to know it. However slang meanings, idiomatic expressions, and related phrases are explained clearly and with usage examples.

Syllabication and Pronunciation

Entry words are presented without syllable breaks, and the word divisions used in the pronunciations provided often include more than one syllable.

Pronunciations are given "where necessary," surprisingly often, but not often enough. Neither a chart of pronunciation symbols nor a pronunciation key is provided, and International Phonetic Alphabet (IPA) symbols are not used. One unquestionably helpful element for the reader is the printing of the accented syllables in capital letters, which highlights the stress and makes the sound easier to "hear." Since most readers depend on a dictionary for authoritative information on pronunciation, this approach to pronunciation represents a serious drawback to its usefulness in schools.

Accessibility

Alternative spellings of words are listed in the main alphabet as separate entries. These entries refer readers to the more generally accepted spelling (where full explication is given).

All entries are arranged letter by letter within a single alphabet. Guide words are included on each page, but there is no thumb indexing. The dictionary does have a convenient table of contents for the appendixes and a user key that is printed on the end-papers in the front and back of the book where it is easy to find. All labels and parts of speech that appear in the entries are spelled out.

Special Features

All the special features of the *Fearon New School Dictionary* are contained in the appendixes. These include lists of the planets, continents, islands, countries, oceans, lakes, rivers, Canadian provinces, U.S. states, prime ministers of Canada, presidents of the United States, fathers of the Confederation (Canada), and sign-ers of the Declaration of Independence. There is also a guide to the metric system. Each list contains other information related to the main topic, such as capitals of states and terms of office. This information is available in other reference sources, but at home or in the office other reference sources are not always available. There are no maps, charts, tables, biographical entries, or essays. Prefixes are listed in the main alphabet. There are no prefix tables.

Graphics and Format

Fearon New School Dictionary is a pocket-sized hardback dictionary with sewn signatures. The binding is sturdy and durable and should hold up under heavy use. The paper is strong and there is little show-through from one side of the page to the other. The lack of illustrations is a drawback, especially for students, since pictures can be extremely useful in elucidating the meaning of many words.

Summary

The *Fearon New School Dictionary* has a number of positive attributes: it is easy to use, its general range of words is relatively broad and broad-minded, it includes informative appendixes, and it provides substantial coverage of contemporary slang and idiomatic expression. However, its deficiencies seriously affect its usefulness in a school, office, or home setting. It does not include extensive information on the origin and development of the idiomatic words, which is what students often need. By excluding abbreviations, symbols, and diacritical marks, the editors have also excluded a wealth of standard dictionary information. No systems for syllabication, pronunciation, plural forms, etymologies, and synonyms have been provided. This dictionary is not recommended as a primary acquisition for library or classroom use.

The Little Oxford Dictionary of Current English

Facts at a Glance

Full title: **The Little Oxford Dictionary of Current English: Sixth Edition**
Publisher: Oxford University Press
Editor: Julia Swannell
Edition reviewed: © 1986

Number of pages: 720
Number of entries: 25,000
Number of words: 34,000
Intended readership: adult
Trim size: 4″ × 6″
Binding: laminated paper over boards

Price: $11.95
Sold to libraries and other educational institutions; also sold in bookstores and by direct mail
ISBN 0-19-861188-9
Seventh edition to be published in late 1994

Introduction and Scope

The Little Oxford Dictionary of Current English is part of the Oxford dictionary series published in England by Oxford University Press (OUP) and sold in the United States. *The Little Oxford Dictionary* closely resembles THE POCKET OXFORD DICTIONARY. Many of its definitions are identical, or nearly so, to those in the POCKET OXFORD; others have obviously been condensed from those in the larger work. Both dictionaries also use the same typographical conventions. However, *The Little Oxford Dictionary* has fewer entries and also lacks the basic etymologies found in the POCKET OXFORD edition.

This is a wholly *English* dictionary; its spellings, pronunciations, and definitions clearly reflect its origins. The work has not been revised for the American market. However, the current (sixth) edition, published in 1986, places special emphasis on quick and easy reference. Although it contains some American words and definitions (**elevator** and the **trunk** of a car, for example), its publishing date prevents it from having many current words. A seventh edition of this work is scheduled for publication in late 1994.

Authority

Published by the highly reputable Clarendon Press of Oxford University, the dictionary's first edition appeared in 1930 under the editorship of George Ostler. The second through fourth editions were edited by Jessie Coulson, a member of the editorial staff of the OXFORD ENGLISH DICTIONARY. Julia Swannell edited the fifth and also the current sixth edition, with the assistance of members of OUP's department.

Comprehensiveness of Entries

The book jacket lists among the work's important features its broad range of contemporary English and the special attention paid to the vocabulary of new technology. The computer-related definition of **bit** is included; some terms dealing with the new video technologies are not. Some contemporary words and phrases, such as **ageism, privatize, surrogate mother, tofu,** and **user-friendly**, appear.

Foreign words that are not fully assimilated into English appear as main entries in bold italics, and their language is noted in abbreviated form in square brackets; for example, [F] for French.

The Little Oxford Dictionary of Current English

❶ Main entry word in boldface type
❷ Italicized part-of-speech label appears before the definition or definitions to which it applies
❸ Usage label, in italics, indicates this definition is restricted
❹ Parentheses enclose explanatory words or phrases
❺ Compound entries follow main entry word, in strict alphabetical order

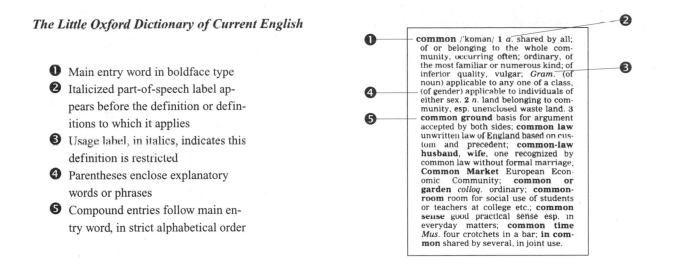

Parts of speech are indicated immediately following the entry word. There are some usage labels, such as *colloq.* for colloquialisms and *sl.* for slang words. Field labels, such as *law,* are provided to identify other specialized word uses. Irregular inflected forms are provided.

There are no illustrative phrases or sentences to enhance definitions such as can be found in many other pocket dictionaries. For Americans seeking to understand unfamiliar British usages, this omission is drawback. Etymologies, synonyms, and antonyms are excluded, but these omissions are not unusual in a work of this scope.

Quality and Currency of Entries

The definitions are concise and clearly written. Senses of words are arranged by frequency of use in Great Britain and are numbered consecutively. Specialized uses are introduced by an abbreviated, italicized label. For example, the third entry for the noun **bill** indicates that the word historically (*hist.*) meant

weapon with hook-shaped blade.

The verb form as well as phrases and compound words are listed under the first and most common sense; these include **bill of exchange** and **billposter.** Adjectives are most often defined by the use of synonymous words rather than a sentence or phrase of definition. None of the Buying Guide's test entries for currency—including *bungee jumping, dis, fax, HDTV, intifada, maquiladora, rap, retrovirus,* and *virtual reality*—appear in this dictionary. Users who are looking for coverage of English as it is currently spoken should consider a more current work, such as the same publisher's CONCISE OXFORD DICTIONARY.

Syllabication and Pronunciation

The work uses the International Phonetic Alphabet (IPA) to indicate pronunciations, and it adds marks for nasalization and an *x* for the Scottish *ch,* as in **loch.** The pronunciation key appears at the front of the volume.

Set off by slash marks, pronunciation is noted immediately following the entry word for most (but not all) words. Accent marks indicate stressed syllables within the pronunciations, but syllabication is not noted. This omission is a drawback for student readers of the dictionary. The pronunciations provided are those of southern England, not standard American English. Only the preferred form of pronunciation is given.

Accessibility

Main entry words appear in boldface type and overhang the text; capital letters are used as appropriate, as for abbreviations and proper nouns. Sub-senses are easily located with their boldface numbers, and run-in entries and compounds also appear in boldface.

The dictionary has paired bold guide words at the top of each double-column page, with a centered page number. This is helpful because some of the work's cross-references cite page numbers. A table of contents lists the dictionary's special features, so the reader will not overlook them.

Special Features

The dictionary's introduction provides a helpful explanation to the reader on how to use the contents effectively. Also provided at the front of the book are a full pronunciation key, a list of abbreviations, and a note on proprietary terms and trademarks. There are three appendixes: "Some points of English usage," "Countries of the world and related adjectives," "The metric system of weights and measures." These features take up only ten pages and are especially useful.

Graphics and Format

There are no illustrations provided in this dictionary. The overall layout of each page is good for a book of this size. The margins are narrow, but the typeface is strong and clear. The board cover, stitching, and head-band make this a sturdy volume that would withstand travel and frequent consultation.

Summary

The Little Oxford Dictionary is a handy pocket-size work that will serve well as a quick reference source for concise British definitions of words in the basic English lexicon. Those who require a small British dictionary will find this a good buy. However, this title is not sufficiently comprehensive or current to be considered as a first choice; this cannot be the *only* British dictionary in a good collection. For such collections, a larger, more comprehensive volume such as THE CONCISE OXFORD DICTIONARY or the OXFORD ENCYCLOPEDIC ENGLISH DICTIONARY will also be needed.

Merriam-Webster's Collegiate Dictionary, Tenth Edition

Facts at a Glance

Full title: **Merriam-Webster's Collegiate Dictionary, Tenth Edition**
Publisher: Merriam-Webster
Editor: Frederick C. Mish
Edition reviewed: © 1993

Number of pages: 1,559
Number of entries: 160,000
Number of illustrations: 700, all in black and white
Intended readership: college to adult
Trim size: 7″ × 9½″
Binding: hardcover

Price: $20.95 (unindexed); $21.95 (thumb indexed)
Sold to libraries and schools; also sold in bookstores
ISBN 0-87779-708-0 (unindexed);
    ISBN 0-87779-709-9 (thumb indexed)
No stated revision policy

Introduction and Scope

The 1993 edition of this successful desk dictionary bears a new title, which contains the *Merriam* name to distinguish the work from other "Webster's" dictionaries. Like its predecessor, the ninth edition, it is intended "to serve the general public as its chief source of information about the words of our language." Although the title indicates student use, office and home use is intended as well. Ten thousand new words or meanings and 100 new illustrations have been added since the ninth edition. Brief verbal illustrations have been added to the synonym paragraphs, and the number of usage

notes has been expanded. Dates of words' first use have been reviewed and revised.

Authority

This volume marks the 150th anniversary of the dictionary publishing program of the well-known and highly respected Merriam-Webster, Inc. The first *Webster's Collegiate Dictionary* appeared in 1898. Designed to be compact and convenient, it was based on the *Merriam-Webster Unabridged* and was the first of a series of desk dictionaries to be published over the past 100 years.

For the tenth edition, the staff, which includes trained lexicographers and linguistic experts, had access to a collection of more than 4.5 million citations collected over a 110-year period. An electronic database of 20 million words of text, drawn from a wide variety of publications, was also available to the staff.

Comprehensiveness of Entries

According to promotional material, *Merriam-Webster's Collegiate Dictionary* contains 160,000 entries, 211,000 definitions, 35,000 verbal illustrations, 35,000 etymologies, 4,400 usage paragraphs and notes, and 700 black-and-white line drawings. This is comparable to the 200,000 entries of THE AMERICAN HERITAGE COLLEGE DICTIONARY and the 180,000 entries in the RANDOM HOUSE WEBSTER'S COLLEGE DICTIONARY.

Of the randomly selected 50 entries from **sacking** to **sadhu,** none could be called "technical," although the work as a whole is quite thorough and up-to-date in its coverage of this type of vocabulary. Several less familiar words from unique fields of knowledge such as religion (**sacrarium, sacristan**), horse riding (**saddlery, saddletree**) and Hebrew (**Sadducean, sadhe**), are included. Three science terms (**sacral, sacroiliac,** and **sacrum**), two sports terms (**sacrifice fly, sacrifice hit**), and an entry with one archaic definition (**sacred**) appear.

Biographical and geographical names are not included in the main lexicon; they are located in separate sections in the end matter. The information in those sections is current, with entries for **Violeta Chamorro,** a unified **Germany, Lithuania** and **Ukraine** as independent republics, and **Boris Yeltsin** as head of Russia. There was no entry for *Michael Jackson.*

Vulgarisms are included and labeled. For example, **bullshit** is entered as a noun and a verb, the dates of first usage are given, and each definition is labeled: "—usu. considered vulgar." Britishisms receive separate entries and are labeled *chiefly Brit* with a cross-reference to the American entry. Some italicized labels, such as *trademark* (**Kleenex**) and *service mark* (**Grammy**), are unique to this dictionary. Taxonomic names of plants and animals are italicized and enclosed in parentheses.

Etymologies are succinct but carefully constructed to give a lot of information in a small amount of space. Set

Merriam-Webster's
Collegiate Dictionary, Tenth Edition

❶ Syllabication shown by a centered dot

❷ Part-of-speech label abbreviated and in italics

❸ Etymology in boldface square brackets

❹ Date of the earliest recorded use in English, in parentheses, precedes boldface number that introduces first sense

❺ Illustration adds to information for the first definition of the first homograph

❻ Usage note, italicized except for boldface entry word, shows variation—both in spelling and meaning

❼ Homographs appear as separate, numbered entries

❽ Cross-reference in small capitals

❾ Usage label in italics

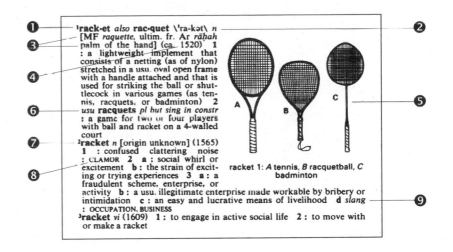

¹**rack·et** *also* **rac·quet** \'ra-kət\ *n* [MF *raquette*, ultim. fr. Ar *rāḥah* palm of the hand] (ca. 1520) **1** : a lightweight implement that consists of a netting (as of nylon) stretched in a usu. oval open frame with a handle attached and that is used for striking the ball or shuttlecock in various games (as tennis, racquets, or badminton) **2** *usu* **racquets** *pl but sing in constr* : a game for two or four players with ball and racket on a 4-walled court

²**racket** *n* [origin unknown] (1565) **1** : confused clattering noise : CLAMOR **2 a** : social whirl or excitement **b** : the strain of exciting or trying experiences **3 a** : a fraudulent scheme, enterprise, or activity **b** : a usu. illegitimate enterprise made workable by bribery or intimidation **c** : an easy and lucrative means of livelihood **d** *slang* : OCCUPATION, BUSINESS

³**racket** *vi* (1609) **1** : to engage in active social life **2** : to move with or make a racket

racket 1: *A* tennis, *B* racquetball, *C* badminton

in square brackets, they precede the definitions and trace a word as far back in English as possible. Most give the Middle English and Old English versions of a word and their definitions. Etymologies of technical terms that do not appear to have originated in English are labeled [ISV] for *International Scientific Vocabulary*. Words related to the entry word are introduced by *akin*. Indented synonym paragraphs begin with the abbreviation **syn** followed by a list of words in small capital letters. Antonyms are not treated.

Usage labels may be temporal, such as *obs* and *archaic;* regional, such as *New Eng., Southern,* and *chiefly Canad;* and stylistic, such as *slang.* For example, within the third definition of **joint,** one finds *slang:* PRISON 2, referring the reader to the second definition of that word. Nonstandard (*nonstand*) indicates that the entry is not used by many people but that it may have some currency (such as **irregardless**). Usage notes may take the place of definitions, as in the following entry: **programme** *chiefly Brit var of* PROGRAM.

According to the book's preface, usage paragraphs have increased in number since the ninth edition and have been extensively revised based on *Webster's Dictionary of English Usage* (first edition, © 1989). They include the historical background, body of opinion, current usage, and relevant examples and quotations.

Illustrative examples for definitions are a mixture of short phrases written by the editors and quotations from literary texts. For example, in the entry **jazz,** users will find "<that wind, and the waves, and all that ~—John Updike>." Under **knead,** one finds "<~*ing* dough>" and "<~*ed* sore neck muscles>." The swung dash stands for the word being illustrated.

Quality and Currency of Entries

The format of the entries is logical and easy to read. The boldface entry word is followed by the pronunciation in reverse slash marks, the part-of-speech label in italics, and the first known date of the word's use in English in parentheses. Definitions, or *senses* follow. A boldface number and a colon introduce each sense; a small letter introduces a *subsense.* Angled brackets contain illustrative phrases. Synonyms and inflected forms appear at the end of the main entry. The following entry illustrates the format:

men·da·cious \men-'dā-shəs\ *adj* [L. *mendac-, mendax* — more at AMEND] (1616): given to or characterized by deception or falsehood or divergence from absolute truth <~ tales of his adventures> **syn** see DISHONEST — **men·da·cious·ly** *adv* — **men·da·cious·ness** *n*

Definitions in this dictionary are accurate and comprehensive. The order of *senses* is historical so that the first use in English is given first. For example, the older meaning of **bewitch,** "to influence or affect injuriously by witchcraft" precedes the modern connotation of "to attract as if by the power of witchcraft: ENCHANT." The use of dates to indicate the senses' first use helps avoid the confusion for users that such order might otherwise cause.

The lexicon does not include some current, popular words, such as *bungee jumping, dis, intifada, maquiladora,* and *virtual reality.* There are, however, definitions for **fax, rap** (as music), and **retrovirus,** and **HDTV** is spelled out in the list of abbreviations in the end matter.

Syllabication and Pronunciation

Entry words are divided by boldface centered dots that indicate acceptable division points. These are intended for typographical use, as single-letter syllables are not set off from the rest of the word: **about, obey.** Other entries with disputed syllabications include **En·glish** and **rhythm.** Division points in entry words may, but do not necessarily, correspond to those in the pronunciations. Syllables are not shown in succeeding homographs unless there are differences in the way they are pronounced. High-set marks indicate primary stress, and low-set marks identify secondary stress. A pronunciation is given for words in open compounds that do not have their own entries: **Mary Jane** \-ʹjān\. Pronunciations are given for inflected forms, but only for the part of the word that changes: **he·ro·ic** \hi-ʹrō-ik\, **he·ro·ical·ly** \-i-k(ə-)lē\. (The syllable in parentheses is pronounced by some but not all people.) A division symbol (÷) precedes pronunciations sometimes considered unacceptable, as in **nu·cle·ar** \ʹnü-klē-ər, ʹnyü-, ÷ -kyə-lər\. Users unfamiliar with this practice may find the inclusion of less acceptable pronunciations among more acceptable ones to be confusing.

The dictionary attempts to reflect regional, educational, and social differences in pronunciation patterns. An abbreviated list of pronunciation symbols appears at the bottom of every right-hand page. An extensive "Guide to Pronunciation" in the front matter details the methods used to ascertain various pronunciations. International Phonetic Alphabet (IPA) equivalents are given in the guide but not in the one-page "Pronunciation Symbols," which is located on the inside back cover for quick access.

Accessibility

Entries are sequenced in alphabetical order, letter by letter: **ABC** and **ABD** appear between **abbreviation** and **Abdias.** Entries with Roman numerals are entered as though they were spelled out; homographs are given separate entries with superscripts. Although readers will have no problem locating information in this dictionary, they must refer to separate sections to locate abbreviations and symbols for chemical elements, foreign words and phrases, biographical names, and geographical entries.

The cross-referencing is commendable. For example, **pullulate** includes cross-references to GERMINATE, SPROUT, SWARM, and TEEM. The entry for **terror** includes references to TREMBLE, SCOURGE, WORRY, BRAT, REIGN OF TERROR, and FEAR.

The word *or* is used to indicate equal variants of an entry: **movable** *or* **moveable.** Unequal variants receive a separate entry with a reference to the preferred entry: **moustache** *var of* MUSTACHE.

Guide words for the first and last entry on each page are located above the upper outside column. An index to key features, such as instructional materials, tables, and essays, is located in the back of the book. A detailed "Explanatory Chart" at the beginning of the dictionary includes references to page numbers in the useful "Explanatory Notes" section that follows. This section explains the parts of the entries in a clear, concise manner. Thumb-indexed and unindexed versions of the work are available.

Special Features

In addition to the explanatory sections of the front matter already described, there is an essay on "The English Language" that contains examples of how etymological decisions are made and how the dictionary was created. The end matter also includes a number of special features, many of which have been updated or changed from the ninth edition. A section entitled "Signs and Symbols" deals with subjects from astronomy to weather that could not be alphabetized and treated in the main body of the dictionary. A "Handbook of Style" includes guidelines for punctuation (updated from the ninth edition), capitalization, and italicization. "Documentation of Sources" provides rudimentary information on footnotes, endnotes (new to this edition), parenthetical references, and lists of sources. In these sections, the editors point users to other style manuals for further assistance, something that would have been useful in THE AMERICAN HERITAGE HIGH SCHOOL DICTIONARY. "Forms of Address" gives guidelines for corresponding with titled individuals. Deleted from the tenth edition are the list of "Colleges and Universities," the Flowchart Symbols from the "Signs and Symbols" section, and the guidelines on the formation of plural words from the "Handbook of Style." All of these changes seem appropriate.

Merriam-Webster also offers a Language Research Service to owners of the dictionary. According to the last page of the volume, a member of the editorial staff will provide a "prompt, accurate, and concise reply" to any written question about the origin, spelling, pronunciation, meaning, or usage of a word, as well as about the dictionary's features.

Graphics and Format

Although illustrations are clear and properly placed next to the entries they illustrate, they are not a key feature of this work. The 700 black-and-white drawings represent plants, animals, furniture, clothing, hardware, and mechanical items. Useful charts and tables, such as "Proofreaders' Marks" and the "Metric System" are appropriately placed throughout the text. Most two-page spreads contain at least one illustration.

Each page is divided into two columns with narrow margins and no wasted space. The typeface is small but easy to read. The cross-references in small capital letters add variety to an otherwise traditional-looking dictionary. The paper is of good quality and show-through from backing pages is minimal. This standard-sized, sturdily bound volume should hold up well under normal use.

Summary

Merriam-Webster's Collegiate Dictionary, tenth edition, continues the tradition of excellence that previous editions earned. It is comprehensive, easy to use, and accurate, although it does not include as many up-to-date entries as THE AMERICAN HERITAGE COLLEGE DICTIONARY, third edition, or the RANDOM HOUSE WEBSTER'S COLLEGE DICTIONARY.

The changes from the ninth edition improve the work's scope and usefulness, and "Webster's tenth" is destined to continue as the standard dictionary of choice for those in the publishing industry and elsewhere. Unlike THE AMERICAN HERITAGE COLLEGE DICTIONARY, *Merriam-Webster's* approach is more descriptive and less focused on graphic appeal. Public and academic libraries will want to include both volumes in their collections. Individuals should choose based on their needs and preferences.

The New Shorter Oxford English Dictionary

Facts at a Glance

Full title: **The New Shorter Oxford English Dictionary**
Publisher: Oxford University Press
Editor: Lesley Brown
Edition reviewed: © 1993

Number of volumes: 2
Number of pages: 4,000
Number of entries: 97,600
Number of illustrations: none
Intended readership: older student to adult
Trim size: 8¾" × 11¼"
Binding: hardcover

Price: $125
Sold in bookstores; also sold by direct mail
ISBN 0-19-861271-0
No stated revision policy

Introduction and Scope

The New Shorter Oxford English Dictionary is, according to its preface, "a historical dictionary of modern English . . . every headword is traced back to the time of its first known use. . . ."

This 1993 dictionary, a two-volume set, applies the historical principles of the OXFORD ENGLISH DICTIONARY (OED) to a shorter, more contemporary lexicon. It claims coverage of "virtually every word or phrase in use in English—worldwide—since 1700." Its 97,600 entries encompass half a million definitions.

Authority

This work takes the place of *The Shorter Oxford English Dictionary,* which has been published since 1933 as a companion to the OED. Rather than simply updating that volume (last published in 1973), the editors have returned directly to the OED to reabridge, reconsider, and rewrite every entry from scratch. They have added new words and definitions, consulted new sources, and included addenda and corrections to the OED that have surfaced since 1989. Both the first edition (1884–1928), with its supplements (1972–1986), and the second edition (1989) of the OED were consulted for this work.

The dictionary's authority rests on the excellent reputation of the reference works and the extensive information files of the Oxford University Press. Editor Lesley Brown has almost 20 years of experience in historical lexicography; the list of linguistic and subject area consultants for the dictionary includes 66 doctors and professors.

Comprehensiveness of Entries

The principal difference between this edition and the OED is the omission of words and phrases obsolete before 1700. Thus, the OED's eight separate entries for the word **humble** have been reduced to two in the *New Shorter OED* at the expense of obsolete definitions such as "to rumble; to mumble, to hum or buzz as a bee"; and "apparently a popular corruption of *homily.*" The now obsolete use of the word as a replacement for the French *umbles,* or entrails, merited a full entry in the OED; that fact is merely noted in the word's etymology in the *New Shorter OED.*

The 50 entries from **bug** to **bullfinch** include six for **bug**; three for **bugger;** the botanical terms **bugloss, bulb,** and **bulbil;** the British expression **Buggins' turn;** the American expressions **bughouse** (slang for a mental institution) and **bugology** (jocular term for entomology); **Bugis,** an Indonesian people; *bugaku,* a Japanese dance form; and **bukshi,** an Anglo-Indian historical word for an army paymaster.

The work's strengths include its etymologies and illustrative quotations from published sources. The former, although thorough, employ numerous abbreviations, such as in the entry **fleet** [OE *flēot* (also *flēote* or *-a*), corresp. to OFris. *flēt,* (M)Du. *vliet,* MHG *vliez,* ON *fljót,* f. Gmc base of FLEET *v.*[1]].

The illustrative quotations are drawn from an impressive array of sources (7,300 according to the book jacket) but have been drastically reduced in number from the OED's 2,412,400 to this work's 83,000. This reduction sometimes severely restricts the user's ability to understand an obsolete meaning by reading several examples. For example, the OED includes "A boxer, a fighter" as a rare definition for the word **pucker,** and illustrates this use with a quotation from James Joyce. No mention of this use is made in *The New Shorter Oxford.* In addition, many words simply go unillustrated: none of the obsolete, mathematical, or chemical definitions for the word **component,** for example, has an illustrative example.

As in the OED, vulgarisms are present and the dictionary has a distinct British slant. The work includes no usage notes, synonym studies, or biographical or geographical entries.

Quality and Currency of Entries

The entries in *The New Shorter OED* are typically similar to those in the OED, except that *The New Shorter OED* gives an approximate date of the word's first occurrence in English instead of illustrative phrases. The date is indicated immediately after the part-of-speech label by an abbreviation, such as *ME* for *Middle English* or *L17* for *late seventeenth century.* A list of these abbreviations appears in the dictionary's user's guide. Definitions are ordered chronologically and are generally clear. The following is a typical entry:

> **festivity** /fɛ ˈ stɪvɪti/ *n.* LME. [9OOFr. *festivit'* or L *festivitas,* f. as prec.: se - ITY.] **1** A festive celebration, a feast; (an occasion of) rejoicing or gaiety. In *pl.,* festive proceedings. LME. †**2** Festive quality or condition; suitability for a festival; cheerfulness. M16-L17.
> **1** E. SUMMERSKILL Weddings, golden weddings, funerals, and other festivities.
> **festiveness** *n.* M20. **festivous** *a.* (now *rare* or *obs.*) = FESTIVE M17

The currency of this work's lexicon is evident in entries such as **bungee jumping** (which appears under **bungee**), **fax, HDTV, intifada,** *maquiladora,* **rap** (as music), **retrovirus,** and **virtual reality.** *Dis,* in the contemporary slang sense of "disrespect," does not appear. Compared with the OED, this work has a better coverage of contemporary words.

Syllabication and Pronunciation

Once again, this dictionary follows the OED's lead. Entry words are not syllabicated, and syllable divisions within the pronunciations are often unclear. Pronunciations use the International Phonetic Alphabet (IPA) and are, according to the user's guide, "those which can safely be regarded as allowable in British English at the present time." Pronunciation keys appear in the user's guide and immediately preceding each volume's main lexicon; an abbreviated version is printed across the bottom of each two-page spread.

Accessibility

Along with affordability, this dictionary's accessibility is probably its most significant selling point. Its 2 volumes are downright handy compared with the OED's 20, and they are thumb indexed. Other features, such as overhanging entry words and stricter sequencing of definitions within entries, also make the work more accessible than its parent volume. As in the OED, entries are in alphabetical order, letter by letter. A small selection of abbreviations appears at the beginning of each letter of the alphabet. Guide words appear at the top of each page.

The 12-page "Guide to the Use of the Dictionary," while comprehensive and thorough, could be easier to use. Subheads are not clearly set off from the text, and examples are buried within dense explanatory paragraphs. A labeled sample definition or page would improve its usefulness.

Special Features

The New Shorter OED includes a few special features. In addition to the aforementioned user's guide, there is a table of abbreviations and symbols, a chart of the Greek and Russian characters used in transliteration, a list of the works cited in the illustrative quotations, and lists of the books of the Bible and the Shakespearean plays referenced in the text.

Graphics and Format

Although the print is somewhat small, the overall format is appealing. The typeface is clear and readable, and the margins are ample. There are no illustrations. The work lies flat when open, is sturdily bound, and should hold up well under regular use. Some show-through is evident, but it is not particularly distracting.

Summary

The New Shorter Oxford English Dictionary is a high-quality reference work. It follows the OED's tradition of including quotations from published literature to illustrate the senses of words as they have changed over time. The work's size, however, sometimes severely limits the scope of these quotations. The lexicon is thorough and up-to-date, but it cannot compete with a good unabridged dictionary.

Libraries that own the OED should note that this work contains information that arose after the OED second edition's publishing date of 1989; thus, it is more current than that work. Scholars who desire comprehensive historical coverage may still want to consider purchasing the COMPACT OXFORD ENGLISH DICTIONARY, a single-volume photoreduction of the OED. Those who seek good international coverage, the authority of the Oxford University Press, and the OED's historical approach, however, will appreciate the affordability and convenience of this unique work.

Oxford American Dictionary

Facts at a Glance

Full title: **Oxford American Dictionary**
Publishers: Oxford University Press (hardcover edition); Avon Books (paperback editions)
Editors: Eugene Ehrlich; Stuart Berg Flexner; Gorton Carruth; Joyce M. Hawkins
Edition reviewed: © 1980, 1986 printing (Oxford)

Number of pages: 832 (hardcover and trade paperback editions); 1,120 (mass market paperback edition)
Number of entries: 35,000
Intended readership: adult
Trim sizes: $5^7/_8'' \times 9''$ (hardcover); $5^1/_4'' \times 8''$ (trade paperback); $4^3/_{16}'' \times 6^7/_8''$ (mass market paperback)

Price: $21 hardcover; $9.95 trade paperback; $4.99 mass market paperback
Sold in bookstores and supermarkets; also sold directly to libraries
ISBN 0-19-502795-7 (Oxford, hardcover);
   ISBN 380-51052-9 (Avon, trade paperback);
   ISBN 380-60772-7 (Avon, mass market paperback).
No stated revision policy

Introduction and Scope

The *Oxford American Dictionary,* first published in 1980 by Oxford University Press (OUP), and issued simultaneously in two paperback editions by Avon Books, was designed to give Americans a concise desk dictionary whose authority matches that of OUP's British dictionaries. Unlike the many other Oxford dictionaries, the *American Dictionary* embodies an American lexicon and uses American spellings.

Authority

The *Oxford American Dictionary* is based primarily the *Oxford Paperback Dictionary* (not available in the United States). Apart from Joyce Hawkins, who compiled that work, its chief editors are American and are not on the OUP staff. These editors include the late Stuart Berg Flexner (editor of THE RANDOM HOUSE UNABRIDGED DICTIONARY, among many other works), Eugene Ehrlich (lecturer in English and comparative literature at Columbia University), and Gorton Carruth, former editor at Funk & Wagnalls. All are eminently qualified for their task and bring wide experience in language studies and reference books to the *Oxford American Dictionary.*

Comprehensiveness of Entries

According to the publisher's jacket blurb, "the *Oxford American Dictionary* contains all the words an American is likely to hear or read in the home, office, or school." Given that it contains only 35,000 entries, however, this claim is not to be taken seriously. Indeed, the "Publisher's Note" at the beginning of the dictionary acknowledges that "this *Oxford American Dictionary* is not intended to be comprehensive or to be a substitute for an encyclopedia or larger dictionary."

The given count of 35,000 entries does not include many derivative words and phrases that appear under these main entries. Biographical and geographical names are included as entries, as well as some British words that are familiar to Americans, such as **Oxbridge** and **pence.**

Quality and Currency of Entries

The *Oxford American Dictionary* is more suited for everyday practical use than for the scholar. Words used in defining difficult or technical entry words are generally much simpler than the entry word itself. For example, the first definition for **psychology** is "the study of the mind and how it works."

The dictionary does not use synonyms to define words "unless they help distinguish shades of meaning." Occasionally, a simple sentence or phrase is included to show how a word might be used in context; such examples are printed in italics. There are no etymologies, although literal translations are given for words of foreign origin. Idiomatic phrases and derivative or compound words are included within the entry for the word from which they derive and are printed in boldface type. For example, the entry for **grace** includes **be in a person's good graces, days of grace, grace note,** and **with good grace.** When it was issued in 1980, the *Oxford American Dictionary* was intended to be a dictionary for the eighties. However, it has not been revised since its initial publication and now shows its age. For example, while it includes such common modern terms as **ayatollah** and

Oxford American Dictionary

❶ Pronunciation enclosed in parentheses

❷ Inflected forms set in boldface type and enclosed in parentheses

❸ Syllabication shown by centered dots

❹ Idiomatic expressions introduced by an open square

❺ Usage notes introduced by an open triangle, set on its side

❻ Usage labels italicized and enclosed in parentheses

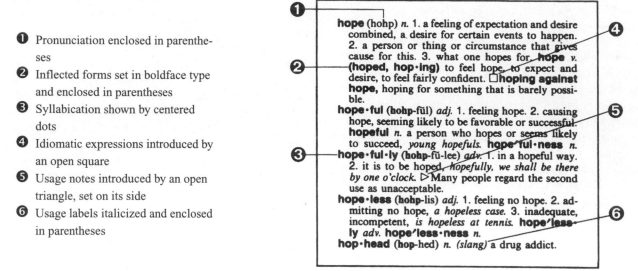

gridlock, it does not include *AIDS, compact disc,* or *yuppie.* The computer term **byte** is included, but *modem* and *floppy disk* are not.

Syllabication and Pronunciation

Main entry words and their inflected and variant forms are divided into syllables by centered dots, showing the acceptable division of the word. Derivative words within an entry include a stress mark to indicate different emphasis in similar words.

Pronunciation is indicated by an easy-to-use system of respelling that includes diacritical marks where necessary. Pronunciations are standard American English.

Accessibility

The excellent design of the *Oxford American Dictionary* enhances its accessibility. Entry words are printed in boldface type, and in a different typeface from the main text, and overhang the text. Different senses of a word are numbered but run on in the text. Different parts of speech, derivative words, and idiomatic words and phrases are all included under the main entry but are printed in the same boldface type as the main entry word, enabling the reader to find them with ease. Guide words, printed flush with the outside margin at the top of each page, indicate the first and last entry word on the page.

Special Features

The most notable feature of the *Oxford American Dictionary* is its usage notes, which are included for about 600 potentially troublesome entries. These give clear guidance for the reader who is not sure of proper usage. The editors proudly point out that this dictionary "dis-

tinguishes between good and bad English" and claim that it "sets high, somewhat conservative standards in usage." This is generally true. For example, although the second sense of the word **disinterested** is given as "uninterested, uncaring," the usage note for this word remarks that "careful writers regard [this] use as unacceptable because it obscures a useful distinction between *disinterested* and *uninterested.*" The usage note for **contact** observes that "careful writers do not use *contact* as a verb. Instead of *contacting* someone, they *call* or *write* or *visit* him." Another usage note emphasizes the distinction between *fewer* and *less.*

Usage notes are indicated by the symbol ▷. A special index lists all the entries that include usage notes. Many entries also carry usage labels. The *Oxford American Dictionary* identifies *informal, slang, old* (for archaic), and *contemptuous.*

Graphics and Format

The *Oxford American Dictionary* is available in three formats: hardcover, trade paperback, and mass market paperback. The hardcover edition will be the first choice for library collections.

The typeface is large and easy to read, especially in the hardcover and trade paperback versions. The page design is clear and uncluttered, with ample white space and margins. The absence of illustrations is not a drawback. The pronunciation key is included in the introductory text. It would have been more accessible on a page by itself.

Summary

The *Oxford American Dictionary* is the first OUP dictionary designed specifically for Americans. With only 35,000 entries, it cannot be considered the first or only choice for either library or individual collections. Also, it is now seriously outdated, and at the time of this review OUP had not announced any plans to revise the work.

However, the *Oxford American Dictionary* still has much to recommend it. It offers basic and clear, if unsubtle, definitions that can be easily understood by the average reader. Moreover, it contains some 600 authoritative usage notes whose conservative stance will be applauded by grammarians. The clear print and excellent page design (particularly in the hardcover and trade paperback editions) is an added bonus.

The *Oxford American Dictionary* does not compete against other Oxford dictionaries. It is sufficiently different from the titles that originated in the United Kingdom that many libraries may want to have both this book and another Oxford work, such as THE CONCISE OXFORD DICTIONARY. It is most closely comparable to THE AMERICAN HERITAGE DESK DICTIONARY and WEBSTER'S NEW IDEAL DICTIONARY, although the comparison is not clear-cut. In any event, this book, ideally suited for everyday use by ordinary Americans, makes a useful supplement to other, more comprehensive dictionaries. The pity is that it is not more comprehensive and up-to-date.

The Oxford Encyclopedic English Dictionary

Facts at a Glance

Full title: **The Oxford Encyclopedic English Dictionary**

Publisher: Oxford University Press

Editors: Joyce M. Hawkins; Robert Allen

Edition reviewed: © 1991

Number of pages: 1,824

Number of entries: about 70,000 (reviewer estimate)

Number of illustrations: about 200 (reviewer estimate) in black and white, plus 16 pages of full-color maps

Intended readership: high school to adult (reviewer estimate)

Trim size: 7″ × 9¾″

Binding: hardcover

Price: $35

Sold in retail outlets; also sold directly by the publisher

ISBN 0-19-861248-6 (plain); ISBN 0-19-861266-4 (thumb indexed)

No stated revision policy

Introduction and Scope

The Oxford Encyclopedic English Dictionary is a combination abridged dictionary/concise encyclopedia published by Oxford University Press (OUP). According to the preface, the work was prepared from the authoritative lexical database assembled for the *Concise Oxford Dictionary* and other dictionaries of current English, supplemented by the encyclopedic resources held by the Oxford English Dictionaries Department.

The editors are Joyce Hawkins and Robert Allen: the former edited the OXFORD AMERICAN DICTIONARY and the latter edited the CONCISE OXFORD. A scholar of Edinburgh University is cited for identifying and creating the geographical encyclopedia entries, but no other academics are noted for their contributions.

With about 70,000 dictionary entries and over 200,000 definitions, the dictionary is limited in scope but examines words in depth. Dictionary entries employ the following sequence: entry word; pronunciation, using the International Phonetic Alphabet (IPA); a summary of all parts of speech applicable to the word; inflections; definitions, listed in order of relative familiarity and importance; phrases and idioms employing the word; derivatives that can be understood from the meaning of the main word; and etymology. Illustrative examples are invented phrases rather than actual quotations. When appropriate, definitions are preceded by usage labels that establish a meaning as regional or specific to a given field.

The work does not include the intensive studies of a word's history through citations that are a hallmark of the OXFORD ENGLISH DICTIONARY (OED). Etymologies, too, are far more limited than those found in the main OED. (Indeed, the dictionary directs the reader to Oxford's etymological dictionaries for full studies of word origins.) There are no synonym or antonym studies. What is provided, though, is clear and understandable.

The lexicon is fairly up-to-date, including entries for **fax, intifada, rap,** and **retrovirus.** The work proclaims its inclusion of scientific and technical terms, and there are good entries for **chaos theory** and **black holes,** but other current terms are treated less well. The entries for **Aids** (sic) and **CD-ROM** are extremely brief, and *HDTV* and *Internet* are absent.

Brief essays of an encyclopedic nature follow some dictionary entries. **Mass,** for instance, ends with two paragraphs on the development of this concept from the Middle Ages to nuclear physics. The entry **Homo** consists almost entirely of an account of current thinking about human evolution.

Supplementing the dictionary entries are about 10,000 encyclopedia entries that provide brief identifications of people (from **Guy Fawkes** to the **Marx Brothers**), places (countries, cities, rivers, mountains), and famous objects (**Mona Lisa, Trianon**) or events (**Great Schism**). Entries for people and places include pronunciations. The encyclopedia entries show a British slant. There are entries for **Kit-Cat Club,** Nancy **Mitford,** and **South Sea bubble** but not for the *Know-Noth-*

ing or *Bull Moose* parties, *Toni Morrison,* or *Teapot Dome.*

Special Features

A major highlight of *The Oxford Encyclopedic* is the section of supplementary encyclopedic information in the back of the book. The section begins with a "Chronology of World Events" that groups historical developments under three headings: "Near East, Mediterranean, and Europe"; "Rest of the World"; and "Culture/Technology." Starting with the year 552 A.D., the first of these headings becomes "Britain and Europe" (the other two do not change). The chronology is useful only to someone who knows something about the event being listed: "*Sherman march* through *Georgia,*" for instance, locates the event in time, but does not explain what happened. A two-page "Chronology of Scientific Developments" appears next, and includes changes in the fields of medical science, telecommunications, computer technology, and space exploration.

Following these chronologies are 32 appendixes, including a listing of countries of the world (including the now-defunct Soviet Union); organizational charts of the British, U.S., United Nations, and European Community governments; genealogical charts of British kings and queens; lists of prime ministers and presidents; scientific and technical information, including mathematical shapes and forms, weights and measures, chemical elements, electronic symbols, astronomical data, and geological, ecological, and anatomical diagrams and charts; alphabets; drawings of architectural features; and the dimensions of the playing fields for several sports. While some of this information is standard dictionary material, other sections (such as a table of hallmarks used for stamping precious metals and a chart of some basic fingerprint patterns) are unusual and make for interesting browsing.

Closing out the volume is a collection of 16 four-color maps. The maps are dated, showing the former Czechoslovakia, U.S.S.R., and Yugoslavia; Germany, however, is depicted as one country.

Graphics and Format

Boldface entry words stand out quite clearly, especially because the subsequent entry information is slightly indented. The typography is extremely clear and easy to follow. Numerals and letters used to distinguish meanings are also in boldface, as are inflections, phrases, idioms, and related words.

Each page has a pair of guide words. They are set in a large typeface and separated from the text by a horizontal line. The pronunciation key appears in the user's guide at the front of the book; an abbreviated version is printed at the foot of each two-page spread, with vowels and consonants alternating spreads. This handy practice

puts the reader only a page turn away from clarification of any symbol.

The book opens flat, but the gutter margins are quite narrow and type tends to get lost inside, especially near the middle section of the lexicon. The paper is of good quality, with limited show-through that is distracting only in the appendixes. Maps are printed on a heavier stock.

Summary

Backed by the authority of OUP, *The Oxford Encyclopedic English Dictionary* is as reliable as a dictionary can be. The encyclopedic material is clear and useful, although the style of the "Chronology of World Events" seems too telegraphic. The scope of the work is not as great as the other encyclopedic dictionaries reviewed here—Webster's Encyclopedic Unabridged Dictionary of the English Language and Webster's Comprehensive Dictionary: Encyclopedic Edition—but it contains a more authoritative lexicon. The British slant of the encyclopedia material may limit its appeal for some users. A library with a collection of more comprehensive semi-abridged dictionaries and full-fledged encyclopedias probably has little need for this work, but it could be a valuable all-in-one reference volume for home or office.

The Oxford English Dictionary, Second Edition

Facts at a Glance

Full title: **The Oxford English Dictionary, Second Edition**
Publisher: Oxford University Press
Editors: John Simpson; Edmund Weiner
Edition reviewed: © 1989, second edition

Number of volumes: 20
Number of pages: 22,000
Number of entries: 290,500
Number of illustrations: none
Intended readership: adult
Trim size: 9" × 12"
Binding: hardcover

Price: $2,750
Sold to libraries; also sold by direct mail
ISBN 0-19-861186-2
No stated revision policy; *OED Additions Series* currently being published

Introduction and Scope

According to the book's preface, the aim of the 20-volume *Oxford English Dictionary* is

The Oxford English Dictionary

❶ Etymology is enclosed in brackets

❷ Quotations, arranged chronologically, illustrate word histories

❸ Field labels are italicized

❹ Cross-references are set in small capitals

❺ Dates, in boldface type, and sources are cited for all quotations

to present in alphabetical series the words that have formed the English vocabulary from the time of the earliest records down to the present day, with all the relevant facts concerning their form, sense-history, pronunciation, and etymology.

The *OED*, as it is commonly called, traces the historical usage of each entry word by citing a series of quotations from printed works in which the word has appeared, starting with the oldest surviving English language texts (ca. 1150) and continuing to the present day. The goal is nothing short of complete documentation of the English language, both as it is currently used and as it has been used in the past.

The *OED* was first published in ten volumes from 1888 to 1928, and was originally entitled *A New English Dictionary on Historical Principles.* Users who noticed mistakes in the published volumes, especially overlooked words or early uses, sent their observations to journals such as *Notes and Queries* or directly to the dictionary's Oxford offices. Supplements to the dictionary were issued in 1933 and in four volumes between 1972 and 1986; the 1989 second edition combines all supplementary material with the original text and adds about 5,000 new items, creating a single comprehensive alphabetized lexicon.

According to its introduction, the work contains "about 290,500 main entries . . . making a total of 616,500 word-forms." There are 137,000 pronunciations, 249,300 etymologies, 577,000 cross-references, and 2,412,400 illustrative quotations.

Authority

The *OED* is the result of work begun in 1858 under the direction of the Philological Society of the University of Oxford, England. The dictionary grew out of the recently popularized idea that historical illustration of a word's use was essential—even tantamount—to a full definition of the word. An 1859 proposal for the project listed several principles for the work, the two most important of which were:

I. The first requirement of every lexicon is that it should contain every word occurring in the literature of the language it professes to illustrate.

IV. In the treatment of individual words the historical principle will be uniformly adopted.

The plan of the Philological Society was to incorporate materials from earlier dictionaries and to add citations from all writers before 1500 and from "as many as possible of the more important writers of later times." (The Early English Text Society was founded in 1864 chiefly to provide reliable editions of medieval English writings for the new dictionary.) By 1884, about 1,300 volunteer readers had collected nearly 3.5 million citations from more than 5,000 British authors; subsequent efforts increased the number of citations to 6 million. The post–World War II supplements included an additional 1.5 million citations and several large specialized word collections.

According to the introduction of the second edition, when editorial work was begun on it in 1983 the files were growing "at the rate of some 120,000 quotations per year." Sources used in the selection of new words included computer databases of research abstracts, newspaper and periodical texts, and legal reports; advance publicity for new dictionaries and the dictionaries themselves; and, as the editors put it, "personal observation by members of the Dictionary Department and other contributors (the historical dictionary's own style of 'oral evidence')."

Comprehensiveness of Entries

The *OED*'s 290,500 main entries, although fewer than the 460,000 claimed by WEBSTER'S THIRD NEW INTERNATIONAL or the 315,000 claimed by the RANDOM HOUSE UNABRIDGED DICTIONARY, represent some 616,000 word forms, including combinations, derivatives, and phrases. A randomly selected sample of the 50 entries from **humanoid** to **humectative** includes the scientific and technical terms **humantin** (zoology), **humate** (chemistry),

humboldtite (mineralogy), and **humectant** (chemistry/medicine).

One can get a sense of the scope of the *OED*'s coverage by considering that the 50 selected entries span three full pages of text. Among them is the word *humble,* which boasts no less than eight separate entries, including obsolete meanings such as "to rumble; to mumble, to hum or buzz as a bee"; "an occasional spelling of UMBLES (itself a later form of NUMBLES, OF. *nombles*), the inwards of a deer or other beast"; and "apparently a popular corruption of HOMILY." All of these definitions are illustrated, of course, by quotations from published sources.

Vulgarisms are present, both as main entry words and as alternate definitions for words with other meanings. Because of the historical nature of the work, British meanings of words and citations from British literature are prominent. In an introductory section entitled "The Future of the *OED,*" the editors acknowledge the dictionary's need for expanded coverage of "the English of North America, which is the greatest source of linguistic change." Close inspection of the work reveals adequate coverage of American expressions, with the noted exception of only the most recent terms. The definitions for **main line,** for instance, include "a principal route, connection, conduit, family, etc. U.S."; and "A large or principal vein, into which drugs can readily be injected; hence, an intravenous injection of drugs; the act or habit of making such an injection. *slang* (orig. U.S.)." Illustrative quotations for the entry include citations from Sidney Perelman, William S. Burroughs, *Hunt's Merchant's Magazine, Detective Fiction Weekly,* and *The New York Times.* More contemporary words of American origin such as *bungee jumping, dis, rap* (as music), and *virtual reality* do not appear, although the computer-related meaning of *virtual* is present.

Etymologies, most of them substantial, are included for all entries. The following examples give a sense of both the range and the depth of scholarship that has gone into this aspect of the *OED:*

> **American Express** orig. *U.S.* [f. the name of the *American Express* Co., whose orig. function was to provide express mail services throughout N. America]

> †**yclepe** . . . [OE *geclipian, gecleopian* to call (in various senses): see Y-3C and CLEPE *v.* Spenser's *ycleepe* is a new back-formation on YCLEPT. In quot. 1901 'ycleping' is an error for 'clipping' (CLIP *v.*[1]).]

Detailed usage labels such as *Biochem., Chiefly U.S., Obs.,* and *Path.* (Pathology), are also present. The dictionary does not include synonym or antonym guides, nor does it include usage notes; the latter are omitted in deference to the illustrative quotations. The *OED* does not include biographical or geographical terms, although derivatives of such words may be found if they have entered the vocabulary: **Germanicism, Hooverville,** and **Lithuanian** all appear, but *Germany, Herbert Hoover,* and *Lithuania* do not.

Quality and Currency of Entries

The *OED*'s word entries and definitions are the result of the most comprehensive historical lexicography project ever conducted. Scholars using the dictionary will certainly be able to unlock the secrets of the most difficult English language passages, although they will need patience to locate the correct sense of a word among the many meanings and illustrative examples provided. A typical entry begins with the unsyllabicated entry word in boldface type, followed by the pronunciation (International Phonetic Alphabet [IPA] system) in parentheses. Obsolete entries and definitions are preceded by †, and nonnaturalized or partially naturalized words by ‖. Part-of-speech and usage labels appear next, along with principal earlier forms or spellings of a word. The etymology is presented in brackets and is followed by the definitions, indicated by indented boldface numbers and letters. Definitions, according to the "General Explanations" section that precedes the main lexicon, occur "in the order in which they appear to have arisen." Synonym notes and studies do not appear.

A list of illustrative quotations follows each definition. These citations are the heart of the *OED,* and their scope is remarkable. A scan of the dictionary's 143-page bibliography reveals works ranging from *Beowulf* and the *Bible* (11 versions are listed) to those of Ray Bradbury, Anthony Burgess, and contemporary poet William John Burley. Salman Rushdie's *Midnight's Children* appears, as does *Poor Richard's Almanac,* a list of some 85 specialized journals, and works by noted word coiners such as James Joyce and Lewis Carroll.

The quotations include, according to the "General Explanations,"

> the earliest and, in obsolete words or senses, the latest, known instances of [a word's] occurrence. . . . They are arranged chronologically so as to give about one for each century, though various considerations often render a larger number necessary. The original spelling is retained, as an essential part of the history of the language.

The *OED*'s coverage of contemporary words is sometimes inadequate. **Fax** and **retrovirus** appear as entries, but *HDTV, intifada,* and *maquiladora* do not. This shortcoming can be attributed to the work's 1989 publication date. Users should also note that the second edition is not strictly a revision of the first edition, but rather an integration of the original work with the supplements. As a result, some of the older material does not reflect recent scholarship.

Syllabication and Pronunciation

Entry words in the *OED* are not syllabicated. Stresses are indicated (by high and low prime marks preceding the stressed syllables) in the pronunciations, but the locations of syllable breaks are not always clear. The prefatory material provides the guidelines that the *OED* has followed for such matters, but syllabication is addressed only in the context of a word's pronunciation:

> Any consonant combinations that make up a single sound are treated as unbreakable (so *o'ccur, para'psychic* but *ac'cede, resig'nation*); single letters symbolizing consonant combinations are perforce unbreakable (so *e'xistence*).

Users could ostensibly locate and follow these rules, but those seeking clear visual information about where words may be broken on a typeset page will not find the *OED* helpful.

Pronunciations are indicated using the IPA, and alternate pronunciations are given for words such as **Derby.** For some entries, the British pronunciation is simply listed first; in others, pronunciation notes are given, such as the following for **rather:**

> The pron. with long vowel . . . is now usual in England; the short sound . . . is common in Scotland (but not *dial.*) and America, and is given by Walker as the standard pron. in his time. . . .

The pronunciation key appears within the prefatory material to volume I and opposite the copyright page of each subsequent volume.

Accessibility

Entries in the *OED* are sequenced in strict alphabetical order, letter by letter. Abbreviations, however, may appear either as main entries unto themselves (**B.B.C.**), or at the end of the entry for the initial letter of the abbreviation (**B.A., B.S., BYOB,** for example, appear at the end of the entry for the letter **B**). Although the prefatory material notes this split, it does not offer any rationale for it.

No instructional material *per se* is provided within the *OED,* although the "General Explanations" include descriptions of "the vocabulary," "classification of the vocabulary," "main words," "subordinate words," "combinations," "derivatives," "ordering of entries," "ordering of senses," and "pronunciation." These sections are precise and thorough, often at the expense of economy and clarity. The novice user will not find them particularly accessible, although collectively they read well as a fascinating treatise on lexicographical principles. A "Key to the Conventions of the Dictionary" is also provided, as are lists of abbreviations and symbols (at the front of each volume) and the previously noted pronunciation keys. The Oxford University Press publishes a separate book, *A Guide to the Oxford English Dictionary,* which covers the *OED* in detail.

Although the second edition, with supplements integrated into the main lexicon, now allows *OED* users to look up each word only once, the work is still the least accessible of dictionaries. Its 20 large volumes preclude casual use, and although guide words appear at the top of each page, the sheer length of the average entry makes speedy word location difficult. Potential purchasers should bear in mind that the *OED* is intended primarily as a specialized reference tool and a historical record of the language, not as a handy "user's dictionary."

Special Features

The 1989 edition of the *OED* features a new introduction as well as the fascinating "History of the *Oxford English Dictionary,*" reprinted from the 1933 edition. Those interested in word origins and lexicography in general will find this supplement interesting reading, as it includes the original 1879 instructions to word collectors, a typical citation slip of the day, and anecdotes such as the following:

> The difficulty of [common words with a long history] had become apparent even in the early period of the work, and formed the subject of comment by Dr. Murray in 1881:
>
>> In returning to me his last batch, Mr. Jacob mentioned to me that the division of the meanings of the verb *Set,* and the attempt to put them in satisfactory order, had occupied him over 40 hours. In examining his results, with 51 senses of the simple verb, and 83 of phrases like *set-out, set-off, set-down,*—134 divisions in all—I do not wonder at the time. I suspect that the Editor will have to give 40 more to it, for the language seems not to contain a more perplexing word than *Set,* which occupies more than two columns of Webster, and will probably fill three of our large quarto pages.
>
> When *set* finally came to be done, more than thirty years later, it took nearer 40 days than 40 hours to digest the mass of examples which had accumulated by that time; the word occupies a column more than 18 pages of the Dictionary, and extends to 154 main divisions, the last of which (*set up*) has so many subdivisions that it exhausts the alphabet and repeats the letters down to *rr.*

Also notable in the "History" is the section on the use of computers in the production of the second edition.

Graphics and Format

The *OED* includes no illustrations. The typeface is clear, although the point size in which the etymological quotations have been set is, of necessity, very small. Entries are quite readable, especially after one becomes familiar with their format. Boldface and italics have been used to good effect, and entries are well spaced from one another.

The text is set in three columns with ample margins all around. Some show-through can be detected, but the paper is of a high quality and the bindings are sturdy. The overall appearance of a typical page is quite attractive.

Summary

Among reference works, the *Oxford English Dictionary* stands in a class of its own. As a historical record of the English language, its quality is unsurpassed. The combining of the supplements with the main lexicon alone makes the second edition worth purchasing; the attractive new typographical format encourages browsing and makes the work as a whole more accessible to the average reader. The *OED* is not, however, intended to be a "user's dictionary" or a desk reference tool; it does not include features such as usage notes, appended reference materials, biographical and geographical entries, or clear syllabications of entry words.

Although the second edition claims 5,000 new entries and a computerized database, the complex nature of the dictionary necessarily makes it difficult to keep up-to-date. The work also maintains a persistent and perhaps unavoidable British bias. While home users may want to consider one of the less expensive abridged versions of the work, such as THE NEW SHORTER OXFORD ENGLISH DICTIONARY (or perhaps the COMPACT OXFORD ENGLISH DICTIONARY, a direct photoreduction of the *OED* into one volume with a magnifying glass included), no serious reference library should be without this unique and important reference tool.

The Oxford Modern English Dictionary

Facts at a Glance

Full title: **The Oxford Modern English Dictionary**
Publisher: Oxford University Press
Editor: Julia Swannell
Edition reviewed: © 1992, 1993 printing

Number of pages: 1,287
Number of entries: 90,000
Number of illustrations: none
Intended readership: high school to adult (reviewer estimate)
Trim size: 5¼" × 8½"
Binding: hardcover

Price: $19.95
Sold in retail outlets; also sold directly by the publisher
ISBN 0-19-861267-2
No stated revision policy

Introduction and Scope

The Oxford Modern English Dictionary is the newest addition to the Oxford line of dictionaries, intended to provide "accessible, up-to-date information about a broad range of modern English vocabulary in a conveniently-sized book." This abridged dictionary contains about 90,000 dictionary entries and more than 130,000 definitions. The volume reviewed was a 1993 printing of a work copyrighted in 1992. The clarity of the definitions should make the work accessible to high school students as well as adults.

Entries employ the following sequence: entry word; pronunciation; a summary of all parts of speech applicable to the word; inflections; definitions, listed in order of relative familiarity and importance; phrases and idioms employing the word; derivatives that can be understood from the meaning of the main word; and etymology. The work uses invented illustrative examples rather than actual quotations. When appropriate, definitions are preceded by usage labels that establish a meaning as regional or specific to a given field. Pronunciations use the International Phonetic Alphabet (IPA). Syllabication is not indicated, although main and secondary stresses are shown.

The scope and nature of the entries is further discussed in the review for THE CONCISE OXFORD, the volume on which this dictionary is based. As befits the intention of this book's editors to provide a handy, brief dictionary, the entries do not have extensive etymologies, nor do they offer synonym or antonym studies. About 400 entries include brief usage notes. These explain the distinctions between confusing words such as *amend* and *emend* or *imprint* and *imprimatur.* Many notes address the question of acceptability of words—**ain't,** we are told, is "usually regarded as unacceptable in spoken and written English." A number of these notes, however, are too weak to be used as guides: according to one usage note, a pronunciation given for **diphtheria** "is considered incorrect by some people"; one meaning of **interface** is "deplored" but only by the vague "some people."

The preface states that the lexicon stresses "the language of every day but also includ[es] the essential vocabulary of science and technology." Entries are indeed fairly up-to-date, especially with regard to new words reflecting popular activities. Included from the Buying Guide's test entries for currency are **bungee jumping, fax, intifada,** and **rap** (as music). The dictionary also has such new words as **hip hop, karaoke, liposuction, PC** (for political correctness), and **user-friendly.** The work is weaker than stated with regard to its coverage of scientific and technical terms, however. The editors omit *air bag, fractal, retrovirus,* and *CAM* (computer-aided manufacturing), although **CAD** (computer-aided design) appears.

There are no biographical or geographical entries, except words applied to groups of people (**Walloon**) or those derived from proper nouns. The selection of such words has a British bent. The dictionary includes **Edwardian, Georgian,** and **Norfolk jacket;** it does not include the American identifier *Jacksonian* or *Eisenhower jacket*. Surprisingly, it does not have either *Newtonian* or *Jungian*.

Special Features

This very brief dictionary is a no-frills affair, simply offering a collection of clear definitions in a basic lexicon. The usage notes discussed above are the only special feature within the main body of the dictionary. An 11-page appendix provides a table of British and American weights and measures and some notes on the proper use of punctuation marks. The work has a user's guide, but no illustrations and no extensive tabular material.

Graphics and Format

Boldface entry words stand out well; the entries themselves are indented from the left margin, which also helps identify the entry word. The typography is clear and easy to read. Boldface type is used for the numbers and letters that distinguish meanings, as well as for variations of entry words such as inflections, phrases, idioms, and related words. All of these items are easily visible, helping the user to locate the information desired.

Each page has a pair of guide words. Having four guide words on every two-page spread greatly aids access. The explanation of pronunciation symbols appears in the front of the book, but nowhere else. This is not unusual in a compact dictionary.

The book opens flat and margins are ample, leaving no problems in reading all text. The small trim size and hardcover binding make the book easy to hold in one hand. The paper is of good quality, with limited show-through.

Summary

Based on the authoritative database of Oxford University Press, *The Oxford Modern English Dictionary* is a fine compact source. It is largely British in its approach, however. A library desiring access to the high quality of Oxford's work would be better off purchasing a more comprehensive and full-featured dictionary; any need for an abridged dictionary would be better met by an American publication, such as THE AMERICAN HERITAGE COLLEGE DICTIONARY, third edition, or MERRIAM-WEBSTER'S COLLEGIATE DICTIONARY, tenth edition. A consumer may find *The Oxford Modern English Dictionary* useful if he or she has a strong desire for a British approach, but for the kind of casual user most likely to buy a work of this scope, an American publication would probably be more helpful.

The Pocket Oxford Dictionary of Current English

Facts at a Glance

Full Title: **The Pocket Oxford Dictionary of Current English: Seventh Edition**
Publisher: Oxford University Press
Editor: R. E. Allen
Edition reviewed: © 1984; 1986 printing

Number of pages: 900
Number of entries: 49,000
Intended readership: adult
Trim size: 4¼" × 7"
Binding: hardcover

Price: $14.95
Sold to libraries and other educational institutions; also sold in bookstores
ISBN 0-19-861133-1
No stated revision policy

Introduction and Scope

The Pocket Oxford Dictionary, part of the Oxford dictionary series published by Clarendon Press, is a nominal abridgment of the CONCISE OXFORD DICTIONARY. At some 900 pages in length, however, it is a substantial reference work in its own right. Both in size and in content, *The Pocket Oxford Dictionary* is weightier than the term "pocket" normally suggests— it would be better described as a smaller-sized desk dictionary.

Although this volume includes "American" words and also gives American spellings as well as British ones, where these differ, *The Pocket Oxford* remains primarily a dictionary of the English language as it is written and spoken in the United Kingdom.

Authority

The first edition of *The Pocket Oxford Dictionary,* issued in 1924, was the result of more than seven years' labor by the redoubtable Latin scholars F. G. and W. H. Fowler. In creating the work as, ostensibly, an abridged version of the CONCISE OXFORD DICTIONARY, their goal was to "keep to the principle that a dictionary is a book of diction, concerned primarily with words and phrases as such," and to achieve "the task of making clear the idiomatic usage of words."

The Pocket Oxford Dictionary has been revised and reissued periodically, most recently in this seventh edition (1984). The current edition was edited by R. E. Allen, with the assistance of the Oxford English Dictionary department. This pocket volume remains perhaps the most authoritative dictionary of its kind.

The Pocket Oxford Dictionary of Current English

❶ Entry word printed in boldface type
❷ Italicized part-of-speech label appears before the definition or definitions to which it applies
❸ Italicized illustrative phrases or sentences show the main entry word in context
❹ Usage label, in italics, shows context in which word or phrase is used
❺ Compound entries follow main entry word
❻ Etymology is in square brackets at the end of the entry and includes cross-reference (indicated by small capitals)

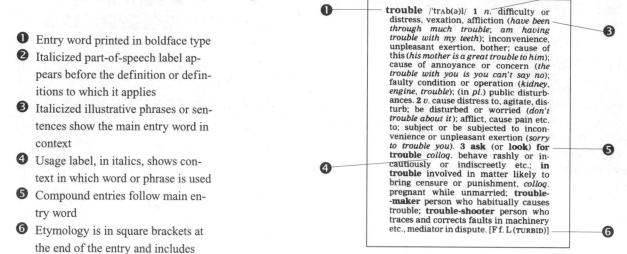

Comprehensiveness of Entries

The Pocket Oxford Dictionary includes a fairly good selection of contemporary words such as **acid rain, AIDS, fibre optics**, and **floppy disc**. But given its 1984 copyright date, many current terms such as *fax, retrovirus,* and *mammogram,* do not appear. Many of the entries are for words common in British but not in American vocabulary, such as **pram, pavement,** and **petrol.** In many instances, compound and derivative words listed under a main entry have application strictly to British English—for example, the entry for **home** includes such compounds and derivatives as **home farm, Home Rule,** and **Home Secretary.** The word **homely** is first defined as "simple, plain, unpretentious," and only second as "*US* (of facial appearance) unattractive."

The Pocket Oxford Dictionary, covering 49,000 words and phrases (including many idioms), is quite comprehensive for a dictionary bearing the appellation "pocket."

Quality and Currency of Entries

Entries in *The Pocket Oxford Dictionary* are unusually comprehensive for a smaller desk dictionary. Different senses of the same word are given with the most important and current senses first.

When appropriate, usage and subject labels are included in the entries. Words that are considered offensive by members of a particular ethnic or religious group (**nigger, wop**) are labeled with a boldface **R** (for racially offensive). The boldface capital letter **D** indicates a disputed use that, although widely encountered, is not generally approved by grammarians and word spe-

cialists (such as the use of *infer* to mean "imply"). Subject or field labels indicate when a word is used in music, law, a particular science, and so forth. The label *US* alerts the reader to words, spellings, and definitions that are peculiar to the United States.

Compound and derivative forms of an entry word, as well as idiomatic phrases, are given within the main entry. Etymologies are given in highly abbreviated form at the end of entries.

The following entry, quoted in full, indicates the style of a typical entry in *The Pocket Oxford Dictionary:*

narrow /'n^ae^rə^ʊ/ **1** *a.* of small width in proportion to length; not broad; confined or confining (esp. *fig.: within narrow bounds*); careful, exact; with little margin (*narrow escape*); narrow-minded. **2** *n.* (usu. in *pl.*) narrow part of a sound, strait, river, pass, or street. **3** *v.* make or become narrower, lessen, contract. **4 narrow boat** canal boat; **narrow-minded** intolerant, prejudiced, rigid or restricted in one's views; **narrow seas** English Channel and Irish Sea. [OE]

Syllabication and Pronunciation

Syllabication is not indicated in the entry word but does appear in the phonetically respelled pronunciations. Whereas previous editions used conventional respelling pronunciation, the current edition employs the International Phonetic Alphabet (IPA). The editor justifies this switch by saying that the IPA affords "greater precision and consistency" and also enables "guidance on pronunciation to be more valid internationally.

American users must be aware that *The Pocket Oxford Dictionary* gives the British, not American, pronunciations of its entry words. This pronunciation is commonly known as *Received Pronunciation* (RP), the standard pronunciation of educated speakers in the south of England. The most obvious (but by no means the only) difference between British and American pronunciation concerns the pronunciation of *a* sounds, as in the words **rather, basket,** and **repatriate**.

Accessibility

The Pocket Oxford Dictionary includes a brief but handy table of contents. Boldface guide words at the top of each page in the main section of the book indicate the first and last entry words on that page. Readers will have to get used to the fact, however, that idiomatic phrases and compound words are generally embedded within main entries. Thus, for example, the reader looking for the definition of *public address system* will find it in the entry **public.** This entry contains not only expressions beginning with the word **public,** but also expressions such as **in public,** which one might expect to find under the entry **in.**

Special Features

The Pocket Oxford Dictionary boasts several special features. The appendixes include a table of weights and measures, featuring both British and American weights and measures (where these vary) and their metric equivalents. Other tables show the Greek and Russian alphabets, books of the Bible, countries of the world, counties of the United Kingdom, and U.S. states. There is also a three-page section on the use of punctuation marks that uses the British system of single quotation marks.

Graphics and Format

With a trim size of 4¼″ × 7″ and a thickness of 2″, the *Pocket Oxford Dictionary* is somewhat larger than the typical pocket dictionary. Each page is divided into two columns. Entry words are in boldface and overhang the text, making them easy to see. Compound words, variant forms, and idioms within the main entry are also printed in boldface. The type is small but legible, and the white space is adequate for a book of this size. The paper is thin and there is show-through, which may annoy some readers. The book is sturdily bound, however, and includes a book jacket.

Summary

Although this edition of *The Pocket Oxford Dictionary* makes a number of concessions to the contemporary language and the contemporary reader, it is still predominantly British in its orientation. Its treatment of vocabulary, spelling, definitions, pronunciation, and usage will serve the British user very well. Unless American readers have a special need for an authoritative British dictionary of this size, they would do better to choose an American paperback dictionary, such as *The Merriam-Webster Dictionary*, based on that publisher's reputable COLLEGIATE DICTIONARY, tenth edition.

Random House Unabridged Dictionary

Facts at a Glance

Full title: **Random House Unabridged Dictionary, Second Edition**
Publisher: Random House
Editor: Stuart Berg Flexner
Edition reviewed: © 1993

Number of pages: 2,520
Number of entries: more than 315,000
Number of illustrations: 2,400
Intended readership: high school to adult
Trim size: 9½″ × 12¼″
Binding: hardcover

Price: $89.95
Sold in bookstores
ISBN 0-679-42917-4
No stated revision policy

Introduction and Scope

The 1993 printing of a work that originally came out in 1987, the second edition of the *Random House Unabridged Dictionary* features a very up-to-date lexicon. Late Editor-in-Chief Stuart Berg Flexner's preface, unchanged from the original 1987 printing, best states the purposes of this volume:

> (1) to provide the user with an accurate, accessible guide to the meanings, spellings, pronunciations, usage, and history of the words in our language . . . (2) to provide a scrupulously up-to-date dictionary of record, a storehouse and mirror of the language that will serve the user not only in the present, but for years to come; (3) to bring to the user the results of the most recent, authoritative research and knowledge from scholars and experts in all fields, edited with care.

This new printing of *Random House* continues its not uncontroversial tradition of recording the most current words possible.

Authority

The *Random House Unabridged Dictionary* was first published in 1966 as *The Random House Dictionary of the English Language,* a mere five years after the pub-

Random House
Unabridged Dictionary, Second Edition

❶ Syllabication indicated by centered dots

❷ Italicized part-of-speech labels followed by inflected forms in boldface type

❸ Variant spelling notes British preference

❹ Etymology appears in brackets following definitions

❺ Run-on entry follows main entry and etymology

❻ Captioned drawing illustrates definition 1

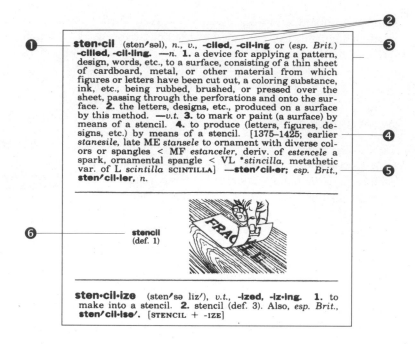

sten·cil (sten′səl), *n., v.,* **-ciled, -cil·ing** or (*esp. Brit.*) **-cilled, -cil·ling.** —*n.* **1.** a device for applying a pattern, design, words, etc., to a surface, consisting of a thin sheet of cardboard, metal, or other material from which figures or letters have been cut out, a coloring substance, ink, etc., being rubbed, brushed, or pressed over the sheet, passing through the perforations and onto the surface. **2.** the letters, designs, etc., produced on a surface by this method. —*v.t.* **3.** to mark or paint (a surface) by means of a stencil. **4.** to produce (letters, figures, designs, etc.) by means of a stencil. [1375–1425; earlier *stanesile,* late ME *stansele* to ornament with diverse colors or spangles < MF *estanceler,* deriv. of *estencele* a spark, ornamental spangle < VL *stincilla,* metathetic var. of L *scintilla* SCINTILLA] —**sten′cil·er;** *esp. Brit.,* **sten′cil·ler,** *n.*

stencil (def. 1)

sten·cil·ize (sten′sə līz′), *v.t.,* **-ized, -iz·ing. 1.** to make into a stencil. **2.** stencil (def. 3). Also, *esp. Brit.,* **sten′cil·ise′.** [STENCIL + -IZE]

lishing of the controversial (to linguistic scholars, at least) WEBSTER'S THIRD NEW INTERNATIONAL DICTIONARY OF THE ENGLISH LANGUAGE, UNABRIDGED. Edited by the late Jess Stein, the 260,000-entry volume was the newest—if comparatively smaller—unabridged dictionary in America. The 1987 second edition had an entry count of 315,000. Flexner, who worked under Stein on the first edition, was best known as editor of *The Dictionary of American Slang,* as well as author of *I Hear America Talking* and *Listening to America.*

The book jacket of the 1993 printing states that over 1,000 new words and meanings have been added and that 1,500 entries and definitions have been updated since the 1987 edition. None of the prefatory or appendix material has been updated for this printing. Flexner is still listed as the editor-in-chief, even though he died in 1990.

The editors list more than 350 consultants, many of whom are academically affiliated or editors of magazines or journals. A list of an additional 49 "Special Consultants" includes writers such as Toni Morrison, Gay Talese, and Alvin Toffler.

Comprehensiveness of Entries

Random House's 315,000 entries place it well below the some 460,000 of the latest printing of its primary competitor, WEBSTER'S THIRD. *Random House*'s entries, though, clearly reflect its 1993 revision date. Computer-related terms and acronyms include **BIOS** (*Basic Input Output System*), **CD-ROM, emoticon** (such as the sideways smile face now seen in many electronic bulletin board communications), **RISC** (*Reduced Instruction Set Computer*), and **SCSI** (*Small Computer System Inter-*

face). Computer-related definitions for **trojan horse** and **virus** are also present. Current science-related entries include the AIDS drug **AZT, DNA fingerprinting, Hubble Space Telescope, Prozac,** and **RU 486.** A random sample of the 50 entries from **glue** to **glyceride** includes the following scientific and technical entries: **glueball, gluon, glutamic acid, gluten, glyburide,** and **glycemia.**

Vulgar terms are present as main entries, and vulgar definitions—usually labeled *Slang* (*vulgar*)—are included for words such as **blow, cock, jump,** and **lay.** Britishisms are likewise present as main entry words such as **colour** and **lorry,** as well as within definitions of words such as **bonnet** and **lift.** Alternate British pronunciations are also given for entries such as **Derby.**

Random House is laden with features that contribute to its reference value. Etymologies are present for many entries—often with a span of dates marking when the word was first recorded in English. In its 1987 printing, *Random House* was the first unabridged dictionary to include these. In fact, many "etymologies" consist solely of dates at the end of an entry. The entry for **Antwerp blue,** for example, concludes "[1825–35]." Etymologies also note Americanisms, as at the end of the **gubernatorial** entry: "[1725–35, *Amer.;* < L *gubernātōr-* (s. of *gubernātor*) steersman, GOVERNOR + -IAL]."

The book jacket claims more than 10,500 synonym lists and 900 synonym studies. Antonyms are also present in many instances. Both are indicated in boldface by **-Syn.** and **-Ant.,** respectively, along with the definition numbers they refer to, as at the conclusion of **mild:**

—**Syn. 1.** soft, pleasant. See **gentle. 3.** temperate, moderate, clement. **4.** bland. —**Ant. 1.** forceful. **3.** severe. **6.** harsh.

Synonym studies are lengthier, more detailed descriptions of synonyms, as at the conclusion of the entry for **join:**

> —**Syn. 1.** link, couple, fasten, attach; conjoin, combine; associate, consolidate, amalgamate. JOIN, CONNECT, UNITE all imply bringing two or more things together more or less closely. JOIN may refer to a connection or association of any degree of closeness, but often implies direct contact: *One joins the corners of a mortise together.* CONNECT implies a joining as by a tie, link, or wire: *One connects two batteries.* UNITE implies a close joining of two or more things, so as to form one: *One unites layers of veneer sheets to form plywood.* **10.** abut, border. —**Ant. 1, 12.** separate, divide.

Random House employs a wide variety of usage labels, including "baby talk," "facetious," and "eye dialect." The work is particularly strong in identifying regionalisms, not just through usage labels for entries such as **bodacious,** which is labeled as *South Midland and Southern U.S.,* but also through special "Regional Variation Notes" that conclude some entries. (Flexner's preface acknowledges the guidance of consultants from such projects as the *Linguistic Atlas of the United States* and the *Dictionary of American Regional English;* an opening essay by Craig M. Carver, "Dialects," includes maps of regions of American English.) The entry for **cottage cheese** concludes with the following:

> —**Regional Variation.** FARMER CHEESE and FARMER'S CHEESE are widely used throughout the U.S. as terms for a kind of COTTAGE CHEESE. This same kind of cheese, with varying curd and sourness, is also called SOUR-MILK CHEESE in Eastern New England; CURD or CURD CHEESE, chiefly in the Northeastern and Southern U.S.; POT CHEESE, chiefly in the Hudson Valley; SMEARCASE, chiefly in the North Midland U.S., and sometimes CREAM CHEESE in the Gulf States.

Other features of *Random House* include "Pronunciation Notes" (discussed below) and some 240 "Usage Notes" at the conclusion of entries. These usage notes are especially susceptible to the charges of "permissiveness" that are leveled at *Random House* by purists, although they are in keeping with the work's generally descriptive philosophy. The note for **anyone,** for example, simply steers users in the right direction:

> —**Usage.** ANYONE as a pronoun meaning "anybody" or "any person at all" is written as one word: *Does anyone have the correct time?* The two-word phrase ANY ONE means "any single member of a group of persons or things" and is often followed by *of: Can any one of the members type? Any one of these books is exciting reading.* ANYONE is somewhat more formal than ANYBODY. See also **each, they.**

In others, as for **cohort,** some history is introduced:

> —**Usage.** A COHORT was originally one of the ten divisions of a legion in the Roman army, containing from 300 to 600 men. The most common use of COHORT today is in the sense "group" or "company": *A cohort of hangers-on followed the singer down the corridor. . . .*

Random House uses only invented phrases for its illustrative examples. According to the book jacket, over 75,000 sample sentences and phrases are included, which is a far cry from the some 200,000 illustrative quotations used in WEBSTER'S THIRD. That volume takes a different approach from *Random House,* using only examples from literature.

Although generally accurate in conveying usage, some of *Random House*'s examples may not be readily recognizable by a nonnative speaker. The second definition of **gratuitous,** "being without apparent reason, cause, or justification" is illustrated by the phrase "a gratuitous insult" rather than the more commonly encountered "gratuitous violence." At other times, one wishes for more. Of the 11 definitions for **isolate,** for example, only one has an illustrative phrase.

Biographical and geographical entries are incorporated within the main lexicon of *Random House* and are up-to-date. **Germany** (as a unified country), **Lithuania** and **Ukraine** (as independent republics), and **Boris Yeltsin** all have entries. There are no entries for *Violeta Chamorro* or *Michael Jackson.* The absence of the former is particularly puzzling, as she was included in the 1992 RANDOM HOUSE WEBSTER'S COLLEGE DICTIONARY.

Quality and Currency of Entries

Main entries in *Random House* appear as syllabicated words in boldface type, followed by the pronunciation in parentheses, the part-of-speech label and usage labels in italics, and any inflected forms in boldface type. Numbered definitions follow, with illustrative sentences in italics. Etymologies and/or dates of the word's first written occurrence come after the definitions in brackets. Any synonym, usage, pronunciation, or regional variation notes conclude the entries.

Definitions are ordered, according to the user's guide, with the most frequently encountered meanings "generally" coming before less common ones within each part-of-speech group. This is in opposition to the practice of WEBSTER'S THIRD, which lists definitions in historical order.

A user must be fairly well-educated to comprehend some of the more technical and scientific entries, though this is not unusual for an unabridged work. The first definition for **marsupial,** for example, begins: "any viviparous, nonplacental mammal of the order Marsupialia." Overall, the definitions are clear, although somewhat shorter than those in WEBSTER'S THIRD. The following entry is typical:

> **frus·trate** (frus′trāt), *v.,* **-trat·ed, -trat·ing,** *adj.* —*v.t.* **1.** to make (plans, efforts, etc.) worthless or of no avail; defeat; nullify: *The student's indifference frustrated the teacher's efforts to help him.* **2.** to disappoint or thwart (a person): *a talented woman whom life had frustrated.* —*v.i.* **3.** to become frustrated: *His trouble is that he frustrates much too easily.* —*adj.* **4.** frustrated. [1400–50; late ME < L

frustrātus, ptp. of *frustrārī,* v. deriv. of *frustrā* in vain] — **frus′trat·er,** *n.* —**frus′trat·ing·ly,** *adv.* —**frus·tra·tive** (frus′trā tiv, -trə-), *adj.*
—**Syn. 1.** balk, foil, circumvent. See **thwart.**

Random House features many up-to-date entries, including **bungee jumping, dis, fax, HDTV, intifada, maquiladora, rap music, retrovirus,** and **virtual reality.** Like its shorter offspring, RANDOM HOUSE WEBSTER'S COLLEGE DICTIONARY, the volume includes an entry for **politically correct** as well as some words that exemplify the practice: **anchorperson** and **chairperson.**

Syllabication and Pronunciation

Primary and secondary stresses are shown using boldface and roman accent marks, respectively, in the pronunciations of both the main entry and the inflections. Inflected forms show syllable divisions for the parts that differ from the main entry, as the above example has shown. Run-on entries receive the same treatment as main entries: complete divisions are noted with syllabication, as well as pronunciation if it is sufficiently different.

Random House favors a pronunciation system using diacritical marks rather than the International Phonetic Alphabet (IPA). As explained in the user's guide, this "orthographically motivated" system makes "efficient use of the knowledge that a native speaker of English has about the language." The editors have added IPA equivalents at the end of the descriptions of the pronunciation symbols in the user's guide. A pronunciation key also appears inside the front cover and on the page opposite the beginning of the letter *A.* A concise pronunciation key appears on the lower right-hand corner of every other right-hand page. The pronunciation system will be easier for the average user than that of WEBSTER'S THIRD, which employs over 75 symbols and fails to give concise pronunciation keys within the main text of the dictionary. Alternative pronunciations in *Random House* are listed in order of frequency, separated by commas:

con·voy (*v.* kon′voi, kən voi′; *n.* kon′voi)

to·ma·to (tə mā′tō, -mä′-)

Random House also uses pronunciation notes at the conclusion of some entries to "discuss the regional distribution, acceptability, or history of various pronunciations of the entry word." The following, for the entry **forte,** is typical:

—**Pronunciation.** In the sense of a person's strong point (*He draws well, but sculpture is his forte*), the older and historical pronunciation of FORTE is the one-syllable (fôrt) or (fōrt). The word is derived from the French word *fort* 'strong.' A two-syllable pronunciation (fôr′tā) is increasingly heard, especially from younger educated speakers, perhaps owing to confusion with the musical term *forte,* pronounced in English as (fôr′tā) and in Italian as (fôR′te).

Both the one- and two-syllable pronunciations of FORTE are now considered standard.

Accessibility

Random House is arranged in strict alphabetical order, letter by letter, with abbreviations fully integrated: **mdse., me, ME, Me, Me., M.E., M.E.A., meacon.** The seven-page "How to Use the Random House Dictionary" provides adequate coverage of the various components of an entry, although it does not include a page of sample entries, as do most other dictionaries. Instead, each portion of an entry is illustrated with its own highlighted example from the lexicon. Under "Parts of Speech," for instance, the following sample entry appears:

ben·ze·noid (ben′zÚ noid′), *Chem.* —*adj.* **1.** of, pertaining to, or similar to benzene, esp. with respect to structure. — *n.* **2.** any benzene compound. [1885–90; BENZENE + -OID]

Boldface guide words appear at the upper outside corners of every page. Red thumb indexes are included for every two letters of the alphabet, the supplements, and the maps.

Special Features

Random House concludes with an abundance of supplements that may prove useful to the home purchaser but will be of little use in libraries. Fully 262 pages are devoted to supplementary material, and an additional 32 pages contain full-color maps. The supplements are: "Signs and Symbols," "Directory of Colleges and Universities," "The Declaration of Independence," "The Constitution of the United States," four concise foreign language-English dictionaries (French, Spanish, Italian, and German), a "Basic Manual of Style," "Words Commonly Confused," and "Words Commonly Misspelled." In addition, the inside back cover includes tables entitled "Weights and Measures" and "Foreign Alphabets." Forty-five charts and tables are scattered throughout the dictionary itself, including "Chemical Elements," "International Phonetic Alphabet," "The Planets," "Roman Numerals," and "Taxonomic Classification."

The beginning of *Random House* features some excellent essays, none changed from the original 1987 printing of the second edition. "Usage: Change and Variation," by Thomas J. Creswell and Virginia McDavid, tackles the question of the role dictionaries should have in determining proper usage. "Dialects," by Craig M. Carver, reflects the emphasis the editors of *Random House* have given to that field.

Graphics and Format

All illustrations (except maps, which appear against a white background) are black-and-white line drawings set off in gray-colored boxes. The illustrations are clear and contribute to the overall attractiveness of the work. *Random House*'s crisp, bright design is more appealing and easier to read than that of WEBSTER'S THIRD. Margins are adequate and the binding is sufficient for a work of this size.

Summary

The *Random House Unabridged Dictionary* remains the most up-to-date unabridged dictionary on the market. Although by simple word count WEBSTER'S THIRD remains a stronger work, *Random House* will appeal to users who require a work that reflects more contemporary English. Although WEBSTER'S THIRD generally features lengthier definitions, some users may be confused by its preference for sequencing them historically, rather than by frequency of use, as *Random House* does. *Random House* includes a number of supplements that may be of value to a home purchaser. Its pronunciation system is easier to use than that of WEBSTER'S THIRD, and it includes pronunciation keys throughout the text. Although it has fewer illustrative quotations than does WEBSTER'S THIRD, *Random House*'s graphic design and typeface make it easier to read.

The revised and updated second edition of *Random House* may not be a necessary purchase for those who already own the 1987 printing of the second edition, but it will certainly make a fine purchase for any individual or library that does not already own it. At just under $90, it remains one of the best buys in reference publishing.

Random House Webster's College Dictionary

Facts at a Glance

Full title: **Random House Webster's College Dictionary**
Publisher: Random House
Editor: Robert B. Costello
Edition reviewed: © 1992

Number of pages: 1,600
Number of entries: 180,000
Number of illustrations: 800, all in black and white
Intended readership: high school to adult
Trim size: 7" × 9½"
Binding: hardcover

Price: $18 (plain edged); $20 (thumb indexed)
Sold in bookstores
ISBN 0-679-41420-7 (plain edged);
    ISBN 0-679-41410-X (thumb indexed)
No stated revision policy

Introduction and Scope

Random House Webster's College Dictionary calls itself "a state-of-the-art compilation of modern words and meanings" and "a reliable, up-to-date guide to information about our vigorous, constantly evolving language." This contemporary, current dictionary is intended for high school students, college students, and adults. Although the work's 1992 publication date makes it slightly older than the 1993 MERRIAM-WEBSTER'S COLLEGIATE DICTIONARY, tenth edition, it lives up to the Random House reputation of including many very recently coined—if not downright trendy—words in its 180,000 entries.

Authority

This work first appeared in 1968 as the College Edition of the *Random House Dictionary of the English Language*. In 1975, it became known as the *Random House College Dictionary*. With the 1991 publication, the name *Webster's* was added to the title. The name change and book cover design caused Merriam-Webster to successfully sue Random House for damages, but Random House was allowed to continue to use the well-recognized lexicographer's name within its title.

This dictionary was the first book to benefit from the Random House Living Dictionary Project, a large database created from the RANDOM HOUSE UNABRIDGED DICTIONARY, SECOND EDITION. As such, the editors were able to update more easily online the new words and senses that make this dictionary so current. Robert B. Costello, the editor-in-chief of this work and senior editor of the second edition of the RANDOM HOUSE UNABRIDGED DICTIONARY, notes in the preface that "new vocabulary can be added instantly" using this system.

Random House Webster's takes the same generally descriptive approach to the language that the editors of the unabridged first edition (the late Jess Stein) and second edition (the late Stuart B. Flexner) took. Forty editors contributed to this work, along with four consultants who are professors in the fields of English and linguistics.

Comprehensiveness of Entries

Random House Webster's entry count of 180,000 places it above the recently published MERRIAM-WEBSTER'S COLLEGIATE DICTIONARY, tenth edition, which has 160,000 entries, but below THE AMERICAN HERITAGE COLLEGE DICTIONARY, third edition, which has about 200,000 entries.

A randomly selected sample of the 50 entries from **riot** to **ritardando** reveals coverage of a wide variety of subjects. Nine technical terms (**riot gun, riot shield, rip cord, riposte, riprap, ripsaw, riptide, RISC, ritardando**), one scientific term (**ripple mark**), and one mathematical term (**rising rhythm**) are defined along with two slang words, one chiefly British entry (**ripping**), an Italian historical period (**Risorgimento**), a

Frankish division, three entries that include idioms, and **Rip Van Winkle.** Although no vulgarisms appear in this sample, vulgar words appear as main entries or within the definitions of other words, where they are usually labeled "Slang (vulgar)." British entry words are labeled *Chiefly Brit.;* British definitions for words with other meanings are labeled *Brit.*

Random House Webster's has several features that enable the user to select the correct use of a word. Synonym studies exist for many entries. They can be quite detailed, as for the entry **irony,** which uses 14 lines to explain **irony, satire,** and **sarcasm.** "See" references at the end of entries also point the reader toward synonym studies. For example, the entry **equip** ends with "—**Syn.** See FURNISH."

Usage notes give the reader information about words that are often confused with other words, such as **principal,** and words that may be incorrectly used in common speech, such as **literally.** Cross-references to the notes are included in related entries.

Random House Webster's employs more than the usual number of descriptive labels, including *Chiefly New Eng.* and *Dial.* for general dialect; field labels including *Math.* and *Music.;* labels of time for obsolete or archaic words and older usages; and many labels of style, including *Informal, Nonstandard, Slang, Disparaging, Offensive, Facetious, Baby Talk, Chiefly Literary, Eye Dialect,* and *Pron. Spelling* (for entries such as **gonna** and **lemme**).

Finally, *Random House Webster's* includes etymologies in brackets at the end of many entries. Following in the path of its parent work, which was the first unabridged dictionary (other than THE OXFORD ENGLISH DICTIONARY) to include etymologies, *Random House Webster's* often records the approximate dates of when many words entered the language. Unfortunately, there is liberal use of abbreviations, as the etymology of **future** demonstrates: "[1325–75; ME *futur* < AF, OF < L *fūtūrus* about to be (fut. participle of *esse* to be)]." In many cases the etymology per se is not included, but dates of first use are. The entry **joystick,** for example, simply concludes with "[1905–10]."

The editors created the illustrative quotations, which appear in italics within the entries. Although most are brief phrases rather than complete sentences, they convey the meanings well. At times, however, their absence is conspicuous. Of the ten definitions for **proposition,** for example, only the fourth is illustrated by a phrase. None of the seven definitions for **propagate** has an example phrase. Such omissions may make the work difficult for use by nonnative English speakers.

Both biographical and geographical entries are included within the main lexicon, and the work is up-to-date here as well with entries for **Violeta Chamorro, Germany** as a unified country, **Lithuania** and **Ukraine** as independent republics, and **Boris Yeltsin** as head of Russia. There is no entry for *Michael Jackson.*

Quality and Currency of Entries

On the whole, entries in *Random House Webster's* are accurate, well organized, and up-to-date. Definitions are ordered so the most common meaning is given first within each part of speech. The definitions are written at a senior high school or higher reading level, but they are clear and often detailed. **Photography,** for example, is defined as:

> **1.** the process or art of producing images of objects on sensitized surfaces by the chemical action of light or of other forms of radiant energy. **2.** CINEMATOGRAPHY. [1839]

Main entries appear as syllabicated words in boldface type, followed by the pronunciation in parentheses, the part-of-speech label and any usage labels in italics, and any inflectional forms in boldface type. The numbered definitions follow with illustrative sentences in italics within the definitions. Etymologies and/or dates of the word's first written occurrence come in brackets at the end of the definitions. Synonym notes, usage notes, and derived entries—when present—conclude the entries. A typical entry follows:

> **in·fec·tious** (in fek′shəs), *adj.* **1.** communicable by infection, as from one person to another or from one part of the body to another. **2.** causing or communicating infection. **3.** tending to spread quickly and generally: *infectious laughter.* **4.** *Obs.* diseased. [1535–45]
> —**in·fec′tious·ly,** *adv.*
> —**in·fec′tious·ness,** *n.* —**Syn.** See CONTAGIOUS.

Given the dictionary's computerized database and relatively recent publication date, it is not surprising that this work is extremely up-to-date. Typical entries include **bungee jumping, dis, fax, HDTV, intifada, maquiladora, retrovirus,** and **virtual reality.** The entry for **rap** (which has 15 definitions) contains a "see" reference to **rap music.** New definitions for old words such as **Trojan horse** and **virus** are also present.

Syllabication and Pronunciation

In this work, syllabication is shown within each entry word. Primary and secondary stresses are indicated by boldface and roman accent marks in the pronunciation of both the main entry and its inflections. Inflected forms show syllable divisions for the parts that differ from the main entry. Run-on entries receive the same treatment as main entries: complete divisions are noted with syllabication. Some examples of syllabication are: **a·bout** (ə bout′), **Eng·lish** (ing′glish *or, often,* -lish), **o·bey** (ō bā′), and **rhythm** (rith′əm).

As in the RANDOM HOUSE UNABRIDGED DICTIONARY, second edition, the pronunciations in *Random House Webster's* employ diacritical marks rather than the International Phonetic Alphabet (IPA). According to the "Pronunciation Guide," this system "reflects underlying sound-spelling relationships in English," whereas the

IPA obscures the underlying relationship between sounds. Forty-five symbols are used as well as seven symbols for "Non-English Sounds." The full pronunciation key appears only in the prefatory material, but an abbreviated version appears in the lower right-hand corner of right-hand pages.

The work uses alternative pronunciations, with the most frequently used form listed first. Only the differing part of the pronunciation is shown, for example: **co·gnac** (kōn'yak, kon'-, kôn'-).

Accessibility

Readers should be able to locate terms easily in *Random House Webster's*. The entries are arranged in strict alphabetical order, letter by letter (**newcomer, new criticism, New Deal, New Delhi, newel**), with abbreviations fully integrated into the scheme (**bozo, bp., B/P, B.P., b.p., BPD, B picture, B.P.O.E.**). Each page of the dictionary has guide words for the first and last entries on the page in boldface type above the outer column.

The 19-page "Using This Dictionary" contains virtually everything the reader will need to know to locate information in the dictionary and includes clearly labeled examples for each explanation. It is often difficult, however, to locate a specific piece of information in this section, perhaps due to its length or the lack of subheadings within each section. A sample two-page spread precedes the user's guide, with each part of an entry labeled.

Alternate spellings are well represented in this work and point the user to the preferred spelling using small capital letters:

> **es·thet·ic** (es thet'ik), *adj., n.* AESTHETIC.
> **mous·tache** (mus'tash, mə stash'), *n.* MUSTACHE.

A thumb-indexed version of the dictionary is available for $2 more than the regular version.

Special Features

Several special features conclude the dictionary. An eight-page "Guide for Writers" contains rules on punctuation, use of italics, capitalization, manuscript preparation, footnotes, in-text citations, and reference lists. A two-page essay entitled "Avoiding Sexist Language" provides guidance on how writers can avoid sexism in word choices and usage. "From Sounds to Spellings" is a two-page table that can be used to find words if readers are unsure of spellings. A one-page index to the features and to selected illustrations from the lexicon ends the volume.

Graphics and Format

Overall, the appearance of *Random House Webster's* detracts from the work's value. Nearly all illustrations are small black-and-white line drawings. Only about a third of the pages have any illustrations at all. When illustrations do appear, however, they are current and helpful.

The design is crowded, the main print size is small, and the use of a variety of typefaces and styles is confusing. The volume lacks the crisp, bright appearance of THE AMERICAN HERITAGE COLLEGE DICTIONARY. Pages are relatively thin and the backing page does, on occasion, show through. Of particular concern are the extremely narrow margins at the gutter of the open page. The text is readable, but the user will often have to press the page flat before reading an entry. The work is sturdily bound, however, and this pressure should not shorten its life.

Summary

The *Random House Webster's College Dictionary* is an up-to-date dictionary that compares favorably with similar works on the market. It has a greater number of up-to-date entries than MERRIAM-WEBSTER'S COLLEGIATE DICTIONARY, tenth edition. *Random House Webster's* sole drawbacks are its relatively small print and unattractive page design—particularly as those features compare with those in THE AMERICAN HERITAGE COLLEGE DICTIONARY. The latter also features a far greater number of illustrations. *Random House Webster's,* however, has the advantage of being based not only on the most up-to-date unabridged dictionary in the English language, but also on a computerized lexicographic database that will ensure that it will always remain current. These features, combined with the clear definitions, usage notes, and synonym studies, add up to a fine collegiate dictionary that will not disappoint its users.

Webster Comprehensive Dictionary: Encyclopedic Edition

Facts at a Glance

Full title: **Webster Comprehensive Dictionary: Encyclopedic Edition**
Publisher: J. G. Ferguson
Editors: S. Stephenson Smith; Robert W. Voorhees; William Morris
Edition reviewed: © 1992

Number of volumes: 2
Number of pages: 1,728
Number of entries: 90,000
Number of illustrations: 1,500, most in black and white
Intended readership: grade 8 and up
Trim size: 8" × 10¾"
Binding: hardcover

Price: contact publisher for price information
Sold door-to-door
ISBN 0-89434-135-9
Next scheduled revision: 1995

Webster Comprehensive Dictionary: Encyclopedic Edition

❶ Syllabication shown by a centered dot

❷ Italicized part-of-speech label precedes definitions to which it applies

❸ Informative illustration includes title and callouts

❹ Scientific name, in italics, given for each variety

❺ Italicized usage label

❻ Etymology enclosed in square brackets at end of entry

❼ Cross-references set in small capitals

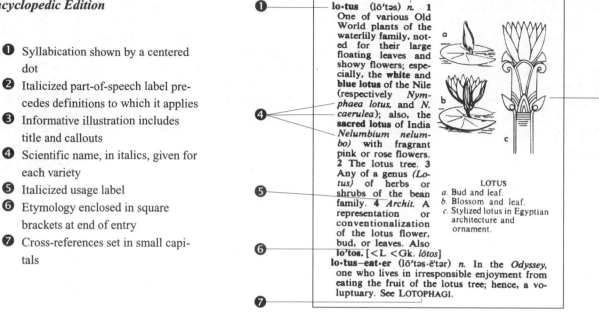

lo·tus (lō′təs) *n.* **1** One of various Old World plants of the waterlily family, noted for their large floating leaves and showy flowers; especially, the **white** and **blue lotus** of the Nile (respectively *Nymphaea lotus,* and *N. caerulea*); also, the **sacred lotus** of India *Nelumbium nelumbo*) with fragrant pink or rose flowers. **2** The lotus tree. **3** Any of a genus (*Lotus*) of herbs or shrubs of the bean family. **4** *Archit.* A representation or conventionalization of the lotus flower, bud, or leaves. Also **lo′tos.** [< L < Gk. *lōtos*]
lo·tus–eat·er (lō′təs·ē′tər) *n.* In the *Odyssey,* one who lives in irresponsible enjoyment from eating the fruit of the lotus tree; hence, a voluptuary. See LOTOPHAGI.

LOTUS
a. Bud and leaf.
b. Blossom and leaf.
c. Stylized lotus in Egyptian architecture and ornament.

Introduction and Scope

The 1992 edition of the *Webster Comprehensive Dictionary: Encyclopedic Edition* contains 1,728 pages divided between two volumes. According to the introduction, the dictionary is designed "to serve the practical and professional needs of all who speak or use the English language."

Authority

The *Webster Comprehensive Dictionary: Encyclopedic Edition* has been published in several editions with various titles, but its base is the *Funk & Wagnalls Standard Dictionary of the English Language,* first published in 1958. In choosing the lexicon for this dictionary, the editors attempted

> to secure the widest possible coverage of both the established word stock of English and of the rapidly expanding vocabularies of the arts, sciences, trades and professions.

The current edition of the *Webster Comprehensive Dictionary* lists a distinguished three-member editorial board: Albert H. Marckwardt, Professor Emeritus of English and Linguistics, Princeton University; Frederic G. Cassidy, Professor of English, University of Wisconsin; and James G. McMillan, Professor of English, University of Alabama. These three were also listed in the 1984 edition, and no information about their level of contribution to more recent versions is provided. Long lists of consulting editors and consultants include "many of the nation's eminent leaders in education, industry, the arts, sciences, and professions." These lists are quite outdated, however, as some of the corpora-

tions mentioned are now defunct and a number of the "leaders" deceased.

Comprehensiveness of Entries

The 90,000 entries in the *Webster Comprehensive Dictionary* make this work less complete than other semi-abridged dictionaries such as MERRIAM-WEBSTER'S COLLEGIATE DICTIONARY, tenth edition, with 160,000 entries, or THE AMERICAN HERITAGE COLLEGE DICTIONARY, with 200,000 entries. The lexicon includes many scientific and technical terms; however, the vocabulary has not been updated to include many of the computer terms that are now commonly used. Vulgarisms are not included.

One strong point of this dictionary is the inclusion of extensive synonym/antonym guides that contain example sentences. Usage labels, usage notes, and full etymologies are also provided for many entries throughout the book. Illustrated examples, provided occasionally, are invented phrases or sentences. These features convey a feel for the English language that most collegiate dictionaries do not.

Biographical entries are included within the main lexicon but have not been recently updated. None of the following receive entries: *Violeta Chamorro, Michael Jackson,* or *Boris Yeltsin.* In addition, the list of U.S. presidents concludes with Ronald Reagan. Geographical entries also appear within the main dictionary but are outdated as well. For example, **Germany** is listed as a divided country, and **Lithuania** and **Ukraine** are labeled "constituent republics" of the Soviet Union. Most of the geographical entries are repeated—in a shorter version—in the gazetteer, which appears at the back of the book. Some of the information in the gazetteer has been updated, such as the status of **Germany** as a unified country.

Quality and Currency of Entries

Main entry words are syllabicated, appear in boldface type, and overhang the text. Following the entry word are the pronunciation, part(s) of speech, and plural or restricted forms with variant spellings. Multiple definitions are numbered. Field and usage labels appear in italics, and etymologies appear in brackets at the end of the entry.

According to the book's introduction, "Either the most relevant or the most general meaning is given first. . . ." The introduction also states, "Where the current sense of a word is more meaningful in the light of its history, however, the original sense is given first."

The definitions in this work are sometimes inadequate and even misleading. For example, in the following entry, the negative aspect of the word **stereotype** is not adequately conveyed in the definition.

> **ster·e·o·type** (ster′ē·ə·tīp′, stir′-) *n.* **1** A plate taken in type metal from a matrix, as of paper, reproducing the surface from which the matrix was made. **2** Stereotypy. **3** Anything made or processed in this way. **4** A conventional or hackneyed expression, custom, or mode of thought. —*v.t.* ·**typed,** ·**typing 1** To make a stereotype of. **2** To fix firmly or unalterably.

The dictionary lacks currency in vocabulary selection. None of the following words are defined in the text: *bungee jumping, dis, fax, HDTV, intifada, maquiladora, rap,* or *virtual reality.*

Syllabication and Pronunciation

Syllabication in both main entries and inflected forms is shown with centered dots. Primary stress is indicated with a bold accent mark and secondary stress with a roman accent mark.

According to the editors, the pronunciation system used in this dictionary "is one which has been determined to be the simplest, most meaningful, and accurate one for the purposes of dictionary transcription." It uses the letters of the alphabet with standard diacritical marks. Alternate pronunciations are provided. The full pronunciation guide is included in the front matter, and an abbreviated key appears at the bottom of every right-hand page.

Accessibility

The entries are sequenced in strict letter-by-letter order: **aide, aide-de-camp, Aidin, AIDS, aiglet.** Guide words appear at the top left and top right corner of every page, with the page number centered between them. Thumb indexes are not provided. Alternate spellings give "see" references.

The explanatory information in the front of the dictionary is quite detailed. However, the majority of this information is presented in essay format, which is much less accessible to the average reader than the more graphically oriented format used in many other dictionaries. The front matter does, however, include a useful single page of sample entries with labels.

Special Features

Webster Comprehensive Dictionary contains several appendixes at the end of the second volume, including lists of abbreviations, quotations, and members of the United Nations; a gazetteer; and essays on grammar, public speaking, and business law and wills. Much of the material in the appendixes is outdated and of questionable value, however. For example, in the essay "Grammar and Usage Handbook," the section on business correspondence discusses typewriter type, carbon paper, and erasing. "The Library Research Paper" instructs the reader on how to use the (noncomputerized) card catalog and cites reference books with copyright dates in the 1950s and early 1960s. These sections fail to even acknowledge the widespread use of computers in homes, schools, offices, and libraries.

Graphics and Format

About 1 in 90 entries is accompanied by a black-and-white line drawing. For the most part, the drawings are clear. The illustrations are labeled, and some include captions with additional information. Within the main lexicon, some charts and tables are shown, including foreign alphabets, meteorological symbols, and U.S. presidents (through Ronald Reagan).

Two sections of photographs and drawings on glossy paper are randomly placed—one section in each volume. The unusual combination of subject matter shown in these sections includes such diverse topics as invertebrates (glass models), architecture, canals, masks of many lands, and U.S.-manned space flights. The illustrations are a mix of black and white and color and, with only a few exceptions, look as though they have not been updated in several decades.

The book's design is reasonably attractive and readable. The dictionary is printed on good-quality paper that is nearly opaque, and the binding is durable and should withstand heavy use. The two-volume format makes this work more difficult to manage than a single-volume dictionary.

Summary

Despite the 1992 copyright, *Webster Comprehensive Dictionary: Encyclopedic Edition* is quite dated. It is similar in scope to THE OXFORD ENCYCLOPEDIC ENGLISH DICTIONARY, but it is not as current as that work. Clearly, this dictionary has not seen a major revision in many years. Unfortunately, this fact alone overshadows any merit that may have previously been found in this reference book. Readers looking for a more contemporary semi-abridged dictionary will find several other works, including MERRIAM-WEBSTER'S COLLEGIATE DICTIONARY, tenth edition, more suitable for their needs.

Webster Comprehensive Dictionary: International Edition

Facts at a Glance

Full title: **Webster Comprehensive Dictionary: International Edition**
Publisher: J. G. Ferguson
Editors: S. Stephenson Smith; Robert W. Voorhees; William Morris
Edition reviewed: © 1992

Number of volumes: 2
Number of pages: 1,536
Number of entries: 90,000
Number of illustrations: 1,500, all in black and white
Intended readership: grade 8 and up
Trim size: 8" × 10¾"
Binding: hardcover

Price: contact publisher for price information
Sold door-to-door
ISBN 0-89434-136-7
Next scheduled revision: 1995

Introduction and Scope

The *Webster Comprehensive Dictionary: International Edition* is nearly identical in content to the WEBSTER COMPREHENSIVE DICTIONARY: ENCYCLOPEDIC EDITION. The only difference is that the *International Edition* does not include about 200 pages of supplementary reference material and two 16-page sections of photographs that appear in the ENCYCLOPEDIC EDITION. Because much of this supplementary material is outdated, its omission in this work is of little importance. For a complete description of the *International Edition,* see the review of the ENCYCLOPEDIC EDITION. Neither work is a recommended purchase, since the lexicons are out-of-date and the entry counts are smaller than those of most semi-abridged dictionaries.

Webster Illustrated Contemporary Dictionary: Encyclopedic Edition

Facts at a Glance

Full title: **Webster Illustrated Contemporary Dictionary: Encyclopedic Edition**
Publisher: J. G. Ferguson
Editor: Sidney I. Landau, Editor-in-Chief
Edition reviewed: © 1992

Number of pages: 1,149
Number of entries: 85,000
Number of illustrations: 970, most in black and white
Intended readership: high school to adult
Trim size: 6¾" × 10"
Binding: hardcover

Price: contact publisher for price information
Sold door-to-door
ISBN 0-89434-139-1
No stated revision policy

Introduction and Scope

The 85,000-entry *Webster Illustrated Contemporary Dictionary* is a revised work that, despite its 1992 copyright date, has not been through a major revision in many years and is beginning to show its age. The dictionary contains an abundance of encyclopedic supplements that may enhance its value for some; most of the supplementary material, however, is either out-of-date or of marginal value.

Authority

The *Webster Illustrated Contemporary Dictionary* has a varied history. The present edition is a revised version of *The Illustrated Contemporary Dictionary* (1978) that, in turn, was based on *The Doubleday Dictionary* (1975). Editor-in-Chief Landau, one of the country's preeminent lexicographers, is the author of *Dictionaries: The Art and Craft of Lexicography* and the editor of *Funk & Wagnall's Standard Dictionary of the English Language.*

Comprehensiveness of Entries

The work's 85,000 entries place it within a category often called "family dictionaries," those smaller than a typical collegiate dictionary yet larger than most paperback editions. Entries are included for some current terms such as **AIDS** and **hard disk,** although *CD-ROM* does not appear and the entry for **compact disc** mentions only its audio storage and playback abilities. The entries from **echelon** to **edifice** include **echidna, echinoderm, economy-sized, ecosystem, ectoderm, eczema,** and **edema.**

The preface makes it clear that the work excludes "offensive racial and religious epithets." Countries and states are included in the main lexicon as well as in a supplemental "Gazetteer." Biographical entries are relegated to a section in the encyclopedic supplements. They include **Michael Jackson** and **Boris Yeltsin,** but not *Violeta Chamorro.* The main lexicon has an entry for **Germany** as a unified country, though not for *Lithuania* or *Ukraine.* The "Gazetteer" calls **Lithuania** a "republic" but refers to the *Ukraine* as **Ukrainian SSR** and a "constituent republic SW USSR." This is typical of the sometimes uneven coverage in this work.

Quality and Currency of Entries

Main entries are presented as boldface syllabicated words, followed by the pronunciation within parentheses, the part-of-speech and usage labels in italics, inflected forms, and the definitions. Idioms appear at the end of an entry, followed by an etymology, run-on derivatives, and a synonym list or usage note. The following entry is typical:

> **dis·ap·prove** (dis′ə·proov′) *v.* **·proved, ·proving** *v.t.* **1** To regard with disfavor or censure; condemn. **2** To refuse assent to; decline to approve. —*v.i.* **3** To have or express an unfavorable opinion: often with *of.* —**dis′ap·prov′al** *n.* — **dis′ap·prov′ing·ly** *adv.* —**Syn. 1** dislike, object to, frown upon, denounce, disparage.

Definitions (arranged by frequency of use) are brief and to the point, and should be understandable to most readers. Illustrative phrases and sentences were written by the editors. The volume includes some contemporary words such as **fax, intifada,** and **retrovirus,** but no entries exist for *bungee jumping, dis, HDTV, maquiladora, rap,* or *virtual reality.*

Syllabication and Pronunciation

Primary and secondary stresses are indicated by boldface and roman accent marks. Syllable divisions are given for both inflected forms and run-on entries. A pronunciation key appears at the beginning of the volume, and an abbreviated version appears at the bottom of every right-hand page. Alternative pronunciations are given, with the first being "usually the most widely used." The following entries are typical: **a·bout** (ə·bout′), **Eng·lish** (ing′glish), **o·bey** (ō·bā′, ə·bā′), and **rhythm** (rith′əm).

Accessibility

Webster Illustrated Contemporary Dictionary is arranged alphabetically, letter by letter, with abbreviations and acronyms included (**frozen custard, FRS, F.R.S., frt., fructify**). Although the user's guide is only four pages long, it sufficiently covers the basic structure of the dictionary. Boldface guide words appear on the inside and outside upper corners of every page.

Special Features

Seventeen "Encyclopedic Supplements" constitute about 20 percent of this volume. Unfortunately, many of these (such as "Business Math" and "Wills and Estate Planning") are of marginal usefulness or out-of-date. "The Library Research Paper," for example, makes no reference to online catalogs and cites several outdated reference works in its list of recommended research

tools. The "Word Processing Glossary" has an entry for **single density** disks but none for *laser printer.* The mixed coverage of the "Gazetteer" has already been mentioned. Future editions of this work should either eliminate or update these supplements.

Graphics and Format

All illustrations—except for a 16-page section of black-and-white and color photographs—are generally unremarkable line drawings. The photographs are dated, and some of the tables contain obsolete data. The table of "Planets," for example, describes Saturn as having 9 moons, although more than 20 are now believed to exist. Neptune is listed as having two moons, even though eight have been discovered.

The volume is sturdily bound. The inner margins are a bit narrow, however.

Summary

Despite the recent publication date of this work, the *Webster Illustrated Contemporary Dictionary* still has many dated portions and has been revised in what seems a hit-or-miss fashion. Although the definitions are generally clear, this work is a dubious purchase, at best.

Webster's Encyclopedic Unabridged Dictionary

Facts at a Glance

Full title: **Webster's Encyclopedic Unabridged Dictionary of the English Language**
Publisher: Random House Value Publishing
Editor: Glorya Hale
Edition reviewed: © 1989, 1993 printing

Number of pages: 1,854
Number of entries: 260,000
Number of illustrations: more than 2,000
Intended readership: high school to adult (reviewer estimate)
Trim size: 8½″ × 11″
Binding: hardcover

Price: $14 (U.S.); $19 (Canada)
Sold in bookstores and other retail outlets; also sold to libraries and schools and through other distributors
ISBN 0-517-6878-1
Next scheduled revision: 1994

Introduction and Scope

Based on the first edition of *The Random House Dictionary of the English Language* (unabridged edition, 1966), this 1,854-page work is intended to serve as a sin-

Webster's Encyclopedic Unabridged Dictionary

❶ Syllabication shown by a centered dot

❷ Italicized part-of-speech label appears before the definition or definitions to which it refers

❸ Scientific name, in italics, given for each variety

❹ Captioned illustration enhances the understanding of definition **1**

❺ Usage label, in italics, shows context of this definition

❻ Cross-reference word is in boldface type

❼ Idiom is in boldface type within the main entry

❽ Example phrase clarifies this meaning

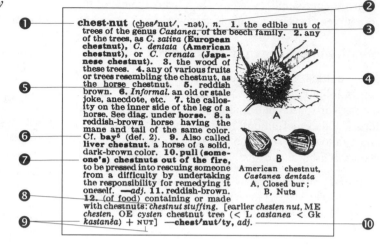

chest·nut (ches'nut/, -nət), *n.* **1.** the edible nut of trees of the genus *Castanea,* of the beech family. **2.** any of the trees, as *C. sativa* (**European chestnut**), *C. dentata* (**American chestnut**), or *C. crenata* (**Japanese chestnut**). **3.** the wood of these trees. **4.** any of various fruits or trees resembling the chestnut, as the horse chestnut. **5.** reddish brown. **6.** *Informal.* an old or stale joke, anecdote, etc. **7.** the callosity on the inner side of the leg of a horse. See diag. under **horse. 8.** a reddish-brown horse having the mane and tail of the same color. Cf. **bay**⁵ (def. 2). **9.** Also called **liver chestnut.** a horse of a solid, dark-brown color. **10. pull (someone's) chestnuts out of the fire,** to be pressed into rescuing someone from a difficulty by undertaking the responsibility for remedying it oneself. —*adj.* **11.** reddish-brown. **12.** (of food) containing or made with chestnuts: *chestnut stuffing.* [earlier *chesten nut,* ME *chesten,* OE *cysten* chestnut tree (< L *castanea* < Gk *kastanéa*) + NUT] —**chest'nut/ty,** *adj.*

American chestnut, *Castanea dentata* A, Closed bur; B, Nuts

❾ Etymology, in square brackets, includes cross-reference in small capitals

❿ Run-on entry in boldface type at the end of the entry, followed by its part-of-speech label in italics

---

gle-volume home reference library. In addition to 260,000 dictionary entries, there are also a number of special features, including a chronology of world history through 1988, a crossword puzzle dictionary, a full-color atlas of the world, a manual of style, a bibliography of major reference works, and lists of U.S. presidents and vice presidents (up to Clinton and Gore). This edition is a 1993 printing of a work with a 1989 copyright date. Its next revision is planned for 1994.

Authority

The 1966 edition of *The Random House Dictionary of the English Language* was the first unabridged English-language dictionary published since the 1961 publication of WEBSTER'S THIRD NEW INTERNATIONAL DICTIONARY. Its editor-in-chief, Jess Stein, and managing editor, Laurence Urdang, had worked on a number of different Random House reference books. The large staff of consultants included such notable names as Theodore Bernstein (usage), Nat Hentoff (jazz), and Henry Steele Commager (U.S. history). The editors characterized the *Random House Dictionary* as "an entirely new dictionary, written in midcentury for twentieth century users." They intended to provide the user with a way "to keep pace with the dynamic growth of his language." The emphasis was on words that were then new to the language. The *Random House Dictionary* was produced with the use of electronic data processing equipment, an innovation at the time. Even with such help, the entire project took about seven years to complete. This original lexicon has been maintained for the *Webster's Encyclope-*

dic Unabridged Dictionary of the English Language, with a few contemporary words added.

Comprehensiveness of Entries

As in the original *Random House Dictionary,* entries provide the "most frequently encountered" meanings first, followed by specialized or archaic definitions. Because the intent was to present words in current use, few archaic or highly technical words are included. Restrictive labels indicating regional, subject-specific, or nonstandard usage are included when appropriate. Example phrases and sentences follow the original plan of using invented phrases rather than actual quotations. This sometimes makes for less-than-lucid explanations. Synonyms and antonyms are provided at the end of many of the entries.

A concise etymology key appears at the bottom of each left-hand page, and a concise pronunciation key is found at the bottom of each right-hand page. The keys translate the symbols used in individual entries. These keys are particularly helpful since there is no guide to the dictionary, as there was in the original *Random House Dictionary.* There are also pronunciation and etymology keys and explanations of foreign-language abbreviations and sounds in the inside covers of the volume.

The randomly selected sample of the 50 entries from **fango** to **Faraday effect** includes **Fanny May,** the nickname for the Federal National Mortgage Association; both **Fano,** a town in central Italy, and its ancient name **Fanum Fortunae;** the ecclesiastical vestment **fanon;** the nautical **fantail stern;** the girl's name **Fantasy; faquir** (*fakir*); and English physicist and chemist

Faraday, Michael, along with **farad, Faraday dark space,** and the **Faraday effect,** all named after him.

Words from many fields are included, and in keeping with the intent of the first edition of the *Random House Dictionary,* particular attention is paid to current words. New words defined in this volume include **glasnost, modem, yuppie,** and **videocassette recorder.**

Biographical and geographical entries are found in the main lexicon. However, *Boris Yeltsin* (as president of Russia), *Lithuania* and *Ukraine* (as independent republics), *Violeta Chamorro* (as president of Nicaragua), *Germany* (as a unified country), and *Michael Jackson* (the singer) are not included.

Quality and Currency of Entries

The main entries begin with a boldface, syllabicated word, followed by the pronunciation in parentheses, an abbreviated part-of-speech label, the plural ending (with pronunciation if necessary), and numbered definitions. If the word is specific to a particular field (for example, biochemistry or anatomy), this is indicated immediately after the part-of-speech label. Illustrative phrases are part of many of the definitions, and etymologies (in brackets) follow. Synonyms, antonyms, and cross-references complete many of the entries.

The most common part of speech is listed first, and the first definition provided is for the most frequently encountered meaning. A typical entry looks like this:

tol·er·ate (tol′ ə rāt′), *v.t.* **-at·ed, -at·ing. 1.** to allow the existence, presence, practice or act of without prohibition or hindrance; permit. **2.** to endure without repugnance; put up with: *I can tolerate laziness, but not sloth.* **3.** *Med.* to endure or resist the action of (a drug, poison, etc.). **4.** *Obs.* to experience, undergo, or sustain, as pain or hardship. [<L *tolerāt(us),* ptp. of *tolerāre* to bear (akin to THOLE[2]; see -ATE[1]] —**tol′ er a′ tive,** *adj.* —**tol′ er a′ tor,** *n.* —**Syn. 2.** support, endure, accept.

Although some effort has been made to add words that have entered common usage since the 1966 publication of the *Random House Dictionary,* the attempt has not been sufficient. None of the following words appear: *bungee jumping, HDTV, intifada, maquiladora,* or *virtual reality. Dis* appears only as a prefix and an abbreviation, not the verb in current usage. Other new words omitted include *futon, camcorder, New Age, laser disc, Chernobyl,* and *perestroika.* **Rap, retrovirus,** and **fax** (as a noun and a verb) are found here, as are **Silicon Valley, POSSLQ, PC** (for personal computer), **CD-ROM,** and **CD** (for certificate of deposit).

Syllabication and Pronunciation

Syllabication and pronunciation are illustrated in the following examples: **a·bout** (<ə> bout′), **Eng·lish** (ing′glish or, often, -lish), **o·bey** (ō bā′), and **rhythm** (ri′ əm). Stressed syllables are indicated by boldface accent marks, and lighter marks show secondary stress.

Accessibility

As previously mentioned, there is no "How to Use the Dictionary" guide in this work, a helpful feature in the original *Random House Dictionary.* Entries are listed alphabetically, letter by letter. Pages are thumb indexed using pairs of letters (*AB, CD,* etc.). Each page is topped with boldface guide words; the first word defined appears at the upper left-hand side, and the last word defined is at the upper right-hand side. Alternate spellings are entered as separate words with the preferred spellings used as definitions: **moustache** is defined as *mustache,* and **esthetics** is defined as *aesthetics.* Under the main entries for **mustache** and **aesthetics,** these alternate spellings are included after the definitions.

Special Features

In addition to the previously noted special features, the volume includes the *Declaration of Independence,* the *Constitution of the United States,* an "Indo-European Language Chart," *The Bad Speller's Dictionary,* and a rhyming dictionary and glossary of poetic terms. The inside back cover features a table of weights and measures, including metric equivalents, and a table of five foreign alphabets. A limitation of the world history chronology appended is that it only goes up to 1988. However, the world atlas section does reflect current changes in the geography of Eastern Europe: the former U.S.S.R. is now shown as a confederation of independent republics, and the former Yugoslavia is shown as separate countries. The manual of style includes a guide to compounding words and a table of Roman numerals. The bibliography of reference works appears not to have been updated since the original *Random House Dictionary,* since the most current years of publication for titles listed are still in the late 1960s. It is unfortunate that many of the special sections included in the first *Random House Dictionary* have been omitted, particularly "Signs and Symbols" and the concise French, Spanish, Italian, and German dictionaries. Their inclusion would have strengthened this work's claim to being an "all-in-one reference center." *The Bad Speller's Dictionary* is an unusual addition to a traditional dictionary. This is a reprint of Krevisky and Linfield's 1967 work. The introduction provided for *Webster's Encyclopedic Unabridged Dictionary* is "The English Language and the Dictionary" by David Yerkes. While certainly an interesting and informative essay, it has replaced a perhaps more useful "Guide to the Dictionary."

Graphics and Format

The typeface used is rather small, although main entry words are printed in boldface. Margins are very small, resulting in crowded three-column pages. There are only about 2,000 illustrations in a work of 260,000 entries; these appear to be the same line drawings used in the original *Random House Dictionary*. Although the paper used is not so thin that backing pages show through, it does not appear to be of a very high quality. This book does lie flat when open. The cover and binding are adequate but may not withstand the heavy use expected for an "all-in-one reference center."

Summary

Although an inexpensive purchase at $14, the lack of substantial numbers of new words in this work is a cause for concern. Since the typical unabridged dictionary offers anywhere from 300,000 to 600,000 words, the 260,000 entries in this one belie the "unabridged" in its title. It has, however, significantly more entries than either THE OXFORD ENCYCLOPEDIC ENGLISH DICTIONARY or most "collegiate" semi-abridged works. The special features are of interest, and add to the overall appeal. The omission of many of the special features that were part of the original volume (noted earlier) also lessen its claim of being an "all-in-one reference center." This might be a helpful purchase for the household without any other reference books, but librarians would do better to spend scarce book budget dollars on a more current and comprehensive dictionary such as THE AMERICAN HERITAGE DICTIONARY (third edition), THE RANDOM HOUSE UNABRIDGED DICTIONARY, or WEBSTER'S THIRD NEW INTERNATIONAL DICTIONARY.

Webster's New Ideal Dictionary

Facts at a Glance

Full title: **Webster's New Ideal Dictionary**
Publisher: Merriam-Webster
Editors: Merriam-Webster staff
Edition reviewed: © 1989, second edition

Number of pages: 671
Number of entries: 60,000
Number of illustrations: 100 (reviewer estimate), all in black and white
Intended readership: student to adult
Trim size: 6¾″ × 9¼″
Binding: hardcover

Price: $11.95
Sold in bookstores
ISBN 0-87779-449-9
No stated revision policy

Introduction and Scope

Conciseness and ease of use characterize this 1989 edition of *Webster's New Ideal Dictionary.* Much of the vocabulary and style is based on *Webster's Ninth New Collegiate Dictionary,* with a considerable reduction in content. The work's 671 pages contain 60,000 entry words and phrases (compared with the *Collegiate*'s 160,000), and 100 illustrations, about one-fifth of the *Collegiate*'s. According to the preface, this work is designed "for ease and speed in getting practical answers to practical everyday questions" and is intended for home or office use.

Authority

Merriam-Webster has offered a line of concise dictionaries for more than 130 years. Predecessors of this work include *Webster's Condensed Dictionary, Webster's Practical Dictionary,* and *Webster's Ideal Dictionary.* This volume draws its authority from the Merriam-Webster name and the reputation of the *Ninth Collegiate* on which its lexicon is based.

Comprehensiveness of Entries

The words selected for inclusion in the *New Ideal Dictionary,* according to the work's preface, are those "most likely to be sought by any person looking for a meaning, pronunciation, or end-of-line division point." Most obsolete, rare, and highly technical words and meanings have been omitted. Dates of first use have been dropped from the corresponding *Webster's Ninth* entries, and simplified definitions are given. For example, the principal definition of the word **honey** in *Webster's Ninth* is "a sweet viscid material elaborated out of the nectar of flowers in the honey sac of various bees." Uses of the word as a verb, an adjective, a term of endearment and a superlative (as in a "honey of a day") are also given. The *New Ideal Dictionary* defines it only as "a sweet sticky substance made by bees . . . from the nectar of flowers."

A randomly selected sample of the 50 entries from **lima bean** to **lingua franca** includes no scientific or technical terms; the least commonly used words among the sample would probably be **limn, limonite,** and **lineament.** Purchasers should not expect this dictionary to provide definitions of difficult, technical, or obscure words.

Some entries have etymologies; most do not. Vulgar entries and offensive definitions have been omitted. Synonym lists are indicated by **syn** at the end of some entries. Usage labels may be temporal, regional, or stylistic; usage notes are brief and to the point, as in **hunker** . . . CROUCH, SQUAT—usu. used with *down.* There are no geographical or biographical entries and no illustrative phrases.

Webster's New Ideal Dictionary

❶ Italicized part-of-speech label appears before the definition or definitions to which it refers

❷ Inflected forms in boldface follow part-of-speech label; syllabication shown by a centered dot

❸ Examples of usage appear in angle brackets, with a roman swung dash standing in for the main entry word

❹ Cross-reference in small capitals

❺ Run-on entries in boldface type

❻ Homographs appear as separate, numbered entries

❼ Sense divider, in italics, introduces meaning related to the preceding sense

❽ Drawing illustrates the first definition of the second homograph

Quality and Currency of Entries

Main entries appear in boldface lowercase letters, followed by the pronunciation in reverse slashes. Part-of-speech and usage labels follow. The numbered senses, in historical order, are introduced by colons; cross-references to other entries are in small capital letters. The following example illustrates many of these features:

> **sec·ond·ary** \'sek- n- der-ē\ *adj* **1** : second in rank, value, or occurrence: INFERIOR, LESSER **2** : belonging to a second or later stage of development **3** : coming after the primary or elementary < ~ schools> **syn** subordinate, collateral, dependent

Because the lexicon is designed to provide a convenient reference for only the most commonly used words, new words and phrases like *maquiladora, bungee jumping,* and *virtual reality* do not appear.

Syllabication and Pronunciation

Entry words have centered dots to indicate end-of-line division points. These do not necessarily correspond to the syllabic divisions in the pronunciation, which are identified with small hyphens. This disparity may prove confusing to the uninitiated user. Primary and secondary stresses are indicated by raised and lowered stress marks in front of the appropriate syllable.

Alternative pronunciations are given, and a "Pronunciation Symbols" page appears at the beginning of the dictionary. Simplified pronunciation keys are provided at the bottom of right-hand pages.

Accessibility

Entries are sequenced alphabetically, letter by letter, including abbreviations. The work is not thumb indexed, but guide words appear at the top of each page. Six pages of detailed "Explanatory Notes" are a reduced version of those in the *Collegiate Dictionary*. They are clearly organized and include several examples to illustrate each feature of the text. A list of abbreviations used in the work also appears in the front matter.

Special Features

The work includes the following special features: lists of "Common English Given Names" and "Foreign Words and Phrases"; the texts of the *Declaration of Independence* and the *Constitution of the United States;* a dated list of the nations of the world and their populations, including East and West Germany and the U.S.S.R.; populations of U.S. cities and states (based on the 1980 census) and Canadian cities and territories; and a table of signs and symbols.

Graphics and Format

There are fewer than 100 illustrations, mostly simple black-and-white line drawings of animals, musical instruments, and architectural features. Their quality and style are consistent throughout the work. The print is clear and very easy to read, with two columns of entries per page. The pages are sturdy and the hardcover binding will withstand years of use.

Summary

Merriam-Webster's *New Ideal Dictionary* is an extremely simplified version of *Webster's Ninth New Collegiate Dictionary,* a classic desktop reference work. The *New Ideal* includes clear, simple definitions of the most commonly used words; it will not help those looking for depth of meaning or technical terminology. Although dated, this sturdy volume is a serviceable, inexpensive alternative to a quality desk dictionary. Families might find it a good purchase for a junior high or high school student, but many buyers will find it worth their money to invest an extra $10 in a more comprehensive and current collegiate dictionary. It is comparable in scope to the AMERICAN HERITAGE STUDENT'S DICTIONARY, which was recently revised and is preferable to the *New Ideal Dictionary* in many respects, including the inclusion of biographical and geographical entries and the quality of the illustrations.

Webster's New World Dictionary, Third College Edition

Facts at a Glance

Full title: **Webster's New World Dictionary, Third College Edition**
Publisher: Prentice Hall (Simon & Schuster)
Editors: Victoria Neufeldt, Editor-in-Chief; David B. Guralnik, Editor-in-Chief emeritus
Edition reviewed: © 1994, revised third edition

Number of pages: 1,574
Number of entries: 150,000
Number of illustrations: 650 (reviewer estimate)
Intended readership: older student to adult
Trim size: 7¼" × 9½"
Binding: hardcover

Price: $18 (plain edged); $20 (thumb indexed); $22 (leatherkraft)
Sold in bookstores; also sold by direct mail
ISBN 0-671-88289-9 (plain edged);
   ISBN 0-671-88243-0 (thumb indexed);
   ISBN 0-671-88572-3 (leatherkraft)
No stated revision policy

Introduction and Scope

Webster's New World Dictionary is a single-volume collegiate dictionary published by Prentice Hall. It ranks with THE AMERICAN HERITAGE COLLEGE DICTIONARY, RANDOM HOUSE WEBSTER'S COLLEGE DICTIONARY, and MERRIAM-WEBSTER'S COLLEGIATE DICTIONARY as one of the finest single-volume desktop references available. With 150,000 entries, this work is noted for its

claim of thorough and contemporary coverage of uniquely American words and phrases, as well as for clear definitions and etymologies. The edition reviewed is an updated 1994 printing of the third edition, first published in 1988.

Authority

The first collegiate edition of *Webster's New World Dictionary* was published in 1953 by a group of lexicographers who wanted to dispense with the authoritarian image of dictionaries and produce a work that would be overtly user-friendly—with relaxed pronunciations and definitions written in contemporary language. The work was widely praised and reprinted, and a second edition emphasizing and identifying Americanisms was issued in 1970. That work became the dictionary of preference for many American newspapers and news agencies, and formed the basis on which the Associated Press and United Press International style manuals were written. The third edition was the first to be edited from a computerized lexicographical database.

David B. Guralnik, the editor-in-chief emeritus of the work, is a well-known lexicographer, and the list of consultants and contributing editors includes more than 40 professors. Other distinguished members of the *Webster's New World Dictionary* staff include Dr. James W. Hartman, pronunciation editor of the *Dictionary of American Regional English,* and Mitford M. Mathews, editor of the *Dictionary of Americanisms,* who passed away in 1985 while the third edition was being produced.

Comprehensiveness of Entries

This work's 150,000 entries place it below the other competitors for the collegiate market: MERRIAM-WEBSTER'S COLLEGIATE DICTIONARY, tenth edition, claims 160,000, RANDOM HOUSE WEBSTER'S COLLEGE DICTIONARY has 180,000, and THE AMERICAN HERITAGE COLLEGE DICTIONARY boasts 200,000. Uniquely American words and phrases are identified in the lexicon by the symbol ★. A randomly selected sample of the 50 entries from **skid** to **ski pants** includes ★**skiddoo,** ★**skid row,** ★**skiffle,** ★**skijoring,** ★**ski jump, skimpy,** ★**skinflick,** ★**skin game, skinhead,** ★**Skinner box,** ★**skinny-dip,** ★**skinpop,** and **skintight.** By comparison, MERRIAM-WEBSTER'S includes 61 entries in the same alphabetical span, including all of the above except for **skinflick** and **ski pants.** AMERICAN HERITAGE encompasses only 47 entry words, omitting **skiddoo** and **skin-pop,** but including **skimobile, skim milk, Cornelia Otis Skinner, Otis Skinner,** and **skin patch,** none of which appear in *Webster's New World.* Finally, RANDOM HOUSE WEBSTER'S omits **skinflick** but includes a full 65 entry words, including multiple entries for several common words such as **skill** and **skip.** Although *Webster's New World* touts its treatment of Americanisms, all of its competitors provide comparable word lists, at least in this example. The contemporary scientific and technical terms **CAD/CAM, retrovirus,** and **CD/ROM** appear, as does a mathematical definition for **chaos.** Vulgarisms are present, both as entry words and as definitions for words with other meanings.

The work is noted for its etymologies, which are particularly thorough and readable. A complex word such as **paraphernalia,** for example, is traced back to its roots through successive derivations:

> ⟦ML, short for *paraphernalia bona,* wife's own goods < LL *parapherna* < Gr, bride's possessions beyond her dower < *para-,* beyond (see PARA-[1]) + *pherne,* a dowry, portion < *pherein,* to BEAR[1]⟧

Even the simple **biscuit** receives a thorough and revealing treatment:

> ⟦ME *bisquit, besquit* < OFr *bescuit* (altered, under infl. of OIt *biscotto*) < ML *biscoctum* < *(panis) bis coctus,* (bread) twice baked < L *bis,* twice (see BINARY) + *coctus,* pp. of *coquere,* COOK⟧.

Usage labels and usage notes are present but infrequent, in keeping with the work's descriptive philosophy. Illustrative phrases, written by the editors, are enclosed within italicized brackets. Synonym guides appear (prefaced with *SYN.*) but are also relatively infrequent.

Biographical and geographical entries are incorporated into the main lexicon. They are quite current, although THE AMERICAN HERITAGE COLLEGE DICTIONARY includes far more. **Lithuania** and **Ukraine** both appear as independent republics, and **Germany** is listed as a unified country. **Boris Yeltsin** appears as the president of Russia; *Violeta Chamorro* and *Michael Jackson* do not appear.

Quality and Currency of Entries

Definitions in *Webster's New World Dictionary,* sequenced in historical order, are notably concise and understandable. **Viscous,** for example, is defined as "having a cohesive and sticky fluid consistency." RANDOM HOUSE WEBSTER'S defines the word as "of a glutinous nature or consistency; sticky; thick; adhesive"; AMERICAN HERITAGE describes it as "having relatively high resistance to flow"; and MERRIAM WEBSTER'S refers the reader to VISCID, which is defined as "having an adhesive quality: STICKY." Occasionally, however, *Webster's New World*'s definitions can become wordy, as in **designated driver:**

> the person in a group who has been designated as the driver of a motor vehicle in which all will be transported and as the one who will abstain from drinking alcoholic beverages while the others may indulge to excess.

A typical entry follows:

> **peach**[1] (pēch) *n.* ⟦ME *peche* < OFr *pesche* < VL *persica* < pl. of L *persicum* < *Persicum* (*malum*), Persian (apple)⟧

> **1** a small tree (*Prunus persica*) of the rose family, with lance-shaped leaves, pink flowers, and round, juicy, orange-yellow fruit, with a fuzzy skin and a single, rough pit **2** its fruit **3** the orange-yellow color of this fruit **4** [Slang] any person or thing that is very good or is well liked

Entries are very current and include **bungee jumping, fax, intifada, maquiladora, rap** (as music), and **virtual reality;** *dis,* in the modern slang sense of "disrespect," and *HDTV* do not appear.

Syllabication and Pronunciation

Webster's New World uses a unique system of indicating syllabication within entry words. A centered dot (·) marks places where a word could be broken at the end of a line of type; a vertical line (|) separates pronounced syllables that should not be typographically broken. For example: **cy|a|no·bac·te·ri|a, man|u·fac·to|ry.** This clear and useful system is also followed in each entry's inflected and derived forms.

Pronunciations in parentheses follow each entry word; according to the "Guide to the Use of the Dictionary," they represent "those widely used by good speakers of American English." Primary and secondary stresses are indicated by boldface and roman primes, and alternate pronunciations are given: **de·fense** (dē fens′, di fens′, dē′fens′). A key to the 54 symbols used appears on the page opposite the inside front cover of the book. A full explanation of each symbol is given in the "Guide to the Use of the Dictionary," and an abbreviated key appears at the bottom of every right-hand page.

Accessibility

The six-page "Guide to the Use of the Dictionary" is detailed but difficult to access, in part because of its small typeface and cramped layout. Although headings in this section ("PRONUNCIATION," "FIELD LABELS," and so on) are printed in capital letters and large type, the rest of the text is tightly spaced, making specific details and examples difficult to locate.

Entries are sequenced in alphabetical order, letter by letter, with abbreviations incorporated into the main lexicon: **glyptograph, gm, GM, G-man, GMAT, Gmc, GMT, gn, Gn, gnar, gnarl.** Guide words appear at the upper outside corners of each page, and alternate spellings simply refer the reader to the preferred one: **moustache** . . . *var. of* MUSTACHE. The dictionary is available in a thumb-indexed version.

Special Features

The appendixes to *Webster's New World Dictionary* include a two-page chart entitled "The Indo-European Family of Languages," a ten-page guide to "Editorial Style," and a five-page list of "Special Signs and Symbols." A color map of "Regional Dialects in the United States" appears on the inside of the front cover, and an extensive list of the abbreviations used in the dictionary appears on the inside of the back cover and the facing page. Other features include essays on "The English Language: Variation, the Dictionary, and the User" by John Algeo, "Etymology" by longtime *Webster's New World* chief etymologist William Umbach, and "The New World Dictionaries: A Historical Overview" by David Guralnik.

Graphics and Format

Graphics and format are principal weaknesses of *Webster's New World Dictionary,* especially when compared with a highly attractive volume such as THE AMERICAN HERITAGE COLLEGE DICTIONARY. The typeface is generally clear and readable; the illustrations, although clearly labeled, are sparse. Perhaps most striking, however, is the cramped look of each page. Top and bottom margins are extremely narrow (less than ¼ inch in places), and the resulting lack of white space is particularly noticeable in the front matter and appendixes. The gutter margin is also too narrow.

Summary

Webster's New World Dictionary is a high-quality desk reference tool, comparable to THE AMERICAN HERITAGE COLLEGE DICTIONARY, RANDOM HOUSE WEBSTER'S COLLEGE DICTIONARY, and MERRIAM-WEBSTER'S COLLEGIATE DICTIONARY. In some respects it is superior to those volumes: its definitions and etymologies are clear, descriptive, and easily understandable; its system of syllabication is unique and helpful; it is quite up-to-date; and it identifies words and phrases that are distinctly American in origin and/or use. These qualities have made it the dictionary of choice for many major newspapers and news agencies in this country.

In other respects, however, *Webster's New World Dictionary* falls somewhat short: its lexicon is not as comprehensive as those of its rivals; most of the American words and phrases that it touts also appear in the other dictionaries, although they are not identified as such; and the narrow margins and sparse illustrations detract from the overall appearance of the pages. At $18, the work is competitively priced. Libraries should include it in their collections; home users will not be disappointed by this work but should be aware of some of its shortcomings. The decision to purchase this volume over one of its rivals will ultimately be a matter of personal preference.

Webster's School Dictionary

Facts at a Glance

Full title: **Webster's School Dictionary**
Publisher: Merriam-Webster
Editors: Merriam-Webster editorial staff
Edition reviewed: © 1986

Number of pages: 1,184
Number of entries: 85,000
Number of illustrations: 953
Intended readership: high school
Trim size: 7" × 9¼"
Binding: hardcover

Price: $15.95; school discount available
Sold in bookstores and other retail outlets; also sold to libraries and schools
ISBN 0-87779-280-1
Revised edition to be published in 1994

Introduction and Scope

The preface to *Webster's School Dictionary* states that it has been written especially for high school students, but the Buying Guide's reviewers feel it is also suitable for junior high readers. Its 85,000 entries range from scientific terms to modern idioms. This dictionary was originally published in 1980 and revised in 1986. It is one of a series of three school titles that include WEBSTER'S ELEMENTARY DICTIONARY and WEBSTER'S INTERMEDIATE DICTIONARY. A revision of this work, with the new title *Merriam-Webster's School Dictionary,* is scheduled for publication in 1994.

Authority

Although no specific credits are given, the dictionary was prepared by Merriam-Webster's highly respected dictionary staff. According to the publisher, the entries were selected from Merriam-Webster's extensive citation files and also from appropriate school texts.

Comprehensiveness of Entries

In addition to the definitions, the dictionary includes etymologies, word histories, a few usage notes, and numerous synonyms. Etymologies appear at the end of the definitions in square brackets. Word histories are longer explanatory notes and are denoted by a small triangle and the word *origin,* underlined and overhanging the following text like an entry word. Anecdotal information is often provided under these word histories.

Synonyms, but not antonyms, are provided; these are indicated by small capital letters following the entry word. In some instances, synonyms are grouped together following the abbreviation *syn.* For example, under the word **opinion,** the list reads: "syn OPINION, BELIEF, CONVICTION. . . ." The different shades of meaning of each of these words are then carefully distinguished in a synonym paragraph, of which there are 530.

Slang terms, such as **bennies** for amphetamine tablets, are labeled, and there are a few other kinds of usage notes throughout the dictionary. For example, the

Webster's School Dictionary

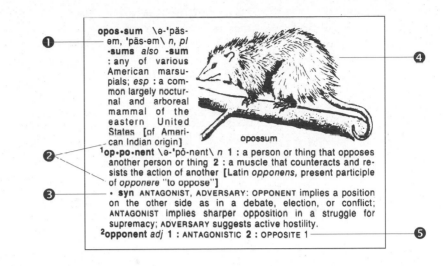

❶ Pronunciations and variants given within back slashes

❷ Etymologies, within boldface brackets, spell out word sources

❸ Synonym study preceded by boldface centered dot and **syn**

❹ Line drawing of animal species placed close to entry word

❺ Meanings cross-referenced to main entry words appear in small capital letters

rhetorical term **asyndeton** is defined as the "omission of the connectives ordinarily expected (as in [Caesar's famous phrase] *I came, I saw, I conquered*)."

Verbal illustrations are included in the dictionary between angle brackets. Phrases appear much more frequently than full sentences, but are adequate for the age level of the intended user.

Quality and Currency of Entries

Information given for entries in *Webster's School Dictionary* includes boldface syllabication, pronunciation, italicized parts of speech abbreviated, numbered definitions, word origins, synonyms, and variant word forms.

Merriam-Webster dictionaries are characterized by a descriptive approach to word definitions, as opposed to the prescriptive definitions found, for example, in the American Heritage dictionaries. Unlike other Merriam-Webster dictionaries, however, this work provides prescriptive guidance in the form of usage notes.

The definitions of a word are in historical order. Unless students are familiar with other Merriam-Webster dictionaries that use this order or have carefully read the front matter, they may be confused, since most dictionaries place the most commonly used definition first.

Some definitions are elaborated more than others. Under **Bible,** for example, the books of both Old and New Testaments are listed. The symbol, atomic number, and atomic weight are noted in a table for chemical elements found under **element.** Comprehensive lists of compound words are given for prefixes, such as **post,** which has 41; **super,** which has 118; and **un,** which receives three pages, each with six columns of words beginning with the **un** prefix. A few foreign words, such as **bête noire** and **joie de vivre,** are included.

Biographical, biblical, mythological, and geographical names are not included in the main lexicon, but are listed in separate appendixes in the back of the dictionary. These listings include boldface syllabication, pronunciation, and brief factual information.

Unfortunately, the 1986 publication date of this dictionary makes it quite dated. Even commonly used words such as *videodisc, VCR,* and *videocassette* are not included. In the "Geographical Names" section, **Germany** is still listed as a "former country . . . constituting two republics"; **Lithuania** is listed as a "constituent republic . . . of U.S.S.R."

Syllabication and Pronunciation

Centered dots indicate syllabication in the entry words. Pronunciation follows and appears between slashes. There are 56 pronunciation symbols used, and these appear on the page preceding the alphabet. There is also an abbreviated pronunciation key at the bottom of the right-hand column on right-hand pages of the lexicon. Variants in pronunciation are given; they are separated by commas and sometimes by semicolons when grouped together. All of the variants are considered acceptable and none is given preference.

Accessibility

Pairs of guide words at the top of each page facilitate locating words in the dictionary. There is no thumb indexing, nor are there thumb guides; even though the dictionary is not too large, these would still be very useful for the intended age group. Words in the main lexicon are listed alphabetically, letter by letter.

Special Features

A guide to using the dictionary is located in the front of the book and is reasonably easy to understand. Clear explanations of how to read the entries in the dictionary are contained in the guide, and include explanations of syllabication, pronunciation, parts of speech, inflected forms, definitions, cross-references, word histories, and synonyms. Under each of these topics, a short lesson is given similar to those found in a grammar handbook.

Appended to the back of the dictionary are abbreviations and symbols for chemical elements; signs and symbols; biographical, biblical, mythological, and geographical names; and a "Handbook of Style," which covers punctuation, italicization, capitalization, and plurals.

Graphics and Format

The overall layout of the page design makes the dictionary quite easy to read, despite the large amount of information given within each entry. Line drawings are used judiciously throughout the book. Most are adequate in size and detail for their purpose. The book lies flat when open, and the binding is sturdy.

Summary

Webster's School Dictionary, published by Merriam-Webster, is an authoritative work. Its entries contain a large amount of information for a school dictionary. However, a more current, comprehensive, and attractive volume such as the 1993 AMERICAN HERITAGE HIGH SCHOOL DICTIONARY represents a better buy despite a slightly higher price. High school students who can use *Webster's School Dictionary* will also be able to use MERRIAM-WEBSTER'S COLLEGIATE DICTIONARY, tenth edition, which is a more comprehensive and up-to-date volume. Students who need a less sophisticated work will find the SCOTT, FORESMAN INTERMEDIATE DICTIONARY more accessible and up-to-date.

Webster's Third New International Dictionary of the English Language, Unabridged

Facts at a Glance

Full title: **Webster's Third New International Dictionary of the English Language, Unabridged**
Publisher: Merriam-Webster
Editor: Philip Babcock Gove, Editor-in-Chief
Edition reviewed: © 1993

Number of pages: 2,764
Number of entries: more than 460,000
Number of illustrations: 3,105 in black and white, 2 color plates
Intended readership: secondary school to adult
Trim size: $9^{1}/_{16}'' \times 12^{9}/_{16}''$
Binding: hardcover

Price: $99.95 (blue sturdite); $100 (blue sturdite with carrying case); $109.95 (imperial buckram)
Sold in bookstores; also sold to libraries and other educational institutions
ISBN 0-87779-201-1 (blue sturdite);
ISBN 0-87779-202-X (blue sturdite with carrying case);
ISBN 0-87779-206-2 (imperial buckram)
No stated revision policy

Introduction and Scope

Webster's Third New International Dictionary is generally accepted as the most authoritative source on modern American English. Although controversy surrounded the publication of the first edition in 1961, the dictionary is now recognized as a superior resource on current American vocabulary and usage. "The basic aim is nothing less than coverage of the current vocabulary of standard written and spoken English," wrote Philip Babcock Gove, the editor-in-chief, in his preface to the first edition. By expanding the dictionary's coverage of scientific and technical terms and updating new uses of old terms to reflect the current state of the language, the editorial staff of the 1993 edition continues to achieve that goal.

Authority

George and Charles Merriam acquired the unsold copies and publishing rights of Noah Webster's *American Dictionary of the English Language* when he died in 1843. An 1847 revision of the work was the first unabridged dictionary produced by G. & C. Merriam Company. Others followed, including *Webster's International Dictionary* in 1890, *Webster's New International Dictionary* in 1909, and *Webster's New International Dictionary, Second Edition,* in 1934. Many people consider the latter to be the bible of the American English language. Merriam-Webster also publishes numerous biographical, geographical, and college dictionaries as well as a thesaurus, a dictionary of synonyms, and other reference books.

Recent promotional material distributed by Merriam-Webster claims that its editorial staff is "the largest group of working lexicographers in North America." A vast majority of the editors listed in the text of *Webster's Third* hold advanced degrees. In addition, over 200 outside consultants contributed their expertise in specialized scientific, technological, and linguistic areas. Between 1934 and 1961 the staff collected more than 6 million citations illustrating the accurate usage of words in modern English. The OXFORD ENGLISH DICTIONARY, Sir William Craigie's *Dictionary of American English,* and Mitford M. Matthew's *Dictionary of Americanisms,* as well as numerous literary works, quotation books, and other refer-

Webster's Third New International Dictionary

❶ Syllabication shown by a centered dot

❷ Italicized part-of-speech label followed by label indicating that this noun has a regular English plural

❸ Drawing illustrates definition 2a of the first homograph

❹ Etymology in boldface square brackets

❺ Examples of usage contained in angle brackets, with a roman swung dash standing in for the main entry word (plural form used, in italics, in the second example)

❻ Capitalization label in italics

❼ Cross-reference in small capitals

❽ Homographs appear as separate, numbered entries

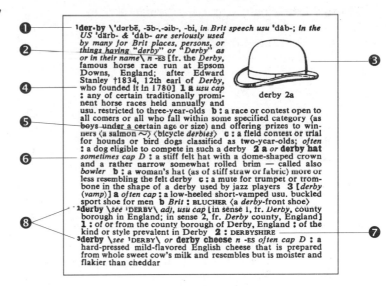

derby 2a

ence works, provided another 10 million citations for the lexicography. The staff continues to collect examples for subsequent revisions, although it labors in anonymity: the dates of employment in the editor list for the 1993 edition stop at 1984. Philip Gove is listed as having worked on the project from 1946 to 1972.

The editors consider themselves to be describers of the language and its usage rather than prescribers of what is acceptable. They therefore use actual quotations from literature to illustrate the use of words in context. These include colloquial and slang definitions as well as the conventional meanings. In addition to defining **head** as a part of the body and a position of leadership, for example, *Webster's Third* includes numerous specialized definitions for the term as it applies to activities as far-ranging as page layout (running heads), fermenting liquid (the head on a glass of beer) and sound recording (the heads on a tape player). It also includes expressions such as "going out of one's head" and "over one's head," contemporary slang and vulgar definitions, and nearly two full pages of compound words and phrases that start with "head."

Comprehensiveness of Entries

Webster's Third is the most comprehensive American unabridged dictionary. Users will generally succeed in finding words here, but it may take some diligence. With 460,000 entries and 2,764 pages, *Webster's Third* is larger than THE RANDOM HOUSE UNABRIDGED DICTIONARY, its principal competitor, which claims 315,000 entries. A sample of the 50 entries in *Webster's Third* from **gaya** to

gazetteer includes five scientific terms related to **gay-lussac;** two plant names, **-gaywings** and **gazania;** and four animal names related to **gazelle.** By comparison, the **gaya** to **gazetteer** section in RANDOM HOUSE contains only 31 entries.

If a word does not appear in the main body of the dictionary, it will probably be listed in the 65-page addendum containing new words. **AIDS, ATM,** and **mouse** (as a computer term) all appear in this section. The dictionary also contains slang words such as **far out, boonies,** and **el cheapo;** terms used in sports and entertainment such as **free agent, air ball,** and **off broadway;** and assorted terms found in daily news reports: **family** as a crime syndicate and **naderism** for consumer advocacy. The editors have done an excellent job of documenting current usage.

Vulgarities (labeled "usu. considered vulgar") seem to be as prevalent as they are in RANDOM HOUSE. Although they do not appear as often in the main body of the text, they appear frequently as main entries in the addendum. Britishisms appear as separate entries (**nappy**), as definitions within entries (**boot**), and as special pronunciations (**derby**).

Detailed etymologies appear immediately after each entry's pronunciation and functional labels. Etymological information is not repeated for subsequent meanings of a word unless the derivation is different. The word **bang,** for example, as it relates to beating, hammering, and producing loud noises, is of Scandinavian origin. When used in reference to hairstyles, however, the word comes from **bangtail;** when used as a reference to the ancient people of Bengal, India, it is of Sanskrit origin.

The origins of scientific terms, although often derived from ancient languages, can be problematic. *Webster's Third* uses the label ISV (International Scientific Vocabulary) for modern scientific and technical words of uncertain origins. The editorial staff's scholarship is evident in derivations of words such as **ondule:**

> [F *ondulé* wavy fr. past part. of *onduler* to wave, ripple, back-formation fr. *ondulation* wave, concentric wave-motion in a liquid or gas, prob. fr. (assumed) NL *undulation-, undulatio* concentric wave motion in a liquid or gas — more at UNDULATION.]

Information about usage is readily available in *Webster's Third.* Unlike RANDOM HOUSE, which uses invented phrases to illustrate definitions, *Webster's* often uses examples from literary works to illustrate nuances in the usage of words. The editors deliberately refrain from designating preferred usage, allowing the reader to use the examples as a guide in making decisions. A randomly selected entry for **hard** on pages 1031–32 includes citations from Henry Garfinkle, W. H. Breen, Clement Attlee, Herman Melville, Arthur Knight, and the *New Republic,* among many others. Carefully defined distinctions precede the citations so that the reader receives a full explanation.

In addition to the definitions and citations, three types of status labels are used with the words: temporal labels, such as *obs* (obsolete) and *archaic;* stylistic labels, such as *slang* and *nonstand* (nonstandard); and regional labels such as *dial* (dialect), *Brit* (British), and *South* (Southern). More than 1,000 synonym articles, designated by *syn,* clarify common words that are often confused. All of these are cross-referenced. Many articles also contain cross-references to related words, printed in small capitals. For **fit out,** one finds FURNISH, EQUIP, OUTFIT, and PREPARE. Readers interested in the development of words will find the system of etymologies, citations, status labels, synonym articles, and cross-references in *Webster's Third* to be extremely useful.

Quality and Currency of Entries

The editors state in the preface that they strive for "the three cardinal virtues of dictionary making: accuracy, clearness, and comprehensiveness." To attain these goals, which can sometimes conflict with each other, they have chosen to add new words currently in use to the lexicon and to omit words that became obsolete before 1775 unless they are found in well-known works by major writers. Definitions are arranged chronologically, with the earliest known meaning of the word listed first. This practice stands in contrast to that of RANDOM HOUSE, which sequences its definitions in order of frequency of occurrence.

Definitions are straightforward, concise, and comprehensive. Readers may occasionally need to look up the words used to define a term. **Endoscopy,** for example, is "examination with an endoscope." An **endoscope** is

> **1:** an instrument for visualizing the interior of a hollow organ or part (as the rectum or urethra) — compare BRONCHOSCOPE, CYSTOSCOPE, OTOSCOPE. **2:** an optical instrument for examining the interior surface of a hole drilled through a pearl and used to distinguish between cultured and natural pearls

Although the reader must use a two-step process, the result is a clear explanation.

Webster's Third strives to present the current state of American English. The addendum before the main body of the dictionary includes entries for **fax, HDTV, rap** as a musical form, and **retrovirus. Bungee** is in the main body of the dictionary, but *bungee jumping* does not appear. **Dis-** is included only as a prefix. There are no entries for *intifada, maquiladora,* or *virtual reality.*

Syllabication and Pronunciation

Webster's Third has made an effort to simplify syllabication. The article on word division in the front matter states:

> The centered periods in boldface main entries indicate places at which a hyphen may be put as the last character in a line of print or writing when the rest of the word must be put at the beginning of the following line. We have made an effort to insert the periods only at places where hyphens would actually be used by publishing houses whose publications show a conscientious regard for end-of-the-line divisions.

This means that a single letter pronounced as a syllable, such as the second *a* in **britannia,** is not set off in *Webster's* (as it is in RANDOM HOUSE). The editors note that a hyphen takes up as much space as a letter, and remind readers that

> Divisions avoided by publishers are sometimes printed in dictionaries probably as a concession to those who believe that syllabic division is a guide to pronunciation. However, it is the pronunciation of a word that governs its orthographic division rather than the other way around.

Another practice avoided here is the division of compound words such as **cardiovascular** so that the last letter of the first element is placed with the second. While RANDOM HOUSE offers the option of dividing at the *i* or the *o, Webster's* divides the word only after the *o.*

Writers using this dictionary to determine the proper division of words with prefixes will have to look up two words, since syllabication is not repeated. To divide **irresponsible,** one must look up **responsible.** This is a minor inconvenience. The following examples demonstrate syllabication practices in *Webster's Third:* **about, en·glish, obey,** and **rhythm.** RANDOM HOUSE divides the same words in this way: **a·bout, Eng·lish, o·bey,** and **rhythm.**

Pronunciations appear immediately after the entry heading, set off by slanted lines. Accent marks denoting stress appear *in front* of the emphasized syllables. A mark above the syllable indicates primary stress and one below the syllable indicates secondary stress. Combined marks before a syllable indicate that the stress varies between primary and secondary.

Where applicable, *Webster's Third* provides several pronunciations of a word to reflect regional differences. The entry for **automobile** includes a full eight options, compared with the three in RANDOM HOUSE. As with usage advice, no pronunciation is designated as preferred. Pronunciation keys appear inside the front and back covers and on one page in the front matter. Unlike in RANDOM HOUSE, no abbreviated versions appear at the bottoms of the pages. Symbols are based on the International Phonetic Alphabet (IPA); the dictionary's front matter includes a detailed explanation of the system.

Accessibility

Webster's Third is easy to use. Detailed instructions and an explanatory chart describing the elements of entries appear in the front matter. Thumb indexes divide the sections; guide words in the upper corners of each page indicate the first and last entries. Entries are alphabetized, letter by letter, and abbreviations are interfiled with words. Variant spellings have their own entries in proper alphabetical sequence: for example, **rime** *var.* of **rhyme;** **esthetic** *var.* of **aesthetic.** The main entry reads **aesthetic or esthetic.** The entry for **moustache** lists *mustache* as a variant spelling. Homographs receive numerical superscripts and are listed historically with the oldest first. Words beginning with *Mc* or *Mac* are treated as if all were *Mac.* Numerals are interfiled as if spelled out: **3-D** appears between **threed** and **three-day fever.** The abbreviations *St.* and *Ste.* are spelled out.

The entry format is simple. The boldface, syllabicated entry word is followed by the pronunciation, then functional labels, inflected forms, and capitalization label where necessary. No entry words are capitalized. The etymology, status labels, subject labels, and subject guide phrases are next. A colon separates this material from the definitions. Boldface Arabic numerals precede the definitions. If illustrative quotations are included, they appear in brackets. Cross-references, *see also* references, and synonym notes appear last. A sample entry follows:

¹**doze** \'dōz\ *vb* -ED/-ING/-s [prob. of Scand origin; akin to ON *dūsa* to doze, *dūs* lull, calm; akin to MLG *dōre* fool, MHG *dōsen* to be quiet, doze — more at DOR] *vt* **1** *archaic*: to make dull : STUPEFY, MUDDLE, CONFUSE **2:** to pass (as time) drowsily — usu. with *away* ⟨*dozing* his life away⟩ ~ *vi* **1a:** to sleep lightly or intermittently **b:** to fall into a light sleep — often used with *off* ⟨*dozed* off in the middle of her reading⟩ **2:** to be in a dull or stupefied condition as if half asleep: be drowsy **syn** see SLEEP.

Special Features

This dictionary has no special sections, but it contains 51 tables illustrating subjects as diverse as various languages and alphabets, weights and measures, gestation periods, and radio frequencies. Individual articles in the front matter provide detailed information on spelling, pronunciation, punctuation, and forms of address.

Although *Webster's Third* contains neither a gazetteer nor a biography section, a great deal of this information is available within the text of the dictionary. The two entries for **athens,** for example, are

1. [fr. *Athens* city-state and cultural center of ancient Greece] . . . a city regarded as a center of culture and intellectual achievement. . . . 2. of or from Athens, the capital of Greece. . . .

This offers basic information and certainly enough for use in a library, where a person doing research could easily consult an atlas or encyclopedia for further details.

Graphics and Format

Webster's Third has seven full-page illustrations, two color plates (illustrating color), and over 3,000 black-and-white drawings accompanying the definitions. Although the smaller drawings are well done and have enough detail to be useful, they are visually less prominent than those in RANDOM HOUSE, which are set at full-column width and separated from the text by horizontal lines.

The book is well designed with adequate margins. Each page contains three columns of text separated by thin vertical lines. Although easy to read, the typeface is small and presents a denser, less accessible overall appearance than that of RANDOM HOUSE. Entry words are in boldface and overhang the text.

The sturdy binding will hold up well. The cover is an attractive navy blue with gold-stamped letters. The book is very large, but it remains flat when opened. Although size will not be an issue in schools and libraries, most homes may lack sufficient shelf and table space for storing and using an oversized dictionary. The book jacket includes information about a special display table with casters that is available for purchase from the publisher.

Summary

Webster's Third is now considered to be the authority for contemporary American English. It contains a wealth of information about the development of the language and the use of words. One can find technical and scholarly words here, as well as slang expressions. A drawback of this dictionary is the fact that new words are listed in a separate section rather than within the main lexicon. In addition, some users will find that the technical and scholarly quality of many definitions makes those definitions difficult to understand. For those users, RANDOM HOUSE may be more suitable, but scholars and those with a serious interest in the English language will prefer *Webster's Third.* It should be the dictionary of choice for libraries, academic institutions, and places where communication in English is important. Noah Webster would be pleased with the evolution of his work.

Webster's II New Riverside University Dictionary

Facts at a Glance

Full title: **Webster's II New Riverside University Dictionary**
Publisher: Houghton Mifflin
Editors: Anne H. Soukhanov, Senior Editor; Kaethe Ellis, Coordinating Editor
Edition reviewed: © 1988

Number of pages: 1,536
Number of entries: 200,000 definitions
Number of illustrations: 400, all in black and white
Intended readership: college to adult
Trim size: 6⁹⁄₁₆″ × 9½″
Binding: hardcover

Price: $17.95
Sold in bookstores; also sold to libraries and other educational institutions
ISBN 0-395-33957-X
No stated revision policy

Introduction and Scope

The 1988 printing of *Webster's II New Riverside University Dictionary* is barely distinguishable from its 1984 predecessor. This compact, one-volume work contains 200,000 definitions and is intended mainly for college students and adults. It is meant to be a functional "user's dictionary," and it contains reader-requested features included on the basis of survey research.

Authority

Webster's II is published by Houghton Mifflin, whose reference books include the esteemed American Heritage family of dictionaries. The staff listing is identical to that of the 1984 version and includes Anne H. Soukhanov as senior editor and Kaethe Ellis as coordinating editor. As with the 1984 version, the lexicon is drawn from and updated by Houghton Mifflin's extensive electronic database.

Comprehensiveness of Entries

The scope of the entries is especially suited to university students and adults, and includes many words from the fields of medicine, science, technology, literature, history, law, business, music, and art. Science, mathematics, and technology are particularly well represented; a typical sequence of entries from **lima bean** to **linchpin** includes the following terms: **limb** (astronomy and botany), **limbate, limbi, limbus, limen, limicoline, limit** (mathematics), **limit point, limnetic, limnology,** and **linac.**

Labels such as *Mus., Computer sci., Anat., Informal, Archaic,* and *Regional* are used effectively throughout the dictionary to delineate specific topics or uses of words. Most main entries have etymologies. One of *Webster's II*'s most appealing features is its "word histories," which rely upon the OXFORD ENGLISH DICTIONARY for information. These paragraphs provide in-depth studies of the origin and development of certain interesting words, such as **jaunty:**

> ▲ *word history:* The English word *jaunty,* like *gentle* and *genteel,* is a borrowing of French *gentil,* "noble." *Jaunty* at one time did mean "genteel" or "well-bred," but it soon developed other senses such as "elegant" and "sprightly." These adjectives were used to characterize those who attempted to behave as if they were well-bred, whether they actually were or not.

Usage notes are clear and concise. Synonyms and antonyms are presented in synonym paragraphs, which follow selected entries.

Quality and Currency of Entries

Main entries are presented in the following format: the syllabicated word in boldface overhanging the text; pronunciation (with alternates) in parentheses; part-of-speech label in italics; partially spelled inflected terms in boldface; etymology in brackets; definitions, preceded by boldface numerals (and sometimes lowercase letters) when more than one definition is given; illustrative phrases (some of them literary) in italics and enclosed in angle brackets; usage notes; and synonym paragraphs. A sample entry, for the word **sordid,** follows:

> **sor·did** (sôr′did) *adj.* [Fr. *sordide* < Lat. *sordidus* < *sordēre,* to be dirty.] **1.** Dirty or filthy : FOUL. **2.** Squalid : wretched <*sordid* slums> **3.** Morally degraded : BASE **4.** Exceedingly avaricious : GRASPING. —**sor′did·ly** *adv.* —**sor′did·ness** *n.*
>
> ★ *syns:* SORDID, BASE, CONTEMPTIBLE, DESPICABLE, LOW, SQUALID, VILE adj.core meaning : having or proceeding from low moral standards <a *sordid* affair that resulted in a scandal>

The definitions, even for many technical terms, are generally clear and accurate. They are not listed in his-

Webster's II New Riverside University Dictionary

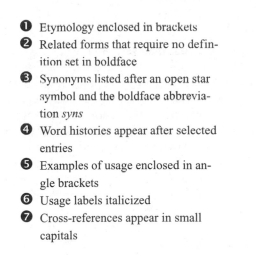

❶ Etymology enclosed in brackets

❷ Related forms that require no definition set in boldface

❸ Synonyms listed after an open star symbol and the boldface abbreviation *syns*

❹ Word histories appear after selected entries

❺ Examples of usage enclosed in angle brackets

❻ Usage labels italicized

❼ Cross-references appear in small capitals

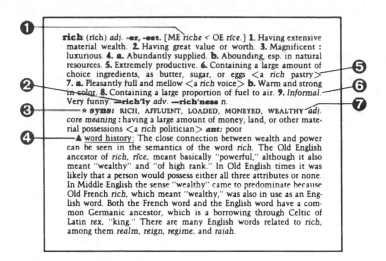

rich (rĭch) *adj.* **-er, -est.** [ME *riche* < OE *rīce.*] **1.** Having extensive material wealth. **2.** Having great value or worth. **3.** Magnificent : luxurious. **4. a.** Abundantly supplied. **b.** Abounding, esp. in natural resources. **5.** Extremely productive. **6.** Containing a large amount of choice ingredients, as butter, sugar, or eggs <a *rich* pastry> **7. a.** Pleasantly full and mellow <a *rich* voice> **b.** Warm and strong in color. **8.** Containing a large proportion of fuel to air. **9.** *Informal.* Very funny. **—rich'ly** *adv.* **—rich'ness** *n.*
✩ **syns:** RICH, AFFLUENT, LOADED, MONEYED, WEALTHY *adj.* **core meaning :** having a large amount of money, land, or other material possessions <a *rich* politician> **ant:** poor
▲ word history: The close connection between wealth and power can be seen in the semantics of the word *rich.* The Old English ancestor of *rich, rīce,* meant basically "powerful," although it also meant "wealthy" and "of high rank." In Old English times it was likely that a person would possess either all three attributes or none. In Middle English the sense "wealthy" came to predominate because Old French *rich,* which meant "wealthy," was also in use as an English word. Both the French word and the English word have a common Germanic ancestor, which is a borrowing through Celtic of Latin *rex,* "king." There are many English words related to *rich,* among them *realm, reign, regime,* and *rajah.*

torical order or by frequency of occurrence; rather, multiple definitions are clustered according to related subsenses. (See previous example of the word **sordid**). Definitions omit vulgar connotations and many slang meanings.

On its book jacket, the work claims to be "today's most up-to-date dictionary," but *Webster's II* is, in fact, quite dated. Although the word **yuppie** has been added since 1984, and an entry exists for **fax** (in noun form only), *bungee jumping, dis, HDTV, intifada, maquiladora, rap, retrovirus,* and *virtual reality* do not appear. *Chernobyl, Glasnost, New Age, NutraSweet, Perestroika,* and *POSSLQ* are missing, as are *camcorder, CD, compact disc, laser disc, VCR,* and *videocassette recorder.*

The sections of biographical and geographical entries at the end of the volume do not include *Violeta Chamorro, Michael Jackson, Boris Yeltsin, Germany* (as a unified country), or *Lithuania* or *Ukraine* (as independent republics). Even major figures at the time of the dictionary's publication such as *Mikhail Gorbachev* and *Sandra Day O'Connor* are not included; similarly, geographic changes such as the renaming of Upper Volta to *Burkina Faso* are not reflected.

Syllabication and Pronunciation

Syllabication is indicated in main entries and derived forms using boldface centered dots. Pronunciations follow main entries and variant forms and are based on the International Phonetic Alphabet (IPA). Alternative pronunciations are given where appropriate. The front matter contains a full pronunciation key; a short key appears at the bottom of the inside columns of each pair of facing pages. The following examples demonstrate the use of syllabication and pronunciation in *Webster's II:* **a·bout** (ə-bout'), **Eng·lish** (ĭng'glĭsh), **o·bey** (ō-bā'), and **rhythm** (rĭth'əm).

Accessibility

A ten-page section entitled "Explanatory Notes" and the helpful "Explanatory Diagram: Major Elements of This Dictionary" provide the reader with valuable information about using *Webster's II.* Entries are ordered in strict alphabetic sequence, letter by letter: **gazelle, gazette, gazetteer, gazpacho, G clef, Gd, Ge, ge-, geanticline.**

The hardcover edition is thumb indexed by pairs of letters, and guide words are printed at the top of each page. Alternate spellings of words are listed independently with a cross-reference to the preferred spelling.

Special Features

The "Concise Guide to Style, Usage, and Diction" provides basic information on capitalization, italicization, and punctuation; problems in English usage; and lists of clichés and redundant expressions.

The section on formatting research papers, business letters, and résumés gives general guidelines and illustrations of correct formats. The list of forms of address includes correct salutations for a wide variety of occupations.

Graphics and Format

Webster's II is attractive and well printed. The guide words and main entry words are large and contrast nicely with the definitions. However, the typeface used for the definitions is not as readable as that found in other dictionaries such as MERRIAM-WEBSTER'S COLLEGIATE DICTIONARY, tenth edition. When the book is lying flat, the gutter margins are too narrow to easily read the inner columns. The cover and binding are sturdy and should withstand heavy use.

The 400 black-and-white line illustrations are crisp and well executed. All are identical to those in the 1984 version.

Summary

Most users would find *Webster's II* adequate and easy to use, with clear definitions and an accessible format. The word history paragraphs enrich the work and encourage browsing.

Because the 1988 version of *Webster's II* is barely different from the 1984 version, owners of the first version should not feel compelled to replace their copies. While *Webster's II* would be sufficient for the needs of most college students and adults, its datedness does not compare favorably with more recently published college dictionaries, such as MERRIAM-WEBSTER'S COLLEGIATE DICTIONARY, tenth edition; THE AMERICAN HERITAGE COLLEGE DICTIONARY; or RANDOM HOUSE WEBSTER'S COLLEGE DICTIONARY—all of which are better buys.

The World Book Dictionary

Facts at a Glance

Full title: **The World Book Dictionary**
Publisher: World Book
Editors: Clarence L. Barnhart; Robert K. Barnhart
Edition reviewed: © 1993

Number of volumes: 2
Number of pages: 2,430
Number of entries: 225,000
Number of illustrations: 3,000, all in black and white
Intended readership: elementary school to adult
Trim size: $8\frac{3}{8}'' \times 10\frac{7}{8}''$
Binding: hardcover

Price: $99; $85 (when purchased with WORLD BOOK ENCYCLOPEDIA); $79 (to schools and libraries)
Sold directly to schools and libraries; also sold door-to-door
ISBN 0-7166-0293-8
Revised annually (approximately 100 new entries added each year)

Introduction and Scope

Especially designed to complement the WORLD BOOK ENCYCLOPEDIA, the two-volume *World Book Dictionary* provides information about the "most important and most frequently used words and phrases in the English language." Like its predecessors, the 1993 edition is aimed at "students of various ages" and "all members of the family." Containing 225,000 entries, it is one of the largest abridged dictionaries of the English language,

especially when its omission of biographical and geographical entries is considered.

Authority

First published in 1963 as the *World Book Encyclopedia Dictionary,* this work has been entitled the *World Book Dictionary* since 1967. From its inception, it has been edited by Clarence L. Barnhart, the noted American lexicographer who developed the Thorndike-Barnhart school dictionaries. His son, Robert K. Barnhart, became managing editor with the 1972 edition and has been co-editor since 1976.

The preparation of this dictionary is actually a cooperative effort of two publishing entities. The Barnharts and the staff of Barnhart Books compile the lexicographical portion, while the staff of the WORLD BOOK ENCYCLOPEDIA is responsible for the illustrations and special articles and for ensuring that the dictionary's contents are consistent with the encyclopedia and appropriate for its users.

An international committee of 46 recognized authorities in the fields of linguistics, phonetics, and English language and literature assisted with the formulation of editorial policies for the *World Book Dictionary.* In addition, more than 100 specialists served as consultants for entries in their fields of knowledge.

Entries and definitions in this work are based on an extensive file of more than 3 million quotations compiled over a period of 35 years. This file is constantly being updated by the dictionary staff and by correspondents throughout the English-speaking world, who record new words, usages, and meanings that appear in a wide variety of newspapers, magazines, journals, and books.

Comprehensiveness of Entries

With its 225,000 entries, the *World Book Dictionary* exceeds the number of entries in three recently revised standard college dictionaries: the 1991 RANDOM HOUSE WEBSTER'S COLLEGE DICTIONARY, third edition (180,000 entries); the 1993 AMERICAN HERITAGE COLLEGE DICTIONARY, third edition (200,000 entries); and the 1993 MERRIAM-WEBSTER'S COLLEGIATE DICTIONARY, tenth edition (160,000 entries).

The *World Book Dictionary* is intended to represent "the working vocabulary of the English language" and covers a wide variety of terms (except in those areas where the editors have deliberately limited coverage, such as obsolete, archaic, and highly technical words). It is particularly strong in foreign words and phrases and in names of plants and animals. Because it is designed to be used in conjunction with the WORLD BOOK ENCYCLOPEDIA, the *World Book Dictionary* omits biographical and geographical entries that would duplicate articles in the encyclopedia. It does, however, include entries for

The World Book Dictionary

❶ Boldface asterisk indicates that the entry word is illustrated

❷ Syllabication shown by a vertical rule between syllables

❸ Italicized part-of-speech labels followed by inflected forms in bold-face type

❹ Italicized illustrative sentences and phrases follow some definitions

❺ Usage label signifies that this meaning is not used in a literal sense

❻ Etymology appears in square brackets following entry definitions and includes cross-reference to related etymology

❼ Illustration with callouts helps to clarify meaning for definition **1a**

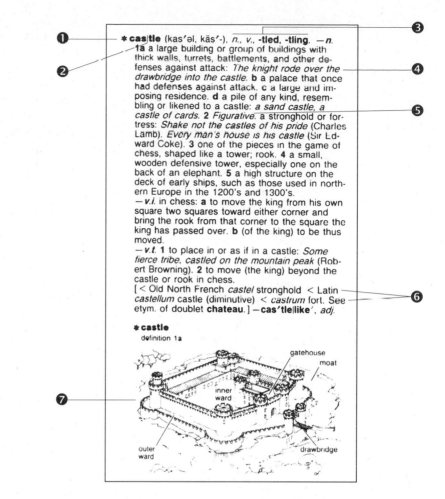

❶ ❷ ❸ ❹ ❺ ❻ ❼

*cas|tle (kas′əl, käs′-), *n., v.,* **-tled, -tling.** — *n.*
1a a large building or group of buildings with thick walls, turrets, battlements, and other defenses against attack: *The knight rode over the drawbridge into the castle.* **b** a palace that once had defenses against attack. **c** a large and imposing residence. **d** a pile of any kind, resembling or likened to a castle: *a sand castle, a castle of cards.* **2** *Figurative.* a stronghold or fortress: *Shake not the castles of his pride* (Charles Lamb). *Every man's house is his castle* (Sir Edward Coke). **3** one of the pieces in the game of chess, shaped like a tower; rook. **4** a small, wooden defensive tower, especially one on the back of an elephant. **5** a high structure on the deck of early ships, such as those used in northern Europe in the 1200's and 1300's.
— *v.i.* in chess: **a** to move the king from his own square two squares toward either corner and bring the rook from that corner to the square the king has passed over. **b** (of the king) to be thus moved.
— *v.t.* **1** to place in or as if in a castle: *Some fierce tribe, castled on the mountain peak* (Robert Browning). **2** to move (the king) beyond the castle or rook in chess.
[< Old North French *castel* stronghold < Latin *castellum* castle (diminutive) < *castrum* fort. See etym. of doublet **chateau.**] — **cas′tlelike′,** *adj.*

*castle
definition 1a

outer ward
inner ward
gatehouse
moat
drawbridge

adjectival forms of geographical names. Thus, **Lithuanian** is included, but not *Lithuania.*

The approximately 50 entries between **damage** and **damp** reflect the diversity of this work. Among these entries are four terms related to biology or chemistry (**daman, dambonite, dammar,** and **damiana**), a French phrase (**dame d'honneur**), a German term (**Dämmerschlaf**), two Latin phrases, and several proper names of peoples and legendary figures (for example, **Damara, Damocles**).

In addition, the *World Book Dictionary* includes a number of terms used primarily in other English-speaking countries, such as **chalk and cheese** (British), **chook** (Australian), and **babiche** (Canadian). Such words are clearly labeled to indicate that they are specific to a particular country.

A variety of other usage or restrictive labels (for example, *Informal, Slang, Substandard,* and *Unfriendly use*) accompany many of the entries. Additional labels (for example, *Music, Law, Chemistry*) indicate words that pertain to a particular profession. Further clarification for some words is provided by a usage note, which follows the definition and is preceded by a bold arrow. Usage notes range in length from an entire paragraph for **ain't** to the following succinct and straightforward note for **anil-**

ity: "**Anility** is a much stronger word than **senility,** tending always to convey a definite feeling of contempt." The *World Book Dictionary* includes a few slang terms referring to bodily functions, but it generally excludes vulgarisms, particularly those relating to sexual activity.

Illustrative examples frequently accompany definitions. Although a number of these examples were created specifically for the dictionary, many are quotations from standard authors, newspapers, or periodicals. A literary example of the form is provided for some literary terms, such as **epigram** and **quatrain.**

Synonyms are identified immediately after the definition to which they apply, except when the editors felt it necessary to make certain distinctions between the terms. In these instances, a useful "synonym study" that explains the special nuances of each term appears at the end of the entry. For example, the synonym study following **hopeless** draws distinctions between **hopeless, desperate,** and **despairing** and provides illustrative sentences for each term.

Many entries are accompanied by etymologies, which appear in brackets following the definition portion of an entry. These word histories are simple to interpret since the editors do not use any abbreviations for languages.

Quality and Currency of Entries

Entries in this dictionary follow an easily understandable format. Each main entry word appears in boldface type and extends one space into the left margin. Entry words, which are marked with vertical lines to show syllabication, are followed by the pronunciation in parentheses. Other elements of the entry appear in the following order as appropriate: italicized abbreviations indicating the parts of speech, inflected forms, definitions (arranged with the most commonly used meaning first and with examples of usage and synonyms directly following the definition to which they apply), etymology, synonym studies, and usage notes. Some entries conclude with cross-references to notes under other headings.

To illustrate the structure of a typical entry, the entire entry for **situate** is reproduced below:

> **sit | u | ate** (sich′ ūāt), *v.,* **-at | ed, -at | ing** *adj.* —**v.t.** to place or locate: *The firehouse is situated so that the firemen can easily reach all parts of town. They situated themselves in three separate chambers* (Thomas Paine). —**adj.** *Archaic except Law.* having its location; placed; situated. [< Medieval Latin *situare* (with English *-ate*[1]) < Latin *situs, -ūs* location]

Definitions in the *World Book Dictionary* are notable for their clarity and reflect the editors' policy of defining words that are more likely to be used by younger readers in simple terms. Carefully selected illustrative examples provide further clarification of the meanings.

Since the *World Book Dictionary* is revised annually, its lexicon is remarkably current. The publishers note that approximately 100 new entries are added each year and that, for the 1993 edition, between 400 and 500 references to East and West Germany and the Soviet Union were revised to reflect the current political situation. Among the recently coined terms in this work are **dis, fax, HDTV, intifada, rap** (as it relates to speech and music), **retrovirus,** and **virtual reality.** The dictionary also includes **buckyball, hypertext, interferon, loose cannon, liposuction, New Age, taxol,** and **palimony.** However, *bungee jumping, maquiladora, LAN, MRI, cyberpunk,* and *ibuprofen* do not appear.

Syllabication and Pronunciation

Because the use of dots to indicate syllabication is confusing to many children, the editors use light vertical lines to separate syllables in main entries. These lines indicate where a word may be hyphenated. (In contrast, the syllabication in the pronunciation component of the entry indicates which parts of a word are pronounced as separate units. For example, the main entry for **rhythm** shows no syllabication since it should not be divided; however, the pronunciation indicates that it is pronounced in two syllables.) Inflected forms of the main

entry word are also syllabicated, although the root word is not repeated. Syllables are not indicated in phrase entries that contain words appearing elsewhere in the dictionary.

The pronunciations indicated are those considered "to be in current use among educated speakers of English in the United States, and in representative areas of Canada." Pronunciation is represented in a simplified version of the International Phonetic Alphabet (IPA), with spaces between syllables and accent marks denoting which syllables are stressed. For words with several acceptable pronunciations, the preferred one is provided first but the variants are given. An abbreviated form of the pronunciation key appears at the bottom of almost every right-hand page, while the complete key is reproduced directly preceding the dictionary section in each volume.

Accessibility

Although consulting a two-volume dictionary is less efficient than handling a single volume, the publishers have done what they can to minimize this disadvantage. The spines and front covers of each volume are clearly marked with the portion of the alphabet that appears within (*A–K* in volume 1; *L–Z* in volume 2), and thumb indexes for single letters or groups of letters identify the appropriate section of the volume. In addition, guide words indicate the first and last words on each two-page spread. All entries, including single words, phrases, abbreviations, and acronyms, are interfiled in a single alphabetical sequence, which is arranged letter by letter. Thus, **newborn** appears between **new blue** and **new broom.**

Cross-references are provided between variant spellings of words, with the full information given under the preferred spelling. For example, the user is referred from **esthetic** to **aesthetic** and from **moustache** to **mustache.**

An excellent 12-page chapter entitled "Using This Dictionary" appears at the end of a lengthy section of preliminary material in volume 1. This chapter identifies symbols and abbreviations used within the dictionary and concisely and clearly explains how to interpret each component of an entry. Generous use of illustrative examples enhances the effectiveness of this section. Due to its location, many users may overlook this explanatory material. For optimal use, it probably should have followed the introductory essay at the front of the volume.

Special Features

A 124-page section at the front of volume 1 contains a variety of useful and well-written supplementary features. Printed on cream-colored paper, this preliminary material is divided into four major sections. The first section, "Using Your Language," includes chapters on the history of the English language, as well as rules for spelling, usage, and punctuation. It also provides vocabulary inventories for grades 3 to 12 and college level. The second section, "How to Write Effectively," gives tips on various forms of writing. Entitled "Using Different Languages," the third section contains a chart comparing eight alphabets, pronunciation guides for various languages, and a guide to important signs and symbols.

The final section, "Using This Dictionary," has already been described.

Graphics and Format

Approximately 3,000 black-and-white line drawings are used to clarify selected definitions. These specially commissioned illustrations accompany entries where readers might have difficulty visualizing a concept and where tables and other diagrams could efficiently convey information. Since illustrations do not always immediately precede or follow the entry they complement, an asterisk appears before the entry to alert the user that an illustration is provided. Among the types of entries frequently enhanced by drawings are architectural features, botanical and zoological terms, musical instruments, types of clothing, and modes of transportation.

These volumes are sturdily bound, but the inner margins are somewhat skimpy. Page layouts are attractive, and the typeface, although small, is clear and easy to read. The use of different kinds of type to differentiate parts of an entry is particularly effective. Although the paper is of good quality, it allows some show-through.

Summary

Due to its two-volume format, this work is more cumbersome to use than its one-volume counterparts. In addition, its price is significantly higher than other "college desk dictionaries," including THE AMERICAN HERITAGE COLLEGE DICTIONARY, MERRIAM-WEBSTER'S COLLEGIATE DICTIONARY, and RANDOM HOUSE WEBSTER'S COLLEGE DICTIONARY. However, the *World Book Dictionary* is considerably larger and more comprehensive than those works, and its yearly revisions ensure a currency that most other dictionaries cannot rival. Although the publisher includes elementary school students as part of the *World Book Dictionary*'s intended audience, the work is better suited to middle school students through adults. The *World Book Dictionary*'s breadth of coverage and the clarity and fullness of its entries make it an excellent choice for home, school, or library purchase.

Chapter 13
Evaluations of Special Dictionaries

Collins COBUILD English Language Dictionary

Facts at a Glance

Full title: **Collins COBUILD English Language Dictionary**
Publisher: HarperCollins
Editor: John Sinclair, Editor-in-Chief
Edition reviewed: © 1987, 1992 printing

Number of pages: 1,728
Number of entries: more than 40,000 entries, with more than 70,000 references
Number of illustrations: none
Intended readership: ESL students, nonnative speakers (especially advanced learners), and teachers
Trim size: 6½″ × 9½″
Binding: hardcover

Price: $40
Sold in bookstores; also sold to libraries and other educational institutions
ISBN 0-00-375021-3
No stated revision policy

Introduction and Scope

The *Collins COBUILD English Language Dictionary* is intended to provide nonnative speakers of English with an easy-to-use resource containing useful information about English words and their most common usages. (The acronym stands for the *Collins-Birmingham University International Language Database.*) In the introduction, Editor-in-Chief John Sinclair states that *COBUILD* "offers accurate and detailed information on the way modern English is used in all kinds of communication." The dictionary's goal—to provide a useful guide to writing, speaking, reading, and understanding English—makes it unusual among English as a Second Language (ESL) dictionaries. The work reviewed is the 1992 printing of the 1987 edition. It contains more than 40,000 entries in 1,728 pages.

Authority

COBUILD was developed and compiled from 1980 to 1987 at the University of Birmingham, England, as part of a language research project commissioned by Collins Publishers. The project made extensive use of a corpus taken from written and spoken sources. More than 20 million words amassed from books, print media, radio and television broadcasts, and other sources were input into an electronic database. This database gave the dictionary's compilers a massive lexicon from which to draw; it also allowed them to study and analyze how the words were used in everyday spoken and written communication. The database was also employed to decide which major uses to include, how the entries should be organized, and which uses and word forms to leave out.

Collins COBUILD
English Language Dictionary

❶ Pronunciation given in International Phonetic Alphabet (IPA)

❷ Superscript numbers indicate range of punctuation variations

❸ Example sentences in italics, preceded by EG

❹ "Extra column" separates notes on grammar and semantic relationships from main entries

❺ Boldface triangle introduces slight variations in usage

❻ Boldface circle denotes idioms

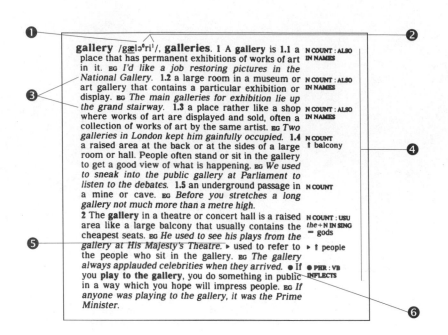

Such analyses give *COBUILD* an authority based on hard, measurable evidence.

Comprehensiveness of Entries

COBUILD's word list is based on the most frequently used words in the English language. No place names or proper names are found in the work, nor are highly technical, dialectal, and obsolete words included. Technical words that are included are defined according to the way they are used in everyday speech. The dictionary also provides usage notes, with recommendations on the level of formality appropriate for various contexts. Vulgarisms appear, but with warnings to avoid using those words in everyday use. The dictionary was compiled in Great Britain but reflects English as an international language; both Britishisms and Americanisms are noted as such.

Definitions are stated in simple language and are always complete sentences. Example phrases and sentences are always taken from actual text. This feature is especially helpful to nonnative users, who often need confirmation of what they think a word means. Related word forms, phrases and expressions that include the entry word, and cross-references are introduced by symbols within main entries. Thus, **furled** appears in the entry for **furl:**

> **furl** . . . When you **furl** something such as an umbrella, sail, or flag, you roll it or fold it up because it is not going to be used. ◊ **furled.** EG *His black umbrella was furled tight.*

One of the most useful and unusual features of *COBUILD* is its description of how combinations of words are related to the meanings and uses of the words. For example, the entry for **hard** contains several subentries, each defining a different sense or idiomatic usage of the word:

> **9** . . . ● Someone who is **as hard as nails** doesn't care at all about how their actions might hurt or affect other people. EG *That man's as hard as nails: he just sat there and laughed!*
>
> **17 Hard** drugs are very strong illegal drugs such as heroin or cocaine.

COBUILD offers ESL students help in understanding word collocations. In addition, the dictionary uses cross-references to help readers find a usage that consists of more than one word.

Quality and Currency of Entries

Entry words are in boldface, followed by numbered definitions. The most common definition appears first, denoted by a number. If a word has different senses (both in meaning and in grammar), a new number is used. If a word has different meanings for each part of speech, the different senses are noted by a decimal, as shown in the following entry:

> **appointment** . . . **1** The **appointment** of someone to do a particular job is the act or process of choosing them to do it. . . . **2** An **appointment** is **2.1** a job or position, usually one involving some responsibility. . . . **2.2** someone who has been chosen for a particular job or position. . . .

COBUILD records current and informal language as it actually occurs in spoken and written texts: examples of such language are **punk, yuppie,** and **bunged up.**

Syllabication and Pronunciation

Entries are not syllabified. All pronunciations are given in the International Phonetic Alphabet (IPA), and stress is shown by putting the vowel sounds in the stressed syllable in boldface. The accent represented is Received

Pronunciation (RP), which was chosen because it is the one most widely used as a norm for teaching purposes. American pronunciations are included when they differ from British ones.

Variations in pronunciation are denoted by superscripts. If there is very little variation in the way a vowel is pronounced, it will appear in boldface with no superscript. If the pronunciation varies significantly (for example, in an unprotected vowel), superscript notations are used to indicate the likely range of variation. A one-page "Pronunciation Guide" is provided in the front matter.

Accessibility

A number of features make this ESL dictionary accessible to the user. A five-page "Guide to the Use of the Dictionary," the aforementioned "Pronunciation Guide," and a one-page guide to "Special Entries" give clear and simple information to help students and teachers alike. In addition, the seven-page introduction is especially informative for teachers and offers both a rationale for and an explanation of the information in the dictionary.

Entries are arranged letter by letter. Special entries appear in boxes, and the language used in the explanations is clear. Guide words are printed at the top of each page.

Special Features

An especially interesting feature is the extra column, separated from the main entries, that includes notes on grammar and semantic relationships. These annotations are easy to understand and helpful for the writer. Notes are provided for each entry. This extra column provides the user with information about word class and the range of syntactic uses, while leaving the text of the main entry simple and accessible.

Grammar notes are abbreviated in small capital letters (for example, N UNCOUNT for *uncountable nouns* and COMB for *combining form*). Each abbreviation used in the grammar notes is explained at its alphabetical place in the dictionary as a boxed "special entry." "Special entry" information is clear and detailed, and makes the dictionary user-friendly.

Semantic relationships are described in the extra column using three symbols: = (meaning the following word is a synonym), ≠ (meaning the following word is an antonym), and ⇑ (meaning the following word has a more general meaning than the entry word).

In addition to explaining the various grammar notes, special entries exist for concepts such as time, measurement, and numbers.

Graphics and Format

The overall design of *COBUILD* is functional, but not terribly appealing. The typeface used is a bit dense, and there are no illustrations. Some users might prefer the more contemporary look of the Longman ESL dictionaries. For advanced ESL learners, however, the value of *COBUILD*'s extensive word list will far outweigh its lack of visual appeal.

Summary

COBUILD is an ESL dictionary that has been long-awaited by ESL teachers and learners who want information about how words are used in modern, everyday English communication. The use of a corpus of millions of words and an electronic database to analyze the patterns of usage makes this dictionary an authority on how words are used in natural texts for communicative purposes. In addition, special information about grammar and semantic relations of words and word collocations make this dictionary a valuable resource for the advanced learner of English who wants to write in English and to refine his or her knowledge of word usage. Despite its British bias, *COBUILD* is the best dictionary available for giving detailed information about the core vocabulary of English, and is recommended for purchase by libraries, ESL teachers, and students.

The Facts On File Junior Visual Dictionary

Facts at a Glance

Full title: **The Facts On File Junior Visual Dictionary**
Publisher: Facts On File
Editors: Jean-Claude Corbeil; Ariane Archambault
Edition reviewed: © 1989

Number of pages: 160
Number of entries: 5,000
Number of illustrations: 800, all in full color
Intended readership: ages 8 to 12
Trim size: 8¼″ × 10″
Binding: hardcover

Price: $18.95
Sold in bookstores; also sold to schools
ISBN 0-8160-2222-4
No stated revision policy

Introduction and Scope

The Facts On File Junior Visual Dictionary is a shortened version of THE FACTS ON FILE VISUAL DICTIONARY, a reference work first published in 1986 by a team of Canadian lexicographers. The goals of that work were to "list all the terms and notions which designate or portray the many elements of everyday life in an industrial, post-industrial or developing society . . . [and] visualize them through graphic representation; i.e., assign to an illustration the role played by the written definition in a conventional dictionary." The *Junior Visual Dictionary* is essentially a picture book, with large, full-color illustrations of objects organized into categories and labeled with the names of their parts.

Quality and Currency of Entries

The illustrations in the *Junior Visual Dictionary* are very up-to-date. A **minivan** is depicted as a type of car, and the **sound reproducing system** illustration includes a **CD player.** A **portable cellular telephone** and a **high-speed train** appear, and the **wallet** on the **personal articles** page in the "Clothing" section has a **Velcro®** **closure.**

The illustrations, generated on a Macintosh computer, are very clear, with bright colors and crisp detail. Although the drawings are not identical to the black-and white illustrations in THE FACTS ON FILE VISUAL DICTIONARY, they are similar. The picture of the sun, for example, has a horizontal cutaway and a single large **prominence** extending down and to the left in both dictionaries.

The labels are for the most part accurate and clear, but occasional problems occur. The **planets of the solar system** illustration includes several of the planets' moons, but neither the illustration nor the labels provide help in distinguishing moons from planets. The guide words for the "Vegetable Kingdom" section read *vegetal kingdom,* and the guitar depicted under the heading **classical guitar** is clearly a country-and-western style instrument.

In general, the vocabulary is appropriate for the 8- to 12-year-old age group. Some words will be challenging: **spicule, faculae,** and **granulation** are all labeled on the illustration of the sun, and the **calyx, sepals, anther,** and **pedicel** are all labeled as parts of a flower. One detects a slight French cultural bias in places such as the full page of cheeses in the "Food" section, which depicts **Camembert, Chèvre, Emmenthal, Gruyère, Petit Suisse,** and **tomme au raisin,** at the expense of *cheddar* and *American.* Some of the "major road signs" on the page of symbols will also be unfamiliar to most American readers.

Accessibility

The Facts On File Junior Visual Dictionary has several features that will make it accessible to young users. The pages in each section are bordered in a pastel shade of blue or green that aids in section location. In addition, a section label appears on the upper outside corner of every page. A two-page alphabetized list of "Themes and Subjects" precedes the illustrations and gives the page number and title of each. An eight-page index includes a single alphabetical listing of all illustrations and their part labels, with the illustration titles in boldface. Finally, a two-page spread at the beginning of the book explains the use of the "Themes and Subjects" list and the index.

Graphics and Format

The dictionary's illustrations are grouped under the following headings: "Animal Kingdom," "Architecture," "Clothing," "Communications," "Do-It-Yourself," "Earth," "Farm," "Food," "Gardening," "Heavy Machinery," "House," "Human Body," "Measuring Devices," "Music," "Optical Instruments," "School," "Sky," "Sports," "Symbols," "Transports," "Vegetable Kingdom," and "Weapons." These categories are essentially the same as those used in the parent work.

Within each section are illustrations of appropriate objects: the three-page "Sky" section, for example, contains illustrations of the planets of the solar system, the sun, the phases of the moon, a comet, and stars. A title appears above each illustration, and the parts of each are labeled; the **electric range** in the "House" section, for example, has lines extending from its parts to labels such as **surface element, cooktop, oven control knob,** and **rack.**

Summary

The Facts On File Junior Visual Dictionary, like its acclaimed parent, THE FACTS ON FILE VISUAL DICTIONARY, is an interesting, high-quality reference tool. It provides 800 full-color, labeled illustrations of objects that children are likely to encounter in an industrialized society, ranging from an aquatic bird to an armchair, from a cordless telephone to a camping tent, and from a mushroom to a motorcycle.

The Facts On File Junior Visual Dictionary's strengths include its clear, current illustrations, its accessibility, and the wide range of items depicted. Although it contains an occasional unclear or mislabeled drawing, the book encourages browsing and will undoubtedly help children expand their vocabularies. It will also be an excellent resource for students of English as a second language. *The Facts On File Junior Visual Dictionary* is highly recommended.

The Facts on File Visual Dictionary

Facts at a Glance

Full title: **The Facts on File Visual Dictionary**
Publisher: Facts On File
Editor: Jean-Claude Corbeil, Editor-in-Chief
Edition reviewed: © 1986

Number of pages: 797

Number of entries: 25,000

Number of illustrations: 3,000 black-and-white drawings

Intended readership: General adult, educators, and students

Trim size: 7⅛″ × 9″

Binding: Laminated paper over boards

Price: $49.95

Sold in bookstores and other retail outlets; also sold to libraries and other educational institutions

ISBN 0 8160 1544-9

No stated revision policy

Introduction and Scope

The Facts On File Visual Dictionary, according to its preface, "is the first basic dictionary of terminological orientation, comprising within a single volume . . . thousands of more or less technical terms" and providing a "reliable modern terminology" for the objects, devices, machines, and tools of daily life—in a visual format. The purpose of the *Visual Dictionary,* according to Jean-Claude Corbeil, the editor in chief, is to graphically "portray the many elements of everyday life in an industrial, post-industrial or developing society . . . which one needs to know to buy an object, discuss a repair, read a book or a newspaper, etc." The Visual Dictionary contains 25,000 terms and concepts, illustrated by 3,000 technical drawings, arranged within 28 thematic chapters. Since all the terms and ideas selected can be graphically presented, no abstract words, adjectives, adverbs, or nouns are included.

Authority

According to the introductory section, some 4,000 to 5,000 references were used in researching and documenting the dictionary, including a variety of dictionaries, encyclopedias, catalogs, and technical documents. Jean-Claude Corbeil is a linguistic specialist. He and his team of Canadian "terminologists" and graphic artists designed this unique reference work following the methodology of systematic and comparative bilingual (French/English) terminological research developed in Quebec in the 1970s. The book was first published in Canada. American English, based on various Merriam-Webster dictionaries and on the 1983 unabridged RANDOM HOUSE DICTIONARY OF THE ENGLISH LANGUAGE, has been used throughout the dictionary.

Graphics and Format

The *Visual Dictionary* is divided into three sections:

- An extensive table of contents, listing all the chapters divided by subcategories. For example:

SPORTS
  Team Games
    Baseball
      Field, catcher, player, bat, glove
    Football
      Playing field . . . , scrimmage . . .
      uniform . . .
    Rugby
      Field, team, ball
    Soccer
      Field, ball. . . .
  Water Sports . . .

- Illustrations depicting the entries
- Three alphabetical indexes (general, thematic, and specialized), which provide three different ways to access the text.

In a series of wide-ranging sections, including "Astronomy," "Geography," "Vegetable Kingdom," "Animal Kingdom," "Food," "House," "Clothing," "Music," "Sports," "Weapons," and "Symbols," black-and-white drawings illustrate various terms and ideas.

Each section is introduced by a title page. The pages that follow are headed with large boldface guide words repeating the section title or a category within it. For example, under **"Sports,"** the headings are **Team Games, Water Sports, Winter Sports,** and so forth. On each page in the section, the subject of the category is presented graphically under a somewhat smaller boldface heading. For example, under **Team Sports: Baseball,** a schematic of a baseball playing field is drawn with each player's position indicated and labeled. Other categories show much more detailed drawings of humans, plants, animals, or objects, with labels for every part shown. Under **Leisure Sports: Mountaineering,** there is a human figure outfitted with, among other things, helmet, helmet lamp, snow goggles, rucksack, rope, and hammer. In another section, **"Do-It-Yourself,"** pages of drawings show tools for carpentry, plumbing, painting, and so forth, with labels providing the name of each tool and its parts.

The general and category indexes are each arranged in four alphabetical columns with page references; italics indicate an illustration, and bold type designates a chapter heading. The general index includes all of the terms in the *Visual Dictionary* in alphabetical order. The thematic indexes list the words and terms alphabetically by sections (for example, **Architecture, Communications, Health, House, Transportation, Weapons**). The specialized indexes place all of the elements or objects depicted on each page within subcategories such as **Athletics, Automobile, Domestic Appliances, Electricity, Men's Clothing, Micro-computer, Skiing.** For example, under **Microcomputer,** 87 concepts and terms related to microcomputers are listed, including **cursor, light pen, joystick, peripherals, input, ROM,** and **computer room.** Where terminological variation exists (that

The Facts on File Visual Dictionary

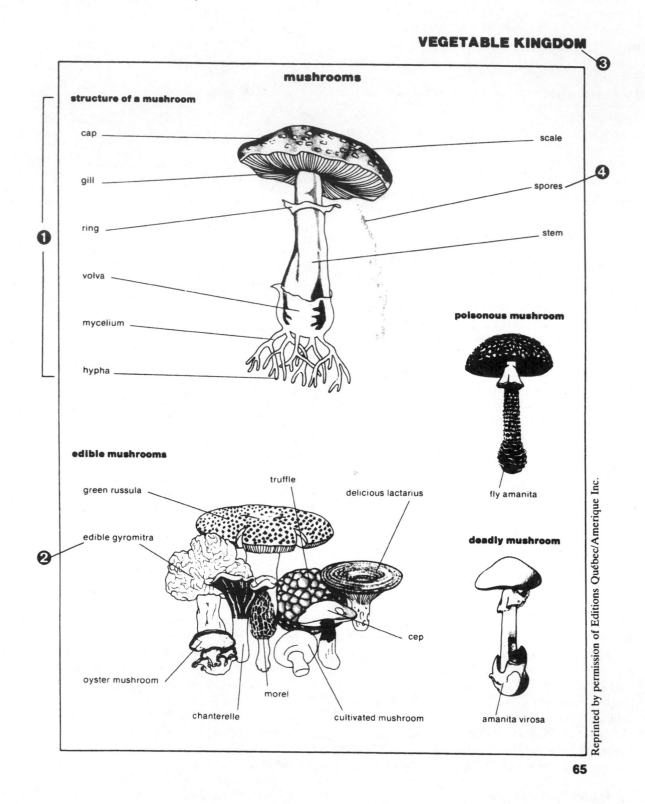

VEGETABLE KINGDOM ❸

mushrooms

structure of a mushroom

cap

scale

gill

spores ❹

ring

stem

volva

poisonous mushroom

mycelium

hypha

fly amanita

edible mushrooms

truffle

delicious lactarius

green russula

deadly mushroom

edible gyromitra

❷

cep

oyster mushroom

amanita virosa

chanterelle

morel

cultivated mushroom

65

❶ Visual definition of term   ❸ Subject heading
❷ Examples of different varieties   ❹ Identification of parts

is, where different words are used for one idea), the most frequently used or best-known terms have been selected.

Quality and Currency of Entries

Although published in 1986, the *Visual Dictionary* remains very up-to-date. In the section **"House Furniture,"** illustrations include an automatic drip coffee maker, a food processor, and a microwave oven. In the **"Communications"** section, the items depicted include a disc camera, a VCR, a video camera, a telephone-answering machine, and telecommunication satellites. Microcomputer systems are shown under **"Office Supplies."** The category **"Energy"** includes graphic representations of various contemporary energy sources, including wind, solar, and nuclear power.

The illustrations are presented from a modern-day perspective (especially clothing, cars, and personal articles) and are simple, accurate, and conceptually clear. Technical graphics were selected because "they stress the essential features of a notion and leave out the accessories."

Accessibility

The *Visual Dictionary* is easy to use in several different ways. Most readers will find that browsing through its intriguing pages will expand one's vocabulary. Basically, however, the *Visual Dictionary* is the book to consult to find out what something is called. Starting with an image in mind, the user would search out the probable appropriate theme in the table of contents and find the reference to an illustration. Turning to that illustration, he or she would find the word. If the user had a word and wanted to know what it looked like or in what category or categories it belonged, he or she would look up the word in one of the indexes and find a reference to the illustrations for the word.

The organization of this dictionary, therefore, allows users to look up an image to find its name or to determine the nature or function of an object in an appropriate context.

Occasionally, there is some confusion in the placement of words or in the illustrations. Some words do not appear where they would be expected: there are no fruits or vegetables listed under **Food;** they are listed in the general index under **Vegetable Kingdom.** A roulette table and a slot machine seem odd choices to include under **Parlor Games.** There are no cross-references between sections. But these are minor quibbles and will not lessen this work's usefulness.

Summary

Although some users may prefer the full-color illustrations of the MACMILLAN VISUAL DICTIONARY, *The Facts On File Visual Dictionary* is a useful reference source for public libraries or for college and even high school libraries. Especially useful for foreign students needing to find the English terms for an object, it is also an excellent resource for educators, and—as the publisher states—for "curious minds of all ages." It will be a valuable addition to any reference collection.

Longman Dictionary of American English

Facts at a Glance

Full title: **Longman Dictionary of American English: A Dictionary for Learners of English**
Publisher: Longman
Editors: Arley Gray; Della Summers; Adrian Stenton; Leah Berkowitz
Edition reviewed: © 1983

Number of pages: 792
Number of entries: 38,000
Number of illustrations: 15 pages of black-and-white drawings
Intended readership: advanced ESL students
Trim size: $5^3/_4'' \times 8^3/_4''$
Binding: paperback

Prices. $15.95
Sold in bookstores; also sold directly to schools
ISBN 0-582-79797-7
No stated revision policy

Introduction and Scope

The *Longman Dictionary of American English* is designed for individuals whose native tongue is not English but who possess an intermediate or advanced fluency in the English language. It is intended to help these users become less dependent upon bilingual dictionaries. It does so by giving not only literal definitions but also connotative values and usage of words and expressions in English.

Authority

Longman is a highly regarded publisher of texts for English as a second language (ESL) instruction as well as for the training of ESL teachers. Consultants for the project include Virginia French Allen, William Crawford, and other recognized authorities in the field, representing major U.S. centers for ESL research and instruction.

Both the selection of main entry words and the controlled vocabulary used in the definitions are based on the Longman Defining Vocabulary, which is a list of 2,000 of the most frequently used words in spoken as well as written English.

Longman Dictionary of American English:
A Dictionary for Learners of English

❶ Syllabication of boldface main entry word shown by centered dots

❷ Pronunciation given in International Phonetic Alphabet (IPA)

❸ Part-of-speech label, in italics, followed by irregular inflected forms in boldface type

❹ Transitive/intransitive verb designations are in brackets, including, in italics, a preposition that often follows this verb

❺ Illustrative sentences in italics

❻ Cross-reference in small capitals

❼ Usage notes elaborate further on the meaning and use of similar words

dec·o·rate /ˈdɛkəˌreɪt/ *v* **-rated, -rating 1** [T *with*] to serve as, or provide with, something added because it is beautiful, esp. for a special occasion: *The streets were decorated with flags.* **2** [I;T] to paint or put paper, etc., on the walls of a house: *How much will it cost to decorate the kitchen?* **3** [T *for*] to give (someone) an official mark of honor, such as a MEDAL

USAGE **Decorate, adorn, embellish,** and **garnish** are all verbs meaning "to add something to, so as to make more attractive." **Decorate,** as in (1) is normally used of places, and often of special occasions: *The children* **decorated** *the house for Christmas;* **adorn** is particularly used of things: *She* **adorned** *herself with jewels;* **embellish** is normally used of things: *The door of the church was* **embellished** *with* CARVINGS; and **garnish** is most often used of cooking: *a baked fish* **garnished** *with pieces of tomato.*

Comprehensiveness of Entries

The dictionary's word list is appropriate for the student of English at the intermediate and advanced levels and for high school and college students using English in mainstream (as opposed to bilingual or remedial) content courses. The list contains a balance of words that students will encounter in formal and informal speech and reading. The jargon of language instruction, used in the introductory exercises and the "Study Notes," is incorporated into the word list.

The work includes more than 5,000 idioms and figurative expressions. Variant forms and comparable and contrasting forms are given and illustrated, expanding the range of the word list still further.

Quality and Currency of Entries

The information is ordered within entries according to the following basic sequence: entry word or phrase; pronunciations, set off by virgules; the part-of-speech label; British spelling or other variant, as appropriate; boldface inflected forms (when irregular or requiring consonant doubling); a boldface numeral (when more than one meaning is defined); the grammar code (explained in the introduction); definition; illustrative sentence or phrase in italics; synonyms; boldface run-ins; cross-references to related words, "Study Notes," and illustrations; and sometimes a paragraph of usage notes, also cross-referenced. Many entries also include cross-references for comparison of words that are logically equal in deep structure but not interchangeable

in surface structure (for example, HOMEWORK and HOUSEWORK).

An important feature of the entries, second in importance to the well-controlled vocabulary, is the usage instructions. Codes and symbols are used to show such language features as noun countability and the objects of phrasal verbs. These points of syntax are essential to native-level language use. Step-by-step instructions in the introduction and a series of thorough "Study Notes" explain the use of these guides. Both the introduction and the "Study Notes" are cross-referenced in the entries.

Another key feature of the entries is the extensive use of illustrative phrases and sentences, at a ratIo of 55,000 illustrations of context to 38,000 entry words.

The work's currency is strong in the area of contemporary idiom, as is appropriate for an ESL dictionary.

Syllabication and Pronunciation

Entry words are syllabified by centered dots; inflected forms and run-ons are not syllabified.

Each entry word is followed by a pronunciation guide enclosed within virgules. The guide takes the form of a respelling in the International Phonetic Alphabet (IPA). IPA symbols are fully explained in the introduction, where a full pronunciation key is provided. In acknowledgment of the sometimes tenuous links between English pronunciation and spelling, "Spelling Notes" are provided that outline the varying ways in which a sound may be spelled.

Accessibility

Boldface guide words are provided for each spread and are set off by rules. The work is heavily cross-referenced, and the "Spelling Notes" offer tips to aid students in finding words they may never have seen or may have only partially heard.

Homographs are listed separately and are designated by superscript numerals following the entry word.

Special Features

A thorough introduction explains the work's features. Also included is a 38-page "Dictionary Skills Workbook," which is cross-referenced throughout the text. The workbook provides exercises for using the dictionary to illustrate the features of grammar and usage that are discussed. Answers are provided at the end of the section.

Affixes are explained, and separate listings for prefixes and suffixes are appended in a section called "Word Building." Explanations and examples are given for ways to change a word's meaning and/or part of speech by using affixes. This is a key skill for the student to master in gaining linguistic fluency. Also provided is a listing of irregular verb forms.

Graphics and Format

The entries are easy to read with their clear typeface and adequate leading. The paper is bright white with no show-through. The margins are narrow, but the entry words are clearly legible, printed in a larger type and in boldface, and overhanging the text.

There are no illustrations for individual entries. However, concepts in the "Study Notes" are illustrated with line drawings, and fifteen full-page drawings are provided. These drawings are in the realistic cartooning style used in most adult ESL texts. They identify objects related to everyday experience and travel. For example, one illustration features items and fixtures in a clothing store; another shows a doctor's office. The illustrations are captioned with the most common spoken variant for each object. The illustration pages are placed adjacent to the page where the relevant main entry appears—that is, the entry for the location (airport, kitchen) or general grouping (electronic items, car parts) illustrated. All of the captions are themselves main entry words, and cross-references to the drawings are provided in their entries.

Summary

The *Longman Dictionary of American English* serves both as a dictionary of the English language and as an instructional text for intermediate and advanced students of English as a second or foreign language. As such, it can be used either as a personal general reference dictionary by nonnative-English speakers or as an auxiliary text for formal instruction.

The *Longman Dictionary of American English* is comparable in scope to the OXFORD ESL DICTIONARY and WEBSTER'S BASIC ENGLISH DICTIONARY. The latter work is not explicitly designed for ESL students and therefore lacks some of the features of the other two dictionaries, such as frequent illustrative examples, The OXFORD ESL DICTIONARY is strikingly similar to the *Longman Dictionary of American English*, even down to the small trim size and the student workbook included in the front matter. The decision to purchase one of these over the other may come down to two factors: price and currency. On both counts, the OXFORD ESL DICTIONARY wins: at $10.95, it is $5 cheaper than *Longman*; copyrighted in 1986, it is also three years younger.

Longman Dictionary of Contemporary English

Facts at a Glance

Full title: **Longman Dictionary of Contemporary English, New Edition**
Publisher: Longman
Editors: Della Summers, Editorial Director; Michael Rundell, Managing Editor
Edition reviewed: © 1987, 1992 printing

Number of pages: 1,229
Number of entries: 56,000
Number of illustrations: 500
Intended readership: advanced nonnative students of English
Trim size: 5¾" × 8½"
Binding: paperback

Price: $25.95; 25 percent discount to schools
Sold in bookstores; also sold directly to schools and universities
ISBN 0-582-84223-9
No stated revision policy

Introduction and Scope

The *Longman Dictionary of Contemporary English* is designed for advanced students and for teachers who need more than a bilingual dictionary. According to the general introduction:

> Dictionaries for learners should present words not as isolated units of meaning, but rather in terms of their function in combination with other words and structures. . . . Consequently, a great deal of attention has been paid to show-

Longman Dictionary of Contemporary English

❶ Syllabication of boldface main entry word shown by centered dots

❷ Pronunciation given in International Phonetic Alphabet (IPA)

❸ Part-of-speech label, in italics, precedes definitions to which it applies

❹ Illustration includes both title, in boldface type, and captions

❺ Example sentences in italics

❻ Idioms, in boldface type, appear at the end of the entry

❼ Usage notes, indicated by a small black square, compare main entry word with a similar word

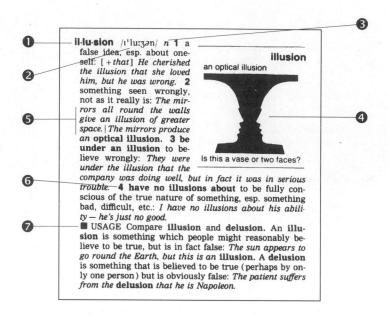

ing the collocational properties of words and the grammatical relations into which they can enter.

Besides definitions, entries contain information on spelling, pronunciation, grammar, and usage. Twenty different "Language Notes" throughout the work discuss general language issues, while 400 "Usage Notes" discuss specific examples. The front matter contains both a "Quick Guide" and a "Full Guide to Using the Dictionary," as well as an explanatory chart showing entry features. The work contains 56,000 main entries in 1,229 pages.

Authority

The work reviewed is the 1992 printing of the 1987 second edition. According to the preface, the editors incorporated responses to the first edition. Furthermore, Longman undertook its own international research projects with educational institutions, which also affected changes.

The words in this dictionary are based on the Longman Citation Corpus. Originally consisting of 25 million words, another 2 million were added for this edition; these were taken from British and American newspapers, as well as citations covering 15,000 neologisms. According to the publisher, the dictionary was compiled by a team of specialist English language teaching (ELT) lexicographers, who worked with a panel of educators headed by the British professor, Sir Randolph Quirk.

Comprehensiveness of Entries

The editors recognize "the international role of English," and their stated intent is to help students use English not only correctly, but also appropriately. Thus,

their word list was created from both spoken and written sources. Entries do not include biographical or geographical words (the latter are treated in a separate list at the end of the book), but they do include abbreviations, acronyms, British and American terms, slang, and vulgarisms.

The word choices are useful. Technical terms such as **DNA, microchip,** and **X chromosome** are included; the slang meanings of **gay** and **crack** are given; and terms such as **gender-bender** and **cost of living** are explained.

Both British and American words, spellings, and abbreviations appear. Users can find information on **Boxing Day** and on **Thanksgiving;** on an **elevator** and on a **lift.** Within entries, synonyms and antonyms are not labeled, but they often appear in usage notes or cross-references.

Entries contain numerous idioms, and phrasal verbs are shown as subentries. Thus the **pick** entry contains **pick a fight, pick at, pick on,** and **pick up.** Most entries present many clear example phrases or sentences. Usage notes explain these examples further. An example under **suppose** is: *I don't suppose you could give me a lift to the station, could you?* The accompanying usage note points out that the word is used "in polite requests."

Quality and Currency of Entries

Main entry words are in boldface type and overhang the text. The entries contain the pronunciation, the part-of-speech label, grammar codes, one or more definitions, and one or more examples. Often they have usage notes as well. Idioms and collocations are included in main entries, but derivatives and compounds have separate entries.

The word **half,** for example, is followed by an entire page of compounds, including **half crown, half measures, half moon,** and **half term.** Each has its own entry.

These two consecutive entries are typical of ones without usage notes:

hill /ˈhɪl/ *n* **1** a raised area of land, not as high as a mountain, and not usu. as bare or rocky: *Sheep were grazing on the side of the hill.* | *The castle stands on a hill.* | *a hill farmer* **2 over the hill** *infml* no longer young

hill·bil·ly /ˈhɪlbɪli/ *n AmE, often derog.* a farmer or someone from a mountain area far from a town

For words with more than one meaning, the most common definition is given first, followed by less common definitions. Most definitions limit themselves to the Longman Defining Vocabulary, a computer-checked core vocabulary of 2,000 words. (The Longman Defining Vocabulary is listed in an appendix.) If words not found in the Longman Defining Vocabulary are used in a definition, they are shown in small capitals, so users will know to look them up separately.

Example sentences and phrases are also written in simple language. If an example might be difficult to understand, its meaning is shown in parentheses. This example is in the entry **tail:** "(*infml*) *I hate it when the driver behind* **sits on my tail.** (=follows my car too closely)."

Grammar codes show part of speech, inflections, and information on whether a noun is countable or a verb is transitive. They also show limitations on a word's use, such as "*usu. sing.,*" and sentence pattern codes.

Syllabication and Pronunciation

Main entry words are divided into syllables. All pronunciations are given in the International Phonetic Alphabet (IPA), with a few additional symbols to indicate differences between British and American pronunciations. Main and secondary stress are shown by superscript and subscript stress marks. Compound words and phrases use a special system that uses dots to represent words and stress marks to show accents. For example, the code for **piece of work** is |ˌ·ˈ··|.

Accessibility

Readers can find words easily in this book. The front matter includes a chart explaining the entries, a "Quick Guide to Using the Dictionary" and a "Full Guide." Both are clear, well organized, and easy to understand. Each page has one guide word at its top outer edge. These are easy to see and read.

Abbreviations and main entries are alphabetized, letter by letter; for example, **P.O., poach, P.O. Box.** Main entries, idioms, collocations, derivatives, and compounds are all set in boldface type. Variant spellings are given main entries with cross-references, unless the spellings are very close in alphabetical order. If two words have a common meaning, both words have main entries and a cross-reference is provided. A double vertical line (‖) indicates British and American differences in spelling and meaning.

Special Features

Special features include new illustrations; grammar codes, mentioned earlier; 20 language notes; and 400 usage notes. The language notes, which appear throughout the dictionary, provide useful information on general topics, such as **Apologies, Politeness,** and **Words followed by prepositions.** One note, on **Tentativeness,** explains, "In English, speakers often show politeness by being indirect and tentative." The note then gives numerous examples of ways to do this.

Usage notes, which are located within entries, provide context information about particular words and their synonyms. One, for example, discusses the phrase **of course,** explaining how the phrase is usually used and when it might seem impolite.

Graphics and Format

The book encourages browsing. The paper looks and feels substantial, and the print is easy to read. Entry words stand out visually; within entries, typographical elements help distinguish components.

The illustrations, consisting of line drawings and photographs, are noteworthy. Many do more than simply illustrate a term. For instance, an illustration of a **laboratory** includes the names of the equipment pictured, such as the *measuring cylinder, tongs,* and *Bunsen burner.* The illustration of chessmen names the various pieces.

Summary

The *Longman Dictionary of Contemporary English* would be a valuable addition to any ESL or general library. It is less academic than the OXFORD ADVANCED LEARNER'S DICTIONARY OF CURRENT ENGLISH and more inviting to look at. The simple but clear definitions and illustrations are excellent—both helpful and user-friendly. The explanations and brief usage notes will help readers really understand the language they are hearing and reading. In addition, the slang and idiomatic uses of words here will appeal to advanced nonnative English speakers. These qualities combine to make this book a worthwhile purchase for teachers, students, and librarians.

Longman Dictionary of English Language and Culture

Facts at a Glance

Full title: **Longman Dictionary of English Language and Culture**

Publisher: Longman

Editors: Della Summers, Editorial Director; Sheila Dignen, Managing Editor; Penny Stock, Editorial Manager

Edition reviewed: © 1992

Number of pages: 1,528

Number of entries: 80,000

Number of illustrations: more than 500

Intended readership: upper intermediate to advanced nonnative students of American English

Trim size: 6" × 9"

Binding: paperback

Price: $29.95; 25 percent discount to schools

Sold in bookstores; also sold directly to universities

ISBN 0-582-08676-0

Revised edition published in 1993

Introduction and Scope

Based on the 1987 edition of the LONGMAN DICTIONARY OF CONTEMPORARY ENGLISH, the *Longman Dictionary of English Language and Culture* contains, according to the preface, an additional "15,000 people, places, events, and institutions in order to provide advanced learners of English with a full reference resource in one book." The book was created to help advanced students of English understand "the words and phrases that make up the complex fabric of English-speaking life and culture." It is a reference in which students can find not only vocabulary words, but also references to **Coca-Cola, Rodeo Drive,** and **Meryl Streep.** It also provides an understanding of words' connotations as well as their denotations.

Besides definitions, entries contain information on spelling, pronunciation, grammar, and usage. The book also has more than 15,000 cultural and encyclopedic entries, more than 400 cultural notes, 16 short feature articles on topics such as baseball and social class in Britain, seven tables, and 32 pages of color photographs, maps, and drawings. The work reviewed is the 1992 first edition. It contains 80,000 main entries in 1,528 pages. A revised edition, published in 1993, was not available at the time of the review.

Authority

This book expands upon the LONGMAN DICTIONARY OF CONTEMPORARY ENGLISH, which is based on the Longman Citation Corpus, a database containing more than 25 million words taken from written and spoken sources. According to the note on the copyright page, the book's additional cultural information

> represents the meaning, connotations, and associations that English-speaking people have, as ascertained by the editorial team on the basis of their professional knowledge and/or citational evidence from newspapers, books, and magazines.

The editorial team included British and American lexicographers, a pronunciation editor, and a geographical consultant.

Comprehensiveness of Entries

The dictionary contains every category of words, including technical and scientific terms, biographical and geographical entries, abbreviations, acronyms, slang, and vulgarisms. The geographical and biographical entries are up-to-date. For instance, **Germany** is described as a unified country, and readers who look up the surname **Jackson** can read about **Andrew, Bo, Glenda, the Reverend Jesse, Michael,** and **Stonewall.**

Word choices tend toward the practical. Although the book does contain technical terms, such as **CD-ROM** and **microchip,** more attention is given to words students might read or hear in everyday life. One quarter-page, for instance, lists the following main entries: **dentistry; denture; denude; denunciation; Denver; Denver, John; Denver boot; deny; deodorant; deodorize;** and **dep** (written abbreviation for **departure**). In addition to including more cultural entries than the LONGMAN DICTIONARY OF CONTEMPORARY ENGLISH, the *Longman Dictionary of English Language and Culture* also contains other entry words and phrases not included in that work, such as **acrophobia, action figure, act of worship,** and **added value.**

Both British and American words, spellings, and abbreviations appear. Within entries, synonyms are written in small capital letters directly after the definition. In addition, synonyms often appear in usage notes or cross-references.

Entries contain phrasal verbs, idioms, well-known sayings, and derived forms. They also contain numerous examples from everyday speech and from literature. Compound words and phrases are not shown as subentries. Instead, they are listed individually.

Grammar notes show part of speech, inflections, and information on whether a noun is countable or a verb transitive. They also show limitations on a word's use, such as "*usu. sing.,*" as well as sentence pattern codes.

Usage and cultural notes add an abundance of helpful information. Usage notes distinguish between synonyms; explain points of grammar, usage, or style; and show differences between British and American English. Cultural notes explain the associations that words

Longman Dictionary of
English Language and Culture

❶ Syllabication of boldface main entry word shown by a centered dot

❷ Two pronunciations, in International Phonetic Alphabet (IPA), are shown, followed by italicized part-of-speech label

❸ Example sentences in italics

❹ Drawing illustrates definition **1** of first homograph

❺ Usage labels in italics

❻ Cross-reference in small capitals

❼ Idioms, in boldface type, appear at the end of the entry

❽ Usage notes, indicated by a triangle on its side, add additional information

❾ Homographs appear as separate, numbered entries

doc·tor[1] /ˈdɒktəʳ‖ˈdɑːk-/ *n* **1** a person whose profession is to attend to and treat sick people: *She wants to be a doctor when she leaves school.* | *You should see|consult a doctor about your earache.* | *Doctor Smith will see you now.* | *Good morning, doctor.* | *You'd better go to the doctor|to the doctor's about your toe.* —see also FLYING DOCTOR **2** a person holding one of the highest degrees given by a university, such as a PHD **3** *AmE* (used when speaking to or about a DENTIST): *My dentist is called Doctor Steen.* **4** *infml* a person whose job is to repair the stated thing: *a radio|bicycle doctor* **5 Is there a doctor in the house?** a phrase which theatre managers are supposed to use if a member of the public is taken ill in the theatre and needs a doctor **6 under the doctor (for)** *BrE infml* being treated by a doctor (for) —see FATHER (USAGE)

▷ USAGE In Britain, medical doctors are called **doctor** but SURGEONS and DENTISTS are called Mr, Miss, Mrs, or Ms followed by their family name. In the US, dentists, medical doctors, and surgeons are called doctor. In both countries holders of a PhD are entitled to be called doctor but rarely use the title outside universities. The title is usu. written **Dr**.◁

doctor[2] *v* [T] *infml* **1** *derog* to change, esp. in a dishonest way: *They were charged with doctoring the election results.* | *It was discovered that the accounts had been doctored.* **2** *euph, esp. BrE* to make (esp. an animal) unable to breed by removing its sex organs; NEUTER[2]: *The cat has been doctored.* **3** *rare* to give medical treatment to

have for native English speakers. A usage note at **hunt,** for instance, explains the difference between **hunting** and **shooting** in Britain; a cultural note explains the conflict between those who love hunting and those who oppose it. The cultural notes in the *Longman Dictionary of English Language and Culture* set it apart from all other English as a second language (ESL) dictionaries on the market.

Quality and Currency of Entries

Main entry words are in boldface type and overhang the text. Entries include the pronunciation, the part-of-speech label (often a grammar code), one or more definitions, example phrases and sentences, and derivatives. They often contain usage notes or cultural notes as well. Main entries may include idioms and collocations, but not compounds, which have separate entries. The following entry is typical:

> **in·vent** /ɪnˈvent/ *v* [T] **1** to make or produce (esp. a new or useful thing or idea) for the first time: *Alexander Graham Bell invented the telephone in 1876.* **2** to think of (a story, like, etc.) esp. in order to deceive; produce (something untrue or unreal): *They invented a very convincing alibi.* | *He invented a hundred reasons why he couldn't go.*
>
> ▷ USAGE You **discover** something that existed before but was not known, such as a place or a fact. You **invent** something that did not exist before, such as a machine or a method: *They discovered oil in the North Sea.* | *Who invented the computer?*

For words with more than one meaning, the most common definition is given first, followed by less common definitions, including those that are literary or technical. Most definitions limit themselves to the Longman Defining Vocabulary, a computer-checked core vocabulary of 2,000 words that are listed in an appendix. Any words not on the list that are used in the definitions are indicated by small capital letters, so that readers can look them up elsewhere in the dictionary.

Syllabication and Pronunciation

Main entries are divided into syllables by centered dots. All pronunciations are given in the International Phonetic Alphabet (IPA), with a few special symbols added to distinguish between British and American pronunciations. Primary and secondary stress are shown by superscript and subscript stress marks. Compound words use a system of dots and stress marks to indicate how the entire phrase should be pronounced. With this system, the code for **personal computer** is: /ˌ··· ˈ··/.

Accessibility

This book is one of the most accessible ESL dictionaries available. A 2-page chart explains the entry format, and a 32-page "Guide to Using the Dictionary" explains how to find words and phrases and fully understand them. These user-friendly tools fully explain the dictionary's rationales and techniques, and provide easy-to-use references for learners of English.

Each page has a guide word located in either the upper left- or right-hand corner. Both words and abbreviations are alphabetized, letter by letter; for example, **Key West, kg, KGB, khaki.** Main entries, idioms, collocations, derivatives, phrasal verbs, and compounds are all set in boldface type. Alternate spellings have separate main entries, with cross-references. If two words have a common meaning, such as **scapula** and **shoulder blade,** each has a main entry and a cross-reference. A double vertical line (‖) indicates British-American differences in spelling and meaning.

Special Features

The special features include 15,000 cultural and encyclopedic entries, 400 cultural notes, special feature pages, and full-page annotated illustrations. Cultural and encyclopedic entries include explanations of such terms as **Twinkie** (the snack food), and the related **Twinkie defense; knock-knock jokes;** and **Harley Davidson.** Special feature pages discuss certain topics in depth. A page on **holidays,** for example, discusses paid holidays, popular vacation spots, and the kinds of places people stay. Full-page color illustrations are mixtures of photographs and drawings, and show American and British homes; scenes from the Wild West; scenes from Shakespeare; television programs; history; pictures of Christmas; and other topics of interest. Many smaller black-and-white photographs and drawings are sprinkled throughout the work. The illustration program is the most extensive of any ESL dictionary, and adds a great deal to its appeal.

Graphics and Format

The book has a clean, attractive appearance. The two-column pages are uncluttered and easy to read. The paper is of good quality, and the binding seems sturdy. The book's paperback cover, however, is not particularly well suited to heavy use. Illustrations include drawings, photographs, and cartoons, and they appear on about a third of the pages. Additional full-page color illustrations are scattered throughout. Most illustrations are useful, although a few, like the cartoon depicting the stereotypical **redneck,** are less valuable.

Summary

The *Longman Dictionary of English Language and Culture* is highly recommended for anyone who is living or who plans to live in England or the United States. It would allow most ESL students to understand English newspapers, television, magazines, and casual conversations. It is equally recommended for libraries and teachers who serve such students. This dictionary, less academic than the OXFORD ADVANCED LEARNER'S DICTION-

ARY OF CURRENT ENGLISH, and COLLINS COBUILD ENGLISH LANGUAGE DICTIONARY, focuses more on the life people live in England or the United States, and less on the structure of their language.

Longman Language Activator

Facts at a Glance

Full title: **Longman Language Activator: The World's First Production Dictionary**
Publisher: Longman
Editors: Della Summers, Editorial Director; Michael Rundell, Managing Editor
Edition reviewed: © 1993

Number of pages: 1,587
Number of entries: 1,052
Number of illustrations: 12
Intended readership: intermediate- to advanced-level nonnative students of English
Trim size: 6″ × 9″
Binding: paperback

Price: $29.95; 25 percent discount to schools
Sold in bookstores; also sold directly to schools and universities
ISBN 0-582-04093-0
No stated revision policy

Introduction and Scope

The *Longman Language Activator* is not an ordinary dictionary. Its editors stress its difference:

> [It] is a dictionary of *ideas* and how to express them in English. This is a new type of dictionary, aimed at helping intermediate to advanced students *produce* language, in other words, to *encode* their ideas. As such, it is a major departure from . . . the traditional role of the dictionary, which is predominantly used by students of English to *decode* the meaning of unknown words.

English offers many choices when someone seeks words to express ideas. This dictionary helps a nonnative speaker choose correct and appropriate words or phrases. Words and phrases are grouped by meanings around 1,052 frequently used concepts, called "Key Words." The Key Words express basic concepts, such as **GOOD/EXCELLENT, GOOD/MORAL,** and **LONG TIME.** This book usually does not list concrete nouns and content words. Entries contain information on pronunciation, usage, grammar, and collocations. They also contain numerous examples. Twelve Key Word pictures, located throughout the work, supply practice and information for users. The work reviewed is the first (1993) edition.

Longman Language Activator

❶ Cross-references to Key Word meanings
❷ Access Map refers reader to Key Word entries
❸ Key Word entry
❹ Numbered meanings list
❺ Submenu
❻ Entry word in boldface type
❼ International Phonetic Alphabet (IPA) pronunciation
❽ Definition uses the Longman Defining Vocabulary
❾ Part-of-speech label in italics
❿ Illustrative examples in italics

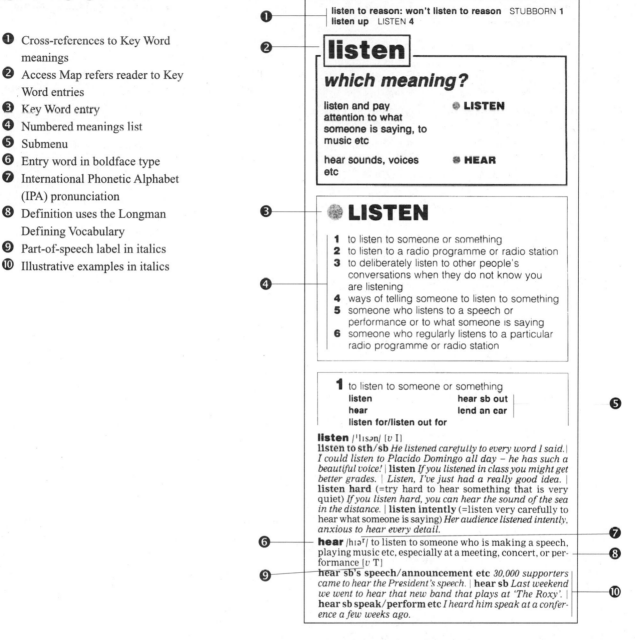

Authority

Longman has been involved with dictionaries for more than two centuries; in 1755, it published Samuel Johnson's dictionary. The *Longman Language Activator* is based on the Longman Corpus Network. This network includes a main corpus of approximately 30 million words taken from books, periodicals, and unpublished materials. It also includes a 10-million word Spoken Corpus and a Learners' Corpus based on actual student writings.

The editors have had previous experience with ESL dictionaries. Summers and Rundell also edited LONGMAN DICTIONARY OF CONTEMPORARY ENGLISH, NEW EDITION; in addition, Summers was one of the editors of LONGMAN DICTIONARY OF ENGLISH LANGUAGE AND CULTURE.

Comprehensiveness of Entries

The *Longman Language Activator* has three main types of entries. The most important of these are the 1,052 Key Word entries. They identify such general concepts and nouns as **BAD, EMPTY,** or **DOCTOR.** Each begins with a list of numbered meanings. The list for the Key Word **DOCTOR,** for example, contains these choices:

1 words meaning a doctor
2 a doctor who has special skills

3 a doctor who treats people who are mentally ill
4 a doctor who treats people's teeth
5 a doctor who treats animals

Below this are separate sections with corresponding numbers. Each section has its own submenu of words and phrases, with entries for each. For instance, the submenu for "**1** words meaning a doctor" contains the following words: **doctor, physician, GP, quack,** and **the medical profession.** The submenu for "**5** a doctor who treats animals" contains **vet** and **veterinarian.**

The entries themselves contain British and American pronunciations, definitions using the Longman Defining Vocabulary (a 2,000-word core of words that are listed at the end of the dictionary), collocations, information about grammar and usage, and numerous examples based on the Longman Corpus Network. A small drawing of an ear indicates words and phrases that are primarily used in spoken English.

The following is the entry for **quack,** found under **DOCTOR:**

> **quack** /kwæk/ an informal word for a doctor who is not very good or for someone who claims to be a doctor but has not been properly trained. [*n* C]
>
> *That quack doesn't know a thing about medicine! | My doctor is one of those quacks who charge the earth for useless treatment.*

In addition to these lengthy Key Word entries, there are many cross-references to specific meanings within a Key Word. For example:

> **raft: a raft of** LOT/A LARGE NUMBER OR AMOUNT **2**
> **rage** ANGRY **5**
> **rage; be all the rage** FASHIONABLE **1**
> **ragged** TEAR **4**

Thus, to find the definition of **rage,** a reader is guided to the fifth meaning of the Key Word ANGRY.

The third type of entry is called an "Access Map." Access Maps ask readers which meaning of a word they seek, offer them choices, and then direct them to the proper Key Word. Students who look up **attack,** for example, choose between "use violence against a person, place etc." and "attack someone with words." They are then directed to the Key Words **attack** and **criticize.**

Quality and Currency of Entries

This book does not contain technical terms, such as *femur;* cultural terms, such as *Broadway;* concrete nouns, such as *basketball;* vulgarisms; or biographical or geographical terms. The introduction directs readers to other books for such words. Nor does this book contain long lists of synonyms, as a thesaurus might. Instead, the menu for each numbered section offers perhaps two to nine words. Most have four or five. These are arranged in order of frequency, with the most general word ap-

pearing first and the most specific last. Thus, the word **decrease** comes before **plummet** and **nosedive,** because it is the more general term.

The definitions are simple to read, because they are written using only the 2,000 words on the Longman Defining Vocabulary list. In a few instances, these words are combined in clear compounds or have simple prefixes or suffixes added.

Syllabication and Pronunciation

Although pronunciation is addressed in this book, it is not emphasized. Entries are not divided into syllables. All pronunciations are given in the International Phonetic Alphabet (IPA), which is shown on the inside front cover. Primary and secondary stress are shown by superscript and subscript stress marks. Both British and American pronunciations are given, separated by double vertical lines.

Accessibility

The book assumes that concepts are related not by a hierarchy (for example, movements, movements of people, movements of people forward, walking), but by a network of relationships. In other words, someone might look up either **food, hunger,** or **eat.** Readers are given several different methods of access. They can either look for a general concept, an idea that needs expression, such as **EAT,** which is a Key Word. Or they can look up a familiar word, such as **snack,** and be directed both to **EAT** and to **MEAL.**

The front matter suggests an additional access strategy: browsing. Whether casual or purposeful, browsing through entries is offered as a useful method of finding and understanding new words.

The front matter contains several essays aimed at teachers. These are followed by the explanatory page and "How to Use the *Longman Language Activator,*" which are aimed at students. These pages explain not only how students could find words and phrases, but also how they could use the book when taking exams.

Special Features

The entire structure of this book, which combines alphabetical organization with conceptual organization, is a special feature, especially when compared with standard dictionaries. Another feature is the use of simple grammar patterns, indicated by codes, and of boldface written examples of such patterns. Both of these help students use words correctly.

The *Longman Language Activator* also distinguishes between written and spoken language. Words and phrases that are primarily spoken or heard are marked with an icon of an ear and identified in the definition with the words "you say." The following examples are listed under the Key Words **SERIOUS SITUATION:**

> **be no laughing matter** . . . if you say that a situation or event **is no laughing matter,** you mean that it is serious
> **be no joke** . . . an informal expression: if you say that a situation or event **is no joke,** you mean that it is difficult or unpleasant

Graphics and Format

Readers familiar with traditional dictionaries may be intimidated at first by this book's format because it is so different from other dictionaries. However, it is clear and easy to read once the user reads the helpful front matter. The two-column layout makes good use of white space, graphic elements, and typographical distinctions. The paperback binding is reasonably heavy, but would not withstand as much heavy use as a hardcover volume.

The book contains no illustrations as such. Instead, it offers 12 Key Word pictures. These are full-page photographs of scenes that are followed by the question "What's the right word?" Each also contains about a half page of text. Many students will undoubtedly look up all 12 pictures just for pleasure.

Key Word pictures allow students to practice choosing an appropriate word. Readers study the picture and think about what it shows and how that might be expressed in English. Then they are told what word 200 English students chose in a survey. Next, they are instructed to read the choices at a certain Key Word and led to the most appropriate choice. This choice is a highly specific word, such as **frisk, jog,** or **shoplift.** The pages end by giving the word that 200 British and American teachers chose, which turns out to be the word deemed most appropriate.

One such Key Word picture shows a man standing outside an open door. He is listening to three people who are talking in another room. Readers are instructed to read the choices at **LISTEN;** one choice leads them to a submenu that contains **listen in, eavesdrop, bug, tap,** and **monitor. Eavesdrop** is circled and its definition shown. Readers are then told that it is the most appropriate word to describe the picture.

Summary

The *Longman Language Activator* is not intended to be used by itself. Instead, it is meant to complement one of Longman's other dictionaries, such as the LONGMAN DICTIONARY OF ENGLISH LANGUAGE AND CULTURE or the LONGMAN DICTIONARY OF CONTEMPORARY ENGLISH, NEW EDITION. For students, teachers, and libraries that already own such dictionaries, this offers a good value. Because the book is unique, it has no competition. It combines the best features of a simple dictionary and a thesaurus, and

it will help nonnative speakers produce correct and appropriate English.

The Macmillan Visual Dictionary

Facts at a Glance

Full title: **The Macmillan Visual Dictionary**
Publisher: Macmillan
Editors: Jean-Claude Corbeil; Ariane Archambault
Edition reviewed: © 1992

Number of pages: 892
Number of entries: 25,000 terms
Number of illustrations: 3,500, all in full color
Intended readership: all ages
Trim size: $7^3/_8'' \times 10^7/_8''$
Binding: hardcover

Price: $45; discount (up to 40 percent) available to schools and libraries
Sold in bookstores and other retail outlets; also sold directly to libraries and schools and by direct mail
ISBN 0-02-528160-7
No stated revision policy

Introduction and Scope

The Macmillan Visual Dictionary is unlike other dictionaries in both content and presentation. According to its introduction, it "closely links pictures and words . . . [and] provides users with the words they need to accurately name the objects that make up the world around them."

The dictionary does not have typical entries. Instead, it has 3,500 computer-generated, full-color illustrations, grouped into 600 subject categories in 28 chapters. The parts of each illustration are labeled, and these 25,000 labels comprise the "lexicon" of the dictionary. The book does not attempt to show all possible objects in a given category (such as **carpentry: tools**); instead it includes typical objects. If several different terms are sometimes used to name an item, a single term was chosen by discussion and consensus. This new book, first published in 1992, is intended for the general public.

Authority

Jean-Claude Corbeil, a linguistic specialist, is the editor-in-chief of *The Macmillan Visual Dictionary,* as well as THE FACTS ON FILE VISUAL DICTIONARY (1986). Corbeil's editorial staff followed a complex research plan (described in the dictionary's introduction) to select the terminology for the illustration labels.

One-hundred seventy-five groups, organizations, and companies (including NASA, IBM, and the Canadian Coast Guard) provided up-to-date technical documents for source material. A total of 4,000 to 5,000 references were consulted in creating the dictionary. These included specialized books by experts in various fields; technical documents, including national standards and official government publications; catalogs and advertisements; encyclopedias; and unilingual, bilingual, and multilingual dictionaries.

Quality and Currency of Entries

Illustrations may show one object, several objects, or detailed scenes. For example, one page includes a single picture of an oyster, another shows numerous kitchen utensils, and a third depicts a busy airport. Headings identify the individual objects shown, and the labels are written around or below each object.

Labels often identify the parts of a single item, such as the **crankshaft** on a gasoline engine or the **shin pad** on an ice hockey player. Dotted lines connect each term with the particular part of the object that it names. In a few instances, the lines are deceptive: one label identifies a garage door as the **garage.** Most often, however, the labels clearly identify specific items.

The full-color illustrations are very up-to-date. The chapter on "Communications" includes pictures of a **videocassette recorder,** a **compact disk player,** and a **video camera.** Under "Office Automation," the illustrations of the parts of a personal computer include a **digitizing pad,** an **optical scanner,** and a **CD/ROM player.**

Most of the pictures are clear, useful, and easy to understand. A few, however, might confuse young readers or students of English as a second language. For example, on the women's clothing pages, users must be able to read and understand the subhead, "Types of Pleats," before they can understand what a **kick pleat** is; the term is printed above a picture of a skirt, near its waistband, not near the pleat itself.

The dictionary's French-Canadian origins sometimes affect the content and nomenclature. For example, team games in the "Sports" chapter include **cricket, rugby,** and **curling.** The table of contents in that chapter includes the heading "Montgolfier," which is later called "Ballooning."

Accessibility

The 16-page table of contents contains chapter headings, subheads, and, in many cases, individual illustration titles. Each chapter is color coded and is preceded by its own list of contents. Small colored tabs and chapter titles printed vertically on the edge of each page aid in subject location. Simply flipping through the book to a chapter is often the easiest way of locating an illustration in this work, although the logic behind the chapter organization is sometimes obscure. The one entitled "Human Being," for instance, is followed by "Farming" and then "Architecture."

The 28-page index is comprehensive but not as accessible as it could be. Main headings appear in boldface, but no further distinctions among entries are given. Five different page references are listed for the word **bed,** for example, with no description of how the word is used in each location. The entry for the word **shoe** refers readers to a picture of a projection screen with a rubber shoe at its base; one must look under **shoe, parts** to find an illustration of the more conventional meaning of the word. Furthermore, compound words are alphabetized strictly according to the first letter of the first word. For example, **personal computer** is listed under the letter *p,* whereas **computer table** is found under *c.* These inconsistencies would have been alleviated by adding cross-references to the index.

Special Features

In addition to the detailed table of contents and index, the work includes a three-page introduction and a two-page usage guide. The guide includes a sample page spread and briefly describes the various elements used in the illustrations. The final section of illustrations in the book, which could be considered a special feature, depicts signs and symbols; it includes the signs of the zodiac, road signs, scientific symbols, and punctuation marks.

Graphics and Format

The Macmillan Visual Dictionary is so attractive and visually appealing that it invites browsing. Many readers will probably forget their initial reason for picking up the book, as curiosity leads them to turn page after page.

The 3,500 computer-generated illustrations are detailed, accurate, and contemporary. The hardcover binding is sturdy, and the paper is shiny and thick enough to enhance the visual content. There is minimal showthrough between pages.

Summary

The Macmillan Visual Dictionary is a unique, attractive reference source. Despite the shortcomings of its index, this dictionary will prove helpful to students, educators, non-English speakers, and people who want to expand their vocabularies.

Very few people could pick up this book and read just a single page. The dictionary will expand the verbal horizons of most readers, who may be delighted to discover the names for many common objects—the **purfling** on a guitar, for example, or the **helix** on a human ear.

Those who already own THE FACTS ON FILE VISUAL DICTIONARY, which contains many of the same illustrations in black and white, might find having the two books redundant. Otherwise, *The Macmillan Visual Dictionary* would be the preferred purchase for the quality of its color illustrations.

Oxford Advanced Learner's Dictionary

Facts at a Glance

Full title: **Oxford Advanced Learner's Dictionary of Current English**

Publisher: Oxford University Press

Editor: A. S. Hornby; A. P. Cowie, Chief Editor, fourth edition

Edition reviewed: © 1989, 1992 printing; fourth edition

Number of pages: 1,579

Number of entries: approximately 57,100

Number of illustrations: more than 1,820, all in black and white

Intended readership: advanced ESL students; adult nonnative speakers

Trim size: 5½" × 8½"

Binding: hardcover

Price: $23.95

Sold directly to libraries and schools; also sold in bookstores

ISBN 0-19-431110-4

No stated revision policy

Introduction and Scope

The *Oxford Advanced Learner's Dictionary* is for foreign students of English who have progressed beyond the basics and who wish to write English as well as read it. According to the book's editor, the content was based on research into those aspects of English that proved most difficult for foreign students to learn. Thus, the work contains an abundance of information on verbs, idiomatic expressions, and fine points of usage. Both British and American meanings and spellings are included. The book assumes that readers have a basic knowledge of English vocabulary and grammar, including grammatical terms.

The work reviewed is the 1992 printing of the 1989 fourth edition. It contains approximately 57,000 main entries in 1,579 pages.

Authority

The original *Oxford Advanced Learner's Dictionary* (first published in 1942) was the brainchild of A. S. Hornby, who believed that true "proficiency in English implied the ability to compose as well as to understand." This fourth edition, edited by Anthony Cowie, follows that tradition but also makes use of recent basic research by the Oxford University Press Lexical Research Unit at the University of Leeds. It also relies on resources of the OXFORD ENGLISH DICTIONARY archive. Phonetic editor Dr. Susan Ramsaran contributes a new element, a treatment of variant pronunciations and of stress in idioms and phrases.

Comprehensiveness of Entries

The *Oxford Advanced Learner's Dictionary* is not aimed at casual users; instead, it is written for people who truly wish to study and understand current English. The book is up-to-date and covers a wide range of common and technical words, abbreviations, and acronyms, such as **ROM** and **microcomputer;** it also includes the entire range of informal English, including idioms, slang, and vulgar or taboo words. The latter are clearly marked so that users do not use them accidentally. The main text does not contain either biographical or geographical entries, but a separate appendix lists the latter.

Entry words use British spelling but also provide American spelling. If an object has both an American and British name, such as **biscuit** and **cookie,** both are listed as main entries, although the definition is British (a **cookie** is defined as "a biscuit").

The entries do not contain either etymologies or synonyms and antonyms that are labeled as such. However, synonyms appear after defining phrases; for instance, the first definition for **fervent,** "showing warmth and sincerity of feeling" is followed by the synonyms *enthusiastic* and *passionate.* Entries contain idioms, derivatives, collocations, and compounds. Users who look up **test,** for example, will discover numerous related uses, including *the acid test, test for, test case, test pilot,* and *test-tube.*

This book is noteworthy for its copious example phrases and sentences, which illustrate different meanings and forms of words. The word **sing,** for instance, has example sentences (one of which is a question) that use *sings, not singing, sang,* and *were singing.* Arrows frequently direct readers to cross-references and usage notes.

Usage notes help readers in several ways. Some explain differences among synonyms or point out alternative or unusual forms. Others explain important nuances in English. One note, for example, points out that certain words have affixes that sound negative but are not. It offers several clear examples: "**Invaluable** means 'extremely valuable.' It is not the opposite of **valuable,** which is **valueless** (or **worthless**)."

Quality and Currency of Entries

A typical entry contains a wealth of information, including pronunciation using the International Phonetic Alphabet (IPA), alternative spellings, idioms, part-of-speech labels, correct collocations, codes showing correct verb patterns, grammatical information, irregular forms, spelling notes, information on derivatives and compounds, and differences between American and

Oxford Advanced Learner's
Dictionary of Current English

❶ Drawings, along with captions, add
to the information for definition **1**

❷ Syllabication shown by a centered
dot

❸ Pronunciation given in International
Phonetic Alphabet (IPA)

❹ Idioms in boldface type

❺ Open arrows and small capitals denote cross-references

❻ Usage label, in italics, in parentheses

❼ Triangle on its side denotes beginning of derivative section

❽ U.S. spelling in italics and parentheses

❾ Compound-word section begins
with the open square symbol

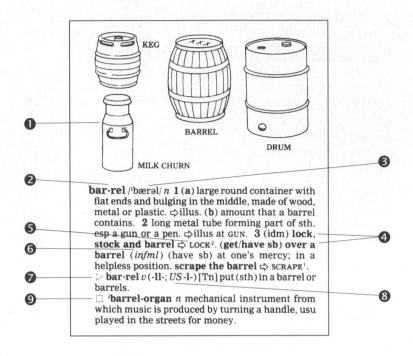

bar·rel /ˈbærəl/ *n* **1 (a)** large round container with
flat ends and bulging in the middle, made of wood,
metal or plastic. ⇨illus. **(b)** amount that a barrel
contains. **2** long metal tube forming part of sth,
esp a gun or a pen. ⇨illus at GUN. **3** (idm) **lock,
stock and barrel** ⇨ LOCK². **(get/have sb) over a
barrel** (*infml*) (have sb) at one's mercy; in a
helpless position. **scrape the barrel** ⇨ SCRAPE¹.
▷ **bar·rel** *v* (-ll-; *US* -l-) [Tn] put (sth) in a barrel or
barrels.
□ **ˈbarrel-organ** *n* mechanical instrument from
which music is produced by turning a handle, usu
played in the streets for money.

British spelling and word usage. In addition, many provide notes about a word's currency, level of formality,
and connotations.

Thirty-two verb patterns are identified by one or
more short codes. *Ln,* for instance, identifies the pattern
of subject-linking verb-subject complement (adjective
or adjective phrase). In a similar way, nouns are also
classified under nine categories, including those *countable* and *uncountable.* In some places, a space-saving
swung dash (~) replaces an entry, or the abbreviation
sb/sth replaces *somebody/something.* Entries are quite
dense, as this one demonstrates:

grit/grɪt/ n [U] **1** tiny hard bits of stone, sand, etc: spread
grit on icy roads ∘ I've got some grit/a piece of grit in my
shoe. **2** quality of courage and endurance: Mountaineering
in a blizzard needs a lot of grit.
▷ **grit** *v* (-tt-) **1** [Tn] cover (sth) with grit; spread grit on
(esp icy roads). **2** (idm) **grit one's ˈteeth (a)** keep one's
jaws tight together. **(b)** (*fig*) summon up one's courage and
determination: *When things get difficult, you just have to
grit your teeth and persevere.*
gritty *adj* (-ier, -iest) full of grit: *cheap gritty bread ∘ a
gritty fighter.* **grit·ti·ness** *n* [U].

The book's currency reflects its 1989 copyright. It contains **fax,** for instance, but not *CD* or *CD-ROM;* **HIV,**
but not *retrovirus;* **rock 'n' roll** but not *rap.*

Syllabication and Pronunciation

Entries are not actually syllabified. Instead, they are divided to show where "a word can be divided when writing or typing." For this reason, short words such as

about are shown with no breaks. Longer words are broken only at sensible divisions. For instance, **meteor** is
broken in only one place: met·eor.

Pronunciations are given in the IPA, with superscript
stress marks indicating primary stress and subscript
marks indication secondary stress. Stress is also marked
in many examples and idioms so that readers will know
how to pronounce them correctly. A British English pronunciation is shown, and the accent chosen is Received
Pronunciation (RP). American variations in pronunciation are identified by the label *US.*

Accessibility

The *Oxford Advanced Learner's Dictionary* has several features that make it accessible. First, a clear, simple five-page "Key to Entries" illustrates important
features of the entries. Following this section, a practical user's guide explains how readers can solve most
common problems they may have while using the dictionary. An appendix entitled "Using the Dictionary—
A Detailed Guide to the Entries" appears at the end of
the book. Finally, the inside front and back covers
contain information that readers will use often: a key
to phonetic symbols, a list of abbreviations, and the
codes used to show noun and adjective classes and
verb patterns.

Entries are arranged letter by letter, and alternate
spellings are entered under each spelling. Every page
has a pair of guide words at the top, although the ones
near the gutter are sometimes difficult to read
quickly.

Special Features

In addition to the detailed entries, the book has 11 separate appendixes. One contains thematically organized illustrations that cover numerous subjects, including wild plants and animals, maps of Great Britain and the United States, and various buildings. Other appendixes contain such useful information as irregular verbs, family relationships, and military rank.

Teachers and curious students will welcome the "Detailed Guide to the Entries" appendix. This fully explains every category of information that the dictionary covers. Pronunciation and grammar are explained clearly and at length. The many sections on how to use the dictionary make the *Oxford Advanced Learner's Dictionary* much more user-friendly than COLLINS COBUILD ENGLISH LANGUAGE DICTIONARY, with its seven-page section.

Graphics and Format

The book has a dense, two-column format that at first appears intimidating. However, such typographical features as the use of boldface type, different type sizes, and graphic elements (circles, squares, swung dashes, and triangles) help readers focus on the information they seek. For example, derivatives are listed together and the section is identified by a small sideways triangle; compound words are listed together, identified by a box. Although few illustrations appear in the text, those that do are generally useful. Often, illustrations have labeled parts, and words with more than one meaning (such as **glasses**) have both meanings illustrated. Considering how few pictures appear, some seem odd choices, such as the contortionist or the ostrich, but most are worth the space they fill.

The paper is of good quality, with some show-through; however, this is apparent mainly where illustrations appear. The hardcover binding seems adequate for a 5½" × 8½" book.

Summary

The *Oxford Advanced Learner's Dictionary* would be a valuable book for any library, ESL teacher, or serious student. Although its extensive coverage can be daunting (the word **put** takes up almost six complete columns), users will almost always find the information they need. Perhaps no single user will make use of every feature in this work, but every feature will probably find an interested audience. The amount and variety of information makes this volume more useful to its intended audience than most dictionaries and also more interesting to browsers. Furthermore, the numerous examples of usage, and the inclusion of idioms, collocations, derivatives, and compounds, will help users understand English as it is actually spoken and written today.

In scope, it is second only to the LONGMAN DICTIONARY OF ENGLISH LANGUAGE AND CULTURE among ESL dictionaries. More comparable, perhaps, to the COLLINS COBUILD ENGLISH LANGUAGE DICTIONARY or the LONGMAN DICTIONARY OF CONTEMPORARY ENGLISH, this work lacks some of the features of the former, but is more scholarly than the latter. It is highly recommended for serious language students who might balk at the higher price of the COLLINS COBUILD.

Oxford-Duden Pictorial English Dictionary

Facts at a Glance

Full title: **The Oxford-Duden Pictorial English Dictionary**
Publisher: Oxford University Press
Editor: John Pheby
Edition reviewed: © 1981, 1984 printing

Number of pages: 820
Number of entries: more than 28,000
Number of illustrations: more than 28,000 in black-and-white plus 6 color plates
Intended readership: grade 9 and up
Trim size: 5" × 7½"
Binding: paperback

Price: $15.95
Sold in bookstores; also sold to libraries and other educational institutions
ISBN 0-19-864155-9
No stated revision policy

Introduction and Scope

The *Oxford-Duden Pictorial English Dictionary* was first published in 1981. According to the work's foreword

> There are certain kinds of information which can be conveyed more readily and clearly by pictures than by definitions and explanations alone: an illustration will help the reader to visualize the object denoted by the word and to form an impression of the way in which objects function in their own technical field or in the everyday life of English-speaking countries.

Thus the work is designed to be useful to the native speaker expanding a technical vocabulary as well as to the learner of English as a second language (ESL). For either, the work can be a practical supplement to a good general dictionary.

The vocabulary is British in slant but American forms are shown in parentheses, preceded by the abbreviation *Am.* Although the British form is given first, both forms are indexed, and the work's British origin should cause

Oxford-Duden
Pictorial English Dictionary

❶ Picture number
❷ Picture title
❸ Numbered drawings illustrate accompanying vocabulary
❹ Headings in boldface type
❺ Common names in parentheses
❻ Usage label in italics

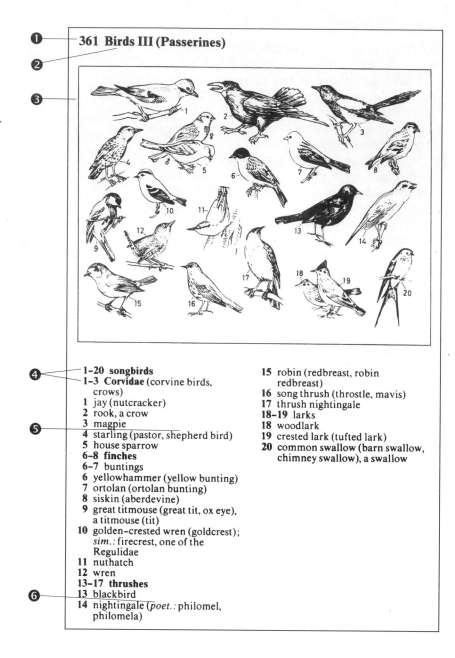

❶ **361 Birds III (Passerines)**

1–20 songbirds
1–3 Corvidae (corvine birds, crows)
1 jay (nutcracker)
2 rook, a crow
3 magpie
4 starling (pastor, shepherd bird)
5 house sparrow
6–8 finches
6–7 buntings
6 yellowhammer (yellow bunting)
7 ortolan (ortolan bunting)
8 siskin (aberdevine)
9 great titmouse (great tit, ox eye), a titmouse (tit)
10 golden-crested wren (goldcrest); *sim.:* firecrest, one of the Regulidae
11 nuthatch
12 wren
13–17 thrushes
13 blackbird
14 nightingale (*poet.:* philomel, philomela)

15 robin (redbreast, robin redbreast)
16 song thrush (throstle, mavis)
17 thrush nightingale
18–19 larks
18 woodlark
19 crested lark (tufted lark)
20 common swallow (barn swallow, chimney swallow), a swallow

few problems for the speaker or learner of American English.

Authority

The work is based on *The Oxford-Duden Pictorial German-English Dictionary,* published in 1980. The current work is the product of "numerous modifications of the text and illustrations of the original work . . . , especially regarding the depiction of everyday objects and situations."

Comprehensiveness of Entries

More than 28,000 objects are named and illustrated in the dictionary. The subjects include "typical scenes in domestic and working life, recreation and sport, flora

and fauna, industry, the arts, science, and technology." These are arranged by categories, such as "Atom, Universe, Earth," "Man and His Social Environment," and "Nature as Environment, Agriculture and Forestry." This arrangement enables the reader to use the book as "a key to the vocabulary of a subject." An alphabetical index lists all the words illustrated, so words can also be accessed as they would be in a conventional dictionary.

Quality and Currency of Entries

The dictionary is remarkable in its range of subjects and the detail and quality of its illustrations. Its value to the ESL learner lies in its excellent coverage of everyday scenes and items.

The native English speaker will also benefit from the work's comprehensiveness and detail, particularly in more technical fields. For example, homeowners attempting to communicate with the plumber or roofer will find extensive vocabularies to describe their problems and preferences. Not only will the reader find vocabularies applicable to daily life and leisure time; a great many sections are devoted to highly technical occupations, such as the production of synthetic fibers and of nuclear energy.

In addition to identifying Americanisms, the entries provide some usage information; 11 abbreviations are explained at the front of the volume. These identify, for example, terms for male (*m.* bull) and female (*f.* cow) animals and their young (*y.* calf).

The black-and-white line drawings in some cases depict complete scenes. The drawings are uniformly clear and carefully detailed, regardless of whether their subject is everyday life or the most specialized field. In addition to the line drawings, the volume contains six superbly reproduced color plates. One of these illustrates **Color** itself; four others depict butterflies, birds (two plates), and deep-sea fauna. A sixth color plate depicts human organ systems. These plates are a valuable addition to the book.

Accessibility

The work is well designed to facilitate accessibility. A detailed table of contents shows the broad category headings in boldface. Listed beneath these are the titles and numbers of the drawings. The easy-to-use alphabetical index lists all the words depicted in the volume as well as their variants. At the top of each page within the lexicon, bold running heads display the picture name and number. Within the index, two boldface guide words appear on each double-page spread, indicating the first and last words on the spread.

Graphics and Format

The illustrations grouped within the broad categories are numbered. Each page or double-page spread shows a list, printed in a two-column format, of words associated with a particular subject. The words are numbered with boldface numerals, each of which corresponds to a numbered item in the illustration. The numbers in the illustration are circled when they refer to the name of an entire construct rather than one of its components. For example, under **Dining Room**, 33 items are named and pictured; these include such objects as a **placemat**, a **wineglass**, and a **coffee cup**. The number 27, referring to the **coffee set**, is circled; numbers for its parts (**coffeepot, sugar bowl,** and so forth) are not. In the list, words that refer to an item whose component parts are also named appear in boldface, and they are usually preceded by the inclusive numerals for the component items. For example, the first item listed under **Dining Room** appears as **1–11 dining set.** Items 1 through 11 include **dining table, table leg,** and **tabletop.** Synonyms for listed words are often given in parentheses after the words.

The alphabetical index is printed in a three-column format. Each word and phrase entered is followed by a boldface numeral indicating the scene in which the item is pictured and a lightface number referring to the item within the picture. Homonyms and uses of the same word in different fields are distinguished by italicized section headings. The abbreviations used for subject fields are explained on the first page of the index.

The dictionary is physically well designed. The typeface used in the lexicon is large and clear; that used in the index, although smaller, is readable. However, because some of the illustrations are small, the embedded numbers may be more difficult for the user to follow. The paperback is exceptionally sturdy and can be opened flat with no danger of loss of pages; it will hold up well with heavy use.

Summary

The Oxford-Duden Pictorial English Dictionary is an excellent, easy-to-use pictorial dictionary. Although some Britishisms are not translated into American usage, its vocabulary includes a wide range of both everyday and technical language; its drawings and color plates are detailed, attractive, and useful.

For the English-language learner, this work will serve as the perfect complement to a good ESL dictionary. The FACTS ON FILE VISUAL DICTIONARY, its larger illustrations and fewer labels is less daunting. However, once the student reaches the intermediate level, the *Oxford-Duden* would be an appropriate choice.

The work also has considerable value for the native speaker, enabling users to expand their vocabularies in many previously unfamiliar areas. The work bears comparison in this regard with THE FACTS ON FILE VISUAL DICTIONARY and THE MACMILLAN VISUAL DICTIONARY, which illustrate a comparable number of words and are also highly useful and well designed. The FACTS ON FILE and Macmillan works are limited in value for the ESL learner because they depict fewer scenes of everyday life and because their size prevent them from being conveniently portable. While the native speaker will find THE FACTS ON FILE and Macmillan works valuable because they were written for an American audience, the easier portability and lower price of the *Oxford-Duden* will make it more attractive to some. It will be useful for larger public and college and university libraries.

Oxford Elementary Learner's Dictionary

Facts at a Glance   °

Full title: **Oxford Elementary Learner's Dictionary**
Publisher: Oxford University Press
Editor: Shirley Burridge
Edition reviewed: © 1981, 1990 printing

Number of pages: 297
Number of entries: 10,000 words and phrases
Number of illustrations: more than 450
Intended readership: beginning ESL students; young
   nonnative speakers
Trim size: 5¼″ × 8″
Binding: paperback

Price: $11.95
Sold directly to libraries and schools; also sold in
   bookstores and other retail outlets
ISBN 0-19-431253-4
No stated revision policy

Introduction and Scope

The *Oxford Elementary Learner's Dictionary* is intended to help students during their first years of learning English. It is purposely simple, yet "allows students to acquire those reference skills so essential for continued and more independent language development." The work reviewed is the 1990 printing of the 1981 edition. It contains 10,000 words and phrases in its 297 pages.

Authority

Although published by the prestigious Oxford University Press, which is known for its numerous scholarly dictionaries, the *Oxford Elementary Learner's Dictionary* provides no information about its editor, Shirley Burridge. No information is given about how the word list was developed.

Comprehensiveness of Entries

In the introduction, the editors state that the 10,000 entries in this dictionary "include all the important words that you need in your daily life and studies." The relatively limited word list of the *Oxford Elementary Learner's Dictionary* makes it one of the most concise ESL dictionaries available. (Webster's Basic English Dictionary, with 32,000 entries, is next.) Entry words include some idioms and slang terms, but no vulgarisms, double entendres, proper names, or place names.

Many entry words are distinctly British. Users will find British spellings (such as **flavour**), British words (for example, **number-plate** instead of *license plate*), and British abbreviations (including **lb** without a final period). Within entries, users will not find etymologies,

synonyms, antonyms, or usage notes. However, many entries do contain examples of words used in typical phrases or sentences.

Quality and Currency of Entries

Definitions are brief, sometimes to the point of inadequacy. For example, **funnel** is defined as a "smokestack," with no mention made of the kitchen utensil. The following entry is typical:

> **spite** /spaɪt/ *n.* (no *pl.*) wish to hurt someone: *She broke her brother's watch out of spite.* **in spite of,** not taking notice of, not caring about: *He slept well in spite of the noise.* **spiteful** *adj.* **spitefully** *adv.*

As the above entry shows, the part of speech is identified, and the information that the noun has no plural is given. If words have irregular plurals, plural forms (such as **trousers**), or small spelling changes with plural forms, those facts are also mentioned. Idioms and derivative forms are also provided.

To show whether a verb is transitive or intransitive, the definitions use such words as *someone* or *something* in the meaning. For instance, the definition of **replace,** a transitive verb, is to "put *something* back in its place again."

The definitions are not particularly current. For example, the entry for **disc** refers to a gramophone [*sic*] record, but not to a computer; **rap** is defined to mean only one action—to strike. However, this is appropriate since the intent of this dictionary is to be basic, rather than comprehensive.

Syllabication and Pronunciation

The *Oxford Elementary Learner's Dictionary* uses the International Phonetic Alphabet (IPA) as a pronunciation guide, and words are pronounced as the British would say them. The only key to the IPA appears on the inside of the book's back cover. The symbols used can be quite confusing for a new user. For students planning to use this publisher's more advanced dictionaries, mastering the IPA will be worthwhile, because both the Oxford ESL Dictionary and the Oxford Advanced Learner's Dictionary use this system. However, students who will use American dictionaries may be confused by the different systems.

Accessibility

A guide word appears at the top of each page. Words and abbreviations are alphabetized letter by letter; for example, the abbreviation **p.m.** comes between **plus** and **pneumonia.**

The four-page introduction clearly explains how to use the dictionary. Its two-column format shows sample entries with explanations beside them. Irregular verb

Oxford Elementary Learner's Dictionary

❶ Selected illustrations, with captions, are grouped together

❷ Pronunciation given in International Phonetic Alphabet (IPA)

❸ Part-of-speech label in italics

❹ Example sentence, in italics, showing entry word in context

❺ Idioms in italicized, boldface type

❻ Compound words at the end of the entry

❼ Homographs shown as separate, numbered entries

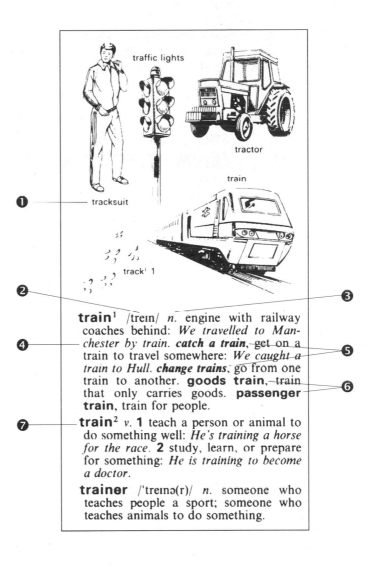

train¹ /treɪn/ *n.* engine with railway coaches behind: *We travelled to Manchester by train.* **catch a train**, get on a train to travel somewhere: *We caught a train to Hull.* **change trains**, go from one train to another. **goods train**, train that only carries goods. **passenger train**, train for people.

train² *v.* **1** teach a person or animal to do something well: *He's training a horse for the race.* **2** study, learn, or prepare for something: *He is training to become a doctor.*

trainer /'treɪnə(r)/ *n.* someone who teaches people a sport; someone who teaches animals to do something.

forms and irregular plural nouns appear both as main entries and with the word from which each is derived. The extra listing allows a user to look up either **had** or **have** to determine the relationship between the two words.

Special Features

The special features include the simple, yet useful, introduction; the large number of example phrases and sentences; the information on irregular spellings; and a key to pronouncing common suffixes. This latter is found on the inside of the front cover and, like the other pronunciation key, uses the IPA, which might confuse a new student of English.

Graphics and Format

The book has a very inviting appearance. The two-column format includes enough white space so that entries are easy to read. Typographical elements are used well throughout. Readers can tell at a glance which words in an entry are examples and which, if any, are idioms. Il-

lustrations always appear in the upper corner of each right-hand page. These illustrations usually appear in groups of three to five and are labeled. When words that have multiple meanings are illustrated, the corresponding meaning is identified by a numeral. One picture, for instance, is labeled "head¹ 1," which refers to the first definition in the first entry for **head.** The pictures themselves are simple, realistic black-and-white line drawings.

Summary

By itself, the *Oxford Elementary Learner's Dictionary* would be of limited usefulness to American users, primarily because of its British words and definitions and its phonetic respellings. Students who master this book's IPA pronunciations will have to learn an entirely different system before they can use an American dictionary, the kind most young students will find in regular classrooms. However, the *Oxford Elementary Learner's Dictionary* would be valuable to a person who already knew British English and who wanted to learn how to use an Oxford dictionary for independent work. It would also provide a good introduction to the more advanced OXFORD ESL DICTIONARY FOR STUDENTS OF AMERICAN ENGLISH.

Oxford ESL Dictionary

Facts at a Glance

Full title: **Oxford ESL Dictionary for Students of American English**
Publisher: Oxford University Press
Editors: A.S. Hornby, with Christina A. Ruse; Dolores Harris and William A. Stewart (American editors)
Edition reviewed: © 1986, 1994 printing

Number of pages: 714
Number of entries: approximately 35,000
Number of illustrations: more than 140
Intended readership: beginning and intermediate non-native students of American English
Trim size: 5⅜″ × 8½″
Binding: paperback

Price: $10.95
Sold directly to libraries and schools; also sold in bookstores and other retail outlets
ISBN 0-19-431403-0
No stated revision policy

Introduction and Scope

The *Oxford ESL Dictionary* is adapted from the *Oxford Student's Dictionary of Current English* (now out of print). It also includes material from the OXFORD ADVANCED LEARNER'S DICTIONARY OF CURRENT ENGLISH. According to the book's preface, the work contains "the more usual words, compounds, and idiomatic expressions" used by "educated Americans" in their conversation and writing. Besides definitions, entries also contain information on spelling, pronunciation, grammar, and usage. A "Dictionary Workbook" at the beginning of the work explains how readers can find and use entries; it also contains brief practice exercises. The work reviewed is the 1994 printing of the 1986 edition. It contains approximately 35,000 main entries in 714 pages.

Authority

This work is published by the prestigious Oxford University Press (OUP), known for its numerous scholarly dictionaries. This volume is an American adaptation of the *Oxford Student's Dictionary of Current English,* which was edited by A. S. Hornby (who also served as the original editor of the OXFORD ADVANCED LEARNER'S DICTIONARY). Members of the English Language Teach-

ing Department of the OUP, New York, worked with American editors to Americanize the *Oxford ESL Dictionary.*

Comprehensiveness of Entries

The editors tried to make this book useful rather than comprehensive. Users will find that the number of entries is comparable to the LONGMAN DICTIONARY OF AMERICAN ENGLISH and to WEBSTER'S BASIC ENGLISH DICTIONARY.

Few strictly scientific or technical words or definitions appear in the OUP work; readers will find both **mouse** and **menu,** for instance, but not their computer-related meanings. This volume includes few vulgarisms, and not the most obscene ones. Instead, it contains only ones that readers are apt to hear, and those are labeled as *taboo.*

Some word choices seem unusual, such as **crosier, plenipotentiary,** and **sloe;** these are seldom read or heard in everyday usage. However, most entry words are more useful. The dictionary avoids all but the most common slang. For example, **junkie** is included, but the drug **crack** is not; however, **hobo,** which is uncommon today, also appears.

American spelling and abbreviations are used, and a note in the preface explains how these are different from those in the British system. Within entries, users will not find etymologies, synonyms, antonyms, or usage notes, except for abbreviations, such as *joc* (jocular), *sl* (slang), and *poet* (poetic). Well over half of the entries contain clear examples of phrases or sentences in context.

Quality and Currency of Entries

A typical entry is easy to read. Entry words are in boldface type and overhang the text. They are followed by the pronunciation, the part-of-speech label, a notation about whether a noun is countable or uncountable, and one or more definitions. Idioms, collocations, derivatives, and compounds follow these. The following entry is typical:

> **in·dex** /ˈīn·deks/ *n* [C] (*pl* ~es, indices /ˈīndə·siz/) **1** something that points to or indicates, esp on a scale of degree or proportion: *increasing unemployment was an ~ of the country's poverty.* **2** list of names, subjects, references, etc in alphabetical order, at the end of a book, or on cards (*a card* ~) in a library, etc. □ *vt* make an index for a book, collection of books, etc.
> **in·dexer** *n* [C] person who prepares an index.
> the 'index 'finger, the forefinger, next to the thumb, used for pointing.

As in this example, definitions are arranged from most to least frequently used. Definitions are clear and are generally at the same level of difficulty as the words themselves.

As a space-saving device, a swung dash (~) is often used in place of an entry word. For this reason, the word

Oxford ESL Dictionary
for Students of American English

❶ Pronunciation shown in International Phonetic Alphabet (IPA), with emphasis on American pronunciation

❷ Italicized part-of-speech label followed by uncountable noun designation in parentheses

❸ Homographs shown as separate, numbered entries

❹ Example phrases in italics, with a swung dash replacing the main entry word

❺ Open square symbol shows a change in the part of speech in an entry

❻ Illustrations include captions

❼ Syllabication shown by a centered dot

❽ Variant plural forms in parentheses

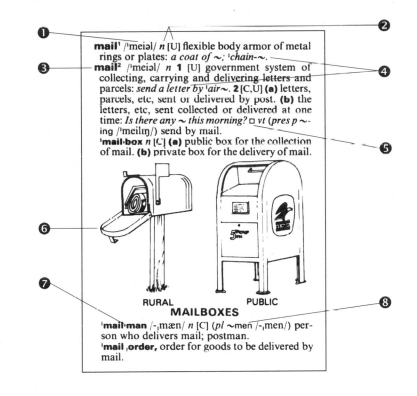

---

history is followed by this example: *a new ~ of Europe.* This system creates some odd forms when derivatives are followed by examples. For instance, the word **admit** is followed by an example using *~ted,* which a reader must decode.

As could be expected of a dictionary with a 1986 copyright date, none of the Buying Guide's test entries for currency appears.

Syllabication and Pronunciation

Main entries are not actually divided into syllables. Instead, they are marked to show where writers can divide them. As a result, words that are not commonly divided during writing, such as **alive** or **enough,** are shown with no breaks.

The *Oxford ESL Dictionary* uses a slightly altered version of the International Phonetic Alphabet (IPA). The changes, which are explained in the preface, reflect American pronunciation. A key to the IPA appears on the inside of the book's front cover.

Accessibility

This dictionary makes it easy for readers to find words. Main entries, idioms, collocations, derivatives, and compounds are all set in boldface type. Variant spellings are shown as main entries with cross-references. Each pair of pages has a pair of guide

words; unfortunately, these appear near the gutter instead of near the outer margins. This placement sometimes makes them difficult to read.

The *Oxford ESL Dictionary* also includes a 30-page "Dictionary Workbook." This provides basic information, such as the English alphabet and how to use it to determine alphabetical order. This feature would be very useful for someone familiar with a different alphabet. The workbook also contains 36 brief exercises that provide practice in various skills, such as finding words that the user does not know how to spell. These exercises would be of value to a home user, but they would be of limited use in a library setting.

Special Features

In addition to the "Dictionary Workbook," mentioned above, special features include six brief appendixes containing what the publishers call "vital cultural information." These tell readers how to understand money, tell time, read and understand numerical expressions (including phone numbers and time of day), and read and write dates and postal abbreviations of states.

Perhaps the most useful feature, however, is the abundance of example phrases and sentences. These are particularly helpful in showing the difference between collocations such as **be carried away, carry on,** and **carry through.**

Graphics and Format

For the most part, the book has a clean, simple look. Typographical elements help distinguish the various elements, and although pages are dense, they are not difficult to read.

The illustrations, however, have a different look. First, they lack uniformity. Some are simple black-and-white line drawings, others look like shaded pencil sketches, and still others are black-and-white photographs. Many are too small to be useful, and some are not near (or even on) the same page as their entry words, nor are they cross-referenced in the entry.

Summary

For most new students of American English, the *Oxford ESL Dictionary* would be a valuable tool. It provides a useful, though somewhat dated, vocabulary, clear definitions, and good examples. The "Dictionary Workbook" would help both students and their teachers, since it includes both information and exercises. The book itself is easy to handle and clear enough for both young and adult students to use. Although students will outgrow this dictionary's somewhat limited vocabulary rather quickly, they will have mastered the basics of dictionary use so that they can move on to the more comprehensive OXFORD ADVANCED LEARNER'S DICTIONARY OF CURRENT ENGLISH.

Webster's Basic English Dictionary

Facts at a Glance

Full title: **Webster's Basic English Dictionary**
Publisher: Merriam-Webster
Editors: Merriam-Webster dictionary staff
Edition reviewed: © 1990

Number of pages: 587
Number of entries: 32,000
Number of illustrations: 600, all in color
Intended readership: beginning ESL students
Trim size: 8″ × 10″
Binding: hardcover

Price: $14.95
Sold in bookstores; also available by mail order directly from the publisher
ISBN 0-87779-150-3
No stated revision policy

Introduction and Scope

Webster's Basic English Dictionary, aimed at students of English as a second language (ESL), is identical to WEBSTER'S ELEMENTARY DICTIONARY. Potential buyers should read the review of that dictionary for details about this work. The dictionary has 32,000 entries, none of which has been changed since the dictionary was first published in 1986 as the *Elementary Dictionary.* Thus, although this dictionary has a 1990 copyright date, it is really a 1986 work.

The scope of this work's lexicon and the comprehensiveness of the definitions place it somewhere between the OXFORD ELEMENTARY LEARNER'S DICTIONARY, a simplified, paperback ESL dictionary with 8,000 entries, and larger hardcover works such as the COLLINS COBUILD ENGLISH LANGUAGE DICTIONARY and the OXFORD ADVANCED LEARNER'S DICTIONARY. Although the work was originally intended for elementary students, adult users will not find the lexicon severely shortened; the names of reproductive organs are included, for example, and the 50 entries from **opera** to **orchard** include words such as **operational, opinionated, oppression, opulent, oracle,** and **oratorical.**

Special Features

Features of this dictionary that will make it useful to ESL students include a controlled vocabulary, clear pronunciations, synonym guides, and short phrases illustrating the uses of words. Unfortunately, some of these features are not as comprehensive as those in dictionaries developed exclusively for ESL students. For example, the OXFORD ELEMENTARY LEARNER'S DICTIONARY has more illustrative examples, many of them full sentences, for each entry word. Usage notes in *Webster's Basic* are minimal, and antonyms are not included.

Pronunciations do not use the International Phonetic Alphabet (IPA). Although the phonetic system used will be more familiar to people who have used other American dictionaries, those from other countries may find the IPA easier to learn and use.

Graphics and Format

The work's color illustrations will be useful to most readers, although some of the labels are not clear. For example, the illustration for **halo** depicts a winged angel holding an open book. Nonnative speakers must read the definition to understand that the word **halo** refers only to the ring of light around the angel's head, and not to the angel itself. Similarly, **rudder** is illustrated by a picture of a woman piloting a sailboat with a rudder. The correspondence between the word and the appropriate part of the illustration is not explicit.

Summary

Webster's Basic English Dictionary is an advanced children's dictionary marketed as an ESL dictionary. As such, it provides a simplified lexicon and easily understood definitions. It lacks some of the features of a typical ESL dictionary such as full illustrative sentences and extensive usage notes. The pronunciations given are

Webster's Basic English Dictionary

❶ Syllabication of boldface main entry word shown by a centered dot

❷ Pronunciation, set off by slashes, follows entry word

❸ Italicized part-of-speech label precedes definitions to which it applies

❹ Cross-references in small capitals

❺ Example sentences, with main entry word in italics, in angle brackets

❻ Run-on entries, in boldface type, appear at the end of the entry

❼ Drawing illustrates definition **1** of the first homograph

❽ Homographs appear as separate, numbered entries

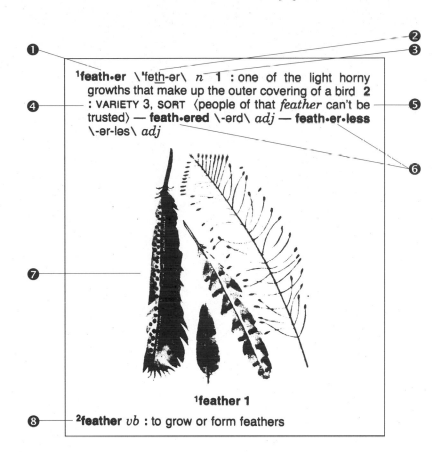

¹feather 1

²feath·er *vb* : to grow or form feathers

clear, but they do not employ the IPA, which may be more familiar to nonnative English speakers. The scope of the lexicon is quite good for the price; its 32,000 words for $14.95 make it a bargain compared with the 40,000-entry Collins COBUILD English Language Dictionary, which retails for $40. Beginning ESL students may find this work useful; adults may prefer the more comprehensive definitions of a standard ESL dictionary such as Collins COBUILD or the Oxford Advanced Learner's Dictionary.

PART FIVE

Electronic Reference Works

Chapter 14
*What to Look for in
Electronic Reference Works*

Librarians and consumers are now faced with an entirely new way of conducting research, based on using computerized, or electronic, reference works. These new tools provide many of the same kinds of information found in traditional print resources. Electronic encyclopedias may contain the text, illustrations, captions, and bibliographies published in their print counterparts. Computerized atlases offer maps and background information similar to that found in standard world atlases. Electronic dictionaries, like their print cousins, contain definitions, etymologies, synonym studies, usage notes, and guides to pronunciation and syllabication.

It would be a mistake, however, to assume that a computerized encyclopedia, atlas, or dictionary is simply an on-screen version of what the user could otherwise consult on the page. The best of such tools offer features that cannot possibly be delivered in print media. Encyclopedias may contain moving pictures as well as still illustrations. Thus animated illustrations can demonstrate the pumping action of the heart, and archival footage can show the first human steps on the moon. To supplement a discussion of Mozart or jazz, brief snippets of representative music are added; to make vivid an entry on the common loon, its eerie call is reproduced. An electronic atlas may allow the user to zoom in on one area of a map or, while looking at a nation's flag, the user can hear a few bars of its national anthem. A computerized dictionary may allow the user to *hear* a word pronounced as well as *see* it written phonetically.

These features can be truly spectacular. They allow a researcher to learn the concepts or terms being explained in more than one way and through more than one sense, a valuable aid because some people learn better by hearing or by viewing graphics than they do by reading text. But these fancy effects may obscure one of the most useful benefits of computerized reference works—they can take advantage of the quick and thorough search capabilities of the computer's processor to allow the user to locate all mentions of a key term or concept in the entire contents of the electronic work. In this way, computerized reference tools may speed the research process considerably, eliminating some of the drudgery without sacrificing the main purpose of research: to explore a topic thoroughly.

Electronic reference works may be revolutionizing the research process. The current generation of students is already learning to be as comfortable, if not more comfortable, working on screen as on paper. Indeed, many of today's children are more at ease with computers than their parents are. Librarians, recognizing the need to provide up-to-date and multifaceted research tools for their patrons, are installing computer reference stations in their libraries in increasing numbers. To be able to advise their patrons on how to take advantage of these reference tools, they are learning to use the programs themselves. However, some librarians entered their field before such computerized capabilities were widespread, and discomfort with such resources still lingers. Similar unease is felt by those consumers who are not yet fully familiar with personal computers, but who have one and are somewhat aware of the attractiveness (in terms of features and cost) of a computerized encyclopedia over a print version.

A bewildering array of questions about the equipment and the reference tools themselves adds to that discomfort. In a rapidly developing, competitive field such as personal computers, librarians and consumers face a fluid situation in which standards are not yet established, and competing approaches are available. The battle between Macintosh and PC-compatibles has been compared to the recent VCR war between Betamax and VHS—only more so.

While this book cannot offer a comprehensive guide to personal computers, it can delineate some of the basic issues involved in shopping for electronic reference works. We can help the prospective purchaser determine whether a given work is suitable to run on the computer equipment available and assess the work's scope and features and the ease with which it can be used. No two computerized reference works are alike. The information included in them differs, the features differ, and, most important, the ease with which the information can be accessed differs. The reviews in this part of the Buying Guide attempt to clarify the differences between competing products, allowing the potential purchaser to consider the advantages and disadvantages of each and to identify those criteria that are most important to him or her.

Characteristics of Electronic Reference Works

In keeping with the parameters established for this Buying Guide, the reviews in this part consider electronic versions of general encyclopedias, world atlases, and general English-language dictionaries. They do not include specialized encyclopedias such as *The American Indian: A Multimedia Encyclopedia,* computerized atlases of the United States such as *U.S. Atlas for Windows,* or electronic word books such as the *Roget's II Electronic Thesaurus,* which is found on the CD sold as *Microsoft Bookshelf.* (We do review THE CONCISE COLUMBIA ENCYCLOPEDIA, THE AMERICAN HERITAGE DICTIONARY, and the HAMMOND WORLD ATLAS, which appear on that CD, as all those products are *general* reference works.)

This part of the Buying Guide is divided into three chapters, each of which is dedicated to a particular kind of computerized reference tool: encyclopedias, atlases, and dictionaries. Note that the reviews of electronic dictionaries are limited to those works that are true dictionaries. Such features as spell checkers, thesauruses, or grammar checkers, whether built into a word-processing program or sold on their own, are not reviewed.

Just as print reference materials differ from one another significantly, so do electronic reference works. Some are available on disk (either CD-ROM or floppy disk); others are provided through an online information service (which requires that the computer have a modem and the user have a subscription to the relevant service). Some are text only; others include elaborate graphics, sound, video, and animation. Some can be accessed any time a computer user has his or her computer turned on—even when working within a standard application program such as a word processor. With these handy tools, a student can do research and outline a term paper at the same time, or a businessperson can check a fact in the database while writing a report. Other electronic reference works do not permit this simultaneous operation, but offer the user the opportunity of saving information from the reference work so that it can be imported into a document created later. Both kinds of works also generally permit users to send information directly from the reference source to a printer.

This ease of cutting and pasting information, of course, raises the issue of proper crediting of information. An unfortunate side effect of this feature is that it may facilitate plagiarism. A middle school teacher who suddenly encounters clear, coherent, encyclopedic prose in a paper from a previously lackluster student will undoubtedly "smell a rat," but all instances of inappropriate use may not be so obvious. Copying cannot be completely prevented, but it would certainly be advisable for a library to post information regarding the proper use of reference material near the relevant computer workstations. Parents with electronic reference tools at home may wish to review these issues with their children as well. (In some cases, the documentation for the electronic work addresses copyright concerns.)

Generally speaking, the works reviewed in these chapters are derived from existing print materials. The print dictionary comes first; the publisher then decides to increase the availability of the work by offering an electronic version. In most cases, the electronic version is published by the same publisher as the print version; there are exceptions, however. Microsoft, the software giant, is entering the CD-ROM market in a big way. It publishes a number of works reviewed here, including ENCARTA, which is an electronic version of the print FUNK & WAGNALLS NEW ENCYCLOPEDIA, and *Microsoft Bookshelf,* which contains the encyclopedia, dictionary, and atlas mentioned above. There are other examples as well. In these cases, the software publisher licenses the data from the original book publisher and then provides the programming skill needed to encode it on disk and build the search engine that enables the user to access that information. In these cases, the software publisher is the source to go to for help in using the program and for updates.

Ease of updating is one significant potential advantage of electronic over print reference works. It is far easier to encode new data for electronic storage, and much less expensive to press CDs or issue new floppy disks than it is to print a new edition of a multivolume encyclopedia. Thus we would expect to see computerized electronic works updated more frequently than their print counterparts—even more often than the print encyclopedia's annual revisions.

Prospective buyers must be aware that the reverse may also be true. A computerized reference work could in fact be *less* current than a print work. For example, a software publisher's license for the content of a print work may apply to one edition only; if the print publisher updates that work but the original license agreement is still in effect, the print version could be more current than the software version. The important point to remember is the basic law of consumerism: *caveat emptor.* Read the fine print and ask the relevant questions before buying an electronic reference work—as you would before making any purchase.

There is a final difference between computerized and print reference materials that are published in multiple volumes—access. Up to 26 patrons can use a 26-volume encyclopedia at one time. An encyclopedia on CD-ROM can be accessed by only one user at a time. It is likely that this will change in the future, as publishers make networking options more available. For now, however, that process is not straightforward, at least in the PC-compatible world. On the other hand, software encyclopedias provide a lot of information in an incredibly easy-to-store package. For home users, this access issue is less problematic.

Structure of Reviews for Electronic Reference Works

Most of the electronic reference works reviewed here are derived from print resources. They begin by taking the text—and perhaps other features—and presenting it in an electronic format. The best computerized resources go well beyond that, however. As noted above, they may supplement the original text with additional kinds of information, such as audio or video or animation, and they can increase the user's own abilities to access the text by providing sophisticated search capabilities.

Because the core of the information is derived from a parent work, however, the reviews in this chapter do not dwell on such factors as authority, clarity, or accuracy. The reader is referred to the detailed examination of these issues in the review of the related print version. The reviews here focus on those issues that are unique to the electronic version of the material. They describe the scope of the work, differentiating it from the print version if necessary. They describe how the computerized

version stacks up in terms of the use it makes of computer capabilities, including audio and video, searching strategies, downloading and printing features, and documentation.

A key characteristic of computerized reference works, of course, is that to use them you must have a computer. Publishers frequently issue more than one version of a computerized reference tool. The most popular versions are available to run under DOS or Microsoft *Windows* (for PC-compatible computers) and on the Apple Macintosh. The same program will not function identically in each of these formats. For reasons of space, however, it is impossible to review all three and indicate the differences in performance. We have focused on reviewing either the DOS or *Windows* version of the program. (Two exceptions are THE SOFTWARE TOOLWORKS WORLD ATLAS and WEBSTER'S NINTH NEW COLLEGIATE DICTIONARY, for which the Macintosh product was reviewed.) The reviewer notes when alternative versions of a program are available; readers considering the purchase of one of these other versions should consult periodicals that may review it.

Facts at a Glance. Each review begins with a list of basic factual information, such as the full title and publisher name; the copyright year and version number; the type of work reviewed (whether on disk or online); the number of entries, words, maps, and illustrations; the intended readership; pricing and ordering information; and the publisher's stated revision policy. This information was all supplied by the publisher and is accurate at the time it was given. When the publisher did not supply the information, the data printed here is followed by the notation (*reviewer estimate*).

Introduction and Authority. The body of each review begins with a description of the work in general terms. Reviewers also note which edition is reviewed, mentioning the copyright year of the edition and its relation to a parent print work.

This section briefly discusses the authority of the work (on the basis of the print work from which it is derived). This includes mention of the publisher's reputation for quality.

Scope and Content. In this section reviewers evaluate how comprehensive the work is in terms of the number of entries, differentiating it, if appropriate, from the parent work. THE RANDOM HOUSE ENCYCLOPEDIA: ELECTRONIC EDITION, for instance, includes the main text section of THE RANDOM HOUSE ENCYCLOPEDIA but not the illustrations in that section or the heavily illustrated section called the "Colorpedia." The review for that electronic work clearly states what material is and is not picked up from the print original. These comments are not intended as criticisms; just because an electronic work does not contain something that is in the print version does not mean that it is undesirable. However, we believe strongly that a potential purchaser should be aware of the actual scope of any work that he or she considers buying.

Reviewers assess the currency of the electronic work by checking for certain standard items. These are the same as those used to assess the currency of print material:

- For encyclopedias, reviewers looked at the entries **Bill Clinton, food pyramid, Hubble Space Telescope, Frida Kahlo, Lithuania, Persian Gulf War,** and **Russia.**
- For atlases, reviewers checked that maps showed the unifications of Germany and Yemen; the breakups of the U.S.S.R., Yugoslavia, and Czechoslovakia; and various current place names, including Kalaallit Nunaat (for Greenland); Myanmar (for Burma); St. Petersburg (for Leningrad); and Yangon (for Rangoon).
- For dictionaries, reviewers looked for the following entries: **bungee jumping, dis, fax, HDTV, intifada, maquiladora, rap, retrovirus,** and **virtual reality.**

Reviewers also comment on how frequently the electronic work is updated, as indicated by the publisher.

Reviewers next describe the structure of the entries. This involves determining whether encyclopedias use longer general entries or the shorter ready-reference type, how complete the entries in a dictionary are, and how balanced the geographical coverage in an atlas is. Here the electronic work is compared with the parent work, noting any differences in scope and features between the electronic and print versions.

Reviews of multimedia works devote a substantial portion of space to discussing the audio, video, and animation features, describing their scope and their quality. An important point here is how easily these features can be accessed.

For those who have not yet seen pictures or video from a computerized electronic work, it is important to point out that there are limitations inherent in converting normal photographs and video to a digitized version. The still images that can be viewed in these programs are generally of reasonable size, usually occupying most of the computer screen, but color images are somewhat grainy, even on a high-quality monitor. (Black-and-white images tend to reproduce better.) This is simply a function of how continuous tone information, like a photograph, is digitized for representation on a computer monitor; digitizing translates the photograph into dots (either black-and-white dots or color dots), and the density of the dots cannot approach the original in terms of clarity. (This process is also affected by the computer's video card and monitor; see *Hardware and Installation,* below.)

The situation in regard to video is even more dramatic. Storing video requires a huge amount of space, and while a CD-ROM has great storage capacity, it is not unlimited. In digitizing video, programmers must delete one of every five frames—the effect is the same as if a film editor snipped out every fifth frame of a movie. The result is a somewhat jerky moving picture, not the smoothly flowing images we are accustomed to seeing on television or at the movies. Video images also tend to be relatively small.

These inadequacies in image conversion should not be considered major obstacles to the enjoyment of an electronic reference work. When we consider that a few years ago animated sequences or video could not even be seen on most personal computers, it is clear that the technology is quickly changing. The quality of these images is already beginning to improve, and it will most likely continue to improve in the future.

Hardware and Installation. In this section the reviewers describe the system requirements needed to run the program. This includes the following points:

- The type of microprocessor
- The amount of RAM (the computer's internal memory) required
- The kind of video card and monitor needed
- The kind of disk on which the program is supplied
- The amount of storage capacity the computer's hard disk must have to run the program
- The kind of CD-ROM drive or modem needed (if appropriate)
- Whether a mouse is needed (or useful)
- The kind of sound cards and speakers needed
- The version of the operating system (DOS, *Windows,* or Macintosh system) required
- Additional software needed

Reviewers will provide this information based on the software publisher's stated *minimum* requirements for each piece of hardware. These minimum requirements are not necessarily established to allow the maximum functioning of the reference tool. If the publisher's minimum for a program is a 16-Megahertz, 80286 computer, there is no question that screen changes and searches will occur more quickly on a faster machine. Different reviewers used different systems as they were evaluating the various programs. These different systems could affect the apparent performance of one program as compared with another—one product could appear to more easily accomplish searches than another simply because it was tested on a faster machine. Comments on performance depend on the capabilities of the equipment used in testing and not exclusively on the result of the program itself; judging one product more favorably than another because of a machine-dependent performance factor is unjust. The reviews are useful guides to a program's *features,* however, and to how easy those features are to use. Judgments of this sort (as of scope) can be made on the basis of the information in these reviews.

In this section, reviewers also comment on how easy it is to install the program the first time and to call it up in subsequent uses. They estimate the amount of time it took for installation to be completed and identify any features that permit the user to customize the program.

Some computerized reference works stay resident in the computer's memory, allowing them to be run whenever a specific key combination (called a *hot key*) is pressed. This section of the review mentions whether the product in question offers this terminate-and-stay-resident (TSR) feature.

Reviewers also comment on how the program presents itself to the user. This includes a description of the user interface (whether it requires the use of commands or function keys or uses pull-down menus) and an explanation of what the screen looks like and how much is displayed. Reviewers comment on how many entries or articles can be viewed at a time and how much text can be displayed from an article. They describe how the user can move within articles and switch from article to article.

Searching Capabilities.

One of the main benefits of computerized reference works is that they greatly facilitate research by speeding up the search for information on a given subject.

Programs often permit more than one kind of search. Users may scan the entire list of article titles or entries for a specific word or concept, or they may instruct the computer to scan the contents of all articles for the mention of that word or concept within the piece. The former kind is like looking in an index for an entry—for example, trying to find which page contains the entry for *John Adams.* The latter is similar to locating all other entries in which John Adams is mentioned.

What distinguishes computerized searching from manual searching is that the computer conducts the search automatically and quickly. On the one hand, the user need not wait (too) long to see what matches are produced. On the other hand, the computer does not use judgment in listing matches. It often produces more matches (called *hits*) than those that have the exact person or thing being searched. Thus, the search for all entries that contain the words *John Adams* could yield a long list of hits, including such articles as *Andrew Jackson* and *Monroe Doctrine* because both mention *John Quincy Adams,* a name that contains the two words requested in the search. Some computerized reference tools also allow the user to activate a near-match capability that will expand the list of matches to those terms that are spelled almost the same as the entered word. The purpose is to aid the user who may have incorrectly typed the search term

or who is not sure of the correct spelling. The result can sometimes be unhelpful, as the searcher must scan through a number of irrelevant nonmatches to find the true hits.

It is important, then, for the user to become familiar with how searches are conducted in a given program—how matches are listed, how near-matches are treated, how the entries in a list can be accessed, and how searches can be focused. Some programs offer the user the chance to conduct *Boolean searches,* in which main terms can be linked to other terms by the use of *and, or,* and *not* to focus or expand the search.

In this section, reviewers describe the program's search capabilities and explain how easy they are to use. The reviewers briefly outline the techniques employed in executing a search and describe the kinds of matches the program generates.

Downloading and Printing.

In this section, reviewers describe features that permit users to select information from the program itself and save it to disk or insert it into a document created in another program. They explain the process followed and evaluate its ease of use. They also point out whether multiple bits of information can be stored and stacked together or manipulated in other ways.

Reviewers also comment on what material can or cannot be printed from the reference tool. Readers should be aware that here, as with the speed of searches, equipment is a major factor in determining a program's performance. The speed and quality of printing are functions not only of the electronic reference work but also of the printer that is attached to the computer.

Documentation.

This section involves an evaluation of the material that the software publisher provides to help the user understand and take advantage of the features in the program. Reviewers describe the extent and nature of the printed material that accompanies the product, assessing how well this documentation explains the program's features and their use.

They also comment on the *help* features, if any, provided on screen. They indicate how easy it is to access online help, the extent to which it covers the program's features, and the usefulness of the assistance that it provides.

Finally, reviewers mention whether the publisher provides a telephone number for users to call to receive troubleshooting help. They also indicate whether the phone calls are toll-free.

Summary.

The evaluation concludes with a summary that recaps the electronic reference work's strengths and weaknesses, commenting on whether the work is a reasonable value for the price and assessing its worth in relation to competing works.

Glossary

For users of this guide who may be unfamiliar with some of the terms employed in these reviews, the following glossary is provided. The terms presented here are those related exclusively to computerized reference products; terms common to print and electronic encyclopedias, atlases, and dictionaries can be found in the glossaries within Chapters 3, 6, and 9, respectively.

Boolean search. A searching strategy that allows researchers to connect more than one term using *and, or,* and *not* in order to narrow or expand the search parameters and help ensure that the matches retrieved are appropriate.

button. A shape that contains a word or words representing a choice within a computer program; by using the **mouse** to click on the button, the user instructs the computer to take the action specified. Also used to refer to one of the two or three selecting switches on a mouse.

byte. The basic unit of computer memory storage, equivalent to the data needed to store one character.

CD-ROM. An abbreviation for *Compact Disc-Read Only Memory,* a kind of storage device similar to the CDs used in audio CD players. These devices can be pressed to hold data for computers with CD-ROM drives to access. (Computers cannot store information on the discs, hence "read only." CD-ROMs can store vast amounts of data—an entire multivolume encyclopedia occupies just about a third of the potential data space on one disc.

click. The pressing of the button on a **mouse,** which instructs the computer to perform an action. Some functions require *double clicking* (two rapid button presses).

command driven. A kind of **interface** in which the user must type commands or use various keystroke combinations to instruct the computer to take actions.

DOS. An acronym for *Disk Operating System,* the program that gives the computer its basic instructions on how to read and write data. Used primarily to refer to the system originally developed for the IBM personal computer and now serving a large number of compatible machines.

download. To take information from a program or an online service and store it in the computer's memory (or on a disk) for later access.

floppy disk. A medium of data storage that holds less information than a hard disk but is transportable. Disks come in different sizes (3½″ and 5¼″) and different types, with variable storage capacities. The size and type to be used with any computer are determined by the kind of floppy disk drive the computer has.

hard disk. A large-capacity memory storage device installed within the computer. Hard disks hold more than **floppy disks** and less than **CD-ROMs;** they are not transportable. Electronic reference works often require a minimum amount of space on the hard disk to load some or all of the program.

hot key. A combination of keys that, when pressed, allow the user to activate a **terminate-and-stay-resident** program even while using an ordinary application program, such as a word processor. Used by some electronic reference works to provide immediate access to their data.

icon. A visual symbol used to represent a kind of database or an action. An electronic reference work may use the icon of a camera to indicate that a photograph related to the entry being displayed is available.

interface. The general structure and methods by which a user navigates through an electronic reference work, accessing its features and exploring its information. Some interfaces are **command driven;** others employ **menus.**

kilobyte. One thousand **bytes;** the measure used to indicate the storage capacity of **floppy disks,** the amount of **RAM,** and the size of files.

Macintosh. One of the three main **platforms** of personal computers. *Windows* and **DOS** are the other types. Programs for Macintosh are generally not interchangeable for use on DOS-compatible machines (although a Macintosh introduced in 1994 does run DOS programs). Many electronic publishers develop versions of the same program appropriate for each platform.

megabyte. One million **bytes;** the measure used to indicate the storage capacity of **hard disks** and **CD-ROMs.**

memory. Computers have two kinds of memory: *ROM,* which is available to the computer at all times and is used to store some basic operating instructions; and **RAM,** which is active only while the computer is on and is used to store programs while they are running and files while they are being used. Electronic reference works often require a minimum amount of RAM to work effectively; these requirements vary from program to program.

menu. A kind of **interface** in which the user is offered a series of optional actions in a list; selecting one option instructs the computer to perform that function.

Microsoft CD-ROM Extensions. A program that instructs the computer's processor in how to enable and access a **CD-ROM** drive.

modem. A piece of equipment used to connect one computer through phone lines to other computers from which it can retrieve data; necessary for using **online** reference works.

monitor. The screen of a computer, which can either be monochrome or full-color. The capacity of a monitor to display graphics clearly and sharply depends on its resolution and on the **video card** within the computer.

mouse. A device connected to a computer by a cable and containing two or three buttons; used to control a pointer that appears on the screen and to instruct the computer to take certain actions; required for some programs.

MPC. The acronym for *Multimedia PC,* an industry standard for PC-compatibles that indicates that a program has certain minimum requirements in terms of processor type, **RAM, hard disk** storage capacity, **video card** and **monitor, CD-ROM** speed, and sound and video capabilities. Also indicates a **DOS**-compatible computer that meets those minimum standards.

multimedia. Any program that includes sound, video, and pictures as well as text.

online. Computer-stored information that can be accessed using a **modem** and communications software; some electronic reference works are available online. Users must first subscribe to the online service; charges generally also include a use fee.

paste. To insert information into an existing file; refers to the ability to retrieve information stored from one program (such as an electronic encyclopedia) into a document being created in another program (such as a report being written on a word processor).

platform. A major type of computer, differentiated from other types by the way the machine works, as determined by the processor and the operating system. The main platforms are **DOS** (also called *PC-compatibles*), **Windows,** and **Macintosh.**

RAM. The acronym for *Random Access Memory,* a type of memory that is active only while the computer is on and is used to store programs while they are running and files while they are being used.

search. The techniques used to look within a computerized database for all mentions of a key word or words.

terminate-and-stay-resident (TSR). A kind of program that can reside within the operating system of the computer, ready to be called up at any time that a special keyboard combination (the **hot key**) is struck, even if a user is running a different program at the time. This feature provides instant access to a reference database whenever a user has his or her computer turned on. TSRs can create difficulties in memory management or conflict with one another, possibly causing the computer to lock up. Advice on these issues in documentation for programs that include this feature is very helpful.

video card. The part of a computer that controls the sharpness and color of a monitor's images. Electronic reference works often require a certain kind of video card to work effectively; these requirements vary from program to program.

Windows. A program that works within **DOS** to provide a graphical environment similar to that of the **Macintosh.** Electronic reference works that run under *Windows* often require that a specified version of *Windows* be present; these requirements vary from program to program.

Chapter 15
Evaluations of Electronic Encyclopedias

Compton's Interactive Encyclopedia

Facts at a Glance

Full title: **Compton's Interactive Encyclopedia**
Publisher: Compton's NewMedia
Edition reviewed: © 1994, version 2.01VW
Type of work: CD-ROM
Platform reviewed: Windows/MPC

Number of entries: 33,000 (encyclopedia); 70,000 (dictionary)
Number of illustrations: 7,000
Intended readership: upper elementary school to adult

Price: $149.95
Sold directly to libraries and schools through distributors
Revised annually

Introduction and Authority

Compton's Interactive Encyclopedia is the CD-ROM version of COMPTON'S ENCYCLOPEDIA, which has been published in book form for the past 70 years. This 1994 electronic version adds to the database with pictures, sound, video clips, interactive U.S. and world history time lines, an atlas, and *The Merriam-Webster OnLine Dictionary* with definitions for 70,000 words.

This edition of the encyclopedia also features "Virtual Workspace," a powerful new tool that makes information gathering, organizing, and storing very productive. With this feature, the publisher takes great advantage of the computer's ability to access and cross-reference the information contained in the database.

Scope and Content

Information in *Compton's Interactive Encyclopedia* is organized to be accessed through ten different entry paths. One approach is to input a search term in the search line that appears immediately upon starting the program. The other nine are featured on a side panel that runs down the right portion of the main menu screen and can be used at any time in the user's search:

- The "Idea Search" button is used to locate articles, pictures, and facts related to a specific topic entered on the topic screen.
- The "Articles" button permits searching through an alphabetical list of article titles.
- The "Multimedia" button allows browsing through listings of all pictures, sounds, videos, slide shows, and animated sequences.
- The "InfoPilot" button calls up a selection of active article windows and groups of article titles that relate to a topic or question.
- The "Topic Tree" button groups all the articles in the encyclopedia by topic and subtopic.
- The "Atlas" button opens access to the database of maps by moving through lists or conducting place name searches.
- The "Timeline" button allows browsing through time lines of world history and U.S. history.

- The "Picture Tour" button displays a randomly chosen selection of images from the encyclopedia, each of which can be used to access the related article.
- The "Dictionary" button opens up an online dictionary that also includes a thesaurus, a list of foreign words, and a list of common English names.

This side panel also includes the "Backtrack" button, which enables the user to retrace his or her steps through previous windows.

Entries take up a full screen with a menu bar displayed on the top and the path bar on the right-hand side. On the bottom of the screen are buttons for going to and retrieving items, accessing online help, and closing articles. There is also an option for simultaneously displaying many entries in multiple windows, which is described elsewhere in this review (see *Searching Capabilities*). The main screen area is somewhat less visually appealing than the screens in THE NEW GROLIER MULTIMEDIA ENCYCLOPEDIA or MICROSOFT ENCARTA, but the interface is generally easy to use. Use of the bottom-of-the-screen "close" button rather than the more typical button in the upper left corner of a window may take getting used to for some *Windows* veterans, but the clear labeling should minimize the amount of time required to become accustomed to this approach.

The content of the work is strong (see the review of COMPTON'S ENCYCLOPEDIA for a full discussion). **Bill Clinton, Lithuania,** and **Russia** are all listed with current information, although given the 1994 copyright of *Compton's Interactive,* it is surprising that the following entries are missing: the *food pyramid* (it still refers to the four food groups), the *Gulf War,* and *Frida Kahlo.* The space travel time line refers to the 1990 launch of the Hubble Space Telescope, but not to any of its problems. The atlas is up-to-date, as it includes the various changes that have recently affected Europe and the Middle East, and its coverage of the whole world seems balanced.

Access to the other search paths in the encyclopedia is always available through the side panel icons described above. Multimedia icons that appear in the left margins of articles indicate the presence of related pictures, sound bits, maps, charts, tables, flags, videos, and cross-references. The system is not perfect, however, since these icons disappear from view as the user scrolls through the article. The system used in THE NEW GROLIER MULTIMEDIA ENCYCLOPEDIA is superior. In that work, icons are always present in a bar just below the entry word.

Pictures with captions, multimedia video clips, animations, slide shows with sound narration, and sounds are available throughout this work and seem to be well chosen and placed. Sounds include such unusual examples as a muezzin prayer and a reading from the "Seneca Falls Declaration." Unfortunately, one of the narrators has a distinct and unappealing lisp.

There are many more multimedia bits than in past editions, and they are divided well among current, scientific, and historical topics. A nice feature of the sound, video, animation, and the slide shows is a status bar below the image that moves during the presentation to indicate the percentage of the show that has been completed. This eliminates user guesswork as to when the clip will end.

The online dictionary and thesaurus is a very useful addition to this already full-featured work. Users can highlight any word in an encyclopedia entry, click the dictionary button, and read the definition of the word. While every word may not be defined, the 70,000 entries in the dictionary give the user a substantial lexicon.

Hardware and Installation

The encyclopedia comes on one CD-ROM disc. The publisher sells Macintosh and *Windows*/MPC versions of the program. We tested the *Windows* version and cannot comment on the similarities or differences of the Macintosh version. Prospective purchasers of that version are advised to consult periodicals for a review.

The *Windows* version requires a multimedia PC with a 386SX/16MHz or better processor, Microsoft *Windows* 3.1 or later, Microsoft CD-ROM Extensions 2.2 or later, and MS-DOS 3.1 or later. The machine needs a minimum of 4 MB of RAM, an SVGA display card and compatible monitor, and a mouse. The MPC-compatible CD-ROM drive should have a sustained transfer rate of 150 KB/sec. To hear audio, the system needs a sound card plus stereo speakers or headphones. A printer is optional but very useful.

Installation is very quick, taking less than five minutes. The computer installs the few files it needs on the hard drive. The program may require a change of the video driver, but this is easily handled within *Windows.*

Searching Capabilities

Compton's NewMedia understands very well that searching capabilities set an electronic encyclopedia apart from its print counterpart. The main menu screen is just waiting for the user to input a topic for searching, and that, indeed, is the most straightforward and quickest way to search for a topic. But there are other methods as well.

In "Idea Search," which appropriately uses a light bulb as its icon, the user inputs a word or phrase that describes a topic or a question to be asked. The computer quickly scans the database for articles, pictures, or short, informative "Fact-Index" entries, creating a list of articles or illustrations related to the request. It then lists them from the most likely to be helpful to the least likely. This is the best place to start looking for information when the user is not sure of which topic to search.

The "InfoPilot" (represented by an airplane) is a more advanced method of navigating through the encyclopedia. Search requests entered in this mode produce displays of a group of five articles. One is the focus entry—the closest match to the search topic. The other four are secondary articles that are related to the first. Each of those four is, in turn, surrounded by four other related articles. Using this route is best for exploring a topic without missing any cross-references.

An organizational tree is the symbol on the "Topic Tree." This search mode organizes articles into topics and subtopics, through which the user can browse. The main list of topics contains 19 categories from "The Arts" to "Technology."

There are also two modes for exploring multiple pieces of data at the same time. The easy method uses the "Backtrack" button to retrace the paths followed in searching, allowing the user to go back as far as five screens to view previously seen articles, pictures, animations, sounds, maps, or path windows.

The expert mode gives the user access to the "Virtual Workspace," which permits managing multiple windows that contain information about a topic of interest. This is similar to the "InfoPilot" feature described above, but in the "Virtual Workspace" the user chooses what appears in the multiple active windows. A user researching a country, for example, could have the main article on the country in one window, a map of the country in another window, the dictionary available for consultation in yet another window, and a slide show or video sequence on a related topic in yet another window. Each window is represented by a block of space in the workspace map, a panel that appears in one section of the screen. The user can click on any of those panels to open that particular window. The feature is like having many books, each open to the topic of interest, sitting on a large desk for instant consultation.

Downloading and Printing

Articles from the encyclopedia can be printed out exactly as they appear. A print button appears on the bottom of the screen and whole articles or excerpts of articles can simply be highlighted and printed. Each article or excerpt appears with a copyright citation at the bottom for easy reference. Atlas maps and time-line segments can be printed out as well; they also have copyright notices. Pictures and still frames from video clips or the slide show cannot be exported or printed out. Unfortunately, the manual includes no information on printing.

Compton's Interactive Encyclopedia also has a "Notebook" feature that can be accessed at any time from the "View" menu (which appears at the top of the screen) and is automatically set to open Microsoft *Write*. (It can be customized to use another word processor as well.) The user can excerpt portions of an article or take notes on a topic and easily switch back and forth between the article and the "Notebook." On this feature, too, the documentation is sparse. Clear instructions are offered on customizing the "Notebook," but not on its use. A brief tutorial helping children on how to take notes would be a good addition.

Documentation

The manual for the encyclopedia contains 72 pages. It is quite thorough, except for the lapses noted in the previous section. It carefully goes through installation instructions and provides an overview of the disc, a guided tour of the features (a great help to the user), and detailed instructions on how to use the various search modes and multimedia features. There is also a comprehensive troubleshooting section. Unfortunately, the manual is not indexed, but the table of contents and the overall organization are clear.

There is a lot of on-screen help as well, written in clear and concise language. An interactive message bar at the bottom of the screen briefly describes the function of whatever button the cursor arrow is pointing to as it roams around the screen. This is a valuable aid to the user.

The publisher also offers technical support over the phone, although not toll free. Hours are business hours (Pacific Time) on weekdays.

Summary

This edition of the *Compton's Interactive Encyclopedia* is certainly competitive with and in some ways superior to its biggest competitors, MICROSOFT ENCARTA and THE NEW GROLIER MULTIMEDIA ENCYCLOPEDIA. Its articles are extensive, the atlas appears to be up-to-date, and it contains more audio, video, and images than earlier editions. Its competitors have not duplicated the easy-to-use searching capabilities. With nine different points of access—including the powerful "Virtual Workspace"—the program provides users of all ability levels with a way to get into the database. It includes an integrated, continuously responsive help system supplemented by more extensive online help. While the encyclopedia does not have a resident word processor, as ENCARTA does, the "Notebook" allows the user to take notes or excerpt segments of articles to use in reports very easily. Finally, the dictionary and thesaurus are valuable features. (These features are also found in ENCARTA, though not in NEW GROLIER.) *Compton's Interactive Encyclopedia* is an excellent resource for home, school, and library use.

The Concise Columbia Encyclopedia, Second Edition (in Microsoft Bookshelf '94)

Facts at a Glance

Full title: **The Concise Columbia Encyclopedia, Second Edition (in Microsoft Bookshelf '94 Multimedia Reference Library)**
Publisher: Microsoft
Edition reviewed: © 1994 (no version number)
Type of work: CD-ROM
Platform reviewed: Windows

Number of entries: more than 15,000
Number of illustrations: more than 1,300
Intended readership: ages 9 and up

Price (for entire *Bookshelf* package): $99.95 (through 12/31/94); $79.95 with school discount; $30 rebate for owners of previous versions
Revised annually

Introduction and Authority

Microsoft Bookshelf '94 is a CD-ROM product that contains seven reference books that can be accessed from a single source. It can be used as a quick reference source from within a word-processing program or anywhere in *Windows,* or as a stand-alone program. The reference works contained in *Bookshelf* include *The Concise Columbia Encyclopedia,* reviewed here, and THE AMERICAN HERITAGE DICTIONARY and THE HAMMOND INTERMEDIATE WORLD ATLAS, reviewed in other chapters of this part of the Buying Guide. Other reference works in *Bookshelf* are *The Original Roget's Thesaurus, The Columbia Dictionary of Quotations, The People's Chronology,* and *The World Almanac and Book of Facts 1994.* Each work is linked to all the others through the "QuickShelf" feature, making *Microsoft Bookshelf* the most varied CD-ROM product reviewed in this guide.

The Concise Columbia Encyclopedia, Second Edition, which is contained on this CD-ROM, is licensed by Microsoft from Columbia University Press. This electronic version reflects the editorial content of the 1991 version of the print CONCISE COLUMBIA, as updated and supplemented with visual material by Microsoft.

Scope and Content

The entries in the *Concise Columbia Encyclopedia,* like those in its parent print work, are of the short, ready-reference type. For some entries, there are also pictures, sounds, or animations. For example, **volcano** includes a text explanation of volcanoes, a pronunciation of the word *volcano,* and a short animated sequence showing how volcanoes are formed. The entry also contains links to **Hawaii, lava,** and **plate tectonics.** The animations are of fairly low resolution and progress slowly; nevertheless, they provide a nice feature that is not present in the print work.

The *Columbia Encyclopedia* is reasonably up-to-date, including entries on **The Hubble Space Telescope,** the **Persian Gulf War,** and **Bill Clinton.** It does not, however, make reference to the *food pyramid* or *Gabriel Garcia Marquez.* In addition, many of the illustrations included are out-of-date, including a picture of Bob Dylan from the 1970s.

Within the text of each entry, there are highlighted words known as *infinite links.* These can be clicked on for connections to other related entries, either in the encyclopedia itself or in the other reference books in *Bookshelf.* Many entries also include a "See Also" button that directs the user to related topics.

Hardware and Installation

Bookshelf comes on a CD-ROM and is currently available in *Windows* and Macintosh formats. The *Windows* version was reviewed; similarities or differences between it and the Macintosh version are unknown. Prospective purchasers of the Macintosh version are advised to consult periodicals for reviews of it.

The minimum hardware and software requirements are a Multimedia PC—386SX or faster—running Microsoft *Windows* 3.1; DOS 3.1; with a VGA card and display and a sound board. The system also must have a CD-ROM drive, a hard drive with 2 MB of available disk space, 4 MB of RAM, and a mouse.

Installation of *Bookshelf* is quite simple, taking under five minutes. The documentation explaining the installation process, however, is almost nonexistent, so if problems should arise, they are difficult to diagnose and remedy.

Searching Capabilities

The Concise Columbia Encyclopedia can be entered in a variety of ways. There is a standard table of contents, including a search window where a word or phrase can be entered. Entries can also be searched using the "Find" window, which displays a list of entries containing the desired term. In addition, users can reference past searches in order to retrieve a search for reuse. The program also includes an "Advanced Find" window. This tool is primarily useful for doing a search in more than one reference work in *Bookshelf.* Its "Help" button accesses useful searching tips and hints.

A feature of *Bookshelf* particularly useful for the encyclopedia is the "Gallery," which allows the user to browse a list of entries that have multimedia features such as sound, pictures, or animations. Unfortunately, this is the only way to ascertain if an entry has this multimedia material. The other multimedia encyclopedias—MICROSOFT ENCARTA, COMPTON'S INTERACTIVE, and THE NEW GROLIER MULTIMEDIA—have a superior approach in that the presence of multimedia material is identified along with the entry itself. Another flaw is that these multimedia features can be retrieved only by scrolling through the listing in the "Gallery," making searching for animations by topic impossible without knowing their headings.

Terms can be combined using the Boolean operators *and, or,* or *not* as well as the connector *near,* which can be user-customized for varying degrees of proximity. For a user who is not familiar with these techniques, however, there is no easy way to access help information without going to the "Advanced Find" box—which is hidden in the menu bar. Once that box is accessed, there is a very thorough explanation of how to use connecting terms, as well as other helpful tips.

The "Find" feature seems to produce matches based on near-spellings, to aid a user who inadvertently misspells a word. A search for *anty,* for instance, retrieved the same 127 items found in the search for *anti.* With no documentation, however, this is not clear to the user beforehand. Nor is there an explanation of how (or whether) this near-match feature could be turned off if a user desired.

Some of the cross-referencing, while intended to link infinitely, only goes in one direction. While examining an article on **Jews,** a user can click on **holocaust** to retrieve that entry but cannot get back to the original entry by clicking on **Jews** in the new article.

Downloading and Printing

Bookshelf comes with the standard cut, copy, and paste features that permit the user to copy text from the entries into the "Notepad" or other applications. In addition, a special "Copy Picture" feature allows the copying and pasting of visuals.

Bookshelf also allows for printing of complete entries, help text, or pictures directly from the program simply by clicking a "Print" button at the bottom of the screen.

Documentation

Almost no documentation comes with *Microsoft Bookshelf '94.* Previous versions included small manuals, but Microsoft decided to eliminate them because members of their target audience—elementary through high school students—tend not to read them. There is a pamphlet that briefly describes installation, system requirements, and information on how to get additional help. There is also extensive online help, although it is not context sensitive. On-screen help can be accessed from any point in the program, but entries can only be consulted through an index listing. Microsoft also offers help via a *CompuServe* forum, on the Internet, and

through a toll-free telephone support line that is open from 6:00 A.M. to 6:00 P.M. (Pacific Time) on weekdays.

While the familiar nature of the reference work makes the *Columbia Encyclopedia* fairly simple to use, the lack of documentation is disturbing. Hidden features, such as key commands that perform special functions, could go unnoticed by a user unless stumbled on through online help. In addition, novice computer users who are not accustomed to multimedia interfaces may find the absence of documentation problematic.

Summary

Microsoft Bookshelf's Concise Columbia Encyclopedia is an interesting, inexpensive reference tool. The entries are clear and easy to use and lend themselves to the multimedia format. The lack of documentation is a serious problem, however, as it makes *Bookshelf* much more difficult for novices to use. Those seeking a more extensive, full-featured electronic encyclopedia would be more interested in ENCARTA, COMPTON'S INTERACTIVE, or THE NEW GROLIER MULTIMEDIA ENCYCLOPEDIA. By including a collection of seven reference sources, *Microsoft Bookshelf* provides a value that other multimedia programs do not possess. It is an excellent tool for writers and works well with a word-processing program. The product seems more appropriate for home use than in the library setting, where the full-fledged electronic encyclopedia is probably more desirable.

Information Finder (Encyclopedia)

Facts at a Glance

Full title: **Information Finder (Encyclopedia)**
Publisher: World Book
Edition reviewed: © 1993, version 2.40
Type of work: CD-ROM
Platform reviewed: DOS

Number of entries: 17,000
Number of illustrations: none
Intended readership: elementary school to adult

Price (for entire *Information Finder* package): $599; $296 (when sold with WORLD BOOK); $149 (annual revision); discount available to schools and libraries
Sold directly to schools and libraries; also sold door-to-door
Revised annually

Introduction and Authority

Information Finder is a CD-ROM version of the text material from the WORLD BOOK ENCYCLOPEDIA and THE WORLD BOOK DICTIONARY. It was prepared and published by World Book itself, which has a long history of providing authoritative reference products. The 1993 edition that was reviewed reflects the 1993 editions of those print works. The CD-ROM program is revised annually.

This review concentrates exclusively on the encyclopedia component of *Information Finder.* Readers who want to learn about the dictionary portion should consult the review of INFORMATION FINDER (DICTIONARY) elsewhere in the Buying Guide.

Scope and Content

Information Finder contains the printed text of 17,000 articles from the WORLD BOOK ENCYCLOPEDIA (1993 edition) and 225,000 entries from the most recent edition of THE WORLD BOOK DICTIONARY.

Encyclopedia entries can be accessed in several ways. Topic searching enables users to browse through an alphabetical index of thousands of topics to locate articles that are most relevant to a desired search. Searching **Bosnia,** for example, reveals a four-and-a-half-page article with suggested cross-references to **Sarajevo** and **Yugoslavia (history).** The screen displays the text of the article on the right and an outline on the left. The "Related Topics" menu allows access to an index of topics relevant to the displayed article; any of those related entries can be quickly opened. A "Quick Facts" feature displays a brief fact listing at the touch of a keystroke.

Based as it is on the 1993 edition of the WORLD BOOK, this electronic version is current through the end of 1992. A lengthy article on **Bill Clinton** covers Clinton's election in November 1992, and articles on **Lithuania** and **Russia** are current through the end of 1992 and include 1993 population estimates. The bibliography on Russia includes 1992 monographs. A detailed piece on the **Persian Gulf War** provides background, an account of the fighting, and a discussion of the consequences. In addition, a "Quick Facts" item covers the period from August 2, 1990, to the end of the war. An article on the **Hubble Space Telescope** describes its launch in 1990 and discusses errors in the telescope's optics. While there is no separate entry for *Frida Kahlo,* she is mentioned in the article on her husband, **Diego Rivera.** The encyclopedia has no entry for *food pyramid,* although it is defined in the dictionary.

A "Notepad" function provides users with a limited word-processing program (features include autowrapping and text-blocking functions). With this feature, researchers can type their own notes or copy information from articles to files that can be imported later into their regular word processor. "Notepad" files can be substantial—up to 64K (about 35 pages) in length.

Although the text is identical to that in the printed WORLD BOOK, *Information Finder* does not reproduce everything in the set. This CD-ROM lacks the color illustrations, maps, and photographs so common in WORLD BOOK. This absence of images is a serious flaw in an oth-

erwise fine product. While the encyclopedia on which *Information Finder* is based is an excellent resource, most purchasers will undoubtedly prefer the highly illustrated multimedia encyclopedias such as COMPTON'S INTERACTIVE, MICROSOFT ENCARTA, or NEW GROLIER.

Hardware and Installation

Information Finder is available in a DOS version only. The publisher plans to offer *Windows* and Macintosh versions in the spring of 1994. Those versions were not reviewed, and we cannot comment on their similarities or differences to the version that was examined. Prospective purchasers are advised to consult periodicals for reviews of those versions.

System requirements are an IBM PC-compatible (XT or better); DOS 3.1 or higher; 640K RAM, with 462K available once *Information Finder* starts; 3 MB of available hard disk space; a monochrome or better card and monitor; a CD-ROM player; MS-DOS CD-ROM Extensions (MSCDEX) version 2.0 if using DOS 3.xx (a higher version of MSCDEX is needed if using DOS 4.xx or higher). A mouse and printer are optional, but recommended.

Installation of *Information Finder* is simple and takes about 15 minutes, including the time spent reading the procedure in the manual. The publisher cautions several times that MSCDEX must already be installed before attempting to install the program. Some other useful cautions give advice on potential conflicts with other programs.

"Quick Setup" installs the retrieval software onto the computer's hard drive. Advanced setup permits the user to customize any of 14 options offered. These options include such items as hardware identification steps; assigning specific locations for temporary work files, bookmarks, and searches; control of print options; the use of italics on the screen for emphasis of text; and requiring a password to exit the program. If the user desires, these options can easily be altered later. This flexibility is an excellent feature for school or public library use.

Searching Capabilities

Information Finder has a number of advantages over its print counterpart provided by the search engine. In addition to basic subject or topic searching, keyword searching using the Boolean operators *and, or,* and *not* is an option. For example, inputting *fastest* and *horse* produces eight hits in three articles. Any one of those articles can be quickly displayed.

Information Finder also has a "Go To" function that allows researchers to use 60,000 cross-references to jump from one related article to another. This function is automatically disabled when a new search is started.

Another special feature is the ability to place up to 25 bookmarks to mark one's place in an article for later retrieval. The "Notepad" feature has already been discussed (see *Scope and Content*).

Downloading and Printing

Anything in *Information Finder* can be printed. Text can be sent directly to the printer or to disk. This print utility is nicely functional: one can choose to print only the portion of the article displayed on screen, a section of an article, the entire article, or an outline of the article. Options within "Quick Facts" windows allow printing of the text in view or all tables. These choices are very helpful for libraries concerned with paper and ink usage.

Downloading is equally simple, just a matter of hitting a keystroke and entering a valid file name and extension. If the file already exists, the program will add to its contents.

Documentation

A 96-page indexed "User's Manual" accompanies *Information Finder*. It contains easy-to-understand directions for installation and information about all the program's special features. There is a helpful glossary as well as the index.

Information Finder also includes a basic tutorial and "Help" screens. Toll-free technical support is available weekdays during business hours (Central Time).

Summary

Information Finder is a valuable reference tool. It provides current information on thousands of topics, is easily accessed by even the most novice searcher, and incorporates a number of special functions that make searching a breeze. Compared with other electronic encyclopedias, like COMPTON'S INTERACTIVE ENCYCLOPEDIA, MICROSOFT ENCARTA, and THE NEW GROLIER MULTIMEDIA ENCYCLOPEDIA, however, *Information Finder* is a lackluster product. With no illustrations, maps, graphs, sound, video, or animation, the program pales in comparison. When these deficiencies are compounded by a steep price—more than that of some of the multimedia products—*Information Finder* becomes quite unattractive. If and when World Book makes the price—or the product—more competitive, this CD-ROM will be worth looking at.

Microsoft Encarta

Facts at a Glance

Full title: **Microsoft Encarta Multimedia Encyclopedia**
Publisher: Microsoft
Edition reviewed: © 1994 (no version number)
Type of work: CD-ROM
Platform reviewed: Windows/MPC

Number of entries: 26,000
Number of illustrations: 8,400
Intended readership: grades 4 to 12

Price: $139
Revised annually

Introduction and Authority

Microsoft Encarta is a CD-ROM product based on the text from the 1993 edition of FUNK & WAGNALLS NEW ENCYCLOPEDIA. Microsoft has enhanced this source material with sound, video footage, interactive charts, an illustrated time line, a game called "MindMaze," and an electronic dictionary and thesaurus. The company has also added to and updated many of FUNK & WAGNALLS' entries. The resulting product is a stimulating encyclopedia specifically designed to aid students in researching topics and writing reports. *Encarta* is not only educational but also fun to use.

Scope and Content

Encarta supplements the text of FUNK & WAGNALLS NEW ENCYCLOPEDIA with many other features. An atlas offers colorful state, country, continent, and world maps. An electronic dictionary and electronic thesaurus allow the user quick access to brief definitions and a bank of synonyms. "MindMaze" is a game that tests a user's knowledge of topics contained in the encyclopedia; it rewards research by giving more points if the player seeks answers from within *Encarta*. Finally, a word-processing program included on the disc allows the user to take notes and write a research paper.

The main body of the work is the encyclopedia. Entries are divided into nine main areas of interest, such as "Performing Arts," "Geography," and "Physical Science and Technology." Each of these areas is then subdivided. "Geography," for instance, is subdivided into 13 categories, including "Countries," "U.S. States," "Maps and Map Making," and "Exploration and Explorers." The categories are split into many entries.

The main window of an entry includes the "Category Frame," which indicates the category to which the entry belongs; the "Article Frame," which displays up to 25 lines of text; an expandable "Gallery Frame," where images are displayed and the presence of linked features (images, sound, and so on) is indicated; and the main button bar, which enables quick access to various features. Long entries include an outline button that gives users an overview of the entry's structure.

Encarta is quite current. There are entries on the **Hubble Space Telescope,** the **Persian Gulf War,** united **Germany** and the republics of the former Soviet Union. Many entries have been revised from the 1993 edition of FUNK AND WAGNALLS, including **Clinton, Bill** and **Bosnia**

and Hercegovina. New entries, such as **ASCII** and **Clinton, Hillary Rodham,** have also been added. Not all entries are as current as these, however. There is no reference to the *food pyramid,* and in the **Black Panther Party** entry, Huey P. Newton (who died in 1989) is listed as still living.

Most entries are long essays supplemented with "see also" references, bibliographies, and "hot links"—high-lighted words that can be clicked on to call up related entries. The section of the **Africa** article that discusses its natural environment, for instance, includes hot links to **plate tectonics,** the **Atlas Mountains,** and the **Rift Valley.**

Most entries are accompanied by icons that indicate the presence of related images, maps, charts, or video or audio material. A partial-screen window displays this material. These can be viewed as they are referred to in the entry or seen separately from the text. Image quality is quite good, and many pictures can be enlarged with a "zoom in" feature.

Maps are clear and colorful but relatively simple, with less detail than is shown in a typical print encyclopedia. Many maps offer the option of zooming in for a more detailed view.

For entries with statistical data, such as population growth of cities, interactive charts are available. The user determines the chart format and may view it in combination with other charts.

The videos include a brief history of the women's rights movement and coverage of the handshake between Yitzhak Rabin and Yasir Arafat in the fall 1993 signing of the Israeli-Palestinian peace agreement. Half of this video footage includes sound as well. *Encarta* has 106 separate video clips. Entries with sound accompaniments include a portion of a song by Bob Marley (in the entry **reggae music**), a snippet from a speech by **Malcolm X,** and name pronunciations for many of the countries in the atlas. There are also speech samples representing 60 languages, with Uzbek, Comanche, and Gaelic among new additions. *Encarta* includes a substantial eight hours of sound.

Hardware and Installation

Encarta was initially released only for *Windows;* a Macintosh version was released in spring 1994. The *Windows* version was examined for this review; prospective purchasers of the Macintosh product should consult journals to read reviews of that particular version before purchasing.

Minimum hardware requirements are an IBM-compatible machine using an 80386SX or higher processor, DOS 3.1 or higher, *Windows* 3.1, 4 MB of RAM, a hard disk, MS-DOS CD-ROM Extensions version 2.2 or later, and a VGA or VGA+ card and display. To fully appreciate *Encarta*'s features, users must have a Multime-dia PC with at least a 30-MB hard disk, an MPC-compatible audio board, and headphones or speakers.

Installation is very straightforward, taking less than 15 minutes. The program notifies the user if the system cannot handle any aspects of *Encarta* (for example, if there is no sound card present).

Searching Capabilities

Encarta offers many ways to access information. The main button bar permits quick access to the table of contents, the atlas, the time line, and the gallery of images. The "Find" button permits more specific searching.

The user can search for a keyword in any area of *Encarta,* or limit the search by category, time frame, type of material (video, text, maps, and so on), or place. The program allows for Boolean searching and includes a "Hints" feature that gives a fuller explanation of how to conduct such searches and how the search engine operates. This guidance is sure to help an inexperienced user.

However, using the information given in the "Hints" box does not always produce the expected results. The window suggests putting the keyword or words in quotation marks to find an exact match. However, searching for *Data General Corporation* by entering "data general" in the "Find" box netted four articles, only one of which was about the company. Similarly, a search for "humanism" retrieved all articles that contained the word *human.* In addition, searching using the atlas was troublesome. If a search word does not appear in the atlas, *Encarta* does not notify the user. Rather, it accesses the next closest alphabetic match. In this way, a search on *Tuuva* retrieved a map containing **Tuscaloosa.** To aid users, these flaws should be fixed in the next version.

An additional feature that can be searched is the "Create Note" feature, whereby a user can add a personal annotation or copy text from an entry into a separate window and name it with a "bookmark," which can be referenced via a bookmark list. The presence of a note is then indicated by an icon attached to the appropriate entry.

Downloading and Printing

Because *Encarta* was designed to be used by students who are writing research papers, it has many features that enable the researcher to use its information. Complete or highlighted text from articles, as well as pictures, can be copied and pasted into the clipboard. The user can also paste information into Microsoft *Write,* a word-processing program that can be opened from within *Encarta.*

Documentation

The documentation provided with *Encarta* is geared toward the primary purpose of the program—to help students write papers. The two short manuals include information on how to paraphrase and how to cite sources as well as descriptions of the program's features. The manuals are filled with full-color screen captures explaining how to use the program's various features. A "Quick Reference" card summarizes the main elements of *Encarta* and how to access them. Librarians should ensure that this card stays near the machine that runs *Encarta*.

The manuals are easy to understand, with clear instructions and helpful illustrations. On the downside, however, is the lack of an index, which hinders users from getting access to information when they don't know what a feature is called. Some features, like the interactive charts, are barely mentioned in the print documentation.

Encarta's "Help" feature makes up for some of the shortcomings of the manuals. It is context sensitive and very comprehensive. It is accessible via an onscreen button, which leads the user to the desired subject or to the table of contents. There is no keyword searching in help, however, which again penalizes the user who does not know what a function is called.

Strangely, especially for a company as involved in the personal computer business as Microsoft is, there is no telephone support available.

Summary

Microsoft Encarta is a fun and easy-to-use reference work that is not only functional but also motivational. Its many access points encourage serendipitous browsing and in-depth study of topics. Its use of multimedia is well balanced and appealing to users with different learning styles. *Encarta*'s range of features far exceeds that of THE NEW GROLIER MULTIMEDIA ENCYCLOPEDIA; features are also better integrated into the work as a whole. The ability of users to personalize the program with their own notes and bookmarks is valuable in a research tool, although it might make the product more difficult to maintain in a multiuser setting such as a library. The search engine needs some improvement, but overall *Microsoft Encarta* is an excellent electronic encyclopedia—superior to its print parent.

The New Grolier Multimedia Encyclopedia

Facts at a Glance

Full title: **The New Grolier Multimedia Encyclopedia**
Publisher: Grolier Electronic Publishing
Edition reviewed: © 1993, version 6.01
Type of work: CD-ROM
Platform reviewed: Windows/MPC

Number of entries: 33,000
Number of illustrations: 4,000
Intended readership: grade 6 to adult

Price: $395; annual update: $97
Sold directly to libraries and schools; also sold through distributors and in computer stores and other retail outlets
Revised annually

Introduction and Authority

The New Grolier Multimedia Encyclopedia is a CD-ROM version of the text of the 1993 ACADEMIC AMERICAN ENCYCLOPEDIA (also published by Grolier), plus additional articles written specifically for this edition. Grolier launched the first version of this CD-ROM product in the mid-1980s and has added numerous refinements and enhancements since then. New to this edition are "Multimedia Maps" and "Knowledge Explorer" features, which provide interesting multimedia introductions to selected topics of interest. Grolier has an excellent reputation for creating quality general-reference works.

Scope and Content

The New Grolier Multimedia Encyclopedia contains the text of 33,000 articles from the 21-volume ACADEMIC AMERICAN ENCYCLOPEDIA. It has many additional features, including 4,000 illustrations, 250 maps, and dozens of sound snippets, animated sequences, and video tracks.

Encyclopedia entries are arranged alphabetically and can be accessed in numerous ways. When the program is opened, an animated logo is displayed. Clicking on the logo opens the encyclopedia window, which reveals 12 files: title list, word search, "Knowledge Tree," a time line, maps, sounds, "Multimedia Maps," "Knowledge Explorer," pictures, videos, animations, and help. Selecting one of those options puts the user in a display screen that includes further choices as well as the main sidebar at the top of the screen. This sidebar provides direct access to the other 11 files as well as additional tools. One button, for instance, moves from a displayed article to a cross-referenced article; others show bookmark and print options.

The interface is clean and clear. *New Grolier* presents options as icons. One attractive feature is that the presence of nontext material (pictures, sound, animation, video) related to an article is displayed in a bar just under the entry word. This bar is visible at all times when scrolling through the entry text, so the user is aware that this material is available. COMPTON'S INTERACTIVE ENCYCLOPEDIA and MICROSOFT ENCARTA, by contrast, put their icons alongside the portion of the entry text to which the multimedia item is related; once the user scrolls past that point, the presence of sound or video may be forgotten.

A complete list of article titles in the encyclopedia can be scanned by clicking the "browse titles" icon or by choosing "browse titles" from the "Search" menu (see *Searching Capabilities* for more information).

The content of the work is quite up-to-date, as searches for **Bill Clinton, Persian Gulf War, Hubble Space Telescope, Frida Kahlo, Lithuania,** and **Russia** revealed; all yielded recently revised or updated information. Many entries, such as **Bill Clinton** and **Bosnia and Hercegovina,** have been updated since the 1993 ACADEMIC AMERICAN ENCYCLOPEDIA was issued. Others, such as **biomathematics** and **Clinton, Hillary Rodham,** have been added to that work's lexicon. The **Persian Gulf War** entry is one of a few "Multimedia Maps" that offer a changing display of images, maps, graphs, and text accompanied by a voice-over narration. (Other subjects include the movements of prehistoric humans and the Roman Empire.) While the overall content of these maps is excellent, the text—in yellow—is difficult to read. The **Hubble Space Telescope** entry includes a 30-second video of the space shuttle.

The "Knowledge Tree" function allows users to access articles from a hierarchical list of topics structured around four branches of knowledge (the arts, geography, nature, and science). The "Timeline" feature allows examination of key world events in chronological order, although the time line display is less visually interesting than that in COMPTON'S INTERACTIVE and far less appealing than that in ENCARTA.

The picture index presents all the pictures in the encyclopedia, organized by subject matter. Pictures are listed by a brief identifier only; COMPTON'S listing, which includes the beginning of the caption, conveys more information.

The map index groups maps into geographic regions from Africa to Oceania. Maps are generally simple but clear and colorful. The maps include cities and rivers; U.S. state maps also include major roads and highways. COMPTON'S and ENCARTA provide greater flexibility by allowing the user to zoom in, enlarging the area displayed to see greater detail.

The animation index presents all the animations in the encyclopedia organized by subject within four categories: human body, mechanical processes, natural processes, and simple machines. Examples are "how eyes can see" and "how levers work." Most animations include brief captions and voice-over narrations.

The video index presents all videos in the encyclopedia organized by subject matter, including animal life, historical events and personalities, plants and fungi, science and technology, space exploration, and U.S. presi-

dents. Persons and events profiled include Jesse Owens at the 1936 Olympic Games and Mahatma Gandhi. Videos range from 15 to 30 seconds and are of varying quality and utility.

The sound index presents all sounds in the encyclopedia organized by type—animal sounds, bird sounds, famous speeches, musical instruments, and musical selections. The 14 famous speeches range from Neil Armstrong's words on the moon to Woodrow Wilson's speech on democratic principles, and they include both original recordings and actors' renderings of speeches. Speeches are all from American history; greater variety would have been better. There are short audio selections from 35 musical instruments ranging from the accordion to the zither. Musical selections include 12 brief excerpts from Bach, Beethoven, Chopin, and others. Sound, video, and animated sequences can be controlled by buttons that allow the user to pause or stop the sequence.

The "Knowledge Explorer" is a collection of audio-visual essays on a variety of general topics ranging from **Asia** to **space exploration.** Samplings of **foundations of science** and **South America** found these to provide excellent introductions to general subjects.

Hardware and Installation

The 1993 edition of *The New Grolier Multimedia Encyclopedia, Windows*/MPC version 6.01, is shipped with a user's guide and one CD-ROM disc. The publisher also sells a Macintosh version of the program, which was not reviewed. We cannot comment on its similarities or differences to the version that was examined. Prospective purchasers are advised to consult periodicals for reviews of that version.

The *minimum* system requirements are as follows: an 80386SX PC-compatible with DOS 3.3, *Windows* 3.1, Microsoft CD-ROM Extensions 2.21, 4 MB of RAM, 1.5 MB available hard disk space, VGA card and monitor (SVGA is recommended), an MPC-compatible CD-ROM drive with minimum 150 KB/sec throughput, and a mouse (which is essential). A *Windows*-compatible printer and drivers are needed to print articles, maps, and selected pictures. A *Windows*-compatible sound card and drivers, along with headphones or speakers, are needed for audio capability.

Installation of *The New Grolier Multimedia Encyclopedia* is a simple process of answering questions; it takes about 15 minutes, including the time spent reading the procedure in the user's guide. The installation program, retrieval software, and database are all on the CD-ROM disc. The CD-ROM drive, sound card, and MSCDEX must be properly installed and configured prior to installing the retrieval software.

During installation, the user is asked if the system includes a compatible sound card. If not, the audio will not be installed. The installation program also asks if *Microsoft Video* should be installed.

Searching Capabilities

A sophisticated multimedia encyclopedia, *New Grolier* has many advantages over its print counterpart. It provides a wide range of approaches to locating information, including searches by title, word, chronology or topic (through the "Knowledge Tree"). Keyword searching using the Boolean operators *and* and *not* is available; searching can be limited to same article, same paragraph, or within a defined number of words. The link to section and next link functions allow the user to move quickly to the next link or cross-referenced topic and back again. While searching a particular topic, all special function indexes—audio, visual, multimedia—can be accessed.

Various forms of truncation can also be used to expand searches. A question mark can be used in searching *wom?n* to get articles on *woman* and *women*. An asterisk can be used for strings of characters. Searching *educat** retrieves all articles related to *education*. Finally, searches can be broadened by using commas. To do a comprehensive search of Greek and Egyptian mythology, a user might search *greek, greece "and" egyptian, egypt and myth**.

To search, the user simply clicks on the "word search" button on the main sidebar or selects "word search" from the search menu. After typing in the search word—for example, *Bosnia*—and any additional clarifying terms, the user selects the word relationship: in the same article, in the same paragraph, or *x* words apart. Our search of *Bosnia* found 61 articles—119 occurrences. Each article with a match is listed, as is the number of instances of the search word in that article.

Downloading and Printing

Several options are available to save and print research results. Searches may be saved in ASCII format for word-processing programs or in a print-to-disk format. The user can save a complete article, a highlighted portion of the article, or a window of text. Specific locations in an article can be marked for future reference by using bookmarks. This reference is then added to a historical bookmark list for later reviewing, printing, or saving to disk. Bookmarks are easily recalled and can be quickly deleted.

Users can print articles, pictures, and maps by selecting "Print" from the file menu or by clicking the "print" button on the main sidebar. The program includes some font control. Because of copyright restrictions, some pictures may not be printed.

The "Save" function allows users to select the hard drive as a destination for downloading. It may be advisable for libraries to have a staff member monitor the hard drive periodically to remove unwanted searches.

Documentation

An indexed 66-page user's guide accompanies the CD-ROM. It contains information on installation; provides a "guided tour" of all the special indexes; has a useful section on developing research strategies; and closes with a series of appendixes illustrating sidebar buttons, menu commands, setting preferences, stop words, and troubleshooting. Information is well organized and very helpful.

New Grolier also provides a wide variety of help screens within the program. These are easily accessed by selecting the question mark on the main sidebar. The "How to" screen suggests how to look up something by subject, browse titles, or select titles from the features menu. Various commands and buttons are described in detail. Technical support is available by calling a toll-free line weekdays during business hours (Eastern Time).

Summary

The New Grolier Multimedia Encyclopedia is one of the most comprehensive and sophisticated of the CD-ROM encyclopedias currently on the market. It has the advantages of the currency and attractiveness of the ACADEMIC AMERICAN ENCYCLOPEDIA while adding a variety of bells and whistles that enhance its depth and attractiveness to students attuned to moving pictures and sound. The addition of the "Knowledge Explorer" and "Multimedia Maps" to this edition greatly enhances the work's appeal.

New Grolier provides content and currency comparable to World Book's INFORMATION FINDER, plus multimedia enhancements similar to COMPTON'S and MICROSOFT ENCARTA. These other two multimedia encyclopedias include an online dictionary, an advantage over *New Grolier*. The word processor resident in ENCARTA and the "Notebook" in COMPTON'S are handy features, but probably not essential—most computer users already have a word-processing program, and *New Grolier* does permit encyclopedia files to be stored for later retrieval. With its clear interface, full-functioned search engine, comprehensive scope, and attractive multimedia components, *The New Grolier Multimedia Encyclopedia* remains an excellent electronic encyclopedia and will prove popular in libraries and homes.

The New Grolier Multimedia Encyclopedia (online)

Facts at a Glance

Full title: **The New Grolier Multimedia Encyclopedia (online)**
Publisher: Grolier
Edition reviewed: © 1994
Type of work: online (accessed on AppleLink)
Platform reviewed: Macintosh

Number of entries: 12,197
Number of illustrations: none
Intended readership: upper elementary school to adult

Price: part of AppleLink service; terms and conditions may vary with other online services
Sold directly to libraries and schools as part of an online service by Apple Computer
Revised annually

Introduction and Authority

The New Grolier Multimedia Encyclopedia is part of the variety of online references available to libraries and schools on AppleLink, Apple Computer's own online service (it was to be renamed *e-World* in the summer of 1994). The same material is also available through other online services.

The content is essentially the 1994 version of THE NEW GROLIER MULTIMEDIA ENCYCLOPEDIA, as available on CD-ROM, except that the online version does not have an atlas or pictures or any of the other audio or video enhancements available on that disk. The encyclopedia is hardly skimpy, however. It contains 80 megabytes of information and allows users of online services—who may not possess a CD-ROM drive—access to a wealth of information that can be quickly looked up.

The authority of the ACADEMIC AMERICAN ENCYCLOPEDIA—the original source of THE NEW GROLIER MULTIMEDIA ENCYCLOPEDIA as well as Grolier's online encyclopedia—is excellent. More information can be found in the review of that print work elsewhere in the Buying Guide.

Scope and Content

Upon opening *The New Grolier Multimedia Encyclopedia (online),* the screen displays three icons that show the division of information within the encyclopedia (or *library,* as it is referred to on screen). These alphabetical divisions are: **A** to **Gila River; Gilbert, Cass** to **Plante, James;** and **plasma** to **zygote.** There are 12,197 documents in the library.

After a user clicks the mouse on one of these divisions, a window appears asking him or her to input an entry for the computer to search. There is also a button for information on library contents; choosing this button results in a message that identifies the division currently open and invites searching. Search categories—for famous persons or places, science, history, the arts, geography, statistics, and "answers to commonly asked questions"—are also shown.

Checking the entries for currency revealed that **Bill Clinton, Gulf War, Lithuania,** and **Russia** were available, but there was no information for the *Hubble Space Telescope, Frida Kahlo,* or the *food pyramid.* Under each entry were many subtopics that could be chosen for further searching. **Russia,** for example, had 269 entries that covered that land from prehistory to the political situation as it stood in 1993. Each entry contains a complete, coherent essay and includes an author's name and a bibliography. Moving back and forth within topics that have already been selected in the encyclopedia is easy with the "Window" feature in the menu bar.

Although lacking illustrations, sound, and video, the encyclopedia is useful. Its search capabilities are very flexible, and the ability to download either whole articles or parts of articles into a memo makes it a helpful resource for collecting ideas.

Hardware and Installation

The encyclopedia comes via modem as part of the AppleLink online service, which is available (for a monthly fee) exclusively for users of Macintosh computers. (For more information about monthly charges and other services available, contact Apple Computer directly.) To use AppleLink, users must have a Macintosh computer equipped with a modem and a hard drive. It requires the installation of AppleLink Version 6.1 on the hard drive and a modem capable of receiving between 300 to 19,200 bps. The software is easy to load and comes with a list of telephone numbers for connecting to the nearest Apple service line.

Searching Capabilities

The basic search screen has been described above. The user-friendly message that invites a search includes mention of the possibility of Boolean searching: "You can use 'and,' 'or,' or 'not' to narrow the search." The searcher can also look for the most up-to-date information by typing a specific date into the boxes labeled "Newer than" and "Older than."

There is also a "Library Help" button. When it is clicked, the service provides a message explaining how to proceed and outlining the various search options. This information can also be printed out for later reference.

Queries can be a simple word—*chocolate*—or phrases—*Mississippi River.* Users can configure seven different operators to receive more specific information about their search topic. These operators include: *and, or, not,* parentheses, field names, range indicators, and value range operators. *And, or,* and *not* function similarly to any Boolean search. Parentheses indicate the order of evaluation of the operators. For example, inputting *(Alamo or Texas) and (Mexico not United States)* retrieves articles that contain either of the first two words and *Mexico,* but not *United States.* Users can also indicate field names such as *Title (Mark Twain)* and find articles with that name in the title.

Range is perhaps the most interesting of the operators and indicates the number of words before or after a term. For example, *Medieval R/10 Europe* searches for articles in which the word *Medieval* appears within ten words before or after *Europe*. A forward range indicator indicates the number of words that one search term appears after the other.

There is also a wild card searching feature that uses an asterisk to stand for a group of letters that might complete the word. Searching on *comput** retrieves articles containing *compute, computing, computer, computed,* and so on.

There are some size limits. A query may not have more than 25 operators, exceed 30 words, or combine more than 50 words or operators. This still gives the user a lot of latitude within which to search.

It is important to note that different online services provide different searching possibilities. The AppleLink service offers full-text searching, which means that the entire contents of the encyclopedia—all the words within entries as well as the entry names themselves—are accessible to the searcher. Services that offer searching for article headings alone give the user less flexibility. This issue should be explored before subscribing to any online service.

Downloading and Printing

Articles from the encyclopedia can be printed out exactly as they appear and taken away by the user for later reference. Users can also take notes from the articles by cutting and pasting clips to a memo within AppleLink that can be printed out later in *TeachText* (the resident word processor on Macintosh computers) or opened in any of the major word-processing packages. Articles can also easily be downloaded into packages that can be sent to other AppleLink users.

Documentation

There is no documentation for this part of the AppleLink service, although there is the online help button (see *Searching Capabilities*). There is also an online address to which memos with comments and questions can be sent on AppleLink.

Summary

While it does not possess the multimedia glitz of the CD-ROM encyclopedias, *The New Grolier Multimedia Encyclopedia (online)* stacks up well. Its articles reflect the text of the parent print work and include bibliographies. It also has a wide variety of searching features that make it a very valuable tool. This is a valuable resource for researchers who want an electronic encyclopedia and have a modem but not a CD-ROM drive.

Another issue arises, however, and that is cost. If an online service charges by time used, it could be that search fees accumulated over a period of time would be enough to justify purchase of the print ACADEMIC AMERICAN ENCYCLOPEDIA—which gives the user an index to aid in searching and thousands of colorful and informative illustrations. If an online encyclopedia is definitely desired, this is a fine one. If that is only one option for accessing encyclopedic information, either a print version or a CD-ROM encyclopedia may be preferable.

The Random House Encyclopedia: Electronic Edition

Facts at a Glance

Full title: **The Random House Encyclopedia: Electronic Edition**
Publisher: Microlytics
Edition reviewed: © 1990 (no version number)
Type of work: floppy disk
Platform reviewed: DOS

Number of entries: 20,000
Number of illustrations: none
Intended readership: middle school to adult

Price: $69.95; discount available to schools and libraries
Sold directly to schools and libraries; also sold by distributors
Revision cycle estimated at every three years

Introduction and Authority

The Random House Encyclopedia: Electronic Edition is a floppy disk version of the text of THE RANDOM HOUSE ENCYCLOPEDIA joined to a search engine called *Infodesk.* It is based on the 1990 edition of the print encyclopedia. Microlytics offers other *Infodesk*-based reference products, including an electronic version of Strunk and White's *The Elements of Style,* that can all be accessed using this common search engine.

Scope and Content

The *Random House Encyclopedia: Electronic Edition* contains about 20,000 articles from the print version's "Alphapedia" and its "Time Chart"; it does not include any material from the print work's "Colorpedia" or atlas.

Entries are grouped into nine main categories: geography; history; philosophy, religion, and mythology; social science; the arts; science; sports and leisure; law; and government. All but law and government are further divided into subcategories. The program also offers a time chart of major events of world history organized under such headings as "The First Civilizations 4000–2000 B.C." and "The Modern World 1950–1989."

Entries can be accessed either by using category and subcategory listings—selecting **geography,** then **countries,** then **France**—or by using the various search capabilities described below.

Based as it is on the 1990 edition of the Random House work, this electronic encyclopedia is current only to 1989. Missing are entries on *Bill Clinton, food pyramid, Gulf War,* the *Hubble Space Telescope, Frida Kahlo,* and independent *Lithuania* or *Russia.* Yemen and Germany are still divided, Czechoslovakia and Yugoslavia united. The work does have entries for **Yangon** (formerly Rangoon) and **Myanmar** (formerly Burma), but other recent name changes are not included.

Entries tend to be brief, as is true of the parent print work. They also employ a telegraphic style, with many abbreviations, which may be difficult for younger users. (For comments on the clarity and accuracy of the entries, see the review of THE RANDOM HOUSE ENCYCLOPEDIA elsewhere in this guide.) There are no bibliographies. Some entries refer to related articles, which can be accessed in a few keystrokes. There are no illustrations, sound, or video. This work is not in the same class as COMPTON'S INTERACTIVE ENCYCLOPEDIA, MICROSOFT ENCARTA, or THE NEW GROLIER MULTIMEDIA ENCYCLOPEDIA. It is most comparable to the text-only electronic encyclopedias found in *Microsoft Bookshelf* and INFORMATION FINDER, although the former adds access to other reference works and the latter is a far more extensive resource.

Hardware and Installation

The encyclopedia comes on floppy disks, the number varying by platform and format. The publisher sells Macintosh and *Windows* versions of the program as well as the DOS version that we tested. Those other versions were not reviewed, and we cannot comment on their similarities or differences to the version that was examined. Prospective purchasers of those other versions are advised to consult periodicals for reviews of those versions.

The DOS version ships with nine 3½″ disks, but 5¼″ disks can be requested. The program must be installed on a hard disk; it cannot be run from the floppy disks. System requirements are a PC-compatible with DOS version 3.3 or higher, 5.8 MB of space on the hard disk, and 480K of available memory. The DOS version of the program does not employ a mouse. The program displays in color.

Installation is simple and fast, taking about 15 minutes. Certain settings—screen colors and printer controls, for example—can be changed subsequent to installation.

The work includes a special program called *Swapinfo* that allows the user to make the encyclopedia a memory-resident program. With this attractive feature, a user can pause in the midst of using an application program—for example, word processing a document— and enter the encyclopedia by hitting a special hot-key combination.

Searching Capabilities

The Random House Encyclopedia: Electronic Edition allows the user to search for information in a number of ways. The "Flash" feature produces a kind of electronic browsing—the program randomly selects entry titles within a given topic area. Two other search capabilities are more advanced.

Using the "Find" key, the user inputs an entry title and that entry is immediately displayed. This search produces matches with *any* article that includes the search word in its title. Thus, *mass* generates hits with **mass** (religion); **mass** (atomic); **mass action, law of; mass production;** and many others. The matches are not always exact, however. Searching for *Mays* generated not only **Willie Mays,** but also **May** (the month), **May beetle, Cape May, Louisa May Alcott, Doris May Lessing, May Sarton, Liza May Minelli,** and **Florence May Chadwick.** In this search mode, the computer does not indicate how many matches have been found; the user must continue scanning the list of hits, which can be quite lengthy. This is an annoying feature.

The "Reverse Dictionary" feature enables the user to search for words that appear within entries. After shifting to this mode, the user can, for instance, type in *state motto* to find how many entries include those words. The answer, 49, seems wrong, but the program is quite correct—**South Carolina** says *state mottoes* because the state has two. To narrow the search, the user can search for two words; the program then matches only those entries that have both words.

The program helps the searcher by accommodating possible spelling errors. If the search word cannot be found in the encyclopedia, the program displays a list of alternatives. The "Reverse Dictionary" also includes a partial word match feature that allows for matches when the correct spelling of the desired word is not known or not input. With partial word match on, typing *egyption* generates matches with *egyptian*. On the other hand, partial word match can lead the researcher astray: the *state motto* search noted above produced matches for **Canada lynx** and **collie** because those entries contain the word *mottled*.

A final research tool is the "bookmark," which enables the user to mark up to 30 articles. Once marked, these articles can be accessed with just a few keystrokes at any time. Entries can be easily placed in and removed from the bookmark.

Downloading and Printing

Articles displayed on screen can be saved into a separate file, which can then be imported into a word-processing document (complete with a copyright line). The program does not allow the user to define a new file name for each saved entry, however; all are placed into the same file.

Articles can be printed, although the program offers few controls over the output. Printouts also display a copyright notice.

Documentation

The manual is quite brief, running under 40 pages. It contains useful and clear instructions about how to install and use the program, along with a number of examples. However, the manual neglects to point out that files created by saving articles to disk can be imported into applications only as DOS files.

The program includes on-screen help as well, although the information is quite basic. The publisher also offers telephone support, but not through a toll-free number. This support is provided weekdays during business hours (Eastern Time).

Summary

For another opinion of this work, see *Booklist (Reference Books Bulletin),* July 1991.

The Random House Encyclopedia: Electronic Edition is a useful on-screen reference tool. The edition reviewed cannot compare with more up-to-date competitors because it lacks currency, although a newer edition could rectify that. It does not compete with the scope or dazzle of the three multimedia encyclopedias: COMPTON'S, ENCARTA, and GROLIER. It also lacks the scope and depth of INFORMATION FINDER, another text-based encyclopedia that has far more content. It is a solid work, however, that offers basic reference information that one can access easily—and conveniently, since it can be used while working in a standard word-processing program. The main benefit of this product is that it provides encyclopedic information to computer owners who do not have a CD-ROM drive. In addition, it is significantly less expensive than the encyclopedias on CD-ROM. With its limited scale, it is more appropriate for home or office than library use.

Chapter 16
Evaluations of Electronic Atlases

Hammond Intermediate World Atlas (in Microsoft Bookshelf '94)

Facts at a Glance

Full title: **Hammond Intermediate World Atlas (in Microsoft Bookshelf '94 Multimedia Reference Library)**

Publisher: Microsoft

Edition reviewed: © 1994 (no version number)

Type of work: CD-ROM

Platform reviewed: Windows

Number of maps: 160

Intended readership: ages 9 and up

Price (for entire *Bookshelf* package): $99.95 (through 12/31/94); $79.95 with school discount; $30 rebate for owners of previous versions

Revised annually

Introduction and Authority

Microsoft Bookshelf '94 is a CD-ROM product containing seven reference books accessible from one source. It can be used as a quick reference tool from anywhere in *Windows,* or as a standalone program. The reference works contained in *Bookshelf* include *The Hammond Intermediate World Atlas,* reviewed here, and THE CONCISE COLUMBIA ENCYCLOPEDIA and THE AMERICAN HERITAGE DICTIONARY, each reviewed in other chapters of this part of the Buying Guide. The review of the CONCISE COLUMBIA lists the other four works in *Bookshelf.*

The *Hammond Intermediate World Atlas* is a collection of maps licensed by Microsoft from Hammond, publisher of THE HAMMOND ATLAS OF THE WORLD and other reputable atlases.

Scope and Content

To the base of maps licensed from Hammond, Microsoft has added over 160 national anthems, 230 flags, pronunciations of place names, and links to the six other reference books included in *Bookshelf.*

Maps can be accessed via a list of options that include searching a table of contents or using a "Find" window that searches for place names anywhere in the atlas. An "Advanced Find" window is primarily useful for searching in more than one reference work in *Bookshelf.*

After a place name is selected, the program displays a map containing the location, although the map may have to be scrolled through to locate the desired place name. From this map, users can access a topographical map of the area as well as a locator map that positions the area in the context of the world. Page buttons at the bottom of the screen allow the user to page back and forth through the atlas, and a "Back" button is used to recall past maps.

After a map has been accessed, place names can be clicked on for pronunciations. Major locations, such as foreign countries and U.S. states, have flags by their names. Clicking on these produces a pop-up box with a picture of the flag and buttons that can be clicked on to bring the user to the relevant encyclopedia entry or almanac listing within *Bookshelf.* Some maps also have a button that will play the country's national anthem. While the anthems are interesting, the sound quality is poor, and there is no way to stop them from playing once started.

The *Hammond Intermediate World Atlas* is fairly current, including Namibia, a united Germany, a united Yemen, and St. Petersburg. It does not, however, make reference to Myanmar or the Taiwan Strait. As with most electronic atlases, the level of detail on the maps is quite low: most smaller towns and cities do not appear. The quality of the cartography is very similar to that of the HAMMOND LARGE TYPE WORLD ATLAS, reviewed elsewhere in this guide. Topographical maps are colorful and reasonably easy to read except for rivers. They include national boundaries, though not country names.

Hardware and Installation

Bookshelf is currently available for *Windows* and Macintosh. The *Windows* version was reviewed; prospective purchasers of the Macintosh version should consult reviews in periodicals to determine how that version of the product performs. System requirements are for a standard Multimedia PC, and installation takes very little time. The review of *Bookshelf*'s version of THE CONCISE COLUMBIA ENCYCLOPEDIA has a detailed discussion of these issues.

Searching Capabilities

Bookshelf's Hammond Intermediate World Atlas can be accessed primarily through a table of contents or the "Find" window to access place names. Places with duplicate names—for example, St. Petersburg, Florida, and St. Petersburg, Russia—are entered as one heading with multiple subheads. The atlas contains no "see also" references or cross-referencing, but they are not necessary. The "Advanced Find" feature searches for place names in the atlas and other *Bookshelf* reference works simultaneously.

The "Gallery" search feature allows users to see a list of all *Bookshelf* entries that contain multimedia elements—animation, sound, or pictures. Since nearly all of the atlas entries contain sound in the form of pronunciations and none contain animations, this feature is not particularly useful for this reference work. Boolean searching is available in *Bookshelf,* but is not necessary for this component.

Downloading and Printing

Bookshelf allows for direct printing of maps, although the reproductions are quite small and difficult to read. City and country labels that have been placed on surrounding bodies of water do not appear on laser printouts, as the bodies of water are printed in black. The flags that appear on pop-up windows can also be pasted into the clipboard and imported into application programs.

Documentation

Almost no documentation comes with *Microsoft Bookshelf '94.* Previous versions have included small manuals, but Microsoft decided to eliminate them since their target audiences—elementary through high school students—tend not to read manuals. The lack of documentation is a problem, however. The program does come with a pamphlet that briefly describes installation, system requirements, and information on how to get additional help. Extensive online help is also provided, but it is not context sensitive. On-screen help can be accessed from any point in the program, although a help index must be consulted to locate an appropriate entry. Microsoft also offers help via a CompuServe forum, on the Internet, and through a toll-free telephone support line available from 6 A.M. to 6 P.M. (Pacific Time) on weekdays.

Summary

Microsoft Bookshelf's Hammond Intermediate World Atlas is an adequate atlas with less-than-adequate documentation. Next to the maps themselves, the best feature of the program is the linkage it provides to related information in the encyclopedia and almanac in *Bookshelf.* The multimedia features make little use of the available technology. Prospective buyers in the market specifically for an electronic atlas may want to look at the other programs reviewed in the Buying Guide. A home user interested in a less full-featured atlas that comes packaged with a variety of other reference sources, however, is likely to be quite satisfied with *Microsoft Bookshelf.* Libraries will find these extra works unnecessary, and the quality of the atlas alone is not worth the purchase price of this set. School libraries especially should consider Brøderbund's PC GLOBE MAPS 'N' FACTS, reviewed elsewhere in this guide.

PC Globe Maps 'n' Facts

Facts at a Glance

Full title: **PC Globe Maps 'n' Facts**
Publisher: Brøderbund
Edition reviewed: © 1993 (no version number)
Type of work: CD-ROM
Platform reviewed: DOS

Number of maps: about 700
Intended readership: grade 4 and up (reviewer estimate)

Price: $49.95
Sold through authorized dealers and directly from the publisher
No stated revision policy

Introduction and Authority

PC Globe Maps 'n' Facts is an electronic atlas published by Brøderbund, a major company in the educational and entertainment software industry. (Brøderbund also publishes the successful "Carmen Sandiego" software series.) The program was originally developed by a company called PC Globe until Brøderbund purchased that company.

Scope and Content

The program includes a variety of resources, including political and physical maps; statistical maps; maps of organizations (NATO, the European Community, the Arab League); time-zone maps; statistics on countries and cities, which can be displayed as tables or charts; tables of the "longest, highest, and largest" rivers, mountains, cities, and so on; flags and national anthems; and currency conversion tabulations. Unlike either the SOFTWARE TOOLWORKS WORLD ATLAS or National Geographic's PICTURE ATLAS OF THE WORLD, this program does not contain photographs, videos, or spoken pronunciations.

Maps and statistical information reflect most of the recent changes in the world. Germany is shown as united and Yugoslavia, Czechoslovakia, and the Soviet Union as divided. Yemen, however, is still shown as two countries. Interestingly, the publisher has retained maps and statistics for the two Germanys, Czechoslovakia, Yugoslavia, and the Soviet Union in their former condition as well as in their newly organized status "to enable users to compare with the new countries." Most recent name changes are included: Cambodia, the Taiwan Strait, Myanmar (for Burma) and Yangon (for Rangoon) all appear. Of the Buying Guide's test entries, only Kalaallit Nunaat (for Greenland) did not appear.

Typical for electronic atlases, the cartography is not as detailed as one would hope. Only major cities are shown, even on the single-country maps, and coastlines often look jagged because of a lack of detail. Although elevation changes are depicted by different colors on the physical maps, their precision is poor compared with that of a print atlas. Maps in this program, however, compare favorably to those in other electronic atlases; unlike those of the PICTURE ATLAS OF THE WORLD, for example, they occupy nearly the entire screen.

Various customizing options are available. When viewing maps, users can calculate the distance between any two points. Users can delete or restore details on surrounding countries for the political and physical maps. They can also hide the legend and map labels. Statistical information can be customized to focus on a particular country in relation to other user-selected countries. Measures can be switched from English units to metric and back again. Currency conversion rates can be updated by the user to ensure that conversion calculations are up-to-date.

A valuable feature allows users to create customized maps—especially useful for students preparing reports. These maps can be saved for later retrieval. Users can control the content, size, color, and position of labels, although information is limited to what already appears in the program's database.

Hardware and Installation

System requirements are an 80386 PC-compatible computer running at 16 MHz or faster with 640K of RAM (although 2 MB are recommended), 2 MB of space on the hard drive, a VGA card and monitor, a CD-ROM drive, and a mouse. Software requirements include DOS 3.3 or higher. This is a DOS, not a *Windows,* program, although it may be run within the *Windows* environment. The publisher recommends that the system also have a sound card.

Brøderbund publishes other versions of the program, including a floppy disk version of *PC Globe Maps 'n' Facts* (which uses 3½" floppy disks) and Macintosh and DOS versions of programs called *MacGlobe* and *PC Globe.* These other versions were not reviewed, and we cannot comment on their similarities or differences to the program that was analyzed. Prospective purchasers interested in these other versions are urged to consult periodicals for reviews of those versions.

Installation is relatively quick and simple. Creating an icon for the program within *Windows* turned out to be a more involved process than described in the documentation, but Brøderbund's telephone support was able to solve the problem.

Searching Capabilities

When the program begins, the user is shown an attractive world political map that is flanked on the left by the various icons that allow access to the database. These icons are strictly pictorial, but any possible confusion is eliminated with a written status line at the bottom of the screen that indicates what each icon represents as the mouse pointer rests on the icon.

Users can also access maps in three other ways. The index feature, which lists all the place names in the database, enables the user to display maps to see a particular geographic feature or city when he or she is unsure of which map is appropriate. The "Maps" menu at the top of the screen allows the user to display a specific country or regional map. Finally, the zoom feature lets the user move back to maps of smaller scale—from countries to regions to the world.

Moving from one country map to another is very easy with this program. Like the PICTURE ATLAS OF THE WORLD, maps of neighboring countries can be accessed simply by clicking on that country's name. Users also have the option at any time of selecting a physical or political map of that country, or skipping to a map of a distant country simply by using the icon menu.

Downloading and Printing

Information in the database—either maps or statistics—can be saved onto disk or printed. Printing options include outputting on a color printer, although the necessary equipment was not available for this review. Graphics being printed can be scaled from 25 to 100 percent of the screen size, a feature that will be particularly useful for students who may want to include a map in a report or project. The program also allows for three different levels of quality in the output. Several black-and-white laser printouts revealed a high level of clarity, especially when the highest-quality print option was selected. Distinctions between levels of shading were clear and place names were easily read.

Documentation

The program comes with an 80-page user's guide that adequately explains its features and functions, although (as noted above) installation to *Windows* was not as straightforward as suggested. The user's guide also provides a glossary of geographic terms and a list of abbreviations.

Classroom teachers can purchase a school edition that includes another booklet, a 48-page teacher's guide that includes 13 activities and a curriculum correlation linking the activities to various academic disciplines.

Free telephone support is available to registered users from 7:00 to 4:30 (Pacific Time) on weekdays, and an online bulletin board can be accessed for free by Brøderbund's customers.

Summary

PC Globe Maps 'n' Facts is a complete, classroom-oriented map package that will aid teachers. It has a good selection of maps that indicate major cities and landforms, as well as numerous charts and tables of information about the countries. Its flexible printing and custom map-making features make it very appropriate for classroom use; home purchasers, however, should consider that it does not include features such as video and audio clips included with products such as SOFTWARE TOOLWORKS WORLD ATLAS. As with nearly all electronic atlases, the lack of detail on the maps themselves prevents this program from being recommended as a serious reference tool for libraries.

PC Globe Maps 'n' Facts is priced very competitively: at $49.95, it is the least expensive of the electronic atlases reviewed in the Buying Guide. It is also very current and is a recommended purchase for students and educators.

Picture Atlas of the World

Facts at a Glance

Full title: **Picture Atlas of the World**
Publisher: National Geographic Society (distributed by Karol Media)
Edition reviewed: © 1992, revised 1994; version 1.1
Type of work: CD-ROM
Platform reviewed: DOS

Number of maps: more than 800
Intended readership: grade 4 and up

Price: $99
No stated revision policy

Introduction and Authority

Picture Atlas of the World, a CD-ROM product, is a full-featured electronic atlas with many multimedia components. The work's intended audience is students in grades 4 to 12 as well as adults. The program was created and published by the National Geographic Society, a renowned publisher of authoritative cartography.

Scope and Content

Picture Atlas of the World contains a variety of elements that make it an entertaining and informative way to explore the world. The program includes more than 800 interactive political, physical, and topographical maps of the world, the oceans, the continents, regions, nations, transportation networks, and specific sites. This program does not allow users to customize maps as they can in other electronic atlases, including PC GLOBE MAPS 'N' FACTS and SOFTWARE TOOLWORKS WORLD ATLAS.

The variety of audio and video features in this electronic atlas adds an encyclopedic element to the work while maintaining a sense of fun. These features include more than 50 video clips, which present visuals, music, and captions covering all continents (some of these clips also include spoken narration); more than 1,200 color photographs with captions, showing people and places; and audio clips with music from around the world and spoken examples of more than 100 languages. The quality of the video and audio features is generally good, although the voices in the spoken segments are sometimes cut off before the end of a sentence.

Other encyclopedic features of this electronic atlas include text descriptions of many countries and locations. Vital statistics of world nations and their smaller subdivisions are also provided. Three animated segments explain latitude and longitude, the principles of cartography, and time zones. These segments are appropriate for younger users as well as adults. In addition, an interactive glossary provides definitions of many of the terms used in the text portions of the atlas.

On starting the program, the user is shown a main menu. With the click of a mouse, users can opt to go through the tutorial, watch narrated animations of geographical concepts, look at a world map, view a list of countries from A to Z, or choose from an index of all the place names appearing in the atlas.

As with other electronic atlases, the maps in this work are fairly simple, showing only major cities and geographic features. This atlas is well balanced, with all areas receiving equal map coverage. Maps and statistical information are quite current. Both Germany and Yemen are shown as united, and the independent republics of the former Soviet Union, Czechoslovakia, and Yugoslavia are presented. Most place names are also current: Myanmar, Yangon, Cambodia, Namibia, and St. Petersburg are all correctly identified. Kalaallit Nunaat, however, is still identified as Greenland.

Hardware and Installation

To run *Picture Atlas of the World,* a user must have a PC-compatible with an 80286 processor or better, at least 2 MB of RAM (with at least 500K of conventional RAM available), a VGA card and monitor, DOS version 4.0 or higher, Microsoft CD-ROM Extensions 2.10 or higher, a CD-ROM drive, an audio adapter, and a mouse. (National Geographic offers a special version of the CD-ROM product that comes bundled with an audio sound board.)

Installation is quite simple, requiring only a few minutes for the user to follow the directions that appear on the screen. Once that process is completed, the program is ready to run. Although National Geographic currently does not offer a Macintosh version of the program, the company plans to market a double-sided disk in January 1995 that will be compatible with both PC and Macintosh systems.

Searching Capabilities

Picture Atlas of the World offers the user a number of ways to access information. The program allows the user to display detailed maps either through the index or by clicking on specific areas of maps that are displayed. For instance, clicking on North America on the world map calls up a map of that continent. Clicking on Canada in the North America map shows that country. Conveniently, the program provides for moving in the reverse direction as well; clicking on locator maps displayed in the corner of continent or country maps brings the user back to the main world map or the related continent map. Some other atlas programs do not provide this ability to move to both greater and lesser detail.

Some maps also show an icon signaling the presence of related maps in the database. Clicking on this icon leads users to maps of the relevant region, a topographical map of the area, a more detailed map of the country, or a transportation map. Other options allow users to

make the names of countries and cities appear on or disappear from continent maps. Finally, users can navigate from one map to another by clicking on the area for a country shown on the map currently displayed. With Afghanistan on screen, for instance, one can easily reveal the map for Pakistan.

Two indexes provide easy access to maps and information. The first—called "Countries A–Z"—provides an alphabetical list of all of the countries shown on the maps. The second is a complete index of all place names that appear in the atlas. If a user clicks on the name of a city, a map appears with the appropriate city highlighted by a red arrow. Both indexes allow users to scroll through each place name or to "drag" the button bar for speedy access to a particular section of the alphabetical list.

Downloading and Printing

Maps and photographs can be saved onto a disk or printed. The manual suggests that saved images can be manipulated and assembled into presentations using an authoring tool from IBM (which was used to create the atlas itself), although it also warns users that the images and maps are copyrighted and cannot be used without authorization. A README file on the CD-ROM disk provides more information about copying than is included in the manual itself. This additional material is helpful, but it would have been easier to use if all related information were located in one source.

The print function in *Picture Atlas of the World* has a serious drawback. It allows users to print only the entire computer screen—including the program icons. Other atlases on CD-ROM, such as PC GLOBE MAPS 'N' FACTS, let users print just the map—a handy feature for students, who may want to include a printout of a map in a school report. In addition, *Picture Atlas of the World* does not have a print option for screens containing statistical information.

Documentation

The disk comes with a 24-page manual that outlines how to navigate through the program. This manual clearly elucidates the main buttons and the features that they lead to. There is also a brief troubleshooting section that addresses some specific problems that may arise (for instance, if the audio does not play). In addition, an interactive tutorial within the program highlights all of the features and shows how to access them. Online help is not provided, but National Geographic does offer a toll-free telephone help line, although it does not specify the times or days that this help is available.

Summary

For another review of the *Picture Atlas of the World,* see *Booklist (Reference Books Bulletin),* November 1, 1993.

The inclusion of videos, photographs, and audio clips of music and spoken languages gives this program more of an encyclopedic quality than Brøderbund's PC GLOBE MAPS 'N' FACTS. As an atlas, however, it has fewer features than either the Brøderbund work or SOFTWARE TOOLWORKS WORLD ATLAS. Unlike those programs, *Picture Atlas of the World* does not allow users to print full-screen maps (without program icons), print screens with statistical figures, or customize maps. The lack of these features limits the program's usefulness—especially for students. Prospective buyers may want to consider SOFTWARE TOOLWORKS WORLD ATLAS, which offers features similar to those found in this work, as well as additional ones—all for a significantly lower price.

The Software Toolworks World Atlas

Facts at a Glance

Full title: **The Software Toolworks World Atlas**
Publisher: Software Toolworks
Edition reviewed: © 1993, version 3
Type of work: CD-ROM
Platform reviewed: Macintosh

Number of entries: more than 300
Number of maps: more than 250 reference and relief maps and 4,000 statistical maps
Number of illustrations: more than 4,000 graphs, 1,000 photographs, and 150 video clips
Intended readership: grade 4 to adult (reviewer estimate)

Price: $69.95; 25 percent discount available to schools
Sold directly to schools; also sold in retail outlets
Revised annually

Introduction and Authority

The Software Toolworks World Atlas is an electronic world atlas available in both floppy disk and CD-ROM format. (The Macintosh CD-ROM version was reviewed.) The program provides an easy-to-use, ready-reference tool for school students from about fourth grade up and for adults. The version reviewed was published in 1993 and is copyrighted by Software Toolworks and Electromap.

Scope and Content

The Software Toolworks World Atlas includes numerous maps, extensive information on world nations and cities, illustrations of national flags, recordings of national anthems, photographs, and video footage. The atlas contains more than 250 color political and topographical maps, including 36 regional and ocean maps and political maps of all the world's nations. It also includes more than 4,000 color statistical maps. The atlas is very balanced; no region receives greater emphasis than another.

The atlas also contains information on more than 300 topics for each nation and data on over 300 cities. This includes information on population, government, climate, legal system, holidays, the economy, exports and imports, industries, communications, currency and exchange rates, and travel information.

The atlas reflects most recent changes in the world, including the unification of Germany and of Yemen, the independence of republics within the former Soviet Union and Yugoslavia, and the division of Czechoslovakia into two nations. Updated place names include Cambodia, Namibia, Taiwan Strait, and St. Petersburg, but Burma, Rangoon, and Greenland have not been updated. The atlas is scheduled for annual (or more frequent) revision; it is hoped that these changes will be reflected in the next version. The DOS, MPC CD-ROM, and *Windows* products are now in version 4. This version adds 50 regional city maps.

Maps are fairly simple, not offering the kind of detail available in print atlases. The choice of detail shown does not always reflect the best judgment. The political map of Spain, for instance, omits Santiago de Compostela, and topographical maps do not include rivers. The great variety of map types provided, however, makes the work very useful.

A valuable feature is the ability to add comments, markers, and labels to any map and data to expand the current database. In this way, users can create their own maps, tailoring the information database to their own needs. This feature may be cumbersome in a library, however.

The atlas has audio and video capabilities that make it fun to use as well as informative. One useful audio feature is the clear pronunciation of the names of all regions, nations, and major cities when their labels are clicked. The atlas also plays the national anthems of most nations—a fun feature for students. A special audio help feature explains the use of various menu commands in clear and simple language. The atlas has two video features—more than 1,000 color photographs of locations in many nations and 150 short, animated videos in color showing major attractions of 47 world cities. In general, the quality of photographs is quite good. The animated videos are of a somewhat poorer quality, with the small image typical of the current generation of CD-ROM products. It is possible to zoom out to a larger size, but doing so makes the quality worse. Audio and video features are easily accessed through both the menu bar and special buttons at the side of each map.

Hardware and Installation

The version of *The Software Toolworks World Atlas* reviewed was for a Macintosh system. It comes on a single CD-ROM disk and can be used with Macintosh II series and up as long as the computer has 2 MB or more of memory, a hard disk, and System 6.05 or higher. To run the animated videos, QuickTime Extensions 1.5 or higher must be installed in the computer's System Folder. The program can be used with either a black-and-white or color monitor, but color is recommended. A mouse is necessary, although many menu items are also command driven.

The publisher also offers a Macintosh floppy disk version of the work as well as floppy and CD-ROM versions for DOS and *Windows*. Versions on floppy disk do not include audio, photographs, or video. These other versions were not reviewed, and we cannot comment on their similarities or differences to the version that was examined. Prospective purchasers of these other versions are advised to consult periodicals for reviews of them.

Installation is very simple, requiring less than five minutes. Only one file needs to be copied to the System Folder; this allows the animated videos to run. To access the program, the user simply inserts the disk into the CD-ROM drive and double-clicks the atlas icon.

The user interface is clear and easy to use. All functions can be launched using the mouse; some menu items are also command driven. In addition to a pull-down menu bar across the top of the screen, a series of buttons appears alongside every map. These buttons allow the user to zoom in and out between nation and regional maps; click back and forth to maps displayed before or after a particular map; and access statistical maps and graphs, information on nations and cities, national flags, national anthems, videos, and still photographs. Information boxes, flag boxes, photograph boxes, and video boxes can be moved on screen to any location. Only one map can be displayed on the screen at a time, but any number of boxes can be opened at the same time.

Searching Capabilities

The Software Toolworks World Atlas employs several modes of access for easy, quick retrieval of information. Using the menu bar, users can scan alphabetical indexes to locate any map as well as any city, river, mountain, sea, or other feature labeled on a map. Users can also search for a place by inputting its name within the appropriate menu item. Graphs, flags, anthems, photographs, and videos can be accessed using the menu bars or the buttons displayed alongside each map.

Regional and national political maps can also be accessed directly from maps displayed on the screen by clicking the labels for regions or nations. The menu bar and special buttons also allow users to move back and forth between maps already displayed. The program keeps track of up to 50 maps in memory.

Downloading and Printing

The user can select any map, graph, flag, or box of information and print it out, save it to disk, or export it to another application. Photographs and video cannot be printed or exported. To print, the user simply selects and displays the desired item and chooses the print command from the "File" menu. The quality of maps, graphs, and flags printed out on a black-and-white laser printer was not very good. (The program was not tested with a color printer.) Colors did not translate well into gray tones, and lettering was difficult to read. This is less of a problem for subject areas of political maps, although the dark gray screen that appears over nonsubject areas makes type difficult to read. Boxed information, which is displayed as simple text, printed very well.

Documentation

The atlas does not come with a printed manual, but one can be ordered from the publisher for $5. Instead, the program has an online manual that can be quickly accessed from any point in the program. The manual is quite comprehensive, straightforward, and easy to use, providing adequate instruction.

The program also includes an audio help function, easily accessible through the Apple menu, that gives clear, simple spoken explanations of the most important submenus under the main menu. This may, however, be distracting in a library setting.

Telephone technical support is available, although not toll free. No hours for this support are given. The publisher is located in California.

Summary

The Software Toolworks World Atlas is a very good multimedia atlas for the price. It is current, comprehensive, and easy to use. Audio and video capabilities make it attractive to younger users, and the ability to expand the database and add markers and labels to maps will appeal to more sophisticated users. The usefulness of the atlas is also enhanced by the ability to print out maps or data and export them to other application programs. This product is recommended for home and school purchase.

Chapter 17
Evaluations of Electronic Dictionaries

The American Heritage Dictionary (in Microsoft Bookshelf '94)

Facts at a Glance

Full title: **The American Heritage Dictionary (in Microsoft Bookshelf '94 Multimedia Reference Library)**

Publisher: Microsoft
Edition reviewed: © 1994 (no version number)
Type of work: CD-ROM
Platform reviewed: Windows

Number of entries: more than 350,000 definitions
Number of illustrations: more than 2,000
Intended readership: ages 9 and up

Price (for entire *Bookshelf* package): $99.95 (through 12/31/94); $79.95 (with school discount); $30 rebate for owners of previous versions
Revised annually

Introduction and Authority

Microsoft Bookshelf '94 is a CD-ROM product that contains seven reference books that can be accessed from a single source. It can be used as a quick reference source from within a word-processing program or anywhere in *Windows,* or as a stand-alone program. The works contained in *Bookshelf* include *The American Heritage Dictionary,* reviewed here. Other *Bookshelf* sources reviewed in this Buying Guide are THE CONCISE COLUMBIA ENCYCLOPEDIA, SECOND EDITION, and the HAMMOND INTERMEDIATE WORLD ATLAS.

Microsoft has licensed this dictionary from Houghton Mifflin, publisher of the well-received American Heritage series of dictionaries. The work licensed for this version of the *Bookshelf* CD-ROM is the third edition (© 1992), the most current available.

Scope and Content

Bookshelf's version of the *American Heritage Dictionary* includes more than 350,000 definitions, supplemented by spoken pronunciations of more than 80,000 words, as well as full-text searching and links to the six other reference books on the disc (see the review of the electronic version of THE CONCISE COLUMBIA ENCYCLOPEDIA for a complete listing of the works in *Microsoft Bookshelf*). Also available to users of this electronic dictionary are more than 2,000 illustrations, both those associated with the dictionary itself and those linked to the encyclopedia and atlas.

Entries in the *American Heritage Dictionary* include brief etymologies, synonym guides, and cross-referencing. Many words also have the extensive usage notes for which the American Heritage series is renowned. The entry **he,** for example, has a lengthy article about the controversy concerning using *he* to refer to indefinite antecedents. There is also a pronunciation key that explains the phonetic pronunciations displayed on the screen.

The *American Heritage Dictionary* is fairly current, including entries on **rap, retrovirus,** and **fax.** It does not, however, make reference to *virtual reality* or *bungee jumping.* In addition, many of the illustrations are out-of-date, including a picture of Gloria Steinem dating back to the mid-1970s.

As with the other works in *Bookshelf,* dictionary entries can be accessed via a tabbed list of options, which includes a table of contents, a "Find" option, and a "Gallery" list of words that have accompanying sounds or images. Also available is the "Advanced Find" window, primarily used for searching in more than one reference work in *Bookshelf.* This feature includes a help button that provides useful searching tips and hints.

Each entry has highlighted words known as *infinite links.* These can be clicked on for pronunciations or connections to other related entries. The entry **belly,** for instance, is linked in this way to **abdomen.**

Hardware and Installation

Bookshelf, provided on CD-ROM, is currently available for both *Windows* and the Macintosh. The Macintosh version of this product was not reviewed, and similarities or differences to the *Windows* version are unknown. Prospective purchasers of the Macintosh version are advised to consult periodicals for reviews of that version.

The minimum hardware and software requirements (the standard needs for a Multimedia PC) and the installation procedures are discussed fully in the review for the electronic CONCISE COLUMBIA.

Searching Capabilities

Bookshelf's American Heritage Dictionary can be entered in a variety of ways. There is a standard table of contents, including a search window where a word or phrase can be entered. Entries can also be searched using the "Find" window, which generates a list of entries containing the desired term. In addition, a user can reference past searches to retrieve and use them again.

A feature of *Bookshelf* that is not specifically applicable to the *American Heritage Dictionary* is the "Gallery" search, which allows the user to browse a list of terms that have specific multimedia features, such as sound, pictures, or animations. Since many dictionary entries contain sound (the spoken pronunciations) and none contain animations, this feature is not useful for this reference work. On the other hand, a user who looks up an entry such as **heart** will certainly be rewarded by seeing the animated sequence showing the heart in action.

Terms can be combined using the Boolean operators *and, or,* and *not,* as well as the connector *near.* This last function can be user-customized for varying degrees of proximity. As noted in the review of CONCISE COLUMBIA, the value of this feature is lessened because there is no documentation explaining it. The only guide to Boolean searching is in the "Advanced Find" box, which is hidden in the menu bar. Once that is found, the on-screen help is thorough.

Searches list near-hits as well as exact matches. Searches for both *ali* and *aly* retrieved the same 35 items, including **Muhammad Ali** and **allegorical** (which contained **ali** in its phonetic representation). By trying to make the search process easier for users who may accidentally misspell a word, Microsoft may be creating a cumbersome set of matches that the more careful typist must scroll through. The lack of documentation on this feature may leave the user quite confused, and there is no information on whether this near-match feature can be turned off. Even more frustrating, the near-match approach does not apply in situations where it may well be desired. Searching for *George Bush* did not generate a match because his entry is under **George Herbert Walker Bush.** A less complicated search engine would be more helpful for the user of *Bookshelf.*

Cross-referencing is also peculiar. The entry for **grouchiest** does not link back to **grouch,** for instance. One group of words that is consistently cross-referenced inadequately is acronyms. Entering *HDTV* produced the information that it stood for **high definition television** but did not produce a link to its full definition.

Downloading and Printing

Bookshelf comes with the standard cut, copy, and paste features, allowing a user to copy text from the entries into the "Notepad" or other applications. In addition, the "Copy Picture" feature allows for the copying and pasting of pictures.

Bookshelf also permits printing of complete entries, help text, or pictures directly from the program simply by clicking a "Print" button at the bottom of the screen.

Documentation

Microsoft Bookshelf '94 contains almost no documentation (simply brief installation instructions), which is a serious flaw—and a departure from past editions. Microsoft decided to eliminate the manual because its target audiences—elementary through high school students—tend not to read them. This seems an ill-advised choice.

There is extensive online help, although it is not context sensitive. Users must access on-screen help by scrolling through the "Help" index. Microsoft also offers help via a *CompuServe* forum, on the Internet, and with a toll-free telephone support line that is open during the day (Pacific Time) on weekdays.

Summary

Microsoft Bookshelf's American Heritage Dictionary is an excellent, low-priced, multifaceted reference tool. The absence of documentation is troubling, but this may not bother a relatively sophisticated computer uscr. As a dictionary, the work is very good. With about 350,000 definitions, it is larger than all competitors except the two unabridged electronic dictionaries—the RANDOM HOUSE UNABRIDGED and THE OXFORD ENGLISH DICTIONARY ON COMPACT DISC—and those works are considerably more expensive. It offers spoken pronunciations, which those works do not, and adds illustrations, which many users will enjoy. The disk has the added bonus of providing six other reference sources. A purchaser looking primarily for an electronic encyclopedia may prefer one of the other offerings on the market to the CONCISE COLUMBIA contained in *Bookshelf,* as they are larger and contain more features. For someone seeking an electronic dictionary, however, the *American Heritage Dictionary* in *Microsoft Bookshelf* is a good buy.

The American Heritage Illustrated Encyclopedic Dictionary

Facts at a Glance

Full title: **The American Heritage Illustrated Encyclopedic Dictionary**
Publisher: Xïphias
Edition reviewed: © 1990–1993, version 4.3
Type of work: CD-ROM
Platform reviewed: DOS

Number of entries: 180,000
Number of illustrations: 4,000
Intended readership: grade 4 to adult

Price: $39.95
Sold through publisher
No stated revision policy

Introduction and Authority

Described in the user's manual as a "multimedia reference work [that] includes over 180,000 definitions and thousands of colorful pictures," the *American Heritage Illustrated Encyclopedic Dictionary* on CD-ROM is based on a print work that was published in 1987 under this title and also as the *Reader's Digest Illustrated Encyclopedia Dictionary,* both now out of print. The book itself drew on the lexicon of the second edition (1982) of THE AMERICAN HERITAGE DICTIONARY, but with occasionally lengthier definitions and the addition of much encyclopedic material.

This electronic edition is released by Xïphias, which has issued other CD-ROM reference products, including three titles in the Time Table of History series. Xïphias has released a 1993–'94 version of *American Heritage Illustrated Encyclopedic Dictionary* on CD-ROM, which was not available at the time of the review.

Scope and Content

Despite having the copyright years 1990–1993 on its jewel case and a README file dated December 12, 1992, this CD-ROM appears to replicate exactly the contents of the earlier book. (The jewel case indicates that the "lexical databases" are copyright 1987.) There are no separate entries, for example, for either *Lithuania* or *Ukraine,* and all articles on Russia refer to the Soviet Union. There are also no entries for *bungee jumping, dis, HDTV, intifada, maquiladora, retrovirus,* or *virtual reality.* The entry for **fax** is simply "a facsimile," and one of the definitions for **rap** is "to improvise words and vocal sounds to musical accompaniment," an overly broad definition that does not clarify.

Entries are presented as they were in the book, including pronunciation, part-of-speech label, inflected forms, idioms, run-on entries, synonyms, usage notes, and etymologies. Most entries (except for compound words) have a "Phonics" button that, when clicked, brings up a key to the pronunciation symbols.

There are about 4,000 color and black-and-white illustrations on the disc. Entries with illustrations are accompanied by a button labeled "Images" that may be clicked to view the illustrations. These displays—which bear no relation to the pictures found in the original print work—are disappointing, however. The resolution of most of the color photographs is poor (although black-and-white images are fine), so many details do not show up. There are also inconsistencies in the *number* of illustrations present for various entries. **Airplane** has 31 illustrations (4 of the *Spirit of St. Louis* alone) and **automobile** has 19, but **polar bear** has 2 and **pig** has 3—both more reasonable numbers. Captions are brief to the point of being useless. One simply reads "*Spruce Goose,*" with no additional information regarding that storied plane. The few captions that are longer are displayed in the same brief time given the shorter captions (though the user can pause). Finally, there is no audio or video connected to the illustrations, an unfortunate feature given the storage capacity of CD-ROM drives.

Entries on countries of the world often feature two images: a map of the world followed by a close-up view of the relevant continent with an arrow pointing to the country. The maps are not entirely useful. Both maps show topographical features but have no labels. They also do not include boundaries, an omission that leaves the user unenlightened as to where the country really is. This lack of detail is particularly confusing, since the intended readership is grade 4 and up. Finally, the maps are as unclear as the photographs.

Hardware and Installation

Minimum hardware requirements for *American Heritage Illustrated Encyclopedic Dictionary* are a PC-compatible (XT or better), 640K of RAM, a CD-ROM drive with audio output, a VGA card and monitor, MS-DOS 3.3 or higher, and Microsoft CD-ROM Extensions 2.1 or later. It is not necessary to have *Windows* to run the dictionary, although it can run under *Windows*.

A mouse is recommended, and makes navigating through the program much easier. Keyboard commands can also be used for many functions, but some of these commands are odd. The "F4" key—not the "ESC" key, as is often the case—doubles as the "Return" button to go back one step, and the "CTRL-ENTER" combination executes a search, not "ENTER" alone; that key, strangely, retypes the last character.

The program is extremely easy to install, since no copying onto the hard drive is required. Instead, the program is simply run by typing in *AHD* at the prompt for the CD-ROM drive. The README file includes instructions for copying certain files onto the hard drive to "speed up some actions," but retrieval time was more than adequate on the 386/33 DX used to test the disc.

Searching Capabilities

Users look up an entry by typing in a word at the "Find" prompt or by selecting the desired letters from the alphabetical display on screen. Typing in the asterisk (*) at the end of letters provides truncation, which the manual misleadingly refers to as *prefix*. Thus, typing in *read** will retrieve entries such as **reading** or **readiness,** as well as such encyclopedia entries as **Reading** (England) and **Sir Herbert E. Read.** Oddly, the space bar has no function in "Search" mode, so when a compound is being searched it must be entered as one word. The proper two-word entry will be retrieved by the system.

After the search is executed, the "Entries Found" screen appears, giving the total number of retrieved entries (up to 1,000). Only ten words appear on screen at a time, but a scroll bar on the right allows the user to peruse the list.

Unfortunately, there is no Boolean capability within the work, which limits the speed of some searches. On the other hand, individual words within compound entries, idioms, plurals, and synonyms will retrieve the main entry with which they are associated. For example, the truncated search *fact** retrieves the main entries **ipso facto** and **point** (where the idiom "in point of fact" appears). This device also works for inflected forms. Such searching capabilities make this work useful for those not used to the variant forms of English words.

Downloading and Printing

A major drawback to this program—particularly in a library setting—is the complete lack of printing or downloading capabilities, which is unusual in a work of this sort. The dictionary can only run as a stand-alone program; it *cannot* be invoked as a terminate-and-stay-resident (TSR) program within a word processor, which somewhat limits its usefulness in a home setting.

Documentation

The 12-page manual that comes within the jewel case is adequate given the relative lack of sophisticated features within the program. However, the README file contains some information not given in the manual—such as the use of various function keys to substitute for the mouse and how to skip over pictures when viewing images.

Within the program, help is offered by audio rather than in print. The messages are retrieved by clicking the "Question Mark" button at the bottom of a screen. This may be annoying in a library and perhaps should not have been used. Audio messages also announce when a search has failed, but this message can be circumvented by pressing the "ESC" key.

Even more annoying, however, is the fact that the README file on the disc points out at least two instances in which "Help" messages are erroneous. This guidance is good to have, but it should appear in the print documentation as well.

Telephone technical support is available, although not toll free. No hours are indicated. The publisher is in California.

Summary

At $39.95, *American Heritage Illustrated Encyclopedic Dictionary* is certainly below average in terms of cost for CD-ROM products. Nevertheless, the lack of printing or downloading capabilities and the mediocre quality of the images make it far from a bargain. About two-and-a-half times as much money will buy *Microsoft Bookshelf,* which includes the third edition of THE AMERICAN HERITAGE DICTIONARY and several other reference works, and features the spoken pronunciations (lacking in this work) of the main entries. More money will also buy the RANDOM HOUSE UNABRIDGED DICTIONARY on CD-ROM, a far more up-to-date and comprehensive work (though one with its own problems). The lack of updating in this product is also a concern. Prospective purchasers should review the 1993–'94 version of the *American Heritage Illustrated Encyclopedic Dictionary* to determine if these problems have been corrected.

Funk & Wagnalls Standard Desk Dictionary

Facts at a Glance

Full title: **Funk & Wagnalls Standard Desk Dictionary**
Publisher: Inductel
Edition reviewed: © 1992, version 2.0
Type of work: floppy disk
Platform reviewed: DOS

Number of entries: 100,000
Number of illustrations: none
Intended readership: grade 6 to adult

Price: $79.95; 20 percent discount available to schools and libraries
Sold directly to schools and libraries; also sold by direct mail and in bookstores and other retail outlets
Next revision planned for January 1994

Introduction and Authority

This dictionary offers an electronic version of the *Funk & Wagnalls Standard Desk Dictionary,* published by Harper and Row in 1984 and now out of print. Inductel also has released floppy disk versions of many McGraw-Hill technical dictionaries and a translating dictionary that covers 26 languages, including English.

Scope and Content

The 100,000 entries in this work reproduce all entries in the print version, along with its dictionary of computer terms, gazetteer, biographical dictionary, abbreviations, and secretarial handbook. This electronic version suffers from the deficiencies of the title on which it is based, among which is lack of currency. There are no entries for *bungee jumping, dis, fax, HDTV, intifada, maquiladora, rap, retrovirus,* or *virtual reality.* Even *AIDS* is not an entry. Further, the quality of the definitions is spotty. Definitions are extremely brief and lack illustrative examples.

The gazetteer and biographical dictionary provide little more than pronunciation guides and brief identification. Both are current up to the 1984 date of the print original but do not reflect significant persons or geographical changes of the past ten years. The "Secretarial Handbook" gives helpful guidance on grammar and usage.

The typical entry in *Funk & Wagnalls* includes all elements in the print work except pronunciations. (The manual promises that these will appear in the future.) Definitions are numbered (ordered by frequency), parts of speech identified, and inflected forms provided. There are no illustrations.

Hardware and Installation

According to the publisher, any PC-XT-compatible (8088 machine) or higher is capable of running this dictionary. System needs are DOS 3.0 (according to the box) or 2.0 (according to the manual) or higher, and 512K (according to the box) or 128K (according to the manual) of RAM; both box and manual agree that 5.6 MB of space is needed on the hard drive. A mouse is not necessary, although the device is supported. The diction-

ary comes on five 3½" high-density disks, so the system must have a compatible drive as well. The publisher does not indicate whether 5¼" disks can be ordered.

A Macintosh version is also available. That version was not reviewed, and we cannot comment on its similarities or differences to the version that was examined. Prospective purchasers of the Macintosh version are advised to consult periodicals for reviews of that version.

Installation is easy, taking only ten minutes. Options such as screen color and use of the mouse are offered upon installation.

The dictionary is capable of running as a terminate-and-stay-resident (TSR) program that can be accessed through a "hot-key" combination when the user is working in an application program such as a word processor. This handy feature allows users to consult a full-fledged dictionary when writing, but it is not without flaws. To run the dictionary as a TSR, most users will need to choose a memory swapping option. Although it mentions this necessity, the manual provides little guidance on an issue that is often confusing in DOS.

Once installed properly, the TSR function works quite well. The user need only have the cursor on a word in his or her word-processing document and press the hot key (which can be customized). The dictionary then pops up and displays the relevant entry. If the word is not included in the database, the dictionary allows the user to type in another word. Pressing the hot key again returns the user to the word processor.

Searching Capabilities

A user may input entries directly from the "Input" line when in the dictionary program. Because the work is case sensitive, the user must capitalize initial letters for names of places and people. (The manual mentions that the work is case sensitive, but does not clearly explain the implications.)

Wild cards can facilitate searches. The ? key may be used for one undefined character and the * key for strings of undefined characters. Therefore, **rou?d** at the "Input" line retrieves **round,** and **rou*** retrieves 47 entries, including **route** and **Round Table.** At least two characters must be present at the beginning of the input to use the ? wild card, but the manual does not document this limit.

Another difficulty is determining exactly what will be retrieved when plurals or other inflected forms are input. This is particularly a problem with verb forms. **Exposed,** for example, retrieves the entry for **expose,** but **exposing** does not.

Downloading and Printing

Users may print by using F3, but must awkwardly access the menu at F2 first. The F2 menu listing also shows options for downloading, including *store, store ASCII, load*

ASCII, and *batch in.* The user can save only to the hard drive, which is not likely to please librarians.

Documentation

The program comes with a 110-page manual relevant to *all* the floppy disk programs Inductel offers. Thus, only two chapters are devoted specifically to *Funk & Wagnalls;* the bulk of the manual discusses common commands for all the programs.

Information in the manual does not always match what the user sees on the screen, and some features are not mentioned in the manual. The description of printing and downloading does not match up with anything displayed on screen. The fact that the user may highlight any word *within* a definition and access the entry for that word (a helpful feature) is undocumented.

Online help is limited. Pressing F1 does little more than state that the program is in database mode and reiterate what is on screen already. Pressing F1 while in the command screen brings up an *input is unknown* message!

At the top of the screen, the user may highlight the option for "Manual" and bring up an online version of the entire manual. Unfortunately, the online manual indicates it is "version 1.0" with a 1987 copyright date; the printed manual is labeled "version 1.2" and bears a 1991 copyright date. (To further the confusion, the program itself is version 2.0, with a 1992 copyright date.) There is no phone number for technical support.

Summary

At 100,000 entries, *Funk & Wagnalls* has a substantial number of entries and provides access to a dictionary for computer users who do not have CD-ROM drives. It does not offer the size or variety of information available in CD-ROM dictionaries, such as THE AMERICAN HERITAGE DICTIONARY (in *Microsoft Bookshelf*), the RANDOM HOUSE UNABRIDGED DICTIONARY, or the *World Book Dictionary* (in INFORMATION FINDER), among other products. *Funk & Wagnalls* operates very quickly—more quickly than a CD-ROM work—and may suffice for some users. But its age, somewhat quirky interface, and confusing documentation detract from this work. This version (2.0) of *Funk & Wagnalls* is not recommended for purchase, but prospective buyers may want to review the new version to see if these problems have been addressed.

Information Finder (Dictionary)

Facts at a Glance

Full title: **Information Finder (Dictionary)**
Publisher: World Book
Edition reviewed: © 1993, version 2.40
Type of work: CD-ROM
Platform reviewed: DOS

Number of entries: 225,000
Number of illustrations: none
Intended readership: elementary school to adult

Price (for entire *Information Finder* package): $599; $296 (when sold with WORLD BOOK); discount available to schools and libraries
Sold directly to schools and libraries; also sold door-to-door
Revised annually

Introduction and Authority

Designed to allow users to search for the definition of an unfamiliar term encountered in the main, encyclopedic portion of *Information Finder,* the dictionary component of this work also allows independent consultation of the dictionary material. It is based on THE WORLD BOOK DICTIONARY, an excellent work since its first appearance in 1963 as the *World Book Encyclopedia Dictionary.*

This review concentrates exclusively on the dictionary component of *Information Finder.* Readers who want to learn about the encyclopedia portion should consult the INFORMATION FINDER (ENCYCLOPEDIA) review elsewhere in this Buying Guide.

Scope and Content

Its 225,000 entries place the 1993 edition of THE WORLD BOOK DICTIONARY virtually in a class by itself—with fewer entries than an unabridged dictionary, but quite a bit more than the usual collegiate dictionary. Its electronic equivalent in *Information Finder* contains all of the entries from the print version, though not the numerous supplementary features. Like its print counterpart, this electronic dictionary contains entries for **dis, fax, HDTV, intifada, rap, retrovirus,** and **virtual reality,** but it lacks entries for *bungee jumping* and *maquiladora.* The work is updated annually.

Besides definitions, this CD-ROM disc has illustrative sentences, idioms (labeled **expr.**), part-of-speech labels, and run-on entries. It lacks many valuable features of the print WORLD BOOK DICTIONARY, however. Usage notes, synonym studies, etymologies, syllabication, and pronunciation are not included. For example, the entry for **ain't** in the print dictionary has a lengthy usage note, but no such note is present in *Information Finder.* The print work has detailed synonym studies, but they are missing here. (Synonyms are provided, but not the book's detailed synonym studies.) Also absent are all of the superb illustrations found in THE WORLD BOOK DICTIONARY, which is surprising given the great storage capacity of a CD-ROM.

The dictionary function in *Information Finder* may be invoked in one of two ways: by highlighting the desired word in an encyclopedia article and double-clicking to bring up the definition; or by simply pressing a function key and inputting a word in the dictionary's word entry window. After the dictionary entry is displayed, the user may search or scroll through more of the dictionary.

When the dictionary is invoked by a user already running the encyclopedia, the entry window is usually positioned so that this new window does not cover the original word—a nice touch. The dictionary window typically displays 6 lines at a time, although the user may increase this display to 16 lines with a keystroke. The main entry word, part-of-speech label, and inflected forms are displayed on the top line, which remains visible while scrolling through the entry. This excellent approach helps the user stay aware of what entry is being viewed. Typefaces of various colors are used to separate the parts of the entry. Definitions, for example, are white, while the illustrative quotations are black and idioms green. Visually, this work is very uncluttered and easy to browse through.

Hardware and Installation

Readers should consult the review of INFORMATION FINDER (ENCYCLOPEDIA) for a discussion of installation and system requirements. Unlike some other electronic dictionaries, this work cannot be used as a "hot-key" program within a word processor.

Searching Capabilities

As previously mentioned, the dictionary may be invoked by pressing the F7 key or by double-clicking on a word in an *Information Finder* article. If no such word exists, the dictionary places the user at the closest entry alphabetically. Words used *within* dictionary definitions may themselves be double-clicked for their entries as well.

Unlike the encyclopedia portion of *Information Finder,* however, the dictionary has no Boolean capabilities, truncation (called "wildcard characters"), or proximity searches.

Downloading and Printing

Dictionary entries can be downloaded onto a disk or printed. The review of the encyclopedia portion of *Information Finder* provides details on these capabilities.

Documentation

Although only 4 pages of the 96-page *Information Finder* manual are devoted exclusively to the dictionary function, this documentation is adequate for this easy-to-use component of the CD-ROM. The only other portions of the manual that the user may need to consult are those on printing and downloading capabilities. Instructions are clear and understandable. Context-sensitive help is available while running the program. Toll-free technical support is available weekdays during business hours (Eastern Time).

Summary

The dictionary in *Information Finder* is a useful, comprehensive, clear reference tool. It is not a recommended purchase, however. The price for the combined encyclopedia and dictionary—even at the lower price of $296 for those who order it along with the print work—is steep for a text-only reference tool. The RANDOM HOUSE UNABRIDGED DICTIONARY, for all its faults, is much less expensive. MICROSOFT BOOKSHELF includes not only a dictionary, but many other resources as well. Two major CD-ROM encyclopedias—MICROSOFT ENCARTA and COMPTON'S INTERACTIVE ENCYCLOPEDIA—provide dictionary components with their multifaceted encyclopedia material. The objection to *Information Finder* is strictly one of price. The dictionary is a fine work (though the absence of some lexicographic features of the parent book is unfortunate), and the user interface and search engine are satisfactory. Until the publisher prices *Information Finder* more competitively or adds more features, however, the product is simply not worth the money.

Macmillan Dictionary for Children—Multimedia Edition

Facts at a Glance

Full title: **Macmillan Dictionary for Children— Multimedia Edition**
Publisher: Macmillan New Media
Edition reviewed: © 1993, version 1.2
Type of work: CD-ROM
Platform reviewed: Windows

Number of entries: 12,000
Number of illustrations: 1,000
Intended readership: ages 7 to 12

Price: $39.95
Sold in computer stores; also sold through the publisher
Next scheduled release due in late 1994

Introduction and Authority

This children's dictionary on CD-ROM is published by Macmillan, well known for its line of children's and student's dictionaries. The lexicon is illustrated by 1,000 color images, including photographs and line drawings. The *Macmillan Dictionary for Children—Multimedia Edition* includes audible pronunciations for all entry words as well as for the words within the definitions. The program also contains three games and 400 sound bites that accompany certain entries. Although the version reviewed had a 1993 copyright date on the package, a credits screen within the program indicated a 1991 copyright date. A new release of this product is due in late 1994; the price will be reduced to $29.95.

Scope and Content

This work is based on the 1989 MACMILLAN DICTIONARY FOR CHILDREN. That work's 35,000 entries were edited down to the 12,000 present in the multimedia version. The decision to curtail the lexicon, despite a CD-ROM's ability to hold large amounts of data, is curious and limits the work's usefulness for older children. Most definitions have been taken verbatim from the print work, and many of the illustrations have been retained for this version. Despite the multimedia version's recent copyright date, the currency of the dictionary is suspect: although **Germany** is defined as a single country, the entry for **Russia** includes the statement, "This country is now called the **Soviet Union.**" None of the Buying Guide's other test entries appears.

The opening screen displays the alphabet in small blocks down the left-hand side. Clicking on a letter brings up a screen displaying illustrations of that letter in ancient alphabets, the first section of a complete list of the dictionary's entry words that begin with that letter, and an additional "index list" of three-letter combinations starting with the selected letter (for example, *Gap, Gas, Gau, Gen, Geo*). Clicking on one of these three-letter combinations brings up the section of the lexicon beginning with that combination. An entry screen can be displayed by clicking on the word from the lexicon list.

Entries are very easy to read. The large-type text section includes the entry word, numbered definitions, illustrative sentences (written by the editors), syllabication in boldface, the pronunciation in parentheses, the part-of-speech label in italics, and variant forms in boldface. No etymologies, synonym/antonym guides, or usage notes are given, but the information from the MACMILLAN DICTIONARY FOR CHILDREN's "Word History" boxes can be retrieved by clicking on an on-screen button included with some of the entries.

Definitions are very brief and are written at an appropriate level. A typical entry follows:

> **gadget** A small, useful tool or device. A bottle opener with a corkscrew at one end is a *gadget.*
> **gad·get** (gaj′ it) *noun, plural* **gadgets.**

Full-color illustrations and photographs accompany many of the entries. The quality of the photographs is often grainy, but the line drawings are very clear.

Three other methods of calling up entry screens make accessibility one of this work's strong points.

Clicking the right-hand mouse button on any word in a definition (such as *corkscrew* in the preceding example) brings up that word's entry screen. All words used in definitions (or their root words) are included in the dictionary's lexicon. If a derived word is selected, the computer displays the root word and asks the user if that word's entry screen should be displayed. In addition, a "Go To" icon (an arrow and target), which is displayed on the screen at all times, allows users to type in a word to be looked up. Words input incorrectly prompt the computer to ask if it should display the word nearest in spelling to the misspelled word. Finally, a "page turn" option in the bottom right-hand corner of each entry screen allows users to search entries alphabetically.

Other on-screen iconic features include "My List," which allows children to select words from the lexicon and place them in a list to be used for quick-reference or in the games that come with the dictionary. The games themselves include a spelling bee game for one or two players; "Hangman"; and "Words Within," which gives children a long word and asks them to type in all the words that can be spelled using some or all of its letters.

Two other special features of this program will make it highly attractive to children. The first is the work's audio capabilities. Clicking the left-hand mouse button on either a word in a definition or an entry word's pronunciation prompts the computer to pronounce the selected word. Other sound effects include 400 "sound bites" that can be played by clicking on buttons that accompany certain entries. Entries with notable sound effects include **pig, moo, gargle, automobile,** and a particularly startling **cannon.** Only the sound clip for **lobby,** a brief snippet of indistinct crowd noises, is difficult to understand.

The second feature is "Zak," an animated cartoon character who appears on certain entry screens. Clicking on the character brings it to life, and it moves across the screen and expresses an emotion related to the entry word. For example, Zak yawns at "boring" words such as **and,** turns a handspring and exclaims "wowee" for words like **alphabet,** cowers at **earthquake,** and sheds a tear at **alcoholism.** Zak is also featured in the "guided tour," a narrated demonstration for novice users about how to look up words. Zak will undoubtedly encourage browsing, as young users will search for entries in which the character appears.

Hardware and Installation

Software requirements include an MS-DOS or PC-DOS operating system, Microsoft *Windows* with multimedia extensions or *Windows* 3.1, and Microsoft MS-DOS CD-ROM extensions (MSCDEX) version 2.2 or later. Hardware requirements include a 386SX processor with a hard drive, 4 MB of RAM, an MPC-compatible CD-

ROM drive, an MPC-compatible audio board, speakers or headphones, an SVGA graphics adaptor and color monitor, and a mouse.

Installation is relatively simple and follows step-by-step instructions included with the disc. One optional step allows users to run the program on only 2.3 MB of RAM, sacrificing the animation sequences and "guided tour" feature.

The publisher also offers a Macintosh version of the work. That version was not reviewed, and we cannot comment on its similarities or differences to the version that was examined. Prospective purchasers of this different version are advised to consult periodicals for reviews of that version.

Searching Capabilities

Other than the ability to search for specific words using the "Go To" feature, no searching features (such as boolean connectors or a special search language) are included with the work. This is not a serious omission in a simple children's dictionary, however.

Downloading and Printing

No print options are available within the program, although some help text files can be printed from the disk's DOS directory. The dictionary can be run only as a standalone program; users cannot access it via a "hot key" from within another program.

Documentation

Apart from a postcard-sized set of installation instructions, no documentation is included with the *Macmillan Dictionary for Children—Multimedia Edition.* Although on-screen help features can be accessed by clicking on comic-strip–style text balloons, the absence of a troubleshooting guide or a printed description of the program's features is a serious omission. The help screens themselves are adequate, but not extensive. User support is provided in the form of a toll-free number that can be called during business hours, Eastern Standard Time.

Summary

The *Macmillan Dictionary for Children—Multimedia Edition* is a unique and attractive reference tool for young learners. Although it does not include documentation or printing options, this program will not only serve as a useful tool for young children but will also spark an interest in words and word games. The lexicon is readily accessible, the sound effects are excellent, and the graphics are very appealing. Children will especially appreciate the color illustrations, word games, and animated cartoon character "Zak," who flits in and out of the program's entry-word screens. Although this dictionary is recommended for children ages 7 to 12, its

12,000-word lexicon somewhat limits its usefulness for children at the upper end of that age bracket. It is highly recommended, however, for younger readers.

The Oxford English Dictionary: Second Edition on Compact Disc

Facts at a Glance

Full title: **The Oxford English Dictionary: Second Edition on Compact Disc**
Publisher: Oxford University Press
Edition reviewed: © 1992
Type of work: CD-ROM
Platform reviewed: Windows

Number of entries: 290,500
Number of illustrations: none
Intended readership: high school to adult

Price: $895
Sold to libraries; also sold by direct mail by the publisher
No stated revision policy; *OED Additions Series* currently being published in print form

Introduction and Authority

The Oxford English Dictionary: Second Edition on Compact Disc contains the full text of the 20-volume OXFORD ENGLISH DICTIONARY (OED) on one CD. The OED is widely recognized as the premier dictionary based on historical principles, illustrating the history and evolution of each English word by reprinting published examples of use dating back to the earliest surviving English-language texts. Readers are urged to consult the review of THE OXFORD ENGLISH DICTIONARY elsewhere in this Buying Guide for more information about the work.

Released in 1992, the CD version contains the text of the 1989 second edition of the OED, the most recent edition.

Scope and Content

Entries are reproduced on the computer screen exactly as they appear in the OED. The parts of an OED entry are attractively displayed in several colors: for example, variant forms appear in blue and usage labels appear in green. These colors can be changed using a pull-down menu; the point size and typeface of the text can also be altered using this menu, making the infamously tiny print of the OED's illustrative quotations easily readable. In addition, users can choose to display either the entire entry or any combination of its etymology, definition, and illustrative quotation list.

An on-screen "map" button allows users to display, in outline form, the structure of an entry that doesn't fit in its entirety on the screen. For example, the map for **subvert,** which includes four obsolete definitions (indicated by †), the first with a subsense, appears as follows:

†1.
    †b.
†2.
†3.
†4.
5.
6.
7.

This function shows how many definitions are included for a word, but with no indication of the meanings attached to this listing, it is of limited value.

The display window allows users to browse through the entry, move to the entries that immediately precede or follow the on-screen entry, or access other entries through use of the "Xref" button or via a search. The "Xref" feature allows users to see the entry for any word used in a displayed entry. For example, the entry **entoproctus** reads "belonging to the *entoprocta,* a class of Polyzoa." By highlighting the term and using this feature, one can quickly display the **Polyzoa** entry in a separate window. Up to four display windows with separate entries can be displayed at the same time. OED users who in the past had to juggle a series of cumbersome volumes to pursue related definitions will appreciate this feature.

Two features of the print OED are not available in the CD-ROM version. One is full text of the bibliography of works cited in the dictionary's illustrative quotations—although a CD-ROM user can call up a list of authors or titles cited and can search all quotations by keyword, date, title, or author. The other is the essay on the history of the OED that prefaces volume I of the print version. The "General Explanations" section of the print version has been replaced in this electronic version by a 71-page booklet, *A User's Guide to the Oxford English Dictionary.*

Remaining true to the spirit of the unembellished OED, the CD-ROM version has no sound capability or graphics.

Hardware and Installation

The *OED on Compact Disc* requires a PC-compatible with an 80386 processor, at least 2 MB of RAM (4 MB are recommended), 1 MB of free hard-disk space, a 3½″ floppy disk drive, a CD-ROM drive, and a VGA card and monitor. Software required includes DOS version 3.0 or higher, Microsoft CD-ROM Extension software (MSCDEX) version 2.0 or higher, and *Windows* 3.0 or higher.

A mouse is needed to install the program and manipulate the windows, but some features can also be controlled from the keyboard. The most notable of these are the pull-down menus that control the program's searching, file manipulation, and text display options.

The publisher also offers a Macintosh version of the work, which it claims is "identical in features, functionality, and screen layout" to the PC version. Prospective purchasers of the Macintosh version are advised to consult periodicals for reviews of that version.

Installation of the program, run from the floppy disk, is easy and follows step-by-step prompts. After installation is complete, the dictionary operates from the CD-ROM drive only; the floppy is no longer necessary. *The OED on Compact Disc* is accessible only from the main *Windows* menu; the program cannot be directly accessed from within another program such as a word processor.

Searching Capabilities

The "Search" option on the program's main menu allows users to access the dictionary in three ways: to look up a word in the traditional manner; to search the entire text of the dictionary for a word or phrase; or to search just the etymologies, definitions, or quotations by categories such as date, author's name, or the language from which an entry word was derived. The broad searching capabilities of *The OED on Compact Disc* are one of its most outstanding features.

Initiating any search produces an on-screen "list window" displaying all words that match the search category. If the search word is typed incorrectly, the list begins with the entry word closest in spelling to the misspelled word. The program allows for slight variations in a word's typography, producing results when the OED entry has different hyphenation, capitalization, or diacritical markings from the keyed-in word. For example, inputting *gumdrop* produced a match with the OED entry **gum-drop.** This feature can be disabled so that only exact matches are displayed.

By selecting the desired word from the list window, the user produces either a display window containing the full text of the OED's entry (for searches with only one result) or a results window containing a summary of the search results (for searches with multiple hits). In the results window, each entry appears as a single line of text. Clicking on the desired line brings up the full display window for that entry.

In addition, the user can search the dictionary's etymologies by language name or by variant form. For example, selecting the *Native American Blackfoot* language from the on-screen list of languages revealed that three OED entry words (**piskun, Sarcee,** and **Siksika**) derive from that language. The dictionary's definitions can be searched for any word or phrase occurring therein, and the illustrative quotations can be searched by any combination of publication date, author, work title, and word or phrase. For example, all entries with an illustrative quotation dating from 1980 to 1988 (the dictionary's most recent) can be found by typing *1980-* in the quotation search window.

Users have other search options as well. They can use wildcard characters in place of one or more letters (crossword puzzle solvers will find this feature handy). A search for *q*z* revealed three possible words: **quartz, quiz,** and **quoz.** Proximity searches allow users to locate instances of two words separated by a specified number of intervening words. For example, searching for *baby #3 bath* produced a list of seven phrases with three words between *baby* and *bath,* most of which had to do with bath water.

Because of idiosyncracies in how entries have been recorded in the OED, users searching the quotation database must ensure that their searches are thorough. Typing in *Joyce, James* produced only one hit. A check of the author list, however, revealed 87 citations credited to *Joyce, J.* Similarly, Shakespeare's quotations are accessible only by using the abbreviation *Shakes.* A title search using *New York Times* produced 8 citations, but *N.Y. Times* yielded 1,700, and another 5 appear as *N. York Times.* A user looking for all citations would have to conduct three searches. These inconsistencies can be vexing, especially to those users who are unfamiliar with the print version of the OED.

Searches can be combined using a query language that employs such Boolean connectors as *and* and *or.* For example, typing in *quo qw=(New York Times) or qw=(N.Y. Times) or qw=(N. York Times) into (Times.quo)* searches for all *New York Times* quotations and saves them in a file entitled *Times.quo.* The necessity of entering and storing these command statements as separate files makes the query process somewhat difficult to master. Users will need to spend some time familiarizing themselves with the capabilities of the program and the idiosyncracies of the OED itself before they can take full advantage of the search feature.

Downloading and Printing

Information from display screens in *The OED on Compact Disc* can be highlighted using the mouse and copied to other *Windows* applications, such as a word-processing program, through a menu. Search result lists must be converted into ASCII files before they can be accessed by another program.

Print features are conspicuously absent from the program. A full screen of information can be printed, but only by first exporting it to a word-processing program using the *Alt* and *Print Screen* keys. This operation preserves the special fonts and characters resident in *The OED on Compact Disc,* but instructions on performing it are not provided with the program. The lack of direct print options is a drawback of the package; libraries installing the dictionary on a machine available to patrons must include a word processor on that machine for users to be able to print search results.

Documentation

Documentation provided with the program includes the thorough and clearly written *User's Guide to the Oxford English Dictionary,* which describes the structure and parts of typical OED entries, and a 123-page spiral-bound instruction manual about the computer version. The manual is comprehensive, providing numerous helpful illustrations of the program's screen displays. In an effort to be detailed, however, it sometimes gives undue prominence to descriptions of the program's special features. For example, "About the *OED2* on CD-ROM," a three-page introductory section, contains inappropriately lengthy descriptions of non-Roman alphabets and special characters. On the other hand, the important section that describes a basic entry-word search is buried 19 pages into the section on "Searching."

Help screens within the program are easy to access from the main menu, and each contains a list of cross-references to related help screens. They are clear but not as comprehensive as the manual.

Summary

The Oxford English Dictionary: Second Edition on Compact Disc is a powerful reference tool that marries valuable search capabilities to a body of content without peer. A brief introduction to its search facilities allows access to the entire text of the OED in a clear, easily browsable format. Many search options are provided here, although idiosyncracies in the text of the dictionary sometimes make specialized searches difficult. In addition, the program's lack of direct print options is a drawback.

Nonetheless, serious students of language with the patience to master the program's search features will find this version indispensable. Of course, they would have to be serious indeed given the very high price of this product—although it is less than half the cost of the print version. That cost savings and the substantial savings in storage space make *The OED on Compact Disc* desirable for libraries and individuals who wish to obtain access to the preeminent English language dictionary.

Random House Unabridged Dictionary, Second Edition

Facts at a Glance

Full title: **Random House Unabridged Dictionary, Second Edition**
Publisher: Random House
Edition reviewed: © 1993 (no version number)
Type of work: CD-ROM
Platform reviewed: DOS, *Windows,* and Mac versions on same disc

Number of entries: 315,000
Number of illustrations: none
Intended readership: high school to adult

Price: $79 (for disc alone); $159 (for both disc and print version)
Sold in software stores and through the publisher
No stated revision policy

Introduction and Authority

This CD-ROM version of the *Random House Un-abridged Dictionary, Second Edition,* was released simultaneously with the print version of that work. It can be purchased along with the book at a price that is lower than the cost of buying the two items separately. The CD-ROM contains the same lexicon as the 1993 edition of the high-quality print work.

Scope and Content

With essentially the entire text of its print counterpart (only prefatory essays are absent), the *Random House Unabridged Dictionary* marks the first American unabridged dictionary to be released on CD-ROM. The disc holds the same contemporary vocabulary as the print work, including entries for **bungee jumping, dis, fax, HDTV, intifada, maquiladora, rap music, retrovirus,** and **virtual reality.** (See the review of the print version for a full discussion of the lexicography.) The publisher has no stated policy as to updating this disc, but the work's promotional material frequently cites the publisher's "Living Dictionary Project"—an electronic database that allows editors to quickly incorporate changes to the work—implying that revisions will be issued periodically.

Entries are taken word for word from the book, and thus include all etymologies, synonym/antonym guides, usage labels, and usage notes. The DOS version does not use varying typefaces, sometimes making it difficult to separate illustrative quotations from definitions proper. Because the *Windows* version employs the book's type variations, it is easier to use.

Only one entry is displayed at a time, although a list of more entries is shown when browsing through the dictionary (6 in the DOS version and 16 in *Windows*). Once a full entry is on the screen, both versions allow the user to move forward to the next entry or back to the previous entry with ease.

One drawback is the absence of the illustrations or tables that appear in the book. Also missing are audible pronunciations of words, a feature present in other CD-ROM dictionaries, such as Webster's Ninth New Collegiate Dictionary and The American Heritage Dictionary in *Microsoft Bookshelf.*

Hardware and Installation

The DOS and *Windows* versions require an 80286 IBM PC or compatible, 2 MB of RAM, and at least 1 MB of space on the hard drive. The *Windows* version requires *Windows* 3.1. A mouse is recommended for both versions. DOS users should find the cursor keys more than satisfactory, but the *Windows* version requires a mouse. The Macintosh version was not reviewed, and we cannot comment on its similarities or differences to the versions that were examined. Prospective purchasers of that version are advised to consult periodicals for reviews of it.

Installation instructions are clearly explained in a small pamphlet that comes with the CD-ROM, and the process takes little time. The installation instructions do not explain how to start the dictionary as a standalone program, however; this is found only by reading the README.TXT file on the CD itself.

The dictionary also functions as a terminate-and-stay-resident (TSR) utility that can be invoked by pressing a hot-key combination while the user is within an application such as a word processor. It displays the entry for the word on which the cursor is resting. If the word is misspelled, the dictionary displays a list of words that most closely resemble it.

Searching Capabilities

Both DOS and *Windows* versions allow the user to directly look up a word in the dictionary, browse through an alphabetically arranged list of words, search for key words within the definition, and search for anagrams of a word. Users can also search for main entries with wild cards, using a question mark for one missing character or an asterisk for multiple characters. Boolean searching may be used in the "Definition" search, but it is slow, especially in *Windows*. Searching for *milk AND honey* in the *Windows* version took over eight minutes to retrieve two hits; the same search in DOS took less than half the time (though that is still quite slow). There is no proximity searching, so the terms searched in a Boolean search can, in fact, appear many words apart from each other in exceptionally lengthy entries. This produces false hits that can cause confusion and slow down the user.

A review in Reference Books Bulletin (*Booklist,* February 1, 1994) revealed several difficulties with searching this CD-ROM, and the comments remain valid. The search for key words in the definitions, for example, yields mixed results. The synonyms portion of the entry, for example, is sometimes searched and other times not. A search for *havoc* in the "Definitions" search retrieves the main entry for **ruin,** since *havoc* is a listed synonym. A search for *timorous,* however, does *not* retrieve the main entry for **nervous,** despite the fact that *timorous* is a listed synonym for that word. The "Definitions" search is also not capable of searching inflected forms or run-on entries unless they appear fully spelled out within the definition. A search on *prelacies* (plural of **prelacy**), for example, yields no hits, as it is not fully spelled out in the main entry.

In the DOS version, the "Anagram" search feature is particularly troublesome. A search on *aunt* retrieves **ANTU**, but also **Toni, Iona, iota,** and **Oita.** A search on *run* retrieves **urn** and **-ian, Ian, IAT, i.t.a., I.T.A., Ito,** and **ITO.** Oddly, the "Anagram" feature works well in *Windows.*

This is not the only discrepancy between the two versions. A "Definitions" search in DOS on the word *advocacy* retrieves 33 hits; the equivalent search in *Windows* produces 19 hits—3 of which the DOS search did not find. Other searches produced similar discrepancies, which is disturbing.

Downloading and Printing

Users cannot print directly from the CD-ROM, although the program is supposed to allow them to move material into a word processor and print from there. This function was tried several times without success in DOS—although it functioned as desired in *Windows.* Since the DOS cut-and-paste features do not seem to work, users will not be able to print from the DOS version at all. There is no downloading capability.

Documentation

A three-page pamphlet that comes within the jewel case of this CD-ROM discusses how to install the program, but otherwise there is no printed documentation for the *Random House Unabridged Dictionary,* which may be intimidating to some users. The DOS version comes with a brief README.TXT file, but all other documentation comes via the F1 "help" key. Help is not context sensitive, although it adequately explains all of the program's features. The *Windows* version features help screens on a wide variety of topics and generally explains the program in much greater detail.

Telephone technical support is available, though the call is not toll free, on weekdays from 7:00 A.M. to 6:00 P.M. (Mountain Time).

Summary

The $79 price for the CD-ROM version of *Random House Unabridged Dictionary* makes it cheaper than the print version. The only other unabridged dictionary available on CD-ROM is the OXFORD ENGLISH DICTIONARY, which caters to a more specialized audience and—due to its very high price—is out of the reach of many prospective purchasers.

This dictionary has a primary advantage in its comprehensive and up-to-date database. Still, this product may be less desirable than other electronic dictionaries. *Mi-*

crosoft Bookshelf, which features several other reference works along with the third edition of THE AMERICAN HERITAGE DICTIONARY, is comparable in price and adds illustrations and audible pronunciations. The latter may also be found in WEBSTER'S NINTH NEW COLLEGIATE. The problems with searching, the sparse documentation, and the worrisome discrepancies between the DOS and *Windows* versions lessen the desirability of the *Random House Unabridged Dictionary* on CD-ROM. It is a promising—but ultimately less than satisfactory—first effort.

Webster's Ninth New Collegiate Dictionary

Facts at a Glance

Full title: **Webster's Ninth New Collegiate Dictionary**
Publisher: Highlighted Data
Edition reviewed: © 1989, version 1.2
Type of work: CD-ROM
Platform reviewed: Macintosh

Number of entries: about 160,000
Number of illustrations: about 600 (reviewer estimate)
Intended readership: high school to adult (reviewer estimate)

Price: $199.95; 35 percent discount available to schools
Sold directly to schools; also sold in retail outlets and by mail order
Content revised on the same schedule as the print version; software updated regularly to meet computer system needs

Introduction and Authority

Webster's Ninth New Collegiate Dictionary, a CD-ROM dictionary, aims to provide instant, easy-to-use access to dictionary entries and definitions for high school and college students as well as adults. This CD-ROM version contains all the text of the print version of the dictionary and thus has the authority of Merriam-Webster behind it. The lexicon licensed from Merriam-Webster by the CD's publisher, Highlighted Data, dates from 1989, however. Merriam-Webster is releasing its own CD-ROM version of the new MERRIAM-WEBSTER'S COLLEGIATE DICTIONARY, tenth edition, in the summer of 1994, which purchasers may wish to consider before making a buying decision.

Scope and Content

Webster's Ninth New Collegiate Dictionary includes approximately 160,000 dictionary entries and 200,000 definitions. Also included are about 600 black-and-white illustrations and 25 tables. The illustrations are informative but not very attractive. The tables, which are quite useful, cover such items as various alphabets and calendars, geologic eras, metric equivalents, foreign currencies, arabic and roman numerals, and the periodic table of elements. Reference material includes an essay on the English language, a section on English spelling and sound correspondences, a guide to pronunciation, a list of abbreviations, astronomical signs and symbols, and a "Handbook of Style." This material is interesting, but the scrolling is very slow.

Version 1.2 of the dictionary, published in 1989, is not very current. Only three of the Buying Guide's ten key words used to judge dictionary currency—**dis, fax,** and **rap**—appeared, and their definitions did not reflect current usage.

Dictionary entries are quite comprehensive. In addition to pronunciations and definitions, the entries include syllabic hyphenation breaks, word etymologies, parts of speech and other functional classifications, variants in spelling, derivations, and inflected forms. The date of the earliest known English usage of the word and the taxonomic names of plants and animals are also provided. Some entries include lists of synonyms, which detail the element of meaning that each shares with the defined word.

Each entry word is accompanied by a spoken pronunciation, which is especially useful for younger users or for difficult words. A helpful feature allows the user to display each entry word in two sizes—standard and large print—both of which are very readable.

Hardware and Installation

The version of *Webster's Ninth New Collegiate Dictionary* reviewed was for a Macintosh system. The product includes a floppy disk containing an application program and the special fonts used in the dictionary as well as a single CD-ROM disc containing the dictionary itself. The program is compatible with both current and older Macintosh computers, from the Mac Plus to the new PowerPCs, as long as the machine has an 800K floppy disk drive and a CD-ROM drive. In addition, 1 MB of RAM is needed to run the dictionary using the Macintosh "Multifinder." A hard drive is recommended, as are good headphones. The program can be run on either a black-and-white or color monitor. Many menu items are command driven, so a mouse is also necessary.

Installation of the program is very simple and takes less than five minutes. The application program on the floppy disk is copied to the hard disk and the special fonts installed in the system folder. (The application can also be accessed directly from the floppy disk if a hard disk is not available.) The dictionary itself resides on the CD-ROM disc. To access the dictionary, the user simply inserts the disc into the CD-ROM drive and double-clicks on the application icon.

Searching Capabilities

Webster's Ninth New Collegiate Dictionary allows users to search for words in several ways. Upon opening the program, a "page" of 36 entry words is displayed, at the top of which are 2 guide words. Clicking once on any word on the page brings up the complete entry. If an entry is accompanied by an illustration, that will be displayed as well.

The user can also access other "pages" in two ways: by clicking on a page-turner icon to browse through prior or subsequent screens or by clicking on one of the A–Z tabs in the "thumbguide" on the right side of the screen. The A–Z tabs allow the user to jump to any letter section of the dictionary (as well as to listings of biographical and geographical entries).

A quicker method to access entries is through the search menu, which permits searching for specific words or phrases. This function does not allow for the use of Boolean operators. Another type of search—random search—seems designed for electronic browsing. Choosing that option simply instructs the computer to display a randomly chosen entry. Users can also search through all the illustrations and tables in the dictionary and can access comprehensive lists of abbreviations, foreign words and phrases, and colleges and universities in the United States and Canada. Clicking on an abbreviation brings up its full form; clicking on a foreign word or phrase brings up its pronunciation (written and spoken) and meaning; clicking on a college or university brings up its location, zip code, and the year it was founded.

Downloading and Printing

The user can easily save or print any definition or illustration. Tables, however, cannot be printed or exported. Definitions print out very well, but many illustrations appear dark and heavy. Exporting definitions or illustrations to another application is also easy. It simply requires copying to the "Scrapbook" and then pasting into the desired document. It is not possible to copy only part of a definition or illustration.

Documentation

Webster's Ninth New Collegiate Dictionary comes with a short printed manual that provides a general overview of how to use the dictionary and some information on troubleshooting. The manual seems quite adequate for anyone using the program. The program does not have an online help feature. However, telephone support is available from Highlighted Data during business hours. Questions were answered satisfactorily and courteously.

Summary

Webster's Ninth New Collegiate Dictionary is only an adequate electronic dictionary, especially considering the high price. It is quite comprehensive and easy to use; searching for words, as well as illustrations, tables, abbreviations, and other features is simple and fast. Unfortunately, the illustrations are informative but not terribly attractive, and no online help is available. The most significant drawback is the dictionary's lack of currency. Purchasers who are particularly interested in currency will probably want to look at other titles.

PART SIX

Large-Print General Reference Works

Chapter 18
Evaluations of Large-Print Reference Works

Hammond Large Type World Atlas

Facts at a Glance

Full title: **Hammond Large Type World Atlas**
Publisher: Hammond
Edition reviewed: © 1994

Number of pages: 144
Number of maps: 51
Number of index entries: 3,100 (reviewer estimate)
Intended readership: visually impaired: young student to adult (reviewer estimate)
Trim size: 9½″ × 12¼″
Binding: hardcover

Price: $32.95; 10 percent discount to schools and libraries
Sold directly to schools and libraries; also sold by direct mail and in bookstores
ISBN 0-8161-5911-4
No stated revision policy

Introduction, Format, and Authority

The *Hammond Large Type World Atlas* is the "only atlas designed especially for Large Print readers," according to the book jacket. First published in 1969 by Franklin Watts, this work features entirely different cartography from that used in other Hammond atlases, in deference to its special format. This one-volume, 144-page work contains 51 easy-to-read maps. The book measures 9½″ × 12¼″ and is easily transportable. It has a sturdy binding and an attractive two-color book jacket. The copyright year is 1994.

Scope and Special Features

Fifty-one three-color maps comprise the body of this atlas. They are set in somewhat drab shades of yellow (countries), blue-green (bodies of water), and red (national boundaries), and each spans a double-page spread. Some geographical bias is evident. For example, the United States is represented by eight maps, compared with one each for Canada and Russia. Europe and North/Central America have 13 maps each. Asia has 11, but South America and Africa have only 5 apiece.

The maps are not as detailed as those of regular-sized print atlases such as THE NEW YORK TIMES ATLAS OF THE WORLD. For example, numerous smaller towns and features such as rivers and mountains are omitted. The maps gain clarity, however, from the uncluttered pages that result from the lack of detail.

Preceding the atlas is the "Gazetteer-Index of the World," which lists 314 continents, countries, states, possessions, and other areas; the area of each in square miles; its population, capital, or chief town; its map page; and its map grid coordinates. Members of the United Nations are indicated. Population figures are "the latest reliable figures obtainable"; those for the United States are based on 1990 census data.

Those map features not included in the Gazetteer-Index appear in the more general index that follows the atlas. When an entry appears on more than one map, grid coordinates and pages indicate the map with the largest scale. Approximately 2,800 entries are included in the general index.

Currency

Maps reflect the political situation of the world as of 1994. For instance, the Czech Republic, Slovakia, unified Germany, unified Yemen, Croatia, Slovenia, Bosnia and Herzegovina, Macedonia, Yugoslavia, and countries such as Latvia and Estonia that were part of the former Soviet Union, are all included.

Currently preferred place names, such as Myanmar (for Burma) and Dhaka (for Dacca), are used; others, such as Yangon (for Rangoon) and Denali (for Mt. McKinley) are not. Full-length official names (for example, Republic of Namibia, Union of Myanmar, Federal Republic of Germany) are not used. Despite these shortcomings, the work's labeling has been improved from the previous (1986) edition. For example, *Beijing* now appears instead of *Peking,* and the vernacular *Braunschweig,* West Germany, has replaced the rarely used Anglicized *Brunswick.*

Accuracy

Bar scales showing miles and kilometers are used to indicate scale, which varies considerably from map to map. Maine, for example, occupies as much page space as does Texas, which appears four maps later in the atlas. Stereographic projection is indicated above the scale for the map of Antarctica only, and no fractional representation of scales is given.

The atlas contains some inaccuracies, not all of which are attributable to its large typeface. On the map of France on page 63, the borders of Monaco are marked in red, but those of Andorra are not. To the east of Andorra a small area is delineated in red, but it is unclear what this area represents. The same area is also marked on page 65 (D1), the map of Spain and Portugal. This mistake was noted in the previous Bowker Buying Guide review of the 1986 edition of this atlas and has not been corrected.

In addition, Sabine Lake, on the border of Louisiana and Texas, has been left uncolored on the map on pages 30–31, although lakes throughout the atlas are colored blue. Also, the gray lines that indicate the boundaries of countries and bodies of water are sometimes not located at the precise point where the map's colors come together. This effect can be seen on the map of Turkey in the Aegean Islands. Although this is largely a page-composition problem, the overall effect reduces the accuracy and attractiveness of the atlas.

Sometimes the large typeface interferes with a map's accuracy. For example, on page 101, the area surrounding Canberra, the capital of Australia, is delineated in red and appears to indicate the Australian Capital Territory. The area immediately to its left is marked with the printed name, but the connection between the two is not clear. A similar problem exists for the U.S. base on Guantánamo Bay in Cuba, on the map on page 40.

Legibility

The paper is opaque and of good quality, and the binding allows the book to lie flat when open. Rather than lose information in the gutter of the book, the publishers have chosen to include a large white margin at the center of each two-page spread that effectively divides each map in half. Unfortunately, this margin is too wide and typographical changes have not been made to accommodate it. For example, the place names for Topeka, Omaha, and Oklahoma, as well as state boundaries and natural features such as the Arkansas River, are all split by an inch of white space on the map of the United States. The book lies flat enough when open that this margin is largely unnecessary.

Map labels are generally easy to read, although there is no legend for map symbols such as those used to indicate capitals, cities, mountains, boundaries, dams, and rivers. Abbreviations also appear without an abbreviations key. Most are obvious, but others such as *Kazakh.* (Kazakhstan), *Maur.* (Mauritania), and *Mal.* (Malawi) may not be. Map labels range in size from 12-point to 28-point type. The index and gazetteer are set in widely spaced lines of 12-point type.

Accessibility

As previously mentioned, the gazetteer-index provides a quick and useful reference to countries, continents, states, possessions, and other major geographical areas. The maps of the atlas are arranged beginning with the world map and the map of North America. They proceed from north to south to east. The order is clear and the progression is easy to follow.

Summary

The Hammond Large Type World Atlas is current and highly legible. As such, it will be a great aid to the visually impaired. Although it is far less detailed than a standard-sized print atlas such as THE NEW YORK TIMES ATLAS OF THE WORLD, this atlas is generally clear and easy to use.

The work has some shortcomings, however. The omission of map legends is a major drawback, and map features are often split by the work's overly prominent center-page margins. Also, more care could have been taken in producing and proofreading this work. Despite these problems, the *Hammond Large Type World Atlas* is unique and highly recommended for those needing a large-print atlas.

American Heritage School Dictionary: Large Print Edition

Facts at a Glance

Full title: **American Heritage School Dictionary: Large Print Edition**
Publisher: Houghton Mifflin
Editor: P. Davies
Edition reviewed: © 1977

Number of volumes: 4
Number of pages: 1,074
Number of entries: 30,000
Intended readership: visually impaired: grades 1 to 9; also useful for older students with learning disabilities
Trim size: 11½" × 13¾"
Binding: hardcover

Price: $269
Sold by the American Printing House for the Blind: Order No. L-0285; also sold by Library Reproduction Service (6 volumes) for $294: Order No. LRS 08170
ISBN 0-3952-4793-4
No stated revision policy

Introduction and Scope

The *American Heritage School Dictionary: Large Print Edition* is similar to the AMERICAN HERITAGE STUDENT'S DICTIONARY reviewed elsewhere in the Buying Guide.

The dictionary has been photoenlarged to 18-point type (guide words and entry words) and 15-point type (definitions). The dictionary has also been enlarged to 18- to 20-point type and is available in six volumes from Library Reproduction Service.

The vocabulary for the *American Heritage School Dictionary* was selected from materials that students would encounter in school. The typefaces used are varied and distinct: the entry word is in sans serif bold, the definition is in serif lightface type, and the illustrative sentences are in italic. All are well designed to enable the visually handicapped student to distinguish each element. Extra-bold centered dots indicate syllable breaks in the entry words. Pronunciation is easy to read, with the accented syllable printed in boldface and also marked with an accent. A short pronunciation key is conveniently provided on each double-page spread. Guide words appear in bold type at the top of each page.

The quality and comprehensiveness of the dictionary are well suited to prepare the student to move up to a higher-level dictionary, such as THE LARGE TYPE AMERICAN HERITAGE BASIC DICTIONARY. Those who can under-stand the BASIC DICTIONARY are strongly encouraged to use it instead of the *School Dictionary*. The *School Dictionary*'s 1977 publication date and prohibitively high price make it a poor choice for most purchasers.

Holt School Dictionary of American English: Large Print Edition

Facts at a Glance

Full title: **Holt School Dictionary of American English: Large Print Edition**
Publisher: Holt, Rinehart and Winston
Edition reviewed: © 1981

Number of volumes: 5
Number of pages: 1,156
Number of entries: 40,000
Number of illustrations: approximately 1,450
Intended readership: visually impaired: ages 9 and up
Trim size: 11½" × 13¾"
Binding: hardcover

Price: $289
Sold by the American Printing House for the Blind: Order No. L-3671
ISBN 0-0305-8999-1
No stated revision policy

Introduction

This large print edition of the *Holt School Dictionary of American English,* photoenlarged from the 1981 edition of that dictionary, is available for upper elementary and middle school students. It has been reproduced in 12- to 19-point type and published in five volumes.

Many of the special features of the dictionary, including maps, charts, and tables, make it a useful reference source and teaching tool. Interesting features such as a glossary of "Persons and Places in Mythology and Folklore," charts of Indian cultures and tribes, and charts of human body systems add to the dictionary's usefulness and appeal.

Definitions are clearly stated, and multiple meanings are indicated by boldface numerals. Idioms and word phrases are listed in boldface under the appropriate main entry word. A useful and convenient short pronunciation key is printed at the bottom of all right-hand pages. This dictionary is similar in scope and price to the AMERICAN HERITAGE SCHOOL DICTIONARY: LARGE PRINT EDITION. Both multivolume works are very expensive and dated. Unfortunately, a more up-to-date large-print children's dictionary is not available. Although it is as dated as both the Holt and American Heritage dictionaries, the single-volume WEBSTER'S NEW ELEMENTARY DICTIONARY is a better buy than either.

The Large Print Version of the Little Oxford Dictionary of Current English

Facts at a Glance

Full title: **The Large Print Version of the Little Oxford Dictionary of Current English**
Publisher: Oxford University Press
Editor: Julia Swannell
Edition reviewed: © 1986, 1993 printing; sixth edition

Number of pages: 674
Number of entries: 23,000 (reviewer estimate)
Number of illustrations: none
Intended readership: visually impaired: secondary school to adult (reviewer estimate)
Trim size: 8″ × 11″
Binding: hardcover

Price: $27.95; 20 percent discount to schools and libraries
Sold directly to libraries and schools; also sold by direct mail and in bookstores
ISBN 0-7089-1679-1
No stated revision policy

Introduction

The Large Print Version of The Little Oxford Dictionary is a reprint of the 1986 pocket-sized THE LITTLE OXFORD DICTIONARY. This one-volume, 674-page hardcover edition contains 23,000 entries. According to the publisher's note, the large-print edition is intended "to fill a 'void' for those readers who are unable to read normal size small print. . . ."

The dictionary is authorized by the Oxford University Press and is published for Ulverscroft, a registered charity whose primary objective is "to assist those who experience difficulty in reading print of normal size." The dictionary is available in the United States from Ulverscroft. Julia Swannell, the editor, also edited the fifth and sixth editions of THE LITTLE OXFORD DICTIONARY.

Scope and Content

Although the dictionary's copyright year is 1986, this version was printed in 1993. However, no new entries were added in this printing, and it does not contain any of the words used to assess currency—*bungee jumping, dis, fax, HDTV, intifada, maquiladora, rap, retrovirus,* and *virtual reality.*

Entries, spellings, pronunciations, and definitions are British unless otherwise noted. For example, **windscreen** is listed instead of *windshield* in this dictionary. The word **tire** is listed as the "US var. of **tyre,**" which is defined as a "rubber covering, usu. inflated, placed round wheel to prevent jarring."

Pronunciations, which employ the International Phonetic Alphabet (IPA), are often, but not always, given following the entry word. They are based on the pronunciation standard in southern England and will not help readers who desire American English pronunciations. Few alternate pronunciations are offered, and the IPA may be difficult for readers who are not used to it. A one-page pronunciation guide is located in the front matter.

Syllable breaks are not given in entries or their pronunciations. Homographs appear as separate entries marked by superscript numbers. Definitions are accurate and reasonably thorough. For example:

> **nest 1** *n.* structure or place in which bird lays eggs and shelters young; breeding-place or lair; snug retreat, shelter; brood, swarm; cluster or accumulation of similar objects.
> **2** *v.i.* make or have nest; (of objects) fit one inside another.
> **3 nest-egg** money saved up as reserve.

The most common definitions are listed first. Others may be preceded by usage labels such as *colloq.* (colloquial), *sl.* (slang), *poet.* (poetical), *arch.* (archaic), *derog.* (derogatory), *fig.* (figurative), or those for specialized areas such as sports, science, and music. Some vulgarities are included, as well as some terms labeled "US slang." There are no biographical or geographical entries, etymologies, or synonyms.

Special Features

Several special features add to this dictionary's usefulness. The two-page "Introduction" describes the parts that make up each entry. This is followed by a useful guide entitled "Abbreviations used in the Dictionary."

"Some points of English usage" is the first of three appendixes that follow the lexicon. It covers commonly mispronounced words, commonly misspelled words, words that are often misused, unusual plural formations, and points of grammar that are often confused. The appendix "Countries of the world and related adjectives," which lists countries, their pronunciations, and adjectives such as *Belgian* and *Polish,* is not current. For example, Germany is still divided, and neither the Commonwealth of Independent States nor the Czech Republic can be found. The final appendix, "The metric system of weights and measures," gives the metric equivalents of U.S. units.

Graphics and Format

The format of this dictionary is functional but not very appealing. There are no illustrations. The pages are set up in a two-column format. Guide words appear in boldface type above each column. Entry words, inflected forms, and phrases and combinations derived from the entry word appear in boldface and are set off from the definitions. Unnaturalized foreign entry words

The Large Print Version of The Little Oxford Dictionary of Current English, Sixth Edition

❶ Pronunciation given in International Phonetic Alphabet (IPA)

❷ Italicized part-of-speech label follows definition number

❸ Usage labels in italics

❹ Prepositions commonly used with the main entry word in this particular sense are italicized and in parentheses

❺ Word combinations involving the main entry word are shown in boldface type following the main definitions

> **treasure** /ˈtreʒə(r)/ **1** *n.* precious metals or gems etc.; hoard of them; thing valued for rarity or associations etc.; accumulated wealth; *colloq.* beloved or highly valued person. **2** *v.t.* store (*up*) as valuable; receive or regard as valuable. **3 treasure-hunt** search for treasure, game in which players seek hidden object; **treasure trove** treasure of unknown ownership found hidden.

appear in boldface italics. Usage labels, technical labels, part-of-speech labels, and prepositions and adverbs commonly used with the entry word are set in italics.

A boldface number precedes the part-of-speech label only if more than one part of speech is given. Definitions, which can be numerous, are otherwise separated only by semicolons. Users may have trouble sifting through some of the long lists of definitions. However, this dictionary is more comprehensive than WEBSTER'S NEW WORLD PORTABLE LARGE PRINT DICTIONARY and THE POCKET DICTIONARY.

The typeface in this dictionary is adequate but not as large as in other large-print volumes. Guide words are set in 14-point type, entry words in 12-point type, and definitions in 11-point type. By comparison, WEBSTER'S NEW WORLD LARGE PRINT DICTIONARY has 18-point guide words, 16-point entry words, and 14-point definitions.

The paper used is opaque and of good quality. The binding allows the book to lie flat, but it may not be sturdy enough to withstand heavy use. However, this volume is easier to handle, transport, and store on a standard shelf than WEBSTER'S NEW WORLD LARGE PRINT DICTIONARY or THE NEW MERRIAM-WEBSTER DICTIONARY FOR LARGE PRINT USERS.

Summary

The Large Print Version of The Little Oxford Dictionary is an accurate, authoritative dictionary of British English. Users should keep in mind that information is not always up-to-date and many current terms are not included. The definitions are thorough, although the dictionary does not contain as many entries as WEBSTER'S NEW WORLD LARGE PRINT DICTIONARY or THE NEW MER-

RIAM-WEBSTER DICTIONARY FOR LARGE PRINT USERS. This dictionary is recommended for those who prefer, or require, large print in a dictionary of British English.

My Second Pictionary

Facts at a Glance

Full title: **My Second Pictionary**
Publisher: Scott, Foresman
Editors: M. Monroe and W. C. Greet
Edition reviewed: © 1964

Number of volumes: 2
Number of pages: 408
Number of entries: 12,500
Intended readership: visually impaired: lower elementary grades
Trim size: 11½" × 13¾"
Binding: hardcover

Price: $153.14
Sold only by the American Printing House for the Blind: Order No. 4-7551
No stated revision policy

Introduction

The large print version of *My Second Pictionary,* edited by M. Monroe and W. C. Greet, is available in 17-point type from the American Printing House for the Blind. The dictionary is aimed toward the skills and interests of younger students and includes familiar words and concepts.

This is one of the dictionaries that the American Printing House for the Blind has reproduced mechanically, "without any attempt to clarify" the illustrations. They note this caveat to prospective purchasers of the dictionary prominently on the order form. Because the process of photographic enlargement can cause some distortion, many illustrations lack clarity, and this may render the picture dictionary of little use to the more seriously visually handicapped. This work has a copyright date of 1964 and is not recommended for purchase.

(See also the review of Scott, Foresman's MY PICTIONARY in this Buying Guide for a description of the publisher's dictionary for still younger children.)

The New Merriam-Webster Dictionary for Large Print Users

Facts at a Glance

Full title: **The New Merriam-Webster Dictionary for Large Print Users**
Publisher: Merriam-Webster
Editor: Frederick C. Mish, Editor-in-Chief
Edition reviewed: © 1989

Number of pages: 1,106
Number of entries: 60,000
Number of illustrations: none
Intended readership: visually impaired: junior high school to adult
Trim size: 8¾" × 11¼"
Binding: hardcover

Price: $40.95; 10 percent discount to libraries, 20 percent discount to wholesalers, sliding scale discount to retailers
Sold directly to libraries, bookstores, wholesalers, and catalogers; also sold by direct mail
ISBN 0-8161-4754-X
No stated revision policy

Introduction

Published by G. K. Hall in conjunction with Merriam-Webster, *The New Merriam-Webster Dictionary for Large Print Users* reproduces the text of the 1989 *New Merriam-Webster Dictionary,* fourth in the line of Merriam-Webster paperback dictionaries started in 1947. It also includes information from *Webster's Ninth New Collegiate Dictionary,* published in 1990. *The New Merriam-Webster Dictionary for Large Print Users* replaces *The Merriam-Webster Dictionary for Large Print Users,* first published in 1975. Definitions were developed by Merriam-Webster's staff of dictionary specialists from a file of more than 13 million usage citations. This one-volume, 1,106-page edition contains 60,000 entries for the visually impaired.

Scope and Content

The entries and definitions in this volume cover a broad range of subjects, including literature, science, mathematics, and sports. However, only two terms used to assess currency—**fax** and **retrovirus**—were found. There are no entries for *bungee jumping, dis, HDTV, intifada, maquiladora, rap,* and *virtual reality.* Biographical and geographical entries, as well as vulgar words and definitions, are not included.

Main entries are followed by pronunciations and part-of-speech labels. More than 2,500 entries contain etymologies before the definitions. Where appropriate, synonyms are listed after the definitions. Four different types of cross-references are used throughout the lexicon: those that provide additional information, a substitution of a definition or sense, a variant, or an inflected form.

Definitions are accurate, thorough, and clear. They are listed in historical order (with older ones first) and are preceded by boldface numerals. Status labels are given for temporal (*obs* for obsolete and *archaic*), regional (*Brit* or *chiefly West*), and stylistic (*Slang*) usage. Definitions may also be followed by usage notes that give supplementary information about idioms, syntax, and semantic relationships.

Homographs appear as separate entries marked by superscript numbers. Variant spellings of equally standard usage are set as joint entries separated by *or*. A secondary variant spelling is separated by the word *also*. Variations that do not closely follow the spelling of the main entry appear as separate entries. Combining forms, prefixes, suffixes, abbreviations, and symbols for chemical elements also appear as main entries.

Guide words are usually the first and last entries on the page. This dictionary's complex system of guide words—which may include variants, inflected forms, and run-ons—is explained on the first page of the "Explanatory Notes" section in the front matter. Although the system is well thought out, readers may find it confusing.

Special Features

The New Merriam-Webster Dictionary for Large Print Users contains many special features. Preceding the lexicon are the "Explanatory Notes," an 18-page guide on how to use the dictionary. This section includes information on entries, pronunciation, labels, inflected forms, capitalization, etymology, usage, abbreviations, and more. It is followed by a one-page list of pronunciation symbols.

Thirteen supplements follow the lexicon. Among them are 14 pages of "Foreign Words and Phrases," a one-page chart of books of the Bible, one page on the metric system and U.S. equivalents, and a two-page

The New Merriam-Webster Dictionary for Large Print Users

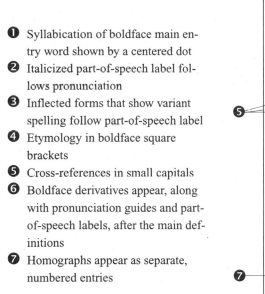

❶ Syllabication of boldface main entry word shown by a centered dot

❷ Italicized part-of-speech label follows pronunciation

❸ Inflected forms that show variant spelling follow part-of-speech label

❹ Etymology in boldface square brackets

❺ Cross-references in small capitals

❻ Boldface derivatives appear, along with pronunciation guides and part-of-speech labels, after the main definitions

❼ Homographs appear as separate, numbered entries

chart of "Weights and Measures." Some of these supplements are dated by today's standards, however, including "Money," "Nations of the World," "Population of Places in the United States," "Population of the United States in 1980," "Population of Places in Canada," and "Population of Canada in 1981." More current state populations are available in large print in the LARGE TYPE AMERICAN HERITAGE BASIC DICTIONARY, REVISED EDITION, and more up-to-date country populations can be found in the HAMMOND LARGE TYPE WORLD ATLAS. Additional sections on "Planets" and "Signs and Symbols" are unique to this large-print dictionary.

Graphics and Format

The two-column format of this dictionary is visually appealing. Entry words and definitions are clear. The typeface is easy to read even though it is smaller than that of WEBSTER'S NEW WORLD LARGE PRINT DICTIONARY. Guide words are set in 18-point type, entry words in 14-point type, and definitions in 12-point type. In comparison, WEBSTER'S NEW WORLD LARGE PRINT DICTIONARY has 18-point guide words, 16-point entries, and 14-point definitions.

Guide words, entries, numbers preceding the definitions, and inflected forms all appear in boldface and are set off from the definitions. Entry words of more than one syllable have centered dots indicating end-of-line divisions. Syllables are also divided within the pronunciations by hyphens. As in other Merriam-Webster dictionaries, primary and secondary stresses are indicated

in the pronunciations by short vertical lines immediately preceding the stressed syllables.

Definitions are preceded by a colon in boldface, and usage notes are preceded by a dash. Labels such as those for parts of speech, usage, and abbreviations are set in italics. Etymologies appear in boldface square brackets. Cross-references are set in small capitals.

Guide words (discussed above) are located at the upper outside corner of each page, and there are no illustrations. The paper is opaque and of good quality. The binding allows the book to lie flat when open and is strong enough to withstand heavy use. The volume should fit on a standard shelf or on a desk.

Summary

The New Merriam-Webster Dictionary for Large Print Users is a well-designed, authoritative, comprehensive, and relatively current dictionary for the visually impaired. Although it is comparable in scope to WEBSTER'S NEW WORLD LARGE PRINT DICTIONARY (Prentice Hall, 1985), the typeface of *The New Merriam-Webster* is not as large as that work's. *Webster's New World* is more dated than *The New Merriam-Webster,* but it is also slightly less expensive. This dictionary meets the standards of the National Association of the Visually Handicapped, however, and in addition, is backed by the authority of the Merriam-Webster name. Although some visually impaired users may prefer the slightly larger print of the *New World* dictionary, they will also find this work to be an excellent purchase.

The Oxford Large Print Dictionary

Facts at a Glance

Full title: **The Oxford Large Print Dictionary**
Publisher: Oxford University Press
Editor: Joyce M. Hawkins
Edition reviewed: © 1988, 1992 printing

Number of pages: 966
Number of entries: 56,000
Intended readership: visually impaired: secondary
    school to adult (reviewer estimate)
Trim size: 8″ × 11″
Binding: hardcover

Price: $35
ISBN 0-19-861234-6
No stated revision policy

Introduction

The Oxford Large Print Dictionary is based on the third edition of *The Oxford Paperback Dictionary,* a work first published in 1979 and well known in England for its clarity. This one-volume, 966-page hardcover edition contains 56,000 entries and 74,000 definitions. The dictionary is "specially designed for those who require an enlarged, easy-to-read page."

The Oxford Large Print Dictionary is published by the Oxford University Press. It was first issued as a large-print edition in 1989 and was reprinted once in 1990 and twice in 1992. The editor, Joyce Hawkins, also edited the OXFORD ENCYCLOPEDIC ENGLISH DICTIONARY and the OXFORD REFERENCE DICTIONARY.

Scope and Content

The content of this dictionary reflects its British orientation. Entry words, spellings, pronunciations, and definitions are British, but some American variations are included. For example, the entry for **windshield** gives no definition except to refer the reader to **windscreen,** the British term for the glass in the front window of a car.

Despite the work's 1992 printing date, no entries appear for *bungee jumping, dis, HDTV, intifada, maquiladora, retrovirus,* or *virtual reality.* Of the terms used to assess currency, only **fax** and **rap** (as music) appear. Although this edition has over 4,000 entries on people, places, and institutions, many of them are outdated by contemporary standards. They would have been up-to-date when the work was copyrighted in 1988. For example, under **Russia,** the second definition is "the USSR." Neither **Lithuania** nor **Ukraine** are listed as independent republics, and *Violeta Chamorro, Michael Jackson,* and *Boris Yeltsin* are absent. The entry for **Germany,** however, reflects that country's reunified status.

The entries are set up with the entry word in boldface type slightly overhanging the text column. Many terms have the syllabicated pronunciation in parentheses, followed by the part-of-speech label, numbered definitions, and usage notes where appropriate.

Pronunciations follow the standard speech of southern England, as described in the pronunciation guide in the front matter. The phonetic pronunciation is given only when a word is difficult to pronounce or recognize, or when it differs from words with the same spelling. Syllable breaks and primary stress are indicated in each pronunciation.

Definitions are accurate and easy to read. Interesting and helpful usage notes about meanings, grammar, and word origins are offered. They are introduced by the symbol ¶. For example, the entry **data** contains the following usage note:

> ¶ This word is now often used with a singular verb (like 'information'), especially in the context of computers, e.g. *the data is entered here,* but it is by origin a Latin plural (the singular is *datum*) and in other contexts should be used (like 'facts') with a plural verb, *these data are from official sources.*

Derived forms of entry words such as plurals, tenses, comparatives, and superlatives are given when these forms are irregular or when the spelling may cause difficulty. Synonyms are not included. Numerous combinations and phrases formed using the entry word are offered. They are preceded by the symbol □. For example, 10 combinations formed with the entry word **blood** are included in that entry block, and 19 combinations and phrases for **blue** are listed there. Specialized definitions, such as slang or informal uses, follow the most common definitions. Vulgarities are included, both as main entries and as definitions for words with other meanings.

Special Features

Special features contribute to the usefulness of this dictionary. A list of abbreviations found in the dictionary precedes the lexicon. The one-page introduction, which includes notes on usage, spelling, derived forms, and proprietary terms, helps readers to understand some of the elements of the dictionary.

Seven appendixes follow the lexicon. The first, "Countries of the World," lists countries, capitals, currencies, and heads of government; however, the information in it is not current by contemporary standards. For example, the Union of Soviet Socialist Republics is included. Next come "Counties of the United Kingdom" and "States of the United States of America." These are followed by "Prime Ministers of Great Britain and of the United Kingdom," "Prime Ministers of Australia, Canada, and New Zealand," and "Presidents of the United States of America"; they are all out-of-date, but would have been appro-

The Oxford Large Print Dictionary

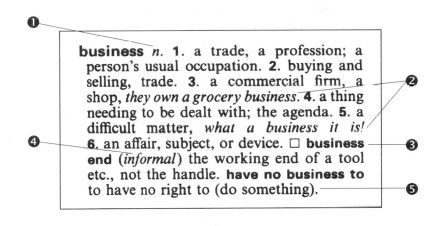

❶ The italicized part-of-speech label precedes the definition to which it pertains

❷ Illustrative sentences appear in italics

❸ Idiomatic expressions, in boldface type, are introduced by an open square symbol

❹ Usage label italicized and in parentheses

❺ Explanatory notes in parentheses

priate in 1988. The final appendix is a fairly comprehensive section on "Weights and Measures."

Graphics and Format

The format of the page, use of boldface and italics, clarity of definitions, and lack of numerous abbreviations all contribute to the readability of this dictionary. Guide words, entry words, and definitions are clear even though the typeface is smaller than that of other large-print dictionaries. Guide words are set in 12-point type, entry words in 10-point type, and definitions in 10-point type. In comparison, THE LARGE PRINT VERSION OF THE LITTLE OXFORD DICTIONARY has 14-point guide words, 12-point entries, and 11-point definitions.

Page numbers are centered at the top of the two-column page. Guide words appear at the top of the page in the outside corners. Entry words, numbers preceding definitions, derived forms (for example, plurals, comparatives, superlatives), and tenses, as well as phrases and combinations formed with the entry word, appear in boldface and are set off from the definitions. Part-of-speech labels and examples of usage appear in italics. Usage labels such as *Amer.* (American), *slang,* and *informal* are enclosed in parentheses and italicized. Technical definitions such as those from the fields of medicine, law, or science are part of the entry block and are not labeled.

Pages are opaque and of good quality. The binding allows the book to lie flat and should be strong enough to withstand heavy use. The volume should fit easily on a standard shelf or on a desk.

Summary

The Oxford Large Print Dictionary is an accurate, relatively current, authoritative, and well-designed dictionary. The typeface is smaller than that of THE LITTLE OXFORD DICTIONARY and WEBSTER'S NEW WORLD LARGE PRINT DICTIONARY, but the design of the page is appealing and the clarity of the definitions is excellent.

This dictionary is highly recommended for the general reader desiring a large-print reference book of British English. The visually impaired may find the typeface of THE LITTLE OXFORD DICTIONARY easier to read, but this dictionary is better designed, easier to use, and with its 56,000 entries (compared with the LITTLE OXFORD'S estimated 23,000), more comprehensive.

The Pocket Dictionary, Large Type Edition

Facts at a Glance

Full title: **The Pocket Dictionary, Large Type Edition**
Publisher: American Printing House for the Blind
Editors: Anne D. Steinhardt, Supervising Editor; Fernando de Mello Vianna, Editorial Director
Edition reviewed: © 1978, 1981 printing

Number of pages: 376
Number of entries: approximately 10,000 (reviewer estimate)
Intended readership: visually impaired: secondary school to adult (reviewer estimate)
Trim size: 11¼″ × 12¾″
Binding: hardcover

Price: $100.87
ISBN 0-395-26661-0; ISBN 0-395-27798-1 (international edition)
No stated revision policy

Introduction

Despite its title, *The Pocket Dictionary,* which measures 11¼″ × 12¾″, is larger than most traditional dictionaries. This one-volume, 376-page dictionary with approximately 10,000 entries is, however, small in scope.

The Pocket Dictionary, Large Type Edition

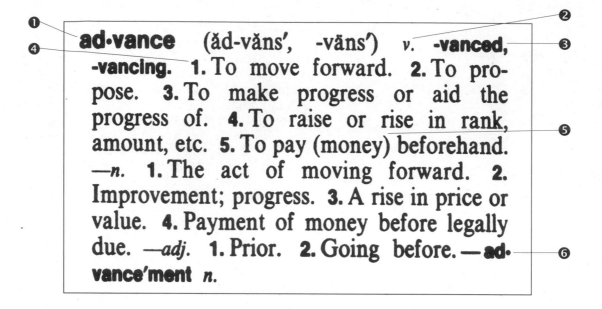

❶ Syllabication of the boldface entry word shown by a centered dot

❷ Italicized part-of-speech label precedes definition to which it pertains

❸ Regular and irregular inflected forms appear in boldface type

❹ Definition numbers are in large, boldface type for easy readability

❺ Explanatory notes in parentheses

❻ Derivatives, in boldface type, appear at end of the entry

The original edition of *The Pocket Dictionary,* copyrighted in 1978, was published as the *Webster's II New Riverside Pocket Dictionary* by Houghton Mifflin. This large-type volume is a reprint of that work, done by the American Printing House for the Blind.

Scope and Content

With a printing date of 1981, it is not surprising that this dictionary does not contain any of the terms used to assess currency: *bungee jumping, dis, fax, HDTV, intifada, maquiladora, rap* (as music), and *virtual reality.* In addition, the lexicon does not include any biographical or geographical entries.

Entries are, however, easy to read. Entry words are divided into syllables by centered dots. The pronunciation for each entry follows in parentheses. The part of speech and derived forms precede the definitions, where appropriate. There are no usage labels, etymologies, or synonyms. Inflected forms often end the entry block.

Homographs appear as separate entries marked by superscript numbers. Common variant spellings are set as joint entries. If one spelling is preferred, the variant spelling appears after the pronunciation and part-of-speech label and is introduced by *Also.*

Definitions are accurate and thorough, but they are not as straightforward as those in other dictionaries. For example, in *The Pocket Dictionary* the definition for **gas** as a noun is:

> **1.** The state of matter distinguished from the solid and liquid states by low density, the ability to diffuse readily, and the tendency to expand. **2.** A substance in this state. **3.** Gasoline.

The definition in Webster's New World Portable Large Print Dictionary reads: "**1** fluid substance that can expand; vapor: some gases are used as fuel **2** gasoline."

With about 10,000 entries, *The Pocket Dictionary* is much less comprehensive than other large-print dictionaries. For example, Webster's New World Portable Large Print Dictionary, a pocket edition, has over 30,000 entries. Webster's New World Large Print Dictionary has over 58,000 entries, and The New Merriam-Webster Dictionary for Large Print Users has 60,000 entries.

Special Features

This dictionary includes several special features. A two-page introductory section, "How to Use This Dictionary," contains helpful information on entry words, variants, inflected forms, labels, and pronunciations.

A four-page section on "Punctuation," which lists common rules, follows the lexicon and is especially useful for writers. Two pages of "Proofreaders' Marks" seem misplaced in a dictionary for the visually impaired. A section on "Weights and Measures" includes U.S. and metric equivalents for customary U.S. units as well as U.S. and metric equivalents for British measures. A "Guide to the Metric System" and a "Metric Conversion Chart—Approximations" follow. The last section, "States of the United States," lists the states, their capitals, the year each was admitted into the Union, and the population of each. The population figures, unfortunately, were current only as of 1981.

A "Rapid Word Finder" appears in the upper outside corner of each page. This consists of a small box containing the first letter of the entry words on that page and a number that corresponds to that letter's sequence within the alphabet. A listing of these pairings at the beginning of the dictionary instructs users to find the number that corresponds to the first letter of the word they are searching for. The assumption of this system seems to be that users will find it easier to locate words numerically, rather than alphabetically; unless one is completely unfamiliar with the alphabet, however, the system will prove only an unnecessary encumbrance.

Graphics and Format

The Pocket Dictionary uses an extra-large typeface that is especially appealing for the visually impaired. Entry words and definitions are set in 18-point type and inflected forms are in 16-point type. Word finders also appear in 16-point type.

The two-column pages are easy to read. Guide words are centered at the top of each page, and page numbers are centered at the bottom. Guide words, word finders, entry words, variant spellings, inflected forms, and the numbers preceding the definitions appear in boldface type. Part-of-speech labels appear in italics.

Pages are opaque and of good quality. The binding allows the book to lie flat. However, the beginning page of the volume reviewed was not well secured to the binding, and it loosened after minimal use. Because of its large size, the book may not fit on standard shelves.

Summary

The extra-large print of *The Pocket Dictionary* is especially appealing for the visually impaired. However, the title of this work is a misnomer, as the dictionary is large and cumbersome. It is neither as comprehensive nor as current as other large-print dictionaries, such as the pocket-sized WEBSTER'S NEW WORLD PORTABLE LARGE PRINT DICTIONARY, WEBSTER'S NEW WORLD LARGE PRINT DICTIONARY, or THE NEW MERRIAM-WEBSTER DICTIONARY FOR LARGE PRINT USERS. Because of these shortcomings, the visually impaired would not be well served by *The Pocket Dictionary* and this book is not recommended for purchase.

The Random House Dictionary: Classic Edition (Large Print Edition)

Facts at a Glance

Full title: **The Random House Dictionary: Classic Edition (Large Print Edition)**
Publisher: Random House
Edition reviewed: © 1983

Number of volumes: 2
Number of pages: 1,082
Number of entries: 75,000
Number of illustrations: more than 600, all in black and white
Intended readership: grade 9 to adult
Trim size: 9″ × 14″
Binding: hardcover

Price: $152
Sold by the Library Reproduction Service: Order No. 14244
ISBN 0-394-53441-7
No stated revision policy

Introduction

The 1983 *Random House Dictionary: Classic Edition* has been specially selected and recommended by the Library Reproduction Service as an "adult level dictionary that would be excellent for high school and college." The two-volume dictionary's text is that of the 1983 Classic Edition of the *Random House Dictionary*, a 75,000-entry work. Its main entries have been enlarged to 16-point type and its definitions to 14-point type.

Scope and Content

As could be expected from a 1983 dictionary, this work contains none of the Buying Guide's test entries for currency. Even relatively common contemporary words such as *AIDS* and *fax* do not appear. The entry list is otherwise standard for a medium-sized adult dictionary.

The entry words, in boldface, are divided into syllables with centered dots. Pronunciation and variants follow. Parts of speech are abbreviated and set in italics, and multiple meanings are numbered in boldface. Usage labels and illustrative phrases are all set in italics, and usage notes are preceded by a bold dash and the word *Usage* printed in boldface. The definitions tend to be very basic, as the following entry illustrates:

lei·sure (lē′zh ər, lezh′ ər), *n.* **1.** freedom from the demands of work or duty. **2.** free or unoccupied time. —*adj.* **3.** free or unoccupied. **4.** having leisure. —**lei′sure·less,** *adj.*

***The Random House Dictionary:
Classic Edition***

❶ Syllabication of boldface main entry word shown by centered dots

❷ Italicized part-of-speech label precedes definitions

❸ Usage labels, in italics, follow definition number

❹ Etymology in boldface brackets

❺ Boldface run-on derivative entries are followed by their part-of-speech labels in italics

❻ Captioned drawing illustrates an entry word

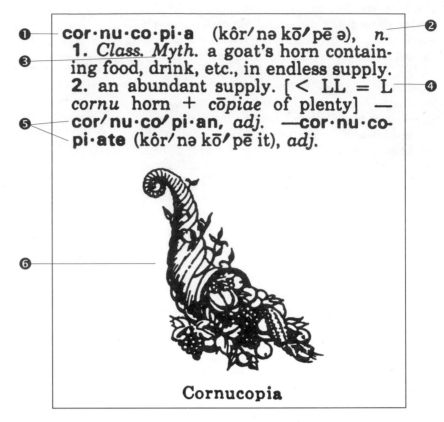

cor·nu·co·pi·a (kôr′nə kō′pē ə), *n.*
1. *Class. Myth.* a goat's horn containing food, drink, etc., in endless supply.
2. an abundant supply. [< LL = L *cornu* horn + *cōpiae* of plenty] —**cor′nu·co′pi·an,** *adj.* —**cor·nu·co·pi·ate** (kôr′nə kō′pē it), *adj.*

Cornucopia

Special Features

Among the advertised features of this large-print dictionary are its "encyclopedic" entries, which include brief biographical and geographical entries. **George Bush,** however, is listed as the "43rd vice president of the U.S. since 1981," and the **Soviet Union** is described as "a country of 15 constituent republics in E Europe and W and N Asia."

A "Basic Manual of Style" at the end of the second volume deals with punctuation and capitalization. Also included are a list of commonly misspelled words; a list of U.S. States with their capitals and postal abbreviations; a chart of North American time zones; a list of countries with their capitals and currencies; a table of the world's largest metropolitan areas; and a table of weights and measures, including metric conversions. Although the population statistics and country names date to 1983, these special features will be useful for the visually impaired.

Graphics and Format

The hardcover *Random House Dictionary* comprises two large volumes. Illustrations are generally clear. The pages are set up in two columns with a center column of white space. While more white space between entries and definitions might be helpful for the visually impaired user, the bold entry word that overhangs the column provides some guidance for the eye.

A central problem with this work is the quality of the typeface. The photoenlargement process unfortunately has made the edges of each character ragged and blurry. In addition, the distinction between the boldface and roman characters has been reduced by photoenlargement. Entry words do not, therefore, stand out from the page as clearly as in typeset large-print dictionaries.

The binding of the work is sturdy and the large pages lie flat when opened.

Summary

The Random House Dictionary: Classic Edition (Large Print Edition) is a two-volume photoenlargement of a 1983 dictionary. As such, users will not find many contemporary words among its 75,000 entries. The large format (9″ × 14″) of this work makes it somewhat awkward to use, and the typeface is fuzzy as a result of the photoenlargement process. Competing works such as THE NEW MERRIAM-WEBSTER DICTIONARY FOR LARGE PRINT USERS and WEBSTER'S NEW WORLD LARGE PRINT DICTIONARY are much less expensive, much more accessible, and (in the case of the Merriam-Webster work) more up-to-date than the *Random House Dictionary.*

Although it has the largest entry count (by only 15,000 over Merriam-Webster) of any of the Buying Guide's large-print dictionaries, *The Random House*

Dictionary: Classic Edition (Large Print Edition) is recommended for purchase only with reservations.

Scott, Foresman Beginning Dictionary: Large Type Edition

Facts at a Glance

Full title: **Scott, Foresman Beginning Dictionary: Large Type Edition**
Publisher: Scott, Foresman
Editors: E. L. Thorndike and C. L. Barnhart
Edition reviewed: © 1979

Number of volumes: 6
Number of pages: 1,406
Number of entries: 28,000
Number of illustrations: approximately 1,200
Intended readership: visually handicapped; upper elementary school students (grades 3 to 6)
Trim size: 11½″ × 13¾″
Binding: hardcover

Price: $290.16
Sold by the American Printing House for the Blind: Order No. 4-2269
No stated revision policy

Introduction

This large-type edition of the *Scott, Foresman Beginning Dictionary,* edited by E. L. Thorndike and C. L. Barnhart, is a resetting of the 1979 *Scott, Foresman Beginning Dictionary.* The type for this edition was entirely reset in 16-point type and all illustrations were redrawn. The dictionary is published in six volumes. It is listed in the reference circular of the National Library Service for the Blind and Physically Handicapped.

This basic dictionary is specifically designed to meet the educational needs of children in the upper elementary grades. However, the superior quality of the word list, definitions, and illustrations, and the large-print format make it useful for developmental reading classes through the high school and adult levels.

Especially helpful features for the visually impaired are the generous use of white space around the varied illustrations and the frequent positioning of etymologies in distinctive boxes labeled "Word History."

The ragged right format guides the eye to the left and is an aid in finding entry words. Extra large boldface guide words at the top corners of each page can be especially helpful for the older elementary student. However, it would have been more helpful to the visually impaired if parts of speech, which are printed in italics, had been printed in boldface to distinguish them from the italicized illustrative phrases. A convenient short pronuncia-

tion key is printed in the upper right corner of each double-page spread.

Since the large-type edition is a resetting of the 1979 edition of the *Scott, Foresman Beginning Dictionary,* it is not current. However, none of its principal competitors (the 1977 AMERICAN HERITAGE SCHOOL DICTIONARY: LARGE PRINT EDITION, the 1981 HOLT SCHOOL DICTIONARY OF AMERICAN ENGLISH: LARGE PRINT EDITION, and the 1975 WEBSTER'S NEW ELEMENTARY DICTIONARY: LARGE PRINT EDITION is significantly more up-to-date. Purchasers should consider that this work, the American Heritage dictionary, and the Holt dictionary cost more than $200 each. Only the two-volume WEBSTER'S NEW ELEMENTARY dictionary is affordable, and its quality is comparable to the other works.

Webster's New Elementary Dictionary: Large Print Edition

Facts at a Glance

Full title: **Webster's New Elementary Dictionary: Large Print Edition**
Publisher: G. & C. Merriam
Edition reviewed: © 1975

Number of pages: 627
Number of entries: more than 32,000
Number of illustrations: 1,200
Intended readership: visually impaired; upper elementary students to high school
Trim size: 13½″ × 10″
Binding: hardcover

Price: $88 (single copy); $78 each (for 2 or more copies)
Sold by Library Reproduction Service: Order No. LRS 08085
ISBN 0–87779–275–5
No stated revision policy

Introduction and Scope

The large-print version of the 1975 edition of *Webster's New Elementary Dictionary* is available from the Library Reproduction Service, a division of the Microfilm Company of California. Reproduced in 18-point type (main entries) and 16-point type (definitions), the more than 32,000 entries are bound in a single large-type unabridged volume.

The dictionary has been developed for students in grades 5 to 8. The clear, precise definitions are easy to understand. Elements such as variant pronunciations, multiple senses, and extensive use of special symbols and pronunciation marks may require some children to seek guidance or special instruction in order to use the dictionary. However, these elements would be useful for bright upper elementary students and would help them prepare for more adult dictionaries. The large type work will be useful for those developmental programs working with junior high and senior high school students.

Guide words are provided at the top of each double-column page; pronunciation keys are printed at the bottom. Page numbers are centered. Synonym paragraphs follow the entry word and are set off from the body of the text by white space and paragraph indentation—a helpful feature for the visually impaired.

A generous number of illustrations helps to break up the pages and attract the eye. For the price, this elementary school large print dictionary is recommended over its competitors, the SCOTT, FORESMAN BEGINNING DICTIONARY: LARGE TYPE EDITION and the AMERICAN HERITAGE SCHOOL DICTIONARY: LARGE PRINT EDITION. (See also WEBSTER'S ELEMENTARY DICTIONARY discussed above in the Buying Guide.)

Webster's New World Large Print Dictionary

Facts at a Glance

Full title: **Webster's New World Large Print Dictionary**
Publisher: Prentice Hall
Editor: Victoria Neufeldt, Editor-in-Chief
Edition reviewed: © 1985, 1989 printing

Number of pages: 1,166
Number of entries: more than 58,000
Number of illustrations: none
Intended readership: secondary school to adult
Trim size: 8¾″ × 11¼″
Binding: hardcover

Price: $34.95
ISBN 0-13-962960-2
No stated revision policy

Introduction

Webster's New World Large Print Dictionary is an abridgment of *Webster's New World Dictionary, Third College Edition* (1988), which contains approximately 150,000 entries. This one-volume, 1,166-page compact school and office edition contains more than 58,000 entries. Victoria Neufeldt, the editor-in-chief, states in the book's foreword that the work is designed for "those who need a dictionary with short, straightforward definitions of the basic vocabulary of today, for easy reference."

Webster's New World Large Print Dictionary replaces *Webster's New World Large Print Dictionary of the American Language: Second Concise Edition* (1979), which was reviewed in the previous Buying Guide.

Scope and Content

Although the copyright year is 1985, the volume reviewed was printed in 1989 and contains material from *Webster's New World Dictionary, Third College Edition* (1988). According to the information on the book jacket, *Webster's New World Large Print Dictionary* is based on the reputable Webster's New World database. The editors of this dictionary also produced the third college edition.

The volume contains a broad range of common scientific, medical, legal, sports, and other technical terms such as **fusion, staphylococcus, logarithm,** and **long jump,** as well as numerous Biblical references. Current words such as **AIDS, air bag, compact disc, floppy disk, HIV, interleukin, IRA, living will, mammography, microchip,** and **punk rock** are included, but more current terms such as *bungee jumping, fax, intifada,* and *retrovirus* are not. British entry words, spellings, and definitions, as well as British slang, are also included.

Guide words are accurate and easy to read. Entries are clear and include frequently used foreign terms. Common variant spellings are set as joint entries. Variant spellings that are similar to the spelling of the entry appear after the definitions; those that differ considerably are cross-referenced. Foreign variations are indicated after the pronunciation of the entry. Homographs appear as separate entries marked by superscript numbers.

Most impressive is the clarity, accuracy, and thoroughness of definitions. Short etymologies appear before the definitions. The most common definitions are listed first; more technical definitions follow. Usage labels are used throughout to indicate colloquial, slang, archaic, obsolete, old poetic, dialectal, British, Canadian, old-fashioned, rare, or vulgar meanings. Run-in entries appear frequently at the end of entries. Numerous prefixes, suffixes, and combining forms increase the number of terms included in the dictionary. No synonym guides are included.

Special Features

Useful special features include a list of abbreviations and symbols used in the dictionary and a section on editorial style containing guidelines on punctuation, italics, numbers, capitalization, abbreviations, and bibliographic citations helpful for the student or adult writer. The "Spellings of English Sounds" section is designed to help a reader determine the spelling of a word by its pronunciation. "The United States," which lists the states, their abbreviations, and capitals, is a helpful student reference. Also included is a "Table of Measures" of the international metric system with common conversion factors and a section of "Special Signs and Symbols."

"Principal Nations of the World" contains a list of countries, their capitals, and populations. This section

Webster's New World
Large Print Dictionary

❶ Syllabication of the boldface main entry word is shown by a centered dot or by a hairline [ ], which indicates a place where, if possible, a word should not be divided

❷ Italic boldface part-of-speech label precedes the definitions to which it pertains

❸ Etymology, in open, double brackets, appears before the definitions

❹ Cross-reference in small capitals, with the appropriate sense in parentheses

❺ Usage label enclosed in brackets

❻ Irregular inflected forms in boldface type following the appropriate part-of-speech label

❼ Run-in derived entry appears in boldface type after the definitions

> **nee·dle** (nēd″l) *n.* ⟦OE *nædl*⟧ **1** a small, slender, pointed piece of steel with a hole for thread, used for sewing **2** a slender rod of steel, bone, etc. used for crocheting or knitting **3** STYLUS (sense *2b*) **4** the pointer of a compass, gauge, etc. **5** the thin, short, pointed leaf of the pine, spruce, etc. **6** the sharp, slender metal tube at the end of a hypodermic syringe — *vt.* **-dled, -dling** [Colloq.] **1** to goad; prod **2** to tease —**nee′dler** *n.*
>
> **nee′dle·point′** *n.* **1** embroidery of woolen threads upon canvas **2** lace made on a paper pattern, with a needle: in full **needlepoint lace**

is quite out-of-date. Population figures for most countries date from the original 1985 printing, and the recent changes in the former Soviet Union and Eastern Europe are not reflected in this volume. A chart of "Area Codes of the United States" and a "Time Chart of World Cities" will be useful to large-print users.

Graphics and Format

There are no illustrations in this volume. Entries and definitions, however, are clear and easy to read. The typeface is larger than that of other large-print dictionaries. Guide words are set in 18-point type, entry words in 16-point type, and definitions in 14-point type. By comparison, THE NEW MERRIAM-WEBSTER DICTIONARY FOR LARGE PRINT USERS has only 14-point entry words and 12-point definitions.

Guide words and entries, as well as parts of speech and their labels, idiomatic phrases, variant spellings, prefixes, suffixes, combining forms, and inflected forms are all in boldface and set off from the definitions. Syllables are divided by either a bold centered dot, which indicates a place where the word can be divided, or a hairline, which indicates a place where the word should not be divided. Usage labels are enclosed in brackets.

Pronunciation guides in parentheses immediately follow the entries. Primary and secondary stress are indicated by boldface and roman stress marks.

The pages are set up in two columns separated by a vertical rule. Guide words are set off in additional white space at the top left-hand corner of the left page and the top right-hand corner of the right page and appear in lowercase boldface type. Page numbers appear near the center of the page across from the beginning guide words.

Pages are opaque and of good quality to eliminate glare. The binding allows the book to lie flat and is sturdy enough to withstand heavy use. The volume should fit nicely on standard shelves or on a desk. According to the book jacket, the work is set according to the type-size standards of the National Association for the Visually Handicapped.

Summary

Webster's New World Large Print Dictionary is a well-designed, highly readable reference work for the visually impaired. It is nearly as comprehensive as THE NEW MERRIAM-WEBSTER DICTIONARY FOR LARGE PRINT USERS. Its slightly larger print makes it more appealing for the visually impaired, although THE NEW MERRIAM-WEBSTER DICTIONARY FOR LARGE PRINT USERS is also a very readable book.

The clarity and thoroughness of *Webster's New World Large Print Dictionary* are enticing features. The work is authoritative, but users should keep in mind that the volume was printed in 1989 and that lexical changes occurring after that time will not be reflected. With only a few exceptions, the dictionary is as current as most other large-print editions (such as the 1989 NEW

MERRIAM-WEBSTER DICTIONARY FOR LARGE PRINT USERS) and is one of the best large-print dictionaries available.

Webster's New World Portable Large Print Dictionary

Facts at a Glance

Full title: **Webster's New World Portable Large Print Dictionary**
Publisher: Prentice Hall
Editors: Michael Agnes, Executive Editor; Jonathan L. Goldman, Project Editor
Edition reviewed: © 1994

Number of pages: 890
Number of entries: more than 30,000
Number of illustrations: none
Intended readership: secondary school to adult
Trim size: 5¼" × 8⅜"
Binding: paperback

Price: $15; $19 (in Canada)
ISBN 0-671-88350-X
No stated revision policy

Introduction

Webster's New World Portable Large Print Dictionary is based on WEBSTER'S NEW WORLD DICTIONARY, THIRD COLLEGE EDITION, and was compiled by its staff. The one-volume, 890-page paperback edition abridges the parent work's 150,000 entries to 30,000. Jonathan Goldman, the senior editor of the dictionary, is also one of the senior editors of the third college edition.

Scope and Content

Given the work's 1994 copyright, it is surprising that of the Buying Guide's test entries only **fax** appears in *Webster's New World Portable Large Print Dictionary*. There are no entries for *bungee jumping, dis, HDTV, intifada, maquiladora, rap, retrovirus,* and *virtual reality.* In addition, the dictionary does not contain any biographical or geographical entries.

Guide words (the only finding aid in the dictionary) are accurate and easy to read. The entry words are clear and syllabicated. Each entry is followed by its part of speech, the plural form if appropriate, and definitions ordered by frequency of use. Any prepositions that commonly occur with a term are set in italics within parentheses. Irregular inflected forms and idiomatic phrases are truncated and syllabicated at the end of entries. An entry that includes many of these elements follows:

> **mean** *v.* **meant** (ment), **mean'ing 1** intend **2** intend to express **3** signify **4** have a certain importance —*a.* **1** low

in quality or rank **2** poor or shabby **3** ignoble, petty, unkind, etc. **4** stingy **5** halfway between extremes —*n.* **1** middle point **2** *pl.* [*sing. or pl. v.*] that by which a thing is gotten or done **3** *pl.* wealth —**by all** (or **no**) **means** certainly (not) —**by means of** by using —**mean'ly** *adv.* —**mean'ness** *n.*

Very few pronunciations are given, and those that appear are often abbreviated, such as **cre den tials** (-shəlz). Both primary and secondary stresses are marked. The key to the pronunciations, a short chart with 25 sounds and examples, is located on the inside front cover.

There are no etymologies, synonym guides, or cross-references. Abbreviated usage labels, such as *obs.* (obsolete), *Mus.* (music), and *Sl.* (slang), appear in brackets next to their appropriate definitions. No vulgar terms are included.

Common variant spellings, such as **dialogue, dialog,** are set as joint entries. Commonly used British terms with variant spellings, such as **colour,** appear as separate entries and are labeled *Br.* (British). Homographs may or may not be listed as separate entries. For example, all three meanings of **bat** are contained in one entry block, but **close** is listed as two entries.

This portable edition is far less comprehensive than WEBSTER'S NEW WORLD LARGE PRINT DICTIONARY, which contains lengthier definitions for its 58,000 entries. In this paperback dictionary, most of the definitions are short and simple, such as: **heron** *n.* wading bird. What has been sacrificed in accuracy and precision is gained in understandability.

Special Features

Several special features precede the lexicon in this large-print edition. "Rules for Forming Plurals" and "Rules for Spelling" contain general rules that seem condescending in a dictionary intended for an adult audience. The section "Abbreviations Used in This Book" includes those for usage labels and parts of speech. No information on using the dictionary is provided.

A section entitled "Abbreviations" follows the lexicon. It lists commonly used abbreviations, such as *AC* for air conditioning and *assn.* for association, as well as abbreviations of titles, states, and some countries.

Graphics and Format

The large print and clarity of this dictionary are especially useful for visually impaired readers. Guide words are set in 18-point type, entry words in 16-point type, and definitions in 14-point type.

Guide words, entry words, parts of speech and their labels, inflected forms, idiomatic phrases, and variant spellings and forms are in boldface. Foreign terms included as entries and labels indicating parts of speech

Webster's New World Portable Large Print Dictionary

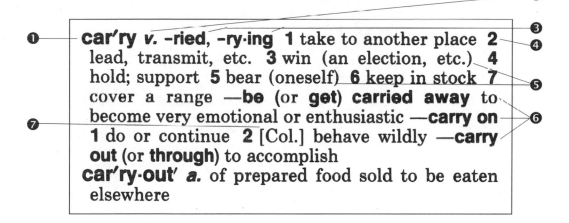

❶ Syllabicated boldface main entry word

❷ Part-of-speech label in italic boldface type

❸ The irregular and regular inflected

forms follow the part-of-speech label and are in boldface type

❹ Definitions numbered in large, boldface type for easy readability

❺ Explanatory notes in parentheses

❻ Run-on entries, in boldface type, follow the main definitions

❼ Usage label enclosed in brackets

are set in boldface italics. Definitions are clearly numbered in boldface type.

Pages use a single-column format. A boldface capital letter is centered above the column to mark the beginning of each letter of the alphabet. The first word on each left-hand page appears as the guide word at the top of the page, as does the last word on each right-hand page.

This dictionary is lightweight and easily transported. It is large enough to lie flat when opened to most of the pages except those at the very beginning and end. There are no illustrations.

Summary

Webster's New World Portable Large Print Dictionary is highly readable and well designed for the visually impaired. Although its definitions are simpler and not as comprehensive as those in WEBSTER'S NEW WORLD LARGE PRINT DICTIONARY, the portable dictionary is accurate and authoritative. It has no real competitors in terms of ease of use. This work will fit nicely in a backpack or briefcase and is a pleasant change from the many cumbersome large-print dictionaries available. Its scope is similar to some of the large-print children's dictionaries, such as the AMERICAN HERITAGE SCHOOL DICTIONARY: LARGE PRINT EDITION. This work, however, does not have a controlled vocabulary and will therefore better serve adult users. This handy paperback carries the seal of approval of the National Association for the Visually Handicapped. It is recommended as a quick-reference tool for the visually impaired.

The Weekly Reader Beginning Dictionary: Large Type Edition

Facts at a Glance

Full title: **The Weekly Reader Beginning Dictionary: Large Type Edition**
Publisher: American Printing House for the Blind
Editor: William Morris, Editor-in-Chief
Edition reviewed: © 1973

Number of volumes: 2
Number of pages: 376
Number of entries: approximately 5,000
Number of illustrations: approximately 600
Intended readership: visually impaired: grades 3 to 5
Trim size: 10⅝″ × 13⅞″
Binding: hardcover

Price: $145.56
Photocopies available from the American Printing House for the Blind: Order No. 4-8883
No stated revision policy

Introduction

This large print edition of *The Weekly Reader Beginning Dictionary* has been photoenlarged from the 1973 edition of *The Weekly Reader Beginning Dictionary.* The original edition of the book was published by Grosset & Dunlap in a trade edition. A school and library edition entitled *The Ginn Beginning Dictionary* was also published originally in 1973 by Ginn and Company, a well-known publisher of educational texts. The work is now published by the American Printing House for the Blind in two volumes. It is also listed in the reference circular of the National Library Service for the Blind and Physically Handicapped.

According to its foreword, *The Weekly Reader Beginning Dictionary: Large Type Edition* is designed for young readers and tells about "words likely to [be met in] day-to-day reading." Teachers and pupils were consulted to find which words they "wanted to know about," and their choice of categories such as animals, games, space travel and food is reflected in the lexicon. Objectives include showing young students "that words can be fun" and helping them "learn to use [words] accurately."

Scope and Content

Although the dictionary was copyrighted in 1973, its basic vocabulary contains the fundamentals needed for today's children in upper elementary grades and into the middle school years. Each entry is clearly defined with a simple word or short phrase appropriate for upper elementary grade readers. Illustrative sentences appear frequently, with the entry word printed in boldface italics. Homographs are treated as separate entries. For example:

> **grave** . . . A place where a dead person or animal is buried.

> **grave** . . . Serious. Bill's brother said it would be a *grave* mistake to drop out of school.

Inflected forms and variants are provided in boldface italic directly under the entry word.

> **care** 1. Protection; charge. Will you take *care* of my bike next week?
>   2. Attention. Cross the busy street with *care*.
>   3. A worry or trouble. Ted doesn't have a *care* in the world.

> **care** To want; to like. Would you *care* to go to the game?
> *cared*
> *caring*

In some instances an illustrative sentence will include another form of the entry word. In this case children will have to gain understanding of meaning by inference. For example, the entry word **satisfy** has the inflected forms **satisfied** and **satisfying** listed, but not the noun *satisfaction*. However, one of the illustrative examples includes the noun:

> To make content; to fill a need. A cool drink of water will **satisfy** my thirst. Susan finds **satisfaction** in listening to records.

The dictionary includes many terms having to do with space, such as **retrorocket, launch pad, moonwalk, aerospaceman** (but not *spacewoman*!), **spaceship,** and **satellite;** however, *computer* is not included.

Graphics and Format

Simple line drawings are used extensively in the generous margins. There are from one to seven illustrated words on each double-page spread. Illustrations are clearly labeled and are placed next to the appropriate word. A number of illustrations (such as those for **washing machine** and **umbrella**) are printed with a background shading that makes the labels difficult to read, especially for readers who are visually impaired. The format of the page, however, is ideal for the visually handicapped. Boldface entry words appear separately in the left-hand margin, with the succeeding definition forming one wide column down the page. Many of the definitions contain more than one meaning of the entry word and are clearly numbered in boldface.

Entry words are set in 24-point boldface type, while definitions are set in 18-point type. Illustration labels are set in 14-point sans serif type.

There are no guide words, syllabication, pronunciations, part-of-speech labels, or etymologies, but these elements are often not included in dictionaries for young readers at these age levels.

Each letter of the alphabet starts on a new page and is illustrated by a large-sized capital and lowercase example of the letter. Page numbers are centered at the top of each page.

While its large size might make it cumbersome for carrying and awkward for standard shelves, its large typeface and clarity are appealing features for the visually impaired student.

Summary

The Weekly Reader Beginning Dictionary is a very basic, simple dictionary geared to the third-to-fifth grade student. The definitions and presentation, however, are sophisticated enough to satisfy the needs of students well into the middle school years. The book is appealing to the eye and accessible, despite some defects in the enlarged illustrations. Visually impaired students and those with certain kinds of learning disabilities, such as dyslexia, would be well served by the clear and appealing layout of this large-print dictionary. The student could logically progress from this dictionary to the AMERICAN HERITAGE SCHOOL DICTIONARY, LARGE TYPE EDITION.

Selected Bibliography

General

American Reference Books Annual (ARBA). Edited by Bohdan S. Wynar. Englewood, CO: Libraries Unlimited, 1970–. Contains reviews of reference books.

ARBA Guide to Subject Encyclopedias and Dictionaries. Edited by Bohdan S. Wynar. Englewood, CO: Libraries Unlimited, 1986.

Balay, Robert. *Guide to Reference Books: Covering Materials from 1986–1990*. (Supplement to the 10th edition.) Chicago: American Library Association, 1992.

Booklist: Including Reference Books Bulletin. Chicago: American Library Association, 1905 . Semimonthly. Contains reviews of reference books.

Bopp, Richard E., and Linda C. Smith. *Reference and Information Services: An Introduction*. Englewood, CO: Libraries Unlimited, 1991.

Choice. Middletown, CT: Association of College and Research Libraries, a division of the American Library Association, 1964–. Monthly. Contains reviews of reference books.

College and Research Libraries. Chicago: Association of College and Research Libraries, a division of the American Library Association, 1939–. Bimonthly. Contains reviews of reference books.

Horowitz, Lois. *Knowing Where to Look: The Ultimate Guide to Research*. Cincinnati: Writers Digest Books, 1984.

Katz, William A. *Introduction to Reference Work*. Vol. 1. Basic Information Sources. 6th ed. New York: McGraw-Hill, 1992.

Lang, Jovian P. *Reference Sources for Small and Medium-Sized Libraries*. 5th ed. Chicago: American Library Association, 1992.

Lee, Lauren K., ed. *Elementary School Library Collection: A Guide to Books and Other Media, Phases 1-2-3*. Newark, NJ: Bro-Dart Foundation, 1994.

Library Journal. New York: R. R. Bowker, 1876–. Semimonthly. "Reference Books of [year]" published annually in April issue. Contains reviews of reference books.

Nichols, Margaret. *Guide to Reference Books for School Library Media Centers*. Englewood, CO: Libraries Unlimited, 1992.

Peterson, Carolyn S., and Ann D. Fenton. *Reference Books for Children*. 4th ed. New York: Scarecrow Press, 1992.

Reference Services Review. Ann Arbor, MI: Pierian Press, 1973–. Quarterly. Contains information of interest about reference books.

RQ. Chicago: Reference and Adult Services Division of the American Library Association, 1960–. Quarterly. Contains reviews of reference books.

Sader, Marion, ed. "The Best in Reference Works, British Literature, and American Literature." *The Reader's Adviser*. 14th ed. Vol. I. New Providence, NJ: R. R. Bowker, 1994.

School Library Journal. New York: R. R. Bowker. Monthly. "Reference Roundup" published annually. Contains reviews of reference books.

Sheehy, Eugene P., comp. *Guide to Reference Books*. 10th ed. Chicago: American Library Association, 1986.

Wilson Library Bulletin. New York: H. W. Wilson, 1914–. Ten issues per year. Contains reviews of reference books.

Wynar, Bohdan S., and Anna G. Patterson. *Recommended Reference Books for Small and Medium-Sized Libraries and Media Centers, 1993*. Englewood, CO: Libraries Unlimited, 1993.

Encyclopedias

ALA Reference Books Bulletin Editorial Board. *Purchasing an Encyclopedia: 12 Points to Consider*. 4th ed. Chicago: American Library Association, 1992.

Collison, Robert, W. E. Preece, and A. W. Read. "Encyclopaedias and Dictionaries." In *The New Encyclopaedia Britannica: Macropedia* 18: 257–286. Chicago: Encyclopaedia Britannica, 1993.

Darnton, Robert. *The Business of Enlightenment: A Publishing History of the Encyclopédie, 1775–1800*. Cambridge: Harvard University Press, 1979.

Hirschberg, Herbert S. "Encyclopedia." In *Encyclopedia Americana* 10: 330–335. Danbury, CT: Grolier, 1993.

Kister, Kenneth F. *Best Encyclopedias: A Guide to General and Specialized Encyclopedias*. 2nd ed. Phoenix: Oryx Press, 1993.

Atlases

American Cartographer. Falls Church, VA: American Cartographic Association, 1974–. Semiannual. Contains reviews of atlases.

Base Line: A Newsletter of the Map and Geography Round Table. Chicago: American Library Association, 1980–. Six issues per year. Contains news and reviews of new atlases.

Brown, Lloyd A. *The Story of Maps.* Mineola, NY: Dover, 1979.

Cartographic Journal. London: British Cartographic Society, 1964–. Semiannual. Contains reviews of atlases.

Geography and Map Division Bulletin. Special Libraries Association. 1947–. Quarterly. Contains reviews of atlases.

Kister, Kenneth F. *Kister's Atlas Buying Guide: General English-Language World Atlases Available in North America.* Phoenix: Oryx Press, 1984.

Robinson, Arthur. *Elements of Cartography.* 6th ed. New York: Wiley, 1993.

Western Association of Map Libraries Information Bulletin. Santa Cruz, CA: Western Association of Map Libraries, 1968–. Three issues per year. Contains reviews of atlases.

Dictionaries

Brewer, Annie M., ed. *Dictionaries, Encyclopedias, and other Word-Related Books.* 3 vols. 4th ed. Detroit, MI: Gale Research Company, 1987.

Chomsky, Noam. *Reflections on Language.* New York: Pantheon, 1976.

Claiborne, Robert. *Roots of English—A Reader's Handbook of Word Origins.* New York: Times Books, 1989.

Collison, Robert, W. E. Preece, and A. W. Read. "Encyclopaedias and Dictionaries." In *The New Encyclopaedia Britannica: Macropedia* 18: 257–286. Chicago: Encyclopaedia Britannica, 1993.

Dillard, J. L. *Black English: Its History and Usage in the United States.* New York: Random House, 1973.

Dillard, J. L. *A History of American English.* White Plains, NY: Longman, 1992.

Gimson, A. C. *An Introduction to the Pronunciation of English,* 4th ed. London: E. Arnold/UK, 1989.

Hartmann, R. R. K. "Dictionaries of English: The User's Perspective." In *Dictionaries of English: Prospects for the Record of Our Language,* edited by Richard W. Bailey. Ann Arbor, MI: University of Michigan Press, 1987.

Hendrickson, Robert. *American Talk: The Words and Ways of American Dialects.* New York: Viking, 1985.

Hindemarsh, R. *Cambridge English Lexicon.* Cambridge: Cambridge University Press, 1980.

"The History of the OED." In *The Oxford English Dictionary,* 2nd ed., prepared by J. A. Simpson and E. S. C. Weiner. xxxv–lvi. (Original Editor James A. H. Murray.) Oxford: Clarendon Press, 1989.

Katzner, Kenneth. *The Languages of the World.* New York: Routledge, 1990.

Kister, Kenneth. "Dictionaries Defined." *Library Journal* Volume 117, June 15, 1992, 43–47.

Kister, Kenneth. *Kister's Best Dictionaries for Adults and Young People: A Complete Guide.* Phoenix: Oryx Press, 1992.

Kučera, Henry. "The Mathematics of Language." In *The American Heritage Dictionary of the English Language, 3rd ed.,* Anne H. Soukhanov, ed., xxxi–xxxiii. Boston: Houghton Mifflin, 1992.

Landau, Sidney I. *Dictionaries: The Art and Craft of Lexicography.* New York: Cambridge University Press, 1989.

Maggio, Rosalie. *The Dictionary of Bias-free Usage: A Guide to Nondiscriminatory Language.* Phoenix: Oryx Press, 1991.

Miller, Casey and Kate Swift. *Words and Women: New Language in New Times.* Updated edition. New York: HarperCollins, 1991.

Murray, K. M. *Caught in the Web of Words: James A. H. Murray and the "OED."* New Haven, CT: Yale University Press, 1977.

Newman, Edwin. *A Civil Tongue.* New York: Bobbs-Merrill, 1976.

Newman, Edwin. *Strictly Speaking: Will American Be the Death of English?* New York: Bobbs-Merrill, 1974.

Pedersen, Lee. "A Natural History of English: Language, Culture, and the American Heritage." In *The American Heritage Dictionary of the English Language, 3rd ed.,* Anne H. Soukhanov, ed. Boston: Houghton Mifflin, 1992.

Pei, Mario. *The Story of Language.* New York: NAL/Dutton, 1984.

Safire, William *On Language.* New York: Times Books, 1981.

Smitherman, Geneva. *Talkin and Testifyin: The Language of Black America.* Wayne State University Press, 1986.

Electronic

Apple Computer. *Inside Macintosh: An Overview.* Reading, MA: Addison-Wesley, 1992.

Benford, Tom. *Welcome to CD-ROM.* New York: MIS Press, 1993.

Fawcett, Heather. "The New Oxford English Dictionary Project." *Technical Communication,* August 1993, 379–382. Project of putting the OED onto CD-ROM.

Granturco, Michael. "An Apple for the Computer." *Forbes,* August 16, 1993, 110. Using computers to teach English.

Magid, Lawrence J. *Cruising Online: Larry Magid's Guide to the New Digital Highways.* New York: Random House, 1993.

Mossberg, Walter. "Parental Guilt Sells Encyclopedias on CD-ROM, Too." *Wall Street Journal,* April 29, 1994, B1.

Neill, George, and Shirley Boes Neill. *Only the Best: Annual Guide to Highest-Rated Multimedia Software for Preschool–Grade 12.* Carmichael, CA: Education News Service.

Parker, Dana, and Bob Starrett. *New Riders Guide to CD-ROM.* Indianapolis: New Riders Publications, 1992.

Rabinowitz, Rubin. "The Ideal CD-ROM Reference Library." *PC,* August 1993, 554–558.

Raskin, Robin, Rubin Rabinowitz, and Don Truette. "27 Good Reasons to Buy a CD-ROM Player." *PC,* December 22, 1992, 345–354. Includes information on CD-ROM encyclopedias.

Schildt, Herbert. *DOS Made Easy.* 4th ed. New York: Osborne McGraw-Hill, 1993.

Shannon, L. R. "Navigating Through Reference Works On Disk." *New York Times,* v. 142, August 3, 1993, B9.

Swart, Edward. "How Are You at Interfacing? You May Like It or Not, But Computers Are Changing the English Language." *Byte,* December 1993, 302.

T.E.S.S. The Educational Software Selector. Hampton Bays, NY: EPIE Institute, 1993.

Turley, James L. *PCs Made Easy.* New York: Osborne McGraw-Hill, 1993.

Waurzyniak, Patrick. "Encarta: Explore New Worlds from the Desk Top." *Byte,* April, 1993, 55–56.

White, Ron. *How Software Works.* Emeryville, CA: Ziff-Davis Press, 1993.

Wiener, Leonard. "Family Encyclopedias on CD-ROM." *U.S. News & World Report,* April 4, 1994, 66.

Williams, Robin. *Jargon: An Informal Dictionary of Computer Terms.* Berkeley, CA: Peachpit Press, 1993.

Publishers and Distributors

American Map Corporation
Subsidiary of Langenscheidt Publishers, Inc.
46-35 54th Road
Maspeth, NY 11378
(718) 784-0055
  The Great World Atlas

American Printing House for the Blind, Inc.
1839 Frankfort Avenue
P.O. Box 6085
Louisville, KY 40206-0085
(502) 895-2405
  *American Heritage School Dictionary: Large
    Print Edition*
  *Holt School Dictionary of American English:
    Large Print Edition*
  My Second Pictionary
  Pocket Dictionary, Large Type Edition
  *Scott, Foresman Beginning Dictionary, Large
    Type Edition*
  *The Weekly Reader Beginning Dictionary: Large
    Type Edition*

Barron's Educational Series, Inc.
250 Wireless Blvd.
P.O. Box 8040
Hauppauge, NY 11788
(516) 434-3311
  *Barron's Junior Fact Finder: An Illustrated Ency-
    clopedia for Children*
  Barron's New Student's Concise Encyclopedia

John Bartholomew & Son, Ltd.
Duncan Street
Edinburgh, Scotland
EH91TA
  Bartholomew Mini World Atlas
  (see HarperCollins)

Brøderbund Software, Inc.
P.O. Box 6125
Novato, CA 94928-6125
(415) 382-4600
  PC Globe Maps 'n' Facts (CD-ROM)

Cambridge University Press
40 West 20th Street
New York, NY 10011-4211
(212) 924-3900
  The Cambridge Encyclopedia
  The Cambridge Paperback Encyclopedia

Cassell Publishers UK
Villiers House
41/47 Strand
London WC2N 5JE
England
  Cassell Giant Paperback Dictionary
  Cassell Student English Dictionary
  (see Sterling Publishing Company, Inc.)

Columbia University Press
562 West 113th Street
New York, NY 10025
(212) 316-7100
  The Columbia Encyclopedia
  The Concise Columbia Encyclopedia
  (see Houghton Mifflin)

Compton's Learning Company
A Division of Compton's MultiMedia Publishing
  Group, Inc.
2 Prudential Plaza
180 North Stetson, Suite 2625
Chicago, IL 60601
(312) 540-5800
  Compton's Encyclopedia and Fact-Index
  Compton's Precyclopedia

Compton's NewMedia
2320 Camino Vida Roble
Carlsbad, CA 92009
(619) 929-2500
  Compton's Interactive Encyclopedia (CD-ROM)

Dorling Kindersley, Inc.
232 Madison Avenue
New York, NY 10016
(212) 684-0404
  My First Dictionary
  My First Encyclopedia

Doubleday
A Division of Bantam Doubleday Dell Publishing
  Group, Inc.
1540 Broadway
New York, NY 10036
(212) 354-6500

The Doubleday Children's Atlas
The Doubleday Children's Dictionary
The Doubleday Children's Picture Dictionary
The Doubleday Picture Atlas

EDC Publishing
A Division of Educational Development Corporation
10302 East 55th Place
Tulsa, OK 74146-6515
(918) 622-4522
The First Thousand Words: A Picture Word Book
Round the World Picture Word Book
Usborne Children's Encyclopedia

Encyclopaedia Britannica, Inc.
310 South Michigan Avenue
Chicago, IL 60604-4293
(312) 347-7000
Britannica Atlas
Children's Britannica
The New Encyclopaedia Britannica
The Young Children's Encyclopedia

Facts On File, Inc.
460 Park Avenue South
New York, NY 10016-7382
(212) 683-2244
The Facts On File Children's Atlas
The Facts On File Junior Visual Dictionary
The Facts On File Visual Dictionary

J. G. Ferguson Publishing Company
200 West Madison Street
Chicago, IL 60601
(312) 580-5480
Webster Comprehensive Dictionary: Encyclopedic Edition
Webster Comprehensive Dictionary: International Edition
Webster Illustrated Contemporary Dictionary: Encyclopedic Edition

Funk & Wagnalls, Inc.
One International Blvd.
Mahwah, NJ 07495-0017
(201) 529-6900
Funk & Wagnalls New Encyclopedia

Gage Educational Publishing Company
A Division of Canada Publishing Corp.
164 Commander Blvd.
Agincourt, Ontario
M1S 3C7, Canada
The Gage Atlas of the World
The Global Atlas
The Macmillan School Atlas

Globe/Fearon
240 Frisch Court

Paramus, NJ 97652
(201) 909-6209
Fearon New School Dictionary

Grolier, Inc.
A Subsidiary of Matra Hachette
Sherman Turnpike
Danbury, CT 06816
(203) 797-3500
Academic American Encyclopedia
The Encyclopedia Americana
Grolier Encyclopedia of Knowledge
The New Book of Knowledge
The New Grolier Multimedia Encyclopedia (CD-ROM)
The New Grolier Multimedia Encyclopedia (on-line)
The New Grolier Student Encyclopedia

Hammond, Inc.
515 Valley Street
Maplewood, NJ 07040
(201) 763-6000
Discovering Maps: A Children's World Atlas
Hammond Atlas of the World
Hammond Atlas of the World, Concise Edition
Hammond International Atlas of the World
Hammond Mini-World Atlas
Hammond Nova World Atlas
Hammond World Atlas: Collector's Edition

Harcourt Brace & Company
6277 Sea Harbor Drive
Orlando, FL 32887
(407) 345-2000
HBJ School Dictionary
The Lincoln Writing Dictionary

HarperCollins Publishers
10 East 53rd Street
New York, NY 10022-5299
(212) 207-7000
Bartholomew Mini World Atlas
Collins COBUILD English Language Dictionary
My First Dictionary
Thorndike-Barnhart Children's Dictionary
Words for New Readers

Highlighted Data
6628 Midhill Place
Falls Church, VA 22043-1833
(703) 533-1939
Webster's Ninth New Collegiate Dictionary (CD-ROM)

Henry Holt & Company, Inc.
115 West 18th Street
New York, NY 10011

(212) 886-9200
The Economist Atlas

Houghton Mifflin Company
222 Berkeley Street
Boston, MA 02116-3764
(617) 351-5000
The American Heritage Children's Dictionary
The American Heritage College Dictionary
The American Heritage Desk Dictionary
The American Heritage Dictionary of the English Language
The American Heritage First Dictionary
The American Heritage High School Dictionary
The American Heritage Picture Dictionary
The American Heritage Student's Dictionary
The Columbia Encyclopedia
The Concise Columbia Encyclopedia
My Big Dictionary
Webster's II New Riverside University Dictionary

Inductel
5339 Prospect Road
San Jose, CA 95129-5028
(408) 866-8016
Funk & Wagnalls Standard Desk Dictionary (CD-ROM)

Bob Jones University Press
1700 Wade Hampton Blvd.
Greenville, SC 29614
(803) 242-5100
The Christian Student Dictionary

Karol Media
350 North Pennsylvania Avenue
Wilkes-Barre, PA 18773-7600
(717) 822-8899
Picture Atlas of the World (CD-ROM)

Kingfisher Books, Inc.
95 Madison Avenue
New York, NY 10016
(212) 686-10060
The Kingfisher Children's Encyclopedia
The Kingfisher Reference Atlas

The Library Reproduction Service of the Microfilm Company of California
1977 South Los Angeles Street
Los Angeles, CA 90011-1096
(213) 749-2463
The Random House Dictionary: Classic Edition (Large Print)
Webster's New Elementary Dictionary: Large Type Edition

Longman Publishing Group
Subsidiary of Addison-Wesley Publishing Company

10 Bank Street
White Plains, NY 10601-1951
(914) 993-5000
Longman Dictionary of American English: A Dictionary for Learners of English
Longman Dictionary of Contemporary English, New Edition
Longman Dictionary of English Language and Culture
Longman Language Activator

Macmillan New Media
124 Mt. Auburn Street
Cambridge, MA 02138
(617) 661-2955
Macmillan Dictionary for Children, Multimedia Edition (CD-ROM)

Macmillan Publishing Company, Inc.
A Division of Paramount Publishing
866 Third Avenue
New York, NY 10022
(212) 702-2000
Beginning Dictionary
Collier's Encyclopedia
Macmillan Dictionary
Macmillan Dictionary for Children
Macmillan Dictionary for Students
The Macmillan First Atlas
Macmillan First Dictionary
Macmillan School Dictionary
The Macmillan Visual Dictionary
(see also Prentice Hall)

Merriam-Webster, Inc.
47 Federal Street
Springfield, MA 01102
(413) 734-3134
Merriam-Webster's Collegiate Dictionary, Tenth Edition
Webster's Basic English Dictionary
Webster's Elementary Dictionary
Webster's Intermediate Dictionary
Webster's New Ideal Dictionary
Webster's School Dictionary
Webster's Third New International Dictionary of the English Language, Unabridged

Microlytics
2 Tobey Village Office Park
Pittsford, NY 14534
(716) 248-9150
The Random House Encyclopedia: Electronic Edition (floppy disk)

Microsoft Corporation
One Microsoft Way
Redmond, WA 98052

(206) 882-8080
>
> *Microsoft Bookshelf* (CD-ROM)
> *Microsoft Encarta Multimedia Encyclopedia*
>   (CD-ROM)

National Geographic Society
1145 17th Street, NW
Washington, DC 20036
(202) 857-7000
>
> *National Geographic Atlas of the World*
> *National Geographic Picture Atlas of Our World*
> *Picture Atlas of the World* (CD-ROM) (see Karol
>   Media)

Oxford University Press, Inc.
200 Madison Avenue
New York, NY 10016
(212) 679-7300
>
> *Atlas of the World*
> *The Compact Oxford English Dictionary*
> *Concise Atlas of the World*
> *The Concise Oxford Dictionary of Current English*
> *The Little Oxford Dictionary of Current English*
> *The New Shorter Oxford English Dictionary*
> *Oxford Advanced Learner's Dictionary of Current English*
> *Oxford American Dictionary*
> *Oxford Children's Encyclopedia*
> *Oxford-Duden Pictorial Dictionary*
> *Oxford Elementary Learner's Dictionary of English*
> *The Oxford Encyclopedic English Dictionary*
> *The Oxford English Dictionary, Second Edition*
> *The Oxford English Dictionary: Second Edition on Compact Disc* (CD-ROM)
> *The Oxford ESL Dictionary*
> *Oxford Illustrated Encyclopedia*
> *Oxford Large Print Dictionary*
> *Oxford Modern English Dictionary*
> *The Pocket Oxford Dictionary of Current English*

Prentice Hall
A Division of Paramount Publishing
15 Columbus Circle
New York, NY 10023
(212) 373-8500
>
> *Webster's New World Children's Dictionary*
> *Webster's New World Dictionary for Young Adults*
> *Webster's New World Dictionary, Third College Edition*
> *Webster's New World Encyclopedia*
> *Webster's New World Encyclopedia, Pocket Edition*
> *Webster's New World Large Print Dictionary*
> *Webster's New World Portable Large Print Dictionary*
> (see also Macmillan Publishing)

Rand McNally & Company
8255 Central Park Avenue
Skokie, IL 60076
(708) 329-8100
>
> *Giant Atlas of the World*
> *The New Cosmopolitan World Atlas*
> *The New International Atlas*
> *Rand McNally Children's World Atlas*
> *Rand McNally Goode's World Atlas*
> *Rand McNally Picture Atlas of the World*
> *Today's World: A New World Atlas from the Cartographers of Rand McNally*
> *World Atlas of Nations*

Random House, Inc.
201 East 50th Street
New York, NY 10022
(212) 751-2600
>
> *The Random House Children's Encyclopedia*
> *The Random House Compact World Atlas*
> *The Random House Encyclopedia, New Revised Third Edition*
> *The Random House Unabridged Dictionary, Second Edition*
> *The Random House Unabridged Dictionary, Second Edition* (CD-ROM)
> *Random House Webster's College Dictionary*
> *The Sesame Street Dictionary*

Random House Value Publishing, Inc.
40 Engelhard Avenue
Avenel, NJ 07001
(908) 827-2664
>
> *Webster's Encyclopedic Unabridged Dictionary*

Reader's Digest Association
Reader's Digest Road
Pleasantville, NY 19570
(914) 769-7000
>
> *Reader's Digest Atlas of the World*
> *Reader's Digest –Bartholomew Illustrated Atlas of the World, Revised Edition*
> *The Reader's Digest Children's World Atlas*

Scott, Foresman & Company
Subsidiary of HarperCollins Publishers
1900 East Lake Avenue
Glenview, IL 60025
(708) 729-3000
>
> *My First Picture Dictionary*
> *My Pictionary*
> *My Second Picture Dictionary*
> *Scott, Foresman Advanced Dictionary*
> *Scott, Foresman Beginning Dictionary*
> *Scott, Foresman Intermediate Dictionary*
> *Thorndike-Barnhart Student Dictionary*

Software Toolworks
60 Leveroni Court
Novato, CA 94949
(415) 883-3000
  Software Toolworks World Atlas (CD-ROM)

Standard Educational Corp.
200 West Madison Street
Chicago, IL 60606
(312) 346-7440
  New Standard Encyclopedia

Sterling Publishing Company, Inc.
387 Park Avenue South
New York, NY 10016-8810
(212) 532-7160
  Cassell Giant Paperback Dictionary
  Cassell Student English Dictionary

Thorndike Press/G. K. Hall
A Division of Macmillan Publishing Company
P.O. Box 159
Thorndike, ME 04986
  Hammond Large Type World Atlas
  The New Merriam-Webster Dictionary for Large
    Print Users

Times Books
Division of Random House, Inc.
201 East 50th Street
New York, NY 10022
(212) 572-4000
  The New York Times Atlas of the World, New Family Edition
  The New York Times Atlas of the World, Paperback Edition
  The New York Times Atlas of the World, Third Revised Concise Edition
  The Times Atlas of the World, Ninth Comprehensive Edition

Troll Associates
100 Corporation Drive

Mahwah, NJ 07430
(201) 529-4000
  My First Atlas
  My First Dictionary
  My First Encyclopedia
  Student Atlas
  Student Encyclopedia
  Young People's Dictionary

Charles E. Tuttle Company, Inc.
153 Milk Street
Boston, MA 02109-4809
(802) 773-8030
  Student Atlas of the World

Ulverscroft Large Print (USA), Inc.
1881 Ridge Road
P.O. Box 1230
West Seneca, NY 14224-1230
(800) 955-9659
  The Large Print Version of the Little Oxford Dictionary of Current English

World Book, Inc.
Subsidiary of Scott Fetzer Co.
525 West Monroe Street
Chicago, IL 60601
(312) 258-4815
  Childcraft—The How and Why Library
  Information Finder (CD-ROM)
  The World Book Atlas
  The World Book Dictionary
  World Book Encyclopedia
  World Book Student Dictionary

Xïphias
8758 Venice Blvd.
Los Angeles, CA 90034
(310) 841-2790
  American Heritage Illustrated Encyclopedia Dictionary (CD-ROM)

Acknowledgments

Page numbers are followed by titles listed in alphabetical order.

Page 82. Reprinted with permission from *Academic American Encyclopedia,* volume 6, page 161. Copyright © 1993 by Grolier Inc.

Page 316. Copyright © 1993 by Houghton Mifflin Company. Reproduced by permission from THE AMERICAN HERITAGE COLLEGE DICTIONARY, THIRD EDITION.

Page 318. Copyright © 1981 by Houghton Mifflin Company. Reproduced by permission from THE AMERICAN HERITAGE DESK DICTIONARY.

Page 321. Copyright © 1992 by Houghton Mifflin Company. Reproduced by permission from THE AMERICAN HERITAGE DICTIONARY OF THE ENGLISH LANGUAGE, THIRD EDITION.

Page 38. Reprinted with permission from *Barron's Junior Fact Finder: An Illustrated Encyclopedia for Children,* page 210, Jean-Paul Dupre. Copyright © 1989 by Barron's Educational Series, Inc.

Page 87. Reprinted with permission from *Barron's New Student's Concise Encyclopedia 2nd ed,* page 20-10, ed. Grace Freedson. Copyright © 1993 by Barron's Educational Series, Inc.

Page 256. From *Beginning Dictionary,* page 550, Editorial Director William D. Halsey. Copyright © 1987 by Macmillan Publishing Company. Reproduced with permission of McGraw-Hill, Inc.

Page 90. From *The Cambridge Encyclopedia,* page 1287, ed. David Crystal. © Cambridge University Press 1990. Reprinted with the permission of Cambridge University Press.

Page 94. From *The Cambridge Paperback Encyclopedia,* page 168, ed. David Crystal. © Cambridge University Press 1993. Reprinted with the permission of Cambridge University Press.

Page 327. Reprinted with permission from *Cassell Student English Dictionary,* page 821, ed. Betty Kirkpatrick. © Cassell 1993 by CASSELL.

Page 41. From *The Green Kingdom,* Volume 5 of *Childcraft—The How and Why Library.* © 1993 World Book, Inc. By permission of the publisher.

Page 45. Reprinted with permission from *Children's Britannica,* 4th edition, © 1994 by Encyclopaedia Britannica, Inc.

Page 292. Reprinted with permission from *The Christian Student Dictionary,* page 309. Copyright © 1982 by Bob Jones University Press.

Page 97. Reprinted with permission from *Collier's Encyclopedia,* volume 7, page 427. Copyright © 1994 by P.F. Collier, L.P.

Page 380. Reprinted with permission from *Collins COBUILD English Language Dictionary,* page 595, ed. John Sinclair. Copyright © 1987 by HarperCollins Publishers.

Page 101. From *The Columbia Encyclopedia, 5th Edition,* 1993, © Columbia University Press, New York. Reprinted with permission of the publisher.

Page 106. Reprinted with permission from *Compton's Encyclopedia and Fact-Index,* volume 5, page 637, Dale Good, Editorial Director. Copyright © 1993 by Compton's Learning Company.

Page 110. From *The Concise Columbia Encyclopedia, 2nd Edition,* 1989, © Columbia University Press, New York. Reprinted with permission of the publisher.

Page 260. Reprinted with permission from *The Doubleday Children's Picture Dictionary,* page 108, Felicia Law. Copyright © 1986 by Grisewood & Dempsey Ltd.

Page 132. Reprinted with permission from *Encyclopaedia Britannica,* 15th edition, © 1994 by Encyclopaedia Britannica, Inc.

Page 113. Reprinted with permission from *The Encyclopedia Americana,* volume 25, page 477. Copyright © 1993 by Grolier Inc.

Page 384. From *Facts On File Visual Dictionary,* page 65. Copyright 1986 by Editions Quebec/Amerique. Author: Jean-Claude Corbeil.

Page 331. Reprinted with permission from *Fearon New School Dictionary,* page 504. Copyright © 1987 by Globe Fearon.

Page 119. Reprinted with permission from *Funk & Wagnalls New Encyclopedia,* volume 3, page 336. Copyright © 1993 by Funk & Wagnalls, Inc.

Page 123. Reprinted with permission from *Grolier Encyclopedia of Knowledge,* volume 8, page 16. Copyright © 1991 by Grolier Inc.

Page 295. Excerpt from HBJ SCHOOL DICTIONARY, Third Edition, copyright © 1990 by Harcourt Brace & Company, reprinted by permission of the publisher.

Page 51. Reprinted with permission from *The Kingfisher Children's Encyclopedia,* page 583, ed. John Paton. Copyright © 1992 by Larousse PLC.

Page 461. Reprinted with permission from *The Large Print Version of the Little Oxford Dictionary of Current English,* page 601, ed. Julia Swannell. Copyright © 1986. Published by Ulverscroft Large Print Books, Ltd.

Page 297. Excerpt from THE LINCOLN WRITING DICTIONARY, SCHOOL EDITION, copyright © 1989 by Harcourt Brace & Company, reprinted by permission of the publisher.

Page 333. Reprinted with permission from *The Little Oxford Dictionary of Current English,* page 105, ed. Julia Swannell. Copyright © 1986 by Oxford University Press.

Page 385. Reprinted with permission from *Longman Dictionary of American English: A Dictionary for Learners of English,* page 177. Copyright © 1983 by Longman ELT.

Page 356. Reprinted with permission from *Webster Comprehensive Dictionary: Encyclopedic Edition,* page 754. Copyright © 1992 by J. G. Ferguson.

Page 407. Reprinted with permission from *Webster's Basic English Dictionary,* page 184. Copyright © 1990 by Merriam-Webster Inc.

Page 282. Reprinted with permission from *Webster's Elementary Dictionary,* page 172. Copyright © 1986 by Merriam-Webster Inc.

Page 360. Reprinted with permission from *Webster's Encyclopedic Unabridged Dictionary of the English Language,* page 254, ed. Glorya Hale. Copyright © 1989 by Random House Value Publishing.

Page 309. Reprinted with permission from *Webster's Intermediate Dictionary,* page 583. Copyright © 1986 by Merriam-Webster Inc.

Page 363. Reprinted with permission from *Webster's New Ideal Dictionary,* page 600. Copyright © 1989 by Merriam-Webster Inc.

Page 150. From WEBSTER'S NEW WORLD ENCYCLOPEDIA, page 110. Copyright © 1992. Reprinted by permission of the publisher, Simon & Schuster, Inc., New York.

Page 154. From WEBSTER'S NEW WORLD ENCYCLOPEDIA, POCKET EDITION, page 706. Copyright © 1993. Reprinted by permission of the publisher, Simon & Schuster, Inc., New York.

Page 471. From WEBSTER'S NEW WORLD LARGE PRINT DICTIONARY, page 656. Copyright © 1985. Reprinted by permission of the publisher, Simon & Schuster, Inc., New York.

Page 473. From WEBSTER'S NEW WORLD PORTABLE LARGE PRINT DICTIONARY, page 119. Copyright © 1994. Reprinted by permission of the publisher, Simon & Schuster, Inc., New York.

Page 367. Reprinted with permission from *Webster's School Dictionary,* page 630. Copyright © 1986 by Merriam-Webster Inc.

Page 369. Reprinted with permission from *Webster's Third New International Dictionary of the English Language, Unabridged,* page 607, ed. Philip Babcock Gove. Copyright © 1993 by Merriam-Webster Inc.

Page 373. Copyright © 1994 by Houghton Mifflin Company. Reproduced by permission from WEBSTER'S II NEW RIVERSIDE UNIVERSITY DICTIONARY.

Page 286. Reprinted with permission from *Words for New Readers,* page 270. Copyright © 1990 by Scott, Foresman and Company.

Page 375. From *The World Book Dictionary.* © 1993 World Book, Inc. By permission of the publisher.

Page 156. From *The World Book Encyclopedia.* © 1993 World Book, Inc. By permission of the publisher.

Page 313. From *The World Book Student Dictionary.* © 1993 World Book, Inc. By permission of the publisher.

Page 288. Reprinted with permission from *Young People's Dictionary,* page 95. Copyright © 1991 by Troll Associates.

Cover Photos

The following publishers have generously given permission to reproduce cover photos of their books, which appear on our cover:

Academic American Encyclopedia, Deluxe Library Edition. copyright 1993 by Grolier Inc.

The American Heritage Dictionary of the English Language, Third edition. Reproduced by permission from the *American Heritage Dictionary of the English Language,* Third Edition. Copyright 1992 by Houghton Mifflin Company.

The Columbia Encyclopedia, 5th edition. Copyright 1993 by Columbia University Press. Reproduced by permission.

The Doubleday Children's Picture Dictionary. Felicia Law, compiler. Copyright 1986 by Doubleday. Reproduced by permission.

The Facts On File Children's Atlas. Copyright 1993 by Facts On File. Reproduced by permission.

Hammond Atlas of the World, third printing. Copyright 1994 by Hammond. Reproduced by permission.

The Kingfisher Children's Encyclopedia. From *The Kingfisher Children's Encyclopedia,* copyright Grisewood & Dempsey Ltd., 1992. Reprinted with permission of Larousse Kingfisher Chambers Inc., New York.

Merriam-Webster's Collegiate Dictionary, Tenth Edition. Copyright 1993 by Merriam-Webster. Reproduced by permission.

My First Encyclopedia. Copyright 1993 by Dorling Kindersley. Reproduced by permission.

New York Times Atlas of the World, New Family Edition. Copyright 1992 by Times Books/Random House. Reproduced by permission.

Oxford American Dictionary. Copyright 1979 by Avon Books. Reproduced by permission.

The Sesame Street Dictionary. Linda Hayward, compiler. Copyright 1980 by Random House, Inc. Reproduced by permission.

Today's World. Copyright 1992 by Rand-McNally. Reproduced by permission.

The World Book Encyclopedia, Vol. 20. Copyright 1993 by World Book Inc. Reproduced by permission.

Index

Titles with full reviews in this Buying Guide appear below in small capital letters. All other titles are in italics. Abbreviations of titles are fully cross-referenced (for example, "AHD. *See* THE AMERICAN ENGLISH DICTIONARY OF THE ENGLISH LANGUAGE (AHD) THIRD EDITION.") Boldface page numbers indicate facsimiles and other illustrations.